MONTE ALBÁN

Settlement Patterns at the Ancient Zapotec Capital

This is a volume in

Studies in Archeology

A complete list of titles in this series appears at the end of this volume.

MONTE ALBÁN
Settlement Patterns at the Ancient Zapotec Capital

RICHARD E. BLANTON

DEPARTMENT OF SOCIOLOGY AND ANTHROPOLOGY
PURDUE UNIVERSITY
WEST LAFAYETTE, INDIANA

WITH CONTRIBUTIONS BY

WILLIAM O. AUTRY, JR.

STEPHEN A. KOWALEWSKI

CARL KUTTRUFF

ELSA REDMOND

CHARLES SPENCER

ACADEMIC PRESS New York San Francisco London

A Subsidiary of Harcourt Brace Jovanovich, Publishers

ACADEMIC PRESS, INC.
111 Fifth Avenue, New York, New York 10003

United Kingdom Edition published by
ACADEMIC PRESS, INC. (LONDON) LTD.
24/28 Oval Road, London NW1

Library of Congress Cataloging in Publication Data

Blanton, Richard E
Monte Albán : settlement patterns at the ancient Zapotec capital.

(Studies in archeology series)
1. Monte Albán, Mexico. I. Title.
F1219.1.011B5 972'.7 77-11917
ISBN 0-12-104250-2

PRINTED IN THE UNITED STATES OF AMERICA

To Alexis

Contents

List of Plates

List of Figures

List of Tables

Preface

Intensive archaeological survey has been used by anthropologists interested in the ancient societies of Highland Mesoamerica for the last two decades, most of such work having been done in the Valley of Mexico. The impetus to adopt this methodology was provided by two related sources. Gordon Willey's survey of the Virú Valley (Willey 1953), a study encouraged by Julian Steward, was one such source. Steward's method of "cultural ecology" seemed to demand a regional approach to discovery and analysis in archaeology, especially insofar as data were needed that contributed to an understanding of changing patterns of resource utilization. According to Steward, this method "pays primary attention to those features which empirical analysis shows to be most closely involved in the utilization of the environment in culturally prescribed ways," or the "cultural core [Steward 1955: 37]."

The other major source of theory that demanded a regional archaeological methodology, in contradistinction to the site-oriented archaeology of more traditional practitioners, was the work of Karl Wittfogel (cf. 1938, 1957) whose Marxist orientation, with its attendant interest in modes of production, required knowledge of changing patterns of land use, in particular those relating to hydraulic agriculture. Wittfogel's writings were disseminated to Mesoamerican archaeologists and their students during the 1940s and 1950s by Paul Kirchoff and, especially, Pedro Armillas (Wolf 1976: 1–4). According to Wolf, as these new sources of theory gradually permeated the thinking of Mesoamericanists,

> new questions were raised for which the extant data were clearly insufficient. What were the characteristics of Mesoamerican agricultural systems? What role did hydraulic agriculture play in prompting or facilitating the growth of large population centers? When was irrigation first introduced? What was the nature of these population centers? When and where did urbanism first arise? How were these urban centers provisioned [pp. 3, 4]?

In 1960, Eric Wolf organized a conference, supported by the National Science Foundation, which was designed to map the future course of anthropological research in the Valley of Mexico, one of prehispanic Mesoamerica's most important centers of cultural evolution. The participants agreed that systematic archaeological surveys would be a useful method for collecting data appropriate for resolving the kinds of questions posed above. Since that conference, several archaeological surveys have been carried out in the Valley of Mexico. These surveys have assumed three different forms, each with its own set of goals: The systematic settlement pattern surveys of Sanders, Parsons, and myself (cf. Sanders 1965; Parsons 1971; Blanton 1972) attempted to discover the changing spatial relations of communities, both with respect to one another and to natural resource zones, allowing inferences concerning the interrelationships of changing patterns of resource exploitation, population dynamics, and political control. In its most elaborate form (Sanders, Parsons, and Logan 1976), following Boserup's (1965) theory, the survey data are used to support the contention that the rise of social stratification and the state are ultimately due to population pressure leading to agricultural intensification, which in turn leads to social differentiation and the need for centralized resource management.

A second tactic employed to resolve the aforementioned problems is the "landscape archaeology" of Pedro Armillas. According to Armillas (1971):

> The basic tenet of landscape archeology is that, through the integration of data on the features of land use that characterized a man-shaped habitat (including settlement, field systems, and hydraulic works, as well as the layout of the web of trackways, causeways, and waterways that linked the components of the regional system), one can perceive the cultural landscape as a reflection of the interplay between the environment, and the technology, structure, and values of the society that shaped it [p. 654].

His work has contributed substantially to our knowledge of the extent, organization, functioning, and productivity of the massive *chinampa* agricultural systems of the Late Postclassic Valley of Mexico (Armillas 1971).

The third approach of the survey archaeologists in the Valley of Mexico is the "urban archaeology" of René Millon and his associates. Their detailed surface survey of the ancient city of Teotihuacan "was designed to focus attention on what kind of an urban center Teotihuacan was and on the relations of Teotihuacanos with the people of other great contemporary centers in Middle America." He felt that an

> accurate, detailed map was an indispensable precondition for any intensive study of urbanization at Teotihuacan. The extent of the urban zone, the density of construction, and the way buildings were disposed within it and related to each other had to be determined if any serious progress was to be made in understanding the society whose members built and lived in this great city [Millon 1973: x, xi].

This study of Monte Albán and the project of which it is a part are outgrowths of the theoretical heritage and archaeological surveys just described. Rather than representing any one of the survey strategies present in the Valley of Mexico research, however, we have borrowed selectively, but not slavishly, from all three, and have added a significant new dimension to both theory and methodology. I refer to our use of regional analysis, a relatively new approach in anthropology based largely on the powerful central place theory of geography (cf. Skinner 1964, 1965a, 1965b; Smith 1974, 1975, 1976). As I outlined it earlier (Blanton 1976b), regional analysis focuses attention on the disposition in space of central institutions—institutions that mediate between specialized subsystems in complex societies. The focuses of central institutional transactions are a society's system of cities and towns—its central place hierarchy. In later chapters I will employ this body of theory and method in developing hypotheses about Monte Albán's origins and its role in the regional system, as well as in drawing a preliminary comparison between the dynamics of civilizations in the Valleys of Mexico and Oaxaca, the latter of which is the setting of Monte Albán.

The Valley of Oaxaca Settlement Pattern Project

This volume describes and analyzes the data collected during the first phase of the Valley of Oaxaca Settlement Pattern Project—which consisted of the detailed mapping and surface collection of the region's major archaeological site, Monte Albán. Much had been known about the site prior to our work—due especially to the efforts of the great Mexican archaeologist, Alfonso Caso—but most of this information pertained to ceramic artifacts found in tombs and to details of architecture and sculpture in and around the site's major cluster of mounded buildings, the Main Plaza. Our goal was to discover what Monte Albán had been like as a city: How many people lived there, and how did that number change through time? What kinds of social units were present, and how are they reflected in the community's spatial organization? What was the city's role in the Oaxaca region—was it primarily a commercial center, an administrative center, or both? What conditions led to the foundation of the city, and to its collapse?

It is understandable that the Valley of Mexico had been chosen as the scene for Mesoamerica's first large-scale regional archaeological surveys, and why it had been the focus of attention at Eric Wolf's conference. Teotihuacan was undoubtedly the largest prehispanic city in the New World, and, of course, the Aztecs, based in the valley, were the major military and commercial force in Mesoamerica when the Spanish arrived. In the Highlands of Mesoamerica, however, one other region had been what Palerm and Wolf (1957) describe as a "nuclear center," i.e., a major locus of innovation and sociocultural change during most of the prehispanic period, the Valley of Oaxaca. Clearly, archaeological studies in the Valley of Oaxaca should contribute as much to an understanding of cultural evolution as would studies in the Valley of Mexico. Monte Albán, located in the valley, is one of Mesoamerica's most important archaeological sites. Its importance in Mesoamerican prehistory is apparent not only from the monumentality and elaborateness of its architecture, but from the large corpus of carved stones found there. According to Joyce Marcus (1976a),

> Monte Albán showed the first Mesoamerican use of the "emblem glyph" or place sign, the bar-and-dot system of numeration, the 260-day ritual calendar (Caso, 1928), the first political conquest records, and the system of naming rulers by their birth dates. Many of these developments anticipated the "indigenous" developments in the Maya region by at least 500 years. The impact and antecedent role of this early urban and militaristic civilization on other Mesoamerican civilizations have been greatly underestimated . . . [p. 137].

Kent Flannery suggested I carry out a settlement pattern survey in the Valley of Oaxaca using the methodology that had been developed during the course of the Valley of Mexico surveys. He envisioned a division of labor between his Oaxaca Human Ecology Project, which is oriented to the exposure of preceramic living floors and Formative villages, and a project that would carry out systematic regional surveys. The valley is an ideal location for such surveys for several reasons:

1. Survey conditions in Oaxaca are similar to those in the Valley of Mexico, so that the methodologies worked out by Millon, Sanders, Parsons, Armillas, and myself would be applicable essentially without modification. Both valleys are semiarid and heavily cultivated so that the natural vegetation does not significantly obscure surface remains, and alluviation is generally not a serious problem. Archaeological sites dating back to as early as 1500 B.C. or even somewhat earlier are, in most cases, easily discoverable on the surface as scatters of sherds and other cultural debris.

2. The ceramic sequence of the Valley of Oaxaca is, in general, well known. Caso, Bernal, and Acosta (1967) (which will often be referred to hereinafter as CBA) published a massive volume on the ceramics of Monte Albán, based on their stratigraphic excavations there over several decades. Participants in Flannery's Human Ecology Project had carried out stratigraphic excavations in several Formative sites, extending the Valley of Oaxaca ceramic sequence back to the beginnings of settled village life, ca. 1500 B.C. (Flannery, Winter, Lees, Neely, Schoenwetter, Kitchen, and Wheeler n.d.). Thus the ceramic sequence from the time of the earliest villages to the Spanish Conquest in the valley was already known.

3. Other work accomplished as part of Flannery's Oaxaca Human Ecology Project has direct relevance to the kinds of problems which interest Valley of Mexico researchers such as myself. Susan Lees (1973) carried out an ethnographic survey of contemporary piedmont villages in the valley to discover the relevance of canal irrigation to varying patterns of political control. Her study may be relevant to an understanding of the process of political centralization in the region, since it is known that piedmont irrigation systems date from as early as the Formative Period. Environmental and land-use studies in the valley have been made by two geomorphologists, Anne and Mike Kirkby (Flannery *et al.* 1967; Flannery *et al.* n.d.). They have systematically divided the valley into a series of physiographic zones, each defined in terms of variables such as slope, soil type, degree of erosion, and the availability of water. Based on their studies of modern land use, they have been able to specify which agricultural techniques are appropriate for each of the physiographic zones, and they have calculated the potential agricultural productivity of each zone. Anne Kirkby (1973) has predicted the demographic characteristics and approximate locations of sites for several of the prehispanic periods, based upon her calculations of changes in maize productivity through time, and knowledge of the climatic history of the valley and the types of agricultural techniques available during each period. These predictions can be of great value because by comparing them with the observed settlement patterns and population densities, period by period, it is possible to make judgments about the extent to which agricultural variables influenced the characteristics of the patterns of settlement and demographic features as compared with the influence of nonsubsistence variables. Studies such as Kirkby's make the Valley of Oaxaca a more desirable locality for an intensive archaeological survey than the Valley of Mexico, where comparable information on change through time in climate, agricultural productivity, and the variable productivity of different environmental zones has not been systematically collected.

The Valley of Oaxaca Settlement Pattern Project was begun during the summer of 1971. Monte Albán was the object of the first season of survey, but two additional summers, 1972 and 1973, were required to complete the detailed surface survey of that ancient city. In addition to working at Monte Albán during the summer of 1972, we began the surface survey of the valley away from the ancient capital. Dudley Varner carried out the survey of the valley's northern arm, the Etla Region (see Figure 1.1, p. 2), an area of roughly 200 km^2, which he was able to complete during the summer of 1973. From January to August 1974, Steve Kowalewski completed the survey of the valley's central region, encompassing some 260 km^2 (see Figure 1.1, p. 2). Our next goal is to survey the valley's expansive southern arm, hopefully to be completed during the winter and summer of 1977. The second volume of our Valley of Oaxaca Settlement Pattern Project series will be a summary and analysis of the data from these latter three surveys.

Acknowledgments

The major sources of funding for the Valley of Oaxaca Settlement Pattern Project have been NSF Grants GS-28547 and GS-38030, through the anthropology office. Further support has been provided from the Research Foundation of the City University of New York (Grants RF-10065 and RF-11145). In addition, the City University of New York Computer Center awarded computation time as well as making key-punch equipment and terminals available.

Ford Foundation grants supplied per diem and travel expenses for several students through the Departments of Anthropology of the University of Michigan and Rice University, Houston, Texas. The Texas Memorial Museum, in Austin, Texas, supplied surveying equipment for the 1971 and 1972 field seasons, a four-wheel-drive vehicle in 1971, and supported four students during the 1972 season. The Departments of Anthropology of Rice University and Hunter College, City University of New York, and the Department of Sociology and Anthropology, Purdue University, supplied field equipment, work and storage space, and secretarial help. Through the efforts of Dr. Blanche Blank and then-chairperson Melvin Ember, a grant was made by Hunter College to pay for the microfilming of the Monte Albán data. These microfilms are in the Regional Center of the Mexican Instituto Nacional de Antropología e Historia (I.N.A.H.) in Oaxaca, for use by visiting scholars.

I thank all those who participated in the Monte Albán survey and analysis. Although there are worse places in the world in which to do archaeological fieldwork, our days on the "hill" were not easy. Locating and mapping ancient features required more climbing up and down than most of us had ever done. The hot Oaxaca sun, bothersome insects, and prickly vegetation often made work uncomfortable. Work in the lab was at times equally tedious. During the summer of 1973, Steve Kowalewski, Chuck Spencer, and Elsa Redmond looked at sherds until they were "blue in the face." Jill Appel worked full-time for over a year preparing the various versions of the Monte Albán base map. Her persistence in the light of all the numerous details that had to be remembered and all the technical difficulties we had is to be admired. The following is a list of project personnel and their years of participation:

Director

Richard E. Blanton 1971–1976

Crew Leaders and Collaborating Archaeologists

Carl Kuttruff 1971–1976	James V. Neely 1971
Steve Kowalewski 1972–1976	Dudley Varner 1971–1973
Margie Lohse 1972–1973	Marcus Winter 1971

Field and Lab Assistants

Brenda R. Allen 1972–1973	Jenna Kuttruff 1971–1976
Paul Neil Allen 1971–1972	Alexis Lee 1973–1976
Bonnie Anderson 1976	Charlotte Lee 1974
Cameron Arcaro 1976	Roger Mason 1972
Tom Arcaro 1976	Joan Mancuso 1976
Jill Appel 1971–1976	Mike O'Brien 1971, 1972
Ira Beckerman 1972–1973	Paco Pinto-Torres 1971
Richard Belding 1971–1972	Michael Rowley 1974
Sharon Belding 1971–1972	Elsa Redmond 1972, 1973
Betty Brown 1972	Dolores Root 1973, 1974
Liz Brumfiel 1971	Mitchell Rothman 1975, 1976
Vincent Brumfiel 1971	Lisa Schiller 1972
Bruce Byland 1972–1973	Yda Schreuder 1972
Valerie Chevrette 1972–1973	Elizabeth Shropshire 1972
Melissa Crowfoot 1972	Charles Spencer 1971–1973
Margaret Curran 1977	Louis Sperling 1973
Gary Feinman 1975–1976	Alice Steinicke 1971
Eva Fisch 1975, 1976	Jane Terry 1976
Laura Henley 1972	Diana Traub 1975, 1976
John Keane 1972	

Of this list special gratitude is owed to Steve Kowalewski, Jill Appel, Carl Kuttruff, and Gary Feinman, whose creativity stimulated me to think about the Monte Albán data in ways I would not have otherwise done. I thank Kowalewski for his useful comments on the first draft of this manuscript.

I am also grateful to two people whose help has been of critical importance. As already mentioned, it was Kent Flannery's idea that such a survey project be started in the Valley of Oaxaca. My hope is that Flannery and the members of his Human Ecology Project will benefit as much from our work as we have from theirs. Dr. Ignacio Bernal, then director of Mexico's Museo Nacional de Antropología, has supplied encouragement and advice at many points. We wish to thank him especially for giving us a copy of the field notes from his original wide-ranging survey of the valley, in which he located and described 274 sites. These notes have facilitated, and will continue to facilitate our survey work because the time required to describe those sites is reduced.

In Mexico, our work was facilitated by those who helped to arrange our permit (*Concesión* No. 5/71), especially Arq. Ignacio Marquina and Arqgo. Eduardo Matos Moctezuma. Manuel Esparza, director of the Oaxaca Regional Center of the I.N.A.H., has facilitated our work in many ways.

I thank William Sanders, who visited Monte Albán with me in 1973 and made some very useful comments. George Cowgill gave me a copy of the Teotihuacan code book, which facilitated the preparation of the computer code for the Monte Albán data. I am also grateful to my archaeological colleagues at Hunter College, C.U.N.Y.: Chris Hamlin and John Speth spent much of their valuable time helping me learn how to use the City University computer, and with Greg Johnson I had useful discussions concerning various aspects of regional analysis. My 4 years at Hunter were very fruitful, due mostly to the stimulation provided by these three people.

During the course of a School of American Research seminar, organized by Kent Flannery, concerning the evolution of Mixtec and Zapotec civilizations, I was able to present some of my ideas on Monte Albán in the presence of Oaxaca specialists. Those discussions also proved to be valuable in the development of this work.

Finally, thanks are due for advice and help to Ignacio Armillas, Donald Brockington, Robert Drennan, Frank Hole, Joyce Marcus, John Paddock, Ronald Spores, Cecile Welte, Marcus Winter, and Robert Fry.

All royalties will go to the Museum of Anthropology, the University of Michigan, Account No. 361541, to be used for the publication of future volumes of our series on the prehispanic settlement patterns of the Valley of Oaxaca, in the series titled "Prehistory and Human Ecology of the Valley of Oaxaca," general editor Kent V. Flannery.

1

Introduction

The Valley of Oaxaca and Monte Albán

SETTING

The Valley of Oaxaca is situated roughly in the center of the Southern Highlands of Mexico, in the modern state of Oaxaca. It contains the largest expanse of relatively flat and therefore agriculturally valuable land in this highland block, totaling over 700 km^2. The valley floor ranges from 1420 to 1740 m in elevation, and the rugged mountains defining the valley's rim rise to more than 3000 m (Kirkby 1973:7). Water is the major limiting factor for valley agriculture because relatively little falls per year (ranging from about 600 mm on the valley floor to 1000 mm or more on the valley divide), because of pronounced year-to-year variability in rainfall, and because evaporation exceeds precipitation during most months, especially at the lower elevations where temperature, slope, and soils are best for farming (Kirkby 1973). Most agriculture, therefore, depends on some combination of canal irrigation, floodwater irrigation, or tapping the water table from wells.

The valley is Y-shaped, with three main subdivisions (Figure 1.1): To the north lies the Etla Valley or Etla Region; extending east is the Tlacolula Valley; the southern and largest valley arm is the Valle Grande, sometimes referred to as the Zaachila arm. Both the Etla arm and the Valle Grande are drained by the Atoyac, a seasonal stream, whereas the Tlacolula arm is drained by the Rio Salado, a similarly ephemeral stream that joins the Atoyac at the confluence of the valley's three arms. Just north of the meeting place of these two drainages is the contemporary capital of the state of Oaxaca, Oaxaca de Juarez (Figures 1.2 and 1.3). Across the Atoyac, west of the modern capital is a series of closely spaced hills, the largest of which is called Monte Albán. These hills, consisting of upturned strata of limestone and consolidated sandstone, rise from roughly 300 m to over 400 m above the valley floor. Even from a distance, dozens of mounds and hundreds of other cultural features can be seen stretching along the tops and sides of the hills. These ruins, which constitute the archaeological site of Monte Albán, apparently represent the ancient counterpart of the modern capital of the region, Oaxaca de Juarez. Unlike the modern city, however, which is situated on the valley floor, the ancient builders of the capital preferred an isolated hilltop location;

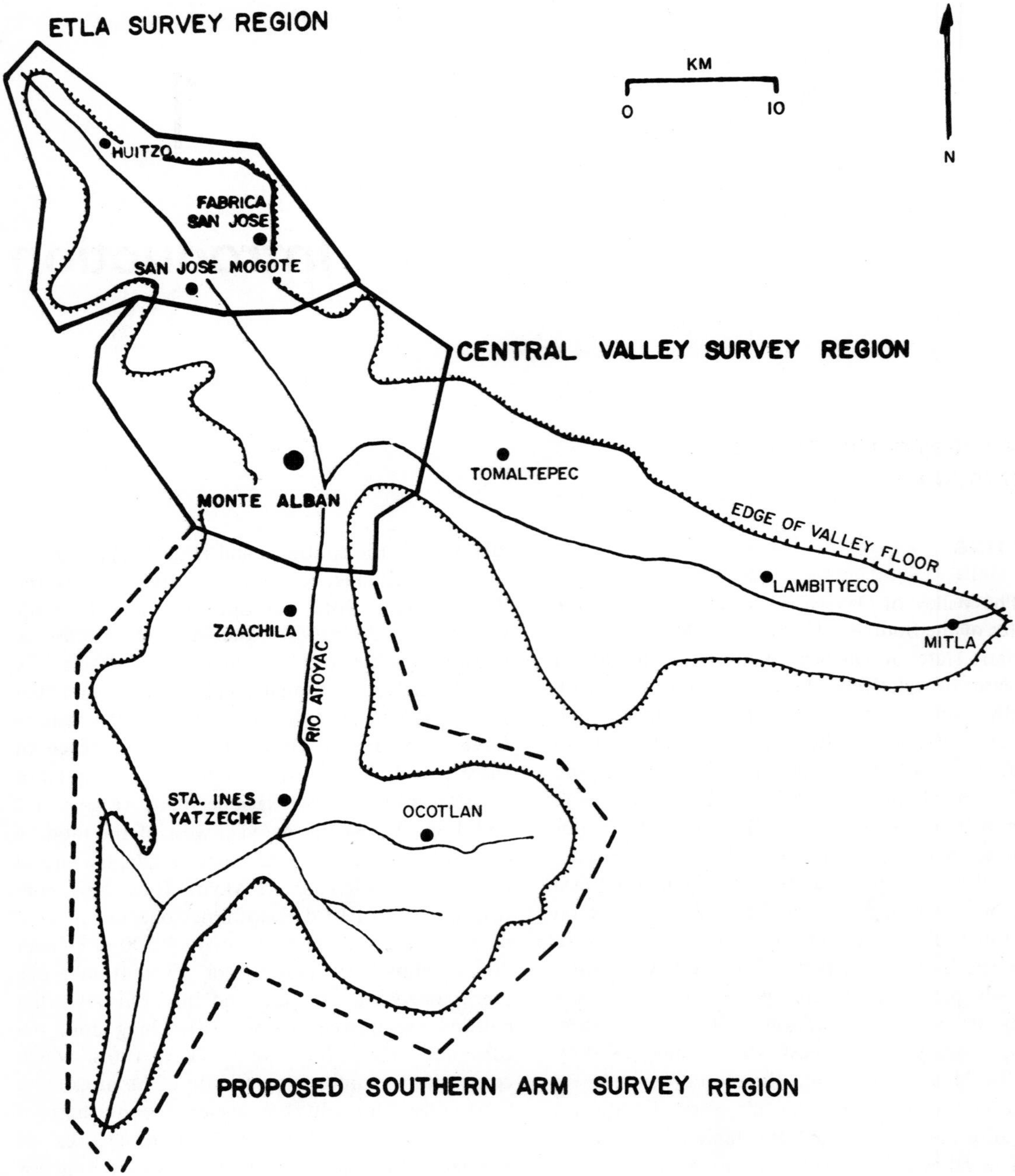

Figure 1.1. The Valley of Oaxaca, showing the survey regions and prominent archaeological sites and modern communities.

the reason for this preference will be discussed in the course of this study.

Several spatially discrete occupation zones make up the archaeological site of Monte Albán, although it was surely a single community in the eyes of its residents. The site, in other words, consists of a closely spaced cluster of hilltop residential zones. Hilltop or hillside locations were so desired by the occupants of the ancient city that once the readily habitable space on the major hill was fully colonized, new settlement took place not on the adjacent flat plain at the hill's base, but on nearby unused hilltops and slopes instead. Monte Albán dominates the group in bulk and elevation. At its highest point there is a rectangular flattened space, referred to as the Main Plaza, measuring some 300 m north–south by 100 m east–west, surrounded by prehispanic mounds larger than any south of Teotihuacan or Cholula (Plates 1 and 2). Surrounding this plaza and its platform mounds are archaeological features extending roughly a kilometer to the south, and nearly 2 km to the north, making up the largest contiguous built-up portion of the total site. This area will be referred to hereafter as "Monte Albán proper" (Figure 1.2). Extending east from Monte Albán proper is a long, rugged ridge called Monte Albán Chico (Figure 1.2). To the north of the main hill there are two smaller protuberances, El Gallo and Atzompa, both covered, as are Monte Albán and Monte

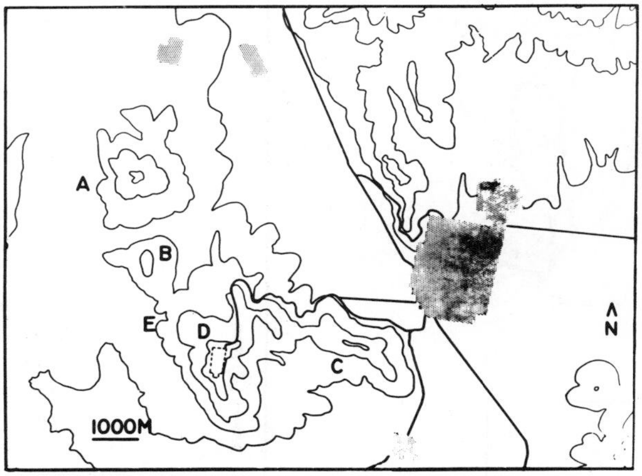

Figure 1.2. The central part of the Valley of Oaxaca. Contour interval is 100 m. The shaded areas are modern communities, the largest of which, in the figure's right center, is the modern capital, Oaxaca de Juarez. The darker lines are major modern roads. The group of mountains to the left of the center of the figure locate the archaeological site of Monte Albán which is composed of Atzompa (A), El Gallo (B), Monte Albán Chico (C), Monte Albán proper (D), and Mogollito, in the vicinity of (E). The dashed lines near the top of Monte Albán proper outline the Main Plaza.

Plate 1. Monte Albán's Main Plaza, looking south from the North Platform. The large mount at the south end of the plaza is the South Platform.

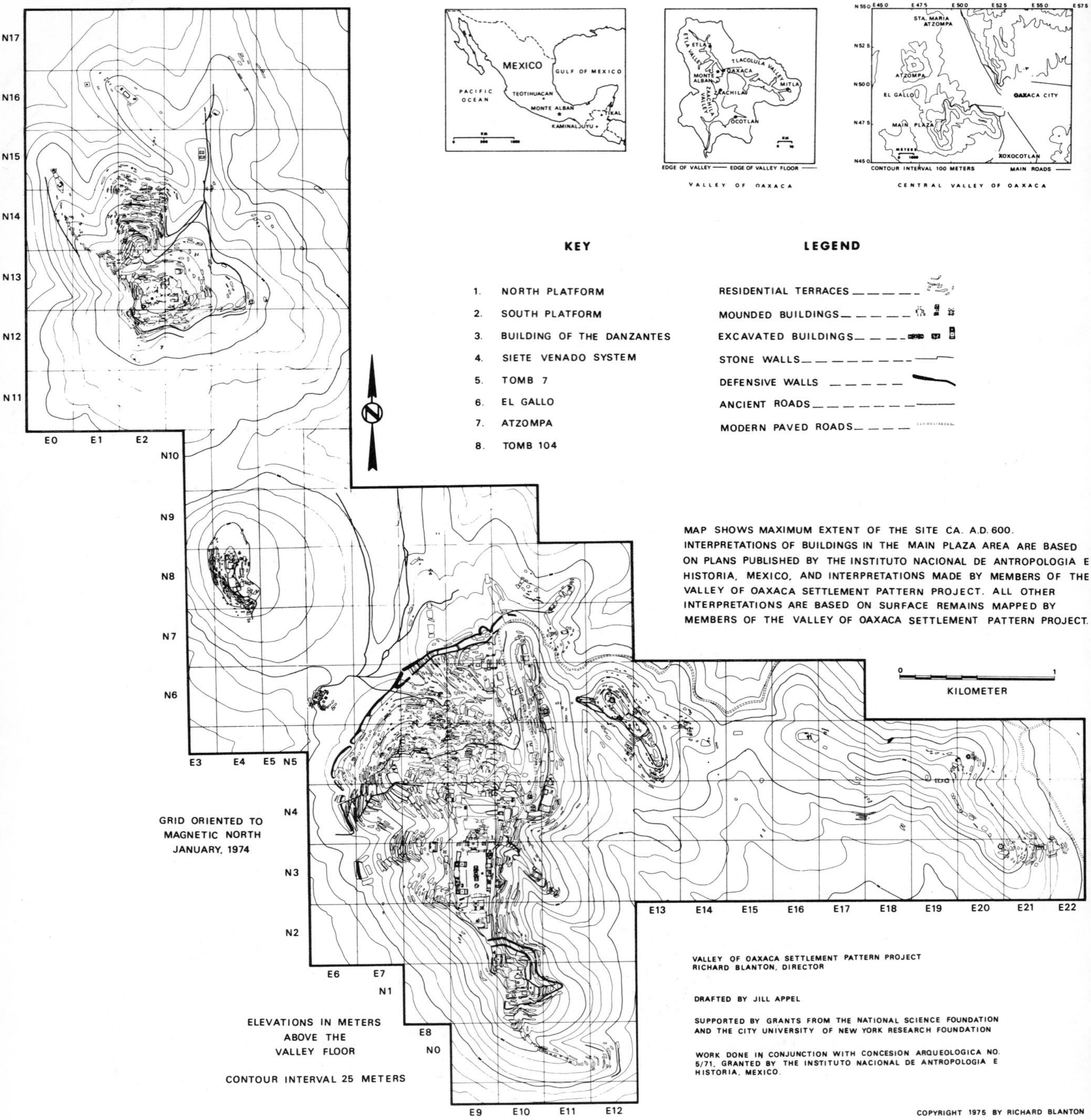

Figure 1.3. Archaeological and topographic map of Monte Albán.

Plate 2. Monte Albán's Main Plaza, looking north from the South Platform.

Plate 3. El Gallo (the nearer hill, to the left) and Atzompa (the farther hill, to the right of center), looking north from Monte Albán proper.

Albán Chico, with archaeological remains (Plate 3). A much smaller, but related group of archaeological features, called Mogollito, is situated at the base and to the northwest of Monte Albán proper (Figure 1.2).

ETYMOLOGY

The source of the name of the hill and site, Monte Albán, is uncertain, nor is it known what the indigenous name was. According to Cruz (1946:157–164), the site is sometimes referred to by local Zapotec speakers as *Danibaan* or 'sacred mountain'. Documents in Xoxocotlan, a Mixtec-speaking community at the base of Monte Albán proper, however, refer to it as the "Hill of the Jaguar" (CBA: 84).[1] According to Joyce Marcus (1976a:131), while there is a small amount of iconographic evidence at Monte Albán favoring the latter interpretation, it is still only conjecture that that was its ancient name. It is at least as likely that in prehispanic Mesoamerica jaguars were a general symbol associated with centers of power (cf. Wolf 1959:78), not to be interpreted as the names of specific places.

[1] CBA refers to Caso, Bernal, and Acosta (1967).

Caso (1970:14) traces the use of the name Monte Albán back to at least the seventeenth century, and suggests that it was derived from the name of one of the site's various owners. A number of the Spaniards who colonized Mexico were named Montalván or Monte Albán, and one in particular was known to have had frequent dealings with the son of Cortés, in whose *Marquesado* Monte Albán was probably included (Caso 1970).

PRIOR ARCHAEOLOGICAL WORK

The monumental ruins at Monte Albán have attracted explorers, antiquarians, and archaeologists for over a century. Three early visitors to the site, in particular, contributed useful information and illustrations, especially pertaining to the corpus of carved stone monuments (Dupaix 1834, 1969; Holmes 1897; and Batres 1902). Scientific archaeology was begun at the site by Alfonso Caso and his associates, particularly Ignacio Bernal and Jorge R. Acosta. Their Monte Albán project, which will be described more fully in later sections of this work, included 18 field seasons from 1931 to 1958. During this time they excavated over 170 tombs, cleared and reconstructed a number of buildings on the Main Plaza, and carried out stratigraphic excavations in several localities. The results of these field seasons have been summarized in a series of reports by Caso (1932, 1935, 1938, 1942), and in one by Acosta (1958). To date, three major works describing the results of this project have been published: Caso and Bernal (1952) reported on the urns and related artifacts; Caso *et al.* (1967) outlined the ceramic sequence and described the ceramic categories; and Caso (1970) described in detail the results of tomb excavations during the first field season, especially the contents of the well-known and spectacular Tomb 7. Reference can also be made to several other short works that have been written utilizing data from the Monte Albán Project (Acosta 1949; Bernal 1949; Sejourné 1960; Flannery and Marcus 1976a; Aveni and Linsley 1972).

Our settlement pattern study of Monte Albán began in 1971 at which time there was clearly a need for a detailed map of the site since no systematic map had ever been made, although Caso's project had produced abundant evidence of the site's large size and its complexity (cf. Bernal 1965:804–805). Prior to beginning the present volume, we had completed three preliminary reports (Blanton 1973, 1976b; Neely 1972), and one article (Blanton 1976a) describing the results of our mapping project. In 1972 and 1973 Marcus Winter carried out excavations in the residential zone of the city (Winter 1974; Winter and Payne 1976). In addition to the excavating and mapping at Monte Albán, there is also a long tradition of work on the epigraphy and iconography of the carved stone monuments there, begun by Caso (1928, 1947). More recently Joyce Marcus, a Maya epigrapher, has turned her attention to the Monte Albán materials (Marcus 1974, 1976a, b).

The following are useful summaries of one or more aspects of the archaeology of the Oaxaca region, including references to the role of Monte Albán in the region: Acosta (1965), Bernal (1965), Caso (1965a, b, c, d), Caso and Bernal (1965), Flannery and Marcus (1976a, b), Marquina (1964: Chapter 5), and Paddock (1966).

Methodology

INTRODUCTION

Our goal was to locate, map, describe, and surface-collect those archaeological features visible on the surface within the bounds of the ancient site of Monte Albán, thus contributing to measurement, inference, and hypothesis testing in the following areas:

1. Establishment of the site's ancient function and nature. In the recent literature, Monte Albán has been referred to as a city (Bernal 1965:804–805), ceremonial or civic–reli-

gious center (Willey 1966:145), elite center (Coe 1962:126), and necropolis(Gorenstein 1975)

2. Determination of changes through time in the extent and density of occupation of the site, and estimation of population based on these data
3. Outline of change through time in the city's internal organization, especially as this contributes to an understanding of changing patterns of political control and social stratification, as well as the city's changing regional role in these areas. Such inferences are based primarily on the patterns of spatial distribution of and variability in buildings categorized as civic and those categorized as residential
4. Elucidation of the nature of craft production and exchange within the community and its regional economic role. Relevant data can be found in the abundance and distribution of features defined as workshops, markets, and roads.

One of the difficulties we encountered during the course of the survey was that of restricting ourselves to the collection of data pertinent to these analytical goals alone since we had a very limited budget and only a short time in which to complete the survey. More information could have been collected in the field but was not, due to these constraints. For example, the architectural renditions of features presented in this volume cannot be considered final versions—in all cases we did them in such a way as to maximize the amount of information collected relevant to the kinds of problems just outlined, but omitted less relevant details.

THE INTERPRETATION OF VARIATION THROUGH TIME

The reader may wonder how change in patterns of behavior in the ancient community can be interpreted, since the data employed are all derived from the surface and should therefore pertain to the latest periods of occupation, prior periods having been buried. Fortunately, the stratigraphic excavations of Caso *et al.* (1967) supplied us with a five-period ceramic sequence. Plotting the distributions of sherds pertaining to these periods reflects the site's change through time in size and morphology. It is true that most of the inferences made pertaining to the city's economic and political organization apply to the period, probably around A.D. 600, that is referred to as Period IIIb, a time when the site reached its maximum size, and when most or all of the buildings now visible on the surface were probably utilized contemporaneously. Again, however, we have depended on the stratigraphic excavations of Caso's Monte Albán Project, and related sources of information, for evidence that the patterns inferable for Period IIIb can or cannot be projected backward in time. Massive abandonment of major buildings, documented by Caso and his associates, and a nearly complete change in the patterns of ceramic distribution pertaining to those periods following Period IIIb suggest that new modes of internal organization appeared and that the city's regional role changed.

FIELD METHODS

At Monte Albán our basic descriptive unit is the terrace, of which there are 2073 in an area of about 6.5 km^2. In a few localities there was evidence of ancient occupation in the absence of terracing. (These localities are referred to as "areas," and are described in Appendix VI.) Normally, however, terraces had to be built by the occupants of Monte Albán to support structures since the entire settlement was built on a series of hilltops. For the most part the structures that had been built atop the terraces, unless they had substantial platform mounds as bases, have eroded, been plowed down, or been covered by soil deposition from higher slopes, leaving evidence for their existence only in the form of wall or floor fragments, soil stains, dense scatters of construction stone, and/or low, often barely perceptible mounds. In some areas of the site, heavy plowing or soil deposition has obscured all of even these forms of evidence for structures. In these cases, since part of the goal of our study was to determine the extent and density of residential occupation of the city, we tried to assess whether or not the terrace had at one time supported residential structures, or whether the terrace was a nonresidential agricultural terrace. Often this was a difficult determination to make. Our assessments hinged on the presence and density of residential debris, especially potsherds and stone tools. A number of terraces were identified (located generally around the fringes of the site proper) that lacked residential structures and debris and that were probably therefore agricultural terraces. These have not been described in detail and will not be included in this report.

The bulk of terraces we mapped and described at Monte Albán we identified as residential terraces, following the criteria described. In some cases, however, terraces evidencing certain kinds of platform mounds may have served civic rather than residential functions. Identifying them as one or the other is, of course, an uncertain procedure when based, as it is here, on surface evidence alone. Excavation will be required to affirm each of our surface assessments of the functions of terraces ultimately, but these assessments will probably be accurate in general. When structures are visible on the surfaces of residential terraces, they are structures that generally resemble aboriginal residences in Mesoamerica—that is, containing one to several rectangular, contiguous rooms, or, often with several rooms situated around a patio. In some cases, these rooms around the patio are elevated on platform mounds. The structures on terraces identified as *civic* in function are different. Specifically, such structures consist of isolated mounds or "open" two-mound groups, adjacent to major roads. They would have lacked the privacy that residential constructions had since traffic flow in and out of such structures would have been unimpeded, permitting general access by the population at large. Civic, as used here, is a general term that refers to features used by the general public. The activities carried out in such places could have included marketing, the performance of rites, and/or the administration of government.

Monte Albán terraces range from as small as 5 m by 10 m or so, containing probably one small structure, to massive terraces as large as 300 m by 100 m, containing dozens of structures. The Main Plaza area, which is bordered by the largest platform mounds on the site, is actually a large terrace measuring roughly 750 m north–south by some 300 m east–west. The range in variation in surface areas of terraces and the spatial distribution of the various size classes of terraces are discussed in detail in Chapter 4.

Following our past practice in the Valley of Mexico surveys, aerial photographs were used in the field to locate terraces and other archaeological features. Detailed photogrammetric maps and plane table maps are of course much more accurate in locating features than are aerial photographs, but also substantially more expensive. Fortunately, especially in Monte Albán proper, terraces are often large and bordered by dense vegetation such that they show up prominently in the aerial photographs. Plate 4 shows the southern extension of Monte Albán proper, including the Main Plaza area, which is visible as a large white rectangle surrounded by platform mounds. Numerous ancient terraces can be seen in this photograph. The next photograph, Plate 5, an enlargement of Plate 4, centering on the area below the Main Plaza (or south, since the Main Plaza is oriented north–south), illustrates how we delineated and numbered archaeological features on the aerial photographs as we located and described them in the field. In some parts of the site, this procedure could not be followed for two reasons:

1. Seams in the aerial photographs at some points obliterated areas where terraces are present. Where this occurred, we made transect maps with

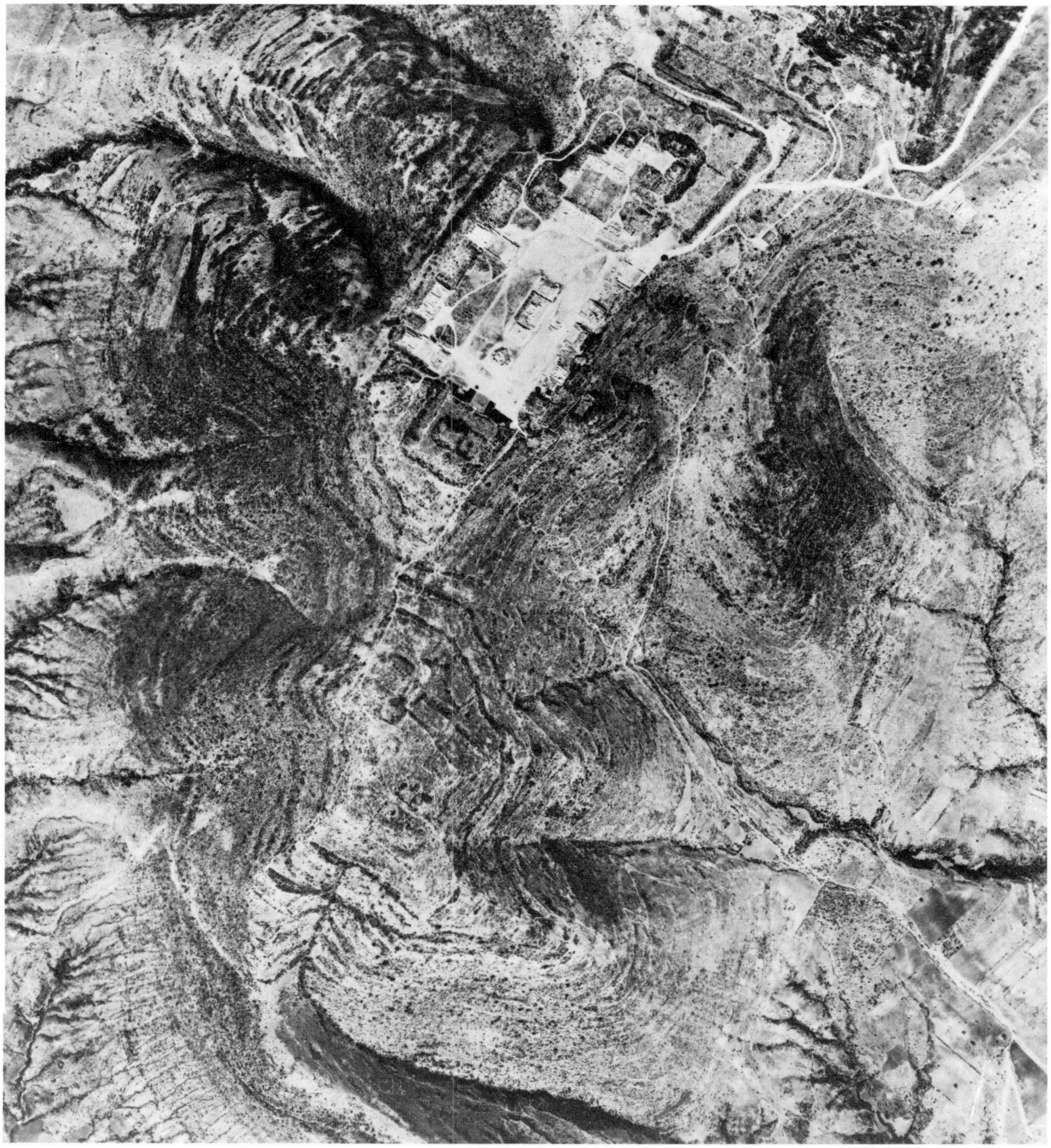

Plate 4. Aerial photograph of the southern extension of Monte Albán proper. The large light area bordered by platform mounds in the upper center of the photograph marks the Main Plaza. The modern paved road leading to the Main Plaza goes off to the upper right corner. The photograph is oriented roughly 45° east of north.

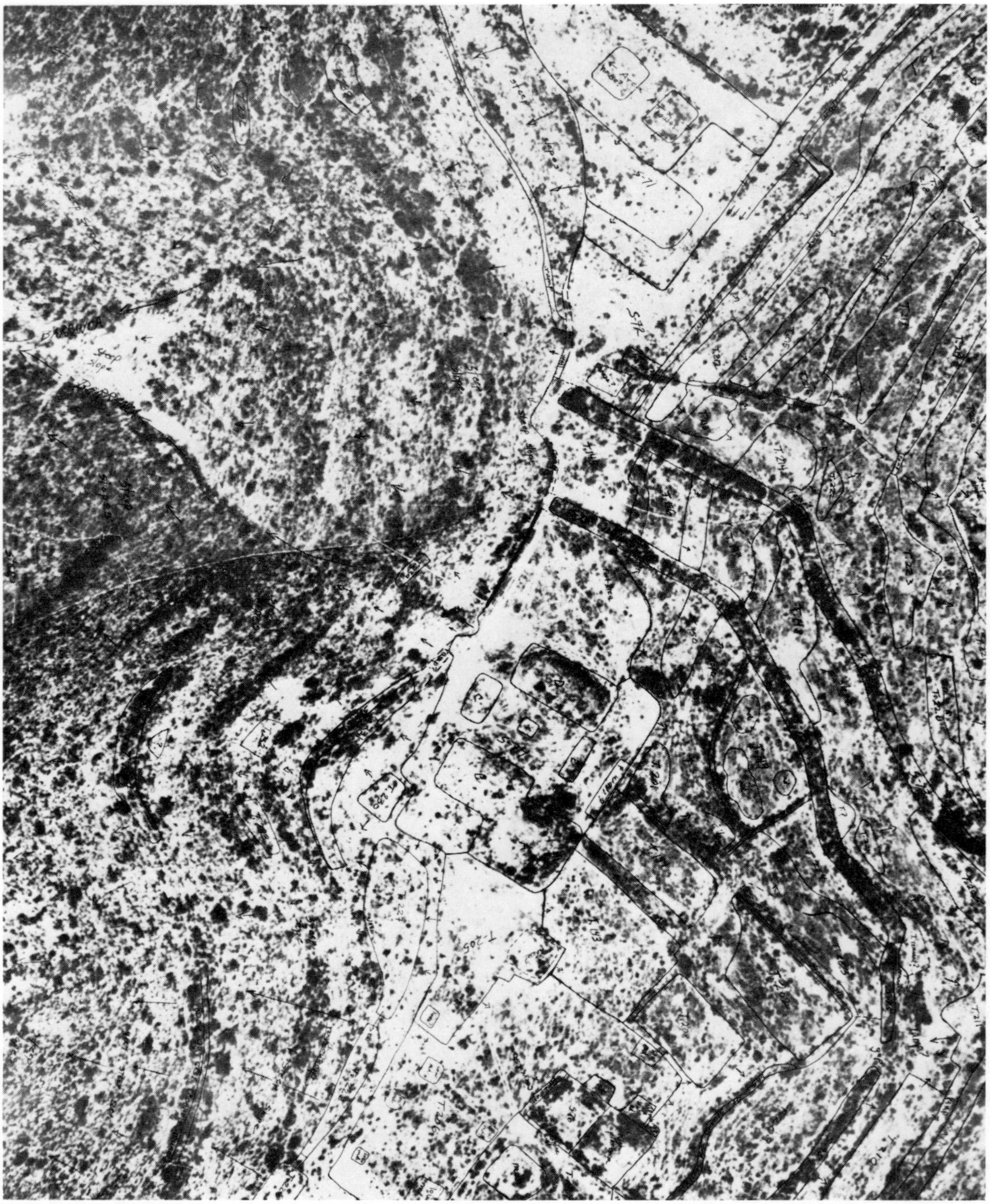

Plate 5. Enlargement of Plate 4, centered on an area just below left center of Plate 4. Archaeological features have been delineated and numbered.

Brunton compasses and tapes to ascertain the locations of the "lost" features.

2. Some terraces do not show up on the aerial photographs. This problem was especially acute on Monte Albán Chico and on Atzompa. For these two areas, the photographs we used in the field were 1:5000 enlargements of the standard 1:20,000 Valley of Oaxaca mosaics produced by the Compania Mexicana de Aerofoto, S.A. At this scale, the resolution is such that small terraces cannot be easily seen. The locations of such terraces on the aerial photographs were approximated according to their proximity to natural features such as trees and *barrancas*, 'drainage features', that do show up. We were fortunate in having a special set of aerial photographs, made by the same company, of Monte Albán proper and El Gallo, at a scale of 1:5000. These were enlarged for field use to a scale of roughly 1:1000. The resolution in this set of photos is much better than the 1:20,000 set, allowing more accurate placement of features.

Once located in the field, and drawn on the aerial photographs, terraces were assigned a number. The terraces on Monte Albán proper, Mogollito, and Monte Albán Chico have a continuous series of numbers from 1 to 1464 (although the following numbers were not used: 442–446, 448–450, 1349, 1366, 1417, and 1424). Terraces in this series are referred to by number only, preceded by the word *Terrace*. The El Gallo terraces have a separate series of numbers ranging from 1 to 139: In this volume, these particular terrace numbers are always preceded by E.G. Atzompa terraces also have a separate series of numbers ranging from 1 to 482: These numbers are preceded by an Az. when referred to here. After assigning a number, the descriptive procedures outlined below were followed for each terrace—unless it was determined that the terrace was agricultural, in which case no description was made nor numbers assigned:

1. A Brunton compass and tape map was made (in some cases pacing was substituted for tapes), usually at a scale of about 1:250 or 1:500, showing the dimensions of the terrace and the location of archaeological features when present. Defining the limits of terraces was often difficult. The outside, or downhill edges of terraces are usually easy to spot because retaining walls have generally remained intact, creating sharp boundaries. The uphill edges of terraces are more difficult to define normally because erosion from slope or terraces above has tended to obscure them. Our procedure was to locate the break in slope, even if only vaguely present, and consider that to be the upper boundary. In many cases this will probably not be found to be the precise ancient upper boundary of the terrace, but there is simply no means now of obtaining a more accurate measurement from the surface. Due to slope wash, this method of defining the upper boundaries of terraces results in general in some underestimate of the real terrace dimensions, but I estimate the error to be less than 5 to 10% for the site as a whole. In those parts of the site where erosion has been most severe, the error in terrace-area measurements is in some cases, no doubt, greater than this.

2. A surface collection was made of 50 to 100 sherds, figurines, and urn fragments. Rims and decorated sherds were emphasized since they are more likely to contain chronological information. For large terraces, larger collections were made. In some areas of the site where only Period IIIb materials are present, not every terrace was surface-collected, or only small collections were made. A total of roughly 1700 surface collections were made from the site, totaling approximately 25,000 diagnostic sherds (an additional 30,000 sherds collected were identified as to type, but have not been used in the preparation of this report since they all represent types lacking chronological diagnosticity). Collections of lithic materials were not normally made, for fear of confusing the results of future systematic random sampling of these items. The density and composition of lithic materials, however, were described in the survey form for each terrace, as well as could be done by surface inspection alone.

3. In most cases terraces and/or features were photographed.

4. A survey form was completed. These forms are based on those used in the Valley of Mexico surveys. The form is reprinted on page 13.

The pottery densities indicated in Section III, Part (*e*) on this form are identical to those defined by the Valley of Mexico researchers (Blanton 1972:18–20).

Field crews normally consisted of two to five people. The crew leader was responsible for locating terraces and drawing them on the aerial photograph after which crew members began the map and the search for artifacts and features. Once this was done, the survey form could be completed, usually by the crew leader. Sherds were then bagged and returned to the lab for washing, sorting, and tabulating.

LABORATORY WORK

In our laboratory in Oaxaca de Juarez, sherds were sorted and identified as to category by Steve Kowalewski, Chuck Spencer, and Elsa Redmond, and then tabulated. For the most part, the sherds were categorized following CBA (Caso *et al.* 1967), but some new categories were defined and some new variants of the CBA categories devised. Because of these changes we decided to employ a new designation system for the ceramic categories and to augment the descriptions of categories present in the original work. Appendix II (by Kowalewski, Spencer, and Redmond) contains the revised descriptions and category numbers, indicating also the CBA designation for each of our new categories, if one could be assigned. In the Hunter College laboratory in New York, these category tabulations were rearranged so that the terrace numbers appeared in numerical order. The counts for all but very rare categories were directly entered onto disc format using the City University of New York Computer Center's "WYLBUR" text-editing system. Once entered and checked, the data were then stored on both card and tape format for later use. Part 1 of Appendix III in this volume was produced by listing this data set on white paper. Part 2 contains the hand-tabulated totals for the rare ceramic categories not included in Part 1.

The next stage consisted of measuring the surface areas of terraces, whole structures, and patios from the field maps, and calculating the volumes of platform mounds. Once this was completed, all the terrace forms and maps were examined and the data coded following the coding scheme described in the introduction to Appendix I, Part 1. Those categories not readily codable (such as comments) are contained in Appendix I, Part 2. In coding the terrace data, Opti-Scan coding sheets were used which were read by the computer center of the University of Pennsylvania and converted to card format. The cards were in turn read by the City University of New York computer, and the data stored on the WYLBUR file, where they were readily available for checking, editing, and analysis. Checking the terrace data involved complete cross-checking with the original sources for some variables, and a sample was checked of all other variables. The results indicate a high degree of accuracy and consistency; the data set is reproduced in Appendix I, Part 1.

THE MONTE ALBÁN MAP

Inside the back cover is a 1:10,000 copy of the final Monte Albán map. (Figure 1.3 on p. 4 is a smaller version of this same map.) Portrayed here are the residential terraces, civic buildings, roads, stone boundary walls, and defensive walls, as well as the modern paved road (in dashed lines). The map represents the community at its height, probably around A.D. 600, when, as far as can be established, all features visible on the surface were contemporaneously in use.

The placement of features on the Monte Albán map is based on tracings from the aerial photographs used in the field, but with some modifications which were necessary for two reasons. First, as mentioned earlier, seams in the aerial photographs eliminated some occupied areas, necessitat-

Survey Form

Terrace, Area number ______ Recorder ______
Square *(i.e., aerial photo number. These are not used in this report.)*
Date______

I. Natural setting of the unit:
  a. Topography
    Gentle slope Small alluvial fan
    Hilltop Ridgetop
    Other Steep slope
  b. Description of soil color, texture, depth, and degree of erosion
  c. Hydrography: springs *barrancas* washes
  d. Vegetation type and abundance:
  e. Special resources:

II. Modern cultural features:
  a. Structures:
  b. Agricultural use:

III. Prehistoric features:
  a. Condition of the unit (erosion, pitting, etc):
  b. Terrace description:
  c. Specialized features (walls, flooring, etc.):
  d. Miscellaneous artifacts—indicate relative abundance:
    Obsidian
    Other chipped stone
    Ground stone
      manos
      metates
      celts
      pestles and mortars
    Figurines
    Spindle whorls
    Pottery discs
    Other
  e. Pottery
    1. Quantity and distribution
      NONE EVEN
      SPARCE LOCALIZED
      MODERATE
      HEAVY
    2. Periodization:

	Present	Some	Well represented	Dominant
Early I				
Late I				
II				
IIIa				
IIIb–IV				
V				
Other				

  f. Depth and nature of the archaeological deposit

IV. Miscellaneous data:

V. Problems, summaries, impressions:

ing that we locate terraces using transects which were inserted during the production of the map by adjusting the locations of adjacent terraces until what appeared to be a good fit was achieved. Second, the tracings from the aerial photographs (which had been enlarged using a "camera lucida" device) were fitted to the site's contour map which was supplied to us by the Mexican *Dirección General de Aeronautica Civil, Depto. de Aerodromos*. It is a photogrammetric map at a scale of 1: 25,000, with 25-m contour intervals, which was enlarged again using the camera lucida, to a working scale of 1:2000; the tracings were fitted from the aerial photographs over it. As is to be expected, there was considerable difficulty fitting the two maps together due in part to distortions and seams in the aerial photographs and to inaccuracies in the photogrammetric map which had been drawn in connection with the construction of the new airport to the south of Oaxaca de Juarez and been designed to serve as a topographic guide for pilots landing there. For this reason, the photogrammetric map was not done with great accuracy in mind, and some errors are present. Where these were obvious, the appropriate changes were made, based on recollection of the topography and/or on the aerial photographs. Most of the discrepancies lay in the area along the lower north slopes of Monte Albán proper.

The next stage in the production of the map entailed reducing the field drawings of archaeological features from their variety of scales down to the working scale of 1:2000. The scaled features were then placed on the map according to the airphoto tracings and the modifications of the tracings, and a penultimate ink tracing was made on large pieces of graph paper at which point the Main Plaza was added to the map. Our version of it is based on two published versions made by Caso's Monte Albán Project (Caso 1970: *Plano Topográfico de Monte Albán Antes de la Exploración*; and Marquina 1964: *Lámina* 86), with some modifications based on information we collected during the course of our field seasons. The placement of the Main Plaza was based both on topographic considerations and according to its placement in the 1:25,000 photogrammetric map. On our map, it was located according to the grid on the photogrammetric map, which was oriented to magnetic north, since we had determined that the orientation of the staircase of the large mound on the south end of the plaza (the South Platform) was within 1° of east–west. At this point an arbitrary grid was superimposed over the entire site, oriented as closely as possible to magnetic north, using the staircase of the South Platform as a baseline.

Each grid square, representing an area 300 m east–west by 400 m north–south, appears in Appendix VII at a scale of 1:2000. These squares are numbered according to their locations east and north of an imaginary original point to the lower left of the map. The Monte Albán map extends 22 squares east and 17 squares north (some squares near the site boundaries are somewhat narrower than the majority). Each grid square is numbered, with the number of squares north of the origin indicated first, followed by the east square number. The Main Plaza, for example, fills most of square N3E9.

With the addition of the grid, the penultimate 1:2000 map was completed. Because this map was so large (extending over about one-fourth of the area of my lab!), we had to cut it up prior to final tracing on white vellum. These final ink-on-vellum sections were then photographically reduced to a scale of 1:10,000. Because of slight distortions in the camera lens, the sections so reduced could not be fitted back together perfectly. This has resulted in a small amount of distortion along the east edge of the E5 row of squares from N6 to N10, and along the west edge of the E12 row from N3 to N6. This composite map was glued to white vellum, the lettering and additional maps added, and again, sent off to the photographer. Several different attempts were then made to insure the right thickness of line, and so on, but finally an acceptable 1:10,000 version was produced. Needless to say, after all the hard work, discouragements, map sections that would not fit together, and so forth, we were extremely happy to see this final version. The last stage was the preparation of the individual grid squares for publication, which involved adding the terrace numbers (see Appendix VII).

LIMITATIONS OF THE MONTE ALBÁN MAP

Obviously a map made in the manner just described has certain limitations. We feel, however, that it is more than adequate for the goals of our project, while at the same time its cost was consonant with our limited budget. The relative placement of features is correct, and the distances between closely spaced features are accurate for our purposes. Because of the possibility of cumulative errors in the placement of features, however, long-distance measurements will undoubtedly be less reliable. There were several junctures in the preparation of the map at which errors could have been introduced:

1. Distortions in the aerial photographs used to locate terraces were undoubtedly present and difficult to assess or correct, due to distortions in the lenses of the cameras used to take and enlarge the photographs, due to seams in the mosaics, and due to vertical distortion where there was considerable topographic relief (areas higher up and closer to the camera look larger than they should).
2. A small amount of distortion is also introduced by the lens in the camera lucida used to enlarge and reduce various components of the map.
3. I have already discussed the inaccuracies encountered in the 1:25,000 photogrammetric map used as a base map.
4. Finally, some errors remained in the 1:2000 working map that were incorporated into the final 1:10,000 version, involving the scales and orientations of several terraces. These errors have all been corrected in the 1:2000 map sheets that make up Appendix VII.

THE DETERMINATION OF SITE BOUNDARIES

For the most part, Monte Albán's boundaries are discrete and easy to pinpoint. The only exceptions to this are along some portions of Monte Albán Chico where terraces are in some cases widely scattered, and along the north-extending ridges of Atzompa, where terraces are similarly widely spaced. A few such scattered terraces and other evidence for occupation also exist north of Monte Albán, in squares N7 and 8, E8 and 9. Because the site boundaries are generally discrete, we had little or no trouble in deciding on our survey boundaries. Usually a strip of at least several hundred meters wide was examined beyond what appeared to be the limit of terracing or other evidence of occupation to assure that the edge had in fact been encountered, and in some cases a much wider area was investigated. Our determination of site boundaries has been substantiated by Steve Kowalewski's survey of the central portion of the Valley of Oaxaca, the area surrounding Monte Albán (Kowalewski 1976). The modern community called *Colonia 3 de Mayo* has grown over some Monte Albán terraces in the vicinity of N4E21 and 22. Here our estimate of the site's boundary may be slightly inaccurate since some ancient terraces have been destroyed. The paucity of prehispanic sherds in the *colonia*, however, suggests that only a small part of the ancient community has actually been destroyed or covered. Similarly, the activities of modern occupants of Sta. María Atzompa on the north slope of the hill of the same name may have destroyed some ancient features. Steve Kowalewski wrote the following description of this area, which includes squares N17, E3 and 4, and the ridge included in these squares as it extends north of the Monte Albán map:

> Pottery is sparse but includes Periods Late I, II, IIIb or IV, V [these are periods in the Monte Albán ceramic sequence, to be discussed below], colonial, and recent. Some [ancient] terracing is evident, but in general the area is quite eroded so that a good map would be difficult. The west slope appears to have been more heavily occupied than the east. There is a mound complex on the ridge top, with very small structures not more than 1 m high. A possible ancient road or terrace edge runs for ca. 100 m or more along the west edge of the ridge top. At least two ancient roads–one on the ridge top, and one further down the west slope–are evident, which were probably the major access ways to the Period IIIb community on the hill-top. Vegetation in this area is just grass, soil generally thin. Near the modern town, especially on the east side of the ridge, fields are separated from one another by roughly ½ m changes in elevation and very small stone alignments. These may be the remains of ancient terraces or simply field boundaries.

To conclude, while there is some evidence for scattered use of this vicinity in prehispanic times, it was probably not an important part of the ancient community here, which, as is evident from the Monte Albán map, was mostly concentrated along the top of the hill.

CHRONOLOGY OF THE WORK

Survey began on Monte Albán, around the edges of the Main Plaza, during the summer of 1971. The following summer, Carl Kuttruff and his crew completed the map of Monte Albán Chico; Steve Kowalewski and his crew completed Atzompa; Charles Spencer and his crew completed El Gallo, while I continued to work on Monte Albán proper. During the summer of 1973, the survey of Monte Albán proper was completed and all sherds identified as to category and tabulated. I made two additional short visits to the site during January 1974, and August 1974, to clean up a few details and correct field maps where scales or orientations had been omitted. Coding and entry into the computer of the ceramic and terrace data sets began during the fall of 1973 and continued through the summer of 1975. The Monte Albán map was completed during the period September 1973 to August 1975, and analyses of the data and the preparation of the 1:2000 map sheets were in progress from the fall of 1975 through the summer of 1976.

A COMPARISON OF THE MONTE ALBÁN SURVEY AND MAP WITH MILLON'S TEOTIHUACAN SURVEY AND MAP

We have attempted in every way possible to make data collection at Monte Albán comparable to that of René Millon's group at Teotihuacan. In part this is impossible because the two sites differ substantially from one another with respect to residential patterns, layout, and other features. There is no evidence of terraces at Teotihuacan, which are the most convenient units of description and surface collection at Monte Albán, since the former city was built in the middle of a flat-bottomed valley. Millon's minimum unit of description at Teotihuacan is the "site," of which there are about 5000 in an area of roughly 20 km^2 (Millon 1973:16). A *site* at Teotihuacan is a structure such as a building or an open space defined by buildings. Each such site was described architecturally and mapped, usually by Brunton compass and tape, and surface-collected. These procedures are very similar to our own at Monte Albán, and the survey forms completed for each Teotihuacan site contain essentially the same information as the Monte Albán survey forms (cf. Millon 1973: Figure 11). The surface collections at Teotihuacan differed from ours in that they systematically included stone implements, whereas ours did not, and it is my impression that in general more sherds were picked up by Millon's crews per site than we picked up per terrace. According to Millon, surface collections from individual sites normally numbered at least 100 sherds (Millon 1973:16). Our average was only 35 sherds collected per terrace that eventually were tabulated. This lower figure is due to two factors: First, collections from the hundreds of small pure Period IIIb terraces tended to be small, since there was no difficulty in establishing periodicity, and, second, some sherds collected in the field proved difficult to categorize once they were washed, and hence were not tabulated.

The major difference between the two surveys lies in the preparation of the maps. Millon contracted a special photogrammetric map of the entire site area, with 1-m contour intervals. The specifications for this map stated that the bulk of contours over the whole site be accurate to within 50 cm, that horizontal accuracy for at least 90% of well-defined features be within 1.25 m, and that all modern cultural features and most of the vegetation be included (Millon 1973:8–12). This map, divided into blocks representing 500 m on a side, and printed on Cronaflex, was used as a field map. While it would obviously have been desirable to have such a detailed and accurate map made of Monte Albán, we feel that a map based largely on aerial photographs, even with the attendant problems, is suitable in the light of the goals of our project.

The publication of the Teotihuacan map also differs from the maps included in this volume. While the 1:10,000 maps of the two sites are very similar in terms of the extent of detail portrayed (I refer to Millon 1973: Map 1), the 1:2000 individual map sheets of Teotihuacan are much more detailed than the 1:2000 maps included in Appendix VII of this volume. The 1:2000 map sheets of Teotihuacan represent the 500-m square sections of the photogrammetric map, and show all modern features. Clear plastic overlays for each of these sheets indicate the interpretations of ancient architectural features made by Teotihuacan Project personnel. The 1:2000 map sheets included in Appendix VII of this volume compare, in a sense, only to the clear plastic overlays in Millon's volume. That is, they show our interpretations of the prehispanic features (including just a few modern cultural features such as roads) along with the gross contour lines derived from the 1:25,000 photogrammetric map.

AN ASSESSMENT OF THE VALIDITY OF OUR METHODOLOGY

One kind of data to be used in this analysis, similar to settlement pattern studies done elsewhere, is that pertaining to the differential distribution of artifacts visible on the surface—I maintain that such distributions reflect differential patterns of deposition of artifacts in the past. For example, elite items should show more frequency of occurrence around elite activity areas. Workshops should appear as concentrations of products produced, used, or discarded in production, e.g., "kiln wasters" around pottery producing sites. Some critics of this methodology question these assumptions, and tend to believe only what comes from in situ contexts, since, they argue, different surface conditions artificially create different patterns in surface artifact densities, irrespective of variability in deposition patterns. For example, a critic would argue that more surface artifacts will be found in areas with sparse vegetation than in areas with dense vegetation, and more artifacts should be found in recently plowed areas, because plowing both removes vegetation and brings artifacts to the surface. Since we recorded the major aspects of the contemporary environment of terraces, including the density of vegetation and recency of plowing, it is possible to evaluate such criticisms. To do this I looked at the distribution of several frequently found artifact classes. Table 1.1 lists the results of the cross-tabulations of these artifact classes (as well as the presence of moderate to dense deposits of pottery) with two features of the modern environment of terraces: the presence of moderate to heavy vegetation and evidence for recent plowing (within 2 years). The expected values for each occurrence of each vari-

Table 1.1. Cross-Tabulations of Selected Artifact Classes with Modern Environmental Conditions

	Observed	Expected	χ^{2a}	Phi[b]
a. Artifact occurrences on terraces with moderate to heavy vegetation				
Obsidian	721	641	83.3*	.2
Other chipped stone	1046	1026	4.8	.05
Manos	313	296	5.8	.05
Metates	145	133	5.2	.05
Figurines	412	379	18.5*	.1
Shell	129	111	14.3*	.08
Urns	171	183	4.8	.05
Moderate pottery density	18	76	225.6*	.33
b. Artifact occurrences recently plowed terraces				
Obsidian	159	150	.9	.02
Other chipped stone	278	240	18.6*	.1
Manos	113	69	40.4*	.14
Metates	32	31	.003	.004
Figurines	101	89	2.5	.04
Shell	18	26	2.9	.04
Urns	51	43	1.8	.03
Moderate pottery density	37	17	28.*	.12

*Signifies statistical significance above the .01 level.
[a]All χ^2 values are rounded to the nearest tenth.
[b]All Phi values are rounded to the nearest hundredth.

able are given; these are the values expected if it were the case that no association or disassociation existed between the pairs of variables. Phi coefficients and χ^2 values have been calculated for each variable pair to aid in the assessment of strengths of relationships between the variables (all of these calculations and those in the remainder of this volume were done by the City University of New York computer, using "SPSS Version 6" statistical programs). The results do not generally support the criticisms of our methodology; they do show, however, that some of the artifact classes that we believe were generally distributed on the site (i.e., utilized in all households) do have some tendency to appear more frequently on recently plowed terraces. Moderate to heavy pottery concentrations, chipped stone tools other than obsidian (mostly the local cherts and quartzite), and manos exhibit this pattern. In part, however, these associations may be misleading. For example, as will be described in Chapter 3, those areas of the site that may have contained mano workshops, as determined by criteria other than density, have a higher than normal density of manos, and today happen to be heavily plowed. Other parts of the site that have also been heavily plowed, for example, over most of El Gallo, and the north slope of Atzompa, have relatively few manos (Chapter 4 contains a discussion of the distribution of workshops).

Both marine shell and obsidian, rare items that I would argue had differential patterns of deposition in ancient times (because they were obtainable only through long-distance trade), fail to conform to the critic's hypothesis. The small χ^2 value that resulted from the obsidian contingency table suggests that its occurrence is statistically independent of plowing. Marine shell actually was noted on fewer than expected plowed terraces because, as I will point out in Chapter 3, much of it was found in and around what were probably shell workshops in an area that happens to be unplowed today. Urns, figurines, and metates, items that were probably used generally by all households, show little statistical association with recency of plowing—further evidence that plowed fields do not reliably contain more types and numbers of artifacts.

Similarly, the results of cross-tabulations of artifact occurrences and vegetation density generally fail to support the critic's hypothesis. Pottery density is the exception and does conform to the critic's argument. That is, moderate to heavy pottery deposits were found less often than expected on terraces with moderate to heavy vegetation. Urns, a general-use artifact category, also show a slight tendency to occur more often on terraces with sparce vegetation than expected. All other artifact categories cross-tabulated here, however, were found more often on terraces with dense vegetation than expected, in general because those areas of the site that had the longest and most dense occupation, in ancient times are also, quite by chance the most densely vegetated areas today. In part this is true because this "core" area is protected by the Mexican government and is less heavily grazed than the remainder of the site. Some portions of Monte Albán that were occupied during only one or two periods and were less densely occupied, also happen to be areas which today are heavily grazed and so have a relatively light vegetation cover.

I conclude that for the most part the differential occurrence of artifacts on the surface of Monte Albán is not attributable to variation in modern conditions that affect surface-collecting, but is due for the most part to differential patterns of artifact deposition in the past.

Contemporary Monte Albán

INTRODUCTION

By comparison with most major Highland Mexican archaeological sites, Monte Albán is in reasonably good condition. Its remote hilltop location and relative agricultural marginality have protected it from intensive recent use, and no human community has been situated on the site since the Conquest. Further, the Mexican government has kept a watchful eye over the site for a number of years, especially that part of it in the vicinity of the Main Plaza. The situation is not entirely a happy one, however. Terraces are being damaged more and more every year due to a combination of plowing, overgrazing, the beginnings of encroachment of *colonias* that are extensions of Oaxaca de Juarez, and pot hunting. The growth of *colonias* threaten Monte Albán especially along the eastern extremity of Monte Albán Chico (squares N4,E21 and 22). This problem also threatens terraces in the vicinity of squares N7 and 8, and E11. To a lesser extent, the modern village of Los Ibañez threatens archaeological features in Mogollito (square N6E6).

THE MONTE ALBÁN SITE SUBDIVISIONS

Before describing the patterns of damage to archaeological features at Monte Albán due to pot hunting, grazing, plowing, and erosion, I will explain the method used to subdivide the site, since the data are summarized according to these subdivisions. The subunits within the site are, I feel, unlike the arbitrary grid squares, cultural units, perhaps comparable to the *barrios* of modern communities in parts of Mexico. I have defined these units on the basis of the distribution of civic and elite residential buildings within the site. Carl Kuttruff first noted that the large mound groups outside the Main Plaza area tend to occur more or less evenly spaced from one another in Monte Albán proper. By mound group we mean two to four platform mounds facing a common plaza or patio, occasionally with a small attached platform. Platform mounds are distinguished from the low mounds that are the remains of residential buildings, but where no intentional platform was constructed. I arbitrarily defined platform mounds as those that today are at least 1 m in elevation—sure evidence that a platform was constructed. These evenly spaced mounds typically do not consist of a single-mound group, but rather a cluster of mound groups, that sometimes include an isolated mound.

The clustered distribution of mound groups can be quantitatively demonstrated through the use of the Clark and Evans "nearest neighbor" statistic (Clark and Evans 1954) which expresses the extent to which points in a space exhibit regular, random, or clustered distribution. To calculate the nearest-neighbor value for mound groups within Monte Albán proper, the distances from the edges of mound groups or isolated mounds to the edges of nearest mound groups or isolated mounds were measured. These measurements considered both horizontal and vertical distances between mound groups or mounds. The statistic is given by:

$$R = \frac{\Sigma r/n}{(2\sqrt{d})^{-1}}$$

where r = the nearest-neighbor values, and d = density (number of points per square unit of measurement). If all points are located in the same place, the R will equal 0 (maximum clustering); if the points are randomly spaced, R will equal 1; and if evenly spaced, R will equal 2.1491 (Clark and Evans 1954). Values less than 1, then, indicate clustering. The nearest-neighbor value derived for mound groups in Monte Albán proper is .723, indicating a tendency to cluster. To identify these clusters, a histogram of the nearest-neighbor values was prepared (Figure 1.4). The bulk of these values occur in a mode below 60 m, and a discontinuity exists between this mode and all other values, above 70 m. I then drew lines around the mounds and mound groups that are 60 m or less from one another. Surprisingly, each of these mound group clusters, with the exception of the cluster that includes the Main Plaza (which was considered to be one mound group), has the same composition. Each consists of one or two closed mound groups that look like elite residences, plus one open single-mound or double-mound group that resembles

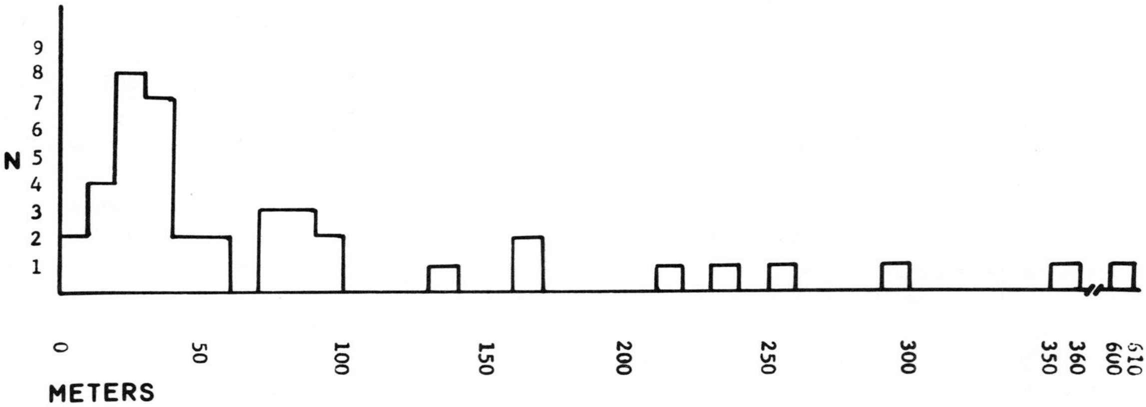

Figure 1.4. Histogram of mound and mound group nearest-neighbor values, Monte Albán proper only.

a civic building. The group of mounds near the Main Plaza are different in that they are all probably elite residences. Terrace 453 (in the northeast corner of N6E9 and adjacent squares) is a single-mound group, but has the same composition as the other mound group clusters, namely an open area between two large mounds plus a space containing two mounds that are closed off from the open area by stone walls. These more isolated features may have been elite residences. Another surprising feature of the mound group clusters is that, as I will demonstrate, each is directly adjacent to a major ancient road, therefore easily accessible; this is especially true from the civic component of each cluster. Furthermore, each mound group cluster is located at or near the center of a group of residential terraces, suggesting the clusters were neighborhood or *barrio* focuses. If one looks at the other parts of the site (Atzompa, El Gallo, Monte Albán Chico, Mogollito), this same pattern is present—that is, groups of residential terraces are in each case dominated by mound clusters consisting of one or more closed groups plus one or more open areas with a single- or double-mound group. One other cluster of mounds is found along the ridge running north along the northeast edge of Monte Albán proper. This group consists of a probable elite residence sitting on a high promontory (Terrace 1460, square N6E11), plus one large and one small isolated mound (Terraces 491 and 1448), on the nearest flat space to the north, adjacent to a major road. The fact that this cluster has the typical composition and is surrounded by a discrete group of residential terraces is suggestive that it be considered a mound group cluster even though it is less clustered than the others.

Figure 1.5 shows the mound group clusters, each outlined with dashed lines. Fifteen such clusters are discernible. As mentioned, each mound group cluster is near the center of a group of residential terraces, suggesting the clusters may have served as the focuses of certain kinds of neighborhood activities. More specifically, if I have been correct in my imputation of elite versus civic functions of the mound groups comprising the clusters, it is possible to infer that the clusters combined elite activities and some civic functions. The elite residences, for example, could have been the residences of top-ranking families of corporate groups perhaps analogous to the Aztec *Calputin*. The civic buildings may have been markets, ritual spaces, or had other similar functions for the adjacent population, requiring the buildings be easily accessible. In the absence of more data, it will not be possible to specify the functions of these buildings with great accuracy, but these seem to be reasonable possibilities.

In order to determine which terraces may have been associated with which mound group clusters, I drew Thiessen Polygons (Bogue 1949), which is a simple geometric method for identifying regions associated with particular features, such as cities, or in this case, mound group clusters (this procedure was not required, obviously, for those parts of the site where mound group clusters and associated terraces are spatially discrete, for example, Atzompa and El Gallo). To derive the polygons surrounding the clusters of mound groups, I drew lines from closest edge to closest edge of the clusters, then identified the polygon boundaries by bisecting these lines. Figure 1.6 shows the polygons thus derived, numbered from 1 through 15. Since this method involves bisecting lines drawn between mound group clusters, the resulting polygons or site subdivisions are smaller where the mound group clusters are more closely spaced, and larger where they are more widely separated. Are the site subdivisions thus derived completely arbitrary, or do they reflect reality? This is a difficult question to answer, but there is some evidence they were meaningful in ancient times. For example, the large outer defensive wall built, apparently, to isolate site subdivision 1 from the rest of the community, falls exactly on the subdivision line separating it from subdivision 2 possibly indicating the presence there of a recognized ancient

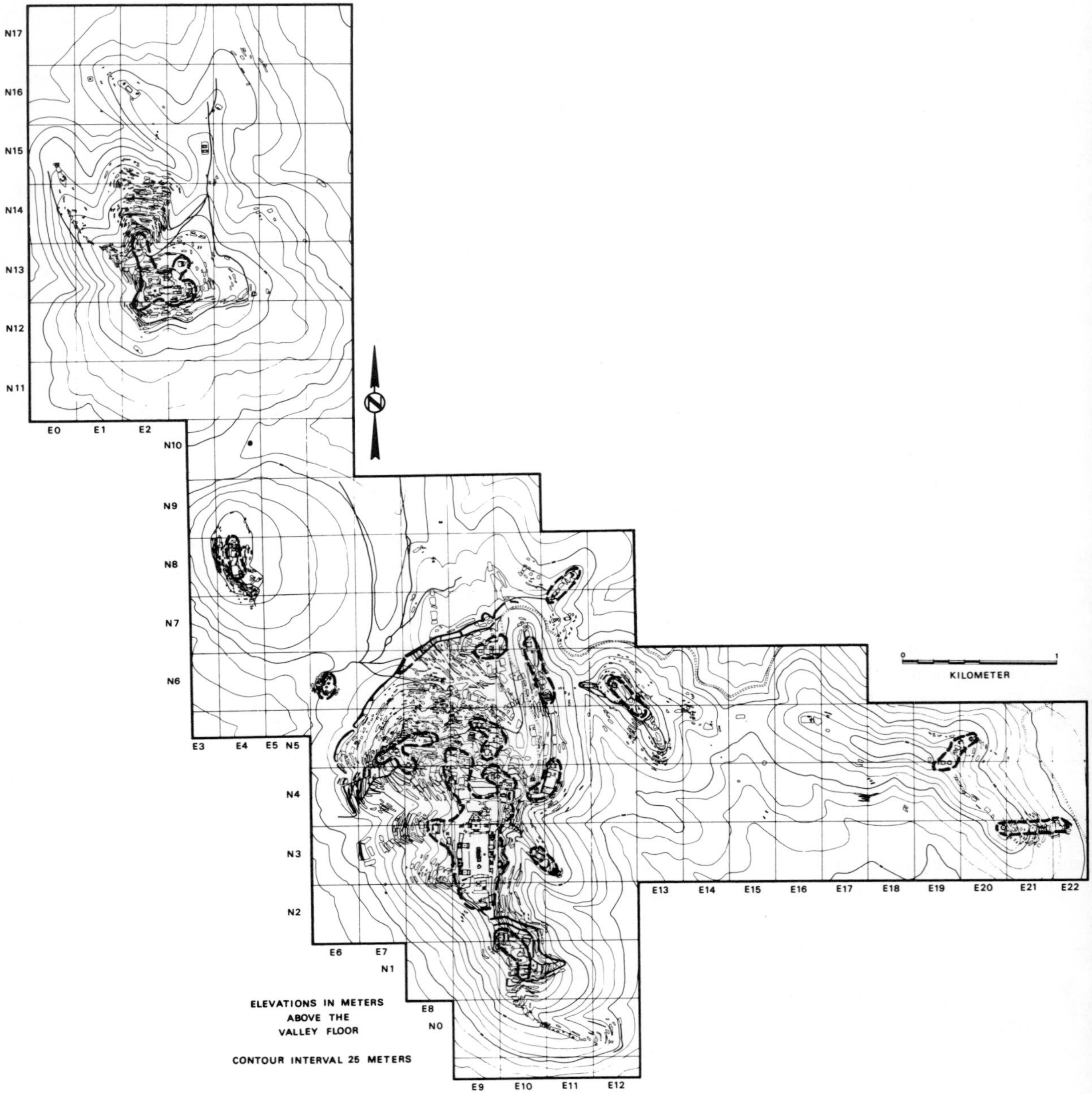

Figure 1.5. Monte Albán mound group clusters (outlined with dashed lines).

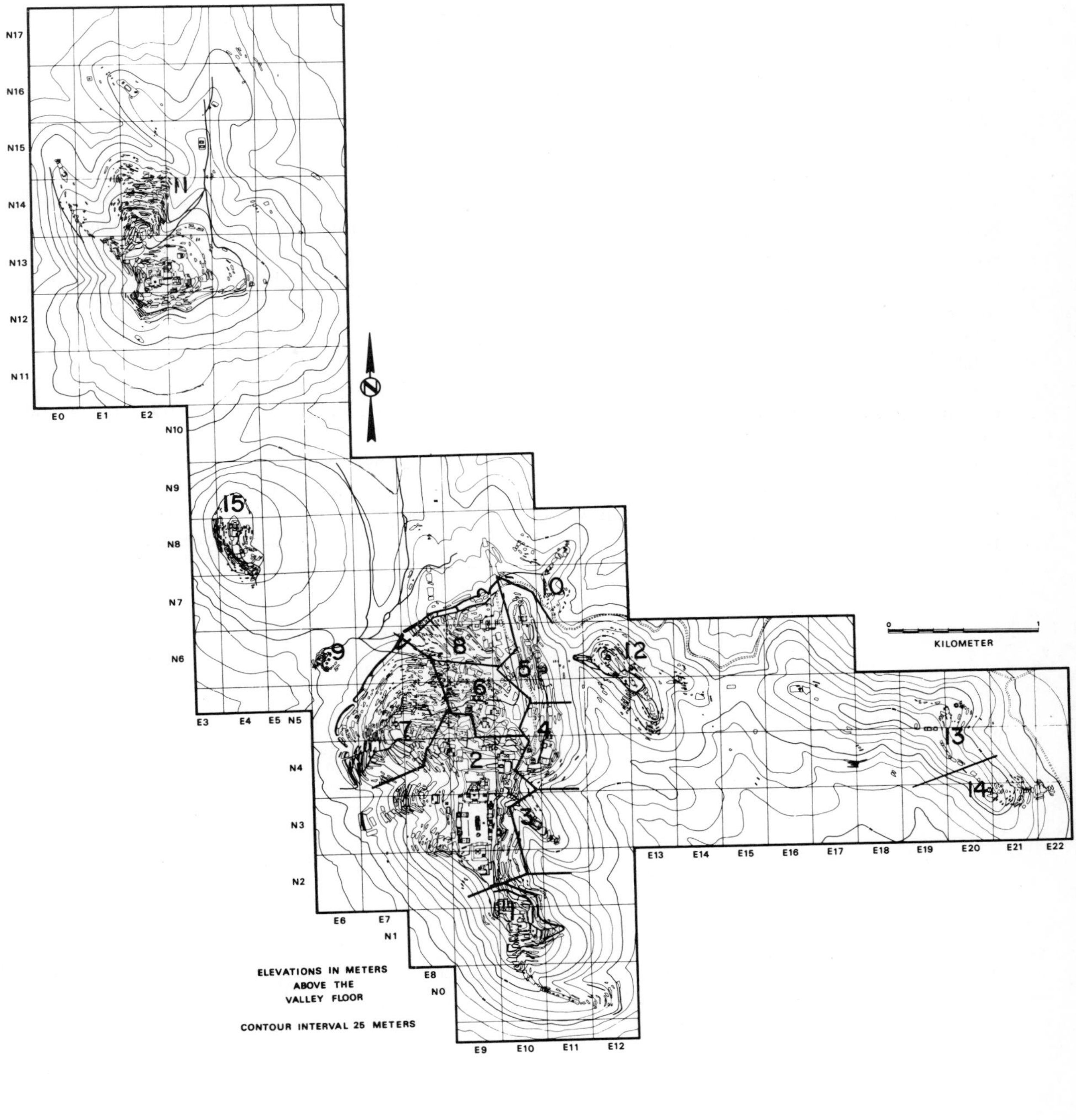

Figure 1.6. The Monte Albán site subdivisions.

boundary line. Along part of the west boundary of subdivision 4, the line falls in an area which was largely unused, even though terraces could have been built there; the same is true of the west boundary of subdivision 5 and the east boundary of subdivision 8—this too is a sparsely used area, perhaps reflecting a real boundary between social units. A wide unused space separates subdivision 10 from subdivision 5. Having drawn the polygon boundaries, I was surprised that the boundary separating subdivisions 4, 5, and 8, on the one hand, from 6 and 7 (and to a lesser extent, 2), on the other, falls roughly along the main *cañada* or 'canyon' which drains the north slope of Monte Albán proper, and which tends to divide it into east and west halves (Figure 1.6). It seems reasonable to suppose that a prominent topographic feature such as this would have been viewed as a convenient social or political boundary in ancient times. Similar topographic breaks correspond to lines separating subdivisions 3 from 2 and 4, and that separating part of subdivisions 2 and 7. While none of these facts proves the reality of the proposed site subdivisions in ancient times, they do, at least, offer some support for their existence.

DAMAGE TO THE SITE DUE TO PLOWING, EROSION, POT HUNTING, AND GRAZING

The terrace data were coded so that they could be summarized by site subdivision, enabling us to begin to examine some of the similarities and differences between these units. The data thus summarized are also useful as a means for illustrating variable patterns of modern land use and damage to the site. Figures 1.7–1.11 show, as percentages of the total number of terraces per site subdivision, the patterns of modern use (grazing and maize agriculture), the percentage of terraces severely damaged due to erosion and/or plowing, pot-hunted terraces, and frequency of excavations. The areas of most damage to terraces are those adjacent to the modern communities of Los

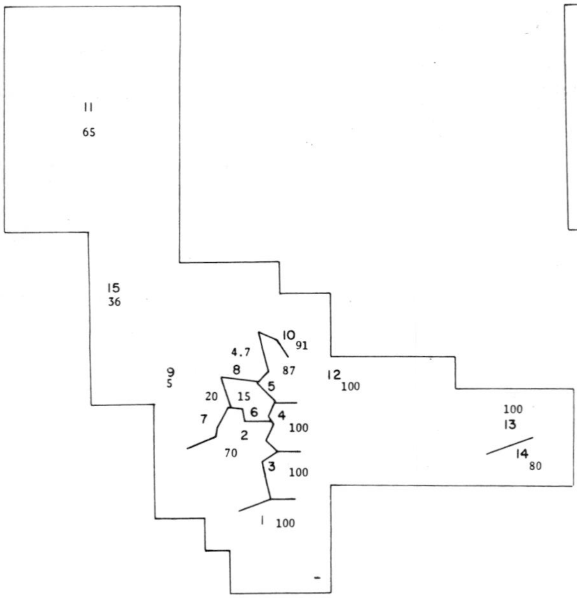

Figure 1.7. Percentage of terraces used primarily for grazing, by site subdivision.

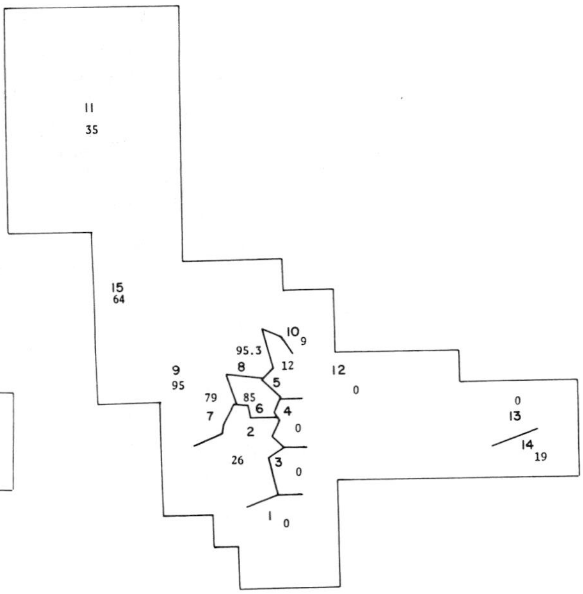

Figure 1.8. Percentage of terraces used today for maize cultivation, by site subdivision.

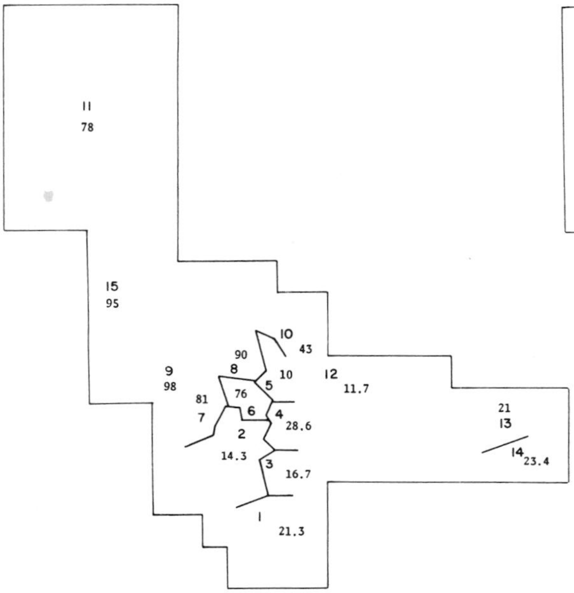

Figure 1.9. Percentage of terraces moderately to heavily damaged due to erosion and plowing, by site subdivision.

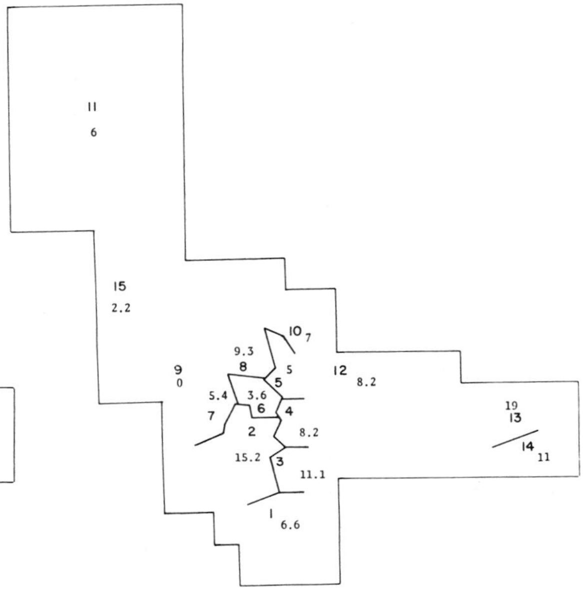

Figure 1.10. Percentage of terraces with evidence of pot hunting, by site subdivision.

Ibañez and Sta. María Atzompa. Extensive use is made today by the residents of these communities of the ancient terraces as agricultural terraces, especially on El Gallo, Mogollito, in site subdivisions 7, 8, and 6, and also on the north slope of Atzompa. In addition, these areas tend to be overgrazed, leading to erosion and further damage to archaeological features; and woodcutting in the vicinity of Atzompa is intensive.

Pot hunting as a source of damage to terraces has a definite pattern. The most seriously potted areas are site subdivisions 2, 3, 13, and 14. Subdivisions 2 and 3 were apparently extensively looted in colonial times, as is to be expected since the largest mounds are found in this general area. Now this zone is protected by the Instituto Nacional de Antropología e Historia (I.N.A.H.), so the frequency of looting has drastically declined. The looting of subdivisions 13 and 14, however, is mostly recent, and is on the rise, no doubt related to the recent growth of the *Colonia 3 de Mayo* and other *colonias* in that area.

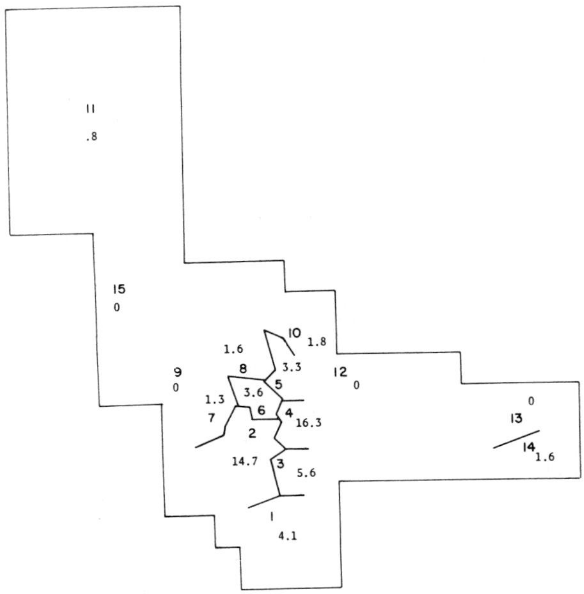

Figure 1.11. Percentage of terraces with evidence of excavations, by site subdivision.

Periodization and Chronology

A detailed description of the ceramic categories used in the preparation of this report will be found in Appendix II. This categorization is based largely on the ceramic typology of Caso *et al.* (1967). We exchanged the letter-plus-number naming scheme used by these authors with a simple numerical scheme to facilitate computer coding and sequencing. Appendix III is a terrace-by-terrace tabulation of the categories. Appendix IV contains the counts for all but rare categories by grid square. Appendix V contains the counts, again for all but rarely occurring categories, by site subdivision.

In this volume, the Monte Albán ceramic collections have been utilized for two limited purposes: First, we have made a series of maps that show Monte Albán's maximum extent at various periods by plotting those categories specific to each period. Period-by-period population estimates have been made based on these maps. Second, and to a very limited extent, we have illustrated patterns of differential distribution of ceramic categories within the site by plotting their densities of occurrence by site subdivision. These plots are intended only to suggest certain distributional patterns, not to prove their existence. The statistical significance of the observed distributions cannot be ascertained since our "grab bag" collection method was oriented to finding the periods represented on each terrace, not to collecting a numerically representative sample of each category present.

THE CERAMIC PERIODS

Caso *et al.* (1967) identified five basic ceramic periods at Monte Albán, two of which, Periods I and III, could be subdivided. The following is a brief introduction to these periods.

Period I

This is the earliest well-represented ceramic assemblage on Monte Albán, having been found on bedrock or sterile soil in several of the Monte Albán stratigraphic excavations (CBA: 89–106). We found only two earlier objects on the surface of the site, a Guadalupe phase (Middle Formative) figurine, and one sherd of the same phase. Caso *et al.* were able to divide Period I into three subperiods: a (the earliest), b, and c (CBA: 96–99). Because only a few new ceramic types appeared as late as subperiod c, and because a number of the very common later Period I types first appeared during subperiod b, especially the ubiquitous G-12 bowls (CBA: 96, Figures 4, 5), we have grouped b and c into one period and refer to it as Period Late I. We refer to Ia as Period Early I. Many of the categories that first appeared during Period Early I continued into Late I. The group of Early I categories I used to identify the limits of the site at that time, thus, had to be a subset of the Period I categories that did not continue into Late I. Fortunately, a group of grayware categories seems to fit this description, especially the G-15s and G-16s in the CBA nomenclature. These are vessels, usually well burnished, with decoration consisting of fine-line incising (for details, see Appendix II). Some categories that appeared later and were in use during Period Late I also have fine-line incised design, and so remain confusing exceptions to the rule. Examples include our categories 1350, 1353, and 1354. Table 1.2 lists the categories I used to plot the extent of the site during Period Early I. Since this is not a plot of all the categories that were actually being used at that time, longer-enduring types being omitted, it reflects the extent, not relative density, of all Early I pottery. Table 1.2 also lists the categories I used to plot the maximum extent of the site during Late I. These categories were chosen because they are not restricted to Period Early I, and do not extend into the subsequent Period II. This list of categories, as is true for all the categories in Table 1.2 for the various periods, excludes rare categories, even those that are chronologically diagnostic.

Period II

Categories used to plot the maximum extent of Monte Albán during this period are listed in Table

1.2. Again, other categories were actually in use during that time that are not listed here, but are categories that were continuations from Period I. Caso *et al.* (1967:281–308) describe a transitional phase between Periods II and the subsequent Period IIIa which is based on the assemblages of several tombs and offerings in which ceramic items pertaining to Periods II and IIIa were found together. Since no categories are particular to this period, however, we cannot discover it in surface collections, and it has not been utilized in our site periodization.

Period IIIa

The categories appropriate for plotting the maximum extent of Monte Albán during Period IIIa are few, consisting mostly of various carved vessels (G-23 in the CBA nomenclature), along with thin orange, and one Teotihuacan-related category with steep sides, flat bottoms, tripod supports, and coffee bean appliqué around the base. No other categories that occur with any substantial frequency are particular to this period. The remaining categories that were being used are ones that persisted into subsequent periods. None of the IIIa diagnostics are frequently found.

A transitional phase between Periods IIIa and IIIb was discovered by Caso *et al.* (1967: 365–378), based mostly on the contents of tombs 103 and 104. Again, as was true for *Transición II–IIIa*, this phase is easy to see in collections of contemporaneous items, since it has the characteristics of both the preceding and following periods, but it cannot be conveniently deciphered from surface collections, and so is not utilized here.

Period IIIb–IV

Caso *et al.* distinguished the Monte Albán ceramic periods up to Period IIIb based largely on variation in vessel shape, finish, design, and paste, and, to a lesser extent, on the relative frequency of occurrences of types. Period IIIb was distinguished from Period IV, instead, on historical grounds, namely, the abandonment of the Main Plaza. As they demonstrate with data from their excavations in the *Plataforma Este* of the Main Plaza (Appendix X, Figure A.X–32), pottery in use when the building was in use scarcely differs from that found in offerings deposited after the building was already in ruins. They therefore group these two periods into one longer period referred to as Period IIIb–IV, as we have. The categories used to plot the extent of Monte Albán during this period are listed in Table 1.2. When we originally did the Monte Albán survey, it looked as though the Monte Albán assemblage could be "pure" IIIb, since none of the categories typical of Lambityeco, a known Period IV community (Paddock, Mogor, and Lind 1968), was noted on the surface. We have subsequently abandoned this opinion, at least for the time being. During the course of his archaeological survey of the central part of the Valley of Oaxaca, Kowalewski identified what he feels were several Period IV ceramic production centers, each with separate distribution spheres unrelated to Lambityeco (Kowalewski 1976: 514–517). The absence of Lambityeco-like materials at Monte Albán, therefore, is not evidence for the absence of Period IV occupation at Monte Albán. The nature of this occupation will be discussed in Chapter 5.

Period V

Here we depart from Caso *et al.* in considering that Period IV pottery pertains to the Zapotec tradition in the valley, contemporaneous with the Mixtec Period V materials. Period V pottery has been found everywhere we have surveyed so far, including in communities that must have been Zapotec, as well as in Mixtec communities. We feel that Period V is simply the valley's Late Postclassic period. Further stratigraphic excavations and C^{14} dates will be required to confirm this interpretation, but we feel it is the most reasonable working hypothesis. Categories used to plot the maximum distribution of Period V Monte Albán are listed in Table 1.2.

Table 1.2. Ceramic Categories Used for Distribution Maps

Early I	
	1332, 1338, 1339, 1340, 1342, 1343, 1344, 1346, 1347, 1348, 1349, 1351, 1356, 1357, 1364, 1365, 1367, 1368, 1370
Late I	
	0016, 0022, 0031, 0032, 0038, 0121, 0122, 0123, 0383, 0384, 0385, 0386, 0387, 0389, 0390, 0391, 0393, 0394, 0395, 0402, 0561, 1262, 1297, 1341, 1345, 1353, 1354, 1355, 1359, 1360, 1361, 1362, 1363, 1366, 1369, 2010, 2042, 2065, 2072, 2076, 2079, 2080
II	
	0001, 0002, 0003, 0004, 0005, 0006, 0021, 0406, 0407, 1419, 1420, 3408
IIIa	
	1264, 1265, 1312, 1421, 3410, 3411
IIIb–IV	
	1120, 1122, 1125, 1126, 1137, 1138, 1140, 1259, 1263, 1422, 2418, 3035, 5085, 5086
V	
	1102, 1104, 1105, 1106, 1107, 1109, 5007, 5329

FIGURINES AND URNS

So few figurine and urn fragments were found during the course of the survey that their utility for delimiting the extent of occupation during the various periods, or for testing hypotheses concerning differences in function and status between the site subdivisions, is probably nearly nil. Carl Kuttruff has described the categories found, and discusses their distributional patterns in Appendix VIII.

CONCLUSION

The Monte Albán ceramic sequence is frustrating to the anthropologist because most of the periods are so long they cannot be used to monitor sometimes even major shifts in ancient population distributions. The impreciseness of the ceramic periods is not the fault of those who first identified them. Caso *et al.*, in fact, have done a magnificent job in making sense out of the stratigraphic confusion that is typically present in ancient buildings at Monte Albán. Although future stratigraphic research will undoubtedly produce a finer periodization, in reality the essence of the problem is inherent in the ceramic sequence itself. Many categories continue apparently unchanged for long periods of time since conservatism was the order of the day. This simultaneously singular and frustrating fact will be one of the subjects discussed in the conclusion of this volume.

CHRONOLOGY

Robert Drennan (in press) recently completed an exhaustive review of the chronology of the Oaxaca region based on existing radiocarbon dates. The chronological chart for the Monte Albán ceramic periods included here (Table 1.3) is based on his conclusions (Drennan,in press: Figure 3). (Dates indicated are in radiocarbon years. Rather than discuss Drennan's methods or the radiocarbon assays themselves, I refer the reader to his fine summary.) One possible problem exists with his chronological scheme, as I see it, that can only be resolved when more radiocarbon determinations have been made. I refer to the fact that Period Late I could possibly be too short. Considering the high density of Late I diagnostics and the relatively large number of diagnostic categories of the period, it seems possible that the period actually lasted longer than is indicated by the existing

Table 1.3. Ceramic Periods and Chronology: The Valley of Oaxaca

Mesoamerican periods	Valley of Oaxaca designations	Approximate chronology[a]
	Monte Albán V	1500
Postclassic	....	950
	Monte Albán IV	
	....	600–700
	Monte Albán IIIb	
Classic	....	450
	Monte Albán IIIa	
	....	A.D. 200
	Monte Albán II	
Late and Terminal Formative	....	200 B.C.
	Monte Albán Late I	
	....	300
	Monte Albán Early I	
Middle	....	500
	Rosario Phase	
	....	600
	Guadalupe Phase	
Formative	....	800
	San Jose Phase	
Early	....	1150
	Tierras Largas Phase	
Formative	....	1400

[a]Dates based on Drennan (in press). Dates are in radiocarbon years.

radiocarbon dates, perhaps occupying part of the long span indicated for Period II.

POPULATION ESTIMATES

It is probably reasonable to assume that virtually all the Monte Albán terraces were in use during Period IIIb. Only a few terraces (those in square N0E12) lack evidence of IIIb–IV pottery. I say that IIIb was the maximum period of occupation: Although we cannot determine the actual extent of the site during Period IV, it is likely that some population declines occurred, since the Main Plaza was abandoned, signaling the beginning of the community's decline in importance. It is probably also a reasonable, though not precise, assumption that residential architecture exposed on the surface by excavation or looting pertains to Period IIIb. Fortunately, the bulk by far of residential features so exposed are in portions of the site that had little or no Period V occupation. Although Period IV residences are more difficult to account for, I will assume that exposed residences pertain to Period IIIb. Appendix X summarizes the data on dimensions of exposed residential architecture, and on structures with platform mounds. In a few cases enough information was available from the surface to allow me to calculate how much surface area of terrace was taken by a residence (for example, if I could be sure that a terrace held only one residence, then the terrace area for that residence is the same as the total terrace surface area). Following both assumptions—that all terraces were occupied in Period IIIb and that the residences exposed on the surface date to the same period—Monte Albán's maximum population can be estimated by calculating the total number of households that could have been contained within the total surface area of residential terraces on the site and by multiplying this figure by some value for average household size. I did this as follows: Of the 2073 terraces we located, mapped, and described, 2006 were identified as residential. Of the 2006, 37 support rooms, or even whole residences, elevated on platform mounds. These will be referred to as *elaborate residences*. Recall that I distinguish elaborate residences from civic buildings based on their relative closure, civic buildings being more open to general traffic flow.

Of the 1969 terraces lacking elaborate residences, 19 had buildings that were preserved or excavated in such a way that I was able to calculate the terrace area taken per house, as just described. In spite of the small size of this sample, the mean figure derived, 311.9 m^2, is probably not unreasonably high or low. This value is consistent with Marcus Winter's finding, in his recent excavations at Monte Albán, that Late Formative "household clusters" (which include the house itself plus the adjacent area used for household activities) extended over an area with a radius of about 10 m (Winter 1974:982). Winter does not provide a comparable value for the area of IIIb–IV household clusters, but does mention that on three juxtaposed terraces the IIIb–IV houses were about 25 m apart (Winter 1974:983).

The buildings I have identified as elaborate residences cover much larger areas. The mean terrace surface area per elaborate residence is 2473.3 m^2, based on a sample of 19 well-preserved examples.

Since those residential terraces at Monte Albán lacking elaborate residences have a total surface area of 902,947 m^2, at 311.9 m^2 per house, the total number of nonelaborate households was roughly 2895. Similarly, there should have been roughly 63 elaborate residences on the 155,300 m^2 of terrace surface area supporting these structures. Using the value of 5 to 10 people per nonelaborate household (cf. Sanders 1965:134), a number roughly between 14,475 and 28,950 is derived. Elaborate residences probably housed more people, since such households tended to have servants (cf. Carrasco 1964). However, it is still not possible to arrive at a reasonable estimate for this period at Monte Albán. Assuming an average of 10–20 in these larger households, the total maximum population of Monte Albán at its height was about 15,000 to 30,000 (that is, assuming all terraces were occupied contemporaneously).

This population figure, derived by estimating the total number of households, is remarkably close to the value that can be derived using the method developed by Sanders (1965:50) for the Valley of Mexico archaeological surveys. According to this method, which Sanders developed based on populations of contemporary rural communities in the Teotihuacan Valley, a compact settlement such as Monte Albán should have a population density in the vicinity of 25 to 50 per hectare. Using this density yields an estimate for the population of Monte Albán of roughly 16,250 to 32,500.

In subsequent chapters the population estimate for Period IIIb will be used as a baseline for estimating the maximum populations of the other periods, and the proportion of the total area of the site occupied during each period will be considered to be proportional to the maximum population for each period. This is a slightly risky procedure since it assumes that the density of terraces on Monte Albán remained unchanged through time. In the absence of suitable data to the contrary, however, no more satisfying assumption can be made.

The Contents of Subsequent Chapters

The following four chapters outline the nature of settlement pattern change and continuity in

Monte Albán from its foundation to the end of the prehispanic sequence. These chapters are largely restricted to consideration of the archaeological data from the city itself, and include relatively little in the way of a summary of events and processes in the region as a whole. I have limited the scope of these chapters because the next volume of the Valley of Oaxaca Settlement Pattern series will present a detailed look at the region archaeologically and at Monte Albán's role in it. The final chapter of this volume will consist of a brief comparison of Monte Albán with its highland Mesoamerican contemporary, Teotihuacan, in order to test the hypothesis, preliminarily, that Monte Albán and Teotihuacan were very different kinds of communities, and that the societies in the regions dominated by each had different dynamic properties.

2

The Origins of Monte Albán

Distribution and Size of Population

Figure 2.1 shows the density of Early I sherds from our surface collections by grid square. In this plot, as in all other pottery density plots, some squares containing only a few terraces are not included, even when sherds were found there. I felt that plotting the density of sherds found on only a few terraces over an entire grid square could give a false impression of the distribution of the pottery of a particular period. For the same reason, we have not plotted the density of sherds found in the two squares containing the Main Plaza (N2E9, N3E9), since we did not make surface collections in that zone. The discussions of activities in the Main Plaza during the various periods will be based on stratigraphic excavations there by Caso's Monte Albán Project. Three concentrations of Early I sherds are apparent in Figure 2.1, two on either side of the Main Plaza in squares N3E8 (and, to a lesser extent in N4E7 and 8), and in squares N3E10 and N4E10 (and, to a lesser extent, in square N4E11), and one south of the Main Plaza, in squares N1E11 and N0E10 (and, to a lesser extent, in N1E10 and N2E10). These concentrations of sherds may reflect discrete residential *barrios*. As I will demonstrate in the next section, the Main Plaza was not a residential zone during this period, confirming the fact that there was an open, residentially unused space between the east and west sherd concentrations. Square N4E9, located between the two concentrations and north of the Main Plaza, was also apparently largely unused during this period. Very few Early I sherds are present from the surface there, and stratigraphic excavations in "Sistema Y" (Terrace 27), a mound group just north of the North Platform, encountered Periods Late I and II on sterile soil (CBA:115–116, 121, 130, 139).

Surrounding these three sherd concentrations are zones of apparently less dense occupation, especially along the north slope of Monte Albán proper. This apparent "core–periphery" pattern is difficult to interpret, and it will be difficult to estimate the population of the site at that time. This pattern may only reflect the fact that some of the Early I categories used in the plot map actually persisted into Period Late I, when the site covered the entire north slope of Monte Albán proper (given the general conservatism of Monte Albán ceramics, this seems highly likely). Another possibility is that the site's population expanded later in Period Early I from the original core area near the top of the hill down onto the site's northern

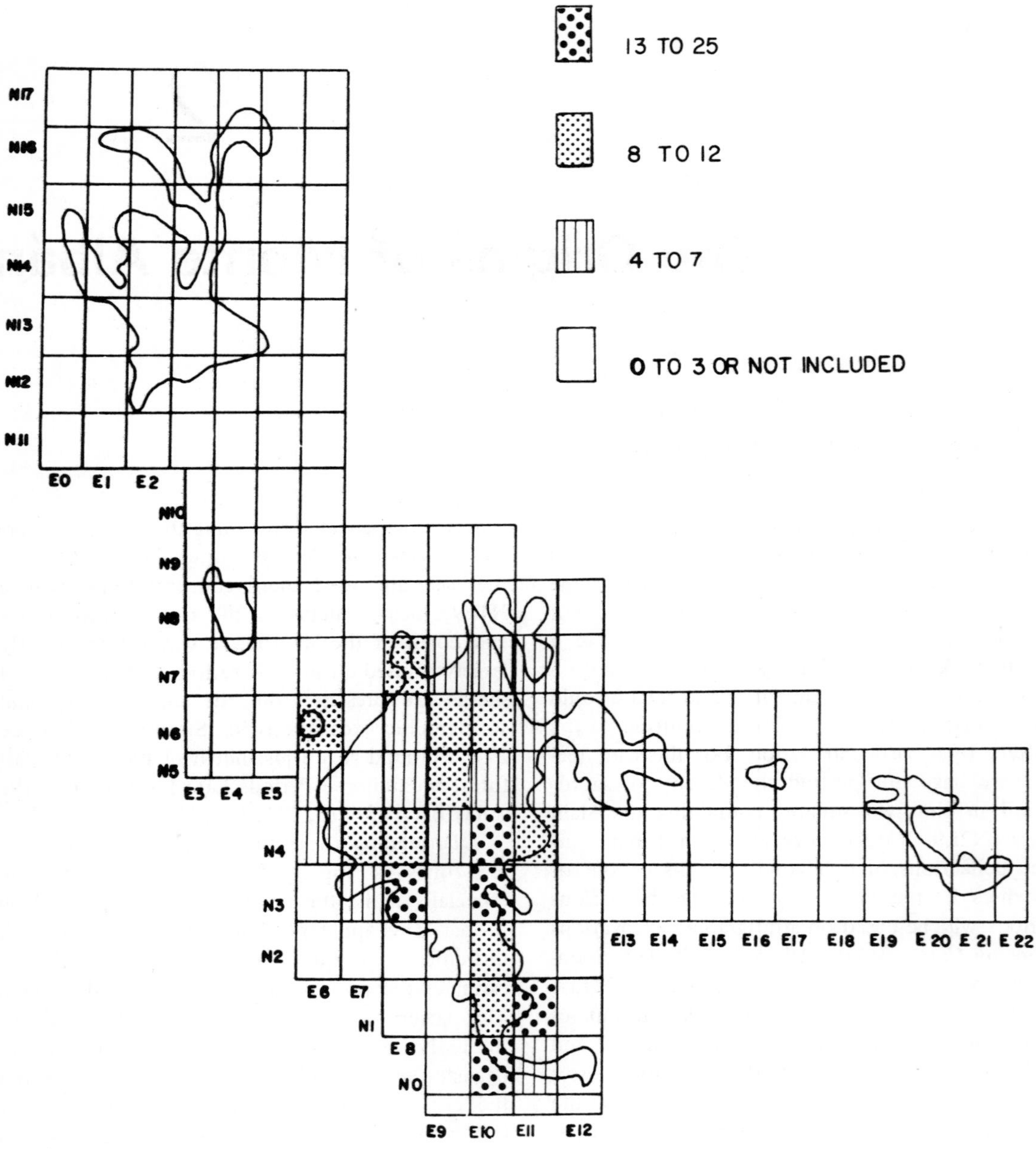

Figure 2.1. Number of sherds collected per hectare of collected terrace surface area, by grid square. Period Early I.

slope. None of these alternatives can be evaluated with the data at hand, although Marcus Winter's excavations in square N5E8 (Terraces 634, 635, and 636) north of the core tend to support the idea that the periphery was occupied during Early I, since he encountered Early I households there (Winter 1974:982).

Relatively dense Early I pottery extends over an area of roughly 69 ha, a little more than one-tenth of the site's maximum extent. If we assume the population density of this area to have been the same as that of the average for Period IIIb, then the population for the core should have been around 1600 to 3200 as a maximum. If the periphery was simultaneously, but less densely occupied, I estimate it may have contained another 1950 to 3900 people, assuming an average of about one-third the population density of the core, over an area of roughly 255 ha. This results in an estimate total of about 3500 to 7000 inhabitants for the period.

The Main Plaza

The Main Plaza of Monte Albán was not a residential zone, apparently, during Period Early I. One definite Early I building has been exposed by excavation, that in the southeast corner of the North Platform (the "P.S.A." excavations, CBA: 95–96). The section of the building exposed consisted of a sloping wall some 2.5 m to 2.75 m in elevation, unlike anything exposed in the Early I household clusters by Marcus Winter (1974:982). Another Main Plaza building was probably first built during this period, but final publication of the excavation results is needed to affirm this. I refer to the so-called "*Danzantes* gallery" found under Mound 1 (Acosta 1965:814–816; Marquina 1964:325; and Appendix X: Figure A.X–32). Other reported Main Plaza excavations lack Early I types and have, instead, Late I or Period II pottery on sterile soil (cf. CBA:137–141, 443–444).

Probably as early as Period Early I, the Main Plaza was a special area, lacking general habitation. Instead, even then, it was an area delineated by buildings that appear to have had civic or elite residential functions. The building discovered under Mound 1 appears to have been a *gallery* of carved stone monuments. These monuments, dating to Periods I and II, show human figures in rubbery, dancelike poses, often accompanied by glyphs (Caso 1947; Villagra 1942; Marcus 1976a). The Mound 1 gallery includes only a small portion of the total of 310 such monuments that have been found in the Main Plaza, since many of them were apparently removed from the gallery and were used for construction in later buildings (Marcus 1976a:126). Although many interpretations of these figures have been offered, that of Michael Coe is the most compelling. According to him:

> [The] distorted pose of the limbs, the open mouth and closed eyes indicate that these are corpses, undoubtedly chiefs or kings slain by the earliest rulers of Monte Albán. In many individuals the genitals are clearly delineated, usually the stigma laid on captives in Mesoamerica where nudity was considered scandalous. Furthermore, there are cases of sexual mutilation depicted on some *Danzantes*, blood streaming in flowery patterns from the severed part. To corroborate such violence, one *Danzante* is nothing more than a severed head [Coe 1962:95–96].

We may infer that, at least in part, the activities in the Main Plaza, probably beginning as early as Early I, had a military theme. More will be said of this fact in the next section.

The Origins of Monte Albán

Monte Albán was one of many new communities founded during Period Early I. In those areas we have surveyed (the Etla and Central Valley regions), 84 Early I sites have been located, representing approximately a fourfold increase over the number of Guadalupe and Rosario phase sites (Kowalewski in press: 13). The bulk of Early I sites fit into one of the following categories: (*a*) towns, such as San José Mogote (Figure 1.1 on p. 2), typically located adjacent to highly productive agricultural land, which were probably the administrative and economic centers of local societies; (*b*) villages, such as Tierras Largas, located adjacent to well-watered deep alluvial soils (Winter 1972); and (*c*) villages, located along major and minor tributary streams, in the piedmont zone, where canal irrigation was possible (Flannery *et al.* 1967). Monte Albán does not fit into these site categories. It was not located with easy access to the deep, well-watered alluvial zone in mind, nor is it adjacent to an irrigable tributary stream. In fact, its location on top of a steep-sided mountain that rises some 400 m above the valley floor suggests the residents' lack of orientation to farming. Based on Kirkby's work (1973: Figure 51, passim), we may infer that the adjacent hill slopes were not suitable for maize cultivation at that time. A group of people interested in farming would presumably have first colonized Monte Albán Chico, especially its eastern extent, which, while providing the advantages of a hilltop, would also have permitted access to the rich alluvial zone near the confluence of the Salado and Atoyac. This ridge, however, was not colonized until Monte Albán Periods IIa and IIIb, some 700 or 800 years later. No natural resource is present on Monte Albán that would have attracted so large a population. In fact, supplying the population's daily water requirements would have been time and energy consuming, since no natural, dependable, substantial sources of water are present on the hill.

Because Monte Albán was situated in such an inaccessible place, it is possible to infer it was not a market or place of redistributive commodity exchange. The hilltop location would have added substantially to the energy and time required to move products. In short, Monte Albán does not fit into any of our Early I site categories, and its location is not a practical one from the point of view of provisioning or economic exchanges. The community was also unusual in being the largest of the period in those regions we have surveyed. The next largest site we surveyed, San José Mogote, may have extended over an area of 41 ha (Varner 1974). Recall that Early I Monte Albán may have extended over a total area of 320 ha, 65 ha of which was relatively densely settled. Lastly, Monte Albán in Period Early I was unusual vis-à-vis other valley communities in having a large and unique group of carved stone monuments. Considering all these facts, I earlier presented the hypothesis that Monte Albán had been founded as a center of regional decision making (Blanton 1976a). The advantage of such an explanation is that it becomes possible to understand the site's bizarre location. Regional capitals of the sort I refer to as *disembedded* (Blanton 1976b), need not be located optimally from the point of view of agricultural or other resources since they are supported by taxation, nor is it necessary for them to be located satisfactorily for marketing or production since such centers usually lack such functions, at least on a regional scale. In fact, such centers are often located purposely in neutral, marginal locations. Washington, D.C. and Brasilia, both disembedded capitals, demonstrate this locational pattern. Brasilia is located in the middle of virgin jungle, and Washington was founded in a completely undeveloped, forested area where, according to Morrison (1965), the "red clay soil . . . became dust in dry weather and liquid cement in every rain, after which swarms of mosquitos spread malaria [p. 360]."

One of the situations in which a new neutrally located capital is likely to be founded arises when a group of autonomous societies join in a confederation or league (Blanton 1976b:257). The locus of league decision making is likely to be neutrally located, away from existing centers of power, because adding the confederacy or league decision-making functions to any one of the existing centers would tend to augment the influence and prestige of that one center at the expense of the other cojoining centers. In addition, such placement would be undesirable from the point of view of residents of the other centers of power since the massing of the purchasing power of elites in that one place would give it commercial advantages, again, at the expense of the other centers (Blanton 1976b:257). Viewed in this way, the location of Monte Albán, central to the Valley of Oaxaca as a whole, but on an isolated hilltop away from any existing center, seems ideal.

Probably the most common cultural setting in which a league or confederacy is likely to be formed appears when a group of autonomous societies in a region face a common external enemy. The center of league decision making, in this case, is likely to be a special-function place oriented to military matters alone. Early Athens may be a reasonable analogy in this regard for Monte Albán. According to Thucydides:

> Most of them had been always used to living in the country. . . . From very early times this way of life had been especially characteristic of the Athenians. From the time of Cecrops and the first kings down to the time of Theseus the inhabitants of Attica had always lived in independent cities, each with its own town hall and its own government. Only in times of danger did they meet together and consult the king at Athens; for the rest of the time each state looked after its own affairs and made its own decisions. There were actually occasions when some of these states made war on Athens [Thucydides, *Peloponnesian War II*: 2; Warner 1954:106].

The contents of the carved stone monuments at Monte Albán seem to support the hypothesis that it was a special-function community, the center of a regional military alliance, not only at the time of its founding but in later times as well. Marcus (1976a) writes:

> The fundamental theme of Monte Albán I through IIIa sculpture can be characterized as pertaining to militarism: The slain captives of Periods I and II, the place signs of conquered towns of Period II, and the names and/or dates, plus place signs, of bound captives of Period IIIa. At other Zapotec sites on the valley floor the themes are quite different. Jaguars and various ritual themes are particularly conspicuous [p. 133].

The absence of ritual iconography in the monumental sculpture of Monte Albán is a singular fact, since we know that most "primitive" administrative institutions are heavily religiously sanctified. This absence of religious themes may reflect more than just the fact that Monte Albán was a special-function community. Institutions such as military leagues might be expected to maintain neutrality, not only locationally, as seems to have been the case for Monte Albán, but also in other respects. Barbara Aswad (1970) has reminded us that Muhammed was initially driven from Mecca because:

> With trading alliances as its primary control and serving for a center of polytheistic tribes upon whose existence it depended, Mecca in fact resisted the innovation of monotheism and the disruption Muhammed was causing. Finally he and his group of followers were forced from its limits. It also seems that the acceptance of another religion such as Christianity would cause a loss of neutrality in Mecca's position as a trade center between the Byzantine and Sassanian Empires [p. 63].

The analogy between Monte Albán and Mecca is not perfect because it is not likely that Monte Albán was a trade center. Instead, the analogy I am trying to draw focuses on the neutrality required of an institution that is supported by a group of otherwise autonomous societies, especially if those societies adhere to a variable mix of beliefs in the supernatural. Religious themes were probably best avoided in the iconography that advertises league activities, such as that in the *Danzantes* gallery.

Early Monte Albán *Barrios*

If Monte Albán had been a center of regional decision making for a regional confederacy, then its Early I settlement pattern may be easily explained. As I mentioned earlier, the core of Early I settlement apparently consisted of three residential areas along three sides of the Main Plaza. Such a pattern could make sense if the population of the city had been composed of representatives from league members. Residents in each *barrio* would have been close to members of others to facilitate communication, but could maintain ethnic identities by living in separate localities on the hilltop. If this hypothesis makes sense, one might expect the ethnic differences between the subdivisions to be reflected in the ceramic assemblages. The entire population of the Valley of Oaxaca and adjacent regions participated in a common ceramic tradition during Period Early I. However, if ethnically distinct groups in the valley were at least in part self-sufficient from the point of view of ceramic production, then we might expect certain subtle differences to appear in the ceramic assemblages from different subregions. For example, one or more categories could, by chance alone, become more popular in one society, while being used less among adjacent groups. Isolated ceramic producers in different areas might be expected to develop distinguishable styles and techniques, even while producing in the context of a single, broad ceramic tradition. Some such differences between ceramic assemblages might be expected to exist at the "microstyle" level (cf. Deetz 1965). If so, their discovery is beyond the scope of our ceramic typology, since no such detailed studies of the categories have been done. I decided to try a simple exercise to see if differences between ceramic assemblages on Monte Albán could be discovered using our ceramic categories alone. Table 2.1 lists the rank-order of the three most popular ceramic categories from the three grid squares that comprise each of the proposed *barrios*. Obviously no vast differences are apparent from area to area in terms of what the most popular ceramic categories are. Categories 1338, 1342, 1364, and 1365 tend to be well represented in each square. Some differences between areas are present, however: For example, categories 1346 and 1347, which manifest "pinched-in," "figure eight" rims, are relatively popular in *Barrio* 1. Similarly, category 1349 is popular in *Barrio* 1, but is not among the top three in the other areas. Category 1367 is a popular type only in *Barrio* 3. If it were true that these three site subdivisions were getting their pottery from ethnically distinct groups, then for reasons mentioned earlier, it should be the case that the three grid squares comprising each of the site subdivisions should evidence more overlap of categories than there is overlap of popular categories between the site subdivisions. To test this hypothesis I simply counted the number of categories that occur at least twice among the three most popular categories within

Table 2.1. The Three Most Frequent Ceramic Categories Found in the Three Period Early I Site Subdivisions

Subdivision	Squares	Categories (rank in parentheses)
1	0111	1338(1), 1342, 1365(2), 1364(3)
	0010	1347(1), 1338, 1357(2), 1346, 1349(3)
	0110	1338(1), 1342, 1365(2), 1349(3)
2	0310	1338(1), 1370(2), 1342, 1364(3)
	0410	1338(1), 1365(2), 1364(3)
	0411	1338(1), 1342, 1357, 1364, 1365(2), 1332, 1351, 1356, 1368, 1370(3)
3	0308	1338(1), 1364(2), 1351, 1370(3)
	0407	1338(1), 1342, 1346(2), 1367(3)
	0408	1338(1), 1367(2), 1342, 1370(3)

each of the site subdivisions, and derived a value for *category overlap* by dividing this number by the total number of categories represented, among the top three, among the three squares. The values derived are: *Barrio* 1 = .5; *Barrio* 2 = .5; *Barrio* 3 = .57. The same procedure was followed to find the proportion of overlapping categories between the site subdivisions. The results are as follows:

Barrio	1	2	3
1	x	.38	.36
2		x	.5
3			x

The mean value for category overlap between squares within the *barrios* is .52, while the mean value of overlap between the site subdivisions is .41. This constitutes a provisional test of the hypothesis that more differences are present between the site subdivisions, in terms of the mix of popular ceramic types, than is present between the squares comprising each of the subdivisions. Admittedly, this is a risky procedure, given the nature of our ceramic collections, but it does lend some credibility to the idea that the Early I site subdivisions were ethnically discrete *barrios* where perhaps the representatives from cojoiners in a regional confederacy resided. The hypothesis can be shown to be wrong if we fail to find matching patterns in popularity of ceramic categories in regions of the valley away from Monte Albán.

Conclusions

I suggest that at roughly 400 or 500 B.C. a panregional polity or a confederacy was formed in the Valley of Oaxaca, manifested by the construction of a new capital on the top of Monte Albán. What is likely to have been a military showcase there, the *Danzantes* gallery, seems to indicate the league had primarily offense–defense functions. This hypothesis seems to account for the following, otherwise confusing, facts:

1. The location of the new capital on an isolated hilltop, apparently without regard for the proximity of sources of water, cultivatable land, or extractable resources. A regional market and/or production center would probably not have been located in such an inaccessible place. As outlined earlier, however, disembedded capitals are typically located in neutral places, away from existing centers of power, in order to avoid augmenting the influence of any one of the existing centers at the expense of the others. Because such centers are supported by tax revenues, they need not be self-sufficient from the point of view of local resources or food.
2. Not only were there more carved stone monuments at the new capital than at any other valley center, but they differed from those of the other centers in portraying exclusively military themes. Monuments from other centers prominently include ritual themes. This makes sense for a neutral institution, since subjects are best avoided for which there may have been no regional concensus; ritual may have been one such area. Although there were undoubtedly rituals and religious beliefs among the population of Monte Albán, carved stone monuments that pertain to league activities were understandably purely militaristic in theme.
3. The population of the newly founded community was not uniformly distributed over the hilltop. Three concentrations of sherds seem to indicate three discrete residential areas. The fact that the ceramic assemblages from these three site subdivisions show more uniformity, in terms of the most frequently occurring types, within the subdivisions than between the subdivisions can be interpreted to mean that the subdivisions were ethnically distinct and as a result got their pottery from separate ceramic production centers. Separate neighborhoods, I argued, would have helped maintain ethnic identities.

This model for the origins of Monte Albán scarcely has the status of an "explanatory sketch." While it seems to account for these disparate and seemingly otherwise inexplicable facts, it has severe limitations. First, we have no idea what societies may have been involved in the development of the regional polity. The fact that there are three site subdivisions tempts me to suggest that the populations of the three arms of the Valley of Oaxaca were involved, but there is no direct evidence of this. In the next stage of our survey project, we hope to throw some light on this problem through the analysis of Early I ceramic assemblages. We might predict, for example, using a simple gravity model (Haggett 1965:35; Olsson 1965) or some comparable statistic, that each site subdivision will show an unpredictably high degree of interaction with a particular valley center or region, the center or region whose representatives lived there. A further and more serious problem with this model is that it has nothing to say about why a regional polity would have formed during Period Early I. Apparently some new military threat appeared at that time that made it worthwhile for several societies to join in a league, in spite of the costs of such a polity, one of which was the construction and maintenance of the new regional capital. What was the source of the new menace? It is not likely, in my opinion, that this military threat was emanating from the Valley of Mexico. The societies in this valley did, in later times, have a strong impact on those in Oaxaca, but not much was happening there, in evolutionary terms, as early as 400 or 500 B.C. Cuilcuilco was possibly a reasonably large and influential center this early (cf. Heizer and Bennyhoff 1958; Palerm 1961:300), but the monumental architecture there is not of a scale sufficient to suggest the presence of a polity so powerful that its effects could have been felt all the way to Oaxaca. In fact, there is no convincing evidence that Cuicuilco's political hegemony extended even over the entire Valley of Mexico (Blanton 1972:53). Teotihuacan, the Valley of Mexico's great regional center of the Classic Period, probably cannot be considered to have been a major power until the Patlachique phase (ca. 150 B.C.) at the earliest (Millon 1973:51; Cowgill 1974).

I recommend that rather than looking to the Valley of Mexico as a source of military intimidation of sufficient scale to have produced political reorganization in Oaxaca, that, instead, we look at the southern highlands region alone. The works of Flannery and his associates (Flannery *et al.* n.d.; Flannery and Marcus 1976a, b), along with the surveys of Varner (1974) and Kowalewski (1976), have amply demonstrated the gradual growth and political centralization of societies in the Valley of Oaxaca during the Early and Middle Formative Periods. Societies in the dozens of smaller, less nuclear valleys in the Oaxaca region, however, were by no means evolutionarily stagnant (cf. Spores 1972:173), although we know relatively little about them. These peripheral societies might increasingly have viewed villages in the comparatively plush Valley of Oaxaca as convenient sources of grain (and labor?). Such invaders would have been difficult to control by small polities in the Valley of Oaxaca due to the surrounding rugged terrain. Eric Wolf argues that one of the reasons for the success of peasant revolutionaries in Morelos during the Mexican Revolution was their ability to escape into mountain redoubts in the rugged territory (Wolf 1969:293). The combined resources of a league, however, might have been sufficient for the pacification of adjacent territories, and, in fact, the revenues produced from forced tributes imposed on conquered groups would probably have served to defray the costs of supporting the confederation and the new capital center.

3

Periods Late I and II

Settlement Distribution

Periods Late I and II can be distinguished ceramically because some categories do not persist past Late I, while some new categories appeared that were specific to Period II. I have combined these two periods into one chapter, however, because the two periods were similar from the point of view of population size and settlement distribution. By Late I the city had expanded to include nearly all of Monte Albán proper (Figure 3.1). Additionally, El Gallo was first colonized (a few Early I sherds are present on El Gallo, but probably represent only a very small occupation), and there was a small occupation on Atzompa in square N14E5. A group of terraces in square N0E12 and adjacent sections of N0E11 (Terraces 1401–1406, 1435–1446) which evidence abundant Late I and II pottery were not surface-collected, and so are not included in Figure 3.1. The situation during Period II was similar, except that a slight decline in population had occurred. El Gallo seems to have been abandoned, and the paucity of sherds at Mogollito suggests a reduced occupation there (Figure 3.2). The occupation of square N14E5 was abandoned, but a few Period II sherds were found on the north slope of Atzompa in squares N16E4 and N15E0. On Monte Albán proper the occupation along the site's edges seems to have been less dense, although, in my opinion, this may be due to the nature of the Period II ceramic diagnostics, rather than a reflection of a real population decline. Most of the categories used to demarcate the Late I extent of Monte Albán are utilitarian categories, probably widely used, while those that are known to have been restricted to Period II are mostly "costly" categories that were probably more frequently utilized by elites. I include here categories 0001, 0002, 0003, 0004, 0006, 0406, 0407, 1420, and 3408 (see Appendix II). This represents 9 out of 12 diagnostics for the Period. The fact that most of the Period II diagnostics are costly undoubtedly explains the much lower sherd densities apparent in Figure 3.2 as compared with the Late I densities. We cannot infer from these data, however, that the population density of the city was reduced during Period II as compared with Period Late I. Likewise, as I will demonstrate below, site subdivision 2, the area dominated by the Main Plaza, seems to have had a larger proportion of elites than the more peripheral subdivisions. This fact may help explain why the boundaries of the city appear to have retreated somewhat during

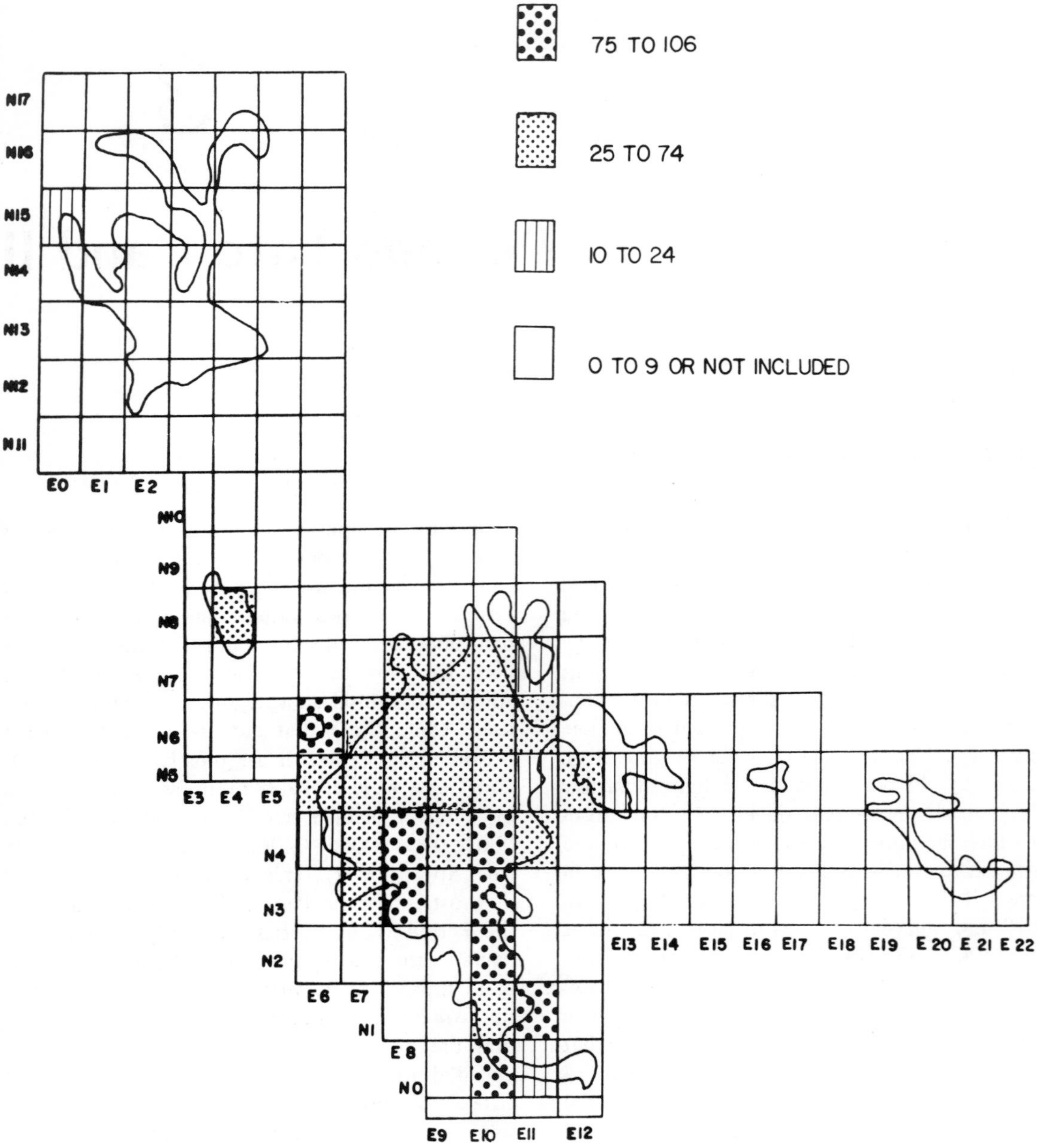

Figure 3.1. Number of sherds collected per hectare of collected terrace surface area, by grid square. Period Late I.

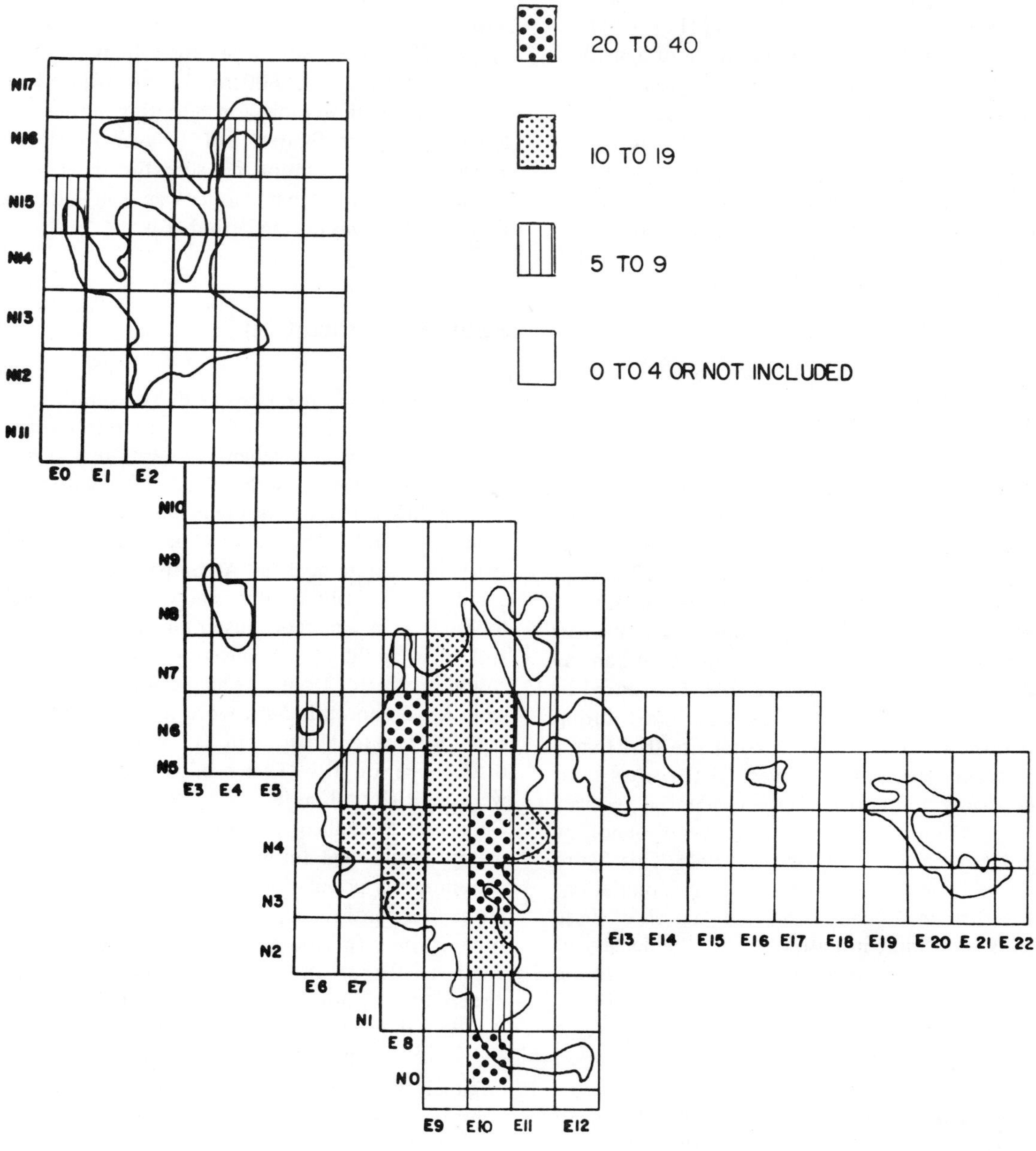

Figure 3.2. Number of sherds collected per hectare of collected terrace surface area, by grid square. Period II.

Period II, since more peripheral households may have been using fewer of the Period II diagnostics. One last point can be made about sherd densities. Those areas in Figure 3.1 that had been densely occupied in Early I have the highest Late I sherd densities. This is to be expected since some of the categories that were in use during Late I and which are therefore useful in plotting the site's maximum extent at that time, had also been used during Early I, especially the following set of cream-paste categories: 0016, 0038, 0387, 0389, 0391, and 0394 (Appendix II).

Population Estimates

Again using the Period IIIb population estimate as a baseline, since roughly 68% of the total site of Monte Albán was occupied during Late I, the population of that period was roughly 10,200 to 20,400. This may be a slight underestimate because terraces are, in general, more densely packed in the area that was occupied during Late I and II than is true for the site as a whole. If counted in terms of surface areas of terraces occupied during Late I, the percentage of the total site that Late I occupation represents is larger. Of the site's total surface area for nonelaborate residential terraces of 902,947 m^2, 662,895 m^2 have evidence of Late I pottery (or 73% of the total). This figure might not be useful for estimating population, however, since we cannot be sure that all of these terraces were built in Late I, or that the density of terraces in Monte Albán proper was great during Late I as it later became during Period IIIb. In the absence of better information, the smaller value will be adopted as a population estimate for Period Late I.

The Period II population extended over a maximum area roughly 64% of that of the site's total area (416 out of 650 ha). I estimate the population, therefore, to have been roughly 9650 to 19,300, as a maximum. Calculated in the other way, that is, using the total surface area of terraces with evidence for Period II occupation (635,540 m^2, or 70% of the site total), then the population estimate derived is 10,800 to 21,600. Again, there is no definitive reason for adopting either the lower or higher figures, but I favor the lower values since we cannot be sure the density of terraces in Monte Albán proper was as high during Period II as it was during Period IIIb.

Spatial Organization

The three concentrations of Early I sherds seem to indicate the presence of three discrete residential *barrios* at Monte Albán during its first period of occupation (along with a smaller concentration at Mogollito). I argued in the introductory chapter that in Period IIIb the city had *barrios*, some spatially discrete such as Atzompa, and some located contiguously to other subdivisions, but each focused on a separate cluster of elite residential and civic buildings. A question that cannot be easily answered from surface evidence alone is whether or not this *barrio* organization had persisted at Monte Albán from its founding in Early I through Period IIIb. Two subdivisions of the city were spatially discrete during Period Late I, El Gallo and Mogollito, and these were nearly completely abandoned during Period II. Otherwise, the community's population during these periods was probably continuously distributed over Monte Albán proper (excluding the area around site subdivision 10); no discrete residential clusters are discernible. If, however, it could be demonstrated that the mound group clusters that were the focuses of the Period IIIb site subdivisions were originally constructed during Periods Late I and II, then it would be reasonable to argue the site subdivisions within Monte Albán proper have considerable time depth.

Unfortunately, so little excavation has been done outside the Main Plaza it is impossible to ascertain the dates of construction of the mound group clusters, with only four exceptions. Within the mounds comprising Terrace 453, the focus of site subdivision 8, three tombs were excavated by Caso and his associates pertaining to Period II (see Appendix I, Part 2). This conforms to our impressions in the field that, where we could superficially inspect the fill of these buildings, little other than Late I and II pottery could be seen. Terrace 1456, the small ball court that is part of the mound cluster in site subdivision 4 has a buiding under it from which a very fancy Period I vessel was excavated, a life-sized head portraying the god *Cocijo* (Caso and Bernal 1952: Figure 30). Tomb 38, a Period II tomb, was found in site subdivision 3's mound group cluster (see Appendix I, Part 2). Again, our field impression, based on the superficial examination of mound fill here, was that these mounds had first been built during the latter portion of the Formative, that is, probably during Late I and/or II. A complete Period II urn was discovered during the excavation of *Siete Venado* (Terrace 1458), part of the mound group cluster of site subdivision 1 (Caso and Bernal 1952: Figure 254).

No other information at my disposal directly indicates a Late I or II date for the construction of the mound group clusters within Monte Albán proper, but one other class of information may be a source of clues. During the coding of the terrace data I noticed a tendency for those mound groups in the areas of the site occupied only during the Classic period to have orientations predominantly 4 to 10° west of magnetic north. On the contrary, those mound groups on Monte Albán proper where there was occupation during Periods Late I and II more often had orientations within 2 or 3° of magnetic north (Table 3.1) (see also Acosta 1965:814). This may reflect the fact that during the Late and Terminal Formative Periods the preferred orientation for buildings was such that they now have close to a north–south magnetic orientation, while during the Classic Period new buildings tended to be built with orientations that now appear as some degrees west of north. The fact that buildings within the site subdivisions that have Late I and II occupations tend to have the same orientations suggests that they may have been built more or less contemporaneously during the latter part of the Formative Period. As will be detailed below, much of the flattening as well as the final definition and construction around the Main Plaza occurred during Periods I and II. Since the predominant orientations of buildings there, as well as the orientation of the Main Plaza as a whole, are roughly magnetic north–south today (cf. Caso 1970: *Plano* I), it is arguable that it was during those periods that the orientations preferred were those that today are north–south.

This is by no means a perfect method for dating buildings since some have orientations that vary considerably from north–south (these are labeled "other orientations" in Table 3.1). Likewise, some buildings that may have been built originally during Period Late I and II were undoubtedly rebuilt during later periods, perhaps in some cases in such

Table 3.1. Orientations of Mound Groups at Monte Albán

a. Mound groups in those areas with Late I and II pottery	
Other	27%
4–10° west of north	10%
Within 2–3° east or west of north	63%
b. Mound groups in those areas with occupations only during Periods IIIa and IIIb–IV	
Other	27%
4–10° west of north	46%
Within 2–3° east or west of north	27%

a way as to conform to the orientation that was currently popular. A number of rooms and patios have been exposed by excavations on Terrace 21. Based on the dates of tombs associated with these features, it seems likely that most were built during Periods IIIa and IIIb (Appendix I, Part 2). It is interesting that, according to the crew supervisor who described this terrace, the predominant orientation of buildings is 6° west of north. In two cases, mound groups that have close to north–south orientations, Terraces 453 (cf. CBA: *Plano* 8) and *Sistema Y*(Terrace 27), have rooms superimposed on them, pertaining to construction phases long after their initial dates of construction, with orientations west of north (Appendix II, Part 2). It was apparently so important to orient rooms in what now appears as west of north, during the Classic Period, that it was done even if the platform mound upon which the room sat was oriented differently.

I conclude preliminarily, based upon what little excavated evidence exists, along with trends in building orientations, that the *barrio* organizational pattern persisted from the time the city was founded until its collapse at the end of Period IIIb, and that the mound group clusters that were the neighborhood focuses in Monte Albán proper during Period IIIb also had that function during Periods Late I, II, and IIIa (except for site subdivision 10).

The Main Plaza and Site Subdivision 2 during Periods Late I and II

During Periods Late I and II a considerable amount of energy was expended in construction in the Main Plaza area. The excavations in the southeast corner of the North Platform (CBA: 90–106), or the P.S.A., where the Early I platform was discovered, demonstrate the magnitude of this activity. Altogether these deep pits exposed roughly 8 to 9 m of fill. By measuring the areas of dated fill exposed in each trench (CBA: *Plano* I), it was possible to estimate roughly the amount of construction there pertaining to each ceramic period. The small Early I building represents only about 2.6% of the fill exposed in the series of pits. Late I fill, however, accounts for roughly 39% of the total construction exposed, and Period II accounts for about 39%. During Period IIIa more construction was done here, amounting to about 21%, but little or no additional work was done during Period IIIb or later. In other words, along the edge of the North Platform that abuts on the Main Plaza, the bulk (roughly 77%) of construction was carried out during the Late and Terminal Formative Periods. Apparently, however, the North Platform had been, until Period II, a much narrower building, north to south, than it is now. Excavations in *Monticulo I Romano* (just to the north of G in Figure 4.3 on p. 61) (CBA:137–141), near the center of the platform, and north of the P.S.A., encountered Period II materials on bedrock. Construction there dating to Period II accounts for roughly 40% of the total exposed. This portion of the North Platform was expanded greatly during the Classic Period–7% of the fill is datable to Period IIIa, and 53% to Period IIIb. The beginnings of expansion of the North Platform northward, however, evidently appeared during Period II.

While the west and north limits of the Main Plaza had been defined in Period Early I (by the *Danzantes* building and the building found in the P.S.A.), by Period II the east edge had been defined as well. Evidence for this is the construction of the *Plataforma Este* (Appendix X, Part 2: Figure A.X–32; CBA:443–444), which has Period II pottery on bedrock. According to Acosta, the leveling of the Main Plaza was nearly completed by the end of Period II (Acosta 1965:818, 829). One would guess that the south end of the plaza would have been defined in the Late or Terminal Formative Periods also, but no excavated evidence bears on the early history of the South Platform.

By the end of Period II, an early version of the Main Plaza ball court had been built (Acosta 1965: 824) (to the left and down from 1 of Figure 4.3), and the arrow-shaped Structure J pertains to this period (Caso 1947) (the building to the north of the South Platform). No other building has been found in Mesoamerica like Structure J, except for the smaller and simpler Mound O at Caballito Blanco, a small site in the eastern arm of the Valley of Oaxaca (Paddock 1966:120). Structure J appears to have been the Period II version of the military showcase, replacing or perhaps supplementing the *Danzantes* building, although some have interpreted the building as an astronomical observatory (Aveni and Linsley 1972). That Structure J functioned as a military showcase seems to be evident based on the presence of 40 carved slabs set into the building's face that Caso identified as "conquest slabs" (Caso 1947; Marcus 1976a:127–131).

Obviously the Main Plaza continued, during the Late and Terminal Formative Periods, to be a special area where the bulk of the community's monumental contruction was evident and where military successes were advertised. By Period IIIb, as I will describe below, the area associated with the Main Plaza, site subdivision 2, was distinct from the other site subdivisions in having a greater number of platform mounds that look like elite residences. This subdivision was not only the center of league activities, then, but was also an elite residential district. This pattern may be one that can be pushed back to include the Late and Terminal Formative Periods. One of the elite residences within site subdivision 2, the only one to have been excavated, was originally built during Periods I and II (I refer here to *Sistema Y*) (CBA: 113–137). The distribution of costly Period Late I and II ceramic categories seems to reflect an unusually high concentration of elite residences in Area 2 (these collections do not include the Main Plaza or its buildings). Of the 42 categories used to produce the Late I plot map (Figure 3.1), 5 were identified as costly (0389, 0394, 1345, 1360, and 1366), because all evidence highly burnished surfaces and/or incised decoration. Two of the 5 categories (or 40%) thus chosen occur with more frequency in site subdivision 2 than in the other subdivisions (Figures 3.3–3.7). Of the remaining noncostly categories, only 7 (or 19%) occur most abundantly in Area 2. The picture is clearer for Period II where of the 12 diagnostics for this period identified as costly (categories 0001, 0002, 0003, 0004, 0005, 0006, 0380, 0406, 0407, 1420, 3408, and 3409) 7 (or 58%) are most frequent in site subdivision 2 (Figures 3.8–3.19). Site subdivision 8, the area focused on Terrace 453 is interesting in this regard. Two of the Period II costly types are most abundant there (0002 and 0005), and 4 others are relatively abundant there (0001, 0004, 0006, 0406). Tomb 77 of Terrace 453 is where Caso found the famous Period II urn that Bernal and he (Caso and Bernal 1952:204, Figure 341) describe as the most beautiful they had en-

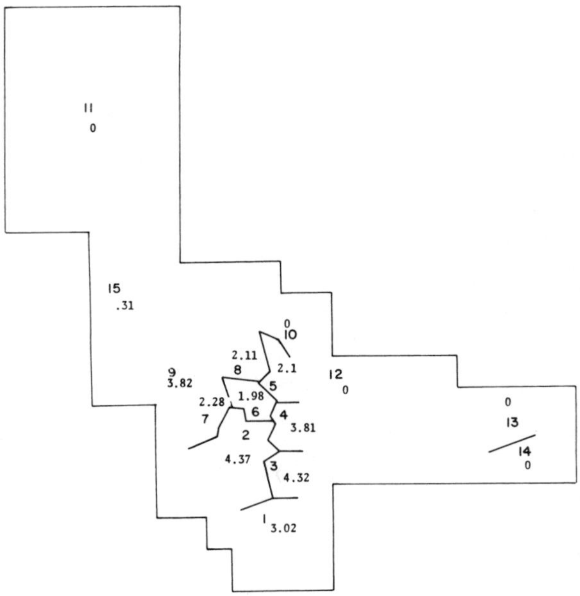

Figure 3.3. Distribution of ceramic category 0389, expressed in sherds per hectare of collected terrace area.

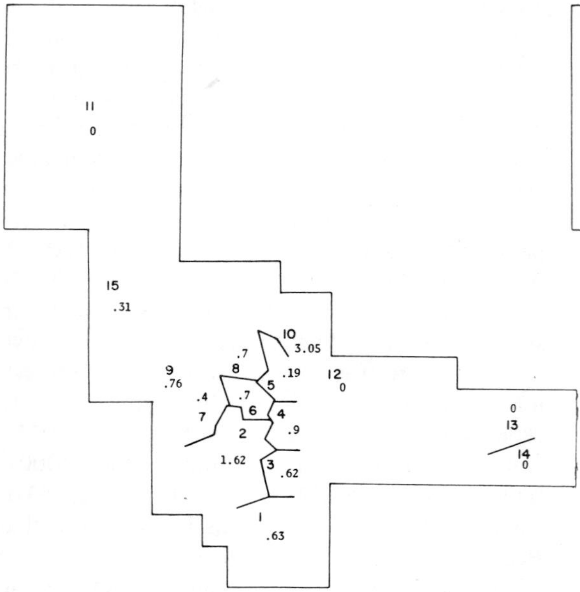

Figure 3.4. Distribution of ceramic category 0394, expressed in sherds per hectare of collected terrace area.

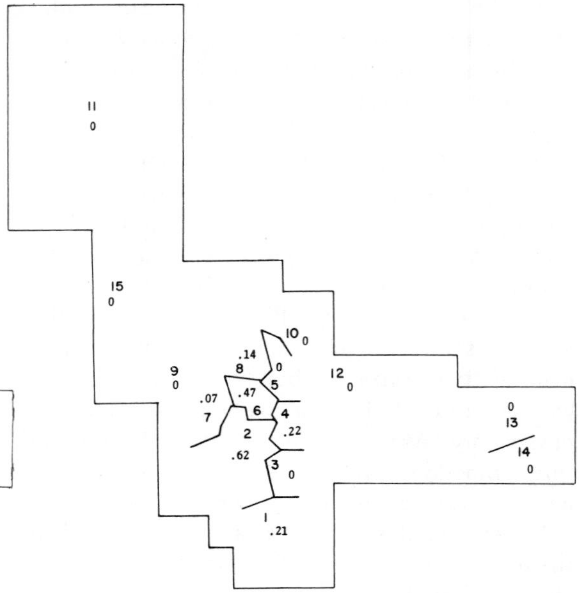

Figure 3.5. Distribution of ceramic category 1345, expressed in sherds per hectare of collected terrace area.

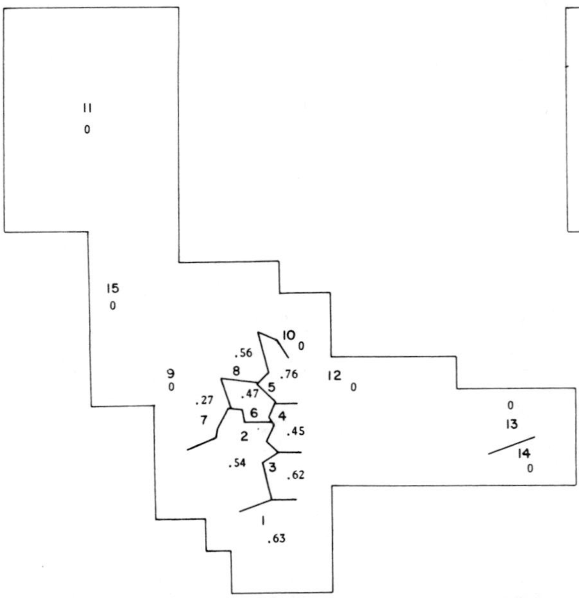

Figure 3.6. Distribution of ceramic category 1360, expressed in sherds per hectare of collected terrace area.

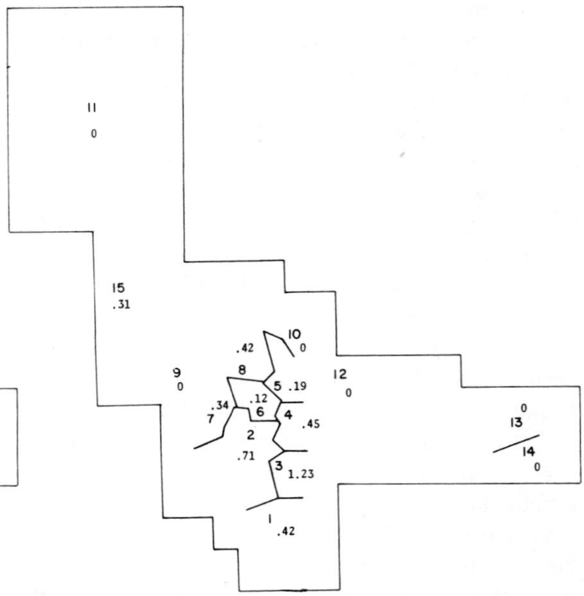

Figure 3.7. Distribution of ceramic category 1366, expressed in sherds per hectare of collected terrace area.

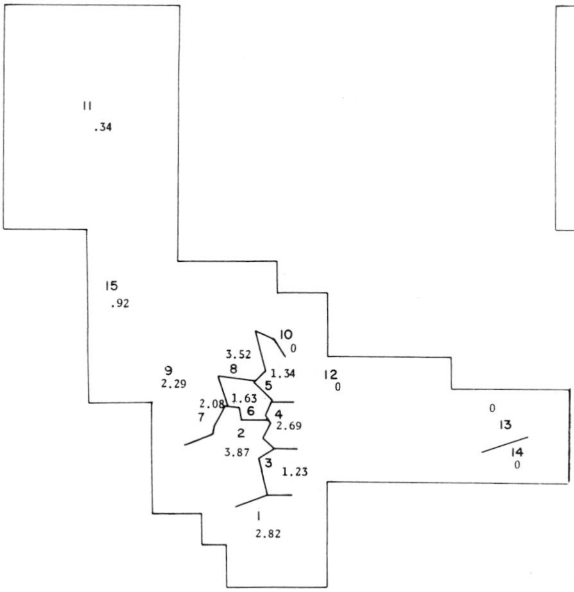

Figure 3.8. Distribution of ceramic category 0001, expressed in sherds per hectare of collected terrace area.

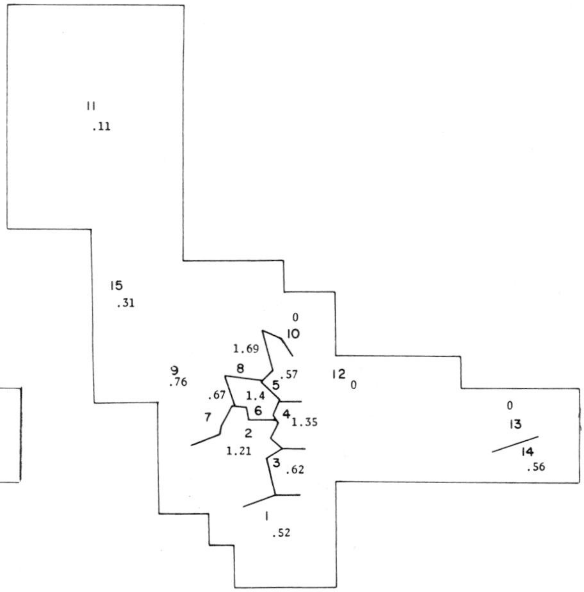

Figure 3.9. Distribution of ceramic category 0002, expressed in sherds per hectare of collected terrace area.

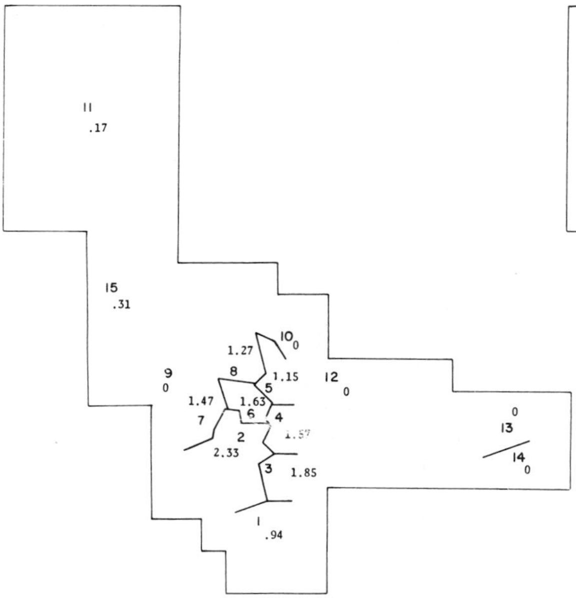

Figure 3.10. Distribution of ceramic category 0003, expressed in sherds per hectare of collected terrace area.

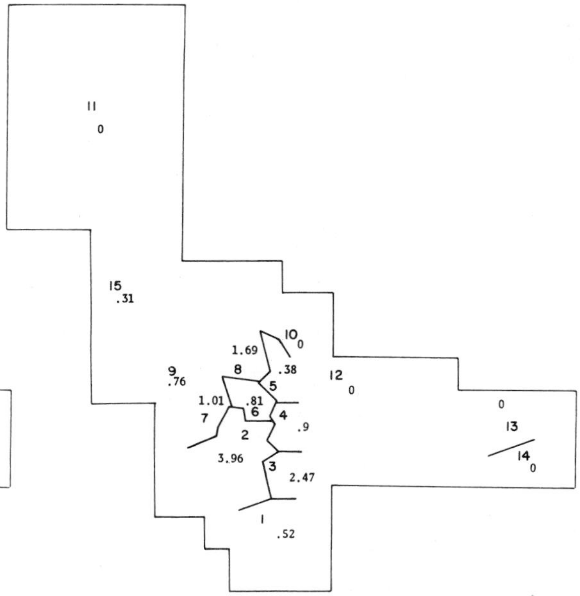

Figure 3.11. Distribution of ceramic category 0004, expressed in sherds per hectare of collected terrace area.

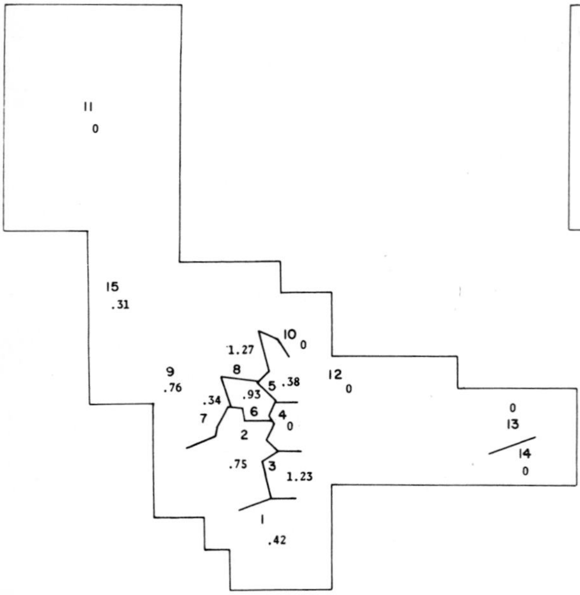

Figure 3.12. Distribution of ceramic category 0005, expressed in sherds per hectare of collected terrace area.

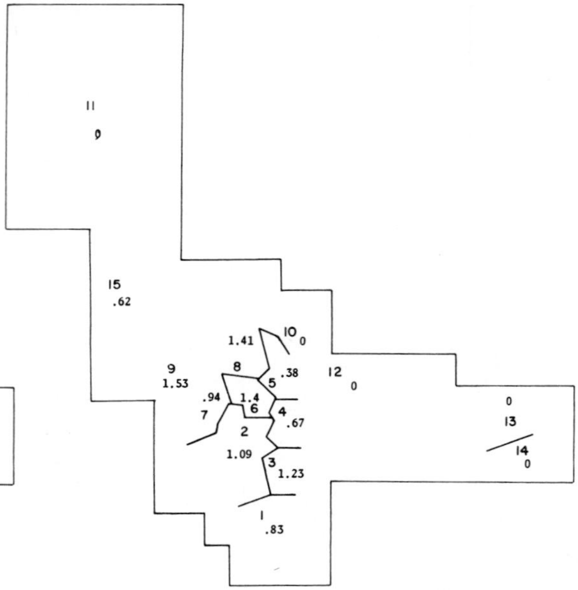

Figure 3.13. Distribution of ceramic category 0006, expressed in sherds per hectare of collected terrace area.

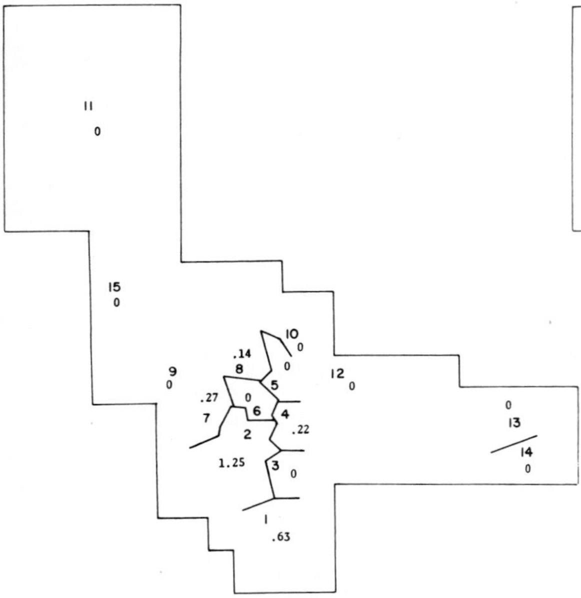

Figure 3.14. Distribution of ceramic category 0380, expressed in sherds per hectare of collected terrace area.

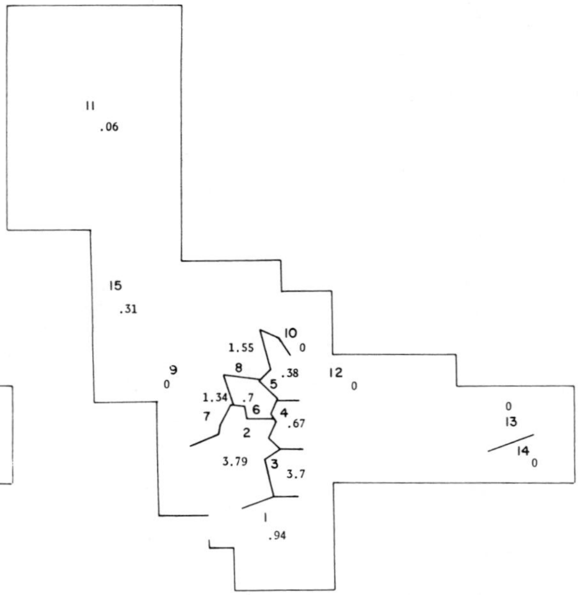

Figure 3.15. Distribution of ceramic category 0406, expressed in sherds per hectare of collected terrace area.

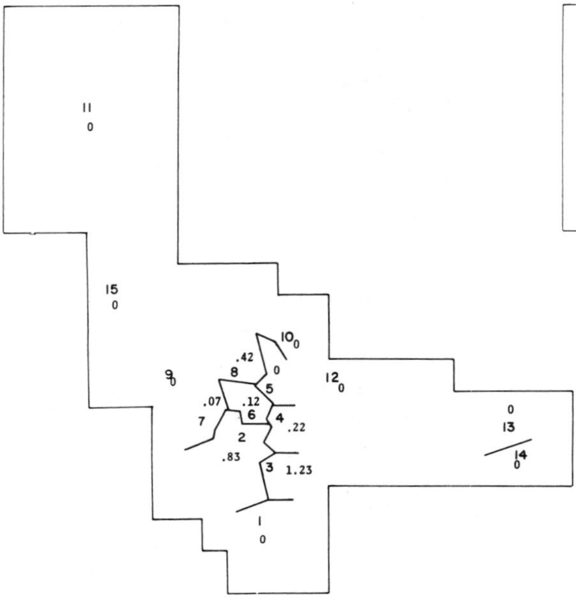

Figure 3.16. Distribution of ceramic category 0407, expressed in sherds per hectare of collected terrace area.

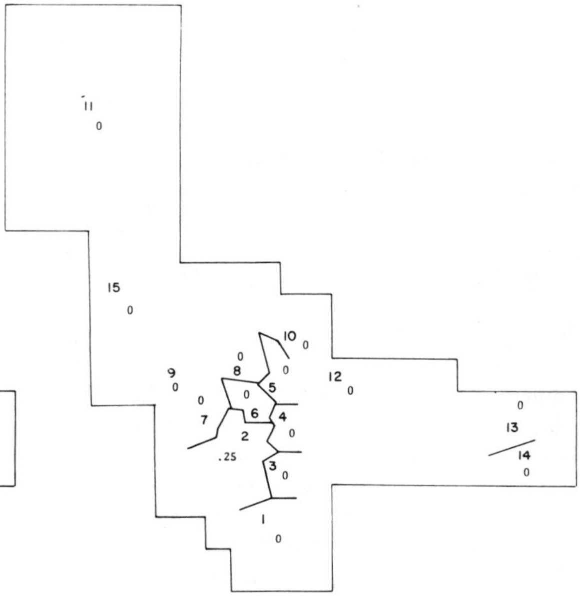

Figure 3.17. Distribution of ceramic category 1420, expressed in sherds per hectare of collected terrace area.

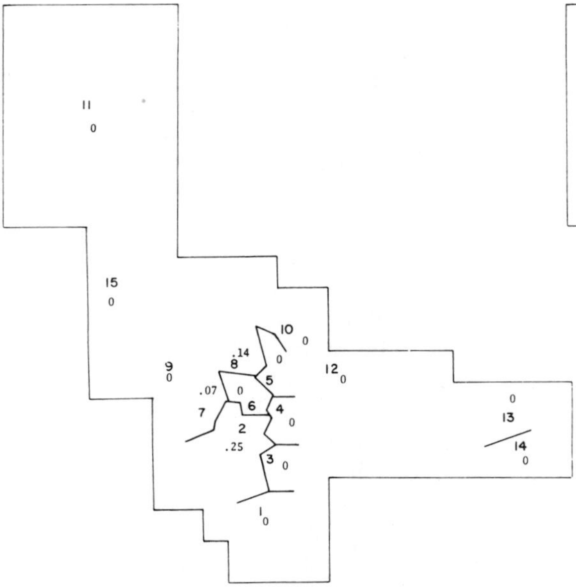

Figure 3.18. Distribution of ceramic category 3409, expressed in sherds per hectare collected terrace area.

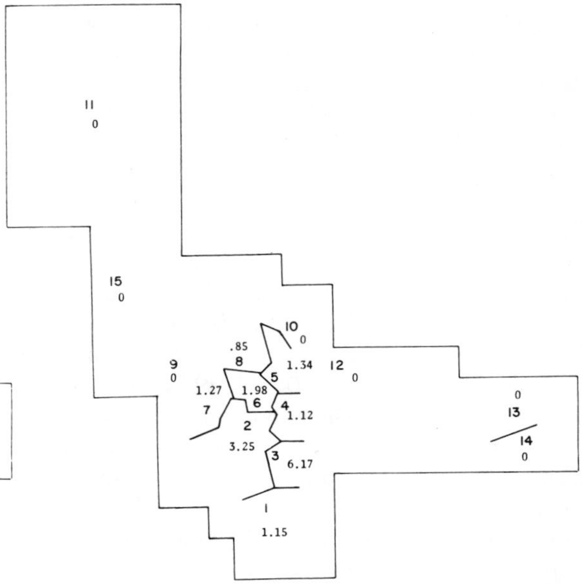

Figure 3.19. Distribution of ceramic category 3408, expressed in sherds per hectare of collected terrace area.

countered at Monte Albán. I conclude that site subdivision 8 may have been a relatively "affluent" neighborhood in Period II.

Defensive Walls of Periods Late I and II

A large defensive wall defines part of the north, northwest, and part of the west boundaries of Monte Albán proper (see Figure 1.3 on p. 4 and the 1:10,000 map). I feel that this wall was built sometime prior to the Classic Period, probably during Periods Late I and/or II. The goal of Carl Kuttruff's excavations in Terrace 1227 was to date this wall, and his evidence does seem to confirm the accuracy of this dating (Appendix IX). We have been unable to date definitively the wall's construction because even where it has been cut through or eroded (for example in square N6E8, where the *cañada norte* has cut across it), there are very few sherds to be found in its fill. This fact alone may be significant, however, because one would think that any large feature built in or around the site in later times would be filled with sherds. Apparently the fill used in the construction of the wall was relatively free of sherds, possibly indicating that people had not been living in the vicinity of the feature prior to its construction. The wall was probably a defensive one, although it may have had as many as two other purposes: Where the wall crossed the *cañada norte* in square N6E8, it apparently created a reservoir some 2.25 ha in surface area which would have held an estimated maximum 67,500 m^3 of water (Neely 1972); its second possible function is one common to such walls in medieval cities. As related by Saalman (1968): "While one tends to think of [walls] in terms of siege, with the militia behind the crenellations pouring boiling oil on ascending invaders . . . the everyday and even more important purpose of the walls should not be neglected: control of entry and exit in peacetime [p. 22]." Whether or not Monte Albán's major wall had this function is unknown, but, as I will argue in the next chapter, there are buildings in several localities on the site that appear to have had *gatelike* functions, indicating, perhaps, an interest among the community's administrators in regulating and/or taxing traffic flow.

The wall begins on the east in square N7E10. The slopes to the east of the wall's terminus here are very steep, probably explaining why no construction was done further in this direction. A large flat platform (Terrace 523) is found along the top of the wall, in this same square, at a point where four major ancient roads converged (Figure 4.4 on p. 65; see pp. 63-66 for a discussion of roads) and crossed the wall. This platform is one of the gatelike features just mentioned which will be discussed further in the next chapter. As the wall extends westward from this platform, it remains only partially a cultural feature. A durable limestone outcrop has created a low cliff several meters in elevation, which the wall's builders took advantage of as a base upon which to construct. A smaller, upper wall begins at the very west edge of square N7E10, and it, too, seems to sit on a natural outcrop. As the wall drops down into the *cañada norte*, however, in squares N7E8 and N6E8, both walls exhibit relief on both sides, and are obviously purely cultural features. The smaller, interior wall is badly eroded, possibly indicating it was built before the larger, outer wall, while the latter wall is in relatively good condition. As it drops down into the *cañada*, the outer wall averages at least 4 to 5 m in elevation, and has a maximum width of about 20 m. Retaining stones are visible along the bases of both walls in this descending stretch, and along the top of the larger wall, stone wall fragments are visible in several localities, as well as stones set in place as though they had been used as paving. Plate 6 shows the double wall along this stretch.

Past the *cañada norte*, in square N6E7, the two walls join. For the remainder of its extent to square N4E6, the builders of the wall used a resis-

Plate 6. Monte Albán's major defensive walls, looking east from near the bottom of the ***Cañada Norte.*** The inner wall, along the right edge of the photograph, is largely eroded. Where the outer, larger wall crosses the ***cañada,*** it would have created a reservoir in the bowl-shaped area in the lower center of the photograph.

tant layer of limestone as a foundation, but evidence of modification of that natural feature during the wall's construction is present (Appendix IX). Due to the presence of the limestone shelf along this stretch, the wall is in some places as high as 9 m! In square N6E7, a major ancient road cuts across Terrace 1226 and the wall. According to the person who wrote the survey form for this terrace, where "the road crosses the defensive wall, there is a ramp, and at this point the wall makes a fairly sharp turn possibly to make the access point easier to defend."

In squares N5E6, N4E6, and N3E7, where large *barrancas* cross it, the wall was discontinuous, which can be explained in two ways: First, the amount of fill that would have been required to span these canyons would be enormous; second, the *barrancas* are so steep sided and deep that they themselves serve as effective barriers to human movement. Therefore, no construction was necessary.

In square N3E7, the isolated segment of wall surrounded north and south by steep *barrancas* is not built on a natural outcrop. It has relief on both sides and appears to be entirely a cultural feature, and as was the case along the slopes beyond the wall's eastern terminus, the hill slopes beyond its southern terminus are very steep (that is, those in squares south and southeast of N3E7), presumably obviating the need for any man-made defensive feature. The wall extends, then, only over that part of the site's northern, northwestern, and western limits where relatively shallow slopes would have invited attack or the free flow of traffic.

Two other smaller walls were discovered at Monte Albán during the course of our survey that were probably built during Periods Late I and/or II. These walls are situated at the very southernmost extreme of Monte Albán proper, in square N0E12 (one of the walls stretches slightly into square N0E11). Again, the walls are bounded north and south by steep slopes, so they served to restrict traffic only along an area of shallow slopes. Both walls were built of stone chunks like a terrace wall, with dirt fill thrown in behind. The smaller wall extends for roughly 130 m, while the larger wall's length is roughly 250 m. A large platform, Terrace 1445, was found at the larger wall's north end, at a point where the slope is shallow enough to have permitted the flow of traffic. This terrace could be a gatelike feature analogous to Terrace 523 on the main defensive wall.

No direct evidence is available to ascertain the date of construction of these two smaller walls, but all of the terraces located just above them evidence predominantly Late I and II pottery (Terraces 1401–1406, 1435–1446). In fact, this small area (mostly square N0E12) is the only locality on Monte Albán where terraces are present but where very few IIIa or IIIb sherds were found. The city's boundary seems to have retreated uphill in this small area after Period II. Since the two walls bound these terraces very nicely, it is tempting to suppose they were built during the time the terraces were occupied.

Late I and Period II Irrigation Features

During 1971 James V. Neely mapped and test-excavated a small irrigation system located along the east slope of Monte Albán proper (Figure 3.20) whose canals are fed by a dam located southeast of the South Platform and by an unidentified source along the south of Monte Albán Chico. These canals fed a series of agricultural terraces between Monte Albán and the modern village of Xoxocotlan (Figure 3.20). In accordance with the results of his test excavations, Neely has established that the canal and terrace system was first begun during Early Monte Albán I, was in peak use during Period Late I, and declined drastically during Period II (Neely 1972; Mason, Lewarch, O'Brien, and Neely n.d.). According to the calculations by Mason *et al.*, the irrigated terraces here would only have produced surplus food for at most several hundred people, so the system is probably not of much significance in understanding the city's growth or in establishing its sources of food.

Periods Late I and II: Conclusions

After its founding, Monte Albán increased rapidly in size, nearly tripling its Early I maximum population sometime during Late I. Most of Monte Albán proper had been occupied by this time, and El Gallo had been colonized. Construction activities in the Main Plaza area were continued, and by the end of the period, over 300 *Danzantes*, signifiers of military victories, had been erected (as far as we know—more probably exist but are now buried). This growth phase ended prior to the subsequent ceramic phase. The paucity of Period II materials at El Gallo suggests it was abandoned, indicating that not only did the growth phase cease but that some declines occurred. Two other features of Periods Late I and II may be evidence that Monte Albán's fortunes changed after its initial success. While the number of conquest monuments erected during Period I exceeds 300, only 40 such stone carvings were produced during Period II (Caso 1947), as far as we know. Second, it appears that it was sometime during Late I or II that walls were built around part of the community's perimeter, including the main wall along its north and west edges. If the purpose of these walls was to defend the community from invaders, then we may infer that Monte Albán's military dominance over the region was weak or nonexistent. Even if the walls served for traffic regulation and taxation, similar to those of medieval towns, rather than for defense alone, this still implies something about Monte Albán's regional status. Surely a capital with an established and dependable tax base, in the form of tributes from conquered regions and/or league participants, would have had no need for the income that might be derived from gate taxes. All things considered, it appears that Monte Albán's regional hegemony and its sources of support were weak or perhaps simply unpredictable during the latter part of the Formative Period. The construction of the large reservoir in the *cañada norte*, and the irrigation system mapped by Neely provide further evidence that there was an attempt on the part of the community's population to achieve more self-sufficiency.

A contrary interpretation of Monte Albán's fortunes during the latter part of the Formative has been made. According to Joyce Marcus (1974):

> It is noteworthy that the 310 or more *Danzantes* which appear during Monte Albán I constitute 80% of the total monument record from that site. In other words, it was during the initial occupation of Monte Albán that the effort devoted to carving monumental figures was the greatest. This early effort probably coincides with the time when the rulers of Monte Albán would have felt the greatest

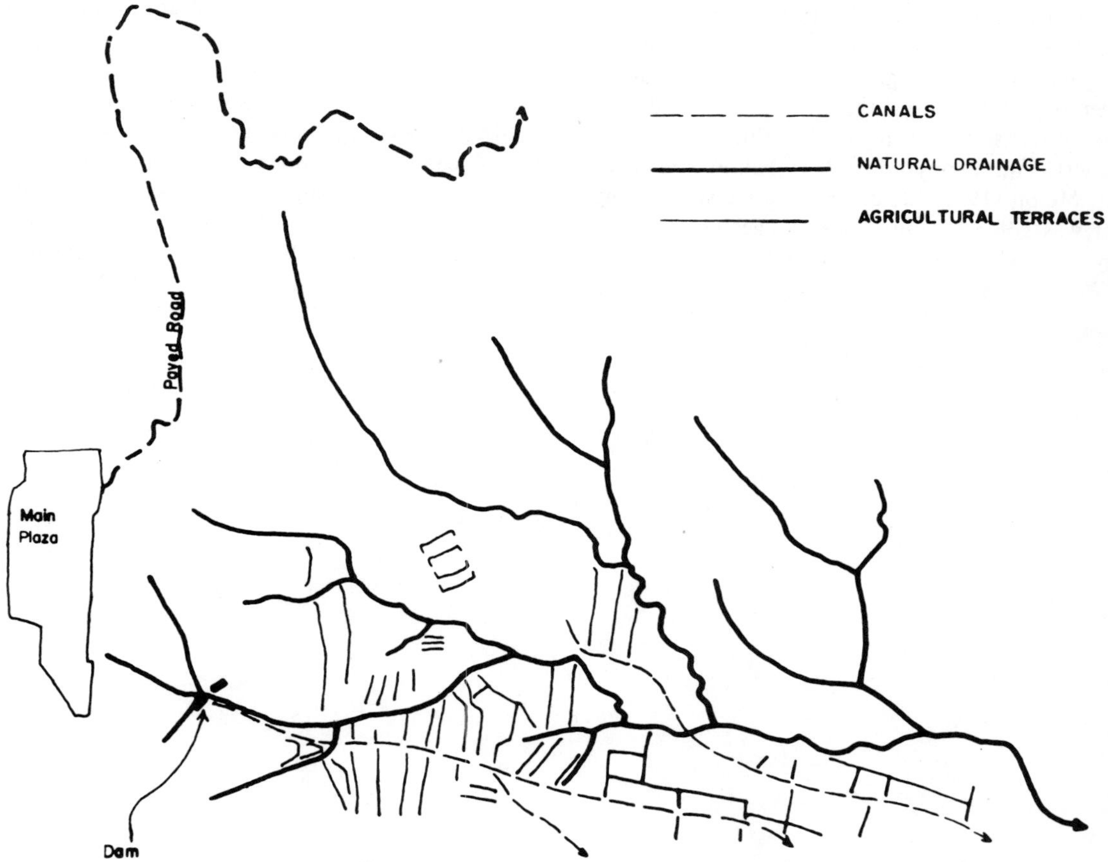

Figure 3.20. The canals and irrigated terraces east of Monte Albán proper, based on Neely (1972: Figure 1).

> need to legitimize their power and sanctify their position. Perhaps by creating a large gallery of prisoners, they were able to convince both their enemies and their own population of their power, although it was not yet institutionalized or completely effective [p. 90].

As Marcus explains, as Monte Albán's power became more institutionalized and more effective, the need to erect monuments to display that power declined. This is an interesting argument for which there may be support in the form of an analogy—the construction of the Pyramid of the Sun at Teotihuacan may illustrate the same principle. This building was constructed largely during the beginnings of the growth of the city's regional hegemony, not during the time of its maximum population size and regional influence (Millon, Drewitt, and Bennyhoff 1965; Millon 1967). In fact, Millon (1973:42) describes the city planning that was going on during Teotihuacan's early history as "audacious" due to its monumental scale.

We know so little about regional organization and its changes through time in Oaxaca that no final judgment can be made concerning which of these two interpretations of Monte Albán's fate in the latter part of the Formative Period is more accurate. In thinking about these problems, however, one is constantly reminded of what Thucydides wrote about early Athens, which is cited in the preceding chapter. First, he said that at certain times the member groups of the Attican league actually went to war against Athens. This seems to imply that the support base of a disembedded league capital can fluctuate greatly since league participants may retain a great deal of local autonomy. Second, Thucydides points out that early Athens was really only important in times of distress. One might expect that the funding of a military league and thus the league capital might be reduced during periods of relative peace. If this were the case, the capital's population might decline and new sources of income might have to be developed, precisely what seems to have happened at Monte Albán just prior to the Classic Period.

4

Monte Albán in Periods IIIa and IIIb—IV

According to the hypothesis presented in the previous two chapters, Monte Albán was the capital of a political institution that had a broad regional scope, but that was limited largely to matters of offense and defense. It seems to follow logically that such an institution might become more powerful, and be better funded during periods of military strife. It is highly likely that beginning about A.D. 200 or 300 it was the case that the level of military tension in Highland Mesoamerica as a whole increased, due to expansionist Teotihuacan. We know that by the Tlamimilolpa phase (ca. A.D. 200–450) Teotihuacan had assumed its more or less final form, and that its influence was beginning to be felt over much of Mesoamerica (Millon 1973:56; Bernal 1966). In part Teotihuacan's presence in Mesoamerica is evident only in the form of stylistic elements or exchanged objects, while in some localities Teotihuacan's influence was more direct, undoubtedly reflecting conquest. The best-documented example of the latter is at Kaminaljuyu, where some of the buildings were rebuilt in the Teotihuacan style (Sanders and Price 1968:168). This occurred during the Esperanza phase there, ca. A.D. 400 (Michels 1973: Table 8). While it cannot be proven with the data at hand, I feel we may safely infer that the rich Valley of Oaxaca would have been a prime target for those in Teotihuacan who were directing the expansion of empire. It seems clear, however, that, unlike Kaminaljuyu, the Valley of Oaxaca and its capital, Monte Albán, never became part of that empire. The stylistic influence of Teotihuacan is present at Monte Albán, both in pottery (cf. Bernal 1965:801, 803) and in architecture (Acosta 1965:824), but, overall, this influence is diffuse and generic, and involves only a few specific ceramic categories (e.g., categories 1421 and 3411). The basic ceramic assemblage at Monte Albán, during Teotihuacan's expansion in Periods IIIa and IIIb, looks nothing like the pottery at Teotihuacan, and no building at Monte Albán was ever built in the precise style of Teotihuacan.

While Teotihuacan's influence is barely identifiable at Monte Albán in the artifactual and architectural senses, it was no doubt present in the form of military threat. This probably more than any other factor explains Monte Albán's growth beginning in Period IIIa (ca. A.D. 200–400), and continuing into Period IIIb (ca. A.D. 400–600). Monte Albán's enhanced status in Period IIIa is also evidenced by the fact that the previously regionally specific styles in carved stone monuments disappeared, while the Monte Albán style became the regional standard (Marcus 1976a:136).

I previously discussed some of the problems with the Period IIIa ceramic assemblage, especially the paucity of good markers, that make it difficult to estimate Monte Albán's population and the city's maximum extent during that time. The evidence we do have from our surface collections, however, suggests that all of Monte Albán proper continued to be occupied during this period, and in addition, that Atzompa was colonized along with that portion of Monte Albán Chico included in squares N5E12, N5E13, and N6E13 (Figure 4.1). The low sherd densities for Period IIIa undoubtedly reflect the scarcity of Period IIIa markers and probably do not necessarily indicate any reduced population density. I estimate that IIIa materials cover an area equivalent to roughly 73% of the maximum area of the site; assuming a population density like that for Period IIIb, the population was probably in the vicinity of 11,000–22,000, an increase of about 12% over that of Period II. The city continued to grow so that sometime during Period IIIb, as far as we can tell from surface evidence, virtually all terraces were occupied (Figure 4.2). Following our previous calculation, the IIIb maximum population was roughly 15,000–30,000, a 27% increase over that of Period IIIa.

It is highly likely that Monte Albán was considerably reduced in population by Period IV, but I cannot estimate the magnitude of the decline since Period IV ceramics at Monte Albán are virtually identical to those of Period IIIb. We do know that the Main Plaza fell into disuse after having reached its zenith in terms of architectural monumentality during Period IIIb (CBA:89, passim).

The Main Plaza in Periods IIIa and IIIb

Construction in the Main Plaza area continued apace through Period IIIa, and by the end of the first half of IIIb it had achieved its final form (Acosta 1965:824–831). Two figures are included here that portray the final form of the Main Plaza. Figure 4.3 presents an architectural rendition of the area, based on several published maps resulting from Caso's Monte Albán project (Caso 1970: *Plano* I; Marquina 1964: *Lámina* 86; Acosta 1965: Figure 1), plus features we noted during the course of our survey. Figure A.X–32 of Appendix X, Part 2, is a simplified sketch of the Main Plaza showing the building designations; Appendix I, Part 2 of this volume contains a detailed summary of references to the Main Plaza excavations (Terrace 1447).

I have argued that throughout Monte Albán's history the Main Plaza was a special area, a military showcase and center of league activities. In the absence of sufficient published information concerning the artifacts uncovered here, however, it is difficult to infer much about the specific features of human activity in this zone. The best I can do is to attempt to infer the characteristics of behavior here based on the inspection of the morphology of its buildings alone. The plaza is bordered north and south by the two largest buildings in the city, the North and South Platforms, which have generally been interpreted as palace and/or public building (North Platform) and temple (South Platform) (cf. Flannery and Marcus 1976a: 215). Although no direct archaeological evidence supports this interpretation, the morphologies of the two buildings seem to corroborate the hypothesis. The South Platform lacks a closed mound group of the sort I have interpreted to be elite residences. The patio formed by the two mounds atop this feature, however, was apparently secluded and of difficult access because of the construction of a wall at point O in Figure 4.3. The feature still does not appear to have been an elite residence because the staircase of the southwest building (according to *Lámina* 87 in Marquina 1964) faces west and not north onto the patio. The South Platform staircase is high, steep, and much narrower than that of the North Platform, and, once one arrives at the top of this staircase, one must continue onward, moving circuitously around the large mound, to enter finally the se-

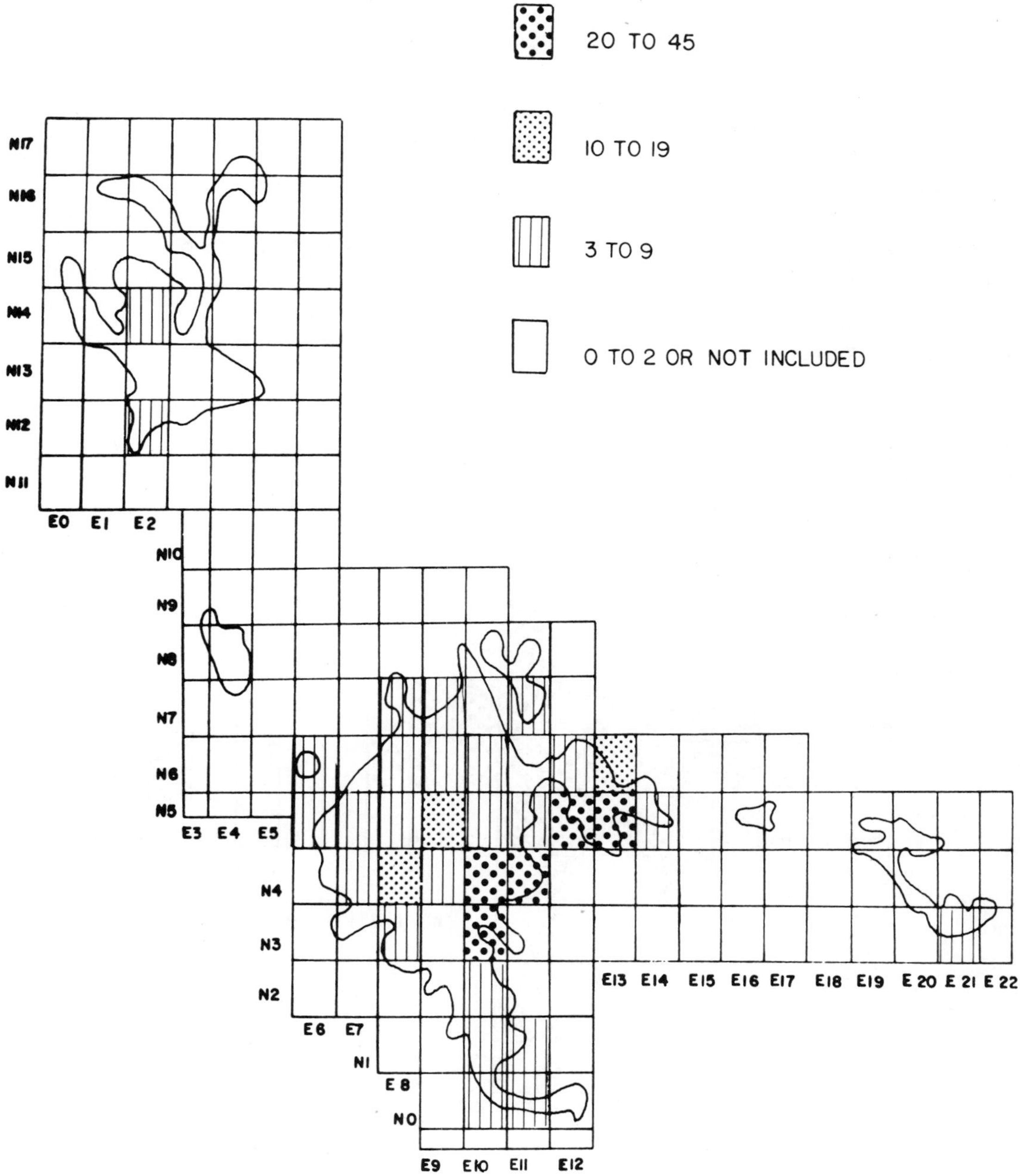

Figure 4.1. Number of sherds collected per hectare of collected terrace surface area, by grid square. Period IIIa.

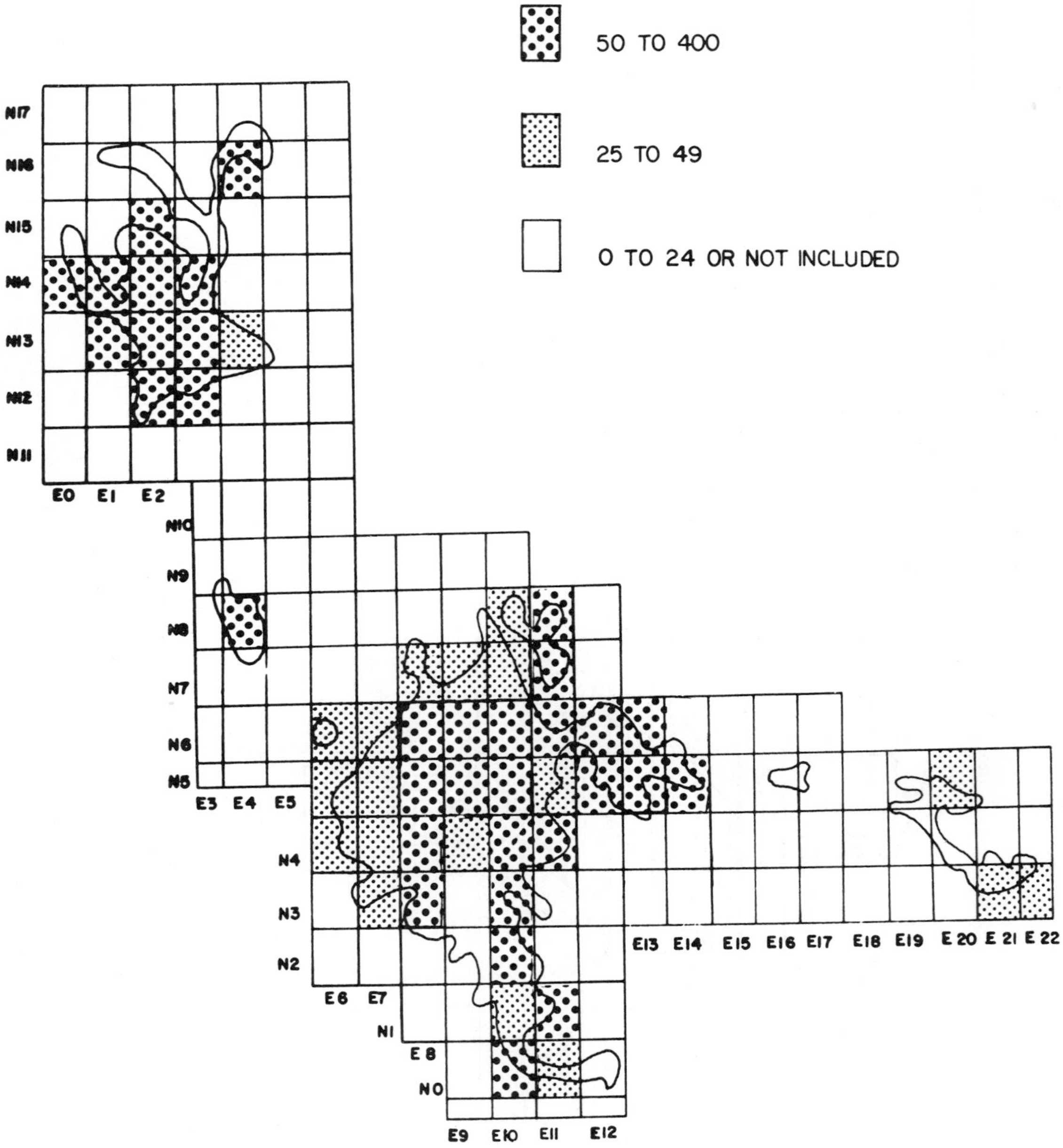

Figure 4.2. Number of sherds collected per hectare of collected terrace surface area, by grid square. Period IIIb–IV.

cluded plaza. Not much can be inferred from this except by contrasting it with the North Platform. The broad North Platform staircase seems to invite passage into the building from the Main Plaza. Once at the top of the staircase, and after passing through narrow colonnaded halls, the visitor would have been awed by the site of a huge sunken patio surrounded by high pyramid platforms (Plate 7). This passageway was a visual display, obviously intended by the architects of the North Platform to create an impression of power. No such display is present on the South Platform, indicating perhaps it was a more secluded building, access to which was not by individuals whom it was necessary to awe or inspire.

Since much more excavation has been carried out in the North Platform, a more detailed set of observations about its probable functions can be made than can be made about the South Platform's function or functions. In order to do this I make the following two assumptions: (*a*) Civic buildings are so defined because they lack any obvious architectural impediments to the general flow of traffic. Elite residences, facing inward on an enclosed patio were designed to restrict traffic flow, or permit the selection of entrants. It follows that the more architectural impediments there are in a building designed to restrict traffic flow, the more "private" a building could be. (*b*) Highest ranking personages in a hierarchically organized society are likely to be isolated more than others because in their daily activities they normally come more into contact with other higher ranking elites than with the general public. These individuals would tend to live and work, then, in buildings with more protective gates to restrict traffic flow than would lower ranking elites or nonelites.

The general accessibility of the North Platform from the Main Plaza ends at the sunken patio. The remainder of the feature is highly secluded, allowing the entry and exit of only selected personnel. The mound group labeled D in Figure 4.3, which looks much like an elite residence (since all its staircases face the patio), is the single most se-

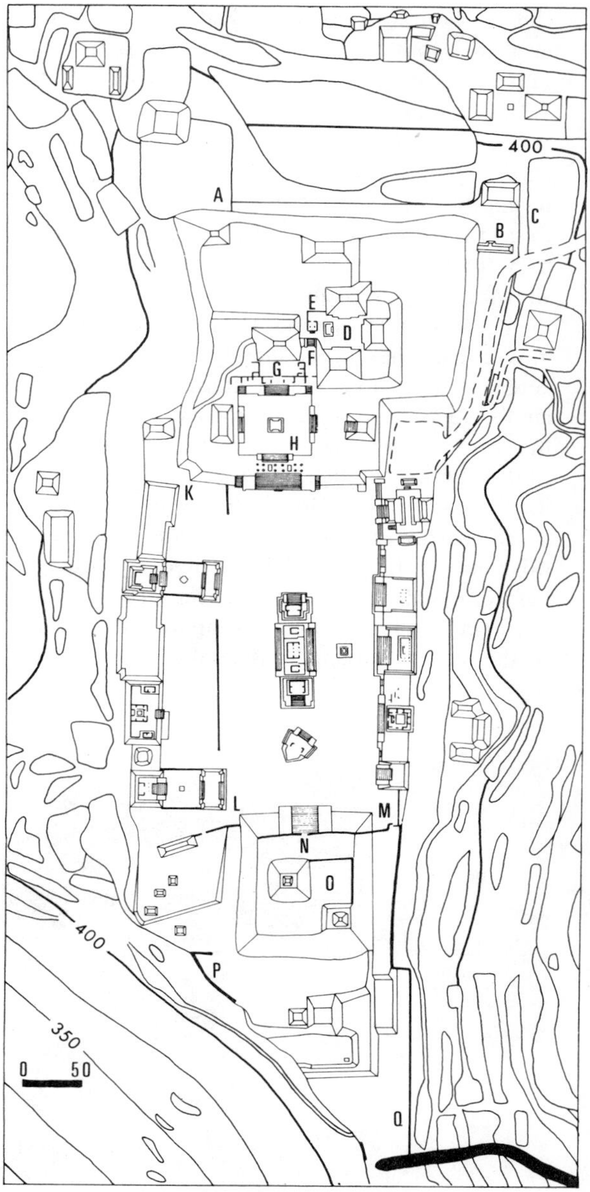

Figure 4.3. Monte Albán's Main Plaza and adjacent terraces. The square outlining the figure is based on the base map grid, and is oriented to magnetic north (north at the top of the figure). Letters are points referred to in the text.

cluded feature on the North Platform, and in fact, in all of Monte Albán. In order to pass from the sunken patio into this feature (following Figure 4.3), one must climb a small staircase at the northeast corner of the sunken patio, pass through a narrow gate into a narrow hallway (F), that leads to another staircase (at this juncture it is possible to go to the left to enter the large flat area north of Montículo I), climb this staircase, then another allowing entry to a small room with two columns, then pass from this room through a narrow door into a hall that turns sharply right (E), finally entering the patio area. An alternative and equally cumbersome route to this same patio takes one up the central staircase on the north edge of the sunken patio, through a narrow gate leading into the patio in front of Montículo I (G), then through a very narrow passage at the northeast corner of this patio leading to hall F, where one proceeds as before. Based on this traffic pattern, I suggest that this highly secluded mound group was the residence of the highest ranking household at Monte Albán, and, further, that the business of these persons could have been conducted in patio G; ambassadors, visiting elites, messengers, or delegations desiring to see the "ruler" of Monte Albán would, after climbing the North Platform staircase and after having been suitably impressed with the sunken patio, have passed through a gate into G, where the ruler could enter discretely and without having to pass through a general-access area, through the small gate directly from hall F and the residence.

The large flat areas to the northwest and east of the "ruler's palace" have been plowed such that no architecture remains, and therefore functional interpretation from surface evidence is not possible. Presumably, though, this would have been ideal space for the population supporting the palace—guards, cooks, craftsmen, and the like.

To conclude this section, what little evidence does exist tends to support the idea of a functional dichotomy between the North and South Platforms, the former a palace and civic building, the

Plate 7. Sunken patio of the North Platform, looking southwest.

latter a secluded building lacking residential functions, a temple perhaps—although there is no evidence specifically supporting that.

Two structures, however, on the Main Plaza probably can be functionally interpreted. The more obvious is the ball court, located off the southeast corner of the North Platform (Figure 4.3). Structure J is a carry-over from Period II, and was apparently built as a military showcase. This leaves a total of 14 other buildings, 6 along the west side of the plaza, 3 in the middle, and 5 along the east side (Figure 4.3). It is striking that during Period IIIb, Monte Albán was made up of 14 *barrios* (plus a fifteenth, the Main Plaza area itself). Perhaps each of these units and/or the societies that each *barrio* may have represented maintained a building on the Main Plaza for the purpose perhaps of housing elites who were the league representatives. Unfortunately, no archaeological evidence exists that ties any one of these buildings to any of the *barrios* at Monte Albán, or to any specific region or community outside the city, so the hypothesis cannot be tested directly, but I will return to this point in a later section in order to elucidate some indirect evidence that may be relevant.

In summary, then, the Main Plaza was apparently a civic and elite residential area, dominated on the north end by a combined civic building and palace, and on the south end by perhaps a temple, although its identification as such is uncertain. Included also are a ball court, a military trophycase, as well as 14 other buildings that may have housed representatives to a military league. Continuing into Period III militarism is the dominant iconographic and epigraphic theme in carved stone monuments. Of nine Period III stelae found in and adjacent to the Main Plaza, six portray bound captives (Caso 1928; Marcus 1976a:131).

Accessibility of the Main Plaza

Prior interpretations of the Main Plaza have tended to portray it as a generally accessible, public area. Paddock, for example, writes of the public pageantry there, visible to all who might choose to stroll through (Paddock 1966:153). Winter and Payne (1976) have argued that the Main Plaza was a distribution point for products produced by craftsmen in the city. Markets are notoriously difficult to identify by direct archaeological evidence, but, in my opinion, the setting and morphology of the Main Plaza strongly argues against this or any interpretation in which it is viewed as a feature open to the general public. First, the Main Plaza as a whole has a closed, segregated appearance, unlike what one would predict for a structure that would have served the general population. All Main Plaza staircases face inward on the plaza; the backs of buildings facing out onto the remainder of the city all are composed of very high nearly vertical walls. By Period IIIb, only three small entryways to the plaza were present (K, L, and M of Figure 4.3), and each of these could easily have been guarded to assure the regulation and control of traffic flow. The modern entrance to the plaza is a ramp built over the northwest corner of the ball-court building, but in ancient times this would not have been a gate since the ball court abuts directly on the corner of the North Platform. The terrace along the east base of the North Platform, upon which the modern road is built, was probably not a traffic artery in ancient times. As far as I can tell, at the point where the modern road enters the parking lot (1 in Figure 4.3), a ramp had to be built by the Mexican government road crews over a vertical ancient wall. Similarly, at the point where the modern road comes up on this terrace (just south of points B and C of Figure 4.3), a similar ramp had to be built. Further evidence that the ramp along the east base of the North Platform was not a roadway in ancient times is the placement of Terrace 24 (B in Figure 4.3), directly in the path of any traffic flow. A similar long, broad terrace is found along the North Platform's north base, but it, too, apparently was not a traffic artery. Some of the residences exposed during Caso's excavation of Terrace 20 (Caso 1938: *Plano* 13) are situated such that they would have blocked any traffic flow here (A in Figure 4.3). Residences were built right up to the north base of the North Platform.

The flow of traffic between buildings within the Main Plaza was facilitated by the broad, flat plaza itself, but traffic between the Main Plaza buildings and features outside was inhibited by steep walls and narrow passageways. This would make sense if the plaza area had been a center of regional decision making by high ranking elites rather than some variety of general-access place. The secludedness of the Main Plaza becomes even more apparent in view of the nature of traffic flow in the city as a whole. Figure 4.4 is a reconstruction of Monte Albán's ancient road system. Only well-defined roads are shown. These are features that extend for hundreds of meters, or even a kilometer or more, easily followed today; and these same features are supported by retaining walls, and, in places, cut into the slope. Figure 4.4 makes the distinction between minor roads and major roads—the difference being one of dimensions. Although it is difficult today to reconstruct the exact width of any of these features, in general the roads defined as major tend to be 3–8 m in width (Plate 8), while minor roads range from about 2 to about 3 m. The hundreds of ramps and trails within the ancient city, some of which are still visible on the surface today, are not indicated. These would not have been major traffic arteries because they tend to be of limited length, perhaps joining together several related terraces, but not allowing the general flow of traffic through the city as a whole. Two roads in Monte Albán proper were probably the major arteries handling traffic flow of the latter type. These are labeled E and F in Figure 4.4. Road E is the more important of the two, running more or less midway through the major residential zone in Monte Albán proper, servicing site subdivisions 6, 7, and 8. Road F runs

Plate 8. Looking east along road I just east of point B of Figure 4.4.

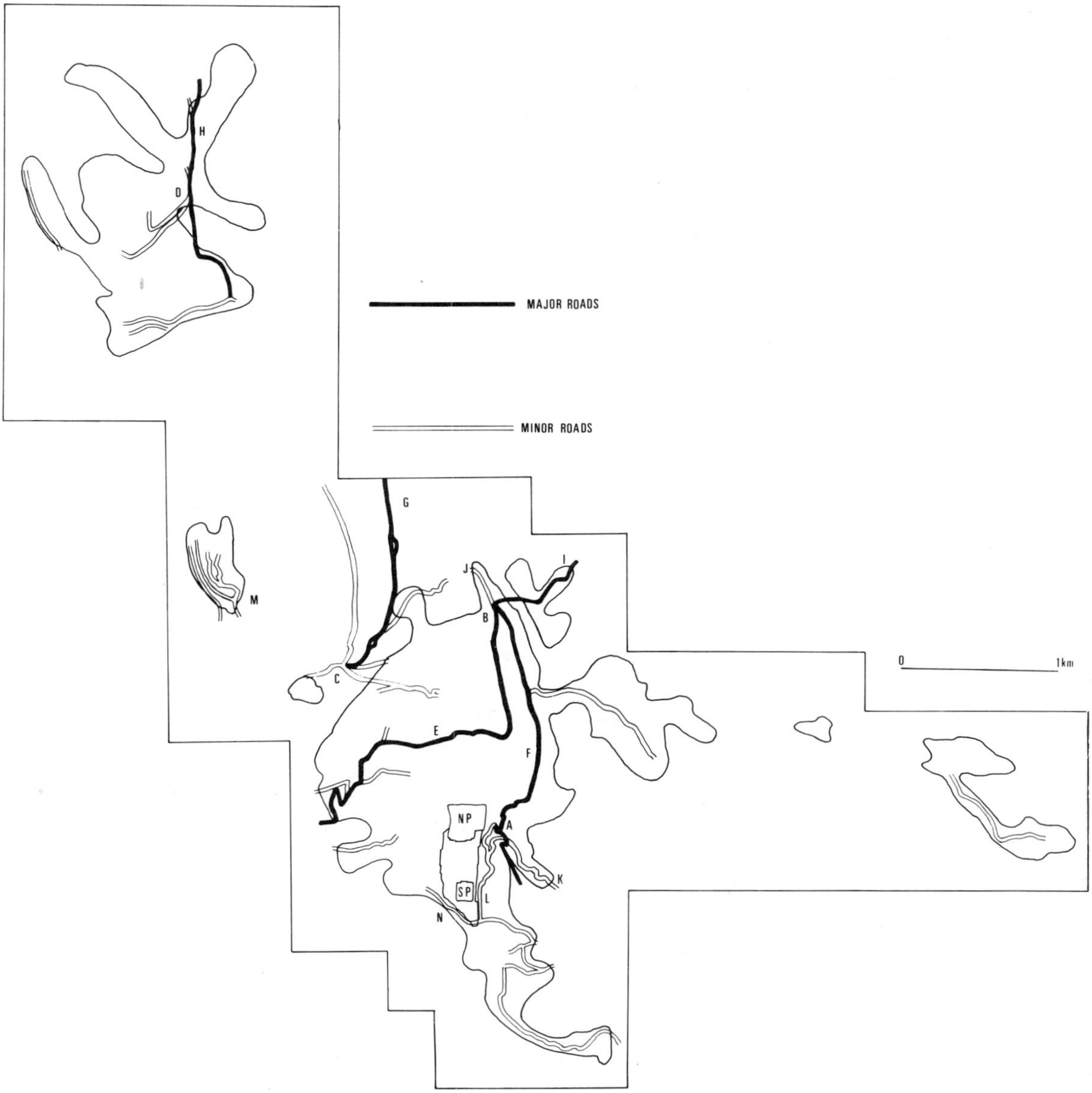

Figure 4.4. Reconstruction of Monte Albán's ancient road system. Letters are at points discussed in the text.

along the north–south trending ridge on which are situated site subdivisions 3, 4, and 5. This road continues south and east out of the city, running in the direction of the modern village of Xoxocotlan while the two other major roads pertaining to Monte Albán are outside Monte Albán proper. Road G of Figure 4.4 was probably the major route between Monte Albán proper and Atzompa, while road H was Atzompa's major internal route.

Four important traffic nodes are apparent in Figure 4.4 (points A, B, C, and D). Node B was the city's most important, in the sense that the most major and minor roads join here. At this point roads E and F join, to form road I and a smaller road J enters the city also at this point. Node B is Terrace 523, a large ramp situated over the defensive wall that I earlier suggested could be a gatelike feature. The other important traffic node within Monte Albán proper is point A of Figure 4.4. This is a lesser node, where road F is crossed by two smaller roads, K and L (L divides into two very narrow ramps at this point).

Two features of Monte Albán's road system form a strong argument that the city was not a marketing community and that the Main Plaza was not a marketplace. First, the Main Plaza apparently was not directly accessible by any of the community's major or minor roads (Figure 4.4). This supports the hypothesis that the plaza was a relatively closed, secluded area, not a public place into and out of which there would have been abundant traffic flow. Secondly, Monte Albán proper lacks the overall spatial patterning often typical of preindustrial market towns, where a spokelike arrangement of roads radiates outward from a central marketing district (cf. Hull 1976 and Krapf-Askari 1969, who include maps of traditional African marketing cities). Traffic nodes of highest accessibility in such cities are near the center of town, at the marketing place. Teotihuacan illustrates this pattern, although it was organized on a grid system. A probable market there, the "Great Compound," at the center of the city sits directly at the intersection of the major north–south and east–west roads (Millon 1973:37). Monte Albán's traffic nodes, by contrast, are all near its edges or are outside the community's boundaries—surely a strange pattern for a market town.

Monte Albán's status as a production–marketing center will be considered more fully below, utilizing the surface evidence for workshop activities. Based only on the road pattern, and on the morphology of the Main Plaza, however, I conclude with some sense of security that Monte Albán was not a marketing center, and that the Main Plaza was not a marketing place.

The Monte Albán *Barrios*

During Monte Albán Period IIIb all 15 of the site's subdivisions were occupied. I assume that this was not the case during Period IV, although there is no direct archaeological evidence at the moment to support this contention. The abandonment of the Main Plaza after Period IIIb implies that the city had lost its role as a regional capital, and this probably meant a loss of much of its population as well. I am probably reasonably safe, then, in the assumption that the morphology of the city as we see it today is a reasonably accurate reflection of what it was like at its height during Period IIIb. Undoubtedly there was some architectural modification of the IIIb city by its later inhabitants, but I have been unable to find any evidence either in the literature or from the surface for major construction pertaining to Periods IV or V. A more serious problem for the analysis that is to follow has to do with patterns of artifact deposition. To a certain extent it is likely that more recent patterns of deposition have "masked" or blended with the earlier patterns. This is a problem that cannot be dealt with at all for Period IV, since we have no idea where people were living within the city at that time, or how many there were. Fortunately, we can identify the location and extent of the Late Postclassic or Period V settlement. Since the city was considerably reduced in area by that time, it will be possible to distinguish to a certain extent deposition patterns pertaining to that period from earlier periods. I will assume that the surface evidence for patterns of artifact deposition at Monte Albán relates largely to Period IIIb and/or earlier periods, except for those areas we know were densely occupied during Period V. Using this hypothesis I will be able to argue that the city changed dramatically in form and function between the time of the abandonment of the Main Plaza and the beginning of Period V.

The following is a description of the 15 site subdivisions as I believe they were in Period IIIb, along with some suggestions about how they may have changed through time and about why there is variability among these units. Probably the most obvious dimension of variability between the site subdivisions has to do with size. Some subdivisions are much larger than others and contain many more terraces. Atzompa, for example, has nearly 500 terraces, while subdivision 13 has fewer than 50. Variability between subdivisions also exists in terms of the monumentality of public and elite residential architecture. Table 4.1 summarizes some of the differences between the site subdivisions, specifically differences in total surface area of residential terraces (elaborate and nonelaborate), population estimates derived from these values, and the total volume of mounded buildings. These three variables, elite population, nonelite population, and total mound volume by site subdivision are interrelated. That is, subdivisions with fewer nonelites have smaller numbers of elites and less in the way of mounded construction, and vice versa. Row 14 of Table 4.1 contains the percentage of each subdivision population that resided on terraces with elaborate residences. The value for subdivision 2 is probably too low since I did not include an estimate of the elite population residing in the Main Plaza (I have no way of estimating the size of that population). The percentages derived show a considerable amount of regularity, the range being from about 1% to about 13%. Most, however, range from 3% to 6%. This regularity manifests itself also as a positive correlation between the nonelite population and elite population estimates, using a rank–order correlation technique. The value for Spearman's r_s derived for these two variables is .74, significant above the .01 level ($Z = 2.77$) (Blalock 1972: 416–418).

Similarly, a positive correlation was derived for the estimates of nonelite population and total mound volume for each subdivision ($r_s = .75$), significant again above the .01 level ($Z = 2.88$). The latter regularity can also be expressed by calculating the total mound volume in each subdivision per capita (cubic meters of fill per person)—see Table 4.1. Most values fall between 3 m^3 and 20 m^3 per person, with two notable exceptions. Site subdivision 3 has a relatively large value. Part of this variation could be due to my methodology rather than to some real difference between this and other subdivisions. It is possible, for example, that the geometric method used to delineate the limits of subdivisions underestimated the area encompassed by this subdivision. It is also possible that Terrace 87, a very large area west of the subdivision 3 elaborate residence, was residential (I classed it as civic in function because it lacks evidence for houses). It is also possible that this subdivision was distinct in this regard. Why this might be so I cannot say, but, will be outlined below, this part of the site is unusual in other regards as well.

Site subdivision 2 is substantially different from the others in terms of cubic meters of mound fill per person (with a value of 229). This may reflect the fact that this subdivision was not simply one of the *barrios*, but, instead, was the center of regional decision making. A high correlation exists between mound volume and nonelite population in the other subdivisions probably because elites in each subdivision depended on their attached population, or some portion of it, for labor in construc-

Table 4.1. Site Subdivision Statistics

	Nonelaborate residential terraces						Terraces with elaborate residences								
Site subdivision	Surface area sum (m^2)	Mean (m^2)	*N*	Standard deviation (m^2)	*V*	Estimated population	Surface area sum (ha)	Mean (m^2)	*N*	Standard deviation (m^2)	Estimated elite population	Total estimated population	Percentage elite population (of total population)	Total mound volume (m^3)	m^3 per capita (of the population lower estimate)
1	76,541	665.6	115	866.2	1.3	1,227–2,454	19,642	6,547	3	5,942.2	79–159	1,306–2,612	6.0%	16,148	12.36
2	194,560 (excludes Main Plaza)	888.4	219	1,066.4	1.2	3,119–6,238	48,599	5,399	9	5,824.9	196–363 (excludes Main Plaza)	3,315–6,630	6.0%	759,498	229.1
3	6,470	431.3	15	670.9	1.56	104–208	3,969	3,969	1	0	16–32	120–240	13.0%	7,682	64.0
4	33,824	768.7	44	1,079.4	1.4	542–1,084	4,694	2,347	2	825.9	19–38	561–1,122	3.4%	6,879	12.3
5	47,587	834.9	57	1,055.9	1.26	763–1,526	1,696	1,696	1	0	7–14	770–1,540	.9%	6,276	8.2
6	62,984	473.6	133	608.5	1.28	1,009–2,018	18,037	6,012	3	2,766.8	73–146	1,082–2,164	6.7%	12,350	11.4
7	151,208	530.6	285	777.8	1.47	2,424–4,848	3,290	1,645	2	298.4	13–26	2,437–4,874	.5%	7,218	3.0
8	55,212	452.6	122	587.5	1.3	885–1,770	15,200	15,200	1	0	61–122	946–1,892	6.4%	9,088	9.6
9	7,014	175.35	40	94.0	.54	112–224	unknown	unknown	1	0	5–10 (probably)	123–246	4.0%	348	2.8
10	11,129	209.9	53	230.4	1.1	179–356	482	482	1	0	5–10	180–260	2.7%	632	3.5
11	145,158	316.2	459	397.0	1.25	2,327–4,654	33,153	4,144	8	4,435.6	134–268	2,461–4,922	5.4%	66,828	27.2
12	31,351	188.9	166	305.8	1.6	503–1,006	1,147	1,147	1	0	5–10	508–1,016	1.0%	2,860	5.6
13	11,702	293	40	321.0	1.1	188–375	1,261	631	2	36.1	5–10	193–386	2.5%	3,688	19.1
14	17,436	285.8	61	311.6	1.1	280–560	1,102	1,102	1	0	5–10	284–568	1.8%	5,125	18.0
15	27,495	205.2	134	329.6	1.61	441–882	3,028	3,028	1	0	12–24	453–906	2.6%	7,460	16.5
Whole site[a]	902,947	458.5	1,969	725.7	1.58	14,475–28,950	155,300	4,313.9	37	4,269.3	633–1266	15,108–30,216	4.2%	912,080	60.4

[a]Includes some not included in the site subdivisions.

tion. Smaller subdivisions therefore had smaller buildings. The public and elite residential buildings in site subdivision 2, however, were probably constructed using the labor of a larger population than that in subdivision 2 alone.

I suggested in the preceding section that 14 of the buildings on the Main Plaza may have been buildings representing each of the 14 site subdivisions (that is, all subdivisions except for subdivision 2). These *representative* buildings, like the mounded buildings in the site subdivisions, vary in size. Figure 4.5 compares the variability of volume of mounded buildings in the 14 site subdivisions and of mounded buildings I call representative buildings, each set ranked from largest to smallest. The two populations exhibit essentially the same pattern of variation. That is, the slope from largest to smallest values for the two populations is approximately the same, except that the largest site subdivision volumes are much larger than the largest volumes of representative buildings, and the smallest volumes for the site subdivision buildings are much smaller than the smallest Main Plaza buildings. This exercise has not tested the hypothesis that each site subdivision had a representative building on the Main Plaza, but it does lend some support to the idea, however, since the variability in volumes of the buildings in these two populations is not greatly different.

A second dimension of variability between the site subdivisions lies in the surface areas of terraces identified as residential (Table 4.1). It occurred to me at first that this variability could be due to topography alone. Terraces built in some subdivisions may have tended to be in more rugged terrain, requiring smaller terraces, but this argument seemed weak because terrace areas are larger, in general, on Monte Albán proper, even where the terrain is steep (for example in site subdivisions 1 and 3), and Atzompa's mean residential terrace area is smaller than those on Monte Albán proper even though there is a wide range of topography at Atzompa, probably roughly approximating the range on Monte Albán proper.

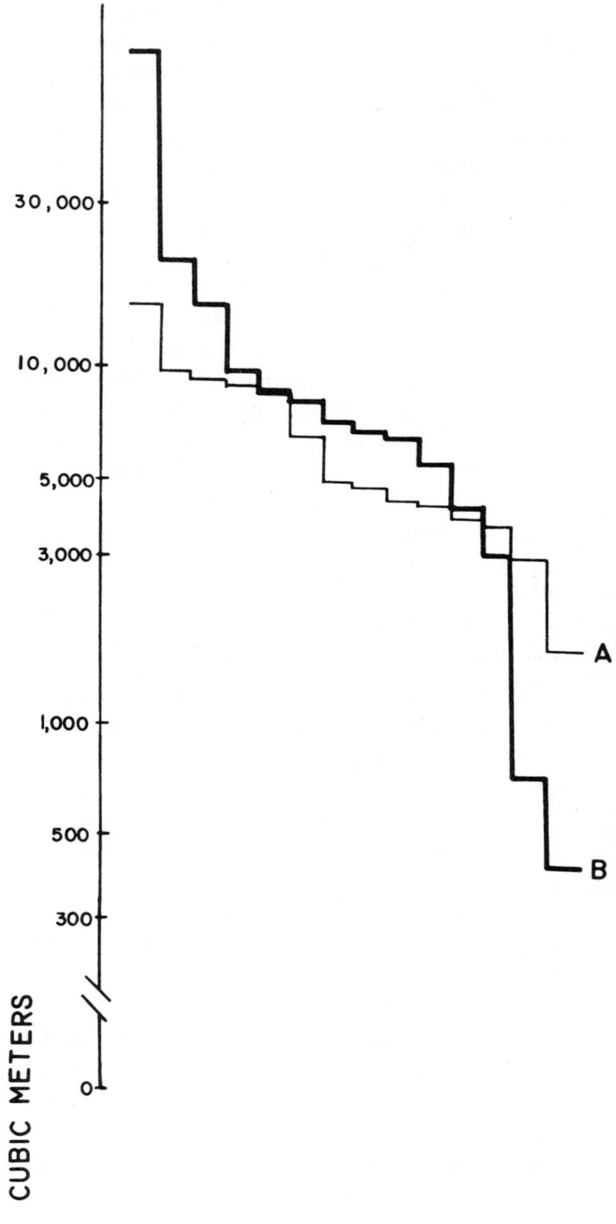

Figure 4.5. Comparison of size variation in mound volumes of ***representative*** Main Plaza buildings (A) and mound volumes of site subdivisions (B), both ranked from largest values to lowest values.

During his survey of the Central Valley of Oaxaca, Kowalewski noted that Periods Late I and IIIb were similar in having a preponderance of small communities, including many isolated residences, hamlets, and small villages (Kowalewski 1976:480, 818). Periods II and IIIa, he notes, were different in that a large proportion of the population resided in larger communities. He interprets this to mean that the kinds of social units involved in production varied through time (Kowalewski 1976:818); during Periods Late I and IIIb, he argues, the basic unit of production was small, perhaps involving individual households. Suprahousehold units, on the other hand, may have been the basic units of production in the region during Periods II and IIIa. If this kind of change through time had occurred also at Monte Albán, it might be possible to explain some of the variability in terrace surface areas between the site subdivisions.

The following evidence seems to support Kowalewski's hypothesis as applied to Monte Albán:

1. Those areas of the site with the longest occupational histories, namely, those subdivisions in Monte Albán proper (except for subdivision 10), should show the greatest variability in residential terrace surface area since, presumably, terraces visible on the surface now represent construction during periods when the basic social units were small as well as during times when the basic social units were larger. Variability should be less than this in surface areas of residential terraces in those portions of the site occupied during only one period. The coefficient of variation *V*, calculated by dividing the standard deviation by the mean, is commonly used for comparing the variability in populations with different means (Blalock 1972: 88). Larger values for *V* indicate more variability. The values for *V* calculated for the Monte Albán site subdivisions support this hypothesis. Those subdivisions with the longest occupational histories, including occupations during Periods Late I and IIIb as well as during Periods II and IIIa, have a mean value for *V* of 1.35. The predominantly IIIb subdivisions (numbers 10, 11, 13, and 14) have a mean value for *V* of 1.1, indicating less internal variability in surface areas of residential terraces.

2. Residential terraces built when basic social units were larger would probably not be destroyed in later periods when the basic social units were smaller. It would have been easier to simply subdivide existing large terraces. The mean residential terrace surface areas in those parts of the site with Periods II and IIIa occupations, then, should be larger than the means for subdivisions occupied predominantly during Period IIIb. This hypothesis is again supported since the mean surface area of residential terraces in areas with Periods II and IIIa occupations is 630.7 m^2, while the mean for those parts of the site with predominantly IIIb occupation is only 276 m^2. The predominance of smaller terraces in the IIIb site subdivisions is easily seen by inspection of the frequency polygons for residential terrace surface areas (Figures 4.6–4.21). Further, there is some evidence that, as I suggested before, large terraces may have been subdivided during Period IIIb, to accommodate smaller social units. Stone walls were noted that subdivide large terraces at the following locations: Terraces 21, 92, 149, 204, and 491.

3. According to the hypothesis, any portion of the site occupied only during Periods Late I and IIIb should show little variability in residential terrace surface area, and the mean terrace surface areas should be smaller than areas including occupations during Periods II and IIIa. Two such locations exist at Monte Albán. El Gallo was founded in Late I, abandoned before Period II, and not reoccupied until Period IIIb. Mogollito (square N6E6) had a roughly similar occupational history, although it was founded sometime during Period Early I. The mean value of *V* for these two areas is identical to the value of *V* for the IIIb subdivisions (1.1), and the mean surface area of residential terraces is actually less than that for the IIIb areas (239.2 m^2).

I conclude that during three periods in the

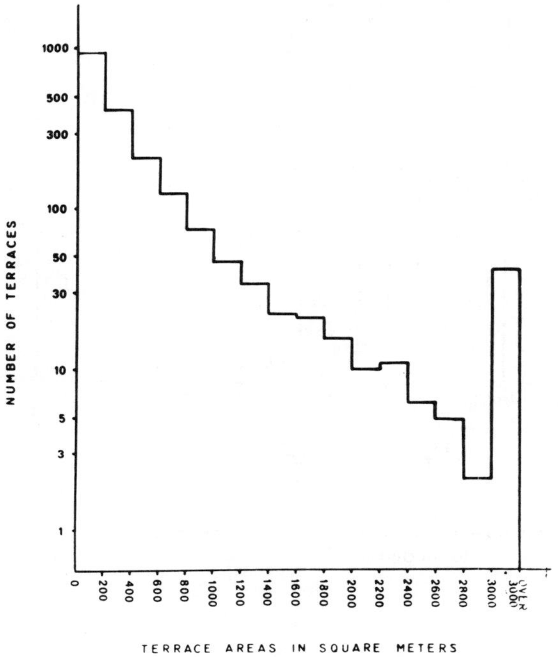

Figure 4.6. Histogram of residential terrace surface areas. Total site.

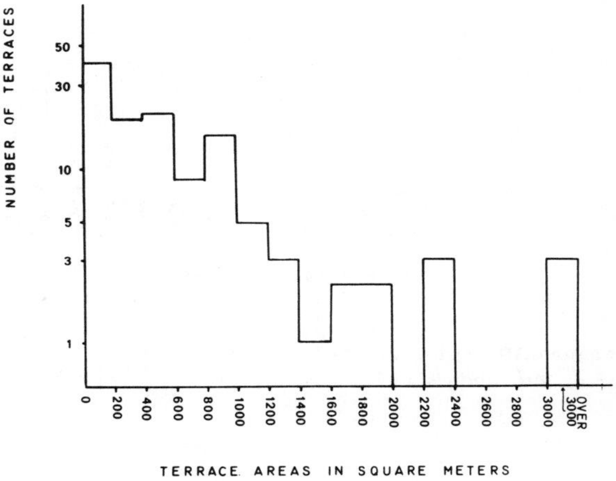

Figure 4.7. Histogram of residential terrace surface areas. Site subdivision 1.

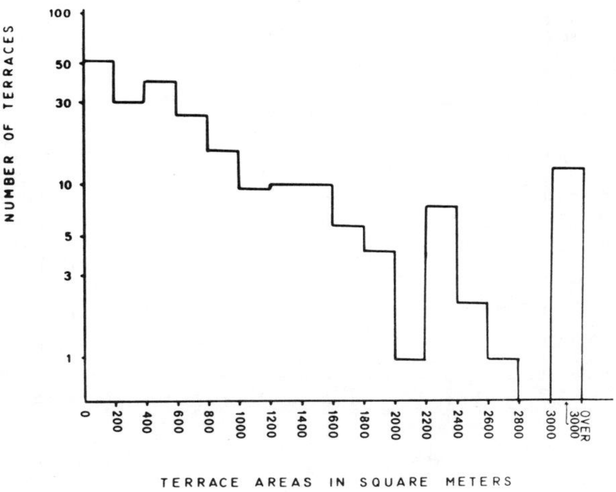

Figure 4.8. Histogram of residential terrace surface areas. Site subdivision 2.

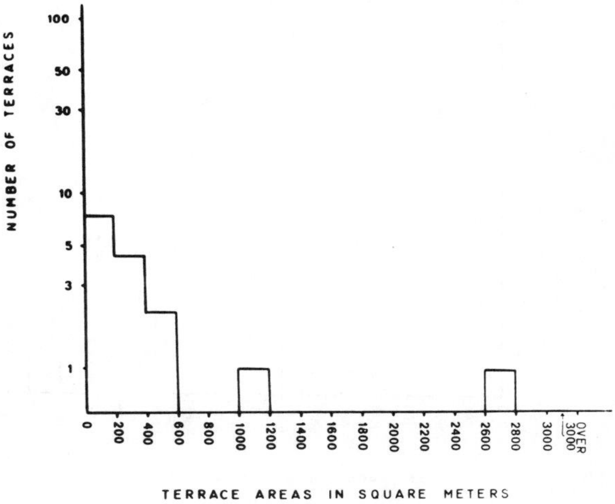

Figure 4.9. Histogram of residential terrace surface areas. Site subdivision 3.

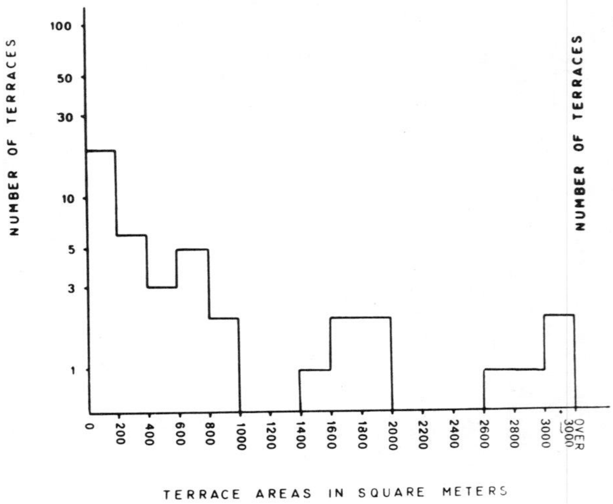

Figure 4.10. Histogram of residential terrace surface areas. Site subdivision 4.

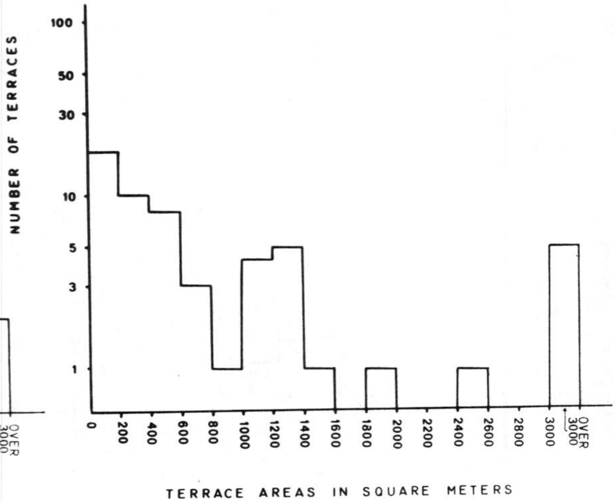

Figure 4.11. Histogram of residential terrace surface areas. Site subdivision 5.

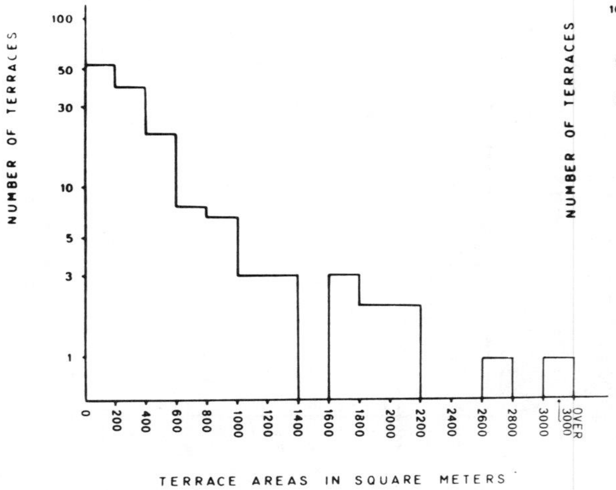

Figure 4.12. Histogram of residential terrace surface areas. Site subdivision 6.

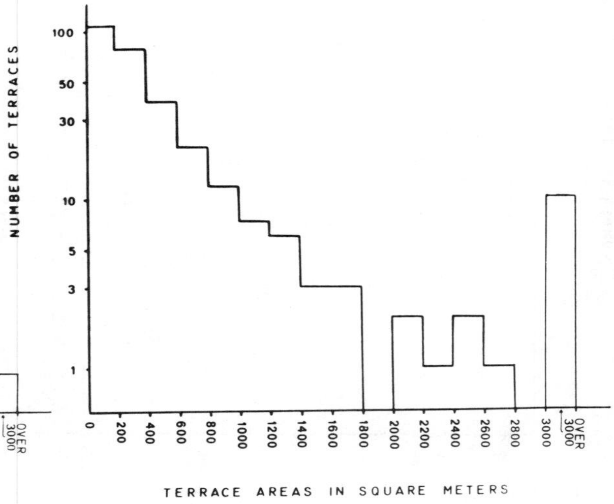

Figure 4.13. Histogram of residential terrace surface areas. Site subdivision 7.

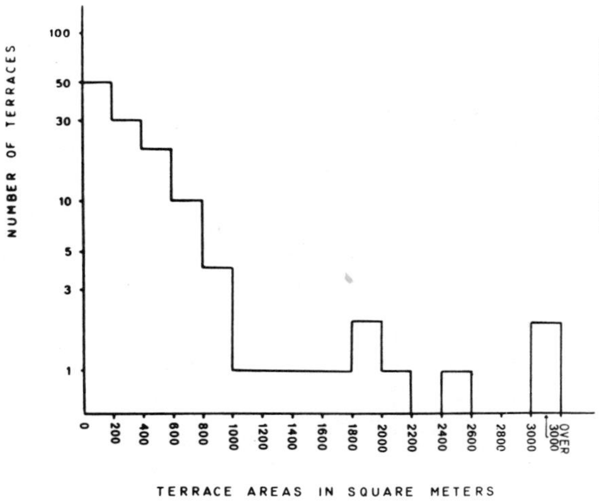

Figure 4.14. Histogram of residential terrace surface areas. Site subdivision 8.

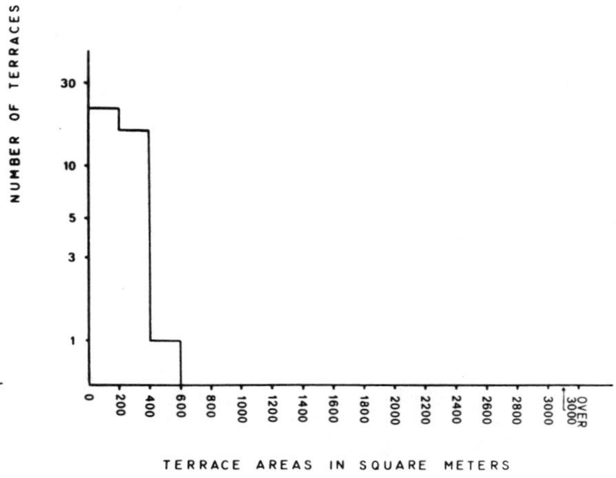

Figure 4.15. Histogram of residential terrace surface areas. Site subdivision 9.

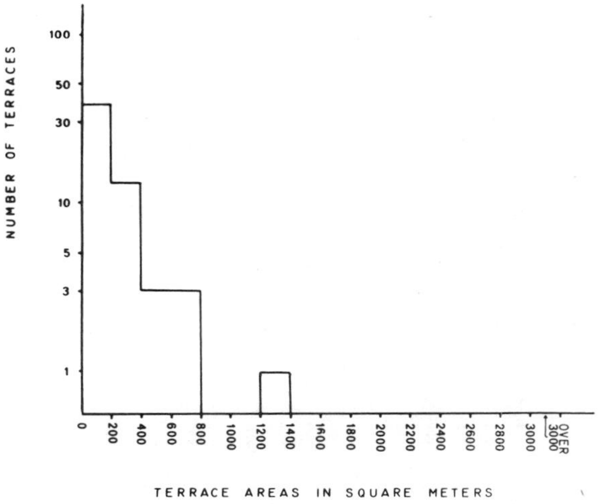

Figure 4.16. Histogram of residential terrace surface areas. Site subdivision 10.

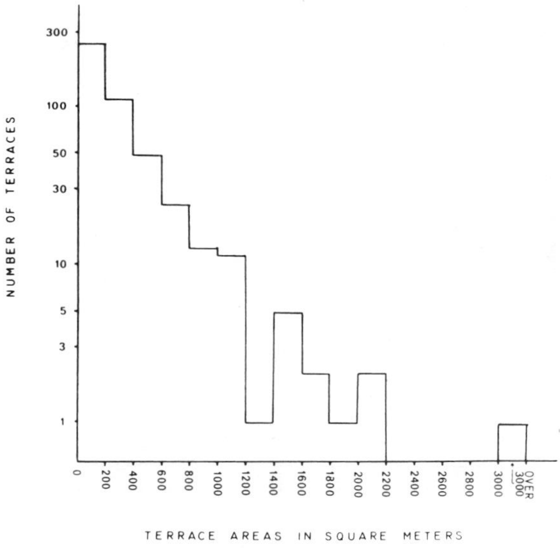

Figure 4.17. Histogram of residential terrace surface areas. Site subdivision 11.

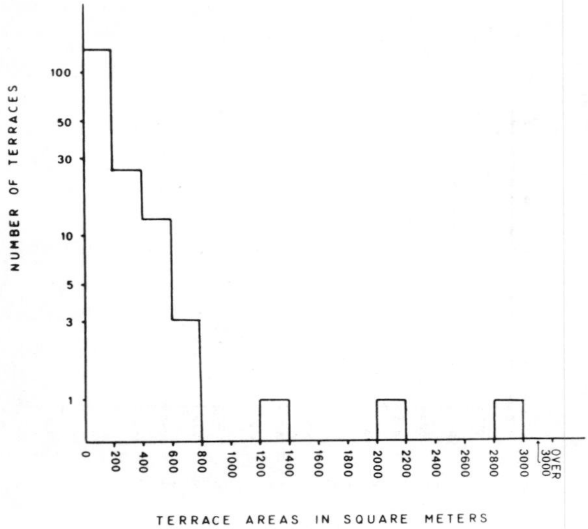

Figure 4.18. Histogram of residential terrace surface areas. Site subdivision 12.

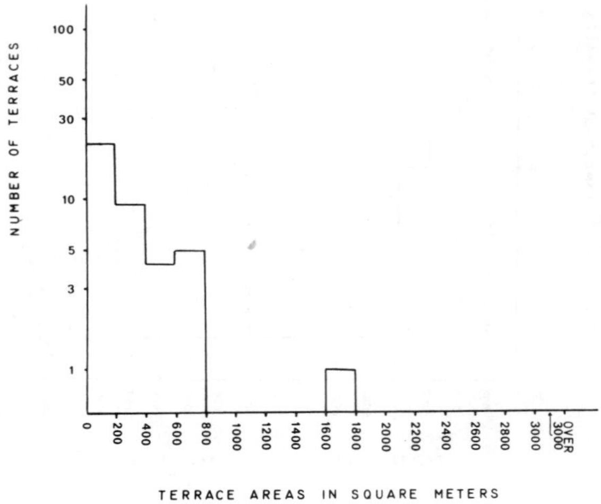

Figure 4.19. Histogram of residential terrace surface areas. Site subdivision 13.

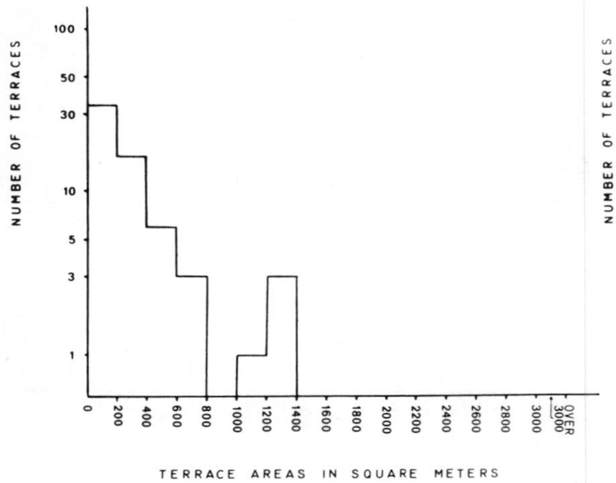

Figure 4.20. Histogram of residential terrace surface areas. Site subdivision 14.

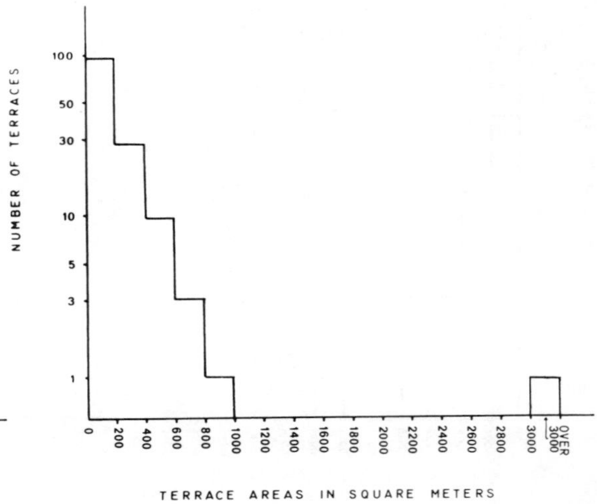

Figure 4.21. Histogram of residential terrace surface areas. Site subdivision 15.

city's history there were two sizes of social groups building and residing on residential terraces. During Periods Late I and IIIb these social units were smaller than the units common in Periods II and IIIa. Exactly what these units were cannot be easily discovered from surface evidence alone, but by far the largest number of terraces in the IIIb areas range from somewhat less than 200 m^2 up to about 400 m^2, suggesting single households as the basic unit (assuming each required roughly 300 m^2 of terrace surface area). The much larger values for residential terrace surface areas in the chronologically mixed portion of the site are more difficult to interpret in terms of the exact composition of social units, but the mean value derived, 630.7 m^2, is roughly double the area presumably needed by each household. Even in these subdivisions, however, the most frequent size class is that near and below 200 m^2, probably single-family terraces.

Descriptions of the Monte Albán *Barrios*

The remaining variability we have been able to discover from surface evidence has to do with certain architectural features and the differential distribution of artifacts. It will be most convenient to relate these differences by describing the site subdivisions one by one:

SITE SUBDIVISION 1

This subdivision is centered on the mound group cluster that includes Terraces 1458 (*Siete Venado*), 1461, and 207. This *barrio* is distinct from the others at Monte Albán proper in having its own set of defensive walls, a double system with an outer, larger wall, and an inner, smaller wall. These walls form roughly a half-circle with the mound group cluster at approximately the center point. Defensive features were not built along the west edge of the area, because the natural slope here is very steep, but the wall built along the outside edge of Terrace 231 and a small wall fragment built just southwest of Terrace 145 are exceptions to this. This system of fortifications seems to have been built late in the city's history, probably toward or after the end of Period IIIb, although the exact date cannot be ascertained. Evidence of the late date of construction of these features lies first in the fact that the walls were built over existing terraces. For example, Terraces 146 and 213 were probably originally one larger terrace divided by the wall; the same thing can be said of Terraces 150, 147, 214, 149, and 148. Second, we carried out a very small excavation on Terrace 225 (N2E10), at a point where the interior edge of the lower wall could be seen clearly resting on the terrace surface (at roughly the middle of the terrace). Figure 4.22 shows the cross section of this small cut. The regularly cut and regularly placed stones of the defensive wall resting on a

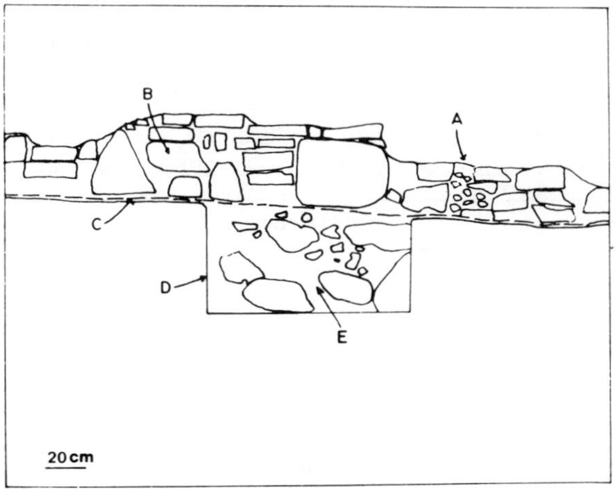

Figure 4.22. Cross section of cut into the outer defensive wall where it crosses Terrace 225 (N2E10). The line labeled (A) is the contemporary surface of the wall. (B) are stones pertaining to the wall construction. (C) is a packed-earth surface, probably the terrace's ancient surface. (D) is the limit of the excavation, and (E) is fill of uncut stones and earth, deposited when the terrace was constructed.

packed-earth surface are easy to distinguish from the irregular stones below that surface that were used as fill during the construction of the terrace. Sherds from the packed-earth surface, and from the fill of the wall itself include some IIIb–IV categories, and two sherds of our category 3030, a probable Period IV diagnostic (Appendix II; Table 4.2). I conclude the wall was built late in Period IIIb or during Period IV.

The interesting feature of the set of defensive walls is that, while providing protection along the relatively shallow slopes to the east and south, the walls would also have served to cut this subdivision off from the remainder of the city. Only a very narrow gap remains at Terrace 145 between the terminus of the walls and the edge of the slope, presumably enabling the restriction of the flow of traffic into and out of the area south of the South Platform.

Two roads within this subdivision converge on the mound group cluster (Figure 4.4), one from the east, the other from the ridge to the south, and pass through gates in the outer wall at Terraces 242 and 250. An additional opening in the wall is present at Terrace 211, and a ramp running just inside the outer defensive wall connects this gate with the east road to the east of Terrace 304. At two of the openings in the outer wall, Terraces 242 and 211, there are small isolated platform mounds. These mounds may have had gatelike functions, perhaps serving as points for traffic control or the collection of gate taxes. A series of such small, isolated mounds or small mound groups exists at Monte Albán, all near the edges of the city, and all located adjacent to ancient roads. I hypothesize that all these features functioned as gates of some sort (I refer to the mounds on Terraces 79, 85, 92, 211, 242, 327, 337, 703, and Atzompa Terraces 136, 137, 392, 413, 419, 431, 462, and 469).

Table 4.2. Summary of Chronologically Diagnostic Sherds Found in the Terrace 225 Excavation

Category	Period	Number
0008	I	1
0032	I	1
0393	I	2
0395	I	1
0402	I	1
1126	III–IV	1
1207	I–IIIa	1
1264	IIIa	1
1366	Late I	1
1367	Early I	1
2010	I	3
2065	I	3
2077	I	1
2079	I	1
2080	I	1
2085	Early I–II	1
3030	IV	2

Little evidence exists from our surface survey and collections that indicates any special productive activities in site subdivision 1, or any unusual patterns of artifact deposition. One possible exception to this is that this area has more evidence for quarrying of the limestone bedrock than the other subdivisions (Figure 4.23). Perhaps some of the produce from this activity was used in the construction of the Main Plaza, since little direct evidence for quarrying has been found near the latter feature. The relative abundance of *pounders* noted in this subdivision may be related to the quarrying (Figure 4.24). (Pounders, as we define them, are fist-sized rocks with rough, abraded edges that look as though they have been used for pounding rock.)

SITE SUBDIVISION 2

This area was unlike the other site subdivisions. The amount (in cubic meters) of mound fill per capita here is well above that for the others, implying that the labor for construction of buildings was drawn from a wider circle than just the immediate population. In addition to the Main Plaza, this subdivision contains a relatively large number of mound groups that appear to have been elaborate residences (Terraces 5, 17, 18, 24, those on 27, 51, 169, 256, and 264). Virtually all the carved stone monuments at Monte Albán come from the Main Plaza or terraces in this subdivision adjacent to it. Of a total of roughly 360 monuments from the site, I know of only two outside subdivision 2, one, a carved lintel from Terrace 1458, in subdivision 1, and the other a fragment of what appears to have been a small stela from the small ball court in subdivision 4.

Several categories of nonceramic artifacts were noted frequently on the surface in subdivision 2, which I believe were more frequently consumed by an elite. The items include marine shell (Figure 4.25), obsidian (Figure 4.26) (both of which could only have been obtained through long-distance exchange), and a group of what I refer to as *unusual rocks and minerals* (Figure 4.27). Included in this category are marblelike manos and metates, greenstone, ignumbrite, serpentine, onyx, jade, jadeite, fossils, magnetite, mica, groundstone beads, alabaster, coral, jasper, ochre, and malachite.

The relatively high concentration of items such as those in site subdivision 2 probably reflects the higher density of elite families here, but also may reflect the fact that more workshops were present here, producing the items used by those living in the Main Plaza and the adjacent group of elaborate residences. Thre is some evidence for the latter in the nature of distribution of features we identified as shell and obsidian workshops. Marine shell and obsidian both occur in very small quantities all over the surface of Monte Albán. Normally, if these items are encountered on a terrace, only one or two fragments are present, a density we refer to as *sparse*. Sparse obsidian was noted on 38% of the Monte Albán terraces, and sparse shell was noted on 6%. On a few terraces abundant shell or obsidian was noted, which usually implies that 10 or more pieces could be sighted in a small area im-

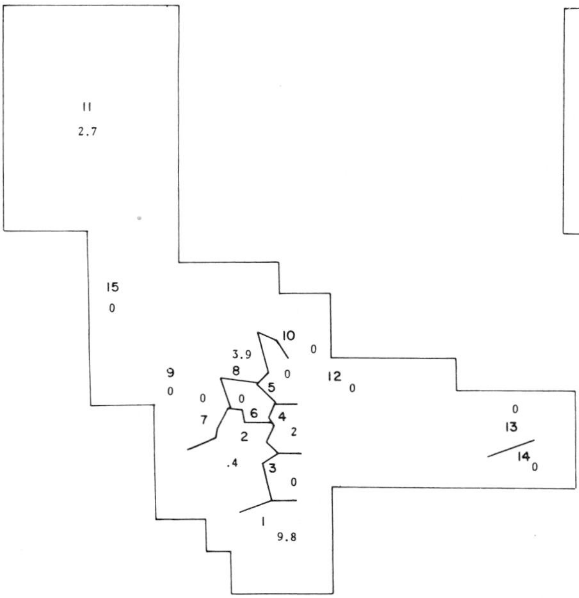

Figure 4.23. Percentage of terraces with evidence for quarrying, by site subdivision.

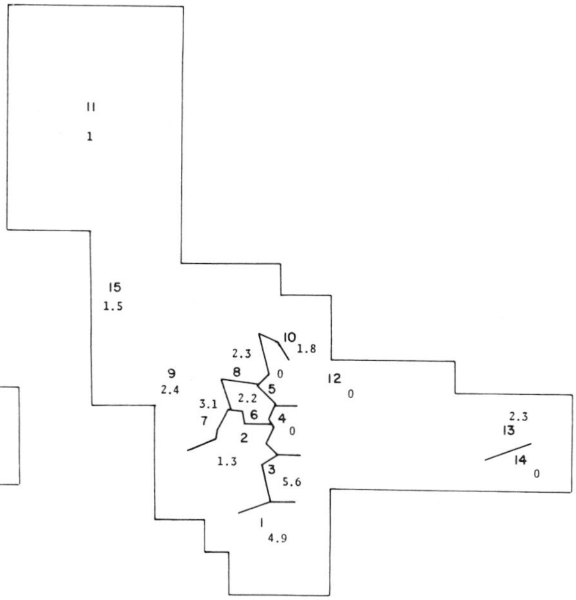

Figure 4.24. Percentage of terraces with pounders, by site subdivision.

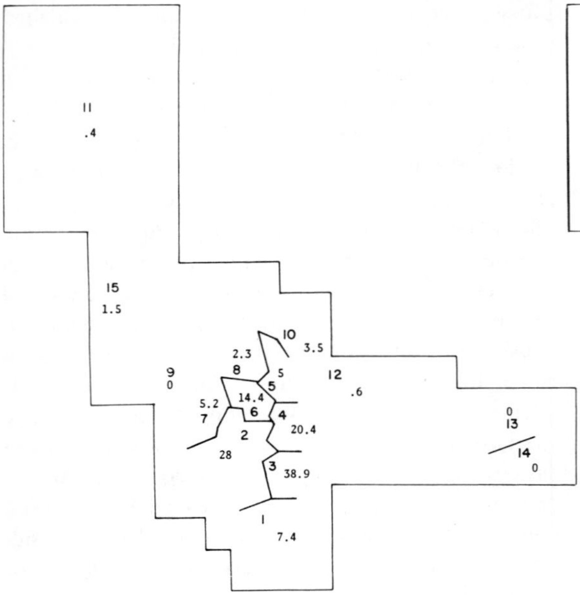

Figure 4.25. Percentage of terraces where marine shell was noted, by site subdivision.

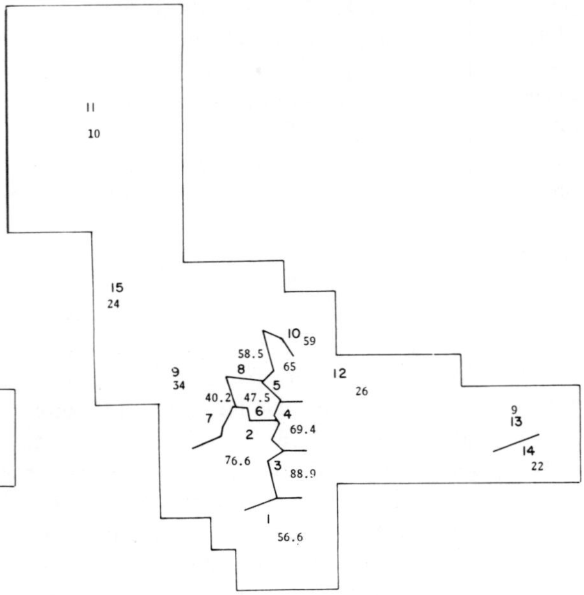

Figure 4.26. Percentage of terraces where obsidian was noted, by site subdivision.

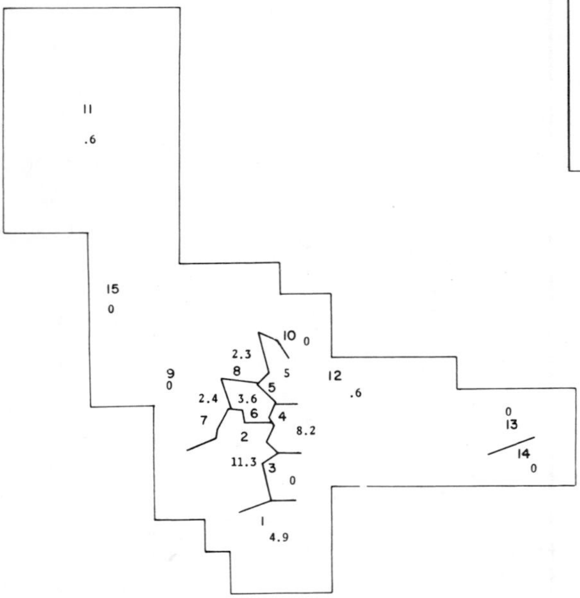

Figure 4.27. Percentage of terraces where unusual rocks and minerals were noted, by site subdivision.

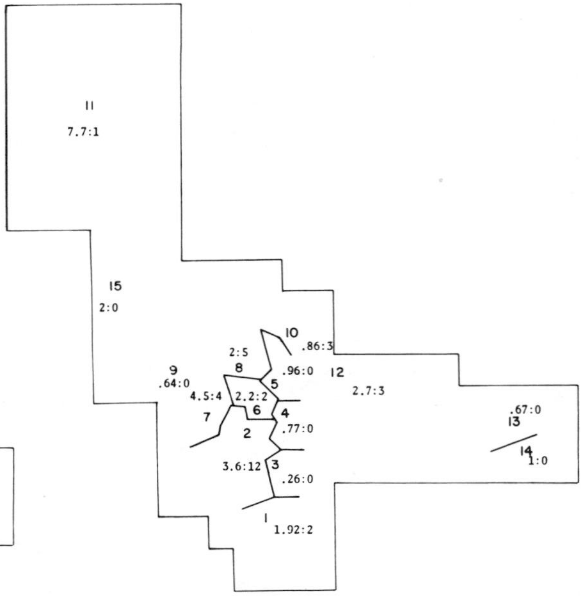

Figure 4.28. Obsidian workshops. The number to the left of the colon is the expected value, based on the percentage of terraces of the whole site in each subdivision. The number right of the colon is the observed number, by site subdivision.

mediately and that if a surface collection were to be made hundreds or even thousands of pieces could be picked up. The latter concentrations have been referred to as workshops. Figure 4.28 shows the distribution of concentrations of obsidian identified as workshops while Figure 4.29 shows the distribution of shell workshops.

If shell workshops had been evenly distributed throughout the population of Monte Albán, then the expected number in each subdivision could be calculated according to the percentage of terraces that each subdivision contains of the total number of terraces on the site. Calculated in this way, the expected number of shell workshops for site subdivision 2 is 1.14–6 shell concentrations were found. All but one of these were found among a group of terraces west of the Main Plaza in the south end of square N3E8. This relatively isolated location, separated from the densely settled zones to the north by a large *barranca*, would only have been a suitable location for the production of marine shell items for use by the population of the Main Plaza.

Obsidian workshops also occur with more than expected frequency in site subdivision 2: 3.6 are expected, but 12 were discovered. In the next section of this chapter I will explore in more detail the nature of obsidian working at Monte Albán. For our purposes in this section, however, the distribution of these workshops does support the idea that both the majority of the consumers and producers, and distributors of this item resided in site subdivision 2.

Since the items just described (obsidian, shell, and unusual rocks and minerals) are nonceramic, there is no means of dating their deposition from our surface evidence alone. It is likely that site subdivision 2 retained its elite orientation from Periods Late I through IIIb, but there is some evidence from our surface collections that the patterns of elite use of ceramic items changed during Period II from the prior patterns. Whether the uses of nonceramic costly items also changed after Period II is unknown. Periods IIIa and IIIb–IV have many fewer costly ceramic categories than prior periods. For Period IIIa I can identify only two such categories, the Teotihuacanoid vessels with coffee bean appliqué (category 1421), and thin orange (category 3411), possibly a tradeware from the Mixteca or Teotihuacan. For Period IIIb no category really fits into the costly group with the possible exception of Fine Orange (category 3030), and this probably pertains to Period IV rather than to IIIb (Appendix II). By far the majority of ceramic items used during Periods III and IV, probably by both elite and nonelite households, especially after Period IIIa, were the dull, gray, poorly made vessels representative of what Caso *et al.* refer to as the "Zapotec Ceramic Tradition [CBA: passim]."

Not only were fewer fancy ceramic categories being used during Period III in general, but our evidence from surface collections seems to indicate that, unlike Periods Late I and II, these items were not necessarily more frequently used by the population of site subdivision 2 (Figures 4.30, 4.31).

One last point can be made concerning the population of site subdivision 2 before the descriptions of the other subdivisions are completed. In

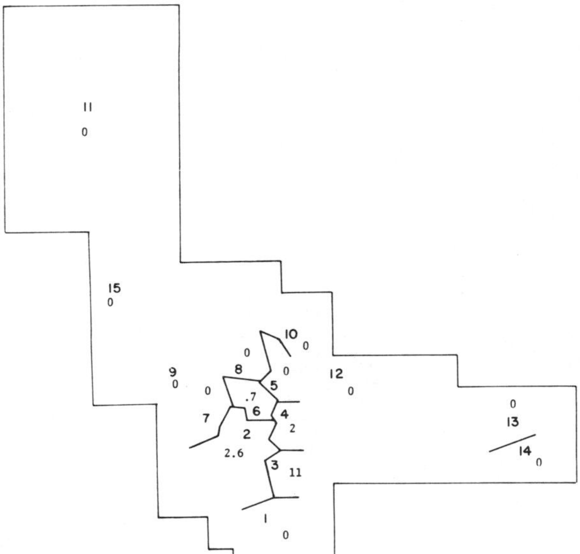

Figure 4.29. Percentage of terraces with evidence for marine shell workshops, by site subdivision.

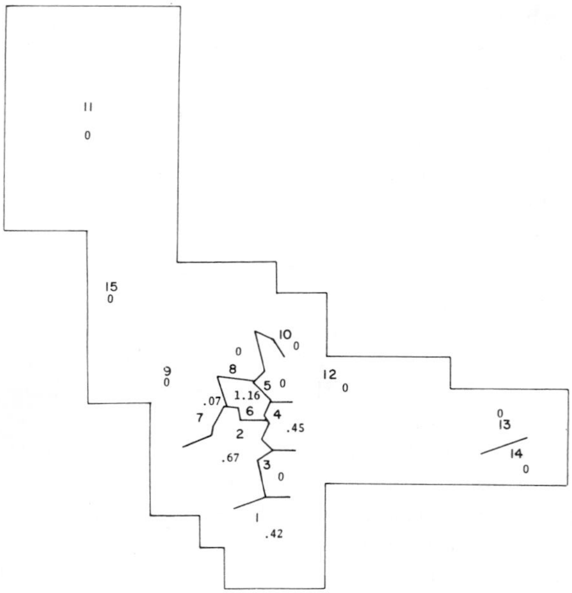

Figure 4.30. Distribution of ceramic category 3411, expressed in sherds per hectare of collected terrace area.

the chapter concerned with the foundation of Monte Albán, I hypothesized that a neutral institution, such as a military league, that serves to join together a group of otherwise autonomous societies, is not likely to be associated with a single deity or set of deities, since the cojoining societies may vary in their supernatural beliefs and ritual practices, such that consensus in such matters would be difficult to achieve. I suggested that this is why militarism is by far the dominant theme in Monte Albán's carved stone monuments, whereas such monuments from other valley centers often have ritual themes. This is not an argument for the nonexistence of ritual or religious beliefs at Monte Albán, but instead one implying that no single supernatural being is likely to be associated with the capital center. There is abundant evidence, in fact, at Monte Albán, for ritual and supernatural beliefs. Caso and Bernal (1952) describe the representations of deities, especially on funerary urns, that they encountered in their stratigraphic excavations in the city. We found urn fragments (Figure 4.32) and figurine fragments (Appendix

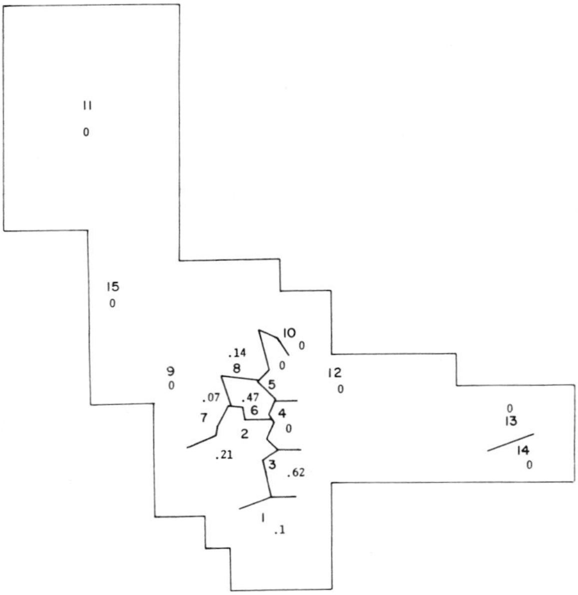

Figure 4.31. Distribution of ceramic category 1421, expressed in sherds per hectare of collected terrace area.

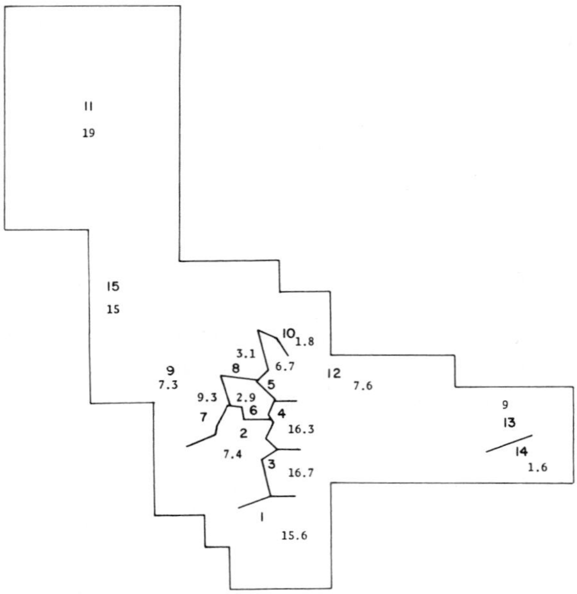

Figure 4.32. Percentage of terraces where urn fragments were noted, by site subdivision.

VIII) throughout the city, suggesting the rituals employing these items were widespread among the general population. The items published by Caso and Bernal (1952) portray a wide range of supernatural beings popular at Monte Albán, duplicating the range from other Oaxacan archaeological sites. As expected, no single deity seems to be associated solely with the capital.

A test of my hypothesis can be carried out using the Caso and Bernal data. The test can by no means be considered definitive since there is no guarantee that the Caso and Bernal sample of items portraying deities is a representative one. The results of the test are interesting nonetheless. I have argued that site subdivision 2 was a special area—the center of league activities. If my hypothesis is correct that there was no state church or single deity associated with the military confederation, then none of the deities identified by Caso and Bernal should occur more frequently in this subdivision than would be expected on probabilistic grounds alone. In order to investigate how deities were distributed at Monte Albán, I went through the Caso and Bernal volume, looking for tomb numbers or other proveniences that could securely be located in terms of our terrace numbering system, then tabulated items according to whether or not they were found in subdivision 2 or other site subdivisions. Only items from Periods IIIa and IIIb–IV were tabulated in order to minimize possible problems having to do with change in the popularity of deities through time, and other chronologically related problems. A total of 76 items could thus be tabulated, most of which were from site subdivision 2, since that was where most of the excavations had been carried out. The ratio of objects from subdivision 2 to those from other subdivisions is 52:24. It seemed that any deity deviating widely from this ratio must have been either strongly associated with, or strongly disassociated with, site subdivision 2. According to the hypothesis, no such significant deviations should occur. To test this, 2 X 2 contingency tables were done for the more frequently occurring deities, tabulating them according to their presence or absence in subdivision 2, and calculating the value of χ^2 for each table. Table 4.3 lists the proveniences of the deities used in these contingency tables. Some of the representations of deities occurred so infrequently that their χ^2 val-

Table 4.3. Proveniences for Selected Deities[a] (Periods III and IV only)

Monte Albán location	Site subdivision	Caso and Bernal (1952)
	Murcielago	
Tomb 92	2	Fig. 119
Montículo O	2	Fig. 119
"Loma de la Cruz"	5	Fig. 123
Edificio de los Danzantes	2	Fig. 124
Tomb 117	2	p. 351
Tomb 122	1	Fig. 125
Tomb 54	5	p. 88
Tomb 108	4	p. 88
Atzompa	11	p. 88
	Diosa de Glifo "2.J"	
Tomb 122	1	Fig. 122
P.S.A.	2	p. 80
Montículo I	2	p. 82
Atzompa	11	p. 83
Tomb 21	2	p. 83

(Continued)

Table 4.3. *(Continued)*

Monte Albán location	Site subdivision	Caso and Bernal (1952)
	Diosa "13 Serpiente"	
Patio of Tomb 104	2	p. 283
Atzompa	11	p. 285
Tomb 103	2	p. 285
Tomb 104	2	p. 285
Sistema Y	2	p. 285
Montículo M	2	p. 285
Tomb 108	4	p. 290
Patio of Tomb 144	4	p. 290
Tomb 128	2	p. 290
	Xipetotec	
Tomb 103	2	p. 252
Tomb 58	2	p. 254
Tomb 139	2	p. 260
North of *Patio Hundido*	2	p. 260
Patio of Tomb 80	2	p. 260
West of T. 453	8	p. 260
	Quetzalcoatl	
Tomb 6	2	p. 146
Tomb 109	4	p. 146
Tomb 104	2	p. 146
Tomb 105	4	p. 146
Tomb 6	2	p. 155
Montículo i	2	p. 158
North of *Patio Hundido*	2	p. 159
Sistema Y	2	p. 159
Atzompa	11	p. 160
Tomb 6	2	p. 155
	Cocijo	
Patio of Tomb 105	4	Fig. 11
Tomb 105	4	p. 36
Tomb 9	2	p. 37
Tomb 103	2	p. 37
Tomb 6	2	p. 37
Tomb 104	2	p. 38
Sistema Y	2	p. 38
Tomb 97	6	p. 38
Tomb 80	2	p. 40
Tomb 103	2	p. 40
Tomb 62	8	p. 40
Tomb 7(2)	2	p. 41
Montículo B	2	p. 41
Sistema Y	2	p. 46
South of South Platform	2	p. 49
Tomb 104	2	p. 50
Atzompa	11	p. 53

[a]From Caso and Bernal (1952).

ues would have been meaningless (for example the *dios con yelmo o máscara de ave de pico ancho* or the deity of glyph L). All deities used in this analysis were relatively rare, requiring the use of the "corrected χ^2" (Blalock 1972:285). The corrected χ^2 values derived are the following: for *Cocijo*, .325; for *Quetzalcoatl*, .22; for *Xipetotec*, .13; for *Diosa "13 Serpiente,"* .062; for *Diosa "2.J,"* .84; and for *Murcielago*, 1.6. As predicted by the hypothesis, none of the deities is strongly associated (or disassociated) with site subdivision 2, and therefore, I contend with the political institution centered there. The highest corrected χ^2 value derived, in fact, was that for the deity *Murcielago* (1.6), a value not significant (with 2 degrees of freedom), even at the .1 level.

SITE SUBDIVISION 3

This subdivision sits on the ridge extending south and east from the North Platform. The mound group cluster dominating the subdivision consists of an impressively large elaborate residence, Terrace 1463, plus a small isolated mound on Terrace 92. This is the site's smallest subdivision, including only 15 nonelaborate residential terraces. Terrace 87, one of the largest within the site, extends northwest from the elite residence. It apparently required considerable energy in its construction as it covers an area of 4706 m^2, and its retaining walls are several meters high in some places. I was unsure how to classify this feature while in the field. Its large size and location adjacent to a major road suggested that it could have been a market or comparable general-access feature. This interpretation seemed to be supported by the absence of any obvious residential architecture visible on the surface, although artifacts are abundant. I now wonder if the absence of residential architecture here indicates a nonresidential function. More recently I have been impressed with the extent to which plowing in colonial times may have destroyed many such features. I first became aware of this problem when I looked at Plates X and XXIV in Batres's *Explorations of Monte Albán, Oaxaca, Mexico* (1902). When these photographs were taken, even the Main Plaza was a cornfield! If Terrace 87 had been a residential area rather than a market or civic area, then the maximum population of the site subdivision would have been roughly 75–150 more than estimated.

Site subdivision 3 is unusual in having a relatively high proportion of terraces with evidence for craft production. While only .8 shell workshops are expected here, based on the percentage of terraces in this subdivision, 3 were noted (Figure 4.29). One *other-lithic* (chert and/or quartzite) concentration was noted that may have been a workshop (Figure 4.33). A relatively large number of terraces contained evidence of artifacts that may have been used in production, including pounders (Figure 4.24), mortars and pestles (Figure 4.34), celt fragments (Fig. 4.35), and what we called *weird* groundstone (Figure 4.36). This latter category includes several kinds of ground-stone artifacts that I felt might have been used in craft production, or in large-scale food production. Since we did not actually collect these items for use analysis, my functional interpretations must remain hypothetical. It seemed, however,that plotting the distribution of weird ground stone might product some information about differences in activities between the site subdivisions in a general sense. Included in this category are oversized or what we called "monster" manos, basin metates with thick square bases, stone discs, stone "doughnuts," stone balls, and all other ground stone labeled "function unknown" by the survey crews. This subdivision also has the highest frequency of occurrence on the site of shell (Figure 4.25), and obsidian (Figure 4.26), although no actual obsidian workshops were noted.

The relatively abundant evidence for artifacts associated with production in site subdivision 3 may be due to the fact that, like the terraces in subdivision 2, there may have been a relatively greater concentration of craftsmen here producing items for consumption by the elite population of the Main Plaza and of the group of elaborate residences near the Main Plaza.

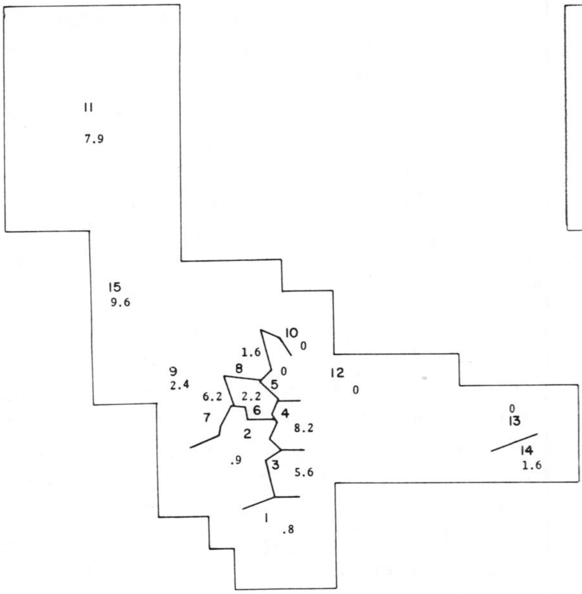

Figure 4.33. Percentage of terraces with concentrations of chert and/or quartzite tools and debris, by site subdivision.

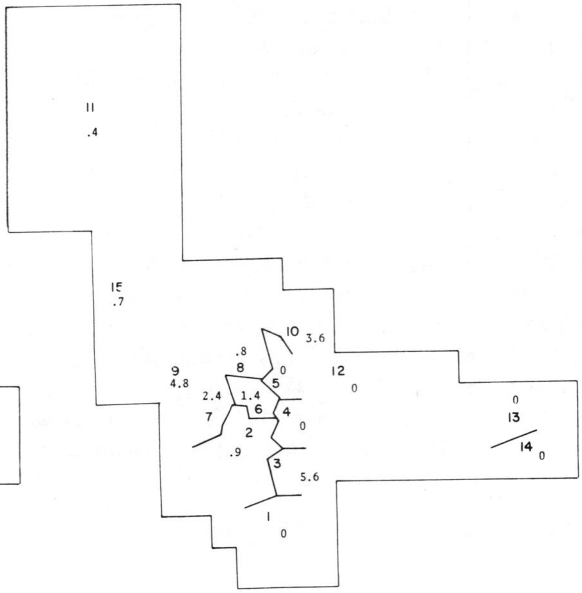

Figure 4.34. Percentage of terraces where mortars and/or pestles were noted, by site subdivision.

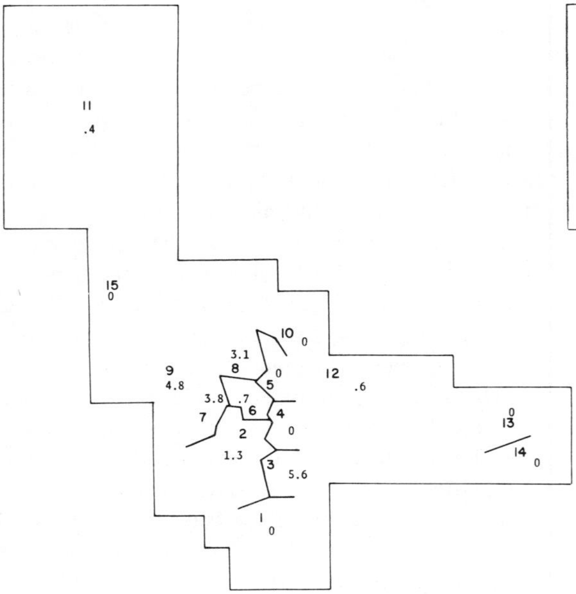

Figure 4.35. Percentage of terraces where celts or celt fragments were noted, by site subdivision.

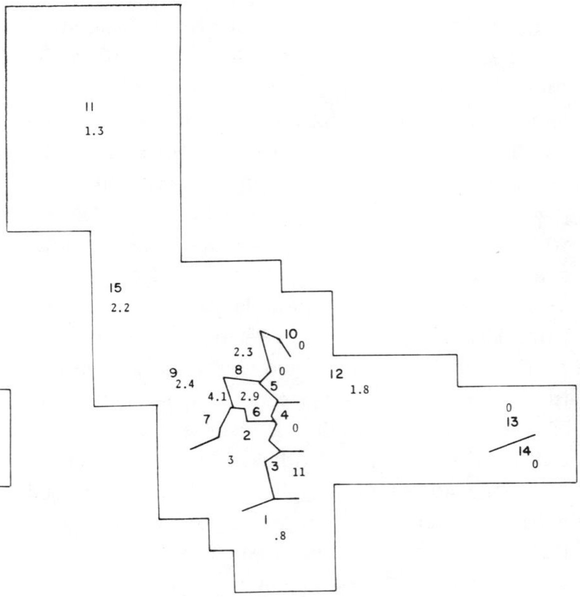

Figure 4.36. Percentage of terraces where unusual ground-stone objects were noted, by site subdivision.

SITE SUBDIVISION 4

This area centers around two elaborate residences, Terraces 1459 and 1462 (where the famous Tomb 105 is located), a ball court, Terrace 1456, and a terrace with two low platforms, accessible by a ramp from the east and south (above Terrace 118), that I interpret as an open civic area. Road F passes through this mound group cluster (Figure 4.4). This subdivision is unusual only in its relative abundance of elite items, namely marine shell (Figure 4.25), Fine Orange pottery (category 3030) (Figure 4.37), and unusual rocks and minerals (Figure 4.27). Other-lithic workshops are relatively abundant here (Figure 4.33).

SITE SUBDIVISION 5

An elaborate residence, Terrace 1460, dominates this group of terraces from a high, steep-sided promontory. The area I proposed as the subdivision's civic zone is downslope from Terrace 1460 to the north, where there are two isolated platform mounds directly adjacent to road F, at Terraces 491 and 1448. This site subdivision has little evidence for craft production or any unusual frequency of occurrence of elite items.

SITE SUBDIVISION 6

The mound group cluster dominating this subdivision consists of two closely spaced elaborate residences (Terraces 174 and 165), plus an isolated platform mound (Terrace 160), and an open double-mound group, Terrace 800. These latter two terraces are directly adjacent to Monte Albán's major traffic route, road E (Figure 4.4). We noted no evidence on the surface here suggesting any strong difference with other subdivisions in terms of production or the consumption of elite items, except that thin orange (category 3411) is relatively abundant here (Figure 4.30).

SITE SUBDIVISION 7

Two elaborate residences, Terraces 278 and 1306, and an open double-mound group, Terrace 938, dominate this part of the site. The latter terrace is directly accessible from Monte Albán's road E (Figure 4.4). As I first mapped it, it looked as if this road passed just north of Terrace 938, access to the terrace being by way of ramps extending from the terrace's east and west ends. After revisiting the site several times, however, this interpretation became less certain because the road north of Terrace 938 is only faintly, if at all, visible; to indicate this, I drew it with dashed lines. It now seems that all traffic on road E may have passed directly through Terrace 938 and the open area to the southwest of the terrace. This open area, between Terrace 938 and the two elaborate residences, called Area 16 (N5E8 and N5E7), is interesting because no terraces are visible within its bounds (although several possible small structures were noted along its northwest edge), even though the slope is relatively gentle here and therefore suitable for terrace construction. Artifacts are as abundant in this area as on adjacent terraces. I

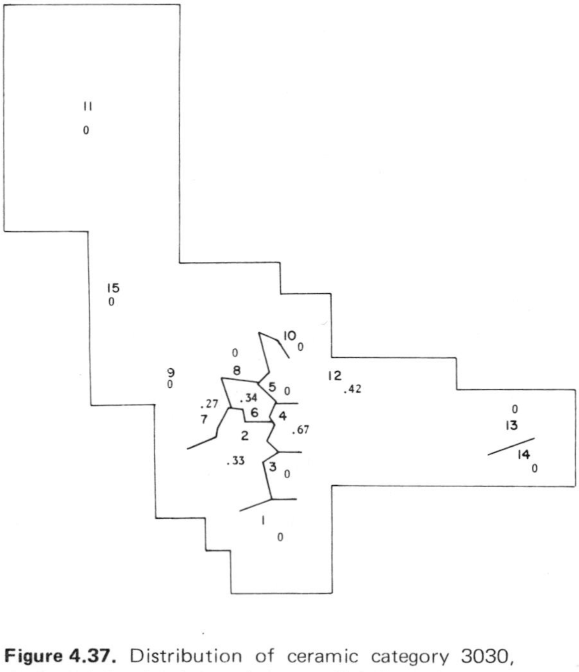

Figure 4.37. Distribution of ceramic category 3030, expressed in sherds per hectare of collected terrace area.

thought at first that recent plowing had destroyed whatever archaeological features might originally have been here, but it later occurred to me that although this portion of the site had been heavily cultivated, it had not destroyed terraces adjacent to the open space. This seems to indicate that in ancient times this was an open space, as it is today, not used for residential construction. Its location, in the middle of a mound group cluster, directly in the path of Monte Albán's major ancient road, and more or less central to a large and densely occupied portion of the site, seemed to suggest that it would have been ideal as a marketing place. With this in mind it was exciting to see that considerable evidence for craft production was noted on the surrounding terraces during the course of our survey. Most of the evidence is in the form of ground-stone artifacts that may have been produced here and/or used in production. The following artifact categories were noted relatively frequently in site subdivision 7: mortars and pestles (Figure 4.34), celts (Figure 4.35), and weird ground-stone objects (Figure 4.36). Two possible mano workshops were noted, identified by our finding concentrations of mano fragments and unfinished mano blanks, as well as two metate workshops (Figure 4.38). The latter were concentrations of the large, square-based basin metates that are much larger than those normally found on residential terraces. Whether these metates were being produced here or used for the production of other products cannot be determined from our surface inspection alone.

Site subdivision 7, in addition to having some evidence for craft production involving ground stone, also has a relatively large number of other-lithic concentrations (Figure 4.33). Most of these are located on terraces just inside the defensive wall and adjacent to road E in squares N4E6 and 7. The reason for their location there is probably the presence, down the ridge some 200 or 300 m to the west, of an outcrop of the same quartzite that is found on the terraces.

To conclude, surface evidence seems to indicate that the population of site subdivision 7 was involved, to a greater extent than the populations of the other subdivisions, in production of ground-stone implements or in production that involved the use of ground-stone implements. The same is true for production involving quartzite. Since the implements themselves cannot be dated by simple surface inspection, one cannot be sure when these productive activities were taking place. It is a possibility that these materials were deposited during Period V, when, as it will be argued later, Monte Albán became a more commercially oriented center than it had been in prior periods. Both site subdivisions 7 and 8 have abundant evidence for occupation during the latter period. However, the most dense concentrations of Period V pottery in subdivision 7 are along the base of the hill, especially on the "megaterraces" just inside the defensive wall, while the bulk of evidence for ground-stone implements and possible workshops is higher up, closer to Terrace 938, the possible market, Area 16, and road E. This should mean that at least some of the evidence for production here

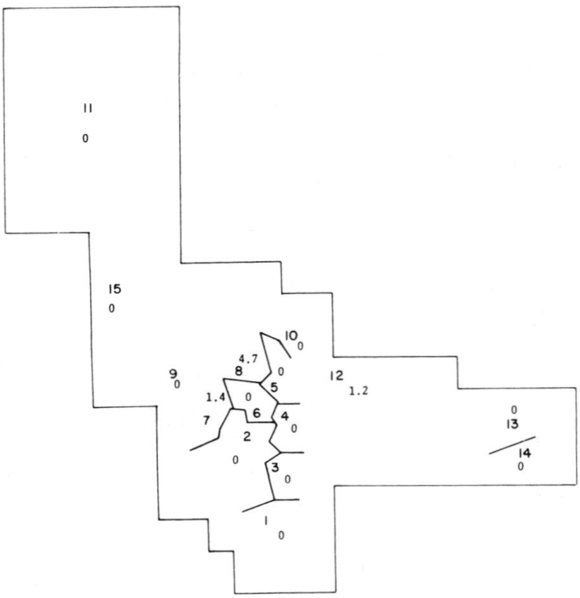

Figure 4.38. Percentage of terraces where mano and/or metate workshops were noted, by site subdivision.

pertains to Periods IIIb–IV and earlier. The other-lithic workshops are in the middle of a dense concentration of Period V pottery.

SITE SUBDIVISION 8

This subdivision focuses on a large complex of mounds, Terrace 453, which is the one referred to by Caso and his associates as *El Pitahayo* (Appendix I, Part 2). The large open area between the double-mound group at the center east of the terrace is accessible from road E (Figure 4.4), and is thus comparable to Terraces 938 and 800. Site subdivision 8, like 7, has relatively abundant surface evidence for craft production. Dating these workshops, however, is a more severe problem here than was the case for subdivision 7, since virtually all of subdivision 8 was heavily occupied during Period V as well as earlier periods back as far as Period I. Like subdivision 7, production here may have involved, in part, the production or use of ground stone, especially manos or metates. A total of six localities were noted that may have been mano or metate workshops, more than any other site subdivision (Figure 4.38). The frequency of occurrence of both manos and metates is also the highest here of the other subdivisions, perhaps reflecting the productive orientation (Figures 4.39, 4.40). Celts are also relatively common (Figure 4.35). The other hypothesized production orientation of site subdivision 8 is obsidian working. The number of obsidian workshops expected here, calculated according to the percentage of terraces represented by the subdivision of the total number, is two; five were noted. It is highly likely, though, that most of these concentrations pertain to Period V, as I will demonstrate below.

SITE SUBDIVISION 9

Terrace 1464 is the presumed civic and elite residential focus of this small subdivision. Little evidence is present on the surface here that would indicate that the behavior of the population was

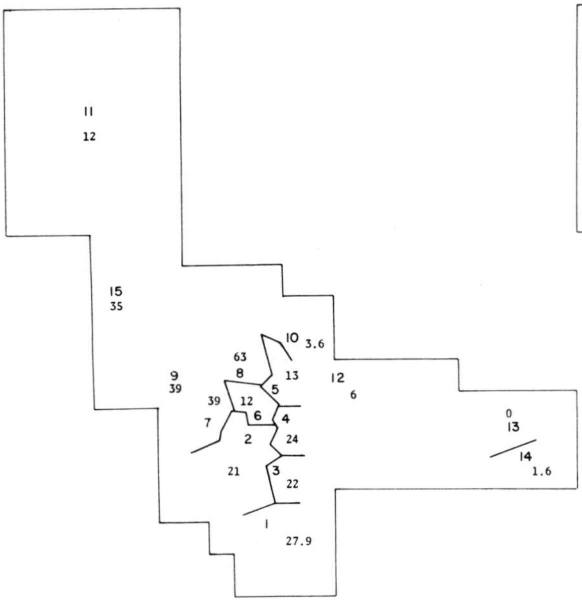

Figure 4.39. Percentage of terraces where manos were noted, by site subdivision.

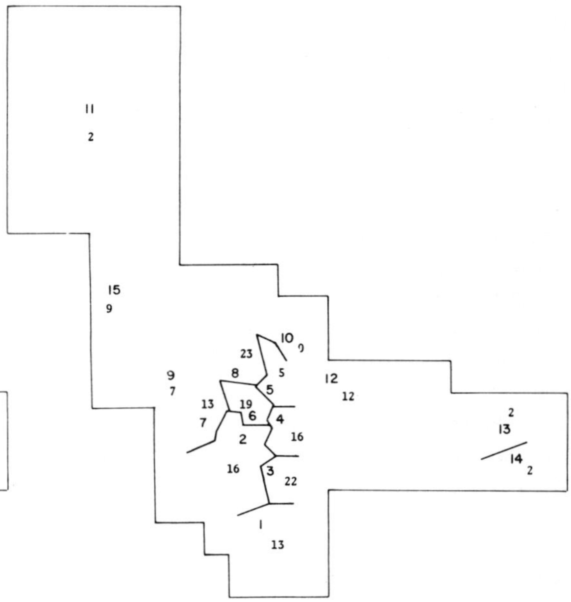

Figure 4.40. Percentage of terraces where metates were noted, by site subdivision.

distinct from that of the other subdivisions. Mortars and/or pestles and celts were noted on a total of four terraces here, a relatively large percentage, but probably not indicative of an important focus of craft production (Figures 4.34, 4.35).

SITE SUBDIVISION 10

This small, spatially discrete area of terraces sits on a small ridge and the adjacent slopes just northeast of the remainder of Monte Albán proper. Occupation here was probably primarily during Periods IIIb–IV and V. A small closed mound group, Terrace 1455 was the area's single elaborate residence. A terrace with an isolated platform mound, Terrace 657, adjacent to road I (Figure 4.4) I interpret to be the subdivision's civic focus, although a second, smaller, but very similar terrace is located below the ridge to the southeast (Terrace 867). Adjacent to the latter feature we noted three obsidian concentrations that may have been workshops. The number of such concentrations is larger than expected for such a small subdivision (Figure 4.28); although their dating cannot be determined, they might pertain to Period V (see below).

One aspect of the Period IIIb–IV ceramic assemblage from this subdivision was different from the other subdivisions, either in terms of the production and/or consumption of one item, *comales* (flat cooking vessels for tortillas) of the type we call *café* (category 2418) (Figure 4.41). These were found with considerably more frequency here than on the other subdivisions. No independent evidence was noted that would demonstrate that this category was being produced here (e.g., kilns or *kiln wasters*), but such evidence may be difficult to come by on the surface and its absence does not prove that such production was absent. Ceramic production of any kind will probably be difficult to detect on the surface at Monte Albán. Marcus Winter discovered two small features in the course of his excavations in the vicinity of Terrace 634 (N5E8) that he interprets as ceramic kilns (Winter and Payne 1976), in an area where we had not noticed any evidence of ceramic production.

SITE SUBDIVISION 11 (ATZOMPA)

Atzompa has a long occupational history, but by far the majority of terraces have evidence for occupation only during Period IIIb–IV. The absence of Fine Orange pottery (our category 3030), a Period IV marker, suggests the occupation was limited to Period IIIb (Figure 4.37). A small amount of Late I and II pottery was also noted (at Az.Terraces 392, 419, and 448), and there is an area just north of the main mound group, in square N14E2 that has some evidence for a Period IIIa occupation (and a few additional IIIa sherds were noted in N12E2).

The mound group cluster at Atzompa is complex, but shows the basic pattern present in the other site subdivisions. That is, it consists of what

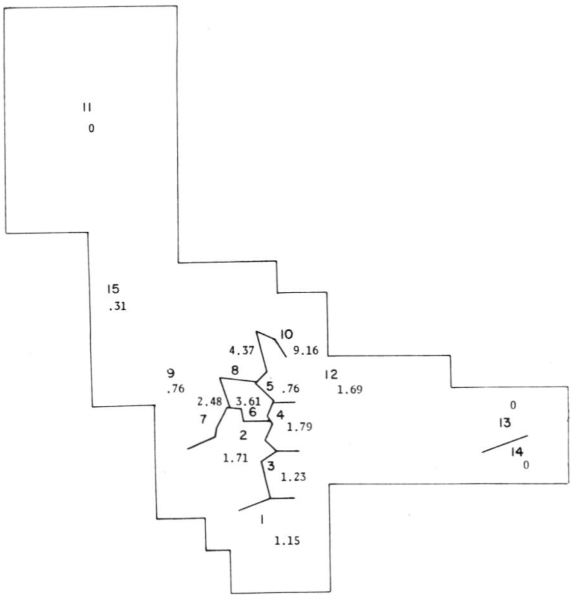

Figure 4.41. Distribution of ceramic category 2418, expressed in sherds per hectare of collected terrace area.

appears to have been an elaborate residence (Az.Terrace 10), plus an open plaza with a double-mound group (Az.Terrace 138), the latter accessible by way of a road. Clustered around this large elite residence are several other elaborate residences and ball courts (Az.Terraces 3, 8, 11, 19, 139, 448). This elite district seems to have been relatively isolated from the remainder of the population; of the roads that are easily discernible on the surface at Atzompa, none leads directly here (Figure 4.4). The major road (H) comes up the ridge from the direction of the modern village of Sta. María Atzompa, but remains along the east edge of the settlement. Smaller routes that connect to H service only those residential zones north and south of the elite district, as well as the open mound group, Az.Terrace 138. Additionally, four large quarries situated around the major residence serve to accentuate the isolation of this mound group and its attached features from the remainder of the community. From the point of view of the isolation of the feature, it is comparable to the Main Plaza at Monte Albán proper. And, like the Main Plaza, large plazas and staircases within this group (including Az.Terraces 8, 10, and the ball courts) facilitate the internal flow of traffic, while little evidence exists for openings or gates that would have facilitated the general flow of traffic from the outside. The east mound of Az.Terrace 10 has broad staircases on both sides, as does the long mound that divides the plaza of Az.Terrace 8 into northern and southern halves; similarly a broad ramp or staircase connects Az.Terrace 8 with the large ball court to the east.

In spite of the similarities between the Az.Terraces 8 and 10 complex, on the one hand, and the Main Plaza, on the other hand, these features were probably not functionally analogous. The Atzompa complex was just another elite residence, or set of elite residences, comparable to those in the other site subdivisions, although built on a substantially larger scale. Whether or not the Atzompa elite residential complex was actually more closed and the elite population there actually more isolated from the general population than was the case in the other subdivisions, or whether this just appears to be the case because of the monumentality of the buildings, cannot be answered with the data at hand.

Atzompa is unlike the other site subdivisions in several regards, only one of which is the monumentality and seeming secludedness of its elite residences. Atzompa also had a much larger total population than the other subdivisions, except for subdivision 2. Atzompa is also unique in being the only *barrio* from which we have evidence that the population participated in a marketing-distribution system at least in part distinct from that participated in by the remainder of the city's population ("marketing-distribution" is hyphenated since there is no direct evidence for how products were distributed, whether through markets alone, or through some degree of administered distribution). Our ceramic category 2418, the *café* comals that are so abundant in site subdivision 10, and which are present over much of the remainder of the site (Figure 4.41), are absent at Atzompa. By contrast, our category 1125, comals with *gris-cremosa* (whitish gray) paste, are abundant at Atzompa but rare to absent on other parts of the site (Figure 4.42). Perhaps the simplest interpretation of this is that the two categories of comals were being produced by two distinct groups of producers whose marketing regions only slightly overlapped. Two other ceramic categories manifest a similar distributional pattern, probably for the same reason (Figures 4.43, 4.44).

These data do not imply that the population of Atzompa was involved totally in a marketing-distribution system different from that of the remainder of the city's population. Our other IIIb–IV ceramic categories are present over all of the site, in more or less equivalent densities. Likewise, it cannot be inferred from these data that Atzompa was economically self-sufficient; relatively little evidence exists for workshops there. One obsidian concentration was noted, but on a terrace that was probably exclusively occupied

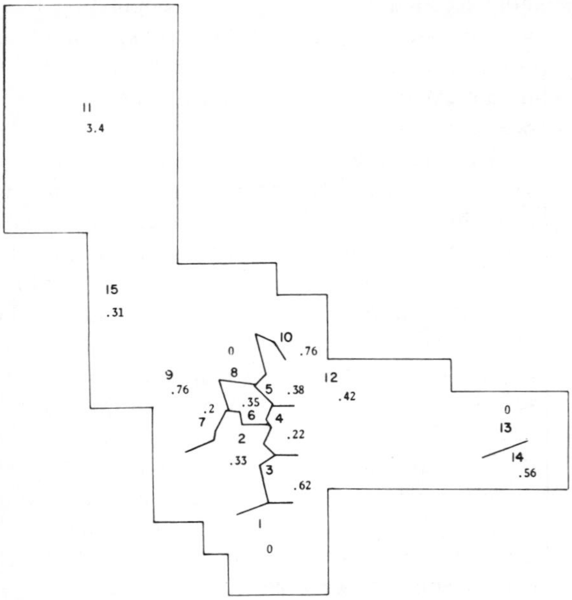

Figure 4.42. Distribution of ceramic category 1125, expressed in sherds per hectare of collected terrace area.

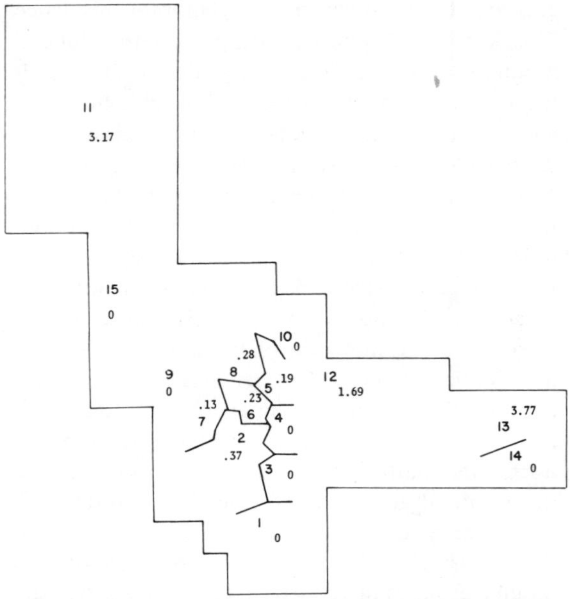

Figure 4.43. Distribution of ceramic category 1259, expressed in sherds per hectare of collected terrace area.

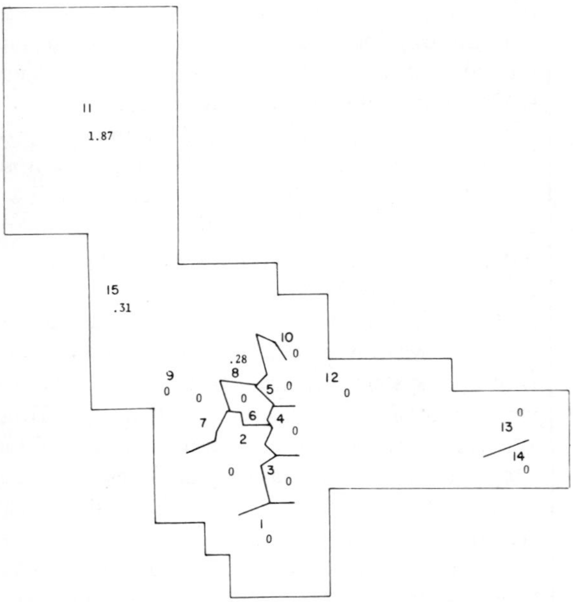

Figure 4.44. Distribution of ceramic category 1137, expressed in sherds per hectare of collected terrace area.

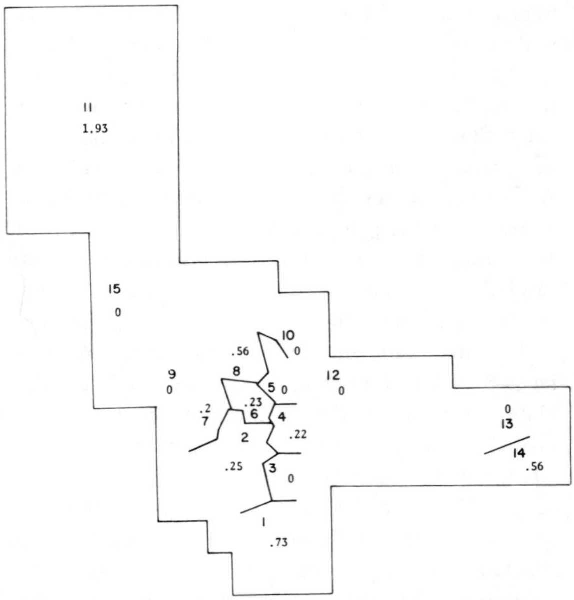

Figure 4.45. Distribution of ceramic category 1310, expressed in sherds per hectare of collected terrace area.

during Period V. (Az.Terrace 430). A total of 38 concentrations of the local cherts and quartzites were noted that may have been workshops, but this represents only 8% of the total number of terraces (Figure 4.33). A relatively high proportion of kiln wasters was found at Atzompa (Figure 4.45)—our category 1310—but it is not clear that this necessarily implies the presence of a strong emphasis on ceramic production. Kiln wasters are usually found near places where pottery is being fired, since misfirings are discarded on the spot, but, according to Kowalewski, Spencer, and Redmond, who examined these sherds, none is so badly flawed that normal use of the vessel would have been impossible. It may be that the distribution pattern of kiln wasters on the site as a whole simply reflects the fact that the population of Atzompa was more often willing or forced to use slightly misfired vessels.

Two last points about the surface archaeological remains at Atzompa: First, a terrace distribution pattern was noted here that is one of our few clues to the existence of a kind of Period IIIb social group larger than the household, but smaller than the site subdivision. In the vicinity of Az.Terraces 215, 303, and 338, several terraces were noted in group formation with a long narrow terrace defining in each case the lower edge of the group (see Appendix I, Part 2 for comments on this pattern). In several other localities at Atzompa clumps of three to five or more terraces were noted that may represent the same multihousehold groups (e.g., in the vicinities of Az.Terraces 72, 410, 433, 452, 468, and 472). Evidence of similar clusters of terraces was also noted at El Gallo, in the vicinities of E.G.Terraces 67 and 106.

The second concluding point concerning Atzompa has to do with water. Two small features were noted at Atzompa that may have been used for water storage, but these were probably much too small to have served the needs of the entire population of the subdivision. One is a small depression in the open area north of Az.Terrace 3 (N13E3). The other is situated in the northwest corner of the subdivision's major residence, Az.Terrace 10. The latter feature is inaccessible from below due to a very steep gradient, implying it was used exclusively by the residents of the household above. Evidently, the majority of the residents of Atzompa could depend on daily deliveries of water for their household needs and for drinking. This implies that defense and self-sufficiency during siege were not important considerations for the people living there, which is corroborated by the absence of any defensive walls at Atzompa. The hilltop location of the subdivision, I argue, was not for defense, but designed to achieve the kind of isolation and locational neutrality required of a part of a disembedded capital.

SITE SUBDIVISION 12

One elaborate residence dominates this subdivision—Terrace 1453; adjacent to it is a large terrace with an isolated platform mound: Terrace 659. I interpret these as the subdivision's mound group cluster. This subdivision was first occupied during Period IIIa, but expanded to its maximum extent during IIIb–IV. Some Period V pottery was also noted (see Figure 5.1 on p. 102). The latter fact is unfortunate in the sense that features visible on the surface could date to anywhere from Periods IIIa through V. It is particularly frustrating to lack any convenient means for dating the rather extensive series of defensive walls encircling the upper part of this subdivision. Another surface indication is present that indicates defense was a problem for the residents here, but again, there is no means for discovering when that was true. Several terraces near the defensive walls (Terraces 682, 683, 688, 695, 696, 698, 700, 701, 710, 711, 722, 733, and 991) have large piles of fist-sized stones that would have been ideal as projectiles.

Little evidence is present on the surface for specialized production by the population of subdivision 12. Two concentrations of metates were noted, representing only 1.2% of the total number of terraces here (Figure 4.38). No other workshops were noted.

SITE SUBDIVISION 13

This small *barrio* has within its mound group cluster an open two-mound group (Terrace 1450) comparable in form to Terraces 800 (N5E9) and 938 (N5E8), and two small elaborate residences (Terraces 1451 and 1452). Its occupation dates exclusively to Period IIIb–IV. No evidence for specialized production was noted.

SITE SUBDIVISION 14

The elaborate residence here (Terrace 1449) sits on a promontory overlooking the remainder of the subdivision. The area's civic focus was the large plaza with an open double-mound group, Terrace 1170. Adjacent to this latter feature, on Terrace 1177, we noted a possible ball court (N3E21). The walls of the court would have been the slope along the edge of Terrace 1170 and a small elongated mound opposite this slope along the outer edge of the terrace. If this feature had been a ball court, it was an unusual one. All the other ball courts at Monte Albán are situated adjacent to elaborate residences (Terraces 1456, 1458, Az.Terraces 3, 8, 448, E.G.Terrace 2), and one is in the Main Plaza. The Terrace 1177 ball court, adjacent to the open plaza of Terrace 1170, was probably the only generally accessible such feature in the ancient city.

SITE SUBDIVISION 15 (EL GALLO)

El Gallo was occupied primarily during Periods Late I and IIIb–IV. These two occupations are roughly isomorphic, although the IIIb–IV residents may have slightly outnumbered the Late I residents, and IIIb–IV pottery is everywhere more dense on the surface. The site's elaborate residence, E.G.Terrace 1, is flanked by a ball court (E.G.Terrace 2) (N8E4). Northeast of E.G.Terrace 1 are several low mounds, arranged in linear order, that may be the remains of a reservoir (N9E4). Charles Spencer estimated the area of the reservoir to have been roughly 1700 m^2. To the south of E.G.Terrace 1 there are three large platforms (E.G.Terraces 3, 120, and 139), each with a small mound in its southeast corner. These terraces are difficult to interpret because they have been plowed in the past, but even so it appears that E.G.Terrace 139 was covered with residential structures, while E.G.Terraces 3 and 120 may have been open (one possible small structure was noted on 120). If so, then E.G.Terraces 3 and 120 may have been the subdivision's civic area. The road pattern at El Gallo, which is exceptionally well preserved, supports this interpretation. The subdivision's major road (M on Figure 4.4), comes directly up from the south slope of the hill in the direction of the group of three large platforms (E.G.Terraces 3, 120, and 139), but only one ramp actually provides access into E.G.Terrace 139. Road M divides before entering 139 into two smaller roads that bypass 139 on its east and west sides. Both of these latter roads lead directly up to E.G.Terraces 3 and 120 (and the related E.G.Terrace 4), as do ramps on the east and west slopes that enter from the north. The area that I propose as the subdivision's civic focus is thus the most accessible point in the subdivision.

Two other roads were identified at El Gallo, both along the densely settled west slope. The higher of the two connects with road M (Figure 4.4) somewhere in the vicinity of E.G.Terrace 40, while the lower road provides an independent route south down the hillslope in the direction of Monte Albán proper.

Charles Spencer, who directed the survey crew at El Gallo, brought to my attention the fact that the El Gallo road system facilitates traffic flow north–south rather than east–west. This means that those terraces away from road M, especially the downhill group on the west slope, seem to lack direct access to the E.G.Terrace 3 and 120 civic area, while retaining access to the south slope of the hill, and, by extension, to Monte Albán proper. According to Spencer's interpretation of the surface ceramic densities, this may have been less the case during Period Late I than it had been during Period IIIb–IV, since the group of relatively isolated terraces downslope to the west had their major occupation during the latter period. The most dense Period Late I material seems to be nearer the top of the ridge. This might be evidence that the mound group cluster had more functions vis-à-vis the population of El Gallo during Period Late I, necessitating direct access to road M, than it had during Period IIIb–IV, when access to the latter road seems to have been less important.

Little evidence was found at El Gallo for a productive specialty, although nearly 10% of the terraces have relatively dense concentrations of the local cherts and quartzites (Figure 4.33).

That portion of El Gallo south and to a certain extent northeast of E.G.Terraces 125 and 119 (E.G.Areas 3 through 8) was probably originally covered with terraces. An estimated 15 terraces have been nearly totally obliterated by recent plowing and the consequent erosion here.

An Overview of Craft Production at Monte Albán

In the preceding section the surface evidence for craft production in each of the site subdivisions was described. In this section I will look in more detail at the nature of obsidian production and will place the evidence for craft production in general in a more diachronic and comparative framework.

While coding the terrace data, I noticed that the nature of obsidian production and consumption in those areas with abundant Period V pottery was different as compared with areas of the site lacking Period V occupation. Specifically, terraces with Late Postclassic occupation tended more often to have sparse obsidian present, and the number of concentrations of obsidian suggesting workshops was higher on these terraces as a group. Additionally, the obsidian concentrations in areas lacking Period V pottery tended to be close to elaborate residences, while those in the Period V zones were not spaced in this way. All of these impressions are supported statistically. The presence of obsidian is strongly associated with the presence of Period V pottery, producing a χ^2 of 58.2 with one degree of freedom, significant at well over the .001 level. Kowalewski found a similar high degree of association between obsidian and Period V sites during the course of his survey (Kowalewski 1976:799). The spacing of obsidian concentrations that may have been workshops with respect to elaborate residences is summarized in Table 4.4. To measure these distances, I followed what I thought looked like the most likely travel route between each two points. Several things are apparent in this table: First, the mean distance from obsidian workshop to nearest elaborate residence is higher for Period V areas than for areas lacking Period V occupation (311 m compared with 176.8 m). The value indicated for Period V should probably be even higher than indicated since the nearest elaborate residence for three of the obsidian concentrations in the Period V zone was probably not in use at that time (I refer to Terrace 1306). Probably the nearest elaborate residence for all of the workshops in question in the area occupied during Period V was Terrace 453 (N7E9). Second, the pattern of spacing of obsidian concentrations with respect to elaborate residences in that part of Monte Albán proper that lack any substantial Period V pottery is unlike the spacing where the late pottery does occur. Seven, or 44% of the obsidian workshops in the non-V area (and therefore, presumably, definitely dating to prior periods), are located nearly equidistant from two to four elaborate residences (Table 4.4). If production of obsidian, prior to Period V, had been primarily for consumption by elites, then locations close to one, or equidistant from several elaborate residences containing such households, would have been optimal. In this regard it is interesting to note that two of the obsidian concentrations, on Terraces 82 and 84, are directly adjacent to traffic node A of Figure

Table 4.4. Distances from Obsidian Concentrations to Nearest Elaborate Residence[a]

Terrace number of obsidian concentration	Distance and terrace number of the elaborate residence(s)[b]
13	160 m, Terraces 17 and 278 (also equidistant to Terrace 169)
22	60 m, Terraces 17 and 18
36	130 m, *Sistema Y*, on Terrace 27
43	110 m, " "
63	40 m, Terrace 51
67	160 m, Terrace 51
71	160 m, Terrace 51
82	280 m, Terrace 51
	260 m, Terrace 1463
	330 m, *Sistema Y*, Terrace 27
	380 m, Terrace 1462
84	240 m, Terrace 1463
	320 m, Terrace 51
	370 m, Terrace 1462
	390 m, *Sistema Y*, Terrace 27
160	70 m, Terrace 165
170	40 m, Terrace 165
	70 m, Terrace 174
178	100 m, Terrace 5
	140 m, Terrace 174
	120 m, Terrace 169
210	220 m, Terrace 1461
217	260 m, Terrace 1458
	270 m, Terrace 51
317	360 m, Terrace 1461
350	460 m, Terrace 264
453[c]	0 m, (has a concentration of obsidian)
454[c]	180 m, Terrace 453
522[c]	240 m, Terrace 453
610[c]	320 m, Terrace 453
1210[c]	340 m, Terrace 453
1226[c]	490 m, Terrace 1306
1227[c]	430 m, Terrace 1306
1228[c]	380 m, Terrace 1306
1236[c]	420 m, Terrace 1306

[a]Monte Albán proper only, excluding site subdivision 10.
[b]Distances measured from center to center of terraces, along the most likely route.
[c]Period V area.

4.4. From this point the two terraces are roughly equidistant, by ancient road, from four elaborate residences. None of the obsidian concentrations in the part of the site with substantial Period V occupation show this pattern; instead, those concentrations are more or less evenly scattered throughout the area of Period V occupation.

These workshop data are difficult to interpret since the Period V occupation of Monte Albán sits on top of terraces occupied during earlier periods, making dating of workshops by surface inspection alone impossible. I interpret this information, however, along with that summarized previously in the site subdivision descriptions, to imply that during and prior to Period IIIb (and IV?), obsidian was a relatively rare product, used primarily by an elite. Most workshops were located in and adjacent to site subdivision 2, where the bulk of the city's elite population resided. Obsidian workshops tended to be located adjacent to one or midway between several elaborate residences. Obsidian was one category of material being worked in and near site subdivision 2 mostly for use by an elite; other products produced and consumed in this same zone included marine shell and the items included in my category of unusual rocks and minerals. A second zone of craft production in the city, again pertaining to Periods IIIb (IV?) and earlier, followed the site's major road (E in Figure 4.4), and was located between and around Terraces 453 and 938, in site subdivisions 7 and 8. Products produced in this zone, like those produced in parts of the site away from Monte Albán proper, were generally consumed utilitarian goods, including manos and metates, and the local quartzites and cherts. By Period V much less production of costly goods is present on the site. Obsidian, by that time, was a widely utilized good, and workshops were no longer optimally situated to produce for elite households alone. Manos and metates and other utilitarian ground stone may have continued to be produced, or used in production, but the dating of these workshops is problematical.

This interpretation is no doubt oversimplified and potentially faulty due to our present inability to date workshops directly and to recognize certain classes of productive activities from surface evidence alone (for example feather working). Even the identification of ceramic workshops has proven to be a problem at Monte Albán. I would predict that utilitarian categories would have been manufactured in the utilitarian production zone along road E, but we found no evidence of that; interestingly, the possible kilns that Winter and Payne argue were used in the production of utilitarian Period IIIb–IV types (Winter and Payne 1976) were found in the vicinity of Terrace 634, adjacent to Terrace 938 and Area 16, the proposed market. This find notwithstanding, it is my impression that there was little ceramic production at Monte Albán. I have already mentioned the absence of concentrations of kiln wasters anywhere on the site's surface. None of the kiln wasters we did find was so damaged that normal use of the vessel would have been precluded. Independent evidence of ceramic production is also difficult to find on the surface at Monte Albán. Only a total of six *polishing stones* or burnishing pebbles were noted during the survey (two in site subdivision 8, two in subdivision 15, and two in subdivision 11). These are quartzite stones with one highly polished edge, identical to the ones I have seen being used for burnishing by the potters in the modern ceramic-producing village of San Bartolo Coyotepec. We located three fragmentary pits that were probably kilns of some sort or roasting ovens on Terraces 377 and 1206, and one outside the site in square N7E7. Each was roughly a meter in diameter at the top (somewhat wider at the bottom), and roughly a meter deep. The bedrock lining in each case was reddened, probably due to high temperatures. No evidence of ceramic firing could be found near the features, however, so their functions are unknown. They could have been used for burning lime for plaster, but, again, no direct evidence indicating this could be found on the surface. An additional problem with these kilns is that there is no sure way of dating them, so they are not definitely even prehispanic.

All things considered, I doubt there was much ceramic production at Monte Albán. In fact, by comparison, there was probably little production within the city of any type. Table 4.5 summarizes the total terrace surface areas and population estimates for terraces where evidence of craft production was noted (based on the value of 311.9 m^2 per household, and 5 to 10 persons per household). These values are largely meaningless since

Table 4.5. Numbers of People Estimated to Have Lived on Terraces Where There Is Evidence for Craft Production

Workshop type	Square meters of terrace area	Population estimate
Obsidian	56,134	900–1800
Shell	8,321	133–266
Mano	2,238	35–70
Metate	1,053	17–34
Other-lithic	53,881	864–1728

they assume all workshops were in operation contemporaneously. The real values for the population involved in craft production at any given point in time would be less. On the other hand, these values are an underestimate in the sense that they reflect only those kinds of productive activities discoverable through surface inspection. The values derived are still of interest, however. The total maximum population of households engaged in production when calculated in this way is roughly 2000 to 4000, which would represent roughly 13% of the total population of the community during Period IIIb–IV. A somewhat more realistic population estimate can be made if obsidian workshops are excluded that are likely to have been in operation during Period V alone. This gives a new total of roughly 1500 to 3000 persons, roughly 10% of the population estimated for Period IIIb–IV.

Monte Albán was definitely a lightweight, from the point of view of craft production, by comparison with its contemporary in the Valley of Mexico, Teotihuacan. Millon and his associates estimate that by roughly A.D. 600, Teotihuacan had a total population engaged in craft production of roughly 30,000, or 25% of the city's total population—400 obsidian workshops pertain to this period, accounting for roughly 10,000 obsidian workers and associated households, as well as 150 to 200 nonobsidian workshops, 100 to 150 of which were obviously involved in ceramic manufacture (Millon 1976:231, 233; Spence n.d.:35). Teotihuacan was clearly the major center of production and marketing in the entire Valley of Mexico (Blanton 1976c). By contrast, I would argue, while some products were being produced at Monte Albán, it is not likely the city was a major regional production or marketing center, at least not prior to Period V. I have already alluded to the fact that Monte Albán's road system is unlike that expected of a market center, and it lacks any large market-like feature comparable to Teotihuacan's Great Compound (Millon 1973:20). This is precisely what is to be expected if Monte Albán had been, as I have hypothesized, a special-function community, a regional political capital, disembedded from the remainder of the region's economic and political central place hierarchy. The population of the capital was probably dependent, in terms of consumer items as well as food, on taxes and the region's marketing and production system, which was spatially separated from the community. I will expand my discussion of this topic in the concluding chapter of this volume.

Household Variability during Period IIIb–IV

According to Marcus Winter (1974), by Period IIIb Monte Albán residences consisted of rooms facing on a central patio, but I doubt this is true for the community as a whole. A number of small terraces far downslope from the mound group clusters had fragments of buildings that look like simple rectangular rooms, lacking a patio. Winter's sample includes only residences with patios probably because it represents only higher ranking individuals who could live near the top of the hill, closer to the civic–ceremonial and marketing features. Within the group of residences with patios, Winter has distinguished three categories which, he argues, reflect the presence of three social classes within the city. His data consist of architectural plans published by Caso and his associates, along with data from his excavations in the vicinity of Terrace 634, totaling 14 residences. The categories identified by Winter are distinguishable in terms of the size and architectural complexity of the patios (Winter 1974: Table 2), as well as the overall size and complexity of the structure and associated burials. His most simple group has a mean area of patios of 12.88 m^2; the next group has somewhat larger patios (the mean equaling 24.94 m^2), and a *banqueta* forming an outer patio around a smaller, inner patio; the largest group consists of palaces such as the *Plataforma Este* on the Main Plaza (Appendix X: Figure A.X–32). The latter group has a mean patio surface area of 112.33 m^2.

During the course of our survey we collected more data pertaining to the metrical attributes of residences. Our sample is larger than Winter's in that we measured room areas and patio areas for mound groups that have not been excavated, as well as for nonmounded residences that have been excavated or extensively looted, but which have not yet been published. Even this larger sample, of course, does not reflect the total variability of residences at Monte Albán, because it is too small, and overrepresents residences of the upper socioeconomic groups whose residences have most often been looted or excavated, and because metrical data are easily derived from elaborate residences whose rooms are elevated on platform mounds and whose patios are defined by mounds. Figures 4.46 and 4.47 are histograms showing the variability in two of the attributes we measured (all patio measurements are of the larger, outside patio when a double patio is present). These data do not support Winter's contention that three categories of residents were present at Monte Albán during Period IIIb. The variability present in this sample suggests more complexity socioeconomically than is encompassed in Winter's tripartite scheme. The patio surface area histogram, for example, can be reasonably divided into at least six modes, at just over 10 m^2, at roughly 16 m^2, at 80–100 m^2 at 280–520 m^2, at 580–780 m^2, and there are nine examples in the over 1000 m^2 category. A possibility exists that some of this variability is due to the fact that some of the

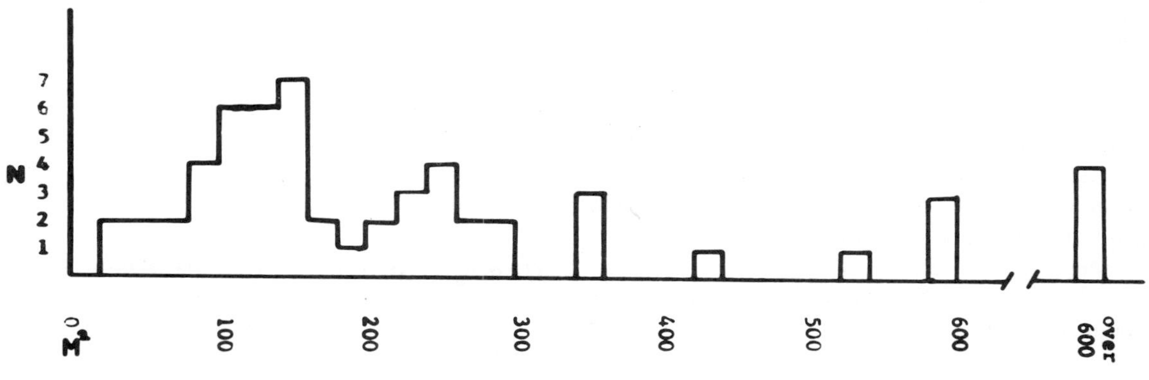

Figure 4.46. Histogram of total room areas for well-preserved residential structures.

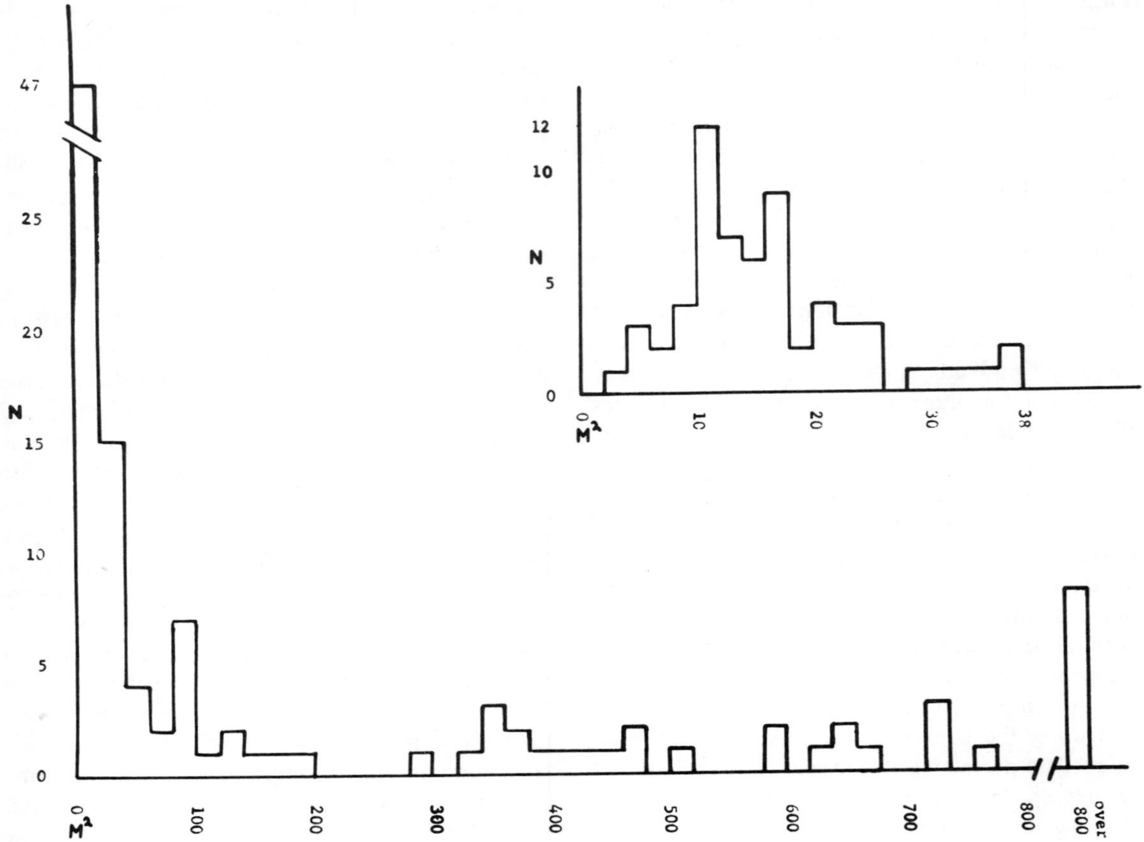

Figure 4.47. Histogram of patio areas. The outside measurement was used in cases of a double patio. The inset histogram is a detail of the variability in the size classes less than 38 m².

residences actually date to periods before or subsequent to IIIb. Since these structures are all on the surface, however, it is likely that most or all were in use during IIIb, when, as far as I can tell, virtually all the Monte Albán terraces were occupied.

Clearly we will need a much larger and better-defined sample of residences before we can begin to unravel the complexity of socioeconomic differentiation at ancient Monte Albán. The surface-collected data pertaining to residential variability, however, do strongly suggest that a simple scheme such as that proposed by Winter will probably be inadequate.

Change through Time in the Use of Space at Monte Albán

During the course of his excavations around Terrace 634 (N5E8), Winter (1974) noted a tendency for houses to become more compact and closed through time. Those he excavated dating to Periods I and II were open–features associated with houses tended to be scattered around them over an area with a radius of about 10 m. By Period IIIb the houses he excavated consisted

> of rooms adjoining the sides of a square central patio with plaster floor. . . . In the examples excavated in 1972 and 1973, ovens were the only features found outside the rooms and patio. The closed household cluster with a central patio as focal point has a centripetal inward orientation which contrasts sharply with the open household cluster [Winter 1974:983].

This "closure" of residences is one aspect of what Winter refers to as the "increasingly formalized use of space" at Monte Albán by Period IIIb (Winter 1974). He also found architectural evidence that traffic flow between households was more rigorously contained by walls and stairways than had been the case in prior periods (Winter 1974).

The surface evidence from Monte Albán tends to confirm the idea that there was more formal use of space, involving more traffic flow regulation, in its later history. We have already discussed the construction of the double-wall system around site subdivision 1, dating to late Period IIIb or Period IV. Persons moving in and out of this area had to pass through the four or five small gates in this wall system, perhaps facilitating traffic control and taxation, as well as defense. I have argued previously that the Main Plaza was a segregated, closed elite administrative place, access to which was only by way of three small and easily controlled entrances. There is some evidence that the degree of closure of the Main Plaza and its buildings increased through time. While examining the modifications to Terrace 25 (N4E10) being made in connection with the construction of a restaurant (!), I noted what appears to have been a staircase that originally would have connected this terrace with the ramp along the east base of the North Platform, in the vicinity of what we call Terrace 24. This staircase was partially exposed under the base of a retaining wall that I.N.A.H. archaeologists were reinforcing. The retaining wall was clearly an aboriginal feature, however, that would have covered the staircase, separating Terrace 25 from features above it at a point where, apparently, traffic originally had moved.

A second, and more obvious bit of evidence that the Main Plaza was becoming more closed in the city's later history is a stone wall built around the South Platform, and the area south and west of it (Figure 4.3). This wall defines an area I refer to as the "South Platform Precinct." The wall is discontinuous, and present today in four segments (between M and Q, at N and P, and south of L, in Figure 4.3). The wall would have restricted the flow of traffic at points where the natural slope is shallow–no wall was built in places with a rapid drop-off, except to the west of L and P. The wall is well preserved especially along the east side of the South Platform. Here it reaches a maximum elevation of roughly 3 m (Plate 9). The wall appears to have been built late in the city's history, but presumably before the Main Plaza was abandoned at the end of Period IIIb. Two facts argue for the lateness of the wall's construction: First, the wall nearly blocks the top of the South Platform staircase (at point N of Figure 4.3), leaving only a small entrance. Presumably a wide staircase would not have been built originally if only such a small access to the top of the platform had been desired. Second, the wall appears to have been built over a ramp located just north of the point where the wall abuts the outer defensive wall around site subdivision 1 (at Q in Figure 4.3). It appears that prior to the construction of the wall, traffic would have flowed freely from road L (Figure 4.3), across the south end of what later became the closed precinct, then on to the group of terraces west of the South Platform by way of ramp N (Figure 4.3). This wall, then, not only served to isolate the South Platform Precinct, but also stopped or at least severely curtailed the flow of traffic along what may have been an important route previously.

In several localities we noted stone walls that appeared to have had the function of separating residential features from traffic arteries and/or civic plazas (Terraces 92, 202, 206, 207, 209, 453, 491, and 938). Unfortunately these features cannot be dated from surface evidence alone and so I cannot be sure they reflect an increasingly formalized use of space and traffic control within the city. The other data just summarized, along with Winter's information, do suggest more closure and isolation of residential and other features through time, perhaps culminating during Period IIIb. Clearly, the Main Plaza was a more isolated place just prior to its abandonment. No well-founded explanation for these phenomena can be put forth at the moment, but Winter (1974) seems to imply that the compactness of houses and more formalized use of space in Period IIIb may have been the result of the increased density of occupation within the city at that time; his evidence indicates that Period IIIb represented the maximum occupation of the terraces he excavated. It is also possible that these data are indicative of a change more fundamental than one related just to the increase in the density of the population. If social relations between households had changed just prior to or during Period IIIb, such that they became more self-contained in certain respects, and required fewer ties to other households, then the more inward-focused, closed residences may have been favored. I have already proposed, based on the terrace surface data, that the residential units that were building and occupying terraces during Period IIIb were smaller than those of preceding periods. The increasing closure of the Main Plaza may also be evidence for changes in social relations in the city toward the end of its tenure as regional capital. The elite who directed the political institution centered on the Main Plaza seemed to want, increasingly, to isolate themselves from the general public, and consequently resided in a veritable fortress with no direct access to the city's major traffic routes, a secluded place accessible only through a few small easily guarded gates.

Plate 9. The South Platform precinct wall, looking south from a point just southeast of M of Figure 4.3.

5

Monte Albán from Its Collapse through Period V

Period V is a disappointingly long ceramic period, within which, at the moment, we have no means of detecting population changes or shifts in the pattern of settlement. The population estimate presented here is based on a measurement of the maximum extent of these materials on the site; whether it reflects the size and layout of the community at any particular point in time is unknown. According to my calculations, substantial Period V deposits are present over roughly 14% of the maximum surface area of Monte Albán. Scattered evidence for occupation during this period is present over another roughly 13% of the site. Using the IIIb population as a baseline, and assuming the scattered areas had roughly one-third the density of the more densely settled areas, I estimate the maximum population for Period V to have been about 2774–5549, a drop of nearly 82% from the IIIb maximum. The population history of the city from the time of the IIIb maximum to Period V is unknown due to the lack of diagnosticity of Period IV pottery. There was probably a substantial population at Monte Albán during Period IV, even though the Main Plaza was abandoned. Of the 138 tombs that Sejourné found suitable for an analysis of funerary ritual symbolism at Monte Albán out of the 172 tombs excavated there by I.N.A.H. archaeologists, 40 pertained to Period IV (Sejourné 1960). Acosta (1965:831) refers to a Period IV "enclave" on the north slope of Monte Albán proper where most of the tombs of the period were found. Only a few sherds collected as part of our survey are known to date to Period IV, our category 3030 (Figure 4.37 on p. 85), and these were found near the top of the hill.

By Period V the bulk of the city's population was living away from the top of Monte Albán proper, along its base, especially in site subdivisions 7 and 8 (Figure 5.1). Locations inside the defensive wall along here were favored. Apparently people wanted to live away from the very top of the hill, but not so far down that they would have been outside the protective walls. Judging from the density of pottery, Terrace 453 and the surrounding subdivision 8 were the center of Period V activities. This is interesting, since Terrace 453 is adjacent to traffic node B of Figure 4.4, the most highly accessible node in the city's road network. This location, closer to the valley floor, and with access to major roads, suggests Monte Albán may have been more commercially oriented during Period V than it had been during prior periods. No independent evidence favoring this idea exists

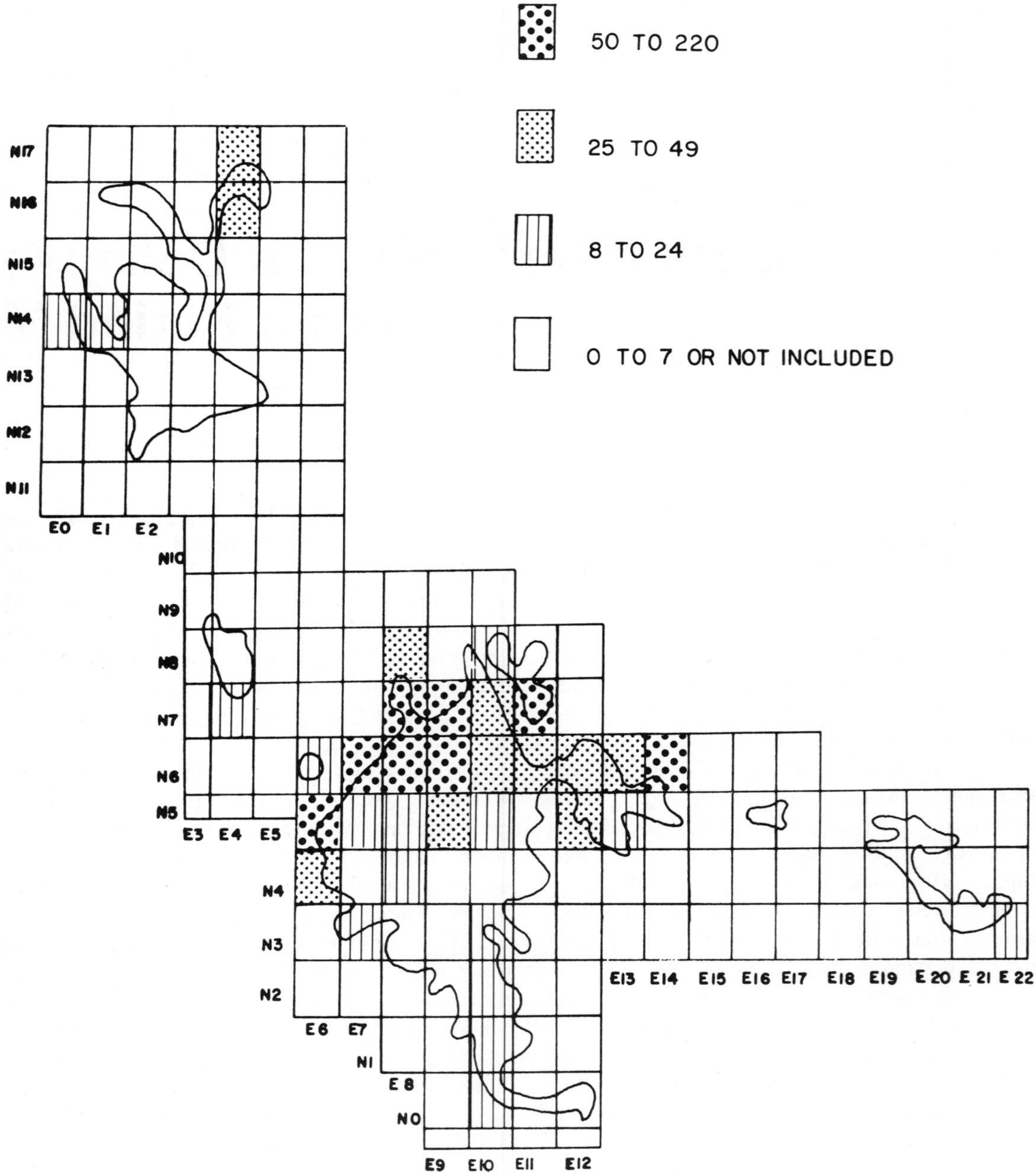

Figure 5.1. Number of sherds collected per hectare of collected terrace surface area, by grid square. Period V.

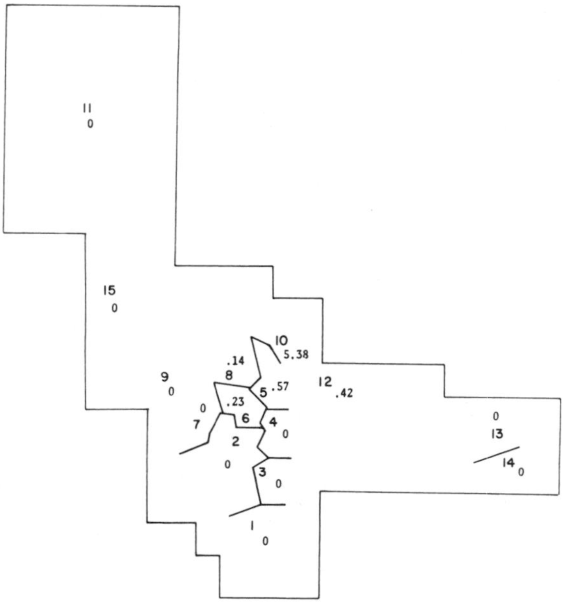

Figure 5.2. Distribution of ceramic category 5000, expressed in sherds per hectare of collected terrace area.

since we have no way of dating the concentrations of artifacts on the surface that we have interpreted as workshops.

Just to the east of the major concentration of Period V pottery around Terrace 453, in subdivision 10, a number of Aztec III black-on-orange sherds were found. Actually a few of these sherds were found in adjacent subdivisions (Figure 5.2), but most came from subdivision 10, especially around Terrace 867 (N7E11). This may have been the location of the Aztec garrison in the Valley of Oaxaca, since little other evidence for the Aztec presence has been found during the course of our surveys (cf. Esparza 1975).

The Collapse of Monte Albán

The abandonment of the Main Plaza no doubt reflected the collapse of the political institution centered there. As I see it, at least two factors may have been causes of the demise: First, and more important, was the fact that, beginning in the seventh century A.D., Teotihuacan was beginning to show signs of downfall. Its Metepec phase (ca. A.D. 650–750) occupation was somewhat reduced compared with the prior phase (Millon 1967, 1973:59), and there is evidence for substantial population declines at that time in the rural Valley of Mexico (Blanton 1972:82–83; Sanders 1965:102). Sometime shortly after A.D. 700, Teotihuacan was massively abandoned, never to regain its status as a key regional center (Millon 1967, 1973:59). It is not likely to have been just coincidental that the Main Plaza was abandoned sometime also during the seventh century A.D. If the regional polity at Monte Albán had grown in importance during Period III in response to the military expansionism of Teotihuacan, then the collapse of that center would have considerably reduced the value of a military alliance in the Valley of Oaxaca. The elite in the cojoining societies in the valley may have increasingly found it not worthwhile to support the capital and the political institution centered there. Any decline in such support would have been disastrous for a political capital lacking a strong economic orientation, and located in an out-of-the-way place. The city was no doubt not self-sufficient.

A second set of problems facing administrative institutions in the Valley of Oaxaca during the Late Classic Period that could have hastened Monte Albán's decline were local ones. Steve Kowalewski argues that rapid population growth during Period IIIb, evident in those areas that have been surveyed, resulted in the "filling up" of all usable agricultural land (Kowalewski 1976:805; in press). In such a situation it is likely that the number of disputes over access to productive land could have increased dramatically, both between individual households and larger territorial units. This would have placed a strain on the adjudicative authorities in the valley, perhaps further reducing their desire to support a military alliance which no longer had a crucial role.

6

Concluding Comments

In earlier chapters I presented a hypothesis concerning the nature of Monte Albán's regional role. In this chapter I will discuss two of the implications of that hypothesis and then briefly summarize my conclusions about Monte Albán and changes there through time.

There are many differences between Monte Albán and Teotihuacan, but the most fundamental, in my view, is the different position each had in the hierarchy of central places in their respective regions. Judging from the settlement pattern data collected in the Valley of Mexico, Teotihuacan seems to have expanded its hegemony through a process of elimination of what had been local centers, usurping their central place functions (Blanton 1972, 1976c). The result was a highly centralized regional system, with most political and economic activities concentrated in the one center. In this mode of regional organization, which geographers refer to as a "primate" settlement distribution (cf. Berry 1961; Blanton 1976b), one large, multifunctional center dominates the region so completely that the growth of lower-order centers is retarded (Blanton 1976b). The primate pattern of the Valley of Mexico's Classic Pèriod was not an isolated event. The dynamics of social systems there after the end of the Formative Period were such that periods with the primate regional mode alternated with periods of less regional centralization. Following the collapse of Teotihuacan there was a period of "balkanization," the so-called "Early Toltec" Period, during which no single center dominated valley affairs; beginning about A.D. 1000, however, another regional center emerged, at Tula, Hidalgo, reestablishing the primate mode (Blanton 1972, 1976c). This center in turn collapsed, followed by another period of regional decentralization, the Early Aztec Period (Blanton 1972, 1976c). Toward the end of the prehispanic sequence, the growth of Tenochtitlan–Tlatelolco seems to provide evidence that another move in the direction of regional centralization was in process.

My hypothesis concerning Monte Albán's function is an argument that regional organization in the Valley of Oaxaca was unlike that in the Valley of Mexico. No primate centers dominated the Valley of Oaxaca the way that Teotihuacan, Tula, and, to a lesser extent, Tenochtitlan–Tlatelolco had dominated the Valley of Mexico. According to this hypothesis, the regional capital in Oaxaca was a special-function community, located in such a

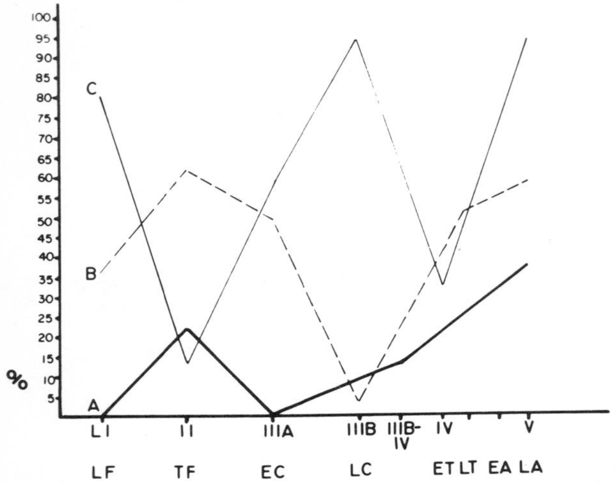

Figure 6.1. Percentage of sites not occupied during periods prior to and subsequent to each period. The Monte Albán ceramic periods are along the top row. Below these are the Valley of Mexico Periods (LF=Late Formative; TF=Terminal Formative; EC=Early Classic; LC=Late Classic; ET=Early Toltec; LT=Late Toltec; EA=Early Aztec; LA=Late Aztec). (A) Sites in the Etla Region; (B) sites in the Valley of Mexico; (C) sites in the Central Valley of Oaxaca Region.

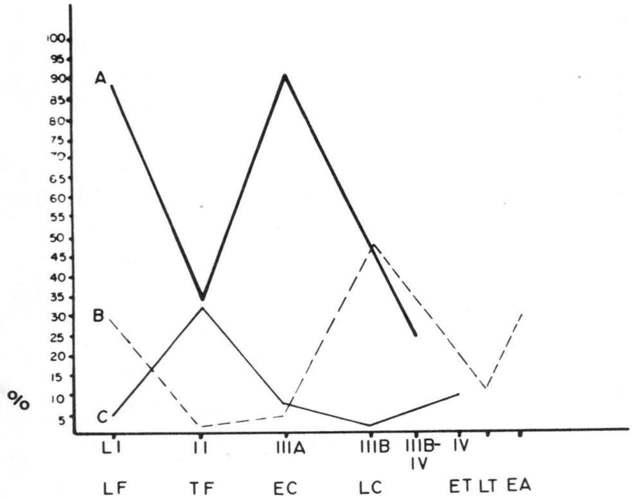

Figure 6.2. Percentage of sites occupied during prior and subsequent ceramic periods. Period indicators are the same as for Figure 6.1. (A) Sites in the Etla Region; (B) sites in the Valley of Mexico; (C) sites in the Central Valley of Oaxaca Region.

way as to avoid "distortion" of the region's existing central place hierarchy. Local polities retained a considerable degree of autonomy. A test implication of this hypothesis is the following: Settlement patterns in the Valley of Oaxaca should show more continuity than those in the Valley of Mexico. In the latter region, each time a new primate center emerged, whole communities were abandoned and new ones formed. Local polities subsequently lost power to the new center and collapsed; rural areas came under the strong control of the center, and demographic shifts occurred. Similarly, entirely new settlement configurations emerged following the collapse of the primate mode. In the Valley of Oaxaca, by contrast, local societies retained more autonomy. The growth or collapse of the regional capital would have had less impact on settlement patterns since it was disembedded from the region's central place hierarchy. This implication of the general hypothesis cannot be fully explored until we have completed more archaeological surveys in the Valley of Oaxaca, but even with the data at hand the hypothesis is largely supported.

In order to demonstrate the degree of settlement continuity in the Valleys of Oaxaca and Mexico, I plotted period by period from the Late Formative to the end of the prehispanic sequence, the percentages of sites in the two regions with no continuity, that is, the percentage of sites that were not occupied during the immediately prior or subsequent ceramic periods (Figure 6.1). I also calculated the percentage of sites that had been occupied during both prior and subsequent ceramic periods (Figure 6.2). To calculate the values for the Valley of Mexico, I combined the data from the Ixtapalapa Region (Blanton 1972) and the Texcoco Region (Parsons 1971). The percentages for the Valley of Oaxaca are expressed separately for the Etla Region (Varner 1974) and the Central Valley Region (Kowalewski 1976). Interestingly, the hypothesis is not confirmed in the Central Valley Region where the degree of settlement pattern continuity is comparable to the rural Valley of Mexico. Apparently Monte Albán had exerted a strong influence on populations very close to it. The predicted greater degree of settlement continuity is apparent in Varner's data, however, in a region further removed from Monte Albán. The Valley of Mexico data show the much stronger impact that regional centers had on rural populations there, especially notable since both the Ixtapalapa and Texcoco Regions are much more distant from the various political capitals (Teotihuacan, Tula, and Tenochtitlan–Tlatelolco) than the Etla Region is from Monte Albán.

A second implication of the general hypothesis concerns the ceramic sequences of these two regions. It has been argued that Monte Albán was not an important center of production and distribution for the region. Presumably the region's production and distribution centers would therefore have been little altered due to Monte Albán's growth or decline. Such a situation would have been quite different from that in the Valley of Mexico where there is considerable evidence for the centralization of production and distribution, especially at Teotihuacan (Blanton 1976c). If it had been the case that a consequence of the primate pattern in the Valley of Mexico was a greater tendency for centralized control of production and distribution, this should have been reflected archaeologically. In the Valley of Mexico, the collapse or reorganization of a polity such as that centered at Teotihuacan might more often be associated with drastic changes in economic systems tightly associated with it. In the Valley of Oaxaca, the growth or collapse of Monte Albán would have been reflected much less in patterns of production and distribution, which perhaps helps to explain the vast differences in the ceramic sequences of the two valleys, a difference immediately apparent to anyone who has worked in both areas. The ceramic sequence in Oaxaca is characterized by continuity of categories and conservatism, as described in various sections of this book. From the Late Formative to the end of the prehispanic sequence there really are only two major changes in ceramic assemblages—that between Periods II and IIIa and that between Periods IIIb–IV and V (CBA: passim). By a major change I mean a nearly complete replacement of ceramic categories, with little or no overlap. In the Valley of Mexico sequence, by contrast, from the Late Formative Ticoman phase to the end of the prehispanic sequence I count 10 major changes in ceramic assemblages (those between the following phases: Ticoman, Tezoyuca–Patlachique, Tzacualli, Miccaotli, Tlamimilolpa, Xolalpan, Metepec, Coyotlatelco, Mazapan, Early Aztec, and Late Aztec) (Blanton and Parsons 1971). Some of these phases are generically similar; for example, the Coyotlatelco and Mazapan ceramics are alike in that red-on-buff types dominate, but anyone who is familiar with these two phases knows there is virtually no overlap of specific categories. I conclude that there was relatively little administrative control of craft production by the political institution centered at the region's capital in the Valley of Oaxaca, and that this was less true in the Valley of Mexico. An event as drastic as the abandonment of the Main Plaza at Monte Albán is not significantly reflected in the valley's ceramic sequence.

A Summary of Ideas about Monte Albán

As I see it, the foundation of a regional political capital at Monte Albán at the juncture of the Middle and Late Formative Periods was due to military tension between societies in the Valley of Oaxaca and those in adjacent regions. A military league in the valley would not only have served to protect, but, through aggressive expansion, could have generated revenues to support the new political institution and its capital. Because cojoining valley polities retained considerable local autonomy (as indicated, for example, by the continued construction of carved stone monuments in regional styles), the new capital had to be placed in such a way as to please everyone involved, and not drastically alter the political or economic status quo. An unused, economically marginal hilltop was chosen as the site, ideal because it was away from existing centers, yet central to the valley as a whole. The new capital grew rapidly from the date of its founding into the subsequent ceramic phase, reaching a population sometime during Period Late I of 10,000 to 20,000 or more. Massive construction was begun in the Main Plaza area, and over 300 monuments were erected testifying to the military prowess of the league.

Sometime during the same ceramic period, however, the city's growth ceased; by the time Period II ceramic diagnostics were being used, El Gallo and Mogollito had been abandoned. Also at approximately this time or during Period II a large defensive work was constructed along the city's exposed north, northwest, and west edges; where this feature crossed a canyon a reservoir was formed. A small irrigation system was built along the community's east slope. All of this seems to suggest that, for a while at least, there had been an attempt made to increase the city's self-sufficiency, and defense from invaders may have been a problem, although it still remains a possibility that the wall functioned only for traffic control and the collection of gate taxes. Another smaller set of walls guarded the city's southernmost flank. In spite of these apparent setbacks, construction continued on the Main Plaza, and more monuments were erected telling of military victories. By the end of Period II, according to Acosta, the Main Plaza had nearly assumed its present shape.

By the beginning of the next ceramic period, IIIa, a new political and economic force was making itself felt througout Mesoamerica, emanating from the Valley of Mexico where a massive city was growing at Teotihuacan, larger than any ever built by American Indians. The government centered there had not only drastically restructured political and economic systems in the Valley of Mexico, but had embarked on a campaign of military expansion in more distant regions. They no doubt had in mind the annexation of the fertile and populous Valley of Oaxaca. At this juncture, the political institution whose setting was the regional capital at Monte Albán was apparently more heavily "funded," in order, no doubt, to stop the expansionist Teotihuacanos. During the long span when Teotihuacan was a prominent feature of the cultural environment of Mesoamerica, the IIIa and IIIb Periods in the Valley of Oaxaca, Monte Albán grew, and more and more massive construction was carried out in the Main Plaza. By Period IIIb the city had reached its maximum population of about 15,000 to 30,000—virtually all terraces visible on the surface today were occupied.

The collapse of Teotihuacan, beginning in the seventh century A.D. and complete by the middle of the eighth, resulted in the demise of its Oaxacan counterpart Monte Albán. The political institution centered there was an expensive one to support, and once it had lost its major reason for existence, was probably no longer provisioned. A disembedded capital, located in a marginal place, is not self-sufficient economically, and so the abandonment of the Main Plaza was accompanied by general population decline. The magnitude of that decline cannot be traced precisely, but we do know that by Period V Monte Albán had a population equivalent to about 18% of its Period IIIb maximum. The abandonment of the Main Plaza seems to have been accompanied also by another round of building of defensive walls—a double system was constructed around site subdivision 1, and a smaller set may have been built around subdivision 12, although the latter set have not yet been dated precisely.

From its foundation until at least Period IIIb, Monte Albán's population had resided in *barrio*-like subdivisions. Three such subdivisions were present in Period Early I, or possibly 4 if Mogollito is counted, probably 10 existed during Period Late I, 8 in Period II, and the site had expanded to include 15 by Period IIIb. One of these, subdivision 2, was special in that it contained the Main Plaza and a group of what appear to have been elite residences surrounding it. The others, I have shown, housed league representatives and their supporting populations. Each subdivision may have had a representative building on the Main Plaza.

Monte Albán was probably not an important regional center of production and exchange, but some production took place there nonetheless. During and prior to Period IIIb, probably, two zones of production existed. One, in the near vicinity of the Main Plaza, was oriented to the manufacture of items for an elite; the other, situated especially in site subdivisions 7 and 8, along the city's major road, involved more of production of utilitarian goods for the general population.

Perhaps the most exciting and theoretically significant result of our survey work in Oaxaca to date is the discovery that this valley's regional organization during much of the prehispanic sequence was apparently very different from the regional organization of the Valley of Mexico where highly centralized states periodically restructured settlement patterns, producing large primate centers that combined much of the region's political control and economic activities. In Oaxaca, no primate center, as far as we know, ever dominated so thoroughly the valley population.

Why the societies in two such regions with roughly similar environmental settings and with similar technologies should have departed so radically in terms of their regional organizations and their evolutionary histories is unknown. While the survey data from Monte Albán raise a number of questions worth investigating in the future, this is perhaps the most important, since it is relevant to an understanding of cultural evolution in a general sense. In order to realize my goal of restricting the topic of this volume largely to the settlement patterns of Monte Albán, however, I will not begin to grapple with this problem here. In future volumes of our settlement pattern series, the discussion of broader topics in cultural evolution in Oaxaca, such as this one, will be our goal.

Appendixes

APPENDIX I

Terrace Data

Part 1. Numerically Coded Data

This appendix includes all terrace data that could be conveniently coded in numerical form. Each terrace fills two rows of numbers (Cards 1 and 2), the first row extending for 79 columns, the second for 44 columns. The column values are identified in the terrace code book that follows:

Monte Albán Terrace Code Book

Column(s) **Card 1**

- 1 — 1 = Monte Albán; 2 = Atzompa; 3 = El Gallo
- 2 — 1 = Terrace (originally this data set included structures and areas as separate designations—now only terraces are included. Structures are described separately in the structure summary as are areas)
- 3–6 — Terrace number
- 7–8 — Card number (01, 02). Space was maintained here for numbers larger than 9 columns in case future versions of this data set include all ceramic information.
- 9 — 0 = No ceramic collection made: 1 = ceramic collection made
- 10–12 — North grid coordinate (not used in this volume)
- 13–15 — East grid coordinate (not used in this volume)
- 16–17 — North square number
- 18–19 — East square number
- 20–21 — Area designation (Thiessen Polygon)
- 22–23 — Recorder: 00 = missing data; 01 = Blanton; 02 = Kuttruff; 03 = Varner; 04 = Kowalewski; 05 = Lohse; 06 = Allen; 07 = Appel; 08 = Beckerman; 09 = Brumfiel; 10 = Byland; 11 = Chevrette; 12 = Keane; 13 = Mason; 14 = O'Brien; 15 = Pinto-Torres; 16 = Redmond; 17 = Schreuder; 18 = Spencer; 19 = other; 20 = Crowfoot; 21 = Smythe; 22 = Schiller; 23 = Henley
- 24–26 — Elevation of the terrace in meters above the valley floor, to the nearest 25 meter line
- 27 — Topography: 1 = near flat; 2 = hilltop; 3 = moderate to steep slope; 4 = flat ridgetop; 5 = missing data
- 28 — Soil type: (this category proved to have little value since most soils are the same gray brown rocky loam, code value 1)
- 29 — Estimated soil depth, meters: 0 = cannot estimate (this category proved to be of little value because normally soil depth could not be estimated)
- 30 — Silting: 1 = none; 2 = some; 3 = heavy; 4 = missing data. Little variability was noted in this category. Most terraces have a small amount of silting, but the category "degree of erosion" proved to be much more valuable for describing the condition of terraces, along with degree of destruction due to plowing
- 31 — Damage due to erosion and plowing: 1 = none; 2 = light; 3 = moderate to heavy; 4 = missing data
- 32 — Spring: 0 = absent; 1 = present; 2 = missing data

33 *Barranca* or wash adjacent: 0 = absent; 1 = present; 2 = missing data
34 Vegetation: 0 = none; 1 = grass only; 2 = grass and brush; 3 = cultivated; 4 = missing data
35 Vegetation abundance: 0 = none; 1 = sparse; 2 = moderate; 3 = heavy; 4 = missing
36 Special resources: 0 = none; 1 = quarryable stone; 2 = other; 3 = missing data (see comments section for description of other)
37 Modern use: 0 = none; 1 = grazing only; 2 = agriculture; 3 = residential; 4 = I.N.A.H.; 5 = road; 6 = missing
38 Recency of plowing: 0 = unknown or none; 1 = cultivated this year; 2 = sometime in the past; 3 = missing data
39 Extent of pot hunting: 0 = none; 1 = some (1 or 2 small pits); 2 = heavy; 3 = missing data
40 Extent of excavation: 0 = none; 1 = some (e.g., the exposure of one or two tombs); 2 = extensive; 3 = missing data
41 Number of unnumbered tombs visible on the surface; 9 = missing data
42 Number of numbered tombs visible on the surface: 9 = missing data
43 Ancient retaining wall fragments visible on the surface: 0 = none; 1 = present; 2 = missing data
44–49 Estimated area of the terrace in square meters
50 Structural wall fragments visible on the surface: 0 = none; 1 = present; 2 = missing data
51 Prevailing wall orientations: 0 = none; 1 = north–south; 2 = 8–10° west of north; 3 = nonstandard; 4 = missing data; 5 = 5 or 6° west of north; 6 = east of north; 7 = west of north; 8 = mixed
52 Presence of well-defined structure or structures less than 1 m in elevation: 0 = none; 1 = present; 9 = missing data (see the structure summary for details)
53 Presence of well-defined structure or structures greater than or equal to 1 m in elevation: 0 = none; 1 = present; 9 = missing data (see the structure summary for details)
54 Estimated function of the terrace: 0 = unknown or missing data (see the structure summary and comments sections–some terraces identified as unknown may have had elite residences); 1 = residential; 2 = mostly elite residential (possibly including some civic ceremonial functions); 3 = probably mostly civic–ceremonial; 4 = ball court; 5 = other (see comments section)
55 Number of measurable patios visible on the surface: 9 = missing data (dimensions will be found in the structure summary)
56 Number of *adoratorios* visible on the surface: 9 = missing data
57 Estimated total number of residences: 0 = no basis for an estimate; 9 = 9 or more (see comments section)
58–63 Total mound volume in cubic meters
64 Plaster floor or floors visible on the surface: 0 = absent; 1 = present; 2 = missing data
65 Evidence of ancient quarrying: 0 = no; 1 = yes; 2 = missing data
66 Surface concentrations of artifacts suggesting a workshop: 0 = none; 1 = some; 2 = probable; 3 = positive; 4 = missing data (for values 1–3, see the workshop summary)
67 Type of workshop: 0 = none; 1 = shell; 2 = obsidian; 3 = mano; 4 = metate; 5 = ceramic; 6 = other-lithic; 7 = other; 9 = missing data
68 Carved stone: 0 = none; 1 = present; 2 = missing data
69 Other features: 0 = none or missing data; 1 = probable hearth; 2 = bench; 3 = mural; 4 = columns; 5 = several (see the comments section); 6 = drainage; 7 = well-preserved staircase; 8 = defense or boundary wall; 9 = other
70 Ancient burning visible on the surface: 0 = absent; 1 = possible; 2 = present; 3 = missing data
71 Number of burials visible on the surface: 0 = none; 9 = missing data
72 Access to known or probable major ancient road: 0 = far; 1 = close; 2 = directly adjacent; 3 = missing data
73 Surface obsidian density: 0 = none; 1 = sparse; 2 = moderate; 3 = abundant; 4 = missing data
74 Obsidian points: 0 = absent; 1 = present; 2 = missing data
75 Obsidian blades: 0 = absent; 1 = present; 2 = missing data
76 Obsidian flakes: 0 = none; 1 = present; 2 = missing data
77 Obsidian cores: 0 = absent; 1 = present; 2 = missing data
78 Miscellaneous obsidian (usually small, unidentifiable fragments): 0 = none; 1 = present; 2 = missing data
79 Color of obsidian: 0 = none or not noted; 1 = gray; 2 = green; 3 = other; 5 = several colors present; 6 = black

Monte Albán Terrace Code Book

Column(s) **Card 2**

1–6 Case number (same as Cards 1–6, Card 1)
7–8 Card number 02
9 Chipped stone blades other than obsidian (usually quartz, flint, or chert): 0 = none; 1 = present;

2 = missing data

10 Other chipped stone points: 0 = none; 1 = present; 2 = missing data

11 Other chipped stone flake tools: 0 = none; 1 = present; 2 = missing data

12 Other chipped stone cores: 0 = none; 1 = present; 2 = missing data

13 Miscellaneous other chipped stone pieces (usually nondescript chunks of quartz, chert, or flint): 0 = none; 1 = present; 2 = missing data

14–15 Number of whole or fragmentary manos: 98 = missing data; 99 = present, but number not indicated

16–17 Number of whole or fragmentary metates: 98 = missing data; 99 = present, but number not indicated

18 Stone bowls: 0 = absent; 1 = present; 2 = missing data

19 Other ground stone: 0 = absent; 1 = present; 2 = missing data or unknown function

20 Published information: 0 = no; 1 = yes; 2 = missing data

21–22 Number of figurines: 98 = missing data; 99 = present but number not indicated in the report

23 Spindle whorls: 0 = absent; 1 = present; 2 = missing data

24 Pottery disks: 0 = absent; 1 = present; 2 = missing data

25 Worked shell fragments: 0 = none; 1 = sparse; 2 = abundant; 3 = missing data

26 Unworked shell fragments (or not obviously worked): 0 = none; 1 = sparse; 2 = abundant; 3 = missing data

27 Kiln wasters: 0 = absent; 1 = present; 2 = missing data

28 Urn fragments: 0 = none; 1 = present; 2 = abundant; 3 = missing data

29 Whistle fragments: 0 = absent; 1 = present; 2 = missing data

30 *Incensario* fragments: 0 = absent; 1 = present; 2 = missing data

31 *Candeleros*: 0 = absent; 1 = present; 2 = missing data

32 Miscellaneous artifacts: 0 = none; 1 = present (see comments section); 2 = missing data

33 Pottery density: 0 = sparse; 1 = sparse to light; 2 = moderate; 3 = heavy; 4 = missing data

34 Surface assessment of Period Ia: 0 = absent; 1 = sparse; 2 = light; 3 = moderate; 4 = missing data

35 Surface assessment of Period Late I: 0 = absent; 1 = sparse; 2 = light; 3 = moderate; 4 = missing data

36 Surface assessment of Period II: 0 = absent; 1 = sparse; 2 = light; 3 = moderate; 4 = missing data

37 Surface assessment of Period IIIa: 0 = absent; 1 = sparse; 2 = light; 3 = moderate; 4 = missing data

38 Surface assessment of Period IIIb–IV: 0 = absent; 1 = sparse; 2 = light; 3 = moderate; 4 = missing data

39 Surface assessment of Period IV (alone): 0 = absent or not distinguishable from IIIb; 1 = sparse; 2 = light; 3 = moderate; 4 = missing data

40 Surface assessment of Period V: 0 = absent; 1 = sparse; 2 = light; 3 = moderate; 4 = missing data

41 Estimated depth of the archaeological deposit in meters: 0 = no basis for an estimate

42 Comment written (if yes, see comments section): 0 = no; 1 = yes; 2 = missing data

43 Presence of ceramic burnisher or comparable: 0 = absent; 1 = present; 2 = missing data

44 Reference in the literature to Monte Albán IV occupation of this terrace: 0 = no; 1 = yes; 2 = missing data

```
1100010111992800409020137512111002201002111000480111011000000000100000010100100
11000102001000002001000001000000111112002100
110002011198265040802023751112200210100000100260213301104000051100000000201000
11000202001000101010010000000001111112000000
110003011196279040902033751111200210101000100146510001000000000000000000001010000
11000302001000202000000000000000101212000000
110004011201277050902033751111100210200000100126500001000000000000000000001000010
11000402000010000000000000000000001111000100
110005011204279050902033751101100210101000000375011042111002488000000000001010000
11000502000010100000000001000000001221100000
110006011203284050902033751111100210101010000234312001000000000100000000002000010
11000602000010001000000000000000001211000000
110007011207280050902033751111100211100000000302900010000000000000000000001010000
11000702000010200000000000000000001212000000
110008011195285040902033751101100210200100000527512101000000000100000000001010000
11000802000000001000000000100000011121200000
110009011192282040902034001101100210100120000115712301100000000000000000001010000
11000902000000001000000000000000001220200000
110010011202271050802183751101100211100000100516100001000000000000000000001000010
11001002000010203000000000000000000221200000
110011011200263040802183751101100210200000100175200001000000000000000000001000010
11001102000010100000010000000000010221200000
110012011193262040802183751102000210100000000160611001000000000000000000001000010
11001202000010100000100000100000101212000000
110013011198258040802183751102100210100100100167711101100000000101200000003000010
11001302000010001000010000000000001201000000
110014011194267040802034001101100211100000000172613011000000133000000000001000010
11001402000010001000000101000000001112000000
110015011194272040902034001101100210100110000057311201200000000100000000001000010
11001502000000001000000000000000000220100000
110016011191268040802064001101100210100102000062513101100000000100000000001010000
11001602000000000001000000000000010221100000
110017011190271040902034001101100210101000000256811132101002146000000000001000010
11001702000010000010010000000000001220100000
110018011185276040902034001101100210400203000138711012401005975100010000001000010
11001802000000000001010000000000001220100000
110019011189275040902064001101100210101121100149512201100000000100000000001000010
11001902000000000001010000000000002201000000
110020011181278040902034001101100210400203100635711202300000000100013000000000000
11002002000000000001000000000000002311000100
110021011185292040902034001101100220100208001797615602990000000100015000100000010
11002102000010001001990000000000000221200010
110022011183271040902034001101100210100000000159912001000000000001200000200000010
11002202010010000000000000000000001221101010
110023011181269040802034001111100211100000000088400001000000000000000000001000010
11002302000000000000000000100000000110000010
110024011179303041002034001101100210400210100211312022100002628100014000100000010
11002402000010000001000001000000001221000000
110025011178308041002034001101100210500110100239000001000000000000000060001000010
11002502000010000000000000000000001221200010
110026011180299040902034001101100210101000000184900001000000000000000000000000000
11002602000010000000000000000000001220000010
110027011188302041002034001101100220400225101175017452819011013100015000100000010
11002702000010000000199000100000010221200000
110028011181313041002034001101100220500110000230411101100000000100000000001000010
11002802000010000000000000000000001221100000
110029011188316041002033751101100220100104100082517201200000000000000000001000010
11002902000010000011000000000000000221100000
110030011179318041002033751101101220100203100068417301300000000100010000100000010
11003002000010000001000000000000001222110001
110031011193311041002033751101101220100203000313617401400000000100010000100000010
11003102000010000001000001000000001221100000
110032011197296040902063751101100220100211000924113013030000000100006000100000010
11003202000000000000100000000000001211000000
110033011200296040902033751101100220100000100083600001000000000000000000001000010
11003302000010000000000001000000001210200000
110034011196300040902063751101100220101010000014111001100000000000000000001000010
11003402000000000000000000100000102120000000
110035011195304041002063753101101220100101100026815101100000000000000000001000010
11003502000010000001000000000000000121100000
110036011199309041002063753101101220101000000212152012000000001012000002000010
11003602000010102000000001000000001211000000
110037011196314041002063503101101220100100100049515201200000000100000000001000010
11003702000010000000000010000000012201000000
110038011197301041002033751101101220100110100049011101101000000100000000001000010
11003802000010000000000001000000001220100000
110039011192316041002063753101101220100102000062111201200000000100000000001000010
11003902000010000011000001000000000220100000
110040011191323041004033503101101220100202100095815115100000000100006000100000010
11004002000010000001000000000000112211004100
110041011193318041002063503101101220100100000046015101101000000000000000001000010
11004102000010000000000001000000002212000100
110042011196317041002063503101101220100000100047300001003000000000000000000000000
11004202000010000000000001000000001121200000
110043011196310041002063753101101221100204100179315501500000000101200000200000010
11004302000010001001000000100000011221101010
1
110044011200300041002033751101101221100100100044811101100000000000000000001000010
11004402000010000000000001000000001211000000
110045011202301051006033751101101220100000100171100001000000000000000000001000010
11004502000010001000010001001000012212000100
110046011204298050906033753101101221100000000140400000000000000000000000000000000
11004602000000001000000000000000001211000100
110047011204304051006033503101101221100000000211900001000000000000000000001000010
11004702000010001000010001000000001112000100
110048011208304051006033503101101221100000000096700001000000000000000000001000010
11004802000010000000000001000000000211000000
110049011209306051006033503101101221100000100030600001000000000000000000001000010
11004902000010001000000001000000001102000000
110050011210308051006033503101101220100000000215000010000000000011000001000010
11005002000010000010000002000000001102000000
110051011131301031002024003101100230102000100223411032100003147100015002101000
11005102010010101010000201000001112212000000
110052011147298030902024001101100230100000100040500001000000000100017001101000
11005202000000000000000000000000001121200000
110053011144300031002024001101100230100000000074700001000000000000000000002101000
11005302001000001000000000010001001212000000
110054011148302031002024003101101220100000100046711001000000000000000000002100100
11005402000010000000000000000000002102000000
110055011151300031002024003101101230100000100031600001000000000000000000002000000
11005502000000000000000000000000001101000000
110056011138298030902024003101100220100000100042000001000000000000000000001000000
11005602000000000000000001000000000101000000
110057011148306031002024001101101220100000100069500001000000000000000000002101100
11005702001000100000001000100001022120000000
110058011148308031002024003101101220100000100067800010000000000000000000001201000
11005802001000000100000000000010011110000000
110059011149309031002023753101101220100000100012500001000000000000000000001000000
11005902000010000000000000000000102201000000
110060011134305031002024003101100221101000100047413101100000000000000000002100100
```

```
110060020000100000000100000000000012212000000
11006101114030203100202400110110022010000010003580000100000000000000000000021001000
11006102001000100010000000000000001212000000
11006201113030503100202400110110022110000010006451110100000000000000000080011001000
11006202000000001000020000000000101222000000
11006301113130403100202400310110022110000010006001300100000000000001208001301100 0
11006302001000000000990100000000101112000000
11006401114230403100202400110110022010000010002451100100000000000000000000020000000
11006402001000100000000000300000011110000000
11006501014430303100202400110110022010000000001880000100000000000000000000010000000
11006502000000100000000000000000000101000000
11006601114530903100202375110110022010000000005181100100000000000000000000011010000
11006602010000000000900000000000001102000000
11006701111629702090202400110110022010000010007630000100000000000001200002301100 0
11006702001000000000000101000001122112000000
11006801112530103100202400110110022010000010002871300100000000000000000000011010000
11006802001000000000000000010000001102000000
11006901111830102100202400110110022010000010010170000100000000000000000000011001000
11006902001000000000990000000000101202000000
11007001112230403100202400110110022010000010000401000010000000000000000000011001000
11007002000110100000000000000000101110100000 0
11007101111930702100202375110110022010000010003910700100000000000002200001300100 0
11007102001000001000000000000000001121200000 0
11007201112630803100202375110110022010000010000912000010000000000000000000012101000
11007202001010000010000000001000001221000000 0
11007301112531203100202350110110022010000010014000000100000000000021008001301100
11007302001000100000990022000000010112000000
11007401112331403100202350110110022010000010011250000100000000000000000000011011000
11007402110000002000990100010000001201000000
11007501116130604100202400310210121010100010017701100100000000000000000000021010000
11007502001000000000000000000000011222100000 0
11007601116230304100202400310110021050000010003580000100000000000000000000011010000
11007602001010000000000000000000101221000000 0
11007701115930203100202400310110121010000010001520000100000000000000000000010000000
11007702001000001000000000000000000110000000 0
11007801116930404100201400210110022010020110004641110210100000010000000011011000
11007802001010100001000001000001112200005100
11007901116730804100201400310110022040111000034801601000000511710000000021000010
11007902001010000010000001000000001210000000
11008001116230904100202400310210022010000010003870000100000000000160000210110 00
11008002001010000000300010000011122210000000
11008101115830803100202400310220122010020010002431400110000000010000000021011000
11008102001000100000990001010001012211000100
11008201115831003100202400310210122010000010002881300100000000010120000230110 00
11008202101000000000990001000001110210000000
11008301115631103100202375310210122010000010001980000100000000000000000000021010000
11008302011000000000000000000000011211000000
11008401115931303100202375310210022110000010002420000100000000000012000023001000
11008402001000000000000000100000101220100000 0
11008501115531303100202375110110122110000000005720001000000000930000000021011000
11008502001010000000000000000000001002100000 00
11008601115731503100202375110210022110000010003750000100100000000000000000021010000
11008602001100001010000000001000012222000000 0
11008701114732103100302375110210122110000010047060000000000000000000090021011010
11008702001010101000990001000000112211000000
11008801113532703100302350110110022010000000000980000100000000000000000000002101000
11008802101000100000000000000000001110000000 0
11008901113333003100302350110110022010000000002668000010000000000002100002301100 0
11008902001010000000001000000000011221100000 0
11009001112933203110302350110110022110000010010480000100000000000011000021011000
11009002001000000000010020000000112201000000
11009101114032003100302350310120122110000000000350000010000000000000000000011010000
11009102000010000000101000000000011101000000
11009201113033503110302325310110022110100000010501601000000046010000000021011000
11009202001000000010010001000000012212000000
11009301112733703110302325310110022010000000005251610100000000000000000000021001000
11009302001000001010000000000000011110000000
11009401112633903110302325310110022110000010002040000100000000000000000000021010000
11009402101100000100010001010000002101000000
11009501112634003110302325310110022110000010004490000100000000000016000021011000
11009502101000100010000011010000012201000000
11009601113232103100302325310120122010000000001200000100000000000000000000001010000
11009602001000000000000000000000001100000000 0
11009701115631903100302375310110122010000010003200000100000000000000000000001011000
11009702000100101000000000010000101212000000
11009801116231104100202375310110022010000010006360000100000000000000000000021011000
11009802001010100000200010100001022110100000
11009901117831904100402375110110022010100010034451100100000000000000000000021010000
11009902001000201000010000010000101211000000
11010001117130804100201400110110022010000010006861600100000000000000000000011010000
11010002001010200000000000000000001100000000 0
11010101117230604100201400110110022050010000012481600100000000000000005001101000 0
11010102000010000000010000001000102210000000
11010201117531104100201400110110022050000010002130000100000000000000000000010000000
11010202000010200000000010000000102211000000
11010301017631304100401400110110022010000000001250000100000000000000000000010000000
11010302000010000000000000000000001110000000 0
11010401117331804100401375310110022010020100002841610110100000001000000011111000
11010402001010001001000000010000101211000000
11010501118233004110409375410110012010000010035570002000000151400000000210100 00
11010502000010000000200110100011112110000000
11010601118932604100402375110120122010000010004501000100000000000000000000010000000
11010602000010000000000000000000001110000000 0
11010701117932704100419375410110012010000000003000000010000000001000000021110000
11010702101010100000000000000000010121000000 0
11010801017632304100401375310110022010000000002340000100000000000000000000011010000
11010802000010000000010000000000101110000000
11010901017532204100401375310120022010000000001500000100000000000000000000011010000
11010902000000000000000000000000001100000000 0
11011001017632504100401375310220022010000000000880000100000000000000000000010000000
11011002001010100000000000000000001110000000 0
11011101117632804100402375310110022010000010006500000100000000000260000100000 00
11011102001000001000000000000000100111000000 0
11011201117332204100401375310110022010000010000840000100000000000000000000011010000
11011202000010002000000000000000000112000000 0
11011301116733204110402375310110022010000000002160000100000000000016000010000000
11011302001000100000000000100000011010000000
11011401117833604110402350310120022110000000002000000100000000000000000000011001000
11011402000000000000200000000001001110000000
11011501117433404110402350310120022110000000001870000100000000000000000000011010000
11011502001000100000000010000000001110000000
11011601117433604110402325310120022110100000008490000100000000000000000000011010000
11011602001010000000020000010000001110000000
11011701118333704110402375310120022010101000000900000100000000000000000000011011000
11011702001100002000010000000000010202000000 0
11011801118934004110402375310120022110000000003520000100000000000000000000011011000
11011802001000000000000000000000001101000000
11011901118333904110402375310120022110000000006920000100000000000000000000011010000
11011902001000000000000100000000112221000000
11012001118734104110402350310110022110000000002000000100000000000000000000011011000
```

```
1101200200100000000000000000000000001110100000
11012101117231404100202375110110022010000010010320000100000000000000000021001000
110121020000102000009900000000000112221000000
11012201116531304100202375310110022110000000022460000100000000000000000021001000
1101220200000000100002000000000000001121000000
11012301116231504100202375310110022110000000001080000100000000000000000021001000
11012302000000000000000001000000101101000000
1101240111623210410021535031011012301000000000083000010000000000000000000100000000
1101240200000000000000000000000000001102000000
110125010160321041002023503101101230100000000062000010000000000000000000100000000
11012502000000000000000000100000011010000000
110126011179343041104023253101200220100000000121000010000000000000000000100000000
1101260200100000000000000000000000001000000000
1101270111823430411040232531012002201000000000074000010000000000000000000000000000
1101270200000000000000000000000000001100000000
1101280111833540411040230031012102201000000000118000010000000000000000000000000000
1101280200001010100000000000000000000220000000
11012901116933804110402300310120022110000000007760000100000000000000000011001000
1101290200100010000000000000000000001110000000
11013001116833104110402325310110022110000000000441700100000000000100000011010000
1101300200101010000000000000000000001111000000
11013101117332504100402350310110022010000010001500000100000000000000000011010000
11013102000000100000000000000000000001000000000
11013201117032204100401350310120022110000010000380000100000000000000000011001000
1101320200100000000000000000000000101111000000
11013301116732804100402325310110022110000010000780000100000000000000000011001000
1101330200100000000000000000000000000101000000
110134011165331041104023003101101220100000000001380000100000000000000000010000000
1101340200001000000001000000000000001110000000
11013501116732304100402325310110022110000000000700000100000000000000010001101000
1101350200100000000000000101000000111100000000
11013601117131704100202375310110022110000010002150000100000000000000000011010000
1101360200000000000010000000000000011111000000
11013701116031603100202375310110022110201000000491100100000000000000000001010000
110137020000000000000000000000000010121000000
110138011158322031003023503101100221100000000002911001000000000000000000900100000000
1101380200100000001000000000000000000111000000
110139011157324031003023503101100220100000000000560000100000000000000000010000000
1101390200000000000000000000000000000101000000
11014001114832503100302375310110122010000000001341000100000000000000000011010000
1101400200001000000000000000000000101100000000
11014101115132703100301350310120022110000000001501100100000000000000000011000010
1101410200001000000000000000000000001100000000
11014201114732803100301350310110022110000010000830000100000000000000000011010000
1101420200001000001000000000000000001100000000
11014301107731101100109400410110022010000010022750000100000000000000000011011000
1101430200101000000000000000000000101111000000
11014401108130902100107400410120022010000010012060000100000000001000000011011000
1101440200001000100000000000000000001211000000
1101450110942980209010140041011001201001000015271310100000000010000900011011000
1101450200001010000000000000000000010221100000
11014601109430102100101400110110022010000010010501000100000000000000000011001000
1101460200001000000000000000000000001111000000
11014701109430402100101400110110022010000000000951100010000000000000000010000000
1101470200001000000000000000000000101111000000
11014801109330702100101400110110022010000010011880000100000000000000000011001000
11014802000010100010010000000000011222100000
11014901108831002100101400110110022010000000018760000100000000000000000011010000
1101490200001000000000000000000000001101000100
11015001109030502100101400110120022010000000000560000100000000000000000011010000
1101500200001000000000000000000000001210000000
11015101120631205100603350310110122010000000003290000100000000000000000011000010
1101510200001000100000000000000000002201000000
11015201120031104100203350310110122010000010004360000100000000000000000011000010
1101520200001000100001000000000000110000000
11015301120331105100603350310110122010000010013920000100000000000000000011000010
1101530200001000000000000000000000001102000000
11015401120231505100603350310110122110000010011250000100000000000000000011000010
1101540200001000000000000010000000001202000000
11015501119932204100403350310110122010020000003071110110100000010000000011000010
1101550200001000000000000010000000101010000000
11015601120432005100403325310110122010011000009171110110000000000000000011000010
1101560200001000000000000010000000111010000000
11015701121731505100603325110110122010010000046221100110000000010000000011000010
110157020000100000000000000000000001021200010
11015801121632405100403325110110022010000010016450000100000000000000000011000010
1101580200001000000000000000000000000100000000
11015901122330505100603325310110022010000010017600000100000000000000000021000010
1101590200001000110000000100000000011100000
11016001122429805090603325310110132021000000025871101000000050900120000230000010
11016002000010000000002000101000010122200000
11016101122432305100603325310110022010010100030401512210000291110000000011000010
11016102000010099011000000000000011221000000
11016201017827304090203400310110122010101010008471000100000000010000000001000010
1101620200000000000000000000000000000100000000
11016301017427504090203400310110122010000010002050000100000000000000000700001000 10
110163020000000000000000100000000000100000000
11016401120727305090203375110110022010000000004241100100000000000000000001000010
110164020000100000000000000000000010201000100
11016501121929905090603350110110122010100000064841101231000366210000000011000010
1101650200001000000000000100000000011211000000
11016601121730605100603325310110122010000010006431300100000000000000000011000010
110166020000000000000000000000000000110000100
11016701120527005080203375110110022110100010042621100100000000000000000001000010
110167020000101000000000000100000000011200000
11016801120626305080203375110110022110101010009691110110000000010000000011000010
1101680200000000000000000000000000001110000000
11016901120926905080203375110110032121100000024901102100000051300000000100000000
1101690200000000000000000000000000011021200000
11017001121429805090603350310110122010012010019601110110000000010220000130000010
1101700200001000000000000010000001011110000000
11017101121029005090603350110110122010011000004371110110000000010000000011000010
11017102000010000001000001000000010121000001
11017201120728705090603375110110122010000000000824000100000000000000000011000010
110172020000000000000000010000000001101000100
11017301120329005090603375110110122010101000010831100100000000000000000011000010
110173020000100010009900010000001011100000100
11017401120929405090603350110110122010102000085131621231000456010000000011000010
1101740200001000000000000000000001111100000000
11017501120128905090603375110110022010010210008101110110000000000000000000000000
11017502000010000000000000000000101110000001
11017601119729004090203375110110122010012010032401120100000000010000000001000010
1101760200001000000000000000000000001100000000
11017701121028105090203375310110132021000000042320000100000000000000000001000010
110177020000100000000000001000000111221000100
11017801121328105090203350110110132021000000033770000100000000000120000130000010
1101780200001000000000000000000001011010100100
11017901121328605090603350110110132021000010018041100100000000000000000011000010
110179020100100000000000001000000012210000100
11018001117926604080203375310110122010000010001910000100000000000000000001000010
```

11018002000010000000000000000000000011112000100
11018101117726604080203375310110122010000000000530000100000000000000000001000010
11018102000000000000000010000000101010001000
11018201117826304080203375310110122022000000005370000100000000000000000001000010
11018202000010000000000000000000011111000010 0
11018301118125804080203375310110132021000000015311300100000000000000000001000010
110183020000100000000010000000011111010000
11018401118526104080203375310110022010101000015541300100000000000000000000100010
1101840200001010000000000000000001121000010 0
11018501118726604080203375310110022010000010006700000100000000000000000001000010
1101850200001000000000000000000000101000100
11018601118226504080203375310110122100000000001181300100000000000016000000000010
1101860200000000010000000000000000101000100
11018701118926004080203375110110022010000000011231300100000000000000000011000010
110187020000100000000000000000001010101000 0
11018801118825604080203375110110032021000000003501300100000000000000000011000010
11018802000000100000000000000000011101010100
11018901118925304080703375110110032021101000004650000100000000000000000011000010
1101890200001000000000000000000001111101010 0
11019001119625104080703375310110032121000000008090000100000000000000000021000010
1101900200001000000099000100000000101010000
11019101119624904080703350310110032021000000006900000100000000000000000021000010
110191020000100000009900010000000111111000000
11019201118924704080703350310110032021000000017190000100000000000000000011000010
110192020000001000000000100000011111100000 0
11019301118425004080703350310110032121101000010210000100000000000000000011000010
11019302000010100000000001000000101100000100
11019401118524604080703350310110132021000000001500000100000000000000000001000010
11019402000010000000990000000000011121100010 0
11019501118124504080703325310110122122000000017390000100000000000000000011000010
1101950200001000000000000100000011110000010 0
11019601118823404070703325310110122122000000003250100010000000000000000021000010
11019602000010000000000000000000111101000000
11019701118823204070703325310110122122000000002015000010000000000000000021000010
11019702000010000000000000000000101111000000
11019801118125104080703350310110122022000000004891300100000000000000000011000010
1101980200000000000000000000000001100000000
11019901117725404080203350310110122110101000017211001000000000000000000001000010
11019902000000000000000100000000111010000 00
11020001116426504080203375310110122010000010003081700100000000000000900010000 10
1102000200000000000000000000000010110000100
11020101108430802100101400310110022010000000001271100100000000000000000011010000
110201020000100000000000000000001111100000 0
11020201108131802100101400110110022010000010009820000100000000000000080011010000
1102020200000010100000000000000001110100000 0
11020301108331802100101400110110022110000010006260000100000000000000000011010000
110203020000100000000000010000000011010000 00
11020401108631602100101375310110022010000010007340000100000000000000080010000000
11020402000010101000010000000000000122110000 00
11020501106530501100102400410110022010010010023401110100000000010000000021011000
110205020000001020009901000000011122320000 00
11020601107131001100101400410110022010000010068001100100000000000000180021010000
11020602000010001000000000000000011111000100
11020701106731501100102400410110022010000010025631301300000029800000000021011000
11020702000000000000000000000000111101000 0
11020801107631501100101400110110022010000000007001100100000000010000000012010000
110208020000100000000100100000000011010000 00
11020901107532001100102400110110022110100000038931300100000000001000000023011000
1102090200001010000000000100001122010000 00
11021001106732401100102375110110022110000010010860000100000000000012000023011000
11021002000010000000010000000000000111110000 0
11021101108532302100102375110110022110000010013131001000000010700000000200000 00
1102110200000000000000000000000000110000000 0
11021201110029802090201400310120022110000000063016001000000000000000090021000010
1102120200001000000000000000000001111100000 0
11021301109830002090202400110120022110000010004501100100000000000000000021011000
110213020000000000000201000100001111110000 00
11021401109930302100201400110120022010000000005481100100000000000000000021000010
110214020000100000000100000000000011000000 10
11021501110330002090202400110120022010000010005620000100000000000000000021010000
1102150200001010000000000000000011111110000000
11021601110230202100201400110120022010000000002000000100000000010000000021001000
1102160200001000000000000000000001111000000
11021701110730302100202400110120022010000010013401100100000000000120000013011000
110217020000100000000000101000000111100010 0
11021801111030002100202400310110022010000010002000000100000000000000000010000000
110218020000000000000000000000000444444400 00
11021901110730502100202375310120022110000010011890000100000000000000000011010000
1102190200001010000001000000000011110100000 0
11022001110530802100202375310120022110100000023461100100000000000000000011010000
1102200200010000010099000000000012111100000 0
11022101109731502100102350310120022010000000001500000100000000000000000011011000
110221020000101000000000001000000111000000 00
11022201109930602100202400310110022010000000003000000100000000000000000010000000
11022202000000000000000000000000111000000 00
11022301109831002100101375310110022010000000007320000100000000000000000012011000
1102230200001000200000000110000012201000000
11022401108831702100102375110110022010000000001000001000000000000000000010000000
1102240200001000000001000000000000111100000 0
11022501108932002100102350110110022010000000005560000100000000000000000011010000
110225020000101000000200000000000111110000 00
11022601109331602100101350310110022110000000007200001000000000000000000010000000
1102260200001010100000000001000000111100000 0
11022701107530101100102400310110022010000010008770000100000000000000000011010000
1102270200001000000001000001000000111100000 0
11022801106630501100102400310110022010000010006320000100000000000000000011010000
110228020000000000000200000000000111010000 00
11022901106230701100102400310110022010101010002341100100000000000000000001101000
1102290200001000000000000000000010111100000 0
11023001107629801090102400310110022010000010003750000100000000000000000011011000
110230020000100000001000000000000111100000 00
11023101107429701090102400310110022010000010008131100100000000000000100111011000
1102310200001000000001000001000000110101010 0
11023201107629401090102400310120022010000000001750300100000000010000000011010000
11023202000000000100000000000000101110100000 0
11023301107229601090102400310120022110000010001880100100000000010000000011010000
1102330200010000000001010001000001011000000 0
11023401107129001090102350310110022010000000005820100100000000000000000011011000
1102340201000000100001000000000000110100000 0
11023501109427602090202350310220022110000000000601300100000000000000000000000000
11023502000000100000000000000000001100000000
11023601109727602090201350310220023110000000001291300100000000000000000001010000
1102360200000000000000100000000000111000000 0
11023701109927702090202350310220023110000000000760000100000000000000000001010000
11023702000000000000000001010000010101000000
11023801110027802090202400310110023110100000001601100100000000000000000000000000
11023802000010000000000000000000101110000000
11023901108429402090101400310120023110000000001331300100000000000000000010000000
11023902000000000000000000000000001110000000 0
11024001106031101100102400110110022110000010001600000100000000000000000021010000

```
110240020100000000000011000000001111101000000
1102410110623160110010240031011002211000001001208000010000000000000000021010000
110241020000100000000000000000010110100000
1102420110593140110010240031011002201011211004351182122000000681000080021010000
110242021000000010110000000000001011110000000
11024301105332301100102400110110022110000010023041120100000000000000000021010000
110243020000101000000000000000010111010100000
1102440110613260110010240011011002211000001001300000010000000000000000080020000000
110244020000100000000100000000000011010100000
1102450110613290110010137511012002211000001000901000010000000000000000020000000
110245020001000000000000110000001111101001 0
1102460110613310111010237511011002211000001000745000100000000000000000020000000
110246020000000000000000001000001110100000 0
11024701106233301110102375110110022010000010005161100100000000000000000020000000
110247021001001000000200000000010111100000 0
1102480110633360111010235011011002211000001000562100010000000000000000021010000
110248020000101010000300000000010011110000 00
1102490110643400111010132511011002201000001000547000010000000000000000080020000000
1102490200001000000000000000000000000000000 0
1102500110683360111010135021011002211000000000910000010000000000000000100210 10000
110250020010100000000000000000001011000000 00
11025101111622730408020337531011012201000000000009811001000000000000000000001000010
110251020000000000000000000000000011010001 00
1102520111572650308020340031011002201000000000036707001000000000100000000 1000010
110252020000100000000000000000000110110100 00
11025301116125404080203350310110022022000000007520000100000000000000000001000010
110253020000000000000000000000011111200010 0
11025401116025103080203350310110022022101000014820000100000000000000000001000010
110254020000100000000000000000011110100010 0
1102550111552520308020335031011002202200000000424000010000000000000000000001000010
110255020000000000000000000000001011100010 0
1102560111432690308020340011011002201001111008762112113000009081000000001000010
110256020000100000010000010000001111110000 01
1102570111462710309020340031011002201000000000751110010000000000000000000001000010
110257020000000000000000000000011111000000 0
11025801113827103090203400310110022010000000007541100100000000000000000001100010
110258020000000000000000000000001011000010 0
11025901113127103090203400310110122010000000101100001000000000000000000001000010
110259020000100000000000100000001110000010 0
110260011144268030802034003101101220101010000023900001000000000000000000001000010
110260020000000000000000000000011110100010 0
110261011140248030802034003101101220100000000010311001000000000000000000001000010
110261020000000000000000000000001111000000 0
110262011148264030802034003101101220100000000067317001000000000000000000001000010
110262020000100000000000000000011201000100
110263011156254030802033503101101220101010000012011001000000000000000000001000010
110263020000100000000000100000000111101000 0
11026401115726003080203375310110122010101010037441101110100164000000000001000010
11026402000010000001000001000000101101010000
1102650111522560308020337531011012201000000000109130010000000001000000001000010
110265020000000100000000000000001010000000 0
110266011164252040802033503101101220100000000005900001000000000000000000001000010
110266020000100000000000000000000110000010 0
11026701116725304080203350310110122010000010001491100100000000000000000000000000000
110267020000000000000000000000000110000000 0
1102680111642500408020335031011012202200000000045800001000000000000000000000000000
110268020000000100000000000000001110100010 0
110269011167249040802033503101101220220000000044000001000000000000000000000000000
110269020000001000000000000000001101000101 00
110270011194245040807033501101100221220000000006280000100000000000000000021000010
110270020000100000000100000000000111211000000
1102710111962470408070335011011002202200000000462000010000000000000000000021000010
110271020000000000009900010000001121110001 00
11027201118825104080703350110110022021000000012640000100000000000000000011000010
110272020001000001000000100000011111100010 0
11027301118125504080203350310110122021000000019960000100000000000000000000000000
110273020000000000000000000000000011111100010 0
11027401119724004070703350110110022022000000004290000100000000000000000021000010
110274020000100000000000100000010111100000 0
11027501119523904070703350110110022022101000039850000100000000000000000021000010
110275020000100010000000001000000111211000100
11027601119223804070703350110110022021000000002600000100000000000000000021000010
110276020000100000000000100000011111001010 0
110277011190236040707033251101100220210000000500513001000000000000000000021000010
110277020000100000000000000000001111110001 00
11027801120124305080703350110110022010000000185611042101002047000000000021000010
110278020000100000000000000000000112110100 00
11027901119122804070703325310110122022000010003260000100000000000000000021000010
110279020000000000000000000000001101110000 00
11028001119022604070703325310120122022000000005821100100000000000000000020000000
110280020000100000000000000000000101020000 00
11028101112327203090203400110110022010101010024381100110000000000000000011000010
110281020000199990000000010000000112110100 00
11028201112326903080203400110110022110101000012761100110000000010000000011000010
110282020000000000000000000000001011110000 00
11028301111927102090203400110110122010000000004071000100000000000000000011000010
110283020000100000000000100000001111100000 0
11028401017722504070703275310110122122000000001610000100000000000000000000000000
110284020000000000000000000000000000000000 00
11028501117423004070703275310110122022000010002660000100000000000000000000000000
110285020000000000000000000000000100000000 0
11028601117222904070703275310110122022000000004840000100000000000000000000000000
110286020000000000000000000000000111000000 00
11028701117122504070703275310110122022000000003000000100000000000000000000000000
110287020000000000000000000000011101000000 0
11028801117222704070703275310110122022000010006470000100000000000000000001000010
110288020000100000000000000000011101000000 0
11028901116922404070703275310110122122000000001200000100000000000000000001000010
110289020000000000000000000000001101100000 0
11029001117122004070703275310110122010000000005560000100000000000000000000000000
110290020000000000000100000000000111000000 0
11029101118121704070703275310110022022000000005050000100000000000000000020000000
110291020000100000100000010000010111110000 00
1102920111832200407070330031011002202200001001528000010000000000000000021000010
110292020000100000000000000000011110100000 0
11029301118622004070703300310110022022000000000912000010000000000000000021000010
110293020000100000000000000000001111010100
11029401118722304070703300110110022022000000016961101100000011500000000021000010
110294020000100000000000000000011111100000 0
11029501119022304070703300110110022022000000006000000100000000000000000020000000
110295020000001000000000000000000100000000 0
11029601116625704080203350310110122022000010018750000100000000000000000001000010
110296020000100000000200000000001111000101 00
11029701115724903080203350310110122022000000021420000100000000000000000001000010
110297020000101000000000000000001011110001 00
11029801116324704080203350310110022022000000003570000100000000000000000001000010
110298020000100000000000000000010111100000 0
11029901115124903080203350310110122022000010009721100100000000000000000001000010
110299020000100000000000000000011111100000 0
11030001115424503080203350310110022022000000003631100100000000000000000001000010
```

1103000200000000000000000000000000111111000000
11030101107033001110102350310110022110000000015513001000000000000000000011001000
1103010210100000000000100000000000101101000000
11030201107133301110102350310110022110000000000820000100000000000000000010000000
1103020210100000000000000000000000101101000000
11030301106732701100102375310110022110000010008090000100000000000120000020000000
1103030200001000100000000010000001111110000000
11030401106932801100102375310110022010000010005550000100000000000000080020000000
1103040200000000000000100000000010011110100000
11030501105934001110102350310110022010000000005880000100000000000000000010010000
1103050210010010000001000001000000111010000000
11030601105533201110102375310110022110001000005931700100000000000120090010000000
1103060200100000000000000100000010111100000000
11030701105132801100102375310110022110000000002331300100000000000120000011010000
1103070200000010000099010000000001111000000000
11030801105132501100101375310110022110000010005761300100000000000120000011000010
1103080200001000000000200000000000011110000000
11030901104832301100102375310110022010000010004440000100000000000000000011010000
1103090200100010000099000000000001111101000000
11031001104832001100102375310110122010000000001600000100000000000000000021010000
1103100200100000000000000000000010111101000000
11031101105531101100101400310110122010000000003611100100000000000000090021011000
1103110200001010000000000000000001010000000000
11031201105331001100101375310110122110000010009261100100000000000130090022011000
1103120200001000000100100000000000112010000000
11031301105130701100102375310220122110100110018801100100000000001110080021010000
1103130200001000100102000001000111110100000000
11031401104630801100102375310120122110000010009781100100000000000000090021010000
1103140200100000000000000010001000101010000000
11031501104730901100101375310120122010000010002891100100000000000000000021000010
1103150200001010000000000100000000111000000000
11031601105031301100101375310120122010000010001741300100000000000000000021000010
1103160200001010000000000000000001111000000000
11031701104330801100102375310220122010000010017061100100000000000101200023010000
1103170200110000000000100000000000101101000000
11031801104731201100101375310120122010000010001101100100000000000000000021001000
1103180200000000000000100000000010111000000000
11031901104131001100102350310120122110000010008221100100000000000100000021001000
1103190210100000000000000000000001111100000000
11032001103931100100102350310120122110000010001311710100100000010000000021011000
1103200200001000000000100000000000011010000000
11032101004231401100101350310120122110000010001650000100000000000000000021010000
1103210200000010000000000000000000100100000000
11032201103731100100102350310120122110100010008051100100000000000000000002100100
1103220200100020200002000000000001011110000000
11032301103831500100102350310110122110000000008860000100000000000000000021011000
1103230210100010000000000000100001110100000000
11032401103331700100102325110120122110000010016791200100000000000120090021010000
1103240210010000000000100000000000011010100000
11032501103632000100101350110120122110000000002100000100000000000000000010000000
1103250200000010000000000000000000110100000000
11032601102932000100102325110110122110000010012001000100000000000000000021011000
1103260200001020000000000101000101120000010000
11032701103132000100101325310110122110000010002001100100000000001000000010000000
1103270200100000000000000000000000120000010000
11032801102931800100102325310110022110000010000991300100000000001100000021001000
1103280200000000000000000000000000110000000000
11032901102532500100102300410110022110000010001771100100000000000000090020000000
1103290200100000000000100000000000011000000000
11033001102232700100102300410110022110000010001961100100000000000000000021010000
1103300200100000000000100000000001111000000000
11033101102232800100101300410120022110000000002101100100000000000000090011010000
1103310200001010000000000000100000012000000000
11033201102132900100102300410110022110000010001881700100000000001000000021010000
1103320200110000000000200000100000011010000000
11033301101833900110102275410110022110000010033201140100000000000000000021010000
1103330210010000000000000000100001011010000000
11033401102333000110101300310120022110000010004500000100000000000000000011001000
1103340200000000000000000000000000111000000000
11033501102133800110101275310120022110000010004300000100000000000000000011010000
1103350200001000000000000000000010011110000000
11033601101634700110102275310110022010000010004300000100000000000000000010000000
1103360200001000000000000000000000011000000000
11033701101434700110102275410110022110100010016041702000000000001000000021011000
1103370200001000000000000000000001011100000000
11033801105832401100102400310110022010000010001961100100000000000000000011011000
1103380201100000000000100000100001111010101000
11033901105532401100102375310110022110000010005931100100000000000000000011011000
1103390200001000000099000000000001111010000000
11034001105733001100102375310110022010000010005120000100000000000000080011010000
1103400200001000000099000000000000111100000000
11034101105532101100102375310110022010000010009861300100000000000000080021010000
1103410200001000000099000101000010110100010000
11034201105733301110102375310110022110001010001830000100000000000120000021001000
1103420200000000000000000000000000111000000000
11034301104632101100102375310120122110000010010770000100000000000000000011010000
1103430200001020000001000000000001111010000000
11034401104432101100102375310110122010000010002000000100000000000000000010000000
1103440200000000000000000000000000111000000000
11034501104232301100101375310110122110000000004101100100000000000000000010000000
1103450200001010000000000000000000110000010000
11034601104532001100102375310110122010000000001001000100000000000000000014222220
1103460222222000000000000000000004444444400000
11034701104631801100101375310110122110000000001420000100000000000000000010000000
1103470200000000000000000000000004444444400000
11034801011127602090202400310110023110000010005481700100000000001000000021010000
1103480200001000000000100000000000110100000000
11034901111427602090201400310110023010000010000691300100000000000000000011010000
1103490200001000000000100000000000111110000000
11035001112326503080202400110110023010110500006271100120000000010120000013011000
1103500200110000000119900010000001111110000000
11035101115924503080203350310110022022000010010860000100000000000000000001000010
1103510200001000000000000000000001011110000000
11035201116424504080203325310110022022000000003055000010000000000000000001000000
1103520200001000000000000000000001011010000100
11035301115624103080203325310110022022000000000608110010000000000000000001000010
1103530200001000000000000000000001001010101000
11035401015124203080203325310110022022000010005660000100000000000000000001000010
1103540200001000000000000000000000110100000000
11035501015224003070203325310110022022100000002881100100000000000000000001000010
1103550200000990000000000000000000001000000000
11035601115024603080203325310110022022000010012680000100000000000000000001000010
1103560200000000000000000000000001111020001000
11035701015723903070203325310110122022000000000952000010000000000000000001000010
1103570200000000000000000000000001011010000000
11035801116524204080203325310110122022000010012250000100000000000000000001000010
1103580200001000000000000000000011111000000000
11035901116123804070203325310110122122000000000946000010000000000000000001000010
1103590200000000000000000100000010110000000000
11036001016423804070203325310110122022000000000575000010000000000000000001000010

```
110360020000102000000000000000000101101000000
11036101115423603070203325310110122122000000138513001000000000000000000001000010
110361020000000000000000000000000101100000000
11036201015423803070203325110110022022101000004481600110000000000000000000001000010
110362020000100000000000000000001101010001000
11036301115024003080203325310110022122000000008160000100000000000000000000001000010
110363020000000000000000000000001100101000000
11036401114923903070203325310110122022000000004120000100000000000000000000001000010
110364020000100000000000000000001110100000000
11036501116023504070203300310110122022000010011751100100000000000000000000000000000
110365020000100000000000000000001110101000000
11036601114923503070203300310110122022000000005200000100000000000000000000001000010
110366020000000000000000000000001101010000000
11036701114923203070203300310110122022000000000957000010000000000000000000000000000
110367020000000000000000000000001111101000000
11036801114723103070203275310110122022000000014620000100000000000000000000000000000
110368020000000000000000000000001101000000000
11036901116423404070203300310110122022000000001360000100000000000000000000000000000
110369020000000000000000000000001101010000000
11037001115723303070203300310110122022000000004240000100000000000000000000000000000
110370020000000000000000000000001110101000000
11037101114622803070203275310110122022000000007530000100000000000000000000000000000
110371020000000000000000000000001010101000000
11037201114522603070203250310110122022000000015620000100000000000000000000001000010
110372020000000000000000000000001101010000000
11037301115122503070203250310110122022000000008400000100000000000000000000001000010
110373020000000000000000000000001000101000000
11037401114321903070203250110110122022100000014890300100000000000000000000001000010
110374020000101000100100010000011111000010000
11037501114321403070203225110120122022000100303300001000000000000000008000100010
110375020000100000000000000000001110101000000
11037601113521703070203225110110122022000000022340000100000000000000000000001000010
110376020000100000000000000000001010001000000
11037701115021503070203225110110122022000000019400000100000000000027091001000010
110377020000100000000000100000001010101000000
11037801114221003070203225110110122022000000024000010100000000000000000000001000010
110378020000100000000000000000001110001000000
11037901118120304060703250110120122022000010032431100100000000000000000800210000010
110379020000101000000000000000001110001000000
11038001117820204060703225310120122022000000023930000100000000000000000000010000000
110380020000000001000000000000000001110010000
11038101117620904060703250110110122022000000025370000100000000000000000000011000010
110381020000100000000000000000001110101000000
11038201117421304070703250310110122022000000008400000100000000000000000000021000010
110382020000000000000000000000001110101000000
11038301117721304070703275310110122022000000003390000100000000000000000000020000000
110383020000000000000000000000001011001000000
11038401113925003080202350310110123010000000017900001000000000000000000000000000000
110384020000100000000100000000000001001000000
11038501113825303080202350310120122010000000002691600100000000000000000000000000000
110385020010000000000600000000001111110000000
11038601113525803080202375310110122110000000007370000100000000000000000000001010000
110386020000100000000200010000001111110000000
11038701111825702080202375310110123110100000006011300100000000000021000001010000
110387020010000000009900020000001011110000000
11038801113326003080202400310110123010000010001781310100100000000000000000001010000
110388020000000000000200010000011011010000000
11038901122831505100602325110110122122000000013490000100000000000000000000021010000
110389020000000010000100000000011111111010000
11039001123431005100602300310110122122000000005560000100000000000000000000011010000
110390020010000010000000000000000111101000000
11039101123630705100602300310110122121000010002360000100000000000000000000011010000
110391020000101000000000101000001111101000000
11039201124231106100502300310110122021000010004880000100000000000000000000011010000
110392020011001000000000000000000011000000000
11039301124130906100602300310110122021000010005740000100000000000000000000011010000
110393020010000000000000000000000001001010000
11039401124030605100602300310110122121000010004750000100000000000000000000011000100
110394020000000010000000000000000011001000000
11039501125330206100802300310110122022000010005960000100000000000000000000011010000
110395020010002010000001000000000001101010000
11039601124331206100502300310110122021000010005490000100000000000000000000011010000
110396020010000000000000000000001111101010000
11039701124431306100502325110110122021000010003040000100000000000000000000021010000
110397020011000000000100000000001111010000000
11039801124731006100502300310110122021000010004630000100000000000000000000010000000
110398020000001000000000000000001111010100000
11039901125130806100502300110110122021000000000431000100000000000000000000011010000
110399020010000000000001000000011111110100000
11040001124931006100502300110110122021000000000081000010000000000000000000021010000
110400020010001000000100000000001011010001000
11040101111926702080202400310110022010100010006801100100000000000000000000021010000
110401020000100000000000100000001111010000000
11040201112326303080202400310110022010000010005981100100000000000000000090011010000
110402020000001000109900010000001111010000000
11040301112326103080202400310110022010000010002401300100000000000000000000011010000
110403020000100020100000010100011111110000000
11040401112726803080202400310110122010000000002401100100000000000000000000010000000
110404020000000000000000000000000001101000000
11040501112926703080202400310110122010000010004260000100000000000000000000010000000
110405020000000000000000000000000001101000000
11040601113026303080202400310110123010000010004931300100000000000000000000010000000
110406020000100000000000000000001110100000000
11040701112926503080202400310110122010000010001261300100000000000000000000010000000
110407020000000000001000000000000001100000000
11040801112625903080202400310110023010000010008001100100000000000000000000010000000
110408020010000000000000001000000110000000000
11040901112225803080202400310120022010000010005931100100000000000021000011010000
110409020010000000000000020000011111110000100
11041001111826302080202400310110023010100010012091100100000000000021000011010000
110410020010000010009900020000011111111000000
11041101112425603080202375310110023010000010000620000100000000000021000011010000
110411020010001000000100020000001011110000000
11041201112525403080202375310110023010000010012600000100000000000000000000011010000
110412020011000000009900100000001111110000000
11041301112625303080202375310220023010000010000660000100000000000011000011010000
110413020010000000000100010000001111000000000
11041401112925303080202375310220022010000000000640000100000000000000000000011010000
110414020000100010000000101000000110000000000
11041501112725003080202350310110022010000010001840000100000000000000000000010000000
110415020010000000000100100000001110100000000
11041601113125003080202350310110022010000010002770000100000000000000000000011010000
110416020011000000000100100000010111010000000
11041701112724903080202350310110022110000000000700000100000000001000000011010000
110417020010000000000300010000011011010000000
11041801113224703080202350310110022010000010008290000100000000000000000000011010000
110418020010000000100200010000011011100000000
11041901113224403080201325310110022110000010006231300100000000000000000000011000010
110419020000100000000100010000000001100000000
11042001020420405060700250310120112010000020015491300099000000002240203034222220
```

```
110420022222989822298223323222444444440120
11042101120820305060701250310120112022000000000033000010000000000000000000000000
1104210200001000000000000000000000001101010000
11042201120720205060701250310130122122000010000760000100000000000000000001001000
110422020000100000000000000000000000101010000
11042301120819905060701250310130122010000010000960000100000000000000000000000000
1104230200001000000000000000000000001101000100
11042401121020105060701250310120122022100010005201110100100000000000000000000000
11042402000010000000000000000100001011010100000
11042501119920404060708250310120122011000010002080000100000000001600000000000000
11042502001100101000000000000000001011010200000
11042601120320305060701250310120122122000010001951300100000000000160000010001000
110426020000102000000100001000001011110200000
11042701120020705060719250310120122122000000001441000100000000000160000010100002
110427020000101010000000000000000010111102000000
11042801120121005060701275310120122022000000000400000100000000000000000000000000
110428020000101010000000000000000000001010000
11042901120520905060701275310120122122000010002100000100000000000000000000000000
1104290200001000000000000000000000001101010000
11043001120321005070719275310120122010000010001201310100100000000000000000000000
1104300200000000000000000000000000000001010000
11043101120321305070708275310120122022000000002000000100000000000160000010010000
1104310200110000200000000000000000100101010000
11043201120421505070701275310120122022000010002020000100000000000160000000000000
110432020000000000000000000100011010010001000
11043301120921505070708275310120122110000000000700000100000000000000000000000000
110433020011000000000000000000000000001010000
11043401121121805070719300310120122110000010002251100100000000000000000000000000
110434020000100000000000000000000000001010000
11043501121022005070708300310120022010000010002350000100000000000160001000000000
1104350200001010000000000000000000001001010000
11043601120620605060719250310120122022000000000934000100000000000000000000000000
110436021000100000100000000000000101011000000
11043701121120605060719250310120122010000010008761300100000000000000000001001000
1104370200110010000001000000000001000010101000
11043801120621505070719275310120022110000010000460000100000000000160000000000000
1104380200101000000000000000000000000101000000
11043901121321005060708275310120022022000000001650000100000000000000000000000000
1104390200110000000000000000000000001101010000
11044001121721105070719275310120122122000000001550000100000000000000000000000000
11044002000010000010000000010000001111010000
11044101122021305070719275310120122110000010001830000100000000000000000000000000
1104410200110000000000000000000000000001010000
11044701130824707080002225310120022010000010004310000100000000000000000011010000
11044702000010000000000000000000000000000010000
11045101127130506100802325110110022022100000015020000100000000000000000011010000
11045102001010000000990000000000011120101010 0
11045201128130607100802325110110022010200000000999100010000000000000000002100001 0
1104520200000010000099000000000001011010101 00
11045301128129707090802300110110022021218110152001113010000904010120000230110 00
1104530200001999900199000000000001112110101 10
11045401126830306100802300110110022022100010031370000100000000010220000301100 00
110454020000199990109900000000000111101010100
1104550112613120610081432511012012202210000002762130100000000048000000002100001 0
1104550200001000000000000000000001012010200 00
11045601125930506100802300110110022021000010018430000100000000000000000011000010
1104560200001020000099000000000001101010000
11045701124531606100514325110110022021000010013020000100000000000000000011000010
1104570200001990000099000000000001011020100 00
11045801123931805100502325110110022010000010010160000100000000000000000011000010
110458020000000000009900000000000011112010000
11045901124932006100514325310110022010000010005060000100000000000000000011010000
1104590200000000000000000000000000111101000 0
11046001125631906100502325310110022010000010003181300100000000000000000010000000
11046002000000100000000000000000001101010000
11046101126131806100502325310110022150100010013801300100000000010000000010000000
1104610200000000000000000000000000001101010000
11046201124030506110502350410110022110000000031011400100000000000000000021000010
1104620200100000000000000000000000001112010100
11046301123633205110502350410110022010000000014000000100000000000000000021000010
1104630200000000009900000000000000110100000 0
11046401122933705110502350410110022010011110033751110110000000001000000020000000
1104640200001000001990000000000000110200000 0
11046501122434005110414350310110022110000000027300000100000000000000000011000000
1104650200000000000000000000000000110200000 0
11046601121730705110402350410110022110000000018001300100000000000000000021000010
1104660200100000000990000000000000111201010 0
11046701121033705110402375410110022010000000019331100100000000000000000021000010
110467020010099000009900000000000011220101 00
11046801120333605110402375410110022010000000006250000100000000000000000021010000
1104680200001000000000000000000000010010001 00
11046901120033005110402375310110022010000010015570000100000000000000000010000000
110469020000100000000200000000000011120001 00
11047001121134005110402350310110022010000010007731300100000000000000000011000010
1104700200000000000000000000000000111020001 00
11047101121033205110414350310110022010000000019380000100000000000000000010000000
1104710200001000000099000000000000022100000 00
11047201121334305110402350310110022010000010004501400100000000000160000010000000
110472020000100000000100000000000001001000100
11047301122133305110414350110110022010000000001750000100000000000000000010000000
1104730200000000000000000000000000002101010000
11047401121432905100402350310110022010000000002150000100000000000000000010000000
1104740200000000000000000000000000001102000000
11047501121232705100414350110110022010000000001630000100000000000000000010000000
1104750200000000000000000000000000002101000000
11047601121732805100402350110110022010000010005571400100000000010000000011000010
1104760200001000000000000000000000001102010100
11047701124433106110514350310110022110000000002310000100000000000000000020000000
1104770200001000000099000000000000012010100 00
11047801123932905100514350310110022010000010015080000100000000000000000020000000
1104780200000000000000000000000000001102010000
11047901124833006100514350310111022110000000000720000100000000000000000011000010
1104790200001000000000000000000000010210100 000
11048001023633805110501350310110022110000010000750000100000000000000000010000000
1104800200000000000000000000000000100101000 000
11048101122932805100514350310110022110000010007180000100000000000000000011000010
1104810200001000000000000000000000001202000000
11048201123833605100502350310110022110000010013980000100000000000000000010000000
1104820200000010100001000000000011120201010 0
11048301125333006110511350310110022010000010005510000100000000000000000021000010
1104830200001000000099000000000000021010000 00
11048401125532506100502350310110022010000010002390000100000000000000000012000010
110484020000100000000100000000011011110000 00
11048501125733006110511350310110022110000000013041300100000000000000000021000000
1104850200001000000000000000000000102101010000
11048601125932905110610350310110022010000010005201300100000000000000000021000010
1104860200001000000000000000000000101102010000
11048701126132406100502350310110022010000010007251400100000000000000000021000010
1104870200001010000000000000000000111101010 100
11048801126132806100502350310110022010000000001911300100000000000000000010000000
```

11048802000010000000010000010000001102010000
11048901126332806100502350310110022010000010001970000100000000000000000011001000
11048902000010000000000000000000001101010000
11049001026532406100511350310110022010000000007850000100000000000000000021000010
11049002000010000000000000000000102101010100
11049101127332306100511325410110022010100000004417000110000001161000008002100001
11049102000010000000010000000000102111010100
11049201127332606100502325310110022110000010026001700100000000000000000011000010
11049202000010100000990000010000111101000000
11049301127432806100502325310110022010000010044291600100000000000000000011000010
11049302000010000000000000000000001111010000
11049401126833106110511325310110022110000000002440000100000000000000000011000010
11049402000010000000990000000000002101000000
11049501126433206110502325310110022010000000003600000100000000000000000011000010
11049502000010000000990000000000001101010000
11049601123632405100502325110110022010000010011401400100000000010000000011000010
11049602000000000000990000010000011101000100
11049701124432206100502325110110022010000010000621400100000000000000000011000010
11049702000000000000000000000000000112000000
11049801124632306100502350310110022010000010001560000100000000000000000011001000
11049802000010000000000000000000001102000000
11049901124932606100502350310110022010000010002400000100000000000000000010000000
11049902000010000000000000000000001101000000
11050001125032306100513350310110022010000010001180000100000000000000000010000000
11050002000000000000000000000000011101000000
11050101126232106100511350310110022110000000011310000100000000000000000011000010
11050102000000000000000000000000021100000000
11050201125432406100502350310110022010000010002001100100000000000000000010000000
11050202000010000000000000000000001202000000
11050301128932107100502325410110022110000010018620000100000000000000000020000000
11050302000000000000990000000000001101010100
11050401129332007100502325410110022110000000004320000100000000000000000021010000
11050402000010000000000000000000001101010000
11050501129232507100502325310110022110000010031570000100000000000000000011010000
11050502000010001000990000000000001101010000
11050601129531907100502325310110022110000000001600000100000000000000000020000000
11050602000000000000000000000000000101010000
11050701129731607100502325310110022110000000003360000100000000000000000021000010
11050702000010000000000000010000000101010000
11050801129029807090802300110120032021102010003150000100000000010000000012000010
11050802000010000010000000000000101211020100
11050901129329707090802300110120032021000010001080000100000000000000000012000010
11050902000010100000000000010000111101010000
11051001128331507100502325310110022010000000003120000100000000000000000010000000
11051002000000000000010000000000000101010100
11051101127831706100502325310110022110000000008200000100000000000000000010000000
11051102000010001000020010000000101101010000
11051201128331907100502325310110022110000000004011300100000000000000000010000003
11051202000010000000000000000000000101010000
11051301128931607100502325310110022110000000011730000100000000000000000021000010
11051302000010000000000001000000001101020000
11051401129831707100502325310110022110000000001000000100000000000000000021000010
11051402000000000000000000000000000101010000
11051501130131807100502325310110022110000000003740000100000000000000000011010000
11051502000010000000000000000000001101010000
11051601129530607100802300110110022110000000005410000100000000000000000020000000
11051602000010100000000000000000001101010000
11051701129630307100802300310120132021000000006450000100000000000000000011000010
11051702000010100000990001000000111101010000
11051801129929607090802300310120132121000000003600000100000000000100000013011000

11051802000010200010010001000000101111010100
11051901130129507090802300310120122122000000005120000100000000000000000011011000
11051902000019900000010000000000101101020000
11052001129729207090802300310120032022000000005600000100000000000000000011011000
11052002001010099010990100000000101101010000
11052101129728807090802300110120032021000000003600000100000000000000000011011000
11052102001000000000990000010001001101010000
11052201129828107090802275110110122122000000025460000100000000000220000013011000
11052202001109999000990100000000001101020100
11052301131030907100502275310120011010000010018721300000000000000000090021001000
11052302000010000000000000000000000000001010100
11052401131430807101002275310110122110000000003431100100000000000000000011010000
11052402000010000000000000000000000000001010100
11052501132430208100002250410110122110100000104301100100000000000000000021011000
11052502001000000000000000000000001101020100
11052601133729708090002250410110122110000010016681100100000000000000000021010000
11052602000010000000000000000000000000000010100
11052701132930508100002250310110022110000000019470000100000000000000000011010000
11052702000000000000000000000000000000000010100
11052801132532108101019250310120111010000000002800000100000000000000000010000000
11052802000000000000000000000000000000001000000
11052901132332508101002250310110111010000010000661300100000000000000000010000000
11052902001000000000000000000000000000001010000
11053001132233008111019250310120121110000010003270000100000000000000000010000000
11053002000000000000000000000000000101010000
11053101133032008101019225310110022010000010002260000100000000000000000011010000
11053102000010000000000000000000000000001010000
11053201133232308101019225310110022010000010002961300100000000000000000011010000
11053202000010000000000000000000000000001010100
11053301133131708101019225110110022010000000003790000100000000000000000011010000
11053302000010000000000000000000000000001010000
11053401132433008101019225310110122010000010000670000100000000000000000010000000
11053402000000000000000000010000000001010000
11053501132632308101019225310121122010000010001080000100000000000000000010000000
11053502000000000000000000000000000000001010000
11053601130933507111002250310110122121000010012260000100000000000000000011010000
11053602000010000000000000000000100001010000
11053701131433507111002250410110032121100000003040000100000000000000000021011000
11053702001100000000000001000000000000001010100
11053801132832308101002225310110022010000010000220000100000000000000000010000000
11053802000010000000000000000000000000001010100
11053901132832508101002225310110022010000010000110000100000000000000000010000000
11053902000010000000000000000000000000001010000
11054001133331808101019225110110022010000000002480000100000000000000000010000000
11054002000010000000000000000000001000001010000
11054101132932808101002225310110122010000010004181300100000000000000000011010000
11054102000010100000010000000000001000001010000
11054201133531908101019225110110022010000010004280000100000000000000000010000000
11054202000010000010020000000000000000001010100
11054301133632208101019225110110022010000000001540000100000000000000000010000000
11054302000010000000000000000000000000001010000
11054401133432508101019225310110022110000010000160000100000000000000000011011000
11054402001000000000000000000000000000001010000
11054501133732008101002225310110122110000010001610000100000000000000000010000000
11054502000010000000000000000000000000001010000
11054601135232208101019200310120122010100010000661300100000000000000000011011000
11054602000010000000000000000000000000001010000
11054701034032508101002200310120122110000010000181400100000000000000000011010000
11054702000010000000000000000000000000001010000
11054801133435208111002250310120021010000000001070000100000000000000000010000000

110548020000000000000200000000000000001010000
11054901133635208111002225310120021010000000000750000100000000000000000010000000
110549020000000000000000000000000000001010000
11055001124838006121211350410110022110000000028250000100000000000000000010000000
110550020010001000000000000000010001001010100
11055101127129006090801300110120032021000000000840000100000000000000000011000010
110551020000100000000100000000000111102010000
11055201126728906090813300110120032021000000000300000100000000000000000011011000
110552020000000001099000000000000101111010000
11055301127628706090813300110120032021000000003930000100000000000000000011000010
110553020010001000099000000000000111201010000
11055401127228506090819300110120032121000010001800000100000000000000000010000000
110554020000000000000000000000000122000100000
11055501127828006090801300110120032121000010012000000100000000000000000011010000
110555020000100010000100000000000101101020000
11055601128128007090813300110120022012000010003641100100000000000014000011010000
110556020000100990009900000000000111111010000
11055701029128807090813300110120022022000000012380000100000000000000000011000010
110557020000100000000000000000000004444444440000
11055801128829007090801300110120032021101010002940000100000000000000000011001000
110558020000101000000001000000000101101010010
11055901128828707090801300110120032021110100000701100100000000000000000011010000
110559020000101000019900000000000100102010000
11056001128628307090801300110120032021101000005531200100000000000000000011000010
110560020000199990000000000000004444444440100
11056101128529307090801300110120032021100010008621100100000000000000000011010000
110561020000100010000100000100001111101010100
11056201128928307090813300110120032022000000007200000100000000000000000011000010
110562020000100000000000000000000101102010100
11056301127928506090813300110120032021201010000901100100000000000017000011011000
110563020010005030100000000100000111201010100
11056401127928606090811300110120032022101000001120000100000000000000000011010000
110564020000000000000000000000000112110010000
11056501128328107090813300110121032022000000003300000100000000000017000113010000
110565020000104030000000000000000101101010000
11056601128328507090801300110120032022000000005250000100000000000017090011011000
110566020000199990000100000000001101001010000
11056701128627707090813300110120032022000000002930000100000000000000000000000000
110567020000102010000000000000000001101010000
11056801128127607090813300110120032122000000002720000100000000000000000001000010
110568020000101000000000000000000001201010000
11056901128427507090813300110120032122000000002420000100000000000000000000000000
110569020000100000000200000000000001111010000
11057001128527307090813300110120032122000000008741700100000000000013000001001000
110570020000105000000000000000000002101010000
11057101128127107090813300110120032122000010003890000100000000000013000000000000
110571020000104000000200000000000001101010000
11057201127927306090813300110120032022000010004170000100000000000000000001010000
110572020000102000000100000000000001101020000
11057301128426907080813275110120032122000000003220000100000000000000000001000010
110573020000002000000000000000000002101010000
11057401128326807080814275110120032022000000005601300100000000000000000001000010
110574020000001000000000000000000001101010000
11057501128927107090814275110120032122000000003840000100000000000000000000000000
110575020000003000000000000000000001102000000
11057601129327207090814275110120032021000000005120000100000000000000000000000000
110576020000001000000000000000000001101010000
11057701128226407080814275310120032122000000003490000100000000000000000000000000
110577020000000000000000000000000001001000000
11057801128126207080814275310120032022000000002500000100000000000000000001000010
110578020000001000000000000000000001100010000
11057901127826106080814275310120022022000000001840000100000000000000000001000010
110579020000000000000000000000000002001010000
11058001027625906080814250310120022122000000002700000100000000000000000001000010
110580020000000000000100000000000001101000000
11058101027225906080814250310120022022000000001100000100000000000000000000000000
110581020000001000000000000000000001001000000
11058201126726206080814250310120022122000000001760000100000000000000000000000000
110582020000000000000000000000000002101000000
11058301127128406090812300110120022022000000005200000100000000000016000001001000
110583020001010001002000000000000101101010000
11058401127427806090814300110120022022000010016351100100000000000000000011000010
110584020010000000000000000000000011102010000
11058501127627906090814300110120022022000010003621100100000000000000000011001000
110585020000003000000000000010000101101020100
11058601127327606090812275310120022122000000004720000100000000000000000001010000
110586020001010000000100000000000101101010000
11058701127127606090819275210120022122000000006030000100000000000000000001011000
110587020000101000000000000000000101111010000
11058801127427206090812275310120022022000000000450000100000000000000000000000000
110588020000000000000000000000000001101000000
11058901127627206090814275310120022022000000000900000100000000000000000001000010
110589020000000000000099000000000000111000000
11059001127627106090814275310120022022000010001390000100000000000000000000000000
110590020000000000000000000000000002101010000
11059101027427006090812275310120022022000000000750000100000000000000000001001000
110591020000100000000000000000000001111010000
11059201027626906080814275310120022122000000000900000100000000000000000000000000
110592020000000000000000000000000000101000000
11059301128626007080819275310120132121000000002400000100000000000008000000000000
110593020000000000000000000000000001101010000
11059401028326507080812275310120022022000000000750000100000000000000000000000000
110594020000100000000000000000001001100010000
11059501128826307080812275310120032021000000006240000100000000000000000000000000
110595020000100000000001000000000001101010000
11059601128525807080814275310120022022000010002440000100000000000000000000000000
110596020000100000000000000000000000101000000
11059701128325707080814275310120022122000000000370000100000000000000000001000010
110597020000000000000000000000000000000001010000
11059801128225507080819250310120022122000000006170000100000000000000000000000000
110598020000000000000000000000000001001010000
11059901128825807080814275310120032021000000001800000100000000000000000000000000
110599020000199990000200000000000001101010000
11060001129326207080802275310120022022000010003241300100000000000000000001010000
110600020011003020000000000000000001101010000
11060101129626407080819275310120022022000010001280000100000000000000000011010000
110601020000102000000100000000000111111010000
11060201130926107080002250310120032121100010003801100100000000000000000011011000
110602020011001000000100000000000101101010000
11060301127226406080814250310120032121000010001920000100000000000000000000000000
110603020000000000099000000000000001101010000
11060401127226606080814275310120022022000010000891100100000000000000000000000000
110604020000000000000000000000000002100010000
11060501126727306090813275310120022122000000000934000100000000000000000001010000
110605020000100020000000000000000101101010000
11060601126028106090813275310120122022000000002051300100000000000000000011010000
110606020010003000000000000000000011100010100
11060701126027806090813275310120122022000000001050000100000000000000000011010000
110607020010000000000000000000000011101020000
11060801126027606090819275310120122022000000001120000100000000000000000011010000

```
1106080200001000000000 100000000000000 1001010000
1106090112662690608 08 102503 1012002202200001000206110010000000000000000011010000
110609020010001000000000000000000101101010000
1106100112632680608 08 142503 1022012212200001000570000010000000000001200001301100 0
110610020000000010000000000000000001101010000
1106110112632810609 08 142753 1012002202200000000240000010000000000000000000001000010
110611020000000000000000000000000101102010000
1106120112672820609 08 142753 1012002212200000000139000010000000000000000000000000000
110612020000000000000000000000000101101020000
1106130112682780609 08 142752 1012002212200000000120000010000000000000000000000000000
11061302000000000000001000000000011111201000 0
1106140112712600609 08 013003 1012002202200001000054000010000000000000000000010000000
1106140200100010100000000000000000001001010000
1106150112692800609 08 012753 1012002202200001000109000010000000000000000000010000000
1106150200001000000000000000000000011111000000
1106160112692730609 08 012753 1012002212200001000188000010000000000001000000001010000
1106160200000000100000000000000000001101020100
1106170112622850609 08 012753 1012012212200001000052000010000000000001000000000000000
11061702000000000000000000000000000 1101010000
1106180112523050610 08 013003 1012003202100001000659000010000000000000000000011011000
110618020010002000100 10000000000101211010000
1106190112553040610 08 053003 1012003202100000000061000010000000000000000000010000000
110619020010000000000000000000000 100102010000
1106200112562940609 08 042753 1012003202100000000065000010000000000000000000011000010
1106200200001000000000000000000001111 01010000
1106210112602980609 08 043003 1012003212100001000572000010000000000001000000011000010
110621020000000000000000000000000 111201010000
1106220112622980609 08 053003 1012003202100000000765000010000000000000000000012011000
1106220200000000001099000000000001 10200010000
1106230112552930609 08 112753 1012003212100000000103000010000000000000000000000000000
110623020000100000000000000000001111 02010000
1106240112662960609 08 193001 1012003202100000001864000010000000000000000000012010000
1106240200001020000000200000000000111100020000
1106250112552900609 08 112753 1012012212200000000348000010000000000001000000000000000
1106250200100000000000000000000001 11201010010
1106260112702950609 08 193001 1012003202100000000297000010000000000000000000011001000
110626020000099000000000000000000 1 1101020000
1106270112572880609 08 112753 1012012202200000000064000010000000000000000000000000000
11062702000000000000000000000000001102010000
1106280112652990609 08 143001 1012003202100001000054000010000000000000000000011100010
110628020000000100099000000000011111 01010000
1106290112752950609 08 083001 1012002202200000000014000010000000000000000000011000010
110629020000000000000000000000001011101020000
1106300112722910609 08 053001 1012002202200000000160130010000000000000000000011011000
11063002000019999000990000000000010110102001 0
1106310112642860609 08 042753 1022002212200001000039000010000000000000000000001000010
1106310201100020000000000000000000 1101010000
1106320112642910609 08 043003 1012012202200001000068000010000000000000000000001000010
1106320200001000000001000000000010120100000 0
1106330112622930609 08 163003 1012012202200000000053000010000000000000000000011000010
1106330200001000000000000000000011121101000 0
1106340112192430508 07 193501 1012012204202001001100130010000000000001600002000000 0
1106340200001000200001000001000011210101010 0
1106350112192380507 07 193501 1012002214202001000443000010000000000000000000021010000
1106350200001000000000100100000001121101000 0
1106360112202430508 07 113501 1012002204202001000874000010000000000000000000021001000
11063602000000101000000000000000001110101000 0
1106370112532710609 06 022503 1012012202200001000048000001000000000000000000020000000
110637020000100000000100000000000000001010010
1106380112502710609 06 112753 1012002212200001000162000010000000000000000000020000000
1106380200001000000000000000000000000101010100
1106390112512740609 06 192753 1012012202200000000216000010000000000000000000020000000
1106390200001000000000000000000000000101010000
1106400112482680608 06 022753 1012012202200001000486000010000000000000000000011011000
11064002000010000010000000000000010111101010 0
1106410112502750609 06 142753 1012012202200001000311000010000000000000000000011000010
110641020000000000000000000000000001101010000
1106420112472750609 06 192753 1012012202200000000240000010000000000000000000012011000
110642020000101000000010100000000010100101000 0
1106430112542770609 08 142751 1012012202200001002100000100000000000000000090010000000
1106430200100000001000000000000110010102010 0
1106440112552850609 08 142751 1012012202200001000490000010000000000000000000010000000
11064402000000000000000000000000000000001010000
1106450112492800609 06 142753 1012012202200000000174000010000000000000000000011001000
110645021000000990000000000000000011100010000
1106460112442790609 06 192753 1012012202200000000035000010000000000000000000000000000
11064602001000000000000010000000000102010000
1106470112722790609 06 193003 1012012202200001000288000010000000000000000000000000000
1106470200001000000000000000000000001101010000
1106480112422710609 06 023003 1012012202200001000244000010000000000000000000000000000
11064802001000100000010000000000010110101000 0
1106490112412710609 06 023003 1012012202200001000106000010000000000000000000000000000
1106490200000000001000000000000000001111010100
1106500113333510 8 111002250 3 1012001111000000000096000010000000000000000000010000000
1106500200000000000000000000000000000000001000000
1106510113273500 8 111002250 3 1012001111000001000713000010000000000000000000011001000
1106510200001000000001000000000000000001010000
1106520113263470 8 111002250 4 1012001111000000000325000010000000000000000000010000000
110652020000100000000000000000000010000101000 0
1106530113263450 8 111002250 4 1012001111000000000720000010000000000000000000011010000
11065302001000000000000000000000101001010000
1106540113313450 8 111002250 3 1012001111000000000144000010000000000000000000010000000
1106540200000000000000000000000000000000001000000
1106550113233430 8 111002250 4 1012001111000000000722000010000000000000000000020000000
11065502001000000000000000000000100001010000
1106560113193400 7 111002250 4 1012001111000000000572000010000000000000000000021010000
110656020000100000000 1000000000010000101010 0
1106570113173380 7 111002250 4 1012001111010000000878110100000000380000000000021001000
110657020000000000000000000000000110101010000
1106580113173400 7 111002250 3 1012001111000000000071000010010000000000000000011011000
110658020000100000100000000000000101001010000
1106590112483840612 12 113504 1011002211000000000204000010000000016700000000011001000
110659020010000000000000010000000000011010000
1106600112373920513 12 023504 1011002211010000001461132200000001990022000013011000
1106600200001010000000000000000000100001010000
1106610112423940613 12 113503 1011002211000001000430000010000000000000000080012010000
11066102000000001000010000010000100111010000
1106620112343930513 12 023504 1011002211000000000131000010000000000000000000014222220
11066202222229898222982233232222000001010000
1106630112343950513 12 023254 1011002211000000000080000010000000000000024000011011000
110663020000000009010000000000000100001010000
1106640112323980513 12 113253 1011002201000001000262000010000000000000000080011000010
110664020000099990000000000010000100001010000
1106650112304010513 12 133253 1011002201000000000440110010000000000000000000010000000
11066502000000001000020000000000100001010100
1106660112284020513 12 023253 1011002211000001000260000010000000000000000000011011000
110666020000001000000200000000000100001010100
1106670112254020513 12 023253 1011002211000001000401000010000000000000000000011011000
1106670200000000000000000000000000000000001010000
1106680112244000513 12 023253 1011002211000001000100000010000000000000000000011011000
```

```
110668020000000000000000000000000000000001000000
11066901121840505131213325310110022110000000012850000100000000000000000011011000
11066902001000100000010000000000000002010100
11067001122739705131202325310110022110100010003601300100000000000000000011011000
11067002000000000000020000000001100011010000
11067101121340505131213300310110022010000000002130000100000000000000000011000010
11067102000000000000010000000000000001010100
11067201121140605131202300310110022010000010003710000100000000000000080021010010
11067202001000000000000000000000000001010000
11067301121540305131210300310110022010000010004800000100000000000000080010000000
11067302000000000000000000000000000011010000
11067401123838805121219350310110022010000010000760000100000000000000080011010000
11067402001000101000000000000000000001000000
11067501124238206121201350310110022110000010000980000100000000000000080010000000
11067502001000000000000000000000000002010000
11067601124338106121201350310110022010000010000400000100000000000000080010000000
11067602000000000000000000000000100002010000
11067701124438106121201350310110022110100000004301300100000000000000000010000000
11067702000000001000000000000000100002010100
11067801123938505121202350310110022010000010001030000100000000000000000010000000
11067802000000000000000000000000000001010000
11067901124138106121219350310110022010000010001140000100000000000000080011010000
11067902001000000000000000000000000001010000
11068001123538705121219325310110022010100010000710000100000000000000000110000000
11068002000000000000000000000000000001010000
11068101124337605121201325310110022110000010000380000100000000000000000010000000
11068102000000000000000000000000000001010000
11068201024337806121201350310110022010000000000180000100000000000000090010000000
11068202000000000000000000000000100002010000
11068301124238006121201350310110022110000010000520000100000000000000090010000000
11068302001000000000000000000000100002010000
11068401124837506121202350310110022010000000001630000100000000000000000011011000
11068402000010000000000000000000000001001010000
11068501124937606121202350310120022110000000000560000100000000000000000011010000
11068502001000000000000000000000000011010000
11068601124637806121202350310110022010000010001030000100000000000000000011010000
11068602001000000000010000000000000001010000
11068701124937006121219325310110022110000010000210000100000000000000000010000000
11068702000000000000000000000000000001010000
11068801124837006121201325310110022110000010000920000100000000000000090010000000
11068802000000100000000000000000000002000000
11068901125037206121219350310120022010000000000430000100000000000000000011001000
11068902000000000000000000000000000001010000
11069001025337306121219350310110022010100010001560000100000000000000090010000000
11069002000000010100000000000000000001010100
11069101025737506121210350310110022010000010000330000100000000000000000010000000
11069102000000000000000000000000000001010000
11069201025837606121210350310110022010000000000510000100000000000000000010000000
11069202000000000000000000000000000001010000
11069301025637406121219350310110022010000010000350000100000000000000000010000000
11069302000000000000000000000000000001010000
11069401025837406121219350310110022010000010000900000100000000000000000010000000
11069402000000000000000000000000000002010000
11069501025037406121201350310110022010100000000941300100000000000000090010000000
11069502000000000000000000000000000002010000
11069601026137406121210350310110022010000010001420000100000000000000090011001000
11069602001000000000000000000000000001010000
11069701126337506121210350310110022110100010001121300100000000000000090011011000
11069702001000000000000000000000100011010000
11069801026037406121210350310110022010000000000501300100000000000000000011010000
11069802000010100000000000000000000001010100
11069901024936806121210325310110022010000000001440000100000000000000000010000000
11069902000000000000000000000000000002010000
11070001025337006121201350310110022110000000000491100100000000000000090010000000
11070002000010000000000000000000100001000000
11070101125236706111202325310110022010100010001100000100000000000000090010000000
11070102000100000000010000000000100001010000
11070201025336506121210325310110022010000010001170000100000000000000080011010000
11070202001000000000000000000000000002010000
11070301025532806111202300410110122010000010009460001010100034000000080020000000
11070302000000000000000000000000000001010000
11070401025336206121202325310110022010000000001310000100000000000000000010000000
11070402000010000000000000000000000000010000
11070501025436406121202325310110022010000010001440000100000000000000000010000000
11070502000010000000000000000000000000010000
11070601125536606121202325310110022110000010001660000100000000000000000010000000
11070602000000000000000000000000000112010000
11070701126036806121219325310110022010000000002410000100000000000000000011001000
11070702000000000000000000000000000001000000
11070801125936906121214350310110022010000000000900000100000000000000000010000000
11070802000000000000000000000000000001000000
11070901026137106121214350310110022010000010001000000100000000000000000010000000
11070902000000000000000000000000000001000100
11071001126337106121202325310110022010000010000680000100000000000000090010000000
11071002001000000000000000000000000001000000
11071101126437206121202325310110022010000010000500000100000000000000090011010000
11071102000000000000000000000000000001000000
11071201026038006121214350310110022110000000001001300100000000000000000010000000
11071202000000000000000000000000000001000000
11071301125837906121202350310110022110000010002601300100000000000000000011010000
11071302000000000000000000000000001001002010000
11071401025638206121219350310110022010000010000240000100000000000000000010000000
11071402000000000000000000000000000001000000
11071501125338306121201350310110022110000010000770000100000000000000000010000000
11071502000000000000000000000000000002010000
11071601125038706121219350310110022110000010000460000100000000000000000010000000
11071602000000000000010000000000000110202000
11071701024739206131210325310110022010000000002050000100000000000000000010000000
11071702000000000000000000000000000001000000
11071801024639106131210350310110022110000010001450000100000000000000080010000000
11071802001000000000000000000000000001010000
11071901024539006131210350310110022010000000000500000100000000000000000011010000
11071902001000000000000000000000000001010000
11072001024738706121210350310110022010000000000500000100000000000000000010000000
11072002000000000000000000000000000001010000
11072101125538606121214325310110022010000010004100000100000000000001200012000010
11072102000010000000000000000000100001010000
11072201126038206121202325310110022110000010002291400100000000000000090011010000
11072202000000000000000000000000000002010000
11072301026737006121202300310110022010000000000460000100000000000000000010000000
11072302000000000000000000000000000002010000
11072401126338306121202300310110022010000010000300000100000000000000000011001000
11072402000000000000010000000000000002010000
11072501125938506121202325310110022110000000000452000100000000000000000011010000
11072502001000000000000000000000100002010000
11072601125638606121202325310120022010000010000330000100000000000000000011001000
11072602000000000000000000000000100002010000
11072701125339106131202300310110122110000010000340000100000000000000000010000000
11072702000000000000100000010000000001000000
11072801125439206131202300310110122010000010000281100100000000000000000011001000
```

1107280200100000000000000000000000000012010000
11072901124339506131202300310120122010000000000160000010000000000000000000000000
110729020000100000000100000000000000002010000
11073001024939406131202300310110022010000000000430000010000000000000000000000000
110730020000000000000000000000000000002010000
11073101124839306131202325310110122010000001000332130010000000000000000001010000
110731020010000000000000000000000000002010000
11073201124439506131202325310110022010000001000460000010000000000000000000000000
110732020000100000000100000000000000002010000
11073301024539706131202300310110122010000001000190130010000000090000000000000000
110733020000000000000000000000000000002010000
11073401024640006131202300310120122010000001000310000010000000000000000001010000
110734020000000000000000000000000000001000000
11073501025439806131202275310120122010000000000260000010000000000000000000000000
110735021010000000000000000000000000002010000
11073601125640006131214275310120122010000000000800000010000000000000000000000000
110736020000000000000000000000000000001000000
11073701026339006131214300310110122010000000000260000010000000000000000000000000
110737020000000000000000000000000000002000000
11073801126439206131202275310120122010000001000240000010000000000000000001011000
110738020000000000000100000000000000002010000
11073901026938706121214275310110022010000000000372000010000000000000000000000000
110739020000000000000000000000000000002000000
11074001027338506121214275310110022010000000000420000010000000000000000000000000
110740020000000000000000000000000000001000000
11074101027537906121202275310110022011000001000052000010000000000000000000000000
110741020000000000000000000000000000002000000
11074201027438106121210275310110022010000001000040000010000000000000000000000000
110742020000000000000000000000000000001000100
11074301124934406110502325310120022010000000000091110010000000000000000010000000
110743020010000000000000000000100120000000000
11074401124834706110502325310120022010000000000108000010000000000000000010000000
110744020110000000000000000000000000002010000
11074501124334706110502325310110022010000000000150110010000000000000000011010000
110745020000000000000000000000001000001010000
11074601124134706110502325310110022010000000000180000010000000000000000011010000
110746020000000000000000000000001000002010000
11074701025235106111202300410110022010000000000077160010000000000000000010000000
110747020000000000000000000000000000002010000
11074801125234306110502325310120021010000000000028110010000000000000000011010000
110748020001000000000000000000000000101000000
11074901025234206110502325310120021110000000000048000010000000000000000010000000
110749020000000000000000000000000000102000000
11075001131724707080002225310110022010000001000681130010000000000000000010000000
110750020010100000000000000000000000000010100
11075101124027205090611300310120122122000000000147000010000000000000000000000000
110751020010001000000000000100000011100010000
11075201124828206090614275310120122022000000000064000010000000000000000000000000
110752020001000000000000000000000001101010000
11075301124628606090614275310120122122000000002100130010000000000000000001000010
110753020001010000000000000000000101101020100
11075401124428806090614300310120122022000000000176000010000000000000000001000010
110754020000000000000000000000000001101020000
11075501124028106090619300310120022122000001000325000010000000000000000000000000
110755020001000000000000000000000101020000000
11075601124027706080611300310120122022000000000157000010000000000000000000000000
110756020000000000000000000000000001001000000
11075701124128806090611300310120122122000000000161000010000000000000000000000000
110757020001000000000000000000000001112010000
11075801124128306090602300310120122122000001000120000010000000000000000000000000
110758020001000000000000000000000001001000000
11075901124229006090614300310120122022000000000294000010000000000000000001000010
110759020000000000000000000000000001101010000
11076001124129406090614300310120132021000000000192000010000000000000000001000010
110760020011002000000100000000000001101010000
11076101124529106090614300310120022022000000000766000010000000000000000001000010
110761020000000000000000000000000001101010000
11076201124929006090614275310120122022000001002623000010000000000000000000000000
110762020000199000000000000000000011112020000
11076301124529706090614300310120132021000000000549130010000000000000000001000010
110763020000000000000000000000000111101020000
11076401124129806090614300310120132021000001000275130010000000000000000001000010
110764020001000000000100000000000101101010000
11076501123929605090619300310120132121000000000480000010000000000000000000000000
110765020000000000000000000000000000102020000
11076601123829705090611300310120032021000001000050000010000000000000000001010000
110766020000000000000000000000000101002010000
11076701123729705090611300310120132021000001000167000010000000000000000000000000
110767020001010000000100000000000110111010000
11076801124129706090619300310120032021000000000094000010000000000000000000000000
110768020000000000000010000000000000001010000
11076901123629805090602300310120132121000001000150000010000000000000000000000000
110769020010000000000000000000000000001010000
11077001023929905090619300310120132021000000000350000010000000000000000000000000
110770020010002000000000000000000100101010000
11077101122630305100614325310120122022000000000140130010000000000000000020000000
110771020000000000000000000000000101002010000
11077201122729805090619325310120132021101010000558000010000000000000000021010000
110772020010100010000200110100000111102010000
11077301122830105100614325310120032021000000000178000010000000000000000020000000
110773020000000000000000000000000100102010100
11077401122929905090602325310120132021000001000242000010000000000000000011011000
110774020001000000100100000000000101112000000
11077501123030105100614325310120032021000000000220000010000000000000000011000010
110775020000000000000990000000000101102010100
11077601123230305100619300310120132021000000000678000010000000000000000011010000
110776020000000000000000000000001001002010000
11077701122930805100614300310120132021000000000093000010000000000000000010000000
110777020000000000000000000000000000101010000
11077801123130205100602325310120032021000001000239000010000000000000000010000000
110778020000000000000000000000000011102000000
11077901123430405100614300310120132021000000000188000010000000000000000010000000
110779020000000000000000000000000001101010000
11078001123329905090619300310120032021000000000077000010000000000000000010000000
110780020001000000000000000000000001102000000
11078101123630305100614300310120132021000000000246000010000000000000000010000000
110781020000000000000000000000000001102010000
11078201123429805090614300310120132021000001000247000010000000000000000010000000
110782020000000000000000000000000001002000000
11078301023828305090614300310120032121000001000109000010000000000000000010000000
110783020000000000000000000000000001002010000
11078401123829005090602300310120132021000001000901000010000000000000000010000000
110784020000000000000100000000000012112000000
11078501123727905090614300310110122022000000000130000010000000000000000010000000
110785020010000000000000000000000001001010000
11078601023629205090602300310120132021000001000284000010000000000000000011010000
110786020001000000000301000100000001102000000
11078701123628205090614300310120022022000000000103000010000000000000000011000010
110787020000000000000000000000000000112010000
11078801123628505090602300310120032021000001000293000010000000000000000011010000

```
110788020011002000000000000000000001102000000
11078901123428005090614300310120122022000000000770000100000000000000000000011000010
110789020000001000000000000000001002010000
11079001123428805090614300310120032021000000001910000100000000000000000000011010000
110790020000000000001000000000101102010000
11079101123429405090614300310120132021000000002130000100000000000000000000010000000
1107910200000000000000000000000000101010000
11079201123129505090614325310120132121000000003070000100000000000000000000011000010
110792020000000000000000000000000001101010000
11079301123528805090619300310120022022000000000480000100000000000000000000011011000
1107930200001010000000000000000000001101010000
11079401123329005090614325310120032021100000012360000100000000000000000000010000000
11079402000000000000000000000000001101202010100
11079501123328205090602325310120132021000010007720000100000000000000000000011011000
110795020010000000000200000000001111112010000
11079601123128405090614325310120132021000000000440000100000000000000000000011000010
1107960200000000000000000000000000101201010000
11079701123028605090614325310120132021000010009800000100000000000000000000011000010
110797020000000000000000000000000101101010000
11079801122929505090614325310120132021000010004040000100000000000000000000010000000
110798020000001000000000000000000101101010000
11079901122828105090602325310120132021000010002990000100000000000000000000011010000
11079902000000000000000000000000001002010000
11080001122828905090601325310110132021000010024520002010000070810000000020000000
1108000200001000000000200000000000101212010000
11080101122429105090619325310120122022000000000750000100000000000000000000020000003
1108010200100000000001000000000101102000000
11080201122528605090601325110120122022000010010881100100000000000000000000020000000
11080202000010002000010000000001111102000100
11080301122328505090619325110120122022000010009211100100000000000000000000010000000
1108030200100000000000000000000000101211000100
11080401122228405090611350110110122022000010003481100100000000000000000000010000000
1108040200001000000001010100000011111102010100
11080501122129105090619325110120122122000010005601100100000000000000000000011010000
110805020010000000000000000000000001110200000
11080601122029105090601350310110122022000000000840000100000000000000000000010000000
11080602000000000000000000000000001102000000
11080701122128405090619350110120122022000000001540000100000000000000000000010100000
1108070200000000000010000000000000000120000000
11080801021929005090611350310120122022000010003120000100000000000000000000010000000
11080802000000000000100000000000000102000000
11080901122028305090601350310120122022000010003200000100000000000000000000010000000
1108090200001000000000000000000101102010000
11081001121928305090601350310120122022000010002800000100000000000000000000010000000
1108100200000000300000000000000011110201000
11081101121728805090601350310120122022000010005620000100000000000000000000010000000
11081102000010001000000000000000011110200000
11081201121728405090619350310120122022000010003360000100000000000000000000011011000
110812020011000000000000000000000111112000000
11081301121528905090611350310120122022000000000830000100000000000000000000010000000
11081302000000100000000000000000101102010000
11081401123427505090613325310120122022000000000230000100000000000000000000011011000
11081402000000000000100000000000001102000000
11081501123327105090611325310120132021000000000900000100000000000000000000010000000
110815020000020000000000000000000001102000000
11081601023227005090601325310120122122000010000870000100000000000000000000010000000
110816020010001000000100000000000001101010000
11081701123227305090611325310120032021000000001250000100000000000000000000011000010
110817020000000000000000000000000010102010000
11081801123127305090619325310120022022000010001600000100000000000000000000010000000
```

```
110818020000000000100100000000000000001102010000
11081901123026905080613325310120132021000000001000000100000000000000000000010000000
11081902000000000000000000000000001002010000
11082001122926805080711325310120122022000000000640000100000000000000000000010000000
110820020000000000000000000000000001101010000
11082101022926705080701325310120132121000000000780000100000000000000000000010000000
11082102000000000000000000000000001101000000
11082201122826705080719325310120132121000010001140000100000000000000000000010000000
11082202000000000000000000000000001002000000
11082301123027305090611325310120132121000010002100000100000000000000000000010000000
1108230200001010000000000000000000101002010000
11082401123027605090619325310120132121000010001920000100000000000000000000011010000
11082402000000000000000000000000001010010000
11082501023627505090611300310120122022000010000420000100000000000000000000000000000
11082502001100000000000000000000001002010000
11082601123727405090619300310120122022000010000300000100000000000000000000000000000
11082602001010000000020000000000101001010000
11082701123827305090601300310120122022000010004541300100000000000016000001011000
1108270200001010000001000000000011201010100
11082801023726905080619300310120122022000010000600000100000000000000000000000000000
11082802001000000000000000000000001102000000
11082901023727105090611300310120122122000010000881300100000000000016000000000000
11082902000010000000000000000000001112010000
11083001123527105090601300310120122122000010001600000100000000000016000001011000
11083002000010000010010000000001101102010000
11083101023427105090619300110120132121000010000640000100000000000000000000000000000
11083102001000100010020000000001101020100000
11083201122827505090601325310110122122000010006261100100000000000000000000011000010
11083202000010001000000100000000111102010000
11083301022927105090611325310110022122000000000940000100000000000000000000010000000
11083302000010100000000000000000001001201000
11083401122826905080619325310120122122000000001280000100000000000000000000010000000
11083402000010000000010000000000101002010000
11083501122626705080713325310110122122000010002371300100000000000000000000010000000
110835020000101000000300000000010010020100100
11083601122727105090611325310120022122000000001691300100000000000000000000010000000
110836020010101010000000000000000001112010100
11083701122426605080713325310120122022000000000870000100000000000000000000010000000
1108370200100000000001000000000000001102010000
11083801122627405090611325310120122022000010001180000100000000000000000000010000000
1108380200100000100001000000000001002010000
11083901122527105090619350310120022022000000003190000100000000000000000000010000000
110839020000000000000300000000011121020100000
11084001022627705090611325310120122022000010001800000100000000000000000000010000000
1108400200000000000000000000000000000120000000
11084101122327405090613350310120122022000000000523000010000000000000000000021000010
110841020000101000100100000000011021010100000
11084201122126905080719350110120122022000000003041300100000000000000000000021010000
1108420200001000001000000000000011110101000
11084301121926805080713350310120022022000010004160000100000000000000000000021001000
11084302001100000000010100000000101102010000
11084401121927405090611350310120122122000000000251000010000000000000000000021000010
11084402000000202000000000000000101102010000
11084501021826305080713350110120022022000010002181700100000000000000000000020000000
1108450200001020000000000000000000100102000100
11084601122027605090619350310120122122000000000570000100000000000000000000010000000
110846020010100010000100000000001111112010000
11084701121727405090211350310120022022000000001561100100000000000000000000011000010
1108470200001000000000000000000000120101000
11084801021726805080213350310120022122000010004160000100000000000000000000011001000
```

```
1108480200000010000000000000000011011020100000
110849011215262050807113503101201221220000000039300001000000000000000000010000000
110849020001000000000000000000000001102000000
110850011286342071110022503101101220100000100008300001000000000000000000001001000
11085002000000000000000000000000000001010000
110851011252340061105023253101201221100000000005013001000000000000000000010000000
1108510200000000000000000000000000001102000000
110852011298335071110022753101100220100000100006217001000000000000000000001010010
11085202000010000000000000000000000001010000
110853011301336071110022503101100220100000100003500001000000000000000000001010000
110853020000000000000000000000000000002010000
110854011303337071110022503101100220100000100005813001000000000000000000001010000
11085402001000000000010000000000000001010000
110855010313338071110022503101100220100000000002110000100000000000000000011010000
11085502000010000000000000000000000001010000
110856011289341071110022503101100221100000000009600001000000000000000000001001000
11085602001000000000000000000000000002010000
110857011290342071110022503101100221100000000007600001000000000000000000000000000
110857020000000000000000100000000100002010000
110858011292344071110022253101101221100000100012100001000000000000000000001000010
110858020000100000000100000000002000003020000
110859011287346071110022253101200221100000100004800001000000000000000000000000000
11085902000000000000000000000000100002010000
110860011290348071110022253101100221100000100008200001000000000000000000001011000
110860020000000000000010000000000100012010000
110861011293349071110022253101200221100000000000870000100000000000000000000000000
110861020000100000000000000000000100002010000
110862011299351071110022253101200220100000100011900001000000000000000000101001000
110862020001000000000100000000000100102010000
110863011301352071110022253101200220100000100010200001000000000000000000001011000
11086302001100000000010000000000000000001010000
110864011303348071110022253101100220101000100027213001000000000001200000301100 0
110864020000100000000000000000000101002020000
110865011303350071110022253101100220100000100012900001000000000001200000301100 0
110865020000100000000000000000000101001010000
110866011300349071110022253101100221100000100004200001000000000000000000000000000
110866020000000000000100000000000111112020000
110867011300346071110022254101100220100000100007900001000000000510000000001001000
110867020010000000000000000000000100002020000
110868011300341071110022503101200220100000100010900001000000000001200000301100 0
110868020000000000000000000000001100002020000
110869011300340071110022503101100221100000100007200001000000000000000000001000010
110869020000100000000000000000000000002020000
110870011299338071110022503101200320210000000017600001000000000000000000101010000
110870020001001000000000000000000100002020000
110871011299337071110022503101200321210000100033600001000000000000000000001001000
110871020010000000000000000000000100002020000
110872011296338071110022503101100221100000000005200001000000000000000000000000000
11087202000000000000010000000000000000002010000
110873011293337071110022503101100220220000000005200001000000000000000000000000000
110873020000000000000000000000000001002020000
110874011273373061212022753101201220100000000002100001000000000000000000001011000
110874020010000000000000000000000100002010000
110875011272376061212022753101100220100000100003200001000000000000000000001010000
110875020000000000000000000000000001102020000
110876010271380061212023003101100221100000100002600001000000000000000000000000000
110876020000000000000000000000000000002020000
110877010244412061312022753101201220100000000005600001000000000000000000010000000
110877020000100000000000000000000000002000000
110878010242410061312022753101201220101000100008200001000000000000000000011010000
110878020000001000000000000000000000002020000
110879010236418051312022754101100221101000100169500001000000076300000000021010000
110879020000000000000001000000000000000002000000
110880010236411051312023003101100220101000100020011001000000000000000000010000000
1108800200000000000000000001000000000002000000
110881010239407051312023003101100220100000100010400001000000000000000000010000000
110881020001100000000000000000000000002010000
110882011241396061312023253101100221100000100070700001000000000001408001 0000000
110882020000000050000000000000000010001202000 0
110883010248423061412102253101101220100000000002500001000000000000000000010000000
1108830200000000000000000000000000000002020010
110884010247426061412022253101100220100000100011000001000000000000000000010000000
110884020000100000000000000000000000001010000
110885010246427061412022503101201220100000000007400001000000000000000000011001000
110885020001100000000000000000000000001010000
110886011244426061412022503101200220100000100002600001000000000000000000010000000
110886020011000000000000000000000100002010000
110887011242424061412022503101200221100000000005100001000000000000000900 10000000
110887020000000000000000000000000100002020000
110888010243421061412022503101200220100000100004000001000000000000000000010000000
11088802000000000000000000000000000000002000000
110889011239424051412022753101100221100000000004450000100000000000000000010000000
110889020010100000000000000001000010000201000 0
110890010239419051312102753101100220100000000005200001000000000000000000010000000
11089002000000000000000000000000000000002000000
110891010238421051412022753101200220100000000004000001000000000000000000010000000
11089102000000000000000000000000000001000000
110892010235424051412022753101100220101000100008700001000000000000000000010000000
110892020010000000000000000000000000002010000
110893010238424051412022753101100221100000000002290000100000000000000000010000000
1108930200001000000001000000000000000002000000
110894010235426051412022501101100220100000000003640000100000000000000000010000000
110894020000100000000000000000000100002010000
110895010235427051412102501101100220100000000005900001000000000000000000010000000
11089502001100000000000000000000000000002000000
110896010233427051412022501101100221100000100008800001000000000000000000010000000
1108960200001000000000000000000000000002000000
110897010235428051412102503101100221100000000004500001000000000000000000010000000
11089702000000000000000000000000000000001000000
110898010232426051412022503101100220100000100015900001000000000000000000010000000
1108980200001000000000100000000000000002000000
110899010230427051412102503101100220100000100010700001000000000000000000010000000
11089902001000000000000000000000000000002010000
110900011216275050902143503101200220220000000013900001000000000000000000010000000
110900020000000000000000000000000101112010000
110901011217273050902143503101200220220000100017713001000000000000000000010000000
110901020000000000000200000000001111100000 00
110902011216275050902143503101200221220000000010900001000000000000000000010000000
110902020000000100000000000000000101102000000
110903011216273050902143503101200221220000100006700001000000000000000000010000000
110903020000100000000300000000000101112010000
110904011215271050902143503101200220220000100008513001000000000000000000011001000
110904020010000000100200000000000111201010000
110905011216277050902143503101201220220000000012400001000000000000000000010000000
110905020000000000000100000000000001002000000
110906011215276050902143503101200220220000000009000001000000000000000000011011000
110906020000001000000100000000000111202010000
110907011213273050902143753101201220220000100006500000100000000000000000010000000
110907020000101020000000000000000101102000000
110908011212271050902143753101200220220000000010700001000000000000000000010000000
```

```
1109080200100010000000000000000000112010000
110909010212267050802193753101200220220000000030000010000000000000000000010000000
11090902000000000000000000000000000201000000
110910011213266050802193503101200220220000100057600001000000000000000000011000010
11091002000000200000010000000000011120100000
110911011214266050807193503101200220220000100088411001000000000000017000010000000
11091102101000000010000000000000101201000000
110912011212253050807193751101200220220000100320000001000000000000000000011011000
1109120200000010000004000000000001012010101000
110913011209260050807123751101200220220000100036000001000000000000000000010000000
1109130200100010000010000010000101102010000
110914011209255050807193751101200220220000100121000001000000000000000000011010000
11091402010000100010020000000000111201000100
110915011209249050807123751101200221220000000036400001000000000000000000010000000
11091502000000100000000000000000111101010000
110916011210246050807193501101200320210000100052000001000000000000000000010000000
11091602001000100000200000000000101102010100
110917011206245050807123751101200320210000000042900001000000000100000000010000000
11091702000000000000000000000000101012010000
110918011207243050807193751101200320210000100079500001000000000000000000010000000
11091802000010000000000000000000101112000000
110919011207258050807123751101200220220000100061600001000000000000000000010000000
11091902000001000000100000100011111010101000
110920011206256050807133751101200220220000100014500001000000000000000000010000000
11092002001000100000000000100001121010000000
110921011205258050807123751101200220220000100010300001000000000000000000011010000
11092102000000200000000100000001112020201000
110922011205260050807193751101200220220000100026400001000000000000000000011001000
11092202001000000000000000100001011020100000
110923011202257050807123751101200220220000100077500001000000000000000000011010000
11092302001000000000000000000001011020100000
110924011204247050807123751101200320210000100121711001000000000000000000010000000
11092402000001000000000100000001011010101000
110925011205249050807193751101200320210000100099413001000000000000000000011001000
11092502000000102000010000000001101112010100
110926011202251050807123751101200320210000000067214001000000000100000000011001000
11092602001100101000000000000000111112010100
110927011205252050807143751101200220221010100072216001100000000100000000010000000
11092702000000100000000000000000101211010100
110928011201253050807123751101200320210000100029000001000000000000000000011011000
11092802001100200000000000000000111012020000
110929011207254050807193751101100320210000100012000001000000000000000000011010000
11092902000000100000000000100001011120200000
110930011221251050807103501101100220100000100013900001000000000000000000021010000
11093002001000000000000000000001010010100000
110931011221254050807143501101200220221000100050400001000000000000000000021010100
11093102000000000000100000000011111120001000
110932011219258050807193501101100221100000000019600001000000000000000000020000000
11093202001000000000100000000000102000000000
110933011222258050807103503101200220220000100130400001000000000000000000011001000
11093302001000100000001000000011111020100000
110934011223251050807143501101200220220000100064900001000000000000000000011000010
11093402001000100000030000000000111020100000
110935011224243050807193501101200220220000100054000001000000000000000000011011000
11093502000010100000020000010001112101010000
110936010213258050807193501101200321210000100021000001000000000001300002101000
11093602000000801000010000000000112201010000
110937010214255050807113501101200320210000100017311001000000000000000000020000000
11093702001000001000000000000000101112000000
110938011219252050807013501101200320210000100605011010110001849000008002101100
11093802000019900000990100000000111112010110
110939011222241050807133501101200221220000100043000001000000000000000000021010000
11093902000001000000200000000000002101010000
110940011223246050807193501101200321210000100025300001000000000000000000021010000
11094002000010100000020000000000112111010000
110941011221249050807013501101200220220000100010500001000000000000000000021010000
11094102000010000010010000000000101200000000
110942011224249050807133501101200221220000100015500001000000000000000000011001000
11094202000010000000000000000000111020000000
110943011225253050807013501101200221220000100068000001000000000000000090011010000
11094302000010001000000000010000110012000000
110944010226248050807113503101200220220000100011500001000000000000000000010000000
11094402000000000000100000000000010010000000
110945011226242050807193503101200220220000000084413001000000000000000000010000000
11094502000010201000010000000001101102010100
110946010226261050807133253101201220220000100018400001000000000000000000010000000
11094602000000000010000000000000110020100000
110947011227255050807113253101201220220000100017500001000000000000000000010000000
11094702000000100000000000000001011102000000
110948010224255050807013501101200221220000100021700001000000000000000000011010000
11094802000010300000000000000001101112000000
110949011223254050807133501101201220220000100026600001000000000002400001000000
11094902000010101000000000000000111110100000
110950011228427051412025003101201221100000000018600001000000000000000000010000000
11095002000000100000000000000000100012000000
110951011227431051412025003101101220100000000012000001000000000000000000010000000
11095102000010000000000000100000000012010000
110952011225436051412022251101100221100000000215114001000000000000000000010000000
11095202000000000000100000000001000020100000
110953011225444051412022253101101221100000100008013001000000000000000000010000000
11095302000000000000000000100000000020001000
110954011223444051412022253101101221100000000019200001000000000000000000010000000
11095402000000000000000000000000000020000000
110955011229439051412022253101101221100000100010914001000000000000000000010000000
11095502000010000000000000000000000020000000
110956010227439051412022253101101221100000000008300001000000000000000000010000000
11095602001000000000000000000000000020000000
110957011212439051412022253101201221100000000004313001000000000000000000010000000
11095702000000000000000000000000000020000000
110958011204445051412022003101101220100000100005100001000000000000000000010000000
11095802000010000000000000100000000020000000
110959010188456041500021503101201320210000000019500001000000000000000000000000000
11095902000000000000000000000000000020100000
110960010163473041500021503101101220100000100015000001000000000000000000000000000
11096002000010000000000000000000000010100000
110961010167474041500001503101422443633300200012024000990000000224920300422222 0
1109610222222989822298223323222444444440222
110962010000000000000190003101100220100000100003300001000000000000000000030000000
11096202000000000000000000000000000020000000
110963011200473051500022003101100220100000000004800001000000000000000000000000000
1109630200000000000000000000000000001000100
110964010349250080800022001101101221100000100087413001000000000000000000011011000
11096402000000000000000000000000000000010000
110965011350255080800022003101101221220000100017200001000000000000000000011011000
11096502001000000000000000000000000000010000
110966011351253080800022003101101221100000100015016001000000000000000000011010000
11096602000000000000000000000000000000010100
110967011216209050607012503101200221220000100019313001000000000000000000000000000
1109670200001000000001000000000000001111000100
110968011217208050607012503101200221220000100015600001000000000000000000000000000
```

```
110968020000101010000000000000000001101000000
110969011217203050607192503101201221220000100013200001000000000000000000001010000
11096902000010200000010000000000101101010000
110970011220208050607012503101201221220000100044200001000000000000000000001010000
1109700200001000101000000000001101101010100
110971011224216050707012753101200221221000100004913001000000000000000000001011000
11097102000010000000000000000001101010000
110972011225214050707192753101201221220000100022413001000000000000000000000000000
11097202000010001000000000010000101101010100
110973011238227050707012753101201221220000100112913001000000000000000000000000000
1109730200001000100000000000000001100010000
110974011233223050707082753101201221100000100011613001000000000000000000001010000
110974020000000000000000000000001101010100
110975011233225050707012753101201221101000100011516001000000000000000000001010000
110975020000100000000000000000001001010000
110976010233229050707013003101201221100000100040011001000000000000000000000000000
11097602000010000000000000000001101000000
110977011227225050707083003101201221100000100020513001000000000000000000000000000
11097702000010100000000000100000110101000
110978011227223050707083003101101221100000100054900001000000000000000000000000000
11097802000010000000000000000000444444440000
110979011213214050707012753101201221220000100145013001000000000000000000000000000
1109790200001000000000000000001011001010000
110980011230226050707083003101201221100000100002313001000000000000000000001001000
110980020000100000000000000000001000000000
110981011230226050707013003101201221100000100003513001000000000000000000000000000
1109810200001000000000000000000000001000100
110982010226226050707013003101201221102000100002800001000000000100000000000000000
110982020000000000000000000000001001010000
110983011221223050707013003101201221100000100011211001000000000000000000001000000
11098302000010000000000000000000010001010100
110984011220224050707013253101201221101000100047313001000000000000000090000000000
110984020000101010100000000000000444444440100
110985010236370051212022753101200220100000100025400001000000000000000000000000000
110985020000000000000000000000000001010000
110986011229373051212192753101100220100000100048200001000000000000000000001011000
110986020000000000000000000010000100001010000
110987010233372051212022753101100220100000000014900001000000000000000000000000000
11098702000000000000000000000000000002010000
110988010234359051112192753101101220100000000029000001000000000000000000000000000
11098802000000000000000000000000000002010000
110989011238376051212023003101100220101000100024000001000000000000000000001001000
11098902001100000000000000000000100112010000
110990010224370051212192503101100220100000100048000001000000000000000000000000000
110990020000000000000000000010000000002010000
110991010238373051212023003101100220100000000030000010000000000000009001000000000
11099102000000000000000000000000000002010000
110992010219386051212022753101100220100000000039200011000000004500000000100000001
11099202000000000000010000000000000002010000
110993010221388051212022753101100220100000000030000001000000000000000000010000000
11099302000000000000000000000000000002010000
110994010220387051212022752101100220100000000040000001000000000000000000010000000
11099402000000000000000000000000000002010000
110995011222388051212193003101100220100000100047000001000000000000000000010000000
11099502000010000000010000000000000002010000
110996010224384051212123003101100220100000000023000001000000000000000000010000000
11099602000000000000000000000000000002020000
110997010218386051212022753101100220100000000012600001000000000000000000010000000
11099702000000000000000000000000000002010000
110998010214384051212192503101100220100000100008500001000000000000000000000000000
110998020000000000000200000000000000001010000
110999010208384051212122503101100221100000000000600000100000000000000000000000000
11099902000000000000000000000000000001000000
111000010224262050807113253101201220220000100034211001000000000000000000010000000
11100002000000100000000000010000011002000000
111001010228261050807113253101201221220000000011400001000000000000000000010000000
11100102000000000000000000000000001002010000
111002011228259050807073253101200220220000000010000001000000000000000000010000000
11100202000000000000000000000000001002000000
111003011228253050807193253101201221220000100039600001000000000000000000011010000
11100302001000100000000000000000101102000100
111004011227247050807193253101201221220000100025000001000000000000000000010000000
11100402020000000000100000000000101102010000
111005011228241050807133253101200221220000000054900001000000000000000000020000000
11100502001000100000200000000000111102010000
111006011231254050807113253101201220220000100020200001000000000000000000010000000
11100602000000000000000000000000001102000000
111007011231250050807113253101201220220000100023500001000000000000000000010000000
11100702000010000000000000000000001002010000
111008011230249050807113253101201220220000000013900001000000000000000000010000000
11100802000010000000000000000000001002010000
111009011229248050807133253101201220220000000010500001000000000000000000010000000
111009020000100010000100000000001001102010000
111010011233252050807193253101201220221010100044800001000000000000000000012010000
1110100200110010100000000000000000001102010000
111011010234259050807073253101201220220000100076500001000000000000013000011000010
11101102000010100000000000000000001000002000000
111012011232263050807193253101201320210000100038400001000000000000000000010000000
111012020010001000000000000000000011102010000
111013011230261050807113253101201220220000100102100001000000000000000000010000000
111013020000100000000000000000000011002000100
111014011237265050807133003101201320210000100031900001000000000000000000001010000
111014020000101000000000000000001001102010000
111015011239264050807073003101201220220000100070000001000000000000000000000000000
11101502000010000100000000000000000000002020000
111016011239260050807133003101201221220000100016000001000000000001600001010000
11101602000000000000000000000000001001102010100
111017010237261050807013003101201221220000100025800001000000000000000000000000000
11101702000010000000010000000000000000012000000
111018011236262050807113003101201220220000100006000001000000000000000000001001000
111018020000000000001000000000000000002000000
111019010230242050807073253101100221100000100028011001000000000000000000010000000
111019020010000000000100000000000010002010000
111020011229239050707013254101200321210000100004000001000000000000000000021001000
1110200200001010100001000000000000101102000000
111021011240266050806133003101201221220000100023213001000000000000000000000000000
111021020000100000000000000000000000002020000
111022011238267050806133003101201221220000100015700001000000000000000000000000000
111022020000000000000000000000000000102010000
111023011242264060806133003101201220220000100006800001000000000000000000000000000
111023020000000000000000000000000001101000000
111024011242264060807133003101201220220000100020800001000000000000000000000000000
111024020000000000000000000000000001102000000
111025011241259060807193003101200320210000100049800001000000000000000000001010000
111025020010000000000000000000000001102010100
111026011239258050807193003101201320210000100012000001000000000000000000001010000
111026020000100010000000000000000001102010000
111027011241268060806193003101201320210000100011200001000000000000000000001001000
111027020010000000000000000000000001102010000
111028011243261060807193003101201321210000100024011001000000000000000000000000000
```

```
11102802000010000000000000000000001102010100
11102901124326506080613300310120022022000010003241400100000000000000000010000000
11102902000010100000010000000000001102000000
11103001124426506080614300310120022122000010001961100100000000000000000010000000
11103002000000000000000000000000000102000000
11103101124226806080613300310120122122000000000850000100000000000000000010000000
11103102000010000000010000000000001001000000
11103201124526606080619300310120132021000000000491100100000000000000000011001000
11103202000000200000010000000001101102000000
11103301124626606080614275310120122022000010003080000100000000000000000010000000
11103302000100000000000000000000001201000000
11103401124426206080719300310120132121000010002400000100000000000000000010000000
11103402001000000000010000000000001102010000
11103501124526006080714300310120132021000010003410000100000000000000000010000000
11103502000000000000000000000000001102000000
11103601124626006080719275310120132021000010005110000100000000000000000011000010
11103602000010000000000000000000001101010000
11103701124725906080719275310120132021000010003391100100000000000000000011010000
11103702001000000000000000000000101111020100
11103801124826506080613275310120132021000010004761100100000000000000000011010000
11103802001000000000000000000000002101000000
11103901125225906080719275110120132021000010013981300100000000000000000021001000
11103902000010000000010000000000001201020000
11104001124925906080719275110120132021000010001601100100000000000000000011000010
11104002000000000000000000000000011001010000
11104101025126406080613275110120132021000010001820000100000000000000000010000000
11104102000000010000000000000000001100010000
11104201025326406080613275110120132021000010004080000100000000000000000010000000
11104202000000010000000000000000001000010000
11104301123223805070719325310120132121000000000650000100000000000000000010000000
11104302000010100000000000000000101102010000
11104401123124405080713325310120032021000010003200000100000000000000000010000000
11104402001010000000010000000001101102010000
11104501122223705070711350310120122022000010001800000100000000000000000010000000
11104502000000000000000000000000100102000000
11104601122523105070713325310120132121000000000202000100000000000000000011001000
11104602000000000000000000000000011202000000
11104701122323605070711350310120132121000000000241000100000000000000000010000000
11104702001009900000010000000000101102010000
11104801022923405070711325310110122022000010001130000100000000000000000010000000
11104802000010001000000000000000001001000000
11104901123323705070719325310120132021000010002920000100000000000000000010000000
11104902000010000100000000000000001102020000
11105001121638905121219275310110122110000000001450000100000000000022000013111000
11105002000010000000000000000000100012010000
11105101021538805121202275310110122010000010001090000100000000000000000010000000
11105102000000000000010000000000000002010000
11105201121839005131219275310110022010000010000831300100000000000000000011000010
11105202000000000000000000000100000012000000
11105301022538705121202300310110122110000010004240000100000000000000000010000000
11105302000000000000000000000000000002010000
11105401122738905121202300310110122010000010001820000100000000000000000010000000
11105402000000000000000000000000100002020000
11105501022939005131202325310110122110000010007040000100000000000000000010000000
11105502000000000000000000000000001102020000
11105601022839305131202325310110122110000000000136000100000000000000000010000000
11105602000000000000000000000000000002020000
11105701021858305191319225310120022110000000000075000100000000000000000000000000
11105702001000000000000000000000000002000000
11105801021958305191312225310120122010000000000040000100000000000000000000000000
11105802000000000000000000000000000001000000
11105901022058005191302225310120022010000000000080000100000000000000000000000000
11105902000000000000000000000000000002000000
11106001021758705191302250310110122110100010001450000100000000000000000000000000
11106002001000000000000000000000000002000000
11106101121759105191319250310110022010100000000041000100000000000000000000000000
11106102000000000000000000000000000001000000
11106201121759505191302250310220022010000000003420000100000000000000000000000000
11106202000000000000000000000000000002000000
11106301021059905191314250310110022010000000000683000100000000000000000010000000
11106302000000000000000000000000000001000000
11106401020859705191312275310120022010000010002101300100000000010000000010000000
11106402000000000000000000000000100002020000
11106501020759705191319275310110022110000000000224000100000000000000000010000000
11106502000000000000000000000000100002010000
11106601020359905191302275310110022110000010001700000100000000000000000010000000
11106602000010000000000000000000000002000000
11106701020659605191314275310110022010000000000090000100000000000000000010000000
11106702000000000000000000000000000002000000
11106801020659305191302275310110022010000000000050000100000000000000000000000000
11106802000000000000000000000000000002000000
11106901020258005191314300210110022110000000004671600100000000000000000000000000
11106902000000000000000000000000000002000000
11107001122251405170002275410110021110100010003780000100000000000000000000000000
11107002001000000000000000000000001102010100
11107101017853604170013175310110022010000010005250000500000000000000000000000000
11107102000000000000000000000000000000010100
11107201017653804170002175310110022122000010004880000500000000000000000000000000
11107202000000000000000000000000000000000100
11107301017553804170002175310110032121000010003250000500000000000000000000000000
11107302000000000000000000000000000000000100
11107401017453704170002150310110032121000010004880000500000000000000000000000000
11107402000000000000000000000000000000000100
11107501017854504180013175310110022022000010001900000500000000000000000000000000
11107502000000000000000000000000000001000100
11107601018754204180013225310110022110000010001201300100000000000000000000000000
11107602000010000000000000000000010002000000
11107701018654304180002200310110022110000010001501100100000000000000000000000000
11107702000000000000000000000000010002000100
11107801016856404180014150310110022010000010005560000500000000000000000000000000
11107802000000000000000000000000000000000100
11107901017056404180014150310110122010000000000283000500000000000000000000000000
11107902000000000000000000000000000000000100
11108001020153605170012275310110022110000000000501000500000000000000000010000000
11108002000000000000000000000000000000000100
11108101019853304170012250310110021110000000000829000100000000000000000000000000
11108102000000000000000000000000000001000100
11108201118954104180002225310110022110000010000500000100000000000000000000000000
11108202000000000000000000000000000002000000
11108301020263105211302150310110022010100010001130000100000000000000000000000000
11108302000100000000000000000000000002000000
11108401020562305201302175310110022110100000000065000100000000000000000000000000
11108402000000000000000000000000000001010000
11108501020762005201319200310120122110000000000085000100000000000000000000000000
11108502001000000000010000000000000002000000
11108601021061705201302200310110022110000010002030000100000000000000000000000000
11108602000000000000000000001000000002000000
11108701121161405201319200310110022110000000000621000100000000000000000000000000
11108702001000000000000000000000000001000000
11108801021361305201319225310110022110100000000254000100000000010000000000000000
```

```
11108802000010000000010000000000100002010100
11108901021461205201319225310110022110000000001290000100000000000000000000000000
1110890200000000000000000000000000000002000000
11109001121661105201319225310110022010000010005280000100000000000000000001001000
11109002000010000000010000000000100012010100
11109101021660905201319225310110022110000000003330000100000000000000000000000000
11109102000010000000000000000000100001010000
11109201020960305201319250310120022110000000001630000100000000000000000000000000
11109202000000000000000000000000000001010000
11109301020760305201319250310120022110000010003800001000000000000000000000000000
111093020000100000000000000100001000020101 00
11109401020760105201302250310110021110000010001590000100000000000000000010000000
1110940200000000000000000000000000000002000000
11109501019759704191302275310110022110000000001200000100000000000000090010000000
1110950200000000000000000000000000000002000000
11109601019059704191319275310110022110000010001420000100000000000000000010000000
1110960200000000000000000000000000000001000000
11109701018859804191319275310110022110000010002030000100000000000000000010000000
1110970200001000000000000000000000000002000000
11109801018659904191302275310110022110100000006000000100000000000000000010000000
11109802000010000000000000000000000000012000000
11109901020460405201319250310110022010000000000400000100000000000000000010000000
1110990200001000000001000000000000000002000000
11110001123724205080719300310120032121000010006450000100000000000000000010000000
111100020010100000000000000000000010110102000 0
11110101123824605080711300310120032121000010003501100100000000000000000010000000
111101020010001000000000000010000001102000000
11110201123724905080719300310120132121000000001430000100000000000000000011010000
11110202000010100000000000000000001101102020000
11110301123324405080719325310110122010000010001091100100000000000000000010000000
111103020000101000000000000000000001002000000
11110401123524705080713325310110022110000010000440000100000000000000000010000000
1111040200001000000000000000000000000002010000
11110501123524405080713325310120022022000010001080000100000000000000000011010000
11110502001100000000030000010000001102010000
11110601123924605080711300310120022022000010000900000100000000000000090001001000
111106020000000000000000000000000000102010000
11110701023924805080719300310120022022000010001070000100000000000000000000000000
111107020010100000000000000000000001002000000
11110801124124806080711300310120022022000010000950000100000000000000000001001000
111108020000100000000000000000000001002000000
11110901124125006080713300310120132121000010001500000100000000000000000000000000
111109020000000000000000000000000001002000000
11111001024024506080701300310120122110000010000180000100000000000000000000000000
111110020000100000000000000000000001001000000
11111101024225106080719300310120132021000000001060000100000000000000000000000000
111111020000030100000000000000000000102000000
11111201024325106080717300310120022110000010000411300100000000000000000000000000
111112020000000000001000000000000000001020000
11111301024424606080711300310120032121000000002080000100000000000000000000000000
1111130200000000000000000000000000000002010000
11111401124625006080711300310120022022000000004641300100000000000000000001001000
111114020010101000000000000000000010110201010 0
11111501024524606080717300310120022110000010001140000100000000000000000000000000
1111150200001000000000000000000000000001010000
11111601124325206080717300310110122110000010003011300100000000000000000000000000
1111160200100000000002100000000000001102010000
11111701024824706080711275310120032121000010002160000100000000000000000000000000
11111702001100100000000000000000001101010000
11111801024824406080717275310120032121000010001370000100000000000000000001000010

1111180200000000000000000000000000000001010000
11111901024324106080713300310120032021000010001850000100000000000000000000000000
111119020000001000000000000000000000000002010100
11112001024524106080711300310120132021000010000670000100000000000000000001001000
1111200200000000000000000000000000000002000000
11112101024623306070717275310120021010000010001880000100000000000000000001010000
11112102000000000000000000000000001002010000
11112201024022506070717275310120032121000010000648000010000000000000000000000000
11112202000000000000000000000000000001001010000
11112301024623106070717275310110021110000010001370000100000000000000000000000000
1111230200000000000000000000000000000001000000
11112401024423106070713275310120022110000010000930000100000000000000000000000000
111124020000000010000000000000000000000000000
11112501124023406070701300310120021110000000000451300100000000000000000000000000
111125020010100000000000000000000000001002010100
11112601023723205070711300310120021110000010000841300100000000000000000000000000
111126020000000000000000000000000000001002010000
11112701023323605070711325310120021010000010000900000100000000000000000000000000
1111270200000000000000000000000000000002000000
11112801029227807090801300310120022022000010000700000100000000000000000000000000
111128020010100000000000000000000001001020100 00
11112901129027907090813300310120022122000010001200000100000000000000000000000000
1111290200100000000000000000000000101102010000
11113001028025107080813250310120022122000000000720000100000000000000000000000000
1111300200100000000000000000000000000001000000
11113101028125407080813250310120022122000010002880000100000000000000000000000000
111131020000000000000000000000000001101000000
11113201027925206080813250310120022122000010000850000100000000000000000000000000
1111320200001000000000000000000000000000000000
11113301127825106080811225310120132121000000006400000100000000000000000000000000
1111330200000100000000000000000000000012010100
11113401127724906080802225310120132121000010006000000100000000000000000000000000
1111340200100000001000000000000000001002010200
11113501127624706080811225310120132121000010005600000100000000000000000001000010
111135020000000001000000000000000001111010100
11113601027325006080811225310120122122000000001650000100000000000000000000000000
111136020000000000000000000000000001101000100
11113701126725706080813225310110122010000010001113000000000000000000000000000000
111137020000000000000000000000000000111010100
11113801027325406080811225310120132021000000007000000100000000000000000000000000
111138020000001000000000000000000001101000100
11113901027425706080811250310120032021000010000740000100000000000000000000000000
11113902000000010000100000000000000100000000
11114001127025906080813225310120022022000010000600000100000000000000000000000000
11114002000010000000010000000000000200010000
11114101027425506080801225310120022122000010001500000100000000000000000000000000
111141020011000000000000000000000000111000100
11114201026724806080719225310120122022000010003681300100000000000000000010000000
1111420201000000000000000000000000000001000000
11114301026424906080719225310120132021000010002510000100000000000000000010000000
1111430200001000000000000000000000000001010000
11114401126024906080719250310120132021000010004570000100000000000000000020000000
111144020010100000000000000000000001000000100
11114501125624906080713275110120132121000000001860000100000000000000000021001000
11114502000010100000000000000000000100000000
11114601025924506080711250110120022110000010000531300100000000000000000021010000
11114602000000000000000000000000000000000010100
11114701025825406080713250110110122010000010000840000100000000000000000010000000
111147020000000000000000000000000000000000000000
11114801126025406080719250110120122022000010004501300100000000000000000012000010
```

11114802000010000000000000000000000102020100
11114901125926106080819250310110122022000010006001300100000000000000000012000010
11114902000010000000000000000000100102010100
11115001020460605201319225310110022010000010000740000100000000000000000000000000
11115002000000000000000000000000000001000000
11115101020760905201302225310110022010000000017940000100000000000000000000000000
11115102000010000000000000000000100002000000
11115201120360805201302225310110022110000000001450000100000000000000000000000000
11115202000010000000000000000000000002000000
11115301120461105201319200310110022110000000006140000100000000000000000001001000
11115302000010001000020000000000101012000100
11115401020061505201319200310110121110000000001890000100000000000000000000000000
11115402000010000000000000000000000001000000
11115501115465503211419150310110122122101000002760000100000000010000000020000000
11115502000010000000000000000000001002000100
11115601015665503211402150310110022010000000001630000100000000000000000020000000
11115602000000000000010000000000001002000000
11115701115665303211419150310110122022100010001430000100000000000000000021001000
11115702000010000000000000000000001002000000
11115801115465403211419175310110122010000000001830000100000000000000000020000000
11115802000010000000000000000000001002000000
11115901115865103211402175310110022110000010006500000100000000000000000020000000
11115902000000000000000000000000000002000100
11116001115465203211419175310110122010000000002610000100000000000000000020000000
11116002000010000000000000000000001002000000
11116101115465003211402175310110022110100010006400000100000000000026000020000000
11116102000010000009900000000000100002000000
11116201015464903211419175310120022110000010003320000100000000000000000020000000
11116202000010000000010000000000000002010000
11116301116064804211402175310110021010000000000610000100000000000000000010000000
11116302000010000000000000000000000102010100
11116401015564703211402200310120121110000000000800000100000000000000000010000000
11116402000010000000000000000000000002000100
11116501015964703211402175310120121010000000000440000100000000000000000010000000
11116502000000000000000000000000000002000000
11116601015564503211420200310111022010000010002010000100000000010000000011010000
11116602000010000000000000000000000002000100
11116701115364403211402200310120022110000010000880000100000000000000000011000010
11116702000010000009900000000000000002000000
11116801015464203211420200310110022010000000000600000100000000000000000010000000
11116802101000000000000000000000000002000000
11116901115565703211402150110110022012000010013980000100000000000000000020000000
11116902000010000009900000000000000102000100
11117001115466403221402125410110022022110010050150001010000337110000800020000000
11117002000010000000000000000000101112020000
11117101016066103221402125310110022122000010004270000100000000000000000010000000
11117102000000000000000000000000000002020000
11117201116266103221420125310110022010100010001940000100000000000000010011001000
11117202000000000000000000000000100002010100
11117301015666803221402125310110022022000000000451000100000000000000000011000010
11117302000000000000000000000000001102010000
11117401115667003221419125310110022022000010003270000100000000000000000011001000
11117402000010000000000000000000001102010000
11117501115367003221402125310120032021000000005830000100000000000000000010000000
11117502000000000000010000000000001102010000
11117601115166903221421125310120032021000010002570000100000000000000000010000000
11117602001000100000010000010000101102000000
11117701115066203221402125310120032021000010022480001000000001980000080011001000
11117702000010000000010000000000102212010000
11117801014966203221420125310120032021000000006120000100000000000000000010000000
11117802000000000000000000000000100002010000
11117901114865503211419150310120122122000010012940000100000000000000000011000010
11117902000000000000010000000000001102010100
11118001014365103211412175310120122022000010004110000100000000000000000011001000
11118002000000000000000000000000100002010000
11118101014765003211421175310120122110000010001610000100000000000000000010000000
11118102000000000000010000000000001102010000
11118201014564403211420200310110022110000010005170000100000000000000000010000000
11118202000010000000010000000000000102010000
11118301014464603211402175310110022110000010001750000100000000000000000010000000
11118302000000000000000000000000000002010000
11118401014464903211402175310110022010000010001250000100000000000000000010000000
11118402000000000000000000000000000002010000
11118501014964903211419175310120122110000010002880000100000000000000000010000000
11118502000000000000000000000000001002000000
11118601014564203211412200310110022010000000000900000100000000000000000010000000
11118602000000000000000000000000100102010000
11118701014564003211402225310110022110000010001200000100000000000000000010000000
11118702000010000000020000000000000002000000
11118801014964803211419175310110022110000010002880000100000000000000000011000010
11118802000010000000000000000000000012010000
11118901014964303211412200310110022110000000000820000100000000000000000010000000
11118902000000000000000000000000000002000000
11119001114764303211402200310110022010000010001000000100000000000000000011010000
11119002000000000000000000000000000002000000
11119101014563703211412225310110022110000010000440000100000000000000000011001000
11119102000000000000010000000000100002000000
11119201014864103211421225310110122110000010000730000100000000000000000010000000
11119202000000000000010000000000000002000000
11119301015064203211419225310110022110000010001250000100000000000000000010000000
11119302000010000000000000000000001102000000
11119401014763603211402225310120022010000010000800000100000000000000000011000010
11119402000000000000010000000000000002000000
11119501014863403211420250310120022110000000000580000100000000000000000010000000
11119502001000000000010000000000100002010000
11119601114863303211420250310110022010000000000720000100000000000000000010000000
11119602000000000000010000000000000012000000
11119701014963903211421225310110022110000000000500000100000000000000000010000000
11119702000000000000000000000000000002000000
11119801016564304211419175310110022100000010000900000100000000010000000010000000
11119802000010000000000000000000000002000000
11119901016464504211419175310110022110000000000790000100000000000000000010000000
11119902000010000000010000000000000002000000
11120001026026606080813250310110122010000010001000000100000000000000000010000000
11120002000000000000000000000000000000000100
11120101026226106080813250310110032021000010000601300100000000000000000011001000
11120102001000000000000000000000000001010100
11120201126225406080811250310120032021000010001111300100000000000000000010000000
11120202000000000000000000000000000110000000
11120301126325706080813250310120132121000010002510000100000000000000000010000000
11120302001000100000000000000000000102000000
11120401126426006080811225310120132021000010001210000100000000000016000010000000
11120402001000000000000000000000000002000000
11120501126325806080813225310120132021000000000290000000000000000000000010000000
11120502000000000000000000000000000000000000
11120601026625406080813225310110122010000000000351300500000000000037001010000000
11120602000000000000000000000000000000000000
11120701126625206080819225310120132021000000001810000100000000000000000011011000
11120702000010000000000000000000000101020000
11120801125926006080819250310120022022000010002621300100000000000000000011001000

136

```
11120802001000000000000001000000100102010100
11120901125926206080811250310120022022000010000630000100000000000000000011001000
1112090200000010000000000000000000002102010000
11121001125926506080811250310120122022000000000591300100000000000220000013010000
1112100200000000000000000000000000002112020000
11121101125826506080813250310120022022000010001040000100000000000000000011010000
111211020000100010000000000000000000102000100
11121201125726506080811250310120022022000010002380000100000000000000000010000000
1112120200000000000000000000000000000002010000
11121301125625806080711250110120122010000010000980000100000000000000000020000000
1112130200000000000000000000000000001102010000
11121401025425906080701275110110023010000010010031301000000053500000000020000000
111214020000100000000000000000000000100000100
11121501125525206080719275110120132021000010003821300100000000000000900010000000
1112150200001000000000000000000000000002020100
11121601125325106080721275110120132021000010002170000100000000000000000010000000
1112160200000010000000000000000000000102000000
11121701125524606080719275110120032121000010009780000100000000000000000010000000
111217020010001000000000000000000000101101020000
11121801025325506080711275110120132021000010003190000100000000000016000011010000
11121802011110300000000000000000000001101010000
11121901025224906080721275310120022022000010010260000100000000000000000011001000
111219020011002020000000000000000000001001000000
11122001125025406080719275310120032021000010002800000100000000000000000011010000
1112200200100010001000000000000000000001101000000
11122101124725206080713275310120132021000010004890000100000000000000000012011000
111221020010000000001000000000001011000020000
11122201025024506080711275310120022022000010003711100100000000000000000010000000
11122202001000100000000000000000000000001010100
11122301125025006080713275310120022022000000001190000100000000000016000011001000
111223020000100000000000000000000000001101000000
11122401124924006080721275310120132021000010001560000100000000000000000010000000
11122402000010000000000000000000000000102010000
11122501125123906070719275310120032121000010000991300100000000000000000010000000
11122502000010100000000000000000000000000000000100
11122601125923206070701250310120132121000010039001100100000000000120900022011102
111226020016001000100101000000001102202020100
11122701125122506070701250310120132121011010028001300100000000000120800012110001
111227020000100020000000000000000000102212020100
11122801124121606070701250310120132121000010031981300100000000000220800013011000
111228020000101000000000000000000000101202020100
11122901123221205070701250310120132121000010021121300100000000000000080011000010
111229020000100010000000000000000000001202020000
11123001025022806070719250310120022110000010000490000000000000000000000010000000
1112300200000000000000000000000000000000000000000
11123101023322005070711275310120122110000010001571300100000000000000000010000000
111231020000000000000000000000000000000001000000
11123201123121505070713250310120122022000010003290000100000000000000000010000000
111232020010000000000000000000000000001000010000
11123301123522005070713275310120022010000010001101300100000000000000000011010002
11123302000000000000000000000000000001100020000
11123401023021805070719275310120022010000010001600000100000000000000000010000000
111234020000100000000000000000000000000001000000
11123501121620005060701250310120132121000010036790000100000000000000080001010000
11123502001000000000020200000000011022020200000
11123601120719605060702250310120132021000010005280000100000000000120800020110000
111236020000100000000001000000000001011010200000
11123701120619905060719250310120032121000010002050000100000000000000000000000000
111237020000000000000000000000000000000001000000
11123801019920004060701250310120132121000010010800000100000000000000080000000000
```

```
1112380200001030000000000000000000000101010000
11123901119020204060711250310120132021000010005570000100000000000160800021001000
111239020011100000100000000000000102212010000
11124001119520804060719250310120132021000000001320000100000000000000000011010000
111240020010101000000100000000000001102000000
11124101019220704060719250310120132121000000001090000100000000000160000010000000
11124102001000000000000000000000100000100|00
11124201119019904060719225310120132021000000001094000010000000000016080011010000
11124202001000000000000000000000000001002020000
11124301119119704060711225310120132021000000002960000100000000000160000010000000
11124302001000100000000000000000000101100020000
11124401019220804060719250310120132121000000002160000100000000000000000010000000
11124402000000100000000000000000000000101010000
11124501018620504060719250310110022010000000002600000100000000000000000010000000
111245020010002000000000000000000000000001000000
11124601018320404060719250310120022110000000003280000100000000000000000010000000
111246020010000000000000000000000000000001000000
111247011180209040607012503101200221220000000045900001000000000001600011000010
1112470200001000000000000000100001001020100000
11124801019521104070719275310130122022000000002890000100000000000000000010000000
111248020000000000000000000000000000000102010000
11124901018920904060711250310120122122000000003400001000000000000000000010000000
1112490200000000000000000000000000000000001010000
11125001016164004211412200310110022010000010000700000100000000000000000010000000
1112500200100000000000100000000000000002010000
11125101115464003211420225310110022110100010001640000100000000001000000010000000
1112510200100000000000000000100000010020100000
11125201115863703211420225310110022010000010000970000100000000000000000011001000
1112520200100000100000000000100001001020100000
11125301115363603211402225310110022110000000003030000100000000000000000010000000
111253020000100000000100000000001000020000000
11125401015463403211420250310110022110000010004190000100000000000000000010000000
1112540200000000000000000000100000000002010000
11125501016264804211419175310110022010000000001170000100000000000000000010000000
1112550200000000000000000000000000000000201  000
11125601016265104211419150310110022010000000002330000100000000000000000010000000
11125602000000000000000000000000000000012000000
11125701016464804211402150310110022010000000001600001000000000000000000010000000
1112570200000000000000000000000000000000002000000
11125801016164304211402200310110022010000000000750000100000000000000000010000000
1112580200000000000000000000000000000000002000000
11125901015864203211419200310110022010000000000480000100000000010000000010000000
1112590200001000000000000000000000000000002000000
11126001115263103211402250310110022010000010013490000100000000000000000020000000
111260020001000000009900000000000100002000000
11126101114963203211412250310110022110000010002280000100000000000000000010000000
111261020010000000000200000100001000020200000
11126201015363003201411250310110022010000000002370000100000000000000000010000000
1112620200000000000000000000000000000000002000000
11126301015863503211419225310110022110000010002670000100000000000000000010000000
111263020000000000000100000000000000002000000
11126401115863203211420225310110022110000010003950000100000000000000000010000000
111264020000000000000100000100011000120000000
11126501116262104201419250310110022010000010002870000100000000000000000010000000
1112650200000000000000000000000000000000002000000
11126601016761804201420250310110022110000000010970000100000000000000000010000000
1112660200000000000000000000000000000000002000000
11126701016961104201402250310120022110000000001170000100000000000000000010000000
1112670200000000000000000000000000000000002000000
11126801017660904201320275310110022110000000003770000100000000000000000010000000
```

```
1112680200000000000000000001000000000002000000
11126901017460904201319275310110022110000000006681300100000000000000000010000000
1112690200000000000000000000000000000002000100
11127001017860504201319275310110022010000000007400000100000000000000000010000000
1112700200000000000000000000000000000002000000
11127101017960204201320275310110022110000000002240000100000000000000000010000000
1112710200000000000000000000000000000002010000
11127201018260104201302275310110022110000000004640000100000000000000000010000000
1112720200000000000000000000000000000002000000
11127301023050005160002275410110022110000000027781102000000028100000000010000000
1112730200001000000000001000100000000002000000
11127401022850405160002275310110022110000000002800000100000000000000000010000000
1112740200001000000000020000000000000002000000
11127501022950805160002275410110022110000010021060000100000000000000000010000000
1112750200001000000109900000000000001002000100
11127601023151405170020275310110022010000010000530000100000000000000000010000000
1112760200000100000000000000010000001002000000
11127701023251405170002275310110022010000010000700000100000000000000000010000000
1112770200001000000000000000000000001002000000
11127801023451405170002275310110022010000010001751100100000000000000000010000000
1112780200000000000000000000000000000002000000
11127901023245805150002200410110022110100010010190000100000000000000000010000000
1112790200101000000000000000000000000002010100
11128001019640204131212250310110022110000000000181000010000000000000000010000000
1112800200100000000000100000000000000002000000
11128101021839905131202300310110022110000000000090000010000000000000000010000000
1112810200000000000000100000000000000002000000
11128201020939405131220275310110022110000000000054000010000000000000000010000000
1112820201000000000000000000000000000002000000
11128301021139505131220275310110022010000010000720000100000000000000000010000000
1112830200100000000000000000000000000002000000
11128401021540005131202300310110022010000000001050000100000000000000000010000000
1112840200000000000000000000000000000002000000
11128501021240205131202300310110022010000010000500000100000000000000000000000000
1112850200000000000000000000000000000002000000
11128601020840405131202300310110022010000000000065000010000000000000000010000000
1112860200000000000000000000000000000002000000
11128701020840705131220300310110022110000000000065000010000000000000000010000000
1112870200001000000000000000000000000002010000
11128801020740605131219300310110022110000010002540000100000000000000000010000000
1112880200000000000009900000000000000002000000
11128901120740405131219300310110022110000010000840000100000000000000000010000000
1112890200000000000009900000000001010012010000
11129001121540905131220300310110022010000010000850000100000000000000000010000000
1112900200000000000001000001000010001200010000
11129101121741205131220300310120022010000010000980000100000000000000000010000000
1112910200000000000000000000000001000120000000
11129201021241105131219300310110022110000000000950000100000000000000000010000000
1112920200000000000001000001000000000002010000
11129301021041205131220300310110022010000010000920000100000000000000000010000000
1112930200000000000000000000000000000002000000
11129401120540405131219300310110022110000010001270000100000000000000008001000000
1112940200001000000099000000000000000012010000
11129501020640105131219300310110022110000010001400000100000000000000008001000000
1112950200000000000009900000000000000002010000
11129601020440805131219275310110022010000000000150000010000000000000000010000000
1112960200000000000000000000000000000002000000
11129701020739705131202275310110022110000010002100000100000000000000000010000000
1112970200000000000000000000000000000002000000
11129801020440305131219275310110022010000010006430000100000000000000009001000000
1112980200000000000000001000000000000002010000
11129901120140805131219275310110022010000010003590000100000000000000000010000000
1112990200001000000009900000000000100002010000
11130001018820904060722250310110022110000010001270000100000000000000000010000000
1113000200000000000000000000000000000001010000
11130101019221104070719275310110122110000000001240000100000000000000000010000000
1113010200001000000000000000100000010020100000
11130201118721104070713275310120032121000000013500000100000000000160000210110000
1113020200001010000000000000000000112202020000
11130301119721304070711275310120022010000010001200000100000000000000000010000000
1113030200010100000000000000000000001002000000
11130401119721404070719275310120122110000000003601300100000000000000000010000000
1113040200100010000000000000000000000002000000
11130501118421204070713275310110122010000000009551300100000000000000000010000000
1113050200001010000000000000100001021020100000
11130601121123505070711350110110022110100000014341101210100217210000000010000000
1113060200001000000000100010000112202000000
11130701121423305070701350310120032021100010006660000100000000000000000010000000
1113070200001000000000100000000001022020000000
11130801120923005070711350310120132021000010002000000100000000000000000010000000
1113080200001000000000000000100001022120100000
11130901120423505070701350310120122122000010050321800100000000000000000011010000
1113090200001010200099001000000111220201010000
11131001120923605070701350110120122122000010005201300100000000000000000010000000
1113100200001010000000000000000111202010100
11131101121922705070711325310120132121000010002341300100000000000000000010000000
1113110200100000000000100000000001010120000000
11131201122323205070716325310120032121000000000900000100000000000000000010000000
1113120200100000000000000000000001012120000000
11131301121823105070716350310120032021000000001170000100000000000000000010000000
1113130200000000000000000000000001020020000000
11131401122323205070716325310120032021000000001000000100000000000000000010000000
1113140200000000000000000000000001022020000000
11131501022023505070716350310120032021000000003000000100000000000000000010000000
1113150200001000000000000000100001022020000000
11131601122523405070716325310120022122000000004030000100000000000000009001101000
1113160200001020000000100000100011022020000000
11131701122123305070716350310120032021000000002410000100000000000000000010000000
1113170200001000000000100000000001022020000000
11131801121423005070701350310120032121000010006441300100000000000000000021010000
1113180200001000100000000000000001022020100000
11131901121422805070701350310120032021000000001460000100000000000000000011010000
1113190200011010000000000000100001012120000000
11132001121823005070716325310120032021000000001560000100000000000000000010000000
1113200200000000100000000000000001010020000000
11132101121322605070716325310120132121000000001290000100000000000000000010000000
1113210200000000000000000000000000020020000000
11132201121222505070716325310120032021000010002211300100000000000000000010000000
1113220200100000000000000000000001020020001000
11132301122022905070704325310120032121000010002570000100000000000000000010000000
1113230200001000001000000000000001020020001000
11132401121222605070701325310120032121000000006300000100000000000000000021010000
1113240200001000001000000000100001022020000000
11132501120322905070701350110120022122000010034611400100000000000000000011000010
1113250200001020100000000000000110221201000000
11132601120622605070704325310120132021000010001830000100000000000000000010000000
1113260200001000000000000000000001012020000000
11132701120522405070704325310120022122000010018561101000000050000160000200000000
1113270200001010001002000000000000020020000000
11132801120322605070704325310120032021000000001950000100000000000000000010000000
```

111328020000101000000000000000000001101002020000
111329011200227050707163253101200320210000100003800001000000000000000000011000010
11132902000010000000000000000000000100202010000
111330011197228040707163253101200320210000000016700001000000000000000000010000000
11133002000010100000000000000000000102202000000
111331011204222050707113253101200320210000100032500001000000000000000000010000000
11133102000010000000000000000000002202000000
111332010205222050707103253101100220100000000007200001000000000000000000010000000
11133202000000000000000000000000000002020000
111333011203221050707163253101200320210000000027200001000000000000000000010000000
11133302000010000010000000000000000121202000000
111334010203220050707103003101200321210000100013000001000000000000000000010000000
11133402000010000000000000000000000002010000
111335011203219050707163003101201221220000100019200001000000000000000000010000000
1113350200001000000000000000000000122000000
111336011197218040707163003101200320210000100076700001000000000000000000010000000
1113360200001010000000000000010000000102000000
111337011201219050707113003101200320210000100024100001000000000000000000010000000
1113370200000000000000000000000000022002000000
111338010192220040707043003101201220220000100007600001000000000000000000010000000
1113380200000100000000000000000000010202000000
111339011194221040707113003101200321210000100015311001000000000000000000010000000
1113390200100010000000000000000000002002000100
111340010199217040707163003101200320210000100012600001000000000000000000010000000
1113400200000000000010000000000000100002000000
111341010193217040707043003101200321210000100010500001000000000000000000010000000
1113410200000000000000000000000001100002000000
111342011196216040707163003101200320210000100144000001000000000000000000011000000
1113420200001000000020000000000000100002000000
111343010207219050707183003101200220100000000006611001000000000000000000010000000
1113430200000000000000000000000000000000000000
111344010209218050707163003101200320210000100084200001000000000000000000010000000
1113440200001000000000000000000000000002000000
111345010206217050707163003101200220220000000004420001000000000000000000010000000
1113450200001000000000000000000000000001000000
111346011206216050707193003101200320210000000003500001000000000000000000011000010
1113460200001000000000000000000000000002000010
111347010209222050707013253101101221101000000012817001000000000000000000010000000
1113470200001000000000000000000000001002000000
111348010211222050707113253101200221101000100008100001000000000000000000010000000
1113480200001000000000000000000000000002010100
111350010203400051312022753101100220100000000009000001000000000000000000010000000
1113500200001000000000000000000000000002000000
111351010201404051312022753101100220100000000019300001000000000000000000010000000
1113510200000000000000000000000000000002000100
111352010202408051312122753101100221100000000014700001000000000000000000010000000
1113520200000000000030000000000000100002000000
111353010199409041312192753101100221100000000008500001000000000000000000010000000
1113530200001000000010000000000000000002000000
111354010197410041312122503101100221100000000002900001000000000000000000010000000
1113540200000000000000000000000000000002000000
111355010200402041312025003101100220100000000010500001000000000000000000010000000
1113550200000000000000000000000000000002010100
111356010203396051312022503101100220100000000013800001000000000000000000010000000
1113560200000000000000000000000000000002000000
111357011253194060609172001101200320210000000021800001000000000000000000010000000
1113570210100000000000000000000000101002000000
111358011255196060609172001101200320210000000031500001000000000000000000010000000
1113580200101000000000000000000000102002020000
111359011253197060609172001101200320210000000004400001000000000000000000010000000
1113590200001010000000000000000001112000020000
111360011250197060609202001101200321210000000025200001000000000000000000011001000
1113600200000000000000000000010000102202000000
111361011252193060609202001101200221220000100013800001000000000000000000010000000
1113610200000000000000000000000000010002010000
111362011253191060609202001101200320210000000020000001000000000000000000010000000
1113620200001010100100000000000000122212010000
111363011106314021002013503101100220100000100013500001000000000000000000010000000
1113630200000000000000000000000000001102000000
111364010113309021002013753101100220100000100007000001000000000000000000010000000
1113640200000100000000000000000000022002000000
111365011112311021002013503101100220100000100023100001000000000000000000010000000
1113650200001000000000000000000000001102000000
111367011262193060609082001101200320210000100015700001000000000000000000010000000
1113670200001000000000000000000000112101020100
111368011263192060609202001101200320210000000008300001000000000000000000010000000
1113680200000000000000010000000000102200000000
111369011261190060609232001101100221100000000013000001000000000000000000010000000
1113690200111000000000000000000001002102000000
111370011262191060609202001101200220220000000018200001000000000000000000011001000
1113700200010200000000000000000000102200000000
111371011259189060609232001101200321210000000010100001000000000000000000011011000
1113710200100010000000000000000000122202000000
111372011262189060609232003101200321210000000009900001000000000000000000011011000
1113720200100010000000000000000000102202000000
111373011263188060609232003101200221220000100006000001000000000000000000010000000
1113730200110100000010000000000000002202000000
111374011260188060609202001101200321210000000005900001000000000000016000010000000
1113740200001010000000100000000000122200000100
111375011258187060609202001101200320210000000029200001000000000000000000011010000
1113750200000000010000100000000000112100010000
111376011260187060609202001101200320210000100015400001000000000000000000011001000
1113760200000100000000000000000000122000000000
111377011263188060609232001101200321210000000021500001000000000000000000011010000
1113770200110010000020000000000000102212000000
111378011261186060609232001101200320210000000015200001000000000000000000011011000
1113780200010202000010000000000000102212010000
111379010258186060609202001101200320210000000003500001000000000000000000010000000
1113790200000000000000000000000000002200000100
111380011255187060609202001101200320210000000011100001000000000000000000011001000
1113800200010000000010000000000000122201020000
111381011255186060609202001101200321210000000011300001000000000000000000011010000
1113810200000000010000000000000000122102000000
111382010259184060609232001101201321210000000023800001000000000000000000011011000
1113820200110000000010000000000000210000000000
111383011262185060609232003101200221100000100028213001000000000000000000010000000
1113830200000100000000000000000000002000000100
111384011255185060609232003101200221220000000020800001000000000000000000011001000
1113840200001010000000000000000000002012000000
111385011256183060609232003101200321210000000029800001000000000000000000011011000
1113850200110000000000010000010000101202000000
111386010257189060609162001101200220220000100006000001000000000000000000010000000
1113860200001000000000000000000000000002000000
111387011257248060609162001101200220220000100026000001000000000000000000010000000
1113870200001000000000000000000000000002000000
111388011253183060609232003101200321210000000019800001000000000000000000010000000
1113880200110000000000000000000000002002010000
111389011256181060609232003101201320210000000035900001000000000000000000010000000
1113890200110000010000000000000000002202000000
111390011253182060609232003101201321210000000011700001000000000000000000010000000

```
11139002000010000000000000000000010220200000O
111391010255180060509212003101201320210000000004000001000000000000000000010000000
11139102000010000000000000000000002100000100
111392011256178060509232003101201320210000000216000010000000000000000000011001000
1113920200001000000000000000000001120000000000
111393011255176060509181753101200320210000000013600001000000000000000000010000000
1113930200000000000000000000000002000000000
111394010255177060509081753101201320210000000021600001000000000000000000010000000
1113940200001000000000000000000000020000000000
111395011253188060609082001101200321210000100006000001000000000000000000010000000
1113950200001010000000000000000012200200000O
111396010253187060609082001101200220220000100010800000100000000000000000010000000
11139602000010000000000000000000002002000000
111397011250189060609082003101200220220000000015000001000000000000000000010000000
11139702000010000000000000000000002002000000
111398011251191060609082001101200320210000100024000001000000000000000000010000000
11139802000010000000000000000000002202010000
111399011250190060609082003101200220220000000025200001000000000000000000010000000
11139902000010000000000000010000022002000000
111400011124340031103173253101100221100000100023600001000000000000000009001101000O
111400020000100000000000000000000000002000000
111401011011353001101012753101100221100000100012000001000000000000000000010000000
11140102000010000000000000000000002002000000
111402011012357001101012503101200220100000100028000001000000000000000000010000000
111402020000100000000100000000001020020000O0
111403010011361001201012503101100221100000100030800001000000000000000000010000000
111403020000100000000100000000000122010000O0
111404011016358001101012503101100220100000100020400001000000000000000000010000000
11140401000010000000000000000000002200000000
111405011012354001101012503101100220100000100018000001000000000000000000010000000
111405010000000000000000000000000002202000000
111406010017360001101012503101200220100000000006600001000000000000000000010000000
11140602000010000000000000000000002200000000
111407010131241030802043253101100221100000100006200001000000000000000000000000000
11140702001000000000000000000000101102000000
111408011123244030802173253101200221100000100006600001000000000000000000000000000
111408020000000000000000000000000102202000000
111409011123247030802043253101100220100000100004000000100000000000000000000000000
111409020000000000000000000000000102202000000
111410010120227030702042253101100221100000100013500001000000000000000000001010000
1114100200000000000000000000000000000002000000
111411011114227020702042253101422443633300200006424990990000000224920393422222O
1114110222222989822298223323222244444444440222
111412010089324021001013503101100220100000000010200001000000000000000000010000000
111412020000100000000100000000001222120000O0
111413010080328011001013503101100220100000000051700001000000000000000000010000000
111413020001101000000000000000000001102000000
111414010092324021001013253101100220100000000048000001000000000000000000010000000
111414020000000000000000000010001001102000000
111415010087331021101013253101100220100000000026000001000000000000000000010000000
111415020000000000000000100000000000111120000O0
111416010087328021001013503101100220100000100035100001000000000000000000010000000
111416020000000000000000000000000000012120000O0
111418010091331021101013003101100220100000000008000001000000000000000000010000000
111418020000000000000000000000000000000010000O0
111419010092329021001013003101100220100000000006000001000000000000000000010000000
111419020000000000000000000000000000001002000000
111420010095319021001013253101100220100000000007500001000000000000000000010000000
11142002000010000000000000000000001022220000O0
111421010101315021002013503101100220100000100010100001000000000000000000010000000

11142102000010000000000000000000001022020000O0
111422010096319021001013253101100220100000000000800001000000000000000000010000000
11142202000010000000000000000000001020020000O0
111423010099316021001013503101100220100000000000800001000000000000000000010000000
111423020010000000000000000000000000021020000O0
111425011255188060609172001101200320210000100007000001000000000000000000010000000
111425020000001000000000000000000000022000000000
111426011226228050707083003101201220101000100072800001000000000000000000000000000
111426020010000000000000000001000000110100000O
111427011090328021001013253101100221100000000019200001000000000001000000010000000
111427020000100000000100000000001100120000O0
111428010347254080800022253101100220100000100006600001000000000000000000011011000
111428020000100000000000000000000000000000020000
111429010312249070800022253101100220100000100018900001000000000000000000010000000
111429020001000000000000000000000000000000020000
111430011249233060707132753101200320210000000008400001000000000000000000010000000
111430020010000000000100000000000002202020000
111431011252235060707132753101200320210000000015000001000000000000000000011001000
111431020000000000000000000000000000002020000
111432011256234060707222501101200321210000000020014001000000000000000000010000000
11143202000010000000010000000000000000202000O
111433011254230060707112503101100220100000000008811001000000000000000000010000000
11143302000010000000000000000000000000100000O
111434010186311041002014003101100220100104100160016001000000000000000000000000000
111434020000000000010000000000000022212000000
111435010008362001201012503101100220100000100014914001000000000100000000010000000
111435020000000000000000000000000000220000000O
111436010013365001201012503101100220100000100028000001000000000000000000010000000
111436020000000000000000000000001002201000000
111437010016363001201012503101100220100000100016000001000000000000000000010000000
111437020000000000000000000000000000000100000O
111438010012368001201012253101100220100000100035000001000000000000000000010000000
111438020000101000000000000000000001210101000O
111439010015369001201012253101100220100000100029414001000000000000000000010000000
111439020000100000000000010000000022000000O0
111440010017370001201012253101100220100000100039200001000000000000000000010000000
1114400200000000000000100000000000000200001000O
111441010011371001201012253101100220100000100018000001000000000000000000010000000
111441020000100000000000000000000021000000O0
111442010010372001201012253101200220100000000014000001000000000000000000010000000
111442020000100000000000000000000021000000O0
111443010019372001201012253101100220100000100079300001000000000000000000010000000
11144302000010000000000000000000002000000000
111444010023374001201012003101100220100000000023114001000000000000000000010000000
111444020000002000000000000000000001220000000O
111445010025378001201012003101100220100000100061600000000000000000000080010000000
1114450200000000000000000000000000000000000000
111446010026369001201012253101100220100000100018000001000000000000000000010000000
11144602000010000000000000000000001100000000
111447010140287030902014251101100220401268116050011693420723646100015001100001O
1114470200001000000100000000000010444444440101
111448011283322071005023254101100220100000000122000013000003443000000000210000010
1114480200001000000000000000000000111110000000
111449011155628032014002504101100210102000000110216012111001556100000000200000000
11144902000010000000990000000000000000010000000
111450011199590041913022754101100221102000100237900013000002222100000000310000010
111450020000000000000000000010000200003010000
111451010213601052013022503101100211100000000006050002210000038310000000031001000
1114510200000000000000000000000000000001010100
111452011215607052013022253101300221102000000006560001210100108310000000030000000
```

```
11145202010010000000020000000001200003030000
11145301125437606121202350210110022010100000011471101211100134600000000001001000
11145302000100000000100000000000000001010000
11145401036826609080002200410110022010100000003331101000000038100000000000000000
11145402000000000000000000000000000001000010100
11145501133035008111002250410130021010010000004821101210100020110000000021010000
11145502010010000000000000000000000101010000
11145601118232404100402375410110022010020010022001101400000209610001500210110000
11145602000010000000000000000000121111000100
11145701118833404110401375410110022010010210051361110120000000101700002101 0000
11145702000010100001000020010000101211000100
11145801108230102100101400410110022010120010132751201211001363510161500210110000
11145802000019900001000000000000010221100 0100
11145901120033604110402375410110022010110010017631101211100326910000500210010000
11145902000000000000000000000000000001001010100
11146001124733406110502350210110022010110010016961201211100271710000000011000010
11146002000000000000001000000000000111010101 00
11146101107131401100101400410110022010110110020161101211100204010000800210100000
11146101000010000001000001000000102222000001
11146201118233304110402375410110022040020110029311810210000000010000500210110000
11146202000010000000100000101000001111000000 1
11146301113832603100301375410110022010110110039691601211000722210000800210110000
11146302000110001001010101000000111100000100
11146401125819206060921200210300220021000010054000321300000034800000000010000000
11146402000010000000000000000000101000010000
21000101152311213031105400410110022110000000007681100100000000000000000000000000
21000102000000000000000000000000001202020100
21000201152111113031105400310110022010000010001810000100000000000000000000000000
21000202100000000000000000000000001102000100
21000301152910413031104400410110022110020010024901212210000055310000520000000000
21000302000010000000000100000000001011120001 00
21000401152610713031104375310110022110000010012400000100000000000000000000000000
21000402000000000000000000000000000000002000000
21000501152610913031116375310110022110000010015280000100000000000000000000000000
21000502000010000000000000000000010000200 0000
21000601152911413031116375110110022110010000021651210110000000010000000110010000
21000602000010000000001000000000100203000000
21000701152311013031116375310110022010000010002100000100000000000160000100000000
21000702000010000000000000000000000100002000010
21000801153109013031118400410110022010020010064211211230000489710000500010000010
21000802000010000000001010000000001002030000 00
21000901153709113031118400310110122010100010007621200100000000010000010000000000
21000902000010000000000000000000010020300010 0
21001001152708213021104400210110022110101010143001201211104589010000500000000000
21001002000010100001000000000000110021300010 0
21001101152207713021104400310110022110100010029181301210000144001000000000000000
21001102000000000000000000000000000000002000100
21001201151807612021105400310110022110000010018000001300000074500000000000000000
21001202000000000000000000000000000000002000000
21001301151307512021104375310110022010000010007850000100000000000160000100000000
21001302001100000000000000010000000020300000 0
21001401153207213021104400310120022127000010008980000100000000000000000000000000
21001402000000100000010000000000010000301000 0
21001501152807113021104375310120022022000010014390000100000000000000000000000000
21001502000010000000000000000000100013000000
21001601153007013021104375310120022022000000005360000100000000000000000000000000
21001602000000000000000000000000010001300000 0
21001701153606813021105375310120022022000000006890000100000000000000000000000000
21001702000000000000000000001000000000200 0000
21001801153206813021104375310120022022000010002970000100000000000000000000000000
21001802000000000000000100000000000100012000000
21001901152109413031105400310110022110000010018681211220000115011000000010000000
21001902000000000000000000000000000000002000000
21002001151808712021105400310110022110000000002260000100000000000100000010000000
21002002001000000000000000000000000100113000000
21002101151709312031104400310110022110000000002000000100000000000000000010000000
21002102000000000000000000000000000000002000000
21002201052110613031105375310120022110000000001161200100000000000000000010000000
21002202000100000000000000000000000000002000000
21002301051509312031104375310110022010000010002360000100000000000000000010000000
21002302000000000000000000000000000000002000100
21002401151506912021105375310120022022100010009100001100000020600000000010000000
21002402000010000000000000000000000000002000000
21002501151507012021105375310110022010000010005520000100000000000000000010000000
21002502000010000000000000000000000000002000100
21002601151707112021105375310110022010000010011200000100000000000000000010000000
21002602000010000000010000000000000000002000100
21002701152007013021105375310110022010000000000680000100000000000000000010000000
21002702000000000000000000000000000000002000000
21002801151807012021104375310110022010000000000730000100000000000000000010000000
21002802000000000000000000000000000000001000000
21002901151407112021104375310110022010000010000960000100000000000000000010000000
21002902000000100000000000000000000000012000000
21003001152807313021104400310110022110000010003521200100000000001000000000000000
21003002000000000000000000000000000000212000000
21003101153207413021105400310110022110000000000320000100000000001000000000000000
21003102000010000000000000000000000000002000000
21003201153907913021105400310110022122000010006761300100000000011000000000000000
21003202000000000000000000000000000100213000100
21003301153908213021108400110110022110000000001360000100000000000000000000000000
21003302000000000000000000000000000000001000000
21003401153908513021105400110110022110000010004571300100000000001000000000000000
21003402000000000000000000000000010000002000000
21003501154308813021105400310110022110000010004640000100000000000000000000000000
21003502000000000000000000000000000000002000000
21003601154108813021105400310110022010000000002580000100000000000000000000000000
21003602000000000000000000000000000000002000000
21003701153908813021104400310110022010000010003200000100000000000000000000000000
21003702000000000000000000000000000000002000000
21003801153709913031105400310110022010000010012001200110000000010000000001010000
21003802100000000000000000000000000000002000100
21003901154509813031104375310110022110100010010881301210000022410000001000000000
21003902000000000000000000000000000000002000000
21004001154510113031104375310110022110000010003520000100000000000000000010000000
21004002000000000000000000000000000000002000100
21004101153907213021108400310110022010000000001160000100000000000000090001000000
21004102000010000000000000000100001001230000 00
21004201154007713021116400310110022010000000000406000010000000000000000001000010
21004202000000000000000000000010000100102000000
21004301154207113021116400310110022010000000000861000010000000000000000010000000
21004302000010000000010100010001100012000100
21004401154107513021116400310110022022000000000338000010000000000000000011000010
21004402000000000000000000000010000100002010000
21004501153507113021105400310110022110000010002730000100000000000000000010000000
21004502000000000000000000000000100000 2000000
21004601153607013021105375310120022022000010005010000100000000000000000010000000
21004602000010000000000000000000000000002000000
21004701154307013021104400310120122022000000003410000100000000000000000010000000
21004702000000000000000000000000000100002000000
21004801154106713021116375310120122022000000001739000010000000000000000010000000
```

21004802000010000000010000010000100012000000
2100490115380651302110437531012002202200001000543000010000000000000000010000000
21004902100001000000000000000000100002000000
2100500115420651302110437531011002202200001001104120121000006960000000010000000
210050020000101000100000000000001000002000100
2100510115430741302110540031012002202200001000227000010000000000000000010000000
21005102000000000000000000000000100002000000
2100520115480691302111637511012013202100001005200000100000000000000000010000000
21005202000010100000030000010001100023000100
2100530115420791302110440031012003202100001000744000010000000000100000000000000
21005302100000000000000000000000100002000000
2100540115440771302110440031012003202100000000378000010000000000000000011010006
2100540200000000000000000010000100012000000
2100550115470781302110537531012003202100001000495000010000000000000000010000000
21005502000000100000000000000000100002000000
2100560115450821302110540031012002201000001000225000010000000000000000010000000
21005602000000000000000000000000000002000000
2100570115480821302110537531012002202200000000722000010000000000000000090010000000
21005702010000001000000000000000100002000000
2100580115480621302111637531012002201000001000384000010000000000000000010000000
21005802000010000000000000000000100002000000
2100590115510661302111637531012002202200001000510000010000000000000000010000000
21005902000010000000010000000000100012000000
2100600115520711302111637531012002202200001001619000010000000000000000010000000
21006002000010000000000100000000100002000000
2100610115540751302111637531012002202200001000455000010000000000000000010000000
21006102000010000000000000010000100012000000
2100620115520661302111637531012012202200000000750000010000000001000000011000010
21006202000010100000020000000000100002000100
2100630115520651302111637531012012202200001000372000010000000000000000011000010
21006302000010100000020000000000100202000000
2100640115440591301111637531012002202200001000756000010000000000000000010000000
21006402000010000000000000000000000002000100
2100650115370621302110537531012002201000000001125000010000000000000000010000000
21006502000000000000000000000000000002000000
2100660115370641302111837531012002202200001001164000010000000000000000010000000
21006602000000000000000000010000000002000000
2100670115341141303110435031012012212200000000269000010000000000000000001010010
21006702000010000000000100000000000002000000
2100680115311171303110435031012002211000001000562000010000000000000000800000000000
21006802010000000000000000000000000002000000
2100690115341171303110435031012002201000001000180000010000000000000000000000000
21006902000000000000000000000000000002000000
2100700115311191303110435031012002201000001000900000010000000000000000000000000
21007002000000000000000000000000000002000000
2100710115331201303111835031011002201000001000156140010000000000000000000000000
21007102000000000000000000000000000002000000
2100720115311321304111832531011002201000001000180000010000000000000000010000000
21007202000000000000000000000000000002000000
2100730115361331304111832531011002201000001000338000010000000000000000010000000
21007302000000100000000000010000000002000000
2100740115411301304110432531012002201000001000123000010000000000000000010000000
21007402000000100000000000000000000002000000
2100750115331341304111832531012002211000001000112000010000000000000000010000000
21007502000000000000000000000000000002000000
2100760115491391304110432531011002211000001000151000010000000000000000010000000
21007602000000000000000000000000100002000000
2100770115191001203110440031011002201000001000334000010000000000000000010000000
21007702000000000000000000000000000002000000
2100780115180991203111637531011002201000001000179000010000000000000000000000000
21007802000010000000000000010000000002000000
2100790115201061203110437531011002211000000000216000010000000000000000010000000
21007902000010000010000000000000000002000000
2100800115211111303111637531011002201000000000160000010000000000000000010000000
21008002000010000000000000010000000002000100
2100810115231161303110837531012002201000001000349000010000000000000000010000000
21008102000010000000000000010000000012000100
2100820115211191303111635031011002211000001000090000010000000000000000010000000
21008202000010000000000000000000000002000000
2100830115161031203111637531012002211000001000099000010000000000000000010000000
21008302000000000000000000000000000002000000
2100840115150971203111637531011002201000001000293000010000000000000000010000000
21008402000000000000000000000000000002000000
2100850115170971203111637531011002201000000001261200100000000000000000010000000
21008502000000000000000100000000000002000100
2100860115160881202110840031011002201000000000204000010000000000000000010000000
21008602000010000000000000000000000001000000
2100870115150861202111640031011002201000001000148000010000000000000000010000000
21008702000010000000000000000000000102000000
2100880115150821202110540031011002201000001000196000010000000000000000010000000
21008802000000000000000000000000100102000000
2100890115130791202111637531011002201000001000194000010000000000000000010000000
21008902000010000000000000010000000002000000
2100900115140781202110537531012002201000001000233000010000000000000000010000000
21009002000010000000000000000000000002000000
2100910115110771202110537531011002211000001000247000010000000000000000010000000
21009102000010100000000000000000000022000000
2100920115120971203110537531011002201000001000684130010000000000000000010000000
21009202000010100000000000000000000002000000
2100930115111011203111637531012002202200001000585120010000000000000000010000000
21009302000010000000010000000000000002000000
2100940115130881202111637531012002211000001001100000010000000000000000011000010
21009402000010000000000000010000100023000000
2100950115120811202111637531012002211000001000880000010000000000000000011000010
21009502000010000000000000010000100002010000
2100960115131021203111037531011002201000001000257170010000000000000000010000000
21009602000000000000000100000000000002000100
2100970115141021203111837531011002211000001000432110010000000000000000080010000000
21009702000010000000000000010000000002000000
2100980115140891202111937531021002211000000000135000010000000000000000010000000
21009802000010000000000000010000000002000000
2100990115100751202110837531011002211200001000240000010000000000000000011000010
21009902000010100000000000000000000002000000
2101000115100811202111637531012002201000001000634000010000000000001600011000010
21010002000010000000000000010000100002000000
2101010115110881202111037531011002211000000000605000010000000000001600010000000
21010102001000100000990000020000100002000000
2101020115090981203111635031012002211000001001508000010000000000001600011000010
21010202000010000000010000010000100002000000
2101030115020841202110835031011002211200000000066000010000000000000000010000000
21010302000000000000000000000000000002000100
2101040115020751202110835031011002202200001000367000010000000000001600010000000
21010402001000000000000000000000000022000000
2101050115040761202110435031012002212200001000331000010000000000000000010000000
21010502011100000000000000010000000002000000
2101060115060821202111635031012002211000000000744130010000000000001600010000000
21010602001109900000000000000000100012000000
2101070115080881202111835031012002211000001000388000010000000000000000010000000
21010702001100100000000000010000000002000000
2101080115080731202110435031011002212200001000720130010000000000000000010000000

```
210108020011000000000000000000000000000000002000000
210109010507072120211043503101100220220000100041900001000000000000160800100000000
2101090200101000000000000000100001000002000000
210110011506071120211043503101100221220000000006360000100000000000000000000011000010
210110020011000000000000000000000000000002000000
21011101150407012021108350310120022122100010008551300100000000000000000000010000000
2101110200111000000000000001000000000002000000
210112011509104120311083503101100221220000000006481300100000000000000000000010000000
210112020011000000000000000000000100002000000
21011301149907612021108350310110022012000010004620000100000000000160000100000000
21011302000010000000000000000000000000002000000
21011401150407112021104350310110022022000010001200000100000000000000000000011000010
210114020011000000000000000000000000000002000000
21011501151006912021104375310110022022000010000700000100000000000000000000010000000
2101150200000000000001000000000001000002000000
21011601151210412031105375310110022110000010002400000100000000000000000000010000000
210116020011000000000000000000000000000002000000
21011701151806212021105350310110022010000010001500000100000000000160000100000000
21011702110010000000000000000000000100002000000
21011801151706412021105350310110022010000000001200000100000000000000000000010000000
2101180200001000000000000000000000000002000000
21011901151506512021104350310120022022000010001100000100000000000000000000010000000
2101190201001000000001000000000100000200000
21012001151306612021105350310120022010000000001260000100000000000000000000010000000
210120020000000000000200000000000100002000000
21012101151107112021118375310110022010000000000850000100000000000000000000010000000
210121020000000000000000000000000000000002000000
21012201151310612031105375310110022110000000000360000100000000000000000000010000000
210122020000000000000000000000000000000002000000
21012301151706512021104375310120022122000010002020000100000000000000000000010000000
2101230200001000000000000000000000000002000000
21012401151706712021105375310110022010000000000250000100000000000000000000011000010
2101240200001000000000000000000011000002000000
21012501151206912021104375310120022010000010001560000100000000000160000100000000
2101250201101000000000000000000000010000200010 0
21012601151611412031105350310110022110000000001114000010000000000000000000010000000
21012602011000000000000000000000100000200000 0
21012701152012613041116350110110022110000000000374000010000000000000000000010000000
21012702000100000000000000000000000000001000100
21012801152213013041108350110110022110000000002330000050000000000116000011000010
2101280200101000000000000000000000000001000100
210129011521139130411183251101100221100000100160013005000000000001000000 10000000
21012902000000000000000000000000000000001000000
21013001151913912041104325310110022110000010012000000100000000000000000000010000000
2101300200000000000000000000000000000002000000
21013101152513913041116325310110022110000010018401400100000000000000000000010000000
210131020000000000000100000100004444444440100
21013201152914413041116325310120022110000000002941300100000000000000000000010000000
2101320200000000010000000000000000000002000100
21013301152813113041105350110110022110000000002230000100000000000000000000010000000
2101330200000000000000000000000000000002000000
21013401153613013041105325310110022110000010000690000100000000000000000000010000000
2101340200000000000000000000000000000002000000
21013501154513913041104325310120022000000000001713001000000000000000900100000000
21013502001000000000000000000001000002000000
21013601052514613041105325110110022110000010009291110000000000000000000800100000000
210136020000000000000000000000000000000000000
21013701052615513051116300310110022110000000004200001000000000780000050010000000
210137020000000000000000000000000000000000000
21013801055707113021116375310110022010000000003220000301000032611000000020000000

2101380200010000000000000000000000000002000000
21013901156007514021108350310120022022000010008000000100000000000000000000010000000
2101390200010000000000000001000010000200010 0
21014001156307414021116350310120022022000010009600000100000000001000000010000000
210140020011000000000000000100011000020001 00
21014101155906913021108375310120022022000010010880000100000000000160000100000000
2101410200101000000000100000100001000020001 00
21014201155606613021116375310120122022000000000450000100000000000000000000010000000
210142020010000000000000000100011000020001 00
21014301156407014021118350310120022022000000001960000100000000000000000000010000000
2101430201100000000000100000000001000002000000
21014401155406313021108375310120022022000010003000000100000000000000000000010000000
21014402101010000000001000001000010001200000 0
21014501156106814021116350310120022022000000001120000100000000000000000000010000000
2101450200110990000000000001000110010200000 0
21014601156306614021108350310120122022000000000840000100000000000000000000010000000
2101460200101990000002000001000010001200000 0
21014701156106214021108350310110022010000010008100000100000000000000000000010000000
2101470200110000000000000000000000000002000100
21014801156506614021104350310120032021000000002900000100000000000000000000011000010
2101480200000000000000000000000000100002000000
21014901155806213021116350310120032021000010001200000100000000000000000000010000000
2101490200100000000000200000000001000002000000
21015001155706413021108350310120032021000010008960000100000000000000000000010000000
21015002001000000000002000000000001000002000000
21015101156607414021116350310120022022000000001020000100000000000000000000010000000
2101510200110000000001000001000010000200010 0
21015201156707414021116350310120022022000000001760000100000000000000000000010000000
2101520200010000000000000000000000100002000000
21015301156807214021116350310120032021000010009900000100000000000000000000010000000
2101530200100000000000000000000011000022000000
21015401156207814021104350310110022010000000005200010110100000001000000010000000
210154020010000010000000000100001000020000 00
21015501156807714021104350310120032021000000001200000100000000000000000000010000000
2101550200110010000000000000000000100022000000
21015601156708014021116350310120022022000000000480000100000000000000000000010000000
21015602001000001000010000000000100122000000
21015701156408014021118350310120032021000000001400000100000000000000000000011001000
2101570200100000000000000000000000000002000100
21015801157007214021104350310120032021000010005600000100000000000000000000010000000
2101580200101010000000000000000000100022000000
21015901156806714021104350310120022022000010001960000100000000000000000000010000000
21015902000000000000100000000000100002000000
21016001157207614021104350310120032021000010007900000100000000000000000000010000000
21016002000100010000100000000000100012000000
21016101157107214021118350310120032021000000000463000010000000000000000000010000000
2101610200000000000000000001000000000002000000
21016201157207014021104350310120032021000010003040000100000000000160000100000000
21016202001100000000010000000000400002000000
21016301157106814021104350310120032021000000000674000010000000000160000100000000
2101630200100000000000000000000000100002000000
21016401157306914021116350310120032021000010002500000100000000000000000000011000010
2101640200100000000000000000000000100002000000
21016501157407614021104350310120032121000010004200000100000000000000000000010000000
2101650200100000000000000000000000100012000000
21016601157008114021118350310120032021000000001470000100000000000000000000010000000
2101660200100000000000000000100011000120001 00
21016701155907813021104350310120122022000010003600000100000000000000900100000000
21016702001000100000000000000000011000022000000
21016801155908013021104350310120122022000010000440000100000000000000000000010000000
```

```
210168020001100000000000000000000100002000100
21016901155907913021104350310120122022000010000750000100000000000000000010000000
2101690200101000000000100000000000100012000000
21017001156408114021104350310120032021000010004670000100000000000000000011010001
21017002100010000000010000010000100012000000
21017101156608314021108325310120022022000010004550000100000000000000000011010000
2101710200111000000000200000000000000012000000
21017201156106314021108350310120122122000010001580000100000000000000000010000000
21017202001110000000010000010000000012000000
21017301156408514021104325310110122010000010004880000100000000000000000010000000
21017302001010000000000000000000000000002000000
21017401156708514021118325310110022010000010001100000100000000000000000010000000
210174020000000000000101000000000000002000000
21017501157108514021108325310120022122000010001550000100000000000000000010000000
2101750201001000000000000000000000100002000000
21017601156908714021108325310120022022000000001870000100000000000000000010000000
210176020000000000000100000000000100002000000
21017701056908814021108300310120022022000000001530000100000000000000000010000000
210177020010100000000000000001000010000200000000
21017801157208614021104325310120022022000010000810000100000000000000000010000000
2101780200000000000000000000000000100002000000
21017901057608714021104300310120022010000010002450000100000000000000000010000000
2101790200000000000000000000000000000001000000
21018001157108814021104300310120022010000010002540000100000000000000000010000000
21018002000000000000000000000000004444444440000
21018101156908814021104300310120022010000000008100001000000000000000000010000000
2101810200000000000000000000000000000002000100
21018201157908614021104300310110022110000000004280000100000000000100000010000000
2101820200000000000000000000000000000002000000
21018301157808914021104300310110022110000010002240000100000000000000000010000000
21018302000000000000000000000000000000002000000
21018401157508914021104300310110022010000010001600000100000000000000000010000000
21018402001010000000000000000000000000002000000
21018501157109014021108300310110022010000000000950000100000000000000000010000000
210185020010000000000100000000000000002000000
21018601158108714021108300310110022110000010001520000100000000000100000010000000
21018602000000000000000000000000000000002000000
21018701158208614021108300310110022110000010000960000100000000000000000010000000
21018702000000000000000000000000000000002000000
21018801158308714021116300310120022010000000000750000100000000000000000010000000
2101880200000010000000000000000000100002000000
21018901158708514021116300310120022022000010007000000100000000000000000010000000
21018902001010000000000000000000000100002000000
21019001158708914021108300310120022022000010003550000100000000000000000010000000
210190020011000000000100000000001100002000000
21019101158208814021108300310110022010000000001300000100000000000000000010000000
21019102001100000000000000000000000000002000000
21019201158709014031116275310120022010000000001310000100000000000000000010000000
21019202000010000000000000000000000000002000000
21019301158809114031116275310120022010000000001470000100000000000000000011001001
21019302000000000000000000000000000000002000000
21019401159209214031116275310110022010000000000680000100000000000000000010000000
2101940201001000000000000000000000100002000100
21019501159409214031104275310120022010000000000890000100000000000000000010000000
2101950200011000000000000000000000200002000000
21019601159609114031116275310110022010000000001990000100000000000000000010000000
2101960200100000000000000000000000100002000100
21019701159709314031108275310110022010000010000540000100000000000000000010000000
21019702000100000000000000000000000000002000100
21019801160009215031104250310120022010000000000850000100000000000160000010000000
2101980200001000000001000000000000000002000000
21019901160309315031116250310120022110000010001200000100000000000000000010000000
2101990200100000000000000000000000100002000000
21020001159809614031116250310120022010000010000570000100000000000000000010000000
2102000200100000000000000000000000100002000000
21020101159509814031100250540442244363330020001892499099000000022492039142222220
2102010222222989822298223323222444444440222
21020201157008314021100325540442244363330010001362499099000000022492039142222220
2102020222222989822298223323222444444440222
21020301157308314021104325310110022010000010000910000100000000000000000010000000
2102030200000000000000000000000000100012000000
21020401057608114021101325310110022010000010001360000100000000000000000010000000
210204020000000000000000000000000100002000000
21020501157508214021104325310120032021000000001810000100000000000000000010000000
2102050200001000000000000001000010000200000000
21020601157708214021105325310110022010201010005451720120200000010000000010000000
2102060200001000001000000000000000100002000000
21020701157607614021105325310120032021000000005880000100000000000000000010000000
210207020100000000000000000100001000022000000
21020801157608414021105325310120032021000000001580000100000000000000000010000000
2102080200100000000000000000000000100012000000
21020901157507514021105325310120032021000000003620000100000000000000000010000000
2102090200001000000000000001000010001200000000
21021001057406914021105350310120032021000000002011300100000000000000000010000000
2102100200000000000000100000000000100002000000
21021101157406814021104350310120032021000000002401300100000000000000000011000010
2102110200100000000000000000000000100002000000
21021201157606714021105325310120032021000010001200000100000000000000000010000000
2102120200001000000000000000000000100002000000
21021301157608014021116325310120022022000010001230000100000000000000000010000000
2102130200001000000000000000000000100002000000
21021401157807714021104325310120032021000010002750000100000000000000000010000000
2102140200001000000000000000000000100002000000
21021501157807114021104325310120032021000000006720000100000000000000000011001000
2102150200100000000000000000000001100002000100
21021601057806614021104325310120032021000000000800000100000000000000000010000000
2102160200001000001000000000000000100002000000
21021701157706514021116325310120132021000010002160000100000000000000000010000000
2102170200101000000000200000000000100002010000
21021801157806214021104325300130031021000000002340000100000000000000000000000000
21021802001000000000000000000000000200003000000
21021901157506314021105325100030031021000010001190000100000000000000000000000000
21021902001000000000000000000000000200003000000
21022001157506214021104325310030030021000010001160000100000000000000000000000000
21022002001000000000000000000000000000001000000
21022101157106114021104325310130031021000010001190000100000000000000000000000000
21022102000000000000000000000000001200003000000
21022201157206014011108325310130022010000010001040000100000000000000000000000000
21022202000000000000000000000000001100002000000
21022301057806014011116325310130021010000010001601400100000000000000000000000000
21022302001000000000000000000000000200003000000
21022401058106014021108325310130021010000010003390000100000000000000000000000000
21022402001000000000000000000000000200003000000
21022501057905914011105325310130021010000000001390000100000000000000000000000000
21022502000000000000000000000000000000001000000
21022601158208014021116325110130021010000010001501000100000000000000000000000000
21022602001000100000000000000000000200003000000
21022701158308314021108325310130121010000010002191100100000000000000000000000000
210227020110000000000100000100002000003000100
21022801158308114021116325310130021010000000001160000100000000000000000000000000
```

210228020110001000000000000000000000001000000
21022901158408214021116300310130021010000010004520000100000000000000000000000000
2102290200000000000001000000000000100001000000
21023001158008014021104325310130021022000010001960000100000000000000000000000000
210230020010000000000100000000000200003000000
21023101158307714021108325310130021022000000001370000100000000000000000000000000
210231020010000000000001000010000100001000000
21023201158407214021108325310130021022000010005330000100000000000000000000000000
210232020010000000000000000020000200003000000
21023301158307114021116325310130021010000010021971100100000000000160000000000000
210233020011000000000200000020000200013000100
21023401158007014021116325310130121110000010016000000100000000000000000000000000
210234020010001000000200000020000200013000100
21023501158206414021108325310130021022000010001610000100000000000000000000000000
210235020000000000000000001000000100002000000
21023601158306414021108325310130021022000010000670000100000000000000000000000000
210236020110000000000100000000000200003000000
21023701058306314021104325310110021110000010001510000100000000000100000000000000
210237020010000000000000000000000100002000000
21023801158306714021108350310130021022000010000961300100000000000000000000000000
210238020100001000000000000010000200003000000
21023901157106514021104350310130131021000000001610000100000000000000000000000000
210239020000100000000200000000000200003000000
21024001157306514021104325310130031021000000000790000100000000000000000000000000
210240020000100000000000000000000200003000000
21024101156806414021104350310130131021000010001850000100000000000000000001001000
210241020000101010000000000010000200013000000
21024201056606414021116350310130131021000000001630000100000000000000000000000000
210242020010101000000000000000001200003000000
21024301156606514021116350310130131021000000002150000100000000000000000000000000
210243021100100000000100000000000200003000000
21024401056606314021104350310130031021000010001160000100000000000000000000000000
210244020011102000000100000000000200003000000
21024501156606214021116350310130131021000000000850000100000000000160000000000000
210245020011002000000000000010000200003000000
21024601156406214021116350310130021010000000000420000100000000000000000000000000
210246020010100000000000000000000200003000000
21024701157405814011116325310130021010000010000450000100000000000000000000000000
210247020000000000000100000000000000001000000
21024801057805614011116300310130021010000000000900000100000000000000000000000000
210248020100000000000000000000000000001000000
21024901058205814011116300310130021110000000000470000100000000000000000000000000
210249020000000000000000000000000000001000000
21025001158405814011116300310130021110000010002210000100000000000000000000000000
210250020000100000000000000000000000001000000
21025101158205614011104300310130021110000000000490000100000000000000000000000000
210251020000000000000000000000000000001000000
21025201158205514011104300310130021010000010000451300100000000000000000000000000
210252020010000000000000000000000000001000000
21025301158205314011116300310130021010000010001100000100000000000000000000000000
210253020000001000000000000000000000001000000
21025401059505214011104275310130121010000000000151300100000000000000000000000000
210254020000000000000000000000000000000000000
21025501058906414021116300310130021010000000000691300100000000000000000000000000
210255020010100000000000000000000000001000000
21025601058706214021116300310130021010000010000280000100000000000000000000000000
210256020000000000000000000000000000001000000
21025701158706514021116300310130121010000010003280000100000000000000000000000000
210257020000000000000000000000000000001000000
21025801159106814021116300310130021010000010000980000100000000000000000000000000
210258020000000000000000000010000000001000000
21025901059206714021104300310130121022000000002180000100000000000160000000000000
210259020011100000000000000000000000001000000
21026001159106314021104300310130121010000000002800000100000000000160000000000000
210260020010100000000000000000000200003000000
21026101159207714021104300310130021021000000000710000100000000000170000000000000
210261020011102000000200000000000200003000010
21026201159107314021104300310130131021000000001450000100000000000160000000000000
210262020011100000000000000000000200003000000
21026301159207114021104300310130131021000000001600000100000000000160000000000000
210263020011100000000000000000000200003000000
21026401159307514021104300310130131021000000003760000100000000000160000000000000
210264020011100000000000000000000200003000000
21026501159108314021116300310130031021000010004520000100000000000160000000000000
210265020010101000000000000010000200003000000
21026601158908614021104300310130021012000010004200000100000000000000000001010006
210266020000100000000000000000001200003000000
21026701059308214021116300310130131021000010000870000100000000000000000000000000
210267020010000000000000000000000000001000000
21026801159308314021116275310130031021000010002330000100000000000000000000000000
210268020010100000000000000020000200003000000
21026901158906714021116300310130021022000000002410000100000000000000000000000000
210269020010100000000000000000000100002000000
21027001158907214021104300310130021022000000000520000100000000000160000001010000
210270020010100000000000000010000100012000000
21027101158806714021116300310130021022000010002860000100000000000160000000000000
210271020010101000000000000010000200003000000
21027201158707214021104300310130121022000010005400000100000000000000000000000000
210272020010101000100000000000000200003010000
21027301158707514021104300310130121022000000003800000100000000000000000000000000
210273020000100010000300000020000200003000000
21027401158807914021116300310130021022000010005690020100200000000160000000000000
210274020010100000000002000100001200003000000
21027501158907914021108300310130121122000010006010000100000000000000000000000000
210275020000103000000200000010000200003000000
21027601158608314021104300310130021122000000002280000100000000000000000000000000
210276020000101000100200000000000200013000000
21027701159108714021108300310130031021000000001820000100000000000000000000000000
210277020100101000000000000010000200003000000
21027801159209014021104275310130031021000000004580000100000000000000000000000000
210278020010100000000000000000000200003000100
21027901159308814021108275310130031021000010005810000100000000000000000000000000
210279020010100000000000000010000200013000000
21028001159508914021108275310130031021000010003220000100000000000000000000000000
210280020000100000000100000010000200003000100
21028101159708914021108275310130021022100010001260000100000000000000000000000000
210281020000101000000000000010000200003000000
21028201159708714021108275310130121022000010001150000100000000000000000000000000
210282020000100000000100000000000100002000000
21028301159508214021104275310130121022000000001220000100000000000000000000000000
210283020000000000000000000000000100002000000
21028401159708814021104275310130021022000010001800000100000000000000000000000000
210284020000000000000000000020000100002000000
21028501059608314021104275310130121022000000001590000100000000000000000000000000
210285020001000000000000000000000000001000100
21028601060008615021104275310130121122000000001610000100000000000000000000000000
210286020000000000000000000000000000001000000
21028701060108615021104275310130121022000000001580000100000000000000000000000000
210287020000003000000000000000000000001000000
21028801160008815021104275310130021110000000000250000100000000000000000000000000

```
21028802000010000000000000000000000000001000000
21028901060408815021104250310130121022000000000439000010000000000000000000000000000
21028902000010000000000000000000000000001000000
21029001060709115031116225310130121010000000000195000010000000000000000000000000000
21029002000000000010000000000000000001000000
21029101159608014021104275310130131121000000000126000010000000000000000000000000000
21029102000000000000000000000000000001000000
21029201059807914021104275310130131021000001000154000010000000000000000000000000000
21029202000000000000000000000000000001000000
21029301159807714021116275310130021021000001000218000010000000000000000000000000000
21029302000000000000000000000000100002000100
21029401160007714021105275310130121110000000000478000010000000000000000000000000000
21029402000010000000000000001000010000200000 0
21029501160207715021116275310130021110000001000624000010000000000016000000000000
21029502101010000000000000000000100002000000
21029601060108115021108275310130021110000001000140000010000000000000000000000000000
21029602000010100000000000000000000001000000
21029701060208115021108275310130021022000000000091000010000000000000000000000000000
21029702000010000000000000000000000001000000
21029801060407715021108250310130121122000000000423000010000000000000000001011000
21029802000010000000000000000000200003000000
21029901060707915021116250310130021010000001000145000010000000000000000000000000000
21029902000000000000010000000000000001000000
21030001159606214021116275310130021010000001000107000010000000000000000000000000000
21030002000010000000000000000000100001010000
21030101059606614021116275310130021010000001000187001010010000000000000000000000
21030102000010000000000000000000000001000000
21030201159706814021104275310130121010000001000126151010010000000000000000000000
21030202000000000000000000000000000001000000
21030301159607214021116275310130031021000001000290000010000000000000000000000000000
21030302000010000000000000000000200003000100
21030401159506814021104275310130031021000001000086000010000000000016000000000000
21030402001000000000000000000000000001010100
21030501159407114021116275310130031021000001000229110010000000000000000000000000000
21030502000010000001000000010000200003000000
21030601159507414021116275310130031021000001000281000010000000000000000000000000000
21030602000010000000010000020001200003000000
21030701159407814021104275310130131021000001000324000010000000000026000000000000
21030702001110000000000000010001200003000000
21030801159807214021105275310130021010000001000197000010000000000016000000000000
21030802000010000000000000000000000001010000
21030901059906414021116275310130021010000001000170111010010000001000000000000000
21030902000000000000010000000000000011000100
21031001160006615021104275310130121010000000000101000010000000000000000000000000000
21031002000010000000010000000000000001000100
21031101060206215021116275310130021010000000000159000010000000000000000000000000000
21031102000010000000000000000000000000000000
21031201160106515021104275310130121010000000000165000010000000000000000000000000000
21031202000010000000010000000000000001000000
21031301060306215021116275310130021010000000000070000010000000000000000000000000000
21031302000010000000000000000000000001000000
21031401159906014021104275310130121010000001000316000010000000000016000000000000
21031402001000000000010000000000000001000000
21031501159905914011116275310130021010000000000119000010000000000000000000000000000
21031502000010000000000000000000100002000100
21031601060005715011116275310130021010000000000539000010000000000000000000000000000
21031602000000000000000000000000000001000000
21031701160005515011108275310130121022000000000083000010000000000000000000000000000
21031702000010000000000000001000010000200000 0
21031801060005315011116250310130121010000000000154000010000000000000000000000000000
21031802000010000000000000000000000001000000
21031901060705015011108250310130121110000001000350000010000000000000000000000000000
21031902000000000000000000000000000001000000
21032001061305315011108225310130021110000001000740000010000000000000000000000000000
21032002000000000000000000000000000001000000
21032101060705515011108250310130021010000001000300000010000000000000000000000000000
21032102000000000000000000000000000001000000
21032201060505715011116275310130021110000000000474000010000000001000000000000000
21032202000000000000010000000000000001000000
21032301061205815011108250310130021010000001000183000010000000000000000000000000000
21032302000000000000000000000000000001000100
21032401061606115021116250310130021010000000000090000010000000000000000000000000000
21032402000000000000010000010000100002000000
21032501061606415021108225310130021010000000000215000010000000000000000000000000000
21032502000000000000000000000000000001000000
21032601161406915021104225310130021010000000000030000010000000000000000000000000000
21032602000000000000000000000000000001000000
21032701061407115021105225310130021010000001000320000010000000000000000000000000000
21032702000000000000010000000000000001000000
21032801161207115021104250310130021010000000000134000010000000000000000000000000000
21032802000010000000000000000001000001000000
21032901161006315021116250310130021010000000000170000010000000000000000000000000000
21032902000000000000000000000000100002000100
21033001161006715021108250310130021022100001000261000010000000000000000000000000000
21033002000100000000010000000000200003000000
21033101060906615021104250310130021110000000000113000010000000000000000000000000000
21033102000000000000000000000000000001000000
21033201160707115021104250310130121022000000000082000010000000000000000000000000000
21033202000010000000010000000000100002000100
21033301160606815021108250310130121022000001000317000010000000000016000000000000
21033302101110100000000000010100200003000000
21033401160606715021108275310130121022100001000214000010000000000026000000000000
21033402001110001000000000000001200013000000
21033501160806515021104250310130021022000000000139000010000000000000000000000000000
21033502000010000000000000000000100002000000
21033601160406815021105275310130021010000000000136130010000000000000000000000000000
21033602101000000000000000010001200003000000
21033701060406515021104275310130021010000000000077000010000000000000000000000000000
21033702000000000000000000000000000001000100
21033801160706315021108275310130021010000001000150000010000000000000000000000000000
21033802000010000000000000000000000001000100
21033901160906115021104250310130021010000000000083110010000000000000000000000000000
21033902000000000000000000000000100002000100
21034001060806015011105275310130021010000000000133000010000000000000000000000000000
21034002000000000000000000000000000001000000
21034101154405813011108350310130021022100000000168000010000000000000000000000000000
21034102000000000000000000010000200003000000
21034201154405613011108350310130021022100001000235000010000000000000000001010000
21034202000000000000010000000000200003000100
21034301154605913011108375310130021022000000000351000010000000000000000000000000000
21034302000010000000020000010000200003000000
21034401154805813011108375310130021022000001000216000010000000000000000001010000
21034402001100000000020000010000200003000000
21034501154905713011108375310130021022000000000083000010000000000000000000000000000
21034502000000000000010000000001200003000000
21034601155105713011104375310130021022000000000090000010000000000000000001010006
21034602000000000000000000000000100002000000
21034701155105613011108350310130031021000000002000000010000000000000000000000000000
21034702000010001000000000010001200003000000
21034801155106013011104375310130021022000000000130000010000000000000000000000000000
```

21034802000010000000000000010001200003000100
21034901155306013011108350310130031021100000001950000100000000000160000001010000
2103490200111010000002000001000200003000000
21035001155405613011108350310130031021000010000450000100000000000000000001010000
2103500200000000010000000000000200003000000
21035101155057130111083503101300310210000000009600001000000000000000000000000000
2103510200000010000000000000000010000200000
21035201155054130111043503101301311210000100015300001000000000000000000000000000
2103520200000000000001000000000000000100000
21035301155605413011108350310130131121000000001790000100000000000000000000000000
2103530200000000000000000010000000001000000
21035401055905413011104350310130131121000000001770000100000000000000000000000000
2103540200001000000000000000000020001300000
21035501155005313011105350310130021010000010001461400100000000000000000000000000
2103550200000000000000000000000000000100000
21035601154705513011108350310130021010000000003351300100000000000000000000000000
2103560200010010000001000001000010000200000
21035701155205313011105350310130021122000010002880000100000000000000000000000000
2103570200100000000000000000000100002000000
21035801055505013011104350310130021110000000003430000100000000000000000000000000
2103580200001000000000000000000000001000000
21035901155705013011108350310130021110000010001151400100000000000000000000000000
2103590200000000000000000010000000001000100
21036001155705213011105350310130021110000010000710600100000000000000000000000000
2103600200000000000000000000000000001000100
21036101055604913011108350310130021110000000000410000100000000000000000000000000
2103610200101000000000000000000000001000000
21036201055604713011108350310130021110000000001660000100000000000000000000000000
2103620200000000000000000000000000001000100
21036301155904113011105325310130021110000010000750000100000000000000000010000000
2103630200001000000000000000001100002000000
21036401156103914011105325310130021110000010000541300100000000000000000010000000
2103640200000000000000000010000200003000100
21036501156203814011105325310130021110000010002460000100000000000000000010000000
2103650200000000000000000000010000200000
21036601056403614011105300310130021110000010000290000100000000000000000010000000
2103660200000000000000000000000000000000100
21036701057003514011105300310130021010000010000530000100000000000000000010000000
2103670200000000000000000000000000001000100
21036801156903214011105300310130021010000010002690000100000000000000000010000000
2103680200000000000000000000010000200010
21036901057103114011108300310130021010000010001261300100000000000000070010000000
2103690200000000000000000000000000001000100
21037001157403114011104275310130021010000010001601100100000000000000000010000000
2103700200100000000000000000000100012000000
21037101157202914001108275310130021010100010004500001000000000001600010000000
2103710200001000000000000000000000001000100
21037201057402814001104275310130021110100010000281400100000000000000000010000000
2103720200000000000000000000000000001000000
21037301057702814001105275310130021110100010003211100100000000001000000011010000
2103730200100000000000000000000000000000000
21037401158002714001117275310130021110000010002060000100000000000000000010000000
2103740200100000000000000000000000001000100
21037501158102514001101275310130021010000010001050000100000000000000000010000000
2103750222222989822098223323222444444440120
21037601058202914001104275310130021110000010000921100100000000000000000010000000
2103760200001000000000000000000000001000100
21037701058103014001117275310130021110000010000600000100000000000000000010000000
2103770200000000000000000000000000001000000
21037801158203014011119275310130021110000010001381300100000000000000000010000000
2103780200000000000000000010000100002000000
21037901058202514001117275310130021110000010000580000100000000000000000010000000
2103790200000000000000000000000000001000100
21038001057303514011104300310130121110000000002613001000000000000000000000000000
2103800200001000000000000000001000001000100
21038101057103514011104300310130021110000010000451300100000000000000000000000000
2103810200000010000000000000000000001000000
21038201057203614011108300310130121110000010000261300100000000000000000000000000
2103820200000000000000000000000000001000000
21038301057703514011104275310130121110000010000630300100000000000000000000000000
2103830200000000000000000000000000001000000
21038401057803614011104275310130121010100010000171300100000000000000000000000000
2103840200000000000000000000000000001000000
21038501058303714011104250310130021010000010001000000100000000000000000000000000
2103850200000000000000000000000000001000000
21038601058402314001119250310130021010000010000320000100000000000000000010000000
2103860200000000000000000000000000001000000
21038701058802314001117250310130021010000010000520000100000000000000000010000000
2103870200000000000000000000000000001000000
21038801059102214001119250310130021010000010001560000100000000000000000010000000
2103880200100000000000000000000000000000000
21038901058401914001117250310130021010000000000490000100000000000000000020000000
2103890200000000000000000000000000000000000
21039001059502014001119250310130021010000010000900000100000000000000000010000000
2103900200000000000000000000000000001000000
21039101058002114001117250310130021110000010000610000100000000000000000020000000
2103910200000000000000000000000000001000000
21039201160402215001104225310130021110100010029641711230000053700160000 20000000
2103920200100000000000000000000001101000100
21039301061001915001119225310130021010000010009131700100000000000000000021000000
2103930200000000000000000000000000001000100
21039401161201815001104225310130021010000010001730000100000000000000000020000000
2103940200001000000000000000000000001000000
21039501061401915001105225310130021010000010000450000100000000000000000010000000
2103950200000000000000000000000000001000000
21039601061301815001104225310130021010000010000441300100000000000000000010000000
2103960200000000000000000000000000001000100
21039701161401715001119225310130021010000010001451300100000000000000000010000000
2103970200000000000000000000000000001000000
21039801061401815001104225310130021010000010000400000100000000000000000010000000
2103980200000000000000000000000000000000000
21039901159702914001117225310130021010000010000700000100000000000000000000000000
2103990200000000000000000000000000001000000
21040001154510313031105375310130021010000010005440000100000000000000000000000000
2104000200001000000000000000000000001000000
21040101154910013031105375310130021010000010006440000100000000000000000000000000
2104010200000000000000000000010000200010 0
21040201154610613031105375310130021010000010001541100100000000000000000000000000
2104020200000000000000000000000000001000000
21040301054210913031105350310130021010000000002950000100000000000000000000000000
2104030200000000000000000000000000000000000
21040401154011313031105350310130021010000010001590000100000000000000000000000000
2104040200000000000000000000000000000000000
21040501053811413031105350310130021010000010001360000100000000000000000000000000
2104050200000000000000000000000000001000000
21040601054011613031105350310130021010000010002230000100000000000000000000000000
2104060200000000000000000000000000000000000
21040701054511413031105350310130021010000010002540000100000000000000000000000000
2104070200000000000000000000000000000000000
21040801155310513031105350310130021110000010003000000100000000000000000000000000

```
21040802000000000000000000000000000001000000
21040901157515114051105250310130021010000010000561700100000000000000000000000000
21040902000000000000000000000000000001000000
21041001157815014051108250310130021110100010000821700100000000000000000000000000
21041002001000100000000000010000000001000000
21041101158115714051108225310130021010100010003341100100000000000000000000000000
21041102000000000000000000000000200003000000
21041201058014914041108250310131021010000010001510000100000000000000000000000000
21041202000100000000000000000000000001000100
21041301148707112021116300310130021010100000000000100130000000150000000020000000
21041302000010000000000001010001000001000100
21041401049607312021116325310130021110000010000380000100000000000000000011010000
21041402000010000000000000000000100002000000
21041501156018014051108200310130121110100010001260000100000000000000000000000000
21041502000100000000000000000000000001000000
21041601057516014051108225310130021010000010001200000100000000000000000000000000
21041602000000000000000000000000000001000000
21041701058314714041108225310131021010000000001260000100000000000000000000000000
21041702000000000000000000000000000001000000
21041801058012014041108275310130021010100010001440000100000000000000000020000000
21041802011010000000000000010000000001000000
21041901162411515031108250410130021010100010035200001310000175900000000020000000
21041902101000000000000000001000110110200010
21042001060011815031104275310130021010000010000790000100000000000000000020000000
21042002000000000000000000000000000001000000
21042101155910713031105350310130021010000010003250000100000000000000000000000000
21042102000010000000000000000000000001000000
21042201055611013031105350310130021110000010001050000100000000000000000000000000
21042202000000000000000000000000000000000000
21042301055611213031105350310130021010000010000410000100000000000000000000000000
21042302000000000000000000000000000000000000
21042401054811913031105325310130121010000010000760000100000000000000000010000000
21042402000000000000000000000000000000000000
21042501155211913031105325310130121010000010002540000100000000000000000020000000
21042502000000000000000000000000200003000000
21042601155409913031105375310130021010000010004840000100000000000000000000000000
21042602000000000000000000000000200003000000
21042701055410113031105375310130021010000000000410000100000000000000000000000000
21042702000000000000000000000000000001000000
21042801155109913031105375310130021010000010000981700100000000000000000000000000
21042802000000000000000000000000100000000000
21042901055209313031105375310130021010000010004361400100000000000000000010000000
21042902000000000000000000000000000000000000
21043001160019014061117150310130021110000010014220000100000000000012000002011001
21043002000001000000000000000000200001030000
21043101165212316041104225410130021010200010016640000101000002360000080020000000
21043102000010000000000000000000000001000100
21043201165012016031104225410130021010200010002100010110100000010000000020000000
21043202000010000000000000000000000001000000
21043301060012014041104250310130021010000010001310000100000000000000000011010000
21043302000000000000000000000000100002000000
21043401060212115041104250310130021010000010001340000100000000000000000010000000
21043402000000000000000000000000000001000000
21043501160412215041104250310130021010000010001460000100000000000000000010000000
21043502000010000000000000000000000001000000
21043601055309013021105375310130021010000000002311100100000000000000000010000000
21043602000000000000000000000000000001000000
21043701055108613021105375310130021110000000003090000100000000000000000010000000
21043702000000000000000000000000000001000100
21043801055609413031105350310130021010000010000510000100000000000000000010000000
21043802000000000000000000000000000000000000
21043901055909413031105350310130021010000010003211300100000000000000000020000000
21043902000000000000000000000000100000000000
21044001156109814031105350310130021022000010002700000100000000010000000010000000
21044002000000000000000000000000200003000000
21044101055810113031105350310130021010100010000600000100000000010000000000000000
21044102000000000000000000000000000000000000
21044201056309814031105325310130021010000010002880000100000000000000000010000000
21044202000000000000000000000000000000000000
21044301056510314031105325310130021010000010000510000100000000000000000010000000
21044302000000000000000000000000000000000000
21044401056710714031105325310130021010000010002130000100000000000000000000000000
21044402000000000000000000000000000000000000
21044501156510714031105325310130021010000010004451400100000000000000000000000000
21044502000000000000000000000000110000200000
21044601056311214031105325310130021010000010003401100100000000000000000010000000
21044602000000000000000000000000000000000000
21044701056411314031105325310130021010000010002440000100000000000000000010000000
21044702000000000000000000000000000000000000
21044801052709713031101400210110021110020010035751701400000020601000050020000000
21044802000000000001000000000000000001000100
21044901054009113031116400210110021010100010011521501400000168010000000000000000
21044902000000000000000000000000200113000100
21045001168914017041104175310130121010000010003840000100000000000000000001001002
21045002000010000000000000000000000001000000
21045101069014117041119175310130121010000010001760000100000000000000000001001000
21045102001000000000000000000000000001000000
21045201068513917041104200310130021010000010004470000100000000000160000001010002
21045202000010000000010000000000100002020100
21045301168813417041119200310130021010000010003410000100000000000000000000000000
21045302000000000000010000010000000001000000
21045401168514517041119175310130021010000010001040000100000000000000000001010002
21045402000010000000010000000000000001000000
21045501068215117051113175310130121010000010003760000100000000000000000000000000
21045502000010000000010000000000100002020000
21045601167614016041119200310130121110000010001290000100000000000000000000000000
21045602000010000000000000000000100000220000
21045701067715416051116175310130121010000010001520000100000000000000000000000000
21045702000010000000000000010000201003030000
21045801167915516051119150310130121110000010001520000100000000000000000001010000
21045802000010000000000000000000000001010000
21045901100000000001104175310130021110000010003470000100000000000000000000000000
21045902000000010000000000000000100000020000
21046001066714316041119200310130121010000010001600000100000000000000000000000000
21046002000000000000000000000000000001000000
21046101162518115061119150310130021010000010002400000100000000000000000001001000
21046102000000010000000000000000000000010000
21046201166406516021117225410130021110100010056001321000000133210000000020000000
21046202000000000000000000000000001001000000
21046301064411516031104225310130021110000010000720000100000000000000000020000000
21046302000000000000000000000000000001000100
21046401066605616011104200310130021110000010001081100100000000000000000010000000
21046402000000000000000000000000000001000000
21046501067005516011117200310130021010000010000990000100000000000000000000000000
21046502000010000000000000000000000001000000
21046601067205416011104200310130021010000010000741300100000000000000000010000000
21046602000000000000000000000000000001000000
21046701067505316011117200310130021010000010000821300100000000000000000010000000
21046702000000000000000000000000000001000000
21046801067305216011104200310130021010000010001041300100000000000000000010000000
```

210468020000000000000000000000000000001000000
21046901067104016011116175310110021110000010008401101300000000690000090010000000
210469020000000000000000000000000000001000100
21047001066804716011104175310130021010000010000751300100000000000000000010000000
210470020001000000000000000000000000001000000
21047101064904716011104150310130021110000010000381300100000000000000000000000000
210471020000000000000000000000000000000000000
21047201065706816021116225310130021110000000001501300100000000000000000010000000
210472020001000000000000000000000000001000000
21047301064008116021117225310130021110000010000631300100000000000000000010000000
210473020000000000000000000000000000001000000
21047401063508415021104225310130021110000010000901300100000000000000000010000000
210474020000000000000000000000000000001000000
21047501063108415021117225310130021110000010001650000100000000000000000010000000
210475020000000000000010000010000000001000100
21047601063308315021117225310130021110000010000600000100000000000000000010000000
210476020000000000000000000000000000001000000
21047701063008315021117225310130021110000010000601300100000000000000000010000000
210477020000000000000000000000000000001000000
21047801066807116021116200310130021010000010001541300100000000000000000000000000
210478020000000000000000000000000000001000000
21047901065208816021117225310130021110000010001500000100000000000000000010000000
210479020000000000000000000000000000001000000
21048001067804916011117175310130021010000010000960000100000000000000000000000000
210480020000000000000000000000000000001000000
21048101059108514021116300310130021021000000003360000100000000000000000002222220
210481022222298982209822332322222000030000000
21048201061506915021104225310130021010000000000220000100000000000000000000000000
210482020000000000000000000000000000001000000
31000101135413208041510325210110022010200010030281101211100592810000000011010000
310001020010101000000000000000000111102000100
31000201135412808041510325210130022010000000000800110140000005410000000020000000
310002020000000000000000000000000001001000100
31000301134913108041510325210130021112000010016001101000000019210000000021010000
310003020010100000000000000000000110002000000
31000401134612908041510325210130021012000000000648000010000000000000000020000000
310004020000000000000000000000000000001000000
31000501134313308041510325210130021010000000000351000010000000000000000020000000
310005020010000000000000000000000000001000000
31000601133413608041510300210130022022000000000456140010000000000000000020000000
310006020001000000000000000000000001002010100
31000701133313408041510300210110022022000000000720000010000000000001600020000000
310007020011002000000000000010001101102010100
31000801133013508041519300310130022122000000000384000010000000000002600021001000
310008020000100000100000000000001001001000100
31000901035213308041510325210130022010000000000217000010000000000000000020000000
310009020001000000000000000000000000001000100
31001001135213508041510325310130022110000010002121400100000000000000000021010000
310010020010000000000000000000000201002020100
31001101135213608041510325310110022110000000000104000010000000000000000020000000
310011020000000000000001000000000100002000000
31001201135413708041510325310110022110000000000089000010000000000000000020000000
310012020000000000000000000000000000001000000
31001301135413808041510325310110022110000000000068000010000000000000000010000000
310013020000000000000000000000000000001000000
31001401135013508041510325310130022010000000000035000010000000000000000020000000
310014020010001000000010000000000201003010000
31001501034413708041510325310130022010000000000203000010000000000000000010000000
310015020001010200000100000000002000030000000
31001601135512508041510325310130022010000010000891100100000000000000000010000000

310016020001000000000000000000000000001000100
31001701135312508041510325310130023010000010000451100100000000000000000010000000
310017020000000000000000000000000000001000100
31001801135012508041510325310130023010000010000691100100000000000000000010000000
310018020000000000000000000000000000000000100
31001901135612408041510325310130032021000010001420000100000000000000000010000000
310019020010100000000000000000000000001000000
31002001035412408041510325310130032021000000000144000010000000000000000010000000
310020020010100000000000000000000200003010000
31002101135012408041510325310130032021000000000221000010000000000000000011010000
310021020010100000000000000001000200003010100
31002201034712508041501325310142044063330000000421100100000000000449203914222220
310022022222298982229822332322224444444440120
31002301135512308041501325310140044063330000001171100100000000000249203914222220
310023022222298982229822332322224444444440122
31002401134312308041513300310130032021000010003901100100000000000000000020000000
310024020000000000000000000010000001102000000
31002501134412408041511300310130032021000010002210000100000000000000000010000000
310025020010000000000000000000000200003000000
31002601134012508041513300310130032021000010001571300100000000000000000010000000
310026020001000000000000000000000001002000000
31002701133812608041511300310130022010000010000701300100000000000000000010000000
310027020000000000000000000000000001002000000
31002801134112608041513300310130032021000010002060000100000000000000000011010000
310028020001030000000000000000000201103000000
31002901133812708041511300310130022022000010002450000100000000000000000000000000
310029020000000000000000000000000101002000000
31003001134112708041511300310130021122000000000076000010000000000000000010000000
310030020001000000000000000000000001002000000
31003101133912808041511325310130021122000000000108000010000000000000000010000000
310031020000020000000000000000000001002000000
31003201133612908041513300310130021122000000000012000010000000000000000010000000
310032020001000000000000000000000001102000000
31003301033712708041511300310130021010000000000176000010000000000000000000000000
310033020001000000000000000000000000001000000
31003401133313108041518300310130031021000000000291000010000000000001600020000000
310034020011100000000000000000000101002000100
31003501133312908041519300310130132021000000000122000010000000000000000010000000
310035020001000000000000000010000001002000000
31003601132713508041519300310130021021000000000270000010000000000001600011000010
310036020010101000100000000000000001002000000
31003701132913508041519300310130021021000000000144000010000000000001700022000010
310037020001000000000000000000000012102000000
31003801132613808041519300310130021021000000000190000010000000000000000020000000
310038021000101000000100000000000001101000100
31003901132813508041519300310130021021000000000024000010000000000000000010000000
310039020001000000000000000000000001001000000
31004001132714108041513300310110021110000000000262000010000000000000000020000000
310040020001000000000000000000000101002000000
31004101132614308041511300310130021022000000000030000010000000000001600021000010
310041020001010000000000000000000000001000000
31004201132513908041513300310130021021000000000114000010000000000001600010000000
310042020001030000000000000000000101002000000
31004301132514208041513300310130021021000000000080000010000000000000000020000000
310043020000100000100000000000000001001000000
31004401132614108041511300310130021121000000000090000010000000000000000010000000
310044020001010000000000000010000000001000000
31004501132414108041513300310130021021000010003220000100000000000000000011010000
310045020010101030000000000010000112002000000
31004601132613408041519300310130031021000010000540000100000000000000000001000010

```
310046020010100000000000000000000001001000000
310047011326136080415183003101300310210000000020300001000000000000000000001000010
31004702000010200000010000000000100000100010
310048011324136080415193003101300310210000000016900001000000000000000000000000000
31004802000010200000000000010001100002000000
310049011324138080415193003101300320210000000012400001000000000000160000010000 10
31004902001100300000000000000000101002010100
310050011322138080415113003101300310210000100043713001000000000000000000000000000
31005002001100000000000000000000100102000000
310051011322141080415133003101301311210000100084400001000000000000000000000000000
31005102000010000010020000000000000102000000
310052011323144080415183003101300310210000000007400001000000000000000000021000010
31005202000010000000000000000000001001000000
310053011324144080415183003101300310210000000006300001000000000000000000021000010
31005302000010000000000000000000101002000000
310054011325144080415183003101301320210000100013800001000000000000000000020000000
31005402000000000000000000000000001001000000
310055011323135080415193003101300210100000100010500001000000000000000000001010000
31005502000010000000000000000000000001000000
310056011321140080415193003101300320210000000021113001000000000000000000000000000
31005602001010000010000000000000000001000000
310057011318138070415162753101300210100000000020013001000000000000000000000000000
31005702000000000000000000010000000001000000
310058011320142070415193003101300311210000000017400001000000000000000000010000000
31005802000010000000020000000000000001000000
310059011319142070415193003101300321210000000005300001000000000000000000010000000
31005902000010000000000000000000001001000000
310060011318142070415192753101300321210000000018700001000000000000000000020000000
31006002001000000000000000010000000001010000
310061011316142070415192753101300211220000000023411001000000000000000000020000000
31006102000010000000000000010000000001000100
310062011321145080415113003101300321210000100007800001000000000000000000020000000
31006202000100101000000100000000000001001000000
310063011322145080415133003101300321210000000015700001000000000000000000021000010
31006302000000000000000000000000001001000000
310064011354122080415183003101300210220000100020000001000000000000000000000000000
31006402000010000000010000000000000001000000
310065011354120080415183003101300320210000000023400001000000000000000000001000010
31006502000010000000000000000000000001000000
310066011352121080415183003101300210100000000009200001000000000000000000000000000
31006602000010000000000000000000000001000000
310067011347122080415183003101300210100000000010400001000000000000000000000000000
31006702000010000000000000000000001001000100
310068011346122080415183003101300210100000000003600001000000000000000000000000000
31006802000010000000000000000000000001000100
310069011352119080415183003101300321210000000013800001000000000000000000000000000
31006902000010000000010000000000101002000000
310070011348120080315183003101300321210000000014500001000000000000260000001010000
31007002000010000000010000000000001001000100
310071011352118080315103003101300320210000000014411001000000000000000000000000000
31007102000010000000000000000000000001000100
310072011348119080315133003101301320210000000040800001000000000000000000000000000
31007202000010300000010000000000001001000000
310073011352117080315113003101301320210000100016400001000000000000000000000000000
31007302000010000000010000000000201003000000
310074011348118080315133003101301320210000000014400001000000000000160000000000000
31007402000010000000000000000000001001000000
310075011350117080315133003101300320210000100031000001000000000000000000000000000
31007502000000000000000000000000000001000000
310076011343120080315183003101300310210000000021500001000000000000000000000000000
```

```
31007602000000000000020000000000001001000000
310077010339120080315183003101300210100000100012800001000000000000000000000000000
31007702000000000000000000000000000001000000
310078011338124080415133003101300320210000000009600001000000000000000000020000000
31007802000010000000000000000000000001000000
310079010348121080415183003101300211100000100009000001000000000000000000000000000
31007902000010000000000000000000000001000000
310080011330131080415193003101301320210000000047300001000000000000000000011000010
31008002000010000000000000010000001001000000
310081010330133080415013003101422443633399200007222990990000000002249203924222220
31008102222229898222982233232222444444440122
310082011327138080415193003101300210210000000026400001000000000000000000011000010
31008202000010100000000000000001001001000000
310083011343122080415163003101300320210000000018000001000000000000000000001001000
31008302001110000000020000000000101002010100
310084011339122080415163003101301320210000000013200001000000000000000000010000000
31008402000010100000000000000000001001000100
310085011343121080415163003101301320210000000009400001000000000000000000000000000
31008502000010000000010010000000100002000100
310086011337122080415163003101301310210000000011500001000000000000000000010000000
31008602100000000000000000000000000001000100
310087010342121080415163003101301320210000000017700001000000000000000000000000000
31008702001010000000010000010000100002000100
310088011338121080415163003101301310210000000013200001000000000000000000000000000
31008802000100000000000000000000100002000000
310089011335127080415163003101300210220000000005800001000000000000000000010000000
31008902000010100000000000000000200003000100
310090011335126080415163003101300210220000000016300001000000000000000000020000000
31009002001000001000000000000000201003000100
310091011332128080415163003101300210220000100006200001000000000000000000010000000
31009102000000000000000000000000000001000000
310092011329130080415163003101301210220000000023000001000000000000000000011000010
31009202000010100000010000000000101002000100
310093011331127080415163003101300210220000000017600001000000000000160000021001000
31009302000010100000000000010000201003000100
310094011328130080415163003101300210220000000013000001000000000000160000021001000
31009402000010100000000000010000201003000100
310095011328126080415163003101300210100000100006013001000000000000000000000000000
31009502000000100000000000010000001001000000
310096011325131080415163003101300210100000100008413001000000000000000000020000000
31009602001010000000000000000000000001000100
310097010323131080415163003101300210220000100003900001000000000000000000020000000
31009702000010000000000000000000100002000000
310098011320133080415163003101300210220000100004700001000000000000000000020000000
31009802001100101000010000000000001001000000
310099011318134070415162753101300210100000100005713001000000000000000000020000000
31009902100000000000000000000000000001000000
310100010316135070415162753101300210100000100004313001000000000000000000020000000
31010002100000000000000000000000000001000000
310101011343128080415163253101300220102010100015011001000000000000000000020000000
31010102000000000000000000000000000001000100
310102011341136080415163253101300220100000000007200001000000000000000000011000010
31010202000010000000000000000000001001000000
310103011339138080415163003101300221100000000025700001000000000000000000011010000
31010302000010100000000000010000000001000000
310104011337138080415163003101300220100000100070211001000000000000000000020000000
31010402001000000000000000000000100002000100
310105011334143080415103003101300210220000000003000001000000000000000000000000000
31010502000010000000000000000000211003000100
310106011358123080415183003101300210100000100033200001000000000000000000000000000
```

```
3101060200001000000000000000000001001000100
31010701136112209041518300310130021010000010001220000100000000000000000000000000
3101070200001000000000000000000001001000000
31010801036712209041518300310130021010000000000660000100000000000000000000000000
3101080200001000000000000000000000001000000
31010901033814408041519300310130032021000000001270000100000000000000000000000000
3101090200001000000000000000000004444444440000
31011001133814108041516300310130031121000000001310000100000000000000000001010000
31011002000010000000000000010000101002000100
31011101033714108041516300310130021010000000002150000100000000000000000000000000
3101110200000000000000000000000000001000100
31011201135113808041519325310130032021000000001060000100000000000000000001010000
31011202000010000000000000010000200003000100
31011301034813808041519325310130032021000000001460000100000000000000000000000000
31011302000010000000000000000000200003000000
31011401134513908041519300310130032021000000001710000100000000000000000001000010
31011402001010100000000000010000200003000000
31011501034313908041518300310130021010000010002090000100000000000000000000000000
3101150200001000000000000000000000001000100
31011601033214208041517300310130021022000000002270000100000000000000000000000000
3101160200001010100000000000000000001001010000
31011701033014308041517300310130021022000000004090000100000000000000000020000000
3101170200000000000000000000000001002010100
31011801033314408041517300310130021022000010001590000100000000000000000010000000
3101180200001010000000000000000001001000100
31011901133114608041517300310130021122000010005191100100000000000000000011010000
3101190200001010000000000000000001001010100
31012001134413108041510325210110022010100010018811101000000018600000000021010000
31012002001010000000000001000000201103010100
31012101132312808041516300310130021010000000000440000100000000000000000000000000
310121020000101000000000000000000000001000000
31012201032612708041516300310130021010000010000240000100000000000000000000000000
3101220200001000000000000000000000001000000
31012301135313908041507325310130022110000010000560000100000000000000000000000000
31012302000000000000000000000000000000000000
31012401135414008041519300310130022110000010004041110100000000000000000000000000
31012402000010000000000000010000000001000000
31012501133214808041517300310130021121000000001390000100000000000000000000000000
3101250200001000000000000000000001001000000
31012601035314108041507300310130022110000010000650000100000000000000000000000000
31012602000000000000000000000000000000000000
31012701135114108041519300310130032021000010001630000100000000000000000000000000
3101270200101000000000000000000000001000100
31012801135014308041507300310130032021000010001060000100000000000000000000000000
31012802000010000000000000010000001001000000
31012901134614208041518300310130032021000000000820000100000000000000000000000000
31012902000010001000010000000000001001000100
31013001035811908031518300310130032021000000004110000100000000000000000000000000
3101300200001000000000000000000000001000100
31013101035511908031518300310130032021000010001140000100000000000000000000000000
3101310200001000000000000000000000001000000
31013201035711808031518300310130032021000000004830000100000000000000000000000000
3101320200001000000000000000000000001000000
31013301035911708031518300310130021110000010000320000100000000000000000000000000
3101330200000000000000000000000000001000000
31013401036411909031512300310130021021000010001090000100000000000000000000000000
3101340200000000000000000000000000001000000
31013501036712109041518300310130021110000000000270000100000000000000000000000000
3101350200000000000000000000000000001000100
31013601036512309041518300310130021010000000000330000100000000000016000001010000
3101360200001000000000000000000000001000000
31013701031314207041516275310130021010000010001601300100000000000000000020000000
3101370200001000000000000000000001001000000
31013801031114207041518275310130021021000000000901300100000000000000000020000000
3101380200000000000000000000000001001000000
31013901133813208041510325210130022010000010036001101100000006130016000020000000
31013902001110502000010000000000202103020100
```

Part 2. Data from Terrace Survey Forms

Included here are data from the terrace survey forms that could not be numerically coded. Included also are all published references to features we could identify in terms of our terrace numbering system. The abbreviation *P.U.S.* means "possible but unmeasurable structure noted." This refers to cases where a structure is probably present, but is so plowed down and/or eroded that no measurements could be made. Many locations mentioned in the various publications of Caso's Monte Albán project could not be tied to our numbering system, e.g., "*estaca* 29," *Monticulo Nopalito, Plataforma de la Oficina, Plataforma de la Tanque*, and others. References to *Tesoro* mean Caso 1970. *Urnas* refers to Caso and Bernal (1952). Entries in quotation marks without source cited are comments by persons who completed the survey forms.

Terrace number

1 Tomb 153: CBA: *Tabla* XVI. Comment: Tomb 153, a IIIb–IV tomb, seems to pertain to a structure earlier than the last-constructed patio. A baby burial was noted in a IIIb–IV pot adjacent to Tomb 153.

2 Grooved, cut greenstone noted.

4 Stone wall along east edge of terrace may be recent.

6 Tomb 134: CBA: *Tabla* XVI.

7 One "grooved stone" noted.

18 Tomb 103, contained bird head in jade: Caso and Bernal 1965:889; Caso 1965: 904–905. Offering in the patio of this tomb described in Caso (1942). Caso (1938) includes a plan of the mound (*Plano* 16), a plan of the tomb (*Plano* 15), and description of glyph "*en la cornisa*." See also CBA: Chapter VIII, passim. Tomb 111: Caso (1942) description of "Old God" vase (Figure 20 and p. 183); Caso (1965b) description of head-shaped brazier; CBA: *Tabla* IV. Tomb 110: Bernal 1949; CBA: *Tabla* XIII.

19 Tomb 172: CBA: *Tabla* XVI.

20 Tomb 104: Caso 1965a:864, 866–867, Figures 27, 28; Caso and Bernal 1965:889. Description of jade in Caso (1965b: 904–905). Description of stone inscription in Caso (1965c). Description of headdress with serpent in Bernal (1949:64, Figure 16); Caso (1938:68–69, *Plano* 13) shows configuration of patio and location on the terrace, *Plano* 17, the tomb (see also Figures 94, 95, 96, 99–102, *Lámina* I); CBA: Chapter VIII, passim. Tomb 118: Caso 1942:183; *Tesoro*: 54; CBA: *Tabla* VII. Comment: Caso (1938: *Plano* 13) shows the remnants of residential architecture over most of the surface of Terrace 20. This indicates that this portion of the ramp north of the north platform was not a road, but rather, a residential zone.

21 Tomb 13: CBA: *Tabla* XVI. Tomb 18: CBA, *Tabla* XVI. Tomb 21: Caso (1965b: 929) describes five copper axes found above this tomb, indicating Monte Albán IV; CBA: *Tabla* XIII. Tomb 138: CBA: *Tabla* XVI. Tomb 139: Bernal 1949: Figures 21, 42,

and 44–48; CBA: *Tabla* XIII. Tomb 140: Bernal 1949: Figure 59; CBA, *Tabla* XVI. Tomb 148: CBA: 281. Features: Several probable drainage features noted in the excavation areas. The terrace is bisected by a rubble wall running east–west. Its date of construction could not be determined. Comments: Much excavation has been carried out here, exposing a number of rooms, patios, and other residential features. Because of the complexity of the stratigraphy and architecture exposed, few statements can be made concerning the contemporaneity of occupation of rooms, traffic patterns, or the like. Most of the tombs excavated here pertain to periods IIIa and IIIb. This probably indicates that most buildings visible on the surface also pertain to those periods. In this light it is interesting to point out that the survey crew noted a general tendency for exposed walls to be oriented roughly 6° west of north, which seems to have been the normal pattern for buildings built during the Classic period.

22 One P.U.S. noted near the south end of the terrace.

23 Two P.U.S. noted, one near the north end, the other near the center of the terrace.

24 Known as *Montículo X*, see Caso (1935: 13–15 and excavation plan). Also Caso (1938:16–18). Caso (1965b:899, Figure 5) describes Offering 1, which contained carved jade (Period II), see also p. 900. A carved stone, the *Lápida de Bazán*, was found on the slope of this terrace (see Caso 1938:18, Figure 25; Caso 1965a, Figure 13; and Caso 1965c:941).

25 Comment: As part of the work on this terrace done during 1974 in connection with the new restaurant, Mexican archaeologists rebuilt the wall separating this terrace from the one above it (Terrace 24). As I interpret it, during this excavation and construction, the bottom of a broad staircase was exposed that originally connected these two terraces. Later, obviously before *Montículo X* was expanded to its current size (since the east edge of this mound extends nearly to the edge of Terrace 24), this staircase was replaced with a vertical wall, now the east retaining wall of Terrace 24. This new wall was probably built after Monte Albán II, when *Montículo X* was expanded. Traffic flow between Terraces 24 and 25 would have ceased, and the north platform area would have become more isolated, in my opinion, as a result of the change.

26 Little evidence of architecture.

27 This terrace contains two features that have been described in the literature. Tomb 7 is described in detail in Caso (1970). (See also Caso 1932; 1935; 1965b:908–914, 918–929, Figures 34–37, 44, 46, 48–57, 63; Caso 1965c:952–953, 956–957, Figures 4, have been used during Monte Albán IV prior to its Monte Albán V reuse (see CBA: 413). The large mound group consisting of three mounds and an *adoratorio* is the one referred to by Caso and Bernal as *Sistema Y.* Stela 16 was found on the west mound of this group (see Caso 1935:18; Bernal 1949: Figure 60; *Tesoro*: 37; and CBA: 113–137, *Planos* 2–6, and Tabla II). *Plano* 2 in CBA seems to be in error in showing an orientation of several degrees west of north for the group. The other architectural plans in CBA indicate a north–south orientation, except for a late (IIIb or IV) room atop the north building. Tomb 10: Caso 1965:868, Figure 29; *Tesoro*: 37; CBA: *Tabla* XVI. Tomb 12: *Tesoro*: 37. Tomb 158: CBA: *Tabla* XVI. Tomb 159: CBA: *Tabla* XVI.

29 Tomb 42: CBA: *Tabla* XVI. Tomb 65: Caso 1935:19–23; CBA: *Tabla* XVI. Tomb 66: Caso 1935:19–23; CBA: *Tabla* XVI. Tomb 67: Caso 1935:19–23; CBA: *Tabla* VII. One piece of alabaster was noted.

30 Tomb 58: Caso (1935:19–23; CBA: 399 and *Tabla* XVI) indicates Monte Albán IV date. Tomb 61: Caso 1935:19–23; CBA: *Tabla* VII. Tomb 72: Caso 1935:19–23, Figure 35. Caso (1965:863) describes murals; Caso (1965c:936) describes Monte Albán II glyphs. Comment: "There are three . . . central patios, apparently contemporaneous, with surrounding rooms, suggesting occupation by at least three . . . families."

31 Tomb 4: Caso 1932:15; Caso 1935:17; *Tesoro*: 24, 29, 38, Figures 15, 16. Tomb 6: Caso 1932:16, carved stone in Figure 24a; Bernal (1949: Figures 30, 38, and 49; *Tesoro*: 30–33, 31) includes description of carved stone (see also Figures 18, 20, 21, 22, 23; CBA: *Tablas* VII, XIII). Tomb 71 (Caso 1935:17, 18).

35 Tomb 48: CBA: *Tabla* XVI.

39 Tomb 40: CBA: *Tabla* XVI. Tomb 74: Caso 1935:19–23; CBA: 281. One "strange piece" of ground stone noted.

40 Tomb 150: CBA: *Tabla* XVI. Tomb 151: CBA: *Tabla* XVI. Comment: Beneath these tombs, exposed by excavation, is a feature we called the "weird structure." The crew director describes it as "a primary structure of a very unusual shape [that] for some reason was built on the steep slopes near the bottom of the *barranca*. Apparently later the structure was filled in and leveled off to form a mound, on which other structures were no doubt built. Two tombs (150 and 151) were built below the floor of the later structure. The only certain part of the later structure still remaining is plaster flooring on top of Tomb 151. During excavation and reconstruction, the tombs were stabilized by rock and mortar walls, which should not be confused with the original construction. A small residence with patio is off to the north of the main structure."

41 "This is a small terrace containing one relatively simple residence."

43 Tomb 45: Marquina 1964: *Lámina* 94. Tomb 46: CBA: *Tabla* XVIII. Tomb 47, Caso (1965b:908; CBA: 399, *Tabla* XVI) indicates the tomb was Monte Albán IV, since it contained both Fine Orange and plumbate. Tomb 57: Caso 1935:19–23; CBA: Tabla VII. Comment: "Small rock shelters were found in the limestone outcrop along the southern edge of the terrace."

45 "This terrace is actually a group of 'subterraces' at slightly different elevations."

46 "This terrace consists of two subunits."

47 "A large terrace with varying elevations."

50 One pestle noted.

51 Four stone balls were found, three in the southwest corner of the patio. The room at the top of the north mound has two circular depressions in the floor, .5–1 m in diameter. One stone disc was found, and one chunk of Oaxaca onyx (travertine).

52 "On the south end there is a large stone with carvings, probably rolled from the Main Plaza."

53 One piece of jasper noted.

58 One serpentine bead found.

61 One sandstone abrader noted and one canal fragment described as "a cut stone with roughed down center" also noted.

67 Mica and obsidian flakes eroding out of east face.

70 One probable Fine Orange sherd found.

72 One possible greenstone celt and one possible mortar noted.

76 One possible hammerstone, and mica fragments noted.

78 Tomb 56: Caso 1935:19–23. One greenstone mano noted, as well as a small amount of mica and a chunk of copper ore (?). Comment: "A deep pit excavated here exposes 4.7 m of fill, and does not seem to reach bedrock. An early wall section was noted near the bottom of this pit."

79 Function: The absence of mounds arround a patio and the small size of the room at the top of the mound seem to argue against this being an elite residence. Since the terrace does occur near the juncture of several important ancient roads, it may have been one of the gatelike features discussed on page 000. The modern I.N.A.H. guard's house is situated on this terrace, facing the mound. One stone ring fragment noted.

80 Possible chert choppers located on north end of terrace.

81 Mica fragments. Comment: "Possible house in northwest corner, but unmeasurable."

82 Mica noted.

84 Mica noted.

85 Function: An isolated mound such as is found here, adjacent to an important road, may indicate a gatelike function as discussed on page 76.

86 Greenstone noted.

87 Function: This is one of the largest artificially constructed flat spaces on Monte Albán. Although abundant artifacts were noted, including hammerstones, manos and metates, as well as pottery, and chipped-stone tools, no evidence of residential architecture was found. The terrace's location, at the confluence of several important roads, and adjacent to an apparent elite residence (Terrace 1463), suggests it may have been a marketlike area. No definite evidence can be offered, however. See page 83 for further discussion. A niche or small tomb is exposed along the south retaining wall.

92 Function: The presence of an isolated mound, with a very small room at the top,

and adjacent to an elite residence and road, suggests a civic or gatelike function. See pp. 20-21, 76 for discussion. One stone disk noted.

93 One possible ground-stone celt fragment noted.

95 One sandstone drain tile noted.

101 Excavations have exposed a stone-lined circular pit roughly 1 m in diameter.

105 Function: This terrace, and the adjacent Terrace 1457, with what appears to be large open spaces, good traffic access (via road F and the large ramp running to the southwest), and locations between two elite residences, suggests some kind of "public" function, perhaps marketing. Miscellaneous artifact: Mica noted.

111 One fragment of mica.

114 One bead or pendant.

135 One small stone with carved surface over roughly 8 cm by 5 cm with a geometric design.

138 One bedrock mortar noted.

142 One polished slate fragment described as "not sure of function" noted.

145 Features: A stone wall roughly 1 m high runs along the west edge of the terrace, between the two large defensive walls. An excavation has exposed a subterranean room, accessible by staircase. The room has well-cut stone and mortar walls and a plaster floor. It is 1.8 m in depth, and 1.8 by 1.17 m in area, the long axis running approximately SW–NE. It was probably originally roofed.

148 Two pieces of serpentine noted and greenstone described as "ground flat" also noted.

149 "This terrace is surrounded by stone walls, with only one opening near the southwest corner. Inside the walls are four low rocky mounds, probably residences."

157 "This is a large, uneven, difficult-to-define terrace, with one excavated structure partially exposed."

160 Function: Terraces with isolated mounds such as this, adjacent to important roads and elite residences, may have had public functions such as markets or gates.

161 Jade mosaic found in the patio area, pertaining to Monte Albán IIIa (see Caso 1942: 185, Figure 22; Caso 1965b:906). Tomb 119: CBA: *Tabla* XVI. Tomb 120: CBA: *Tabla* XVI. One-half of a large ground stone noted, "like a flat doughnut roughly 40 cm in diameter."

164 One P.U.S. noted.

166 Two P.U.S. noted.

171 Tomb 43: Caso 1938:32; Caso 1965b:897, Figure 1–a description of jade earplugs; CBA: *Tabla* IV. Tomb 97: Caso (1938: 32–33) indicates a Monte Albán IV date (see also CBA: *Tabla* XVI).

172 One P.U.S. noted.

173 Four P.U.S. noted.

175 Tomb 160: CBA: *Tabla* VII. Tomb 161: CBA: *Tabla* XVI.

177 Two P.U.S. noted.

178 One P.U.S. noted.

179 Two P.U.S. noted.

180 One probable structure roughly 25 m^2 noted.

181 One probable structure noted, roughly 14 m^2 in area.

182 One P.U.S. noted.

184 One structure, roughly 25 m^2 noted, and one measurable structure noted.

185 One P.U.S. noted.

186 One P.U.S. noted. Large ground-stone pieces noted, also one large chunk of ignumbrite; "not local."

188 One P.U.S. noted.

189 One P.U.S. noted.

193 Two P.U.S. noted.

194 One P.U.S. noted.

195 Two P.U.S. noted.

200 Features: Possible steps and a fragment of a stone floor. One P.U.S. noted.

205 Mica noted. Two possible structures, 72 m^2, 112 m^2.

206 Carved stone noted adjacent to Terrace 1461. The north end of this terrace, between Terraces 1461 and 205 is an artificial flat, open surface. The south end of the terrace has five low, probably residential, mounds (areas: roughly 100, 64, 90, 100, and 100 m^2). A stone wall between the two northernmost mounds could have served to restrict the flow of traffic from the "public" area around Terraces 1461 and 207, thereby assuring the privacy of the residential area.

211 This terrace contains a low mound adjacent to a break in the defensive wall, possibly indicating a gatelike function.

212 A low, level area running east–west across

the terrace may have been a road or ramp.
215 One hammerstone noted.
217 Low mound, possible structure noted, 92 m.
231 A series of walls, exidence of a structure, were noted eroding out of the northwest edge of the terrace *under* the defensive wall.
232 One Oaxaca onyx bowl fragment, and one fragment of mica noted.
240 Mica noted.
242 Tomb 122: CBA: *Tabla* XVI. One piece of either drain tile or decoration piece noted.
243 Chunk of chalk or limestone noted.
248 One quartz hammerstone noted.
251 One possible structure noted, 33 m.
253 One P.U.S. noted.
254 One P.U.S. noted.
255 One P.U.S. noted.
256 Tomb 92: Caso 1938:33; Monte Albán IV (CBA: *Tabla* XVI).
258 One P.U.S. noted.
259 One P.U.S. noted.
260 Two P.U.S. noted.
262 Two P.U.S. noted.
264 The tomb here is probably Tomb 2, judging from the map of tombs in *Tesoro*, Figure 9 (see also *Tesoro*: 22, 26–28, Figures 10, 11, 13; Caso 1932:14; and CBA: *Tabla* XVI).
266 One P.U.S. noted.
268 Two possible structures noted, each ca. 50 m^2 in area.
269 One P.U.S. noted.
271 One P.U.S. noted.
272 One possible structure noted, ca. 25 m^2 in area. One unidentifiable piece of ground stone noted.
273 One P.U.S. noted.
275 Two P.U.S. noted.
276 One P.U.S. noted.
277 One P.U.S. noted.
291 One chunk of magnetite noted. Also one grooved abrading stone noted.
293 One P.U.S. noted.
296 One P.U.S. noted.
297 Two P.U.S. noted.
304 One hammerstone noted.
306 Small dry cave in limestone outcrop above the terrace.
311 Stone floor noted.
312 Circle of stones less than 1 m in diameter noted, possibly a stone-lined pit. A drilled hole in a limestone outcrop roughly 3 cm across and 3 cm deep, "apparently the start of a quarrying operation." One mano or pounding stone noted.
313 Tomb 1: Caso 1932:14; *Tesoro*: 21, 26, Figure 9. One hammerstone noted.
314 "At approximately the center of the south edge there is an irregularly shaped piece of limestone with a square hole pecked into it to a depth of about 5 cm. The square is roughly 30 cm square." One chert hammerstone noted.
318 Mica present.
324 "Quarry for limestone blocks located on north end of terrace."
326 Several mica fragments noted. "The terrace was covered with three sunken areas that were patios, probably indicating three residences."
327 Probably two residences represented. "A good terrace to excavate due to its preservation and small size. May be pure Late I and II."
329 A ramp bisects the terrace, running NW–SE. Steps noted on this ramp. "Limestone outcrops present–may have been quarried."
331 Wall fragments and a stone floor noted.
335 One fragment of mica noted.
337 May have gatelike function?
338 One P.U.S. noted.
341 One possible structure noted, ca. 160 m^2.
345 One possible structure noted, ca. 96 m^2.
350 Tomb 79: Caso 1938: 32; CBA: *Tabla* XIII. Tomb 80: Caso 1938:33; CBA: *Tabla* XVI. Tomb 81: Caso 1938:32. Tomb 87: Caso 1938:33. One grooved abrading stone noted.
52 Two P.U.S. noted.
353 One P.U.S. noted.
356 One P.U.S. noted.
358 Fragment of mica noted.
362 One possible structure noted, roughly 56 m^2?
374 A grooved stone abrader and an earspool noted.
377 A probable kiln with stokehole has been dug into the arroyo bank on the northwest side of the terrace. The kiln is rock lined, and has a maximum diameter of about 2 m. The stokehole is roughly 1.5 m below the top of the kiln. "No kiln wasters or other fired material noted."
380 One celt fragment noted.
388 Serpentine pebbles noted.

389 One chunk of magnetite noted.
396 Mica noted.
400 "Retaining wall fragments in this area suggest the main road would have been roughly 8 m wide."
402 One metate or mortar carved into a large rock near the edge of the terrace. One possible bedrock mortar and one greenstone celt fragment noted.
403 Ground-stone piece, possibly an abrader, and mica fragments noted.
409 Mica noted. A possible structure is 61 m^2.
410 Jadeite bead noted.
416 One serpentine pebble noted.
417 One serpentine pebble noted.
418 One grooved abrading stone. One cylinder ca. ¼ inch diameter by 1 inch long of travertine or Oaxaca onyx.
420 Consists of three possible houses above a possible walkway that may be the eroded remnant of a road running along the slope.
423 A large gap in the defensive wall just below this terrace seems to be a recent feature, made by animals herded to and from grazing.
432 One probable pounding stone noted. Evidence exists in this area of more terraces, but serious erosion prohibits secure identification and description.
436 One celt noted.
437 Two probable houses noted, 49 m^2 and 76 m^2.
440 One greenstone pestle found in the center of the terrace.
451 Three P.U.S. noted.
452 Probable residences exposed by numerous potholes.
453 *El Pitahayo*, Tomb 70: Caso 1935:23; CBA: *Tabla* VII. Tomb 77: Caso (1935:23, Figures 45–46, 48) described as "very rich"; *Urnas*: Figures 249, 251–252, 341, one urn "the most beautiful at Monte Albán"; Marquina: *Lámina* 94; CBA: *Tabla* VII, *Plano* 8. Tomb 78: Caso 1938:32; Caso 1965b:898; CBA: *Tabla* VII, *Plano* 8. One quartzite burnishing stone noted. The orientations of mounds, though somewhat difficult to assess accurately, seem to be largely congruent with the cardinal directions. Walls exposed at the tops of the mounds, however, range from a few to 10° west of north. This may reflect the original construction of the mounds in Late I or II, and their use up until the later periods, when the west-of-north orientations were common. The three numbered tombs pertain to Monte Albán II. This, plus the fact that Kuttruff noted mostly Period II and some of Late I ceramics in the fill of mounds, tends to support this idea. According to Kuttruff "mounds were probably constructed during M.A.II, although there is a considerable amount of M.A.V debris in the fields." A very large unnumbered cruciform tomb was noted in the central mound group. Since such a tomb was not mentioned in any of the published references it seems the tomb may have been looted after the I.N.A.H. excavations here.
454 Two P.U.S. noted.
462 Two P.U.S. noted.
464 Tomb 54: Bernal 1949: Figure 54; CBA: *Tabla* XVI. Three P.U.S. noted.
466 Three P.U.S. noted.
467 "A rectangular sloping area . . . with six leveled areas that could have served as the locations for residential structures."
468 One P.U.S. noted.
469 Two P.U.S. noted.
470 Three P.U.S. noted.
474 One P.U.S. noted.
476 Two P.U.S. noted. Road cut here exposes roughly 2 m of stratigraphy, including three superimposed plaster floors.
482 Three P.U.S. noted.
484 Small ochre fragment noted.
487 Three P.U.S. noted.
490 Two P.U.S. noted.
491 The small isolated mound, large open area, and probable access to a main road suggest a possible public function. It is interesting to note that a probable residence in the southwest portion of the terrace was separated from the probable road by a stone wall—perhaps to assure privacy.
496 Three P.U.S. noted. Nearly 3 m of stratigraphy exposed in a road cut, including walls and floors.
503 A sloping area with microterraces with probably six or seven residences.
508 Two P.U.S. noted. One celt fragment noted.
510 One P.U.S. noted, two others likely.
518 One P.U.S. noted. One complete and two fragments of greenstone celt noted.
520 One piece of cut and polished stone noted.
521 "Fragment of spherical crystalline object that had been drilled."
522 Three or four P.U.S. noted.

523 This large terrace is actually part of the major defensive wall, and may have had gate functions. A large staircase in the northwest corner leads to the major road in the direction of site subdivision 10, and both major roads in Monte Albán proper seem to converge on this terrace. Additionally, another ancient road, that passes through Terrace 555, converges on this point. A few wall fragments were noted on the terrace surface, but no direct architectural evidence is present, other than the staircase that supports this functional suggestion.
524 Two P.U.S. noted.
525 A large terrace with 14 P.U.S. arrayed along an ancient road.
526 Multilevel terrace with three P.U.S. noted on flattened areas.
527 "Three level areas at more or less regular intervals along the terrace are probably the locations of single house structures."
532 One P.U.S. noted.
537 One P.U.S. noted.
538 One P.U.S. noted.
540 One pottery disc that may have been used as a scraper.
541 One quartzite hammerstone noted.
542 One P.U.S. noted. One mortar noted.
550 Multilevel terrace with at least six or seven P.U.S. noted.
559 Tomb 90: Caso 1938:33, was looted earlier.
560 At least two P.U.S. noted.
561 Two P.U.S. noted.
562 One P.U.S. noted.
563 Probably single residence. Three bowl or mortarlike metates and five manos suggest a workshop? One full grooved axe noted.
565 Three metate and four manos present suggests a workshop? Also present: A groundstone "ring," 7.5 mm thick by 15 cm diameter.
566 Sandstone slab floor noted. One quartzite pounding stone noted. Several mortarlike metates and several manos suggest a workshop.
583 One celt noted.
585 Two P.U.S. noted.
594 One piece of mica noted.
606 One P.U.S. noted.
616 Small caves cut into bedrock above the terrace, possibly a limestone quarry(?).
618 One polishing stone noted.
622 Celts noted.
628 One metate noted with parallel striations, possibly for some special kind of grinding.
629 One hammerstone noted.
634–636 We noted at least two P.U.S. on Terrace 634. Winter has excavated nearly all of this terrace, as well as Terraces 635 and 636 (see Winter 1974).
638 One P.U.S. noted.
640 One P.U.S. noted. One small, unidentifiable piece of ground stone noted.
643 The arroyo walls along this area were built up with stones in ancient times. An ancient dam across this arroyo is situated just northwest of the terrace. One hammerstone noted. One ground piece of malachite noted.
649 One P.U.S. noted. "Ground rock" noted.
656 Two P.U.S. noted.
658 One bedrock mortar noted.
663 One celt noted.
665 Two P.U.S. noted.
666 One P.U.S. noted, with a small attached room.
669 Two P.U.S. noted.
670 One jadeite bead noted.
671 One P.U.S. noted.
676 "Located on the ramp running along the 'defensive wall' at this point. Apparent fragments of this wall are present in the form of a line of rocks along the outside edge of the terrace."
682 "A large pile of roughly shaped stones along the back of the terrace is enigmatic. Were these quarried here, or stored for use in defense?"
683 "Another pile of stones, as is present on Terrace 682."
688 "Lower defensive wall runs along the outside edge of the terrace. Here the defensive wall is 1.5 m in width, but its original height cannot be estimated. A pile of stone rubble present, as on Terraces 682 and 683."
690 Sunken area present is probably a patio. One deep metate fragment noted.
695 Rubble pile noted, like those on Terraces 682, 683, and 688.
696 Rubble pile noted, like those on Terrace 682, etc.
697 "On the NW edge there is a substantial rubble wall—comparable in size to the 'upper defensive wall'."
698 Rubble pile noted, like those on Terrace 682, etc.
700 Rock rubble pile, like those found on Terrace 682, etc.

701 Rock rubble pile like those found on Terrace 682, etc.
709 One P.U.S. noted.
710 Two rock rubble piles, like those found on Terrace 682, etc.
711 One rock rubble pile noted, like those on Terrace 682, etc.
713 One large quartzite bead noted.
721 One quartzite drill noted.
722 Rock rubble pile noted, like those on Terrace 682, etc. "Several" P.U.S. noted.
733 Rock rubble pile noted, like those on Terrace 682, etc.
742 One P.U.S. noted.
743 One fossil noted.
750 Two probable houses, 107 m^2 and 45 m^2, noted.
753 One P.U.S. noted.
767 Two hammerstones noted.
773 One P.U.S. noted.
774 Two celt fragments noted.
775 One P.U.S. noted.
776 One hammerstone noted.
794 One chunk of mica noted. One P.U.S. noted.
800 Open double-mound group, adjacent to a major road. May be a public building.
802 One Fine Orange sherd noted. One P.U.S. noted.
803 Two P.U.S. noted.
804 One P.U.S. noted.
818 One piece of ground stone noted and described as "nature unknown."
827 One P.U.S. noted.
830 One pestle noted. One grooved grinding tool also noted.
831 One ground sandstone tool noted.
835 One chunk of mica noted, and one P.U.S. noted.
836 "Numerous chunks" of limestone present.
839 One quartzite pounding stone noted.
841 "One worked sherd that had apparently been used as a polisher." One small mano or pestle also noted.
842 One possible pestle noted and described as "either a pestle or a small mano."
845 Probably a one-house terrace.
848 One "hammerstone" noted.
867 Isolated mound on a large terrace. Possible public building or gatelike function?
868 "Possible colonial sherds noted."
879 Isolated mound on a large flat terrace. Possible public building or gatelike function?
887 "Maguey roasting pit present on east end of the terrace–could not determine whether it is modern or ancient."
904 One celt piece noted.
911 Large circular mortarlike feature suggests some special productive activity. It is 30 cm in height, has a diameter of 65 cm, and has a depression 15 cm deep by 20 cm diameter.
912 Two P.U.S. noted.
914 One P.U.S. noted. One ground-stone tool, "possibly a mano or a pestle."
916 One P.U.S. noted.
919 One hammerstone fragment and three P.U.S. noted.
921 One P.U.S. noted.
924 Two P.U.S. noted.
925 One "grinding stone" noted.
926 One P.U.S. noted.
927 One partially excavated P.U.S. noted.
931 One hammerstone and one P.U.S. noted.
933 One hammerstone noted.
935 One mano fragment noted, "very fancy, highly polished, almost marblelike in quality."
938 An open two-mound group, accessible from the main Monte Albán road. Possibly a public area, but function cannot be ascertained from surface evidence alone. Stone walls and/or steep retaining walls isolate the terrace from those east, west, and north, but there is easy access to the large, open area called Area 16, and ramps provide direct access to the road that passes through Monte Albán proper in this area. A stonewall extending east from the east mound may have served to divide traffic flow into two streams–one leading to the main area between the mounds, the other into what appears to be a more secluded area to the northwest of the east mound, surrounded north and south by stone walls, with a steep retaining wall to the east. The ramp leading up to the terrace in this area divides into two ramps, one leading to the one side of this wall, the other ramp to the other side. Faint traces of an *adoratorio* were noted between the mounds.
941 One greenstone celt noted.
943 A limestone outcrop here looks quarried.
945 One quartzite pounding stone and one P.U.S. noted.
946 One ground stone noted and described as, "function unknown; ground depression on both sides."
947 "Two hemispherical stones, each 10 cm in radius."
948 Ground-stone "doughnut" fragment found,

roughly 3.5 cm thick, with an estimated outside diameter of about 11 cm, made of nicely smoothed gray green granite.

953 One P.U.S. noted.

961 Folder missing.

963 One P.U.S. noted.

966 One 25 m^2 structure noted.

967 Two P.U.S. noted.

970 One fragment of a granite ball and two P.U.S. noted; one pestle also noted.

972 Two P.U.S. noted.

974 One P.U.S. noted.

979 One "toy" metate noted.

981 One P.U.S. noted.

983 One P.U.S. noted.

984 One bell-shaped pit is exposed. One mano fragment and one celt also noted.

991 Rock rubble pile noted like those on Terrace 682, etc.

1003 One P.U.S. noted. Looks like a one-house terrace.

1009 "Huge *olla* rim fragment found, rim 6″ high–not collected because it would not fit in the sherd bag."

1011 Two hunks of nonlocal granite stone noted of the sort used for manos.

1013 One P.U.S. noted.

1014 Two pieces of partially worked sandstone noted.

1015 One chunk of greenstone noted and described as having "a flat, round face."

1016 One pestle and many "partially worked sandstone and limestone balls present."

1025 One P.U.S. noted.

1028 One P.U.S. noted.

1037 One P.U.S. noted.

1044 One" possible pounder" noted.

1049 One ground stone noted and described as being "polished on one side; function unknown."

1070 One P.U.S. noted.

1071–1075 These are possibly recent, not ancient, terraces.

1077 Two bedrock mortars and one P.U.S. noted.

1078–1081 These terraces are possibly agricultural only, indicated by the paucity of remains noted.

1088 One P.U.S. noted.

1090 One P.U.S. noted.

1093 Probably a one-house terrace.

1095 "Possible *jaguey* (small modern reservoir) on south end of terrace."

1102 One bedrock mortar noted.

1106 Small remnant of stone wall in circular pattern, no scale indicated.

1114 "Wall fragments 16 or 17 m to the west may represent the original length of the terrace."

1119 One P.U.S. noted.

1125 "The terrace was identified on the basis of finding one probable corner fragment, and the fact that the slope has apparently been modified slightly to create a flat space. Erosion is so bad here, however, that the identification may be wrong. The slopes throughout this area are steep and badly eroded, and some terraces have probably completely disappeared."

1133 One P.U.S. noted.

1134 One celt fragment noted.

1135 "Retaining wall fragments indicate this was built as a terrace, but it would have been flooded when the reservoir was full. The same is true for Terrace 1134." One pestle fragment noted.

1136 One P.U.S. noted.

1137 The wild suggestion was made that this is a remnant of an early dam put across the *barranca*. Only excavation can tell.

1141 "All terraces in this immediate area are on natural outcrops, have a few retaining walls, and have little pottery. This area may have been used only for agriculture, or may have been occupied only briefly during Monte Albán II and then in IIIb (although a little IIIa was found). Several odd fragments of retaining walls, not associated with recognizable terraces were noted."

1144 "The probably ancient road that passes here is roughly 2 m wide."

1146 One P.U.S. noted.

1148 One P.U.S. noted.

1149 One P.U.S. noted.

1153 One P.U.S. noted.

1155 One P.U.S. noted, with a sunken central area, probably the patio.

1159 One P.U.S. noted.

1163 "Probably a one-house terrace."

1166 One P.U.S. noted.

1169 "Apparently some recent leveling and reuse of the area by residents of the *Colonia 3 de Mayo*."

1170 Very large open area with two mounds, suggestive of a public building.

1172 "Recent excavation has revealed a nicely built ancient retaining wall 1.5 m high."

1177 A low mound on the south edge of this terrace creates a space reminicent of a ball court, with the slope of Terrace 1170 acting as the court's other wall.

1179 Two P.U.S. noted.

1200 "Probably part of Terrace 1149."

1201 One P.U.S. noted.

1205 No pottery present. Function therefore uncertain.

1206 This terrace contains a possible kiln, a circular feature roughly 1.5 m in diameter and roughly 1.5 m in depth. The lip is stone lined. A lime coating 5 cm thick noted at one point. The walls have been reddened and blackened by the heat. Possibly a plaster kiln. No kiln wasters present.

1208 One P.U.S. noted.

1211 "May actually be two terraces."

1214 A possible public building, with direct access to the road passing east–west by means of a ramp.

1215 A possible stone dam noted across the small *barranca* to the east. Age unknown. One P.U.S. noted.

1220 One mano fragment and one celt fragment noted.

1222 One P.U.S. noted.

1225 One P.U.S. noted.

1226 Two quartzite pounders noted. "A main road crosses this terrace. Where this road crosses the defensive wall there is a ramp. The defensive wall makes a fairly sharp turn where the ramp is located, possibly to make the access point easier to defend." One mano and two celts noted.

1227 One P.U.S. noted.

1228 Four P.U.S. noted.

1230 A flat area carved out of bedrock, but no sherds or other cultural materials present.

1235 One probable quartzite pounder noted.

1239 One possible celt fragment noted.

1241 One pounding stone that looks like a celt. This terrace may be an extension of 1240.

1264 "One large chunk of fired clay with no specific shape."

1269 Three P.U.S. noted.

1273 Another of the large, difficult-to-define terraces in this area. Two mounds present. A public area?

1275 Difficult-to-define terrace that shows relatively little evidence of construction. One "crude" celt fragment noted.

1279 Two P.U.S. noted.

1290 One P.U.S. noted.

1298 One rock rubble pile like those noted in Terrace 682, etc.

1309 Two basin metates noted, square in shape, although their basins are round. "This is a broad, sloping area with probably about eight houses visible at the surface, each of which is a low mound or subterrace."

1310 One P.U.S. noted.

1316 One worked sherd noted, and a soil discoloration that may indicate a midden or house.

1322 One P.U.S. noted.

1323 "Two soil discolorations on lower edge, but contour suggests one structure, in the upper center of the terrace." One celt also noted.

1324 One celt fragment noted.

1325 One ground-stone travertine "doughnut" fragment, dimensions not given.

1327 An isolated mound on a large terrace, on a major road. Possibly had gatelike functions? One possible celt fragment noted.

1328 One piece of ignumbrite noted.

1333 One possible celt noted.

1339 One P.U.S. noted.

1341 "One white smooth stone disc, 2 mm thick, 1.5 cm in diameter."

1348 One P.U.S. noted.

1351 Two P.U.S. noted.

1355 One P.U.S. noted.

1359 One hammerstone noted.

1362 One pestle fragment noted.

1367 Two P.U.S. noted.

1369 "One ground-stone piece with highly polished flat surface and utilized edge."

1374 Function uncertain–could have been an agricultural terrace?

1375 One celt fragment noted.

1379 Soil discoloration may indicate P.U.S.

1381 One pestle noted.

1383 One P.U.S. noted.

1389 One "possible celt blank" noted.

1391 One P.U.S. noted.

1400 Limestone–shale outcrop above terrace has a small rock shelter.

1411 Missing folder.

1414 One human tooth found.

1434 Tomb 3: Caso 1932b:14; Caso 1935:17; Caso 1942:177; Marquina 1964: *Lámina* 94; CBA: *Tabla* XIII; *Tesoro*: 24, 28–29, Figures 13, 14. Tomb 8: Caso 1932b:32; Caso 1935:17; CBA: *Tabla* VII. Tomb 9: Caso 1932b:32; Caso 1935:17; Bernal 1949: Figure 25; Caso 1965b:903, Figure 13b; CBA: *Tabla* XIII. Tomb 30: Caso 1935:17; CBA: *Tabla* XVI.

1436 One chert pounding stone.

1445 A large platform at the north end of a defensive wall. Possible gatelike functions? This would have been the only reasonable point for traffic to flow past the wall because the wall's southern terminus is on a very steep slope.

1447 **Main Plaza**

Published information for buildings

Ball-Court: Caso 1935:11–13, Figures 24–26; Caso 1938:14; Marquina 1964: 318–322, *Fot.* 132, *Lámina* 88.

Adoratorio between Mounds p and h: Caso 1935:7; Acosta 1949. Structures g, h, and i: Caso 1938:10; Marquina 1964: *Láminas* 86, 91; Caso 1965:862; Caso 1965b:901, 903, Figures 7, 8.

Structure J: Caso 1938:10–14, 62; Caso 1942:173–174, Figures 13, 14; Caso 1947, passim; Marquina 1964:327–333, *Láminas* 86, 92; Caso 1965c:936–938, Figures 12, 13; Aveni and Linsley 1972; Marcus 1976: 127–131.

Mound 1 (*Danzantes* building): Dupaix 1834: Plates XXIII, XXIV; Dupaix 1969, Vol. II: *Lámina* 20, Figure 66; Holmes 1897: Part II: 223–224, Figure 71; Batres 1902:32, Plan 2, Plates XIV, XV; Caso 1928: passim; Caso 1935:7, 8, 10–11; Caso 1938:5, 66; Caso 1942:171–173; Villagra 1942; Caso 1947; Marquina 1964:322, 324, 326, *Láminas* 86, 89; Acosta 1965:814; Marcus 1976:125–127.

Mound m: Caso 1938:66–68, *Plano* 12; Caso 1942:171, Figure 10; Acosta 1958: 24–26; Marquina 1964:312–313, 322, 326, *Láminas* 86, 90, *Fot.* 140; Caso 1965b:909, Figure 23.

North Platform: Batres 1902:31, Plates VIII, XI, XII; Caso 1928, passim; Caso 1932:11–14; Caso 1935:5–7; Caso 1938: 14–16, 63–66; Caso 1942:174–181, Figures 15, 16; Bernal 1949: Figure 17; Acosta 1958: Figure 5; Marquina 1964:314, 316–318, 350; Acosta 1965:846; Caso 1965b: 901, 903, 905–906, 908, 910–911, Figures 9, 13, 17, 18, 20, 24, 25, 27, 30; Caso 1965c:941; CBA: 89–106, 137–141, *Plano* I, passim; Caso 1970:20–23, Figures 1–3, 5, 6.

Mound p: Bernal 1949: 66, *Lámina* V.

Plataforma Este: Marquina 1964:322; CBA: 443–444, *Plano* 10.

South Platform: Holmes 1897: Part II: 220, Plate XXVII; Batres 1902: Plates II, III, IV, XVIII; Caso 1928; Caso 1938:5; Acosta 1958:12, Figures 9, 10, 14–16, 26–29; Marquina 1964:318, 349, *Lámina*, 86; Caso 1965:856.

System IV: Caso 1942: Figures 11, 12; Marquina 1964:312–313, 322, 326; *Lámina* 86, *Fot.* 139; Acosta 1965: Figures 6, 7.

Published information for Main Plaza tombs: Tomb 60: Caso 1935:8, 9; Caso 1942:177, Marquina 1964:325; CBA: *Tabla* XIII. Tomb 69: Caso 1935:10; Bernal 1949: Figures 36, 52, 61; Marquina 1964:325, *Lámina* 94. Tomb 116: CBA: *Tabla* XVI. Tomb 117: CBA: *Tabla* XVI. Tomb 123: Caso 1965a:868–869. Tomb 128: Marquina 1964: *Lámina* 94; CBA: *Tabla* XIII. Tomb 135: Marquina 1964, *Lámina* 94; CBA: *Tabla* VII. Tomb 152: CBA: *Tabla* IV. Tomb 162: CBA: *Tabla* VII. Tomb 164: Bernal 1949: Figure 58; CBA: *Tabla* XIII. Tomb 166: CBA: *Tabla* VII.

Miscellaneous artifacts: Mica present on North Platform, especially abundant south of the main mound group.

1451 Probably an elite residence. Although it is only a two-mound group, the south edge of the patio faces a steep wall, limiting access to the patio.

1452 One hammerstone noted.

1454 No sherds from the mound, so dating is difficult. Sherds in the general vicinity are mostly Monte Albán V.

1456 *Juego de Pelota del Plumaje* or Ball Court Number 2: Caso 1942:183. A stone column was exposed in the north bank of the court, whose function is unknown, probably pertaining to an earlier building. Some mica noted. A carved stone fragment was noted in the floor of the court. The modern paved road to the Main Plaza cuts into the base of this terrace, exposing a vertical maximum of 2.4 m of stratified deposits. Most of the exposed material consists of tan fill, in some places with charcoal bands, but plaster floors and vertical cut-stone walls are also present. No obvious interpretation of these materials could be made.

1457 Tomb 108: Caso 1938:92–95, *Plano* 19; CBA: *Tabla* XIII. Tomb 109: Caso 1938: 92–95, Figure 107, *Plano* 19; CBA: *Tabla* XII. One P.U.S. noted, as well as three roughly measurable structures (227 m^2, 86 m^2, 61 m^2), two of which have been partially excavated. Possible other-lithic and shell work.

1458 *Siete Venado*: This is a large mound group with ball court attached on the east side. A large flat area north of the group is included in this description, an area bounded on the north by one of the large defensive walls and on the west by a smaller stone wall no more than 1 m high. This area had some evidence of stone walls, and may have had low buildings on it that have been plowed down. Near the southwest corner of this area two large shaped basalt stones were found, originally one piece, that together, no doubt, weigh more than a ton. It looks as though some stone-working project was under way that was never completed A pit in the smaller south mound exposes roughly 6 m of fill. This same mound has a carved stone beam at the north edge of the room atop the staircase (Caso 1942: 185; Acosta 1958: Figure 35). West of this same mound, in what appears to be back dirt, is a heavy concentration of worked milky quartz that looks to me like a possible redeposited workshop. A Period II urn was encountered in excavations here (*Urnas*: Figure 254).

1459 "Large stone lintel, 2.5 m long, noted on top of west mound." A rock rubble pile at the south end of the patio was probably originally a stone wall that would have restricted access into the patio area.

1460 The south and west mounds of this group were probably built to provide privacy for the patio area, since their top surfaces are much too narrow to serve as rooms.

1461 Tomb 99: Caso (1938:33) indicates it is Monte Albán IV; CBA: *Tabla* XVI. A two-mound group with attached small mound north of the larger mound. Privacy of the patio area was assured by the construction of a stone wall.

1462 *El Quetzal*, or *Sistema de la Piedra de la Letra*. Tomb 105: Caso 1938:83–92, *Plano* 18, Figure 104, *Láminas* IIa, b, III, IV, V; Caso 1942:177; Marquina 1964:343–346, *Láminas* 97, 98; Caso 1965a:863, 865, Figure 26; Caso 1965b:929, Figure 62; description of Monte Albán IV copper rattles: Caso 1965c:941. Caso (1942:185) describes replacing the lintel over the entrance to the structure, a stone piece weighing 5 tons.

1463 Tomb 38: CBA: *Tabla* VII. The presence of an *adoratorio* is uncertain due to plowing. The stone wall along the south edge of the patio is probably ancient, to limit access and provide privacy. Much of the pottery collected here was Early I, Late I and II, including a collection from the east mound, from the fill, that was mostly Early I, Late I, with some II possible.

Az.Terrace Number

1 A depression may be the patio area of a residence.

2 One P.U.S. noted.

3 Consists of an excavated large house, attached ball court to the south, and a plaza and mound to the north. A possible reservoir was noted just downhill and N60°E from the mound.

8 Includes three mounds and a large excavated house.

9 "Sunken area approximately 20 m west of the northwest corner may indicate a courtyard."

10 Caso (1942:185–187) discusses excavation of the main mound and *adoratorio*, probably this feature, as well as two patios that *could* be Az.Terraces 3 and 8. A probable reservoir was noted on the northwest corner of the main (north) mound. Two worked sherds noted.

11 A depression noted west of the west mound may be a small attached residence.

23 One P.U.S. noted. "Structures in this area are small and very few."

25 Function uncertain. Few artifacts noted.

26 Three depressions noted that may be patios.

32 Two raised areas and one sunken area noted–probably several residences?

38 One possible residence with sunken area–294 m^2. Two other P.U.S. noted.

40 One depression noted, a possible patio.

41 Stone-lined circular pit noted, .5-m diameter by 2 m deep.

43 One worked sherd and one P.U.S. noted.

45 One worked sherd noted.

50 One large square stone with a circular depression ground into it. Stone measures 59 cm by 33 cm, and is 26 cm thick. "Atzompa seems to have several small plazas created by building with only one or two mounds, but using a steep terrace slope to enclose another side. (e.g., Az.Terrace 39) Why? Trying to save money?" One celt fragment noted.

52 One diorite shaft straightener noted. "It was

decided to make one surface collection over the entire terrace area despite different elevations and subareas, because of all the plowing and erosion. Patches of lighter soil and heavier concentrations of rocks may represent former structures."

57 "Adjacent to Az.Terrace 57 upslope to the south is a rock alignment running perpendicular to the terrace–about 10 stones–steps?"
62 "Two areas noted where remains of plaster can be seen."
80 "This terrace may have been used as a road."
81 This may have been part of an ancient road.
85 One possible structure noted, 78 m^2.
96 One P.U.S. noted.
103 Is a naturally flat area due to an outcrop, but is probably a terrace because of the presence of midden.
119 One hammerstone noted.
124 One fragment of an obsidian eccentric.
125 Disposition of retaining stones suggests this terrace was much wider at one time.
126 Three projectile points, "probably washed down from above."
127 Limits and residential function questionable.
128 "I feel this was an industrial area because of the abundance of broken rocks and lithics, the proximity of the quarried bedrock outcrop, the presence of ramps leading away from the possible quarry, and the extreme paucity of ceramic remains."
129 "I hesitate to call this a residential terrace. The shape, lack of structural features, and paucity of ceramics argue against it. The abundance of broken rock and quarried rock outcrops seem to point to this being an industrial area similar to Az.Terrace 128."
131 One possible structure noted, 150 m^2.
132 One P.U.S. noted. One ground-stone tool noted–"function unknown."
135 "Approximately 16 m below . . . is a squarish (40 cm) 18 cm deep hole pecked into the bedrock." One worked sherd noted.
136 Isolated mound at the site's extremity, probably at a point of traffic flow. A gate-like feature?
137 Same possible function as Az.Terrace 136. Stone floors and a possible staircase noted.
138 A large open area accessible by major road, with double-mound group. A public area?
139 Two P.U.S. noted.
140 Fragment of a toy *olla*. Two areas of soil discoloration, may be a house or middens.
141 One P.U.S. noted.
142 "On one of the scattered rocks there is a 5 cm diameter hole 2 cm deep that may have been a door hinge." One P.U.S. noted.
145 "Two to three fragments of a chili-grinder noted."
147 "May have served as a ramp or road."
151 Two P.U.S. noted, as raised, discolored areas.
153 One IIIa *sahumador* noted.
157 "May be a ramp instead of a residential terrace."
166 Two worked sherds (scrapers) noted. One P.U.S. noted.
167 "At the south end of the terrace there is a shallow, meter-wide 'canal'." One worked sherd noted.
168 "Terraces 167, 168, 169 are three terraces in a row, same general size and configuration. Do other similar units exist?"
181 "Has a high bank that looks like as much as 2 m of fill. Terraces in this area constructed by both cutting and filling. Clear, long retaining walls not seen, but stones in construction fill are often apparent and serve to retard erosion."
194 "More than usual number of *ollas* present."
196 "More than usual number of *ollas* present."
197 "More than usual number of *ollas* present." One P.U.S. noted.
201 Missing folder.
202 Missing folder.
206 One ground stone fragment noted and described as, "function unknown."
215 Eight scrapers found. "This field fits a pattern noted in this area: an obvious lower bank, plowed and eroded down, with one terrace along the bottom and one or two terraces above, which may look more like low mounds than terraces. Might this mean residences above and field below, or is this just due to the recent plowing and land ownership pattern?"
216 One possible mortar noted.
221 One worked sherd noted.
222 One "10-sided stone dice" noted.
227 One P.U.S. noted.
233 May actually be two terraces.
234 Five P.U.S. noted.
242 One worked sherd noted, used as a scraper.
261 Possible other-lithic workshop and ceramic work? One "polishing stone for pottery" noted.

266 One worked sherd noted, used as a scraper.
272 One greenstone celt noted.
274 One hammerstone noted.
276 One small greenstone noted.
278 One P.U.S. noted.
280 "A local farmer came by and we struck up talk, and aside from telling us about the founding of Atzompa by a king after the flood, he very explicitly pointed out that all the terraces in this field were ancient houses. We asked why all these fields were so broad and long, and he replied that it was because of all those houses. He said that he has noted walls and '*cimiento*' on the mounds in this field."
285 One P.U.S. noted.
290 One ground-stone basin noted and described as "carved into bedrock."
293 "A friendly *milpero* deftly pointed out where his plough had torn down ancient structures in this area."
300 One possible plumbate sherd noted.
303 Another example of a long, skinny terrace at the base of two to four more normally shaped terraces. Are these some kind of functional/residential units?
304 Same as Az.Terrace 303.
306 One fragment of a "day or year" glyph noted.
307 One shaft straightener noted.
309 One possible structure noted, 82 m^2.
310 One P.U.S. noted, in the form of a depression that may have been a patio.
315 Possibly a ramp rather than a residential terrace.
323 One P.U.S. noted.
328 One hammerstone noted.
329 One P.U.S. noted.
332 "Terraces in this area are harder to interpret than in higher zones and less rich in artifacts. Are these the slums?"
334 One worked sherd noted.
336 One worked sherd noted.
337 "The area north (downslope) is extremely complex and strange. It consists of several narrow longish things that look like ramps, one above the other about 1 m in elevation above the last one. These look very small for structures, and are crowded together. There is a lot of cut stone, and these features do have retaining walls. They are certainly not ramps."
338 One P.U.S. noted. See notes for Az.Terrace 339.
339 "Terraces 338 and 339 are a 'structure–sidewalk' case since they have a narrow ramp below them."
342 One possible structure noted, 25 m^2.
345 One "stucco polishing stone" noted.
347 "A definite Period IV diagnostic *ollita* noted."
348 One ground-stone "stucco polisher" noted. Note how crowded the terraces are at the top of the ridge."
350 Some ground stone noted.
359–360 "In both 359 and 360 there are equally placed clumps of vegetation near the centers of both terraces, possibly indicating patio depressions that catch and hold moisture better than other places."
362 One P.U.S. noted.
363 One hammerstone noted.
364 One P.U.S. noted.
366 One P.U.S. noted.
367 One P.U.S. noted.
368 Two P.U.S. noted.
369 Two possible structures noted, each 25 m^2.
371 Two possible structures noted, 56 m^2 and 107 m^2.
374 Three P.U.S. noted.
375 Two P.U.S. noted.
376 One P.U.S. noted.
379 One P.U.S. noted.
380–382 Two shale scrapers noted (Terrace 380). Another group of three closely spaced, similar, possibly related terraces. "There may be more terraces on the sides of these ridges, but they are difficult to locate because of small size and unimpressiveness. If they do not have some kind of retaining or structure walls they are not being recorded."
392 "Consists of four structures grouped arround a plaza plus a possible 'high status residence', but less mounded to the north. The position on the point of the ridge was probably the governing factor in the location of this complex. Perhaps the group easily visible on the ridge to the east is of equivalent function and date." The crew member argues that access to the mound group could have been easily controlled. "We can not be sure of dates for structures we see now, but there surely was a Late I–II occupation here. Whether the present mounds are actually a IIIb reoccupation is unclear."
393 Five P.U.S. noted.
396 "This area is quite interesting for the num-

ber of terraces, lack of artifacts, and plenty of structural evidence."

401 One P.U.S. noted.

412 Many *ollas*.

413 Two jade beads noted. Isolated circular mound, possibly with gatelike functions? "It seems similar to the isolated structures along the southeast corner of Atzompa."

419 Open two-mound group on the major road running north–south. Possibly had gatelike functions? As was true for Az. Terrace 392, this group has a Late I–II component as well as a IIIb component, but the date of mound construction cannot be ascertained on the basis of surface evidence alone.

431 "Small but fairly complicated civic or ceremonial group." Another gatelike structure?

437 "Terrace back is an outcrop of reconsolidated limestone that could have been used as plaster in construction on Atzompa."

448 The main Atzompa ball court. Caso (1942: 185) mentions the excavation here, but gives no details. "Niches are visible in the NE and SW corners. The platforms along the north, east, south and west edges have exposed plaster floors and walls. The excavations have encouraged erosion–e.g., a portion of the north inner wall is falling away, and several large rocks have fallen into the northwest corner of the court."

449 Small ball court.

452 Oxidized sherds noted. Some possible Late Monte Albán IV or Early Monte Albán V present.

462 Large platform with low mounds, dominating what was probably a road along this ridge. May have had gatelike functions, and is perhaps the analogy of Az. Terraces 419 and 392.

463 "In this area the contemporary Atzompa people have dug shallow pits to extract *cal* for cement. Sometimes these pits are used for catching rainwater."

469 Isolated mound. Possible gatelike function? Stone floors are visible.

475 A "water sign" glyph was noted.

E.G.Terrace Number

1 Main El Gallo mound group.

2 El Gallo ball court.

3 Large open area with an isolated mound and no evidence for other structures. Possibly a public area?

6 One P.U.S. noted.

7 One polishing stone (?) and one P.U.S. noted.

8 One hammerstone, one slate tabular polishing stone with grooves in both sides (2 cm × 5 cm × 5 cm), and one P.U.S. noted.

9 One P.U.S. noted.

10 One P.U.S. noted.

16–18 These terraces look residential in that they have shaped stone walls, but have almost no pottery (one or two IIIb–IV sherds noted per terrace).

21 One P.U.S. noted.

22 Folder missing.

23 Folder missing.

34 One P.U.S. noted.

36 One "strange piece" of ground stone noted.

37 Possible other-lithic and obsidian work?

38 Two P.U.S. noted.

43 One "small, miscellaneous piece" of ground stone noted.

47 One worked sherd noted, with a hole drilled in it. One P.U.S. noted.

48 This recorder tended to indicate the normal chert or obsidian density as "moderate," but did not mean to imply the presence of workshops. One retouched sherd noted.

49 One P.U.S. noted.

51 One pestle noted.

56 One piece of ground stone noted.

61 One P.U.S. noted.

67–68 "E.G.Terraces 67 and 68 may be a structure–sidewalk case, with Terrace 68 a kind of ramp below 67, upon which the structure would have sat."

70 One P.U.S. noted.

71 One P.U.S. noted.

81 Missing folder.

82 One hammerstone noted.

83 One P.U.S. noted.

84 One P.U.S. noted.

85 One P.U.S. noted.

86 One P.U.S. noted.

87 One P.U.S. noted.

89 One P.U.S. noted.

90 May have been part of a road or ramp.

92 Two P.U.S. noted.

93–94 May have been parts of a road or ramp.

96 One P.U.S. noted. The ramp or road of which E.G. Terraces 90, 93, and 94, are part of probably passes over this terrace, but leaves room for a small structure.

101 One P.U.S. noted.

104 Two P.U.S. noted.

105 One P.U.S. noted.

106 An example of the "structure–sidewalk" arrangement (a thin ramp runs along the base of the terrace). One P.U.S. noted.
110 One P.U.S. noted.
111 May be a road fragment.
112 One P.U.S. noted.
115 One P.U.S. noted.
117 Possibly two terraces. One P.U.S. noted.
118 One P.U.S. noted.
119 One P.U.S. noted.
120 One P.U.S. noted. May have been largely an open area.
127 One P.U.S. noted.
129 One P.U.S. noted.
130 One P.U.S. noted.
135 Classification doubtful. Few sherds or other artifacts present.
139 Five P.U.S. noted.

APPENDIX II

Description of Ceramic Categories

STEPHEN A. KOWALEWSKI
CHARLES SPENCER
ELSA REDMOND

Introduction

The basic work on Monte Albán ceramics is still *La Cerámica de Monte Albán* (Caso, Bernal, and Acosta 1967—hereafter referred to as CBA). This appendix in no way supersedes that study. But the requirements of dealing with surface potsherds instead of whole vessels necessitate special treatment. Often our ceramic categories are identical to types defined in CBA. In every possible case we have attempted to show the relationship between our categories and the established types. The present study is an update, a reorganization, and an index to CBA, and it should be read with a copy of that fine work at hand. The temporal placements of many of the categories described here are tentative, based on information available to us in 1974.

The body of data that follows is not to be taken as a statistically reliable representation of variability in Monte Albán ceramics. Our primary purpose in analyzing the collections from the Monte Albán Survey was to date changes in the settlement pattern of the urban center. We wanted to classify the sherds according to types that could be fitted into the existing Monte Albán ceramic sequence, so that a provenience could be dated according to gross time periods of the sequence.

In May 1973 we began to label all the sherds in each collection by their provenience. We had the industrious assistance of our coworkers Ira Beckerman, Valerie Chevrette, Dolores Root, and Louise Sperling, who tediously labeled and tabulated over 25,000 diagnostic sherds. All of the sherds were dumped together and sorted into established paste types. Further subdivisions were made according to subjective impressions of consistently cooccurring paste, form, and decorative attributes. These are our *ceramic categories*. The number of critical attributes used in defining the category varies considerably. Some very specific categories are defined by six or more attributes; other simpler or more general categories are defined by only two or three. The system of classification is thus designed to be flexible enough to express and exploit varying levels of information carried in different ceramic types and complexes. After checking and describing, every occurrence of a type was recorded on a tabulation sheet attached to the category description form. Most of the work was completed by August of 1973. The entire typology was checked and somewhat simplified in July of 1974, and again in January 1977. We are grateful to Dr. Marcus C. Winter for his help during the analysis.

In the ceramic category descriptions that follow, we used the following terms:

I. Attributes of paste
   A. *Gris* (category numbers begin with 1)
      1. Fine (sand tempered)
      2. Coarse or *gris-cremosa* (diorite tempered)
   B. *Crema* (category numbers begin with 0)
   C. *Amarillo* (category numbers begin with 3)
   D. *Café (category numbers begin with 2)*
      1. Fine (sand tempered)
      2. Coarse (diorite tempered)

The four major terms of paste correspond exactly to the paste categories of the same name established by Caso *et al.* (1967:18–19). (All page and figure references in this appendix refer to CBA, except where noted. See also pp. 477–484 for Shepard's discussion of these pastes and the two subtypes of *gris* and *café*.) Except where noted, all references to *gris* paste in the category descriptions mean fine- or sand-tempered *gris*.

II. Attributes of form
   A. General shape modes
      1. Bowl
      2. Jar (*olla*-necked; *tecomate*-neckless)
      3. Bottle
      4. Comal, plate
   B. Specific shape modes
      1. Wall profiles
         a. Outleaned: e.g., Figures 317(a), 320(a)
         b. Convex or hemispherical: e.g., Figures 176(a), 266(a), 379(a)
         c. Composite silhouette: e.g., Figure 378
         d. Cylindrical: e.g., Figure 218
         e. Globular: e.g., Figures 308, 309, 388, 389
      2. Rim Profiles
         a. Direct: e.g., Figures 11 (first row, third from left), 285(b)
         b. Flaring: e.g., Figure 4 (first row, first from left; third row, first and third from left)
         c. Outcurving: e.g., Figures 8 (third row, third from left), 22 (first row, seventh from left)
         d. Everted: Figures 8 (fifth row, fourth and fifth from left)
      3. Wall thickness: Generally in this report "thin" means less than 0.5 mm, and "thick" means 1 cm or more

III. Attributes of surface finish
   A. Unburnished, unslipped surfaces: These correspond to Shepard's (1968:187) terms "unslipped and unpolished" surfaces. They are further divided into four subtypes.
      1. Plain: No treatment given to the surface other than the shaping required to form the vessel.
      2. Wiped: Surface is treated by rubbing what Shepard (p. 187) calls a "yielding tool" (such as a hand, cloth, or leather) over the surface while the clay is still plastic leaving visible, smooth striations. Figure 13f on page 189 of Shepard is an example of this kind of finish.
      3. Scraped: The surface is treated by dragging a hard and usually sharp-edged tool, such as a sherd, obsidian blade, or shell, across the surface of either a plastic or leather-hard vessel. Figure 13c (Shepard: 189) is an example of scraping on a plastic surface, while Figure 13d on the same page illustrates the results of scraping when the vessel is leather-hard. Except where noted, all references to "scraped" in the category descriptions mean scraped when vessel is leather-hard.
      4. Smoothed: Surface is treated by rubbing when leather-hard with a hard, smooth tool to produce a "tactually smooth" surface (Shepard: 187, 190).
   B. Burnished (unslipped) surfaces: These correspond to Shepard's "polished, unslipped" surfaces (p. 191). They are produced by rubbing when leather-hard with a hard, smooth tool until a luster results. In this study the following subtypes are occasionally used when it is felt that the distinction has importance for the definition of a ceramic category.
      1. Well burnished: Burnishing that leaves no obvious rubbing marks
      2. Streaky burnishing: Burnishing that does leave obvious rubbing marks
      3. Lightly burnished: Burnishing that only occurs in isolated streaks across the vessel surface
      4. Pattern burnished: Burnishing that is purposely decorative
   C. Slipped surfaces: These correspond exactly to "slipped surfaces" as defined by Shepard (pp. 191–193). The following is a list of CBA slip types that have been incorporated into this study:
      1. C-5: White slip on *crema* paste (p. 46)
      2. C-6: Brown slip on *crema* paste (p. 46)

3. C-20: Black slip on *crema* paste (p. 46)
4. K-5: Graphite slip on *café* paste (pp. 51–52)
5. K-6: Black slip on *café* paste (p. 52)
6. A-13: White slip on *amarillo* paste (p. 60)
7. C-4: Red slip on *crema* paste (p. 46). In this study, however, C-4 is referred to as red "paint."
8. C-7: Red on orange "double-slip" on *crema* paste–described in of CBA (p. 47). In this study, however, C-7 is referred to as red on orange (or red on streaky red and orange, or streaky red and orange) "paint."
9. K-3: Red slip on *café* paste (p. 50). In this study, however, K-3 is referred to as red "paint."

D. Smudging: Corresponds exactly to "smudging" as defined by Shepard (pp. 88–90).

E. Differential firing or fire-clouding: A localized discoloration of the surface finish produced during the firing process either purposely or accidentally. Shepard calls this effect "fire-clouding [p. 92]."

IV. Attributes of decoration

A. Plastic decoration (see Figure A.II–1)

1. Incising: This corresponds exactly to "incising" as defined by Shepard (1968). We differentiate between two basic kinds of shallow incising executed before the firing of the vessel when the paste is leather-hard or softer.
   a. Fine-line incising: Done with a tool having a very sharp point, such as a maguey thorn or bone needle. The lines tend to be less than 1 mm wide and less than 1 mm deep.
   b. Wide-line incising: Executed with a tool having a relatively duller point, such as the polished end of an antler or piece of bone. The lines vary in width from 1 mm to about 3 mm, depending on the particular tool employed, and are generally 1.0–1.5 mm deep, or less.
2. Carving: This is done with a sharp tool resembling a knife or a gouge, such as an obsidian blade. Deep incisions are made, usually more than 1 mm in depth and from 1 mm to as much as 5 mm in width, with most being about 2–3 mm wide and 1.5–3.0 mm deep. Carving results in the actual removal of clay in order to form the design, whereas fine-line and wide-line incising generally cause the clay to be displaced or squeezed to the side as the tool makes its pass.
3. Scratching: This is executed with a sharp-pointed tool, such as a maguey thorn, after the vessel is completely dry or after firing. The outer, burnished layer of the finish is scratched off, exposing the underlying paste. Shepard's Figure 14d (p. 197) is a good example of a scratched surface; the term she assigns to it is "post-firing incision [p. 196]."
4. Appliqué: A separate piece of clay is shaped and attached to a vessel, usually for decorative purposes.
5. Modeling: This corresponds exactly to what Shepard (p. 195) terms "modelling or hand manipulation . . . used for high-relief decoration and for representation of human and animal figures."

B. Painting: The paint types used here correspond to the descriptions and illustrations in CBA.

Figure A.II–1. Glossary of incised motifs: (*a*) line with dip; (*b*) half-moon with dot; (*c*) parallel double line with scallops; (*d*) parallel triple line with scallops; (*e*) combing; (*f*) loops; (*g*) curls; (*h*) closed fish tail; (*i*) open fish tail; (*j*) single wavy line; (*k*) joined wavy line; (*l*) vertical slashes; (*m*) opposed diagonal lines; (*n*) cross-hatching; (*o*) horizontal Vs; (*p*) inverted Vs; (*q*) double-line breaks; (*r*) sets of vertical and horizontal lines; (*s*) grecas (step-fret).

Category Descriptions

Category: 0001
CBA designation: Probably C-7 (p. 47, Figure 208[a])
Periodization: II
Paste: *Crema*
Vessel form:
General shape mode: Bowl
Specific shape mode: Outleaned, flaring rim
Surface Treatment: Interior and exterior burnished
Decoration:
Painting: Exterior completely covered with specular red paint. This goes over the rim and to about 1 cm below the rim interior. Rest of interior is painted orange or streaky red and orange.

Category: 0002
CBA designation: C-11 (68, Figures 208[b], 209[b])
Periodization: II
Paste: *Crema*
Vessel form:
General Shape Mode: Bowl
Specific Shape Mode: Outleaned wall, flaring rim
Surface Treatment: Interior and exterior burnished
Decoration:
Plastic Decoration: Fine-line scratching on exterior body. Various motifs, but that shown in Figure 209(b) is the most common. The lines are usually less than .5 cm apart and are about 1 mm wide.
Painting: All of exterior is covered with dark red paint, specular in every case. The paint goes about 1 cm over the rim interior. The rest of the interior is painted orange or streaky red and orange.

Category: 0003
CBA designation: C-7 (pp. 47, 230, *Lámina* X[a])
Periodization: II
Paste: *Crema*
Vessel form:
General shape mode: Bowl
Specific Shape Mode: Outleaned wall, cylindrical. Some with narrow everted rim. Thin. Probably all with hollow feet.
Surface treatment: Interior and exterior burnished
Decoration:
Painting: Red paint (occasionally specular) on streaky red and orange, or orange, background. Exterior is never solid red, but instead, blotches or designs of red occur on an orange background. Rims are often red.

Category: 0004
CBA designation: C-11 (p. 68; *Lámina* X[b],[c])
Periodization: II
Paste: *Crema*
Vessel form:
General shape mode: Bowl
Specific shape mode: Thin (less than 1 cm thick), cylindrical, probably all with hollow feet
Surface treatment: Interior and exterior burnished
Decoration:
Plastic Decoration: Scratching on exterior body—large rectangular shapes, usually with 0.5–1.0 cm or more between the lines. The lines themselves are 1–3 mm wide.
Painting: Entire vessel is painted streaky red and orange, or orange. Red paint, sometimes specular, is painted over this finish, often in conjunction with the scratchings.

Category: 0005
CBA designation: C-11 (p. 68, *Lámina* X[b],[c], Figure 205[b])
Periodization: II
Paste: *Crema*
Vessel form:
General shape mode: Bowl
Specific shape mode: Thin, usually cylindrical
Surface treatment: Interior and exterior burnished
Decoration:
Plastic Decoration: Scratching on exterior
Painting: Red paint on orange, or streaky red and orange, on the interior and exterior
Stucco: None
Comments: This is a miscellaneous C-11 category for sherds that do not fit easily into 0004 or 0002, because of their small size or poor preservation.

Category: 0006
CBA designation: C-11, C12 (pp. 68, 230, 231, *Lámina* X[a]–[e])
Periodization: II
Paste: *Crema*
Vessel form:
General shape mode: Bowl
Specific shape mode: Thin, cylindrical, with hollow feet
Surface treatment: Interior and exterior burnished
Decoration:
Plastic decoration: May or may not be present
Painting: May or may not be present

Category: 0008
CBA designation: C-2 (p. 45)
Periodization: I
Paste: *Crema*
Vessel form:
General shape mode: Comal

Surface treatment:
Top: Wiped, painted
Bottom: Plain, sometimes wiped
Decoration:
Painting: C-2 on top surface. Sometimes solid, sometimes with wide bands of red on plain background.

Category: 0016
CBA designation: C-4 (p. 46)
Periodization: I
Paste: *Crema*
Vessel form:
General shape mode: Bowl
Specific shape mode: Wide everted rim. Rim is usually more than 3 cm wide.
Surface treatment:
Interior: Burnished
Exterior: Variable
Decoration:
Painting: Thickly applied garnet red (C-4), on interior and/or exterior.

Category: 0018
CBA designation: C-4 (p. 46; Figure 21–fourth row, fourth from left)
Periodization: I
Paste: *Crema*
Vessel form:
General shape mode: Bowl
Specific shape mode: Outleaned wall with narrow (1.5–3.0 cm wide) everted rim
Surface Treatment: Interior and exterior burnished
Decoration:
Painting: C-4 on interior and exterior

Category: 0021
CBA designation: C-7 (pp. 47, 240, Figure 214[a])
Periodization: II
Paste: *Crema*
Vessel form:
General shape mode: Bowl
Specific shape mode: Exterior rim flange
Surface treatment: Interior and exterior burnished
Decoration:
Plastic decoration: Appliqué flange
Painting: C-7 on interior and exterior

Category: 0022
CBA designation: C-2 (p. 45)
Periodization: I
Paste: *Crema*
Vessel form:
General shape mode: Brazier
Specific shape mode: Thick (greater than 1 cm), outleaned wall. Direct, beveled rim
Surface treatment: Interior and exterior wiped or lightly burnished.
Decoration:
Painting: C-2 style of thin red painting in stripes around the rim and on interior bands perpendicular to the rim; also on exterior
Comments: Some have traces of burning.

Category: 0023
CBA designation: C-6, C-7 (pp. 46–47, Figure 218[a]–[d])
Periodization: II
Paste: *Crema*
Vessel form:
General shape mode: Cylinder
Specific shape mode: Exterior shelf about 3 cm below rim (for a lid?)
Surface treatment: Interior and exterior burnished
Decoration:
Plastic decoration: Sometimes with scratching on exterior
Painting: When it occurs, streaky red-on-orange C-7, on interior or exterior

Category: 0031
CBA designation: C-2 (p. 45; *Lámina* VII[a],[b])
Periodization: I
Paste: *Crema*
Vessel form:
General shape mode: Jar
Specific shape mode: Miscellaneous body sherds
Surface treatment:
Interior: Wiped
Exterior: Wiped, occasionally streaky burnished
Decoration:
Painting: C-2 style of painting (thinly applied red) on exterior

Category: 0032
CBA designation: C-2 (p. 45)
Periodization: I
Paste: *Crema*
Vessel form:
General shape mode: Bowl
Specific shape mode: Miscellaneous body sherds
Surface treatment:
Interior: Wiped or slightly burnished
Exterior: Variable
Decoration:
Painting: C-2 thin red paint

Category: 0038
CBA designation: C-2 (p. 45)
Periodization: I
Paste: *Crema*
Vessel form:
General shape mode: Bowl
Specific shape mode: Everted rim. Form is like Figure 20 (second row, fourth from left)

Surface treatment:
Interior: Wiped (almost always) or lightly burnished
Exterior: Usually wiped
Decoration
Painting: C-2 (thin red) painting on top of rim. Occasionally painted bands on bowl interior, or on exterior to "break" in rim

Category: 0056
CBA designation: C-2, C-4 (p. 46)
Periodization: I
Paste: *Crema*
Vessel form:
General shape mode: Jar
Specific shape mode: Rim sherds of *tecomates* (neckless jars). Form is like Figures 151, 153
Surface treatment:
Interior: Wiped or plain
Exterior: Burnished
Decoration:
Painting: C-2 or C-4 red paint over all of exterior

Category: 0057
CBA designation: C-7 (p. 47)
Periodization: Late I–rare; II–most abundant; IIIa–rare
Paste: *Crema*
Vessel form:
General shape mode: Bowl
Specific shape mode: Convex wall, outleaned wall, cylindrical
Surface treatment: Interior and exterior burnished
Decoration:
Painting: C-7 (streaky red or reddish orange paint over orange base)

Category: 0121
CBA designation: C-2 (p. 45, *Lámina* VII[a])
Periodization: I
Paste: *Crema*
Vessel form:
General shape mode: Jar
Specific shape mode: *Olla* with outleaned neck
Surface treatment:
Interior: Plain or wiped
Exterior: Wiped
Decoration:
Painting: C-2 (thinly applied red paint) on exterior

Category: 0122
CBA designation: C-2 (p. 45, *Lámina* VII[b])
Periodization: I
Paste: *Crema*
Vessel form:
General shape mode: Jar
Specific shape mode: *Olla* with curved-back neck
Surface treatment:
Interior: Plain or wiped
Exterior: Wiped
Decoration:
Painting: C-2 on exterior

Category: 0123
CBA designation: C-2 (p. 45)
Periodication: I
Paste: *Crema*
Vessel form:
General shape mode: Jar
Specific shape mode: Fragments of *olla* necks for which rim profile is unknown
Surface treatment:
Interior: Plain or wiped
Exterior: Wiped
Decoration:
Painting: C-2 on exterior

Category: 0374
CBA designation: C-1 (p. 45)
Periodization: Monte Albán I, II. C-1 occurs in Periods I and II, but similarities in rim from between this category and C-2 *ollas* (0121, 0122) suggest a Period I date.
Paste: *Crema*
Vessel form:
General shape mode: Jar
Specific shape mode: *Olla* with straight or curved-back neck and neck fragments with indeterminate rim profile
Surface treatment:
Interior: Plain or wiped
Exterior: Usually wiped, sometimes lightly burnished

Category: 0375
CBA designation: C-1 (p. 45, Figure 18–second row, fourth from left)
Periodication: I–II
Paste: Crema
Vessel form:
General shape mode: Bowl
Specific shape mode: Outleaned wall, direct rim
Surface treatment:
Interior: Wiped or lightly burnished
Exterior: Plain or scraped

Category: 0376
CBA designation: C-1 (p. 45, Figure 18–first row, seventh from left)
Periodization: I–II
Paste: *Crema*
Vessel form:
General shape mode: Bowl

Specific shape mode: Interior and exterior wiped or lightly burnished

Category: 0377
CBA designation: C-1 (p. 45, Figure 18–third row, third from left)
Periodization: I–II
Paste: *Crema*
Vessel form:
General shaped mode: Potstand
Specific shape mode: Base
Surface treatment:
Interior: Wiped
Exterior: Lightly burnished, wiped

Category: 0378
Periodization: I–II
Paste: *Crema*
Vessel form: Miscellaneous rim or body sherds
Surface treatment: Interior or exterior burnished
Decoration:
Plastic decoration: May or may not exist
Painting: Specular red paint on one or both sides

Category: 0379
Periodization: I–II
Paste: *Crema*
Vessel form:
General shape mode: Comal
Surface treatment:
Top: Burnished
Bottom: Wiped or plain

Category: 0380
CBA designation: C-20 (p. 47, *Lamina* II[k],[l])
Periodization: I–II, but more characteristic of II
Paste: *Crema*
Vessel form:
General shape mode: Bowl
Specific shape mode: Various
Surface treatment: Interior and exterior burnished, black slip

Category: 0381
CBA designation: C-2 (p. 45, Figure 19–first row, first from left)
Periodization: I
Paste: *Crema*
Vessel form:
General shape mode: Brazier (?) grip
Surface treatment: Wiped and painted
Decoration:
Painting: C-2 red paint

Category: 0382
CBA designation: C-2 (p. 45, Figure 19–third row, first from left)
Periodization: I
Paste: *Crema*
Vessel form:
General shape mode: Plate
Surface treatment:
Top surface: Streaky burnished or wiped
Bottom surface: Plain or wiped
Decoration:
Painting: C-2 paint in stripes around rim and in bands across the top surface.
Comments: Some of these could be comals (0008)

Category: 0383
CBA designation: C-2 (p. 45)
Periodization: I
Paste: *Crema*
Vessel form:
General shape mode: Brazier
Specific shape mode: With potstand base
Surface treatment: Interior and exterior plain or wiped lightly burnished
Decoration:
Painting: C-2 (thin red paint) on interior and exterior
Comments: Some examples show evidence of burning.

Category: 0384
CBA designation: C-2 (p. 45, Figure 19–second row, fifth from left)
Periodization: I
Paste: *Crema*
Vessel form:
General shape mode: Bowl
Specific shape mode: Small, outleaned wall, direct rim
Surface treatment:
Interior: Wiped
Exterior: Wiped or plain
Decoration:
Painting: Interior has C-2 stripe at rim

Category: 0385
CBA designation: C-2 (p. 45, Figure 19–second row, fourth from left)
Periodization: I
Paste: *Crema*
Vessel form:
General shape mode; Bowl
Specific shape mode: Small, thin (less than 1 cm thick) convex wall
Surface treatment:
Interior: Wiped or sometimes lightly burnished
Exterior: Rough or sometimes wiped

Decoration:
Painting: C-2, on interior only

Category: 0386
CBA designation: C-2 (p. 45)
Periodization: I
Paste: *Crema*
Vessel form:
General shape mode: Miscellaneous C-2 rim sherds
Surface treatment: Interior and exterior usually wiped, sometimes lightly burnished
Decoration:
Painting: C-2 on interior or exterior

Category: 0387
CBA designation: C-4 (p. 46, Figure 21—third row, second, third, and fourth from left; fourth row, first and second from left)
Periodization: I
Paste: *Crema*
Vessel form:
General shape mode: Bowl
Specific shape mode: Shallow, ("Suchilquitongo") dish, with nubbin feet. Flat or beveled rim
Surface treatment:
Interior: Top of rim is burnished. Interior of bowl below rim is wiped
Exterior: Burnished
Decoration:
Plastic decoration: A "fillet" on the exterior about 0.5 to 1.5 cm below rim. This is an appliqué strip of unpainted, unburnished clay, with punctations, hachures, or crisscross slashes. There is considerable variation in its size, position, and plastic treatment, but the fillet is the key feature distinguishing this category from 0390.
Painting: C-4 paint on top of rim and about 1 cm down the exterior, or to the top of the fillet
Comments: 0388 (C-1 conical feet) probably go with these rims.

Category: 0388
CBA designation: C-1 and some C-2
Periodization: I
Paste: *Crema*
Vessel form:
General shape mode: Bowl
Specific shape mode: Solid conical support (nubbin foot) from shallow bowl
Surface treatment: Usually wiped
Decoration:
Painting: Occasionally some C-2 painting
Comments: These may fit with 0387.

Category: 0389
CBA designation: C-4 (p. 46, Figure 21 [top row])
Periodization: I
Paste: *Crema*
Vessel form:
General shape mode: Bowl
Specific shape mode: Thick (0.8–1.5 cm), outleaned wall. Rim outcurving, flaring, or direct
Surface treatment:
Interior: Burnished
Exterior: Usually wiped, occasionally burnished
Decoration:
Plastic decoration: Single, wide (1–3 mm) incised line on interior about 1.5–2.0 cm below rim
Painting: C-4, occasionally specular, applied after incising to interior, occasionally to exterior

Category: 0390
CBA designation: C-4 (p. 46, Figure 21 [fourth row, third from left; fifth row, fifth from left])
Periodization: I
Paste: *Crema*
Vessel form:
General shape mode: Bowl
Specific shape mode: Shallow dish, flat or beveled rim
Surface treatment:
Interior: Top of rim burnished. Interior of bowl wiped
Exterior: Burnished
Decoration:
Painting: C-4 paint on top of rim, and on exterior to at least 1 cm below rim. In some cases the entire exterior is painted.

Category: 0391
CBA designation: C-4 (p. 46)
Periodization: I
Paste: *Crema*
Vessel form:
General shape mode: Bowl
Specific shape mode: Thick (more than 1 cm), outleaned wall. Outcurving rim
Surface treatment:
Interior: Burnished
Exterior: Usually wiped, sometimes lightly burnished
Decoration:
Painting: C-4 on interior

Category: 0393
CBA designation: C-4 (p. 46)
Periodization: I
Paste: *Crema*
Vessel form:
General shape mode: Bowl

Specific shape mode: Miscellaneous, and very small rim sherds. Some have eccentric rims.
Surface treatment: Variable
Decoration:
Painting: C-4 (thickly applied; garnet red paint). Some have white slip.

Category: 0394
CBA designation: C-4 (p. 46; *Lámina* VII[c])
Periodization: I
Paste: *Crema*
Vessel form:
General shape mode: Jar
Specific shape mode: Narrow necked bottle
Surface treatment:
Interior: Generally untreated, although may be burnished, wiped, or white slipped for 2–3 cm below interior rim.
Exterior: Burnished
Decoration:
Plastic decoration: Occasionally one or two very widely spaced (10 cm apart) incised horizontal lines running at an angle across the body. Incised before painting.
Painting: C-4 covers exterior and rim, to about 1 cm below rim on interior.

Category: 0395
CBA designation: C-4 (p. 46)
Periodization: I
Paste: *Crema*
Vessel form: Indeterminate and miscellaneous body sherds
Surface treatment: Variable
Decoration:
Painting: C-4 on one or both sides

Category: 0396
CBA designation: C-4 (p. 46)
Periodization: I
Paste: *Crema*
Vessel form:
General shape mode: Potstand
Specific shape mode: Basal or juncture pieces. Form resembles Figure 158.
Surface treatment:
Interior: Wiped
Exterior: Burnished
Decoration:
Painting: C-4 on exterior

Category: 0397
CBA designation: C-5 (p. 46)
Periodization: I
Paste: *Crema*
Vessel form: Miscellaneous
Surface treatment: Variable, white slip on one or both sides
Decoration:
Plastic decoration: Variable, but usually none
Painting: None except for white slip

Category: 0398
CBA designation: C-5 (p. 46; Figure 22, *Lámina* II[d],[e])
Periodization: I
Paste: *Crema*
Vessel form:
General shape mode: Bowl
Specific shape mode: Wide (greater than 2 cm) everted rim
Surface treatment:
Interior: Burnished, slipped white
Exterior: Wiped or plain

Category: 0399
CBA designation: C-5 (p. 46; Figure 22 [first row, first from left])
Periodization: I
Paste: *Crema*
Vessel form:
General shape mode: Bowl
Specific shape mode: Outleaned wall, direct rim
Surface treatment:
Interior: Burnished, stripe (2–3 cm wide) of white slip at rim
Exterior: Variable

Category: 0400
CBA designation: C-5 (p. 46, Figure 22 [first row, seventh from left])
Periodization: I
Paste: *Crema*
Vessel form:
General shape mode: Bowl
Specific shape mode: Outcurving rim
Surface treatment:
Interior: Burnished, probably slipped and slightly smudged
Exterior: Burnished or wiped
Decoration:
Plastic decoration: Fine-line incising on rim. Motifs are various but resemble those of Early I *gris* pottery.

Category: 0401
CBA designation: C-4, C-5 (p. 46, Figure 22 [first row, seventh from left])
Periodization: I
Paste: *Crema*
Vessel form:

General shape mode: Bowl
Specific shape mode: Outcurving rim
Surface treatment:
Interior: Burnished, and slipped
Exterior: Often burnished
Decoration:
Painting: Exterior often has C-4. Otherwise unpainted. Interior has 1–3 cm wide stripe at rim, with C-5 white slip below.

Category: 0402
CBA designation: C-5 (p. 46; Figure 22 [second row, second from left])
Periodization: I
Paste: *Crema*
Vessel form:
General shape mode: Bowl
Specific shape mode: Narrow (less than 2 cm wide) everted rim
Surface treatment:
Interior: Burnished and slipped white. Some have dark smudging marks.
Exterior: Burnished and slipped white. Usually no smudging

Category: 0403
CBA designation: C-6 (pp. 46, 230)
Periodization: Early I–II. C-6 is more abundant in II. Convex outleaned wall bowls occur in Ia–II; cylindrical bowl occurs in II.
Paste: *Crema*, often fine
Vessel form:
General shape mode: **Bowl**
Specific shape mode: (*a*) convex wall, Figure 23 (second row, third and seventh from left); (*b*) cylindrical, Figure 203, (*c*) outleaned wall, Figure 23 (first row, first and fourth from left; (*d*) miscellaneous.
Surface treatment: Interior and exterior burnished. Surface color is gray brown or sometimes cream, often with orange or black fire-clouding.

Category: 0404
CBA designation: C-7 (p. 47)
Periodization: Ic–rare; II–abundant; IIIa–rare
Paste: *Crema*
Vessel form:
General shape mode: Comal
Surface treatment:
Top: Burnished
Bottom: Plain or wiped. Some have evidence of burning.
Decoration:
Painting: C-7 on upper surface

Category: 0405
CBA designation: C-7 (pp. 47, 358, Figure 293[b])
Periodization: II–IIIa
Paste: *Crema*
Vessel form:
General shape mode: *Sahumador.*
Specific shape mode: Bowl has large (approximately .5 cm) perforations.
Surface treatment: Interior and exterior burnished.
Decoration:
Painting: C-7

Category: 0406
CBA designation: C-11 (p. 68; Fig. 205(b), *Lámina* X [b], but without red paint)
Paste: *Crema*
Vessel form:
General shape mode: Bowl
Specific shape mode: Thin, cylindrical, with hollow feet
Surface treatment: Interior and exterior burnished and smudged. Finish is gray brown, sometimes with orange fire-clouding.
Decoration:
Plastic decoration: Scratching on exterior (penetrates the smudged surface layer to the underlying paste). Scratches are 1–3 cm wide.
Painting: None on vessel surface, but red paint is usually rubbed into the scratch marks.

Category: 0407
CBA designation: C-12 (p. 68, *Lámina* X[d])
Periodization: II
Paste: *Crema*
Vessel form:
General shape mode: Bowl
Specific shape mode: Cylindrical, with hollow feet
Surface treatment: Interior and exterior burnished and smudged. Finish is dark in color. Similar to C-20
Decoration:
Plastic decoration: 1–2 mm wide scratches on exterior, which penetrate the smudged surface to the underlying paste.
Painting: None on vessel surface. Red paint is often rubbed into the scratch marks.
Comments: Distinguished from 0406 only by darker surface color

Category: 0561
CBA designation: C-2 (p. 45)
Periodization: I
Paste: *Crema*
Vessel form:
General shape mode: Jar
Specific shape mode: *Tecomate* (neckless jar)

Surface treatment:
Interior: Wiped or plain
Exterior: Wiped
Decoration:
Painting: C-2 on exterior

Category: 1102
CBA designation: G-3M (p. 448, Figure 376)
Periodization: V
Paste: *Gris*
Vessel form:
General shape mode: Bowl
Specific shape mode: Hollow supports from hemispherical or composite silhouette bowls with tripod supports
Surface treatment: Interior and exterior burnished
Decoration:
Plastic decoration: None, or modeled and excised. Motifs include serpent or earth monster heads, bird beaks, deer hooves, and other animal feet.

Category: 1103
CBA designation: G-3M (p. 448)
Periodization: V
Paste: *Gris*
Vessel form:
General shape mode: Bowl
Specific shape mode: Composite silhouette *molcajete*, some with hollow, tripod supports
Surface treatment: Interior and exterior burnished
Decoration:
Plastic decoration: Interior base has deep, parallel or parallel-opposed line incising.

Category: 1104
CBA designation: G-3M (p. 448, Figures 376, 379[a]–[c])
Periodization: V
Paste: *Gris*
Vessel form:
General shape mode: Bowl
Specific shape mode: Hemispherical, thin, direct or slightly incurving rim
Surface treatment: Interior and exterior burnished

Category: 1105
CBA designation: G-3M (p. 448, Figures 377, 378)
Periodization: V
Paste: *Gris*
Vessel form:
General shape mode: Bowl
Specific shape mode: Composite silhouette
Surface treatment: Interior and exterior burnished

Category: 1106
CBA designation: G-3M (p. 448, Figure 379[d],[e])
Periodization: V
Paste: *Gris*
Vessel form:
General shape mode: Bowl
Specific shape mode: Outleaned wall, direct rim, flat or sometimes slightly rounded base
Surface treatment: Interior and exterior burnished

Category: 1107
CBA designation: G-3M (p. 448)
Periodization: V
Paste: *Gris*
Vessel form:
General shape mode: Bowl
Specific shape mode: Shallow hemispherical or composite silhouette
Surface treatment: Interior and exterior burnished. Both surfaces are white, except for gray, differentially fired band from rim 2–3 cm down the exterior.

Category: 1109
CBA designation: G-1M, G-3M (p. 448, Figures 386, 387)
Periodization: V
Paste: *Gris*
Vessel form:
General shape mode: Jar
Specific shape mode: Thin, globular *olla*. Neck and rim form variable
Surface treatment:
Interior: Plain or wiped, and burnished at mouth
Exterior: Burnished
Decoration:
Plastic decoration: Sometimes pattern burnished

Category: 1111
CBA designation: G-1 (pp. 23–24, 218–219, Figures 103, 183)
Periodization: I–II
Paste: *Gris*
Vessel form:
General shape mode: Plate
Specific shape mode: Shallow, miniature
Surface treatment:
Interior: Burnished
Exterior: Plain
Decoration:
Plastic decoration: Appliqué tails, fins, feet

Category: 1120
CBA designation: G-1 (Figures 358[a],[f], 360)
Periodization: IIIb–IV. Probably more frequent in IIIb
Paste: *Gris*
Vessel form:

General shape mode: Jar
Specific shape mode: Large, thick or medium-thick, globular *olla*. Tall, outleaned neck, direct rim. Some have solid round or strap handle attached at neck and shoulder.
Surface treatment:
Interior: Wiped
Exterior: Wiped and rough

Category: 1122
CBA designation: G-35 (pp. 385–393, Figure 320[a])
Periodization: Probably IIIb
Paste: *Gris*
Vessel form:
General shape mode: Bowl
Specific shape mode: Flat base, outleaned wall, *cajete cónico* with direct rim. The rim was reinforced on the exterior with an additional strip of clay that was only carelessly smoothed down.
Surface treatment:
Interior: Burnished
Exterior: Always rough in appearance, but in places may be lightly burnished.

Category: 1123
CBA designation: G-1, G-35 (pp. 434–436, Figure 366)
Periodization: III–IV
Paste: *Gris*
Vessel form:
General shape mode: Sahumador
Specific shape mode: Hollow tubular handle; small, fairly deep bowl, with small perforations in bowl
Surface treatment:
Interior: Wiped or burnished
Exterior: Rough

Category: 1125
Periodization: IIIb
Paste: *Gris-cremosa*
Vessel form:
General shape mode: Comal
Specific shape mode: Shallow, slightly convex wall, direct rim. The plate rests on a thicker, rough (occasionally pebble-pitted) base that begins about 3 cm below the rim. Rim diameter 44–50 cm.
Surface treatment:
Interior: Burnished
Exterior: Wiped and rough

Category: 1126
CBA designation: G-35 (pp. 385–395, Figure 317)
Periodization: III–IV
Paste: *Gris*
Vessel form:
General shape mode: Bowl
Specific shape mode: Conical *cajete*. Flat base, outleaned wall, direct rim
Surface treatment:
Interior: Burnished
Exterior: Plain or rough. Rim sometimes wiped

Category: 1137.
CBA designation: G-35
Periodization: IIIb
Paste: *Gris*
Vessel form:
General shape mode: Bowl
Specific shape mode: Medium thick, nearly vertical walled, direct or sometimes flat rim
Surface treatment:
Interior: Burnished
Exterior: Variable

Category: 1138
CBA designation: G-35 (pp. 385–393, Figure 317[e]–[h])
Periodization: IIIb
Paste: *Gris*
Vessel form:
General shape mode: Bowl
Specific shape mode: Flat base, outleaned wall, direct rim. Wall comes up from base nearly vertically for about 1 cm, than slants out (*base incipiente*).
Surface treatment:
Interior: Burnished
Exterior: Rough. Rim sometimes wiped

Category: 1140
CBA designation: G-35 (Figures 320, 322)
Periodization: III–IV
Paste: *Gris*
Vessel form:
General shape mode: Bowl
Specific shape mode: Flat base, outleaned wall, conical *cajete*. May have hollow or solid nubbin tripod supports, or no supports.
Surface treatment:
Interior: Walls burnished, bottom wiped
Exterior: Variable, but usually rough in appearance
Decoration:
Plastic decoration: "Stick polished" (sloppy lines on the interior base made with the burnishing tool)

Category: 1141
CBA designation: G-1 (Figure 245 [38])
Periodization: I–IV
Paste: *Gris*
Vessel form:
General shape mode: Jar
Specific shape mode: *Tecomate*–globular

Surface treatment:
Interior: Generally wiped, some rims burnished
Exterior: Generally rough or wiped

Category: 1143
CBA designation: G-1, G-3
Periodization: I–IV(?)
Paste: *Gris*
Vessel form:
General shape mode: Bowl
Specific shape mode: Very thick (15–20 mm), cylindrical or outleaned wall *apaxtli*. Rim diameter at least 50 cm, rim form varies considerably
Surface treatment:
Interior: Burnished
Exterior: Variable

Category: 1144
Periodization: Unknown
Paste: Surface color black
Vessel form:
General shape mode: Bowl
Specific shape mode: About 90% of this type in our collections have outleaned walls, with direct or slightly flaring rims. There are a few convex wall bowls and several miscellaneous forms.
Surface treatment:
Interior: Burnished
Exterior: Streaky burnished

Category: 1194
CBA designation: G-21 (pp. 67, 347, Figures 43, 223[d])
Periodization: II–rare in IIIa
Paste: *Gris*
Vessel form:
General shape mode: Bowl
Specific shape mode: Flat base; thick, outleaned walls; flat, direct rim
Surface treatment:
Interior: Usually burnished or smoothed
Exterior: Variable
Decoration:
Plastic decoration: Either (*a*) two crude, parallel lines, incised when clay was nearly dry, on interior of rim; or (*b*) crude, widely spaced lines, made when clay was nearly dry, in rough designs on interior base; or (*c*) rim and base incising may occur on same vessel.

Category: 1207
CBA designation: G-12 (pp. 25, 225, 347; Figure 4 [all two-line examples except fourth row, first from left])
Periodization: Ib–IIIa
Paste: *Gris*
Vessel form:
General shape mode: Bowl
Specific shape mode: Outleaned walls, flat base. Wall thickness variable, rim direct or flaring
Surface treatment:
Interior: Burnished
Exterior: Burnished, wiped, or scraped
Decoration:
Plastic decoration: Two wide-incised parallel lines on interior below rim

Category: 1227
CBA designation: G-12 (pp. 25, 225, Figure 4 [fourth row, first from left])
Periodization: Ib–II
Paste: *Gris*
Vessel form:
General shape mode: Bowl
Specific shape mode: Outleaned wall, flat base, wall thickness variable, narrow everted rim
Surface treatment:
Interior: Burnished
Exterior: Burnished, wiped, or scraped
Decoration:
Plastic decoration: Two wide-incised, parallel lines on interior below rim

Category: 1241
CBA designation: G-12 (pp. 25, 225, 347, Figure 4 [second row, second from left; third row, fifth from left])
Periodization: Ib–IIIa
Paste: *Gris*
Vessel form:
General shape mode: Bowl
Specific shape mode: Outleaned wall; flat base; direct, flaring, or narrow everted rim. Thickness variable
Surface treatment:
Interior: Burnished
Exterior: Burnished, wiped, or scraped
Decoration:
Plastic decoration: One wide-incised line on interior below rim

Category: 1258
CBA designation: G-12 (pp. 25, 225, 347, Figure 4 [first row, first from left; third row, first and fourth from left])
Periodization: Ib–IIIa
Paste: *Gris*
Vessel form:
General shape mode: Bowl
Specific shape mode: Outleaned wall; flat base; direct, flaring, or narrow everted rim. Wall thickness variable.
Surface treatment:
Interior: Burnished

Exterior: Burnished, wiped, or scraped
Decoration:
Plastic decoration: Three parallel, wide-incised lines on interior below rim.

Category: 1259
Periodization: IIIb (?)
Paste: *Gris*
Vessel form:
General shape mode: Bowl
Specific shape mode: Vertical, or nearly vertical wall, large flange on interior rim. Rim diameter ranges from 48–68 cm. Thickness about 1.6 cm.
Surface treatment:
Interior: Wiped
Exterior: Burnished, wiped, or scraped

Category: 1262
CBA designation: G-5 (p. 25; Figure 3)
Periodization: Ia–Ic
Paste: *Gris*
Vessel form:
General shape mode: Bowl
Specific shape mode: Outleaned wall, generally thick or medium thick
Surface treatment:
Interior: Burnished around rim. Some have rest of interior wiped while others have entire body burnished and a gray slip around the rim.
Exterior: Burnished

Category: 1263
CBA designation: G-35
Periodization: III–IV. More frequent in IIIb than in IIIa.
Paste: *Gris*
Vessel form:
General shape mode: Bowl
Specific shape mode: Hollow, hemispherical, tripod supports for G-35 bowls
Surface treatment:
Interior: Plain
Exterior: Plain or smooth

Category:, 1264
CBA designation: G-23 (pp. 80, 312, 317, Figure 271[a],[b])
Periodization: IIIa
Paste: *Gris*
Vessel form:
General shape mode: Bowl
Specific shape mode: Outleaned wall, direct or slightly flaring rim, flat base
Surface treatment:
Interior: Burnished
Exterior: Burnished, scraped, or smoothed
Decoration:
Plastic decoration: Carved on exterior when leather-hard

Category: 1265
CBA designation: G-23 (pp. 80, 312, 317; Figures 266–270)
Periodization: IIIa
Paste: *Gris*
Vessel form:
General shape mode: Bowl
Specific shape mode: Hemispherical
Surface treatment:
Interior: Burnished
Exterior: Burnished, scraped, or smoothed
Decoration:
Plastic decoration: Carved on exterior when leather-hard

Category: 1268
CBA designation: G-1
Periodization: Ic–IV
Paste: *Gris*
Vessel form:
General shape mode: Bowl
Specific shape mode: Steep, medium thick, slightly convex wall. Basal form is unknown. Rim beveled on interior.
Surface treatment:
Interior: Wiped
Exterior: Scraped, with a band of wiping on rim

Category: 1274
CBA designation: G-35
Periodization: IIIa–IIIb
Paste: *Gris*
Vessel form:
General shape mode: Bowl
Specific shape mode: Solid, nubbin supports from flat base, tripod support, outleaned wall bowl
Surface treatment: Smoothed

Category: 1275
Periodization: Unknown
Paste: *Gris, café*
Vessel form:
Specific shape mode: Roughly round disc made by abrading or chipping potsherd. About 3–6 cm in diameter. A few have a perforation in center.
Surface treatment: Variable.

Category: 1277
CBA designation: G-1
Periodization: III–IV

Paste: *Gris*
Vessel form:
Specific shape mode: 1–2 cm long, conical, solid spike attached to outside of outleaned bowl, interior flanged vessel, *olla*, or other form
Surface treatment: Plain

Category: 1297
CBA designation: G-12 (pp. 25, 26, 96, 176, 180, Figures 5 [first three rows], 130, 131)
Periodization: Ib–Ic
Paste: *Gris*
Vessel form:
General shape mode: Bowl
Specific shape mode: Flat base, outleaned wall
Surface treatment:
Interior: Burnished
Exterior: Usually scraped, but varies from burnished to scraped
Decoration:
Plastic decoration: Fine-line incising on interior base, probably done with a comblike object with sharp points, when clay was nearly dry. The most typical design is a series of alternating sets of concentric circles and concentric wavy lines.

Category: 1310
Periodization: Unknown
Paste: *Gris*
Vessel form: Variable
Surface treatment: Variable
Comments: Kiln wasters. Sherds that have bubbles or cracks of the kind resulting from firing a vessel that is not completely dry. In all cases, it appears that the flaw would not have been serious enough to prevent normal use of vessel.

Category: 1312
CBA designation: G-23 (pp. 312–317)
Periodization: IIIa
Paste: *Gris*
Vessel form: Miscellaneous and indeterminate
Surface treatment:
Interior: Variable
Exterior: Burnished, scraped, or smoothed
Decoration:
Plastic decoration: Carved on exterior when leather-hard

Category: 1319
CBA designation: G-15 (pp. 32, 193, Figures 162[c]–[g], 163)
Periodization: I
Paste: *Gris*
Vessel form:
General shape mode: *Sahumador*
Specific shape mode: Miniature. Hollow handle. Everted rim, sometimes scalloped or with tabs.
Surface treatment:
Interior: Burnished
Exterior: Burnished and/or smoothed
Decoration:
Plastic decoration: Wide-line incising on rim

Category: 1330
Several categories were accidentally combined. Disregard distributional data for this category number.

Category: 1331
CBA designation: G-17 (pp. 25, 32)
Periodization: I
Paste: *Gris*
Vessel form:
General shape mode: Bowl
Specific shape mode: Rim everted and scalloped
Surface treatment: Interior and exterior burnished
Decoration:
Plastic decoration: Wide-line incising on both rim and interior wall, one wide line along inner edge of rim, one single wide line just below rim on interior wall, vertical slashes emphasizing every node of the scalloped rim.

Category: 1332
CBA designation: G-16, G-17 (pp. 32, 35)
Periodization: Ia
Paste: *Gris*
Vessel form:
General shape mode: Bowl, plate
Specific shape mode: Everted rim bowl; plate with occasional scalloped rim. Figure 10 (third row, second from left)
Surface treatment: Interior and exterior burnished
Decoration:
Plastic decoration: Fine-line incised cross-hatching on everted rim. In some cases, wide-line incising outlining rim scallops.

Category: 1333
CBA designation: G-15 (pp. 25, 32)
Periodization: I
Paste: *Gris*
Vessel form:
General shape mode: Bowl
Specific shape mode: Flat base, everted rim with notches in rim
Surface treatment:
Interior: Burnished

Exterior: Smoothed and/or burnished
Decoration:
Plastic decoration: Wide-line incising on rim and exterior: line breaks, plain lines, or wavy lines.

Category: 1334
CBA designation: G-17 (pp. 32, 35)
Periodization: I
Paste: *Gris*
Vessel form:
General shape mode: Bowl
Specific shape mode: Shallow, with everted, notched rim
Surface treatment: Burnished
Decoration:
Plastic decoration: Punctations above rim notches. Wide-line incising often present: one line on rim and one on interior below rim.

Category: 1335
CBA designation: Unknown
Periodization: I
Paste: *Gris*
Vessel form:
General shape mode: Bowl
Specific shape mode: Flat base, wavy or crinkled rim
Surface treatment: Interior and exterior burnished
Decoration:
Plastic decoration: Sometimes two lines incised around rim

Category: 1336
CBA designation: G-15 (pp. 26, 32, Figure 8 [fourth row, fourth from left; fifth row, first from left])
Periodization: I
Paste: *Gris*
Vessel form:
General shape mode: Bowl
Specific shape mode: Shallow, with narrow, everted rim
Surface treatment:
Interior: Burnished
Exterior: Burnished or smoothed
Decoration:
Plastic decoration: Wide-line incising on rim and interior wall: scallops and plain and perpendicular lines. Occasional additional fine-line incising

Category: 1337
CBA designation: G-15 (pp. 25, 32, Figure 8 [fourth row, first and fourth from left])
Periodization: I
Paste: *Gris*
Vessel form:
General shape mode: Bowl
Specific shape mode: Shallow, with narrow, everted rim
Surface treatment:
Interior: Burnished
Exterior: Burnished, smoothed, or scraped
Decoration:
Plastic decoration: Wide-line incising, with plain lines on rim, and parallel wavy lines or line breaks on interior wall

Category: 1338
CBA designation: G-17 (pp. 32, 33, 35, Figures 12 [first row, first from left; second row, first and second from left; third row, first and third from left], 114, 115)
Periodization: Ia
Paste: *Gris*
Vessel form:
General shape mode: Plate
Specific shape mode: "Fish plate." Shallow, rim everted or outcurving
Surface treatment:
Interior: Burnished
Exterior: Plain or burnished
Decoration:
Plastic decoration: A variety of fine-line and wide-line incising and modeling techniques applied to rim, and sometimes to interior wall and base: tails, wings, fins, scales, or faces of fish or birds

Category: 1339
CBA designation: G-16 (p. 32, Figure 10 [third row, first from left])
Periodization: Ia
Paste: *Gris*
Vessel form:
General shape mode: Bowl, plate
Specific shape mode: Shallow bowl, plate with wide everted rim
Surface treatment: Interior and exterior burnished
Decoration:
Plastic decoration: Parallel wide-line incising on rim. Fine-line incising between wide lines: parallel wavy lines, grecas, or one wavy line.

Category: 1340
CBA designation: G-16, G-17 (pp. 32, 33, Figure 11 [second row, first from left])
Periodization: Ia
Paste: *Gris*
Vessel form:
General shape mode: Bowl
Specific shape mode: Shallow; thick wall; thick, squarish, everted rim

Surface treatment:
Interior: Burnished
Exterior: Wiped
Decoration:
Plastic decoration: Plain and parallel wide-line incising, and opposed lines, parallel wavy lines, cross-hatching, or plain perpendicular lines

Category: 1341
CBA designation: Unknown
Periodization: I
Paste: *Gris*
Vessel form:
General shape mode: Bowl
Specific shape mode: Outleaned wall, flat base; or composite silhouette. Everted rim
Surface treatment:
Interior: Burnished
Exterior: Burnished, scraped, or smoothed

Category: 1342
CBA designation: G-15, G-16 (p. 32; Figure 8 [fifth row, fourth from left])
Periodization: Ia
Paste: *Gris*
Vessel form:
General shape mode: Bowl
Specific shape mode: Flat base, outleaned wall; or composite silhouette. Wide everted rim
Surface treatment: Interior and exterior burnished
Decoration:
Plastic decoration: Wide- and fine-line incising on rim: parallel wide lines, fine-line cross-hatching, wide-line half-moon with dot, wide-line single-line scallops, single wavy line, wide sets of vertical and horizontal lines, fine-line parallel scallops, or scalloped rim with broken wide lines along scalloped outer edge with added dots at every node.

Category: 1343
CBA designation: G-15, G-16 (p. 32, Figure 8 [fifth row, fourth from left])
Periodization: Ia
Paste: *Gris*
Vessel form:
General shape mode: Bowl
Specific shape mode: Flat base, outleaned wall; or composite silhouette. Everted rim
Surface treatment: Interior and exterior burnished
Decoration:
Plastic decoration: Wide- and fine-line incising on rim: combinations of single wide line, concentric parallel wide lines, wide-line sets of vertical and horizontal lines, scalloped rim with broken wide lines, fine-line parallel double-line scallops, fine-line half-moon with dot, single wavy line, opposed diagonal fine lines.

Category: 1344
CBA designation: G-16 (p. 32, Figure 11 [second row, first from left])
Periodization: Ia
Paste: *Gris*
Vessel form:
General shape mode: Bowl
Specific shape mode: Everted rim
Surface treatment: Interior and exterior burnished
Decoration:
Plastic decoration: Fine-line cross-hatching on rim. Sometimes zones are marked by wide-line incising.

Category: 1345
CBA designation: G-15 (p. 32, Figure 9 [third row, first from left])
Periodization: I
Paste: *Gris*
Vessel form:
General shape mode: Bowl
Specific shape mode: Cylindrical, in some cases slightly outleaned; thin wall; direct rim; some with flange on exterior wall
Surface treatment: Interior and exterior burnished
Decoration:
Plastic decoration: Two parallel wide lines incised below rim on exterior. Additional wide-line motifs: plain lines, stepped lines, or combinations of line breaks and dots

Category: 1346
CBA designation: G-15 (pp. 26, 32, Figure 9 [fourth row, third from left])
Periodization: Ia
Paste: *Gris*
Vessel form:
General shape mode: Bowl
Specific shape mode: Steep wall. Rim flaring or outcurving, occasionally "pinched" so that mouth has figure eight form.
Surface treatment:
Interior: Burnished
Exterior: Burnished or smooth
Decoration:
Plastic decoration: Fine-line incising on interior and exterior walls: combinations of two parallel lines, double- or triple-line scallops, two joined wavy lines, groups of opposed diagonal lines and curls, or open and closed fish tails.

Category: 1347
CBA designation: G-15, G-16 (pp. 26, 32)
Periodization: Ia
Paste: *Gris*
Vessel form:
General shape mode: Bowl
Specific shape mode: Rim thick and "pinched-in," and flat, outcurving, or flaring.
Surface treatment: Interior and exterior burnished
Decoration:
Plastic decoration: Fine- and wide-line incising on interior and exterior walls: combinations of one or two parallel lines, opposed diagonal lines, or wavy lines.

Category: 1348
CBA designation: G-15 (pp. 26, 32, Figure 133[b,d–f])
Periodization: Ia
Paste: *Gris*
Vessel form:
General shape mode: Bowl
Specific shape mode: Hemispherical, thin wall
Surface treatment: Interior and exterior burnished
Decoration:
Plastic decoration: On rim or just below on exterior. Wide-line incising: parallel lines just below rim on exterior. Fine-line incising: line breaks, parallel lines just below rim on exterior, one wavy line, or curls

Category: 1349
CBA designation: G-15, G-16, G-18 (pp. 26, 32, 35, Figure 141)
Periodization: Ia
Paste: *Gris*
Vessel form:
General shape mode: Bowl
Specific shape mode: Composite silhouette, tripod mammiform hollow supports, rim flange
Surface treatment: Interior and exterior burnished
Decoration:
Plastic decoration: Fine-line incising on some rims: straight lines, wavy lines, opposed diagonal lines

Category: 1350
CBA designation: G-15, G-18 (pp. 26, 32, 35, 175, 176, Figure 138[c])
Periodization: I
Paste: *Gris*
Vessel form:
General shape mode: Bowl
Specific shape mode: Composite silhouette, tripod supports, rounded, everted rim
Surface treatment: Interior and exterior burnished
Decoration:
Plastic decoration: On rim and/or interior wall. Wide-line incising: parallel lines, sometimes with slashes or dots. Fine-line incising: parallel lines, sets of opposed diagonal lines, or cross-hatching. Wide- and fine-line incising may be combined on same rim. Specific motifs include half-moon with dot, and closed fish tail.

Category: 1351
CBA designation: G-15, G-18 (pp. 26, 32, 35, Figures 8 [fifth row, second from left], 138[d],[e])
Periodization: Ia
Paste: *Gris*
Vessel form:
General shape mode: Bowl
Specific shape mode: Composite silhouette, tripod supports, outcurving rim
Surface treatment: Interior and exterior burnished
Decoration:
Plastic decoration: Fine-line incising on end of outcurving rim and on exterior angle of base: combinations of wavy and concentric lines, diagonal slashes

Category: 1352
CBA designation: G-3, G-18 (pp. 24, 25, 175, 176, Figure 128 [i])
Periodization: I
Paste: *Gris*
Vessel form:
General shape mode: Bowl
Specific shape mode: Composite silhouette, plain rim
Surface treatment: Interior and exterior burnished
Decoration:
Plastic decoration: One basal profile has notches (scallops?)

Category: 1353
CBA designation: G-12, G-15 (pp. 25, 26, 32; Figure 8 [fifth row, third from left])
Periodization: Ib–Ic
Paste: *Gris*
Vessel form:
General shape mode: Bowl
Specific shape mode: Flat base, outleaned wall, flaring or outcurving rim
Surface treatment:
Interior: Burnished
Exterior: Scraped or smoothed
Decoration:
Plastic decoration: Two to three parallel lines below rim on interior wall; additional fine-line combing in sporadic locations on interior wall

Category: 1354
CBA designation: G-12, G-15 (pp. 25, 26, 32, Figure 4

[fourth row, second from left]
Periodization: Ib–Ic
Paste: *Gris*
Vessel form:
General shape mode: Bowl
Specific shape mode: Flat base, outleaned wall, flaring or outcurving rim
Surface treatment:
Interior: Burnished
Exterior: Scraped or smoothed
Decoration:
Plastic decoration: Both fine and wide line: one wavy line above parallel G-12 lines

Category: 1355
CBA designation: G-12, G-15 (pp. 25, 26, 32)
Periodization: Ib–Ic
Paste: *Gris*
Vessel form:
General shape mode: Bowl
Specific shape mode: Flat base, outleaned wall, flaring rim
Surface treatment:
Interior: Burnished
Exterior: Scraped or smoothed
Decoration:
Plastic decoration: Parallel wide lines below rim on interior with additional wide-line motifs above: line breaks, lines with dips, punctations, or vertical slashes. A few examples also have fine line "combing."

Category: 1356
CBA designation: G-12, G-15 (pp. 25, 26, 32)
Periodization: Ia
Paste: *Gris*
Vessel form:
General shape mode: Bowl
Specific shape mode: Flat base, outleaned wall, some with outcurving rim
Surface treatment: Interior and exterior burnished
Decoration:
Plastic decoration: Two or sometimes three wide lines incised below rim. Fine-line incising above or between wide lines: line breaks, two curving lines, diagonal lines, cross-hatching

Category: 1357
CBA designation: G-15, G-16 (pp. 26, 32, Figure 8 [first row, third from left; second row, third from left])
Periodization: Ia
Paste: *Gris*
Vessel form:
General shape mode: Bowl
Specific shape mode: Flat base, outleaned wall, flaring rim
Surface treatment:
Interior: Burnished
Exterior: Wiped or smoothed
Decoration:
Plastic decoration: One or two parallel wide lines on interior, 2–3 cm below rim. Fine-line incising above: long diagonal lines, or zones of diagonal lines or cross-hatching

Category: 1358
CBA designation: G-15, G-16 (pp. 26, 32)
Periodization: Ia
Paste: *Gris*
Vessel form:
General shape mode: Bowl
Specific shape mode: Flat base, outleaned wall, rim thick and flat, direct or flaring
Surface treatment: Interior and exterior burnished
Decoration:
Plastic decoration: Wide- and fine-line incising. Wide-line grooves along flat edge of rim, or parallel lines just below rim on interior. Fine-line opposed diagonal lines, single wavy lines, or curls

Category: 1359
CBA designation: G-5 (p. 25)
Periodization: I
Paste: *Gris*
Vessel form:
General shape mode: Bowl
Specific shape mode: Flat base, outleaned wall, direct or flaring rim
Surface treatment:
Interior: Burnished stripe along rim, rest is wiped
Exterior: Scraped or smoothed
Decoration:
Plastic decoration: Band of pattern burnishing 1–2 cm below rim on interior: parallel wavy or diagonal lines. Mistermed "negative painting"

Category: 1360
CBA designation: G-13 (p. 26, Figure 158)
Periodization: I(a)
Paste: *Gris*
Vessel form:
General shape mode: Bowl
Specific shape mode: Flat, potstand, or annular base; outleaned wall; direct or flaring rim.
Surface treatment: Interior and exterior burnished
Decoration:
Plastic decoration: Concentric parallel lines on inte-

rior and exterior walls or on the base, or lines spiraling to center of interior side of flat base

Category: 1361
CBA designation: G-15 (pp. 26, 32)
Periodization: I
Paste: *Gris*
Vessel form:
General shape mode: Bowl
Specific shape mode: Flat base, shallow, outleaned wall, direct rim
Surface treatment:
Interior: Burnished
Exterior: Wiped
Decoration:
Plastic decoration: Two parallel wide lines below rim on interior and occasionally below rim on exterior, and fine-line parallel double-line scallops on interior wall

Category: 1362
CBA designation: G-15 (pp. 26, 32)
Periodization: I
Paste: *Gris*
Vessel form:
General shape mode: Bowl
Specific shape mode: Flat base, outleaned wall, outcurving rim
Surface treatment:
Interior: Burnished
Exterior: Plain, wiped, or scraped
Decoration:
Plastic decoration: Shallow, wide-line incising on interior rim: straight lines above and below wavy line, parallel double- or triple-wavy lines on interior wall

Category: 1363
CBA designation: G-15 (pp. 26, 32, Figure 8 [first row, third from left; third row, first from left])
Periodization: I
Paste: *Gris*
Vessel form:
General shape mode: Bowl
Specific shape mode: Flat base, outleaned wall, outcurving rim
Surface treatment:
Interior: Burnished
Exterior: Scraped or smoothed
Decoration:
Plastic decoration: Two parallel wide-line incised lines, and fine-line incising above: zoned cross-hatching, wavy line, or diagonal lines

Category: 1364
CBA designation: G-15, G-16 (pp. 25, 32, Figure 8 [second row, first from left; first row, first from left])
Periodization: Ia
Paste: *Gris*
Vessel form:
General shape mode: Bowl
Specific shape mode: Flat base, outleaned wall, outcurving rim
Surface treatment:
Interior: Burnished
Exterior: Plain and/or smoothed
Decoration:
Plastic decoration: Fine-line incising below rim in 3–4 cm area delineated by one or two parallel lines: opposed diagonal lines, cross-hatching, parallel double- or triple-wavy lines, parallel double or triple scallops, parallel line breaks, or punctations

Category: 1365
CBA designation: G-15, G-16 (pp. 26, 32, Figure 9 [first row, first from left])
Periodization: Ia
Paste: *Gris*
Vessel form:
General shape mode: Bowl
Specific shape mode: Flat base, outleaned wall, flaring or outcurving rim
Surface treatment:
Interior: Burnished
Exterior: Burnished, scraped, or smoothed
Decoration:
Plastic decoration: Fine-line incising below rim (not "zoned"): cross-hatching, one wavy line, diagonal lines, double-line breaks, or parallel double-line scallops

Category: 1366
CBA designation: G-16, G-17 (pp. 32, 35, 185, Figures 12 [first row, second and third from left; third row, second from left], 145)
Periodization: Ic
Paste: *Gris*
Vessel form:
General shape mode: Bowl, plate
Specific shape mode: Shallow bowl, plate with slightly everted or outcurving, scalloped rim
Surface treatment:
Interior: Burnished
Exterior: Scraped
Decoration:
Plastic decoration: Wide-line incising on rim, interior wall, or nodes of scallops. Some also have fine-line cross-hatching on scalloped rim and interior wall.

Category: 1367

CBA designation: G-15 (pp. 26, 32; Figures 149[a], 171)
Periodization: Ia
Paste: *Gris*
Vessel form:
General shape mode: Jar
Specific shape mode: *Tecomate*. Small, thin
Surface treatment:
Interior: Wiped or plain, and partly burnished
Exterior: Burnished
Decoration:
Plastic decoration: Wide-line incised parallel lines just below rim. Fine-line parallel lines just below rim: curls, line breaks, or one wavy line

Category: 1368
CBA designation: G-16 (p. 32; Figure 10 [second row, second from left])
Periodization: Ia
Paste: *Gris*
Vessel form:
General shape mode: Jar
Specific shape mode: Medium size, with gradually forming neck and curved-back rim
Surface treatment:
Interior: Burnished around rim, wiped
Exterior: Burnished
Decoration:
Plastic decoration: Fine-line incising, often in zones, on exterior: opposed diagonal lines, cross-hatching, or curls.
Painting: Some have red paint rubbed into incised areas.

Category: 1369
CBA designation: G-15, G-16 (pp. 26, 32)
Periodization: I
Paste: *Gris*
Vessel form:
General shape mode: Jar
Specific shape mode: Straight-necked, thin, small
Surface treatment:
Interior: Plain or wiped
Exterior: Burnished
Decoration:
Plastic decoration: Fine-line incising on exterior: parallel scallops, or zones of opposed lines. Some have wide-line incising: wavy lines around rim, or plain lines.

Category: 1370
CBA designation: G-15, G-16 (pp. 26, 32)
Periodization: Ia
Paste: *Gris*
Vessel form:
General shape mode: Bowl
Specific shape mode: Cylindrical or outleaned wall, direct or outcurving rim
Surface treatment: Interior and exterior burnished
Decoration:
Plastic decoration: Fine-line zoned incising on exterior: cross-hatching, opposed or wavy lines

Category: 1371
CBA designation: G-17, G-18 (pp. 32, 35, 149, Figure 86)
Periodization: I
Paste: *Gris*
Vessel form:
General shape mode: Bottle
Specific shape mode: Miniature
Surface treatment:
Interior: Plain
Exterior: Burnished
Decoration:
Plastic decoration: Appliqué *Cocijo* face, sometimes hands

Category: 1372
CBA designation: G-17 (pp. 32, 35)
Periodization: I
Paste: *Gris*
Vessel form: Variable. Jar, bowl, plate
Surface treatment:
Interior: Burnished
Exterior: Burnished, some wiped
Decoration:
Plastic decoration: Wide- and fine-line incising: curls, swirls, hollow dots, or cross-hatching.

Category: 1373
CBA designation: G-15, G-16 (pp. 26, 32, Figures 149[b], 150)
Periodization: Ia
Paste: *Gris*
Vessel form:
General shape mode: Potstand
Specific shape mode: Basal rim
Surface treatment:
Interior: Wiped
Exterior: Burnished
Decoration:
Plastic decoration: Wide- and fine-line incising on exterior: opposed diagonal lines, punctations, cross-hatching, grecas, or concentric rings

Category: 1419
CBA designation: G-4 (pp. 78, 80, Figure 52)
Periodization: II

Paste: *Gris*
Vessel form:
General shape mode: Bowl
Specific shape mode: Slightly convex wall, thick, flat rim, outleaned wall
Surface treatment: Interior and exterior burnished. Differentially fired, "white rim black ware"; 1–2 cm wide, cream colored band on interior rim, extending 2–4 cm down exterior

Category: 1420
CBA designation: G-11 (p. 61; *Láminas* III–V)
Periodization: II
Paste: *Gris*
Vessel form:
General shape mode: Bowl
Specific shape mode: Outleaned wall, flat base
Surface treatment: Interior and exterior burnished
Decoration:
Stucco: Postfiring coat of stucco, painted in rose and probably other colors

Category: 1421
CBA designation: Figure 289
Periodization: IIIa
Paste: *Gris*
Vessel form:
General shape mode: Bowl
Specific shape mode: Flat base, steep, outleaned wall. Basal flange, and sometimes hollow tripod supports
Surface treatment: Interior and exterior burnished
Decoration:
Plastic decoration: Coffee bean appliqué in band below basal flange
Painting: Occasional traces of red paint on exterior

Category: 1422
CBA designation: G-1
Periodization: IIIb–IV
Paste: *Gris*
Vessel form:
General shape mode: Bowl
Specific shape mode: Flat base, outleaned or occasionally convex wall *molcajete* ('grater bowl'). Medium thick (7–12 mm)
Surface treatment:
Interior: Plain
Exterior: Plain or rough
Decoration:
Plastic decoration: Closely spaced, deeply incised parallel or opposing lines

Category: 1999
Several categories were accidentally combined. Disregard distributional data for this category number.

Category: 2009
CBA designation: K-2 (p. 50, Figure 26)
Periodization: Ib–V
Paste: *Café*
Vessel form:
General shape mode: Jar
Specific shape mode: Necked *olla*
Surface treatment:
Interior: Variable
Exterior: Wiped or scraped
Decoration:
Plastic decoration: Roughly scraped or incised while wet ("raked")

Category: 2010
CBA designation: K-3 (p. 50, Figure 27 [fourth row, first from left])
Periodization: I(a?)
Paste: *Café*
Vessel form:
General shape mode: Bowl
Specific shape mode: Thick (at least 1 cm); outcurving rim.
Surface treatment:
Interior: Burnished
Exterior: Usually wiped
Decoration:
Painting: K-3 dark red on interior

Category: 2011
CBA designation: K-19 (p. 51, Figure 31 [second row, second and third from left])
Periodization: Ib–II
Paste: *Café*
Vessel form: Comal
Surface treatment:
Top: Burnished (often streaky). Dark brown
Bottom: Plain or wiped

Category: 2013
CBA designation: K-1, K-19 (pp. 49, 51)
Periodization: Shape mode (*a*) I–III; (*b*) Ic–II; (*c*) Ib–II
Paste: *Café*
Vessel form:
General shape mode: Jar
Specific shape mode: *Olla*—(*a*) curved-back neck, K-1, Figure 25 (third from left); (*b*) straight neck, thin, K-19, Figure 31 (first row, eighth from left); (*c*) straight neck, thick, K-19, Figure 31 (second row, first from left); (*d*) indeterminate
Surface treatment:
Interior: Rough or wiped. Shapes (*b*) and (*c*), rim burnished; (*a*) wiped
Exterior: Variable. Shapes (b) and (c), rim burnished; (*a*) wiped

Category: 2014
Periodization: Shape mode (*a*) V; (*b*) IV–V
Paste: *Café*
Vessel form:
General shape mode: Comal
Specific shape mode: (*a*) Rim has upturned lip; (*b*) rim thickened top and bottom.
Surface treatment:
Top: Burnished
Bottom: Plain or wiped

Category: 2015
Periodization: Unknown
Paste: *Café*
Vessel form:
General shape mode: Comal
Specific shape mode: Miscellaneous, mainly body sherds
Surface treatment:
Top: Usually burnished
Bottom: Plain or wiped

Category: 2040
CBA designation: K-12 (p. 51, Figure 30 [first and second from left])
Periodization: Ic–II
Paste: *Café*
Vessel form:
General shape mode: Bowl
Specific shape mode: Rim has lip on interior
Surface treatment:
Interior: Wiped
Exterior: Wiped or plain

Category: 2042
CBA designation: K-3 (p. 50)
Periodization: Ic
Paste: *Café*
Vessel form:
General shape mode: Bowl
Specific shape mode: Exterior flange about 1 cm below rim.
Surface treatment: Interior and exterior burnished
Decoration:
Plastic decoration: Appliqué flange about 1 cm below rim on exterior
Painting: Red paint in splotches or stripes on interior, top of rim and flange, and sometimes on exterior

Category: 2052
CBA designation: K-8 (p. 51)
Periodication: I–II
Paste: *Café*
Vessel form:
General shape mode: Bowl
Specific shape mode: Thin (less than 1 cm), outleaned wall, direct rim
Surface treatment:
Interior: Burnished
Exterior: Burnished or wiped

Category: 2061
CBA designation: K-8, K-19 (p. 51; Figures 215–217)
Periodization: II
Paste: *Café*
Vessel form:
General shape mode: Cylinder, bowl
Specific shape mode: Variable
Surface treatment: Wiped or burnished, usually interior and exterior burnished
Decoration:
Plastic decoration: Cylindrical bowls (K-8?) have 2–3 mm wide scratching on exterior, as in Figure 205(a),(b).

Category: 2064
CBA designation: K-3 (p. 50, Figure 27 [fourth row, third from left])
Periodization: Ic
Paste: *Café*
Vessel form:
General shape mode: Bowl
Specific shape mode: Narrow (less than 2 cm wide) everted rim
Surface treatment:
Interior: Burnished
Exterior: Usually burnished
Decoration:
Painting: Sometimes red K-3 paint on top of rim

Category: 2065
CBA designation: K-3 (p. 50)
Periodization: I
Paste: *Café*
Vessel form: Miscellaneous body sherds
Surface treatment: Variable
Decoration:
Painting: Red, K-3

Category: 2072
CBA designation: K-3 (p. 50, Figure 27 [first row, first from left])
Periodization: I
Paste: *Café*
Vessel form:
General shape mode: Bowl
Specific shape mode: Beveled rim
Surface treatment: Variable
Decoration:
Painting: Sometimes present (K-3 red)

Category: 2073
CBA designation: K-8 (p. 51)

Periodization: I–II
Paste: *Café*
Vessel form:
General shape mode: Jar
Specific shape mode: Thin (about 5 mm)
Surface treatment:
Interior: Usually wiped
Exterior: Usually burnished

Category: 2076
CBA designation: K-3 (p. 50)
Periodization: I
Paste: *Café*
Vessel form:
General shape mode: Jar
Specific shape mode: Variable
Surface treatment:
Interior: Plain, wiped
Exterior: Burnished, sometimes wiped
Decoration:
Painting: Red paint, both thickly and thinly applied

Category: 2077
CBA designation: K-3 (p. 50, Figure 27 [fourth row, second from left])
Periodization: I
Paste: *Café*
Vessel form:
General shape mode: Bowl
Specific shape mode: Thick (more than 1 cm), outleaned wall, flaring rim
Surface treatment:
Interior: Burnished
Exterior: Wiped or lightly burnished
Decoration:
Painting: K-3 red over all of interior

Category: 2078
CBA designation: K-8 (p. 51, Figure 29 [first row, third and fifth from left])
Periodization: Ic–II
Paste: *Café*
Vessel form:
General shape mode: Bowl
Specific shape mode: Thin (less than 1 cm), outleaned wall, flaring rim
Surface treatment:
Interior: Usually burnished
Exterior: Usually wiped

Category: 2079
CBA designation: K-8 (p. 51, Figure 29 [first row, second and fourth from left])
Periodization: I
Paste: *Café*
Vessel form:
General shape mode: Bowl
Specific shape mode: Thick (at least 1 cm), outleaned wall, flaring rim
Surface treatment:
Interior: Burnished
Exterior: Usually wiped

Category: 2080
CBA designation: K-3 (p. 50)
Periodization: I
Paste: *Café*
Vessel form: Miscellaneous rims
Surface treatment: Variable
Decoration:
Painting: Red paint, usually K-3

Category: 2083
CBA designation: K-14 (p. 85, Figure 57 [fourth row, second from left])
Periodization: IIIb
Paste: *Café*
Vessel form:
General shape mode: Bowl
Specific shape mode: Incipient annular base of conical *cajete*
Surface treatment:
Interior: Wiped or burnished
Exterior: Usually plain

Category: 2085
CBA designation: K-8 (p. 51; Figure 29 [second row, third and fifth from left])
Periodization: Ia–II
Paste: *Café*
Vessel form:
General shape mode: Bowl
Specific shape mode: Thin (less than 1 cm), convex wall
Surface treatment:
Interior: Burnished
Exterior: Burnished, streaky burnished, or wiped

Category: 2086
CBA designation: K-14, K-22 (pp. 85, 86; Figures 57, 58)
Periodization: IIIb–IV
Paste: *Café*
Vessel form:
General shape mode: Bowl
Specific shape mode: Conical *cajete*
Surface treatment:
Interior: Wiped or burnished
Exterior: Usually plain

Category: 2411
CBA designation: K-3 (p. 50, Figure 27 [fifth row, first–third from left])
Periodization: I
Paste: *Café*
Vessel form:
General shape mode: Bowl
Specific shape mode: Shallow, "Suchilquitongo" dish, flat or beveled rim
Surface treatment:
Interior: Wiped below rim, burnished on top of rim
Exterior: Wiped
Decoration:
Plastic decoration: Some have fillet on exterior.
Painting: K-3 on top of rim
Comments: Similar to 0387

Category: 2412
CBA designation: K-1
Periodization: I
Paste: *Café*
Vessel form:
General shape mode: Bowl
Specific shape mode: Solid nubbin support
Surface treatment: Plain, wiped
Comments: May be with 2411

Category: 2413
CBA designation: K-8 (p. 51)
Periodization: I–II
Paste: *Café*
Vessel form:
General shape mode: Bowl
Specific shape mode: Outleaned wall, direct rim, small exterior rim flange
Surface treatment: Interior and exterior burnished

Category: 2414
CBA designation: K-5 (pp. 51, 52, Figure 32)
Periodization: Ic–II
Paste: *Café*
Vessel form:
General shape mode: Bowl
Specific shape mode: Variable
Surface treatment:
Interior: Burnished
Exterior: Variable
Decoration:
Painting: Graphite "slip" on interior and sometimes exterior

Category: 2415
CBA designation: K-6 (p. 52, Figure 33)
Periodization: Ib
Paste: *Café*
Vessel form:
General shape mode: Bowl
Specific shape mode: Outleaned wall, flaring or narrow everted rim
Surface treatment:
Interior: Burnished
Exterior: Wiped
Decoration:
Plastic decoration: Lines incised through slip
Painting: Black or dark brown slip on interior, rarely on exterior

Category: 2416
CBA designation: Unknown
Periodization: II
Paste: *Café*
Vessel form:
General shape mode: Bowl
Specific shape mode: Outleaned wall, direct rim
Surface treatment: Interior and exterior burnished
Decoration:
Painting: Dark red, 1 cm wide stripe on rim interior

Category: 2417
CBA designation: K-19 (pp. 51, 248, 249, Figure 227)
Periodization: II
Paste: *Café*
Vessel form:
General shape mode: *Sahumador*
Specific shape mode: Flat, with usually large (1.5 cm) holes
Surface treatment:
Interior: Usually burnished
Exterior: Usually wiped

Category: 2418
CBA designation: Unknown
Periodization: IIIb–IV
Paste: *Café*
Vessel form:
General shape mode: Comal
Specific shape mode: Raised "shelf" on underside several centimeters in from rim. Rim direct or with upturned lip
Surface treatment:
Top: Burnished
Bottom: Plain or wiped

Category: 3030
CBA designation: A-7 (p. 86, Figure 328[a,b])
Periodization: Late IIIb–Early IV.
Paste: *Amarillo* ("Imitation Fine Orange")
Vessel form:
General shape mode: Bowl, cylinder

Specific shape mode: Various thin wall, including convex wall bowl and barrel-shaped cylinder
Surface treatment: Interior and exterior burnished
Decoration:
Plastic decoration: Usually none, but incising and/or carving sometimes present on exterior

Category: 3033
CBA designation: A-4 (pp. 59, 60, Figure 38)
Periodization: I–II
Paste: *Amarillo*
Vessel form:
General shape mode: Bowl
Specific shape mode: (*a*) with annular or ring base; (*b*) convex wall; (*c*) outleaned wall, direct or flaring rim.
Surface treatment: Interior and exterior burnished
Decoration:
Painting: Occasional red or streaky red on annular base bowl, otherwise none

Category: 3035
Periodization: Unknown. IIIb?
Paste: Either very light *gris* or whitish *amarillo*, orange surfaces
Vessel form: Indeterminate, thin
Surface treatment: Interior and exterior burnished
Decoration:
Painting: Streaky orangish paint?

Category: 3066
CBA designation: A-2 (p. 59, Figure 37 [fourth row, fourth from left])
Periodization: Ic, more abundant in II
Paste: *Amarillo*
Vessel form:
General shape mode: Bowl
Specific shape mode: With hollow supports
Surface treatment:
Interiorr: Wiped
Exterior: Burnished
Decoration:
Painting: Red pain occurs on some examples

Category: 3408
CBA designation: A-9 (p. 70; *Lámina* IX [b],[c], Figures 48, 49)
Periodization: II
Paste: *Amarillo*
Vessel form:
General shape mode: Bowl
Specific shape mode: Convex wall, outleaned wall, cylindrical
Surface treatment: Interior and exterior burnished
Decoration:
Painting: Red paint on exterior or interior

Category: 3409
CBA designation: A-11 (p. 70, Figure 51)
Periodization: II
Paste: *Amarillo*
Vessel form:
General shape mode: Bowl
Specific shape mode: Variable
Surface treatment: Interior and exterior burnished
Decoration:
Plastic decoration: Incising
Painting: Sloppily applied, streaky orange paint

Category: 3410
CBA designation: A-8 (p. 83, Figure 56)
Periodization: IIIa
Paste: *Amarillo*
Vessel form:
General shape mode: Bowl, *tecomate* (?)
Specific shape mode: Convex, outleaned, cylindrical, hemispherical
Surface treatment: Interior and exterior burnished
Decoration:
Plastic decoration: Carving on exterior

Category: 3411
CBA designation: A-3 (pp. 83–84, Figure 275)
Periodization: IIIa
Paste: *Amarillo* (thin orange)
Vessel form:
General shape mode: Bowl
Specific shape mode: Variable
Surface treatment: Interior and exterior burnished

Category: 5000
Periodization: Late V
Paste: Very fine, compact, uniformly orange (5 YR 6/6–5/6)
Vessel form:
General shape mode: Bowl
Specific shape mode: (*a*) Low profile bowl or plate; (*b*) flat or round base, sometimes with solid slab supports
Surface treatment:
Interior: Burnished
Exterior: Burnished or wiped
Decoration:
Plastic decoration: Incised perpendicular cross-hatching on interior of base of shape (*b*)
Painting: Shape (*a*): dark red (2.5 YR 4/4), squiggly lines on interior of five examples, fine black concentric lines on interior of sixth; shape (*b*): dark red squiggly lines on slab supports
Comment: Probably Aztec

Category: 5007
CBA designation: *Cerámica policromada* (pp. 465–475, *Láminas* XIII–XXX)
Periodization: Late V
Paste: Fine *café* or oxidized *gris*
Vessel form: Variable. Convex wall bowl; restricted rim, barrel shape; cylinder, flaring rim; long, hollow support; jar; *incensario*. Bowl most common
Surface treatment: Interior and exterior burnished
Decoration:
Painting: Red, black, and orange designs on heavy, cream colored base. A thin, red slip was often applied to bowl interiors.

Category: 5329
Same as 5007. Combine distributional data.

APPENDIX III

Ceramic Tabulations

Part 1. Tabulations by Terrace

This Appendix presents raw counts of the ceramic tabulations by terrace. Each ceramic category has 52 lines, or cards of data. For each line, the first column is a meaningless number, always a "1." The next four columns indicate the ceramic category number. Following that, two columns indicate the card number. The proveniences present on each card or line are listed in the following pages; each provenience fills two columns—a value of two, for example, is indicated by "02." For some terraces, however, more than one collection was made, and originally these were tabulated separately. I have decided not to indicate these separate proveniences, so some terraces are listed more than once. In these cases, then, in order to calculate the total number of sherds of a category occurring on a terrace, all the values should be summed. A few proveniences could not be securely located after they had been tabulated. Each of these is indicated "deleted."

Card 1 1, 2, 3, 4, 5, 6, 7, 8, 9, 10, 11, 12, 13, 14, 15, 16, 17, 18, 19, 20, 20, 21, 21, 21, 21, 22, 23, 24, 25, 26, 27, 27

Card 2 27, 27, 27, 27, 27, 27, 27, 27, 27, 27, 27, 27, 28, 29, 30, 31, 32, 33, 34, 35, 36, 37, 38, 39, 40, 41, 42, 43, 44, 45, 46, 47

Card 3 48, 49, 50, 51, 52, 53, 54, 55, 56, 57, 58, 59, 60, 61, 62, 63, 64, 66, 67, 68, 69, 70, 71, 72, 73, 74, 75, 76, 77, 78, 79, 80

Card 4 81, 82, 83, 84, 85, 86, 87, 88, 89, 90, 91, 92, 93, 94, 95, 96, 97, 98, 99, 100, 101, 102, 104, 105, 106, 107, 111, 112, 113, 114, 115, 116

Card 5 117, 118, 119, 120, 121, 122, 123, 124, 126, 127, 128, 129, 130, 131, 132, 133, 134, 135, 136, 137, 138, 139, 140, 141, 142, 143, 144, 145, 146, 147, 148, 149

Card 6 150, 151, 152, 153, 154, 155, 156, 157, 158, 159, 160, 161, 164, 165, 166, 167, 168, 169, 170, 171, 172, 173, 174, 175, 176, 177, 178, 179, 180, 181, 182, 183,

Card 7 184, 185, 186, 187, 188, 189, 190, 191, 192, 193, 194, 195, 196, 197, 198, 199, 200, 201, 202, 203, 204, 205, 206, 207, 208, 209, 210, 211, 212, 213, 214, 215

Card 8 216, 217, 218, 219, 220, 221, 222, 223, 224, 225, 226, 227, 228, 229, 230, 231, 232, 233, 234, 235, 236, 237, 238, 239, 240, 241, 242, 243, 244, 245, 246, 247

Card 9 248, 249, 250, 251, 252, 253, 254, 255, 256, 257, 258, 259, 260, 261, 262, 263, 264, 265, 266, 267, 268, 269, 270, 271, 272, 273, 274, 275, 276, 277, 278, 279

Card 10 280, 281, 282, 283, 285, 286, 287, 288, 289, 290, 291, 292, 293, 294, 295, 296, 297, 298, 299, 300, 301, 302, 303, 304, 305, 306, 307, 308, 309, 310, 311, 312

Card 11 313, 314, 315, 316, 317, 318, 319, 320, 322, 323, 324, 325, 326, 327, 328, 329, 330, 331, 332, 333, 334, 335, 336, 337, 338, 339, 340, 341, 342, 343, 344, 345

Card 12 346, 347, 349, 350, 351, 352, 353, 356, 358, 359, 361, 363, 364, 365, 366, 367, 368, 369, 370, 371, 372, 373, 374, 375, 376, 377, 378, 379, 380, 381, 382, 383

Card 13 384, 385, 386, 387, 388, 389, 390, 391, 392, 393, 394, 395, 396, 397, 398, 399, 400, 401, 402, 403, 404, 405, 406, 407, 408, 409, 410, 411, 412, 413, 414, 415

Card 14 416, 417, 418, 419, 421, 422, 423, 424, 425, 426, 427, 428, 429, 430, 431, 432, 433, 434, 435, 436, 437, 438, 439, 440, 441, 442, 443, 444, 447, 601, 451, 452

Card 15 453, 453, 454, 455, 456, 457, 458, 459, 460, 461, 462, 463, 464, 465, 466, 467, 468, 469, 470, 471, 472, 473, 474, 475, 476, 477, 478, 479, 481, 482, 483, 484

Card 16 485, 486, 487, 488, 489, 491, 492, 493, 494, 495, 496, 497, 498, 499, 500, 501, 502, 503, 504, 505, 506, 507, 508, 509, 510, 511, 512, 513, 514, 515, 516, 517

Card 17 518, 519, 520, 521, 522, 523, 524, 525, 526, 527, 528, 529, 530, 531, 532, 533, 534, 535, 536, 537, 538, 540, 541, 542, 543, 544, 545, 546, 548, 550, 551, 552

Card 18 553, 554, 555, 556, 558, 559, 560, 561, 562, 563, 564, 565, 566, 567, 568, 569, 570, 571, 572, 573, 574, 575, 576, 577, 578, 579, 582, 583, 584, 585, 586, 587

Card 19 588, 589, 590, 593, 595, 596, 597, 598, 599, 600, 601, 602, 603, 604, 605, 606, 607, 608, 609, 610, 611, 612, 613, 614, 615, 616, 617, 618, 619, 620, 621, 622

Card 20 623, 624, 625, 626, 627, 628, 629, 630, 631, 632, 633, 634, 635, 636, 637, 638, 639, 640, 641, 642, 643, 644, 645, 646, 647, 648, 649, 650, 651, 652, 653, 654

Card 21 655, 656, 657, 658, 659, 660, 661, 662, 663, 664, 665, 666, 667, 668, 669, 670, 671, 672, 673, 674, 675, 676, 677, 678, 679, 680, 681, 683, 684, 685, 686, 687

Card 22 688, 689, 697, 701, 706, 707, 708, 710, 711, 713, 715, 716, 721, 722, 724, 725, 726, 727, 728, 729, 731, 732, 736, 738, 743, 744, 745, 748, 750, 751, 752, 753

Card 23 754, 755, 756, 757, 758, 759, 760, 761, 762, 763, 764, 765, 766, 767, 768, 769, 771, 772, 773, 774, 775, 776, 777, 778, 779, 780, 781, 782, 784, 785, 787, 788

Card 24 789, 790, 791, 792, 793, 794, 795, 796, 797, 798, 799, 800, 801, 802, 803, 804, 805, 806, 807, 809, 810, 811, 812, 813, 814, 815, 817, 818, 819, 820, 822, 823

Card 25 824, 826, 827, 830, 832, 834, 835, 836, 837, 838, 839, 841, 842, 843, 844, 846, 847, 849, 850, 851, 852, 853, 854, 856, 857, 858, 859, 860, 861, 862, 863, 864

Card 26 866, 867, 868, 869, 870, 871, 872, 873, 874, 875, 882, 886, 887, 889, 900, 901, 902, 903, 904, 905, 906, 907, 908, 910, 911, 912, 913, 914, 915, 916, 917, 918

Card 27 919, 920, 921, 922, 923, 924, 925, 926, 927, 928, 929, 930, 931, 932, 933, 934, 935, 938, 939, 940, 941, 942, 943, 945, 947, 949, 950, 951, 952, 953, 955, 957

Card 28 958, 963, 965, 966, 967, 968, 969, 970, 971, 972, 973, 974, 975, 977, 978, 979, 981, 983, 984, 986, 989, 995, 1002, 1003, 1004, 1005, 1006, 1007, 1008, 1009, 1010, 1012

Card 29 1013, 1014, 1015, 1016, 1018, 1020, 1021, 1022, 1023, 1024, 1025, 1026, 1027, 1028, 1029, 1030, 1031, 1032, 1033, 1034, 1035, 1036, 1037, 1038, 1039, 1040, 1043, 1044, 1045, 1046, 1047, 1049

Card 30 1050, 1052, 1054, 1061, 1062, 1070, 1082, 1087, 1090, 1100, 1101, 1102, 1103, 1104, 1105, 1106, 1108, 1109, 1114, 1116, 1125, 1129, 1133, 1134, 1135, 1137, 1140, 1144, 1145, 1148, 1149, 1152

Card 31 1153, 1155, 1157, 1158, 1161, 1163, 1167, 1169, 1170, 1172, 1174, 1175, 1176, 1177, 1179, 1190, 1196, 1202, 1203, 1204, 1205, 1207, 1208, 1209, 1210, 1211, 1212, 1213, 1215, 1216, 1217, 1220

Card 32 1221, 1223, 1224, 1225, 1226, 1226, 1226, 1226, 1227, 1227, 1227, 1228, 1228, 1229, 1229, 1232, 1233, 1235, 1235, 1235, 1235, 1235, 1235, 1236, 1237, 1239, 1240, 1242, 1243, 1247, 1251, 1252

Card 33 1253, 1260, 1261, 1264, 1265, 1289, 1290, 1291, 1294, 1299, 1302, 1303, 1304, 1305, 1306, 1307, 1308, 1309, 1310, 1311, 1312, 1313, 1314, 1316, 1317, 1318, 1319, 1320, 1321, 1322, 1323, 1324

Card 34 1325, 1326, 1327, 1328, 1329, 1330, 1331, 1333, 1335, 1336, 1337, 1339, 1342, 1346, 1357, 1358, 1359, 1360, 1361, 1362, 1363, 1365, 1367, 1368, 1369, 1370, 1371, 1372, 1373, 1374, 1375, 1376

Card 35 1377, 1378, 1380, 1381, 1383, 1384, 1385, 1387, 1388, 1389, 1390, 1392, 1393, 1395, 1397, 1398, 1399, 1400, 1401, 1402, 1404, 1405, 1408, 1411, 1409, 1427, 1425, 1426, 1427, 1430, 1431, 1432

Card 36 1433, Area 1, Area 2, deleted, deleted, Area 5, deleted, Area 7, Area 8, Area 9, Area 10, Area 11, Area 12, Area 13, Area 14, Area 15, Area 16, T. 1464, Area 18, Area 19, Area 20, Area 21, T. 1464, T. 1464, T. 1464, T. 1464, deleted, T. 1463, T. 1456, T. 1462, T. 1457, deleted

Card 37 deleted, T. 1458, T. 1459, deleted, T. 1448, T. 1455, T. 1453, deleted, T. 1452, T. 1450, T. 1449, T. 1464, deleted, Tomb 90, Tomb 153, deleted, deleted, deleted, T. 225 excavation, Az 1, Az 2, Az 3, Az 4, Az 5, Az 6, Az 7, Az 8, Az 8, Az 9, Az 10, Az 11, Az 12

Card 38 Az 13, Az 14, Az 15, Az 16, Az 17, Az 18, Az 19, Az 20, Az 21, Az 24, Az 25, Az 26, Az 27, Az 28, Az 29, Az 30, Az 31, Az 32, Az 33, Az 34, Az 35, Az 36, Az 37, Az 38, Az 39, Az 40, Az 41, Az 42, Az 43, Az 44, Az 45, Az 46

Card 39 Az 47, Az 48, Az 49, Az 50, Az 51, Az 52, Az 53, Az 54, Az 55, Az 56, Az 57, Az 58, Az 59, Az 60, Az 61, Az 62, Az 64, Az 65, Az 66, Az 67, Az 68, Az 69, Az 70, Az 71, Az 72, Az 73, Az 74, Az 75, Az 76, Az 77, Az 78, Az 79

Card 40 Az 80, Az 81, Az 82, Az 83, Az 84, Az 85, Az 86, Az 87, Az 88, Az 89, Az 90, Az 91, Az 92, Az 93, Az 94, Az 95, Az 96, Az 97, Az 98, Az 99, Az 100, Az 101, Az 102, Az 103, Az 104, Az 105, Az 106, Az 107, Az 108, Az 110, Az 112, Az 113

Card 41 Az 114, Az 115, Az 116, Az 117, Az 118, Az 119, Az 120, Az 121, Az 122, Az 123, Az 124, Az 125, Az 126, Az 127, Az 128, Az 129, Az 130, Az 131, Az 132, Az 133, Az 134, Az 135, Az 139, Az 140, Az 141, Az 142, Az 143, Az 144, Az 145, Az 146, Az 147, Az 148

Card 42 Az 149, Az 150, Az 151, Az 152, Az 153, Az 154, Az 155, Az 156, Az 157, Az 158, Az 159, Az 160, Az 161, Az 162, Az 163, Az 164, Az 165, Az 166, Az 167, Az 168, Az 169, Az 170, Az 171, Az 172, Az 173, Az 174, Az 175, Az 176, Az 178, Az 180, Az 181, Az 182

Card 43 Az 183, Az 184, Az 185, Az 186, Az 187, Az 188, Az 189, Az 190, Az 191, Az 192, Az 193, Az 194, Az 195, Az 196, Az 197, Az 198, Az 199, Az 200, Az 201, Az 202, Az 203, Az 205, Az 206, Az 207, Az 208, Az 209, Az 211, Az 212, Az 213, Az 214, Az 215, Az 217

Card 44 Az 218, Az 219, Az 220, Az 221, Az 222, Az 226, Az 227, Az 228, Az 229, Az 230, Az 231, Az 232, Az 233, Az 234, Az 235, Az 236, Az 238, Az 239, Az 240, Az 241, Az 243, Az 245, Az 246, Az 247, Az 250, Az 251, Az 252, Az 253, Az 257, Az 258, Az 260, Az 261

Card 45 Az 265, Az 266, Az 268, Az 269, Az 270, Az 271, Az 272, Az 273, Az 274, Az 275, Az 276, Az 277, Az 278, Az 279, Az 280, Az 281, Az 282, Az 283, Az 284, Az 288, Az 291, Az 293, Az 294, Az 295, Az 300, Az 302, Az 303, Az 304, Az 305, Az 306, Az 307, Az 308

Card 46 Az 310, Az 312, Az 314, Az 315, Az 317, Az 326, Az 328, Az 329, Az 330, Az 332, Az 333, Az 334, Az 335, Az 336, Az 338, Az 339, Az 341, Az 342, Az 343, Az 344, Az 345, Az 346, Az 347, Az 348, Az 349, Az 350, Az 351, Az 352, Az 353, Az 355, Az 356, Az 357

Card 47 Az 359, Az 360, Az 363, Az 364, Az 365, Az 368, Az 370, Az 371, Az 374, Az 375, Az 378, Az 392, Az 394, Az 397, Az 399, Az 400, Az 401, Az 402, Az 404, Az 408, Az 409, Az 410, Az 411, Az 413, Az 415, Az 419, Az 421, Az 425, Az 426, Az 428, Az 430, Az 431

Card 48 Az 432, Az 435, Az 440, Az 445, Az 450, Az 453, Az 454, Az 456, Az 458, Az 459, Az 461, Az 462, deleted, deleted, deleted, deleted, deleted, deleted, deleted, deleted, deleted, deleted, EG 1, EG 2, EG 3, EG 4, EG 5, EG 6, EG 7, EG 8, EG 10, EG 11

Card 49 EG 12, EG 13, EG 14, EG 16, EG 17, EG 18, EG 19, EG 21, EG 23, EG 24, EG 25, EG 26, EG 27, EG 28, EG 29, EG 31, EG 32, EG 34, EG 35, EG 36, EG 37, EG 38, EG 39, EG 40, EG 41, EG 42, EG 43, EG 44, EG 45, EG 46, EG 47, EG 48

Card 50 EG 49, EG 50, EG 51, EG 52, EG 53, EG 54,

EG 55, EG 56, EG 57, EG 58, EG 59, EG 60, EG 61, EG 62, EG 63, EG 64, EG 65, EG 66, EG 67, EG 68, EG 69, EG 70, EG 71, EG 72, EG 73, EG 74, EG 75, EG 76, EG 78, EG 80, EG 82, EG 83

Card 51 EG 84, EG 85, EG 86, EG 88, EG 89, EG 90, EG 91, EG 92, EG 93, EG 95, EG 96, EG 98, EG 99, EG 101, EG 102, EG 103, EG 104, EG 105, EG 106, EG 107, EG 110, EG 112, EG 114, EG 119, EG 121, EG 123, EG 124, EG 125, EG 127, EG 128, EG 129, EG 2

Card 52 EG 3, EG 120, EG 139, EG 120, EG 139, EG Area 3, EG Area 4, EG Area 6, EG Area 7, EG Area 8, deleted

10001010000010002000001010100010000010000000000000010000000000000203010000
10001020100000100010000000000000100000200000000101000103010000000001000000
10001030100000500000000001040000000201030000010000000010000000104000010101
10001040000010001000000000000000000000100000101000000020000000000000000201
10001050000000010001010000000000000000001000001010000000100000102000000000
10001060000000000000000000000001000000000100000000000001000002000000000001
10001070000000000001000201010000010000000000000000000000000102000000020000
10001080200000010000010000000000100000100000000000000000100000000201000100
10001090000010000000000000000000101000000000000000000001010100000101000010000
10001100000000000000000000000000000000000000010000000000000000102000000101
10001110001010000000000000000000000001000002000000000000000010000000000000000
10001120000010000000000100000000000000000000000000000000000000000000000000200
10001130001000000030000010000010000000000000000002010000000000001000102000 0
10001140100010000000000000000000000000000000000000000000000000000000000100
10001150200010002000000002000200000000000001000000000000101000001000000000
10001160000000000000000000000000000000000000001000000000003000000000000000000
10001170000000100000000000000000000000000000000000000000000000000000000000001
10001180200000100000000000000000000000000001000000100000000000000000000000000
10001190000000000000000000000000000000000000000000000000000000000000000020103
10001200000000000001000100000000000101000000000000000000000000010000000000000
10001210000000000000000000000000000000000000000000000000000000000000000000000
10001220000000000000000000000000000000000000000000000000000000000000000000000
10001230000000010000000000000000000000100000000000000000000000000000000000000
10001240000000000000000000000000000000001000000000000000010000000000000000000
10001250000000100000000000000000010000000000000100000000000000000000000000000
10001260000000000000000000000000000000000000000000000000000000000000000000000
10001270001000000010000000000000000000000000000001010100000000000000000000000
10001280000000000000000000000000000000000000000000000000000000000000000010000
10001290000000000000000000000000000000000000000000000000010000000100000100
10001300000000000001000000000000000000000000000000001000000000000000000000000
10001310000000000000000000000000000010000000000000000000000000000000000000000
10001320000000000000000000000000000000000000000000000000000000000000000020000
10001330000000000000000000000000000000000000000000102000000000000000010000000000
10001340000000000000000000000000000000000000000000000000000000000010001000000
10001350000000000000000000000000000000000000000000000000000000000000000000000
10001360000000000000000000000000000000000000000000000000000001000000020000000000
10001370002000100000001000000000000000000000000000000000000000000100000100010000
10001380000000000000000000000000000000000000000000000000000000000000000000000
10001390000000000000000000000000000000000000000000000000000000000000000000000
10001400000000000000000000000000000000000000000000000000000000000000000000000
10001410000000000000000000000000000000000000000000000000000000000000000000000
10001420000000000000000000000000000000000000000000000000000000000000000000000
10001430000000000000000000000000000000000000000000000000000000000000000000000
10001440000000000000000000000000000000000000000000000000000000000000000000000
10001450000000000000000000000000000000000000000000000000000000000000000000000
10001460000000000000000000000000000000000000000000000000000000000000000000000
10001470000000000000000000000000000010000000000000000000000000000000000000000
10001480000000000000000000000000000000100000000010000000000000000000000000000
10001490000000000000000000000000000000000000000000000000000000000000000000000
10001500000000000000000000000000000000000000000000000000000000000000000000000
10001510000000000000002000000000000000000000000000000000000000000000000000000
1000152000001000000000000000000
10002010000010002000001000100000000000000000000000000000000100000000000000
10002020000000000000000000000000000000000102000000000100000100010000000001
10002030000000100000000010000000000000001000000000000000000000000000000000000
10002040000000000100000000000000000000000010001000100000000000000000000000
10002050000001010000000000000000000000100000001000000000000000000000000000
10002060000000100010000000000001010300000000001000000010100000000000000000
10002070000000000001030000000000100000000000000000000000000000000000000000
10002080000000000000000100000000000000000000000100000000000000000000000000000
10002090000000000001000000000000000000000000000000000000000000000000301010000000
10002100000000000000000000000000000000000000000000000000000000000000000000100
10002110000000000000000000000000000000000010000000000000000000001000000000000
10002120000010000000000000000000000000000000000000000000000000000000000000000
10002130000000000000000000000000000000000000000100010000000000020000000000
10002140000000000000000000000000000000000000000000000000000000000000000000100
10002150000030000000000000000010000000000000000000000000000000000000000000000
10002160000000000000000000000000001000000010000000000000000000000000000000000
10002170000000000000000000000000000000000000000000000000000000000000000000000
10002180000000010000000000000000100000000000000000000000000000000000000000100
10002190000000000000000000000000000000000000000000000000000000000000000010000
10002200000010000002000000000000000000000000000000000000000000000000000000000
10002210000000000000000000000000000000000000000000000000000000000000000000000
10002220000000000000000000000000000000000000000000000000000000000000000000000
10002230000000000000000000000000000000000000000010000000000000000000000000000
10002240000000000000000000000000000000000100000000000000000000000010000000000
10002250000000000000000000000000000000000000000000000000000000000000000000000
10002260000000000000000000000000000000000000000000000000000000000000000000000
10002270000000000000000000000000000000000000000000000000000000000000000000000
10002280000000000000000000000000000000000000000000000000000000000000000000000
10002290000000000000000000000000000000000000000000000000000000000000000000000
10002300000000000000000000000000000000000000000000000000000000000000000000000
10002310000000000000000000000000000001000000000000000000000000000000000000000
10002320000000000000000000000000000000000000000000000000000000000000000000000
10002330000000000000000000000000000000000000000000000000000000000000000000000
10002340000000000000000000000000000000000000000001000000000000000000000000000
10002350000000000000000000000000000000000000000000000000000000000000000000000
10002360000000000001000000000000000000000000000000000000000000000001000000002
10002370000000000000000000000000000000000000000000000000000000000000100000000
10002380000000000000000000000000000000000000000000000000000000000000000000000
10002390000000000000000000000000000000000000000000000000000000000000000000000
10002400000000000000000000000000000000000000000000000000000000000000000000000
10002410000000000000000000000000000000000000000000000000000000000000000000000
10002420000000000000000000000000000000000000000000000000000000000000000000000
10002430000000000000000000000000000000000000000000000000000000000000000000000
10002440000000000000000000000000000000000000000000000000000000000000000000000
10002450000000000000000000000000000000000000000000000000000000000000000000000
10002460000000000000000000000000000000000000000000000000000000000000000000000
10002470000000000000000000000000000001000000000000000000000000000000000000000
10002480000000000000000000000000000000000000000000000000000000000000000000000
10002490000000000000000000000000000000000000000000000000000000000000000000000
10002500000000000000000000000000000000000000000000000000000000000000000000000
10002510000000000000000000000000000000000000000000000000000000000000000000000
1000252000100000000000000000000
10003010000020000010001000101000100010000000000100020000000030001020001 00
10003020100000000020000000000000000000101000000001010001010100000100010000
10003030001000101000000002000000000000000000000100000000100000000000000000001
10003040000000000000200000000000000000000000000001000200000200010000000000000
10003050100000000000100000000000000000000000100010001000000000101000000000
10003060000000000000000000000000200010000020000000000000000000100000000000000
10003070000000000000101000000001000100000000000000000000000000000000000000000
10003080000000000000000000000000001000000000000000000000010000010000000000
10003090000000000000000000000000000000000100000000000000000000010001000100
10003100000000000000000000000000000100010000010000000000000000000000000000000
10003110000000100000100000000000000000000000000000000000000001000001000000000
10003120000000000000000000000000010000000000000000000000000000000000000000000
10003130000000000001000200000000000000000000000000001000000000000100000000000
10003140000000000000000000000000000000001000000000000000000000000000000000000
10003150200000000010000010000000000000000000000000000000000000000000000000000

1000316000000000300000000001000000000000000000000000000000100000000000000000
1000317000002000000000000000000000000000000000000000000000000000000000000
1000318000000000000000000000000000000000100000000000000000000000000000000
1000319010000000000000000000000000000000000000000000000000000000100000000
1000320000000000000010000000001000000000000000000000000000000000000000000
1000321000000000000000000000000000000000000000000000000000000000000000000
1000322000000000000000000000000000000000000000000000000000000000000000000
1000323000000000000000000000000000000000000000010000000000000000000000000
1000324000001000000000000000000000000000000000000000000000000000000000000
1000325000000000000000000000000000000000000000000000000000000000000000000
1000326000000000000000000000000000001000000030000000000000000000000000000
1000327000100000000000000000000100000000000000000000000000001000000000000
1000328000000000000000000000000000000000000000000000000000000000000000000
1000329000000000000000001000000000000000000100000000100010100000000000000
1000330000000000000000000000000000000000000000000000000000000000000000000
1000331000000000000000000000000000000000000000000000000000000000300000000
1000332000000000000000000000000000000000000000000000000000000000000000000
1000333000000000000000000001000000000000100010000000000000000000000000000
1000334000000000001000000000000000000000000000000000000000000000000000000
1000335000000000000000000000000000000000000000000000000000000000000000000
1000336000000010000000000000000000000000100000000000000000000000000000000
1000337000000010000000000000000000000000000000000000000000000000000000000
1000338000000000000000000000000000000000000000000000000000000000000000000
1000339000000000000000000000000000000000100000000000000000000000000000000
1000340000000000000000000000000000000000000000000000000000000000000000000
1000341000000000000000000000000000000000000000000000000000000000000000000
1000342000000000000000000000000000000000000000000000000000000000000000000
1000343000000000000000000000000000000000000000000000000000000000000000000
1000344000000000000000000000000000000000000000000000000000000000000000000
1000345000000000000000000000000000000000000000000000000000000000000000000
1000346000000000000000000000000000000000000000000000000000000000000000000
1000347000000000000000000000000100000000000000000000000000000000000000000
1000348010000000000000000000000000000000000000000000000000000000000000000
1000349000000000000000000000000000000000000000000000000000000000000000000
1000350000000010000000000000000000000000000000000000000000000000000000000
1000351000000000000000000000000000000000000000000000000000000000000000000
100035200000000000000000000000
1000401000000000000000000000000000000100000000010500000000000000000300000000
1000402000000000000000000000000001000000000000000001020000000000000000000000
1000403000000010000000000000000000000001000000000200000000001010000010000
1000404000000010001000000001000000000000000101000300010000000000000000000
1000405000000000000000000000000000000100000000000000010000000000000000000
1000406000000000000000000000000000000010000000000000001000000010200000000
1000407000000000000000000001000000010000010000000001000000000000000000000
1000408000000000000000000000000000000000000000000000000000000000000000000
1000409000000000000000001000000000000000000000000000100010000020000020000
1000410000000000000000000000000000000000000000000000000000000000000000200
1000411000000000000000001000000000000000010000000000000000000000000000000
1000412000000000000000000000000000000000000000000000000000000000000000000
1000413000000000000000000000000000000000000020000000000000000000000000000
1000414000000000000000000000000000000000000000000000000000000000000000101
1000415020000000000000000000000000000000000000000000000000000000000000100
1000416000000000000000000000000000000000000000100000300000000000000000000
1000417000000000000000000000000000000000000000000000000000000000000000000
1000418000000010000000001000100000000000000100000000000000000000000000000
1000419000000000000000000000000000000000000000000000000000000000100000000
1000420000000000000000000000000000000000000000000000000000000000000000000
1000421000000000000000000000000000000000000000000000000000000000000000000
1000422000000000000000000000000000000000000000000000000000000000000000000
1000423000000000000000000000000000000000000000000000000000000000000000000
1000424000001010100000000000000000000000000000000000000000000000000000000
1000425000000000000000000000000000000000000000000000000000000000000000000
1000426000000000000000000000000000000000000000000100020101000000000000000
1000427000000000000010000000000000000000000000000000000000000000000000000
1000428000000000000000000000000000000000000000000000000000000000000000000
1000429000000000000000000000000000000000000000000101000100000000000000000
1000430000000000000000000000000000000000000000000000000000000000000000000
1000431000000000000000000000000000000000000000000000000000000000200000000
1000432000000000000000000010000000000000000000000000000000000000000000000
1000433000000000000000000000000000000000000010000000000000000000000000000
1000434000000000000000000000000000000000010000000000000000000000000000000
1000435000000000000000000000000000000000000000000000000000000000000000000
1000436000000000000000000000001000000000000000000000000000000000200000100
1000437000000000000000100000000000000000000000000000000000000000000000000
1000438000000000000000000000000000000000000000000000000000000000000000000
1000439000000000000000000000000000000000000000000000000000000000000000000
1000440000000000000000000000000000000000000000000000000000000000000000000
1000441000000000000000000000000000000000000000000000000000000000000000000
1000442000000000000000000000000000000000000000000000000000000000000000000
1000443000000000000000000000000000000000000000000000000000000000000000000
1000444000000000000000000000000000000000000000000000000000000000000000000
1000445000000000000000000000000000000000000000000000000000000000000000000
1000446000000000000000000000000000000000000000000000000000000000000000000
1000447000000000000000000000000000000000000000000000000000000000000000000
1000448000000000000000000000000000000000000000000000010000000000000000000
1000449000000000000000000000000000000000000000000000000000000000000000000
1000450000000000000000000000000000000000000000000000000000000000000000000
1000451000000000000000000000000000000000000000000000000000000000000000000
100045200000000000000000000000
1000501000000000000000001000001000100000000000020100000000000000000000000
1000502010000000000000000000000000000000000000000100000100000000000000000
1000503000000020000000000010100000100000000001010000000000000000000000000
1000504000000000000010000000000000000000000000000000000000000000000000000
1000505000000000000000000000000000000000000000000000000000000000000000000
1000506000000000000000000000000000010000000000000000000010000000200000100
1000507000000000000000000000000000000000000000000000000000000010001000000
1000508000000000000000000000000000000000000000000000000100000000000000000
1000509000000000000000000000000000000000000000000000000000000000000000000
1000510000000000000000000000001000000000000000000000000000000000000000000
1000511000000000000000000000100000000000010000000000000000000000000000000
1000512000000000000000000000000000000000000000000000000000000000000000000
1000513000000000000000000000000000000000000000000100000000000000000000000
1000514000000000000000000000000000000000000000000000000000000000000000000
1000515010000000000000000000000000000000000000000000000000000000000000000
1000516000000000100000000010000000000000000000000000000000000000000000000
1000517000000000000000000000000000000000000000000000000000000000000000000
1000518010000000000000000000000000000000000100010000000000000000000000000
1000519000000000000000000000000000000000000000000000000000000000100000101
1000520010000000001000000000000000000000000000000000000000000000000000000
1000521000000000000000000000000000000000000000000000000000000000000000000
1000522000000000000000000000000000000000000000000000000000000000000000000
1000523000000000000000000000000000000000000000000000000000000000000000000
1000524000000000000000000000000000000000000000000000000000000000000000000
1000525000000000000000100000000000000000000000000000000000000000000000000
1000526000000000000000000000000000000000000000000000000001000000000000000
1000527000000000000000000000000000000000000000000000000000000000000000000
1000528000000000000000000000000000000000000000000000000000000000000000000
1000529000000000000000000000000001010000000001000000000100000000000000000
1000530000000000000000000000000000000000000000000000000000000000000000000
1000531000000000000000000000000000000000000000000000000000000000100000000

```
10005320000000000000000000000000000000000000000000000000000000000000000000000000
10005330000000000000000000000000000000000000000000000000000000000000000000000000
10005340100000000000000000000000000000000000000000000000000000000000100000000000
10005350000000000000000000000000000000000000000000000000000000000000000000000000
10005360000000000000000000000000010000000000000000000000000000000000001000000000
10005370000000000000000000000000000000100000000000000000000000000000000000000000
10005380000000000000000000000000000000000000000000000000000000000000000000000000
10005390000000000000000000000000000000000000000000000000000000000000000000000000
10005400000000000000000000000000000000000000000000000000000000000000000000000000
10005410000000000000000000000000000000000000000000000000000000000000000000000000
10005420000000000000000000000000000000000000000000000000000000000000000000000000
10005430000000000000000000000000000000000000000000000000000000000000000000000000
10005440000000000000000000000000000000000000000000000000000000000000000000000000
10005450000000000000000000000000000000000000000000000000000000000000000000000000
10005460000000000000000000000000000000000000000000000000000000000000000000000000
10005470000000000000000000000000000000000000000000000000000000000000000000000000
10005480000000000000000000000000000000000000000000000000000000000000000000000000
10005490000000000000000000000000000000000000000000000000000000000100000000000000
100055000000000000000000000000000000000000000000000000000000000000000000000000000
10005510000000000000000000000000000000000000000000000000000000000000000000000000
100055200000000000000000000000000
10006010000000000000000000000101000000000000000100020200000000000000000010000000
10006020000000000000000000000001000000000000000100000000000000000000000000000200
10006030000000000200100000100000000010100000000000000000000000000000200000000000
10006040000100000000000000000000000010000000000000001010000001000000000000000000
10006050000000000000000000000000000000000000000000001000000000000000000000000000
10006060000000000000000000000000002000000000010100000000000000000000000000000000
10006070000000000010000000000100000000000000000000000000000000000000000000000000
10006080000000000010000000000100000000000000000000000000000000001000000000000000
10006090000000000000000000000000000000000000000000000000000000000000000010000000
10006100100000000000000000000000010000000000000000000000000000000000000000000101
10006110000000000000000000000000000000100000010000001000000000001000000000000000
10006120000001000000000000000000000000000000000000000000000000000000000000000100
10006130000000000000000000000000000000000000000000000000000000000000000000000000
10006140000000000000000000000000000000000000000000000000000000000000000000000400
10006150000000000200100001000000000000000000000000000000100000000000000000000000
10006160000000000000000001000000000000000000000000000000000010000000000000000000
10006170000000000000000000000000000000000000000000000000000000000000000000000000
10006180000000000000000000000000000000000000000000000101000000000000000000000000
10006190000000000000000000000000000000000000000000000000000000000000000000000000
10006200000000000000000000000000000000100000000000000000000000000000000000000000
10006210000000000000000000000000000000000000000000000000000000000000000000000000
10006220000000000000000000000000000000000000000000000000000000000000000000000000
10006230000000000000000000000000000000000000000000001000000001000000000000000000
10006240000000000000000000000000000000001000000000000000000000000000000000000000
10006250000001000000000000000000000000000000000000000000000000000000000000000000
10006260000000000000000000000000000000000000000000000000000000000000000000000000
10006270000000000000000000000000000000000000000002010000000000000000000000000000
10006280000000000000000000000000000000000000000000000000000100000000000000000000
10006290000000000000000000100000000000000000000000000000000001010000000000000000
10006300000000000000000000000000000000000000000000000000000000000000000000000000
10006310000000000000000000000000000000000000000000000000000000000000001000000000
10006320000000000000000000000000000000000000000000000000000000000000000000000000
10006330000000000000000000000000000000000000000100000000000000000000000000000000
10006340000000000000000000000000000000000010000000000000000000000000000000000000
10006350100000000000000000000000000000000000000000000000000000000000000000000000
10006360000000000000000000000000000000000000201000000000000000000000001000000100
10006370000000000000000000000000000000000000000000000000000000000000000000000000
10006380000000000000000000000000000000000000000000000000000000000000000000000000
10006390000000000000000000000000000000000000000000000000000000000000000000000000

10006400000000000000000000000000000000000000000000000000000000000000000000000000
10006410000000000000000000000000000000000000000000000000000000000000000000000000
10006420000000000000000000000000000000000000000000000000000000000000000000000000
10006430000000000000000000000000000000000000000000000000000000000000000000000000
10006440000000000000000000000000000000000000000000000000000000000000000000000000
10006450000000000000000000000000000000000000000000000000000000000000000000000000
10006460000000000000000000000000000000000000000000000000000000000000000000000000
10006470000000000000000000000000000000000000000000000000000000000000000000000000
10006480000000000000000000000000000000000000000000000000000100000000000010000000
10006490000000000000000000000000000000000000000000000000000000000000000000000000
10006500000000000000000000000000000000000000000000000000000000000000000000000000
10006510000000000000000000000000000000000000000000000000000000000000000000000000
100065200000000000000000000000000
10016010002000000000000000000000000000000000000100000100000000000000000000000000
10016020000000000000000000000000000000000000000000000000101000000010000000000000
10016030000000000000000000000001000000000000000000000000000000000000000000000000
10016040000000000000000000000100000000000000000000000000000000000000000000000000
10016050000000000000000000000000000000000000000000000000001000001000000000000000
10016060000000000000000000000000000000001000000000000000000000000000000000000000
10016070000000000000000010002000000200000000000000000001000000001000000000001010
10016080000000000000000000000001000100000100000000000000000000000000000000000000
10016090000000000000000000000100000000000000010000000000001000001000000000000000
10016100000001000000000000000000000000000000000000000000000000000000101010000000
10016110000000010000010000000010000000000000000000000000000000000000000000000000
10016120000000000000000000001000000000000000000000000000000000000000000000000000
10016130000000000000000000000000000000000000010000000000000000000000000020000000
10016140000000010000000000000000000000000000000000000000000000000000000000000000
10016150100000000000000000000000000000000000000000000000000000000000000000000000
10016160000000000000000000000000000000000000000000000000000000000000000000000000
10016170000000000000000000000000000000000000000000000000000000000000000000000000
10016180000000000000000000000000000000000000000000000000000000000000000000000000
10016190000000000000000000000000000000000000000000000000000000000000000000000000
10016200000000000000000000000100000000000000000000000000000000000000000000000000
10016210000000000000000000000000000000000000000000000000000000000000000000000000
10016220000000000000000000000000000000000000000000000000000000000000000000000000
10016230000000000000000000000000000000000000000000000000000000000000000000000000
10016240000000000000000000000000000000000000010000000000001000000000000000000000
10016250000000000000000000000000000000000000010000000000000000000000000000000000
10016260000000000000000000000000000000000000000000000000000001000000000010100000
10016270100000000000000000000000000000000000100000100020000000000000000000000000
10016280000000000000001000000000000000000000000000000000000000000000000000000000
10016290100000000000000000000000000000000000000000000000000000000000000000000000
10016300000000000000000000000000000000000000000000000000000000000000000000000000
10016310000000000000000000000000000000000000000000000000000000000000000000000000
10016320000000000000000000000000000000000000000000000000000000000000000000000000
10016330000000000000000000000000000000000000000000000000000001000000000000000000
10016340100000000000000000000000000000000000000000000000000000000000000000000000
10016350000000000000000000000000000000000000000000000000000000000000000000000000
10016360000000000000000000000000000000000000010000000000000000000000000000000100
10016370100000100000000000000000000000000000000000000000000000000000000000000000
10016380000000000000000000000000000000000000000000000000000000000000000000000000
10016390000000000000000000000000000000000000000000000000000000000000000000000000
10016400000000000000000000000000000000000000000000000000000000000000000000000000
10016410000000000000000000000000000000000000000000000000000000000000000000000000
10016420000000000000000000000000000000000000000000000000000000000000000000000000
10016430000000000000000000000000000000000000000000000000000000000000000000000000
10016440000000000000000000000000000000000000000000000000000000000000000000000000
10016450000000000000000000000000000000000000000000000000000000000000000000000000
10016460000000000000000000000000000000000000000000000000000000000000000000000000
10016470000000000000000000000000000000000000000000000000000000000000000000000000
```

```
10016480000000000000000000000000000000000000000000000000000000000000000000000000
10016490000000000000000000000000000000000000000000000000000000000000000000000000
10016500000000000000000000000000000000000000000000000000000000000000000000000000
10016510000000000000000000000000000000000000000000000000000000000000000000000000
100165200000000000000000000000000
10021010000020000000000000000000000000000000000000000000000000001000000000000000
10021020000000000000000000000000000000000000000000000000000000000000000100000000
10021030100000000000000000000100000000000000000000000000000000000000000000000000
10021040000000000000000000000000000000000000000000000000000000000000000000000000
10021050000000000000000000000000000000000000000000000000000000000000000000000000
10021060000000000000000000000000000000010000000000000000000000000000000000000000
10021070000000000000001000001000000000000000000000000000000000000000000000000000
10021080000000000000000000000000000000000000000000000000000000000000000000000000
10021090000000000000000000000000000000000000000000000000000000000000000000000000
10021100000000000000000000000000000000000000000000000000000000000000000000000000
10021110000000000000000000000000000000000000000000000000000000000000000000000000
10021120000000000000000000000000000000000000000000000000000000000000000000000000
10021130000000000000000000000000000000000000000000000000000000000000000000000000
10021140000000000000000000000000000000000000000000000000000000000000000000000000
10021150000000000000000000000000000000000000000000000000000000000000000000000000
10021160000000000000000000000000000000000000000000000000000000000000000000000000
10021170000000000000000000000000000000000000000000000000000000000000000000000000
10021180000000000000000000000000000000000000000000000000000000000000000000000000
10021190000000000000000000000000000000000000000000000000000000000000000000000000
10021200000000000000101000000000000000000000000000000000000000000000000000000000
10021210000000000000000000000000000000000000000000000000000000000000000000000000
10021220000000000000000000000000000000000000000000000000000000000000000000000000
10021230000000000000000000000000000000000000000000000000000000000000000000000000
10021240000000000000000000000000000000000100000000000000000000000000000000000000
10021250000000000000000000000000000000000000000000000000000000000000000000000000
10021260000000000000000000000000000000000000000000000000000001000000000000000000
10021270000000000000000000000000000000000000000000000010000000000000000000000000
10021280000000000000000000000000000000000000000000000000000000000000000000000000
10021290000000000000000000000000000000000000000000000000000000000000000000000000
10021300000000000000000000000000000000000000000000000000000000000000000000000000
10021310000000000000000000000000000000000000000000000000000000000000000000000000
10021320000000000000000000000000000000000000000000000000000000000000000000000000
10021330000000000000000000000000000000000000000000000000000000000000000000000000
10021340000000000000000000000000000000000000000000000000000000000000000000000000
10021350000000000000000000000000000000000000000000000000000000000000000000000000
10021360000000000000000000000000000000000000000000000000000000000000000000000000
10021370001000000000000000000000000000000000000000000000000000000000000000000000
10021380000000000000000000000000000000000000000000000000000000000000000000000000
10021390000000000000000000000000000000000000000000000000000000000000000000000000
10021400000000000000000000000000000000000000000000000000000000000000000000000000
10021410000000000000000000000000000000000000000000000000000000000000000000000000
10021420000000000000000000000000000000000000000000000000000000000000000000000000
10021430000000000000000000000000000000000000000000000000000000000000000000000000
10021440000000000000000000000000000000000000000000000000000000000000000000000000
10021450000000000000000000000000000000000000000000000000000000000000000000000000
10021460000000000000000000000000000000000000000000000000000000000000000000000000
10021470000000000000000000000000000000000000000000000000000000000000000000000000
10021480000000000000000000000000000000000000000000000000000000000000000000000000
10021490000000000000000000000000000000000000000000000000000000000000000000000000
10021500000000000000000000000000000000000000000000000000000000000000000000000000
10021510000000000000000000000000000000000000000000000000000000000000000000000000
100215200000000000000000000000000
10022010000000010000010000010000000000000000000000002100000000000000000000000000
10022020000000010010000010000000002000001000000000000000001000101000000000000000
10022030000000000000000000000010000000010000000000000000000000000000000000000000
10022040000001000000000000000000010000001000000000000000000000000000000000000000
10022050000000000000100000000000000000000000000000000000000000000000001000000000
10022060000100000000000000000000000000000000000000000000010000000000000000000000
10022070000000000000000100010000000000000000000000000000000000000000000000000000
10022080000000000000000000000000000000000000000000000000000000000000001000000000
10022090000000000000101000000000002000000000000000100000000000000000000000000000
10022100000000000000000000000000000000000200000000000000000000000000000000000001
10022110000000000000000000001000000001000000000000000000000000000001000000000000
10022120000000000000000000400010000000000000001000000000000000000000000000000000
10022130000000000000000000000000000000000100000000000000000000000000000000000000
10022140100000000000000000000000000000000000000000000000000000000000000000000000
10022150000000100000000000000000000000000000000000010000000000000001000000000000
10022160000020000000000000000000000000000000000100000000000000000000000000000000
10022170000000000000000000000000000000000000000000000000000000000000000000000000
10022180000000000000010000010000000000001000100000000000000000000000000000000001
10022190000000000000000000000000000000000000000000000000000000000000000000000001
10022200000000000000000000000000000000000000000000000000000000000000000000000000
10022210000000000000000000000000000000000000000000000000000000000000000000000000
10022220000000000000000000000000000000000000000000000000000000000000000000010001
10022230000000000000000000000000000000000000000000000000000000000000000000000000
10022240001000000000000000000000000000000000000000000000000000000000000000000000
10022250000000000000000000000000000000000000000000000000000000000000000000000000
10022260000000000000000000000000000000000000000010000000000000000000000000000000
10022270100000000000000000000000000000000000000000010100000000000000000000000000
10022280000000000000000000000000000000000000000000000000000000000000000000000000
10022290000000000000000000000000000000000000000000000000000000000000000000000000
10022300000000000000000000000000000000000000000000000000000000000000000000000000
10022310000000000000000000000000000000000000000000000000000000000000000000000000
10022320000000000000000100000000000000000000000000000000000000000000000000000000
10022330000000000000000000000000000000000000000000000000000000000000000000000000
10022340000000000000000000000000000000000000000010000000000000000000000000000000
10022350000000000000000000000000000000000000000000000000000000000000000000000001
10022360000000000000000000000000000000000000000000000000000000000000300000000000
10022370000000000000000000000000001000000000000000000000000000000000000000000000
10022380000000000000000000000000000000000000000000000000000000000000000000000000
10022390000000000000000000000000000000000000000000000000000000000000000000000000
10022400000000000000000000000000000000000000000000000000000000000000000000000000
10022410000000000000000000000000000000000000000000000000000000000000000000000000
10022420000000000000000000000000000000000000000000000000000000000000000000000000
10022430000000000000000000000000000000000000000000000000000000000000000000000000
10022440000000000000000000000000000000000000000000000000000000000000000000000000
10022450000000000000000000000000000000000000000000000000000000000000000000000000
10022460000000000000000000000000000000000000000000000000000000000000000000000000
10022470000000000000000000000000000000000000000000000000000000000000000000000000
10022480000000000000000000000000000000000000000000000000000000000000000000000000
10022490000000000000000000000000000000000000000000000000000000000000000000000000
10022500000000000000000000000000000000000000000000000000000000000000000000000000
10022510000000000000000000000000000000000000000000000000000000000000000000000000
100225200000000000000000000000000
10031010100010000005030000000000000001010000000000040300000000001000001000000000
10031020001000000000000000000000000000000000001040000010100000010203010100000100000
10031030000000000000000000000000001000003000004000300010000000000000102010001000200
10031040001000000000000100000000001000000000000000020101000100010001000000000000
10031050100010000000000000000000000000000000000100000000000000000000002000000000
10031060000000000000020101000000000000000000000000000100000100020100000000000000
10031070000000000001000001000000100000001000000000000001000200000000000001010000
10031080001000200000000000000010000000000000000000001000100000000000002000000000
10031090000010000000000000000000000102000000000000000000000000000000000000000000
10031100000000000000000000000000000000000000000000000001000000000000000000000000
10031110001000001000000000000000000000000000000000000001000000000000000101000101
```

```
10031120004020000000000000000000000000000000000000000000000100000000000000000000
10031130000000010000000000000000010000001000000010000000000000000003020000000001
10031140000001000000000000000000000000000000000000000000000000000000000000000000
10031150300010000000000000000001000100020000000000000000000000010000000000000000
10031160000005000100000100000000000010000000000100000000000001000000000000000000
10031170000000000000000000000000000000000000000000000000000000000000000000000001
10031180100000000000000000000002000000000000000100000000100000000000000000000001
10031190000000000000000000000000100000000000000000000000000000000000000000000000
10031200000001000000000000000000000000000000000000000000100000000000000000000000
10031210000000000000000000000000000000000000000000000000000000000000000000000000
10031220000000000000000000000000000000000000000000000000000000000000000000000000
10031230000000000000000000000000000000000000000000000000000000000000000000000000
10031240000000000000000000000000000010000010000000000000000000000000001000100000
10031250000020000010001000001000100000000000000000000000000000000000000000000000
10031260000000000000000000000000000000000000000000000000000000000000100010001000
10031270000000000000000000000000000000000000000000000000000000000000000000000000
10031280000000000000000000000000000000000000000000000000000000000000000000000000
10031290000000000000000000000000100000000000000000000000000000000000000000000000
10031300000000000000000000000000000000000000000000000000000000000000000000000000
10031310000000000000000000000000000000000000000000000000000000000000000000000000
10031320000000000000000000000000000000000000000000000001000000000000000000000000
10031330000000000000000000000000000000000000001000030200000000000001000000000000
10031340100000000000000000000000000100000000000000000000000000000000000000000101
10031350000000000000000000000000000100000000000000000000000000000000000000000000
10031360000000000000000000000000000100000000000001000000000000000000000010001000001
10031370001000010000000010000000001000000000000000000000000000000000000000000000
10031380000000000000000000000000000000000000000000000000000000000000000000000000
10031390000000000000000000000000000000000000000000000000000000000000000000000000
10031400000000000000000000000000000000000000000000000000000000000000000000000000
10031410000000000000000000000000000000000000000000000010000000000000000000000000
10031420000000000000000000000000000000000000000000000000000000000000000000000000
10031430000000000000000000000000000000000000000000000000000000000000000000000000
10031440000000000000000000000000000000000000000000000000000000000000000000000000
10031450000000000000000000000000000000000000000000000000000000000000000000000000
10031460000000000000000000000000000000000000000000000000000000000000000000000000
10031470000000000000000000000000000000000200000000000000100000100000000000000000000
10031480000000000000000000000000000000000000000000000000000000000000000000000000
10031490000000000000000000000000000000000000000000000000000000000000000000000000
10031500000000010000000000000000000000000000000000000000000000000000000000000000
10031510000000000000000000000000000000000000000000000000000000000000000000000000
10031520000010000000000000000000
10032010100040202000004000000010000010103000000003020000000000000200000200010000
10032020100000000001000000000001020000000000101000100000000000100010000000000000
10032030000701000300000000000000000100000000000010000000000000000000020101010202
10032040101000001030100020100020100020101070501010001000102000000000000000020202
10032050000010003010300010000000000000000100010000010201000002000001000300010000
10032060300020000010100000100000010000001010000000000100000100010000000000000101
10032070100000000000000000000000000000100000000001010003020003010000000000000103
10032080001000400000000020002000100000000000000200030001000201010203000100000100
10032090000000000000000000001000000000000202000201000000000000000001000000000000
10032100000000000000000000000000000000000000000000000000100010100000000000000000001
10032110101030000010006000500010101010101000100000000000000001040101010002000100
10032120000004010000000000100000000000000000000000000000001000000000000000000001
10032130000000000000000010000010004020201020100000400000000000000001000200020300000
10032140202000200000000000000000000000001010000000000000000000000000000001000101
10032150400000301010100010000020100030101000001000010000001000000000010000000000
10032160001000100000100010001000100000000000000000000000002000000000000000000001
10032170000000000000000000000000000000000000000000000000001000000000000000000001
10032180100000001000000000003000101000000000100000000000000001000000000001000000
10032190000000000000000000000000100000000000000000000000001010000000000000020000
10032200100000100000000000001020000000000010000000000000001000000000000000000000
10032210100000000000000000000000000000000000000000000000001000000000000000000000
10032220000000000000000000000000000000000000000000000000000000000100000000010000
10032230000000000000000000000000000002000001000001000000010002000100000000000000000
10032240000000000000000000000000000001000000001000000010000000000000010001000101000100
10032250001040100000101000001020000001000001000000000000000000000000000000000000
10032260000000000000000000000000000000000000000000010000000200000001030102010001000000
10032270000000100000000010000000000000001000000000101000001000000000000000000000
10032280000000101000200000000000000020000000000000000000000000000000001000000000
10032290000000002000000000000000000000000000000000000000000000000000000000000000
10032300000000000000000000100010000000000000000000000000000000000000000000000000
10032310000000000000000000000000000000000000000000000000000000000000000100000000
10032320000000100000010200000000000100001000000000000000000000000000000000000000
10032330000000000000000000000000000000000000000000000101000010103020101010000000000
10032340000001010000000000000000000000000000000000000000000000200010000000000100
10032350001000000000100000000100000001000000000000100000000000000000000000000000
10032360002000100000000000000000000000000000000000000000100000000000001000000020100010003
10032370003010600000001000000010000000000000100000000000000000000000000000000000
10032380000000000000000000000000100000000000000000000000000000000000000000000000
10032390000000000000000000000000000000000000100000000000000000000000000000000000
10032400000000000000000000000000000000000000000000000000000000000000000000000000
10032410000000000000000000000000000000000000000000000000000000000000000000000000
10032420000000000000000000000000000000000000000000000000000000000000000000000000
10032430000000000000000000000000000000000000000000000000000000000000000000000000
10032440000000000000000000000000000000000000000000000000000000000000000000000000
10032450000000000000000000000000000000000000000000000000000000000000000000000000
10032460000000000000000000000000000000000000000000000000000000000000000000000000
10032470000000000000000000001000000000000000000000000000000000000000000000000000
10032480000000000000000000000000000000000000000000000000000000000000000100000000000
10032490000000000000000000000000100000000010000000101000000000000000000000000000
10032500000001000000000000000000000010000000000000000000000000000000000000000000
10032510000000000000000000000000000000000000010000000000000000000000000000000000
10032520000050000000000000000000
10038010000000000000000000000000000000000000000000001010000000000000000001000000
10038020000000000000000000000000000000000000000000000000000000000000000000000000
10038030000101000000000000000000000000000000000000000000000000000000000000000000
10038040000000100000000000000000000000001000000000000000000000000000000000000000
10038050000000000000000000000000000000000000000000000000000000000000000000000000
10038060000000000010000000000100000000000000000000000000000000000000000000000000
10038070000000000001000000000030000000000000000000000000000000000000000000000000
10038080000000000000000000000000000000010000000001000000000000000000000000000000
10038090000000000000000000000000000000001000000000000000000000000000000000000100
10038100000000000000000000000000000000000000000000000000000000000000000000000000
10038110000000000000000010000000000000000000000000000000000000000000000000000000
10038120000100010000000100000001000000000000000000000000000000000000000000000000
10038130000000000000000000000000000000000000000000000000000000000000000100000000
10038140000000000000000000000000000000000000000000000000000000000000000000000000
10038150000000000000000000000000000000000000000001000000000000000000000000000000
10038160000000000000000000000000000000000000000000000000000000000000000000000000
10038170000000000000000000000000000000000000000000000000000000000000000000000000
10038180000000000000000000000000000000000000000000000000000000000000000000000000
10038190000000000000000000000000000000000000000000000000000000000000000000000000
10038200000000000000000000000000000000000000000000000000000000000000000000000000
10038210000000000000000000000000000000000000000000000000000000000000000000000000
10038220000000000000000000000000000000000000000000000000000000000000000000000000
10038230000000000000000000000000000000000000000000000000000000000000000000000000
10038240000000000000000000000000000000000000000000000000000000000000000000000000
10038250000010000000000000000000000000000000000000000000000000000000000000000000
10038260000000000000000000000000000000000000000000000000000000000000000100000000
10038270101000000000000000000000000000000000000000200000000000000000000000000000
```

```
10038280000000000000000000000000000000000000000000000000000000000010000000000000
10038290000000000000000000000000000000000000000000000000000000000000000000000000
10038300000000000000000000000000000000000000000000000000000000000000000000000000
10038310000000000000000000000000000000000000000000000000000000000000000000000000
10038320000000000000000000000000000000000000000000000000000000000000000000000000
10038330000000000000000000000000000000000000000000000000000000000000000000000000
10038340000000000000000000000000000000000000000000000000000000000000000000000000
10038350000000000000000000000000000000000000000000000000000000000000000000000000
10038360000000000000000000000000000000000000000000000000000000000000000000000000
10038370000000000000000000000000000000000000000000000000000000000000000000000000
10038380000000000000000000000000000000000000000000000000000000000000000000000000
10038390000000000000000000000000000000000000000000000000000000000000000000000000
10038400000000000000000000000000000000000000000000000000000000000000000000000000
10038410000000000000000000000000000000000000000000000000000000000000000000000000
10038420000000000000000000000000000000000000000000000000000000000000000000000000
10038430000000000000000000000000000000000000000000000000000000000000000000000000
10038440000000000000000000000000000000000000000000000000000000000000000000000000
10038450000000000000000000000000000000000000000000000000000000000000000000000000
10038460000000000000000000000000000000000000000000000000000000000000000000000000
10038470000000000000000000000000000000000000000000000000000000000000000000000000
10038480000000000000000000000000000000000000000000000000000000000000000000000000
10038490000000000000000000000000000000000000000000000000000000000000000000000000
10038500000000000000000000000000000000000000000000000000000000000000000000000000
10038510000000000000000000000000000000000000000000000000000000000000000000000000
10038520000000000000000000000000
10057010101000000000000000003010000010002010000000040001020001000100000006000100
10057020000020000000000000000000000000001020002010200000000000010100001010200001
10057030000001080001010002010000000001010000000102000000002000000201000000001010
10057040000002020000000000000000001000000000000101040406010102000200000000000100
10057050000010001000200000000000000000000100001020000000000000000000000400020001
10057060000000000010100000000040000002000000000000000000000000040304000301000000
10057070000000000000000001000000000010000000100000000000000000000000000000010000
10057080000000000000000000000000000000001000002000000000000001000000100000000100
10057090000001000001000001000000000020000000000000000000000000000101010001000000
10057100000001000000000000000020000000000001000000000000000000000000000201000002
10057110000000000000030000000000000000001000001000000000000000000000000101000001
10057120000020400000000000000000000000000000000000000000000000000000000000000000
10057130000000000000000000000000000000000000000000000000000000000002040001000000
10057140100000000000000000000000000000000000000000000000000000000000000000000100
10057150200000000000000000020000000000000000000000201000000000000000000000000000
10057160000000000000000000000000000000000000000000000000000001000000000000000000
10057170000000000000000000000000000000000000000000000000000000000000000000000000
10057180000000000000000000000000000000000000000000000000000000000010000000010000
10057190000000000000000000000000001000000000000000000000000000000000000000000000
10057200000000100000000100000000001000000000000000000000000000000000000000000000
10057210000000000000000000000000000000000001000000000000000000000000000000000000
10057220000000000000000000000000000000000000000000000000000000000000000000000000
10057230000000000000000000000000000000000000000000020000000000000001000000010000
10057240001000000000000000000000000000000002000000000000000000000000000000000000
10057250000000000000000000000000000010000100000000000000000000000000000000000000
10057260000000000000000000000000000000000000000000000000101000000000000000000000
10057270000000000000000000020001000001000000000000000020000000000000000000000000
10057280000000000000000000000000000000000000000000000000000002000000000000000000
10057290000000000000000000000000000000000010000000000000000000100000000000000100
10057300000000000000000000000000000000000000000000000000000000000000000000000000
10057310000000000000000000000000000000000000000000000000000000000000000300000000
10057320000101000000000000000203000000000000000000000000000000000000000000000000
10057330000000000000000000000000000000000000000030000000000000000000000000000000
10057340000000000000000000000000000000000000000000000000001000000000000000000000
10057350000000000000000000000000000000000000000001000000000000000000000000000000
10057360000020000000000000000000000000000000001000100000000020000000001120001010 2
10057370202000100000000004000000000000000000010000000000000000000000000000010000
10057380000000000000000000000000000000000000000000000000000000000000000000000000
10057390000000000001000000000000000000000000000000000000000000000000000000000000
10057400000000000000000000000000000000000000000100000000000000000000000000000000
10057410000000000000000000000000000000000000000000000000000000000000000100000000
10057420000000000000000000000000000000000000000000000000000000000000000000000000
10057430000000000000000000000000000000000000000000000000000000000000000000000000
10057440000000000000000000000000000000000000000000000000000000000000000000000000
10057450000000000000000000000000000000000000000000001000000000000000000000000000
10057460000000000000000000000000000000000000000000000000000000000000000000000000
10057470000000000000000000000000000000300000000000000000000000000000000000000000
10057480000000000000000000000000000000000000000000000000000000000000000000000000
10057490000000000000000000000000000000000000000000000000000001000000000000000000
10057500000000000000000000000000000000000000000000000000000000000000000000000000
10057510000000000000000000000000000000000000000000000000000000000000000000000000
10057520000001000000000000000000
10121010100000000010001040100000000000001010000000000000000100000000000004000400
10121020100000000000200000000000000010001010101000000040000002020101000000000000
10121030000100060000000000000000000000001010000000000010100000000000000000020000
10121040000000000001000001000000000002000000001020000000002000000000000000000000
10121050200001000000200000000000101000000000000000001000100010000000000000000000
10121060001000001000000000000000000000001000001000000000000010001010100000000001 00
10121070100000000000001001030002010200000000000000000000000100000000000001000102
10121080003000400000000100000001000000001000100010000000101000100000000000000000
10121090000000000001020003010102000060001000200000000000000002000002010000000000
10121100000101000000000000000000000000000001000000000010000000000000000000100000 1
10121110000000000000001000000000000000000100010000000000000000010000000000020000
10121120000000000000001000100000101000000000010000000000000000000002010100010100
10121130000000000000000000000000000010001000200010400000000000000010100201010000
10121140001000000000000000000000000000000000000000000000000000000000000000000101
10121150200030001000000000000000000000000100000101000000000001000000000000000000
10121160000000000000000100000000100000000000000000000000002000000000000000000000
10121170000010000000000000000000000000000000000000000000000000000000000000000000
10121180001000100000201010001000000000000001020000000010000000000000000000000000
10121190000000000000000000000000000000002010000000000000000000000000000000020100
10121200000000000000000000000201040000000010000000000000000000000000000000000000
10121210000000000000000000000000000000000000000000000000000000000000000000000000
10121220000000000000000000000000000000000000000000000000000000000000000000000000
10121230000000000000000001000000000000000000000000100010000000000000000000000000
10121240000000000000010000000000000000000001000101000000000000000000000101000000
10121250000000001000000000010103030500000000000000000000000000000000000000000000
10121260000000000000000000000000000000000000010000000000000000010001000202000000
10121270100000000000100000000000000010000000010200010001030003000000000000000000
10121280000000000000000000000000000000000000000000000000000000001010001000000000
10121290000000000000100000000000000000000000000000000000100010000000000000000000
10121300000000000000000000000000000010000010001010100000000000000000000000000000
10121310000000000000000001000000000000000000000000000000000000000000000000000001
10121320001000000000000001000101000000010000000100000000000000000040000000000000
10121330000000000000000000000000100000000000000030000000000010000000000000000000
10121340100010000000000000000000000010000000010000003000000101000000000101010100
10121350000010000000000000000000401000000000000000000000000000000000000000010100
10121360001000101000000000000000501010000000000000000000000000000000010100000001
10121370200000001010000000000000002000000100000000000000000000000000000000000000
10121380000000000000000000000000000000000000000000000000000000000000000000000000
10121390000000000000000000000000000000000000000000000000000000000000000000000000
10121400000000000000000000000000000000000100000000000000000000000000000000000000
10121410000000000000000000000000000000000000000000000000000000000000000000000000
10121420000000000000000000000000000000000000000000000000000000000000000000000000
10121430000000000000000000000000000000000000000000000000000000000000000000000000
```

```
10121440000000000000000000000000000000000000000000000000000000000000000000000000
10121450000000000000000000000000000000000000000000000000000000000000000000000000
10121460000000000000000000000000000000000000000000000000000000000000000000000000
10121470000000000000000000000000000000000000000000000000000000000000000000000000
10121480000000000000001000000000000000000000000000000000000000000000000000010000
10121490000000000010000000000000000000000000000000001000100000000000000000000000
10121500000000000000000000000000000000000000000000000000000000000000000000000000
10121510000000000000000000000000000000000000000000000000000000000000000000000000
10121520000000010101000000000000
10122010000002000000000000000101000000000000000000010000000000000000000000000000
10122020000001010001000000020000100000001000000100000000001000000000000000000000
10122030000000010000000000000000000000000000000000000000000100000000000000000000
10122040000000000000000000000000000000000000000001000001020001000100000000000000
10122050000000000000000000000000000000001000000000000000000000000000000100000000
10122060000000000000000000000000001000000000000000000000000000000010000000000001
10122070000000000000000000000000000010000000000000000000000100000000000000000100
10122080000000000010000000000001000000000000000000000000000000000000000000000000
10122090000000000000000000000000001040001000000100000000000100000000000001010100
10122100000000000001000000000000000001000000000000000000000000000000000001000001
10122110000001000000000000000000000000000000000000000000000001000000000000000000
10122120000000000000000000030000000000100000000000000000000000000000000000000000
10122130000000000000000000000000000010100010000000000000100000001000000100000000
10122140000000000000000000000000000000000000000000000000000000000000000000000000
10122150000001000000000000000000000000000000000000000000000000000000000000000000
10122160000001000000000000000000000000000000000000000000000000000010000000000001
10122170000000000000000000000000000000000000000000000000000000000000000000000000
10122180000000000000001000000100000000001010000000000000100000000000000000010000
10122190000000000000000000000000000000000000000001000000000000000000000100000101
10122200000001000000000000000000000000100000000000000000000000000000000000000000
10122210000000000000000000000000001000000000000000000000000000000000000000000000
10122220000000000000000000000000000000000000000000000000000000000000000000000000
10122230000000000000000000000000000000000000000000000000000000000000000000000000
10122240000000000000000000000000000000001000000000000010000000000000000000000000
10122250000000000000000000001000000100000000101000000000000000000000000000000000
10122260000000000000000000000000000000000000000000000000000000000000000100000000
10122270000001000000000000000000000000000000000000000010000000000000000000000000
10122280000000000000000010000000000000000000000000000000000000000000030000000000
10122290000000000000000000000000000000000000000000000000000001000000000000000000
10122300000000000000000000000000000000000000000000000000000000000000000000000000
10122310000000000000000000000000000000000000000000000000000000000000000000000000
10122320000000000000000000000000000000000000000000000000000000000000000000000000
10122330000000000000000000000000000000000001000000000000003000010100000000000000
10122340000000000000000000000000000000000000000000002000005000100020000000000301
10122350000000000000000000000000000001000000000000000000000000000100000000000000
10122360000100000000100000000001000000000000000000000000000000000000000000010000
10122370000100000000100000000000001000000000000000000000000000000000000000000000
10122380000000000000000000000000000000000000000000000000000000000000000000000000
10122390000000000000000000000000000000000000000000000000000000000000000000000000
10122400000000000000000000000000000000000000000000000000000000000000000000000000
10122410000000000000000000000000000000000000000000000000000000000000000000000000
10122420000000000000000000000000000000000000000000000000000000000000000000000000
10122430000000000000000000000000000000000000000000000000000000000000000000000000
10122440000000000000000000000000000000000000000000000000000000000000000000000000
10122450000000000000000000000000000000000000000000000000000000000000000000000000
10122460000000000000000000000000000000000000000000000000000000000000000000000000
10122470000000000000000000000000000000000000000000000000000000000000000000000000
10122480000000000000000000000000000000000000000000000000000000000000000000000000
10122490000000000000000000000000000000000000000000000000000000000000000000000000
10122500000000000000000000000000000000000000000000000000000000000000000000000000
10122510000000000000000000000000000000000000000000000000000000000000000000000000
10122520000000000000000000000000
10123010000000000000000000010000010000001000000000100000000010000000000000000000
10123020100010000000000000000000000030100010000010100000100000100000000000010100
10123030000000010001000000000000000000000100000000100000000000000100000000000000
10123040000010001000000000000000000002010000000002000000000000000001000000000000
10123050000000000000000000000000000000000000000000010001000000000000000000000000
10123060000000000000000000000000000000000000000000000000000001000000100000000000
10123070000000000000000000000000000000100000000000000000001000000000000000000000
10123080000000000000001000100000000000000100000000010000010000000000000000000000
10123090000000000000000000000000001000000000000010000000000000000000000000000000
10123100000000000000000000010000000000000000000000000000001000000000000000000001
10123110000000000000000000000000000000100000000000000000000000000000000100000000
10123120000000000000000000020000010102000100000000000000000000000000000000000100
10123130000000000000000000000000010100000000000000000010000000000000000102010100
10123140000000000000000000000000000000000000000000000000000000000000000000000000
10123150000003000000000000000000000100000000000000000000000000000000000100000000
10123160100010000000000000000000000000000000000000000000000000000000000000000000
10123170000001000000000000000000000000000000000000000000000000000000000000000000
10123180100000000000000000000000000000000000000000000000000000000000000000000000
10123190000000000000000000000000000000001000000000000000000000000001000000000000
10123200000001000000000010001000000000000000000000000000000000000000000000000000
10123210000000000000000000000000000000000000000000000000000000000000000000000000
10123220000000000000000000000000000000000000000000000000000000000000000000000000
10123230000000000000000000000000000000000000000000000000000000000001000200000000
10123240000000000010000000000000000101000000000000000000001000000000000000000000
10123250100000000000000000000000030000000000000000000000000000010000000000000000
10123260000000000000000000000000000000000000010000000000000000000000000000010000
10123270000000000000000000000000000000000000000101000100000000000000000000000000
10123280000000000001000000000000000000000000000000000000000000000001000000000000
10123290000000000000000000000000000000000000000000000000000000000000000000000000
10123300000000000000000000000001000000000000000000000001000000000000000000000000
10123310000000000000000000000001000000000000000000000000000000000000000000000000
10123320000000000000000000000020000000000000000000000000000000000000000000000000
10123330000000000000000000000000000000000000000000000000001000010000000000000000
10123340000000000000000000000000000000000010000000010000000000000000000001010000
10123350000100000000000000000001000000000000010000000000000000000000000000010000
10123360000200010000000000000001000000000000000000000000000000000000000000000000
10123370000200000000000010000000000000100010000000000000000000000000000000000000
10123380000000000000000000000000000000000000000000000000000000000000000000000000
10123390000000000000000000000000000000000000000000000000000000000000000000000000
10123400000000000000000000000000000000000000000000000000000000000000000000000000
10123410000000000000000000000000000000000000000000000000000000000000000000000000
10123420000000000000000000000000000000000000000000000000000000000000000000000000
10123430000000000000000000000000000000000000000000000000000000000000000000000000
10123440000000000000000000000000000000000000000000000000000000000000000000000000
10123450000000000000000000000000000000000000000000000000000000000000000000000000
10123460000000000000000000000000000000000000000000000000000000000000000000000000
10123470000000000000000000000000000000000000000000000000000000000000000000000000
10123480000000000000000000000000000000000000000000000000000000000000000000000000
10123490000000000000000000000000010000000000000000000001000000000000000100000000
10123500000000000000000000000000000000000000000000000000000000000000000000000000
10123510000000000000000000000000000000000000000000000000000000000000000000000000
10123520000000010100000000000000
10374010000001000100000000100000010000000010000001000101000010000000000000000000
10374020000000000000000000000000000000000000100000000000000000000000010000000000
10374030000000000000000000000100000000100000000000000101000000000001000000000001
10374040000000000000000000000000000000000000000001000000000000000000000000000000
10374050000000000000000000000000000000000000000000000000000000100010000000000000
10374060000000000000000000000000000000000000000000000000000000000100000000000000
10374070000000000000000000000000000000000000000000000000001000000000000000000000
```

```
10374080000000000000000000000000000000000000000000000000000000000000000000010000
10374090000000000000000000000000000000000000000100000000010000000000000000000000
10374100000000000000010000000000000000000000000000000101000000000000000000001000
10374110000000000000000000000000000000000000000100000000000000000100000000000000000
10374120000000000100000000000000000010100000000000000010000000201000000000000000
10374130000000000100000000000000000000000100000100000000000000010001010100000000
10374140000000000000000000000000000000000000000000000000000000000000000100000101
10374150100010101000000000000000000000000000000000000000000000000000000000000000
10374160000010000000000000000000000000000000000000001000000000000000000100000000
10374170002000000100000000000000000000000000000000000000000000000000000000010000
10374180000000000002000000000000100000100000000000000000000000000001000100000000000
10374190000000000000000000000000001000000000000000100010000000000000000000010000
10374200000000000000000001000000000000000000000020100000000000000000000000000000
10374210000000000000000010000000010000000000010000000000000000000000000000000000
10374220000010000000000000000000000000000000000000000000000000000000000000010000
10374230000000000000000000000000000000000000000000000000000000000000000000000000
10374240000000000100000000000000000010000000000000000010000000000100000000000000
10374250000000000000001010000000000000000000010000000000000000010100000000000000
10374260000000000000000000000000000000000000000000000000000000000000000000000100
10374270100000000000000000000000000000000000000000100000000001010000000000000000
10374280000000000000000000000000000000000010000000000000000000000000000000000000
10374290000000000000000010000000000000000000000000000000000000000000000000000000
10374300000000000000000000002000200000000000000000000000000000000000000000000000
10374310000000000000000000000000000000000000000000000000000000100000000000000001
10374320000000100000000000000000000000000000000000000000000000000000000000000000
10374330000000000000000000000000000000000000002000000000000000000000000000000000
10374340000000000000000000000000000000000000000000000000000000000000000001000000
10374350000010100000000000000000000000001000000000000000000000000000000000000001
10374360001000000000000000001000100000000000000000000000000000000000000100000000
10374370001000000000000000000000000000000000000000000000000000000000000000000000
10374380000000000000000000000000000000000000000000000000000000000000000000000000
13074390000000000000000000000000000000000000000000000000000000000000000000000000
10374400000000000000000000000000000000000000000000000000000000000000000000000000
10374410000000000000000000000000000000000000000000000000000000000000000000000000
10374420000000000000000000000000000000000000000000000000000000000000000000000000
10374430000000000000000000000000000000000000000000000000000000000000000000000000
10374440000000000000000000000000000000000000000000000000000000000000000000000000
10374450000000000000000000000000000000000000000000000000000000000000000000000000
10374460000000000000000000000000000000000000000000000000000000000000000000000000
10374470000000000000000000000000000000000000000000000000000000000000000000000100
10374480000000000000000000000000000000000000000000000000000000000000000000000000
10374490000000000000000010000000000000000000000000000000000000000000000000000000
10374500000000000000000000000000000000000000000000000000000000000000000000000000
10374510000000000000000000000000000000000000000000000000000000000000000000000000
103745200000000000000000000000000
10375010000000000000000000000000000000000000100000000001000000000000000000000000
10375020000000000000100010000000000010000000000000000000000000000000000000000000
10375030000000100000000000000000000000000000000000001000000000000000000010000000
10375040000000000000000000000000010000000000000000000200000000002000000000000000
10375050000000000000000000000000000000000000000000000000000000000000000000000000
10375060000000000101000000000000000000000000000000000000000000000000000200000000
10375070000000000000000000000000000000000000000000000000000000000000000000000000
10375080000000000000000000000000000000000000000000000001000000000000000000
10375090000000000000000000000000000000000000000000000000000000000000000000000000
10375100000000000000000000000000000000000000000000000000000000000000000000000000
10375110000000000000000000000100000000000000000001000000000000000000000000000000
10375120000000000000000000000000000000000000000000000000000000000000000000000000
10375130000000000000000000000000000000000000000000000000000000000000000000000000
10375140000000000000000000000000000000000000000000000000000000000000000000000000
10375150000000000000000000000001000000000000000000000000000000000000000000000000
10375160000000000000000000000000000000000000000000000000000000000000000000000000
10375170000000000000000000000000000000000000000000000000000000000000000000000000
10375180000000000000000000000000000000000000000000000000000000000000000000000000
10375190000000000000000000000000000000000000000000000000000000000000000000000001
10375200000000000000000000000000001000000000000000000000000000000000000000000000
10375210000000000000000000000000000000000000000000000000000000000000000000000000
10375220000000000000000000000000000000000000000000000000000000000000000000000000
10375230000000000000000000000000000000000000000000000000000000000000000001000000
10375240000000000000000000000000000000000000000000000000000000000000000000000000
10375250000000000000000000000000000010000000000000000000000000000000000000000000
10375260000000000000000000000000000000000000000000000000000000000000000000000000
10375270000000000000000000000000000000000000000000000000000000000000000000000000
10375280000000000000000000000000000000000000000000000000000000000000000000000000
10375290000000000000000000000000000000000000000000000000000000000000000000000000
10375300000000000000000000000000000000000000000000000000000000000000000000000000
10375310000000000000000000000000000000000000000000000000000000000000000000000000
10375320000000000000000000000000000000000000000000000000000000000000000000000000
10375330000000000000000000000000000000000000000000000000000000000000000000000000
10375340000000000000000000000000000000000000000000000000000000000000000000000000
10375350000000000000000000000000000000000000000000000000000000000000000000000000
10375360000000000000000000000000000000000000000000000000000000000000000200000000
10375370000000000000000000000000000000000000000000000000000000000000000000000000
10375380000000000000000000000000000000000000000000000000000000000000000000000000
10375390000000000000000000000000000000000000000000000000000000000000000000000000
10375400000000000000000000000000000000000000000000000000000000000000000000000000
10375410000000000000000000000000000000000000000000000000000000000000000000000000
10375420000000000000000000000000000000000000000000000000000000000000000000000000
10375430000000000000000000000000000000000000000000000000000000000000000000000000
10375440000000000000000000000000000000000000000000000000000000000000000000000000
10375450000000000000000000000000000000000000000000000000000000000000000000000000
10375460000000000000000000000000000000000000000000000000000000000000000000000000
10375470000000000000000000000000000000000000000000000000000000000000000000000000
10375480000000000000000000000000000000000000000000000000000000000000000000000000
10375490000000000000000000000000000000000000000000000000000000000000000000000000
10375500000000000000000000000000000000000000000000000000000000000000000000000000
10375510000000000000000000000000000000000000000000000000000000000000000000000000
103755200000000000000000000000000
10376010000000000000000000000000000000000000000000000000000000000000000000000000
10376020000000000000000000000000000000000000010000000000000000000000000000000000
10376030000000000000000000000001000101000000000000000001000000000000000000000000
10376040000000000001000000000000000000100000000000100000100000000000000000000000
10376050000000000000000000000000000000000000000000000000000000000000000000000000
10376060000010001000000000000000000000000000000000000000000000000000000000000000
10376070000010000000000000000000000000000000000000000000000000000000000000000000
10376080000000000000000000000000000000000000000000000000000000000000000000000000
10376090000000000000000000000000000000000000000000000000000000000000000000000000
10376100000000000000000000000000000000000000000000000000000000000000000000000000
10376110001000000000000000000000000000000000000000000000000000000000000000000000
10376120000000000000000000010000000000000000000000000000000000000000000000000000
10376130000000000000000000000000000000000000000000000000000000000000000000000000
10376140000000000000000000000000000000000000000000000000000000000000000000000000
10376150100000000000000000000000000000000000000000000001000000000000000000000000
10376160000000000000000000000000100000000000000000000000000000000000000000000000
10376170000000000000000000000000000000000000000000000000000000000000000000000000
10376180000000000000000000000000000000000000000000000000000000000000000000000000
10376190000000000000000000000000000000000000000000000000000000000000000000000000
10376200000000000000000000000000000000000000000000000000000000000000000000000000
10376210000000000000000000000000000000000000000000000000000000000000000000000000
10376220000000000000000000000000000000000000000000000000000000000000000000000000
10376230000000000000000000000000000000000000000000000000000000000000000000010000
```

10376240000000000000000000000000000000000000001000000000000000000000
10376250000000000000000000000000000000000000000000000000000100000000
10376260000000000000000000000000000000000000000000000000000000000000
10376270000000000000000000000000000000000000000000000000000000000000
10376280000000000000000000000000000000000000000000000000000000000000
10376290000000000000000000000000000000000000000000000000000000000000
10376300000000000000000000000000000000000000000000000000000000000000
10376310000000000000000000000000000000000000000000000000000000000000
10376320000000000000000000000000000000000000000000000000000000000000
10376330000000000000000000000000000000000000000000000000000000000000
10376340000000000000000000000000000000000000000000000000000000000000
10376350000000000000000000000000000000000000000000000000000000000000
10376360000000000000000000000000000000000000000000000000000000000000
10376370000000000000000000000000000000000000000000000000000000000000
10376380000000000000000000000000000000000000000000000000000000000000
10376390000000000000000000000000000000000000000000000000000000000000
10376400000000000000000000000000000000000000000000000000000000000000
10376410000000000000000000000000000000000000000000000000000000000000
10376420000000000000000000000000000000000000000000000000000000000000
10376430000000000000000000000000000000000000000000000000000000000000
10376440000000000000000000000000000000000000000000000000000000000000
10376450000000000000000000000000000000000000000000000000000000000000
10376460000000000000000000000000000000000000000000000000000000000000
10376470000000000000000000000000000000000000000000000000000000000000
10376480000000000000000000000000000000000000000000000000000000000000
10376490000000000000000000000000000000000000000000000000000000000000
10376500000000000000000000000000000000000000000000000000000000000000
10376510000000000000000000000000000000000000000000000000000000000000
1037652000000000000000000000
10377010000000010000010000001000000000000000000000000000000000000000
10377020000010000000000000000000001000000000000000000000000000000000
10377030000000000000000000000000001000000100000000000000000000000200
10377040001000000000000000000000000000000000001000000000000200000000000
10377050000000000000000000000000000000000000000000000000000000000000
10377060000000000000000000000000000000000000000000000000000000000000
10377070000000000000000000000000000000000000010000000100000100000000000000
10377080000000000000000000000000000000000000000000000000000000000000
10377090000000100001000000000000000000001000000010000000000000000000
10377100000000000000000000010000000000000000000000000000000000000000
10377110001000000000000000000000000000100000000000000000000000000000
10377120000000000000001000000001000000000000000000000000000000000000
10377130000000000100000000000000000000000000000000000000300000000000
10377140000100000000000000000000000000000000000000000000000000000000
10377150000000000000000000000100000000000000000000000000000000000000
10377160000000000000000000000000000000000000000000000000000000000000
10377170000000000000000000000000000000000000000000000000000000000000
10377180000000000000000000000000000000000000000000000000000000000000
10377190000000000000000000000000000000000000000000000000000000000000
10377200000000000000000000000000000000000000000000000000000000000000
10377210000000000000000000000000000000000000000000000000000000000000
10377220000000000000000000000000000000000000000000000000000000000000
10377230000000000001000000000000000000000000000000000000000000000000
10377240000000000000000000000000000000000000000000000000000000000000
10377250000000000000000000000000000000000000000000000000000000000000
10377260000000000000000000000000000000000000000000000000000000000000
10377270000000000000000000000000000000000000000000000000000000000000
10377280000000000000000000000000000000000000000000000000000000000000
10377290000000000000000000000000000000000000000000000000000000000000
10377300000000000000000000000000000000000000000000000000000000000000
10377310000000000000000000000000000000000000000000000000000000000000

10377320000000000000000000000000000000000000000000000000000000000000
10377330000000000000000000000000000000000000000000000000000000000000
10377340000000000000000000000000000000000000000000000000000000000000
10377350000000000000000000000000000000000000000000000000000000000000
10377360000000000000000000000000000000000000000000000000000000000000
10377370000000000000000000000000000000000000000000000000000000000000
10377380000000000000000000000000000000000000000000000000000000000000
10377390000000000000000000000000000000000000000000000000000000000000
10377400000000000000000000000000000000000000000000000000000000000000
10377410000000000000000000000000000000000000000000000000000000000000
10377420000000000000000000000000000000000000000000000000000000000000
10377430000000000000000000000000000000000000000000000000000000000000
10377440000000000000000000000000000000000000000000000000000000000000
10377450000000000000000000000000000000000000000000000000000000000000
10377460000000000000000000000000000000000000000000000000000000000000
10377470000000000000000000000000000000000000000000000000000000000000
10377480000000000000000000000000000000000000000000000000000000000000
10377490000000000000000000000000000000000000000000000000000000000000
10377500000000000000000000000000000000000000000000000000000000000000
10377510000000000000000000000000000000000000000000000000000000000000
1037752000000000000000000000
10378010000000000000000000000000000000000000000010000000000000000001
10378020000000000000001000200020000000000000000000001000000000000000
10378030000001000000000000020000020002000000000000000001000100000000
10378040000001010000000000000000000000000100000100010000000000010000
10378050000000000000000000000000000000000000000000000000000000000000
10378060000101000001000000000000003000000000000000000002000001000000
10378070000000000000001000000000020000000000000000100000000000000000
10378080100000000000000000000000000000000000000000000000000000000000
10378090000000000000001000000000000000000000000001000000000100000000
10378100000000000100000000100000000000000000000000000000000101000000
10378110000000000000000000000000000000000000000000000000000000000000
10378120000000000000100000000000000000000000000000000000000000000000
10378130000001000000000000000000000000001000000000000000010000000000
10378140000100000000000000000000000000000000000000000000000000000100
10378150000000000000000010000000000000000000000000000000000000000000
10378160000000000000000000000000000000000000000000000001000000000000
10378170000000000000000000000000000000000000000000000000000000000000
10378180000001000000000000000000000000000000000000000000000000000000
10378190000000000000000000000000000000000000000000000000001000000000
10378200000000000000000000000000000000000000001000000000000000000000
10378210000000000000000000000000000000000000000000000000000000000000
10378220000000000000000000000000000000000000000000000000000000000000
10378230000000010000000000000000000000000000000000000000000000000000
10378240000000000000000000001000000000000000000000000000000000010000
10378250000020000000000000000000000000001000000000000000000000000000
10378260000000000000000000000000000000000010000000002000000000000000
10378270001000000000000000000001000000000000000000000000000000000000
10378280000000000000000000000000000000000000000000000000000000000000
10378290000000000000000000000000000000000000000000000000000000000000
10378300000000000000000000000000000000000000000000000000000000000000
10378310000000000000000000000000000000000000000000000000000000000000
10378320000000000000000000000000000000000000000000000000000000000000
10378330000000000000000000000000000000000000000000000000000000000000
10378340000000000000000000001000000000000000000000000000000000000000
10378350000010000000000000000000000000000000000000000000000000000000
10378360000000000000000000000000000000000000000000000000000000000000
10378370200000000000000000000000000000000000000000000000000000000000
10378380000000000000000000000000000000000000000000000000000000000000
10378390000000000000000000000000000000000000000000000000000000000000

```
10378400000000000000000000000000000000000000000000000000000000000000000000000000
10378410000000000000000000000000000000000000000000000000000000000000000000000000
10378420000000000000000000000000000000000000000000000000000000000000000000000000
10378430000000000000000000000000000000000000000000000000000000000000000000000000
10378440000000000000000000000000000000000000000000000000000000000000000000000000
10378450000000000000000000000000000000000000000000000000000000000000000000000000
10378460000000000000000000000000000000000000000000000000000000000000000000000000
10378470000000000000000000000000000000000000000000000000000000000000000000000000
10378480000000000000000000000000000000000000000000000000000000000000000000000000
10378490000000000000000000000000000000000000000000000000100000000000000000000000
10378500000000000000000000000000000000000000000000000000000000000000000000000000
10378510000000000000000000000000000000000000000000000001000000000000000000000000
103785200000000000000000000000000
10380010000000000000000000000000000000000000000000000900070000000000000010000020
10380020000000000000100000000000200010100000000000000000000000200000000100000000
10380030000000000000000000000000000000000000000000000000000000001000001010102000
10380040001000000000000000000000000000000000000000000000000000000000000000000000
10380050000000000000000000000000000000100000000000000000000000000000000000000000
10380060000000000000000000000000000000000000000000000000000000000000000100000000
10380070000000000000000000000000000000000000000000000000000100000000000000000000
10380080000000000000000000100000000000000000000000000000000000000000000000000000
10380090100000000000000000000000000000000000000000000000000000000000000000000000
10380100000000000000000000000000000000000000000000000000000000000000000001000000
10380110000000010000000100000000000000000000000000000000000000000000000000000000
10380120000000000000000000000000000000000000000000000000000000000000000000000000
10380130000000000000000000000000000000000000000000000000000000000001000000000000
10380140000000000000000000000000000000000000000000000000000000000000000000000000
10380150100000000000000000000000000000000000000000000000000000000000000000000000
10380160000000000000000000000000000000000000000000000000000000000000000000000000
10380170000000000000000000000000000000000000000000000000000000000000000000000000
10380180000000000000000000000000000000000000000000000000000000000000000000000000
10380190000000000000000000000000000000000000000000000000000000000000000000000000
10380200000000000000000000000000000000000000000000000000000000000000000000000000
10380210000000000000000000000000000000000000000000000000000000000000000000000000
10380220000000000000000000000000000000000000000000000000000000000000000000000000
10380230000000000000000000000000000000000000000000000000000000000000000000000000
10380240000000000000000000000000000000000000000000000000000000000000000000000000
10380250000000000000000000000000000000000000000000000000000000000000000000000000
10380260000000000000000000000000000000000000000000000000000000000000000000000000
10380270000000000000000000000000000000000000000000000000000000000000000000000000
10380280000000000000000000000000000000000000000000000000000000000000000000000001
10380290000000000000000000000000000000000000000000000000000000000000000000000000
10380300000000000000000000000000000000000000000000000000000000000000000000000000
10380310000000000000000000000000000000000000000000000000000000000000000100000000
10380320000000000000000000000000100000000000000000000000000000000000000000000000
10380330000000000000000000000000000000000000000010000000000000000000000000000000
10380340000000000000000000000000000000000000000000000000000000000000000000000000
10380350000000000000000000000000000000000000000000000000000000000000000000000000
10380360000000000000000000000000000000000000000000000000000000000000000100000000
10380370000000000000000000000000000000000000000000000000000000000000000000000000
10380380000000000000000000000000000000000000000000000000000000000000000000000000
10380390000000000000000000000000000000000000000000000000000000000000000000000000
10380400000000000000000000000000000000000000000000000000000000000000000000000000
10380410000000000000000000000000000000000000000000000000000000000000000000000000
10380420000000000000000000000000000000000000000000000000000000000000000000000000
10380430000000000000000000000000000000000000000000000000000000000000000000000000
10380440000000000000000000000000000000000000000000000000000000000000000000000000
10380450000000000000000000000000000000000000000000000000000000000000000000000000
10380460000000000000000000000000000000000000000000000000000000000000000000000000
10380470000000000000000000000000000000000000000000000000000000000000000000000000
10380480000000000000000000000000000000000000000000000000000000000000000000000000
10380490000000000000000000000000000000000000000000000000000000000000000000000000
10380500000000000000000000000000000000000000000000000000000000000000000000000000
10380510000000000000000000000000000000000000000000000000000000000000000000000000
103805200000000000000000000000000
10383010000000000000000000000000000000000000100000000001000000000000000020000000
10383020000000000001000000000100000010000001000000000000000000000000000100000000
10383030000000000000000000000000000000000000000000000000000100000000000000000000
10383040000000000000000000000000010000000000000000000000000000000010000000000000
10383060001000000000000000000000000000000000000000000000000000000000000000000000
10383050000000000000000000000000000000000000000000000000000000000000000000000000
10383070000000000000000000000000000000101000000000000010000000000000000000000000
10383080000000000000000000000000000000001000100000000000000000000000000001000000
10383090000000000000000000000000000000000000000000000000000000000000000000000000
10383100000000000000000000000000000000000000000000000000000000000010000000000000
10383110000000000000000000000000000000000000000000000000000000000000000000000000
10383120000000000000000000003000000000000000000000000000000000000000000000000000
10383130000000000101000000000000000000001000000000000000000000000000000000000000
10383140100010000000000000000000000000000000000000000000000000000000000000000000
10383150000000000100000000000000000000000000000000000000000000000000000000000000
10383160000010000000000000000000010000000000000000000000000000000000000000000000
10383170000000000000000000000000000000000000000000000000000000000000000000000001
10383180000000000000000000000000010000000000000000000000000000000000000000000000
10383190000000000000000000000000000000000000000000000000000000000000000000010000
10383200000000000000000000000000000000000000000100000000000000000000000000000000
10383210000000000000000000000000000000000000000000000000000000000000000000000000
10383220000000000000000000000000000000000000000000000000000000000000000000000001
10383230000000000000000000000000000000000000000000000000000000000000000000000000
10383240000000000000000000000000000000000000000000000000000000000000000000000000
10383250000000000000000000000000000000200000000000000000000000000000000000000000
10383260000000000000000000000000000000000000000000000000000101000100000000000000
10383270001000000000000000000000000000000000000000000000000000000000000000000000
10383280000000000000000000000000000000000000000000000000000000000000000000000000
10383290000000000000000000000000000000000000000000000000000000000000000000000000
10383300000000000000000000000000000000000000000000000000000000000000000000000000
10383310000000000000000000000000000000000000000000000000000000000000000000000000
10383320000000000000000000000000000000000000000000000000000000000000000000000000
10383330000000000000000000000000000000000000000000000000000000000000000000000000
10383340000000000000000000000000000000000000000000000000000000000000000000000000
10383350000000000000000000000000000000000000000000000000000000000000000000000000
10383360000000000000000000000000000000000000000000001000000000000000010000000000
10383370000000000000000000000000000000000000000000000000000000000000000000000000
10383380000000000000000000000000000000000000000000000000000000000000000000000000
10383390000000000000000000000000000000000000000000000000000000000000000000000000
10383400000000000000000000000000000000000000000000000000000000000000000000000000
10383410000000000000000000000000000000000000000000000000000000000000000000000000
10383420000000000000000000000000000000000000000000000000000000000000000000000000
10383430000000000000000000000000000000000000000000000000000000000000000000000000
10383440000000000000000000000000000000000000000000000000000000000000000000000000
10383450000000000000000000000000000000000000000000000000000000000000000000000000
10383460000000000000000000000000000000000000000000000000000000000000000000000000
10383470000000000000000000000000000000000000000000000000000000000000000000000000
10383480000000000000000000000000000000000000000000000000000000000000000000000000
10383490000000000000000000000000000000000000000000000000000000000000000000000000
10383500000000000000000000000000000000000000000000000000000000000000000000000000
10383510000000000000000000000000000000000000000000000000000000000000000000000000
103835200000000000000000000000000
10384010000000000000100010000000000000000000000000000000000000000000000100000000
10384020000000000000000000000000000010000001000000000000010000000000000000000000
10384030000000000000000000000000000000000000000000000000000000000000000000000000
```

```
10384040000000000000000000000000000000000000000000000000000000000000000
10384050000000000000000000000000000000000000000000000000000000000000000
10384060001000000000000000000000000000000000000000000000000000000000000
10384070000000000000000000000000000000000000000000000000000000001010000
10384080001000000000000010000000000000000000000000000000001000001000000000
10384090000000000000000000000000000000000000000000000000000000100010000
10384100000000000000000000000000000000000000000000000000000000000000000
10384110000000000000000000000000000000000000000000000000001010000000000
10384120000000000000000000000000000100000000000000000000000000000000000
10384130000000000000000000000000000000000000000000000000000000000000000
10384140000000000000000000000000000000000000000000000000000000000000000
10384150000000000000000000000000000000000000000000000000000000000000000
10384160000000000000000000000000000000000000000000000000000000000000000
10384170000000000000000000000000000000000000000000000000000000000000000
10384180000000000000000000000000000000000000000000000000000000000000000
10384190000000000000000000000000000000000000000000000000000000000000000
10384200000000000000000000000000000000000000000000000000000000000000000
10384210000000000000000000000000000000000000000000000000000000000000000
10384220000000000000000000000000000000000000000000000000000000000000000
10384230000000000000000000000000000000000000000000000000000000000000000
10384240000000000000000000000000000000000000000000000000000000000000000
10384250000000000000000000000000000000000000000000000000000000000000000
10384260000000000000000000000000000000000000000000000000000000000000000
10384270000000000010000000000000000000000000000000000000000000000000000
10384280000000000000000000000000000000000000000000000000000000000000000
10384290000000000000000000000000000000000000000000000000000000000000000
10384300000000000000000000000000000000000000000000000000000000000000000
10384310000000000000000000000000000000000000000000000000000000000000000
10384320000000000000000000000000000000000000000000000000000000000000000
10384330000000000000000000000000000000000000000000000000000000000000000
10384340000000000000000000000000000000000000000000000000000000000000000
10384350000000000000000000000000000000000000000000000000000000000000000
10384360000000000000000000000000000000000000000000000000000100000000000
10384370000000000000000000000000000000000000000000000000000000000000000
10384380000000000000000000000000000000000000000000000000000000000000000
10384390000000000000000000000000000000000000000000000000000000000000000
10384400000000000000000000000000000000000000000000000000000000000000000
10384410000000000000000000000000000000000000000000000000000000000000000
10384420000000000000000000000000000000000000000000000000000000000000000
10384430000000000000000000000000000000000000000000000000000000000000000
10384440000000000000000000000000000000000000000000000000000000000000000
10384450000000000000000000000000000000000000000000000000000000000000000
10384460000000000000000000000000000000000000000000000000000000000000000
10384470000000000000000000000000000000000000000000000000000000000000000
10384480000000000000000000000000000000000000000000000000000000000000000
10384490000000000000000000000000000000000000000000000000000000000000000
10384500000000000000000000000000000000000000000000000000000000000000000
10384510000000000000000000000000000000000000000000000000000000000000000
10384520000000000000000000000
10385010000000001000001000001000001010000000000000000010001000100000100
10385020000000000000000000000000001000000000000000001000000000000100030000
10385030000000100000000000100000000000000000000000000000000000000000100
10385040000000100000000020000000001000000000100000000000000000000000000
10385050000000000000000000000000000000000000000000000000000000000000000
10385060000000000010000000000000000000000000000000000000000000000000000
10385070000000000000000000000000000000000000000000000000000000000000000
10385080000000001000000000000000000000000000000000000000000000000000000
10385090000000001000000000000000100000000000000010001010000000100010000
10385100000000000000000010000000001000000000100000000000000000000000000
10385110000000000000000000000000000000001000000000000000000000000000000
10385120000000002000001000000000000000000000000000000000000000000000000
10385130000010001000000000000000000000000000000000000000000000000010000
10385140000000000000000000000000000000000000000000000000000000000000000
10385150000000000000000000000000000010100000000000000000100000000000000
10385160000000000000000000000000000000000000000000000000000000000000000
10385170000000000000000000000000000000000000000000000000000000000000000
10385180000000000000000000100000000000000000000000000000000000000000000
10385190000000000000000000000000000000000000000000000000000000000000000
10385200000000000010000000000000101000000000000000000000001000000000000
10385210000000000000000000000000000000000000000000000000000000000000000
10385220000000000000000000000000000000000000000000000000000000000010000
10385230000000000000000000001000000000000000000000000000000000000010000
10385240000000001000000000000000000000000000000000000100000000000000000
10385250000020000000000000002010000010000000000000001000000000000000000
10385260000000000000000000000000000000000000000000000001000000000000001
10385270001000000000000000000000000000001000000000000000001000000000000
10385280000000000000001000000000000000000000000000000001000000000000000
10385290000000000000000000000000000000000000000000000000000000000000000
10385300000000000000000000000000000000000000000000000000000000000000000
10385310000000000000000000000000000000000000000000000000000000000000000
10385320000000000000000000000000000000000000000000000000000000000000000
10385330000000000000000000000000000000004000000000000000000000100000000
10385340000000000000000000000000000000000000000000000000000000000000000
10385350000000000000000000001000000000001000000000000000000000000000000
10385360000000000000000000000000000000000000000000000000000000200000000
10385370000000000000000000000010001000000000000000000000000000000000000
10385380000000000000000000000000000000000000000000000000000000000000000
10385390000000000000000000000000000000000000001000000000000000000000000
10385400000000000000000000000000000000000000000000000000000000000000000
10385410000000000000000000000000000000000000000000000000000000000000000
10385420000000000000000000000000000000010000000000000000000000000000000
10385430000000000000000000000000000000000000000000000000000000000000000
10385440000000000000000000000000000000000000000000000000000000000000000
10385450000000000000000000000000000000000000000000000000000000000000000
10385460000000000000000000000000000000000000000000000000000000000000000
10385470000000000000000000000000000000000000000000000000000000000000000
10385480000000000000000000000000000000000000000000000000000000000000000
10385490000000000000000000000000000000000000000000000000000000000000000
10385500000000000000000000000000000000000000000000000000000000000000000
10385510000000000000000000000000000000000000000000000000000000000000000
1038552010000000000000000000
10386010401030003020006050401010300060502000100010300010002000104030601
10386020101000100010000000000020503000303060000010201010402020001010102
10386030001000700000100010400010200010401010001040001000101020001030205
10386040000040400020100010301000002010000030103000102020000020000000101
10386050100000107000100000000000000010000000002000002000101000703030001
10386060104010000000001000001020103000000010201000105000401010100020101
10386070100000003020305000600010000010001010000010202010001000001000203
10386080203000202000001010100010100000000010001000000000007020201000001
10386090001010102000101010100010200010002030000020004040101040103010200
10386100100000000000000000000000101000004000001000101010001010001010001
10386110000010100000201010102000001000101000000000000010401020002000000
10386120100020303020003070001000204000000010300000101000001000001000000
10386130000000200000001000000000001020200030104020001000002030302010102
10386140300010000000000000000000000000000000000000000000000000001000000
10386150400030201010000000301000001000000000000000101000101000000010100
10386160100010000000101000000000000000000000001010000000000000101000010000
10386170000000001000000000000000000000000000000000000000000000000000001
10386180000020101000102000201010000010202000000000000000000000100000002
10386190000000000000000000100000000000000010000000000010000000000020106
```

```
10386200000001010000200000000010201020200000000000000010000000000000000000000000
10386210000001000000000000000000000000000000000000000000000000000000000000000000
10386220000000000000000000000000000000000000000000000000000000000000000000000000
10386230000000000000000000000000000000000000000000000000000001000000000002000000
10386240000102000000001000000000000000001000100000000010002000000000000000000000
10386250000104000000000000100020204020000000010000000000000000000000000000000000
10386260000000000000000000000000000000001000300000000010000200010200030000000000
10386270000000000000203000400000002020000000010004020100000200010000000000000000
10386280000000000000000000000000000000000000000000000000000000201000000000020000
10386290000000000000000000000000000100000000100000000000000000001000003000100001
10386300000000000000000000000010000000000000000000000000010000000000000000000000
10386310000000000000000000000000000000000000000000000001000000001000000000000000
10386320000000000200000000000202000000000000000000000000001000000000000000000000
10386330000000000000000000000010000000020300020100010100030000000000000000000000
10386340101000000000000000020000000000000000000000001010100010000000000001000501
10386350000001000000001000000003000000000000000000000000000000000000000000000100
10386360000101000000000001010100010100000000020000010000002010000000030001020101
10386370105000000000000000000000000001000000000000000000000000000000000000000000
10386380000000000000000000000000000000000000000000000000000000000000000000000000
10386390000000000000000000000000000000000000010000000000000000000000000000000000
10386400000000000000000000000000000000000000000000000000000000000000000000000000
10386410000000000000000000000000000000000000000000000000000000000000000000000000
10386420000000000000000000000000000000000000000000000000000000000000000000000000
10386430000000000000000000000000000000000000000000000000000000000000000000000000
10386440000000000000000000000000000000000000000000000000000000000000000000000000
10386450000000000000000000000000000010000000000000000000000000000000000000000000
10386460000000000010000000000000000000000000000000000000000000000000000000000000
10386470000000000000000000000000000000000000000000000000000000000000000000000000
10386480000000000000000000000000001000000000000000000000000001000000000000000010000
10386490000000000000000000000000000000202000000000000000000000000000000000000000
10386500000000000001000000000000000000000000000000000000000000000000000000000000
10386510000000000000000000000000000000001000000000000000000000000000000000000001
10386520000000200000000000000000
10387010000000000000100000000000001000000000000100000000000000000000000000000000
10387020000000000000000000000000000000000000000000000000001000000001010000000001
10387030000000000000000000000000000010000000000100000000000000000000001000000000
10387040000000000000000000000000000000000000000000000000000001000000000000000000
10387050100000010000000000000000000000000000000000000000000000000000000000000000
10387060000000000000000000000000000000000000000010000000000000000010001000000001
10387070000000000000000000201000000010000000000000000000000000000000000000000000
10387080000000000000000010000000000000000000100000000000000000000000000000000000
10387090000000000000000000000100000010000000000000000000001000100000000000030100
10387100000000000000000000000000000000000000000100000000101000000000000000000000000
10387110000000000000000000000000000000000000000000000000000000000000000000000000
10387120000000000000000000000000000010000000000000000000000000000000000000000000
10387130000000000000000000000000000000000001000000000000000000000010000000000000
10387140000000000000000000000000000000000000000000000000000000000000000000000100
10387150000001010000000000000100000000000010000000000000000000000000000000000000
10387160000000000000000000000000000001000000000010000000000000000000000000000000
10387170000000000000000000000000000000000000000000000000000000000000000000000000
10387180000000000000000001000001000000000000000000000000000000000000001010000000
10387190000000000000000000000000000000000000000000000000000000000000000000000000
10387200000000000000000000000000000000000000000000000000000000000000000000000000
10387210000000000000000000000000000000000000000000000000000000000000000000000000
10387220000000000000000000000000000000000000000000000000000000000000000000000000
10387230000000000000000000000000000000000000000000000000000000000000000000000000
10387240000000000000000000000000000000000000010000000000000000000000000000000000
10387250000001000000000000000000000000000000000000000000000000000000000000000000
10387260000000000000000000000000000000000000000000000000000002000000000000000000
10387270101000000000000000000000000000000000000000000000000000000000000000000000
```

```
10387280000000000000000000000000000000000000000000000000001000000000100000000000
10387290000000000000000000000000000000000000000000000000000000000000000000000000
10387300000000000000000000000000000000000000000000000000000000000000000000000000
10387310000000000000000000000000000000000000000000000000000000000000000000000000
10387320000000000000000000000000000000000000000000000000000000000000000000000000
10387330000000000000000000000000000000000000000000000000000100000000000000000000
10387340000000000000000000000000000000000000000000000000000000010000001000000100000
10387350000000000000000000000000000000000000000000000000000000000000000000000000
10387360000000000000010000000000002000000000000000000000000000010000000000000000
10387370000001000000000000000000010000000000000000000000000000000000000000000000
10387380000000000000000000000000000000000000000000000000000000000000000000000000
10387390000000000000000000000000000000000000000000000000000000000000000000000000
10387400000000000000000000000000000000000000000000000000000000000000000000000000
10387410000000000000000000000000000000000000000000000000000000000000000000000000
10387420000000000000000000000000000000000000000000000000000000000000000000000000
10387430000000000000000000000000000000000000000000000000000000000000000000000000
10387440000000000000000000000000000000000000000000000000000000000000000000000000
10387450000000000000000000000000000000000000000000000000000000000000000000000000
10387460000000000000000000000000000000000000000000000000000000000000000000000000
10387470000000000000000000000000000000000000000000000000000000000000000000000000
10387480000000000000000000000000000000000000000000000000000000000000000000000000
10387490000000000000000000000000000000000000000000000000000000000000000000000000
10387500000000000000000000000000000000000000000000000000000000000000000000000000
10387510000000000000000000000000000000000000000000000000000000000000000000000000
10387520000000000000000000000000
10389010000000000000100030201000000000000010000010100000000000000000000004000101
10389020001000010000000010000000000040101010100000000000100010200000000000010100
10389030000000010100000000000010000000001010000000010000000000000000000000000002
10389040100000000010103000001000000000001000000000000000000303000300000000000000
10389050100000000200000000000000000000000000000100000000000000000000000000000000
10389060100000000000000010000000002010001000000100000010100001000001000000000000
10389070000000010100000000010400010100000000001000000001010000000000000002000002
10389080000000000100000300000000000000000000000000000000000000000200010100010000
10389090000000000020102000002010001010001000100000000100000010100002000400000000
10389100100000020000000000000000001000300020000000000000000000100020001000000100
10389110000000000000001000100000000000002000102000000000000000000000000101000001
10389120000001000000001020700010001000000000000001000000001000000000000000000000
10389130000100000000010000000001000000001020000000010001000000000000030001020001
10389140000001010000000000000000000000000000000000000000000000000000000000000000
10389150100001010100000000100000000200000000000000000010000010001010000000000000
10389160000000000000001000000000000000000000100010000000000000000000000000000000
10389170000002000000000000000000000000000000000000000000000000000000000000000000
10389180000001000000000000010100000000000000000000000000000000000000000000000000
10389190000000000000000000000000000000000000000000000000202000000000000000000100
10389200000000000000000000000000000000000000000000000000000000000000000000000000
10389210000000000000000000000000000000000000000000000000000000000000000000000000
10389220000000000000000000000000000000000000000000000000000000000000000000010000
10389230000000000000000000000000000000000000000000000000000000000000000000000000
10389240000002000000000000000000000000000000000000000000001000000000000000000000
10389250000000000000000010000000000000000010000000000000000000000000000000000000
10389260000000000000000000000000000000000000000000000000000001010101000301000000
10389270101010000100000002010000000000000000000000000000000000000000000000000000
10389280001000000000000000000000000000000000000000000000000000000000000100000000
10389290000000000000000000000000000000000000000000000000000000000000001000100000
10389300000000000000000000000000000000000000000000000000000000000000000000000000
10389310000000000000000000000000000000000000000000000000000000000000000000000000
10389320000000000000000000000000000000000000000000000000000000000000000000000000
10389330000000000000000000000000000000000000003000000000000010000000000000001000
10389340000000000000001000000000000000000000000000000000001000000000000000000000
10389350000000000000000000000000000000000000010000000000000000000000000000000000
```

10389360000000000000100000000000000000000000010000000000000100000000000201000000
10389370002010000000000000000000200000000000000000000000000000000000000000000000
10389380000000000000000000000000000000000000000000000000000000000000000000000000
10389390000000000000000000000000000000000000000000000000000000000000000000000000
10389400000000000000000000000000000000000000000000000000000000000000000000000000
10389410000000000000000000000000000000000000000000000000000000000000000000000000
10389420000000000000000000000000000000000000000000000000000000000000000000000000
10389430000000000000000000000000000000000000000000000000000000000000000000000000
10389440000000000000000000000000000000000000000000000000000000000000000000000000
10389450000000000000000000000000000000000000000000000000000000000000000000000000
10389460000000000000000000000000000000000000000000000000000000000000000000000000
10389470000000000000000000000000000000000000000000000000000000000000000000000000
10389480000000000000000000000000000000000000000000000000000000000000000000000000
10389490000000000000000000000000000000000000000000000000000000000000000000000000
10389500000000000000000000000000000000000000000000000000000000000000000000000000
10389510000000000000000000000000000000000000000000000000000000000000000000000000
10389520000000000100000000000000
10390010000000000000100000000100000000000000000000000000000000000000000100000000
10390020000000000000000000000000000000000001000000000000000000000000000000000000
10390030000000030000000000000000000100000000000000000000000000000000000000000001
10390040000001000000000000000000000000001000000100000000000000000000000000000000
10390050000000000000000000000000000000000000000000000000001000000000000000000100
10390060000000000000000000000000000000000001000000000000000000000000010000000001
10390070000000000000000000000101000000000000000000000000000000000000000000000000
10390080000100000000000000000000000000000000000100000000000000000200000000000000
10390090000001000000000010000000000100000000010000000000001000010000000000020000
10390100000000000000000000001000100000000000000000000000000000000000000000000100
10390110000000000000010000000000000001000000100000000000000000000000000000000000
10390120000001000000000000100000000000100000000000000000000000000000000000000000
10390130000000000000200010000000000000100000000000000000000000000300010000000000
10390140000001010000000000000000000000000000000000000000000000000100000000000000
10390150200000000100000000000000000000100000000000000000000000000000000000010000
10390160000000000000000000000000000000100010000000000000002000000000000000000000
10390170000000000000000000000000000000000000000000000000000000000000000000000000
10390180100000000000000000000101000000000000000000000000000000000000000000000000
10390190000000000000000000000000000000000000000000000000000000000000000000010000
10390200000000000000000000000000101000000000000000000000000000020000000000000000
10390210000000000000000000000000000000000000000000000000000000000000000000000000
10390220000000000000000000000000000000000000000000000000000000000000000000000001
10390230000000000000000000000000000000000000000000000000000000000000000000000000
10390240000000000000000000001000000000000100000000000000000000000000000000000000
10390250000000000000000000000000000000000000000000000000000000000000000000000000
10390260000000000000000000000000000000000000000000000000100000000000001000000000
10390270200000000000000000010000000000001000000001000010000000000000000000000000
10390280000000000000000000000000000000000000000000000000000000000000000000000100
10390290000000000000000000000000000000000000000000000000000001000000000000000000
10390300000000000000000000000000000000000000000000000000000000000000000000000000
10390310000000000000000000000000000000000000000000000000000000000000000000000000
10390320000000000000000000000000000000000000000000000000000000000000000000000000
10390330000000000000000000000000000000001000000100000000000000000000000000000000
10390340000000000000000000000000000000000000000000000000000000000000000000000000
10390350000000010000000000000000000000000000000000000000000000000000000000000000
10390360000000000000000000000000000000100000000000000000000000000000000000000300
10390370000000000000000000000000001000000000000000000000000000000000000000000000
10390380000000000000000000000000000000000000000000000000000000000000000000000000
10390390000000000000000000000000000000000000000000000000000000000000000000000000
10390400000000000000000000000000000000000000000000000000000000000000000000000000
10390410000000000000000000000000000000000000000000000000000000000000000000000000
10390420000000000000000000000000000000000000000000000000000000000000000000000000
10390430000000000000000000000000000000000000000000000000000000000000000000000000
10390440000000000000000000000000000000000000000000000000000000000000000000000000
10390450000000000000000000000000000000000000000000000000000000000000000000000000
10390460000000000000000000000000000000000000000000000000000000000000000000000000
10390470000000000000000000000000000000000000000000000000000000000000000000000000
10390480000000000000000000000000000000000000000000000000000000000000000000000000
10390490000000000000000000000000000000000000000000000000000000000000000000000000
10390500000000000000000000000000000000000000000000000000000000000000000000000000
10390510000000000000000000000000000000000000000000000000000000000000000000000000
10390520000000000000000000000000
10391010000000000000000000000000000000000000000000000000100000000000000010000000
10391020000000000000000000030000000000000010000000000000000000000000000000010000
10391030000000000000000000000000000000000000000000000000000000000001000000010000
10391040000000000001000000000000000000000000000000000000000000000101000000000000
10391050000000000000000000000000000000000010000000000000000000000000000010000100
10391060101000000000000000000000000000000000000000000000001000000000000000000001
10391070000000000000000000000201000000000000010000000000000000000000000000000000
10391080000000000000000000000000000000100000000000000000000000000000000000000000
10391090000000000000000000000000000000000000000000000000000000000000000000010000
10391100000000000000000000000000100000000000000000100000000000100000001000000000
10391110000000000000000000000000000000000000000000000000000000000000000000000000
10391120000000000000000000010000000010000000000000000000000000000000000000000000
10391130000000000000000000000000000010000000000000020000000000000000000000000000
10391140000000000000000000000000000000000000000000000000000000000000000000000100
10391150000000000010000000000000000000000000000000000000000000000000000000000000
10391160000000000000000000000000000000000000000000000000000000000000000000000000
10391170000000000000000000000000000000000000000000000000000000000000000000000000
10391180000000000000000000010000000000000000000000000000000000000000000000000000
10391190000000000000000000000000000000000000000000000000001000000000000010000000
10391200000000000000000000000000000000000000000000000000000000000000000000000000
10391210000000000000000000000000000000000000000000000000000000000000000000000000
10391220000000000000000000000000000000000000000000000000000000000000000000000000
10391230000000000000000000000000000000000000000000000000000000000000000000000000
10391240000002000000000000000000000000000000000000000000000000000000000000000000
10391250000000000000000000000000000000000000000000000000000000000000000000000000
10391260000000000000000000000000000000000000000000000000000000000000000000000000
10391270000000000000000000000000000000000000000000000000000000000000000000000000
10391280000000000000000000000000000000000000000000000000000000000000000000000000
10391290000000000000000000000000000000000000000000000000000000000000000000000000
10391300000000000000000000000000000000000000000000000000000000000000000000000000
10391310000000000000000000000000000000000000000000000000000000000000000000000000
10391320000000000000000000000000000000000000000000000000000000000000000000000000
10391330000000000000000000000000000000000000000001000000000000000000000000000000
10391340000000000000000000000000000000000000000000000000000000000000000000000000
10391350000000000000000000000000000000000000000000000000000000000000000000000000
10391360000000000000000000000000000000000000000000000000000000000000000000010000
10391370000000010000000000000000000000000000000000000000000000000000000000000000
10391380000000000000000000000000000000000000000000000000000000000000000000000000
10391390000000000000000000000000000000000000000000000000000000000000000000000000
10391400000000000000000000000000000000000000000000000000000000000000000000000000
10391410000000000000000000000000000000000000000000000000000000000000000000000000
10391420000000000000000000000000000000000000000000000000000000000000000000000000
10391430000000000000000000000000000000000000000000000000000000000000000000000000
10391440000000000000000000000000000000000000000000000000000000000000000000000000
10391450000000000000000000000000000000000000000000000000000000000000000000000000
10391460000000000000000000000000000000000000000000000000000000000000000000000000
10391470000000000000000000000000000000000000000000000000000000000000000000000000
10391480000000000000000000000000000000000000000000000000000000000000000000000000
10391490000000000000000000000000000000000000000000000000000000000000000000000000
10391500000000000000000000000000000000000000000000000000000000000000000000000000
10391510000000000000000000000000000000000000000000000000000000000000000000000000

```
10391520000000000000000000000
10393010001020101010000010100000201000000000101000100010200000003000100
10393020000000000002000100000030200020200000100000000000201000001000101
10393030000000200010000000100000000000001000001000000000000000010000010101
10393040000000000000200020000010000000000000000000000000000000000000000
10393050100000001000000000000000010000000000001010000000000000000101000201
10393060001000000000000000000000000000000000000000000002000000000001000000
10393070000000000001010002010000000100000000000000000000200010000000000010001
10393080000000100000001000000000101000000020000000000000000000000000000001
10393090000000001000000010200010000000000000000000000000002000102010100
10393100000000101000000000000000000010202010200000000000000101000000000001
10393110000000000000000000000000001000000000000000000000000100000000000001
10393120001000100000000002000000010000000000000000000000000100000000000000
10393130000000000000000000000000000001000100000000100000001000001000000
10393140001000000000000000000000000000000000000000000000000000000000100
10393150000000000101000000000000000000000000000000000000000000000000000
10393160000000000000000000000100000000000000000000000100000000000000000000
10393170000000000000000000000000000000000000000000000000000000000000001
10393180000010000000000100000000100000100000000000000000000000000000010000
10393190000000000000000000000000000000000000000000000000000000000000001
10393200000000000000000000200000100000000000000000000000000000000000000
10393210000000000000000000000000000000000000000000000000000000000000000
10393220000000000000000000000000000000000000000000000000000000000000000
10393230000000000000000000000000000000000000000000000000000000000000000
10393240000000000000000000000010000000100000000000000000000000000101000000
10393250000000001000000000000010200000000000000000000000000000000000000
10393260000000000000000000000000000000000000000001000200000100000000001000000
10393270000000000001000002000100000000000000000100000000000000000000000000
10393280000000000000000000000000000000000000000000000000000000000000000
10393290000000000000000000000000000000000000000000001000000000000000000
10393300000000000000000000000000000000000000000000000000000000000000000
10393310000000000000000000000000000000000000000000000000000000000000000
10393320000000000000000001000000000000000000000010000000000000000000000000
10393330000000000000010000000000000000000000100000000001000000000000000000
10393340000000000000000000000000000000000000000000000000000000000000000
10393350000000000000000000020100000000000000000000000000000000000000000
10393360000000000000000000000000000000000000100000000000001000000010000000100
10393370003000001000000000000000000000000000020000000000000000000000000000
10393380000000000000000000000000000000000000000000000000000000000000000
10393390000000000000000000000000000000000000000000000000000000000000000
10393400000000000000000000000000000000000000000000000000000000000000000
10393410000000000000000000000000000000000000000000000000000000000000000
10393420000000000000000000000000000000000000000000000000000000000000000
10393430000000000000000000000000000000000000000000000000000000000000000
10393440000000000000000000000000000000000000000000000000000000000000000
10393450000000000000000000000000000000000000000000000000000000000000000
10393460000000000000000000000000000000000000000000000000000000000000000
10393470000000000000000000000000100000000000000000000001000000000000000000000
10393480000000000000000000000000000000000000000000000000000000000000000
10393490000000000000000000000000000000000000000000000000000000000000000
10393500000000000000000000000000000000000000000000000000000000000000000
10393510000000000000000000000000000000000000000000000000000000000000000
10393520000000000000000000000
10394010000010001000000010000000100000000000010000000000100010001010000000
10394020000000000000000000000010100000100000000000000000001000000000010000
10394030100000100000000000001000000000100000000100000000200000000000000010000
10394040002000000000000000000010000000000000000000000000000000000000000
10394050000000101000000000000000000000002000000000000000000000000000000
10394060000000000000000000000000000000000000000000000000100000000000000
10394070000000000000000000000000000000000000000000000100000000000000001
10394080001000100000000000000000000000000000000000000100000101000000000000
10394090000000000000001000000000000000001000100000000000000000000000000010000
10394100000000000000000000000000000000010000000000000000000000000000001000000
10394110000000100000000000000000000000000000001000000000000000000000000000
10394120000010100000000002000000000000000000000000000000001000000000000000000
10394130000000000000000000000000000000000000000101000000000000001000000
10394140000000000000000000000000000000000000000000000000000000000000001
10394150000000000000000000000000000000000000000000000000000000000010000
10394160000000000000000000000000000000000000000000000000000000000000000
10394170001000000000000000000000000000000000000000000000000000000000000
10394180000000000000000000000000000000000000000000000000000000000000000
10394190000000000000000000000000000000000000000000000000000000001000100
10394200000000000000000000000000000000000000000001000100000000000000000000
10394210000000000000000000000000000000000000000000000000000000000000000
10394220000000000000000000000000000000000000000000000000000000000000000
10394230000000000000000000000000000000000000000000000000000000000000001
10394240000000000000000000000000000000000000000000000000000000000000000
10394250000010000000000000000000100000000000000000000000000000000000000000
10394260000000000000000000000000000000000000000000000000000000000000000
10394270000000000000000000000000000000000000000000000000000000000000000
10394280000000000000000000000000000000000000000000000000000000000000000
10394290000000000000000000000000000000000000000000000000000000000000000
10394300000000000000000000000000000000000000000000000000000000000000000
10394310000000000000000000000000000000000000000000000000000000000000000
10394320000000000000000000000000000000000000000000000000000000000000000
10394330000000000000000000000000000000000000001000100010001000000000000000
10394340100000000000000000000000000000000000000000000100000000000000000000
10394350000000000000000000000000000000000000000000000000000000000000000
10394360001000000000000000000000000000000000000000000000000010000000000
10394370000000000000000000000000000000000000000000000000000000000000000
10394380000000000000000000000000000000000000000000000000000000000000000
10394390000000000000000000000000000000000000000000000000000000000000000
10394400000000000000000000000000000000000000000000000000000000000000000
10394410000000000000000000000000000000000000000000000000000000000000000
10394420000000000000000000000000000000000000000000000000000000000000000
10394430000000000000000000000000000000000000000000000000000000000000000
10394440000000000000000000000000000000000000000000000000000000000000000
10394450000000000000000000000000000000000000000000000000000000000000000
10394460000000000000000000000000000000000000000000000000000000000000000
10394470000000000000000000000000000000000000000000000000000000000000000
10394480000000000000000000000000000000000000000000000000000000000000000
10394490000000000000000000000000000000000000000000000000000000000000000
10394500000000000000000000000000000000000000000000000000000000000000000
10394510000000000000000000000000000000000000000000000000000000000000000
10394520000000100000000000000
10395010100000001020005040300000103010000000001000100000001000000000000
10395020000000000001000000000100010001000100000000000010001020000000000003
10395030000000501000100010300020100000100000301000100020100000000010001
10395040100000003010000000000010000000001020300010002020002000000002000
10395050000000001000000000000000000000100000100000000000000000101010000
10395060100000000010100000000100000000000000000000000100000100010000000
10395070000000001000000000000000001000000010000010101010001010000000010002
10395080001000200000000100000000000000010000000001000001000001000100010000
10395090001010000000000401000000000000000000001000000000000000000000000000
10395100000000000000000000000000000000000000000000000102000000001000100
10395110000020200000100000000200000200000000000020000000020000000000000
10395120000010000000000002000000010000000000000000000100000000000000000
10395130000000100010001000000010100010001000000002000001000104000103000
10395140100010100000000001000000000000000000000000000000000000000000000
10395150000000101000000000000000000000000002000001000001000000010000000
```

```
10395160001010000000000000000000000000001000000000000000000000000000000
10395170000000000000000000000000000000000000000000000000000000000000000
10395180101000000000000000000000000000000001000000000001000000000000000
10395190000000000000000000000000000000000000000000000000100000000000010000
10395200000000000030000000000000000000000000000000000000000000000000000
10395210000000000000000000000000000000000000000000000000000000000000000
10395220000000000000000000000000000000000000000000000000000000000000000
10395230000000100000000000000000000000000000001000000000000000000000000
10395240000000000000000000000000000000000100000001000000000000010000000000
10395250000500000000000000000000000000000000000000000000000000000000000
10395260000000000000000000000000000000000000000000000100000001000000020000
10395270100000000000002010000000000000000000000000101000000000000000000000
10395280000000001010000000000000000000200000000000000000000000000010000
10395290000000000000000000000000000000000000000000000000000001000000000000000
10395300000000000000000000000000000000000000000000000000000000000000000
10395310000000000000000000000000000000000000000000000000000000000000000
10395320000000000000000000001000000000000000000000000000000000000000000
10395330000000000000000000000000000001020002000000000000000100010000000000
10395340000000001000000000000000000000000000000000000000000000000000000
10395350000000000000000000000000000000000000000000000000000000000000001
10395360000000000000000000000000000000000000000000000000000000000000102020000000
10395370001000001000000000000010000000000200010000000000000000000000000
10395380000000000000000000000000000000000000000000000000000000000000000
10395390000000000000000000000000000000000000000000000000000000000000000
10395400000000000000000000000000000000000000000000000000000000000000000
10395410000000000000000000000000000000000000000000000000000000000000000
10395420000000000000000000000000000000000000000000000000000000000000000
10395430000000000000000000000000000000000000000000000000000000000000000
10395440000000000000000000000000000000000000000000000000000000000000000
10395450000000000000000000000000000000000000000000000000000000000000000
10395460000000000000000000000000000000000000000000000000000000000000000
10395470000000000000000000000000000000000000000000000000000000000000000
10395480000000000000000000000000000000000000000000000000000000000000000
10395490000000000000000000000000000000000000000000000000000000000000000
10395500000000000000000000000000000000000000000000000000000000000000000
10395510000000000000000000000000000000000000000000000000000000000000000
10395520000000000000000000000
10402010000000000000000000000000000001000000000000000000000000000001000100
10402020000000000010000000000000100000000000000000100010000000000000000
10402030000000000000000000000000100000000000000010000000100000000000000
10402040000000000000000000000000000000000000000000100000101000000000001
10402050000000000000000000000000000000000000000000000000000000000000000
10402060000000001000000000000000000000000000000000000000000000001000000
10402070000000000000100000200000000000000000000000000000001000000000000001
10402080000000000000000000000000000000000000000000000000000000000000000
10402090000000000000000000000000000000000000000000000000000000000000000
10402100000000000000000000000000000000000000000000000000000100010000000
10402110000000000000000000000000000000010000000000000000000000000000000
10402120000000000000000000000000100000000000000000000000000000000000000
10402130001000000000000000000000000000000000000000000000000000100010000
10402140100000000000000000000000000000000000000000000000000000000000000
10402150000000000000000000000000000000000000000000000000000000000000000
10402160000000000000000000000000000000000000000000000000000000000000000
10402170000000000000000000000000000000000000000000000000000000000000000
10402180000000000000000000000000000000000000000000000000000000000000000
10402190000000000000000000000000000000000000000000000000000000000000000
10402200000000000000000000000000000000000000000000000000000000000000000
10402210000000000000000000000000000000000000000000000000000000000000000
10402220000000000000000000000000000000000000000000000000000000000000000
10402230000000000000000000000000000000000000000000000000000000000000000
10402240000000000000000000000000000000000000000000000000000000000000000
10402250000000000000000000000000000000000000000000000000000000000000000
10402260000000000000000000000000000000000000000000000000000000000000000
10402270000000000000000000000000000001000000000000000000000000000000000
10402280000000000000100000000000000000000000000000000000000000000000000
10402290000000000000000000000000000000000000100000000000000000000000000
10402300000000000000000000000000000000000000000000000000000000000000000
10402310000000000000000000000000000000000000000000000000000001000000000
10402320000000000000000000000000000000000000000000000000000000000000000
10402330000000000000000000000000000000000000000010000000000000000000000
10402340100000000000000000000000000000000000000000000000000000000000000
10402350000000000000000000000000000000000000000000000000000000000000000
10402360000000000000000000000000000000000000000000000000000000000000000
10402370000000000000000000000000000000000000100000000000000000000000000
10402380000000000000000000000000000000000000000000000000000000000000000
10402390000000000000000000000000000000000000000000000000000000000000000
10402400000000000000000000000000000000000000000000000000000000000000000
10402410000000000000000000000000000000000000000000000000000000000000000
10402420000000000000000000000000000000000000000000000000000000000000000
10402430000000000000000000000000000000000000000000000000000000000000000
10402440000000000000000000000000000000000000000000000000000000000000000
10402450000000000000000000000000000000000000000000000000000000000000000
10402460000000000000000000000000000000000000000000000000000000000000000
10402470000000000000000000000000000000000000000000000000000000000000000
10402480000000000000000000000000000000000000000000000000000000000000000
10402490000000000000000000000000000000000000000000000000000000000000000
10402500000000000000000000000000000000000000000000000000000000000000000
10402510000000000000000000000000000000000000000000000000000000000000000
10402520000000000000000000000
10403010100030000010003010100000002030400030306030400000001000209000600
10403020003010100010001010002030300000304010102010003010100000100000000
10403030000000601010000020200000402000200000600000100000001000302010500
10403040002010002000200040000000101000100050200030001040103000000020000
10403050200000001010300000000000000030200000000300000200000100020000000
10403060001010001020000000000030005000000010100000203020302000000000000
10403070000010001000000000100000101000000000100000000200000000000001040300
10403080001000000000100000000000010000000000000000000200010102000000100
10403090000000000000020300000100000000000100030000000201010001000000100
10403100000000000100000000000000000001000000000000000000000000000000200
10403110000000000000100000000000000200000200010000000000000000000000000
10403120000040200000000010000000000000000000000000000000000000000000000
10403130000000001000000000000010000000000000000010001000001040202000000001
10403140001000000000000000000000000000000000000000000000000000000000100
10403150100010000000000000000000000000000000000000000000000000000000000
10403160001010100000000000000000001010000000000000002000000000000000001
10403170000010000000000000000000000000000000000000000000000000000000000
10403180001000000000000002000000000000000000000000000000000000000000000
10403190000000000000000000000010000000200000000000000000000000001000103
10403200000000000101000000000000000000000000000000000000000000000000000
10403210000000000000000000000000000000000000000000000000001000000000000
10403220000000000000000000000000000000000000000000000000000000000000000
10403230000000000000000000000000000201000000000000000001000000000000000
10403240000000000000001000000000000010100000000000100000000000000000000
10403250000030000000000000000000000000000001000000000000000000000000000
10403260000000000000000000000000000000000000100000001000000000000000000
10403270002000000000000000000002000000000000000000000000000000000000000
10403280000000000000000000000000000000000000000000000000000000000000000
10403290000000000000000000000000000000000000000000000101000000000000000
10403300000000000000000000000000000000000000000000000000000000000000000
10403310000000000000000102000000000100000000000000010000000000000000000
```

```
10403320000000000000000000000000000000000000000000000000000000000100000000
10403330000000000000000000000000000000000000000000000000000000000000000001
10403340000000000000000000000000000000000000000000000000000000000000000000
10403350000000000000000000000000000000000000000000000000000000000000000000
10403360000000000000000001000000000010000010000000000000000000000060500000100
10403370000100030000000200000000000010000000100000000000000000000000000020000
10403380000000000000000000000000000000000000000000000000000000000000000000
10403390000000000000000000000000000000000000000000000000000000000000000000
10403400000000000000000000000000000000000000000000000000000000000000000000
10403410000000000000000000000000000000000000000000000000000000000000000000
10403420000000000000000000000000000000000000000000000000000000000000000000
10403430000000000000000000000000000000000000000000000000000000000200000000
10403440000000000000000000000000000000000000000000000000000000000000000000
10403450000000000000000000000000000000000000000000000000000000000000000000
10403460000000000000000000000000000000000000000000000000000000000000000000
10403470000000000000000000000000000000000000000000000000000000000000000001
10403480000000000000000000000000000000000000000000000000000000000000000000
10403490000000000000000000000000000000000000000000000000000000000000000000
10403500000000000000000000000000000000000000000000000000000000000000000000
10403510000000000000000000000000000000000000000000000000000000000000000000
1040352000000000000000000000000
10404010000000000000000010201010001000100000000000000300020100000000000100
10404020000010000200010000000101010200010000000010000010200000000000000010200
10404030000000000000000020100000001000100010000000000000000000301010000000100
10404040100000100000100000000000000000000000000000200030200030000000000000000
10404050200000000000000000001000000000010000000000000000000000000000000000000
10404060100000010010000000000000000103010000000000000001000200000301010000000
10404070000000300000000010000000000000000000000000100000000000000000000000000
10404080000000000000000000000001000000000000000000000000000010000000000000000
10404090000000010000000001000000101000000000000000000000000200000201000000000
10404100000000000000000000000020100000000010000000000000000000000000200000001
10404110000000000000000000000000000000000000000000000000000000000000000000000
10404120000000000000000000000000000000000000000000000000000000000000000000000
10404130000000000200000000000000000000000000000000100000000000000000100010000
10404140100000000000000000000000000000000000000000000000000000000000000000000
10404150000000000000000102000000000000000000000000000001000000000000000000000
10404160000000000000000000000000000000000001000000000000000000000000000000000
10404170000000000000000000000000000000000000000000000000000000000000000000000
10404180000010000000000000000000000000000000000000000000000000000000001000100
10404190000000000000000000000000000000000000000000000000000000000000000000001
10404200000000010000000000000000000000000000000000000000000000000000000000000
10404210000000000000000000000000000000000000000000000000000000000000000000000
10404220000000000000000000000000000000000000000010000000000000000000000000000
10404230000000000000000000000000000000000000000000000000000000000000000000101
10404240000100000000000000000000000000000000000000000000100000000000000000000
10404250000000000000000000000000000000000000000000000000000000000000000000000
10404260000000000000000000000000000000000000000000000010000010000000000000000
10404270000000000000000000000001000000000000000000000000000000000000000000000
10404280000000000000000000000000000000000000000000000000000000000000000000000
10404290000000000000000001000000000200000000000000000000000000000000000000000
10404300000000000000000000000000000000000000000000000000000000000000000000000
10404310000000000000000000000000000000000000000000000000000000000000000000000
10404320000000000000000000000001000000000000000000000000000000000000000000000
10404330000000000000000000000000000000001000001000000000000000000001000000000
10404340000000000000000000000000000000000000000000000000000000000101000100000000
10404350000000000000000000000000000000000000000000000000000000000000000000000
10404360000000000000000000000000000000000100000000100000000000000000100000101
10404370000000000000000100000000000000000000000000000000000000000000000000000
10404380000000000000000000000000000000000000000000000000000000000000000000000
10404390000000000001000000000000000000000000000000000000000000000000000000000
```

```
10404400000000000000000000000000000000000000000000000000000000000000000000000
10404410000000000000000000000000000000000000000000000000000000000000000000000
10404420000000000000000000000000000000000000000000000000000000000000000000000
10404430000000000000000000000000000000000000000000000000000000000000000000000
10404440000000000000000000000000000000000000000000000000000000000000000000000
10404450000000000000000000000000000000000000000000000000000000000000000000000
10404460000000000000000000000000000000000000000000000000000000000000000000000
10404470000000000000000000000000000000000000000000000000000000000000000000000
10404480000000000000000000000000000000000000000000000000000000000000000000000
10404490000000000000000000000000000000000000000000000000000000000000000000000
10404500000000000000000000000000000000000000000000000000000000000000000000000
10404510000000000000000000000000000000000000000000000000000000000000000000000
1040452000000000000000000000000
10406010100000000000010000000010000010109010001000501000101010001040000101
10406020000000000010002000001010601000000000101000000000100000101000000000
10406030000000020200000000001000001010100000000200020000000000000501000202000
10406040004000000000010000100000000000000000100000000300000000010000000000000
10406050000000100020000000000000000000000000000000100000000000100000100010000
10406060000000000000000000000000000000000001000000000100010001000001000100000000
10406070001000000000100000000000000000000000000000001000000000000000001010000
10406080000000000000010000010000000000010000000000000000000000000000100000000
10406090000000000000000002000000000000000000000000000000000201000001020000000
10406100000000000000000000010000020101000000000000000000000000000000000000001
10406110000000000000000001000000000000001000000000000000000000000000000000000
10406120000000000000000000000000000000000000000000000000000000000000000000000
10406130000000000000000000000000000000000000020000010000000000001000000000000
10406140000000000000000000000000000000000000000000000000000000000000000000000
10406150100000000000000000000000000000000000000000000000000000000000000000000
10406160000000000100000000000000000000000001000000000000001000000000000000000
10406170100000001000000000000000000000000000000000000000000000000000000000000
10406180001000000000000000000000000000001000000000000000000010000000000000000
10406190000000000000000000000000000000000000000000000000000000000000000000003
10406200000000000000100000000000000000000000000000000000000000000000000000000
10406210000000000000000000000000000000000000000000000000000000000000000000000
10406220000000000000000000000000000000000000000000000000000000000000000000000
10406230000000000000000000000000000000000000000000000000000000000000000000000
10406240000000010000000000000000000000000000000000000000000000000000000000000
10406250000000000000000000000000000000000002000000000000000000000000000000000
10406260000000000000000000000000000000000000010000000000000000000000000000100
10406270000000000000000001000000001000000000000000000000000000000000000000000
10406280000000000000000000000000000000000000000000000000000000000000000000000
10406290000000000000000000000000000000000000000001000200000000000000000000000
10406300000000000000000000000000000000000000000000000000000000000000000000000
10406310000000000000000000000000000000000000000000000000000000000100000000
10406320000000000000000000000000000000000000000000000000000000000000000000000
10406330000000000000000000000000000000000000000000000000000000000000000000000
10406340100000000000000000000000000000000000000000000000000000000000000000000
10406350000000000000000000000000000000000000000000000000000000000000000000000
10406360000000000000000000000000000000000000000000000000000000000200000100
10406370000000200000000000000000000000000000000000000000000000000000000000000
10406380000000000000000000000000000000000010000000000000000000000000000000000
10406390000000000000000000000000000000000000000000000000000000000000000000000
10406400000000000000000000000000000000000000000000000000000000000000000000000
10406410000000000000000000000000000000000000000000000000000000000000000000000
10406420000000000000000000000000000000000000000000000000000000000000000000000
10406430000000000000000000000000000000000000000000000000000000000000000000000
10406440000000000000000000000000000000000000000000000000000000000000000000000
10406450000000000000000000000000000000000000000000000000000000000000000000000
10406460000000000000000000000000000000000000000000000000000000000000000000000
10406470000000000000000000000000000000000000000000000000000000000000000000000
```

```
10406480000000000000000000000000000000000000000000000000000000000000000
10406490000000000000000000000000000000000000000000000000000000000000000
10406500000000000000000000000000000000000000000000000000000000000000000
10406510000000000000000000000000000000000000000000000000000000000000000
10406520000000000010000000000
104070100000000000000000000000000000001000000041000000000000000101000000
104070200000000000000010000010002000000000000000000000000000000100000000
104070300000001000000000000000000000000000001000000000000000000000000000
104070400030000000002000000000000000000000000000000000000000000000000000
10407050000000000000000000000000000000000000000000000000000000000000000
104070600000000000100000000000000000000000000000000000000000000000000000
10407070000000000000000000000000000000000000000000000000000000000000000
10407080000000000000000000000000000000000000000000000000000000000000000
104070900000001000000000000000000000000000000000000000000000000000000000
10407100000000000000000000000000000000000000000000000000000000000000000
10407110000000000000000000000000000000000000000000000000000000000000000
104071200000001000000000000000000000000000000000000000000000000000000000
104071300000000000100000000000000000000000000000100000000000000000000000
10407140000000000000000000000000000000000000000000000000000000000000000
104071502000000000000000000000000000000000000000000000000000000000000000
10407160000000000000000000000000000000000000000000000000000000000000000
10407170000000000000000000000000000000000000000000000000000000000000000
104071800000000000000000000010000000000000000000000000000000000000000000
10407190000000000000000000000000000000000000000000000000000000000000000
10407200000000000000000000000000000000000000000000000000000000000000000
10407210000000000000000000000000000000000000000000000000000000000000000
10407220000000000000000000000000000000000000000000000000000000000000000
10407230000000000000000000000000000000000000000000000000000000000000000
10407240000000000000000000000000000000000000000000000000000000000000000
10407250000000000000000000000000000000000000000000000000000000000000000
10407260000000000000000000000000000000000000000000000000000000000000000
10407270000000000000000000000000000000000000000000000000000000000000000
10407280000000000000000000000000000000000000000000000000000000000000000
10407290000000000000000000000000000000000000000000000000000000000000000
10407300000000000000000000000000000000000000000000000000000000000000000
10407310000000000000000000000000000000000000000000000000000000000000000
10407320000000000000000000000000000000000000000000000000000000000000000
104073300000000000000000000000000000000000100000000000000000000000000000
10407340000000000000000000000000000000000000000000000000000000000000000
10407350000000000000000000000000000000000000000000000000000000000000000
10407360000000000000000000000000000000000000000000000000000000000000000
104073700000001000000000000000000000000000000000000000000000000000000000
10407380000000000000000000000000000000000000000000000000000000000000000
10407390000000000000000000000000000000000000000000000000000000000000000
10407400000000000000000000000000000000000000000000000000000000000000000
10407410000000000000000000000000000000000000000000000000000000000000000
10407420000000000000000000000000000000000000000000000000000000000000000
10407430000000000000000000000000000000000000000000000000000000000000000
10407440000000000000000000000000000000000000000000000000000000000000000
10407450000000000000000000000000000000000000000000000000000000000000000
10407460000000000000000000000000000000000000000000000000000000000000000
10407470000000000000000000000000000000000000000000000000000000000000000
10407480000000000000000000000000000000000000000000000000000000000000000
10407490000000000000000000000000000000000000000000000000000000000000000
10407500000000000000000000000000000000000000000000000000000000000000000
10407510000000000000000000000000000000000000000000000000000000000000000
10407520000000000000000000000
10561010000000000000000000000000000000000000000000000000000000000000000
105610200000000000000000000000100000000000000000000000000000000000000000
10561030000000000000000000000000000000000000000000000000000000000000000
10561040000000000000000000000000000000000000000000000000000000000000000
10561050000000000000000000000000000000000000000000000000000000000000000
10561060000000000000000000000000000000000000000000000000000000000000000
10561070000000000000000000000000000000000000000000000000000000000000000
10561080000000000000000000000000000000000000000000000000000000000000000
10561090000000000000000000000000000000000000000000000000000000000000000
10561100000000000000000000000000000000000000000000000000000000000000000
10561110000000000000000000000000000000000000000000000000000000000000000
10561120000000000000000000000000000000000000000000000000000000000000000
105611300000000000000000000000000100000000000000000000000000000000000000
10561140000000000000000000000000000000000000000000000000000000000000000
10561150000000000000000000000000000000000000000000000000000000000000000
10561160000000000000000000000000000000000000000000000000000000000000000
10561170000000000000000000000000000000000000000000000000000000000000000
10561180000000000000000000000000000000000000000000000000000000000000000
10561190000000000000000000000000000000000000000000000000000000000000000
10561200000000000000000000000000000000000000000000000000000000000000000
10561210000000000000000000000000000000000000000000000000000000000000000
10561220000000000000000000000000000000000000000000000000000000000000000
10561230000000000000000000000000000000000000000000000000000000000000000
10561240000000000000000000000000000000000000000000000000000000000000000
105612500000000000000000000000000100000000000000000000000000000000000000
105612600000000000000000000000000000000000000000000000100000000000000000
10561270000000000000000000000000000000000000000000000000000000000000000
10561280000000000000000000000000000000000000000000000000000000000000000
10561290000000000000000000000000000000000000000000000000000000000000000
10561300000000000000000000000000000000000000000000000000000000000000000
10561310000000000000000000000000000000000000000000000000000000000000000
10561320000000000000000000000000000000000000000000000000000000000000000
10561330000000000000000000000000000000000000000000000000000000000000000
10561340000000000000000000000000000000000000000000000000000000000000000
10561350000000000000000000000000000000000000000000000000000000000000000
105613600010000000000000000000000000000000000000000000000000000000000000
10561370000000000000000000000000000000000000000000000000000000000000000
10561380000000000000000000000000000000000000000000000000000000000000000
10561390000000000000000000000000000000000000000000000000000000000000000
10561400000000000000000000000000000000000000000000000000000000000000000
10561410000000000000000000000000000000000000000000000000000000000000000
10561420000000000000000000000000000000000000000000000000000000000000000
10561430000000000000000000000000000000000000000000000000000000000000000
10561440000000000000000000000000000000000000000000000000000000000000000
10561450000000000000000000000000000000000000000000000000000000000000000
10561460000000000000000000000000000000000000000000000000000000000000000
10561470000000000000000000000000000000000000000000000000000000000000000
10561480000000000000000000000000000000000000000000000000000000000000000
10561490000000000000000000000000000000000000000000000000000000000000000
10561500000000000000000000000000000000000000000000000000000000000000000
10561510000000000000000000000000000000000000000000000000000000000000000
10561520000000000000000000000
111020101000000000000000000000001000000001000000000000000000000100000000
111020200000001000000000100000000000000010000000000000000000000000000000
111020300000001000000000000000000000010000000000000000000000001000000000000
111020400000000000000000000000000000000000000000000000000000000000000000
111020500000000000100000000000000000000000000000000000101000101000000000000
111020600000000000000000000000100000000000000000000000100000000010000000
111020700000010102010000000000000000000000000000000000020002000000000000
111020800000000200000000001000000000010100000000000000000000000000010000
111021000000000000000000000010100000000000000000000001000000000010000000
111020900000000000000000000000000000000000000010000000000001000000000000
111021100010000000000000000001000010000000000000000000001000000000000001
```

1110212000000000000000000000000000000000000001010003010400010400010000
1110213000000200020100000000020000000000000000000000000001010000000000
1110214000000000000010104020301000000000000020001000100000000000000402
1110215110002020000000002000000000000000010000000000000000000000000000
1110216010000000100000000000000000000000001000002000204010101000000000
1110217001503041100000200000001000000000000010100000000000000000020002
1110218010102000101040100000002000100000003000600010000001000100020000
1110219000000020001000000030105000010000000000010101010002000101000002
1110220000000040000000000030102000010000010000010000000000000000000000
1110221000001000200000000000010000010000000000000000000000000000000000
1110222000100000000000000000000000004000000000000010000000000010000010002
1110223010100010000010003010001000000000000000000000000000000000000000
1110224000000000000000001000002000000000000001000000000000020000010001
1110225000001000101000001000102000002000000000000000000001000000000100
1110226000100010100000000000100000000000000000000000000000000000000000
1110227010000000000010002000001000000000000000000000000000000000000000
1110228000000000000040000010000010000000000000000000000000000000000200
1110229000102000000010000000000000000000000000000003010101000100000000
1110230000000000000000000101010000000000001000100000000000001000000000
1110231000000001000000010000000000000000010000000000010100000001000000
1110232030000000000000/00010000040000010202030000000050000000100000000
1110233000000000000000000000000000000000000000000000000010000000000000
1110234000001000000000000000000000000001000001000000000000000000000000
1110235000001000000000000000100000000000000001000000000000000000060004
1110236020000000000060203080000005000102000306020000010000000100000000
1110237000000000000000000000000005000000000000000000000000000000000000
1110238000000000000000000000000000000000000000000000000000000000000000
1110239000000000000000000000000000000000000000000000000000000000000000
1110240000000000000000000000000000000000000000000000000000000000000100
1110241000000000000000000000000000000000000000000000000000000000000000
1110242000000000000000000000000000000000000000000000000000000000000000
1110243000000000000000000000000000000000000000000000000000000000000000
1110244000000000000000000000000000000000000000000000000000000000000000
1110245000000000000000000000000000000000000000000000000000000000000000
1110246000000000000000000000000000000000000000000000000000000000000000
1110247000000000000000000000000000000000000000000000000000000000000000
1110248000000000000000002000000000000000000000010000000000000000000000
1110249000000000000000000000000000000000000000000000000000000000000100
1110250000000000000000000000000100000000000000000000000000000000000000
1110251000000000000000000000000000000000001000000000000000000000000000
11102520000000000000000000001
1110401000101000001000000000001010100010000010000020000000000000000100
1110402000000030000000001000000000010000100000000001000000000000000102
1110403000000000100000000000000200010100000000000000000101000100010000
1110404000000000000040000000002000000000100000000000000000000000000001
1110405000000000001000000000000001000000000000000000201010002000000001
1110406000000001010000000010000000000000000000000100000000010100000100
1110407000000000000000000000000000000000000100000000020200000000010001
1110408000000020000010000100000105000000000000000002000102000004000000
1110409000001000000000000000000000000000000000000100000000000000000001
1110410000000000000000000000000100000000000000000010000000000000000000
1110411000000000000000000000000000000000000000000000000100000000000000
1110412000001000000000000000100000100010000010202000200030000002030000
1110413000100000002000100000004030100010001000000000000000010000010004
1110414000001000000000001000300010100000000000000000000000000001000005
1110415050003000002000001010002010000200000000000000000000000000010000
1110416010102000000000101000000000030001010100000100040001020000000000
1110417001601010401010402000000000000100010000000001000000000200030003
1110418040003010207000002040003000003020001000301000000000000001000000
1110419000000030000000000010107010000000000010000401010000000100080207

1110420010001020002000400020000000000002020202010003010102000000000000
1110421000200000301020000020000000000101010000010001000001000000010100
1110422000100000000000000000000000000000000000000000000000000000000010004
1110423030000010002000103030301000000010007000201000100010100000000200
1110424010100000000002000002000300000000010000010102010001000300010001
1110425010201000201010100010101000003000000000000000000100010000030203
1110426010003020201000002000000000000100000000000000000000000000000000
1110427020001000000010002000101000000000100000000000010001000000000000
1110428010000000000000001000001020001000001020002000000001000000000000
1110429000301000000030100010000010101000000000000200000500010100000000
1110430000000000000000003000200000100000003010100010000000100000030200
1110431000000000000001010001000001000000000101000001000200010000000503
1110432040000000000000200000800000010103000000000000050000000202000001
1110433000000000000000000000000000000000000100000000000001000000000000
1110434000000000000000000000000000000000000000000000000000000000000000
1110435000000000000000000000000000000000000000000000000000000000030001
1110436050701010004000700030402020600101000004000000010000000100010102
1110437000500000100010000000000000004000000000000000000000001000000000
1110438000000000000000000000000000010000000000000000000000001000000000
1110439000000000001000000000000000000000000000000000000000000000000000
1110440000000000000000000000000000000000000000000000000000000000000000
1110441000000000000000000000000000000000000000000000000000000000000000
1110442000000000000000000000000000000000000000000000000000000000000000
1110443000000000000000000000000000000000000000000000000000000000000000
1110444000000000000000000000000000000000000000000000000000000000000000
1110445000000000000000000000000000000000000000000000000000000000000000
1110446000000000000000000000000000000000000000000000000000000000000000
1110447000000000001000000000000000000000000000000000000000000000000500
1110448000000000000000002020100000000000000000000000000000001000000000
1110449000000000000000100000000000000000000000000001000000000000000000
1110450000000000000000000000000000000000000000000001000000000000000000
1110451000000000000000000000000000000000000000000000000000000001000000
11104520000000000010000000001
1110501000100000001000000101000000000000000000000000000000000001000000
1110502000000010000000000000000000000000000000000000000000000000000000
1110503000000000000000000010000000000000000000000000000000000000000001
1110504000000000000000000000000000000000100000000000000000000000000001
1110505000000000000000000000000000000000000000000000000010000000000000
1110506000000000000000000000000000000000000000000001000000000000000000
1110507000000010001000000000000000000000000000000000000101000000000000
1110508000100000000000001000010000000000000000000000000000000000000000
1110509000000000000000000000000100000000000000000000000000000000000000
1110510000000000000000000001010000000000000000100000000000000000000100000100
1110511000000000000000101000000000000000000000000001000103000000000000
1110512000000000000000000000000000000000000001010000000100010102020000
1110513000001010004000100000000000000100000000000000000000001000000000 2
1110514000001010100000202050000000010000000001000000000001000402000205
1110515110005000000010000000000000000000000000000000010000000000000100
1110516020301000000000003000000000010000030000000005020001010000010100
1110517013201020501020502000000000010000010201000000200000000100000001
1110518050408030101020302010109000202000020005010002010001000201040002
1110519000003010000000203020200000201000201000000102020002010100000309
1110520000002010004010400010100001000002010001020203000001000000000100
1110521000200030200000000000010000000100010000010000000000010100000000
1110522000000000000000000000000200020000000000010000010000010000000105
1110523030000010000010200020401000000000000000010001000001000000010100
1110524000000000100000000010003000000000000001000101000000000001000000
1110525000000000200000100010101000003000000000000000000100000101000101
1110526010100010000000000000000100000100010000000000000000010000010000
1110527020100000000000000001010000000000100000000000000000000000000000

11105280000000000000000000001000000000006000000000102000000000000000000000000000
11105290102010000000000000020000101020101000000000010000010000000000000000000000
11105300000100000000000000000000000300010001000101000000000000000010000030000
11105310000000000000000000001000000000001000000000000000000001010200010000000100
11105320300000000000000000000200010011000001000402000000000004000100000000000001
11105330000000000000000000000000000000000000000000001000000002000000000000000001
11105340000000000000000000000000000000001010000000000000000000000000000000000000
11105350001000000000000000000000000000000000000000000000000000000000000000080002
11105360105020100020010010412000101010001000306010000000000000000000000101000001
11105370001000000000000002000100000000008000000000000000000000000000000000010000
11105380000000000000000000000000000000000000000000000000000000000000000000000000
11105390000000000000000000000000000001000000000000000000000000000000000000000000
11105400010000000000000000000000000000000000000000000000000001000000000000000000
11105410000000000000000000000000000000000000000000000000000000020000000000000100
11105420000000000000000000000000000000000000000000000000000000000000000000000000
11105430000000000000000000000000000000000000000000000000000001010000000000000000
11105440000000000000000000000000000000000000000000000000000000000000000000000000
11105450000000000010000000000000000000000000000000000000000000000000100000000000
11105460000000000000000000000010000000000000000010000000000000100000000000000000
11105470000000000000100000000000000000000000000000000000000000000000000000000200
11105480000000000010000010100000000000000000000100000000000000000000000001000000
11105490000000000000000000000010000000000000000010000000000000000000000000000000
11105500000000000000000000000000000000000000000000000000001010000000000010000000
11105510000000000000000000000000000000000000000000000000000000000000000000000000
11105520000000000000000000000000
11106010000000000000100000000001000000000000000000000000000000000000000000000200
11106020000000000000100000000001000000000000000000000000000001000000000000000000
11106030000000002020100000000000000000000000000001000000000000000000000000000000
11106040000000000000001000000000000000000000000000000000001000000000000000000000
11106050000000000000001000000000000000000000000000000000000000000010100000000000
11106060000000000010000000000000000000000000000000000000000000000000000000000100
11106070000000000000000000000000000000000000000000100000100000000000000000000000
11106080000000000000000000000000000010102010000000000000000000000000000000000000
11106090000000000000000000000000000000000000000000000000000000000000000000000000
11106100000000010000000000000000000000000000000000000000000000000000000000000000
11106110000000000000000000000000000000000000000000000000000000000000000000000000
11106120000000000000000000000000000000000000000000000001000000000000000100000000
11106130000000000000000000000000000000000000000010000000000000000010000000000000
11106140000000000000000000000001000000000000000000000000000000000000000000000001
11106150200010002000100010000000000000000000000000000000000000000000000000000000
11106160100000000000000000000000000001000000000100000000000000000100000000000000
11106170005000101000000000000000000000000000000000000000000000000000000000000001
11106180000010000000001010000000010000010100000000000000001000000000000000000001
11106190000000000000000000000010100000000000000000000000001000100010001000000000
11106200000000000000010000000000000000000000100000300000100000000000000000000000
11106210000000000000010000000000000000000000000000000000000000000000000000010001
11106220000000000000000000000000000000000000000000000000000000000000000001000001
11106230100000000000000000000003000200000000000000000000100000000000000000000000
11106240000010000000000000000000000000000000010000000000000100000000000000000000
11106250000000000000000000000010000000000001000000000000000000000000000000000000
11106260000000000000000000001000000000000000000000000000000100000000000000000001
11106270000010000000000000000000000000000000000000000000000000000000000000000000
11106280000000000000000000000000000000000000000000000000000000000000000000000000
11106290001000000000000000000000000000000000000000000000001000001000000000000000
11106300000000000000000000000000000000000000000000000000000000000000000000000000
11106310000000000100000000000000000000000000000001000000000000000000010000010000
11106320000000000000000000000001000030000000000000000000010000000000000000000000
11106330000000000000000000000000000000000000000000000000000000000000000000000000
11106340000000000000000000000000000000000000000000000000000000000000000000000000
11106350000000000000000000000000000000000000000000000000000000000000000000000000
11106360001000000000000000000000400000000000000000000000000000000000000200010001
11106370000000010000000010000000000000002000000000000000000000000000000000000000
11106380000000000000000000000000000000000000000000000000000000000000000000000000
11106390000000000000100000000000000000000000000000000000000000000000000000000000
11106400000000000000000000000000000000000000000000000000000000000000000000000000
11106410000000000000000000000000000000000000000000000000000000000000000000000000
11106420000000000000000000000000000000000000000000000000000000000000000000000000
11106430000000000000000000000000000000000000001000000000000000000000000000000000
11106440000000000000000000000000000000000000000000000000000000000000000000000000
11106450000000000010000000000000000000000000000000000000000000000000000000000000
11106460000000000000000000000000000000000000000000000000000000000000000000000000
11106470000000000000000000000000000000000000000000000000000000000000000000000100
11106480000000000000000000000000000000000000000000000000000000000000000000000100
11106490000000000000000000000000000000000000000000000000000000000000000000000000
11106500000000000000000000000000000000000000000000000000000000000000000000000000
11106510000000000000000000000000000000000000000000000000000000000000000000000000
11106520000000000000000000000000
11107010000000000000000000000000000000000000000000000000000000000000000001000000
11107020000000000000000000000000000000000000000000000000000000000000000000000000
11107030000000000000001000000000000000000000000000000000000000000000000000010000
11107040000000000000000000000000000000000000000000000000000000000000000000000000
11107050000000000010000000000000000000002000000000000000000000000000000000000000
11107060000000000000000000000000000000000000000000000000000000000000000000000000
11107070000000000000000000000000000000000000000000000000000000000000000000000100
11107080000000000000000000000000000000000000000000000000000000000001000000000000
11107090000000000000000000000000000000000000000000000000000000000000000000000100
11107100000000000000000000000000000000000000000000000000000000000000000000000000
11107110000000000000000000000000000000000000000000000000000000000000000000000000
11107120000000000000000000000000000000000000000000000000000000002000000010000000
11107130000000000000000010000000000000000000000000000000000000000000000000000000
11107140000000000000000000000000000000000000000000000000000000000000000000000001
11107150700000000000000000000000000000000000000000000000000000000000000000000100
11107160000000000000000000000000000000000000000000000000000002000000000000000000
11107170001000000000000000000000000000000000000001000000001000000000002000000000
11107180101020101000101010101010100000101000100000000000000000000000000000030000
11107190000000201000000000001000000000000000000000000000100000000000000000000000
11107200000000000100000200010000000000000000000000000000000000000000000000000000
11107210000000000000000000000000000000000000000000000000000000001000000000000000
11107220000000000000000000000001000000000000000000000000000000100000000000000002
11107230000000000000000000000000000000000100000100000000000000000000000000000000
11107240000000000000000000000000000000000000000000000002000000000100000000000000
11107250000000000000002000000000000000000000000000000000000000000000000000000000
11107260000000000000000000000000000000000000000000000000000000000000000000000000
11107270000000000000000000000000010100000000000000000000000000000000000000000000
11107280000000000000000000000000000000000000000000000000000000000000000000000000
11107290000000000000000000000000000100000000000000000000000000000000000000000000
11107300000000000000000000000000000000000000000000000001000000000000000000000000
11107310000000000001000000000000000001000000000000000000001000001000000000000000
11107320000000000000000000000000000100000000000000000000000000000100000000000000
11107330000000000000000000000000000000000000000000000000000000000000000000000000
11107340000000000000000000000000000000000000000000000000000000000000000000000000
11107350000000000000000000000000000000000000000000000000000000000000000000010000
11107360000000000001000000000040401020000000000000010000000000000000000000010000
11107370000000000000000000000000000000000000000000000000000000000000000000000000
11107380000000000000000000000000000000000000000000000000000000000000000000000000
11107390000000000001000000000000000000000000000000000000000000000000000000000000
11107400000000000000000000000000000000000000000000000000000000000000000000000000
11107410000000000000000000000000000000000000000000000000000000000000000000000000
11107420000000000000000000000000000000000000000000000000000000000000000000000000
11107430000000000000000000000000000000000000000000000000000000000000000000000000

```
1110744000000000000000000000000000000000000000000000000000000000000000000
1110745000000000000000000000000000000000000000000000000000000000000000000
111074600000000000001000000000000000000000000000000000000000000000000000
111074700000000000000000000000000000000000000000000000000000000000000000
111074800000000000000000100000000000000000000000000000000000000000000000
111074900000000000000000000000000000000000000000000000000000000000000000
111075000000000000000000000000000000000000000000000000000000000000000000
111075100000000000000000000000000000000000000000000000000000000000000000
11107520000000000000000000000
111090100000000000000000000000000000000000000000000000000000000000000000
111090200000000000000000000000000000001000000000000000000000000000000000
111090300000000000000000000000000000000000000000000000000000000000000000
111090400000000000000000000000000000000000000000000010000000000000000000
111090500000000000000000000000000000000000000000000000000000000000000000
111090600000000000000000000000000000000000000000000000000000000000000000
111090700000000000000000000000100000000000000000000000000000000000000000
111090800000000010000000000000000000000000000000000000000000000000000000
111090900000000000000000000000000000000000000000000000000000000010000000
111091000000000000000000000000000000000000000000000000000000000000000000
111091100000000000000000000000000000000000000000000000000000000000000000
111091200000000000000010000000000000000000000000000000000000000000000000
111091300000000000010000000000000000000000000000000000000000000000000000
111091501000000010000000000000000000000000000000000000000000000000000000
111091700030000000000000000000000000000000001000000000100000000000000000
111091800000000000000000000000100000000000000000000000000000001000000000
111091900000000000000000000020100000000000000000000000000001000000000002
111092000000000000000000000000000000000000000000000000000000000000000000
111092100000000000000000100000000000000000000000000000000000001000001000
111092200000000000000000000000000000000000000000000000000000000000000000
111092300000000000000000000010000000000000000000000000000000000000000000
111092400000000000000010000000000000000000000000000000000000000000000000
111092500000000000000000001000000000000000000000000000000000000000000000
111092600000000000000000000000000000000000000000000000000000000000000000
111092700000000000000000000000000000000000000000000000000000000000000000
111092800000000000000000000000001000000000000000000000000000000000000000
111092900000000000000000000000000000000000000001000000000000000000000000
111093000000000000000000000000000000000000000000000000000000000000000000
111093100000000000000000100000000000000000200000000000000000000000000000
111093200000000000000000000000000000000000000000000000100000000000000000
111093300000000000000000000000000000000000000000000000000000000000000000
111093400000000000000000000000000000100000000000000000000001000000000000
111093500000000000000000000000000000000000000000000000000000000000000000
111093600000000000000000000000001000001000001010000000001000000000000000
111093700000000000000000000000000000000000000000000000000000000000000000
111093800000000000000000000000000000000000000000000000000000000000000000
111093900000000000000000000000000000000000000000000000000000000000000000
111094000000000000000000000000000000000000000000000000000000000000000000
111094100010000000000000000000000000000000000000000000000000000000000000
111094200000000000000000000000000000000000000000000000000000000000000000
111094300000000000000000000000000000000000000000000000000000000000000000
111094400000000000000000000000000000000000000000000000000000000000000000
111094500000000000000000000000000000000000000000000000000000000000000000
111094600000000000000000000000000000000000000000000000000000000000000000
111094700000000000000000000000000000000000000000000000000000000000000000
111094800000000000000000000000000000000000000000000000000000000000000000
111094900000000000000000000000000000000000000000000000000000000000000000
111095000000000000000000000000000000000000000000000000000000000000000000
111095100000000000000000000000000000000000000000000000000000000000000000
11109520000000000000000000000
11120010614030204060402000802080210070401000202000306030003000002000501
11120020100002000000000000200000100010104010100010100010202010100010005
1112003010100040301010002010001000400010001000030200000002000000000000
11120040300000001010400010102020002000001000000030002010000000002010002
11120050300010301030101000201000202000201000203000102010105000001000103
11120060002000403000000000101000100000100010301020002010002010100000100
11120070000000200010302000000000000000030200000000000100000102010000010 2
1112008000200000010101000104040100010102010400010401000000030102020200
11120090000000000202000100000100000000000200000103010000000000101000200
11120100030002000000010000000200010100000002020103030003010101010103010 0
11120110100020000000201010200000000000010000030200000100020201010004000 1
11120120002060001000201000003020200000200000000100000001000000000000000 0
11120130301040201000305010001020001010200030102000005000001030302010001
11120140001010100000100010000010100000203000102000100000000000000100030 2
11120150300030201030402050200040400020204010104000003010201000201030302
11120160302030404000002020101020503010100020000000001020001010101010100
11120170405070200000001000000020204030202030400020302020302020000020100
11120180101000000010001000001020000000000000000200000100010001040001000 1
11120190000000000000000000000100000000000010000020000010000000200010101 00
11120200000010000000100020102000001000003000101000000000101000101040300
11120210006010302010100000200010000030200010100000000000010100010000000 0
11120220000030201000001010100020102030102000301030000005000108000000000 0
11120230002000000010301010103020000010200010200000103030105020000000001
11120240201000000010101020101010102000100000001020401010002010300000001
11120250101000101000100000202000101010101000000010001050505040302020302
11120260301030502050200010200030501020001020000000000000000000000000001
11120270000000000010002000000010002010100000101000000000000001000101000 0
11120280700020000000001000000010000020000000000010001030100010201020102
11120290101000002020103000403000201000000000000100000000000000301000102 01
11120300000000000000000003010103000303010100000000202010000000000000000 0
11120310101000003000100000001000100000101000000000000101000301000100000 0
11120320000000000000000000010200000000000000004000000000000000000100030002 0001
11120330000010002010000010002010201010002000200010000010200010002000200
11120340201030200000000000000000010000000001000000001000000001000000001 0000
11120350100000000000000000000000000200000100000000000000100000500050000
11120360103000200000000000000000000010000000000000000000000000101020408
11120370004000200030001000101000001040002000003000200010101010000020301
11120380000050001000400010102010000020400000100010000000101010200030001
11120390001020201030106030000040002010001000101000000001000101010300000 0
11120400000000010001000200030300010100010102010100020001030101000100001
11120410100000005030203010001010102010102030402030201000400000202000202
11120420001010001000102010003010102020000000201020002000201020001020000
11120430001000200020104020102050307030102030000000205010003000001030401
11120440200000200010200010200020002010201010101000201000000010001000101
11120450106000001020701020201020102010201000101000403000203000100000100
11120460202030001000302000301000101030203010001010003040100030001010103
11120470000030101020101010000000003010001020003000101000102000000000200
11120480000002030101020100000000020000000001010903020001010400010102 01
11120490000001010203030302020300010003020100000000000020002030100000102
11120500102000000000000000001020101030000010102000200010301000000010001
11120510101000001030002010201010202010100000000020101010301010000000300
111205200010002010202010100
11122010511000208030703000507060108030201010102000500030002000002000500
11122020000000200030000010200000100000004060000000103000002010003110304
11122030602010300010100000001000000020202020100010101010001000000000000
11122040001010001040500030201010000020000000001000004020001020001000102
11122050100000000000000000001020001000000000100010002010500000000020501
11122060002000604020204000501030200000400000000200030101000101010000000 0
11122070101010000010201000000000000000000101010000010001010500010100000 0
```

```
1112208000000030100000100010301020000010202020001010000020206030107000 1
11122090000030001020201010100000200000003010000030202000000000001000000
11122100000100200000000000000000010001000000010100010201010100000010204
11122110200010100000000030300000100000100010001000001000302000400020003
11122120000010002010104000000104000003010100000100010000010000000102010 0
1112213000040101020001010001010000000002000101020501010200010000000020000
1112214010602000000000000001000100010001000000000000000000000000001000100
1112215020000010204000004000200030003030101000003000002010000010201000 1
11122160201020301000000000000001000100000000000200010000010200000000 10001
1112217000200020100000000000000001000001000002030000000000100020100000000
1112218010001010000000200000000100010000010000000000000000000200000000 0
1112219000000000000000000100000000000000000000000000001010000000200000000
1112220000001000000000000302000100010000000000001010000000100000003060200
1112221010203020000000000000001000000000000000000100000000010100000000000
1112222000100000000000000000000100000002010000000000000000000020000000000
1112223000101000100000000201000001040000000200020500020000001020000030100
1112224040100000000000000010001010601000000000000001020000000000000200000000
1112225010100000103030300000100020302030001000100010101020103010201010 2
1112226030102010302000000000010000000001000100010003000000001020000000001
1112227000400000000000000010000000000020000010001000001000001000000000000
1112228000000000000000000100000000000000000000020000000202020000010200 01
1112229020102000000000010000010000000100000000000000000000000000400000001
1112230000000000000000000001000000000000001000000000000000000001000000000
1112231000001010000000000000100000000000000000000010000000001000200000000 0
1112232000000000000000000000000000000000000000000000000000000000000000000
1112233000000000100000000010001000000000000003000000000100010000000000001
1112234010002020100000000000000000000000000000000000000000000000000000000
1112235000000000000000000000000000000100000000000000020000000000000010100
1112236010100000030000000000000000000000000000000000000000000000300020212
1112237000502020104000700000100000000000001000000000200000000001000000020 1
1112238000301000000000000000010000000000000000001000000000000000502000201 00
1112239010000000002000101000000000010201010002000000010000010100000000 0
1112240000000000101000000000000000001020100000000005000001000003000100000 0
1112241000100000000000000001000000000000000001000001000001020000010100000 0
1112242000000005000003000000000000000002000000010000000203000000000000000
1112243000000000100010100000000102000100000000010100020000000001020100 00
1112244010000000000000001030000000000100010000000000000000000000000000000
1112245000100000002000000020000000100020100010100000201000001000100000 0
1112246000000000100000000000000001000100000100000000000000030001000000000 0
1112247000100010201000000000000000000000000000000000000000000000000000000
1112248000001000000000010000000000001000001000001030001000101010100000000
1112249010000000000000200000100000201010001000101000000000000000000000100
1112250000200010001000000000000000000000002000000000000000100000000000002
1112251000100000200010101010001000000000000000001000100000000000000000000100
11122520001000002000101000200
1112301000000000001010000000000001000000000000000000000000000000001000100
1112302000000000000000000010000010000000000000000000000000000000100000000
1112303000000000010000000000000100000200000000100000001000000000000000000
1112304000000000000000000000000000000000000020000000100000001000000000 0
1112305010000000000000000000000000000000000010000000000000000000000000000
1112306000000000100000000000002010000000000010000000000000000300010000000 0
1112307000000000000001000000000000000000000000000000000000000000000000000
1112308000000000000000000001010000000000000010000000000000010000200000 0
1112309000000000000020000010000010000000000000000000000000000001000001000 0
1112310010003000000000000000010100000000000000000000000000000101000000000
1112311000000000000000001000000000000000100000000000000000000000000000000
1112312000000000100000200000000000000000101010001000000000000000000001020000
1112313010001000100000000000000000000000100000000010000000000000000000000
1112314000000000000000000000000000000000000000000000000000000000000000100
1112315000000000001000001000000010000000000000000100000000000000000000000
1112316000000000000000000000000100010000200000000000000000010000000000001
1112317000000000000000000000000001000000000000001000000000000000000000001
1112318000000000000100000000000000000001000000000000000000000000000000000
1112319000000000000000000000000000000000000000000000000000000000000000000
1112320000000000000000000000000001000000000000000000000000000000000010000
1112321000000000000000000000000000000000000000000000000000000000000000000
1112322000000010000000000000001000000010000000000001000000000000000000000
1112323000000000000000000000000001000000000000000000000000002010000000000
1112324000000010000000000000000000000000100000000000000000000000000000000
1112325000000000000000000000000000000000000000000000000000000001000000000
1112326000001000000000000000000000000000000000000000001000000000100000000
1112327000000000100000000000000100000000000100000000000000000000000000000
1112328000000000000000000000000000000000000000000000000000001000101000000
1112329010000000000101000000000000000000000000000000000000000000100000000
1112330000000000000000000000000000000000000000010000000000000000000000000
1112331000000000000000000000000000000000000000000000000000000001000000000 0
1112332000000000000000000000000000000000000000000000000000000000000000000
1112333000000000000000000000001000000000000000000000000000000000000000000
1112334000000000000000100000000001000000000000000000000000000000000000000
1112335000000000000000000000000000000000000000000000000000000000000000000
1112336000000000000000000000000000000000000000000000000000000000000000000
1112337000000000000000000000000000000000000000000000000000000000000000000
1112338000000000000000000100000000000000000000000000000000000000000010000
1112339000100000000000000000000001000000000000000000000000000000000000000
1112340000000000000000000000000000000000000000000001000000000000000000000
1112341000000000000000000000000000000000000000000100000000000000200000001
1112342000000000000000000000000000000001000000000000000000000000001000000
1112343000000000000000100000000000000002010000000000000000000000000000100
1112344020000000000000000000000000000000000000000000000000000000000000001
1112345000000000000000000000000000000000000000000000000000000000000000000
1112346000100000000000000000001000000000000000000000000000000100000000000
1112347000000000000000000000000000010000000000000000000000000000000000000
1112348000000000000000000000000000000000000000000201000000000000000000001
1112349000000000000000000000000000000000000000000000000000000000000000100
1112350000100000000000000000000000000000000000000001000000000000000000000
1112351000000000100010001000000000000001000000000000000101000000000000000
11123520001000000000000010000
1112501000000000000000000000000000000000000000000000000000000000000000000
1112502000000000000000000000000000000000000000000000000000000000000000100
1112503000000000000000000000000001000000000000000000000000000000000000000
1112504000000000000100000000000000000000000000000000000000000000000000000
1112505000000000000000000100000000000000000000000100000000000000000000000
1112506000000000000000000000000000000000000000000000001000000000000000000
1112507000000020000000000000000000000000000000000000000000000000000000000
1112508000000000000000000000000000000000000000000000000000000000000000000
1112509000000000000000000000000000000000000000000000000000000000000000000
1112510000000000000000000000000000000001000000000000000000000000000000000
1112511000000000000000000000000000000000000000000000000000000000000000000
1112512000000000000000000000000000000000000000000000000000000000000000000
1112513000000000000001000000000000000000000000000100000002000000000000000 00
1112514000000000000000000000000000000000000000000000000000000000000000000
1112515000000000000000002000000000000000000000000000000000000000000000000
1112516000000000000000000000000000000000000000000000000000000000000000000
1112517000000000000000000000000000000000000000000000000000000000000000000
1112518000000000000000000000000000000000000000000000000000000000000000000
1112519000000000000000000000000000000000000000000000000000000000000000000
1112520000000000000000000000000000000000000000000000000000000000000000000
1112521000000000000000000000000000000001000000000000000000000000000000000
1112522000000000000000000000000000000000000000000000000000000000000000000
1112523000000000000000000000000000000000000000000000000000000000000000000
```

220


```
11125240000000000000000000000000000000000000000000000000000000000000000
11125250000000000000000000000000000000000000000000000000000000000000000
11125260000000001000000000000000000000000000000000000000000000000000100
11125270000000000000000000001000000000000000000000000000000000000000000
11125280000000000000000000000000000000000000000000000000000000000000000
11125290000000000000000000000000000000000000000000000000000000000000000
11125300000000000000000000000000000000000000000000000000000000000000000
11125310000000000000000000001000000000000000000000000000000000000000000
11125320000000000000000000000000000000000000000000000000000000000000000
11125330000000000000000000000000000000000010000000000000000000000000000
11125340000000000000000000000000000000000000000000000000001000000000000
11125350000000000000000000000000000000000000000000000000000000000000000
11125360000000000000000000000000000000000000000000000000000000000000000
11125370000000000000000000000000000000000000000001000000000000000100000
11125380000010100000000000000000000000000000000000000000010201050101000
11125390000000000040001010000000100020000000000000100000000000000000000
11125400000000000000000010100000001000000000000000000000000000100000000
11125410001000000000000000000000000000000000000000000000000000000010000
11125420001000000100020001000000000200000100000000000000000000000000000
11125430000000000000000000001000000000000000100000000020000000000000100
11125440000000000000000000100010001000000000000000000000000000000000001
11125450000000000000000000000000000000000000000000000000000000000010000
11125460000000002000000000001000000000000000000000000000200000000000000
11125470000000000000000000000000000000001000000000000000000000100000000
11125480000000000000000200010000000000000000000001000000000000000000000
11125490000000000000000000000000000000000000000000000000000000000000000
11125500000000000000000000000001000000000000000000000000000000000000000
11125510000000000000000000000000000000000000000000000000000000000000000
11125520000000000000000000000
11126011017141031211204050609080414040901030401010606020207000203010600
11126020102030500070001020401070003060412040201010104050102040502071408
11126030403000807050401010302000202030302030302050203020104050000000302
11126040100030100052101100501030302020008010302050210010005020000020203
11126050604030501010000010001020401010004000100010004010415040201070407
11126060201030605020209000202010103040101030204020103050304020202000100
11126070101000102000100020000000000020100040900000002010002020001020001
11126080503000708000408010504030002040101030102030500010303090305080101
11126090100010105020401010100010600020003010001010102010100000000000200
11126100005010100000100010001020204000404050205030303020001020201030304
11126110105000100000002070301000104000000000202010100030608010301070100
11126120002060101020303000101030301080200000000020000020101010101010300
11126130111100305040405000102010201030300030303020204010503040406020203
11126140007000200000000000100000100000001000000010000000000010003010100
11126150400020200020802050103010401000904030001010300020100020200040300
11126160401040306000101010100010108030300010101000001050407010100010001
11126170004000202000002000001020301010005030401040004010400010203010001
11126180300010002000000050102030003020000000000020000000100000000020201 03
11126190100020100000000000500000000010101000000040109000002000502000001
11126200300000001000101020000000001020000010001000000010102010104060401
11126210500030101010101020000020002010000000203000301000002000000000100
11126220100030203000001030201000000040101010101030200000001020000010000
11126230102000100020000000204030406000100060403030305050003000102000102
11126240101030001030200030301000502000302020002000505010104020202000002
11126250101010005030501010504030508010701030100010001050101030304060202
11126260202020906020101000101040001000102040200010203000300020102020106
11126270201000002010401050200040202030201020202000104020100000000102010 0
11126280000000100010000000000000001000000100000202000000030203000100030000
11126290104010103010003010101010400010101010001010001000000010201000101
11126300100000001000000030101000001000200020001000101000100000000000201
11126310102000001000201050000010203030000000000010000020102010100000100
```



```
11126320000000000000000000000000101000000000000000000000001000100000103 0001
11126330003010001000100010101080000020102010502000101000301030200000100 02
11126340200010200010002010101000100000000000000000100000100010104000100
11126350501000200000000000000000000000103000201000001010300000000010200 0400 04
11126360008010300030002000000000100000102000000000000000000000702041920
11126370107020401010107040202010000000010010104060709060104110007080306
11126380110060406110305010505010201000301010104020103041002382005250412
11126390503031105160608140206050309051305001002040204030103040303010000
11126400605030001020002050303040405030701020202200609030118110805070503
11126411004000203041306020404030104000101040706020109011704090502060607
11126420206060601060602040603010806131605040303050714131101050402020104
11126430103020002030804040002030701010402040305050311130603020503100703
11126440202010307040102000700070005030204010402000302010101000000000209
11126450703020512041007050303060403030401010301010300030106080205030500
11126460301020105010205010500060101000405020307030101090401020300020601
11126470200020603040100030000000101020602000000010001000104040306030100
11126480001040302020003030000050112040000080101260303010301060200050604
11126490200070301010001000204000102060303060102010001050102010200000403
11126500107020300060000000100030203000103000503000303040403000101020102
11126510204030303000002020001020001000203020100020101030100000303020100
1112652010201040302050105060 2
11137010000000000000000000000000000000000000000000000000000000000000000
11137020000000000000000000000000000000000000000000000000000000000000000
11137030000000000000000000000000000000000000000000000000000000000000000
11137040000000000000000000000000000000000000000000000000000000000000000
11137050000000000000000000000000000000000000000000000000000000000000000
11137060000000000000000000000000000000000000000000000000000000000000000
11137070000000000000000000000000000000000000000000000000000000000000000
11137080000000000000000000000000000000000000000000000000000000000000000
11137090000000000000000000000000000000000000000000000000000000000000000
11137100000000000000000000000000000000000000000000000000000000000000000
11137110000000000000000000000000000000000000000000000000000000000000000
11137120000000000000000000000000000000000000000000000000000000000000000
11137130000000000000000000000000000000000000000000000000000000000000000
11137140000000000000000000000000000000000000000000000000000000000000000
11137150000000001000000000000000000000000000000000000000000000000000000
11137160000000000000000000000000000000000000000000000000000000000000000
11137170000000000000000000000000000000000000000000000000000000000000000
11137180000000000000000000000000000000000000000000000000000000000000000
11137190000000000000000000000000000000000000000000000000000000000000000
11137200000000000000000000000000000000000000000000000000000000000000000
11137210000000000000000000000000000000000000000000000000000000000000000
11137220000000000000000000000000000000000000000000000000000000000000000
11137230000000000000000000000000000000000000000000000000000000000000000
11137240000000000000000000000000000000000000000000000000000000000000000
11137250000000000000000000000000000000000000000000000000000000000000000
11137260000000000000000000000000000000000000000000000000000000000000000
11137270000000000000000000000000000000000000000000000000000000000000000
11137280000000000000000000000000000000000000000000000000000000000000000
11137290000000000000000000000000000000000000000000000000000000000000000
11137300000000000000000000000000000000000000000000000000000000000000100
11137310000000000000000000000000000000000000000000000000000000000000000
11137320000000000000000000000000000000000000000000000000000000000000000
11137330000000000000000000000000000000000000000000000000000000000000000
11137340000000000000000000000000000000000000000000000000000000000000000
11137350000000000000000000000000000000000000000000000000000000000000000
11137360000000000000000000000000000000000000000000000000000000000000000
11137370000000000000000000000000000000000000000001000000000000000000000
11137380001010000000000000000000000000000000000000000000000000300000000
11137390001000000000001000000000000000000000000000000000000000000010000
```

1113740000000000000000000000010000200000000000010000000010000100000000002
1113741000000000000000000000000000000000000000000000000010000101000000001
1113742000000000101000000000000000000200010000000000000000000000000000000
1113743000000000000000000000001000000000000000000000000000000000000001000000
1113744000000000001000000000000000000000000000000000000000000000000000001
1113745000000000000000000000000000000000000000000000000000000000001000000
1113746000000000000000000000000000000000000000000000000100000000000000100
1113747000000000000000000000000000000000000000000000000000000000000000000
1113748000000000000000000000000000000000000000000000000000000000000000000
1113749000000000000000000000000000000000000000000000000000000000000000000
1113750000000000000000000000000000000000000000000000000000000000000000000
1113751000000000000000010000000000000000000000000000000000000000000000000
111375200000000000000000000000
1113801020103000000201000000010101020100001000000000000000100000001000000
1113802000000000000000000000000000000100010000000000000000000100000000001
1113803010000002000100000010000000000001000000000000000000001010000001000
1113804000000000000000000100000100000000000000000010000000000000000000001
1113805000000000100000000000000000000000000000100000010000000000000000100
1113806000001000000000000000000000000000000000000000000000000000100000000
1113807000000000000000000000000000000000000000000000100000001000000020000
1113808000000000000000000030000000000000001000000000000000000000000001010
1113809000100000000000000010000000000000000000000000000000000000000000000
1113810001000000000000000000100000000000000000000000000000000200000001000
1113811000000000000000000020001000000000000000000000000000000000000000000
1113812000000001000000000000000000000000000000000000000000000000001000000
1113813000000000001000200000200000010101000000000001020000000010000000000
1113814000000030000000000010000000000001000000000000000000000000000000001
1113815010000010000010001000020000000000000000000000000000000010000000000
1113816000000000000000000000000000000000100000000000000002000100000000000
1113817000101000000000000000000002010000000000000000000000000000000000000
1113818010000000000000000000000000000000000000000000000000000000000000000
1113819000000000000000000000000000000000000000000000000000000000001000000
1113820000000000010001000000100000000000000000000000000001000001020000000
1113821000001000000000000000000000000000000000000000000000000000000000000
1113822000000000000000000000100000000000000000000000000000000000000000000
1113823000000001000000000000000000001000000100010000000000000000000010000
1113824020001000000000000000000000000000000000000000000100000000000000001
1113825000100000100000000001000000000000000100000000000000000000000000000
1113826000000000100000000000000000000000000000000000000000000000000000000
1113827000000000000000000000000100000000000000000000000001000000000000000
1113828000000000000000000000000000000000000000000000000000000000000000000
1113829000100000000000000000000000200000000000000000000000000000000010000
1113830000000000001000000000000000000000010000000000000000000000000000000
1113831000000000000000000000000000000000000000000000000000000000000000000
1113832000000000000000000000000000000000000000000000000000001000000000000
1113833000000000000000000000000000000000000010000000000000101000000000000
1113834000000000000000000000000000000000000000000000000000000000000000000
1113835000000000000000000000000000000000000000000000010000000000000000000
1113836000001000000000000000000000000000000000000000000000000000000000003
1113837000100010000000000000000000000000100000000001000000000000000000000
1113838000000000000000000000000000000100000000000000000001000000000000000
1113839000001000000001010001000000000000000000000000000000000000000000000
1113840000000000000000000000000000000000000000000000000000000000000000000
1113841000000000000000000000000000000000000100000000000000000000000000000
1113842000000000000000000000000000000000000000000000000000100000000000000
1113843000000000000000000010000000000100000000000000000100000000001000000
1113844000100000000000000000000000000000000000000000000000000010000000000
1113845000000000000001000000000000000000010000000000000000000000000000001
1113846000000000000000000000000000000000000000100000000000000000000001000000
1113847000000000000000000000000000000000000100000001000000000000000000000
1113848010000100000000000000000000000001000000000000000000001000000000000
1113849010000100010000000100000100000100000001000000100000010000001000000
1113850010000000000000000000000000001000000000000000000001000000010000000
1113851000000000010000000100010000000000100000000000000000000000000000000
11138520002000000000000000000
1114001000010000020000000100000001001000000000000000010000000000000000000
1114002000000000000000000000000000000000000000000000000000000000000000000
1114003000000100010000000100000200010000000000000000000000000000000000000
1114004000000000000001000000000000000000000000000000000100000000000000000
1114005000000000000000000000000000000000000000000000000000000000000000001
1114006000000000000000000000000000000000000000000000000000000000000000000
1114007000000000000000000000000000000000000000000000000000000000000000000
1114008000000000000000000000000000000000000100000000000010001020001000000
1114009000000000000000000000000000000000000000000000000000000000100000000
1114010000010000000000000100000000000000000001000000000000000000000010000
1114011000000000000000000000000000000000000000000000000000000000000000000
1114012000001000000000000000000000000000000000000000000000000000000000000
1114013000000000100000000000001000000000000000010000000000000000001000000
1114014000000000000000000000000000000000000000000000000000000000000000000
1114015000000000000000000000000000000000000000000000000000000000000000001
1114016000000000000000000000000000000000000000000000000000000000000000000
1114017000000000000000000000000000000000000000000000000000000000000000000
1114018000000000000000000000000000000000000000000000000000000000000000000
1114019000000000000000000000000000000000000000000000000000000000000000000
1114020000000000000000000000000000000000000000001000000000000000000000000
1114021000000000000001000000000000000100000000000000000000000000000000000
1114022000000000000000000000000000000000000000000000000000000000000000000
1114023000000000000000000000000000000000000000000000000000000000000000000
1114024000000000000000000000000000000100000000000000000000000000000000001
1114025000000000000000000000000000000000000000000000000000000000000000000
1114026000000000000000000000000000000000000000000000000000000000000000100
1114027000000000000000000000000010000000000000000000000000000000000000000
1114028000000000000000000000000000000000000000000000000000000000000000000
1114029000000000000000000000000000000000000000000000000000000000000000000
1114030000000000000000000000000000000000000000000000000000000000000000000
1114031000000000000000000000000000000000000000000000000000000000000000000
1114032000000000000000000000000000000000000000000001000000000000000000000
1114033000000000000000000000000000000000000000000000000000000000000000000
1114034000000000000000001000000000000000000000000000000000000000000000000
1114035000000000000000000000000000000000000000000000000000000000000010000
1114036000000010000000000000000000000000000000000000000000000000000000200
1114037000000000000000001010000000000000000000000000000001000000000000000
1114038000100000000000000000000000000000000000000000000000000000000000000
1114039000001000000000000000000000000000000000000000000000000000000000000
1114040000000000000000000000000000000000000000000000000100000000000000000
1114041000000000000000000000000000000000000000000000000000000000000000000
1114042000000000000000000000000000000000000000000000000000000000000000000
1114043000000000000000000000000000000000000000000000000000000000000000000
1114044000000000001000000000000000000000000000000000000000000000000000000
1114045000000000000000000000000000000000000000000000000000000000000000000
1114046010000000000000000000001000000000000000000000000000000000000000000
1114047000000000000000000000000000000000000000000000000000000000000000000
1114048000000000000000000000000000000000000000000000000000000000000000000
1114049000000000000000000000000000000000000000000000000000000000000000000
1114050000000000000000000000000000000000000000000000000000000000000000000
1114051000000000000000000000000000000000000000000000000000000000000000000
11140520000000001000000000000
1114101010300001020100000000000000000000000000000000000001020000000000000
1114102000000000000000000000000000000000010000000000010000000000001010100
1114103010000000000000000000000000000000000000000000000000000000000000000

11141040000000000100000000010000000000000000000001000000000000000000000000000000
11141050000000000000000000000000000000000000000000000000200000000000000000000000
11141060000000000000000000000000000000000000000000010000000000000000000010000000000
11141070001000000000000000000000000001000000000000000000001000000000000000000000000
11141080000000000000000000000000010000000000000000000100000000000000000000000000
11141090000000000000000000000000000000000000000000000000000010000000000000000000
11141100010000000000000000000000000001000000000000000101000000010000000000000001000000000
11141110000000000000000000000002000101000000000000000000000000000000000000000000
11141120000000000000000000000001010000000100000000000000000000000000000000000010000000000
1114113000000000000000000000000000000000000000010100000000000000000100000000000001010000000000
11141140000000000000000000000000000000000000000000000000000000000000000000000000
11141150000000000000000000000000000000000000000000000000000000000000000000000000
11141160000000000000000000000000000000000000000000000010000001000000000000000000
11141170000010000000000000000000000000000000000000000000000000000000000000000000
11141180000000000000000000000010000000000000000100000000000000000000000000000000001000000
11141190000000000000000000000000000000000000000000000000000000000000000000000000
11141200000000000000000000000000000000000000000000000000000000000000000010000000000
11141210000000000000000000100000000000000000000000000000000000000000000000000000
11141220000000000000000000000000000000000000000000000000000000000000000000000000
1114123000000000000000000000000001000000000000000000000000000101010000000000000000001000000000000
11141240000000000000000000000000000000200000000000000000000000000000000100000000000001
111412500000000000000000000010000000000000000000000100000000000000000000000000001000000000000
11141260000000000000000002000000000000000000000000000000000000000000000000000000001000000
11141270000000000000000000000000000000000000001000000000000000000000000000000000
11141280000000000000000000000000000000000000000000000000000000000000000000000000
11141290000000000000000000000000000000000000000010000000010000000000000000000001000000000
11141300000000000000000000000000100000000000000000000000000000000000000000000001000000000
11141310100000000000000000000000000000000000000000000000000000000000000000000000
111413200000000000000000000000000000000000000000000001000000000000000000010000000000000000001
11141330000001000000000000000000000000001000000000000000002000000000000000000000000000000
11141340000000000000000000000000000000000000000000000000000000000000000000000000
11141350000000000000000000000000000000000000000000000000000000000000000000000000
11141360002000000000000000000000000000000000000000000000000000000000000000000000000100
11141370000000000000000000000000000000200000000000000000000000000000000000000000
111413800010000000001000000000000000000000000000000000000000000000000000000000000000000100
11141390000000000000100000000000000000001000000001000000000000000000000000000000
11141400000000000000000000000000000000000000000000000000000000000000000000000000
11141410000000000000000000000000000000000000000000000000000000001000000000000000000
11141420000000000000000000000000000000000000000000000000000000000000000000000000
11141430000000000000000000000000000000000000000000000000000000000000000000010000000000
111414400000000010000000000000020000000001000000000000000000000000000000000000000
111414500000000000000000010000000000000000000000000000000000000000000000000000000010000
11141460000000000010000000010000000000000000000000000000000000000000000000000000
111414700000000000000000000000000000100000000000000000000000000000000000000000000000000100
11141480000000000000000000000000000000000000000000000000000000000000000000000000
111414900000000000000000010001000000000000000000000000000000000000000000000000000000001
11141500000000000000000000000000000000000000000000000000000000000000000000000000
11141510000000000000000000000001000000000000000000000000100000000000000000000000
111415200000000100000000000000000
11143010000201020000040000000200000201000000000000000000002000000010000
11143020100001000000000000000001010100010500010002020200000000100020100
11143030000000100000100020100000000000101000000000000000010002000000001
11143040002000100020300010100010000000000010000010101020000010000010100
111430502000001020101000000010000000100010000000000000000304010300020201
11143060001010000010002000000101000000000000000000000200000100000000101
111430700000000000100000000000000000000000010000010100000000202000000001
11143080100000000000102000000000101010000000000000000000000000100000201
11143090100010000010000010001000100000000000000000000000000000000000000
1114310010102030000000000000000010100010003000100000002010101000100010001
111431101000000000000100010000000000000000001000201000000000202000100010001
11143120000001010000001000000000000000000000000000000100000000000000000000000000
11143130002000010000000020000100000000100000000000000000001000000000010000000000
11143140000000000100000000000001010000000000000000000000100000000000000000000101
11143150200001000000000000000100000100000000010000000000000000001000000000000010000
1114316000000000000000000010000000000000000000000000000001000000000000010000000010000
11143170000001000100000000000000000000000000000000000000000000000000000000000000
11143180000000000010200001000000000000000000000000200000000000000000000000000000
11143190000000000000000000000000000000000010000001000000000010000000000000000000000
11143200000000000000000000001000000000000000100000000000000000000000000000000000000
11143210000000000000000000000000010101000000001000000100000000000000000000000000000
11143220000000000000000000000000000000000000000000000000000000000000000000000000
111432300000000000000000000000000000000000000000000000100010101010000000000000000010000
1114324000000100010101000000000000000000100000000000000000100000000000000100000000000000
11143250000000000000000000000000000000000000000000000000000000000000000000000000
111432600000000000000000000000000001000000000000000000000000000000000000000000000001000000010200
111432700000000000000000000000001000001000010000020100000000001000000000000000000000000
11143280000000000000000000000000000000000000000000000000000000000000000000000000
11143290000000000000000000000000000000000000000000000000000000000000000000010000000000
11143300000000000000000000000000000000000000000000000000000000000000000000000000
111433100000000000000000000010000200000000000000000000030000000000000000000000000000000000000100
111433200000000000000000000000000000000000000000000003010000000000000000000000000010000
11143330000000000000000000000000001000000000000000000001000000000000000000000000000
11143340101000000000000000000000000000000000001000000000000000000000000000000000000
11143350000000000000000000000000000000000000000000000000000000000000000000000000
111433600000000000000000000000000000000000000000000100000000000000000010000000000000000010202
1114337010010000000000000000000001000000000000000000000100000000000000101000100000000000000
111433800000000000000000000000000000000000000000100000000000000000000000000000100010001
1114339000000100000010000001000000000000100020000200000000000000000000000100000010000
1114340000000000000000000000000000000001000100000101010000002020000000000000000000001000000000000
1114341000010000000000000000000000000000000000100000000000000000000010100000000000000000100000010000
11143420000000000000000001000100000000000000002000000001000000000000000000000000000
1114343000000000000000000000000000000000000000000000000000000010000000000000000000000000000200
111434400001000200000000000000100020000000000000000001000100000001000000000000000000000000000100
1114345000000000000010002000010000000000000000000000000000010000000000000000000000000000010000
11143460100000000000000000000000000000000000000000000000000000000000000000000000
11143470000000000000000000000000000000000000000010000000000000000000000000000000000
11143480000000000000000000000000000000000000000000000000010000000000000000000000000000001
11143490000000000000000000000000000000000000000000000000000000000000000000000000
1114350000000000000000000000000000000100000000000000000000000000000000000000000000
11143510000000000000000000000000000000000000000000000000000000000000000000000000
111435200000000000000000000000000
11144010200010001000000100000000000000000100000000000000101000104000000101000000000000000100
111440201000100000100010100000000000000100000000101010000000000000000000000000001000001000000000000
1114403000000300000100000000000200000000000001000000000000000010000000001000000000000000000010100
1114404010000000101030000000000000000000000000200010100000000000020003100003000300010001000000
11144050000000000000000000000000000000000000000000000000200000000000000000000000000
1114406000000000000000000010000000101000000000000000000000100000200010001000000000000000000
11144070000000000000000000000000000000000000000000000000100000000000000000000000000
111440800000010002000000000000000000000000001000000300000000000000000000000000000000
11144090000000000000000000000000000000000000000000000000000000300000000000000000000
111441000000010000000000000000000000000000200100000010000000000000000000000000000000
11144110100000000000000000000000000000000000000000000000000000000000000000000000
11144120000001030000000000000000000000000000000000000000000000000000000000000010000
111441300000000000103000000000000000000000000000001010100000000000100000000000000000000001
11144140000000000000000000000000000000000000000000000000000000000000000000000000
11144150000000000000000000000000000100000000000000000000000000100000000000000000000000000
11144160000000000000000000000000000000000000000000000000100000000000000000000000000
11144170000000000000000000000000000000000000000000000000000000000000000000000000
111441800000010000000000000000000000000000000000000000000000000000000000000000000000000001
111441900000000000000000000000000000000010000000000000000000000000000000000000000

```
11144200000000000000000000000000000000000000100000000000000000000000000
11144210000000100000000000000000000000100000000000000000000000000000000
11144220000000100000000000000000000000000000000000000000000000100000000
11144230000000000000000000000000000000000000000000000000000000000000000
11144240001010000000000000100000000000000000001000000000000000000000000
11144250000000000000010000000000000000000000000000000000000000000000000
11144260000000000000000000000000000000000000000000000000000000000000000
11144270000010000000000000000000000000000000000000000000000000000000000
11144280000000000000000000000000000000000000000000010000000000000000000
11144290000000000000000000000000000000000000000000000000000000000000000
11144300000000000000000000000000000000000000000000000000000000000000000
11144310000000000000000000000000000000000000000000000010000000000000000
11144320000000000000000000000000000000000000000000000000000000000000000
11144330000000000000000000001000000000000000000000000000000000000000000
11144340000000000000000000000000000000000000000001000000000000000000000
11144350000000000000000000000000000000000000000000000000000000000000000
11144360000000000000000000000000000000000000000000000000000002000000300
11144370000000100000002000100000000010000000000000100000000000000010000
11144380000000000000000000000000000000000000000000000000000010100000000
11144390200000000000000000000000000000000000000000000000000000000000000
11144400000000000000000000000000000000000000000000000000000000000000000
11144410000000000000000000000000000000000000000000000000100000000000000
11144420000000000001000000000000000000000000000000000000000000000000000
11144430000000000000000000000000000000000000000001010000000000000000000
11144440000000000000000000000000000000000000000000000000000000000000000
11144450300000000000000000000000000000000000000000000000000000000000000
11144460000000000000000000000000000000000000000001000000000000000000000
11144470000000000000000000000000000000000000000000000000000000000000000
11144480000000000000000000000000000000000000000000000000000000000000100
11144490000010000000000000000000000000000000000000000000000000000000100
11144500000000000000000000000000000000000000000000000000000000000000000
11144510000000000000000000000000000000000000000000000000000000000000000
11144520000000000000000000000
11194010101010102020400020101020200030000000200000200000005000200010300
11194020100000000000000000000000100000101000001020002010103000100010100
11194030000000301000001000200000202000100020500020000000100030000000102
11194040502010000010300010200000100010001050201060101020000000000000000
11194050200010006010200000002010000000100000000000000000401000100020301 00
11194060102000201000000000000000201040000000001000000000300000001000101000200
11194070000020002010000020000000101000000000100000000000000020100000000100
11194080000000000000001010001010000010100010000000000000201010100010102
11194090000000000000000000400000001010000000000000000010001000200010100 00000
11194100003020000000200000000100010103010100010101000102020000010103
11194110000000000000101000100000000000000000000000000000102000102000000 02
11194120102020200000001000000000000000000000000000100000000000000000100
11194130002010100000000000000000001000000000000000001010000000000000000000000
11194140000000000000000000100000000000000000000000000000000000000000001
11194150000000002010000000100000000000000000000000101000000000000000001000000
11194160100010001000100000000000000000000000000000002000001000000000000
11194170000000000000000000000000000000000000000000000000000000000000001
11194180000000000010001000001000000000100000000000000000000000100010001 00
11194190000000000000000010000000000000000000000000000000000000100010001
11194200000000000000000000000000000000000000000000001000000000000000000
11194210000000000000000000000000000000000000000000000000000000000000000
11194220000000000000000000000000000000000000000000000000000000000000000
11194230000000000000000000100000000000000000001000000000000000000020000
11194240100000101000000000000000001000000000000000000000000000000000000
11194250000000000000000000000000100010000000000000000000000000000000000
11194260000000000000000000000000000000000000000000000020100020000000101
11194270000030000000000000000000101000002000000000000000000000000000000
```

```
11194280000000000000000000000000000000000000000000000000000000000000000
11194290000000000000000000000000000000000010000000000010000000000000000
11194300000000000000000000000000000000000000001000100000000000000000000
11194310000000000000000000000000000000000000000000000000000000000000000
11194320000000000000010000000000000000000100000000000000000000000000000
11194330000000000000000000002000000010000000100000000010000000000000000
11194340000000000010000000000000000000100000001000000000001000000000000
11194350000000000000100000000000000000000000001010000000000000000000000
11194360001000000020000000000000001000000000000000000000000000001000200
11194370000000010000020000000100000000000000000000000000000000000000000
11194380000000000000000000000000000000000000000000000000000000000000000
11194390000000000000000000000000000000000000000000000000000000000000000
11194400000000000000000000000000000000000000000000000000000000000000000
11194410000000000000000001000000000000000000000000000000000000000000000
11194420000000000000000000000000000000000000000001000000000000000000000
11194430000000000000000000000000000000000000000000000000000000000000000
11194440000000000000000000000000000000000000000000000000000000000000000
11194450000000000000000000000000000000000000000000000000000000000000000
11194460000000000000000000000000000000000000000000000000000000000000000
11194470000000000000000000000000000000000000000000000000000000000000000
11194480000000000000000000000000000000000000000000000000000000000000000
11194490000000000000000000000000000000000010000000000000000000000000000
11194500000000000000000000001000000000000010000000000000000000000000000
11194510000000000000000000000000000000000000000000000000000000000000000
11194520000000000000000000000
11207010606060812080613011317080605070305040504010604050112010312061000
11207020204000000020003040003041005090905040401050310080711050505060307
11207030400011901050105040704050504050702030602040106030105170203110112
11207040803050106090900020600010200010004080401130306090105010002040302
11207050700100211040500000102000201060004010605000305010401020505020400
11207060208040403030103000004070211000100020203000512040205050604000306
11207070101010404020501040108040201040201000302010202030104020104030807
11207080304000308000405010103020105010302010204020201030201030300020500
11207090301040200010500040200070301000003030000010206081010030507060100
11207100100020201030303000403020107010906030201050704010304000200020503
11207110101020500010001010104000104000203000104010001020503030601010005
11207120101080401030204040001030100010200000001010003030000030205000000
11207130115010103070101000000020205020302010505000103060007120204030005
11207140305040200000001010100000001000000000100000100010000000002000301
11207151800070409020102060101000002030200010100020202000100010001080206
11207160002030009000504030101000201010302050100010104020103010200010202
11207170103020506000400000000000000000000000000010000000100000000000002
11207180402020302010102070301010005010403030005010000000001010200000100
11207190000020001000000000401030001010001000201030003010001000300060208
11207200100020203060202010104010500010101030001000000000304000000000000
11207210000010100000000000000000000000000000000000000000000000000000000
11207220000000001000100000001000000000000000000000001000000000000000000
11207230000000301000002000101000004000000000101010000030001000003000000
11207240101050201020204000100030102050101000000010000020102010200000001
11207250101000002030101000002050303000201000000000100000000000000010101
11207260200000000000000000000000000000002000002000200000020001000200010100
11207270202000001030101010001020100010105000104000200000001000000000000
11207280000000004020002000100000000000000000000000000000002030001010000200
11207290000010100010000010000000002010101010203020102090200000300020100
11207300000000000000000000001010000000002000000000001000001020102000000100
11207310000020100000002000100010201000000000000000000000101000004000000 0
11207320101000100000100020003000200010000120300000200010101010005000000
11207330000000100000000000001000000000000010302010203000200000200010000000000
11207340100020000000100010000020000000002040003000000000102020001000100
11207350201000100000000010102000000000000000001000000010002040000000100060102
```

```
11207360006020100010000030402050002010403000104020002080100060904022012
112073701060207010000060000000400000101010001010000000001000000000010001
112073800000000000000000000000000000000000001000000000000000000000000000
112073900000000000000000000000000000000000000010000000000000000000000000
112074000000000000000000000000000000000000000000000000000000000000010000
112074101000000000000000000000000000000000000000000000000000000000000000
112074200000000000000000000000000000000000000000000000000000000000000000
112074300000000000000000000000000000000000000000000000000000000000000000
112074400000001000000000000000000000000000000000000000000000000000000000
112074500000000000000000000000000000000000000000000000000000000000000000
112074600000000000000000000000000000001010000000000000010000000000000000
112074700000000000000000000000100000000000000000000000000002000000000000
112074800000000100000000000000000000000000000000000003000200000301040100
112074900000101020101000000000010000003000010101020100000000010200000000
112075001010105000100000000000000000300000000000101010003000001000000001
112075101000000000000000010000000000000100000100000200010000000000010000
11207520001010301010000000000
112270100020000010000010100000001010102000000000000100000000300010201000
112270200000000000200000000000000000010000101000000001010600020100020000
112270300000000400010000000010000000000000000001000000000000001020000101
112270400000001010000000000000000000001000102000100000000010100000000000
112270500010000010100000000000000000000000000010000000000000000010101010
112270600000100010003000000000010003000000000000000010001010100000000100
112270701000100000000000000000001000000001000000000000000000000000000201
112270800000001000000000000000001000200000000000000000000020100010000000
112270900000000000001010100000101000000000000000000001000100010002010001
112271000000000000000000000000001020001000000010000000002000100000000001
112271100000000000000000000000000001000000000000200000000101010000010000
112271201000200000000000001000000000200000000000000000010100000000101000
112271300000000101000000000000000100000102010001000000000000000002000301
112271400000100000000000000000000000000000000000000000000000000000000010
112271501000301000100010100000000000000000000001000000000000000020100000
112271600000500030003000001000000102010002010001010000000000100010000010
112271702000201020000000000000000000000000000000000000000000000000000000
112271800010000000000000300000100000101000000001010000000000100000000000
112271900000100000000000000000000000000000000000001000000000000000000000
112272001000000000000000000000000000000000000000100000000000010100000000
112272100000000000000000000000100000000000000000000000000000000000010000
112272200000000000000000000000000000000000000000000000000000000000000000
112272301000000000000000000000000000000000000000000000000000000000010000
112272400000400000000010000000101000100000000000000000000000000000000000
112272500000000000000000000000000010000000000000000000000000000000000000
112272600000000000000000000000000000000000010000000100000000000000000000
112272700000000000000000000000020000000000000000000000000000001000000000
112272800000000020000010000000010000000000000000000000000000000000000000
112272900000000000000000000000000000000000000000100000000000100000200000
112273000000000000000000000000000100020000000000000100000000000100000000
112273100010000000000000000000000000100000000000000000000001000000000000
112273201000000000000000001000001000000000200000000000000001000000000000
112273300000000000000000000000000000000000000000100100000101000000000000
112273400000000000000000000000000000000000000000000000000000000000100000
112273500001000000000000000000000000000000000000000000000000000000040001
112273600030102000100000201000100000000000000000000000010001000102000102
112273700010100010201000000000000000000000000000000000000000000000000000
112273800000000000000000000000000000000000000000000000000000000000000000
112273900000000000000000000000000000000000000000000000000000000000000000
112274000000000000000000000000000000000000000000000000000000000000000000
112274100000000000000000000000000000000000000000000000000000000000000000
112274200000000000000000000000000000000000000000000000000000000000000000
112274300000000000000000000000000000000000000000000000000000000000000000
112274400000000000000000000000000000000000000000000000000000000000000000
112274500000000000000000000000000000000000000000000000000000000000000000
112274600000000000000000000000000000000000000000000000000000000000000000
112274700000000000000000000000000000000000000000000000000000000000000000
112274800000000000000000000000000000000000000000000000000000000000000100
112274900000000000000000000000000000000100000000010000000000000000000000
112275000000000000000000000000100000000000010000000000000000000000000000
112275100000000000000000000000000000000000000000000000000000000000000000
11227520000000100000001000000
112410101010200040202000000000000000200010101010000020100000100000000200
112410200000000000000200000000001010000000000000000200000201010100000000
112410301000103000100000000000010001000001000000001000100000000300000300
112410401010101000001000100000000000100000000100000100010000000000000000
112410501000001020100000000000000000000000000000002000000010000000001000
112410600010002000000000000000000010001000000010000000100010000000200000
112410700000100000000000000000000000000010000000000020000000000000010001
112410800000000000000000001010000000000000000000000000000000002000000200
112410900000000000000000100000001000000010000000000000300000000000010001
112411000000000001000002000000000000010000000000000001010000000000000000
112411100000000000000000001000000000000100000001000000000000000100030000
112411201000100010100000000000000000000000000000000000000000000000000200
112411300000000001010100000000000000000010000000000000000000000010000000
112411402010000000000000000000000001000000000100000000000000000000000000
112411500000102000000000000000000000000000000000000001000000000000000000
112411600000000001000002000000000000000000000001000000000000000000000000
112411700010000020000000000000000000000000000000000000000000000000000001
112411800000000000000000100000002000100010000000100000000000000000000000
112411900000000000000000000000000000000000000000000100000100000000000000
112412000000000000000000000000000000000000000000100000000000000000000000
112412100000000000000000000000000000000000000000000000000000000000000000
112412200000000000000000000000000000000000000000000000000000000000000000
112412300000000000000000000000000000000000000000000010000000000000000000
112412400010000000000000000000000000010000000000000000000000000000010000
112412500000000000000000100000000000000000010000010000000000000000000000
112412600000000100000000000000000000000000000000000000000000000000000000
112412700000000000000000000000000000000000000101000000000000000000000000
112412800000000001000000000000000000000000000000000000000000000000000000
112412900000000000000000000000000000000000000000000000100000000000000000
112413000000000000000000000000000000000000000000000000000000000000000000
112413100000000000000000000000010000000000000000000000000000000000000000
112413200010100000000000000000000000001000000000000000000000000100000100
112413300000000000000000000000000010000000000000000000000001000000000000
112413400000000000000000000000000000000000000001000000000000000000020000
112413501000000000000000000000000000000000020000000000000000010000000000
112413600010201000200000000000000000000000000000000000000000000020001000
112413700010001000000001000000000000000000000000000000000000000000000000
112413800000000000000000000000000000000000000000000000000000000000000000
112413900000000000000000000000000000000000000000000000000000000000000000
112414000000000000000000000000000000000000000000000000000000000000000000
112414100000000000000000000000000000000000000000000000000000000000000000
112414200000000000000000000000000000000000000000000000000000000000000000
112414300000000000000000000000001000000000000000000000000000000000000000
112414400000000000000000000000000000000000000000000000000000000000000000
112414500000000000000000000000000000000000000000000010000000000000000000
112414600000000000000000000000000000000000000000000000000000000000000000
112414700000000000000000000000000000000000000000000000000000000000000000
112414800000000000000000000000000000000000000000000000000000000000000100
112414900000000000000000000000000000000000000000000000000000000000000000
112415000000000000000000000000000001000000000000000000000000000000000000
112415100000000000000000000000000000000000000000000000000000000000000000
```

```
112415200000000000000001000000000
11258010000000000010101020002000000000000010000000000000000000000100000000000100
11258020000000000000000000000000000000000000200010002010000000000010000000001000 1
11258030100000000000000200000100000000000000000000000000000000000100000001010001
11258040001000000000001000000000000001000000000200000000000100000000000000000100
11258050000000000000000000001000000000000000000000101000000000101000000010100010 0
11258060101000000000000000000000000000000000000000000000000401000000000001000100
11258070000000000000000000001010000000000000000000000000000000000002000000000002
11258080001000201000101000000000000000000000001000100000000000000000000001010000
11258090000001000000000000010100000100000000000000000000000010202050100000000000
1125810000000000000100000000100000000000001 01.0000001010000000000000001010000 00
11258110001000000000000000010003000000000001000000001000000000010101020000000000
11258120000000000010000000000001000002000000000000000010001000000000000000000000
11258130000000000000010000000000000001000100000100000000100000000001010001010000
11258140100030000000000000000000000000000000000000000000000000000000000000000001
11258150200020001000000000000000001000000000000000010000020000000000000001000000
11258160000000000100010001000000010001000100000000100000000010001000000100000100
11258170101000000000000000000000000000000000000000000000000000000000000010000000 0
11258180000000000000001000201000000000000000000000001000100000000000000000000000
11258190000001000000000000000000000000000000000001000000000000000000000000010000
11258200000000000000000000000001000100000010000000000000000000000010000000000000 0
11258210000000000000000000000000000000000000000000000000000000000000000000000000
11258220000000000000000000000000000000000000000000000000000000000000000000000000
11258230000000000010001000000000000000000000000000000010000000000000000000000000
11258240100000000000000000000000000000000000000000000000000000000000000000010000
11258250000000000000000000000000000000000000000100000000000000000000000000000001
11258260000000000000000000000000000000000000000000000000000000000000000000000001
11258270000000000000000001000000000000000001000100020000001010010000000000000000
11258280000000000000000000000000000000000000000000000000000000000100000000000000
11258290000000000000000000000000000000000000000100000000100020000000000000000100
11258300000000000000000000000000000000000000000000000000000000000000000000000000
11258310000000000000000000000000000000100000000000000000000000000000000000000000
11258320000000000000000000000000000000000000000000000000000000000001000001000000 0
11258330000000000000000000000000000000000000000000000000100000000000000000000001
11258340000000000000000000000000000000000000000100000000000000000000000010000000
11258350000000000000000000000000000000000000000000000000000000000000000010000010100
11258360001010000010000000000101000000000000000001000200000000001000101000000201
11258370000000000010000000000000000000000000000000000000000000000000000000000000
11258380000000000000000000000000000000000000000000000000000000000000000000000000
11258390000000000000000000000000000000000000000000000000000000000000000000000000
11258400000000000000000000000000000000000000000000000000000000000000000000000000
11258410000000000000000000000000000000000000000000000000000000000000000000000000
11258420000000000000000000000000000000000000000000000000000000000000000000000000
11258430000000000000000000000000000000000000000000000000000000000000000000000000
11258440000000000000000000000000000000000000000000000000000000000000000000000000
11258450000000000000000000000000000000000000000000000000000000000000000000000000
11258460000000000000000000000000000000000000001000000000000000000000000000000000 0
11258470000000000000000000000000000000000000000000000000000000000000000000000000
11258480000000000000001000000000010000000000000000000000000000000000000000010000
11258490000000000000000000000000000000000000000001000000000000000100000000000000
11258500100000000000000000000000000000100000000000000000000000000000000000000100
11258510000000000000100000000000000000000000000000000000000000000000000010000000 0
112585200000000000000000000000000
11259010100000000000000000010001000000000000000000000000000000000000000000000000
11259020000000000000000000000000000000000000000000000000000001000000000000000000
11259030000000000000000000000000000000000000000000000000000000000000000000000000
11259040000000000000000000000000000000000000000000000000000000000000000000000000
11259050000000000010000000000000000000000000000000000000000000000000000000000000
11259060000000000000000000000000000000000000000000002000000000000100000000000000
11259070000000000000001000000000000000000000000000000000000000000000000000000000
11259080000000000000000000000000000000000000000000000000000000000000000000000000
11259090000000000000000001000000000000000000000000000000000000000000000000000000
11259100000000000000000000000000000000000000000000000000000000000000000000000000
11259110000000000000000000000000000000000000000000000000000000000000000000000000
11259120000000000000000000000000000000000000000000100000000000000000000000000000
11259130000000000000000000000000000000000000000000000000000000000000000000000000
11259140000000000000000000000000000000000000000000000000000000000000000000000000
11259150000000000000000000000000000000000000000000000000000000000000000000000000
11259160000000000000000000000000000000000100000000000000000000000000000000000000 0
11259170100010000000000000000000000000000000000000000000000000000000000000000000
11259180000000000000000000000000000000000000000000000000000000000000000000000000
11259190000000000000000000000000000000000000000000000000000000000000000000000000
11259200000000000000000000000000000000000000000000000000000000000000000000000000
11259210000000000000000000000000000000000000000000000000000000000000000000000000
11259220000000000000000000000000000000000000000100000000000000000000000000000000
11259230000000000000000000000000000000000000000000000000000000000000000000000000
11259240000000000000000000000000000000000000000000000000000000000000000000000000
11259250000000000000000000000000000000000000000000000000000000000000000000000000
11259260000000000000000000000000000000000000000000000000000000000000000000000000
11259270000000000000000000000000000000000000000000000000000000000000000000000000
11259280000000000000000000000000000000000000000000000000000000000000000000000000
11259290000000000000000000000000000000000000000000000000000000000000000000000000
11259300000000000000000000000000000000000000000000000000000000000000000000000000
11259310200000000000000000000000000000000000000000000000000000000000000000000000
11259320000000000000000000000000000000000000000000000000000000000000000000000000
11259330000000000000100010100000000000000000000000000000000000000000000000000000
11259340100000000000000000000000000000000000000000000000000000000000000000000000
11259350000000000000000000000000000000000000000000000000000000000000000000000000
11259360000000000000000000000000000000000000000000000000000000000000000000000000
11259370000000000000000000000000000000000000000000000000002000000000000000010000
11259380001010100000000000000000000000000000000000000000000000001000000000100010 0
11259390000000000010100000000000000010101020000000000000000000000000000000000000
11259400000000000000000000000000000000000000000000000010000000000000010001000 0
11259410000000000000000000000001000000000000010000000000000000020001000000000000
11259420101000000000100000000100010002000100000000000000000000020001000000000000
11259430000000000010000010000000000000000000000000010000000000000000000000000200
11259440000000000001000000000010101010000000000010000000000000000100000000000000
11259450000000000000010000000010000000000000000000000000000000000000000000000000
11259460000000000000000000002000100000000000000010000000000000010000000000000000 0
11259470000010000000000000000000000000000000000000000000000000000000000000000000
11259480000000000000000000000000000000000000000000000010000000000000000000000000
11259490000000000000000000000000000000000000000000000000000000000000000000000000
11259500000000000000000000000000000000000000000000000000000000000000000000000000
11259510000000000000000000000000000000000000000000000000000000000000000000000000
112595200000000000000000000000000
11262010000000000010100010100000000000002010000000000000100000000000000000000000
11262020100000000000000000000000000000001010101000000000100010101000000000000000
11262030000000000000001000000001000100000000000001000000100000000000000000000001
11262040000000000000001000001000000000000000000000000000000000000000000000000000
11262050000000010000000000000000000000000000000001000000000000000000000000000000
11262060000000000000100000000000000000001000000000010100000000000000000000000000
11262070000000000000000000000000000000000000000001000000002000000000000000000001
11262080000000001010000000000000000000000000000000000000001000000002000000000000
11262090100000000000000000000000000000000000000000000010000000000000000000000001
11262100000000000000000000000000000000000000000000000000000000100000000000000000 0
11262110000000000000000000000000000000000000000000000000000000100000000000000000 0
11262120000000000000000000000000000000001000000000000000000000000000000000000000
11262130100010100000000000000000000000000000101000000000000000000000000000020000
11262140000000000000000000000000000000000000000000000000000000000000000000000000
11262150000000000000000000000000000000000000000000000000000000000000000000000000
```

```
11262160000001000000000010000000000000000000001000000000000010000000000000000000000
11262170000000000000000000000000000000000000000000000000000000000000000000000000
11262180000000000000102000000000000000100000000000000000000000000000000000000000
11262190000000000000000000000000000000000000000000000000000000000000000000000000
11262200000000000000000000000000000000000000000000000000000000000000000000000000
11262210000000000000000000000000000000000000000000000000000000000000000000000000
11262220000000000000000000000000000000000000000000000000000000000000000000000000
11262230000000000000000000000000000000000000000000000000000000000000000000000100
11262240000000000000100000000000000000000000000000000000000000000000000000000000
11262250000000000000000000000000000000000000000000000000000000000000000000000000
11262260000000000000000000000000000000000000000000000000000000000000000000000000
11262270000000000000000000001000001000000000000000000000001000000000000000000000
11262280000000000000000000000000000000000000000000000000000000000000000000000000
11262290000000000000000000000000000000000000000000000000000000000000000000000000
11262300000000000000000000000000000000000000000000000000000000000000000000000000
11262310000000000000000000000000000000000000000000000000000000000000000000000000
11262320000000000000000000000000000000000000000000000000000000000000000000000000
11262330000000000000000000000000000000000000000000000000000000000000000000000000
11262340000000000000000000000000000000000000100000000000000000000000100000000000
11262350000000000000000000000000000000000000000000000000000000000000000000000000
11262360001000000000000000000000000000000000000000000000000000000000000001000000
11262370000000010000000000000000010000000000000000000000000000000000000000000000
11262380000000000000000000000000000000000000000000000000000000000000000000000000
11262390000000000000000000000000000000100000000000000000000000000000000000000000
11262400000000000000000000000000000000000000000000000000000000000000000000000000
11262410000000000000000000000000000000000000000000000000000000000000100000000000
11262420000000000000000000000000000000000000000000000000000000000000000000000000
11262430000000000000000000000000000000000000000000000000000000000000000000000000
11262440000000000000000000000000000000000000000000000000000000000000000000000000
11262450000000000000000000000000000000000000000000000000000000000000000000000000
11262460000000000000000000000000000000000000000000000000000000000000000000000000
11262470000000000000000000000000000000000000000000000000000000000000000000000000
11262480000000000000000000000000000000000000000000000000000000000000000000000000
11262490000000000000000000000000000000000000000000000000000000000000000000000000
11262500000000000000000000000000000000000000000000000000000000000000000000000000
11262510000000000000000000000000000000000000000000000000000000000000000000000000
11262520000000000000000000000000
11263010001000000101000010000001000000000000000000100000000001000000000000000000
11263020000000000000000000000000000000000000001000000000000100000000000000000010
11263030000000000000100010000000010100000000000000000000000000020000000000000000
11263040000000000000000002000000100001000000100000000000002020000000000000000000
11263050100000010101000000000000000000000000000000000000000100000000000000002
11263060000000000000000010000000000000000000000000000000000000000000000000000000
11263070000000000000000000000000000010200000000000000000000000000000000000000000
11263080002000000000001000010001010000000000000000000010000000010000000000010000
11263090000000000000000000000100000000100000000000000000000000001000000100000001
11263100100000000000000000000000000000010000000000000100010000000000020001000001
11263110001000000000000000000000000000000000000000000100000000000000000000000002
11263120000000000000000000000000000010000000000000000000000000000000100000100020 0
11263130000000010000000000000000000000000000000002000000000000000000000001010101
11263140000000000000000000000000000000000000000000000000000000000000000000000000
11263150000000000000000000000000000010000000000000000000000000000000000000000000
11263160000000000000000010000000000000000000000000000000000000000000000100000000
11263170000000010000000000000000000000000000000000000000000000000000000000000000
11263180000000000000000000000000000000000000000000000000000000000001000000000100
11263190000000000000000000000000000000000000000000000000000000000000010000000100
11263200000000000000000000000000000000000000000000000000000000000100000000000000
11263210000000000000000000000000000010000200000000000010000000000000000000000100
11263220000000000000000000000000000000000000000000000000100000000000000000000000
11263230000000000000000000000000000000000000000000002000000002000000000000000000
```

```
11263240000000000000000000000000000000000000000000000000000000000000000000000000
11263250000000000000000000000000000000000000000000000000000000000000000000000000
11263260001000000000000000000000000000000000000000100000000000000000000000000000
11263270000000000000000000000000000000000000000000000000000000000000000000000000
11263280000000000000000000000000001000000002000000000000000000000000000000000000
11263290000000000000000000000000000000000000000000000000000000000000000000000000
11263300000000000000000000100000000000000000000000000000000000000000000000000000
11263310000001000100000000000100000000100000000000000000000000000000000000000000
11263320000000000000000000000000000000000000000000000000000000000000000000000001
11263330001000200000000010000000000000000000000000000000000000000000000000000000
11263340000000000000000000000000000000000000000000000000000000000000000000000000
11263350000000000000000000000000000000000000000000000000000000000000000000000000
11263360000000010000000000000000000000000000000000100000000000000000000002
11263370000000000000000000000000000000000000000000000000000000000000000000000000
11263380000000000000000000000000000000000000000000000000000000000000000000000000
11263390000000000000000000000000000000000000000000000000000000000000001000000000
11263400000000000000000000000000000000001000000000000000200000000000000000000000
11263410000000000000000000000000000000000000000000000000000000000000000001000000
11263420000000000000000000000000000000000000000000000000000000000000000000000000
11263430000000000000000000000000000000000000000000000000000000000000000000000000
11263440000000000000000000000000000000000000000001000000000000000000000000000000 0
11263450000000000000000000000000000000000000000000000000000000000000000000000000
11263460000000000000000000000000000000000000000000000000000000000000000000000000
11263470000000000000000000000000000000000000000000000000000000000000000000000000
11263480000000000000000000000000000000000000000000000000000000000000001000000000
11263490000000000000000000000000000000000000000000000000000000000000000000000000
11263500000000000000000000000000010000000000000100010000000000000000000001000000
11263510000000000000000000000000010000000000000000000000000000000000000000000000
11263520000000000000000000000000
11264010300010207030002000003000001000100010000010200030000000000000000109010302
11264020000100020000000010000000401010100101040000000000000000000000030004000000
11264030000003010202000204000200010501010000000000000000000000000000050101000402
11264040001020001030300010000010100000000000000000100020102030200000000000000002
11264050100010003030100000101010000000004000000401020100000000000010101000000100
11264060200000101000000000030400000000000000020001010102000004000004000101000101
11264070000001000000002010200000000000000000000001000000010109010000010100000100 04
11264080001000000000000000010100000100000000100000300020100000000000010000020000
11264090000000001000000010100010100000000000000000000000010102010001010002 00
11264100001000000000000000200000101000000000000000101000100000000000000010000000 00
11264110100000100000200010000000000000000000000000000000001000000000000000000000 0
11264120000000100000001000000000000000000000000010000000000000010000000000000000
11264130001000001000001000000010000000000000000000020000000010000000010201010000
11264140000000000000000000000000000000000000000000000000000000000000000000000000
11264150100010000000000000010000000000000000000000200000000000000000000000000000 02
11264160000000000000000000000100000000000000000000000000000000000000000000000000
11264170002000100000000000000000000000000000000000000000000000000000000001010001
11264180200000101000101000000000000101000000000001000000000000000000000000000000
11264190000000000000000101000000000000000000000000000000000201000000000000000000
11264200000000000000000001000000001000000000000000000000000000000000000000000000
11264210000000020002000001000100000000000000000700000200010000000000001010200010000
11264220000010000000000000000000000000000000000000000000000000000000000000000000
11264230000000000000000000001000000000000010000000000000000000000000000000000000
11264240001010000010100000000200000100000000000000000001000000000000000000000000
11264250000000000000000000000000000001000000000000000000000000000000000000000000
11264260100000000000000000000000000100000000000000000001000000000000000000010002
11264270000010000000001000201000000000000000100000000000000000001010000000000000
11264280000000000000000000000000000100000000000001000000000000000000000000000000
11264290000000000000000000000000000000000000000000000000000000000000000000000000
11264300000000000000000100000000000000000000000000000000010000001000000000000000
11264310100000000000000100000000000000000000000000000000000000000001000100000000 0
```

```
11264320000000000000000001000001000000000000000100000000000000000001000100000000
11264330000000000001000000002010000000000000010000010100000000000000000000000000
11264340100000000100000100000000000000000000000000002000000000000000000000000000
11264350101000100000000000000000000000000000000000000100000000000000000000000000
11264360000000002000100000000000000000000000020000000000000000000000000101021103
11264370101000000000000001000000000000000000000001000000000000020000000000000000
11264380000000000000000000001000000000000000000000000000000000000000000001000000
11264390000000000000000000000000000000000000000000000000000000000000000000000000
11264400000000000000000000000001000000002000000000000000000000001000000000000000
11264410000000000000000000000000000000000000000000000000000000000000000100000000
11264420000000000000000000000000000000001000000000000000000000000000000000000000
11264430000000000000000000000000000000000000000000000000001000000000000000000000
11264440000000000000200000000000000000000000000000000000000000000000000000000000
11264450000000000000000000000000000000000000000000000000000000000000000000000000
11264460000000000000000000000000000000000100000000000000000000000000000000000000
11264470000000000000000000000000000000000000000000000000000000000000000001000000
11264480000000000000000000000000000000000000000000000000000000000000000000000000
11264490000000000000000000000000000000000000100010000000000000000000000000000000
11264500000000000000000000000000000000000000000000000000000000000000000000000000
11264510000000000000000000000000000000000000000000000000000000000000000000000000
11264520000000000000000001000000
11265010000001000100000010002010000000000000000200000001000000000000001020000000
11265020000000010100000000000000000000000002000000000000000000000000000001000000
11265030000000001010200000000010000000004020000000000000000102000000100000000103
11265040000000000010101000000010003000000000000102000000000203000000000000000001
11265050000002000000002000000001000000001000000100000000000000000000000101000300
11265060100000000000000000000000300000010000000000001000000200000010000000000001
11265070100000000000000000000010100000100000000000000006030000000100000001010000
11265080000000100000000000000000000000000000000000000000000101000000000000010000
11265090000000000000000000000000000002000000000000000000000000000000000001010000
11265100000000000001000000000000000000000000000000100010000000000000000001000000
11265110000000000000000000000000000000000000000000000000000000000000201000000000
11265120000001020000000000000000000000000000000000000000000000000000000000000000
11265130010100000000000000000000000000000000000100010100010000000000000001000000
11265140001000000000000000000001000000000000000000000000000000000000000000000000
11265150000000000000000000000000000000000001000000001000000000000000000100000000
11265160000000000000000000000000000000000000000000000000000000000000000001000000
11265170100000000000000000000000000000000000000000000000000000000000000000000000
11265180100000000000000000000000000000000001000000000000000000000000000000000100
11265190000100000000000000000000000000000000000000000010200000000000000000000001
11265200000000000000000001000001000000000000000000000000000000000000000000000000
11265210000000000000000000000000000000000002000000000000000000000000000000000000
11265220000000000010001000000000000000000000000002000000000000000000000000000000
11265230000000000000000000100000000000000000000000100000000000000000000001000100
11265240000000000000010000000000000000000000000000000000001000000000000000000000
11265250000000000000000000000000000000100000000000000000000000000000001000000000
11265260000000000000000000000000000000000000000000000000000000000000000000000001
11265270000000000000010000000000010100000000001000100000000010000000001000000000
11265280000000000000000000000000000000000000000000000003000000000000000000000000
11265290000000000000000000000000000000000000000000000001000000000000000000000000
11265300100000000000000000000000000000000000000000000000000000102000000000000000
11265310000000000000000000000000000001000000000000000000000000000000000000000000
11265320000000000000000000000000000000000000000000000000000000000000000000000000
11265330000000000000100010000000000000000000000000000000000000000000020000000000
11265340000000000000000000000000000000000000000001000000000000000000000000000000
11265350000000000000000000000000000000000000000000000000000000000000000000000000
11265360000000000000000000000000000000000000000000000000000000000000000000000300
11265370102000100000000100000000000000000000000000000000000000000000000000000000
11265380000000000000000000000000000000000000000000000000000000000000010000000000
11265390000000000000000000000000000000000000000000000000000000000000000000000000
```

```
11265400000000000000000000000000000000000000000000000000000000000000000100000000000
11265410000000000000000000000000000000000000000000000000000000000000000001000000
11265420000000000000000000000100000000000000000001000000000000000000000000000000
11265430000000000000000000000000000000000000000000000000000001000000000000000000
11265440000000000000000000000000000000000000100000000000000000000000000000000000
11265450000000000000000000000000000000000000000000000000000000000000000000000000
11265460000000000000000000000000000000000000000000000000000000000000000000000000
11265470000000000000000000000000000000000000000000000000000000000000000000000000
11265480000000000000000000000000000000000000000000000000000000000000000000000000
11265490000000000000000000000000000000000000000000000000000000000000000000000000
11265500000000000000000000000000000000000000000000000000000000000000000000000000
11265510000000000000000000000000000000000000000000000000000000000000000000000000
11265520000000000000000000000000
11268010200010103030400010101000102000000000000000000000101010001000000002000300
11268020000000010001000000000001000000100010000010000000000000000001000400000002
11268030001010301020100020101010001020003000000010000000000000000000000000000000
11268040000000000000020600070001030100010000001010001010000000000002010000000001
11268050204000201000000010000000000000000000000001020000000100030100000000030001
11268060000001000000000010000000000000000010000000000000000000000200000100000000
11268070101010100010000000000000000000000000000000010105000000000010000000000001
11268080201000000100000020001010200000003010100000010001000000000001000000000300
11268090000000000000101000000100000001010100000000000000001000000000000000000002
11268100000000000000000100000000000000000000000000000303000000000000020102010104
11268110402000000000020201010001010000000000000000000000000000000002000100010002
11268120000000000100000101010000000000000000000000000000000000000101000001020004 00
11268130002000000000000100000000001010101000000000000000100000001000001000000000
11268140200010000010000000000010000010001000000000000000000000000000000000000000
11268150000000000102010000000000000000000100000000000000100000000200020000000002
11268160000000000000000101000101000200000100000000000000000000000000000000000002
11268170000000100000000000000000000000001000000001000000000000000000000000010001
11268180100000000001010100000000000000000000000000000000000000000000000000000000
11268190000000000000000000000000000000000000000000000000000000000000000000000000
11268200000000000000000000000000002000010000000000001000000000000000000000000100
11268210002000201000020003000201000000030001000001000000000000003000000000000000
11268220000000000100000000000000020000000101000000200000000000000000000000000000
11268230000000000000000000000000001000000000001000100000000000000000000000010001
11268240000010000000000000000000020001000000000000010001000000000000010000000101
11268250000000000000000000000000010000000010000000000000000000000000000001000000
11268260001010100000000000000100000102000000000000000000000000000001000001010000
11268270000000000001000000000000000000000001000001000100010102000000101000000
11268280000000000001000000000000000000000000000003010000000000010100010000000
11268290000000100000100000000100010000000100000001000101010000000000000000000201
11268300000000000000000000000000000000000000101000000000000000000000000000000000
11268310101010101000002010100010202050000000000000010000000000000000000000000000
11268320000000000000000000000000000000000000001000000000000000000000001000000001
11268330000002020401000201040100000100010003010000010000000000000000000000010000
11268340000000000000000000000000010000000000000100010000000000000100010001000000
11268350200000000000000000000000000000000000000000000000000000000000000000020000
11268360002000000000000000100000000000000000000000000000000000000000000300010308
11268370100000000100000010202000000000000000100000000000000000000000000000000000
11268380000000000000000000000000000000000000000000000000000000000000000100000000
11268390000000000000000000000000000000000000000010000000000000000000000000000000
11268400000000000000000000000000000000000000000000000000000000000000000000000000
11268410000000000000000000000000100000000000000000000000000000000001000000000000 0
11268420000000000000000000000000000000000000000000000000000000000000000000000000
11268430000000000000000000000000000000000000000000000000000000000000000000000000
11268440000000000000000000000000000000000000000010000000000000000000000000000000
11268450000000000000000000000000000000000000000000000000000000000000000000000000
11268460000000000000000000000000000000000000000000000000000000000000000000000000
11268470000000000000000000000000000000000000000000000000000000000000000000000000
```

11268480000000000100000000000000000000000000000010000000000000001000000
11268490000000000000000000000000100000000000001000000000020001000000000
11268500101000000000000000000000000000000000000010000000100000000000000
11268510000000010000000000000010000000000000000000100000000000000000000
11268520000000000000000010000
11274010100010102000100000000000101000000000000000200000000000000010000
11274020000000100000000000002000000000000000000000100010000000000000000
11274030001000100000000000000000000000100000000000000000000000020000001
11274040100000000000200010000000001000000000000000001000000000000010000
11274050100000002010000000000000100010000000000000000010100010000000100
11274060000000000000001000101020001000000000000000000000000000000000001
11274070000000000000001000000000000000000000000000000010000000100000100
11274080000000100000000000000000000000000000001000000000100010100010100
11274090000000000000100010000000000000000000000000001000000000000010000
11274100000000000000100000000000000000000000100000001000000000101000000
11274110000000000000200000000000000000000000000000000000000000000010000
11274120000010000000101000000000000000000000000000000000000000000000000
11274130000000000000020000000000000000000000000000001000000000000010000000
11274140000000000000000000000000000000000000000000000000000000000000101
11274150000000001000000000000000100000000000000000000000000000000000000
11274160000000000000000010100000000000000000000010000010000000000000000
11274170000000000000000000000000000000000000000000000000000001000000
11274180000000000010000000001000000010000000000000100000000000000000000
11274190000000000000000000000000000000000000100000000000000000000000000
11274200000000000000000000000000000000000000000000000000000000000000000
11274210000000001000000000000010000000100000000000000000001000000010000
11274220000010000000000000000010000000000000000000000000000000000000000
11274230000000001000000000000000000000000000000000000010000000000000001
11274240000000000000010100000000001000000000000000200000000000000000000
11274250000000000000000000000000001000000000000000000000000000000010000
11274260000000000000000000001000000010000000000000000000000000000000000
11274270000000001000000000000000000010000000000000001000000000000000000
11274280000000000000000000000000000010000000000000000000000000000000000
11274290000000000000000000000000000000000000000000001000000000000000000
11274300000000000000000000000000000000000000000000000000000000000000000
11274310000000001000001020000000001000000000000000000000000000000000000
11274320000000000000000000000000000000000000000000000010000000000000000
11274330000000000000000000100000000000000000000010000000000000000000000
11274340000000000000000000000000000000100000000000000000000000000000000
11274350000000000000000000000000000000000000000000000000000000000000001
11274360000000000000000000000000000000000000000000000000000000000000201
11274370000000100000001000000000000000000000000000000000000000000000000
11274380000000000000000000000000000000000000000000000000000000000000000
11274390000000000000000000000000000000000000000000000000000000000000000
11274400000000000000000000000000000000000000000000000000000000000000000
11274410000000000000000000000000000000000000000000000000000000000000000
11274420000000000000000000000000000000000000000000000000000000000000000
11274430000000000000000000000000000000000000000000000000000000000000000
11274440000000000000000000000000000000000000000000000000000000000000000
11274450000000000000000000000000000000000000000000000000000000000000000
11274460000000000000000000000000000000000000000000000000000000000000000
11274470000000000000000000000000000000000000000000000000000000000000000
11274480000000000000000000000000010000000000000000000000000000000000000
11274490000000000000000000000000000000000000000000000000001000000000001
11274500000000000000000000000000000000000000000000000000000000000000000
11274510000000000000000000000000000000000000000010000000000000000000000
1127452000000000000000000000000
11277010000000000000000000000000000000000000101000000000000000000000000
11277020000010000000000000000000000000000000000000000000000000000000000
11277030000000000000000000000000000000000000000000000000000000000000001
11277040000000000000000000000000000000000000000000000000000000000000000
11277050000000000000100000000000000000000000000000001000000000000000000
11277060000000000000000000000000000000000000000000000000000000000000000
11277070000000000000001000000000000000000000000000000000000000000000000
11277080000000000000000000000000000000100000000000000000000000000000000
11277090000000000000000000000000000000000000000000000000000000000000000
11277100000000000000100000000000000000000000000000000000000000000000000
11277110000000000000000000000000000000000000000000000000000000000000000
11277120000000000000000000000000000000000000000000000000000000000000000
11277130000010000000000000000000000000000000100000000000100000000000000
11277140000000000000000000000000000000000000000000000000000000000000000
11277150000000000000000000000000000000000000000000000000000000000000000
11277160000000000000000000000000000000000000000000000000000000000000000
11277170000000000000000000000000000000000000100010000000000000000000000
11277180100000000000000000000000000000000000000000000000000000000000000
11277190000000000000000000000000000000000000000000000000000000000000000
11277200000000000000000000000000000000000000000000000000000000000000000
11277210000000000000000000000000000000000000000000000000000000000000000
11277220000000000000000000000000000000000000000000000000000000000000000
11277230000000000000000000000000000000000000000000000000000000000000000
11277240000000000000000000000000000000000000000000000000000000000000000
11277250000000000000000000000000000000000000000000000000000000000000000
11277260000000000000000000000000000000000000000000000000000000000000000
11277270000000000000000000000000000000000000000000101000000000000000000
11277280000000000000000000000000000000000000000000000000000000000000000
11277290000000000000000000000000000000000000000000000000000000000000000
11277300000000000000000000000000000000000000000000000000000000000000000
11277310000000000000000000000000000000000000000000000000000000000000000
11277320000000000000000000000000000000000000000000000000000000000000000
11277330000000000000000000000000000000000000000000000000000000000000000
11277340100000000000000000000000000000000000000000000000000000000000000
11277350000000000000000000000000000000000000000000000000000000000000000
11277360000000000000000000000000000000000000000000000000000000000000000
11277370000000000000002000000000000000000000000000000000000000000000000
11277380000000000000000000000000000000000000000000000000000000000000000
11277390000000000000000000000000000000000000000000000000001000000000000
11277400000000000000000000000000000100000000000000000000000000000000000
11277410000000000000000000000000000000000000000000000000000001000000
11277420000000000000000000000000001000000000000000000000000000000000000
11277430000000000000000000000000000000000000000000000000000000000000000
11277440000000000000000000000000000000000000000000000000000000000000000
11277450000000000000000000000000000000000000000000000000000000000000000
11277460000000000000000000000000000000000000000000000000000000000000000
11277470000000000000000000000000000000000000000000000000000000000000000
11277480000000000000000000000000000000000000000000000000000000000000000
11277490000000000000000000000000000000000000000000000000000000000000000
11277500000000000000000000000000000000000000000000000000000000000000000
11277510000000000000000000000000000000000000000010000000000000000000000
1127752000000000000000000000000
11297010402010302050201000004010002020101000201010200000103000200010300
11297020000000300020002010000010200000100010000020001020101010500010101
11297030400010200000102000001000102010302010300010002000000070201050003
11297040202010002020500020200010104020006050000010000020000000000030000
11297050201020103010200000001010100000010000001000002010001000100010200
11297060101000100000000000001020001000000002010000001020000000101000300
11297070100000001000202000102000000100000101020001020000000020301020403 03
11297080102000402000000200000100000100000020000000000000000000103000100
11297090000000000000000000000020400000000000101000001010200020300000100
11297100000000000000001000101000000000100010101010002000001020101020200
11297110000000000000001000101000000000100000103000000020302020701020001

```
11297120001020101010102000000000010000010000000000000010300000010003010302
112971301000102010000010000000000001000002010001010304010002000201010100
1129714000000000000000000000000000000000000000000000010000000000101000201
11297150200020000000201010101000000000020000000000001000000000000000000003
11297160100020005000503000000001010000010001000100000000000000000300010001
11297170100000000000000100000000000000000000000000000000000000000000000003
11297180000000000101040101010200000000001000100010100010000010000001000000
11297190000000103000000000040001000001000000000010000000000000001000030103
11297200300010100000000102000000000000000000201000000010001010100000000000
11297210100000000000000000000000000000000000000000000000001000000000000000
11297220000000000000000000000000000010000000000000000000000100000000000000
11297230000000001000000000000000000010000000000000000000000000000001000001
11297240100030000000000010000000000000002000000000101010000000000001010100
11297250000000000000020100000101040000010000000000000000000000000000000000
11297260000000100000000000000000000000001000000010100000000020000000000
11297270001000000000000000201000100000000001000000001000002000000000000000
11297280001000002000101010100010000000000000000000000000010100000000000100
11297290000000000002000010100000100000000000010000000100000000000000010201
11297300000000000002000000100000000000000000000000000000001000000000000000
11297310000000000100000000000000000100000000000000000001000000000100000000
11297320000000100000000100010100010000000106000000001000000002000000200000
11297330000000000001000000000010100010100010200000000000000001000001000000
11297340100000000000000000010000000000000000000100010000000000000100000100
11297350000000001000000000000000000100000100010001000000000000000000030101
11297360002050200000000000000100020000000000000020200010001020000010002020
11297370006010301000000000000000000000000000000000000000000000000000000000
11297380000000000000000000000000000000000000000000000000000000000000000000
11297390000000000000000000000000000000000000000000000000000000000000000000
11297400000000000000000000000000000000000000000000000000000000000000000000
11297410000000000000000000000000000000000000000000000000000000000000000001
11297420000000000000000000000000000000000000000000000000000000000000000000
11297430000000000000000000000000000000000000000000000000000000000000000000
11297440000000000000000000000000000000000000000000000000000000000000000000
11297450000000000000000000000000000000000000000000000000000000000000000000
11297460000000000000000000000000000000000000000000000000000000000000000000
11297470000000000000000000000000002000000000000000000000000000000000000000
11297480000000000000000000000000000000000000000000000000001000001000000000
11297490000000000000001000100010000000000000000101000001000000000003000000
11297500300000100000000000000000000000000000100000000000000000000001010000
11297510000000000001000102010001000000000000000100000000000001000000000000100
112975200030000000001000010100
11312010100010000001000000010000000000000100000000000001000100000000000000
11312020000000000000000000000000000000010000000000000000000000000000000000
11312030000000101000000000000000100000001010000000000000000000000000000000
11312040000010000000000000000001000000000000000000000000000000000000000000
11312050000000000000000000000000000000010000000000000000000000000000000000
11312060000000000000000000000000000000000000000000000000000000000000000100
11312070000000000000000000000000000000010000000000000000000000000000000000
11312080000000000000000000000000000000000000001000000000000000000000000000
11312090000000000000000000000000000000000000000000000000000000000000000000
11312100000000000000000000000000000000000000000000000000000000001000000000
11312110000000000000000000000000000000000000000000000000001000000000000000
11312120000000000000000000000000000000000000000000000000000000000000000000
11312130000000000000000000000000000000000000000000000000000000000000000000
11312140000000000000000000000000000000000000000000000000000000000000000000
11312150000000000000000000000000000000000000000000000000000000000000000000
11312160000000000000000000000000000000000000000000000000000000000000000000
11312170000000000000000000000000000000000000000000000000000000000000000000
11312180000000000000000000000000000000000000000000000000000000000000000001
11312190000000000000000000000000000000000000000000000000000000000100000000
11312200000001000000000000000000000000000000000000000000000000000000000000
11312210000000000000000000000000000000000000000000000000000000000000000000
11312220000000000000000000000000000000000000000000000000000000000000000000
11312230000000000000000000000000000000000000000000000000000000000000000100
11312240000000000000000000000000000000000000000000000001000000000000000000
11312250000000000000000000000000000000000000000000000000000000000000000000
11312260000000000000000000000000000000000000000000000000000000000000000100
11312270000000000000000000000000000000000000000000000000000000000000000000
11312280000000000000000000000000000000000000000000000000000000000000000000
11312290000000000000000000000000000000000000000000000000000000000000000000
11312300001000000000000000000000000000000000000000000000000000000000000000
11312310000000000000001000000000000000000010000000000000000000000000000000
11312320000000000000000000000000000000000000000000000000000000000000000000
11312330000000000000000010000000000000000000000000000000000000000000000000
11312340000000000000000000000000000000000000000000000000000000000000000000
11312350000000000000000000000000000000000000000000000000000000000000000000
11312360000000000000000000000000000000000000000000000000000000000000000000
11312370000000000000000100000000000000000000000000000000000000000000000000
11312380000000000000000000000000000000000000000000000000000000000000000000
11312390000000000000000000000000000000000000000000000000000000000000000000
11312400000000000000000000000000000000000000000000000000000000000000000000
11312410000000000000000000000000000000000000000000000000000000000000000000
11312420000000000000000000000000000000000000000000000000000000000000000000
11312430000000000000000000000000000000000000000000000000001000000000000000
11312440000000000000000000000000000000000000000000000000000000000000000000
11312450000000001000000000000010000000000000000000000000000000000000000000
11312460000000000000000000000000000000000000000000000000000000000000000000
11312470000000000000000000000000000000000000000000000000000000000000000000
11312480000000000000000000000000000000000000000000000000000000000000000000
11312490000000000000000000000000000000000000000000000000000000000000000000
11312500000000000000000000000000000000000000000000000000000000000000000000
11312510000000000000000000000000000000000000000000000000000000000000000000
1131252000000000000000000000000
11330011406050006020105020608020203010102020205040905050104000204000501
11330020102010400070002010000020106010402020201040103030401030500030002
11330030000001100020401010401010201040702020801030500010102010201050003
11330040004020100031100030001050001020006060105050205070005000000010104
11330050500010111040200010002000103010100020102020005010301010401020200
11330060301010001000102000203020100040100010101000106030102020200000000
11330070102000102000001010001010100010001020200020205000205000403030300
11330080304000305000301020001010101020001010202000002000200040101040101
11330090000010003000300030100030403000102000100000102010002000103010001
11330100202020000010100000200010001000001010201030502020002030002010102
11330110002010100000001020000000000000010200010201000002020405030302000
11330120100090000000000301000002010000020000000201000102000100000300050
11330130002010307010102000100010401000203030304000101000105090504000002
11330140302040000000000100010100000000001000000000000000000000000000001
11330150200010000010200030001010201010101010100000200000101010104010 3
11330160200000105000302000201010002000001010101000100020303030000010001
11330170204000004000000000000000000000000000000000000000000000000000010001
11330180002010102010302020203010001000002030003020400000000000020000000 00
11330190001010100000000000000010200000000101000200000100010001020300010104
113302001000203020101000160000000101010100020000020100000000200000000000000
11330210000000005030700020103020200040800010000030103010212020501040000
11330220002000201000000000040100000200010100010002020000000010000000010001
11330230001000101000100000000000010000000010200000100000100010000000000202
11330240102040001000200010001010100000000300000000000010101010002000000000
11330250100000000010000000000101000201000100000000000000000000000000000000
11330260000000001000000000000080101000002010001000000001000100010000020002
1133027010101000100020000010101020000000010102010000020100020000000000000
```

11330280000000000000000010000010000000000100000000020000000003000000000000
11330290000000101000101000000010100000102010000001000000000302000 10100
11330300100000000010000020000000000010000000000000000000001010000000000
11330310101000002000101050000000010402000100000000000000001000001000000000
11330320100000100000000000000200000000000000401010101000000020000001000103
11330330001030003030201020104000001020000010000000000101020200000000000000
11330340000000000000003000001000000000000100000100000000000100000000000000
11330350101010100000000001010100000100000000000000000010000000000000020000
11330360005020200000001010000000001000101000000000000000000100021103041809
11330370012030401000203040700000000000000000000001000000000000000000040000
11330380000000100000000000000000000000000000000000000000000000000000000000
11330390000000000000000100000000000000000000000000000000000000000000000000
11330400000000000000000100000200000000000000000000001000001000100000000010000
11330410000000000000000000000000000000000000000000000000000000000000000000
11330420000000000000000000000000000000000000000000000000000000000000000000
11330430000000000000000000000010000000000000000000000000000000000000010000
11330440000000000001000000001000100000000000000000000001000000000000000000
11330450000000000100000000000000100000000000000000000000000000000000000000
11330460000000000000000000000000000000000000000000000000000000000000000000
11330470000000000000000000000010000000000000000000000000000001000100000100
11330480000000000000000101000000000000000000000001000001000000010000000000300
11330490000000100000000000000201000001000000000000000100010001000002000001
11330500101010100000000000010000000000000000000000000000000000000000010001
11330510000010000000000000000000000000000000002000100000000000000000000000
11330520000000203000000000100
11332010000000000000000000000000000000000000000000000000000000000000000000
11332020000000000000000000000000000000000000000000000000000000000000000000
11332030000000000000000000000001000000000000000000000000000000000000000000
11332040000000000000000000000000000000001000000000000000000000000000000001
11332050000000000000000000000000000000000000000000000000000000000000000000
11332060000000000000000000000000000000000000000000000000000000000000000000
11332070000000000000000000000000000000000000000000000000000000000000000000
11332080000000100000000000000000000000000000000000000000000000000000000000
11332090000000000000000000000000000000000000000000000000000000000000000000
11332100000000000000000000000000000000000000000000000000000000000000000000
11332110000000000000000000000000000000000000000000000000000000000000000000
11332120000000000000000000000000000000000000000000001000100000000000000000
11332130000000000000000000000000000000000000000000000000000000000000000000
11332140000000000000000000000000000000000000000000000000000000000000000000
11332150000000000000000000000000000000000000000000000000000000000000000000
11332160000000000000000000000000000000000000000000000000000000000000000000
11332170000000000000000000000000000000000000000000000000000000000000000000
11332180000000000000000000000000000000000000000000000000000000000000000000
11332190000000000000000000000000000000000000000000000000000000000000000000
11332200000000000000000000000000000000000000000000000000000000000000000000
11332210000000000000000000000000000000000000000000000000000000000000000000
11332220000000000000000000000000000000000000000000000000000000000000000000
11332230000000000000000000000000000000000000000000000000000000000000000000
11332240000000000000000000000000000000000000000000000000010000000000000000
11332250000000000000000000000000000000000000000000000000000000000000000000
11332260000000000000000000000000000000000000000000000000000000000000000000
11332270000000000000000000000000000000000000000000000000000000000000000000
11332280000000000000000000000000000000000000000000000000000000000000000000
11332290000000000000000000000000000000000000000000000000000000000000000000
11332300000000000000000000000000000000000000000000000000000000000000000000
11332310000000000000000000000000000000000000000000000000000000000000000000
11332320000000000000000000000000000000000000000000000000000000000000000000
11332330000000000000000000000000000000000000000000000000000000000000000000
11332340000000000000000000000000000000000000000000000000000000000000000000
11332350000000000000000000000000000000000000000000000000000000000000000000
11332360000000000000000000000000000000000000000000000000100000000000000000
11332370000000000000000000000000000000000000000000000000000000000000000000
11332380000000000000000000000000000000000000000000000000000000000000000000
11332390000000000000000000000000000000000000000000000000000000000000000000
11332400000000000000000000000000000000000000000000000000000000000000000000
11332410000000000000000000000000000000000000000000000000000000000000000000
11332420000000000000000000000000000000000000000000000000000000000000000000
11332430000000000000000000000000000000000000000000000000000000000000000000
11332440000000000000000000000000000000000000000000000000000000000000000000
11332450000000000000000000000000000000000000000000000000000000000000000000
11332460000000000000000000000000000000000000000000000000000000000000000000
11332470000000000000000000000000000000000000000000000000000000000000000000
11332480000000000000000000000000000000000000000000000000000000000000000000
11332490000000000000000000000000000000000000000000000000000000000000000000
11332500000000000000000000000000000000000000000000000000000000000000000000
11332510000000000000000000000000000000000000000000000000000000000000000000
11332520000000000000000000000000
11338010000010000000101000200010003000000000100000000000200000102000000
11338020000000100000000000000000000001000000000000000000010300000000000000
11338030000000600000101000100000200000000000100010101010000020000010000
11338040000000101010100000100000000010000000000000000000200000000000010000
11338050100000000000020000000000000000001000001010000000000000000010002000001
11338060001000000000000000000000000200000000000000000000000000000000000000
11338070000000000010000000000000200000000000001000000020200000000010001 0000
11338080000000000000000000100000000000001000000000000000000000100000000010000
11338090100000000000000010100010200000000000000000000000000200010200000000
11338100100010100000000000000000000000000001000100020100000000000010000000 0
11338110000000100000000000001000000000000001000002000000000100000101000001
11338120003010200000000001000000003000001000101000000020000000000000000100
11338130000000100020000000000000000000000010002000000000000002000101020101
11338140200000100000000000000100000000000000000000000000000000010000000100
11338150200000000100000000000000000000000000000000100000000000000000000000
11338160000000000100010201000000100000000000001000000000000000000000000000
11338170000000002000000000000000000000000000000000000000000000000000000001
11338180000000000010000000000000000000001000200010000000000000000100000000
11338190000000000000000000000000000000000000000000001000000000000000000101
11338200000010000000000000000000000000000000000000010200000000000000000000
11338210000000000000000000000000000000000000000000000000000000000000000000
11338220000000000000000000000000000000000000000000000000000000000000010000
11338230000000000000000000000000000000000000100010000000000000000000000000
11338240000010000000000000000000100000100000000010001000000000000001000000
11338250000000000000000000000010000000000000000000000000000000000000000000
11338260000000000000000100000000000000010000000010000000000000000000000000
11338270000000000000000000000000000000000000000000000000101000000000000000
11338280000000000000000000000000000000000000010000000000000000000000000000
11338290100000000000000000000000000000000000000000000000000000000000000000
11338300000000000000000000000000000000000000000000000000000000000000000000
11338310000000000000000000000000000000000000000000000000000000000000000000
11138320001000000000000000000000000000000000001000000000000000000100000000000
11338330000000000000000000000200000000000000001000000000000000010000000000000
11338340000000000000000000000000000000000000000002000001000000000000000000
11338350000000100000000000000000000000000000000000000000000000000000000010000
11338360000001000000000000001000003000000001010000000000000000000000002000000000
11338370002010000000000000000000000000000000000000000000000000000000000000
11338380000000000000000000000000000000000000000000000000000000000000000000
11338390000000000000000000000000000000000000000000000000000000000000000000
11338400000000000000000000000000000000000000000000000000000000000000000000
11338410000000000000000100000000000000000000000000000000000000000000000000101
11338420000000000000000000000000000000000000000000000000000000000000000000
11338430000000000000000000000000000000000000000000000000000000000000000000

11338440000000000000000000000000000000000000000000000000000000000000000000000000
11338450000000000000000000000000100000000000000000000000000000000000000000000000
11338460000000000000000000000000000000000000000000000000000000000000000000000000
11338470000000000000000000000000000000000000000000000000000000000001000000000000
11338480000000000000000000000000000000000000000000000000000000000000000000000100
11338490000000000000000000000000000000000000000000000000010000000000000000000000
11338500000000000000000000000000000000000000000000000000000000000000000000000000
11338510000000000000000000000000000000000000000010000000000000000000000000000000
113385200000000000000001000000000
11339010000000000000000000000000000000000000000000000000000000000000000000000000
11339020000000100000000000000000000000000000000000000000000000000000000000000000
11339030000000000000000000000000000000000000000000000000000000000000000000000000
11339040000000000000000000000000000000000000000000000000000000000000000000000000
11339050000000000000000000000000000000000000000000000000000000000000000000000000
11339060000000000000000000000000000000000000000000000000000000000000000000000000
11339070000000000000000000000000000000000000000000000000000000000000000000000000
11339080000000000000000000000000000000000000000000000000000000000000000000000000
11339090000000000000000000000000000000000000000000000000000000000000000000000000
11339100000000000000000000000000100000000000000000000000000000000000000000000000
11339110000000000000000000000000000000000000000000000000000000010000000000000000
11339120000000000000000000000000000000000000000000000000000000000000000000000000
11339130000000000000000000000000000000000000000000000000000000000000000000010100
11339140000000000000000000000000000000000000000000000000000000000000000000000000
11339150000000000000000000000000000000000000000000100000000100000000000000000000
11339160000000000000000000000000100000000000000000000000000000000000000000000000
11339170000000000000000000000000000000000000000000000000000000000000000000000000
11339180000000000000000000000000000000000000000000000000000000000000000000000000
11339190000000000000000000000000000000000000000000000000000000000000000000000000
11339200000000000001000000000000000000000000000000000000000000000000000000000000
11339210000000000000000000000000000000000000000000000000000000000000000000000000
11339220000000000000000000000000000000000000000000000000000000000000000000000000
11339230000000000000000000000000000000000000000000000000000000000000000000000000
11339240000000000000000000000000000000000000000000000000000000000000000000000000
11339250000000000000000000000000000000000000000000000000000000000000000000000000
11339260000000000000000000000000000000000000000000000000000000000000000000000000
11339270000000000000000000000000000000001000000000000000000000000000000000000000
11339280000000000000000000000000000000000000000000000000000000000000000000000000
11339290000000000000000000000000000000000000000000000000000000000000000000000000
11339300000000000000000000000000000000000000000000000000000000000000000000000000
11339310000000000000000000000000000000000000000000000000000000000000000000000000
11339320000000000000000000000000000000000000000000000000000000000000000000000000
11339330000000000000000000000000000000000000000000000000000000000000000000000000
11339340000000000000000000000000000000000000000000000000000000000000000000000000
11339350000000000000000000000000000000000000000000000000000000000000000000000000
11339360000000000000000000000000000000000000000000000000000000000000000100000000
11339370000000000000000000000000000000000000000000000000000000000000000000000000
11339380000000000000000000000000000000000000000000000000000000000000000000000000
11339390000000000000000000000000000000000000000000000000000000000000000000000000
11339400000000000000000000000000000000000000000000000000000000000000000000000000
11339410000000000000000000000000000000000000000000000000000000000000000000000000
11339420000000000000000000000000000000000000000000000000000000000000000000000000
11339430000000000000000000000000000000000000000000000000000000000000000000000000
11339440000000000000000000000000000000000000000000000000000000000000000000000000
11339450000000000000000000000000000000000000000000000000000000000000000000000000
11339460000000000000000000000000000000000000000000000000000000000000000000000000
11339470000000000000000000000000000000000000000000000000000000000000000000000000
11339480000000000000000000000000000000000000000000000000000000000000000000000000
11339490000000000000000000000000000000000000000000000000000000000000000000000000
11339500000000000000000000000000000000000000000000000000000000000000000000000000
11339510000000000000000000000000000000000000000000000000000000000000000000000000
113395200000000000000000000000000
11340010000000000000000000000000000000000000000000000000000000000000000000000000
11340020000000000000000000000000000000000000000000000000000000000000100000000000
11340030000000000000000000000000000000000000000000000000000000000000000000000000
11340040000000000000000100000000000000000000000000000000000000000000000000000000
11340050000000000000000000000000000000000000000000000000000000000000000000000000
11340060000000000000000000000000000000000000000000000000000000000000000000000000
11340070000000000010000000000000000000000000000000000000000000000000000000000000
11340080000000000000000000000000000000000000000000000000000000000000000000000000
11340090000000000000000000000000000000000000000000000000000000000000000000000000
11340100000000000000000000000000000000000000000000000000000000000000000000000000
11340110000000000000000000000000000000000000000000000000000000000000000000000000
11340120000000000000000000000000000000000000000000000000000000000000000000000000
11340130000000000000000000000000000000000000000000000000000000000000000000000000
11340140000000000000000000000000000000000000000000000000000000000000000000000000
11340150000000000000000000000000000000000000000000000000000000000000000000000000
11340160000000000000000000000000000000000000000000000000000000000000000000000000
11340170000000000000000000000000000000000000000000000000000000000000000000000000
11340180000000000000000000000000000000000000000000000000000000000000000000000000
11340190000000000000000000000000000000000000000000000000000000000000000000000000
11340200000000000000000000000000000000000000000000000000000000000000000000000000
11340210000000000000000000000000000000000000000000000000000000000000000000000000
11340220000000000000000000000000000000000000000000000000000000000000000000000000
11340230000000000000000000000000000000000000000000000000000000000000000000000000
11340240000000000000000000000000000000000000000000000000000000000000000000000000
11340250000000000000000000000000000000000000000000000000000000000000000000000000
11340260000000000000000000000000000000000000000000000000000000000000000000000000
11340270000000000000000000000000000000000000000000000000000000000000000000000000
11340280000000000000000000000000000000000000000000000000000000000000000000000000
11340290000000000000000000000000000000000000000000000000000000000000000000000000
11340300000000000000000000000000000000000000000000000000000000000000000000000000
11340310000000000000000000000000000000000000000000000000000000000000000000000000
11340320000000000000000000000000000000000000000000000000000000000000000000000000
11340330000000000000000000000000000000000000000000000000000000000000000000000000
11340340000000000000000000000000000000000000000000000000000000000000000000000000
11340350000000000000000000000000000000000000000000000000000000000000000000000000
11340360000000000000000000000000000000000000000000000000000000000000000000000000
11340370000000000000000000000000000000000000000000000000000000000000000000000000
11340380000000000000000000000000000000000000000000000000000000000000000000000000
11340390000000000000000000000000000000000000000000000000000000000000000000000000
11340400000000000000000000000000000000000000000000000000000000000000000000000000
11340410000000000000000000000000000000000000000000000000000000000000000000000000
11340420000000000000000000000000000000000000000000000000000000000000000000000000
11340430000000000000000000000000000000000000000000000000000000000000000000000000
11340440000000000000000000000000000000000000000000000000000000000000000000000000
11340450000000000000000000000000000000000000000000000000000000000000000000000000
11340460000000000000000000000000000000000000000000000000000000000000000000000000
11340470000000000000000000000000000000000000000000000000000000000000000000000000
11340480000000000000000000000000000000000000000000000000000000000000000000000000
11340490000000000000000000000000000000000000000000000000000000000000000000000000
11340500000000000000000000000000000000000000000000000000000000000000000000000000
11340510000000000000000000000000000000000000000000000000000000000000000000000000
113405200000000000000000000000000
11341010000000000020000020000001000000000000000000000000000000000100000200000000
11341020000000000000000000000000000000000001000000000000000000000000000000010000
11341030000000000000000000000000000000000000000001000000000000000001000000000000
11341040000000000000000000000000000000000000000000000000000000000000000000000000
11341050000000000000000000000000000000000000000000000000000000000000000000000100
11341060000000000000000000000000000000000000000000000000000000000001000000000000
11341070000000000000000000000000100000000000000000000000000000000000000000010000
11341080000000000000001010000000000000000000010000000000000000000000000000000000
11341090000000000000000000000000000000000000000000000000000000000000000000000000

11341100000000000000000000000000000000000000000000000000000000100000000000
11341110000000000000000000000000000000000000000000000000000000000100000000
11341120000000000000100000000000010000000000000000000000000000000000000000
11341130000000200000000000000000000000000000000000000000000000000000000000
11341140000000000000000000000000000000000000000000000000000000000000000000
11341150000000000000000000000000000000000000000000000000000000000000000000
11341160000000000000000000000000000000000100000000000000000000000000000000
11341170000000000000000000000000000000000000000000000000000000000000000000
11341180000000000000000000000000000000000000000000000000000000000000000100
11341190000000000000000000000000000000000000000000000000000000000000000000
11341200000000000000000000001000000000000000000000000000000000000000000000
11341210000000000000000000000000000000000000000000000000000000000000000000
11341220000000000000000000000000000000000000000000000000000000000000000000
11341230000000000000000000000000000000000000000000000000000000000000000000
11341240000000000000000000000000000000000000000000000000000000000000000000
11341250000000000000100000000100000000000000000000000000000000000000000000
11341260000000000000000000000000000000000000000000000000000000000000000000
11341270000000000000000000000000000000001000000000000000000000000000000000
11341280000000000000000000000000000000000000000000000000000000000000000000
11341290000000000000000000000000000000000000000000000000000000000000000000
11341300000000000000000000000000000000000000000000000000000000000000000000
11341310000000000000000000000000000000000000000000000000000000000000000000
11341320000000000000000000000000000000000000000000000000000000000000000000
11341330000000000000000000000000000000000000000000000000000000000000000000
11341340000000100000000000000000000000100000000000000000000000000000000000
11341350000000000000000000000000000000000000000000000000000000000000000000
11341360001000000000000000000000000000000000000000000000000000000000000000
11341370001000001000000000000010000000000000000000000000000000000000000000
11341380000000000000000000000000000000000000000000000000000000000000000000
11341390000000000000000000000000000000000000000000000000000000000000000000
11341400000000000000000000000000000000000000000000000000000000000000000000
11341410000000000000000000000000000000000000000000000000000000000000000000
11341420000000000000000000000000000000000000000000000000000000000000000000
11341430000000000000000000000000000000000000000000000000000000000000000000
11341440000000000000000000000000000000000000000000000000000000000000000000
11341450000000000000000000000000000000000000000000000000000000000000000000
11341460000000000000000000000000000000000000000000000000000000000000000000
11341470000000000000000000000000000000000000000000000000000000000000000000
11341480000000000000000000000000000000000000000000000000000000000000000000
11341490000000000000000000000000000000000000000000000000000000000000000000
11341500000000000000000000000000000000000000000000000000000000000000000000
11341510000000000000000000100000000000000000000000000000000000000000000000
113415200000000000000000000000
11342010000020000000000000000000000000000000000000000000000000000000000000
11342020000000000000000000000000000001000000000000000000000100000000000000
11342030000000000000000000000000000000000000000000000101000100010000000000
11342040100000000000030000000001000000000000000000000000000000000000000100
11342050000000001000000000000000000001000000000000000000000000000000000000
11342060000010000000000000000000000000000000000000000000000000000000000000
11342070000000000000000000000010101000000010000000000000000000010000000000
11342080000000100000000000000000000000000000000000000000000000000000000000
11342090000000000000000000001000100010000000000000000000000000000000010000
11342100000000000000000000000010001000000000000000000000000000000000000000
11342110000000000000000000000000000000000000000010000000001010100000000000
11342120000000000000000010000000100000000000000000000010000000001000000000
11342130000000000010000000000000010000010000000000000000000000000000000000
11342140000000000000000000000000000000000000000000000000000000000000000000
11342150000000000000000010000000000000000000000010000000000000000100000000
11342160000000000000000000000000000000000000100000100000000000000000000002
11342170000000000000000000000000000000000000000000000000000000000000000000
11342180100010000000000000000000000000000100000000010000000000000000000000
11342190000000000000000000000000000000000000000000000000000000000000010000
11342200000000000000000000000000100000000000000000000000000000000000000000
11342210000000000000000000000000000000000000000000000000000000000100000000
11342220000000000000000000000000000000000000000000000000000000000000000000
11342230000000000000000000000000000000000000000000000000000000000000000000
11342240000200000000000000000000000000000100000100000000000000000000000000
11342250000010000000000000000100000000000000000000000000000000000000000000
11342260000000000000000000000000000000000000000000000000000000000100000000
11342270100000000000000000000000001000000010000000000000000000000000000000
11342280000000000000000000000000000000000000000000000000000000000000000000
11342290000000000000000000000000000000000000000000000000000000000000000000
11342300000000000000000000000000000001000000000000000000000000000000000000
11342310000000000000000000000000000000000000000000000000000000000000000000
11342320000000000000000000000000000000000000000000000000000000000000000000
11342330000000000000000000000000000000000000000000000000000000000000000000
11342340000000000000000000000000000000000000000000000000000000000000000000
11342350000000100000000000000000000000000000000000000000000000000000000000
11342360000000000000000000000000000000000000000000000000000000000000000100
11342370000000000000000000000000000000000000000000000000000000000000000000
11342380000000000000000000000000000000000000000000000000000000000000000000
11342390000000000000000000000000000000000000000000000000000000000000000000
11342400000000000000000000000000000000000000000000000000000000000000000000
11342410000000000000000000000000000000000000000000000000000000000000000000
11342420000000000000000000000000000000000000000000000000000000000000000000
11342430000000000000000000000000000000000000000000000000000000000000000000
11342440000000000000000000000000000000000000000000000000000000000000000000
11342450000000000000000000000000000000000000000000000000000000000000000000
11342460000000000000000000000000000000000000000000000000000000000000000000
11342470000000000000000000000000000000000000000000000000000000000000000000
11342480000000000000000000000000000000000000000000000000000000000000000000
11342490000000000000000000000000000000000000000000000000000000000000000000
11342500000000000000000000000000000000000000000000000000000000000000000000
11342510000000000000000000000000000000000000000000000000000000000000000000
113425200000000000000000000000
11343010001000000000000000010000000000000000000000100000000000000000000000
11343020000000000000000000000000000001000000000000000000000100000000000000
11343030000000000000000000000000000000000000000000100000000000000000000000
11343040000000100000000000000000000000000000000000000000000000000000000000
11343050000000000000000000000000000000000000000000000000000000000000000000
11343060000000000000000000000000000000000000000000000000000000000000000000
11343070000000000000000000000000000000000000000000000000000000000000010000
11343080000000000000000000000000000000000000000000000000000000000000000000
1134309000000000000000000000000020100000000000000000000000000000000100010000
11343100000000000000000000000000000000000000000000000000000000000000000000
11343110000000000000000000000000000000000000000000000000000000000000000000
11343120001000000000000000000000000001000000000000000000000000000000000000
11343130000000000000000000000000000101000000000000000000000000000000000000
11343140000000000000000000000000000000000000000000000000000000000000000000
11343150000000000000000000000000000000000000000010000000000000000000000000
11343160000000000000000000000000000000001000000000000000000000000000000000
11343170000000000000000000000000000000000000000000000000000000000000000000
11343180000000000000000000000000000000000000000000000000000000000100000000
11343190000000000000000000000000000000000000000000000000000000000000000000
11343200000000000000000000000001000000000000000000000000000000000000000000
11343210000000000000000000000000000000000000000000000000000000000000000000
11343220000000000000000000000000000000000000000000000000000000000000010000
11343230000000000000000000000000000000000000000000000000000000000000000000
11343240000000000000000000000000000000000000000000000000000000000000000000

```
11343250000000000000000000000000000000000000000000000000000000000000000000000000
11343260000000000000000000000000000000000000000000000000000000000000000000000000
11343270000000000000000000000000000000000000000000000000000000000000000000000000
11343280000000000000000000000000000000000000000000000000000000000000000000000000
11343290000000000000000000000000000000000000000000000000000000000000000000000000
11343300000000000000000000000000000000000000000000000000000000000000000000000000
11343310000000000000000000000000000000000000000000000000000000000000000000000000
11343320000000000000000000000000000000000000000000000000000000000000000000000000
11343330000000000000000000000000000000000000000000000000001000000000000000000000
11343340000000000000100000000000000000000000000000000000000000000000000000000000
11343350000000000100000000000000000000000000000000000000000000000000000000000000
11343360001000000000000000000000000000000000000000000000000000000000000000000000
11343370000000000100000000000000000000000000000000000000000000000000000000000000
11343380000000000000000000000000000000000000000000000000000000000000000000000000
11343390000000000000000000000000000000000000000000000000000000000000000000000000
11343400000000000000000000000000000000000000000000000000000000000000000000000000
11343410000000000000000000000000000000000000000000000000000000000000000000000000
11343420000000000000000000000000000000000000000000000000000000000000000000000000
11343430000000000000000000000000000000000000000000000000000000000000000000000000
11343440000000000000000000000000000000000000000000000000000000000000000000000000
11343450000000000000000000000000000000000000000000000000000000000000000000000000
11343460000000000000000000000000000000000000000000000000000000000000000000000000
11343470000000000000000000000000000000000000000000000000000000000000000000000000
11343480000000000000000000000000000000000000000000000000000000000000000000000000
11343490000000000000000000000000000000000000000000000000000000000000000000000000
11343500000000000000000000000000000000000000000000000000000000000000000000000000
11343510000000000000000000000000000000000000000000000000000000000000000000000000
11343520000000000000000000000000
11344010000000000000000000000000000000000000000000000000000000000000000000000000
11344020000000000001000000000000000000000000000000000000000000000000000000000000
11344030000000000000000000000000000000000000000000000000000000000010000000000000
11344040000000000000000000000000000000000000000000000000000000000000000000000000
11344050000000000000000000000000000000000000000000000000000000000000000000000000
11344060000000000000000000000000000000000000000000000000000000000000000000000000
11344070000000000000000000000000000000000000000000000000000000000000000000000000
11344080000000000000000000000000000000000000000000000000000000000000000000000000
11344090000000000000000000000000000000000001000000000000000000000000000000000000
11344100000000000000000000000000000000000000000000000000000000000001000000000000
11344110000010000000000000000000000000000000000000000000000000000000000000000000
11344120000000000000000000000000000000000000000000000000000000000000000000000000
11344130000000000000000000000000000000000000000000000000000000000000000000000000
11344140000000000000000000000000000000000000000000000000000000000000000000000000
11344150000000000000000000000000000000000000000000000000000000000000000000000000
11344160000000000000000000000000000000000000000000000000000000000000000000000000
11344170000000000000000000000000000000000000000000000000000000000000000000000000
11344180000000000000000000001000000000000000000000000000000000000000000000000000
11344190000000000000000000000000000000000000000000000000000000000000000000000000
11344200000000000000000000000000000000000000000000000000000000000000000000000000
11344210000000000000000000000000000000000000000000000000000000000000000000000000
11344220000000000000000000000000000000000000000000000000000000000000000000000000
11344230000000000000000000000000000000000000000000000000000000000000000000000000
11344240000000000000000000000000000000000000000000000000000000000000000000000000
11344250000000000000000000000000000000000000000000000000000000000000000000000000
11344260000000000000000000000000000000000000000000000000000000000000000000000000
11344270000000000000000000000000000000000000000000000000000100000000000000000000
11344280000000000000000000000000000000000000000000000000000000000000000000000000
11344290000000000000000000000000000000000000000000000000000000000000000000000000
11344300000000000000000000000000000000000000000000000000000000000000000000000000
11344310000000000000000000000000000000000000000000000000000000000000000000000000
11344320000000000000000000000000000000000000000000000000000000000000000000000000
11344330000000000000000000000000000000000000000000000000000000000000000000000000
11344340000000000000000000000000000000000000000000000000000000000000000000000000
11344350000000000000000000000000000000000000000000000000000000000000000000000000
11344360000000000000000000000000000000000000000000000000000000000000000000000000
11344370000000000000000000000000000000000000000000000000000000000000000000000000
11344380000000000000000000000000000000000000000000000000000000000000000000000000
11344390000000000000000000000000000000000000000000000000000000000000000000000000
11344400000000000000000000000000000000000000000000000000000000000000000000000000
11344410000000000000000000000000000000000000000000000000000000000000000000000000
11344420000000000000000000000000000000000000000000000000000000000000000000000000
11344430000000000000000000000000000000000000000000000000000000000000000000000000
11344440000000000000000000000000000000000000000000000000000000000000000000000000
11344450000000000000000000000000000000000000000000000000000000000000000000000000
11344460000000000000000000000000000000000000000000000000000000000000000000000000
11344470000000000000000000000000000000000000000000000000000000000000000000000000
11344480000000000000000000000000000000000000000000000000000000000000000000000000
11344490000000000000000000000000000000000000000000000000000000000000000000000000
11344500000000000000000000000000000000000000000000000000000000000000000000000000
11344510000000000000000000000000000000000000000000000000000000000000000000000000
11344520000000000000000000000000
11345010002000000000000000000000000000000000000000000000000000000001000000
11345020000000000000000000000000000000000000000000000001000000000000000000001000
11345030000000100000000000000010000000000000000001000000000000010101000000000000
11345040000000000000000000000000000000000000000000010000000000000000000000000000
11345050000000000000000000000000000000000000000000000000000000000000000000000000
11345060000000000000000000000000000000000000000000000000000001000000000000000000
11345070000000000000000000000000000000000000000000000000000000000000000000000000
11345080000000100000000000000000000000000000000000000000000000000000000000000000
11345090100000000000000000000000000000000000000000000000000000000001000000000000
11345100000000000000000000000000000000000000000000000000000000000000000000000000
11345110000000000000000000000000000000000000000000000000000000000000000000000000
11345120000000000000000000000000000000000000000000000000000000000000000000000000
11345130000000000000000000000000000000000000000000000000000000001000000001000000
11345140000000000000000000000000000000000000000000000000000000000000000000000000
11345150000000000000000000000000000000000000000000000000000000000000000000000000
11345160000000000000000000000000000000000000000000000000000001000000000000000000
11345170000000000000000000000000000000000000000000000000000000000000000000000000
11345180000000000000000000000000000000000000000000000000000000000000000000000000
11345190000000000000000000000000000000000000000000000000000000000000000000000000
11345200000000000000000000000000000000000000000000000000000000000000000000000000
11345210000000000000000000000000000000000000000000000000000000000000000000000000
11345220000000000000000000000000000000000000000000000000000000000000000000000000
11345230000000000000000000000000000000000000000000000000000000010000000000000000
11345240000010000000000000000000000000000000000000000000000000000000000000000000
11345250000000000000000000000000100000000000000000000000000000000000000000000000
11345260000000000000000000000000000000000000000000000000000000000000000000000000
11345270000000000000000000000000000000000000000000000000000000000000000000000000
11345280000000000000000000000000000000000000000000000000000000000000000000000000
11345290000000000000000000000000000000000000000000000000000000000000000000000000
11345300000000000000000000000000000000000000000000000000000000000000000000000000
11345310000000000000000000000001000000000000000000000000000000000000000000000000
11345320000000000000000000000000000000000000000000000000000000000000000000000000
11345330000000000000000000000000000000000000000000000000000000000000000000000000
11345340000000000000000000000000000000000000000000000000000000000000000000000000
11345350000000000000000000000000000000000000000000000000000000000000000000000000
11345360000000000000000000000000000000000000000000000000000000000000000000000100
11345370001000000000000000000000000100000000000000000000000000000000000000000000
11345380000000000000000000000000000000000000000000000000000000000000000000000000
11345390000000000000000000000000000000000000000000000000000000000000000000000000
11345400000000000000000000000000000000000000000000000000000000000000000000000000
```

```
11345410000000000000000000000000000000000000000000000000000000000000000000000000
11345420000000000000000000000000000000000000000000000000000000000000000000000000
11345430000000000000000000000000000000000000000000000000000000000000000000000000
11345440000000000000000000000000000000000000000000000000000000000000000000000000
11345450000000000000000000000000000000000000000000000000000000000000000000000000
11345460000000000000000000000000000000000000000000000000000000000000000000000000
11345470000000000000000000000000000000000000000000000000000000000000000000000000
11345480000000000000000000000000000000000000000000000000000000000000000000000000
11345490000000000000000000000000000000000000000000000000000000000000000000000000
11345500000000000000000000000000000000000000000000000000000000000000000000000000
11345510000000000000000000000000000000000000000000000000000000000000000000000000
11345520000000000000000000000000
11346010000000000000000000010000000000000000000000000000000000000000000100000000
11346020000000000000000000000000000000000000000000000000000000000000000000000000
11346030000000000000000000000000000000000100000000000000000000000000000000000000
11346040000000000000010100000000000000000000000000000000000000000000000000000000
11346050000000000000000000000000000000000000000000000000000000000000000000000000
11346060000000000000000000000000000000000000000000000000000100000000000000000000
11346070000000000000000000010000010000000000000000000000001000000000000010001000
11346080000000000000000000000000000000000000000000000000000000000000000000000100
11346090000001000000000000000000000000000000000000000000000000000000001010100000
11346100000000000000000000000000000000000000000000000000010000000000100000000000
11346110000000000000000000000000000000000001000000000000000000000000000000000000
11346120000000000000000001000000000000000000000000000000000000000000000000000000
11346130000000000000000000000000000000000000000000000000000000000010000000000000
11346140000000000000000000000000000000000000000000000000000000000000000000000000
11346150000000000000000000000000000000000000000000000000000000000000001000000000
11346160000000000000000000000000000000000000000000000000000000000000000000000000
11346170000000000000000000000000000000000000000000000000000000000000000000000000
11346180000000000000000000000000000000000000000000000000000000000000000000000000
11346190000000000000000000000000000000000000000000000000000000000000000000010000
11346200000000000000000000000000000000000000000000000000000000000000000000000000
11346210000000000000000000000000000000000000000000000000000000000000000000000000
11346220000000000000000000010000000000000000000000000000000000000000000000000000
11346230000000000000000000000000000000000000000000000000000000000000000000000000
11346240000000000000000000000000000000000000000000000001000000000000000000000000
11346250000000000000000000000000000000000000000000000000000000000000000000000000
11346260000000000000000000000000000000000000000000000000000000000000001000000000
11346270000000000000000000000000000000000000000000000000000000000000000000000000
11346280000000000000000000000000000000000000000000000000000000000000000000000000
11346290000000000000000000000000000010000000000000000000000000000000000000000000
11346300000000000000000000000000000000000000000000000000000000000000000000000000
11346310000000000000000000000000000000000000000000000000000000000000000000000000
11346320000000000000000000000000000000000000000000000000000000000000000000000000
11346330000000000000000000000000100000000000000000000000000000000000000000000000
11346340000000000000000000000000000000000000000000000000000000000000000000000000
11346350000000000000000000000000000000000000000000000000000000000000000000000000
11346360000000000000000000000000000000000000000000000000000000000000000000000000
11346370000000000010000000000000000000000000000000000000000000000000000000000000
11346380000000000000000000000000000000000000000000000000000000000000000000000000
11346390000000000000000000000000000000000000000000000000000000000000000000000000
11346400000000000000000000000000000000000000000000000000000000000000000000000000
11346410000000000000000000000000000000000000000000000000000000000000000000000000
11346420000000000000000000000000000000000000000000000000000000000000000000000000
11346430000000000000000000000000000000000000000000000000000000000000000000000000
11346440000000000000000000000000000000000000000000000000000000000000000000000000
11346450000000000000000000000000000000000000000000000000000000000000000000000000
11346460000000000000000000000000000000000000000000000000000000000000000000000000
11346470000000000000000000000000000000000000000000000000000000000000000000000000
11346480000000000000000000000000000000000000000000000000000000000000000000000000
11346490000000000000000000000000000000000000000000000000000000000000000000000000
11346500000000000000000000000000000000000000000000000000000000000000000000000000
11346510000000000000000000000000000000000000000000000000000000000000000000000000
11346520000000000000000000000000
11347010000000000000000000000000000000000000000000000000000000000000000000000000
11347020000000000000000000000000000000000000000000000000000000000000000000010000
11347030000000000000000000000000000000000000000000000000000000000000000000000000
11347040000000000000000000000000000000000000000000000000000000000000000000000000
11347050000000000000000000000000000000000000000000000000000000000000000000000000
11347060000000000000000000000000000000000000000000000000000000000000000000000000
11347070000000000000000000000000000000000000000000000001000000000000000001000000
11347080000000000000000000000000000000000000000000000000000000000000000000000000
11347090000000000000000000000000000000000000000000000000001000100000000000000000
11347100000000000000000000000000000000000000000000000000000000000000000000000000
11347110000000000000000000020000000000000000010000000000000000000000000000000000
11347120000000000000000000010000000010000000000000000000000000000000000000000000
11347130000000000000000000000000000000001000000000000000000000000000000000000000
11347140000000000000000000000000000000000000000000000000000000000000000000000000
11347150000000000001000001000000000000000000000000000000000000000000000000000000
11347160000001000000000000000000000000000000000000000000000000000000000000000000
11347170000000000000000000000000000000000000000000000000000000000000000000000000
11347180000000000000000000000000000000000000010000000000000000000000000000000000
11347190000000000000000000000000000000000000000000000000000000000000000000010001
11347200000000000000000000000000000000000000000000000000000000000000000000000000
11347210000000000000000000000000000000000000000000000000001000000000000000000000
11347220000000000000000000000000000000000000000000000000000000000000000000000000
11347230000000000000000000000000000000000000000000000000000000000000000000000000
11347240000000000000000000000000000000000000000000000000000000000000000000000000
11347250000000000000000000000000000000000000000000000000000000000000000000000001
11347260000000000000000000000000000000000000000000000000000000000000000000000000
11347270000000000000000000000000000000000000000000000000000000000000000000000000
11347280000000000000000000000000000000000000000000000000000000000000000000000000
11347290000000000000000000000000000000000000000000000000000000000000000000000000
11347300000000000000000000000000000000000000000000000000000000000000000000000000
11347310000000000000000000000000000000000000000000000000000000000000000000000000
11347320000000000000000000000000000000000000000000000000000000000000000000000000
11347330000000000000000000000000000000000000000000000000000000000000000000000000
11347340000000000000000000000000000000000000000000000000000000000000000000000000
11347350000000000000000000000000000000000000000000000000000000000000000000000000
11347360000000000000000000000000000000000000000000000000000000000000000001000000
11347370000000000000000000000000000000000000000000000000000000000000000000000000
11347380000000000000000000000000000000000000000000000000000000000000000000000000
11347390000000000000000000000000000000000000000000000000000000000000000000000000
11347400000000000000000000000000000000000000000000000000000000000000000000000000
11347410000000000000000000000000000000000000000000000000000000000000000000000000
11347420000000000000000000000000000000000000000000000000000000000000000000000000
11347430000000000000000000000000000000000000000000000000000000000000000000000000
11347440000000000000000000000000000000000000000000000000000000000000000000000000
11347450000000000000000000000000000000000000000000000000000000000000000000000000
11347460000000000000000000000000000000000000000000000000000000000000000000000000
11347470000000000000000000000000000000000000000000000000000000000000000000000000
11347480000000000000000000000000000000000000000000000000000000000000000000000000
11347490000000000000000000000000000000000000000000000000000000000000000000000000
11347500000000000000000000000000000000000000000000000000000000000000000000000000
11347510000000000000000000000000000000000000000000000000000000000000000000000000
11347520000000000000000000000000
11348010000000000000000000000000000000000000000000000000000000000000000000000000
11348020000000000000000000000000000000000000000000000000000000000000000000000000
11348030000000000000000000000000000000000000000000000000000000100000000000000000
11348040000000000010000000000000000000000000000000000000000000000000000000000000
```

```
11348050000000000000000000000000000000000000000000000000000000000000000000
11348060000000000000000000000000000001000000000000000000000000000000000000
11348070000000000000000000000000000000000000000000000000000000000000000000
11348080000000000000000000000000000000000000000000000000000000000000000000
11348090000000000000000000000000000000000000000000000000000000000000000000
11348100000000000000000000000000000000000000000000000000000000000000000000
11348110000010000000000000000000000000000000000000000000000000000000000000
11348120000000100000000000000000000000000000000000000000000000000000000000
11348130000000000000000000000000000000000000000000000000000000000000000000
11348140000000000000000000000000000000000000000000000000000000000000000000
11348150000000000000000000000000000000000000000000000000000000000000000000
11348160000000000000000000000000000000000000000000000000000000000000000000
11348170000000000000000000000000000000000000000000000000000000000000000000
11348180000000000000000000000000000000000000000000000000000000000000000000
11348190000000000000000000000000000000000000000000000000000000000000010000
11348200000000000000000000000000000000000000000000000000000000000000000000
11348210000000000000000000000000000000000000000000000000000000000000000000
11348220000000000000000000000000000000000000000000000000000000000000000000
11348230000000000000000000000000000000000000000000000000000000000000000000
11348240000000000000000000000000000000000000000000000000000000000000000000
11348250000000000000000000000000000000000000000000000000000000000000000000
11348260000000000000000000000000000000000000000000000000000000000000000000
11348270000000000000000000000000000000000000000000000000000000000000000000
11348280000000000000000000000000000000000000000000000000000000000000000000
11348290000000000000000000000000000000000000000000000000000000000000000000
11348300000000000000000000000000000000000000000000000000000000000000000000
11348310000000000000000000000000000000000000000000000000000000000000000000
11348320000000000000000000000000000000000000000000000000000000000000000000
11348330000000000000000000000000000000000000000000000000000000000000000000
11348340000000000000000000000000000000000000000000000000000000000000000000
11348350000000000000000000000000000000000000000000000000000000000000000000
11348360000000000000000000000000000000000000000000000000000000000000000000
11348370000000001000000000000000000000000000000000000000000000000000000000
11348380000000000000000000000000000000000000000000000000000000000000000000
11348390000000000000000000000000000000000000000000000000000000000000000000
11348400000000000000000000000000000000000000000000000000000000000000000000
11348410000000000000000000000000000000000000000000000000000000000000000000
11348420000000000000000000000000000000000000000000000000000000000000000000
11348430000000000000000000000000000000000000000000000000000000000000000000
11348440000000000000000000000000000000000000000000000000000000000000000000
11348450000000000000000000000000000000000000000000000000000000000000000000
11348460000000000000000000000000000000000000000000000000000000000000000000
11348470000000000000000000000000000000000000000000000000000000000000000000
11348480000000000000000000000000000000000000000000000000000000000000010000
11348490000000000000000000000000000000000000000000000000000000000000000000
11348500000000000000000000000000000000000000000000000000000000000000000000
11348510000000000000000000000000000000000000000000000000000000000000000000
113485200000000000000000000000
11349010000000100000000000000001000000000000000000000000000000000001000000
11349020000000000000000000000000000000000000000001000000000000000000000000
11349030000000000000000000000000000000001010000000000000010000000000000000
11349040000000000000000000000000000000000000000000000000000000000000000000
11349050000000001000000000000000000000000000000000000000000000000000000000
11349060000000000000000000000000000000000000000000000000000000000000000000
11349070000000000000000000000000000000000000000000000000000000000000000000
11349080000000000000100000000000000000000000000000000000000000000000000000
11349090000000000000000000000000000000000000000000000000000000000000000000
11349100000000000000000000000000000000000001000000000000000000000000100000000
11349110100000100000000000000000000000000000100000000000000000000000000000
11349120000000000000000000000000000000000000000000000000000001000000000000000
11349130000000000001000000000000000000000000000000000000000000000010000000000
11349140100000000000000000000000000000000000000000000000000000000000000000
11349150000000000000000000000000000000000000000000000000000000000000000000
11349160000000000000000000000000000000000000000000000000000000000000000000
11349170000000000000000000000000000000000000000000000000000000000000000000
11349180000000000000010000000000000000000000000000000000000000000000000000
11349190000000000000010000000000000000000000000000000000100000000000000000000
11349200000000000000000000000000000000000000000000000000000000000000000000
11349210000000000000000000000000000000000000000000000000000000000000000000
11349220000000000000000000000000000000000000000000000000000000000000000000
11349230000000000000000000000000000000000000000000000000000000000000000000
11349240000000000000000000000000000100000000000000000000000000000000000000
11349250000000000000000000000100000001000000000000000000000000000000000000
11349260000000000000000000000000000000000000000000000000100000000000000000
11349270000000000000000000000100000000010000000000000000000000000000000000
11349280000000000000000000000000000000000000000000000000000000000000000000
11349290000000000000000000000000000000000000000000000000000000000000000000
11349300000000000000000000000000000000000000000000000000000000000000000000
11349310000000000000000000000000000000000000000000000000000000000000000000
11349320000000000000000000000000000000000000000000000000000000000000000000
11349330000000000000000000000000000000000000000000000000000000000000000000
11349340000000000000000000000000000000000000000000000000000000000000000000
11349350000000000000000000000000000000000000000000000000000000000000000000
11349360000000000000000000000000000000000000100000000000000000000000000000200000
11349370000000000000000000000000000001000000000000000000000000000000000000
11349380000000000000000000000000000000000000000000000000000000000000000000
11349390000000000000000000000000000000000000000000000000000000000000000000
11349400000000000000000000000000000000000000000000000000000000000000000000
11349410000000000000000000000000000000000000000000000000000000000000000000
11349420000000000000000000000000000000000000000000000000000000000000000000
11349430000000000000000000000000000000000000000000000000000000000000000000
11349440000000000000000000000000000000000000000000000000000000000000000000
11349450000000000000000000000000000000000000000000000000000000000000000000
11349460000000000000000000000000000000000000000000000000000000000000000000
11349470000000000000000000000000000000000000000000000000000000000000000000
11349480000000000000000000000000000000000000000000000000000000000000000000
11349490000000000000000000000000000000000000000000000000000000000000000000
11349500000000000000000000000000000000000000000000000000000000000000000000
11349510000000000000000000000000000000000000000000000000000000000000000000
113495200000000000000000000000
11351010000000000000000000000000000000000000000000000000000000000000000000
11351020000000000000000000000000000000000000000000000000000000000000000101
11351030000000000000000000000000000000000000000000100000001000100000000000
11351040000000000000000000000000000000000000000000000000100000000000000000
11351050000000000000000000000000000000000000000000000000000000000000000000
11351060000000000000000000000000000000000000000000000000000000000000000001
11351070000000000000000000000000000000000000000000000000000000000000000000
11351080000000000000000000000000000000000000000000000000000000000000000000
11351090000000000000001000100000000000000000000000000000000000000000000000
11351100000000000000001000000000000000000000000000000000000000000000000000
11351110000000000000000000000000000000000000000000000000000000000000000000
11351120000000000000000000000000000100000000000000000000000000000000000000
11351130100000000000010000000000000000000001000000000000000000000000010000
11351140000000000000000000000000000000000000000000000000000000000000000000
11351150000010000000010000000000000000000000000000000000000000000000000000
11351160000000000000000000000000000000000000000000000000000000000000000000
11351170000000000000000000000000000000000000000000000000000000000000000000
11351180000000000000000000000000000000000000000000000000000000000000000000
11351190000000000000000000000000000000000000000000000000000000000000010100
11351200000000000000000000000000000000000000000000000000000000000000000000
```

```
113512100000000000000000000000000000000000000000000000000000000000000000000000000
113512200000000000000000000000000000000000000000000000000000000000000000000000000
113512300001000000000000000000000000000000000000000000000000000000000000000000000
113512400000000000000000000000000000010000000000000000000000000000000000000000000
113512500000000000000000000000000000000000000000000000000000000000000000000000000
113512600000000000000000000000000000000000000000000000000000000000000000000000000
113512700000000000000000000000000000000000000000000000000000000000000000000000000
113512800000000000000000000000000000000000000000000000000000000000000000000000000
113512900000000000000000000000000000000000000000000000000000000000000000000000000
113513000000000000000000000000000000000000000000000000000000000000000000000000000
113513100000000000000000000000000000000000000000000000000000000000000000000000000
113513200000000000000000000000000000000000000000001000000000000000000000000000000
113513300000000000000000000000000000000000000000001000000000000000000000000000000
113513400000000000000000000000000000000000000000000000000000000000000000000000000
113513500000000000000000000000000000000000000000000000000000000000000000000000000
113513600001000000000000000000001000100000000000000000000000000000000000000000000
113513700000000000000000000000000000000000000000000000000000000000000000000000000
113513800000000000000000000000000000000000000000000000000000000000000000000000000
113513900000000000000000000000000000000000000000000000000000000000000000000000000
113514000000000000000000000000000000000000000000000000000000000000000000000000000
113514100000000000000000000000000000000000000000000000000000000000000000000000000
113514200000000000000000000000000000000000000000000000000000000000000000000000000
113514300000000000000000000000000000000000000000000000000000000000000000000000000
113514400000000000000000000000000000000000000000000000000000000000000000000000000
113514500000000000000000000000000000000000000000000000000000000000000000000000000
113514600000000000000000000000000000000000000000000000000000000000000000000000000
113514700000000000000000000000000000000000000000000000000000000000000000000000000
113514800000000000000000000000000000000000000000000000000000000000000000000000000
113514900000000000000000000000000000000000000000000000000000000000000000000000000
113515000000000000000000000000000000000000000000000000000000000000000000000000000
113515100000000000000000000000000000000000000000000000000000000000000000000000000
11351520000000000000000000000000
113530100000000000000000000000001000000000000000000000000000000000000000000000000
113530200000000000000000000000000000000000000000000000000000000000000000001000000
113530300000000000000000000001000000000000000000000000000000000000000000000000000
113530400000000000000000000000000000000000000000001000000000000000000000000000000
113530500000000000000000000010000000000000000000000000000000000000000000000000000
113530600000000000000000000000000000000000000000000000000000000000000000000000000
113530700000000000000000000000000000000000000000000000000000000000000000000000000
113530800000000000000000000000000000000000000000000000000000000000010001000100000
113530900000000000000000000000000000000000000000000000000000000000000000000000000
113531000000000000000000000000000000000100000000000000000000000000000000000000000
113531100000000000000000000000000000000000000000000000000000001000000000000000000
113531200000000000000000000000000000101000000000000000000000000000000000000000000
113531300000000010000000010000000000000000000000000000000000000000000000000000000
113531400000000000000000000000000000000000000000000000000000000000000000000000000
113531500010000000000000000000000000000000000000000000000000000000000000000000000
113531600000000000000000000000000000000000000000000000000000010000000000000000000
113531700000000000100000000000000000000000000000000000000000000000000000000000000
113531800000010000000000000000000000000000000000000000000000000000000000000000000
113531900000000000000000000000000000000000000000000000000000000000000000001000000
113532000000000000001000000000000100000000000000000001000000000000000000000000000
113532100000000000000000000000000000000000000000000000000000000000000000000000000
113532200000000000000000000000000000000000000000000000000000000000000000000000000
113532300000000000000000000000000000000000000000000000000000000000000000100000000
113532400000000000100000000000000000000000000000000000000000000000010000000000000
113532500000000000000000000000000000000000000000000000000000000000000000000000001
113532600000000000000000000000000000000000000000000000000000000000000000000000000
113532700000000000000000000000000000000000000000000000000000000000000000000000000
113532800000000000000000000000000000000000000000000000000000000000000000000000000
113532900000000000000000000000000000000000000000000000000000000000000000000000000
113533000000000000000000000000000000000000000000000000000000000000000000000000000
113533100000000000000000000000000000000000000000000000000000000000000000000000000
113533200000000000000000000000000000000000000000000000000000000000000000000000000
113533300000000000000000000000000000000000000000000000000000000000000000000000000
113533400000000000000000000000000000000000000000000000000000000000000000000000000
113533500000000000000000000000000000000000000000000000000000000000000000000000000
113533600000000001000000000000000000000000000000000000000000000000000000000000000
113533700000000000000000000000000000000000000000000000000000000000000000000000000
113533800000000000000000000000000000000000000000000000000000000000000000000000000
113533900000000000000000000000000000000000000000000000000000000000000000000000000
113534000000000000000000000000000000000000000000000000000000000000000000000000000
113534100000000000000000000000000000000000000000000000000000000000000000000000000
113534200000000000000000000000000000000000000000000000000000000000000000000000000
113534300000000000000000000000000000000000000000000000000000000000000000000000000
113534400000000000000000000000000000000000000000000000000000000000000000000000000
113534500000000000000000000000000000000000000000000000000000000000000000000000000
113534600000000000000000000000000000000000000000000000000000000000000000000000000
113534700000000000000000000000000000000000000000000000000000000000000000000000000
113534800000000000000000000000000000000000000000000000001000000000000000000000000
113534900000000001000000000000000000000000000000000000000000000000000000000000000
113535000000000000000000000000000000000000000000000000000000000000000000000000000
113535100000000000000000000000000000000000000000000000000000000000000000000000000
11353520000000000010000000000000
113540100000000000000000000010000000000000100000000000000000000000000000000000000
113540200000000000000000000000000000000000000000000000000000001000000000000000000
113540300000000000000000000000000000000000000000000000000000000000000000000000000
113540400000000000000000000000000000000000000000000000000000000000000000000000000
113540500000000000000000000000000000000000000000000000000000000000000000000000000
113540600000000000000000000000000000000000000000000000000000000000000001000000000
113540700000000000000000000000000000000000000000000000000000000000000000000000100
113540800000000000000000000000000000000000000000000000000000000000000000000000000
113540900000000000000000000000000000000000000000000000000000000000000000100000000
113541000010000000000000000000000000000000000000000000001000000000000000000000000
113541100000100000000000000000000000000000000000000000000000000000000000100000000
113541200000000000000000000000000000000000000000000000000000000000000000000000000
113541300000000000000000000000000000000000000000000000000000000000000000100000000
113541400000000000000000000000000000000000000000000000000000000000000000000000000
113541500000000000000000000000000000000000000000000000000000000000000000000000000
113541600000000000000000000000000000000000000000000001000000000000000000000000000
113541700000000000000000000000000000000000000000000000000000000000000000000000000
113541800000000000000000000000000000000000000000000000000000000000000000000000000
113541900000000000000000000000000000000000000000000000000000000000000000001000000
113542000000000000000000000000000000000000000000000000000000000000000000000000000
113542100000000000000000000000000000000000000000000000000000000000000000000000000
113542200000000000000000000000000000000000000000000000000000000000000000000000000
113542300000000000000000000000000000000000000000000000000000000000000000000000000
113542400000000000000000000000000000000000000000000000000000000000000000000000000
113542500000000000000000000000000000000000000000000000000000000000000000000000000
113542600000000000000000000000000000000000000000000000000000000000000000000000000
113542700000000000000000000000000000000000000000000000000000000000000000000000000
113542800000000000100000000000000000000000000000000000000000000000000000000000000
113542900000000000000000000000000000000000000000000000000000000000000000000000000
113543000000000000000000000000000000000000000000000000000000000000000000000000000
113543100000000000000000000000000000000000000000000000000000000000000000000000000
113543200000000000000000000000000000000000000000000000000000000000000000000000000
113543300000000000000000000000000000000000000000000000000000000000000000000000000
113543400000000000000000000000000000000000000000000000000000000000000000000000000
113543500000000000000000000000000000000000000000000000000000000000000000001000000
113543600000000000000000000000000000000000000000000000000000000000000000000000000
```

```
113543700010000000000000000000000000000000000000000000000000000000000000
113543800000000000000000000000000000000000000000000000000000000000000000
113543900000000000000000000000000000000000000000000000000000000000000000
113544000000000000000000000000000000000000000000000000000000000000000000
113544100000000000000000000000000000000000000000000000000000000000000000
113544200000000000000000000000000000000000000000000000000000000000000000
113544300000000000000000000000000000000000000000000000000000000000000000
113544400000000000000000000000000000000000000000000000000000000000000000
113544500000000000000000000000000000000000000000000000000000000000000000
113544600000000000000000000000000000000000000000000000000000000000000000
113544700000000000000000000000000000000000000000000000000000000000000000
113544800000000000000000000000000000000000000000000000000000000000000000
113544900000000000000000000000000000000000000000000000000000000000000000
113545000000000000000000000000000100000000000000000000000000000000000000
113545100000000000000000000000000000000000000000000000000000000000000000
11354520000000010000000000000
113550101010000000000000010001000000000000000000000000000000000000000000
113550201000000000000000000000000000000000000000000000000000000000000000
113550300000000000000000000000001000000000000000000000000000000000000000
113550400000000000000000010000000000000000000000000000000000000000000100
113550500000001000000000000000000000000000000000000000100000000000010000
113550600000000000000000000000000000000000000000000000000000000000000000
113550700000000000000000000000000000000000000000000000000000000000000000
113550800000000000000000000100000001000000000000000000000000000000000000
113550900000000100000000000000001000000000000000000000000000000000000000
113551001000000000000000000000000000001000000010100000000000000000000000
113551100000000000000000000000000000000000000000000000200000000000000000
113551200000000000000000000000000100000000000000000010000000100000000000
113551300000000000000000000000000000000000000000000000000000000000000000
113551400000000000000000000000000000000000000000000000000000000000000000
113551500000000000000000000000000100000000000000000000000000000000000000
113551600000000000000000000000000000001000000010000000000000000000000000
113551700000000000000000000000000000000000000000000000000000000000000000
113551800000000000000000101000000000000000000000000000000000000000000000
113551900000100000000000000000000000000000000000000000000000000000000000
113552000000100000000000000000000000000000000000000000000000000000000000
113552100000000000000000000000000000000000000000000000000000000000000000
113552200000000000000000000000000000000000000000000000000000000000000000
113552300000000000000000000000000000000000000000000000000000000000000000
113552400000000000000000000000000000000000000000000000000000000000000000
113552500000000000000000000000000000100000000000000000000000000000000000
113552600000000000000000000000000000000000000000000000000000000000000000
113552700000000000000000000000000000000000000000000000000000000000000000
113552800000000000000000010000000000000000000000000000000000000000000000
113552900000000000000000000000000000000000000000000000000000000000010000
113553000000000000000000000000001000001000100000000000000000000000000000
113553100000000000000000000000000000000000000000000000000000000000000000
113553200000000000000000000000000000000000000000000000000000000000000000
113553300000000000000000000100000000000000000000000000000000000000000000
113553400000000000000000000000000000000000000000000000000000000000000000
113553500000000000000000000000000000000000000000000000000000000000000000
113553600000000000000000000000001000000000000000000000000000001000002000
113553700000000000000000000000000000000000000000000000000000000000000000
113553800000000000000000000000000000000000000000000000000000000000000000
113553900000000000000000000000000000000000000000000000000000000000000000
113554000000000000000000000000000000000000000000000000000000000000000000
113554100000000000000000000000000000000000000000000000000000000000000000
113554200000000000000000000000000000000000000000000000000000000000000000
113554300000000000000000000000000000000000000000000000000000000000000000
113554400000000000000000000000000000000000000000000000000000000000000000

113554500000000000000000000000000000000000000000000000000000000000000000
113554600000000000000000000000000000000000000000000000000000000000000000
113554700000000000000000000000001000000000000000000000000000000000000000
113554800000000000000000000000001000000000000000000000000000000001000000
113554900000000000000000000000000000000010000000000000000000000000000000
113555001000000000000000000000000000000000000000000000000000000000000100
113555100000000000000000000000000000000000000000100000000000000000000000
11355520000000000000000000000
113560100000001000000000000000000010000000000000000000000000000000000000
113560200000000000000000000000000000000000000000000000000001000001010000
113560300000000000000000000000000000000000000001000000000000000000000000
113560400000000000000000000000000000000000000001000000000000000000000000
113560500000000000000000000000000000000000000000000000000000000000000100
113560600000000000000000000000000010000000000000000000000000000000000000
113560700000000000000000001000001000000000000000000000000000000000000000
113560800000000000000000000000000000000000000000000000000000000000000000
113560900000000000000000000000000000000000000000000000000000000000000000
113561000000000000000000001000000000000000000000000000000000000000000000
113561101000000000000000000000000000000000000000000000000000000000000000
113561200000000000000000000000000000000000000000000000000000000100000000
113561300000000000000000000000000000000000000000000000000001000100000000
113561400000000000000000000000000000000000000000000000000000000000000000
113561500000000000000000001000000000000000000000000000000000000000000000
113561600000000000000000000000000010000000000000000000000000000000010000
113561700000000100000000000000000000000000000000000000000000000000000000
113561800000000000000000000000000000000000000000000000000000000000000000
113561900000000000000000000000000000000000000000000000000000000000020000
113562000000000000000000000000000000000000000000000000000000000000000000
113562100000000000000000000000000000000000000000000000000000000000000000
113562200000000000000000000000000000000000000000000000000000000000000000
113562300000000000000000000000100000000000000000000000000000000000000000
113562400000000000000000000000000000000000000000000000000000000000000000
113562500000000000000000000000000000000000000000000000000000000000000000
113562600000000000000000000000000000000000000000000000000000000000000000
113562700000000000000000000000000000000000000000000000000000000000000000
113562800000000000000000000000000000000000000000000000000001000000000000
113562900000000000000000000000000000000000000000000000000000000000000000
113563000000000000000000000000000000000000000000000000000000000000000000
113563100000000000000000000000000000000000000000000000000000000000000000
113563200000000000000000000000000000000000000000000000000000000000000000
113563300000000000000000000000000000000000000000000000000000000000000000
113563400000000000000000000000000000000000000000000000000000000000000000
113563500000000000000000000000000000000000000000000000000000000000000000
113563600000000000000000000000000000000000000000000000000000000000000100
113563700000000000000000000000000000000000000000000000000000000000000000
113563800000000000000000000000000000000000000000000000000000000000000000
113563900000000000000000000000000000000000000000000000000000000000000000
113564000000000000000000000000000000000000000000000000000000000000000000
113564100000000000000000000000000000000000000000000000000000000000000000
113564200000000000000000000000000000000000000000000000000000000000000000
113564300000000000000000000000000000000000000000000000000000000000000000
113564400000000000000000000000000000000000000000000000000000000000000000
113564500000000000000000000000000000000000000000000000000000000000000000
113564600000000000000000000000000000000000000000000000000000000000000000
113564700000000000000000000000000000000000000000000000000000000000000000
113564800000000000000000000000000000000000000000000000000000000000000000
113564900000000000000000000000000000000000000000000000100000000000000000
113565000000000000000000000000000000000000000000000000000000000000000000
113565100000000000000000000000000000000000000000000000000000000000000000
11356520000000000000000000000
```

```
11357010000000000000000000000000000000000000000000000000000000000100000000000000000
11357020000000000000000000000000000000000000000000100000000000010000000000000000000
11357030000000000000000000000000000000000000000000001000000001000000000000000000000
11357040000000000000000000000000000000001000000000000000000000000000000000000000000
11357050100000000000000000000000000000000000000000000000000000000000000000000000001
11357060000000000000000000000000000000000000000000000000000000000000000000001000000
11357070100000000000000000000000000000000000000000000000000000000000000000000000000
11357080000000000000000000000000000000000000000000000000000000000000000000000000000
11357090000000000000000000000000000000000000000000000000000000000000000000000000000
11357100000000000000000001000000000010000000000000000000000000000000000000000000000
11357110000000000000000000000000000000000000001000000000010000000000000000000000000
11357120000000000000000000000000000000000000000000000000000000000000000000000000000
11357130000000000000000000000000000000000000000000000000000000000000000000000000000
11357140000000000000000000000000000000000000000000000000000000000000000000000000000
11357150100000000000000000000000000000000001000000100000000000000000000001000000000000
11357160000000000000000100000010000000000000000000000000000000000000000000000000000
11357170000100000000000000000000000000000000000000000000000000000000000000000000000
11357180000000000000000100000000000000000000000000000000000000000000100000000000000000
11357190000000000000000000000000000000000000000000000000000000000000000000000000000
11357200000000000000000000000000000000000000000001000000000000000000000000000000000
11357210000000000000000000000000000000000000000000000000000000000000000000000000000
11357220000000000000000000000000000000000000000000000000000000000000000000000000000
11357230000000000000000000000000000000000000000000000000000000000000000000000000001
11357240000000000000000000000000000000000000000000000000000000000000000000000000000
11357250000000100000000000000000010001000000100000000000000000000000000000000000000
11357260000000000000000000000000000000000000000000000000000000000000000000000000000
11357270000000000000001000000000000000000000000000000100000000000000000000000000000
11357280000000000000000000000000000000000000000000000000000000000000000000000000000
11357290000000000000000000000000000000000000000000000000000000000000000000000000000
11357300000000000000000000000000000000000000000000000000000000000000000000000000000
11357310000000000000000000000000000000000000000000000000000000000000000000000000000
11357320000000000000000000000000000000000000000000000000000000000000000000000000000
11357330000000000000000000000000000000000000000000000000000000000000000000000000000
11357340000000000000000000000000000000000000000000000000000000000000000000000000000
11357350000000000000000000100000000000000000000000000000000000000000000000000000000
11357360000000000000000000000000000000000000000000000000000000000000000000000000100
11357370000100000000000000000000000000000000000000000000000000000000000000000000000
11357380000000000000000000000000000000000000000000000000000000000000000000000000000
11357390000000000000000000000000000000000000000000000000000000000000000000000000000
11357400000000000000000000000000000000000000000000000000000000000000000000000000000
11357410000000000000000000000000000000000000000000000000000000000000000000000000000
11357420000000000000000000000000000000000000000000000000000000000000000000000000000
11357430000000000000000000000000000000000000000000000000000000000000000000000000000
11357440000000000000000000000000000000000000000000000000000000000000000000000000000
11357450000000000000000000000000000000000000000000000000000000000000000000000000000
11357460000000000000000000000000000000000000000000000000000000000000000000000000000
11357470000000000000000000000000000000000000000000000000000000000000000000000000000
11357480000000000000000000000000000000000000000000000000000000000000000000000000000
11357490000000000000000000000000000000000000000000000000000000000000000000000000000
11357500000000000000000000000000000000000000000000000000000000000000000000000000000
11357510000000000000000000000000000000000000000000000000000000000000000000000000000
11357520000000000000000000000000
11359010000000000000000000000000000000000000000000000000000000000000000000000000000
11359020000000000000000000000000000000000000000000100000000000000000000000000000000
11359030000000000000000000000000000000000000000000001000000100000000000000000000000
11359040000000000000000000000000000000000000000000000000000000000000000000000000000
11359050100000000000000000000000000000000000000000000000000100000000000000000000000
11359060000000000000000000000000000000000000000000000000000000000000000000000000000
11359070000000000000000000000000000000000000000000000000000000000000000000000000000
11359080000000000000000000000000000000000000000000000000000000000000000000000000000
11359090000000000000000000000000000000000000000000000000000000000000000000000000000
11359100000000000000000000000000000000000000000000000000000000000000000000000000000
11359110000000000000000000000000000000000000000000000000000000000000000000000000000
11359120000000000000000000000000000000000000000000000000000000000000000000000000000
11359130000000000000000000000000000000000000000000000000000000000000000000000000000
11359140000000000000000000000000000000000000000000000000000000000000000000000000000
11359150000000000000000000000000000000000000000000000000000000000000000000000000000
11359160000000000000000000000000000000000000000000000000000000000000000000000000000
11359170000000000000000000000000000000000000000000000000000000000000000000000000000
11359180000000000000000000000000000000000000000000000000000000000000000000000000000
11359190000000000000000000000000000000000000000000000000000000000000000000000000000
11359200000000000000000000000000000000000000000000000000000000000000000000000000000
11359210000000000000000000000000000000000000000000000000000000000000000000000000000
11359220000000000000000000000000000000000000000000000000000000000000000000000000000
11359230000000000000000000000000000000000000000000000000000000000000000000000000000
11359240000000000000000000000000000000000000000000000000000000000000000000000000000
11359250000000000000000000000000000000000000000000000000000000000000000000000000000
11359260000000000000000000000000000000000000000000000000000000000000000000000000000
11359270000000000000000000000000000000000000000000000000000000000000000000000000000
11359280000000000000000000000000000000000000000000000000000000000000000000000000000
11359290000000000000000000000000000000000000000000000000000000000000000000000000000
11359300000000000000000000000000000000000000000000000000000000000000000000000000000
11359310000000000000000000000000000000000000000000000000000000000000000000000000000
11359320000000000000000000000000000000000000000000000000000000000000000000000000000
11359330000000000000000000000000000000000000000000000000000000000000000000000000000
11359340000000000000000000000000000000000000000000000000000000000000000000000000000
11359350000000000000000000000000000000000000000000000000000000000000000000000000000
11359360000000000000000000000000000000000000000000000000000000000000000000000000000
11359370000000000000000000000000000000000000000000000000000000000000000000000000000
11359380000000000000000000000000000000000000000000000000000000000000000000000000000
11359390000000000000000000000000000000000000000000000000000000000000000000000000000
11359400000000000000000000000000000000000000000000000000000000000000000000000000000
11359410000000000000000000000000000000000000000000000000000000000000000000000000000
11359420000000000000000000000000000000000000000000000000000000000000000000000000000
11359430000000000000000000000000000000000000000000000000000000000000000000000000000
11359440000000000000000000000000000000000000000000000000000000000000000000000000000
11359450000000000000000000000000000000000000000000000000000000000000000000000000000
11359460000000000000000000000000000000000000000000000000000000000000000000000000000
11359470000000000000000000000000000000000000000000000000000000000000000000000000000
11359480000000000000000000000000000000000000000000000000000000000000000000000000000
11359490000000000000000000000000000000000000000000000000000000000000000000000000000
11359500000000000000000000000000000000000000000000000000000000000000000000000000000
11359510000000000000000000000000000000000000000000000000000000000000000000000000000
11359520000000000000000000000000
11360010000000000000000000000000101000000000001000000000000000000000000000000001000000
11360020000000000000000000000000000000000000000000000000000000000000001000100000000
11360030000000000000000000000000000000000000000000010000000000000000000000000000000
11360040000000000000000000000000000000000000000000000010000000000100000000000000000
11360050000000000000000000000000000000000000000000000000000000000000000000010000000
11360060000000000000000000000000000000000000000000000000000000000100000000000000000
11360070000000000000000000000000000000000000001000000000000000000000000000000000001000
11360080000000000000000000000000100000010000000000000000000000000000000000000000000
11360090000000000000000000000000000000000000000000000000000000000000000000000000100000
11360100000000000000000000000000000000000000000000000000001000000000100000000000000000
11360110000000000000000000000000000000000000000000000000000000000000000000000100010000
11360120000000000000000000000000000000000000000000010000000000000001000000000000000000
11360130000000000000000000000000000000000000000000000000010000000000000000000000000000
11360140000000000000000000000000000000000000000000000000000000000000000000000000000
11360150000000000000000000000000100000000000000000000000000000000000000000000000000
11360160000000000000000000000000000000000000000000000200000000000000000000001000000000
```

```
11360170100010000000000000000000000000000000000000000000000000000000000000000000
11360180000000000000000000000000000000000000000100000000000000000000000001000000
11360190000000000000000000000000000000000000000000000000000000000000000000000000
11360200000000000000000000000000000000000000000000000000000000000000000000000000
11360210000000000000000000000000000000000000000000000000000000000000000000000000
11360220000000000000000000000000000000000000000000000000000000000000000000010000
11360230000000000000000000000000000000000000000000000000000000000000000000000000
11360240000000000000000001000000000000000000000000000000000000000000000000000000
11360250000010000000000000000000000000000000000000000000000000000000000000000000
11360260000000000000000000000000000000000000000000000000000000000000000000000000
11360270000000000000000000000000000000000000000000000000000000000000000000000000
11360280000000000000000000000000000000000000000000000000000000000000000000000000
11360290000000000000000000000000000000000000000000000000000000000000000000000000
11360300000000000000000000000000000000000000000000000000000000000000000000000000
11360310000000000000000000000000000000000000000000000000000000000000000000000000
11360320000000000000000000000000000000000000000000000000000000000000000000000000
11360330000000000000000000000000000000000000000100000000000001000000000000000000
11360340000000000000000000000000000000000000000000000000000000000000000000000000
11360350000000000000000000000000000000000000000000000000000000000000000000000000
11360360000000000000000000000000000000000000000000000000000000000000000001000000
11360370000000000000000000000000000000000000000000000000000000000000000000000000
11360380000000000000000000000000000000000000000000000000000000000000000000000000
11360390000000000000000000000000000000000000000000000000000000000000000000000000
11360400000000000000000000000000000000000000000000000000000000000000000000000000
11360410000000000000000000000000000000000000000000000000000000000000000000000000
11360420000000000000000000000000000000000000000000000000000000000000000000000000
11360430000000000000000000000000000000000000000000000000000000000000000000000000
11360440000000000000000000000000000000000000000000000000000000000000000000000000
11360450000000000000000000000000000000000000000000000000000000000000000000000000
11360460000000000000000000000000000000000000000000000000000000000000000000000000
11360470000000000000000000000000000000000000000000000000000000000000000000000000
11360480000000000000000000000000000000000000000000000000000000000000000000000000
11360490000000000000000000000000000000000000000000000000000000000000000000000000
11360500000000000000000000000000000000000000000000000000000000000000000000000000
11360510000000000000000000000000000000000000000000000000000000000000000000000000
11360520000000000000000000000
11361010000000000000000000000000000000000000000000000000000000000000000000000000
11361020000000000000000000000000000000000000000000000000000000000000000000000000
11361030000000000000000000000000000000000000000000000000000000000000000000000000
11361040000000000000000000000000000000000000000000000000000000000000000000000000
11361050000000000000000000000000000000000000000000000000000000000000000000000000
11361060000000000000000000000000000100000000000000000000000000000000000000000000
11361070000000000000000001010000000000000000000000000000000000000000000000000000
11361080000000000000000000000000000000000000000000000000000000001000000000000000
11361090000000000000000000000000000000000000000000000000000000000000000000000000
11361100000000000000000001000000000000000001000000000002000000000000000000000000
11361110000000000000000000000000000000000000000000000000000000000000000000010000
11361120000000000000000000000000000000000000000000000000000000000000000000000000
11361130000000000000000000000100000000000000000000000000000000000001000000000000
11361140000000000000000000000000000000000000000000000000000000000000000000000000
11361150100000000000000001000000000000000000000000000000000000000000000000000000
11361160000000000000000000000000000000000000000000000000000000000000000000000000
11361170000000000000000000000000000000000000000000000000000000000000000000000000
11361180000000000000000000000000000000000000000000000000000000000000000000000000
11361190000000000000000000000000000000000000000000000000000000000000000000010000
11361200000000000000000000000000000000000000000000000000000000000000000000000000
11361210000000000000000000000000000000000000000000000000000000000000000000000000
11361220000000000000000000000000000000000000000000000000000000000000000000000000
11361230000000000000000000000000000000000000000000000000000000000000000001000000
11361240000000000000000000000000000000000000000000000000000000000000000000000000
11361250000000000000000000000000000000000000000000000000000000000000000000000000
11361260000000000000000000000000000000000000000000000000000000000000000000000000
11361270000000000000000000000000000000000000000000000000000000000000000000000000
11361280000000000000000000000000000000000000000000000000000000000000000000000000
11361290000000000000000000000000000000000000000000000000000000001000000000000000
11361300000000000000000000000000000000000000000000000000000000000000000000000000
11361310000000000000000000000000000000000000000000000000000000000000000000000000
11361320000000000000000000000000000000000000000000000000000000000000000000000000
11361330000000000000000000000000000000000000000000000000000000000000000000000000
11361340000000000000000000000000000000000000000000000000000000000000000000000000
11361350000000000000000000000000000000000000000000000000000000000000000000000000
11361360000000000000000000000000000000000000000000000000000000000000000000000000
11361370000000000000000000000000000000000000000000000000000000000000000000000000
11361380000000000000000000000000000000000000000000000000000000000000000000000000
11361390000000000000000000000000000000000000000000000000000000000000000000000000
11361400000000000000000000000000000000000000000000000000000000000000000000000000
11361410000000000000000000000000000000000000000000000000000000000000000000000000
11361420000000000000000000000000000000000000000000000000000000000000000000000000
11361430000000000000000000000000000000000000000000000000000000000000000000000000
11361440000000000000000000000000000000000000000000000000000000000000000000000000
11361450000000000000000000000000000000000000000000000000000000000000000000000000
11361460000000000000000000000000000000000000000000000000000000000000000000000000
11361470000000000000000000000000000000000000000000000000000000000000000000000000
11361480000000000000000000000000000000000000000000000000000000000000000000000000
11361490000000000000000000000000000000000000000000000000000000000000000000000000
11361500000000000000000000000000000000000000000000000000000000000000000000000000
11361510000000000000000000000000000000000000000000000000000000000000000000000000
1136152000000000100000000000000
11362010000000000100010000000000000000000000000000000000000000000000000000000000
11362020000000000000000000001000000000000000010000000000000000000000000000020000
11362030000000000000000000000000000000000000000000000000000001000000000000000000
11362040000000000000000000000000000000000000001000100000000000000100000000000000
11362050000010000000000000000000000000000000000000000000001000000000000100000000
11362060000000000000000000000000000000000000000000000000000000000000000000000000
11362070000000000000000000000000000000000000000000000000000000000000000000000000
11362080000000000000000000010000000000001000000000000000010000000000000000000000
11362090000000000000000010000000000000001000000000000000000000000000000000000000
11362100000000000000000000000000000000001000000000000000000000010002000000000000
11362110000000000000000000000000000000000010000000000000000000000000000000000001
11362120000000000000000000000000000000000001000000000000000000000000000000000000
11362130000000000000000000000000000000000000000010201000000000000000000000000000
11362140000010000000000000000000000000000000000000000000000000000000000000000000
11362150000000000000000000000000000000001000000000000000000000000000000000000000
11362160000000000000000000000000000000000000000000000000000000000000000000000000
11362170000000000000000000000000000000000000000000000000000000000000000000000000
11362180000000000000000000010000000000000000000000000000000000000000000000000000
11362190000000000000000000000000000000000000000000000000000000000000000000000000
11362200000000000000000000000000000000000000000000000000000000000000000000000000
11362210000000000000000000000000000000000000000000000000000000000000000000000000
11362220000000000000000000000000000000000000000000000000000000000000000000010000
11362230000000000000000000000000000000000000000000000000001000000000000000000000
11362240000000000000000000010000000000000000000000000000000000001000000000000000
11362250000000000000000000000000000000000000000000000000000000000000000000000000
11362260000000000000000000000000000000000000000000000000000000000000000000000000
11362270000000000000000000010000000000000000000000000000000000000000000000000000
11362280000000000000000000000000000000000000000000000000000000000000000000000000
11362290000000000000000000000000000000000000000000000000000000000000000000000000
11362300000000000000000000000000000000000000000000000000000000000000000000000000
11362310000000000000000000000000000000000000000000000000000000000000000000000000
11362320000000000000000000000000000000000000000000000000000000000000000000000000
```

```
11362330000000000000000000000000000000000000000000000000000000000000000000000000
11362340000000000000000000000000000000000000000000000000000000000000000000000000
11362350000010000000000000000000000000000000000000000000000000000000000000000000
11362360000000000000000000000000000000000000000000000000000000000000001000000000
11362370000000000000000000000000000000000000000000000000000000000000000000000000
11362380000000000000000000000000000000000000000000000000000000000000000000000000
11362390000000000000000000000000000000000000000000000000000000000000000000000000
11362400000000000000000000000000000000000000000000000000000000000000000000000000
11362410000000000000000000000000000000000000000000000000000000000000000000000000
11362420000000000000000000000000000000000000000000000000000000000000000000000000
11362430000000000000000000000000000000000000000000000000000000000000000000000000
11362440000000000000000000000000000000000000000000000000000000000000000000000000
11362450000000000000000000000000000000000000000000000000000000000000000000000000
11362460000000000000000000000000000000000000000000000000000000000000000000000000
11362470000000000000000000000000000000000000000000000000000000000000000000000000
11362480000000000000000000000000000000000000000000000000000000000000000000000000
11362490000000001000000000000000000000000000000000000000000000000000000000000000
11362500000000000000000000000000000000000000000000000000000000000000000000000000
11362510000000000000000000000000000000000000000000000000000000000000000000000000
11362520000000000000000000000000
11363010000000000000000000000001000000000000000000000000000000000100000100000000
11363020000000000000000000000000000000000000100000000000000010000000000000000000000
11363030000000000000100000000000000000000000000100000101000000000001000000000000
11363040000000000000100000000000000000000000000000000000000100000000000000000000
11363050000200000000000000000000000000000000000000000000000000000000000000000000
11363060000000000000000000000000000000000000000000000000000000000000000000000000
11363070000000000000000000000000000000000000000000000000000000000000000000000000
11363080000000000000000000000000000000000000000000000000000000000000000000000100
11363090000000001000000000000000000000000000000000000000000000000000000010000000
11363100000000000000000000000000001000000000000000000000000000000000100000000000
11363110000000000000000000000000000000000000000000000000000000001000000000000000
11363120000000000000000000000000000010000000000000000000000000000000000000000000
11363130000000000000000000000000000000000000000000000000000000000000000000000000
11363140000000000000000000000000000000000000000000000000000000000000000000000000
11363150100000000000000000000000000000000000000000000000000000000000000010000000
11363160000000000000000000000000000000000000000000000000000000000000000000000000
11363170000000000000000000000000000000000000000000000000000000000000000000000000
11363180000000000000000000000000000000100000000000000000000000000000000000000000
11363190000000000000000000000000000000000000000000000000000000000000001000000000
11363200000000000000000000000000000000000000000000000000000000000000000000000000
11363210000000000000000000000000000000000000000000000000000000000000000000000000
11363220000000000000000000000000000000000000000000000000000000000000000000000000
11363230000000000000000000000000000000000000000000000000000000000000000000000000
11363240000010000000000000000000000000000000000000001000000000000000000000000000
11363250000000000000000000000000000000000000000000000000000000000000000000000000
11363260000000000000000000000000000000000000000000000000000000000000000000000000
11363270000000000000000000000000000000000000000000000000000000000000000000000000
11363280000000000000000000000000000000000000000000000000000000000000000000000000
11363290000000000000000000000000000000000000000000000000000000000000000000000000
11363300000000000000000000000000000000000000000000000000000000000000000000000000
11363310000000000000000000000000000000000000000000000000000000000000000000000000
11363320000000000000000000000000000000000000000000000000000000000000000000000000
11363330000000000000000000000000000000000000000000000000000000000000000000000000
11363340000000000000000000000000000000000000000000000000000000000000000000000000
11363350000000000000000000000000000000000000000000000000000000000000000000000000
11363360000000000000000000000000000000000000000000000000000000000000001000000000
11363370000000000000000000000000000000000000000000000000000000000000000000000000
11363380000000000000000000000000000000000000000000000000000000000000000000000000
11363390000000000000000000000000000000000000000000000000000000000000000000000000
11363400000000000000000000000000000000000000000000000000000000000000000000000000
11363410000000000000000000000000000000000000000000000000000000000000000000000000
11363420000000000000000000000000000000000000000000000000000000000000000000000000
11363430000000000000000000000000000000000000000000000000000000000000000000000000
11363440000000000000000000000000000000000000000000000000000000000000000000000000
11363450000000000000000000000000000000000000000000000000000000000000000000000000
11363460000000000000000000000000000000000000000000000000000000000000000000000000
11363470000000000000000000000000000000000000000000000000000000000000000000000000
11363480000000000000000000000000000000000000000000000000000000000000000000000000
11363490000000000000000000000000000000000000000000000000000000000000000000000000
11363500000000000000000000000000000000000000000000000000000000000000000000000000
11363510000000000000000000000000000000000000000000000000000000000000000000000000
11363520000000000000000000000000
11364010100000000000000000000100020000000000000000000000000000000000000000010000
11364020000000000000000000000000000101000100000010000000000000000000000001000000000
11364030000000000000000000000000000000000000000001000000001000000000000000000000
11364040001000200010000100000000000000000000000001000000000000010100000000000001
11364050100000000000000000000000000000000000000010000000000000000000000000000000
11364060000000000000100000000000000000000000000000000000000000000000000000000000
11364070000000000000000000000000000000000000000000000000000000000000000000000000
11364080000000000000000000000000000000000000000000000000000000000000000000000000
11364090000000000000001000000000000000000000000000000000000000000000000000000000
11364100000000000000001001000000000000000000000000000000000000200000000000001000
11364110000000000000000000000000000000000000000000000000000000000100000000000000
11364120000010010000000000000000010000000000000000000000001010001000000000000000
11364130000000000000000000000000000010000010000000000000001000001010000000000000
11364140000000000000000000000000000000000000000000000000000000000000000000000000
11364150000000000000000000000000000000000000000000000000000000000000000000000000
11364160000000000000000000000000000000000000000000000000000000000000001000000000
11364170000000000000000000000000000000000000000000000000000000000000000000000000
11364180100010000000000000000000000000000000000000000000000000000000000000000000
11364190000000000000000000000000000000000000000000000000000000000000000000010102
11364200000001001000000000000001000000000000000000000000000000000000000000000000
11364210000000000000000000000000000000000000000000000000000000000000000000000000
11364220000000000000000000000000000000000000000000000000000000000000000000000000
11364230000000000000000000000000000000000000000000000000000000000000000000000000
11364240000000000000000000000000000000000000000000000001000000000000000000000000
11364250001000001000000000000000000000000010000000000000000000000000000000000000
11364260000000000000000000000000000000000000000000000000000000000000000000010000
11364270000000000000000000000000000000000000000010000000000100000000000000000000
11364280000000000000000000000000000000000000000000000000000000000000000000000000
11364290000000000000000000000000000000000000000000000000000000000000000000000000
11364300000000000000000000000000000000000000000010000000000000000000000000000000
11364310000000000000000000000000000000000000000000000000000000000000000000000000
11364320000000000000000000000000000000000000000000000000000000000000000000000000
11364330000000000000000000000000000000001000000000000000000000000000000000000000
11364340000000000000000010000000000000000000000000000000000000000000000100000001
11364350000100000000000000000000000000000000000000000000000000000000000000000001
11364360000000000000000000000000000000000000000000000000000000000000001010000000
11364370000000000000000000000000001000000000000000000000000000000000000000000000
11364380000000000000000000000000000000000000000000000000000000000000000000000000
11364390000000000000000000000000000000000000000000000000000000000000000000000000
11364400000000000000000000000000000000000000000000000000000000000000000000000000
11364410000000000000000000000000000000000000000000000000000000000000000000000000
11364420000000000000000000000000000000000000000000000000000000000000000000000000
11364430000000000000000000000000000000000000000000000000000000000000000000000000
11364440000000000000000000000000000000000000000000000000000000000000000000000000
11364450000000000000000000000000000000000000000000000000000000000000000000000000
11364460000000000000000000000000000000000000000000000000000000000000000000000000
11364470000000000000000000000000000000000000000000000000000000000000000000000000
11364480000000000000000000000000000000000000000000000000000000000000000000000000
```

```
11364490000000000000000000000000000000000000000000000000000000000000000000000000
11364500000000000000000000000000000000000000000000000000000000000000000000000000
11364510000000000000000000000000000000000000000000000000000000000000000000000000
11364520000000000000000000000000
11365010000000000000010101000100000000000000000000000000000000000000000000010100
11365020000000000000000000000000000000000000002000100010000000010001000100000000000000
11365030000000000000000000000000001010000000000000000000000000000100000001000001000001
11365040100000000000001000000000000000000000000100000000000000000000000000000000
11365050000001000000000000000000000000000000000000100000000001000000000000000000000
11365060000000000000100010000000000000000000000000000000000000000000000000000000
11365070000000000000000000000000001000000000000000000000000000000000000000000000
11365080000000000000000000000000000000000000000000000000000000000000000000000100
11365090200000000000000000000000000000000000000000000000000000100010000000000000
11365100000000000000000000000000000000000000000000000000000000000000000000000000
11365110200000000000000000000000000000000000000000001000000000000100010000000000
11365120000000000000000000000000000000000010000000000000000000000000000000000010000
11365130000000000000001000000000000000100000000000000000000010000000000000000000
11365140000000000000000000000000000000000000000000000000000000000000000000000100
11365150000000000000001000010000000000000000000000000000000000000000000000000000
11365160000000000000000000000000000000000000000000000000000000000000000000000000
11365170000000000000000000000000000000000000000000000000000000000000000000000000
11365180000000000000000000000000000000000000000000000000000000000000000000000000
11365190000000000000000000000000000000000000000000000000100000000000000000000000
11365200000000000000000000000000000000000001000000000000000000000000000000000000000
11365210000000000000000000000000000000000000000000000000000000000000000000000000
11365220000000000000000000000000000000000000000000000000000000000000000000000000
11365230000000000000000000000000000000000000000000000000000000000000000000000000
11365240000000000000000000000000000000000000000000000000000000000000000000000000
11365250000000000000000000000000000000001000000000000000000000000000000000000000000
11365260000000000000000000000000000000000000000000000000000000000000000101000000
11365270100000000000000000000000000000000000000000000000000000000000000000000000
11365280000000000000000000000000000000000000000000000000000000000000000000000000
11365290000000000000000000000000000000000000000000000000000000000000000000000000
11365300000000000000000000000000000000000000000000000000000000000000000000000000
11365310000000000000000000000000000000000000000000000000000000000000000000000000
11365320000000000000000000000000000000000000000000000000000000000000000000000000
11365330000000000000000000000000000000000000000000000000000000000000000000000000
11365340000000000000000000000000000000000000000000000100000000000000000000000000001
11365350000000000000000000000000000000000000000001000000000000000000000000000000000000
11365360000000000000000000000000000000000000000000000000000000000000000000000100
11365370000000000000000000000000000000000000000000000000000000000000000000000000
11365380000000000000000000000000000000000000000000000000000000000000000000000000
11365390000000000000000000000000000000000000000000000000000000000000000000000000
11365400000000000000000000000000000000000000000000000000000000000000000000000000
11365410000000000000000000000000000000000000000000000000000000000000000000000000
11365420000000000000000000000000000000000000000000000000000000000000000000000000
11365430000000000000000000000000000000000000000000000000000000000000000000000000
11365440000000000000000000000000000000000000000000000000000000000000000000000000
11365450000000000000000000000000000000000000000000000000000000000000000000000000
11365460000000000000000000000000000000000000000000000000000000000000000000000000
11365470000000000000000000000000000000000000000000000000000000000000000000000000
11365480000000000000000000000000000000000000000000000000000000000000000000000000
11365490000000000000000000000000000000000000000000000000000000000000000000000000
11365500000000000000000000000000000000000000000000000000000000000000000000000000
11365510000000000000000000000000000000000000000000000000000000000000000000000000
11365520000000000000000000000000
11366010000000000000000000000000001000000001000000000000000000000000000000000000
11366020100000001000000000001000100000000000000000000000000000000000000000000100
11366030000000000000000000000000000000000000000000000000000000000000000000000000
11366040000000000000000000000000001000000000000000000000000000000000000000000000100
11366050000000000100000000000000000000000000000000000000000000000000000000000000
11366060000000000000000000000000000000000000100000000000000000000000000000000000
11366070000000000000000000000000010000000000000000000000000000000000000000000001
11366080000000000000000000000000000000000000000000000000000000000000000000000000
11366090100000000000000000000101000000000000000000000000000000000100000000000000
11366100100000000000000000000000000000000000000000000000000000000000000000000000
11366110000000000000000000000001000000000000000000000000000000010000010000000000
11366120000001000000000000010000000000000000000100010000000000000000000000000000
11366130000000000000000000000000000000000000100000000000000000000000000000000000
11366140000000000000000000000000000000000000000000000000000000000000000000000000
11366150100000000000000000000000000000000000000000000000000001000000000000000000
11366160000000000000000000000000000000000000000000000000000000000000000000000000
11366170000100000000000000000000000000000000000000000000000000000000000000000000
11366180000000000000000000000000000000000000000000010000000000000000000000000000
11366190000000000000000000000000000000000000000000000000000000000000000000000000
11366200000000000000000000000000000000000000000000000000000000000000000000000000
11366210000000000000000000000000000000000000000000000000000000000000000000000000
11366220000000000000000000000000000000000000000000000000000000000000000000000000
11366230000000000000000000000000000000000000000000000000000000000000000000000000
11366240000000000000000000000000000000000000000000000000000000000000000000000000
11366250000000000000000000000000000000000000000000000000000000000000000000000000
11366260000000000000000000000000000000000000000000000000000000000000000000000000
11366270002000000000000000000000000000000000000000000000000000000000000000000000
11366280000000000000000000000000000000000000000000000000000000000000000000000000
11366290000000000000000000000000000000000000000000000000000000000000000000000000
11366300000000000000000000000000000000000000000000000000000000000000000000000000
11366310000000000000000000000000000000000000000000000000000000000000000000000000
11366320000000000000000000000000000000000000000000000000000000000000000000000000
11366330000000000000000000000000000000000000000000000000000000000000000000000000
11366340000000000000000000000000000000000000000000000000000000000000000000000000
11366350000000000000000000000000000000000000000000000000000000000000000000000000
11366360000000000000000000000000000000000000000100000000000000000000000001000000000
11366370000000000000000000000000000000000000000000100000000000000000000000000000
11366380000000000000000000000000000000000000000000000000000000000000000000000000
11366390000000000000000000000000000000000000000000000000000000000000000000000000
11366400000000000000000000000000000000000000000000000000000000000000000000000000
11366410000000000000000000000000000000000000000000000000000000000000000000000000
11366420000000000000000000000000000000000000000000000000000000000000000000000000
11366430000000000000000000000000000000000000000000000000000000000000000000000000
11366440000000000000000000000000000000000000000000000000000000000000000000000000
11366450000000000000000000000000000000000000000000000000000000000000000000000000
11366460000000000000000000000000000000000000000000000000000000000000000000000000
11366470000000000000000000000000000000000000000000000000000000000000000000000000
11366480000000000000000000000000000000000000000000000000000000000000000000000000
11366490000000000000000000000000000000000000000000000000000000000000000000000000
11366500000000000000000000000000000000000000000000000000000000000000000000000000
11366510000000000000000000000000000000000000000000000000000000000000000000010000
11366520000000000000000000000000
11367010000000000000000000000000010001000000000010000000000000000000000000001000000
11367020100000200000000000000000000000000000000000001000000000000000000000000000000
11367030000000000000000000000000000000200000000001010000000000000000001000000000002
11367040000000000000000000000000000000001000000000000000000000000000000000000000000
11367050000000000000000000000000000000000000000000000000000000000000000000000100
11367060000000000010000000000000000000000000000000000000001000000000000000000000
11367070000000000000000000000000000000000000000000000000000000000000000000000100
11367080000000000000000000000000000000001000000000000000000000000000000000000000010000
11367090000000000010000000000000000000000000000000000000000000001000000000000000
11367100000000000000000020000000000000000000000000000000000000000000000000000000
11367110000000000000000000000000000000000000000000000000000000000000000000000000
11367120000000000010000000000000000000000000001000000000000000000000000000000000
```

```
1136713000000000000100000000000000000000000000000001000000000000000
1136714000010000000000000000000000000000000000000000000000000000000
1136715000001000000000000000000000000000000000000000000000000000000
1136716000000000000000000000000000001000000000000000000000000000000
1136717010000000000000000000000000000000000000000000000000000000000
1136718000000000000000000000000000000000000000000000000000000000000
1136719000000000000000000000000000000000000000000000000000000000000
1136720000000000000000000000000000000000000000000000000000000000000
1136721000000000000000000000000000000000000000000000000000000000000
1136722000000000000000000000000000000000000000000000000000000000000
1136723000000000000000000000000000000000000000000000000000001000000
1136724000000000000000000000000000000000000000000000000000000000000
1136725000000000000000000000000000000000000000000000000000000000000
1136726000000000000000000000000000000000000000000000000000000000000
1136727000000000000010000000000000000000000000000000000000000000000
1136728000000000000000000000000000000000000000000000000000000000000
1136729000000000000000000000000000000000000000000000000000000000000
1136730000000000000000000000000000000000000000000000000000000000000
1136731000000000000000000000000000000000000000000000000000000000100
1136732000000000000000000000000000000000000000000000000000000000000
1136733000000000000000000000000000000000000000000000000000000000000
1136734000000000000000000000000000000000000000000000000000000000000
1136735000000000000000000000000000000000000000000000000000000000000
1136736000000000000000000000000000000010000000000000000000000000000
1136737000100000000000000000000000001000000010000000000000000000000
1136738000000000000000000000000000000000000000000000000000000000000
1136739000000000000000000000000000000000000000000000000000000000000
1136740000000000000000000000000000000000000000000000000000000000000
1136741000000000000000000000000000000000000000000000000000000000000
1136742000000000000000000000000000000000000000000000000000000000000
1136743000000000000000000000000000000000000000000000000000000000000
1136744000000000000000000000000000000000000000000000000000000000000
1136745000000000000000000000000000000000000000000000000000000000000
1136746000000000000000000000000000000000000000000000000000000000000
1136747000000000000000000000000000000000000000000000000000000000000
1136748000000000000000000000000000000000000000000000000000000000000
1136749000000000000000000000000000000000000000000000000000000000000
1136750000000000000000000000000000000000000000000000000000000000000
1136751000000000000000000000000000000000000000000000000000000000000
113675200000000000000000000
1136801000000000000010000000000000000000000000000000000000000000000
1136802000000000000000000000000000000001000001000000000000000010000
1136803000000000000100000000000000000000001000001000100000000000000
1136804000000000000000000000000000000000000000000000000000000000000
1136805000010000000000000000000000000000000000000000000000000000000
1136806000000000000000000000000000000000000000000000000000000000000
1136807000000000000000000010000000000000000000000000000000000000000
1136808000000000000000000000000000000000000000000000000000000000000
1136809000000000000000000000000000000000000000000000000000000000000
1136810000000000000000000000000000000000000000000000000000000000000
1136811000000000000000000000000000000000000000000000000000000000000
1136812000000000000000000000000000000000000000000000000000000000000
1136813000000100000000000000000000000000000100000000001000000000000
1136814000000000000000000000000000000000000000000000000000000000000
1136815030000000000000000000000000000000000000000000000000000000000
1136816000000001000000000000000000000000000000000000000000000000000
1136817000000000000000000000000000000000000000000000000000000000000
1136818000000000000000000010000000000000000000000000000000000000000
1136819000000000000000000000000000000000000000000000000000000000000
1136820000000000000000000000000000000000000000000000000000000000000
1136821000000000000000000000000000000000000000000000000000000000000
1136822000000000000000000000000000000000000000000000000000000010000
1136823000000000000000000000000000000000000000000000000000000000000
1136824000000100000000000000000000100000000000000000000000000000000
1136825000000000000000001000000000000000000000000000000000000000000
1136826000000000000000000000000000000000000000000000000000200000000
1136827000000000000000000000000000000000000000000000000000000000000
1136828000000000000000000000000000000000000000000000000000000000000
1136829000000000000000000000000000000000000000000000000000000000000
1136830000000000000000000000000000000000000000000100000000000000000
1136831000000000000000000000000000000000000000000000000000000000000
1136832000000000000000000000000000000000000000000000000000000000000
1136833000000000000000000000000000000020000000000000000000000000000
1136834000000000000000000000000000000000000000000000000000000000000
1136835000000000000000000000000000000000000000000000000000000000000
1136836000000000000000000000000000000000000000000000000000001000000
1136837000000000000000000000100000000000000000000000000000000000000
1136838000000000000000000000000000000000000000000000000000000000000
1136839000000000000000000000000000000000000000000000000000000000000
1136840000000000000000000000000000000000000000000000000000000000000
1136841000000000000000000000000000000000000000000000000000000000000
1136842000000000000000000000000000000000000000000000000000000000000
1136843000000000000000000000000000000000000000000000000000000000000
1136844000000000000000000000000000000000000000000000000000000000000
1136845000000000000000000000000000000000000000000000000000000000000
1136846000000000000000000000000000000000000000000000000000000000000
1136847000000000000000000000000000000000000000000000000000000000000
1136848000000000000000000000000000000000000000000000000000000000000
1136849000000000000000000000000000000000000000000000000000000000000
1136850000000000000000000000000000000000000000000000000000000000000
1136851000000000000000000000000000000000000000000000000000000000000
113685200000000000000000000
1136901000000000000000000000000000100000000000000000000000000000000
1136902000000000000000000000000000000000000000000100000000000000000
1136903000000000000000000000000000000000000000000000000010000000000
1136904000000000000000000000000000100000000000000000000000000000000
1136905000000000000000000000000000000000000000000000000000000000000
1136906000000000000000000000000000000000000000000000000000000000000
1136907000000000000000000000000000000000000010000000000000000000000
1136908000000000000000000000000000000000000000000000000000000000000
1136909000000000000000000000000000000000000000000000000000000000000
1136910000000000000000000000000000000000000000000000000000000000000
1136911000000000000000000000000000000000000000000000000000000000000
1136912000000000000000000000000000000000000000000000000000000000000
1136913001000000000000000000000000101000000000000000000010101000000
1136914000000000000000000000000000000000000000000000000000000000000
1136915000000000000000000000000000000000000000000000000000000000000
1136916000000000000000000000000000000000000000000000000000000000000
1136917000000000000000000000000000000000000000000000000000000000000
1136918000000000000000001000000000010000000000000000000000000000000
1136919000000000000000000000000000000000000000000000000000000010000
1136920000000000000000000000000000000000000000000000000000000000000
1136921000000000000000000000000000000000000000000000000000000000000
1136922000000000000000000000000000000000000000000000000000000000000
1136923000000000000000000000000000000000000000000000000000000000000
1136924000000000000000000000000000000000000000000000000000000000000
1136925000000000000000000000000000000000000000000000000000000000000
1136926000000000000000000000000000000000000000000000000000000000000
1136927000000000000000000000000000000000000000000000000000000000000
1136928000000000000000000000000000000000000000000000000000000000000
```

```
11369290000000000000000000000000000000000000000000000000000000000000000000000000
11369300000000000000000000000000000000000000000000000000000000000000000000000000
11369310000000000000000000000000000000000000000000000000000000000000000000000000
11369320000000000000000000000000000000000000000000000000000000000000000000000000
11369330000000000000000000000000000000000000000000000000000000000000000000000000
11369340000000000000000000000000000000000000000000000000000000000000000000000000
11369350000000000000000000000000000000000000000000000000000000000000000000000000
11369360000000000000000000000000000000000000000000000000000000000000000000000000
11369370000000000000000000000000000000000000000000000000000000000000000000000000
11369380000000000000000000000000000000000000000000000000000000000000000000000000
11369390000000000000000000000000000000000000000000000000000000000000000000000000
11369400000000000000000000000000000000000000000000000000000000000000000000000000
11369410000000000000000000000000000000000000000000000000000000000000000000000000
11369420000000000000000000000000000000000000000000000000000000000000000000000000
11369430000000000000000000000000000000000000000000000000000000000000000000000000
11369440000000000000000000000000000000000000000000000000000000000000000000000000
11369450000000000000000000000000000000000000000000000000000000000000000000000000
11369460000000000000000000000000000000000000000000000000000000000000000000000000
11369470000000000000000000000000000000000000000000000000000000000000000000000000
11369480000000000000000000000000000000000000000000000000000000000000000000000000
11369490000000000000000000000000000000000000000000000000000000000000000000000000
11369500000000000000000000000000000000000000000000000000000000000000000000000000
11369510000000000000000000000000000000000000000000000000000000000000000000000000
113695200000000000000000000000000
11370010000000000000000000010100000000100000000000000000000010000000010000000000
11370020000000000000000000000000000000000000000000000000000000010000010000000000
11370030000000000000000000000000000000000000000000100000001000001000000000000001
11370040000000000000000100010000000000000000000000021000000000000000101000000000
11370050000000000000000000000000000000000000000000010000010000000000000000000000
11370060000000000000000000000001000010000000000000000000000000000000000001000000
11370070000000000000000020000000000000000000000000000000000000000000000100000000
11370080000000000000000000000000000000000000000100000000000000000000000100000000
11370090000000000000000000000000000000000000000000000000000000000000000000000000
11370100000000000000000000000000000000000000000000000000000000010000000000000000
11370110000000000000000000000000000000000000000000000000000000000000000000000000
11370120000000000000000000000000000000000000000000000000000001000000000000000100
11370130100000000000000000000000000000100000000001000000000000000000000000000000
11370140100000000000000000000000000000000000000000000000000000000000000000000000
11370150000000000000000000000000000000000000000100000000000000000000000000000000
11370160000000000000000000000000000000000001000000000000000000000000000000000000
11370170000000000000000000000000000000000000000000000000000000000000000000000000
11370180000000000000000000000000000000000000000000000000000000000000000000000000
11370190000000000000000000000000000000000000000000000000000000000000000000000000
11370200000000000000100000000000000000000000000000000000000000000000000000000000
11370210000000100010000000000000000000000000000000000000000000000000000000000000
11370220000000000000000000000000000000000000000000000000000000000000000000000000
11370230000000000000000000000000000000000000000100000000000000000000000000000000
11370240000000100000000000000000100000000000000000000000000000000000000000000000
11370250000000000000000000000000000000000001000000000000000000000000000000000000
11370260000000000000000000000000000000000000000000000000000000000000000000000000
11370270000000000000000000000000000000000000000000000000000000000000000000000000
11370280000000000000000000000000000000000000000000000000000000000000000000000000
11370290000000000000000000000000000000000000000000000010000000000000000000000000
11370300000000000000000000000000000000000000000000000000000000000000100000000000
11370310000000000000000000000000100000000000000000000000000000000000000000000000
11370320000000000000000000000000000000000000000000000000000000000000000000000000
11370330000000000000000000000000000000000000000000000000000000000000000000000000
11370340000000000000000000000000000000000000010000000000000000000000000000000000
11370350000000100000000000000000000000000000000000000000000000000000000000000000
11370360010000000000000000000000000000000000000000000000000000000000000200010000
```

```
11370370010000000000000000000000000000000000000000000000000000000000000000000000
11370380000000000000000000000000000000000000000000000000000000000000000000000000
11370390000000000000000000000000000000000000000000000000000000000000000000000000
11370400000000000000000000000000000000000000000000000000000000000000000000000000
11370410000000000000000000000000000000000000000000000000000000000000000000000000
11370420000000000000000000000000000000000000000000000000000000000000000000000000
11370430000000000000000000000000000000000000000000000000000000000000000000000000
11370440000000000000000000000000000000000000000000000000000000000000000000000000
11370450000000000000000000000000000000000000000000000000000000000000000000000000
11370460000000000000000000000000000000000000000000000000000000000000000000000000
11370470000000000000000000000000000000000000000000000000000000000000000000000000
11370480000000000000000000000000000000000000000000000000000000000000000000000000
11370490000000000000000000000000000000000000000000000000000000000000000000000000
11370500000000000000000000000000000000000000000000000000000000000000000000000000
11370510000000000000000000000000000000000000000000000000000000000000000000000000
113705200000000000000000000000000
11419010000000000000000000000000000000000000000000000000000000000000000000000000
11419020000000000000000000000000000000000000000000000000000000000000000000000000
11419030000000000000000000000000000000000010000000000000000000000000000000000000
11419040000000000000000000000000000000000000000000000000000000000000000000000000
11419050000000000000000000000000000000000000000000000000001000000000000000000000
11419060000000000000000000000000000000000000000000000000000000100000000000000000
11419070000000000000000000000000000000000000000000000000000000000100000000000000
11419080000000000000000000000000000000000000000000000000000000000000000000000000
11419090000000000000000000000000000000000000000000000000000000000000000000000000
11419100000000000000000000000000000000000000000000000000000000000000000000000000
11419110000000000000000000000000000000000000000000000000000000000000000000000000
11419120000000000000000000000000000000000000000000000000000000000000000000000000
11419130000000000000000000000000000000000000000000000000000000000000000000000000
11419140000000000000000000000000000000000000000000000000000000000000000000000000
11419150000100000000000010100000000000000000000000000000000000000000000000300001
11419160100020000010001000000000000000000000000001000000000000000000100000000000
11419170000000000000000000000000000000000000000000000000000000000000000000000000
11419180000000000000000000000000000000000000000000000000000000000000000000000000
11419190000000000000000000000000000000000000000000000000000000000000000000000000
11419200000000000000000000000000001000000000000000000000000000000000000000000000
11419210000000000000000000000000000000000000000000000000000000000000000000000000
11419220000000000000000000000000000000000000000000000000000000000010000000000000
11419230000000000000000000000000000000000000000000000000000000000000000000000000
11419240000000000000000000000000000000000000000000000000000000000000000000000000
11419250000000000000000000000000000000000000000000000000000000000000000000000000
11419260001010000000000000000000000000000000000000000000000000000000000000000000
11419270000000000000000000000000000000000000000000000000000000000000000000000000
11419280000000000000000000000000000000000000000000000000000000000000000000000000
11419290000000000000000000000000000000000000000000000000000000000000000000000000
11419300000000000000000000000000000000000000000000000000000000000000000000000000
11419310000000000000000000000100000000000000000000000000000000000000000000000000
11419320100000000000000000000000000000000000000000000000000000000000000000000000
11419330000000000000000000000000000000000000000000000000000000000000000000000000
11419340000000000000000000000000000000000000000000000000000000000000000000000000
11419350000000000000000000000000000000000000000000000000000000000000000000000000
11419360000000000000000000000000000000000000000000000000000000000000001000000000
11419370000000010000000000000000000000000000000000000000000000000000000000000000
11419380000000000000000000000000000000000000000000000000000000000000000000000000
11419390000000000000000000000000000000000000000000000000000000000000000000000000
11419400000000000000000000000000000000000000000000000000000000000000000000000000
11419410000000000000000000000000000000000000000000000000000000000000000000000000
11419420000000000000000000000000000000000000000000000000000000000000000000000000
11419430000000000000000000000000000000000000000000000000000000000000000000000000
11419440000000000000000000000000000000000000000000000000000000000000000000000000
```

```
11419450000000000000000000000000000000000000000000000000000000000000000
11419460000000000600000000000000000000000000000000000000000000000000000
11419470000000000000000000000000000000000000000000000000000000000000000
11419480000000000000000000000000000000000000000000000000000000000000000
11419490000000000000000000000000000000000000000000000000000000000000000
11419500000000000000000000000000000000000000000000000000000000000000000
11419510000000000000000000000000000000000000000000000000000000000000000
11419520000000000000000000000
11420010000000000000000000000000000000000000000000000000000000000000000
11420020000000100000000000000000000000000000000001000000000000000000000
11420030000000000000000000000000000000100000000000000000000000000000000
11420040000000000000000000000000000000000000000000000000000000000000000
11420050000000000000000000000000000000000000100000000000000000000000000
11420060000000000000000000000000000000000000000000000000000000000000000
11420070000000000000000000000000000000000000000000000000000000000000000
11420080000000000000000000000000000000000000000000000000000000000000000
11420090000000000000000000000000000000000000000000000000000000000000000
11420100000010000000000000000000000000000000000000000000000000000000000
11420110000000000000000000000000000000000000000000000000000000000000000
11420120000000000000000000000000000000000000000000000000000000000000000
11420130000000000000000000000000000000000000100000000000000000000000000
11420140000000000000000000000000000000000000000000000000000000000000000
11420150000000000000000000000000000000000000000000000000000000000000000
11420160000000000000000000000000000000000000000000000000000000000000000
11420170000000000000000000000000000000000000000000000000000000000000000
11420180000000000000000000000000000000000000000000000000000000000000000
11420190000000000000000000000000000000000000000000000000000000000000000
11420200000000000000000000000000000000000000000000000000000000000000000
11420210000000000000000000000000000000000000000000000000000000000000000
11420220000000000000000000000000000000000000000000000000000000000000000
11420230000000000000000000000000000000000000000000000000000000000000000
11420240000000000000000000000000000000000000000000000000000000000000000
11420250000000000000000000000000000000000000000000000000000000000000000
11420260000000000000000000000000000000000000000000000000000000000000000
11420270000000000000000000000000000000000000000000000000000000000000000
11420280000000000000000000000000000000000000000000000000000000000000000
11420290000000000000000000000000000000000000000000000000000000000000000
11420300000000000000000000000000000000000000000000000000000000000000000
11420310000000000000000000000000000000000000000000000000000000000000000
11420320000000000000000000000000000000000000000000000000000000000000000
11420330000000000000000000000000000000000000000000000000000000000000000
11420340000000000000000000000000000000000000000000000000000000000000000
11420350000000000000000000000000000000000000000000000000000000000000000
11420360000000000000000000000000000000000000000000000000000000000000000
11420370000000100000000000000000000000000000000000000000000000000000000
11420380000000000000000000000000000000000000000000000000000000000000000
11420390000000000000000000000000000000000000000000000000000000000000000
11420400000000000000000000000000000000000000000000000000000000000000000
11420410000000000000000000000000000000000000000000000000000000000000000
11420420000000000000000000000000000000000000000000000000000000000000000
11420430000000000000000000000000000000000000000000000000000000000000000
11420440000000000000000000000000000000000000000000000000000000000000000
11420450000000000000000000000000000000000000000000000000000000000000000
11420460000000000000000000000000000000000000000000000000000000000000000
11420470000000000000000000000000000000000000000000000000000000000000000
11420480000000000000000000000000000000000000000000000000000000000000000
11420490000000000000000000000000000000000000000000000000000000000000000
11420500000000000000000000000000000000000000000000000000000000000000000
11420510000000000000000000000000000000000000000000000000000000000000000
11420520000000000000000000000
11421010000000000000000000000000000000000000000000000000000000000000000
11421020000000000000000000000000000100000000000000000000000000000000000
11421030000000000000000000000000000000000000000000001000000000000000000
11421040000000000000000000000000000000000000000000000000000000000000000
11421050000000000010000000000000000000000000100010000000000000000000000
11421060000000000000000000000000000000000000000000000010000000000000000000000000
11421070000000000000000000000000000000000000000000000000000000000000000
11421080000000000000000000000000001000000000000000000000000000000000000
11421090000000000000000000000000000000000000000000000000010000000000000
11421100000000000000000000000000000000000000000000000000000000000000000
11421110000000000000000000000000000000000000000000000000000000000000000
11421120000000000000000000000000000000000000000000000000000000000000000
11421130000000000000000000000000000000000000000000000000000000000000000
11421140000000000000000000000000000000000000000100000000000000000000000
11421150100000000000000000000000000000000000000000000000000000000000000
11421160000000000000000000000000000000000000000000000000000000000000000
11421170000000000000000000000000000000000000000000000000000000000000000
11421180000000000000000000000000000000000000000000000000000000000000000
11421190000000000000000000000000000000000000000000000000000000000000000
11421200000000000000000000000000000000000000000000000000000100000000000
11421210000000000000000000000000000000000000000000000000000000000000000
11421220000000000000000000000000000000000000000000000000000000000000000
11421230000000000000000000000000000000000000000000000000000000000000000
11421240000010000000100000000000000000000000000000000000000000000000000
11421250000000000000000000000000000000000000000000000000000000000000000
11421260000000000000000000000000000000000000000000000000000000000000000
11421270000000000000000000000000000000000000000000000000000000000000000
11421280000000000000000000000000000000000000000000000000000000000000000
11421290000000000000000000000000000000000000000000000000000000000000000
11421300000000000000000000000000000000000000000000000000000000000000000
11421310000000000000000000000000000000000000000000000000000000000000000
11421320000000000000000000000000000000000000000000000000000000000000000
11421330000000000000000000000000000000000000000000000000000000000000000
11421340000000000000000000000000000000000000000000000000000000000000000
11421350000000000000000000000000000000000000000000000000000000000000000
11421360000000000000000000000000000000000000000000000000000000000000001
11421370000000000000000000000000000000000000000000000000000000000000000
11421380000000000000000000000000000000000000000000000000000000000000000
11421390000000000000000000000000000000000000000000000000000000000000000
11421400000000000000000000000000000000000000000000000000000000000000000
11421410000000000000000000000000000000000000000000000000000000000000000
11421420000000000000000000000000000000000000000000000000000000000000000
11421430000000000000000000000000000000000000000000000000000000000000000
11421440000000000000000000000000000000000000000000000000000000000000000
11421450000000000000000000000000000000000000000000000000000000000000000
11421460000000000000000000000000000000000000000000000000000000000000000
11421470000000000000000000000000000000000000000000000000000000000000000
11421480000000000000000000000000000000000000000000000000000000000000000
11421490000000000000000000000000000000000000000000000000000000000000000
11421500000000000000000000000000000000000000000000000000000000000000000
11421510000000000000000000000000000000000000000000000000000000000000000
11421520000000000000000000000
11422010101010000000000000102000001000000000000000000000001000000000000
11422020000000000100000000000000000000000000000000000000000000001000100
11422030000000100000000000101000000000300000000000002000100000000000000
11422040000000000000000000000000000000001000100000001000001000000000000
11422050000000100000000000000000000000000000000000000000000001000000000
11422060000000100000000000001000002000000000100000001020000000001000000
11422070000000000000001000000010100010001000100000000000100000000000000
11422080000000000000000000000000000000101000000000000000000000100000000
```

```
11422090000000000000000000000000000000000000000000000000000000000001010001010100000
11422100100000000000000000001000000010000010001010100000000000000000000000001010000
11422110000000000000000000000000000000000000000000000000100000000000000100000000000
11422120000000000000000000000000000000000000000000000000000000000000100000000001010100
11422130000000000000000000000000000000000000000000000000000000000010000000001000000000001
11422140000000000000000000000000000000000000000000000100000000000000000000000000000000
11422150000000000101000000000001000000000000000000000000000000000000000000000000
11422160000000000000000000000000000000000000000000000000000000000000002000000000000
11422170000000000000000000000000000000000000000000000000000000000000000000000000
11422180000000000000000000000000000000000000000000000000000000000000000000000000
11422190000000000000000000000000000000000000000000000000000000000000000000000000
11422200000000000000000000000000000000000010000000000000000000000000000000000000
11422210000000000000000000000000000000000000001000000000000000000000000001000101000000
11422220000000000000000000000000000000000000000000000000000000000000000000000000
11422230000000000000000000000000000001000000000000000000000000000000000000000000
11422240000000000000000000000000000000000100000000000000000000000000000100000000000000
11422250100000000000000000000000000000000000000000000000000000000000000000000000000
11422260000000000000000000000000000000000100001000000000000000000000000000000000002000000
11422270000000000000000000000000000000000000000000000000000000000000000000000000
11422280000000100000000000000000000000000000000000000000000000000000001000000000000000010000
11422290000000000000000000000000000000000000000000000000000000000000000000000000
11422300000000000000000000000000000000000000000000000000000000000001000000000000000
11422310000000000000000000000000000000000000000000000000000000000000000000000000
11422320000000000000000000000000000000000000000000000000000000000000000000000000
11422330000000000000000000000000000000000000000100000000000000000000000000000000000
11422340000000000000000000000000000000000000000000000000000000000000000000000000
11422350000000000000000000000000000000000000000000000000000000000000000000000000
11422360001000000000000000100000000000000000000000000010000000000000000000000000000000000102
11422370000001000000000000000000000000000000000000000000000000000000000000000000
11422380000000000000000000000000000000000000000000000000000000000000000001000000000
11422390000000000010000000000000000000000001000000000000000000000000000000000000000
11422400100000000000000000000000000000000000000000000000000000000000000000000000
11422410000000000000000000000010000000000000000000000000000000000000000000000000001000000000020000000
11422420000001000000000000000000000000000000000000000000000000100000000000000000000000
11422430000000000000000000000000000000000000000000000000000000000010000000000000000000
11422440000000000000000000000000000000000000000000001000000000000001000000000000000000000000
11422450000000000000000000000000000000000000000000000000000000000000000000000000
11422460000000000000000000000000000000000000000000000000000000000000000000000000
11422470000000000000000000000000000000000000000000000000000000000000000000000000
11422480000000000000000000000000000000000000000000000000000010000000000000000000000000000
11422490000000000000000000000000000000000000000000000000000000000000000000000000
11422500000000000000000000000010102000000000000000000000000000000000000000000010100000000010000000000000000000
11422510000000000000000000000000000000000000100000000000000000000000000000000000001000000000000001000000000
11422520000000000000000000000000
11999010000000000000000000000000000000000000000000000000000000000000000000000000
11999020000000000000000000000000000000000000000000000000000000000000000000000100
11999030000000000000000000000000000000000000000000000000000000000000000000000000
11999040000000000000000000100000000000000000000000000000000000000000000000000000000
11999050000000000000000000000000000000000000000000000000000000000000000000000000
11999060000000000000000000000000000000000000000000000000000000000000000000000000
11999070000000000000000000000000000000000000000000000000000000000000000000000000
11999080000000000000000000000000000000000000000000000000000000000000000000000000
11999090000000000000000000000000000000000000000000000000000000000000000000000000
11999100000000000000000000000000000000000000000000000000000000000000000000000000
11999110000000000000000000000000000000000000000000000000000000000000000000000000
11999120000000000000000000000000000000000000000000000000000000000000000000000000
11999130000000000000000000000000000000000000000000000000000000000100000000000000000000000000
11999140000000000000000000000000000000000000000000000000000000000000000000000000
11999150000000000000000000000000000000000000000000000000000000000000000000000000
11999160000000000000000000000000000000000000000000000000000000000000000000000000
11999170000000000000000000000000000000000000000000000000000000000000000000000000
11999180000000000000000000000000000000000000000000000000000000000000000000000000
11999190000000000000000000000000000000000000000000000000000000000000000000001000000000
11999200000000000000000000000000000000000000000000000000000000000000000000000000
11999210000000000000000000000000000000000000000000000000000000000000000000000000
11999220000000000000000000000000000000000000000000000000000000000000000000000000
11999230000000000000000000000000000000000000000000000000000000000000000000000000
11999240000000000000000000000000000000000000000000000000000000000000000000000000
11999250000000000000000000000000000000000000000000000000000000000000000000000000
11999260000000000000000000000000000000000000000000000000000000000000000000000000
11999270000000000000000000000000000000000000000000000000000000000000000000000000
11999280000000000000000000000000000000000000000000000000000000000000000000000000
11999290000000000000000000000000000000000000000000000000000000000000000000000000
11999300000000000000000000000000000000000000000000000000000000000000000000000000
11999310000000000000000000000000000000000000000000000000000000000000000000000000
11999320000000000000000000000000000000000000000000000000000000000000000000000000
11999330000000000000000000000000000000000000000000000000000000000000000000000000
11999340000000000000000000000000000000000000000000000000000000000000000000000000
11999350000000000000000000000000000000000000000000000000000000000000000000000000
11999360000000000000000000000000000000000000000000000000000000000000000000000000
11999370000000000000000000000000000000000000000000000000000000000000000000000100000
11999380000001010000000000000000000000000000000000000000000000000000000010103000100
11999390000000000000000010000000000000000000100020000000000000000000000000000000000000000000
11999400000000000000000000000000000000010100000000100000000000000000000000000000001000000000
11999410001000000000000000000000000000000000000000000000000000000000000000000000
11999420001000000100000000100000000000100000001000000000000000000000000000000000000
11999430000000000000000000000000000000000000000000000000000100000000000000100000000000000000
11999440000000000000000000000000000000000010001000000000000000000000000000000000000000000001
11999450000000000000000000000000000000000000000000000000000000000000000000000010000
11999460000000000000000002000000000000000000000000000000000000000000000000001000000000000000
11999470000000000000000000000000000000000000000000010000000000000000000000000000001000000000
11999480000000000000000000000000000000000000000000000000000000000000000000000000
11999490000000000000000000000000000000000000000000000000000000000000000000000000
11999500000000000000000000000000000000000000000000000000000000000000000000000000
11999510000000000000000000000000000000000000000000000000000000000000000000000000
11999520000000000000000000000000
12009010100010001000000100000000000000000000000100000000000000020101000100000000000300
12009020000000000000000000200010000100002000200000000000000000000000000102000000000000000000
12009030000000001000100000000000000000000000000000700000000000000000000000000000020100
12009040000000000200004000000000100000000000010004000000000000000000000201000000000100
12009050000000001010002000000000000000000000000000000001000000000000000000010000000000010000
12009060000000000000000000000000000000001000500000000000000000000100000000000020100000000010200
12009070000000001000000000000000000010000000000000000000000000000000000001010000000000000000000000
12009080000000001000000000000000000010000010000000000000000000001000000000001020100020001000000000000
12009090000000000000000000000000000000000000000000000000000000000000001020000101020200000000
12009100000000000000000000000000000000000000000000000000000000000000000000000020000
12009110010000000000000000000000000000000000000000000100000000000000000001000000000000000000000000000100000000
12009120004000000000000000000000000000000000000000000000000000000000000000000000000
12009130001000100000000000000000000000000000000000000000000000000000000000001000000000000000
12009140000000000000000000000000000000000000000000000100000000000000000000000000000000
12009150100000000000000000000000000000000000000000000000000000000000000000000000
12009160000000000000000000000000000000000000000000000000000000000000000000000000
12009170000000000000000000000010000000000000000000000000000000000000000000000000000000
12009180000000000000000000000000000000000000000000000100000000000010000000000000000000000000000
12009190000000000000000000000000000000000000000100000000000000000000000000000000000000
12009200000000000000000000000000000000000000000000000000000000000000000000000000000010000
12009210000000000000000000000000000000000000000000000000041000000000000000000001000000000000000000000000101000000
12009220000000000000000000000000000000000000000000000000000020000000000000000000000000000000000010000
12009230000000000000000000000000000000000000000000000000000000000000000000000100
12009240000000000000000000000000000000000000000000000000000000000000000000000000
```

```
12009250000000000000000000000000000000000000000000000000000000000000000000000000
12009260000000000000000000000000000000002000000000000000000000000000000000000000
12009270000000100000000000000000000000000000000000000000000000000000000000000000
12009280000000000000000000000000000000000000000000000000000000000000000000000000
12009290000000000000000000000000000000000000000000000000000000000000000000000000
12009300200000000000000000000000000100000000000000000000000000000000000000000000
12009310000000000000000000101010000000000000000000000000000000000000000000000000
12009320000000000000000000000000000000000000000000000000000000000000000000000100
12009330000000000000000000000010000000000000000000000000000000000000000000000000
12009340000000000000000000000000000000000000000000000000000000000000000000000000
12009350000000000000000000000000000000000000000000000000000000000000000000000000
12009360000000000000000000000000000000000000000000000000000000000000000000000105
12009370101000000000001000000200000000000000000000000000000000000000000000010000
12009380000000010000000000000000000000000000000000000000000000000000000000000000
12009390000000000000000000000000000000000000000000000000000000000000000000000000
12009400000000000000000000000000000000000000000000000000000000000000000000000000
12009410000000000000000000000000000000000000000000000000000000000000000000000000
12009420000000000000000000000000000000000000000000000000000000000000000000000000
12009430000000000000000000000000000000000000000000000000000000000000000000000000
12009440000000000000000000000000000000000000000000000000000000000000000000000000
12009450000000000000000000000000000000000000000000000000000000000000000000000000
12009460000000000000000000000000000000000000000000000000000000000000000000000000
12009470000000000000000000000000000000000000000000000000000000000000000000000000
12009480000000000000000000000000000000010000000000000000000000000000000000000000
12009490000000000000000000000000000000000000000000000000000000000000000000000000
12009500000000000000000000000000000000000000000000000000000000000000000000000000
12009510000000000000000000000000000000000000000000000000000000000000000000000000
12009520000000000000000000000000
12010010000000000000000000000000010000000000000000000000000000000000000000100100
12010020001010000000000000000000000001000010000000000000001000000000010000000000
12010030000000000000000000000000010000000000000000000000000000000000000200000000
12010040001000000000000000000000000000000000000000000000010000000000000000000000
12010050000000000000000000000000000000000000000000000001000000000000000001000000000
12010060000000000000000000000000000100000000000000000000000000000000000000000000
12010070000000000000000000001010000101010000000000000001000000000000000000000000000
12010080000000010100000000000000000000000000000000000000000000000000000000020000
12010090000000000000000000000000000000000000000000000000000000000001000000100000000
12010100000000000000000000000000000000001000100000000000000000000000000000000000
12010110100000000000000000000000000000000000000000000000000000000010000000010000
12010120000010000000000010000010100000000000000000000000000000000000000000000000
12010130000000000000000000100000000000000000000000000000000000000000000000000000
12010140100000000000000000000000000000000000000000000000000000000000000000000001
12010150100000000000000000000000000100000000000000000000000000000000000000000000
12010160000000000000000000000000000000000000000000000000000000200000000000000000
12010170000000000000000000000000000000000000000000000000000000000000000000000000
12010180000000000000000000000000000000000000000101000000000000000000000000000000
12010190000000000000000000000000000000000000000000000000100000000000000000000000
12010200100010000000000000000000000101000000000000000000000000000000000000000000
12010210000000000000000000000000000000000000000000000000000000000000000000000000
12010220000000000000000000000000000000000000000000000000000000000000000000000000
12010230000000000000000000000000000000000000000000000000000000000000000000000000
12010240000000001000000000000000000000000100010000000000000000000000000000000000
12010250000000000000000000000000000100000000000100000000000000000000000000000000
12010260000000000000000000000000000000000000000001000000000001000000000000000000
12010270100010000000000000002000000010000000000000000000000000000000000000000000
12010280000000000000000000000000000000000000000000000000000000000000000000000000
12010290000000000000000000000000000000000000000000000000000000000000100000000000
12010300000000000000000000000000000000000000000000000000000000000000000000000000
12010310000000000000000000000000000000000000000000000000000000000000000000000000
12010320000000000000000000000000000000000000000000000000000000000000000000000000
12010330000000000000000000000000000000000000000000000000000001000100000000000000
12010340100000100001000000000000000000000000000000000000000000000000000000000000
12010350000000000000000000000000000000000000000000000000000000000000000000000000
12010360000000000000000000000001000001000000000000000000000000000000001000100100
12010370000000000000000000000000000100000000000000003000000000000000000000000000
12010380000000000000000000000000000000000000000000000000000000000000000000000000
12010390000000000000000000000000000000000000000000000000000000000000000000000000
12010400000000000000000000000000000000000000000000000000000000000000000000000000
12010410000000000000000000000000000000000000000000000000000000000000000000000000
12010420000000000000000000000000000000000000000000000000000000000000000000000000
12010430000000000000000000000000000000000000000000000000000000000000000000000000
12010440000000000000000000000000000000000000000000000000000000000000000000000000
12010450000000000000000000000000000000000000000000000000000000000000000000000000
12010460000000000000000000000000000000000000000000000000000000000000000000000000
12010470000000000000000000000000000000000000000000000000000000000000000000000000
12010480000000000000000000000000000000000000000000000000000000000000000000000000
12010490000000000000000000000000000000000000000000000000000000000000000000000000
12010500000000000000000000000000000000000000000000000000000000000000000000000000
12010510000000000000000000000000000000000000000000000000000000000000000000000000
12010520000000000000000000000000
12011010000000000000000000000000000000000000000001010401000000001000000000000200
12011020000000000000000000000000000000000000101000000000000000000000000000000000
12011030000000000000000000000000000000000000000000000000000000000000001000000000
12011040000000000000000000000000000000000000000000000000100000000000000000000000
12011050000000000000000000000000000000000000000000000000001000000000000000000000
12011060000000000000000000000000000000000000000100000000000000000000000000000000
12011070000000000000000000000000010000000000000000000000000000000000010000000000
12011080000000000000000000000000000000000000000000000000000000000000000000000000
12011090000000000000000000000000000000000000000000000000000000000000000000000000
12011100100000000000000000000000000000000000000000000000000000000000000000000000
12011110000000000000000000000000000000000000000000000000000000000000000000000000
12011120000000000000000000000000000000000000000000000000000000000000000000000000
12011130000000010000000000000000000000000000000000000000000000000000001000000000
12011140000000000000000000000000000000000000000000000000000000000000000000000000
12011150000000000000000000000000000000000000000000000000000000000000000000000000
12011160000000000000000000000000000000000000000000000000000000000000000000000000
12011170000000000000000000000000000000000000000000000000000000000000000000000000
12011180000000010000000000000000000000000000000000000000000000000000000000000000
12011190000000000000000000000000000000000000000000000000000000000000000000000000
12011200000000000000000000000000000000000000000000000000000000000000000000000000
12011210000000000000000000000000000000000000000000000000000000000000000000000000
12011220000000000000000000000000000000000000000000000000000000000000000000000000
12011230000000000000000000000000000000000000000000000000000000000000000000000100
12011240000000010000000000000000000000001000000000000000000000000000000000000000
12011250000000000000000000000000000000000000000000000000000000000000000000000000
12011260000000000000000000000000000000000000000000000000000000000000000000000000
12011270000000000000000000000000000000000000000000000000000000000000000000000000
12011280000000000000000000000000000000000000000000000000000000000000100000000000
12011290000000000000000000000000000000000000000000000000000000000000000000000000
12011300000000000000000000000000000000000000000000000000000000000000000000000000
12011310000000000000000000000000000000000000000000000000000000000000000000000000
12011320000000000000000000000000000000000000000000000000000000000000000000000000
12011330000000000000000000000000000000000000000100000000000000000000000000000000
12011340000000000000000000000000000000000000000000000000000000000000000000000000
12011350000000000000000000000000000000000000000000000000000000000000000000000000
12011360000000000000000000000000000000000000000000000000000000000000000000000000
12011370000000000000000000000000000000300000000000000000000000000000000000000000
12011380000000000000000000000000000000000000000000000000000000000000000000000000
12011390000000000000000000000000000000000000000000000000000000000000000000000000
12011400000000000000000000000000000000000000000000000000000000000000000000000000
```

```
12011410000000000000000000000000000000000000000000000000000000000000000000000000
12011420000000000000000000000000000000000000000000000000000000000000000000000000
12011430000000000000000000000000000000000000000000000000000000000000000000000000
12011440000000000000000000000000000000000000000000000000000000000000000000000000
12011450000000000000000000000000000000000000000000000000000000000000000000000000
12011460000000000000000000000000000000000000000000000000000000000000000000000000
12011470000000000000000000000000000000000000000000000000000000000000000000000000
12011480000000000000000000000000000000000000000000000000000000000000000000000000
12011490000000000000000000000000000000000000000000000000000000000000000000000000
12011500000000000000000000000000000000000000000000000000000000000000000000000000
12011510000000000000000000000000000000000001000000000000000000000000000000000000
12011520000000000000000000000000
12013010100010001000002010001000000300000000601100101000001000002000202
12013020000001000100010001000203030103020000002030000040001010201000200
12013030000004000100000100030102010301000203010000000201010000003000201
12013040105010000000000030100000001020002020001020202000101000000000001
12013050100010002000000000000100020100010000020400000101000000000000000
12013060005000200000000000000001000200000300010300000300000200010000010 2
12013070100000001020202030001030101010000000100010000000000000000010201
12013080100000104000000010001000000000000000101020015020000010200000000
12013090001020101020102030000020500020001000100010000040301000000000001
12013100000030000010000000000020000000102020201000000000000000020102000 1
12013110000000000001010200030000020000040000020000000001010001010200001
12013120002020002000001030000000040001010000010100000100010001000100020 2
12013130000010003000101000100000000201000101010002000000005000001010101
12013140001010200000000200000000010000000100000000000010000000000000000 1
12013150300000202040000005030201000000000000000101010100020002010001000 2
12013160100000000000000000002020001000201010000000002000101010004000001
12013170000010105000002000000000000000000000100000000000000000000000000 0
12013180101010100010100000200010000000102000000000100020001000100000000
12013190000020000000000000000030000010100000000030104010003020100020100
12013200000010000000200000003000002000000000000000000001010000000000000
12013210100000002010000000000000000000000000000000001000000010000000 0
12013220000000000000000000000000000000000000000000000100000000000 0
12013230000000100000200000000010101000000000000010100010001000000000100
12013240100020100000000000000000000010301000000001000000000100000000000
12013250101000000000000000020000010000010100000100000000000000000000001
12013260000000000000000000000000000000000010002010002030000010200000 0
12013270000000000000000000000010000000000000000000100000000000000000000 0
12013280000000001010201000100000000000000000000000000000001000000000000
12013290000000000000000000001000000000000500000000000000000000000010000
12013300000000000000000000000010000000000000001000000000000000000000100
12013310000000000000000010301000000000000000000000002000001000300000001
12013320000000000000000101000000000000000300000000000000000010000000 0
12013330000000000000000000010000010000000301000002010100000000000000000
12013340000000000000000000000000000000001020001000000000000100000000100 01
12013350100000101000000000000300000000000100000000000000000000000010000
12013360000000200020000100020000000000100000000000000000100010100000102
12013370301010300000000100000100000200000000100000000000000000100000000 00
12013380002000000000000000000000000000000000000000000000000000000000000 0
12013390000000010000000000000000000000000000000000000000000000000000000 0
12013400000000000000000000000000000000000000000000000000000000000000000 0
12013410000000000000000000000000000000000000000000000000000000000000000 0
12013420000000000000000000000000000000000000000000000000000000000000000 0
12013430000000000000000000000000000000000000000000000000000000000000000 0
12013440000000000000000000000000000000000000000000000000000000000000000 0
12013450000000000000000000000000000000000000000000000000000000000000000 0
12013460000000000000000000000000000000000000000000000000000000000000000 0
12013470000000000000000000000000000000000000000000000000000000000000000 0
12013480000000000000000100000000000000001000000000000000000000000000000000100
12013490000000000000000000000000000001010000000000000000000000001000000000000
12013500002000000000000000000000000010000000100000000000000000000000000000002
12013510000000000000000000000000000000000000000010000000000000000000000000000
120135200000000000000000000001
12014010000010000000000100000200000000000001000100000000000000000100000000
12014020000000100000000000000020100000010000000000001000000000000000000 0
12014030000000000000100000200000000100000000010000000000000100000000000
12014040000000001000000000000000100000000000000000100000000000000000000
12014050000000000000000000000000000000000000000000000000010000000000 0
12014060000000000000000000000000001000000001000000000000000000001020000000000
12014070000000000000000000000000100000000000000000000000000000100000000000 0
12014080000000101000000000000001000000000000000000000000000000102000100000
12014090001000000000000000000001000000000000010000000000000001000000000000
12014100100000000000001000000000000100010000000000000000000000000100000001
12014110000000000000000000000000000000000100000000000000000001010000000000 0
12014120000100000000000000000000000000000100000000000000000003000101020202 00
12014130003000100010101000000001000000000001000101000000000200000000000 1
12014140100000000000000000000100000000000000000000010000000000000000101000400
12014150200010103000001000000100000000000000000000000000000000000000000000000
12014160000000100000001010000010001000000102000000102030100000200000000000
12014170005000101000003010001000000010200010000000003000000000500000000 0
12014180001000000030200010001030001000001000000100010000000000201030101
12014190000000301000000000101050000000000000000000000100000300000000010004
12014200000000100000000000000000010000000100000200000100000100000000000 0
12014210000000030000000000000000000000101000000000000000000000000000001000000
12014220001000000000000000000000000000000000000000000000000000102000000000 1
12014230100000000000020001010100000000000000000000000000000001000000001000 0
12014240000000000000100000000003000100000000000000000000000000000200000000
12014250100000004010000000000102000000000010000000100000000000000000000010100
12014260001000000000000100000000000000010100000100000100000000000000000000000
12014270000000000000000100020100000000200000000000000000000000000000000000
12014280000000000000105000000001000000000000101000000000000000000000000000 0
12014290000000100000000000000000000200000000000000000000100000100000000000 2
12014300100000000000000000201030000000000000040001000000000000000000000000100
12014310000000000000002000000000000000100000101000000000000010200000000000200
12014320300000000000000202010200050000000000100000001000100010000000000000
12014330000000000000000000000100000000100000000000000000000000020100000000 0
12014340000000000000000000000000000000000000000000000000000000000000000000 0
12014350000000000000000101000000102000000000000000000000000000000000030004
12014360100000000050004000102010000000000000010000000000000000000000010001
12014370101000000000000100010000000000020000000000000000000000000000000000 0
12014380000000000100000000000000000000000000000000000000000000000000000000 0
12014390000000000000000000000000000000000000000000000000000000000000000000 0
12014400000000000000000000000000000000000000000000000000000000000000000000 0
12014410000000000000000000000000000000000000000000000000000000000000000000 0
12014420000000000000000000000000000000000000000000000000000000000000000000 0
12014430000000000000000000000000000000000000000000000000000000000000000000 0
12014440000000000000000000000000000000000000000000000000000000000000000000 0
12014450000000000000000000000000000000000000000000000000000000000000000000 0
12014460000000000000000000000000000000000000000000000000000000000000000000 0
12014470000000000000000000000000000000000000000000000000000000000000000000 0
12014480000000000000000000000000010000000000000000000000000000000000000000 0
12014490000000000000000000000000000000000000000000000000000000000000000000 0
12014500000000000000000000000000000000000000000000000000000000000000000000 0
12014510000000000000000000000000000000000000000000000000000000000000000000 0
120145200000000000000000000002
12015010000000200000000000000000000000000000000000100000000000000000000000
12015020000010100000000000000000000000000000000001000001000000000000001
12015030000000100000000000101000000000000000000000100000000001000000000100
12015040000000000000000000001000001000000000000000001010000000000000000
```

```
12015050000000000000000000000000000000000001010000001000000002000000001010000000
12015060000001010000000000000000000000000000000001000000001000000100000000000000
12015070000000000020000001000000001000000000000000000000000100000000000000000000
12015080000000000000000001000000000000000001000000000000000000000100000000000000
12015090010000000000000000000000000101000000000000000000000000000000000000000000
12015100000000000000000000000000000000200001000000000000000000000000002000000001
12015110000000000000000000000000000000000000000100000000000000000000000000000000
12015120000002010000000000000001010100000000000000000000000000010000000000000000
12015130000000000000000000000000000000000000000000001010000000000000000001010000
12015140000000000000000000000000000000000000000000000000000000000000000000000000
12015150000000000010000000100000000000000001000000000000000000000000000000000000
12015160000100000000000000000001000000000000000000000010000000000000000000000000
12015170000000000000000000000000000000000000000000000000000000000000000000000000
12015180000000000000000000000000000000000000000000000000000000000000000000000000
12015190000000000000000000000000000000000000000000000000000000000000000000000000
12015200000000000001000000000000000000000000000000000000000001000000000000000000
12015210000000000000000000000000000000000000000000000000000000000000000000000000
12015220010000000000000000000010000000000000000000000000000000000000000000000000
12015230000000000000001000000000000000001000001000000000000000000000000000000000
12015240000000000000000000000100000000000001000000000000000000000000001010000000
12015250100000000000000000000000000000001000000000000000000000000000000000000000
12015260000000000010000000000000000000000000000000000000000001000000000000000000
12015270000000000000000000000000000000000000000000000000000000000001000000000000
12015280000000000000000000000000000000000000000000000000000000000000000000000000
12015290000000000000000000000000000000000000000000000000000000000000000000000000
12015300000000000000000000000000100000000000000000000000000000000000000000000000
12015310000000000000000000000000000000000000000000000000000000000000000000000000
12015320000000000000000000000000000000000000000000000000000000000000001000000000
12015330000000000000000000000000000000000000000000000000000000000000000000000000
12015340000000000000000000000000000000000000000000000000000000000000000000000000
12015350000000000000000000000000000000000000000000000000000000000000000000000000
12015360000000000000000000000000000000000000000000000000000000000000000000000000
12015370000000000000000000000000000000000100010000000000000000000000000000000000
12015380000000000000000001000000000000000000000000000000000000000000000000000000
12015390000000000000000000000000000000000000000000000000000000000000000000000000
12015400000000000000000000000000000000000000000000000000000000000000000000000000
12015410000000000000000000000000000000000000000000000000000000000000000000000000
12015420000000000000000000000000000000000000000000000000000000000000000000000000
12015430000000000000000000000000000000000000000000000000000000000000000000000000
12015440000000000000000000000000000000000000000000000000000000000000000000000000
12015450000000000000000000000000000000000000000000000000000000000000000000000000
12015460000000000000000000000000000000000000000000000000000000000000000000000000
12015470000000000000000000000000000000000000000000000000000000000000000000000000
12015480000000000000000000000000000000000000000000000000000000000000000000000000
12015490000000000000000000000000000000000000000000000000000000000000000000000000
12015500000000000000000000000000000000000000000000000000000000000000000000000000
12015510000000000000000000000000000000000000000000000000000000000000000000000000
120155200000000000000000000000000
12042010000001000000000000000000000000000000000000000000000000000000000000000000
12042020000000000000000000000000000000100000000000000000000000000000001000000000
12042030000000000000000000000000000000001000000000000000000000000200000000000000
12042040000000000000100000000000000000000000000000000000000000000000000000000000
12042050000000000000000000000000000000000000000000000000000000000000000000000000
12042060000000000000000000000000000001000000000000000000000000000000020000000000
12042070000000000000000000000000000000000000000000000000000000000000000000000000
12042080000000000000000000000000000000000000000000000000000000000000000000000000
12042090000000000000000000000000000000000001000000000000000000000000000000000000
12042100000000000000000000000000000000000000000100000000000000000000000000000000
12042110000000000000000000000000000000000000000000000000000010000000000000000000
12042120000000000000000000001000000000000000000000000000000000000000000000000000
12042130000000000000000000000000000000000000000000000000000000000000000000020001
12042140000000000000000000000000000000000000000000000000000000000000000000000000
12042150000001000000000000000000000000000000000000000000000000000000000000000000
12042160000000000000000000000100000000000000000000000000000100000000000000000000
12042170000000000010000000000000000000000000000000000000000000000000000000000000
12042180000000000000000100000010000000000000000000000000000000000000000000000000
12042190000000000000000000000000000000000000000000000000000000000000000000000000
12042200000000000000000000000100000000000000000000000000000000000000000000000000
12042210000000000000000000000000000000000000000000000000000000000000000000000000
12042220000000000000000000000000000000000000000000000000000000000000000000000000
12042230000000000000000000000000000000000000000000000000000000000000000000000000
12042240000001000000000000000000000000000000000000000000000000000000000000000000
12042250000000001000000000000000000000000000000000000000000000000000000000000000
12042260000000000000000000000000000000000000000000000000000100000000000000000000
12042270000000000000000000000000000000000000000000000000000000000000000000000000
12042280000000000000000000000000000000000000000000000000000000000000000000000000
12042290000000000000000000000000000000000000000000000000000000000000000000000000
12042300000000000000000000000000000000000000000000000000000000000000000000000000
12042310000000000000000000000000000000000000000000000000000000000010000000000000
12042320000000000000000000000000000000000000000000000000000000000000000000000000
12042330000000000000000000000000000000000000000000000000000000000000000000000000
12042340000000000000000000000000000000000000000000000000000000000000000000000000
12042350000000000000000000000000000000000000000000000000000000000000000000000000
12042360000000000000000000000000000000000000000000000000000000000000000000000000
12042370000000000000000000000000000000000000000000000000000000000000000000000000
12042380000000000000000000000000000000000000000000000000000000000000000000000000
12042390000000000000000000000000000000000000000000000000000000000000000000000000
12042400000000000000000000000000000000000000000000000000000000000000000000000000
12042410000000000000000000000000000000000000000000000000000000000000000000000000
12042420000000000000000000000000000000000000000000000000000000000000000000000000
12042430000000000000000000000000000000000000000000000000000000000000000000000000
12042440000000000000000000000000000000000000000000000000000000000000000000000000
12042450000000000000000000000000000000000000000000000000000000000000000000000000
12042460000000000000000000000000000000000000000000000000000000000000000000000000
12042470000000000000000000000000000000000000000000000000000000000000000000000000
12042480000000000000000000000000000000000000000000000000000000000000000000000000
12042490000000000000000000000000000000000000000000000000000000000000000000000000
12042500000000000000000000000000000000000000000000000000000000000000000000000000
12042510000000000000000000000000000000000000000000000001000000000000000000000000
120425200000000000000000000000000
12052010000000000010000000000000000000000000000000000000000001010000002020000000
12052020000000000000000000000000000000000100000000010000000000000000000000000100
12052030000000001000000000000000000000000001000000100000000000000000001000000000
12052040000000000000000000000000000000000000000000000001000000000000000000000000
12052050000000000000000000000000000000000000000000000000000000000001000000000000
12052060000000000000000000000000000000000000000000001000000000000000000000000000
12052070010000000000000000010000000000000000000000000000000000000001000000000000
12052080000100000000000010000000000000000000000000000000000000000000000000000000
12052090000000000000000000000000001000000000000000000000000020100000000000000000
12052100000000000000000000000000000000000000000000000000000000000000000000000000
12052110000100020000001000000000000000000000000000000000000000010000000000000000
12052120000000000000000000010000000000000000000000000000000000000000000000010001
12052130000000000010000000000000000000000000000100000000000100000000000000000000
12052140000000000000000000000000000000000000000000000000000000000000000000000000
12052150000000000000000000000000000010001000000000010000010100000000002000000000
12052160000000000010000000000000000000000000000000000000000000000010000010000000
12052170000000000000000000010000000000000000000000000000000100000000000000000000
12052180000000000010000000200010000000000000000000000000101000000000000000000000
12052190000000000000000000000000100000000000000000000000000000000000001020100000
12052200010000000001000000000000010000000000000000000000000000000000000000000000
```

```
12052210000000000000000000000000000000000000000000000000000000000000000000000000
12052220000000000000000000000000000000000000000000000000000000000000000000000000
12052230000000000000000000000000000000000000000000000000000000000000100000000000
12052240000000000000000000000000000000001000000000000000100000010000100000000000
12052250000000000000000000000000000000000000000000000000000000000000000000000000
12052260000000000000000000000000000000000000000001000000001000000000000000000000
12052270000000000000010000100000000000000000000000100000000000000000000000000000
12052280000000000000000000000000000000000000000000000000000000000000100000000000
12052290000000000000000000001000010000000000000000000000000000000000000100010000
12052300000000000000000000000000000000000000000000000000000000000000000000000000
12052310000000000000000000100000000000000000000000000000000000000000000000000000
12052320000000000000000000000001000000000000000000000000000000000000000000000100
12052330000000000000000000000000000000000000000000000000000000000000000000000000
12052340000000000000000000000000000000000000000000000000000000000000000000000000
12052350000000000000000000000000000000000000000000000000000000000000000000000000
12052360000000000000000000000001000000000000000000000000000000000000000100000000
12052370000000000000010000000000000000000000000000000000000000000000000000000000
12052380000000000000000000000000000000000000000000000000000000000000000000000000
12052390000000000000000000000000000000000000000000000000000000000000000000000000
12052400000000000000000000000000000000000000000000000000000000000000000000000000
12052410000000000000000000000000000000000000000000000000000000000000000000000000
12052420000000000000000000000000000000000000000000000000000000000000000000000000
12052430000000000000000000000000000000000000000000000000000000000000000000000000
12052440000000000000000000000000000000000000000000000000000000000000000000000000
12052450000000000000000000000000000000000000000000000000000000000000000000000000
12052460000000000000000000000000000000000000000000000000000000000000000000000000
12052470000000000000000000000000000000000000000000000000000000000000000000000000
12052480000000000000000000000000000000000000000000000000000000000000000000000000
12052490000000000001000000000000000000000000000000000000000000000100000000000000
12052500000001000000000000000000000000000000000000000000000000000000000000000000
12052510000000000000000000000000000000000000000000000000000000000000000000000000
12052520000000000000000000000000
12065010000000000000000000000000000000000000000000001000000000000000000000000001000000
12065020000000000000000000000000000010000000000000000000000000000000000000000000
12065030000000000000000000000000000000000000000001000000000000000000010000000000
12065040102000000000000000010000000000001000000000000000000000000000000000000000
12065050000000000000000000000000000000000000000000000000000000000000000000000000
12065060000000010000000010000000000000000000000000000000000000000000000000000000
12065070000000000000000000000000000000000000000000000000000002000200000001010000
12065080000000000000000000000000000000000000000000000000000000000000000000000100
12065090000000000000000000000000000000000000000000000000000000000000000000000000
12065100000000000000000000000000000000000000000000000000000000000000000000000000
12065110000000000000000000000000000000000000100000000000000000000000000000000000
12065120000000000000000000000000000000000000000000000000000000000000000000000000
12065130000000000000000000000000010000001000000000000010000000010000000000000000
12065140000001010000000000000000000000000000000000000000000000000000000000000000
12065150100000000000000000000000000000000000000000000000000000000000000000000000
12065160000000000000000000000000000000000000000000001000000000000000000000000000
12065170000000000000000000000000000000000000000000000000000000000000000000000000
12065180000000000000000000000000000000000000000000000000000000000000000000000000
12065190000000000000000000000000000000000000000000000000000000000000001000000000
12065200000000000000100000000000000000000000000000000000000000000000000000000000
12065210000000000000000000000000000000000000000000000010000000000100000000000000
12065220000000000000000000000000000000000000000000000000000000000000000000000000
12065230000000000000000000000000000000000000000000000000000000000001000000000000
12065240000000000000000000000000000000000000000000000000001000000100000000000000
12065250000000000000000000000000000000000000000000000000000000000000000000000000
12065260000000000000000000000000000000000000000000000000001000100000000000000000
12065270000000000000000000000000000000000000000000000000000000000000000000000000
12065280000000000000000000000000000000000000000000000000000000000000001000000000
12065290100000000000000000010000000000000000000000000000000000000000000000000000
12065300000000000000000000000000000000000000000000000000000000000000000000000000
12065310000000000000000000000000000000000000000000000000000000000000000000000000
12065320000000000000000000000000000000000000000000000000000000000000000000000000
12065330000000000000000000000000000000000100000000000000100000000000000000000100
12065340000000000000000000000000000000000000000000000000000000000000000000000000
12065350000000000000000000000000000000000000000000000000000000000000000000000000
12065360000000000000000000000000000000000000000000001000000000000000100000000000
12065370000000000000000000000000000000000000000003000000000000000000000000000000
12065380000000000000000000000000000000000000000000000000000000000000000000000000
12065390000000000000000000000000000000000000000000000000000000000000000000000000
12065400000000000000000000000000000000000000000000000000000000000000000000000000
12065410000000000000000000000000000000000000000000000000000000000000000000000000
12065420000000000000000000000000000000000000000000000000000000000000000000000000
12065430000000000000000000000000000000000000000000000000000000000000000000000000
12065440000000000000000000000000000000000000000000000000000000000000000000000000
12065450000000000000000000000000000000000000000000000000000000000000000000000000
12065460000000000000000000000000000000000000000000000000000000000000000000000000
12065470000000000000000000000000000000000000000000000000000000000000000000000000
12065480000000000000000000000000000000000000000000000000000000000000000000000000
12065490000000000000000000000000000000000000000000000000000000000000000000000000
12065500000000010000000000000000000000000000000000000000000000000000000000000000
12065510000000000000000000000000000000000000000000000000000000000000000000000000
12065520000000000000000000000000
12072010000000000000000000000000000000000000000001000000000000000000000000000000
12072020000000000000000000000000000000000000000000000000000000000000000000000000
12072030000000000000000000000000000000000000000000000000000000000001000000000000
12072040001000000000000000000000000000000000000000000000000000000000000000000000
12072050000000000000000000000000000000000000000000000000000000000000000000000000
12072060000000000000000000000000000000000000000000000000000010000000000000000000
12072070000000000000000000000000000000000000000000000000000000000000000000000000
12072080000000000000000000000000000000000000000000000000000000000000000000000000
12072090000000000000000000000000000000000000000000000000000000000000000000000000
12072100000000000000000000000000000000000000000000000000000000000000000000000000
12072110000000000000000000000000000000000000000000000000000000000000000000000000
12072120000000000000000000000000000000000000000000000000000000000000000000000000
12072130000000000000000000000000000000000000000100000000000000000000000000000000
12072140000000000000000000000000000000000000000000000000000000000000000000000000
12072150000000000000000000000000000000000000000000000000000000000000000000000000
12072160000000000000000000000000000000000000000000000000000000000000000000000000
12072170100000000000000000000000000000000000000000000000000000000000000000000000
12072180000000000000000000000000000000000000000000000000000000000000000000000000
12072190000000000000000000000000000000000000000000000000000000000000000000000000
12072200000000000000000000000000000000000000000000000000000000000000000000000000
12072210000000000000000000000000000000000000000000000000000000000000000000000000
12072220000000000000000000000000000000000000000000000000000000000000000000000000
12072230000000000000000000000000000000000000000000000000000000000000000000000000
12072240000000000000000000000000000000000000000000000000000000000000000000000000
12072250000000000000000000000000000000000000000000000000000000000000000000000000
12072260000000000000000000000000000000000000000000000000000000000000000000000000
12072270000000000000000000000000000000000000000000000000000000000000000000000000
12072280000000000000000000000000000000000000000000000000000000000000000000000000
12072290000000000000000000000000000000000000000000000000000000000000000000000000
12072300000000000000000000000000000000000000000000000000000000000000000000000000
12072310000000000000000000000000000000000000000000000000000000000000000000000000
12072320000000000000000000000000000000000000000000000000000000000000000000000000
12072330000000000000000000000000000000000000000000000000000000000000000000000000
12072340000000000000000000000000000000000000000000000000000000000000000000000000
12072350000000000000000000000000000000000000000000000000000000000000000000000000
12072360000000000000000000000000000000000000000000000000000000000000000000000000
```

```
12072370000000000000000000000000000000000000000000000000000000000
12072380000000000000000000000000000000000000000000000000000000000
12072390000000000000000000000000000000000000000000000000000000000
12072400000000000000000000000000000000000000000000000000000000000
12072410000000000000000000000000000000000000000000000000000000000
12072420000000000000000000000000000000000000000000000000000000000
12072430000000000000000000000000000000000000000000000000000000000
12072440000000000000000000000000000000000000000000000000000000000
12072450000000000000000000000000000000000000000000000000000000000
12072460000000000000000000000000000000000000000000000000000000000
12072470000000000000000000000000000000000000000000000000000000000
12072480000000000000000000000000000000000000100000000000000000000
12072490000000000000000000000000000000000000000000000000000000000
12072500000000000000000000000000000000000000000000000000000000000
12072510000000000000000000000000000000000000000000000000000000000
120725200000000000000000000
12076010000000000000000000000000200000000000000000100000000100001
12076020000000000000000000000000000000000000001000000000000000000
12076030000000000000000000000000000000000000000000000000000000000
12076040000000000000000000000000000000000000000000000000000000000
12076050000000000000000000000000000000000000000000000000000010000
12076060000001000000000000000000000000000000000000000000000000000
12076070000000010000000000000000000000000000000000000000000000000
12076080000000000000000000000000000000000000000000000001000000000
12076090000000000000000000000000000000000000000001000000000000001
12076100000000000000000000000000000000000000000000000000000000000
12076110000000000000000000000000000000000000000000000000100000000
12076120000000000000100000000000000000000000000000000000000000000
12076130000000000000000000000000000000000000000000000000000000000
12076140000000000000000000000000000000000000000000000000000000000
12076150000100000000000000000000000100000000000000000000000000000
12076160000000000000000000000000000000000001000000100000000000000
12076170000000010000000000000000000000000000000000000000000000000
12076180000000010001000000000000000000000000000000000000000000000
12076190000000000000000000000000000000000000000000000000000000000
12076200000000000000000000000000000000000010000000000000000000000
12076210000000000000000000000000000000000000000000000000000000000
12076220000000000000000000000000000000000000000000000000000000000
12076230000000000000000000000000000000000000000000000000000000000
12076240000000000000000000000000000000000000000000000000000000000
12076250000000000000000000000000000000000000000000000000000000000
12076260000000000000000000000000000000000000000101000000000000000
12076270000000000000000000000000000000000000000000000000000000000
12076280000000000000000000000000000000000000000000000000000000000
12076290000000000000000000000000000000000000000000000000100000000
12076300000000000000000000000000000000000000000000000000000000000
12076310000000000000000000000000000000000000000000000000000000000
12076320000000000000000000000000000000000000000000000000000000000
12076330000000000000000000000000000000000000000000000000000000000
12076340000000000000000000000000000000000000000000000000000000000
12076350000000000000000000000000000000000000000000000000000000000
12076360000001000000000001000000000000000000000000000000000000000
12076370100000000000000000000000000000000000000000000000000000000
12076380000000000000000000000000000000000000000000000000000000000
12076390000000000000000000000000000000000000000000000000000000000
12076400000000000000000000000000000000000000000000000000000000000
12076410000000000000000000000000000000000000000000000000000000000
12076420000000000000000000000000000000000000000000000000000000000
12076430000000000000000000000000000000000000000000000000000000000
12076440000000000000000000000000000000000000000000000000000000000
12076450000000000000000000000000000000000000000000000000000000000
12076460000000000000000000000000000000000000000000000000000000000
12076470000000000000000000000000000000000000000000000000000000000
12076480000000000000000000000000000000000000000000000000000000000
12076490000000000000000000000000000000000000000000000000000000000
12076500000000000000000000000000000000000000000000000000000000000
12076510000000000000000000000000000000000000000000000000000000000
120765200000000000000000000
12078010000010000101000100000002000000000000000100000000102000100
12078020000020000000000100001000000000100000010000000000000000000
12078030000010000000000010000000010100001000000000000010000010000
12078040000000001000000000000001000000000000000000000000000000000
12078050000100000000000000000000000000000000000000000000000000100
12078060000000001000000000000000000000000000000000000000000000100
12078070000000000000000100000100000000000000000000000000000000000
12078080000000000000000000000000000000000000000000010000000000000
12078090000000000000000000000100000000000000000001000001000000100
12078100000101001000000000000000001000000000000000000000000000000
12078110000000000000000000000002000000000100000000010000100000000
12078120000000000000000001000000000000000000000001000000000000000
12078130000100000000000000000100000000000001000002000000000000000
12078140000000000000000000000000000000000000000000000000000000001
12078150000100000000000000000000000000000000000000000001000100000
12078160000000000000000000000000001000100000000000000000000000000
12078170002010000000000000000000000000001000000000000000000000000
12078180102000000000010100010000000000100000000000001000000000100
12078190000000000001000000000000000000000001000000000003000000001
12078200000000000000000101000000100000000000000000000000000000000
12078210000000100000000000000000000000000000000000000000000000000
12078220000100000000000000000000000000000000000020000000000000000
12078230000000000000000000000001000000000000000000000000001000000
12078240000101000000000000000000000000000000000100000000000000000
12078250100000000000000000000000000000000000000000000000000000000
12078260000000000000000000000000000000000000000000000000000000000
12078270010000000000000000000001000000010001000000000000000000000
12078280000000000000000000000000001000000000000000000000001000100
12078290000000000000000000000000000000101000000000000000000010000
12078300000000001000000000000000000100000000000000000000000000000
12078310000000000000000000000000000000000000000100010100000000000
12078320000000000000000001000000000000000000000000000000000000000
12078330000000000000000000000000000010101000000100000000000000000
12078340000000000000000000000000000000000000000000000001000000000
12078350000000001000000000000001010000000000000000000000000000000
12078360010001000000000000100000000000000000000000000001010000000
12078370101000000000000000010000000000000000000000000000000000000
12078380000000000000000000000000000000000000000000000000000000000
12078390000000000000000000000000000000000000000000000000000000000
12078400000000000000000000000000000000000000000000000000000000000
12078410000000000000000000000000000000000000000000000000000000000
12078420000000000000000000000000000000000000000000000000000000000
12078430000000000000000000000000000000000000000000000000000000000
12078440000000000000000000000000000000000000000000000000000000000
12078450000000000000000000000000000000000000000000000000000000000
12078460000000000000000000000000000000000000000000000000000000000
12078470000000000000000000000000000000000000000000000000000000000
12078480000000000000000000000000000000000000001000000000000000000
12078490000000000000000000000000000000000000000000000000000000000
12078500000100000000000000000000000000000000000000000000000000000
12078510000000000000000000000000000000000000000000000000000000000
120785200000000000000000000
```

```
12079010000000001000000000000000000000000000000000000000000000010000000000000100
12079020000000000000000000000000000000000000000000000000000000000000001000000000
12079030000000000000000000000000000000000000000000000000000000000000000000000100
12079040000000000000000000000000000000000000000000010000000000001000000000000000
12079050000000000000000000000000000000000000000000000000000000000000000000000000
12079060000000000000000000000000000000000000000000000000000000000100000000000000
12079070000000100000000000000000000000000000000000000000000000000000000000000000
12079080000000000100000010000000000000000000000000000000000000000000000000000000
12079090000000000000001000000000001000000000000000000000000000010000000000000000
12079100000000000000000000000000000000000000001000000000000000000000000000000000
12079110000000000000000000000000000000100000000000000000000000000000000000010000
12079120000000000000000000100000000000000000000000000000000000000000000000000000
12079130003000000000000000000000010000000000000000001000000000000000000000000000
12079140000000000000000000000000000000000000000000000000000000000000000000000000
12079150000000000000000000000000000000000000000000000000100000000000000000000000
12079160000000000000000000000000000000000000000000000000000000000000000000000000
12079170010000000000000000000000000000000000000000000000000000000000000000000000
12079180010010000000000000000000000000000000000000000000201000000000000000000000
12079190000000000000000000000000000000000000000000000000001000000000000000000000
12079200000000000000000000000000000000100000000000000000000000000000000000000000
12079210000000000000000000000000000000000000000000000000000000000000000000000000
12079220000000000000000000000000000000000000000000000000000000000000000000000000
12079230000000000000000000000000000000100000000000000000000000000001000000000000
12079240000000000000000000000000001000000000000000000000000000000001000000000000
12079250000000000000000000000000000000000000000000000000000000000000000000000000
12079260000000000000000000000000000000000000000000000000000000000000000000000000
12079270000000000000000000000000000000000000000000000000000000000000000000000000
12079280000000000000000000000000000000000000000000000000000000000000000000000001
12079290000000000000000000100000000000000000000000000000000000000000000000000000
12079300000000000000000000000000000000000000000000000000000000000000000000000000
12079310000000000000000000000001000000000000000000000000000000000000000000000000
12079320000000000000000010000000000000000000000100000000100000000000000000000000
12079330000000000000000000000000000000000000000000000000000010000000000000000000
12079340000000000000000000001000000000000000000000000000000000000000000000000001
12079350000000000000000000000000000000000000000000000000000000000000000000000000
12079360000000000000000000000000000000000000000000000000000000000000000000000000
12079370000000000000000000000000000000000000000010000000000000000000000000000000
12079380000000000000000000000000000000000000000000000000000000000000000000000000
12079390000000000000000000000000000000000000000000000000000000000000000000000000
12079400000000000000000000000000000000000000000000000000000000000000000000000000
12079410000000000000000000000000000000000000000000000000000000000000000000000000
12079420000000000000000000000000000000000000000000000000000000000000000000000000
12079430000000000000000000000000000000000000000000000000000000000000000000000000
12079440000000000000000000000000000000000000000000000000000000000000000000000000
12079450000000000000000000000000000000000000000000000000000000000000000000000000
12079460000000000000000000000000000000000000000000000000000000000000000000000000
12079470000000000000000000000000000000000000000000000000000000000000000000000000
12079480000000000000000000000000000000000000000000000000000000000000000000000000
12079490000000000000000000000000000000000000000000000000000010000000000000000000
12079500000000000000000000000000000000000000000000000000000000000000001000000000
12079510000000000000000000000000000000000000000000000000000000000000000000000000
12079520000000000000000000000000
12080010000001000000000000000000000000010000000000001000000100000000000000000000
12080020000101000000000000000000000000000000000000000000000000000000000000000000
12080030000000000000000000000000000000100000000000000000000000000000000000010001
12080040000000000000000000000000000000000000000000000000000000000000000000000000
12080050000000000000000000000000000000000010000000000000000000000000000000000000
12080060000000000000100000000001000000000000000000000000000000000000000000000100
12080070000000001000000000000000000000000000000000000000000000000100000000000100
12080080000000000000000000000000000000000000000100000000000000000000001000000000
12080090000000000000000000000000000000000000000000000000002000000002000000010000
12080100000000000000000000000000000000000000000000000000000000000010000000000000
12080110000000000000000000000000000000000000000000000000000000010000000000000000
12080120000000000001000000000000000100000000000000000000000000000000000000000000
12080130000000000010000000000000010100000000000000000000000000000000101000000000
12080140000001000000000000000000000000000000000000000000000000000000000000000100
12080150010000000000000000000000000000000000000000000000000000000000000000000000
12080160010000000000000000000002000000000000000000000000000000000000000000000000
12080170000000000000000000000000000000000000000000000000000000000000000000000000
12080180000000020000002000000000000000000000000000000000000000000100000000000101
12080190000000000000000000000000000000100000000000000000001000000000000000000001
12080200000000000000000000000000000000000000000000000000000000000000000000000000
12080210000000000000000000000000000000000000000000000000000001000000000000000000
12080220000000000000000000000000000000000000000000000000000000000000000000000000
12080230000000000000000000000000000000000000000000000000000000000000000000000000
12080240000000000000000000000000000000000000000000000000100010000001000000000000
12080250000000000000000001000000000000000000000000000000000000000000000000000000
12080260000000000000000000000000000000000000000000000000000001000000000000000000
12080270000000000000000000000000000000000001000000000000000000000000000000000000
12080280000000000000000000000000000000000000000000000000000000000000000000000001
12080290000000000000000000000000000000000000000000000000000000000000000000000000
12080300000000000000000000000000000000000000000001000000000000000000000000000000
12080310000000000000000000000000000000000000000000000000000000000000000000000000
12080320000000000000000000100000000000000000000000000000000000000000000000000000
12080330000000000000000000000001000000000001000000000010000001000000000000000000
12080340000000000000000000000000000000000000000000000000000000000000000000000000
12080350000000000000000000000000000000000000000000000000000000000000000000000000
12080360000000000000000000000000000000000000000000000000000000000000000000000100
12080370002000000000000000000000000000000000000100010000000000000000000000000000
12080380000000000000000000000000000000000000000000000000000000000000000000000000
12080390000000000000000000000000000000000000000000000000000000000000000000000000
12080400000000000000000000000000000000000000000000000000000000000000000000000000
12080410000000000000000000000000000000000000000000000000000000000000000000000000
12080420000000000000000000000000000000000000000000000000000000000000000000000000
12080430000000000000000000000000000000000000000000000000000000000000000000000000
12080440000000000000000000000000000000000000000000000000000000000000000000000000
12080450000000000000000000000000000000000000000000000000000000000000000000000000
12080460000000000000000000000000000000000000000000000000000000000000000000000000
12080470000000000000000000000000000000000000000000000000000000000000000000000000
12080480000000000000000000000000000000000000000000000000000000000000000000000000
12080490000000000000000000000000000000000000000000000000000000000000000000000000
12080500000000000000000000000000000000000000000000000000000000000000000000000000
12080510000000000000000000000000000000000000000000000000000000000000000000000000
12080520000000000000000000000000
12085010000000000000000000000000000000000000000000000000000000000000000010000000
12085020000000000000000000000000010000000000000000010000000000000000000000000100
12085030000000000000000000000000000000001000000000000000000000000000000000000000
12085040000000000000001000100000000000000000000000000000000000000100000000000000
12085050000000000000000000000000000000000000000000010000000000000000000000000000
12085060000000000000000000000000010000000000000000001000000000000000000000000000
12085070000000000000000000000000000000100000000000001000000000000000000000000000
12085080000000000000000000000000000000000000000000000000000000000000000000000000
12085090000000000000000000000000000000000000000000001000000000000000000000000000
12085100000000000000000000000000000000000000000000000000000000000001000000000000
12085110000000000000000000000000000000000000000001010000000000000000000000000000
12085120000001000000100000000000000000000000000000000000001000100000000010000000
12085130000000000000000000000000000000000000000000000000000000000000000000000000
12085140000000000000000000000000000000000000000000000000000000000000000000000000
12085150000000000000000000000000000000000000000000000000000000000000000000000000
12085160000000000000000000000000000000000000000000000000000001000000000000000000
```

120851700000000000000000000000000000000000000000001000000000000000000000000000
120851800000000000010000000000000000000000000000000000000000000000000000000
120851900000000000000000000000000000000000000000000000000000000001000000000
120852000000000000000000000000000000000000000000000000000000000000000000000
120852100000000000000000000000000000000000000000000000000000000000000000000
120852200000000000000000000000000000000000000000000000000000000000000000000
120852300000000000000000000000000000000101000000000000000000000000000000000
120852400000000000000000000000000000000000000000000000000000000000000000000
120852500000000000000000000000000000000000000100000000000000000000000000000
120852600000000000100000000000000000000000000000000000000001000000000000000
120852700000000000000000000000000000000000000000000000000000000000000000000
120852800000000000000000000000000000000000000000000000000000000000000010000
120852900000000000000000000000000000000000000000000000000000000000000000000
120853000000000000000000000000000000000000000000000000000000000000000000000
120853100000000000000000000000000000000000000000000000000000000000101000000
120853200000000000000000000000000000000000000000000000000000000000000000000
120853300000000000000000000000000000000000000000000000000000000000000000000
120853400000000000000000000000000000000000000000000000000000000000000000000
120853500000000000000000000000000000000000000000000000000000000000000000000
120853600000000000000000000000000000000000000000000000000000000000000000000
120853700010000000000000000000000000000000000001000000000000000000000000000
120853800000000000000000000000000000000000000000000000000000000000000000000
120853900000000000000000000000000000000000000000000000000000000000000000000
120854000000000000000000000000000000000000000000000000000000000000000000000
120854100000000000000000000000000000000000000000000000000000000000000000000
120854200000000000000000000000000000000000000000000000000000000000000000000
120854300000000000000000000000000000000000000000000000000000000000000000000
120854400000000000000000000000000000000000000000000000000000000000000000000
120854500000000000000000000000000000000000000000000000000000000000000000000
120854600000000000000000000000000000000000000000000000000000000000000000000
120854700000000000000000000000000000000000000000000000000000000000000000000
120854800000000000000000000000000000000000000000000000000000000000000000000
120854900000000000000000000000000000000000000000000000000000000000000000000
120855000000000000000000000000000000000000000000000000000000000000000000000
120855100000000000000000000000000000000000000000000000000000000000000000000
120855200000000000000000000001
124140101000000000001000000001000000000000000000000000000000000000000000000
124140200000000000000000000000000000000000000001000000000000000000000000000
124140300000001000000000000000000000000000000000000000000000000000000000000
124140400000000000000000000000000000000000000000000000000000000000000000000
124140500000000000000000000000000000000000000000000000000000000000000000000
124140600000000000000000000000000000000000000000000000000000000000000000000
124140700000000000000000000000000000000000000000000000000000000000000000000
124140800000000000000000000000000000000000000000000000000000000000000000000
124140900000000000000000000000000000000000000000000000000000000000000000000
124141000000000000000000000000000000000000000000000000000000000000000000000
124141100000000000000000000000000000000000000000000000000000000000000000000
124141200000000200000000000000000000000000000000000000000000000000000000000
124141300000000000000000000000000000000000000000000000000000000000001000000
124141400000000000000000000000000000000000000000000000000000000000000000000
124141500000000000000000000000000000000000000000000000000000000000000000000
124141600000000000000000000000000000000000000000000000000000000000000000000
124141700000000000000000000000000001000000000001000000000000000000000000000
124141800000000000000000000000000000000000000000000000000000000000000000000
124141900000000000000000000000000000000000000000000000000000000000000000000
124142000000000000000000000000000000000000000000000000000000000000000000000
124142100000000000000000000000000000000000000000000000100000000000000000000
124142200000000000000000000000000000000000000000000000000000000000000000000
124142300000000000000000000000000000000000000000000000000000000000000000000
124142400000000000000000000000000000000000000000000000000000000000000000000
124142500000000000000000000000000000000000000000000000000000000000000000000
124142600000000000000000000000000000000000000000000000000000000000000000000
124142700000000000000000000000000000000000000000000000000000000000000000000
124142800000000000000000000000000000000000000000000000000000000000000000000
124142900000000000000000000000000000000000000000000000000000000000000000000
124143000000000000000000000000000000000000000000000000000000000000000000000
124143100000000000000000000000000000000000000000000000000000000000000000000
124143200000000000000000000000000000000000000000000000000000000000000000000
124143300000000000000000000000000000000000000000000000000000000000000000000
124143400000000000000000000000000000000000000000000000000000000000000000000
124143500000000000000000000000000000000000000000000000000000000000000000000
124143600000000000000000000000000000000000000000000000000000000000000000001
124143700000001000000010000000000000000000000000000000000000000000000000000
124143800000000000000000000000000000000000000000000000000000000000000000000
124143900000000000000000000000000000000000000000000000000000000000000000000
124144000000000000000000000000000000000000000000000000000000000000000000000
124144100000000000000000000000000000000000000000000000000000000000000000000
124144200000000000000000000000000000000000000000000000000000000000000000000
124144300000000000000000000000000000000000000000000000000000000000000000000
124144400000000000000000000000000000000000000000000000000000000000000000000
124144500000000000000000000000000000000000000000000000000000000000000000000
124144600000000000000000000000000000000000000000000000000000000000000000000
124144700000000000000000000000000000000000000000000000000000000000000000000
124144800000000000000000000000000000000000000000000000000000000000000000000
124144900000000000000000000000000000000000000000000000000000000000000000000
124145000000000000000000000000000000000000000000000000000000000000000000000
124145100000000000000000000000000000000000000000000000000000000000000000000
124145200000000000000000000000
124180100000000000200000000000010001010000000000000000000000000000000000100
124180200000000000000000000000000001020101000000000000010100010000010000000
124180301000000300000000000000000001000000000000100000000000000000000000000
124180400000000000000000000000000000000000001000000000000000000000000000000
124180500000000000000000000000000000000001000000100000000100000000000000100
124180601000000030100100000104000000000010000000000000000000000000000000000
124180700000001000000000000000000000000000000000100000000000000000000000000
124180800000000000000000000000000000000000010000010000000000000000000000000
124180900000000000100000000000010000000000000000000000000000000000000020000
124181000010000000000000000100000000000010010000100000000000000000100010000
124181100010000000000000000000000000000000000000040000000000000000000000000
124181200000000000000000101000010000000000000000000000000001000000000000100
124181300000100000000010000000000000000000000000000000000000000000000000001
124181400020000000000000000000000000000000000000000000000000000000000000100
124181501000000000000000000000000000000001001010000000000000000000000010100
124181600020000000000000000000000000001000000000000000010000000000001000100
124181700040010000200000000000000000000000001000000001000000000000000000001
124181800000000000100001000000020000000000001000001010000000000000000000000
124181900000100000000000010000000000001000000000000000020000000001000000101
124182000000002000000000000001000100000000000100000000100000020000000000000
124182100000001010000000000000000000001000000000000000000000000000001000000
124182200000000000000000000000000000000000000000000000000000000000000010000
124182301000000000000000000000000000000000000000200000000000000100000000000
124182400000100000000000000001000100000000000000001000000000010000000000000
124182500000010000010200000100000101000000001000100000001000100000000000001
124182600000100000010000000000000000000000000200000000010001000000000000000
124182700000000000000000000000020000000000000000100000000000000000000000000
124182800000000000000000020000000000000000000000000000000000000000000000000
124182901010100000000000000000000000000000000000000000000000001000000000000002
124183000000000000000000000020100000000000000000000000000000000000000010000
124183100000000000000000000000000000000000000010000000000000002000000000000100
124183201000000000000000000101000100000000000000000000000000000000000000000

```
12418330000000000000000000000000000010000010000000001000201000000000
12418340000000010000000000000000000000000000000000000000010000000000
12418350000000000000000000000000000000000000000000000000000000010001
12418360000000000000000000000000000000000000000000000000000000010200
12418370000000000000000000000100002000100010000000000000000000000000
12418380000000000000000000000000000000000000000000000000000000000000
12418390000000000000000000000000000000000000000000000000000000000000
12418400000000000000000000000000000000000000000000000000000000000000
12418410000000000000000000000000000000000000000000000000000000000000
12418420000000000000000000000000000000000000000000000000000000000000
12418430000000000000000000000000000000000000000000000000000000000000
12418440000000000000000000000000000000000000000000000000000000000000
12418450000000000000000000000000000000000000000000000000000000000000
12418460000000000000000000000000000000000000000000000000000000000000
12418470000000000000000000000000000000000000000000000000000000000000
12418480000000000000000000000000000000000000000000000000000000000000
12418490000000000000000000000000000000000000000000000000000000000000
12418500000000000000000000000000000000000000000000000000000000000000
12418510000000000000000000000000000000000000000000001000000000000000
124185200000000000000000000
13033010000001001040100001020000200001010000001010102000000020002000
13033020000000000001000010001010100010000000100010000000003000000001
13033030000060100000000001000000000201000100010000100001000020000300100
13033040000000002000000000000000000000000100000100020000010000000101
13033050100000000020000001000000100010002000000001010000010100000001
13033060000000000000000000201010101000201000002020100000202000010201
13033070000001020000100000000000000000000000001000000000000000000000
13033080000000000000202000000000000000000000000000000000010000000000
13033090000000000100002000001010000000000000000000300020000010101000
13033100000000000000000000000000000000000010000100000000000000000000
13033110000000000000000100000000000000100000000000000000000000000000
13033120000020200000100000000000000000000000000000000000000001000000
13033130000001000000000000000001010000010000000000000000001000000000
13033140100000000000000000000000000000000000000000000000000000000000
13033150100300010000200010000000001000000101000000000000000000000000
13033160000000010000000000000000000000000010101010000000000000000001
13033170001000102000000000000000000000000000000000000000000100000000
13033180000001000000000000000000000000000000000000100000000000000000
13033190000000000000000000000000000000000000000000000000010001000000003
13033200000000000001000000000000000000000000000000000000000000000000
13033210000000000000000000000000000000000000000000000000010000000000
13033220000001000000000000000000000000000000000000000000000000000000
13033230000000000000000000000000000000000010000000000000000000000000
13033240000000000200000010000000000010000000000000001000100000000000
13033250000000000000000000000001000100000100000000000001010000010000000000
13033260000001000000000000000000000000000020000000000000000000000010000
13033270000000000000000000000010000000000000000000000001000000000000000
13033280000000000000000001000000000000000000001000000000000000000000000
13033290000000000000000001000000101000000000000010100000000000000000000
13033300000001000000000010000000000000000000001000000000100000000000000
13033310000000000000000001000000000000000000000000000000000000101000000
13033320000000000000000000000000010000000000000000000000000000000000000
13033330000000000000000000000000000001000000000000000000000000000010000
13033340000000000000000000000000000000000001000000000000000000000000000
13033350000000000000000000000000000000000000000000000000000000000010000
13033360100010000010000001000000000000000000000000001000000000000000601
13033370102000000101010000000000000010000000000000000000000000000000
13033380000000000000000000000000000000000000000000000000000000000000
13033390000000000000000000000000000030000000000000000000000000000000
13033400000000000000000000000000000000000000000000000000000000000000
13033410000000000000000000000000000000000010000000000000000000000000
13033420000000000000000000000000000000010000000000000000000000000000
13033430000000000000000000000000000000000000000000000000000000000000
13033440000000000000000000000000000000000000000000000000000000000000
13033450000000000000000000000000000000000000000000000000000000000000
13033460000000000000000000000000000000000000000000000000000000000000
13033470000000000000000000000000000000100000000000000000000000000000
13033480000000000000000000000000000000000000000000000000000000000000
13033490000000000000000000000000000000000000000000000000000000000000
13033500000000000000000000000000000000000000000000000000000000000000
13033510000000000000000000000000000000000000000000000000000000000000
130335200000000000000000001
13035010000000010001020300000000200000000000000000000000000000000000
13035020000000000000000000000000002000101000000000000000100000000100000001
13035030000001000001010000010000001040001010000000000000000000000000001
13035040010000000020000000001000100000001000200000000201000000000000000
13035050000000000020000000100000000000000000000000000200000000000000000
13035060000000000000000010300000000000000000000000000200110004000000000000
13035070000002000000000000000000000000000000000000000000000000000000
13035080000000000000000000000000001000000000001010000000000000000000000
13035090000000000000000000000000001010000000000000000000000010001000000000
13035100000000000000000000000000000000000000000000000000000000000000
13035110000000000000000000000000000000000000000000000000010000000000
13035120000100000000000000000000000000000000000000000000000000000000
13035130000000000000000000000000000000100000000000000010000000000000
13035140000000000000000000000000000000000000000000000000000000000000
13035150000100000000000000000000000000000000000000000000000000000000
13035160000000000000000000000000000000000000000000000000000000000000
13035170000000000000000000000000000000000000000000000000000000000000
13035180000000000000000000000000000000001000000000000000000000000000
13035190000000000000000000000000000000000000000000000000000000000100
13035200000000000000000000000000000000000000000000000000000000000000
13035210000000000000000000000000000000000000000000000000000000000000
13035220000000000000000000000000000000000000000000000000000000000000
13035230000000000000000000000000000000000000000000000000000000000000
13035240000101000100000000000000000000000000000000000000000000000000
13035250000000000000000000000000000000000000000000000000000000000000
13035260000000000000000000000000000000000000000000001000000000000000
13035270000000000000000000000000000000000000001000000000000000000000
13035280000000000000000000000000000000000000000000000000010000000000
13035290000000000000000000000000000000000000000000000000000000000000
13035300000000000000000000000000000000000000000000000000000000000000
13035310000000000000000000000000000000000000000000000000000000000001
13035320000000000000000000000000000000000000000000000000000000000000
13035330000000000000000000000000000000000010000000000010000000000000000
13035340000000000000000000000000000000000000000000000000000000000000
13035350000000000000000000000000000000000000000000000000000000000000
13035360000000000000000000001000000000000000000000000000000000060000
13035370003020000000000000000000000000000000000000000000000000020001
13035380000000000000000000000000000000000000000000000000010100010000
13035390000000000100000000000000000000100000000000000000000000000000
13035400000000000000100000000000000000000000000000000000000000000000
13035410000000000000000000000000000000000000000000000000000000010000
13035420000100000005000000010000100010000000000100000000000000000000
13035430000000000000000000000000000000000000000010001020100000000000
13035440000000010000000000020000000000000000000000000000000000000000
13035450000000000000000000000000100000000000000000000000000000000000
13035460000000000000000000000000000000000000001000000000000000000000000
13035470000000000000000000000000000000010000000000000000000000000000
13035480000000000000000000000000000000000010000000000000000000000000
```

```
13035490000000000000000000000000000000000000000000000000000000000000000000000000
13035500000000000000000000000000000000000000000000000000000000000000000000000000
13035510000000000000000000000000000000000000000000000000000000000000000000000000
13035520000000002010000000000000
13408010001020001020001000000000000000100000000000000100010000000000000001000504
13408020100000000000000000000000002010000000100000000000000000100010001020002000
13408030000000400000000000000000002020001000100000000000201000000000002000001000
13408040004000003000300010000000000000000000000000000000000200000100000000000000
13408050000010001000000000000000000000000000000000000000000200000000000000000000
13408060000100000000000000000000000000100000200000000000000000002010000200000000
13408070000100000000000001000000000000000001000000001000000000000000000000000000
13408080000000002000000000000101000000000000000000000000001000000003000000000000
13408090000000000000000030000000000000000000000000000000000000001020100000201000
13408100000010000000000000000000000000000000000000000000000000000000000000000000
13408110000000200000000000000010001000100000000000000000000000000000000000000000
13408120000000020000000000000000000000000000000000000000000000000000000000000000
13408130000000000000000000000000000010000010000000200000000000000001010102000000
13408140000000000000000000000000000000000000000000000000000000000000000000000000
13408150100100000000000100010000000000000000000000000000000000000000000000000000
13408160000000000000000000000000001000000000010000000000000100000100000000000000
13408170000000000000000000000000000000000000000000000000000000000000000000000000
13408180000000001000000000000000000000000000000000000000000000000000000000000000
13408190000000000000000000000000000000000000000000000000000000000000000000000100
13408200000000000000000000000000000000000000000000000000000000000000000000000000
13408210000000000000000000000000000000000000000000000000000000000000000000000000
13408220000000000000000000000000000000000000000000000000000000000000000000000000
13408230000000000000000000000000000000000000000000000000000000000000000000000000
13408240000000000000000000001010001000000000010000000000000000000000000000000000
13408250000000000000000000000000100000100010000000000000000000000000000000000000
13408260000000000000000000000000000000000000000001000100000000000000000000000001
13408270000000000000002000100000100000000000000000000000001000000000000000000000
13408280000000000000000000000000000000000000000000000000000000000000000000000000
13408290000000000000000000000000000200000100000000000001000000000000000000000000
13408300000000000000000000000000000000000000000000000000000000000000000000000000
13408310000000000000000000000000000000000000000000000000000000000000000000000100
13408320000000000000000000000000000000000000000000000000000000000000000000000000
13408330000000000000000000000000100000000000000000200000000000000000001000000000
13408340000000000000000000000000000000000000000000000000000000000000000000000000
13408350000000000000000000000000000000000000000000000000000000000000000000000000
13408360000000000001000000000000000000000000000000000000000000000000010400000000
13408370100000002000000000000000000000000000000000000000000000000000000000000000
13408380000000000000000000000000000000000000000000000000000000000000000000000000
13408390000000000000000000000000000000000000000000000000000000000000000000000000
13408400000000000000000000000000000000000000000000000000000000000000000000000000
13408410000000000000000000000000000000000000000000000000000000000000000000000000
13408420000000000000000000000000000000000000000000000000000000000000000000000000
13408430000000000000000000000000000000000000000000000000000000000000000000000000
13408440000000000000000000000000000000000000000000000000000000000000000000000000
13408450000000000000000000000000000000000000000000000000000000000000000000000000
13408460000000000000000000000000000000000000000000000000000000000000000000000000
13408470000000000000000000000000000000000000000000000000000000000000000000000000
13408480000000000000000000000000000000000000000000000000000000000000000000000000
13408490000000000000000000000000000000000000000000000000000000000000000000000000
13408500000000000000000000000000000000000000000000000000000000000000000000000000
13408510000000000000000000000000000000000000000000000000000000000000000000000000
13408520000000000000000000000000
13410010000000000102000000000000000000000000000000000000000100000000000001000000
13410020000000002000000000000000000000000000000000000000000000000000000100010000
13410030200000000000010100001000000000000202000000000000000000000000002000000100
13410040001010000000000200000000000000000000000000000001010001000000000000010000
13410050300000100000100000000000000000000000000000000000000000000000000000000000
13410060000000001000000000000000000000000000000000000000000010000000000000000101
13410070000000000000000000000000100000000000000000000000000010000000000000010000
13410080000000000000000000001000000000000000000000000000000000000000000000000000
13410090000000000000000001000000000000000000000000000000000000000002010000000001
13410100000001000000000000000000100000000000000000000000000000000000000001000000
13410110000000000000000000000000000000000000000000000000000000000000000000000000
13410120000000000000000000000000100000000000000000000000000000000000000000000000
13410130000000000000000000000000000000000000000000000000000000000000000001000000
13410140000000000000000000000000000000000000000000000000000000000000000000000000
13410150000001000000000000100000000000000001000000000000000000000000000000000000
13410160000000000000000000000000000000000000000000000000000000000000000000000000
13410170000000000000000000000000000000000000000000000000000000000000000000000000
13410180000000001000000000000010000000000000000000001000000000000000000000000000
13410190000000000000000000000000000000000000000000000000000000000000000000000000
13410200000000001000000000000000000000000000000000000000000000000000000000000000
13410210000000000000000000000000000000000000000000000000000000000000000000000000
13410220000000000000000000000000000000000000000000000000000000000000000000000000
13410230000000000000000000000000000000000000000000000000000000000000000000000000
13410240000001000000000000100000000000000001000000000000000100000000000000000000
13410250000000000000000000000000000000000000000000000000000000000000000000000000
13410260000000000000000000000000000000000000000000000000000000000000000000000000
13410270100100000010000001000000000000000000000000000000000000000000000000000000
13410280000000000000000000000000000000000000000000000000000000000000000000000000
13410290000000000000000000000000000000000000000000000000000000000000000000000000
13410300000000000000000000000000000000000000000000000000000000000000000000000000
13410310000000000000000000000000000000000000000000000000000000000000000000000000
13410320000000000000000000000000000000000000000000000000000000000000000000000000
13410330000000000000000000000000000000000000000001000000000000000000000000000000
13410340000000000000000000000000000000000000000000000000000000000000000000000000
13410350000000000000000000000000000000000000000000000000000000000000000000000000
13410360000000000000100000000000000000000000000000000000000000000000000000000000
13410370000000000000000000000000000000000000000000000000000000000000000000000000
13410380000000000000000000000000000000000000000000000000000000000000000000000000
13410390000000000000000000000000000000000000000000000000000000000000000000000000
13410400000000000000000000000000000000000000000000000000000000000000000000000000
13410410000000000000000000000000000000000000000000000000000000000000000000000000
13410420000000000000000000000000000000000000000000000000000000000000000000000000
13410430000000000000000000000000000000000000000000000000000000000000000000000000
13410440000000000000000000000000000000000000000000000000000000000000000000000000
13410450000000000000000000000000000000000000000000000000000000000000000000000000
13410460000000000000000000000000000000000000000000000000000000000000000000000000
13410470000000000000000000000000000000000000000000000000000000000000000000000000
13410480000000000000000000000000000000000000000000000000000000000000000000000000
13410490000000000000000000000000000000000000000000000000000000000000000000000000
13410500000000000000000000000000000000000000000000000000000000000000000000000000
13410510000000000000000000000000000000000000000000000000000000000000000000000000
13410520000000000000000000000000
13411010000000000000000000000000100000000000000000000000000000000000000000000000
13411020000000000001000000000000000001000000000000000000000000000000000000000100
13411030100000000000000000000000001000100000000000000000000000000000000000000001
13411040201000000000000000000000000000000000000000000000000000000000000000000000
13411050000000100000000000000000000001000000000000000000000000000000000000000000
13411060000000000000000000000001000000030000001000100001000000001000000100000000
13411070000000000000000000000000000000000000000000000000000000000001000000000000
13411080000000000000000000000000000000000000000000000000000001000000000000000000
13411090000000000000000000101000000000000000000000000000000010000000000000000000
13411100000000000000000000000000000000000000000000000000000000000000000000000100
13411110000000000000000000000000000000000000000000000000000000000000000000000000
13411120000000000000000000000000000000000000000000000000000000000000000000000000
```

```
13411130000200000000000000000000000000000000000000000000000000000000001000000000000
13411140000000000000000000000000000000000000000000000000000000000000000000000000
13411150000000000000000000000000000000000000000000000000000000000000000000000000
13411160000000000000000000000000000000000000000000000000000000000000000000000000
13411170000000000000000000000000000000000000000000000000000000000000000000000000
13411180000000000000000000000000000000000000000000000000000000000000000000000000
13411190000000000000000000000000000000000000000000000000000000000000000000000000
13411200000000000000000000000000000000000000000000000000000000000000000000000000
13411210000000000000000000000000000000000000000000000000000000000000000000000000
13411220000000000000000000000000000000000000000000000000000000000000000000000000
13411230000000000000000000000000000000000000000000000000000000000000000000000000
13411240000000000000000000000000000000000000000000000000000100000000000000000000
13411250000000000000000000000000000000000000000000000000000000000000000000000000
13411260000000000000000000000000000000000000000000000000000000000000000000000000
13411270000000000000000000000000000000000000000000000000000000000000000000000000
13411280000000000000000000000000000000000000000000000000000000000000000000000000
13411290000000000000000000000000000000000000000000000000000000000000000000000000
13411300000000000000000000000000000000000000000000000000000000000000000000000000
13411310000000000000000000000000000000000000000000000000000000000000000000000000
13411320000000000000000000000000000000000000000000000000000000000000000000000000
13411330000000000000000000000000000000000000000000000000000000000000000000000000
13411340000000000000000000000000000000000000000000000000000000000000000000000000
13411350000000000000000000000000000000000000000000000000000000000000000000000000
13411360000000000000000000000000000000000000000000000000000000000000000000000000
13411370000100000000000001000000000000000000000000000000000000000000000000000000
13411380000000000000000000000000000000000000000000000000000000000000000000000000
13411390000000000000000000000000000000000000000000000000000000000000000000000000
13411400000000000000000000000000000000000000000000000000000000000000000000000000
13411410000000000000000000000000000000000000000000000000000000000000000000000000
13411420000000000000000000000000000000000000000000000000000000000000000000000000
13411430000000000000000000000000000000000000000000000000000000000000000000000000
13411440000000000000000000000000000000000000000000000000000000000000000000000000
13411450000000000000000000000000000000000000000000000000000000000000000000000000
13411460000000000000000000000000000000000000000000000000000000000000000000000000
13411470000000000000000000000000000000000000000000000000000000000000000000000000
13411480000000000000000000000000000000000000000000000000000000000000000000000000
13411490000000000000000000000000000000000000000000000000000000000000000000000000
13411500000000000000000000000000000000000000000000000000000000000000000000000000
13411510000000000000000000000000000000000000000000000000000000000000000000000000
13411520000000000000000000000000
15007010000000000000000000000100000000001000000000000000000000000000000000000000
15007020000100000000000000000000000000100000000100000000000000000000000000000001
15007030000000000000000000000000000000000000000001000000000000000001000000000000000000000
15007040000000000000000000000000000000000000000000000000000000000000000000010000
15007050000000000000000000000000000000000000000000000000100001000000100000000000000
15007060000000000000000000000000000000000000000000000000000100000000000000000100
15007070000000000000100000000000010000000000000000000000000000000000000000000000
15007080000000000000000000000000000000200000000000000000000000000000000101000000
15007090000000000000000000000000000000000000000000020000000000000000000000010000
15007100000000000000000000000000000000100000000000000000000000000000000000000000
15007110000000000000000000000000000000000000010000000000000000000001000000000000000
15007120000000000000000000000000000000000000000000000000000000000001000000000010000
15007130000000000000001000000000000000000000000000000000000000000000000000000000
15007140000100000000000000000000000000000000000000000000000000000000000000000000
15007150200030001000000010100000000000000000000000000000000000000000000000000100
15007160100000100000000000000000001000000000100100010000101000020200000010004000000
15007170000701010100000301010000000000000000000000000000000000040100000000200000002
15007180100010100000000000000200000010000000000000000000100000000000000100000000000000000
15007190000000010000100000000200000000001000000000001000000000010000000000101000002
15007200100000000000000100100000000000000000010000000000000000000100000000000000
15007210000000000100000000000000000000000000000000000001000000000000000200000000
15007220000000000100000000000000000000000000000000000000000000000000000000001000200
15007230000000000000000000001000000000000000000000000000000000000000000000000000
15007240000000000000000000000000000000000000000000000001000000000000000200000000
15007250000000000000000000000000000000001200001000000000000000000000000010001000000000000
15007260000000200000000000000000200000000000000000000000100000000000000000000000000000
15007270000000000000000000000000000000100000010000000000000000000000000000000000
15007280000000000000001000000000020101000000000001000000100000000000000000000000000000100
15007290000000000000000000000000000000001010000000000000000000100000000001000000000000000
15007300000000000000000000001000000000000000000000000000000000000000000000000000
15007310000000000000000000000000100000000000000000000000000000000000000101010000000200020 0
15007320200000000000000000000000101000000000100000000000000000000000000000000000
15007330000000000000000000000000000000000000000000020000000000000000000001000000000001
15007340100000000000000000000000000000000000000000000000000000000000000000000000
15007350000000000000000000000000000000000000000000000000000000000000000000060000
15007360201000000000000000000000100030000000000000000020100000000000000000000000000
15007370000000000000000000000000000000000000000010000000000000000000000000000000
15007380000000000000000000000000000000000000000000000000000000000000000000000000
15007390000000000000000000000000000000000000000000000000000000000000000000000000
15007400000000000000000000000000000000000000000000000000000000000000000000000000
15007410000000000000000000000000000000000000000000000000000000000000000000000000
15007420000000000000000000000000000000000000000000000000000000000000000000000000
15007430000000000000000000000000000000000000000000000000000000000000000000000000
15007440000000000000000000000000000000000000000000000000000000000000000000000000
15007450000000000000000000000000000000000000000000000000000000000000000000000000
15007460000000000000000000000000000000000000000000000000000000000000000000000000
15007470000000000000000000000000000000000000000000000000000000000000000000000000
15007480000000000000000000001000000000000000000000000000000000000000000000000000
15007490000000000000000000000000000000000000000000000000000000000000000010000000000
15007500000000000000000000000000000000000000000000000000000000000000000000000000
15007510000000000000000000000000000000000000000000000000000000000000000000000000
15007520000000000000000000000001
15329010000000000100000000000000000000000000000000000000000000000000000000000000
15329020000000000000000000000100000000000000000000000000000000000000000100000000
15329030000000000000000000000000000000100000000010000000000000000000000000000000
15329040000000000100000000000000000000000000000000000000000001000000000000000000
15329050000000000000000000000000000000000000000000000000000000000000100000000000000
15329060000000000000000000000000000000100000000000000000000000000000300000000000
15329070000000000100000000000000000000000000000000000000000000000000100000000000
15329080000000000000000000000000000000000000000000000000000000000000000100000100
15329090000000000000000000000000000000001000000000000000000000000000000000000001000000
15329100000000000000000000000000000000001000000000000000000000000000000000000000000000
15329110000000000000000000000000000000000000000000000000000000000000000000000000
15329120000000000000000000000000000000000000000000000000000000000000000100000000
15329130000000000000000000002000000000000010000000000000000000000000000000000000000000001
15329140000000000000000000000000000000000000000000000000000000000000000000000100
15329150500010000100000000200000000000000000000000000000000000000000000000000000
15329160000001000200000000000000000000000000000000000000000040200000100000000000
15329170000000700000000000000001010000000000000000000000000000000000000000000000
15329180000000100000000000000201000000000000000000000000000000000000000000010000
15329190000000000000001000000000000000100000000100000000000001000000000000000000000000100000203
15329200000000000000000000001000000000000000000000000000000010000100000000000000000000
15329210000000000000000000000000000000000000000001000010000000000000000000000000000000000100000000000
15329220000000000000000000000000000100000000000000000000100000000000000000000000001000001
15329230000000000000000000000000000000000020000000000000000000001000000000000000000000000000
15329240000000000000000000000000000000000010300000000000000000000001000000000000000000000000000
15329250000000000000000000000000000000000020000000000000000000000000000000000000000100010000000
15329260001000000000000000000000000000000000000000000000000000000000000000000000
15329270100000000000000000000000000000000000000000000000000000000000000000000000
15329280000000000000000000000000000000000000000000000000000000000000000000000000
```

256

```
15329290000000000000000000000000000000000000000000000000000000000000000
15329300000000000000000000100000000000000000000000000000100000000000000
15329310000000000000000000000000000000000000000000000000000010001000000
15329320100000000000001000001000000000000010000000000000000000000000000
15329330000000000000000000000000000000000000000000000000001000000000000
15329340000000000000000000000000000000000000000000000000000000000000000
15329350000000000000000000000000000000000000000000000000000000000000000
15329360100000000000000000000000001000101000002000000000000000100000000
15329370000000000000100000000000000000100000000000000000000000000000000
15329380000000000000000000000000000000000000000000000000000000000000000
15329390000000000000000000000000000000000000000000000000000000000000000
15329400000000000000000000000000000000000000000000000000000000000000000
15329410000000000000000000000000000000000000000000000000000000000000000
15329420000000000000000000000000000000000000000000000000000000000000000
15329430000000000000000000000000000000000000000000000000000000001000000
15329440000000000000000000000000000000000000000000000000000000000000000
15329450000000000000000000000000000000000000000000000000000000000000000
15329460000000000000000000000000000000000000000000000000000000000000000
15329470000000000000000010000000000000000000000000000000000000000000000
15329480000000000000000000000000000000000000000000000000000000000000000
15329490000000000000000000000000000000000000000000000000000000000000000
15329500000000000000000000000000000000000000000000000000000000000000000
15329510000000000000000000000000000000000000000000000000000000000000000
15329520000000000000000000000
```

Part 2. Tabulations of Rare Ceramic Categories

Categories	Proveniences
0008	Monte Albán Terraces 19, 25, 27(2), 31, 39, 45, 80, 92, 98, 99, 102, 119, 147, 174(2), 192, 225 excavation, 246, 254, 259, 322, 324, 330, 364(2), 366, 396, 413, 518, 630, 911, 914, 1047, 1463
0018	Monte Albán Terraces 3, 71, 155, 189, 220, 254, 257, 270, 272, 273, 327, 353, 358, 412, 427, 456, 553, 563, 799, 935, 941, Area 11
0023	Monte Albán Terraces 107, 165, 192, 225, 296, 297, 329, 409, 410, 941, 1457
0054	Monte Albán Terraces 161, 391, 622, 827, 919
0056	Monte Albán Terraces 18, 27, 177, 396, 842, 910, Area 1
0379	Monte Albán Terraces 371, 659, 1450, Area 15, Az.Terrace 211
0381	Monte Albán Terraces 8, 152, 182, 191, 313, 386, 396, 457, 904, 919, 1388
0382	Monte Albán Terraces 1, 39, 75, 78, 99, 103, 107(2), 175, 193, 215(2), 241, 350, 466, 611, 827, 915, 1004, E.G.Terrace 139
0388	Monte Albán Terraces 18, 85, 95, 117, 146, 315, 358, 453, 568, 1012, 1371, Area 1
0396	Monte Albán Terraces 17, 37, 71, 155, 161, 171, 193, 223, 257, 259, 298, 299, 327, 343, 415, 469, 585, 636, 812, 844, 938, 1310
0397	Monte Albán Terraces 3, 20, 21, 24(2), 27(2), 28(2), 44, 71, 106, 137(2), 150, 192, 259, 273, 410, 419, 464, 564, 838, 941, 1208, 1318, 1456, 1462
0398	Monte Albán Terraces 24(3), 25, 27, 61, 99, 107, 123, 189, 190, 212, 242, 395, 398, 415, 622, 846, 1456, 1460
0399	Monte Albán Terraces 25, 36, 40, 78, 795
0400	Monte Albán Terraces 8, 27, 161, 358, 409, 416, 606, 751, 1456
0401	Monte Albán Terraces 8, 22, 37, 71, 75, 80, 105, 134, 151, 192, 206, 219, 220, 269, 275, 276, 330, 358(3), 419, 466, 555, 841, 921, 1309, 1324, 1331, 1464
0405	Monte Albán Terraces 107, 165, 166, 314, 452, 573, 839, Az.Terraces 43, 52, 55(2), 153(2), 333, 334
1103	Monte Albán Terraces 1, 183, 188, 198, 206, 248(2), 273, 276, 379, 380, 381(2), 399, 400, 421, 425, 427(3), 443, 444(4), 445(2), 449, 451, 452, 453(4), 454, 456(2), 473, 479, 487(2), 506(2), 507, 508, 509, 519(7), 521, 522(3), 524, 525(3), 534, 536, 537(2), 541, 554(3), 560, 563, 564, 571(2), 574, 576, 584, 586, 601, 602(2), 622, 626, 635, 640, 657, 663, 664, 665, 667, 677, 680, 685, 687(2), 701, 716, 721, 724, 763(3), 790, 791, 844, 847, 850, 854, 863(2), 866, 867, 868, 869(2), 930, 1015(2), 1025, 1027, 1039, 1145, 1221, 1226(2), 1228(2), 1236, 1302, 1308, 1369, 1509, Areas 2, 5(2), 8, 10(2), 16, E.G.Terrace 83
1111	Monte Albán Terraces 47, 482, 553, 1359
1275	Monte Albán Terraces 1, 7, 14, 51(2), 57, 63, 74(2), 87, 92, 183, 213, 271, 333, 372, 377(2), 455, 456, 462, 522, 532, 558, 569, 639, 768, 785, 804, 843, 933, 1047, 1208, 1235, 1306, 1336, 1447, Area 9, Az.Terraces 6, 135, 330, 331, 352, E.G.Terraces 14, 17
1319	Monte Albán Terraces 17, 1463
1331	Monte Albán Terraces 260, 272, 291, 305, 791, 1392, 1450
1333	Monte Albán Terraces 80, 844, 849, 932
1334	Monte Albán Terraces 80, 168, 177, 329, 553, 1337, E.G.Terraces 3, 54
1335	Monte Albán Terrace 508
1336	Monte Albán Terraces 8, 67, 191, 219, 273, 451, 455, 763, 832
1337	Monte Albán Terraces 52, 260, 297, 558, 618, 919
1350	Monte Albán Terraces 67, 105, 219, 309, 493, 552, 556, 626, 634, 1012, 1448, 1463(2)
1352	Monte Albán Terraces 193, 312
1358	Monte Albán Terraces 98, 132, 268, 343, 454, 475, 772
1371	Monte Albán Terraces 147, 522
1372	Monte Albán Terraces 27, 58, 270, 313, 409, 1377
1373	Monte Albán Terraces 15, 122, 133, 149, 341, 900, 1129, Az.Terrace 211
2040	Monte Albán Terraces 21, 59, 101, 151, 176, 296, 417, 559, 924
2061	Monte Albán Terraces 204, 621, 1213, E.G.Terrace 59
2064	Monte Albán Terraces 6, 29, 89, 104, 147, 269, 277, 312, 358, 403, 407, 488, 839, 1026, 1102, 1305, 1448, Area 13
2073	Monte Albán Terraces 24, 25, 27, 37, 57, 82, 182, 630, 631, 1027, 1047, 1213, 1474
2077	Monte Albán Terraces 27(3), 32, 48, 53, 67(2), 98, 133, 184, 189, 206(2), 208, 212, 213, 225 excavation, 229, 252, 257(2), 276, 294, 327, 383, 388, 451, 453(3), 454, 471, 559, 560, 602, 918, 924, 1318

2083 Monte Albán Terraces 131, 140, 351, 460, 1022, 1324, Az.Terrace 150

2086 Monte Albán Terraces 21, 26, 30, 33, 37, 43, 56, 57, 61, 68, 70, 83, 104, 148, 281, 315, 326, 333, 341, 387, 390, 394, 403, 414, 488, 517, 533, 559, 675, 713, 804, 850, 869(2), 874, 882, 1018, 1020, 1213, 1252(2), 1447, 1452, 1457, Az.Terraces 342, 425, E.G.Terraces 28, 66, 93, 94

2411 Monte Albán Terraces 35, 51, 62(2), 104, 160, 189, 190, 232, 237, 244, 249, 275, 309, 416, 636, 842, 914

2412 Monte Albán Terraces 27(2), 31, 51, 87, 104, 150, 244, 259, 329, 536, 835, 919

2413 Monte Albán Terraces 9, 20, 243, 323, 409, 610, 677, 1390, Area 3

2415 Monte Albán Terraces 9, 26, 28, 31, 185, 229, 241, 257, 270, 274, 313, 466, 508, 767, 920, 1447

2416 Monte Albán Terraces 20, 27, 64, 72, 75, 188, 315, 403, 503, 560, 570, 628, 1309, 1447, 1460

2417 Monte Albán Terraces 10, 20, 80, 82, 265

3030 Monte Albán Terraces 6, 39, 45, 70, 73, 74, 104, 161, 190, 225 excavation (2), 254, 273, 277, 351, 467, 661, 802, 912, 1314, 1457

3066 Monte Albán Terraces 13, 19, 20, 160, 188, 225, 417, 454, 573, 803, 841, 901, 1302

3409 Monte Albán Terraces 8, 21, 55, 59, 182, 187, 272, 555

APPENDIX IV

Sherds per Hectare of Collected Terrace Area, by Grid Square

This tabulation includes only those ceramic categories that are relatively frequent. Immediately following this paragraph, the sequence in which the categories occur by card or line is listed. The first number in each line is a meaningless number. The next four lines indicate the grid square, with the north grid number indicated first, the east grid number second. Square N1E7, for example, is indicated here as "0107." Each value occupies five columns, with two decimal places indicated. They should be read, then, as "000.00." For reasons that are too complicated to explain here, this data set ended up with some extra columns between the grid square number and the ceramic values. Four rows of "0" follow the grid square number, followed, in turn, by the card number. There are 12 cards or lines per grid square. Again, for reasons I will not go into here, these were done such that a card "1," for example, has two cards "01" and "02." The order in which the ceramic categories are tabulated in Appendix IV is the following:

0001	0002	0003	0004	0005	0006	0016	0021	0022	0031	0032	0038
0057	0121	0122	0123	0374	0375	0376	0377	0378	0380	0383	0384
0385	0386	0387	0389	0390	0391	0393	0394	0395	0402	0403	0404
0406	0407	0561	1102	1104	1105	1106	1107	1109	1120	1122	1123
1125	1126	1137	1138	1140	1141	1143	1144	1194	1207	1227	1241
1258	1259	1262	1263	1264	1265	1268	1274	1277	1297	1312	1330
1332	1338	1339	1340	1341	1342	1343	1344	1345	1346	1347	1348
1349	1351	1353	1354	1355	1356	1357	1359	1360	1361	1362	1363

1364	1365	1366	1367	1368	1369	1370	1419	1420	1421	1422	1999
.	.	.	.	.	.	.	.	.	.	.	.
2009	2010	2011	2013	2014	2015	2042	2052	2065	2072	2076	2078
.	.	.	.	.	.	.	.	.	.	.	.
2079	2080	2085	2414	2418	3033	3035	3408	3410	3411	5007	5081
.	.	.	.	.	.	.	.	.	.	.	.
5082	5083	5084	5085	5086	5329						
.	.	.	.	.	.	.	.	.	.	.	.

```
101110000101004100000000000000000000000000000000000000000000615004100000
101110000102006150020500000002050041000000000000000000000205002050000000
101110000201000000184400205004100020500205006150000000820000000020500000
101110000202000000000000000000000410000000000000000000000000020490143400000
101110000301000000245900000004100000000205014340000001639067620041000615
101110000302006150000000410002050020500205018440020500000008200000003279
101110000401000000102500000000000000000000000000000000002050061500000000000
101110000402000000000000000000000410002050000000000000000004100000000020500205
101110000501004100061500205000000000000000000205000000000000000000205000000000
101110000502000000000000000000000820002050020500000000000020500000000000000000
101110000601000000020500000000000000000000205000000000000000000000000000000000
101110000602000000000000000000000000205
101090000101004700047000000000000000000000004700000000000000000470023470047 0
101090000102009390140900000004700000000000000000000000000000000093900000
101090000201000000047000470000000047000000009390000000470000000000000000
101090000202004700000000000000000939000000000001409000000000000042250286000000
101090000301000000469500000004700047000470004700140901409042250000000000
101090000302009390000000000000000000018780000002347000000004700093900000002817
101090000401000000047000000000000047000000000000000000000000000000000000
101090000402000000000000000000000000000000470000000000000000000000000000047000000
101090000501000000000000000000000000000000470000000000000000000000000093900000
101090000502000000000000000000000470000000047000000000000000000000000000000000
101090000601000000047000000000000047000000009390000000000000000000000000000000
101090000602000000000000000000000000000000
102010000101002860004800095000950000000095001430000000000000000239008110000000
102100000102002390052500143000950009500000000480004800048000480009500095
102100000201000480147900048002860009500143002860019100429000480028600143
102100000202002860000000000000000191003820009500095000480004801002010500048
102100000301000000438900000001910004800048005730019100668034350028600239
102100000302004290000000143003340038200334006680009500048012880000002242
102100000401000480042900000000000014300095000480000000048000480004800000
102100000402000480004800000000480009500048000950000000095000000009500048
102100000501000480004800000000950000000048000480000000000000000048001430000 0
102100000502001430014300000005730014300143000000014300000000000000000480004 8
102100000601000950004800048000000009500334000000033400048000000004800000
102100000602000000000000000000000000000000
101100000101002620003300098000330001600065001150001600049001640063800033
101100000102002290011500098000820006500000000160003300049000650001600065
101100000201000000067000000002620006500033001960008200294000490018000065
101100000202000490000000000000001640037600164000490001600000008010107900115
101100000301000000171700000001150008200065003760003300474014880024500180
101100000302001960000000082001640036000278005230019600000007520003301226
101100000401000000026200016000000004900065000160003300016000330000000016
101100000402000480000000065000330003300016000160000000033000330004900033
101100000501000330006500033000490000000000000330001600000000160008200000
101100000502001800008200016003110018000082000000009800065000000003300065
101100000601000160008200033000000006500049000820008200033000490008200000
101100000602000000000000000000000000033
100100000101005020016700000003340033400334001670000000334000000284300000
100100000102003340050200000001670016700334000000016700000000000000000000
100100000201001670133800000010030033400000001670000000669001670083600000
100100000202003340000000000000003340000000334000000000000000000133801505 00334
100100000301000000334500000005020000000334006690000000334030100016700334
100100000302008360000000000000000000016700000013380000000000000008360000001171
100100000401000000033400000000000000000000000000000000000000000016700502 00000
100100000402001670000000000000000000000000000000334000000000000000000016700000
100100000501000000000000167000000000000000000000000000000000033400000000000
100100000502003340000000000000020070016700167000000000000016700000000000000334
100100000601001670000000167000000000000000334000000050200000000000016700000
```

```
100100000602000000016700000000000000000000
100110000101001420000000000000000000000000000000014200000000000000000001420028500000
100110000102000000000000000000000000014200000000000000000000000000000000000
100110000201000000014200000000000000000000000000000000142002850000000000000000
100110000202000000000000000000014200000000001420000000000000000000042800285000 00
100110000301000000128200000000000000000000000000142000000004280128200285 00142
100110000302001420000000000000001420028500000000000000000000000000997000000 0713
100110000401000000028500000000000000000000142000000000000000000000000000000000
100110000402000000000000000000000000000000000000000000000000000000000000
100110000501000000014200000000000000000000000000000000000000000001420000 0
100110000502001420000000000000002850000000000000014200000000000000000000000142
100110000601000000000000000000142000000005700000000000000000000000000000000000
100110000602000000000000000000142000000000000000
104110000101002870011500172001150000000115000570000000000000000011500631 00000
104110000102003440028700057000000000000000000000000000000000005700000000000000000
104110000201000000051600229002870017200057001720005700229000570051600334
104110000202001150000000000000000000001720005700057000570000001606010320005 7
104110000301000570367000000000570017200057007450040100573042430028700172
104110000302002290000000057002290131900573008030028700000010890005702810
104110000401000570028700000000000000000011500000000000000000005700000000000000000
104110000402000000005700000000000000000022900057001150005700057000000000570011 5
104110000501001150011500057000000005700000000570000000000000000000017200000
104110000502001720005700000004590005700115000000000000000000000000000000000057
104110000601000000005700000000000000000017200573005730057300344001150005700000
104110000602000000000000000000000000057
103110000101002850000000000000002850000000028500285000000005700085501709000000
103110000102002850057000000008550000000285002850000000000000000000028500000
103110000201002850170900000005700028500000002850028500285000000057000000
103110000202002850000000000000000000000570000000000000000000000000017090170900000
103110000301000000455800000002850000000000000000570011400114003419002850028 5
103110000302002850000000285008550057001139017090028500000028490028502279
103110000401000000057000000000000000000028500000000000000000000000000000000000
103110000402000000000000000000000000285000000002850000000000000000000000000000
103110000501000000000000000285002850000000028500000000000000000000000000000000
103110000502002850000000000000011390028500570000000000000000028500000000000000285
103110000601000000000000000000000000000000570000000000000000000000000000000000
103110000602000000028500285000000000000000
103100000101007030014800185002960029600296000740003700111005550099900074
103100000102012210055500037002960018500148001480007400037001110000000000
103100000201002590162800074004810022200037000370018500962000740159100407
103100000202005920022200000002220059200111002220003700000001480151700148
103100000301001110432900000002960025900148006660070301221059560048100666
103100000302004070000000185000370136900555015540029600037016280018503996
103100000401000370070300037000370000000222000370003700222001110000000074
103100000402001850003700074000000007400037000000007400074000000011100185
103100000501002220018500037001110011100000002960011100037000370029600037
103100000502006290011100037016650022200259001480011100148000370000000222
103100000601000370003700148000370029600555005550103600407001850011100000
103100000602000000000000037000740000000148
104100000101006590017000414003010005700113000570001900188006220090400038
104100000102009040064000301002450007500170000370013200207003200015100075
104100000201001510145000075006030007500188004900018800490001700152500490
104100000202007350015100019000750022600075001320009400038008100069700188
104100000301000000248600000001510000000057005090041400998050090052700471
104100000302002450003800207000940139400414004520024500057011300000002580
104100000401000190032000019000190007500094000380001900057000190001900000
104100000402000570001900019000190001900057000190000000075000000007500094
104100000501001880026000094001700003800038001700000000057000570009400000
104100000502005270018800094010550013200132000380013200057000190005700260
104100000601000750011300075000190020700584002640050900188000570003800019
```

104100000602000190001900000000000000000000000038
104070000101001740014500174001450002900116000580000000029000290011600087
104070000102001450028900174001450005800000000000005800174000000002900087
104070000201001160052100116003470014500058002610002900029000000011600174
104070000202002320000000000000580008700058000000000000029004920011600232
104070000301000000083900000000290005800087001450008700376016500028900261
104070000302002890000000029002610023200116003180005800029004630000000724
104070000401000000023200029000000000000116000870000000000001160000000000
104070000402000000005800058000290008700029000580000000058000580002900058
104070000501000580002900029000870000000000000000000000000000000026100000
104070000502001740008700029003470017400058000000002900000000000002900087
104070000601000290011600029000000011600087000290011600087000000005800000
104070000602000000000000000000580000000058
105080000101001860004700124000620001600109001550003100078000930038800109
105080000102001710052800155000930018600016000000001600093000160007800031
105080000201001090089900140003260018600000002170001600248000160017100093
105080000202000470000000031003260048100388000620007800000011330108600186
105080000301000310311800000000930007800140002330003100388018770014000186
105080000302002790000000078000470046500171004030010900031006050004700853
105080000401000000014000016000000006200078000160001600016000160001600000
105080000402000780000000000000160004700031000470000000016000000003100000
105080000501000620007800062000470003100000000160000000000000000010900000
105080000502000470014000031003410023300062000000012400047000000003100140
105080000601000470004700047000000023300202000620020200109000310010900000
105080000602000000000000000000000000000078
104080000101002330016300163000700007000070001860004700209002320027900070
104080000102003020046500139000700007000023000470013900070000000011600023
104080000201002090169700163005580011600139004180009300325000930048800232
104080000202003950004700000001860016300302000930000000023016730139400070
104080000301000700251000000001860004700186002560018600651039280037200256
104080000302002330007000070000700055800139003250013900023008370009301441
104080000401000000020900000000230009300093000230000000070000470004700000
104080000402000470002300023000230009300070000470000000000000470004700023
104080000501000700007000116001160004700000000930000000000000230025600000
104080000502002090016300023009060016300139000470011600000000000009300163
104080000601000470013900023000470013900511001630018600116000230011600023
104080000602000000002300000000000000000023
106060000101002590008600000000860008600173000000000000173003460086400000
106060000102003460155601383006050034600000000000000000086000000000000000
106060000201002590146900432004320017300000003460008600086000000000000259
106060000202000000000000000004320008600259000000000000259005190008600000
106060000301000860207400000000000000000000001730008600432034570034600519
106060000302003460000000259000860043200086006050008600000008640000001037
106060000401000860034600000000000017300086000860000000000000000000000000
106060000402000860000000000000000000000000000000860000000000000000008600000
106060000501003460025900000000000008600000001730000000000000000000000000
106060000502000000000000000012970043200000000000000000000000000000000432
106060000601000860000000000000000008600173000000000000000000000000000000
106060000602000000000000000000000000000000
108040000101001070003600036000360003600071000000000000000000007100464000 00
108040000102000710025000000001790003600000000000007100000000000000000000
108040000201000360039300036000000000000000000000003600000000000000000000
108040000202000360000000000001070021400107000360000000000003750153600393
108040000301000000771400036006790003600214000360010700071022500021400107
108040000302002860000000000001790010700000004640010700036011790000001107
108040000401000000014300000000000003600000000000000000000000000000000036
108040000402000000000000107000710017900036000000000000000000003600036000 00
108040000501000000000000036000000000000000000000000000000000000021400000
108040000502000000000000036004290007100000000360010700036000000000000071
108040000601000360000000036000000003600036001070000000000000000000710000 0

108040000602000000003600000000000000000000
007040000101000000000000000000000000000000000000000000000000000000000000
007040000102000000000000000000000000000000000000000000000000000000000000
007040000201000000000000000000000000000000000000000000000000000000000000
007040000202000000000000000011110000000000000000000000000666700000000000
007040000301011110111100000000000000000000011110000001111000000111100000
007040000302000000000000000011110000000000000000000000000000000000001111
007040000401000000000000000000000000000000000000000000000000000000000000
007040000402000000000000000000000000000000000000000000000000000000000000
007040000501000000000000000000000000000000000000000000000000000333300000
007040000502000000000000000000000000000000000000000000000000000000000000
007040000601000000000000000000000000000000000000000000000000000000000000
007040000602000000000000000000000000000000
008030000101000000000000000000000000000000000000000000000000000000000000
008030000102000000000000000000000000000000000000000000000000000000000000
008030000201000000000000000000000000000000000000000000000000000000000000
008030000202000000000000000000000006540196100000000000000000457500654000654
008030000301000001176500000006540000000000000000000000000003922000000000 0
008030000302000000000000000000000000000006540000000000000000000000000000
008030000340100000000000000000000000000000000000000000000000000000000000
008030000401000000000000000000000000000000000000000000000000000000000000
008030000501000000000000000000000000000000000000000000000000000065400000
008030000502000000000000000000000000000000000000000000000000000000000000
008030000601006540000000000000000000000000000000000000000000000000000000
008030000602000000000000000000000000000000
106070000101000000000000000000960000000000000000000000019100000003820000 0
106070000102004780047800000002870009600000000000000000000000009600000000 00
106070000201000000066900000000000000000000009600000000019100000000000000 96
106070000202000000000000000017210191202390003820019100000010520028700000
106070000301000000086000000000000000960000000000000000000960162500669000 96
106070000302001910000000000000000001910000000019100096000000008600000000 382
106070000401000000009600000000000000000000000000000000000000000000000000
106070000402000000000000000000960000000000000000000000000000000000000000
106070000501000960000000000000000000000000000000000000000000000000000000
106070000502000000000000000002860200800000000000000000960000000000000000 0096
106070000601000960009600000000000000478001910000000000000000000000956000 00
106070000602000000000000096000000000000287
106080000101001240000000495003090030900248000000000000000000000620018600 000
106080000102004950043300062000000024800000000000000000000000620006200000
106080000201000000037100000000000000620000000000620000000000620012400186 00186
106080000202002480000000000010520278501485003090018600186014230049500124
106080000301000000191800062001860000000186001240012400248033420030900186
106080000302002480000000000000620030900248006190006200000008050000000990
106080000401000000006200000000000000000000000000000000000000006200000000 00
106080000402000000000000000000000000620000000000000000000000006200000000 00
106080000501000620000000000000620006200000001240006200000000000000620000 0
106080000502000000000000000009280117600000000620006200062000000000620043 3
106080000601000620018600124000000004950049500062003090000000000000805000 62
106080000602000000000000000000000000000248
106090000101004290019800099000330016500066000330006600132002310056100000
106090000102000990042900198001980029700033000000003300066000000013200000
106090000201001320095600099002310023100033001980009900264000000039600198
106090000202001650003300000013520283603297005610056100198014510069200033
106090000301000000230800000001980003300099001320009900264031320033000132
106090000302002970000000000001320023100330001320009900033009890006601715
106090000401000000003300033000000006600099000660003300000000330006600033
106090000402000660009900132000330009900099000000000000000000330003300000
106090000501002970003300000000000000000033000660003300000000330006600000
106090000502000000009900000012860102200132000660013200033000000000000297
106090000601000990013200033000000042900165000330003300066000000052800000

```
106090000602000000000000000000330000000429
106110000101000000000000000001930019300000000000000000001930058000000000000
106110000102000000000000000003870000000000000000000000000000000000000000
106110000201000000005800000001930000000000000000000000019300000000000000
106110000202000000000000000003870038701354001930019300000040620116100000
106110000301000000270800000000000000000000000000193001930116100387 00000
106110000302001930000000000000000000000000019300387000000019300000 01547
106110000401000000019300000000000000000193000000000000000000193000000000
106110000402000000000000000000000000000000000000000000000000000000000000
106110000501000000000000000000000000000000000000387000000000000000000000
106110000502000000000000000005800077400000001930038700000000000000000580
106110000601000000019300000000000019300000000000000000000000000058000000
106110000602000000000000000000000000000000
105110000101001440004800000000000000000000480000000000000480014400479 00048
105110000102001440014400000000480000000048000480004800000000000000000000
105110000201000960019200048001440004800000000000000000192000000004800048
105110000202000000000000000000480028700144000000000000000011490081500096
105110000301000000148500000001440000000000000960004800096007660004800000
105110000302001920000000000000480014400096000960004800000001920000000527
105110000401000000004800048000000000000000480004800000000000000000000000
105110000402000000000000000000480000000096000000000000000000000004800000
105110000501000000000000000000000000000000000480000000000000000004800000
105110000502000000004800000002870004800096000000019200000000000004800000
105110000601000480000000000000000024000144000000000000480000000000000000
105110000602000000000000048000000000000000
107090000101002650003300199002650009900033000330000000099001660033100000
107090000102000990043000132001320023200000000330000000033000330000000000
107090000201000330062900033001320013200033001320003300066000000016600000
107090000202001990006600000024820208503243004960066200166007280043000066
107090000301000000119100000001660000000199003310000000199025150049700265
107090000302002980006600166000330033100066001320013200000004630000001224
107090000401000000026500000000000000000000000330000000066000000003300000
107090000402000330000000099000000003300033000990000000099000330003300066
107090000501000000000000066000330009900033000000000000000000330003300000
107090000502000990016600132007280102600000000990013200033000330013200199
107090000601001320016600066000000046300265000330009900033000000072800033
107090000602000000003300000000000000000728
107100000101000720000000000001440000000000000000000000007200072001440000 0
107100000102000000014400144000000021600000000000000000000000000000000000
107100000201000000028700000001440000000000001440007200072000000007200000
107100000202000000000000000005030079001006001440007200000006470050300072
107100000301000000086200000000720000000072002160007200216013650050300072
107100000302004310000000000000720000000072002160014400000006470000001006
107100000401000000007200000000000007200287000720000000000000720000000072
107100000402000000000000000000720007200072000000000000216000000000000000
107100000501000720000000000000000000000000000000014400000000000000000000
107100000502000720007200000006470050300072000000007200072000000007200144
107100000601000000000000000000000028700359000000000000000000000079000000
107100000602000000000000000000000000000144
107080000101001860000000000000000018600373000000000000000003730037300000
107080000102003730018600000000000037300000000000000000000000000018600000
107080000201000000055900000000000018600000000000000000000000000018600186
107080000202000000000000000005590040900726005590093201118011180037300000
107080000301000000260900000000000000000000000000000000000186046580037300186
107080000302007450000000000000000005590000000000000000000003354000000001863
107080000401000000037300000000000018600000000000000000000000000000000000
107080000402001860000000000000000000000000000018600000000000000000000000
107080000501000000000000186000000000000000000000000000000000000000000000
107080000502001860000000000009320298100000000000000559001860000000000000186
107080000601000000000000000000000018600000000000000186000000149100000
107080000602000000000000000000000000000932
105070000101002030000000101000340003400034000680000000000003040067600000
105070000102001350027100203000680010100000000000000000000000340000000000
105070000201002030071000034002370010100034001010016900338000680003400101
105070000202000340003400000003040040600507000000000000034015550054100068
105070000301000340158900000001690003400068001010000000101012510027100101
105070000302001010003400000001010020300068005070006800034006090000000778
105070000401000000010100000000000003400034000680000000000000000000000000
105070000402000000003400000000000000000068000000000000680000000000000000
105070000501000680000000000000000000000068000000000000000000000006800000
105070000502000340020300034003720033800000000000003400101000000000000203
105070000601000340010100000000000040600135000680010100034000000033800000
105070000602000000000000000000340000000135
105060000101000000000000000000000000000000001160000000000001160058000000
105060000102000000011600116001160000000000000000000000000000000000000000
105060000201001160000000000000000000000000001160000000232001160000000000
105060000202000000000000000002780150702435002320000000116011600023200000
105060000301000000005800000001160011600232009280000000232033630058000116
105060000302000000000000000000000011600116003480011600000013920000001392
105060000401000000023200000000000000000000000000000000000000000000000000
105060000402000000011600000001160000000000000000000000000000000000000000
105060000501000000000000000000000000000000000000000000000116000000000000
105060000502000000000000000013920127600000000000000000000000000000000000
105060000601002320000000000000000000000116000000000000000000000023200000
105060000602000000000001160000000000000232
106100000101002500021900188000630006300282000310000000125003760072000000
106100000102000940031300219001880018800000000000000000125000000012500000
106100000201000000068800219003130012500125001250003100250000000025000094
106100000202000630000000031005010097000438002190003100031017840097000282
106100000301000630231500031002500006300063002190003100313029100106400282
106100000302003130003100125000310018800000004380006300000009700003101283
106100000401000000025000000000000000000031000940009400000000000000012500000
106100000402000000000000031000000000000031000630006300000000000000031 00031
106100000501000630009400031000630003100063000630025000000000000000125 00031
106100000502000000000000000010010065700063000310015600094000000003100188
106100000601000310009400031000000009400407000310025000094000000034400000
106100000602000000000000000003100000000313
104060000101001830000000000000000000000000000000000000000000000000000000
104060000102000000055000000000000000000000000000000000000000000000000000
104060000201000000018300000000000000000000000000000000009200000000920000 0
104060000202000000000000000009160091600733000920018300000006410027500275
104060000301000000073300000001830000000000000920009200000013740027500183
104060000302001830000000000000920018300000003660000000000007330000000550
104060000401000000009200000000000000000092000000000000000000000000000000
104060000402000000000000000000000000000092000000000000000000000000000000
104060000501000000009200000000000000000092000000000000000000000018300000
104060000502000000000000000001830055000092000000000920000000000000000000
104060000601000000000000092000000000000092000000000000000000000009200000
104080000602000000000000000000000000000092
103070000101000000000000052000000000000000000000000000000520005200052000 00
103070000102000000020600000001030025800000000000000000000000000000000000
103070000201000000046400052002060000000052001030005200103000520000000000
103070000202000000000000000005670061800206000520010300000004640046400155
103070000301000000108200000000000000000010300052000000000520082400103000 00
103070000302001550005200052001030005200000001550000000000003610000000515
103070000401001030036100000000000005200103000000000000000000000005200000
103070000402000520000000052000000010300000000000000001030000000000000052
103070000501001550005200103000000000000000000520000000000000000005200000
103070000502000000005200000005670025800155000000000000000000000000000103
103070000601000000005200103000000000520000000000000000000520000000005200000
```

```
103070000602000000000000052000000000000000
103080000101003540005900118000290002900000001180000000147002950067700088
103080000102003530094200295002360017700000000000017700088000290008800000
103080000201001180135500088006180026500088002360020600501001180058900265
103080000202000880005900000000290020600147000290000000029013250164900383
103080000301000880368100000002360011800147004120038300530035630035300265
103080000302003530002900118002360044200353004120020600088009130000002238
103080000401000000061800059000000002900029000290002900059000590000000029
103080000402000290008800000000290008800059000000000000029000880017700029
103080000501001470002900029000590005900088000880000000059000000014700029
103080000502000590008800029001180026500206001180005900118000000002900177
103080000601001770008800029000880023600206000880035300088000590008800000
103080000602000000000000000000000002900029
102090000101014090060400604000000060400201004020000000201020120382300201
102090000102030180181100201006040000000201000000020100402000000000000402
102090000201000000321900000014090020100000010060080502415002010402400201
102090000202010060020100000000000140900201006040000000000048290402400402
102090000301000001187100000012070040200000024150020101409122740000000604
102090000302008050000000604006040261601409026160100600000032190020108048
102090000401000000080500000000000040200000002010000000000002010020100000
102090000402000000000000000000000000000000002010020100402000000020100000
102090000501004020000000402002010020100000004020000000000002010060400000
102090000502028170040200000006640080500805000000020100604000000020100604
102090000601000000020100201002010020101207004020040200201002010000000000
102090000602000000000000201000000020100000
103090000101005190017300519001730000000173003460000000000003460051900000
103090000102010380034600173003460000000000000000000000000000000000000000
103090000201000000051900173005190000000000005190000000346000000103800692
103090000202003460000000000000000017300346005190000000000012110155700173
103090000301000000380600000003460017300000006920034601038003460017300173
103090000302001730000000000001730121100346008650017300346003460034601730
103090000401000000034600000000000000000034600346000000000000000000000000
103090000402000000017300000001730000000000000000000000000000000000000000
103090000501000000000000173000000000000000000000000000000000000000000000
103090000502000000017300000006920034600173000000017300000000000000000000
103090000601001730000000000001730034600519000000000000000000017300000000
103090000602000000000000173000000000000173
105090000101001480018500148001850009200092000560003700092002030048100019
105090000102004810035100092002590014800056000370000000166000190001900000
105090000201001850090600074002400007400056002400005600259000000048100019
105090000202002030000000000003140096100425001480007400037013860140500240
105090000301000370347500000002590003700185002400020300351025880033300185
105090000302001290005600074000740051800240003700018500000005550003701202
105090000401000190025900000000000000370011100019000000003700037000000000
105090000402000370003700056000190001900019000740000000074000370005600037
105090000501000740001900019000370007400000001110000000000000560020300019
105090000502002030007400056007020048100166001110014800056000190001900129
105090000601000740009200056000190025900444002770025900092001480031400000
105090000602000000000000019000000000000203
104090000101001200009600216001680009600168000480007200072003600043200048
104090000102004320014400096001200016800240002400000000240003840024000000
104090000201000720095000024001200000000240002400014400216000240086400168
104090000202003120033600000000480012000000000000000000000008640067200000
104090000301000000187200000001680004800096003120028800312019680024000216
104090000302000720002400144000720024000096002160009600048003840009601296
104090000401000000009600000000000024000480002400000000000002400000000000
104090000402000000000000000000000000000000000480002400048000000002400024
104090000501000480009600000000240002400024000480002400000000000048000000
104090000502001920000000216006480009600024000240007200024000240002400048
104090000601000240007200000000000004800192000720012000024000240002400000

104090000602000240000000000000000000000000
105100000101002420009100242000000000000091000300003000061000910042400091
105100000102001820018200030000160000000030000910003000091000000006100030
105100000201001520048500061002420012100061000910009100212000300021200152
105100000202000000003000000001210033300273000910003000030016360193900091
105100000301000300297000000002730000000091004550003000030022420030300303
105100000302002120000000030000610027300030003640021200000004240000001061
105100000401000000009100061000000003000061000000000000061000000003000030
105100000402000300009100060000000000000030000300000000030000300009100030
105100000501000000006100030000300003000000000000009100000000000003000000
105100000502000300006100000006360009100121000000006100061000000003000030
105100000601000300006100030000000039400121000610012100121000610006100030
105100000602000300000000000000000000000091
002080000101004020080300000008030000000000000000000000000080300803000000
002080000102016060000000000000000080300000000000000000803000000000000000
002080000201000000281100000012050000000000004020000001606000000080300402
002080000202012050000000000004020080300402004020000000000024100040200000
002080000301000000281100000004020000000402000000040200000052200080300402
002080000302008030000000402000000040200402000000000000000004020000004819
002080000401000000000000000000000000000000000000000000000000000000000000
002080000402004020040200000000000000000000000000000000000000040200000000
002080000501004020000000000000000040200000000000000000000000000040200000
002080000502000000000000000004020040200000000000040200000004020000000000
002080000601000000040200000000000000000040200402004020000000402000000000
002080000602000000000000000000000000000000
008080000101000000000000000000000000000000000000000000000000000000000000
008080000102000000000000000000000000000000000000000000000000000000000000
008080000201000000000000000000000000000000000000000000000000000000000000
008080000202000000000000000000000000000000000000000000000625000000000000
008080000301000000312500000000000000000000000000000000000000000000000000
008080000302000000000000000000000000000000000000000000000000000000000000
008080000401000000000000000000000000000000000000000000000000000000000000
008080000402000000000000000000000000000000000000000000000000000000000000
008080000501000000000000000000000000000000000000000000000000031250000000
008080000502000000000000000000000000000000000000000000000000000000000000
008080000601000000000000000000000000000000000000000000000000031250000000
008080000602000000000000000000000000000000
008090000101000000000000000006000060000000000000000000000000060000000000
008090000102000000359300600006000119800000000000000000000000000000000000
008090000201000000179601198000000000000000000000000000000000060000000000
008090000202000000000000000077840658711377023950479000000000000000000000
008090000301000000000000000000000000000000000000000000000083830239500000
008090000302011980000000000000000000000000600000000000017960000000600
008090000401000000239500000000000000000000000000000000000000000000000000
008090000402000000060000000000000060000000000000000000000000000000000000
008090000501000000000000000000000000000000000000000000000000000000000000
008090000502000000119800000017960299400000000000119800000000000060000600
008090000601000000000000000000000000000000600000000000000000029940000000
008090000602000000000000000000000000000000
108110000101000000000000000000000000000000000000000000000000002460000000
108110000102000000000000246000000000000000000000000000000000000000000000
108110000201000000000000000000000000000000000000000000000000000000000000
108110000202000000000000000002460000000246000000000000000394104187000493
108110000301000000763600000012320000000000000000000000000000049300000
108110000302000000000000000002460000000246002460000000246000000000000000
108110000401000000000000000000000000000000000000000000000000000000000000
108110000402000000000000000000000000000000000000000000000000000000000000
108110000501000000000000000000000000000000000000000000000000000000000000
108110000502002460000000000002460024600000000000000000000000000000000000
108110000601000000000000000002460000000246000000000000000000000000000000
```

```
108110000602000000000000000000000000000000
108100000101000000000000000000000000000000000000000000000000000000670000000
108100000102000000000000000000000000000000000000000000000000000000000000
108100000201000000000000000000000000000000000000000000000000000000000000
108100000202000000000000000001340060100802000000020400067020710033400000
108100000301000000187100000000670000000000000000000000000000040100000000000
108100000302000670000000000000000000000000670000000067000670000000000000000000000000
108100000401000000000000000000000000000000000000000000000000000000000000
108100000402000000000000000000000000000000000000000000000000000000000000
108100000501000000000000000000000000000000000000000000000000000000000000
108100000502000000000000000001340100200000000000000670000000000000000000000
108100000601000000000000000000000000013400067000000000000000000000000000053400000
108100000602000000000000000000000000000067
107110000101000000000000000000000000000000000000000000000000000016500000
107110000201000000000000000001650033100000001650000000000000000000000000
107110000201001650016500000000000000000000000000000000000000000000000000
107110000202000000000000000013220347102314000000016500165112400661200496
107110000301001651057900000003310000000496000000016500000013220000000165
107110000302001650000000000000000016500165001650148800165001650016500000000165
107110000401000000016500000000000000000000000000000000000000000016500000
107110000402000000000000000016500000000000000000000000000000000000000000
107110000501000000000000000000000000000000001650033100000000000000000000
107110000502000000000000000004960082600165000000000000000000000000000000000165
107110000601000000000000000331001650132200661000000000000000000000000006610000000
107110000602000000000000000000000000000496
006140000101000000000000000000000000000000000000000000000000000000000000
006140000102000000000000000000000000000000000000000000000000000000000000
006140000201000000000000000000000000000000000000000000000000000000000000
006140000202000000000000000000000000000125000000000000000000099990000000000
006140000301000005000000000000000000000000000000000000000000000000000000
006140000302000000000000000000000000000000250000000000000000000000000000000000025000
006140000401000000000000000000000000000000000000000000000000000000000000
006140000402000000000000000000000000000000000000000000000000000000000000
006140000501000000000000000000000000000000000000000000000000000000000000
006140000502000000000000000000000000000000000000000000000000000000000000
006140000601000000000000000000000000000000000000000000000000000000000000
006140000602000000000000000000000000000000
105120000101000000000000000000000000000000000000000000000000000000000000
105120000102000000000000000000000000000000000000000000000000000000000000
105120000201000000000007520000000000000000000000000000000000000000000000000
105120000202000000000000000000000000022560075200000000000000000000150403008000000
105120000301000000451100000000000000000000000000000752000000000000000000000
105120000302000000000000000000000000150403008060150075200000007520000012030
105120000401000000000000000000000000000000000000000000000000000000000000
105120000402000000000000000000000000000000000000000000000000000000000000
105120000501000000000000000000000000000000000000000000000000000000000000
105120000502015040000000000000000075200752000000000000000000000000075200000000000000000000
105120000601000000075200000000000000000000000000000075200000000000000000000
105120000602000000000000000000000000000000
106120000101000000000000000000000000000000000000000000000000000010500000
106120000102000000000000000000000000021000000000000000000000000000000000000
106120000201000000000000000000000000000000000000000000000000000010500000
106120000202000000000000000007340115300734003150021000210002830063000315
106120000301000000356400000001050000000000000000000105000000031500210000000
106120000302000000000000000002100073400210007340031500000001050000003983
106120000401000000000000000000000000000000001050000000000000000000105001050000000
106120000402000000000000000000000000000000000000000000000000000000000000
106120000501000000000000000000000000000000000000000000000000000031500000
106120000502006300000000000000000105002100021000000001050010500000000000000000105
106120000601000000000000000001050021000210000000000000000000000000000000063000000
```

```
106120000602000000000000000105000000000000000315
105130000101000000000000000000000000000000000000000000000000000000000000
105130000102001500000000150000000044900000000000000000000000000000000000000
105130000201000000000000000000000000000000001500000000000000000000000000
105130000202000000000000000002990089800449000000000000000150019460029900000
105130000301001500194600000000000000000150000000074900150000000000000000015000000
105130000302000000044900000005990209600599026950044900000001500029905240
105130000401000000000000000000000000000000000000000000000000000000000000
105130000402000000000000000000000000000000000000000000000000000000000000
105130000501000000000000000000000000000000001500000000000000000000000000029900000
105130000502008980000000000000000015000299000000000000000000000000000000000000
105130000601000000000000000000000000001500000000000000000000000000000000000150
105130000602000000000000000000000000000150
106130000101000000000000000000000000000000000000000000000000000000000000
106130000102000000000000000000000000000000000000000000000000000000000000
106130000201000000000000000000000000000000000000000000000000000000000000000000485
106130000202000000000000000009710097100971004850048500000063110048500485
106130000301000000485400000000000000048500000004850000000000000000048500000000000
106130000302000000048500000004850097100971024270048500000004850000009709
106130000401000000000000000000000000000000000000000000000000000000000000
106130000402000000000000000000000000000000000000000000000000000000000000
106130000501000000000000000000000000000000000000000000000000000048500000
106130000502000000000000000000000000000000000000000000000000000000000000
106130000601000000000000000000000000000000000000000000000000000000000000
106130000602000000000000000000000000000971
005140000101000000000000000000000000000000000000000000000000000000000000
005140000102000000000000000000000000000000000000000000000000000000000000
005140000201000000000000000000000000000000000000000000000000000000000000
005140000202000000000000000000000000002960000000000000000000000000000003254000000000000
005140000301000000147900000000000000000000000000000000000000000000000000000000000
005140000302000000000000000000000000002960029601183000000000000000000000000000000
005140000401000000000000000000000000000000000000000000000000000000000000
005140000402000000000000000000000000000000000000000000000000000000000000
005140000501000000000000000000000000000000000000000000000000000029600000
005140000502005920000000000000000000000000029600000000000000000000000000000
005140000601000000000000000000000000000000000000000000000000000000000000
005140000602000000000000000000000000000000
005190000101000000000000000000000000000000000000000000000000000000000000
005190000102000000000000000000000000000000000000000000000000000000000000
005190000201000000000000000000000000000000000000000000000000000000000000
005190000202000000000000000000000000000000000000000000000000000000000000
005190000301000000263200000000000000000000000000000000000000000000000000000000000
005190000302000000000000000000000000000000000000000000000000000000000000
005190000401000000000000000000000000000000000000000000000000000000000000
005190000402000000000000000000000000000000000000000000000000000000000000
005190000501000000000000000000000000000000000000000000000000000000000000
005190000502000000000000000000000000000000000000000000000000000000000000
005190000601000000000000000000000000000000026320000000000000000000000000000000
005190000602000000000000000000000000000000
105200000101000000000000000000000000000000000000000000000000000000000000
105200000102000000000000000000000000000000000000000000000000000000000000
105200000201000000000000000000000000000000000000000000000000000000000000
105200000202000000000000000000000000000000002020000000000010120000000000
105200000301000000222700000000000000000000040500405000000020200000000000000000000
105200000302000000040500000002020040500000010120000000000000000000002834
105200000401000000000000000000000000000000000000000000000000000000000000
105200000402000000000000000000000000000000000000000000000000000000000000
105200000501000000000000000000000000000000000000000000000000000000000000
105200000502004050000000000000000000000002020000000000000000000000000000000000
105200000601000000000000000000000000000000000000405000000000000000000000000000000000
```

266

```
105200000602000000000000000000000000000000
103220000101001160011600000000000000000000000000000000000000000000000000
103220000102000000000000000001160000000000000000000000000000000000000000
103220000201000000000000000000000000000000000000000000000000003480000000
103220000202000000000000000001160034800232000000011600116002320011600000
103220000301001160127600000000000000000000000580000000000006960011600116
103220000302001160000000000002320011600116008120034800000001160000001160
103220000401000000000000000000000000000000000000000000116000000000000000
103220000402000000000000000000000000000000000000000000000000000000000000
103220000501000000000000000000000000000000001160011600000000000000000000
103220000502002320000000000000580000000000000000000116000000000000000000000
103220000601001160000000000000000000000001160000000000000000000011600000
103220000602000000000000116000000000000000
103210000101000000000000000000000000000000000000000000000000000000000000
103210000102000000000000000000000000000000000000000000000000000000000000
103210000201000000000000000000000000000000000000000000000000001150000000
103210000202000000000000000001150023000115001150011500000013780034400000
103210000301000000195200000000000000000000230002300000000000034400115000000
103210000302000000000000000005740011500000021810023000000001150023002181
103210000401000000000000000000000000000000000000000000000000000000000000
103210000402000000000000000000000000000000000000000000000000000000000000
103210000501000000000000000000000000000000000000000000000000000000000000
103210000502002300000000000000115003440000000000000115000000000000000000000
103210000601000000000000000000000000000000000000000000000000000000000000
103210000602000000000000000000000000000000
017040000101000000000000000000000000000000000000000000000000000000000000
017040000102000000122000000000000000000000000000000000000000000000000000
017040000201000000000000000000000000000000000000000000000000000000000000
017040000202000000000000000000000243901220000000000000000000609800000000000
017040000301012200487800000012200000000000000000000000000001220000000000
017040000302012200000000000000000000000000122000000000000000000000000000
017040000401000000000000000000000000000000000000000000000000000000000000
017040000402000000000000000000000000000000000000000000000000000000000000
017040000501000000000000000000000000000000000000000000000000000000000000
017040000502000000000000000012200000000000000000000000000000000000000000
017040000601000000000000000000000000000000000000000000000000012200000000
017040000602000000000000000000000000000000
015030000101000000000000000000000000000000000000000000000000000000000000
015030000102000000000000000000000000000000000000000000000000000000000000
015030000201000000000000000000000000000000000000000000000000000000000000
015030000202000000000000000000000000000000002680000000000000214500000001072
015030000301000000375300000000000000000000000000000000000000053600000000000
015030000302000000000000000000000000000000000000000000000000000000000268
015030000401000000026800000000000000000000000000000000000000000000000000
015030000402000000000000000000000000000000000000000000000000000000000000
015030000501000000000000000000000000000000000000000000000000000000000000
015030000502000000000000000000000000000000000000000000000000000000000000
015030000601000000000000000000000000000000000000000000000000000000000000
015030000602000000000000000000000000000000
015000000101003050030500305000000000000000000000000000000006100030500000
015000000102009150000000000000000000000000000000000000000000000000000000
015000000201000000000000000000000000000000003050000000000000000000000000
015000000202000000000000000000000000000000000000000000000000095400000000305
015000000301000000030500000000000000000003050000000000000000030500000000000
015000000302000000000000000000000000000000000000000000000000060700000000305
015000000401000000000000000000000000000000000000000000000000000000000000
015000000402000000000000000000003050000000000000000000000000000000000000
015000000501000000000000000000000000000000000000000000000000000000000000
015000000502000000000000000000000000000000000000000000000000000000000000
015000000601000000000000000000000000000000000000000000000000000000000000
015000000602000000000000000000000000000000
014000000101000000000000000000000000000000000000000000000000000000000000
014000000102000000000000000000000000000000000000000000000000000000000000
014000000201000000000000000000000000000000000000000000000000000000000000
014000000202000000000000000000000000000000000000000000000000036140000000000
014000000301000000481900000000000000000000000000000000000000000000000000
014000000302000000000000000000000000000000000000000000000000000000000000
014000000401000000000000000000000000000000000000000000000000000000000000
014000000402000000000000000000000000000000000000000000000000000000000000
014000000501000000000000000000000000000000000000000000000000000000000000
014000000502000000000000000000000000000000000000000000000000000000000000
014000000601000000000000000000000000000000000000000000000000000000000000
014000000602000000000000000000000000001205
013040000101000000000000000000000000000000000000000000000000001130000000000
013040000102000000000000000000000000000000000000000000000000000000000000
013040000201000000000000000000000000000000000000000000000000000000000000
013040000202000000000000000000000000000000000000000000000000029310045100113
013040000301000000045100000001130000000000003380000000000000000000000000000
013040000302000000011300000001130000000000000001130000000113000000000000000
013040000401000000000000000000000000000000000000000000000000000000000000
013040000402000000000000000000000000000000000000000000000000000000000000
013040000501000000000000000000000000000000000000000000000000000000000000
013040000502000000000000000000000000000000000000000000000000000000000000
013040000601000000000000000000000000001130000000000000000000000000000000
013040000602000000000000000000000000000000
113030000101001160003900000000000000000000000000000000000000390003900000
113030000102000000000000000000000000000000000000000000000000000000000000
113030000201000390000000000000000000000000000000000000000000000000000000
113030000202000000000000000000000000039000390000000000000000096500193000000
113030000301002320548300039001160003900000001540003900000001160000000000
113030000302000000011600000000000000116000000000000000390000000000000000077
113030000401000000000000000000000000000000000000000000000000000000000000
113030000402000000000000000000000000000000000000000000000000000000000000
113030000501000000000000000000000000000000000000000000000000000390011 6
113030000502000390000000000000000770000000000000000000000000000000000000000
113030000601000000000000000000000000000000000039000000000000000000000000000
113030000602000000003900000000000000000000
113020000101000410000000020000000000000000000000000000000000000020000000
113020000102000610000000000000000000000000000000000000000000000000000000
113020000201000000000000000000000000000000000000000000000000000410002 0
113020000202000200000000000000000000000041001020002000020000000132400693 00102
113020000301004480716900163001020004100143002440012200000000410000000000
113020000302000000034600020000000000000041000410006100000000000000000143
113020000401000000000000000000000000000000000000000000000000000000000000
113020000402000000000000000000000000000000000000000000000000000000000000
113020000501000000000000000000000000000000000000000000000000001220026 5
113020000502000410000000000000000610002000000000000000000000000000000000
113020000601000000000000000000000000000000610016300000000000000000000000000
113020000602000000000000000000000000000000
112020000101000000000000000000000000000000000000000000000000000000000000
112020000102000000006100000000000000000000000000000000000000000000000000
112020000201000000000000000000000000000000000000000000000000000000000000
112020000202000000000000000000000000006100061000000000000000061027540104000061
112020000301002451162800367000610006100000006730000000061001840000000000
112020000302000000024500000001840030600061000000000000000610000000000000428
112020000401000000006100000000000000000000000000000000000000000000000000
112020000402000000000000000000000000000000000000000000000000000000000000
112020000501000000000000000000000000000000000000000000000000000610024 5
112020000502000000000000000000000000000610000000000000000000000000000000
112020000601000000000000000000000000000000001220000000000000000000000000000
```

```
112020000602000000000000000000000000000000
012030000101000000000000000000000000000000000000000000000000000000000000
012030000102001370000000000000000000000000000000000000000000000000000000
012030000201000000000000000000000000000000000000000000000000000000000000
012030000202000000000000000000001370000000000000000000000000012360041200137
012030000301001370467000412000000000000000000550000000000000000000000000
012030000302000000000000000000000000000000000000000000000000000000000000
012030000401000000000000000000000000000000000000000000000000000000000137
012030000402000000000000000000000000000000000000000000000000000000000000
012030000501000000000000000000000000000000000000000000000000000000000000
012030000502000000000000000000000000000000000000000000000000000000000000
012030000601000000000000000000000000000000000000000000000000000000000000
012030000602000000000000000000000000000000
013010000101000000000000000000000000000000000000000000000000000000000000
013010000102000000000000000000000000000000000000000000000000000000000000
013010000201000000025500000000000000000000000000000000000000000000000000
013010000202000000000000000000000000000000509000000000000000068700178100255
013010000301005091501300509005090000000000000000000255000000000509000000000
013010000302002550050900000000000000000000000000000000000000000000000000
013010000401000000000000000000000000000000000000000000000000000000000000
013010000402000000000000000000000000000000000000000000000000000000000000
013010000501000000000000000000000000000000000000000000000000000000000255
013010000502000000000000000000000000000000000000000000000000000000000000
013010000601000000000000000000000000000000000002550000000000000000000000
013010000602000000000000000000000000000000
114020000101000000000000000000000000000000000000000000000000000000000000
114020000102000260000000000000000000000000000000000000000000000000000000
114020000201000260002600000000000000000000000000000000000000000005100000
114020000202000000000000000000000001290002600000000000000036250126000206
114020000301004111254500309001800026001540061700000000000000000000000000
114020000302000000059100026000510010300103000260000000000510002600077001 80
114020000401000000007700000000000000000000000000000000000000000000000000
114020000402000000000000000000000000000000000000000000000000000000000000
114020000501000000000000000000000000000000000000000000000000000015400231
114020000502000000000000000000000000000000000000000000000000000000000000
114020000601000000000000000000000000000000026004880000000000000000000000
114020000602000000000000000260000000000026
014030000101000000000000000000000000000000000000000000000000000000000000
014030000102000000000000000000000000000000000000000000000000000000000000
014030000201000000000000000000000000000000000000000000000000000000000000
014030000202000000000000000000000000000000000000000000000000001575803030
014030000301012121697000606012120000000000000606000000000000000000000606
014030000302000000000000000000000000000000000000000000000000000000000606
014030000401000000000000000000000000000000000000000000000000000000000000
014030000402000000000000000000000000000000000000000000000000000000000000
014030000501000000000000000000000000000000000000000000000000000000000606
014030000502000000000000000000000000000000000000000000000000000000000000
014030000601000000000000000000000000000000000000000000000000000000000000
014030000602000000000000000000000000000000
014010000101000000000000000000000000000000000000000000000000000000000000
014010000102000000000000000000000000000000000000000000000000000000000000
014010000201000000064100000000000000000000000000000000000000000000000000
014010000202000000000000000000000006410064100000000000000044870320500000
014010000301012821923100000006410000001282000000000000000000000000000000
014010000302000000064100000000000000000000000000000000000000000000000000
014010000401000000000000000000000000000000000000000000000000000000000000
014010000402000000000000000000000000000000000000000000000000000000000000
014010000501000000000000000000000000000000000000000000000000000000001282
014010000502000000000000000000000000000000000000000000000000000000000000
014010000601000000000000000000000000000000000000000000000000000000000000
014010000602000000000000000000000000000000
014050000101000000000000000000000000000000000000000000000001666000000000000
014050000102000000000000000000000166600000000000000000000000000000000000
014050000201000000000000000000000000000000016660000000000000000000000000
014050000202000000000000000000000833303333016660000000000000833300000000000
014050000301000000666600000016660000001666000000000000000000000000000000
014050000302000000000000000000000000000000000000000000000000000000001666
014050000401000000000000000000000000000000000000000000000000000000000000
014050000402000000000000000000000000000000000000000000000000000000000000
014050000501000000000000000000000000000000000000000000000000000000000000
014050000502000000000000000000000000000000000000000000000000000000000000
014050000601000000000000000000000000000000000000000000000000000000000000
014050000602000000000000000000000000000000
116040000101000000000000559000000000000000000000000000000000000000000000
116040000102000000000000000000000000000000000000000000000000000000000000
116040000201000000055900000000000000000000000000000000000000000055900000
116040000202000000000000000011170111701117000000055900000016760055900000
116040000301011170335200000005590000000000000000000000000000000000000000
116040000302000000000000000000000000000000000000000000000000000000001117
116040000401000000000000000000000000000000000000000000000000000000000000
116040000402000000000000000000000000000000000000000000000000000000000000
116040000501000000000000000000000000000000000000000000000000000055900000
116040000502000000000000000000000000000000000000000000000000000000000000
116040000601000000000000000000000000000000000000000000000000000000000000
116040000602000000000000000000000000000000
015020000101000000000000000000000000000000000000000000000000000000000000
015020000102000000000000000000000000000000000000000000000000000000000000
015020000201000000000000000000000000000000000000000000000000000000000000
015020000202000000000000000000000000000001180000000118000000248200047300236
015020000301001180461000000000000000236001180011800000000000000000000118
015020000302001180035500000000000000118000000000000000000000000000000000
015020000401000000000000000000000000000000000000000000000000000000000000
015020000402000000000000000000000118000000000000000000000000000000000000
015020000501000000000000000000000000000000000000000000000000000000000000
015020000502000000000000000000000118000000000000000000000000000000000000
015020000601000000000000000000000000000000000000000000000000000000000000
015020000602000000000000000000000000000000
```

APPENDIX V

Sherds per Hectare of Collected Terrace Area, by Site Subdivision

The first two columns of each line or card indicate the site subdivision number. Subdivision 5, for example, is indicated by "05." The next two columns list only the card number, of which there are 12 for each site subdivision. Following that the ceramic values are listed, with five columns reserved for each ceramic category. As in Appendix IV, each value has two decimal places, so should be read as "000.00." The order of ceramic categories included is the same as the order in Appendix IV, and is as follows:

0001	0002	0003	0004	0005	0006	0016	0021	0022	0031	0032	0038
0057	0121	0122	0123	0374	0375	0376	0377	0378	0380	0383	0384
0385	0386	0387	0389	0390	0391	0393	0394	0395	0402	0403	0404
0406	0407	0561	1102	1104	1105	1106	1107	1109	1120	1122	1123
1125	1126	1137	1138	1140	1141	1143	1144	1194	1207	1227	1241
1258	1259	1262	1263	1264	1265	1268	1274	1277	1297	1312	1330
1332	1338	1339	1340	1341	1342	1343	1344	1345	1346	1347	1348
1349	1351	1353	1354	1355	1356	1357	1359	1360	1361	1362	1363
1364	1365	1366	1367	1368	1369	1370	1419	1420	1421	1422	1999
2009	2010	2011	2013	2014	2015	2042	2052	2065	2072	2076	2078
2079	2080	2085	2414	2418	3033	3035	3408	3410	3411	5007	5081
5082	5083	5084	5085	5086	5329						

```
0101002820005200094000520004200083001250001000063001980084500031
0102003020017700083000940009400031000100004200031000630005200052
0103000100084500031003020009400063002500006300375000420021900073
0104000940000000000001880031300156000940001000000010110116800563
0105000000239800000001770008300094005530006300594020960026100209
0106002920000000083001670040700261006780015600010008130002101429
0107000000034400010000000006300052000100002100021000630004200010
0108000420000000042000420006300021000420000000063000210008300031
0109000420008400042000420000000010000420001000000000100011500000
0110001770007300010004590014600115000100008400063000000003100083
0111000310007300052000000011500146000730011500031000420007300000
0112000000001000021000000000000042
0201003870012100233004170007900117002610003300150003580060400067
0202005000051600158001870014200042000420008700154001540008300042
0203001120136100100004370012500079003580016200445000870086600287
0204004000012500008001500025800104000830002900017012160108700204
0205000330288100000001920007900117003790027500662038090037100321
0206002620003700146001540073300271004410016700037009330007101994
0207000210035000012000080007900092000460001200062000420001200012
0208000580004200025000210005400042000250001200054000210006700050
0209001080009600071000870004600029000830000800025000210013700008
0210002710012500075010780022500146000670010000062000000004200158
0211000670007900046000330017100366001870032900137000670006200008
0212000080000800012000080000800054
0301001230006200185002470012300123001230000000123001230086400000
0302008640037000000002470012300185000620000000000000000006200000
0303003090074100000004320012300000003090006200247000000098800123
0304003700012300000001850074100123001850000000000012350129600000
0305000620456800000001850006200185005560055600864029010024700370
0306003090000000123003700049400309016050037000062016670006203148
0307000000030900062000620000000247000000000000000000620000000000
0308001230000000062000000012300000000620006200062000000012300123
0309001230012300123000620000000062003700012300000000620006200000
0310004320000000062007410006200247000000006200123000000000000123
0311000620000000123000000012300185003700061700123000000012300000
0312000000006200062000000000000062
0401002690013500157000900000000067000220000000045003360071700045
0402004480035900157000670002200067000450006700090000220002200000
0403001120056100112003810009000090001120009000471000670053800291
0404000670002200000000220015700067000450006700022012110094200135
0405000220262300000000670006700045004260033600381028700038100157
0406001790000000090001350087400404004930015700000005380002201883
0407000220024700045000000000000090000450000000022000000002200000
0408000000002200000000220011200022000900002200045000000006700067
0409001790011200045000220004500000001570000000000000000013500000
0410001570004500000004480004500112000000009000000000000002200045
0411000220006700022000000017900448002690011200157000450002200000
0412000000000000022000000000000022
0501001340005700115000380003800038000190000000095002860040100000
0502000380013400095000950007600019000190001900038000000005700000
0503000000043900076002100007600019000760001900134000000007600076
0504000380000000019002100057300344001150001900000016980078200172
0505000380198500000001720001900057001530005700172018510068700095
0506002480001900076000570007600038003630007600000007250000001298
0507000000015300019000000003800115000760000000000000380007600019
0508000000001900000000190003800057000760000000076000190001900019
0509000570005700019000190001900038000380026700000000000007600000
0510000000001900000008020034400057000190011500038000000001900134
0511000000007600000000000007600210000000013400019000000030500019
0512000000000000000000000000000115
0601001630014000163000810009300140000350003500047001750044200035
0602003260026800058001630011600047000350002300093000000004700012
0603001860064000047001980010500058001510007000221000230036100210
0604000700001200000004190123400733002210010500058015020153700140
0605000350326000000002560002300175003030015100349025730026800198
0606002210002300058000810037300151003140019800000005700002301129
0607000120021000000000000002300081000120000000047000350001200012
0608000350004700058000120001200035000470000000047000350007000023
0609000470002300012000350005800000000700000000000000470016300012
0610001050005800035006640040700175000350008100070000000002300093
0611000700005800058000000036100279001400019800105001160016300000
0612000000000000023000000000000175
0701002080006700147001010003400094001210002000047001210034900074
0702002140052300154001010011400013000000000700080000270004000020
0703001270079800094002880013400040001880004000181000540012100107
0704001340007000007006370074400724000870006000034010520055000161
0705000200156800000001070004700101002210006000261001950028800174
0706002280001300027000940028800121003890008700034000690007000811
0707000000016100013000000002700087000270000700007000470001300000
0708000200002000013000200004700034000400000000027000340000700013
0709000600006000034000400003400000000270001300000000070015400000
0710000870015400027005430052900040000000010700040000000002000141
0711000600008700047000000024800188000470012700060000070028200007
0712000000000000013000200000000121
0801003520016900127001690012700141000280002800099002250049300000
0802001130043700197001690028200014000140000000056000140005600000
0803000280081700113002110012700070001690007000169000000026900070
0804001550004200000017460198602859004370059200211011690059200085
0805000000170400028001550002800070002390005600282029010049300254
0806002960002800070000700036600197001550012700014008170004201338
0807000000025400014000000002800099000280001400014000140004200014
0808000560004200099000140005600042000560000000056000280001400042
0809001270002800042000280007000042000280001400000000140002800014
0810000420012700014009720102800028000990018300056000000007000352
0811001130018300042000000043700282000420008500085000000066200028
0812000000001400014000000000000563
0901002290007600000000760007600153000000000000153003050076300000
0902003050137401221005340030500000000000000000076000000000000000
0903002290129800382003820015300000003050007600076000000000000229
0904000000000000000003820007600229000000000000229004580007600000
0905000760183200000000000000000000001530007600382030530030500458
0906003050000000229000760038200076005340007600000007630000000916
0907000760030500000000000015300076000760000000000000000000000000
0908000760000000000000000000000000000760000000000000000007600000
0909003050022900000000000007600000001530000000000000000000000000
0910000000000000000011450038200000000000000000000000000000000382
0911000760000000000000000007600153000000000000000000000000000000
0912000000000000000000000000000000
1001000000000000000000000000000000000000000000000000000022900000
1002000000000000076000760015300000000760000000000000000000000000
1003000760007600000000000000000000000000000000000000000000000000
1004000000000000000006870206101832000000030500153087020473300382
1005000760923700000006110000000229000000007600000007630015300076
1006001530000000000000760015300076000840015300153001530000000076
1007000000007600000000000000000000000000000000000000000007600000
1008000000000000076000000000000000000000000000000000000000000000
1009000000000000000000000000000000000760015300000000000000000000
1010001530000000000003050137400076000000007600000000000000000076
1011000000000000153001530091600458000000000000000000000106900000
1012000000000000000000000000000305
```

```
1101000340001100017000000000000000000000000000000000000280001700000
1102000450001100000000000000600000000000000000000000000000000000000
1103000110002300000000000000000000000110000000000000000000002800006
1104000060000000000000230008500119000230001700006024240077600147
1105003400828400187001420004000102003450007900011000910000000011
1106000170031700011000340008500004000040000600023000170001700170
1107000000002800000000000000000000000000000000000000000000000000
1108000000000000000000000000110000000000000000000000000000000000
1109000000000000000000000000000000000000000000000000000009100193
1110000170000000000000340001100006000000000000000000000000000000
1111000000000000000000000000000000340018100000000000000000000600000
1112000000000600006000000000000000011
1201000000000000000000000000000000000000000000000000000004200000
1202000420000000042000000021200000000000000000000000000000000000
1203000000000000000420000000000000000004200000000000000000004200042
1204000000000000000000551011020067800169001270012703220005510169
1205000420309300000000420008400042002540012700000001690012700000
1206000000016900000002970118600551018640038100000001690008504915
1207000000000000000000000000000000420000000000000000420004200000
1208000000000000000000000000000000000000000000000000000000000000
1209000000000000000000000000000000000000084000000000000002970000
1210006780000000000002120033900127000000004200084000000000000084
1211000000004200000000420016900127000000000000000000000029700042
1212000000000000004200000000000254
1301000000000000000000000000000000000000000000000000000000000000
1302000000000000000000000000000000000000000000000000000000000000
1303000000000000000000000000000000000000000000000000000000000000
1304000000000000000000000000018900000000000000000009430000000000
1305000000226400000000000377003770000000189000000000000000000000
1306000000037700000001890037700000009430000000000000000000002642
1307000000000000000000000000000000000000000000000000000000000000
1308000000000000000000000000000000000000000000000000000000000000
1309000000000000000000000000000000000000000000000000000000000000
1310003770000000000000000001890000000000000000000000000000000000
1311000000000000000000000003770018900000000000000000000000000000
1312000000000000000000000000000000
1401000560005600000000000000000000000000000000000000000000000000
1402000000005600000000005600000000000000000000000000000000000000
1403000000000000000000000000000000000000000000000000000022600000
1404000000000000000001130028200169000560011300056007910028200000
1405000560158200000000000000000113003950000000000000062100113000056
1406000560000000000000452001130005601525002820000000011300113001638
1407000000000000000000000000000000000000000005600000000000000000
1408000000000000000000000000000000000000000000000000000000000000
1409000000000000000000000000000000000000000560005600000000000000000
1410002260000000000000339001690000000000000011300000000000000000000
1411000560000000000000000000000560000000000000000000000000560000000
1412000000000000005600000000000000
1501000920003100031000310003100062000000000000000000620039800000
1502000610021400000001530003100000000000000000000000000000000000
1503000310033600000000310000000000000000000310000000000000000000000
1504000310000000000001220021400183000310000000000036090134600367
1505000310743100031006120003100183000610009200092021100021400092
1506002450000000000001830009200000004280009200031010090000000979
1507000000012200000000000000310000000000000000000000000000000031
1508000000000000092000620015300031000000000000000000310003100000
1509000000000000031000000000000000000000000000000000000030600000
1510000000000000031003670006200000000310009200031000000000000062
1511000620000000031000000003100031000920000000000000000000620000000
1512000000000310000000000000000000
```

APPENDIX VI

Area Descriptions

Area 1 (N4E12): Covers roughly 1 ha, around the point indicated on the grid square sheet. Located on gentle slope on a piedmont spur. Consists of a scatter of mostly Period I and II sherds, including some Period V. Chert is abundant. No architecture noted.

Area 2 (N4E12): Covers roughly 1 ha, around the point indicated on the grid square sheet. Located on gentle slope on a piedmont spur. Consists of a scatter of mostly Period I and II sherds. No architecture noted.

Area 5 (N6E10): Plowed zone, so no architecture is visible on the surface. This is flat ground, so terracing would not have been necessary for residential construction. Pottery is light to moderate in density, and Periods I, II, IIIb–IV, and V were noted. Sparse obsidian is present, and one probable pottery burnisher was noted.

Area 6 (N7E10); Area of scattered sherds, but no terraces or residential features were noted. This is interesting since the slope is gentle and would have allowed such construction. The absence of terraces here could be due to the fact that this is the border between site subdivisions 8 and 5.

Area 7 (N7E9): Located on gentle piedmont slope below the outer defensive wall, extended over several hectares around the point indicated on the grid square. No terracing present, but one small wall fragment was noted. Sparse ceramics, chert, and obsidian noted. Most pottery dates to Period V, but a few sherds noted dating to periods I, II and IIIb–IV.

Area 8 (N8E9): Covers roughly 1 ha on a gently sloping piedmont spur. No terracing, but several wall fragments were noted. The moderately dense pottery includes Periods I through V. Numerous blades and flakes of obsidian were noted, as well as some quartzite and chert, and two manos and one metate.

Area 9 (N8E9): Plowed field of less than 1 ha along the east slope of a piedmont spur. No terracing is present, but some wall fragments were noted. Obsidian is well represented, and some quartzite, one mano, one metate, and a jadeite bead were noted. Pottery is of moderate density, and includes Periods I, IIIb–IV, and V.

Area 10 (N8E9): Large plowed area, including several hectares in the vicinity of the point indicated on the grid square sheet. Shallow slope, along the top of a piedmont spur. No terracing is present, but a few wall fragments were noted. Obsidian is well represented, and quartzite, chert, one mano, one metate, and a hammerstone were noted. Moderate pottery includes Periods I and V.

Area 11 (N8E9): A 1 ha plowed field on flat ground along a ridge top. No terracing or wall fragments noted. Obsidian, quartzite, and chert tools noted, along with two metates and two pestle fragments. Light-to-moderate pottery includes mostly Periods Late I and V.

Area 12 (N9E8): A plowed field of less than 1 ha along a ridgetop. No terracing is present, but two low mounds may have been residences. Several fragments of obsidian and chert are present, along with a celt fragment. The moderately dense pottery includes Periods Late I, IIIb–IV, and V.

Area 13 (N8E9): A long, plowed rectangular area, along the top of a ridge. No terracing is present but four or five possible house locations were noted. One of these locations, according to the author of the site report, may have been a workshop for chert and obsidian. Also noted in the area as a whole were one mano, one metate, one mortar, a worked sherd, and two projectile points, one of quartzite, and one of obsidian. The moderately dense pottery includes mostly Periods Late I and V.

Area 14 (N6E9): A small agricultural field adjacent to the bottom of the *cañada norte*. No terracing present, but sparse ceramics include Periods I, IIIb–IV, and V.

Area 15 (N6E9): An agricultural field near the bottom of the *cañada norte.* Three or four possible house mounds noted. Moderate-to-dense pottery includes Periods I, II, IIIb–IV, and V.

Area 16 (N5E7, N5E8): A large, open, cultivated area lacking terracing. Three possible residential mounds were noted along the area's west edge, north of Terrace 1306. Otherwise no evidence for architecture is present on the surface. This may have been a marketplace (see the discussion, pp. 85, 86). All periods are represented on the surface.

Area 18–21 (N7E8): These areas are located along a flattish ridgetop north of the defensive wall. Little or no terracing noted, but wall fragments and house mounds are present. Pottery is light to moderate in density, and consists mostly of Period V, along with some Late I and IIIb–IV. Areas 18 and 19 may have been stone working areas involving both obsidian and chert/quartzite.

The El Gallo Areas–3–8 (N8E4): This is a heavily plowed zone that probably originally contained terraces and/or residences. Pottery is sparse to moderate, and consists mostly of Period IIIb–IV, along with some Period Late I.

APPENDIX VII

Monte Albán Grid Square Maps, 1:2000 Map Squares

Each square represents one of the Monte Albán grid squares, the grid square number indicated in the lower left corner. The conventions used to indicate archaeological features are the same as those indicated on the 1:10,000 map and on Figure 1.3. Dark, thick lines represent walls. Platform mounds show the top and bottom areas to scale. Ancient roads are indicated by solid parallel lines and modern roads by parallel dashed lines. The squares are organized, following the Monte Albán map, from west to east, starting with the southernmost row (i.e., row N0).

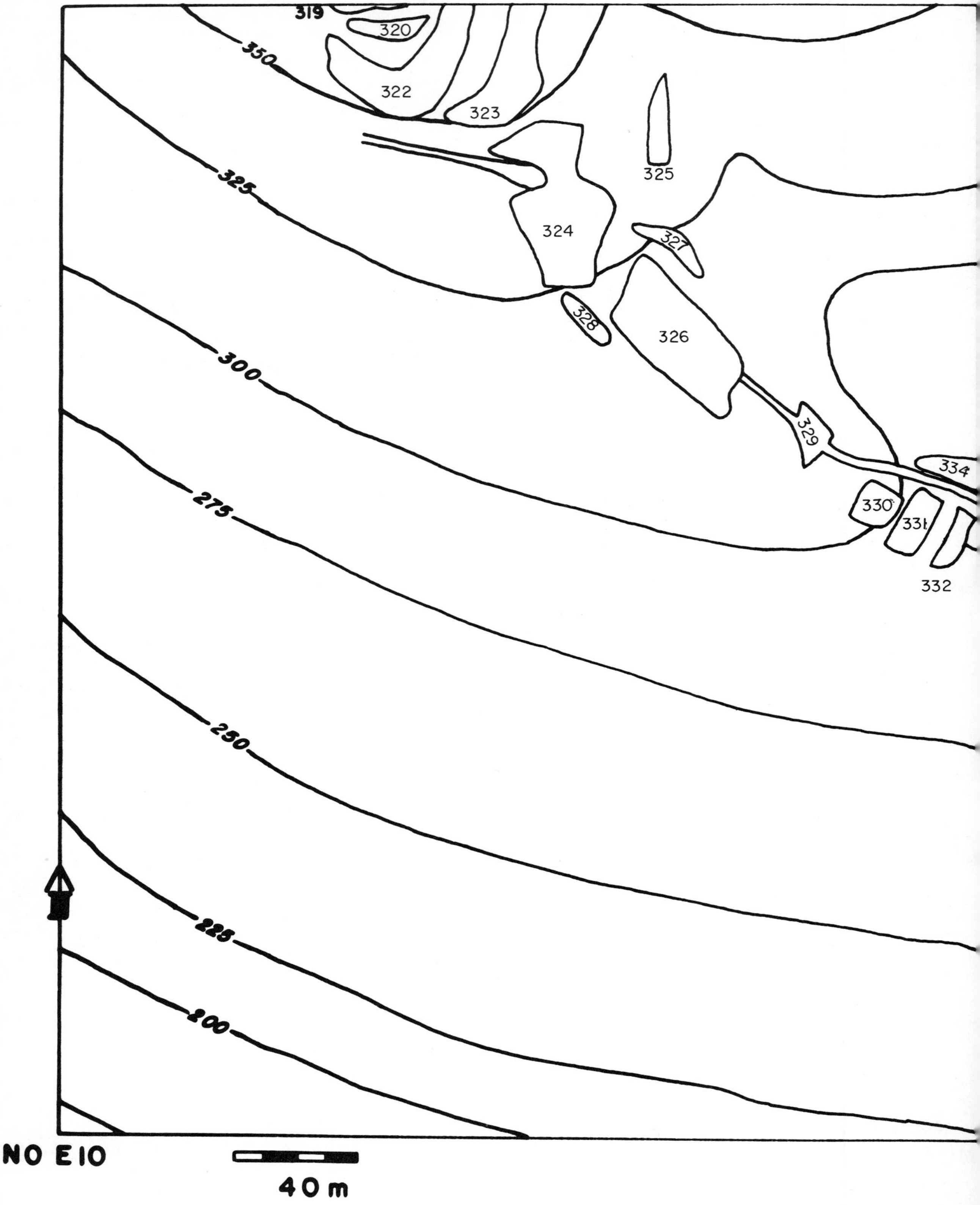
319
320
350
322
323
325
325
324
327
328
326
300
329
334
330
331
332
275
250
225
200
N0 E10
40 m

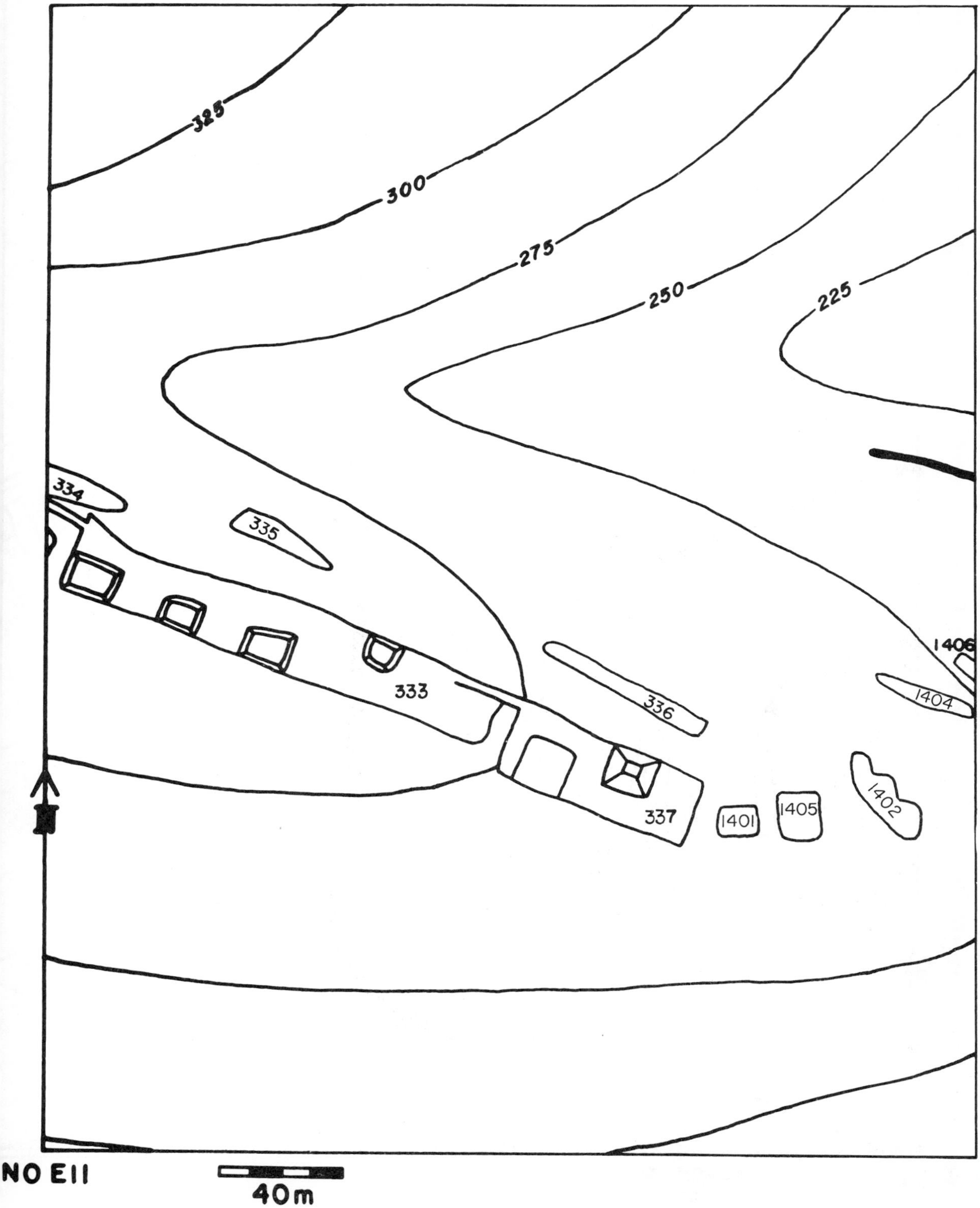
325
300
275
250
225
334
335
333
336
337
1401
1405
1402
1404
1406
N
N0 E11
40m

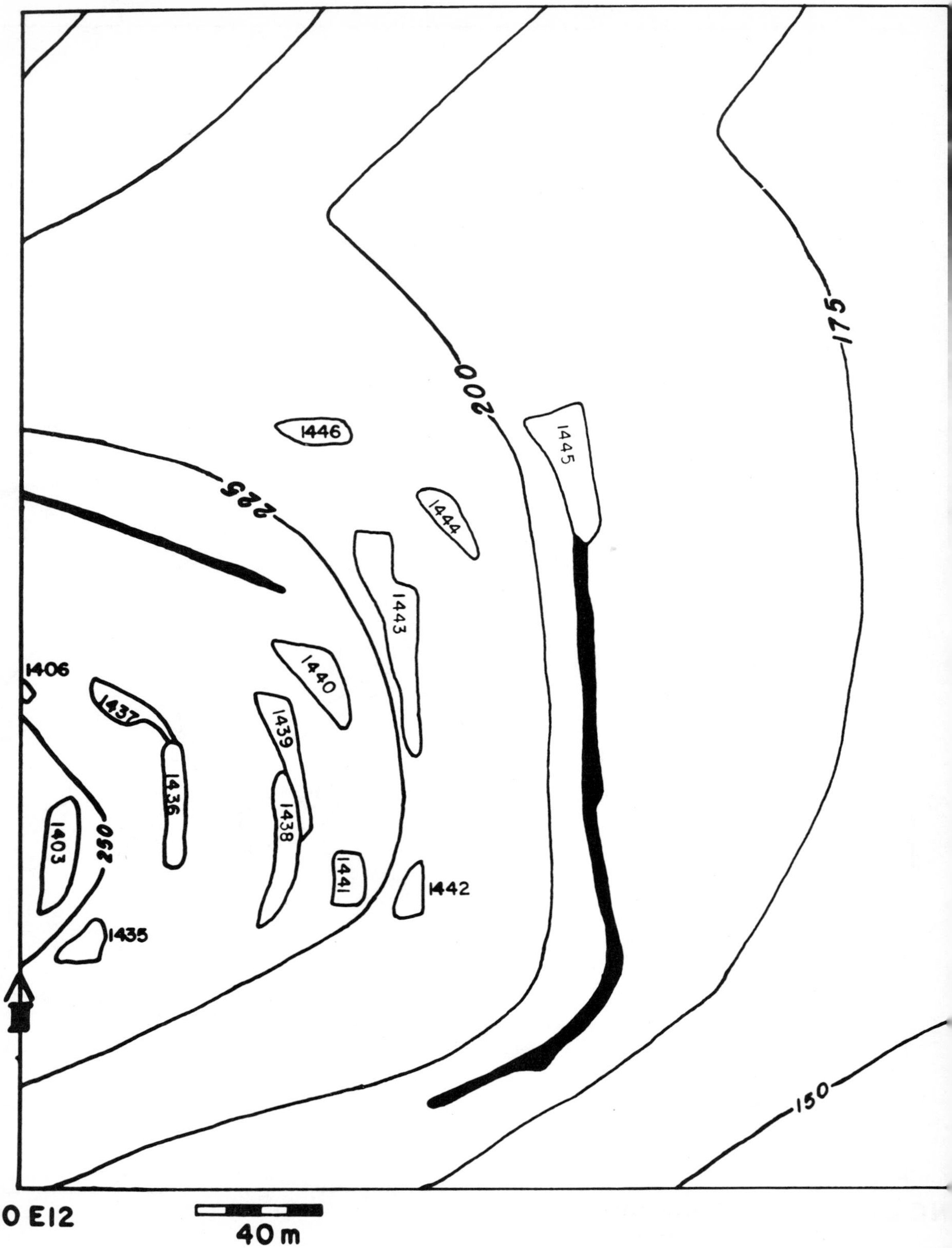
200
175
150
225
250
1446
1445
1444
1443
1440
1406
1437
1439
1436
1403
1438
1441
1442
1435
NO E12
40 m

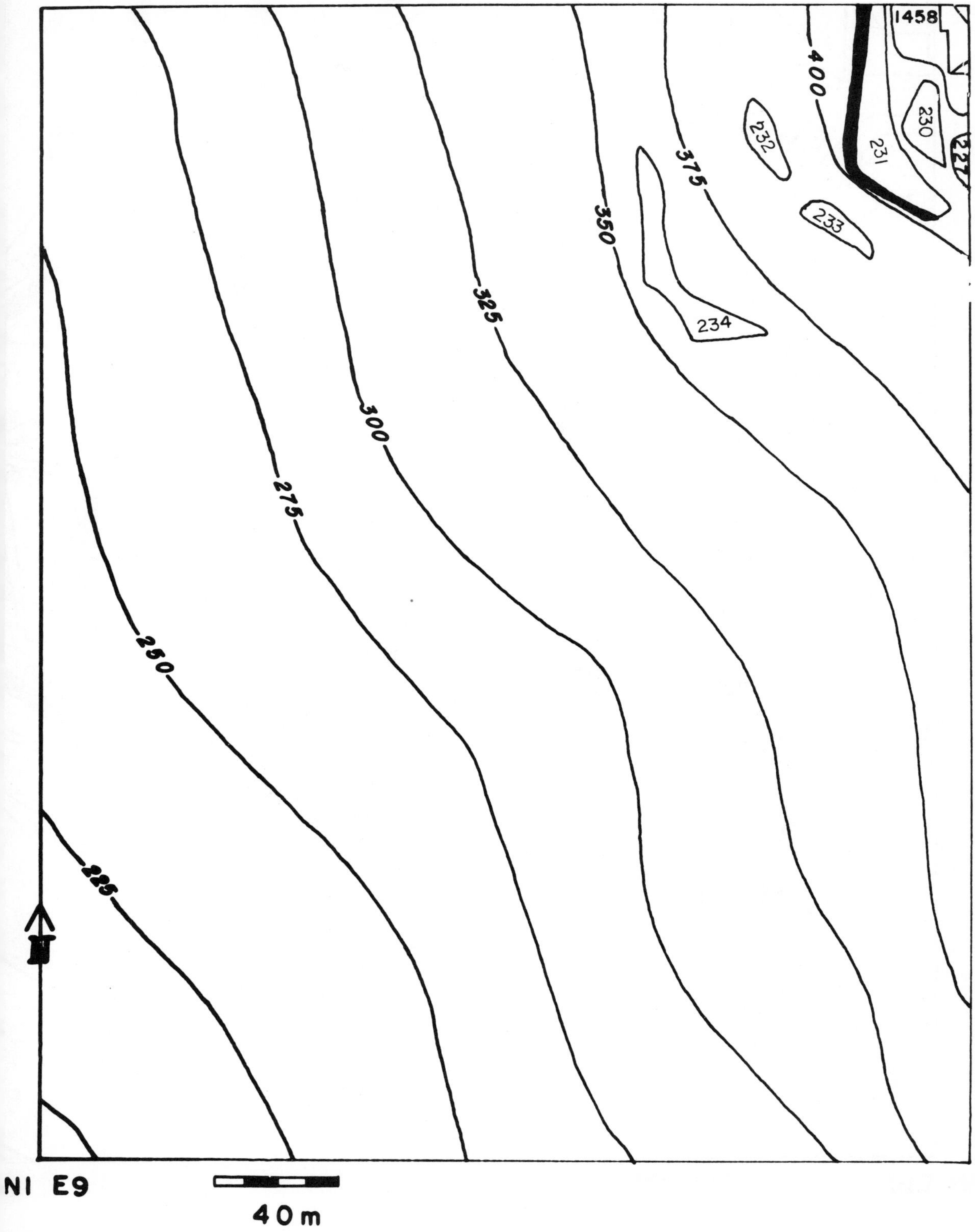
1458
400
375
350
325
300
275
250
225
232
230
231
233
234
N1 E9
40m

202
1413
143
210
208
205
350
227
209
206
301
1461
304
207
303
228
243
400
241
244
229
240
245
242
338
340
339
311
341
N
312
313
308
307
316
310
309
375
315
318
343
314
347
346
317
344
350
345
321
319
323
N1 E10
40 m

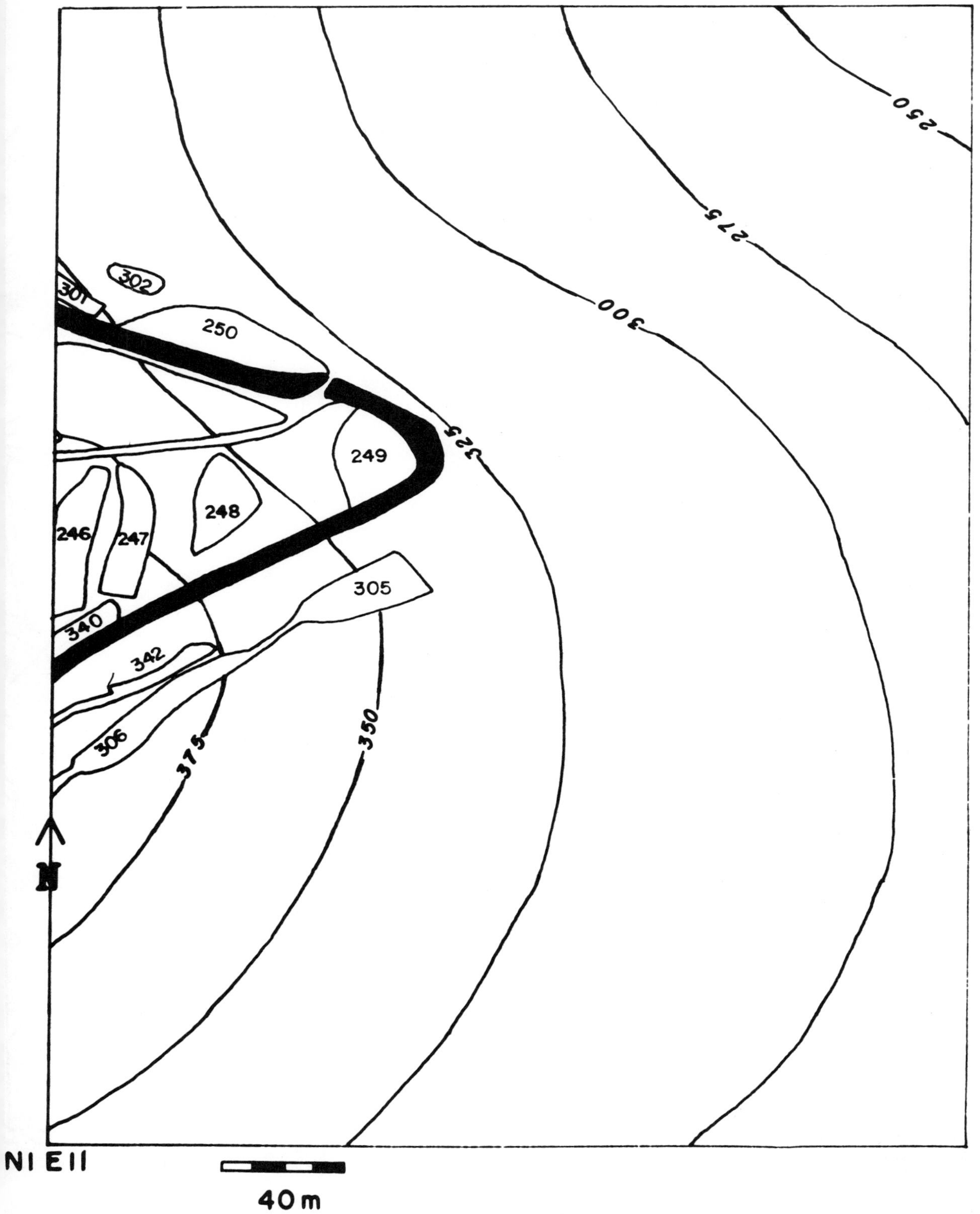

250
275
300
325
350
375
302
301
250
249
248
246
247
305
340
342
306
N
N1 E11
40 m

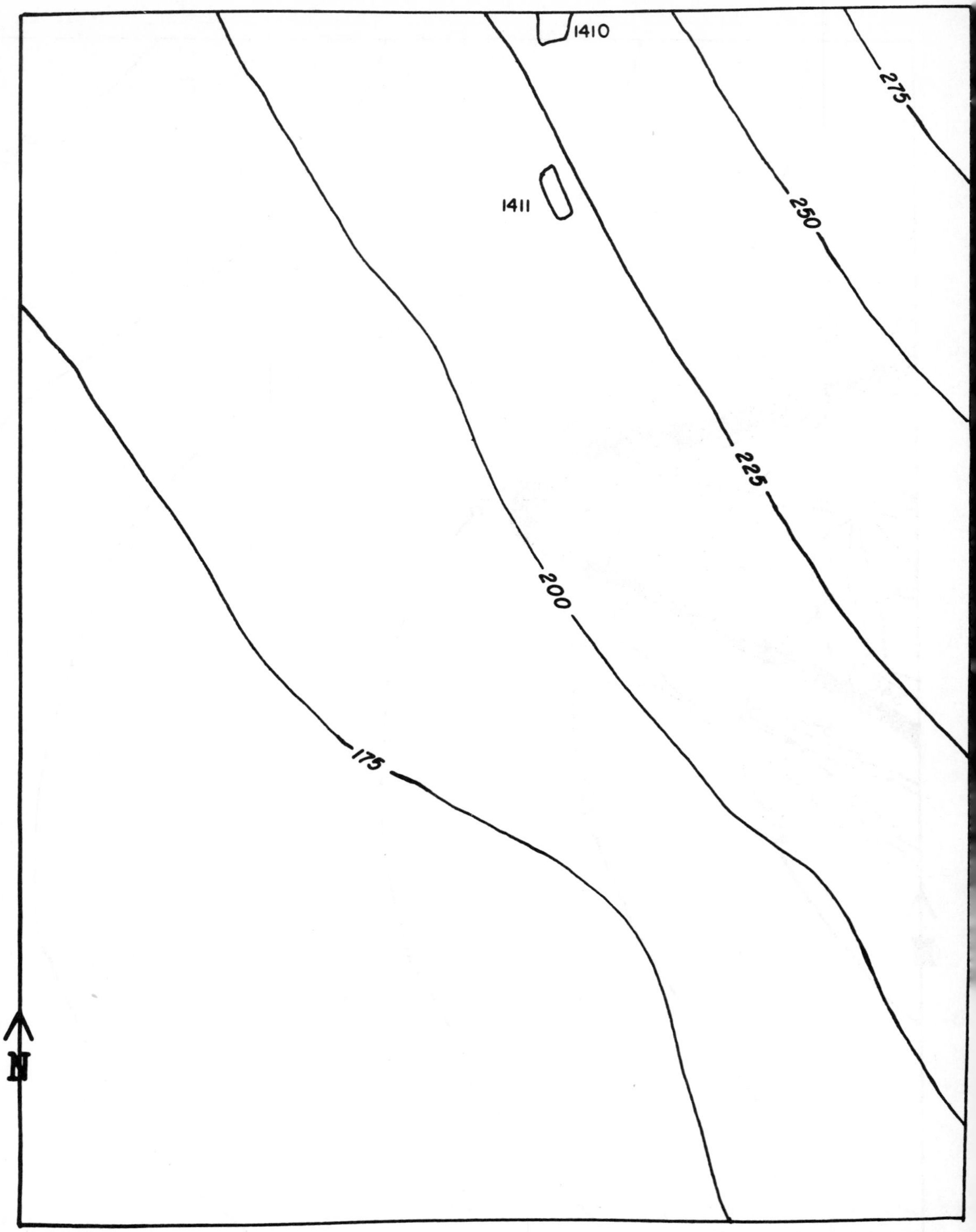

N2 E7

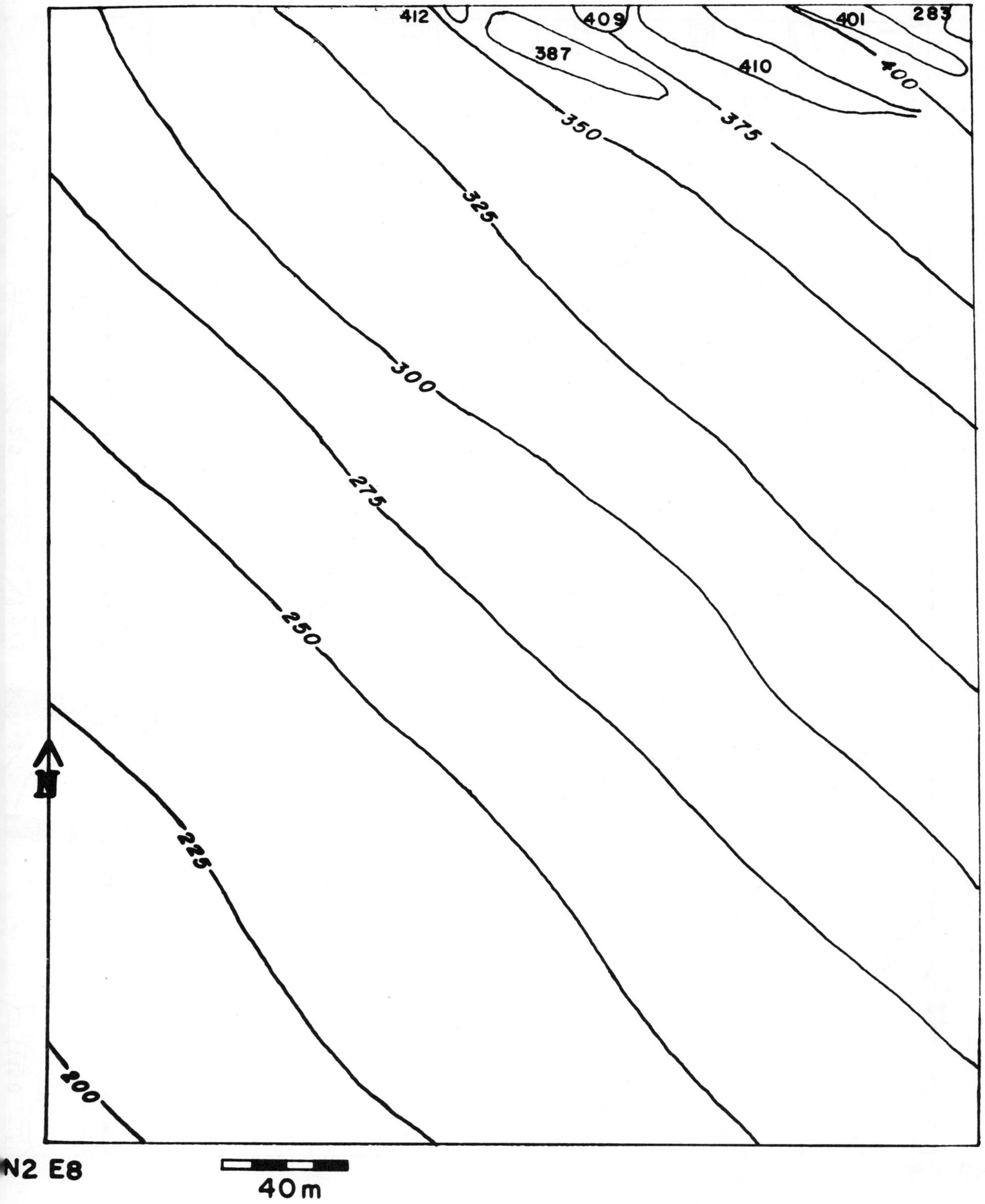

412
409
401
283
387
410
400
350
375
325
300
275
250
225
200
N
N2 E8
40 m

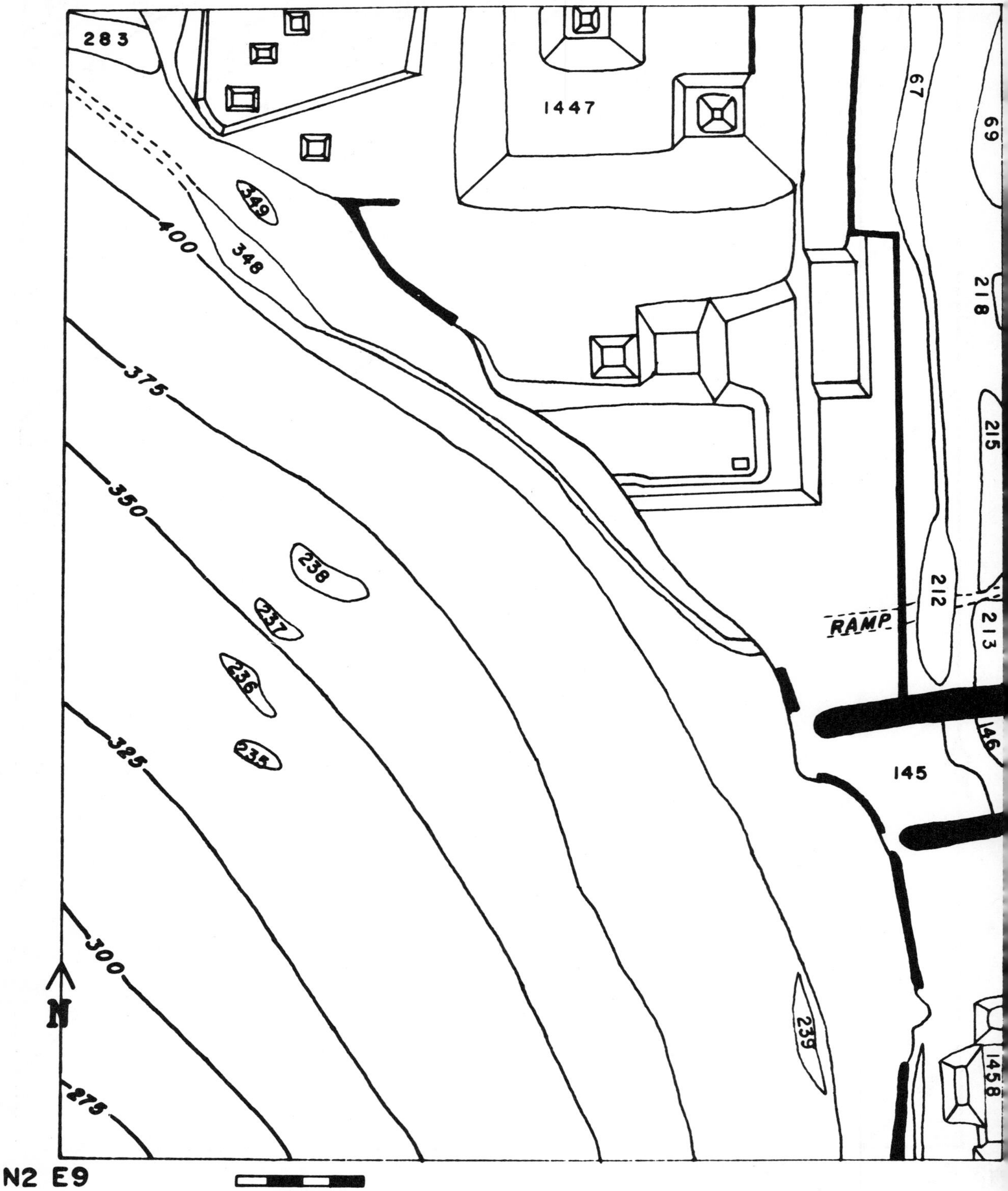
283
1447
67
69
349
400
348
218
375
215
350
238
237
212
RAMP
213
236
325
235
146
145
300
N
239
1458
275
N2 E9
40m

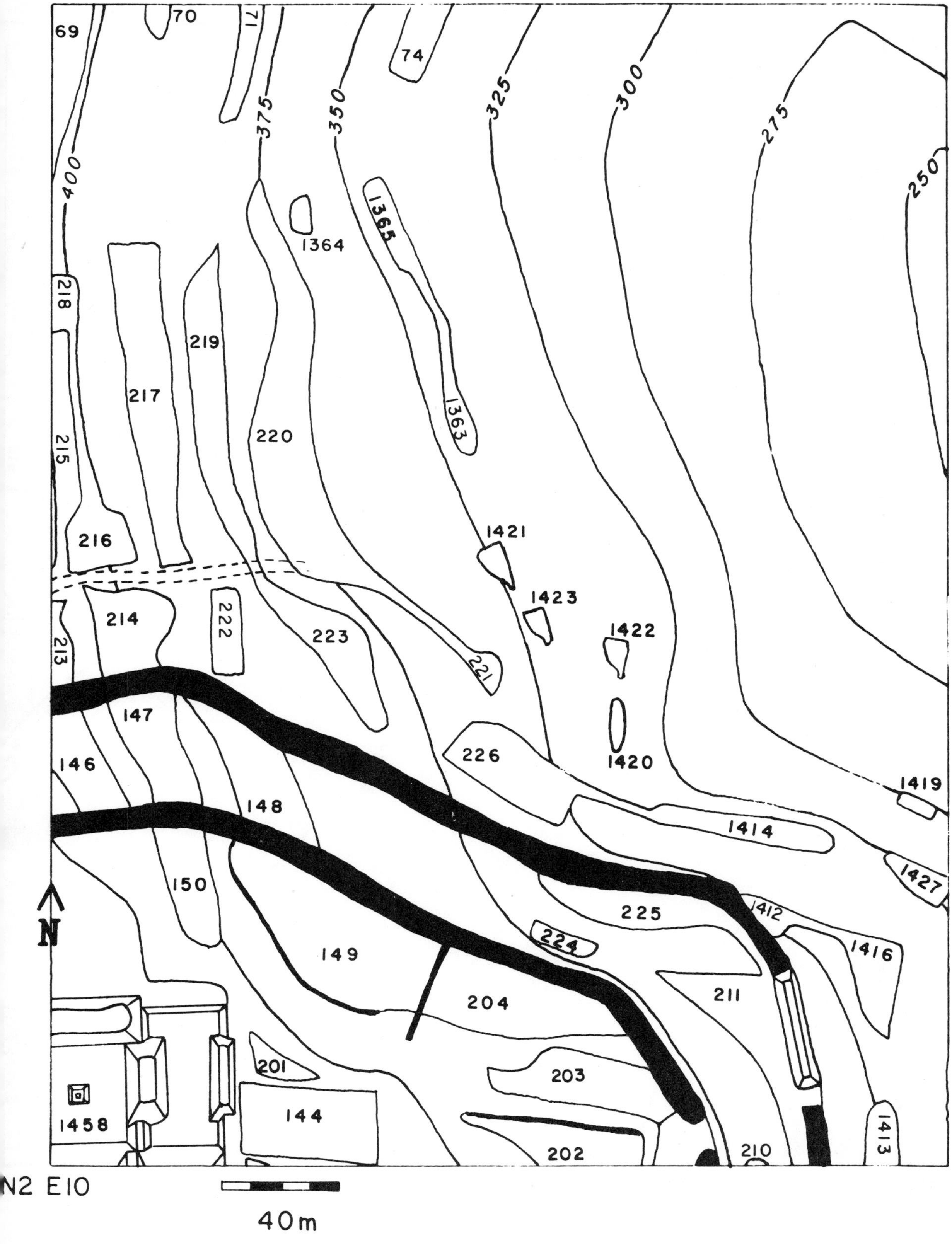
69
70
71
74
400
375
350
325
300
275
250
1364
1365
1363
218
219
217
220
215
216
1421
1423
1422
214
222
223
221
213
147
146
226
1420
1419
148
1414
150
1427
225
1412
149
224
1416
204
211
201
203
1458
144
202
210
1413
N
N2 E10
40m

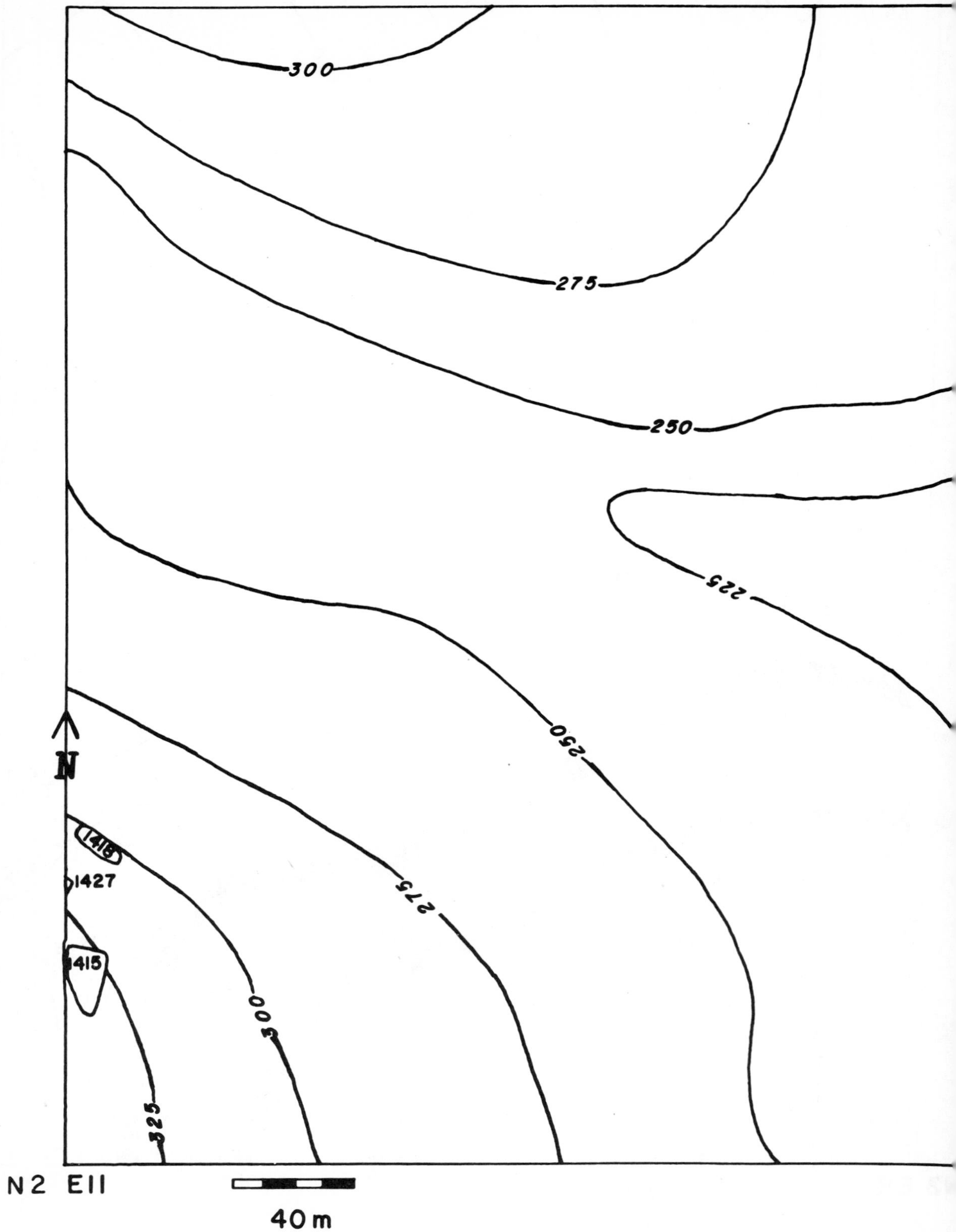

300
275
250
225
250
275
300
325
1418
1427
1415
N
N2 E11
40 m

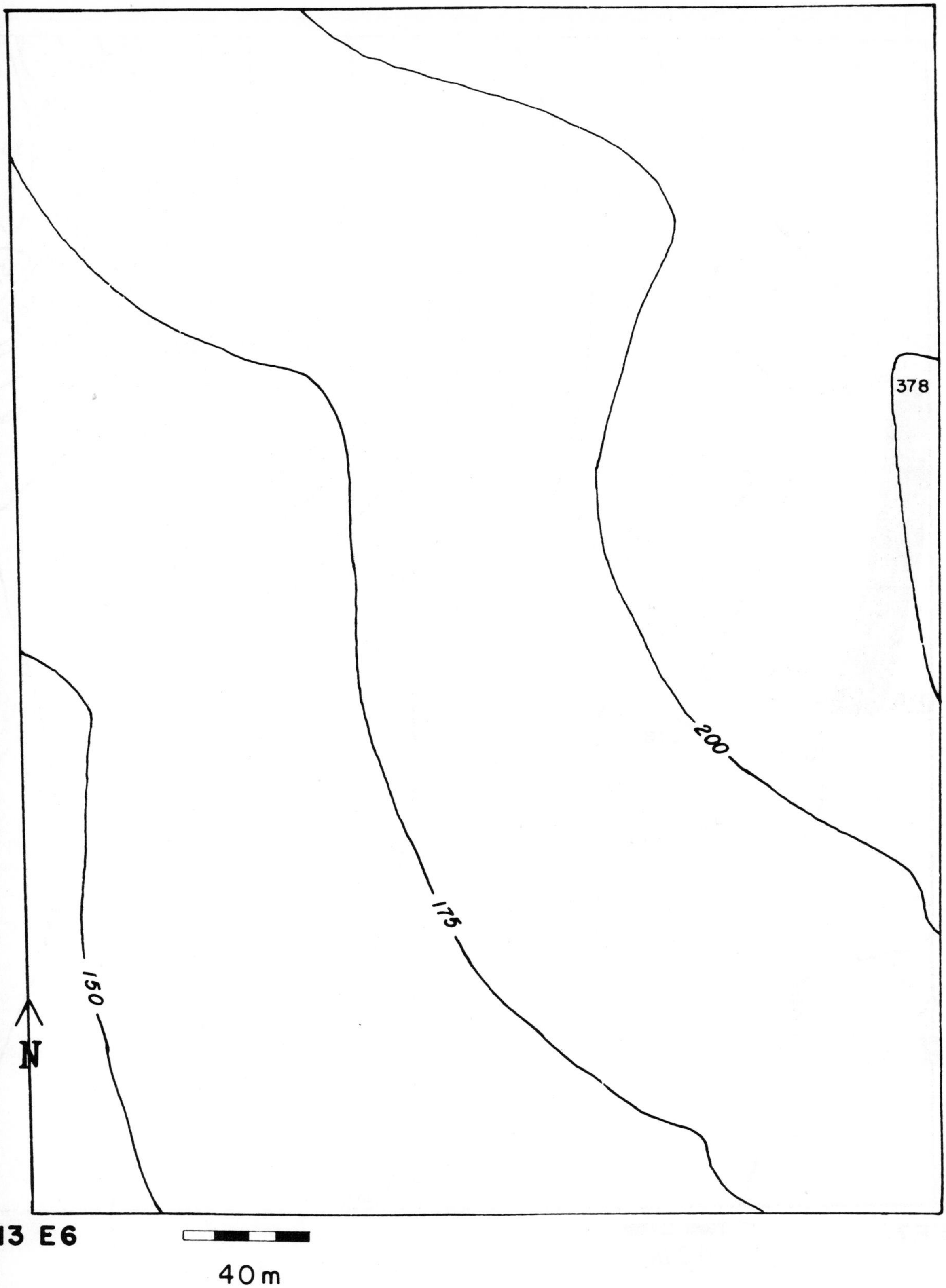

N3 E6

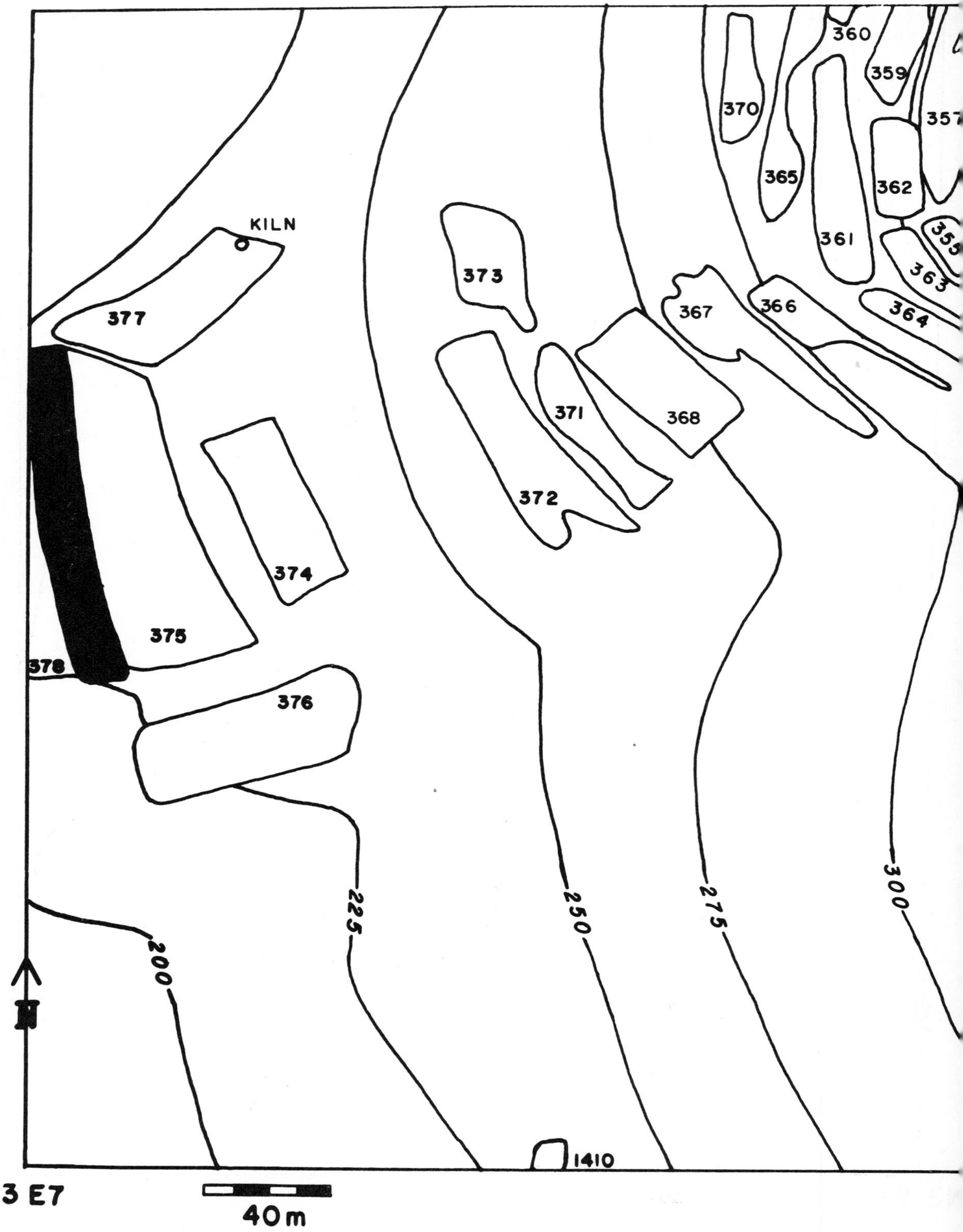

KILN
377
378
375
374
376
373
372
371
368
367
366
370
365
361
362
360
359
357
355
363
364
1410
200
225
250
275
300
N
40m

N3 E7

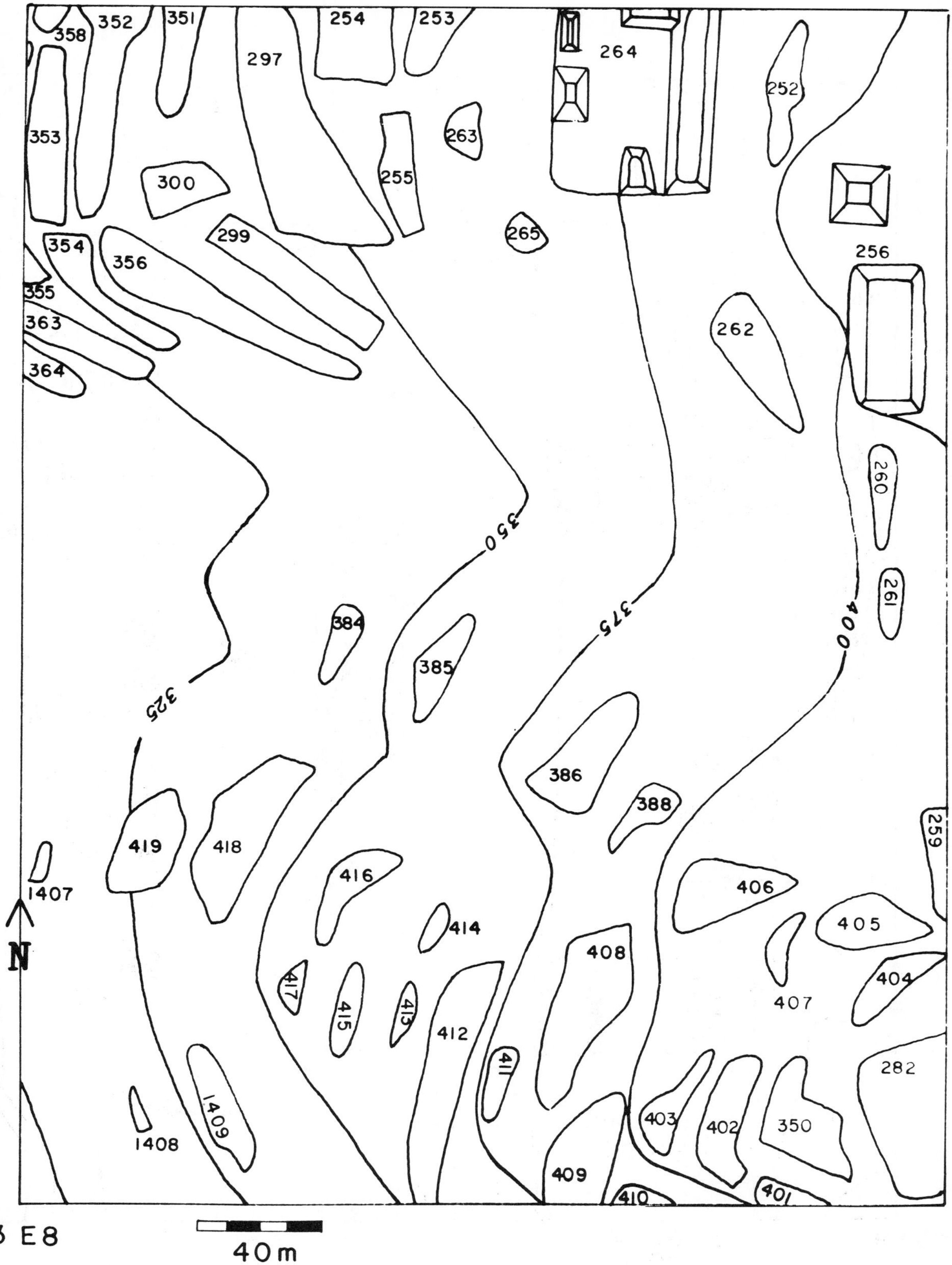

358
352
351
297
254
253
264
252
353
263
300
255
299
265
354
356
256
355
363
262
364
260
350
261
375
400
384
385
325
386
388
259
419
418
416
406
1407
414
405
N
408
417
415
413
404
407
412
411
282
1409
403
402
350
1408
409
410
401
40m

N3 E8

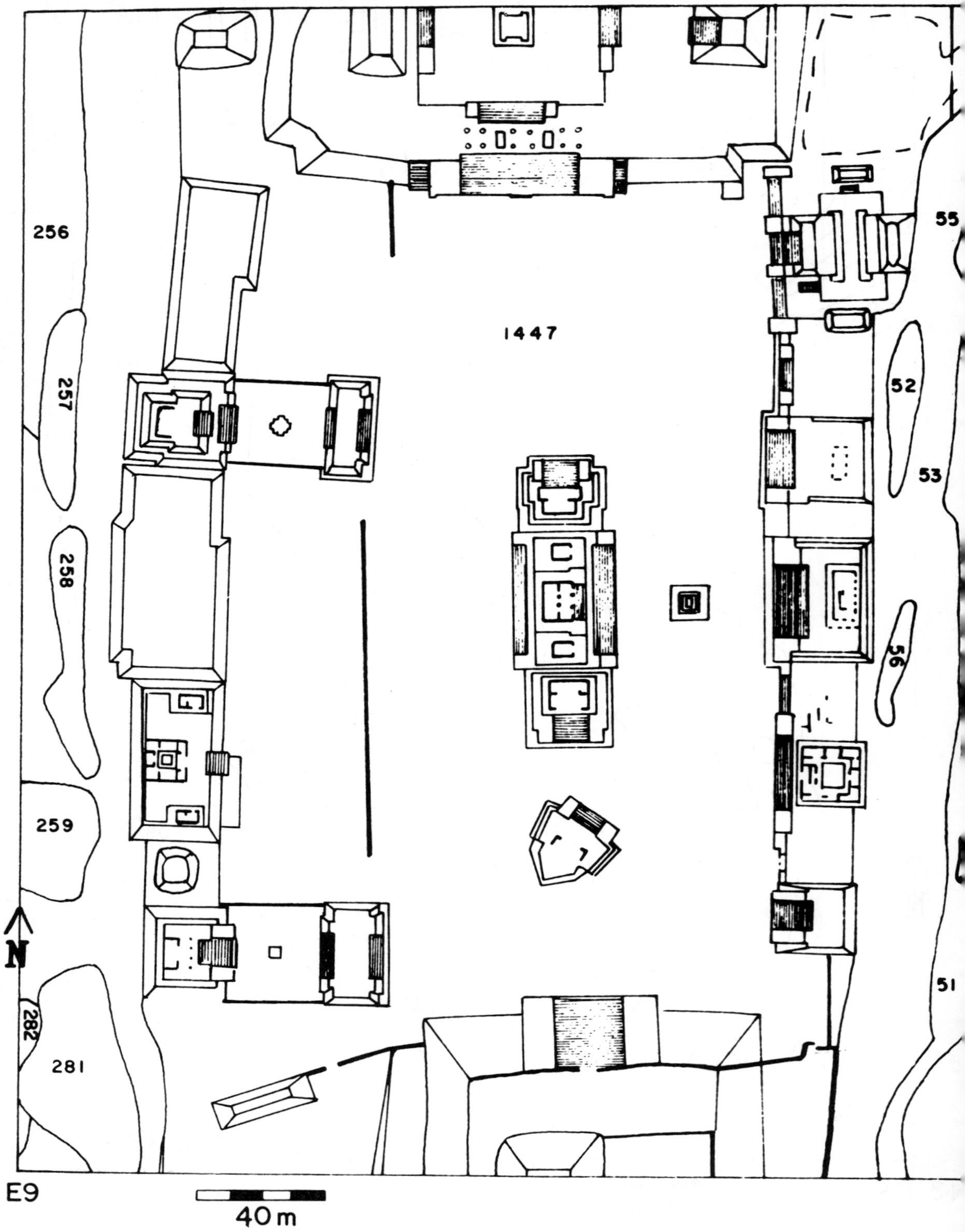

N3 E9

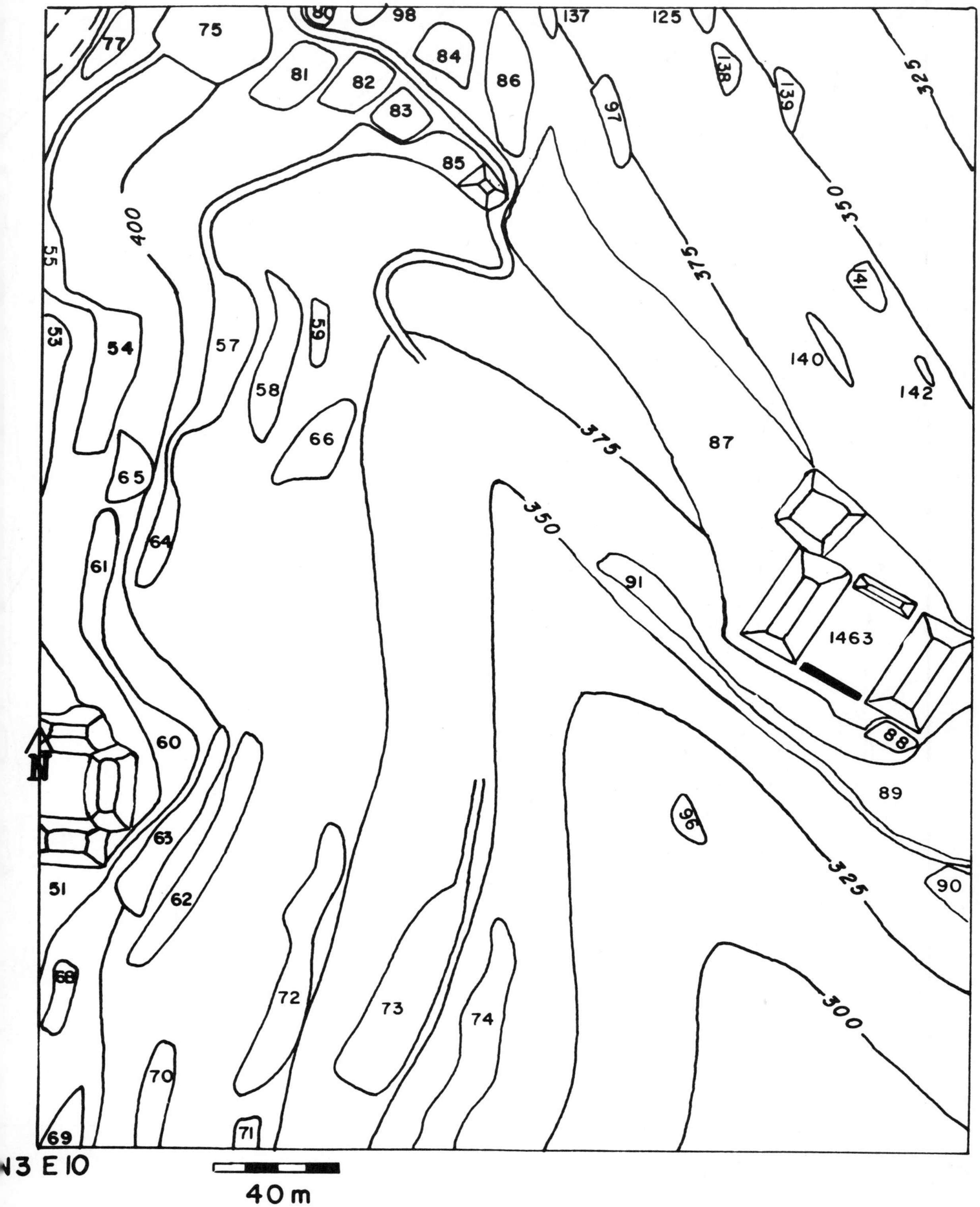
75
77
80
98
137
125
325
84
81
82
86
138
139
83
97
85
350
400
55
375
141
53
54
57
59
140
142
58
66
375
87
65
350
64
61
91
1463
60
N
88
89
63
96
325
51
62
90
68
72
73
74
300
70
69
71
N3 E10
40 m

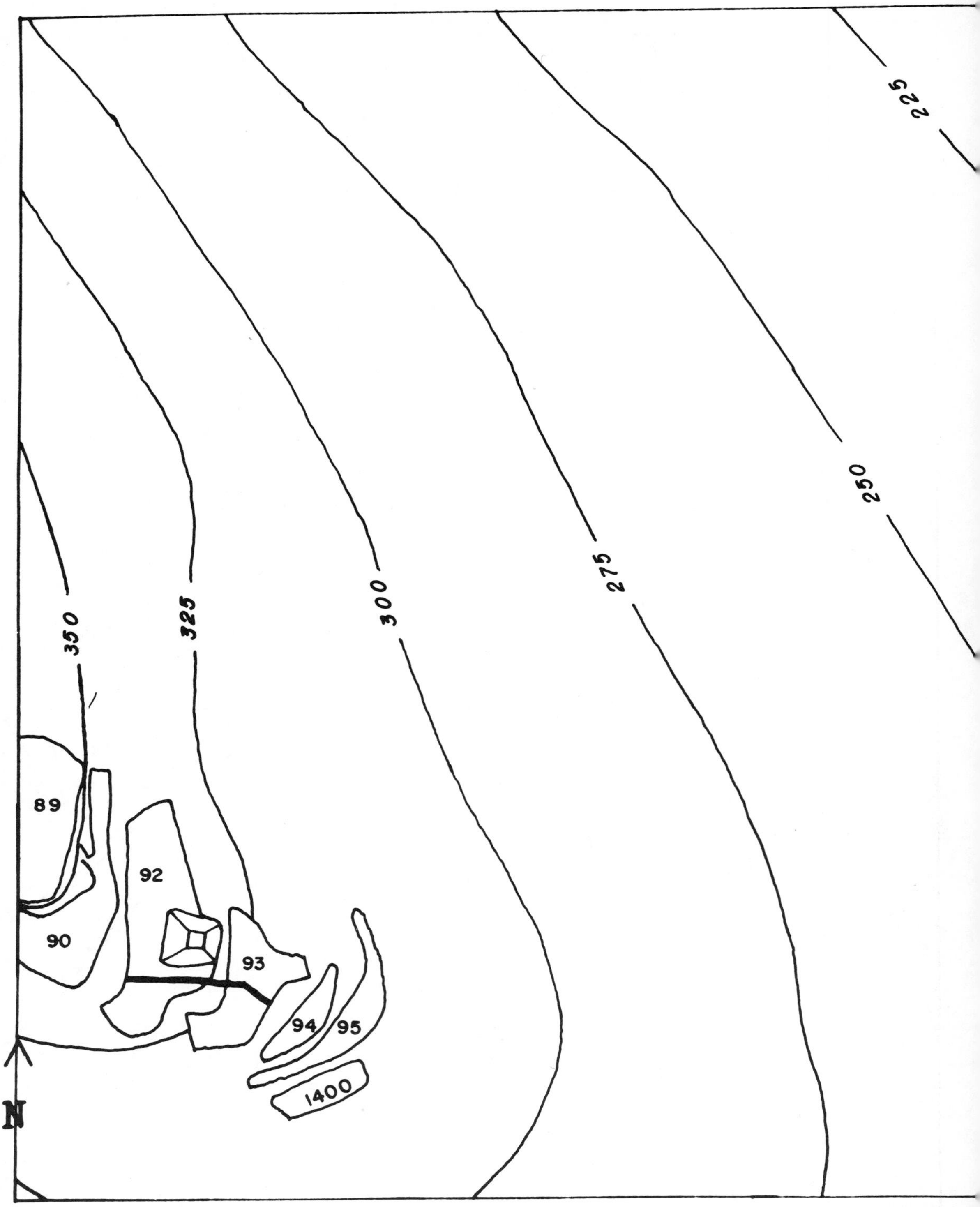

N3E11

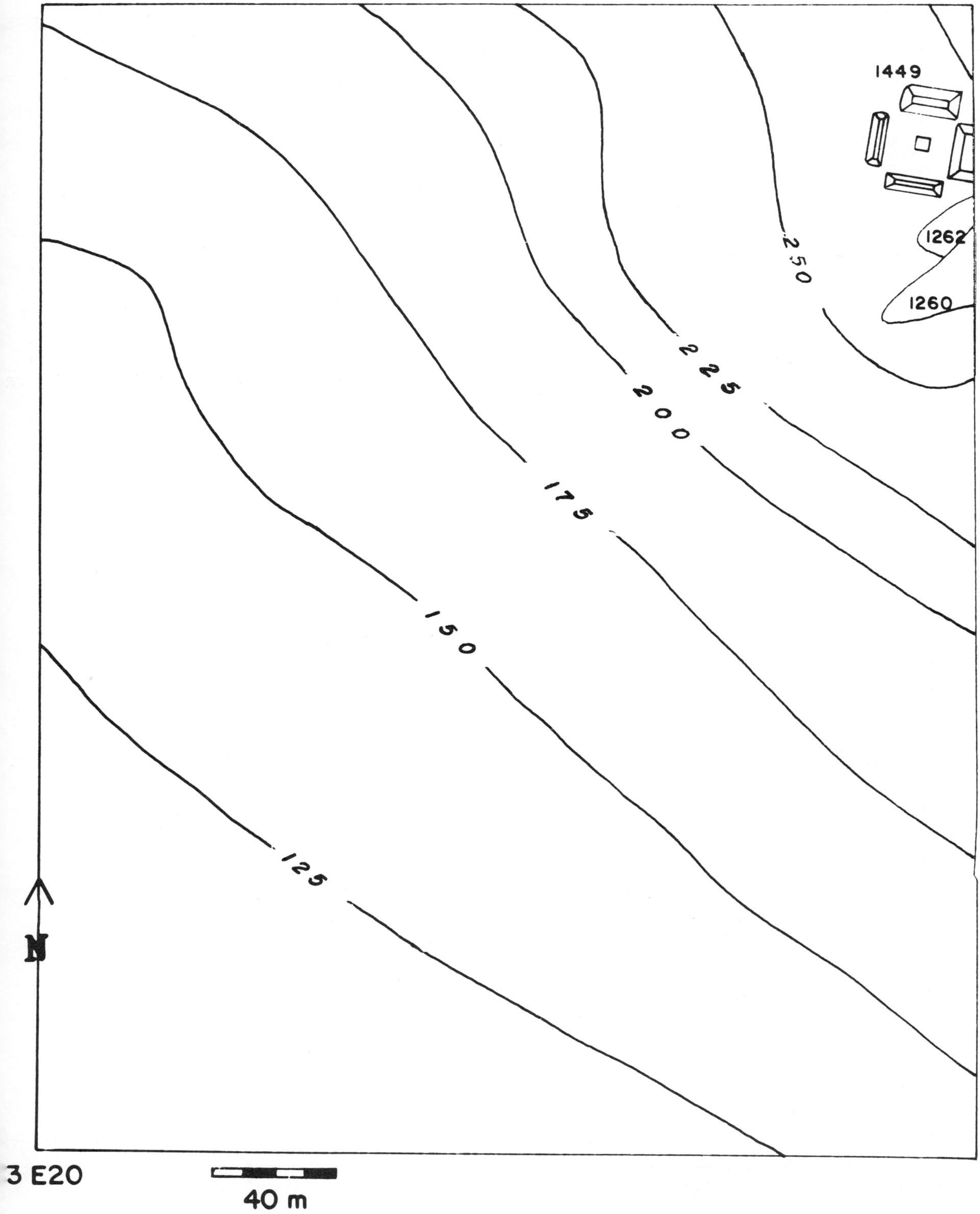
1449
1262
1260
250
225
200
175
150
125
N
3 E20
40 m

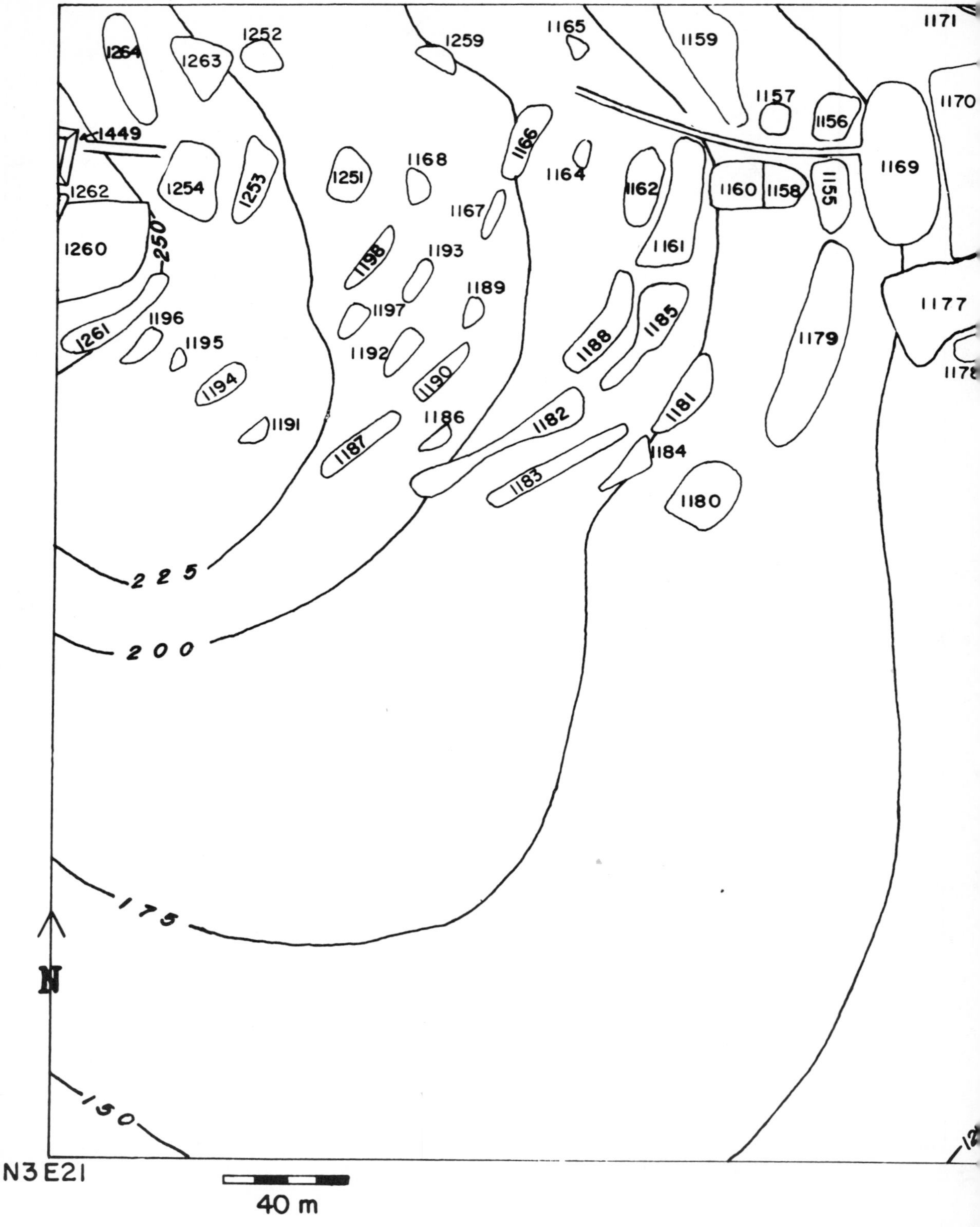

1264
1263
1252
1259
1165
1159
1171
1157
1156
1170
1449
1254
1253
1251
1168
1166
1164
1162
1160
1158
1155
1169
1262
1167
1260
250
1198
1193
1161
1189
1177
1197
1196
1261
1195
1192
1188
1185
1179
1194
1190
1178
1191
1186
1182
1181
1187
1184
1183
1180
225
200
175
150
N
N3E21
40 m

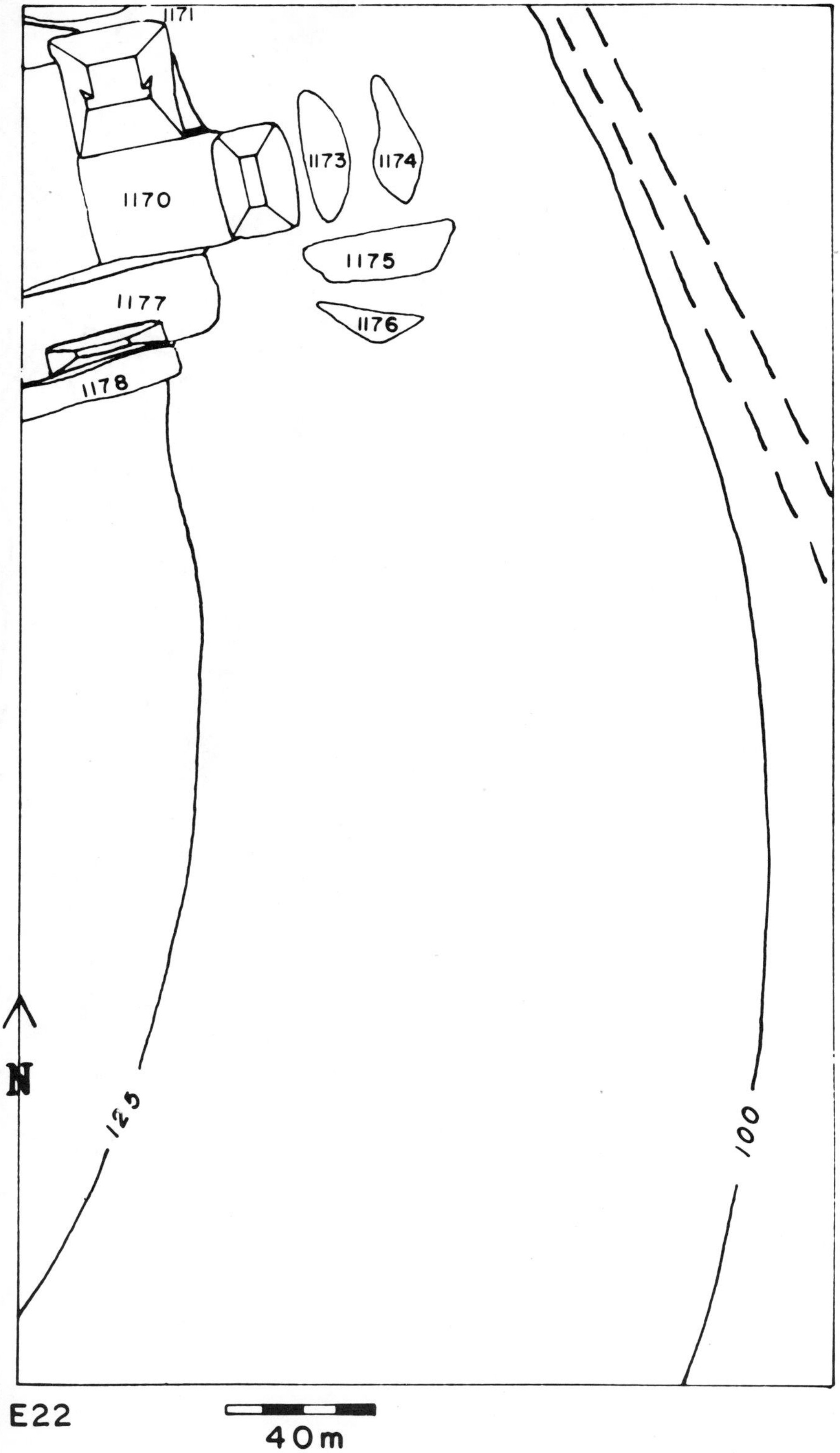

N3 E22

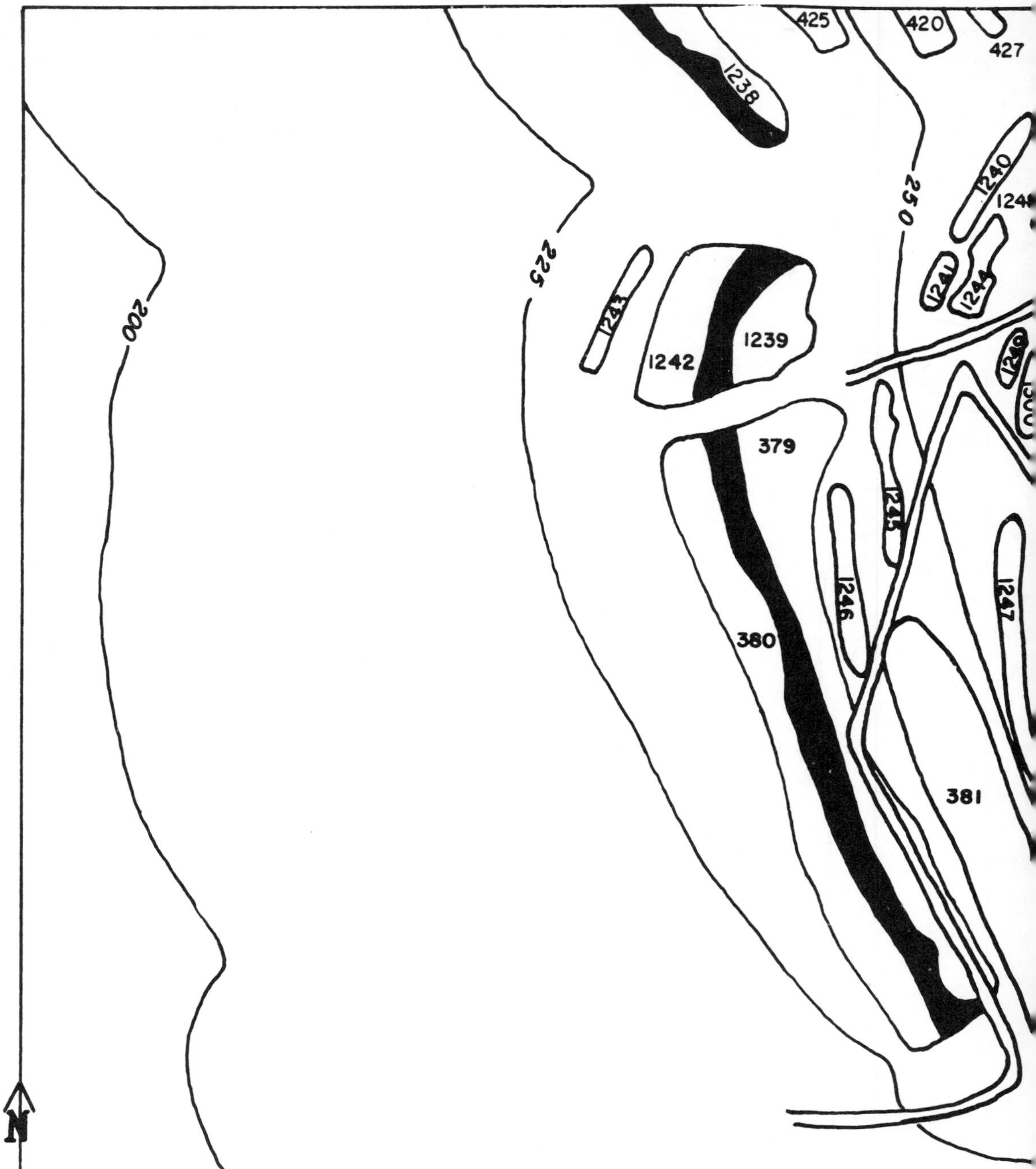
425
420
427
1238
1240
250
225
200
1243
1242
1239
1241
1244
379
1245
1246
1247
380
381
N

N4 E6

40m

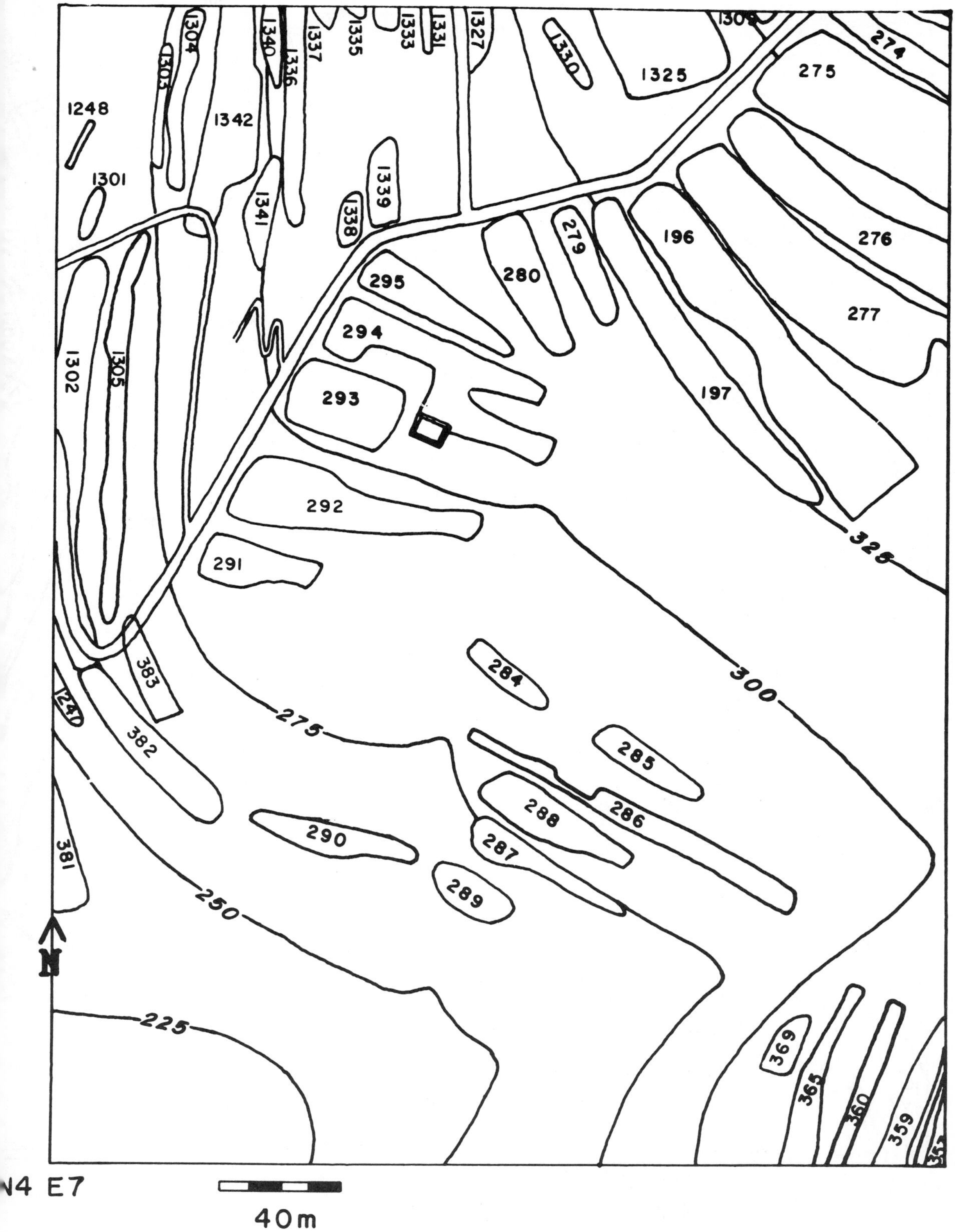
1304
1303
1340
1336
1337
1335
1333
1331
1327
1330
1325
274
275
1248
1342
1301
1341
1339
1338
279
280
196
276
295
294
277
1302
1305
293
197
292
328
291
284
300
383
275
382
285
286
288
290
287
381
289
250
N
225
369
365
360
359
N4 E7
40m

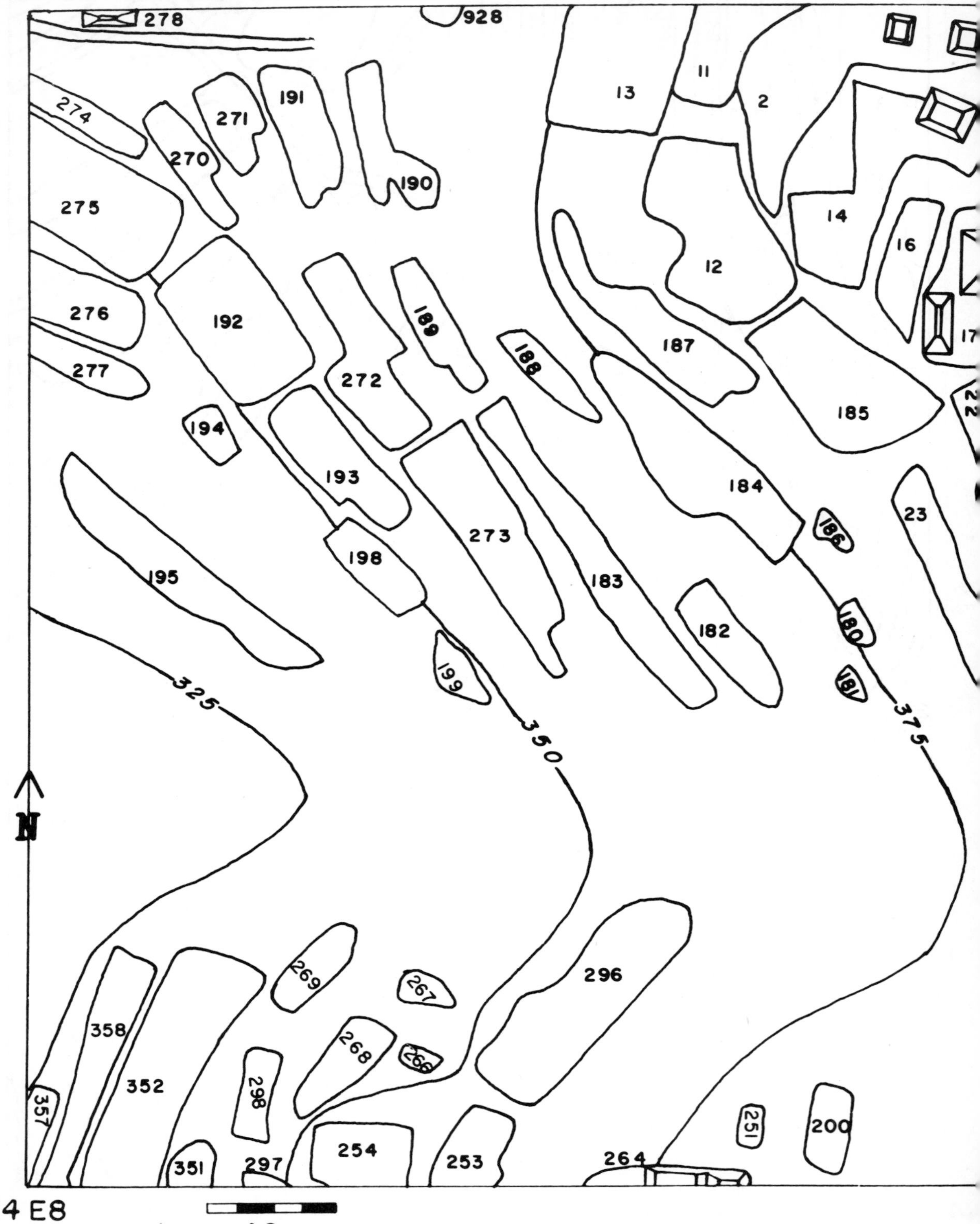

278
928
274
271
191
270
190
275
13
11
2
14
16
12
192
276
189
188
187
17
277
272
185
194
193
184
23
273
186
198
195
183
182
180
199
181
325
350
375
N
296
269
267
358
268
266
352
298
357
251
200
254
264
351
297
253

N4 E8

40 m

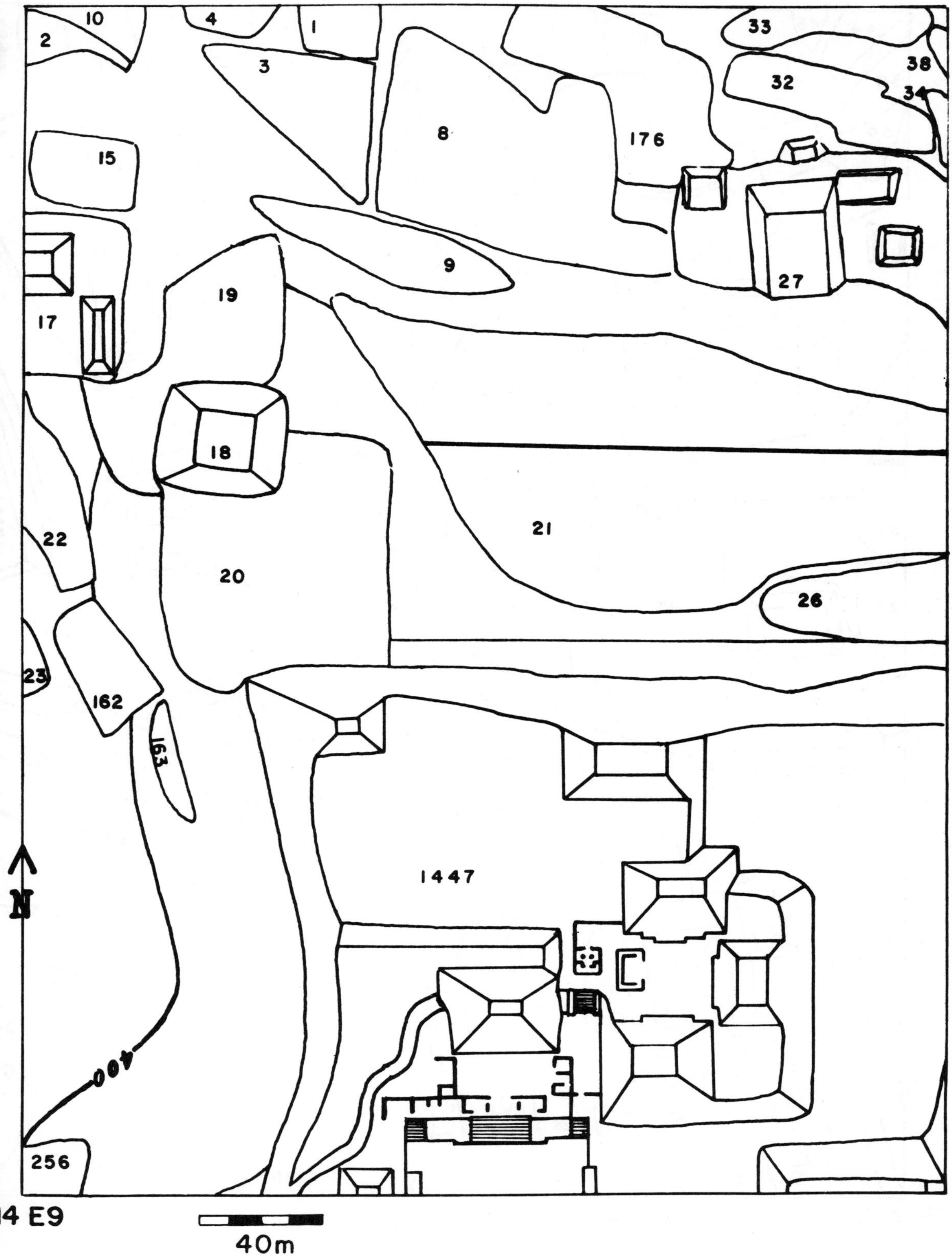
10
4
1
33
2
3
38
32
34
8
176
15
9
27
17
19
18
21
22
20
26
23
162
163
1447
N
400
256
40m

N4 E9

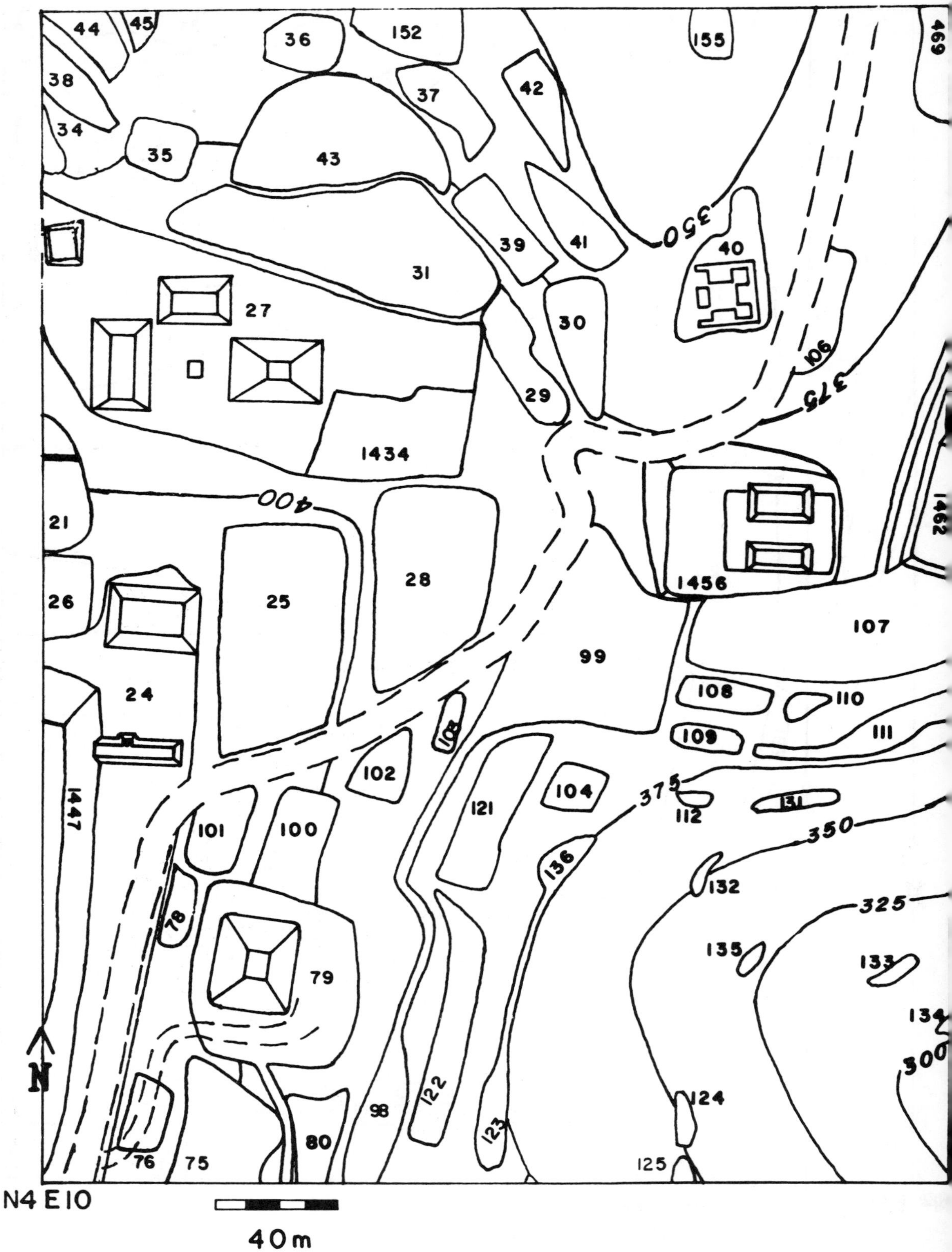

44
45
36
152
155
469
38
37
42
34
35
43
350
40
39
41
31
27
30
106
375
29
1434
400
21
1462
28
25
26
1456
107
99
24
108
110
103
109
111
102
104
375
131
1447
121
112
101
100
350
136
132
78
325
135
133
79
134
N
300
122
124
98
123
80
76
75
125
N4 E10
40m

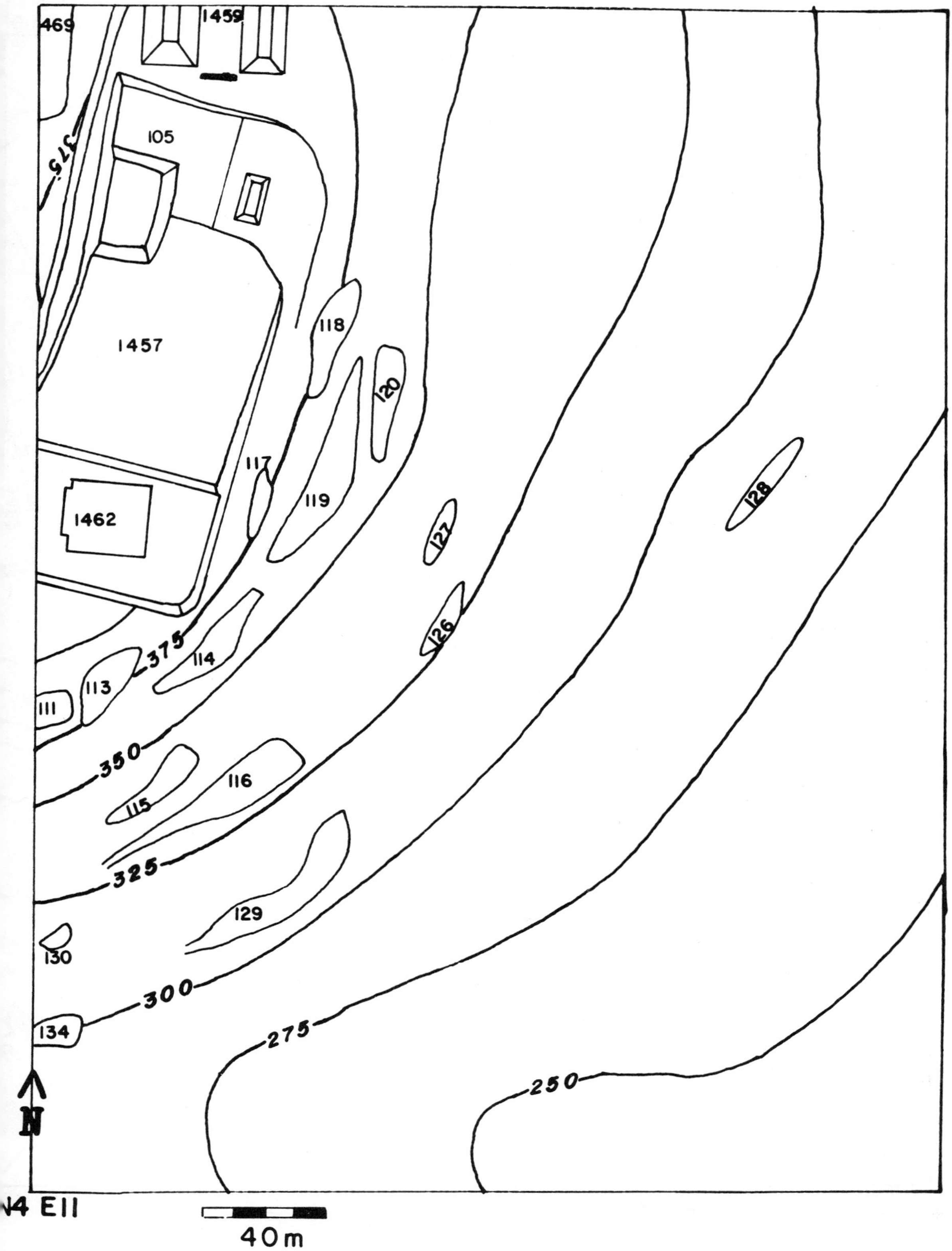
469
1459
105
375
1457
118
120
117
119
1462
128
127
126
375
114
113
111
350
116
115
325
129
130
300
134
275
250
N
N4 E11
40 m

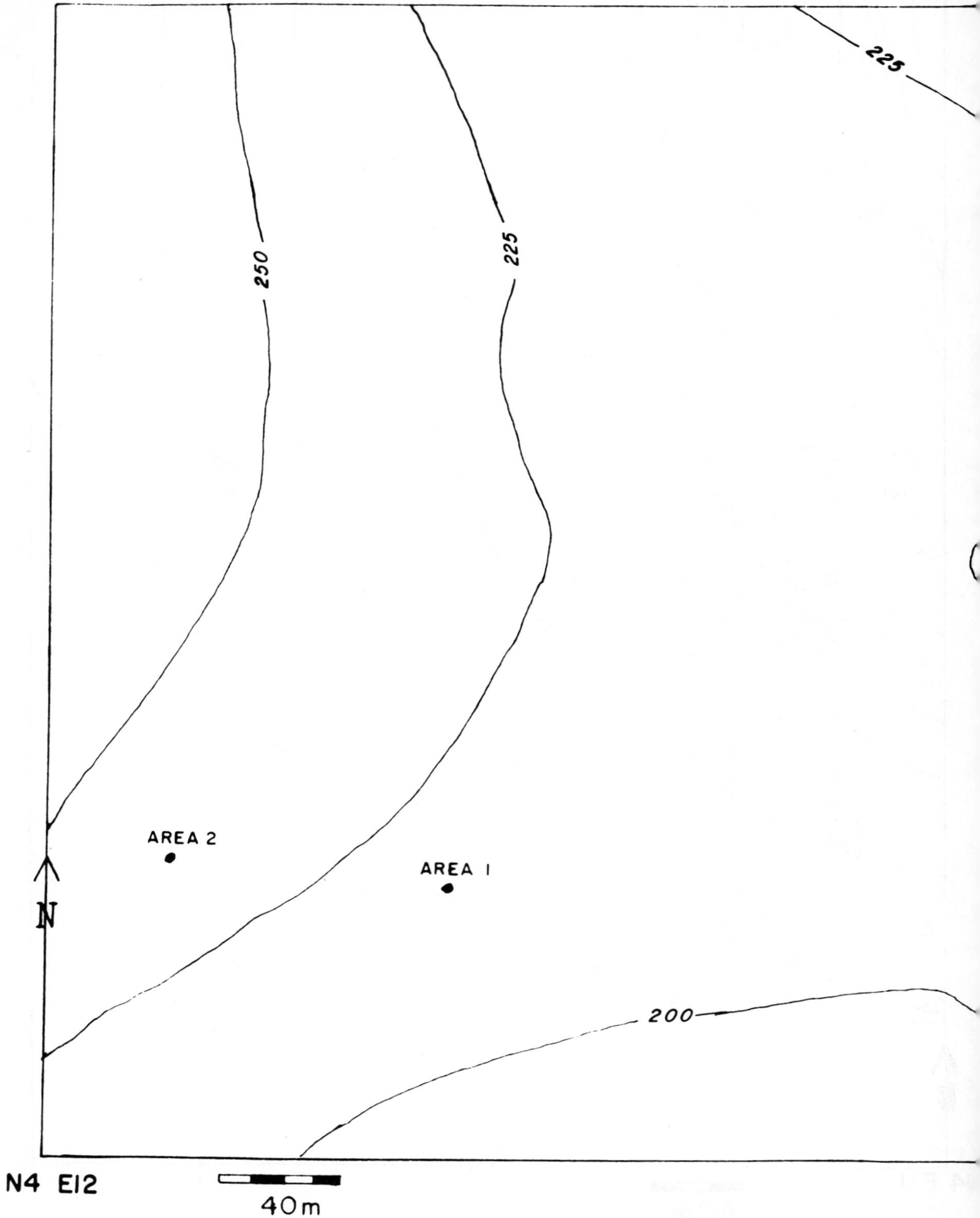
225
250
225
AREA 2
AREA 1
N
200
N4 E12
40m

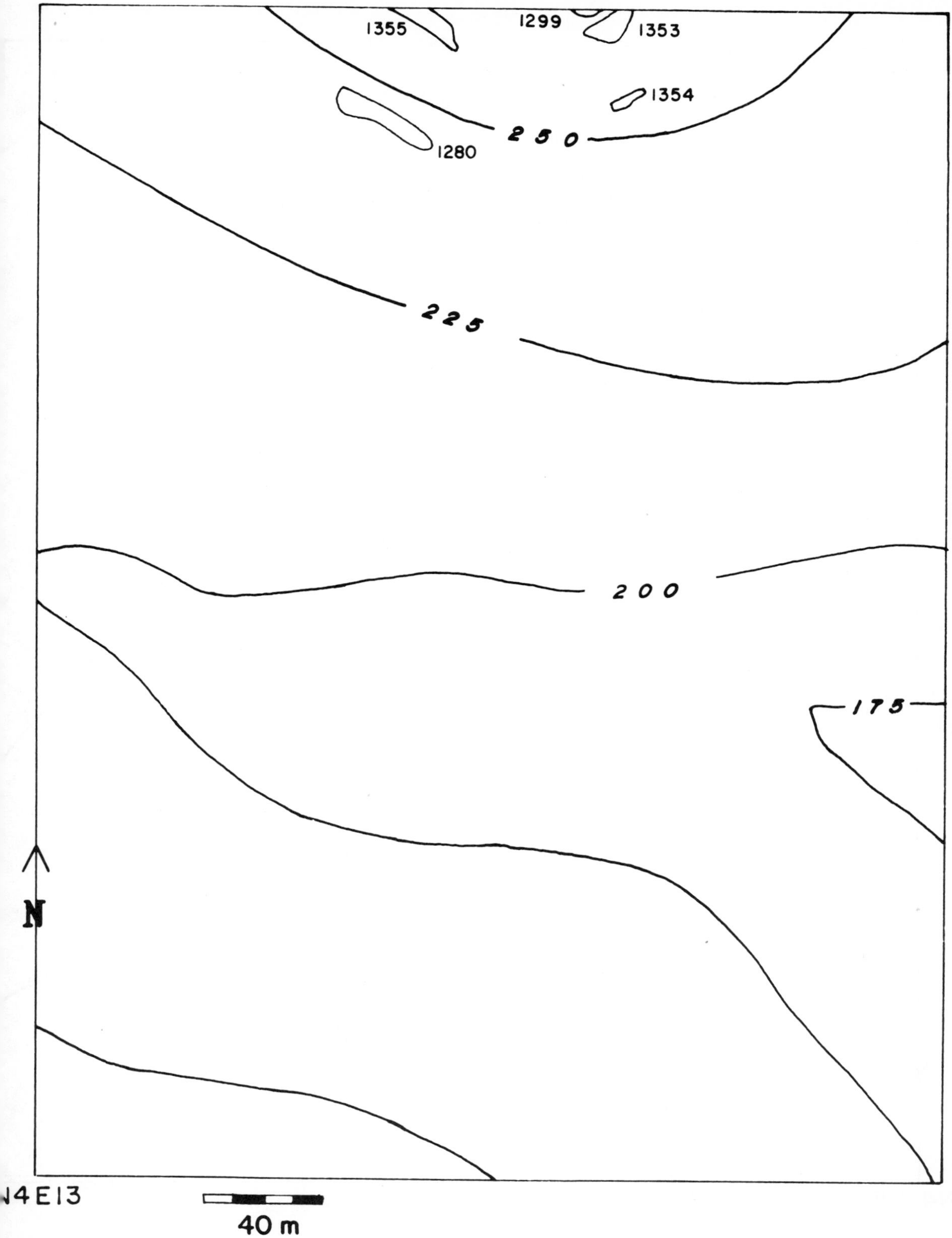
1355
1299
1353
1354
1280
250
225
200
175
N
N4E13
40 m

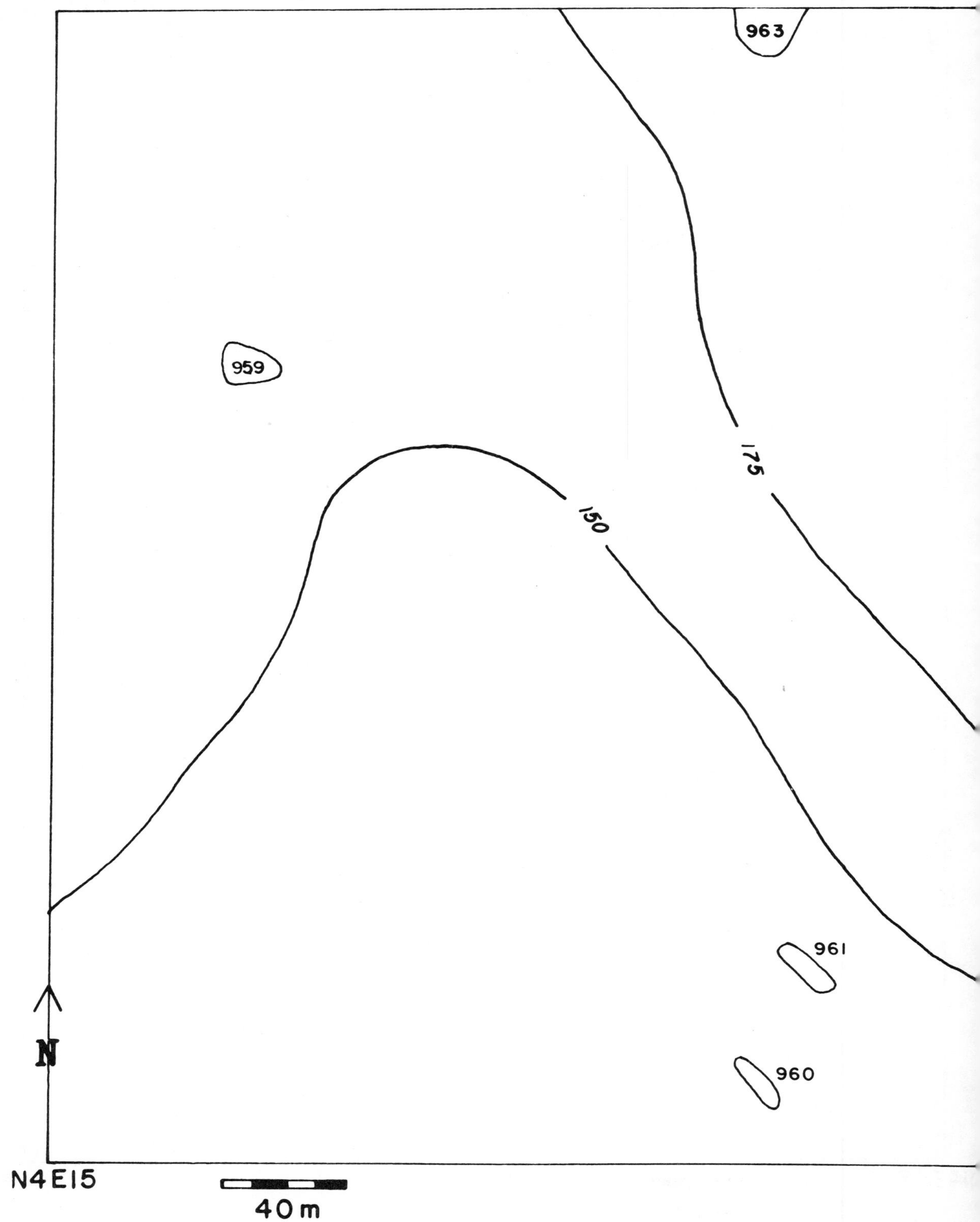
963
959
175
150
961
960
N
N4E15
40 m

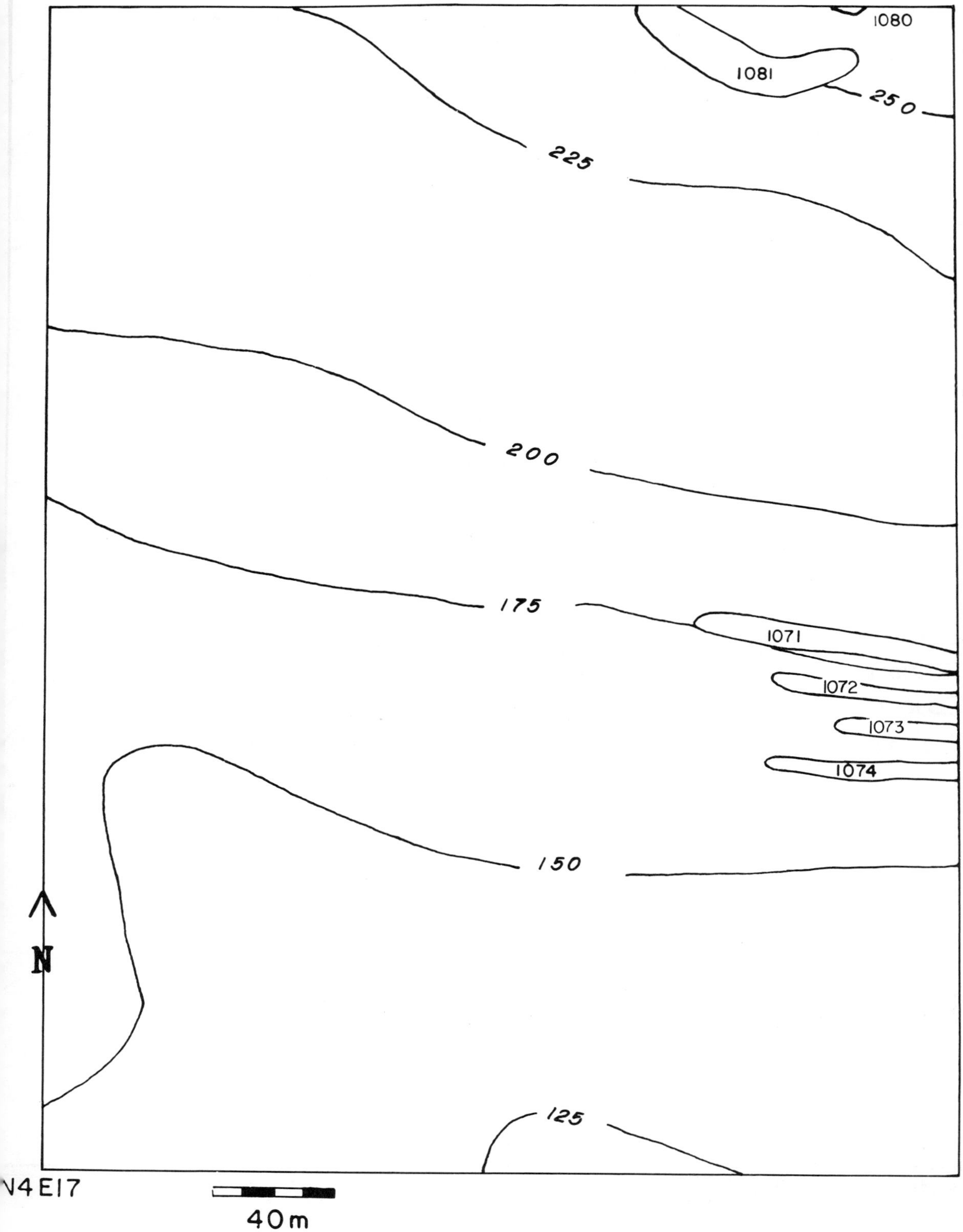
1080
1081
250
225
200
175
1071
1072
1073
1074
150
N
125
4 E17
40m

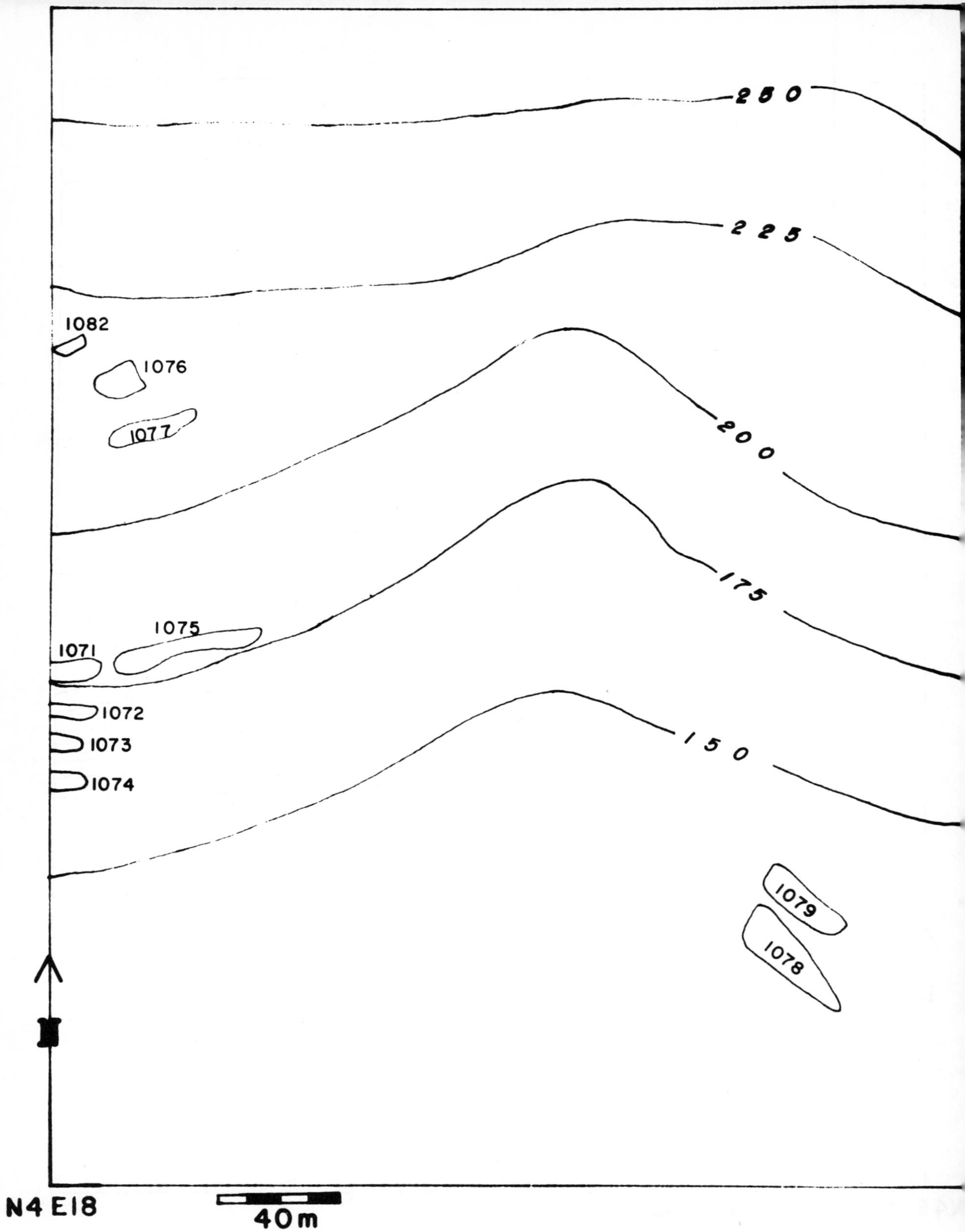

250
225
200
175
150
1082
1076
1077
1075
1071
1072
1073
1074
1079
1078
N4 E18
40m

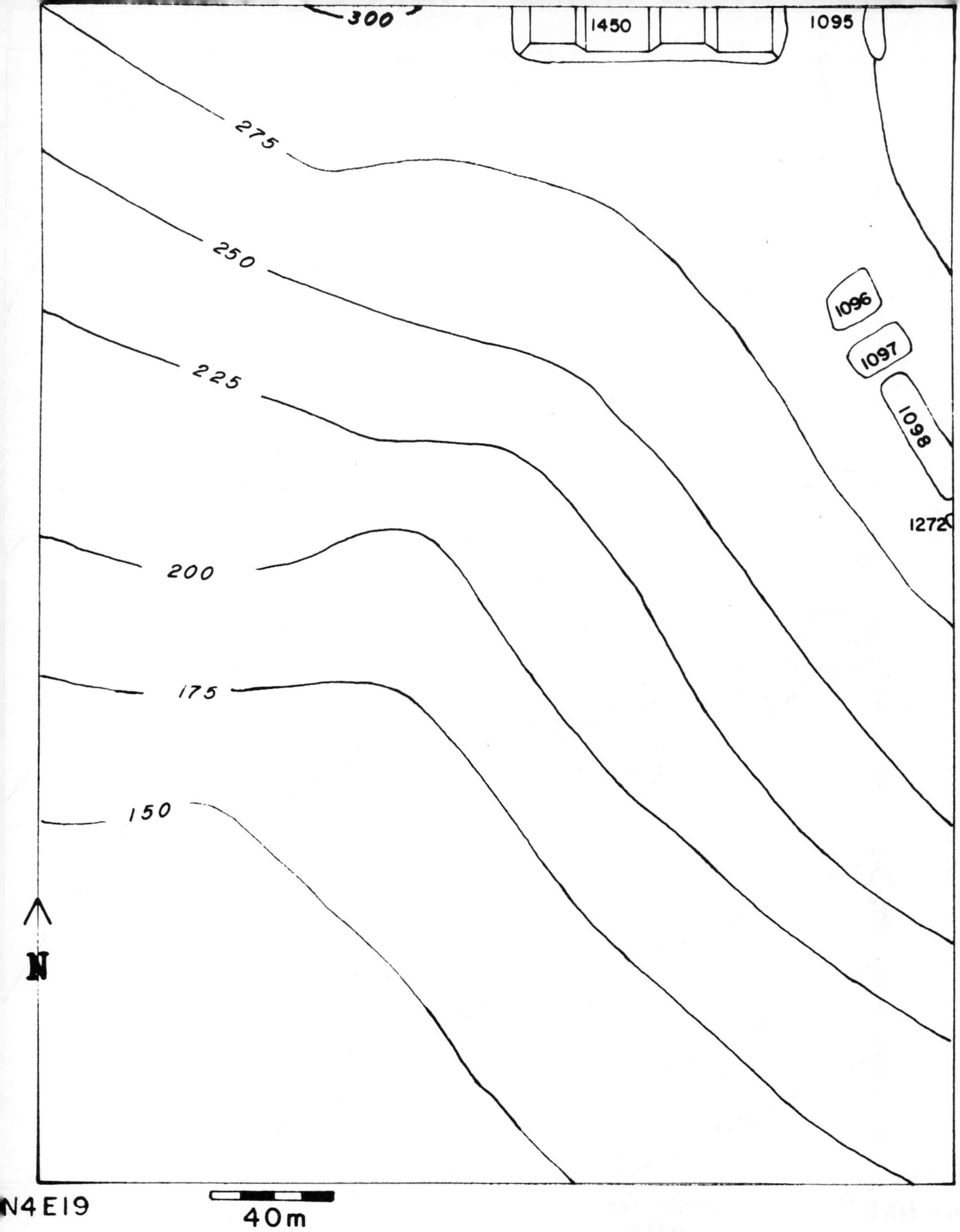
300
1450
1095
275
250
225
200
175
150
1096
1097
1098
1272
N
N4E19
40m

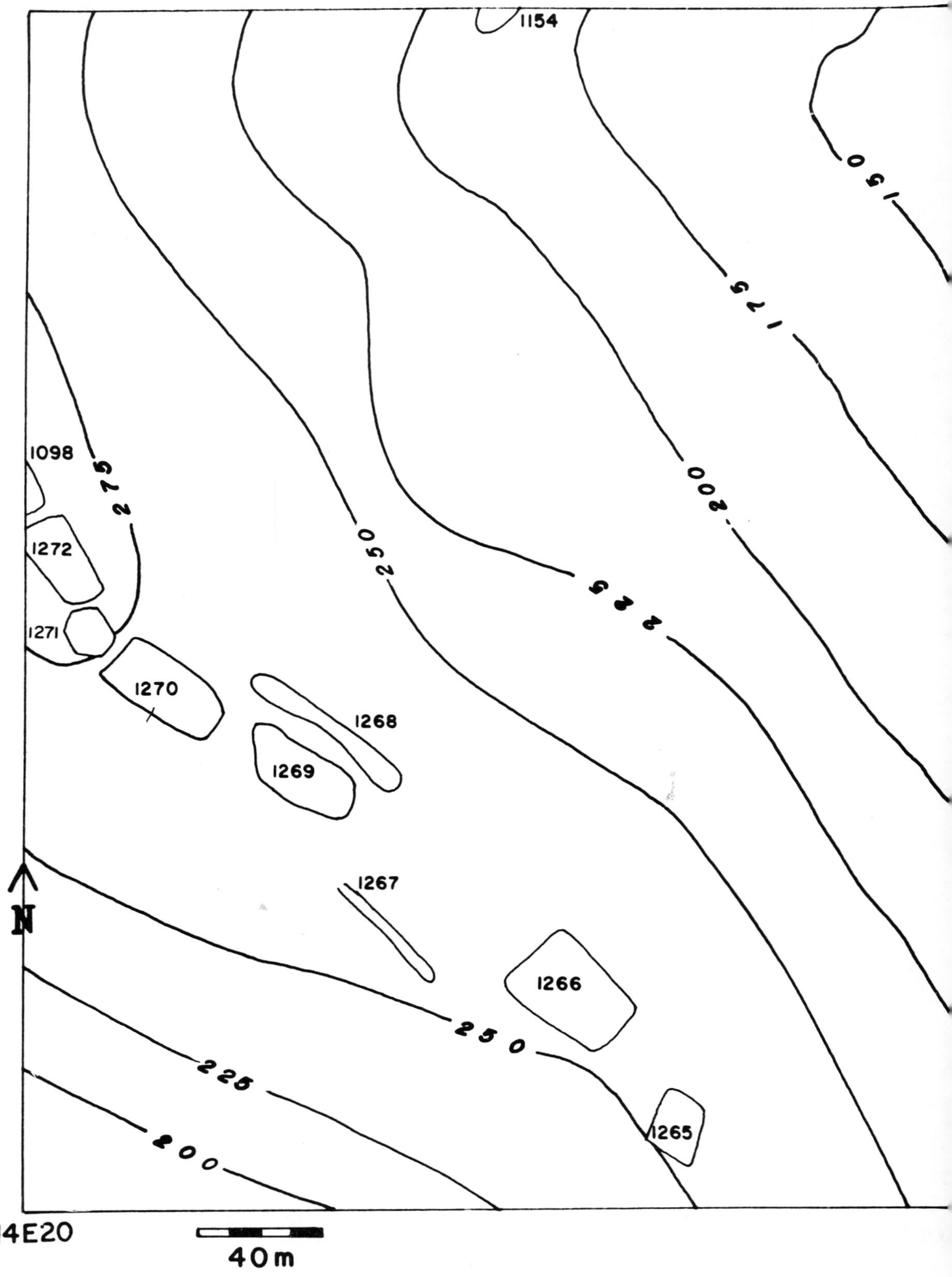
1154
150
175
200
225
250
275
1098
1272
1271
1270
1268
1269
1267
1266
1265
250
225
200
N
N4E20
40m

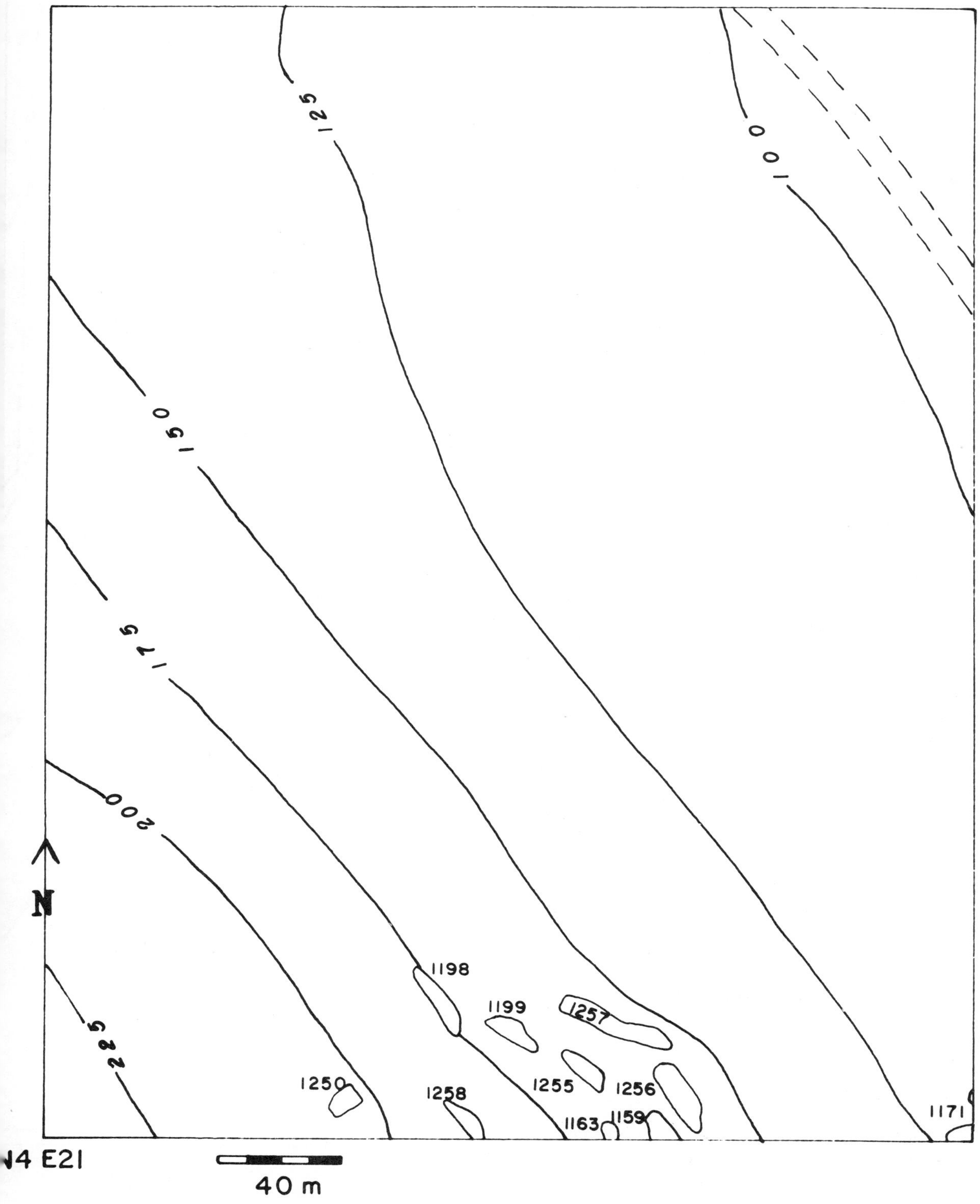
125
100
150
175
200
225
N
1198
1199
1257
1250
1258
1255
1256
1163
1159
1171
4 E21
40 m

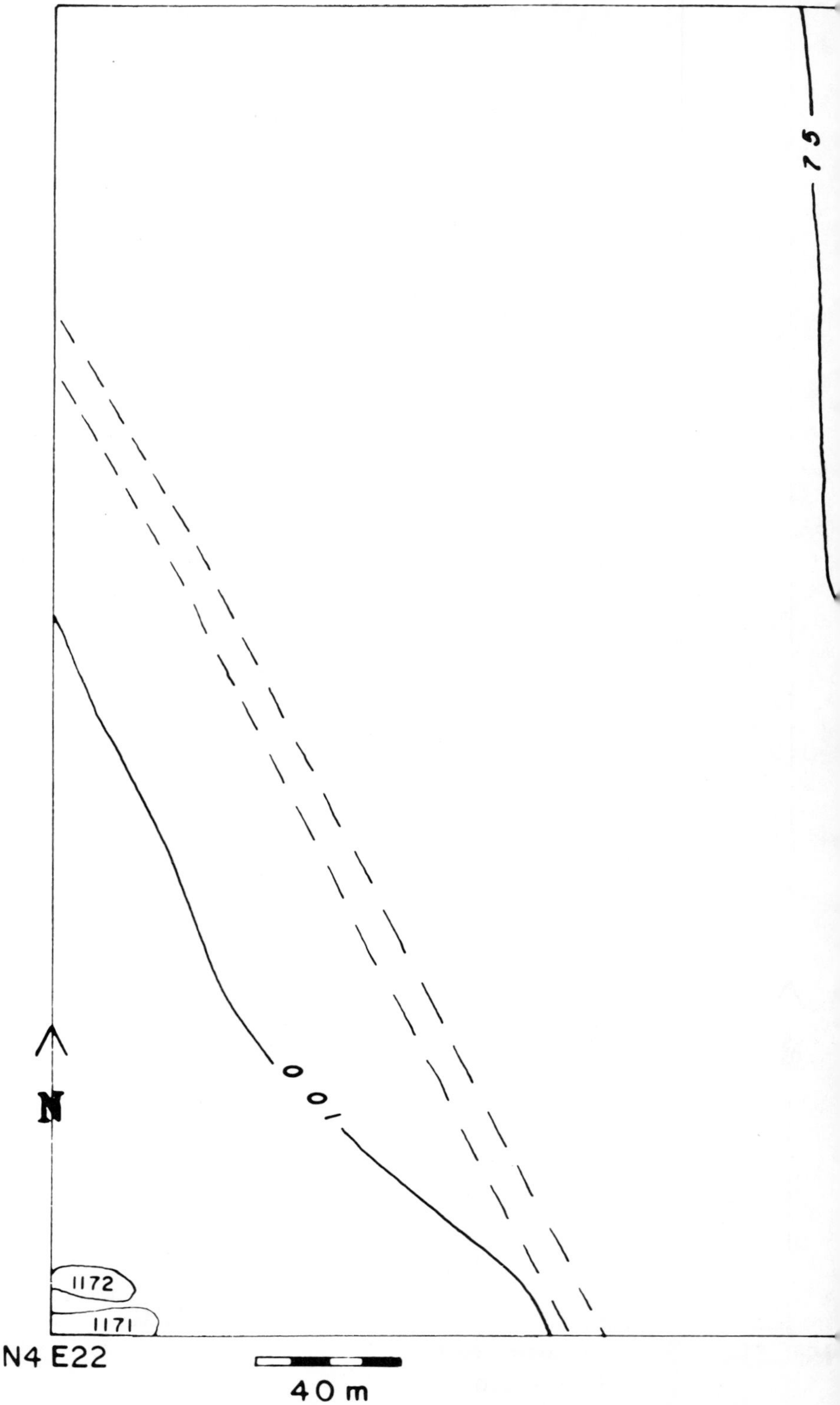

75
100
N
1172
1171
N4 E22
40 m

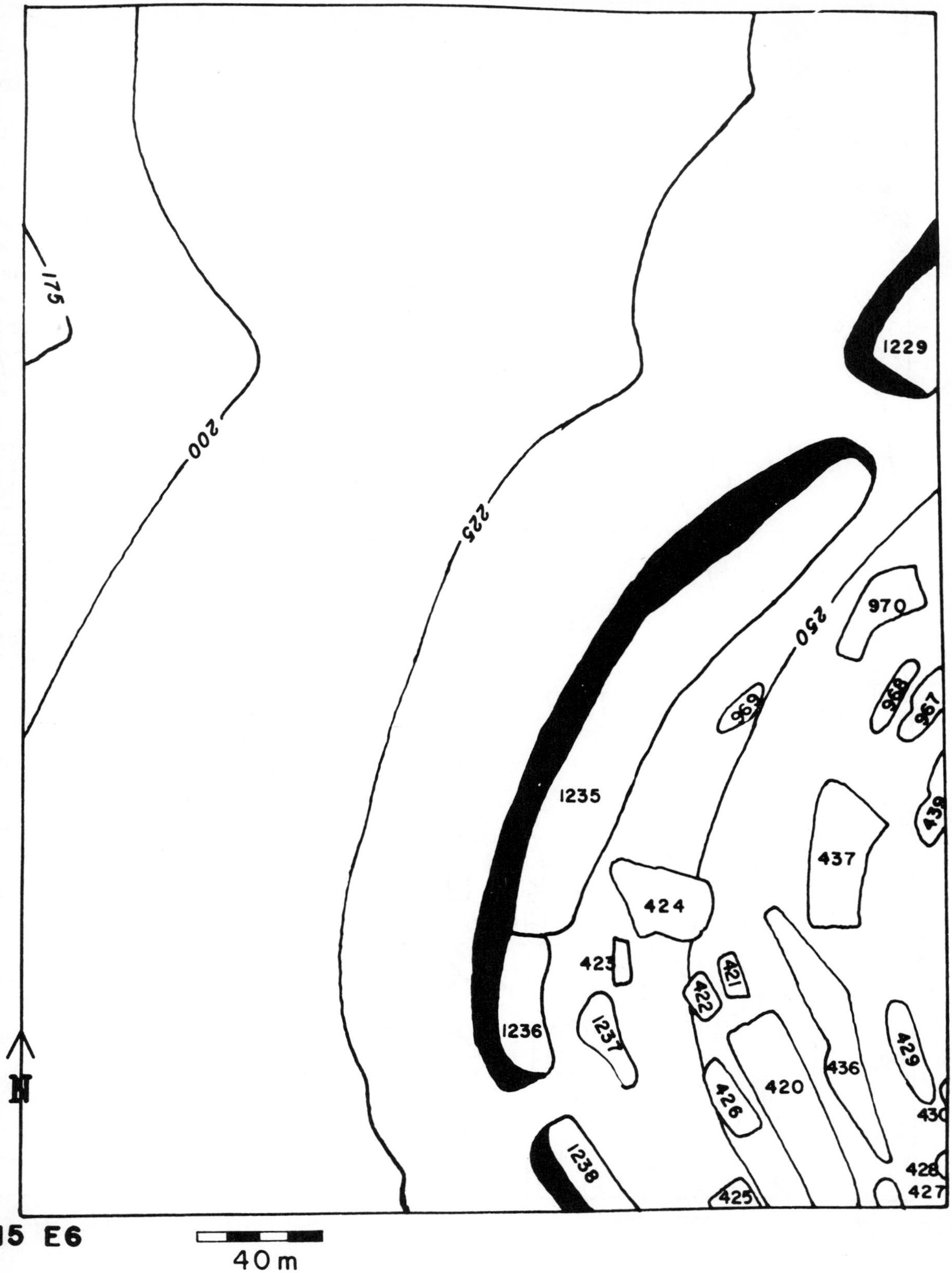

175
200
225
250
1229
1235
1236
1237
1238
970
968
967
969
439
437
424
423
421
422
420
426
436
429
430
428
427
425
N
40 m

N5 E6

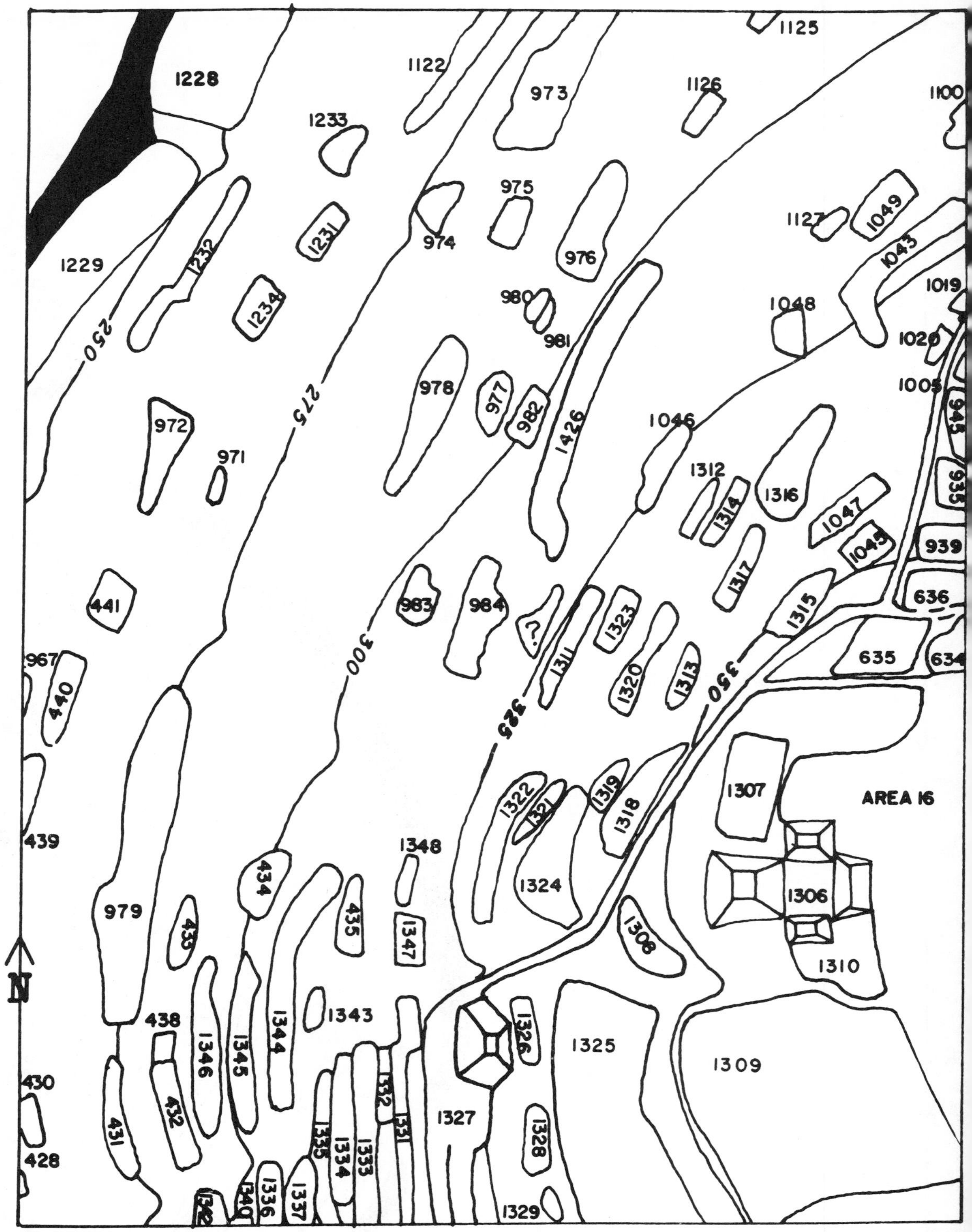
1125
1228
1122
973
1126
1100
1233
975
974
1231
1127
1049
1229
1232
976
1043
1019
980
1234
981
1048
1020
250
1005
978
977
982
275
1426
1046
945
972
971
1312
1314
1316
935
1047
1045
939
441
983
984
?
1323
1317
1315
636
300
635
634
967
440
1311
1320
1313
350
325
1307
AREA 16
1322
1321
1319
1318
439
1348
434
435
1347
1324
1306
979
433
1308
1310
N
438
1346
1345
1344
1343
1326
1325
1309
430
431
432
1332
1331
1327
1328
1335
1334
1333
428
1342
1340
1336
1337
1329

N5 E7

40 m

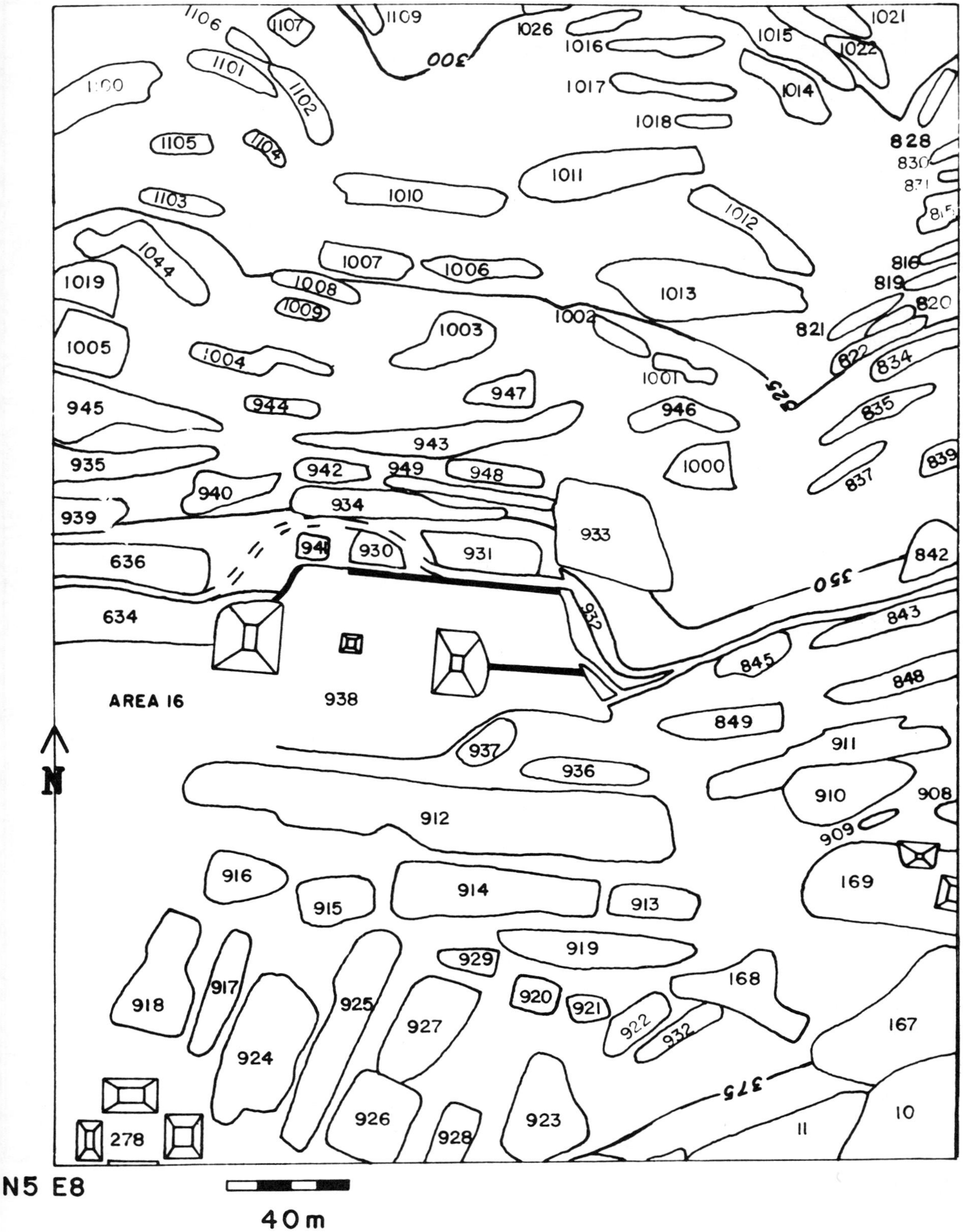
1106
1107
1109
1026
1016
1021
1015
1022
300
1101
1100
1102
1017
1014
1018
1105
1104
828
830
1011
1010
1103
1012
1044
1007
1006
816
1019
1008
1013
819
1009
820
1002
1003
821
1005
1004
822
834
1001
947
325
945
944
946
835
943
935
942
949
948
1000
837
839
940
934
939
933
941
930
931
842
636
350
932
634
843
845
AREA 16
938
848
849
N
937
911
936
910
908
912
909
916
169
914
913
915
919
929
168
917
920
918
925
921
167
927
922
932
924
375
926
923
10
278
928
11
N5 E8
40 m

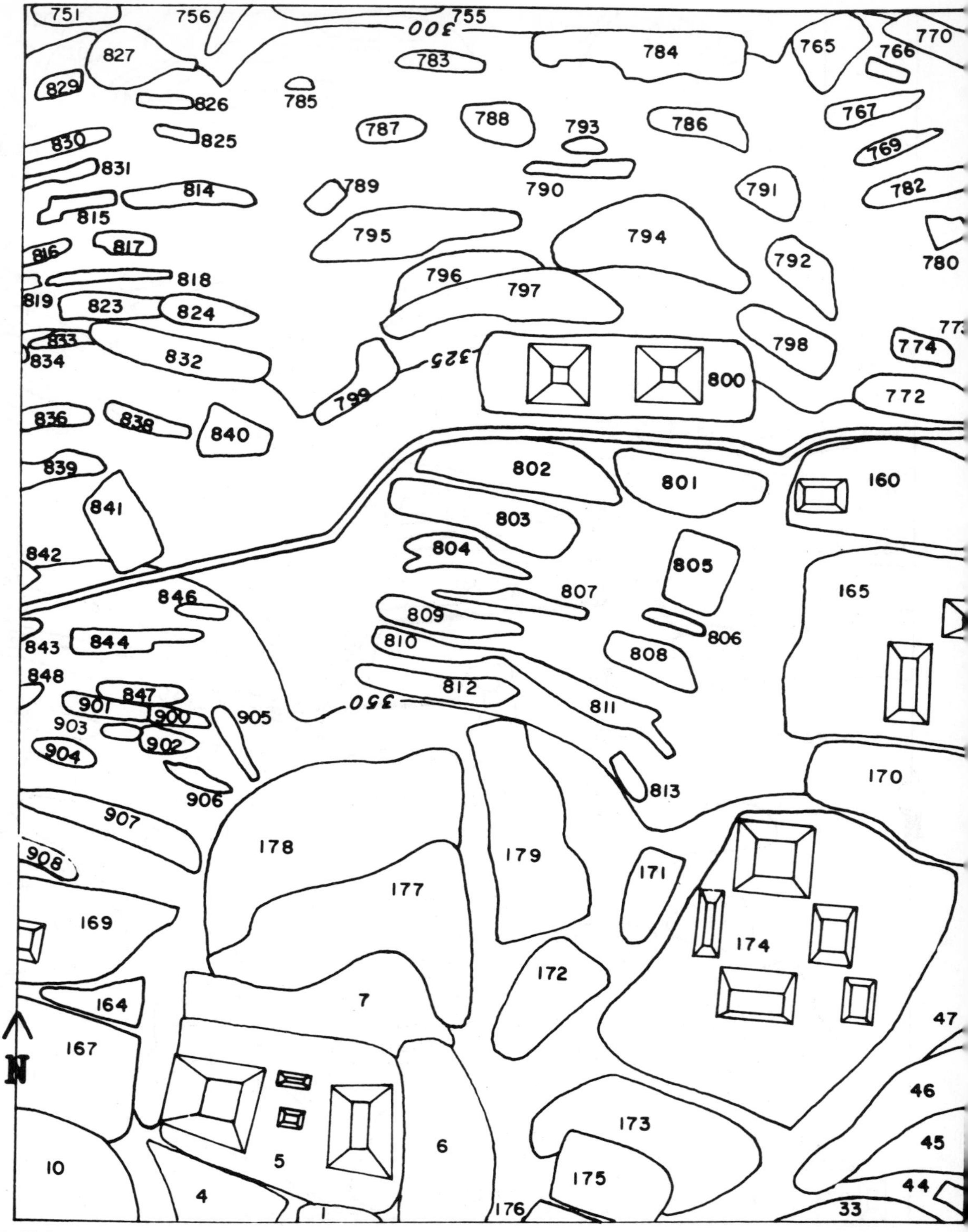
751
756
755
300
827
783
784
765
766
770
829
826
785
767
830
825
787
788
793
786
769
831
814
789
790
791
782
815
795
794
817
816
792
780
818
796
797
819
823
824
798
774
833
834
832
325
800
772
836
838
840
799
839
802
801
160
841
803
804
805
842
846
807
165
809
806
843
844
810
808
848
847
812
901
900
905
350
811
903
902
904
813
906
170
907
178
179
908
171
177
169
174
172
7
164
47
167
N
46
173
6
45
10
5
4
175
44
1
176
33

N5 E9

40 m

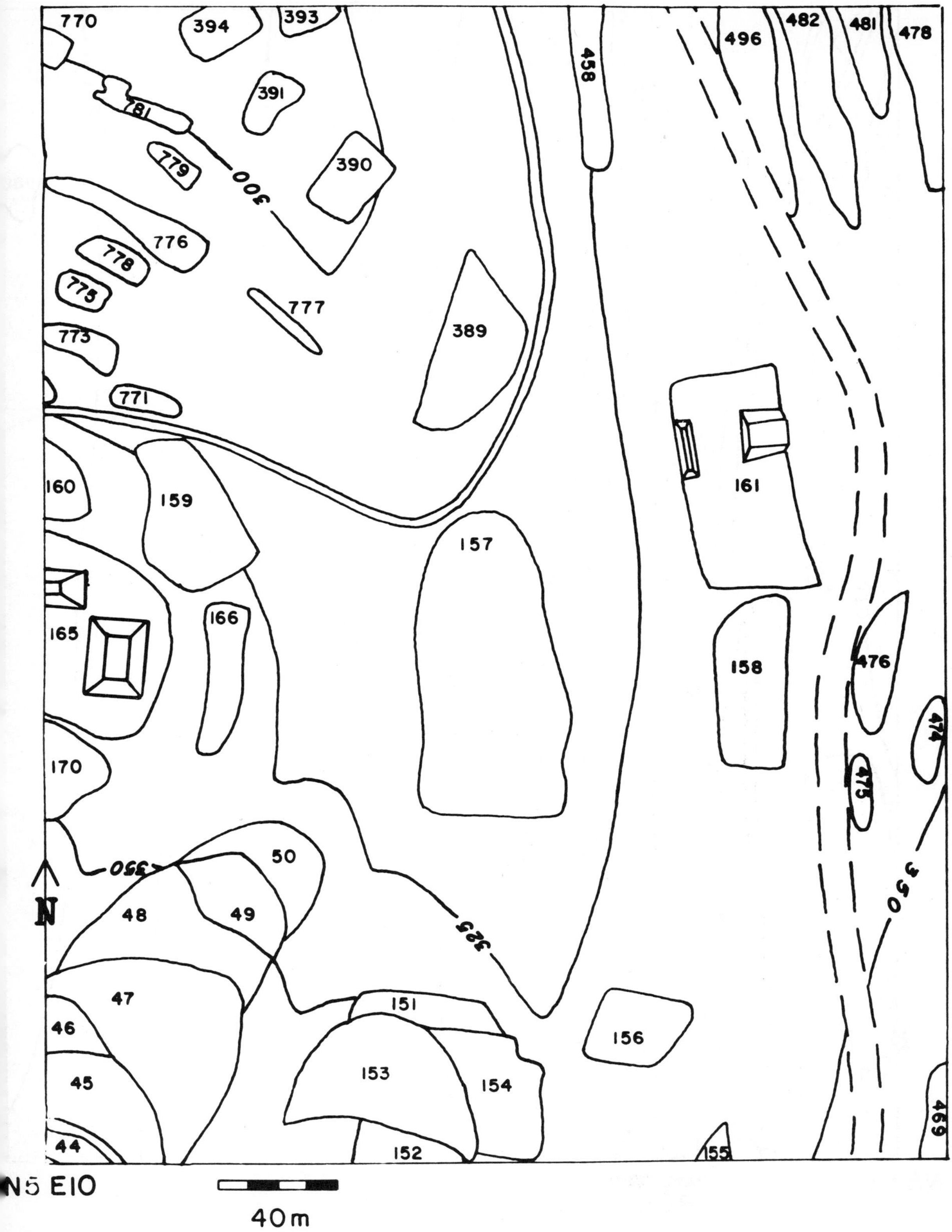

770
394
393
496
482
481
478
458
391
781
779
390
300
776
778
775
777
389
773
771
160
159
161
157
165
166
158
476
474
170
475
50
350
N
48
49
350
325
47
151
156
46
153
45
154
469
44
152
155
N5 E10
40 m

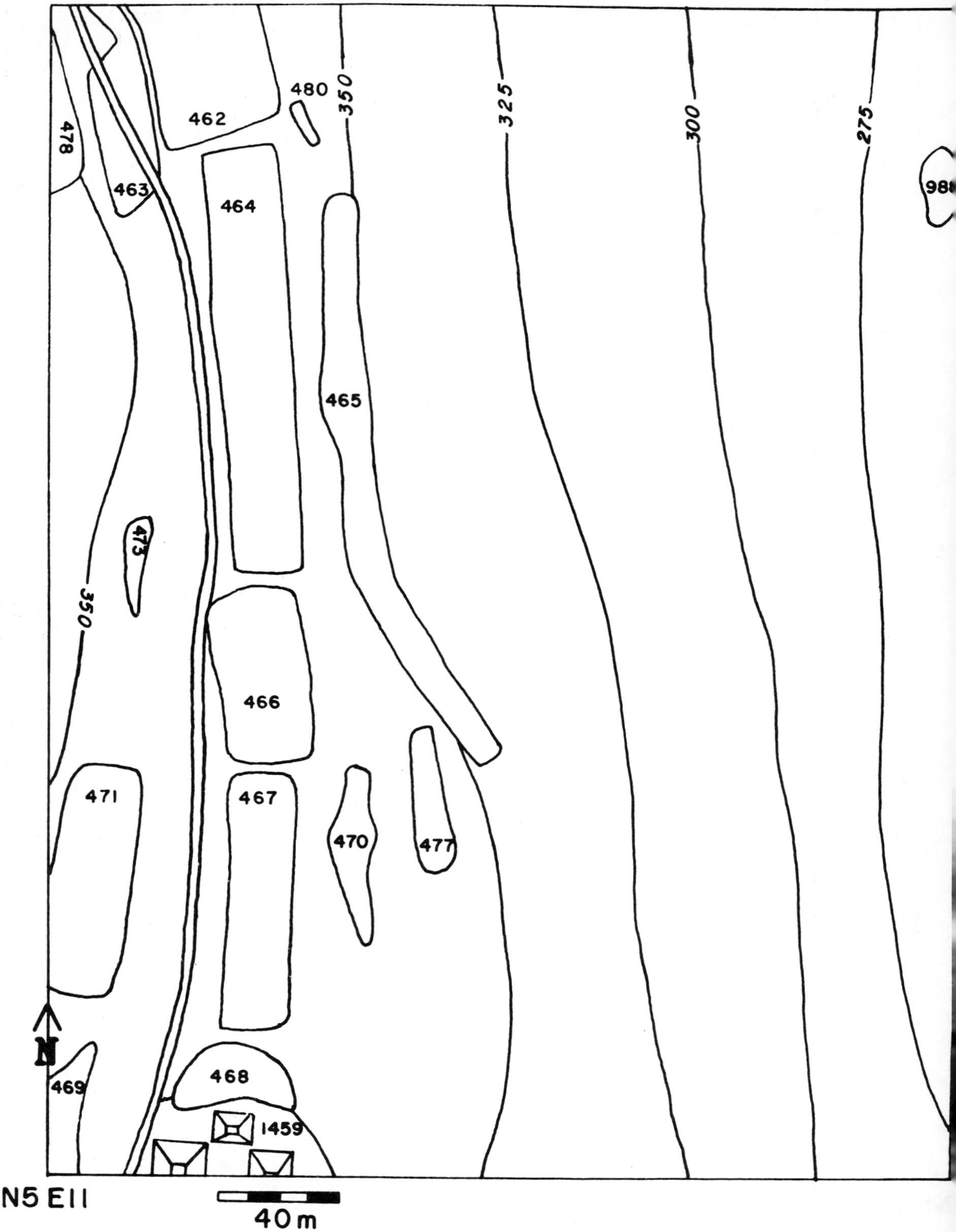

462
480
350
325
300
275
478
463
464
98
465
473
350
466
471
467
470
477
N
468
469
1459
N5 E11
40 m

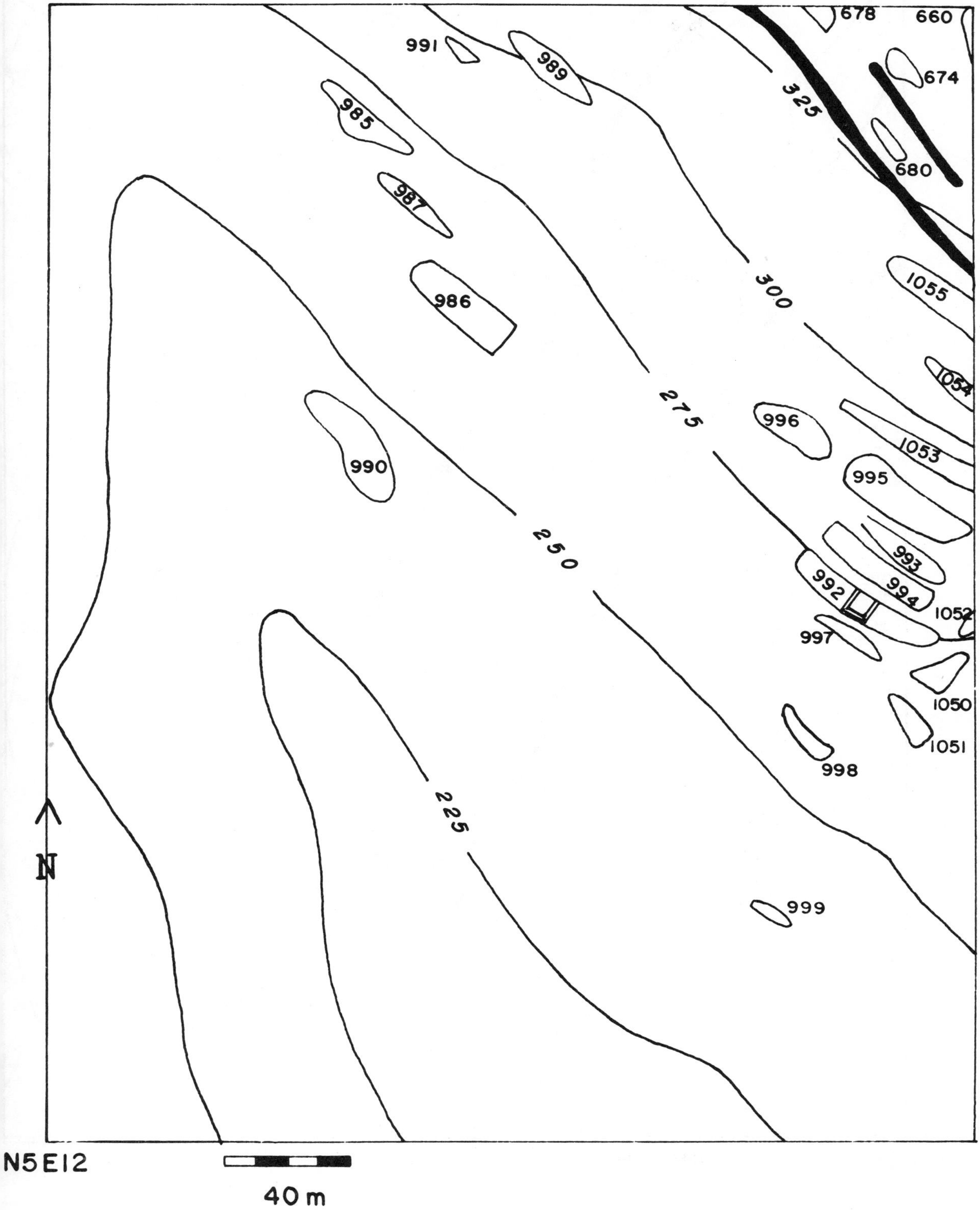
678
660
991
989
674
985
325
680
987
986
300
1055
1054
275
996
1053
990
995
250
993
992
994
1052
997
1050
1051
998
225
N
999
N5E12
40 m

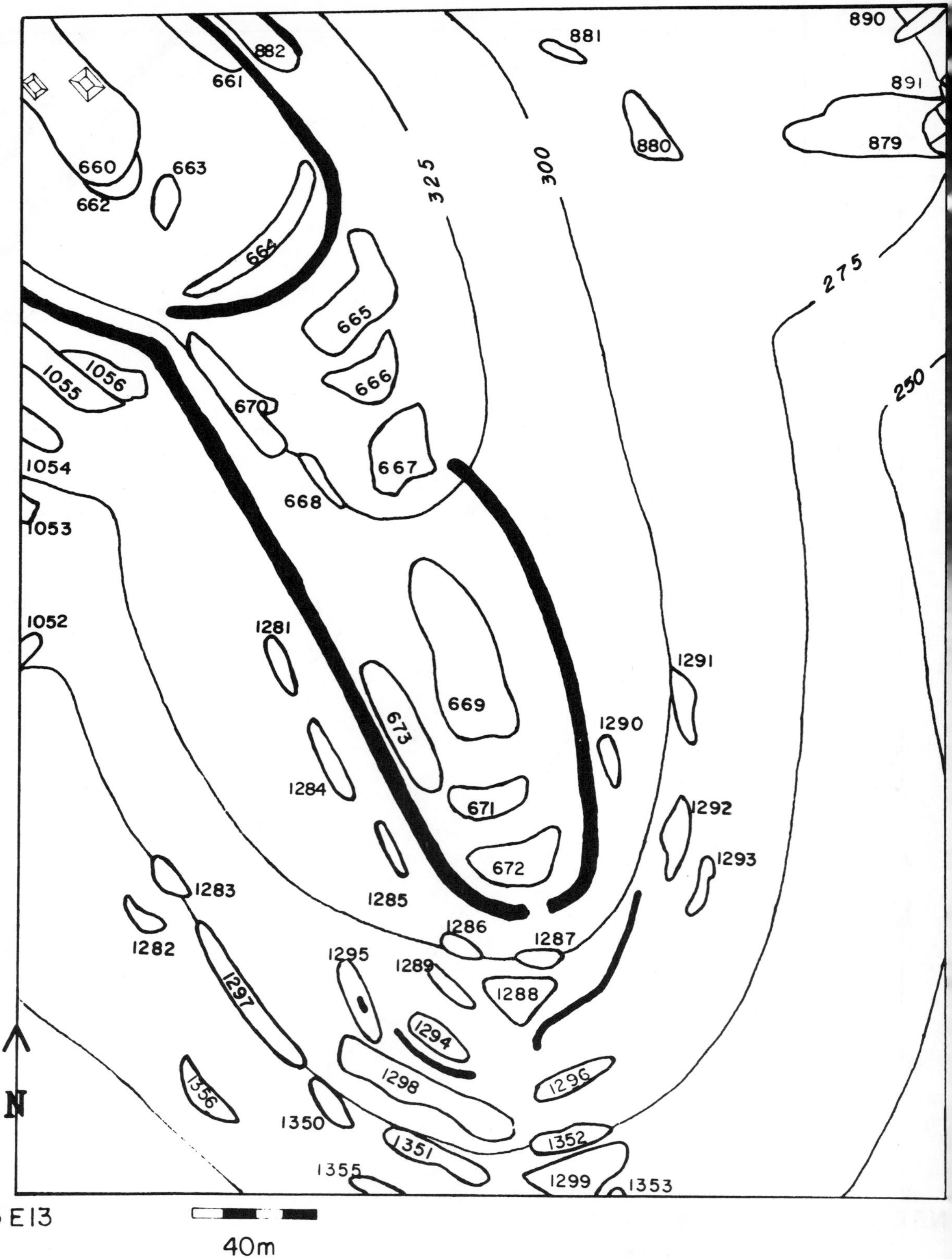

882
881
890
891
661
879
880
660
663
662
325
300
664
275
665
1056
1055
666
250
670
1054
667
668
1053
1281
1052
1291
669
673
1290
1284
671
1292
672
1293
1283
1285
1286
1282
1287
1295
1289
1297
1288
1294
1298
1296
1356
1350
1352
1351
1355
1299
1353
N

N5 E13

40m

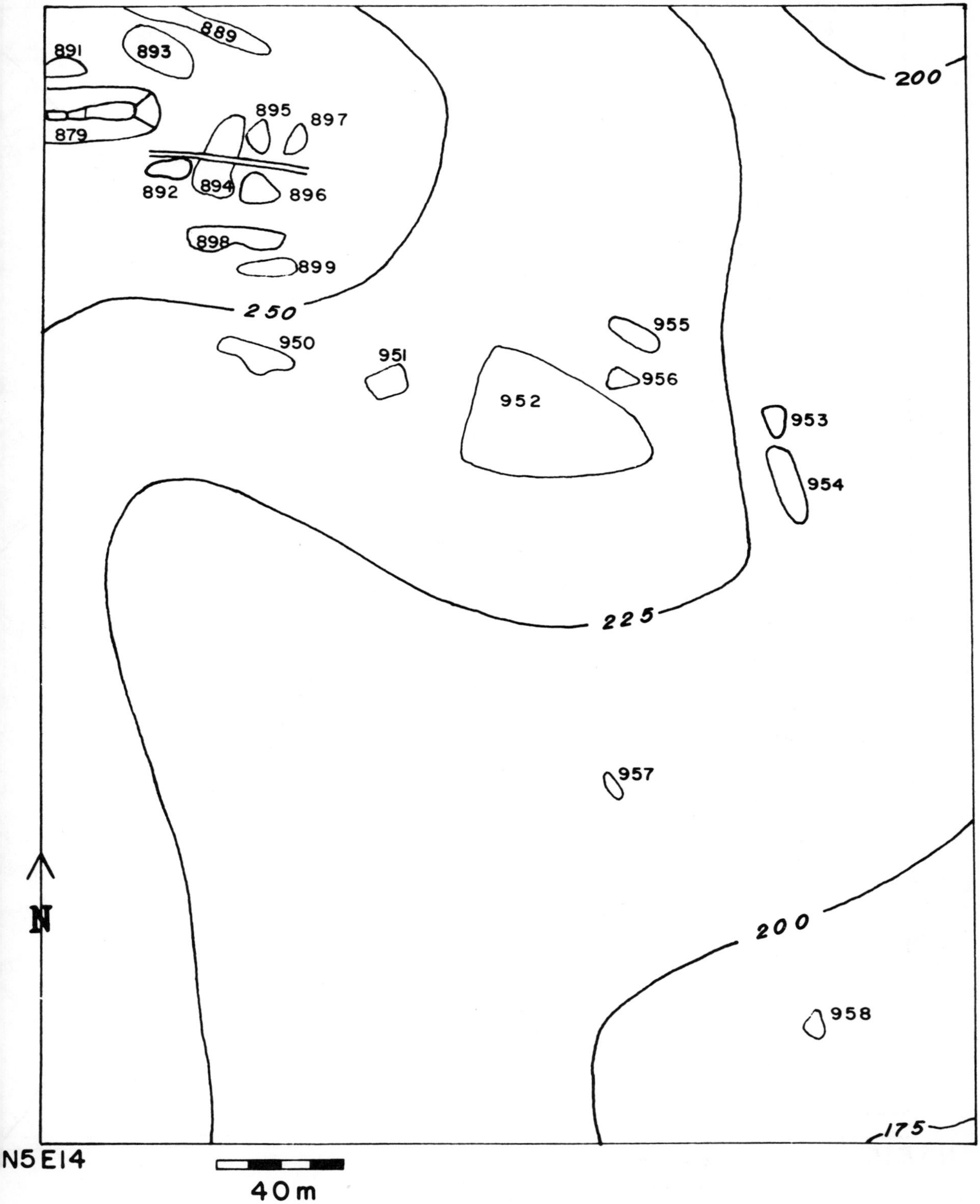
889
891
893
879
895
897
892
894
896
898
899
250
200
950
951
952
955
956
953
954
225
957
N
200
958
175
N5 E14
40 m

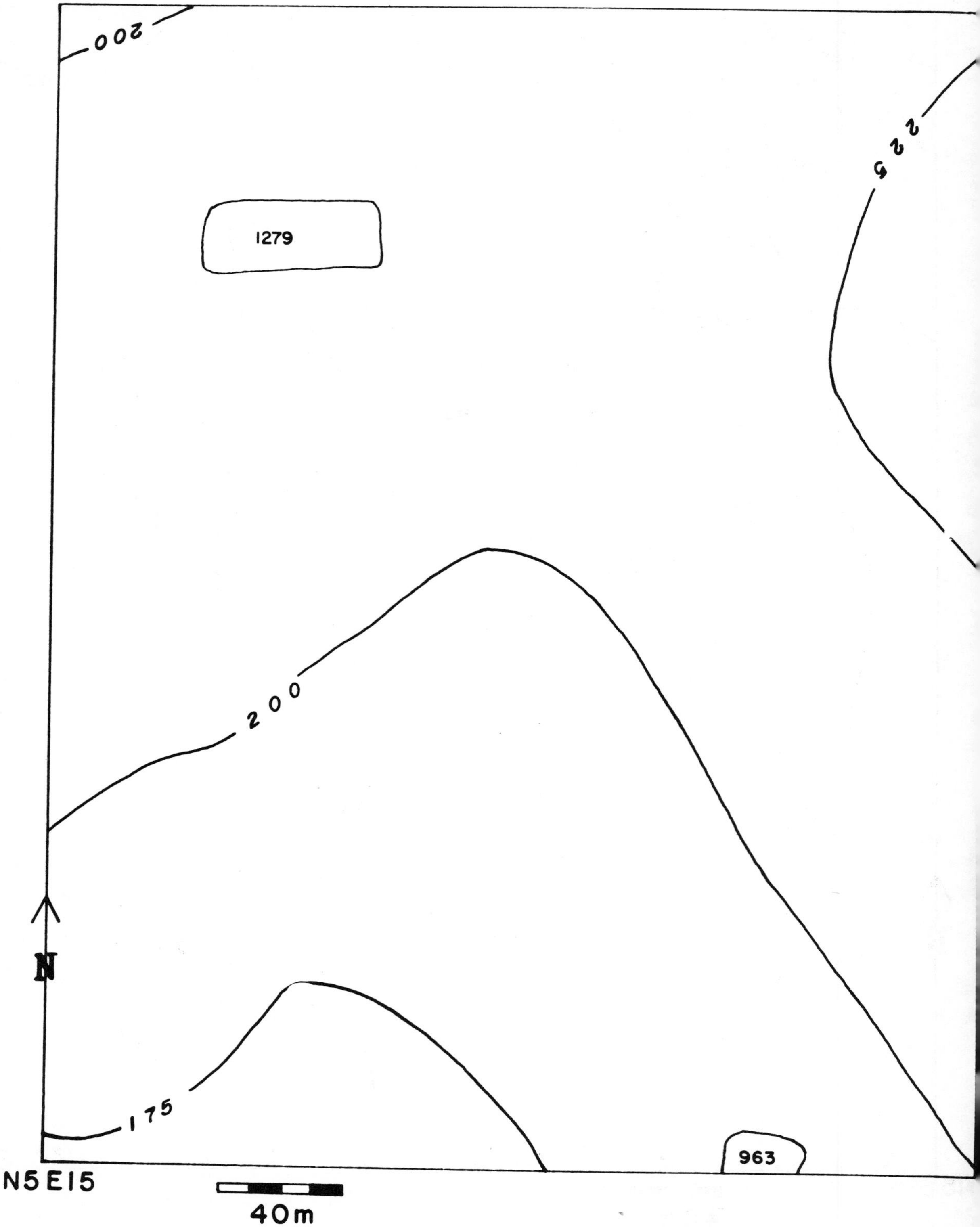
200
225
1279
200
N
175
963
N5 E15
40m

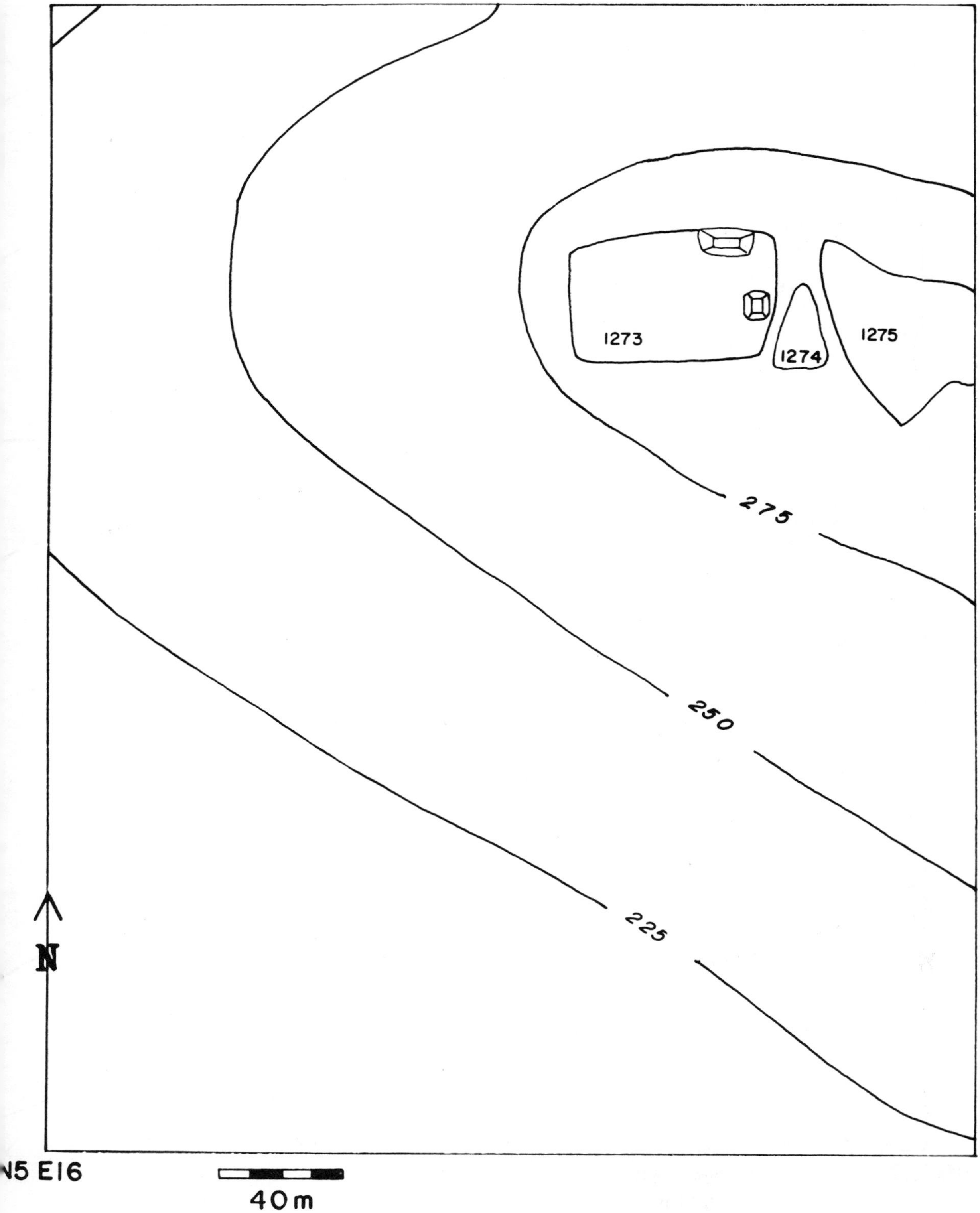

1273
1274
1275
275
250
225
N
N5 E16
40m

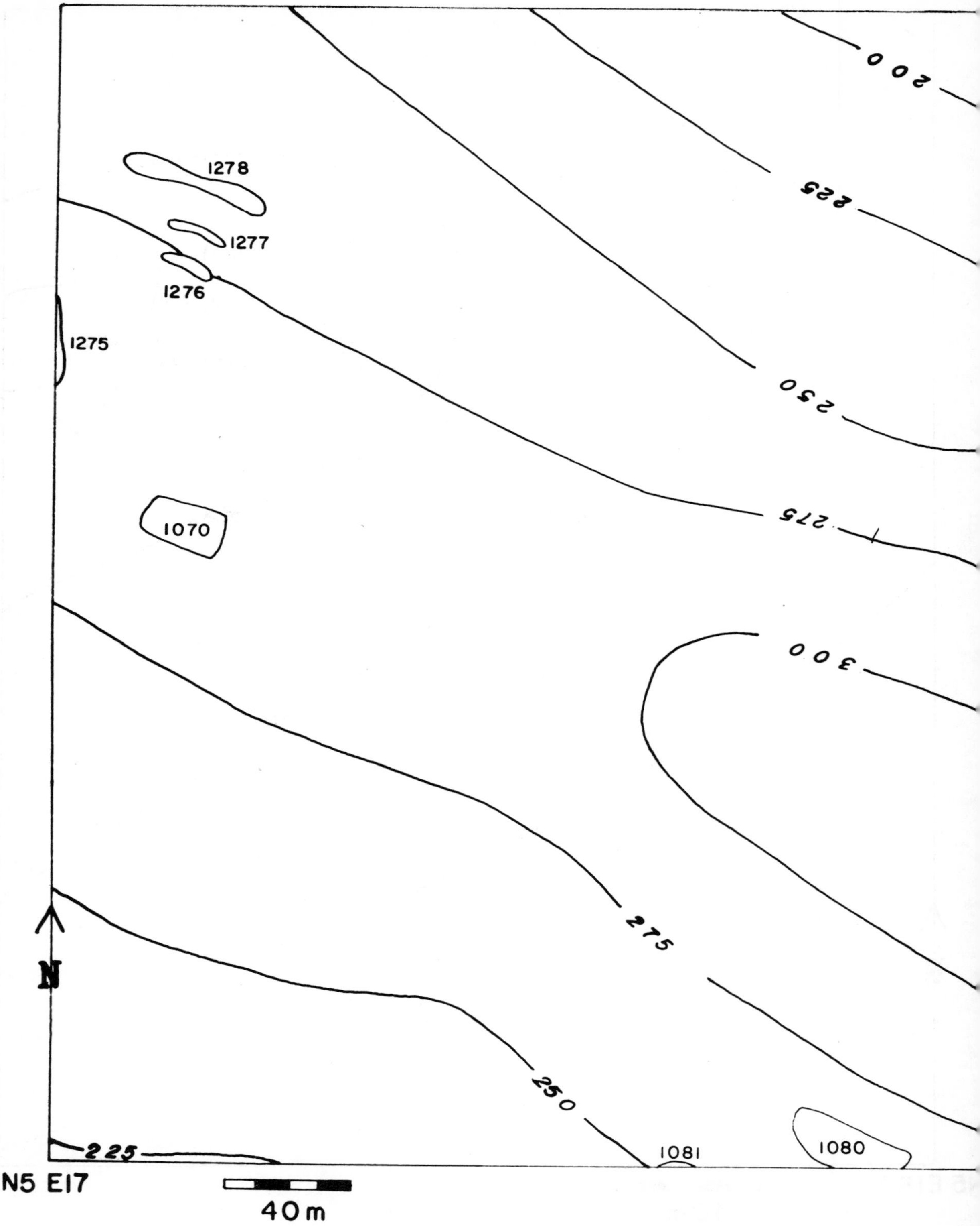

200
225
250
275
300
275
250
225
1278
1277
1276
1275
1070
1081
1080
N
N5 E17
40 m

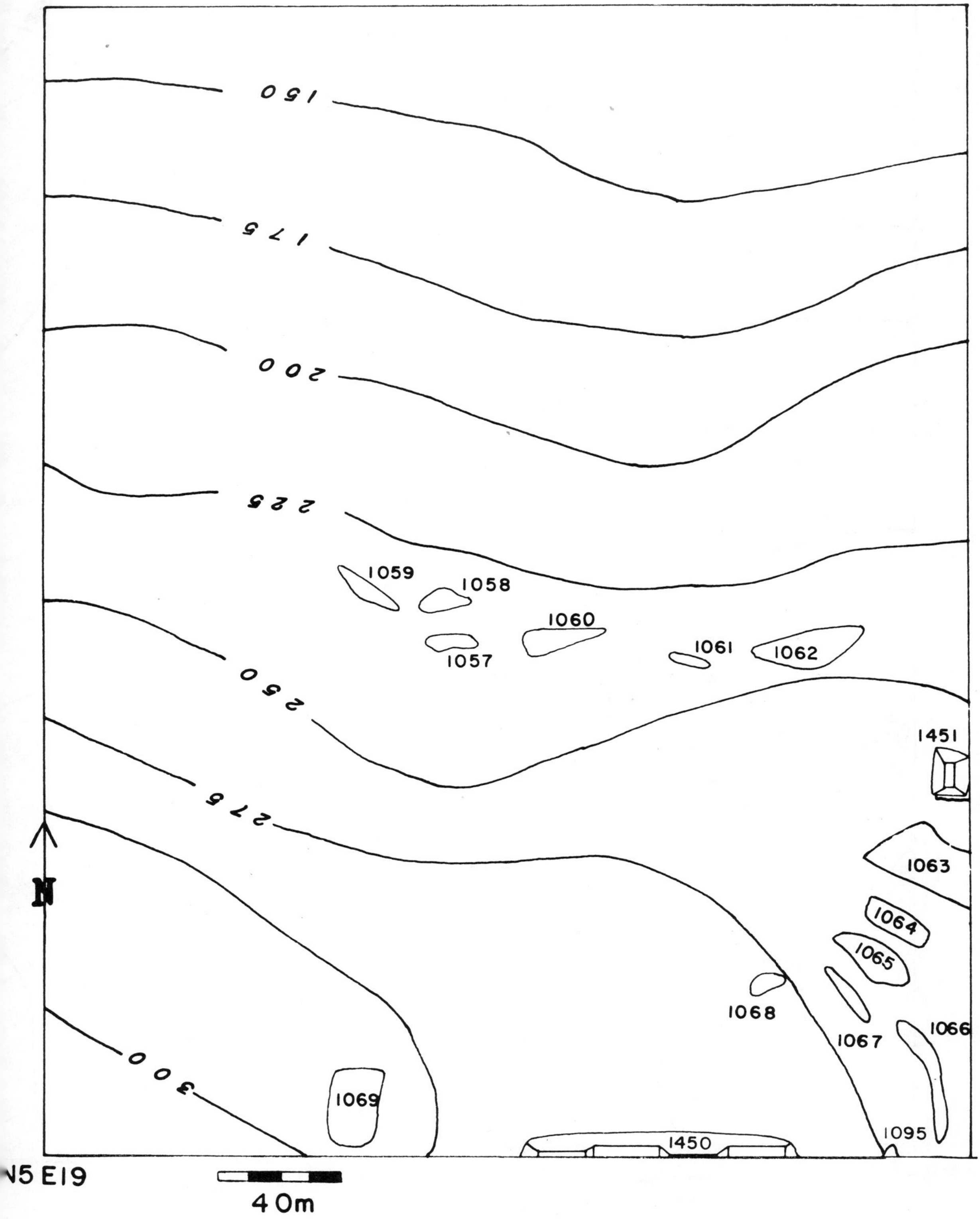

150
175
200
225
250
275
300
1059
1058
1060
1057
1061
1062
1451
1063
1064
1065
1068
1067
1066
1069
1450
1095
N
N5 E19
40m

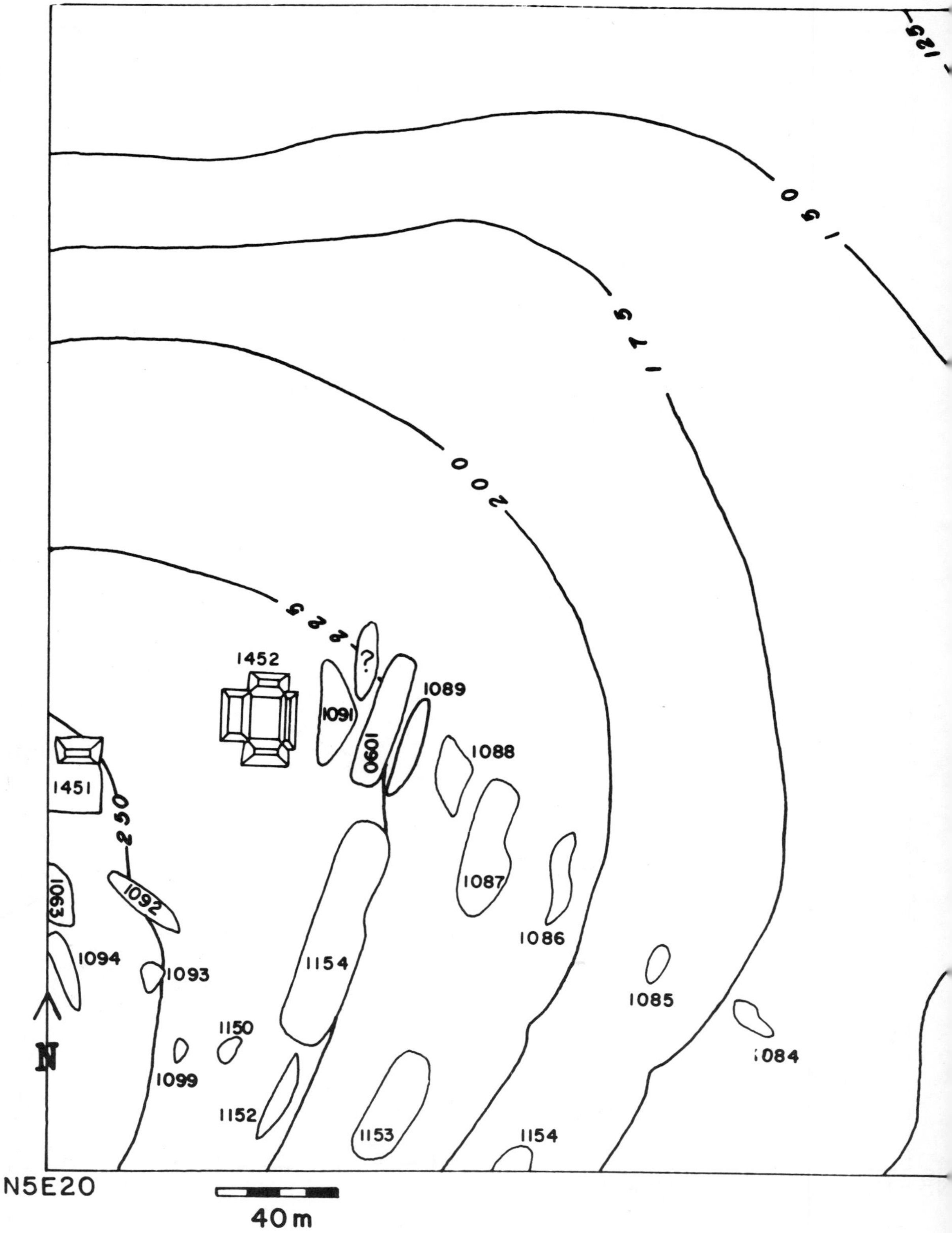

125
150
175
200
225
250
1452
1451
1091
1090
1089
1088
1087
1086
1085
1084
1092
1093
1094
1063
1099
1150
1152
1153
1154
1154
N
N5E20
40 m

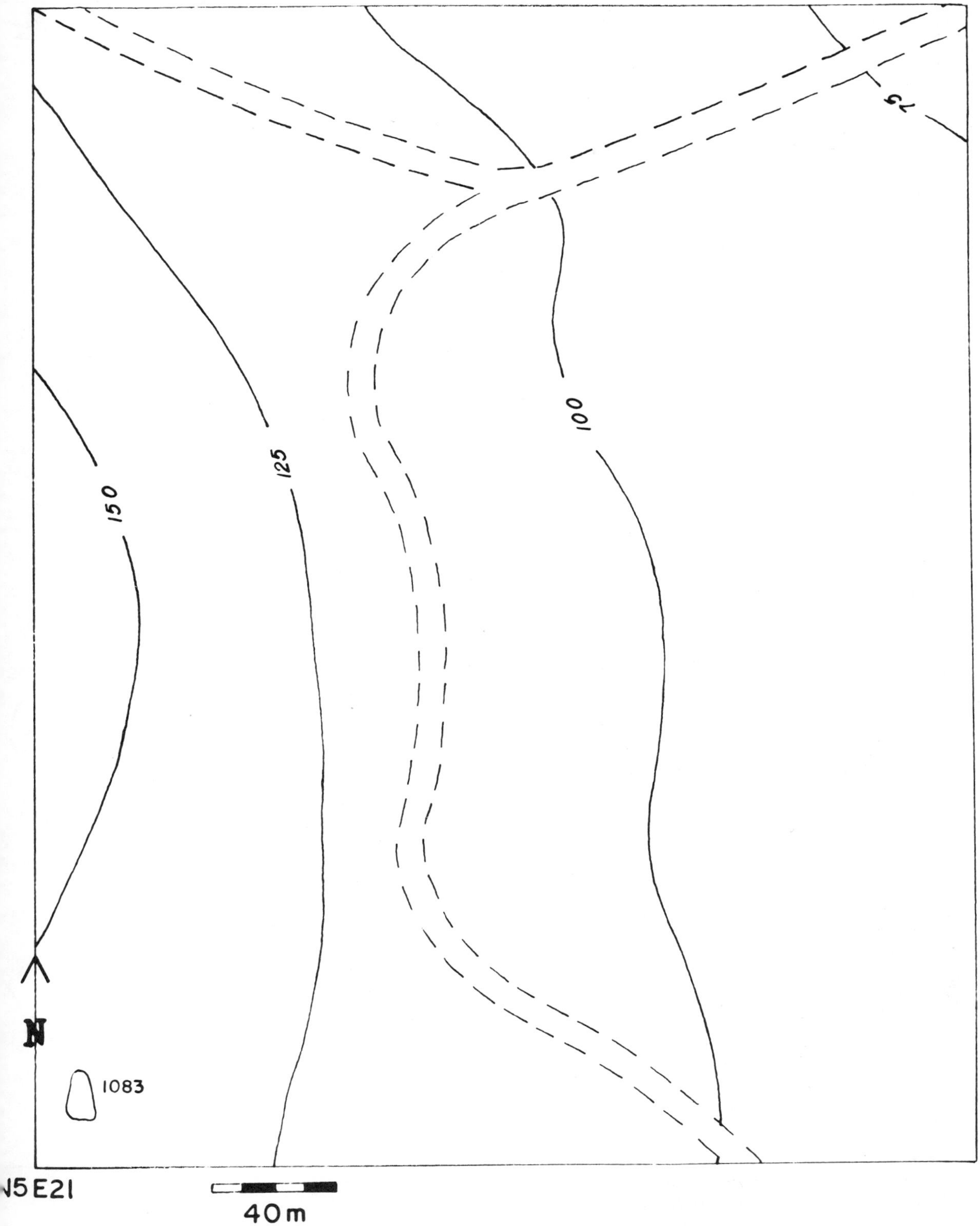
150
125
100
75
N
1083
N5 E21
40m

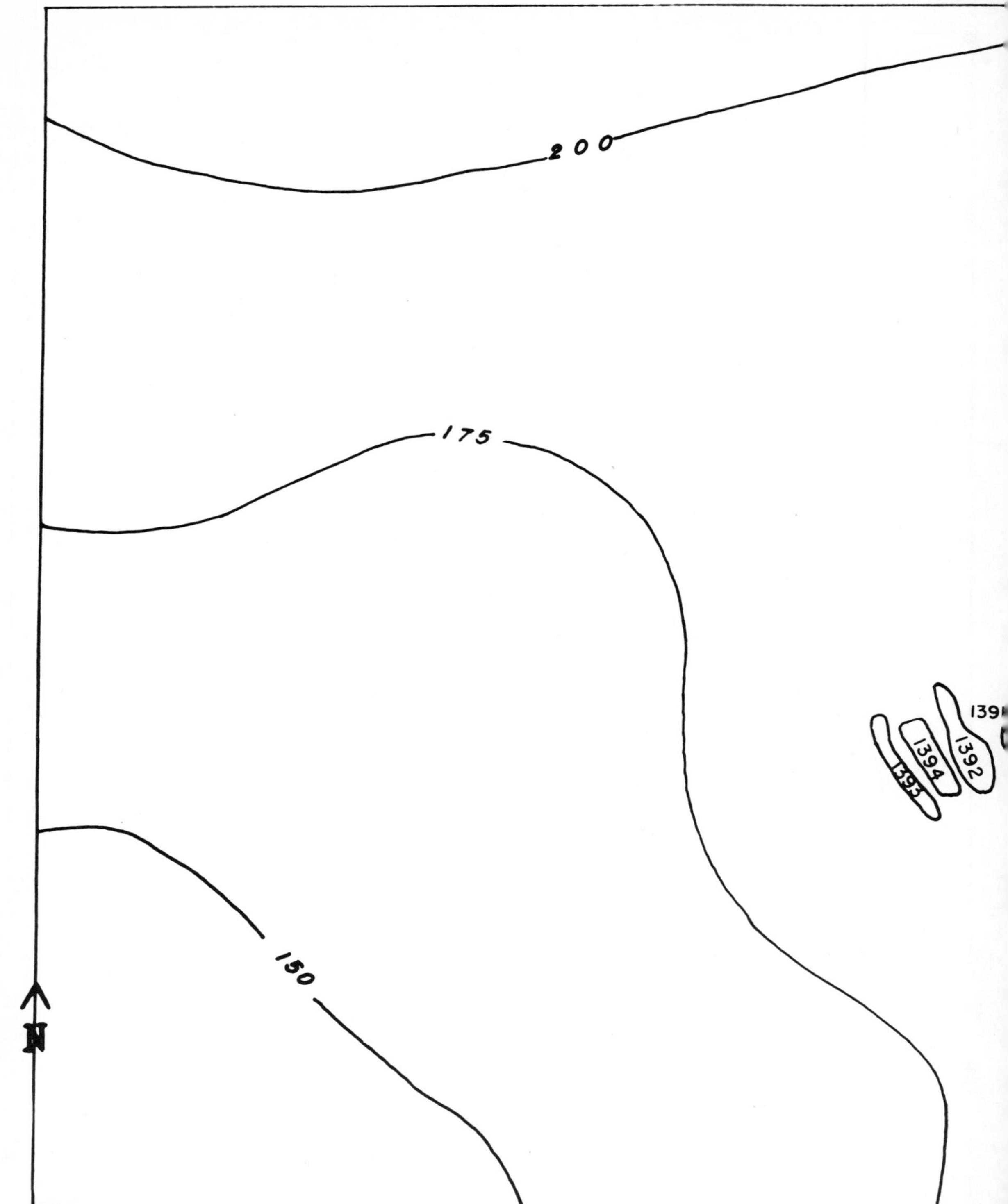

200
175
150
1391
1392
1394
1393
N
N6E5
40 m

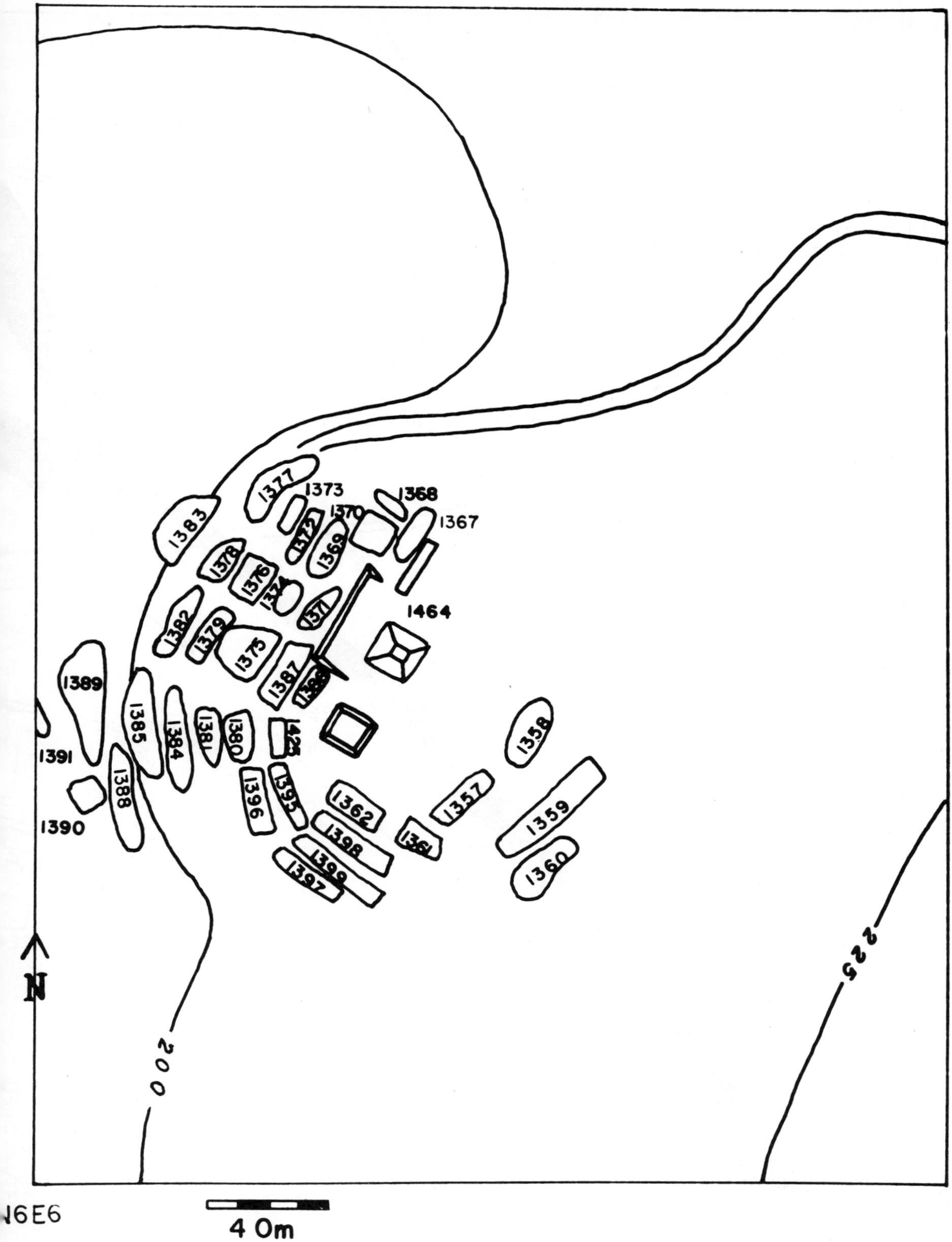
1377
1373
1368
1370
1367
1383
1372
1369
1378
1376
1374
1371
1464
1382
1379
1375
1387
1386
1389
1385
1384
1381
1380
1425
1358
1391
1388
1396
1395
1362
1357
1359
1390
1398
1361
1399
1397
1360
N
200
225
N6E6
40m

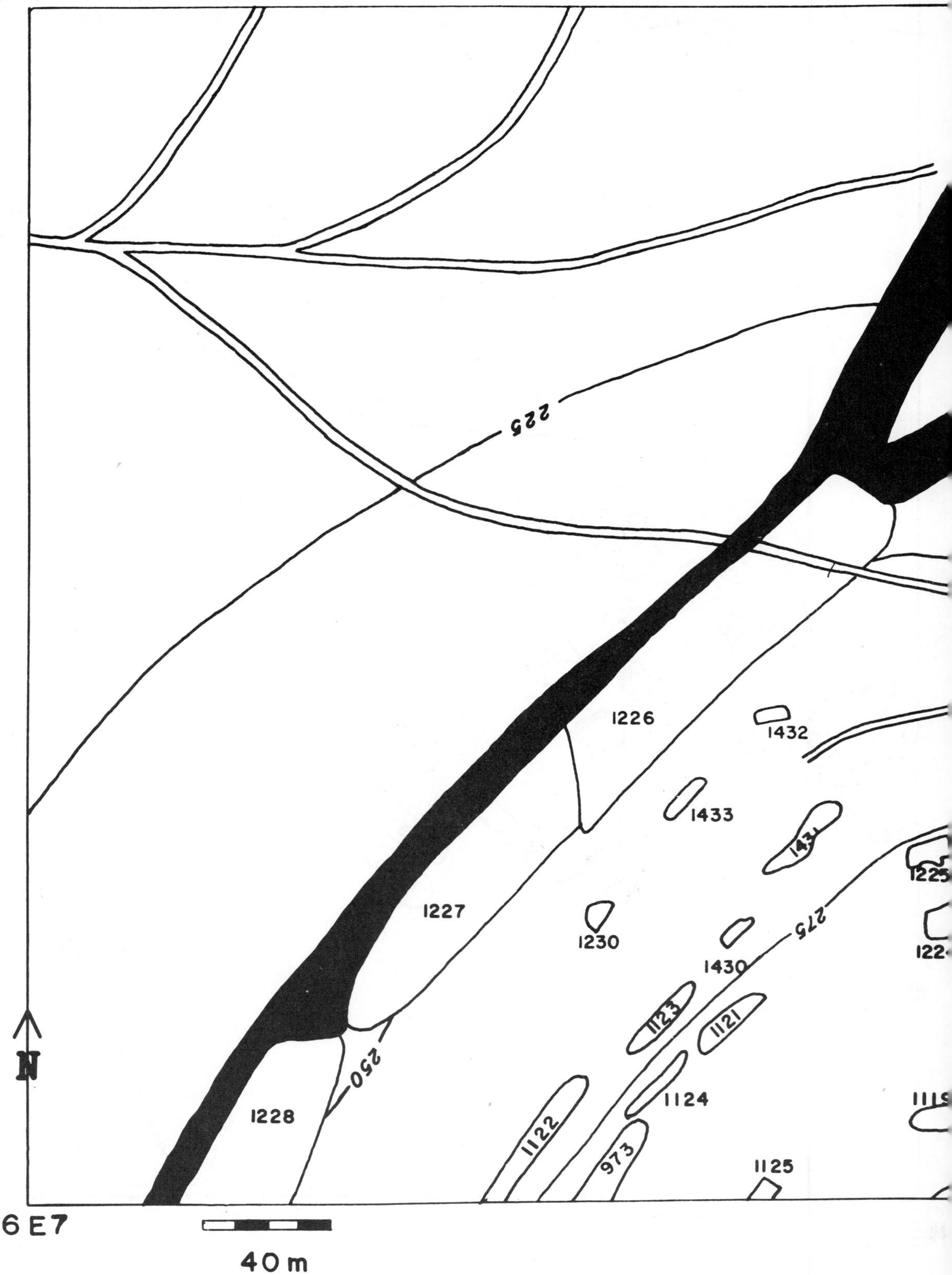

225
1226
1432
1433
1227
1230
1430
275
1123
1121
1124
1122
973
1125
1228
250
N
N6 E7
40 m

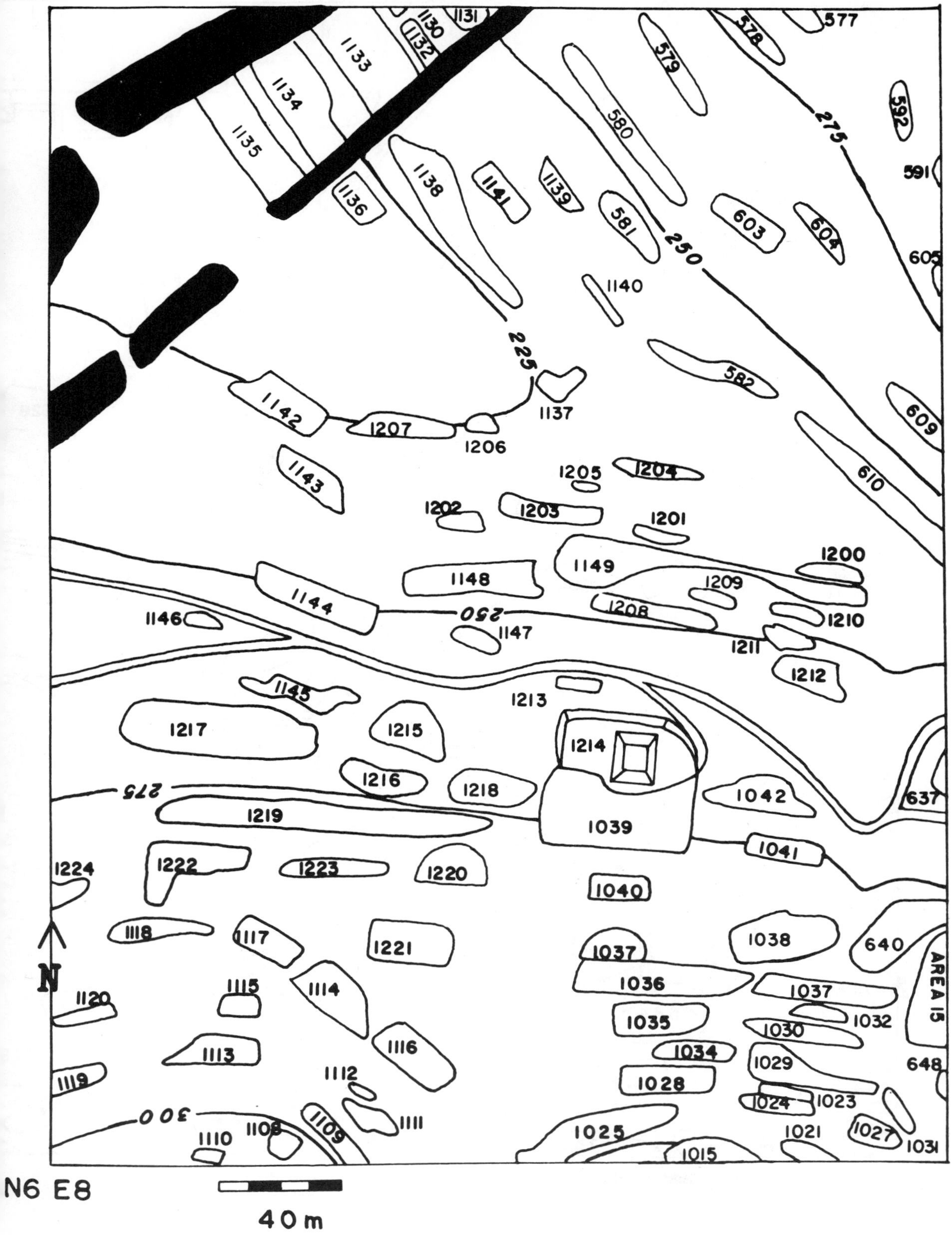

N
N6 E8
40 m

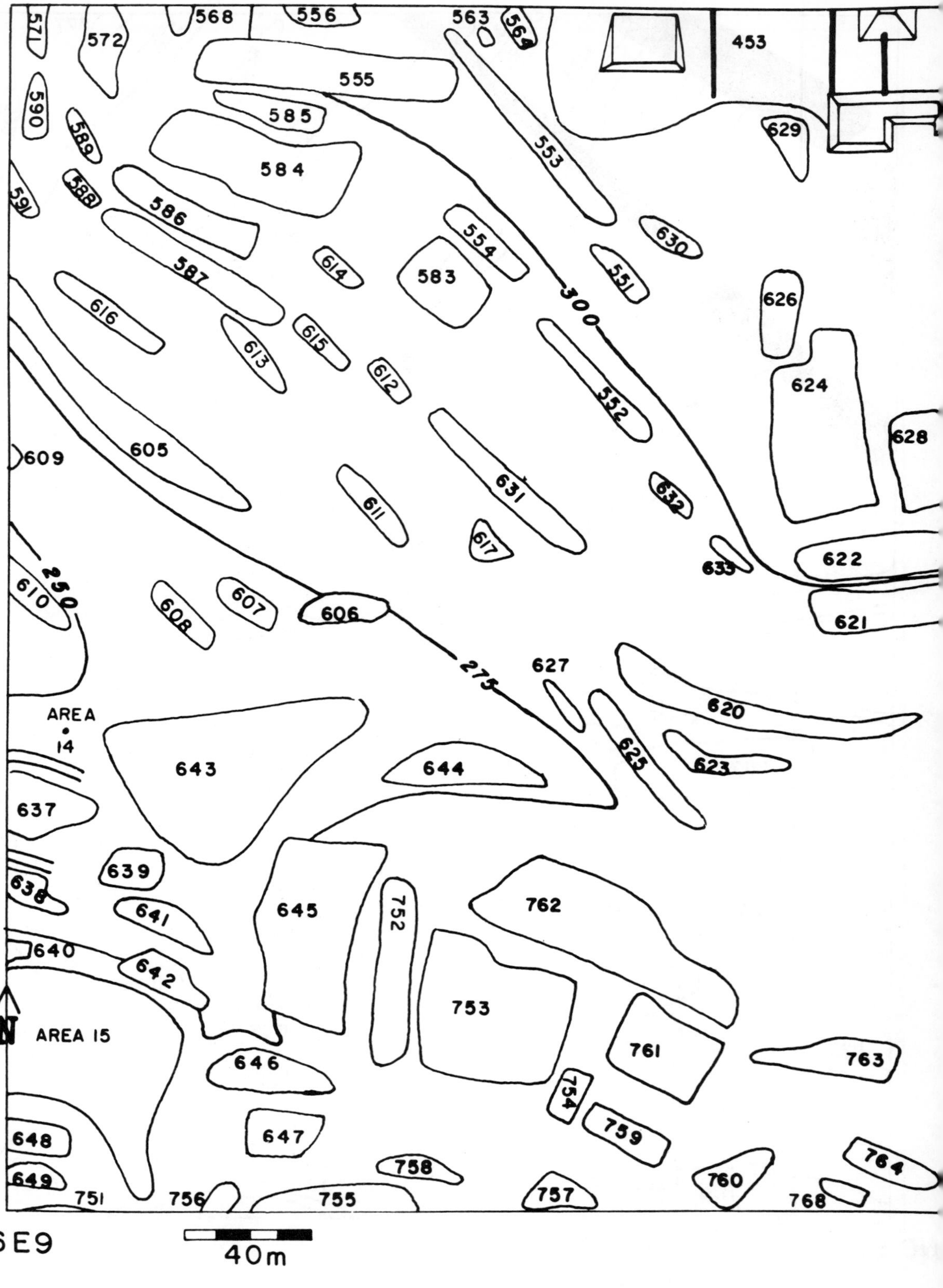
571
572
568
556
563
564
453
555
590
585
589
584
553
629
588
591
586
630
554
614
583
551
587
300
616
626
613
615
612
552
624
628
605
609
631
632
611
617
633
622
250
610
608
607
606
621
275
627
620
AREA
14
643
644
625
623
637
639
762
638
641
645
752
640
642
753
N
AREA 15
761
763
646
754
648
647
759
764
758
760
649
751
756
755
757
768
40m

N6E9

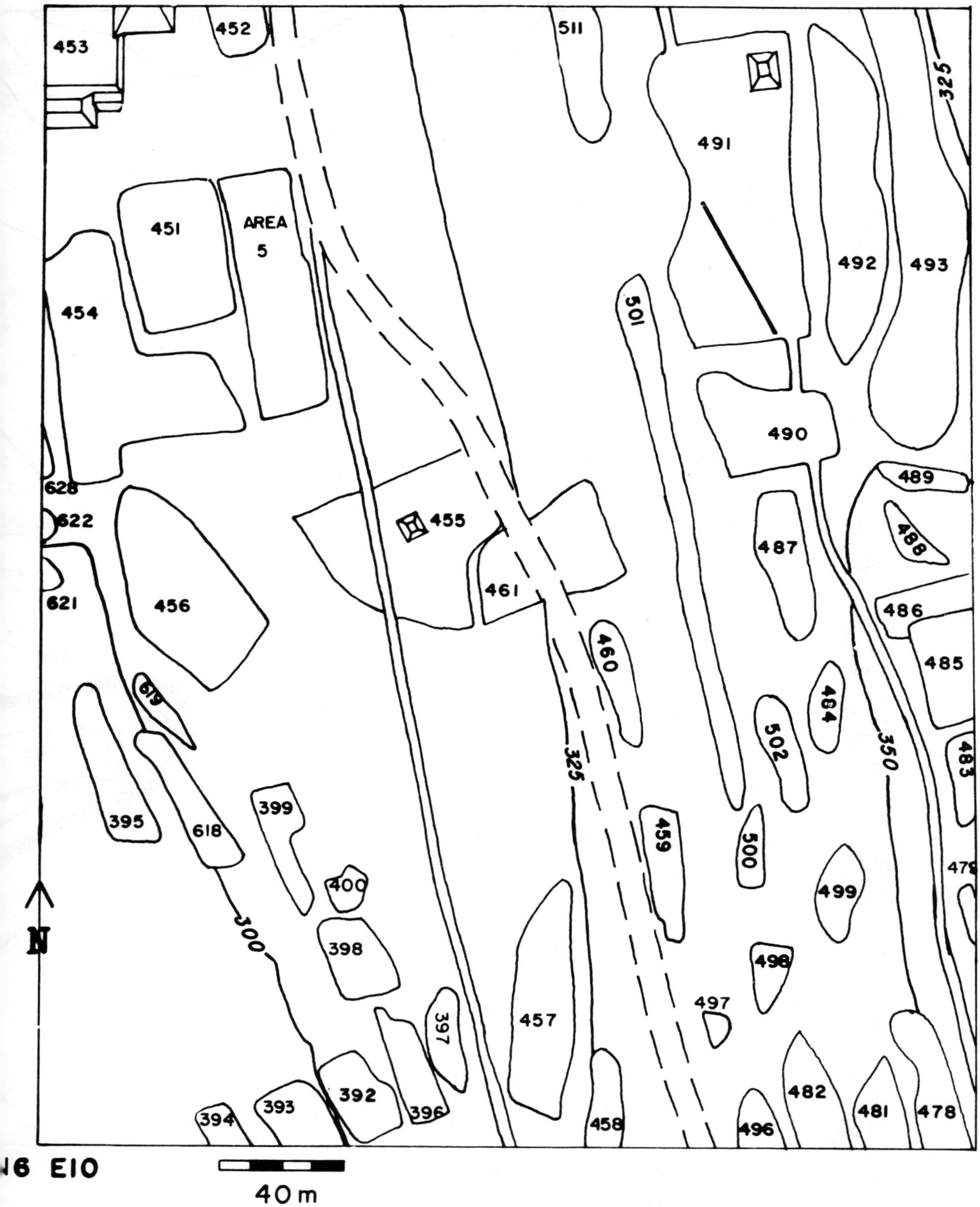
453
452
511
325
491
451
AREA 5
454
492
493
501
490
628
622
455
489
488
461
487
621
456
486
460
485
619
484
502
350
483
325
399
395
618
459
500
479
400
499
N
398
300
498
497
397
457
482
481
478
392
393
396
394
458
496
16 E10
40 m

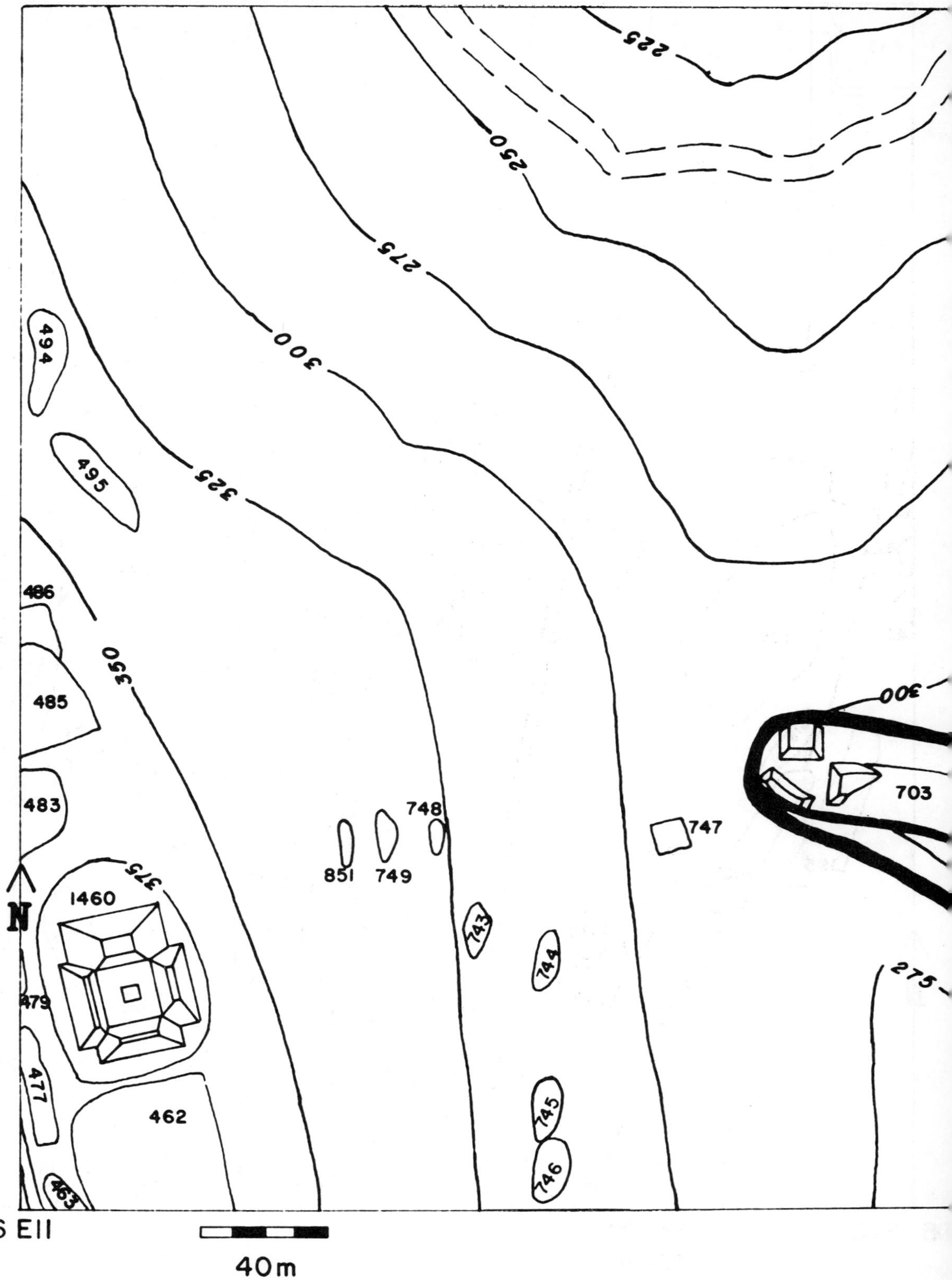

225
250
275
300
325
350
375
494
495
486
485
483
1460
479
477
462
463
851
749
748
743
744
745
746
747
703
300
275
N
40m

N6 E11

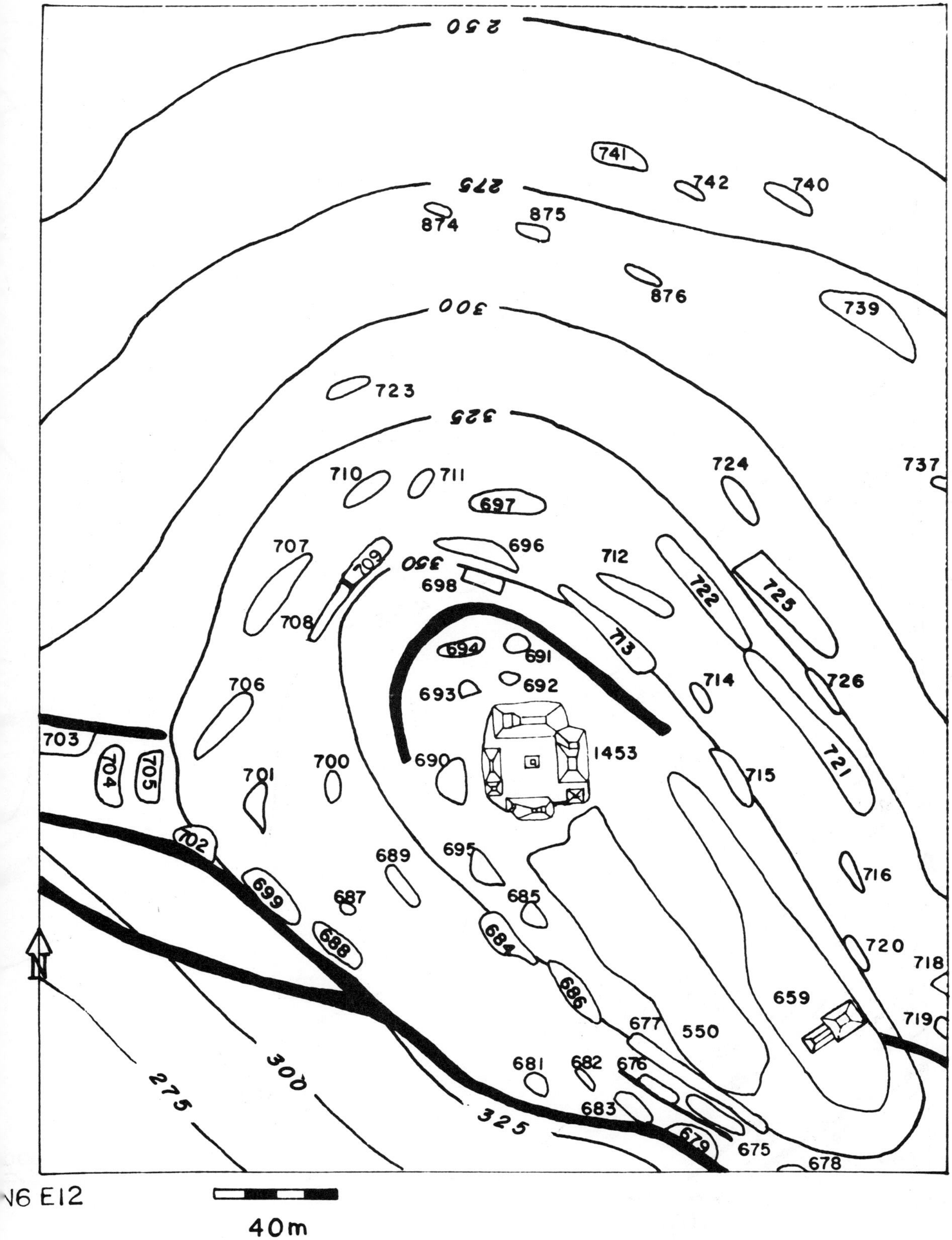
250
741
275
742
740
874
875
876
300
739
723
325
724
737
710
711
697
707
709
350
696
712
698
722
725
708
694
691
713
706
693
692
714
726
703
1453
704
705
701
700
690
715
721
702
689
695
716
699
687
685
684
720
688
718
N
686
659
677
550
719
681
682
676
300
275
683
325
679
675
678
N6 E12
40m

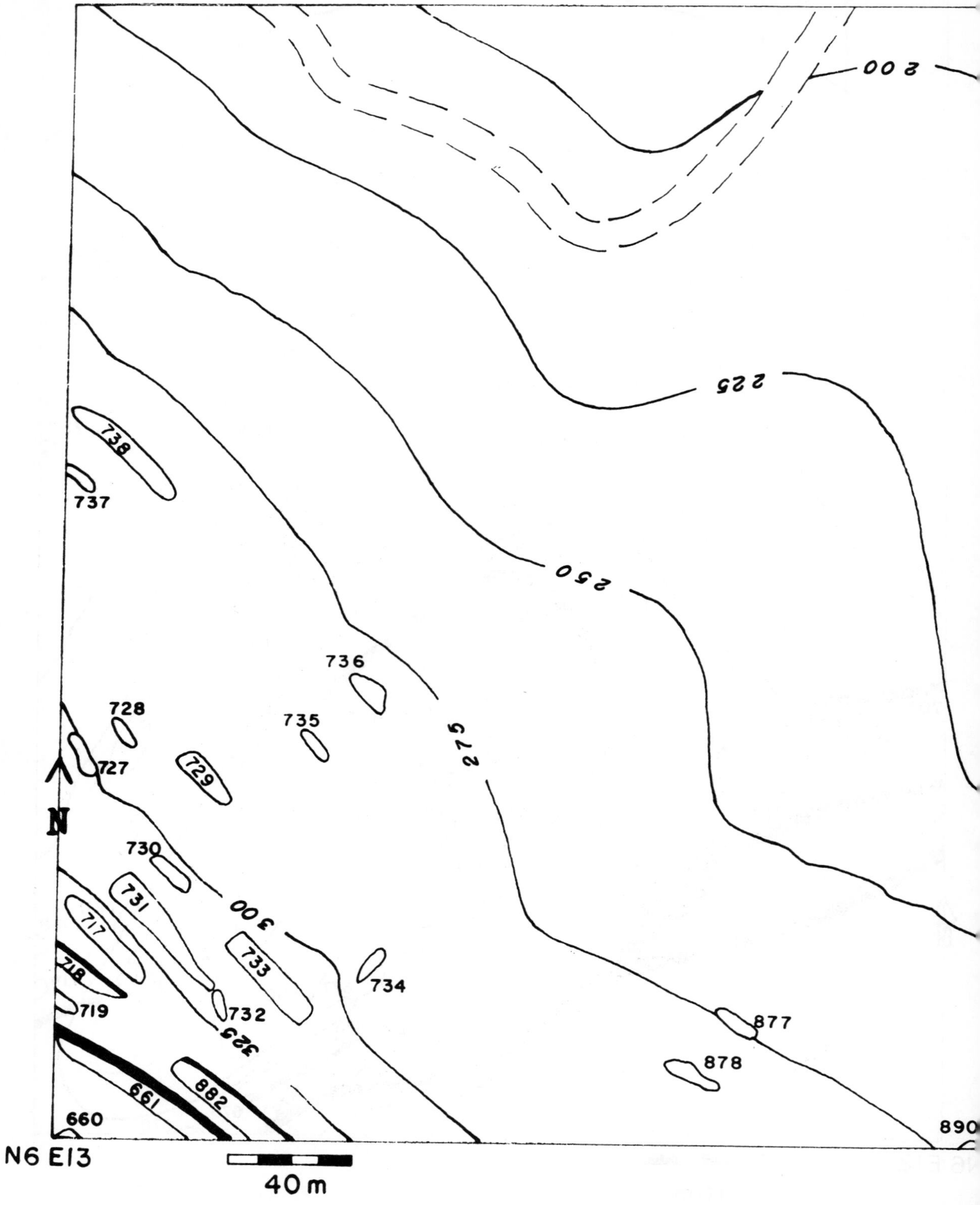
200
225
250
275
300
325
738
737
736
735
728
727
729
730
731
717
718
719
732
733
734
877
878
661
882
660
890
N
N6 E13
40 m

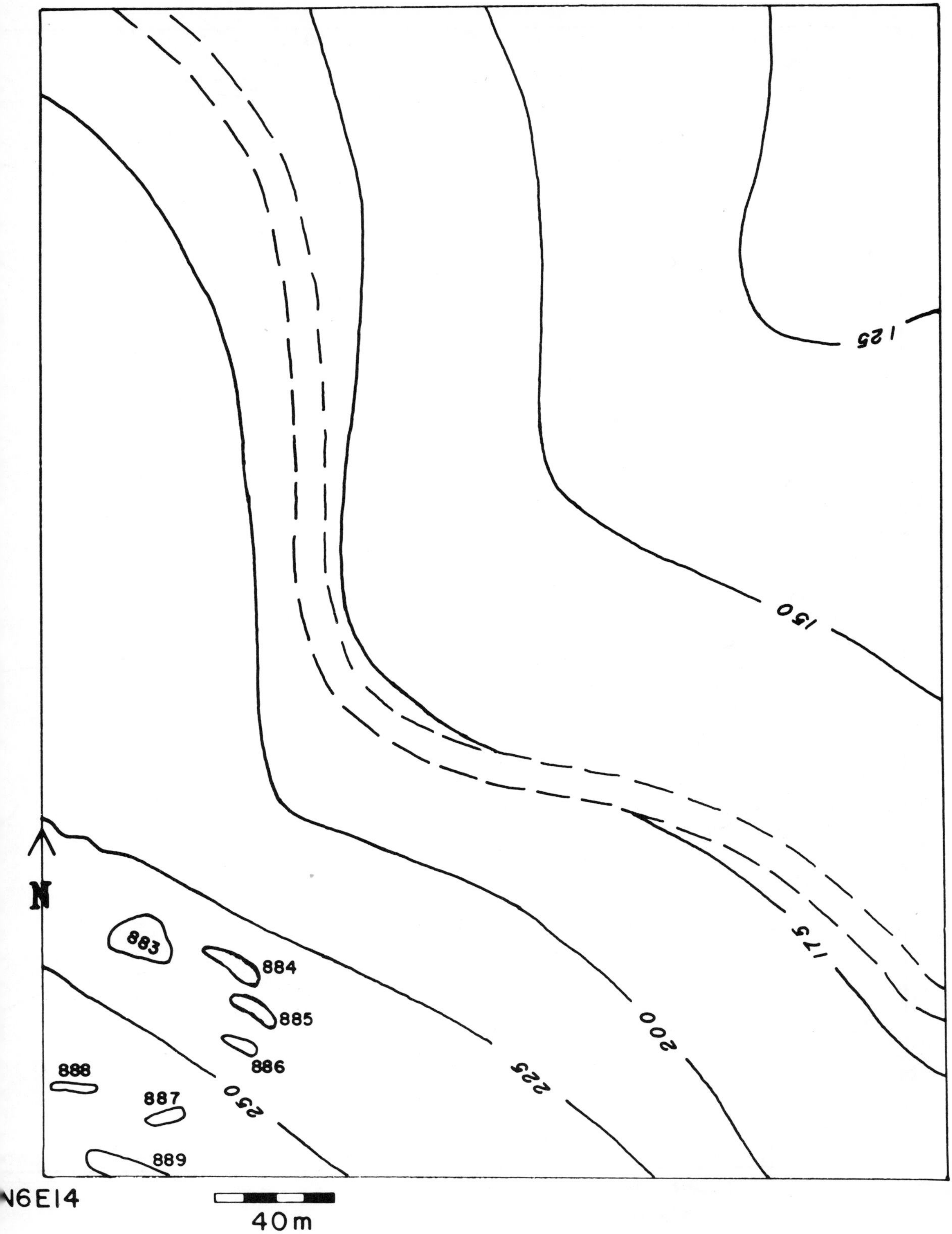
N
125
150
175
200
225
250
883
884
885
886
887
888
889
N6E14
40m

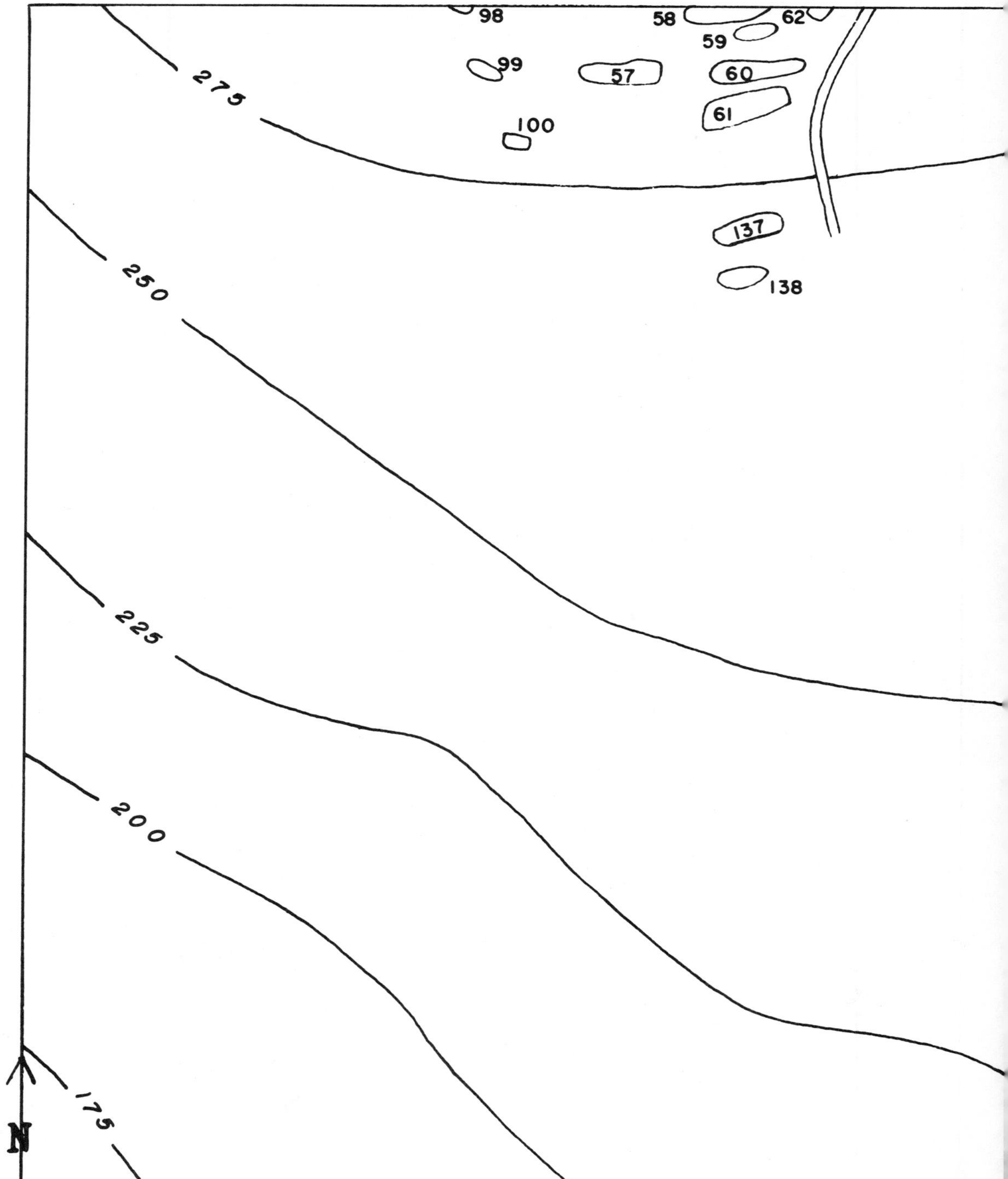

N7E4

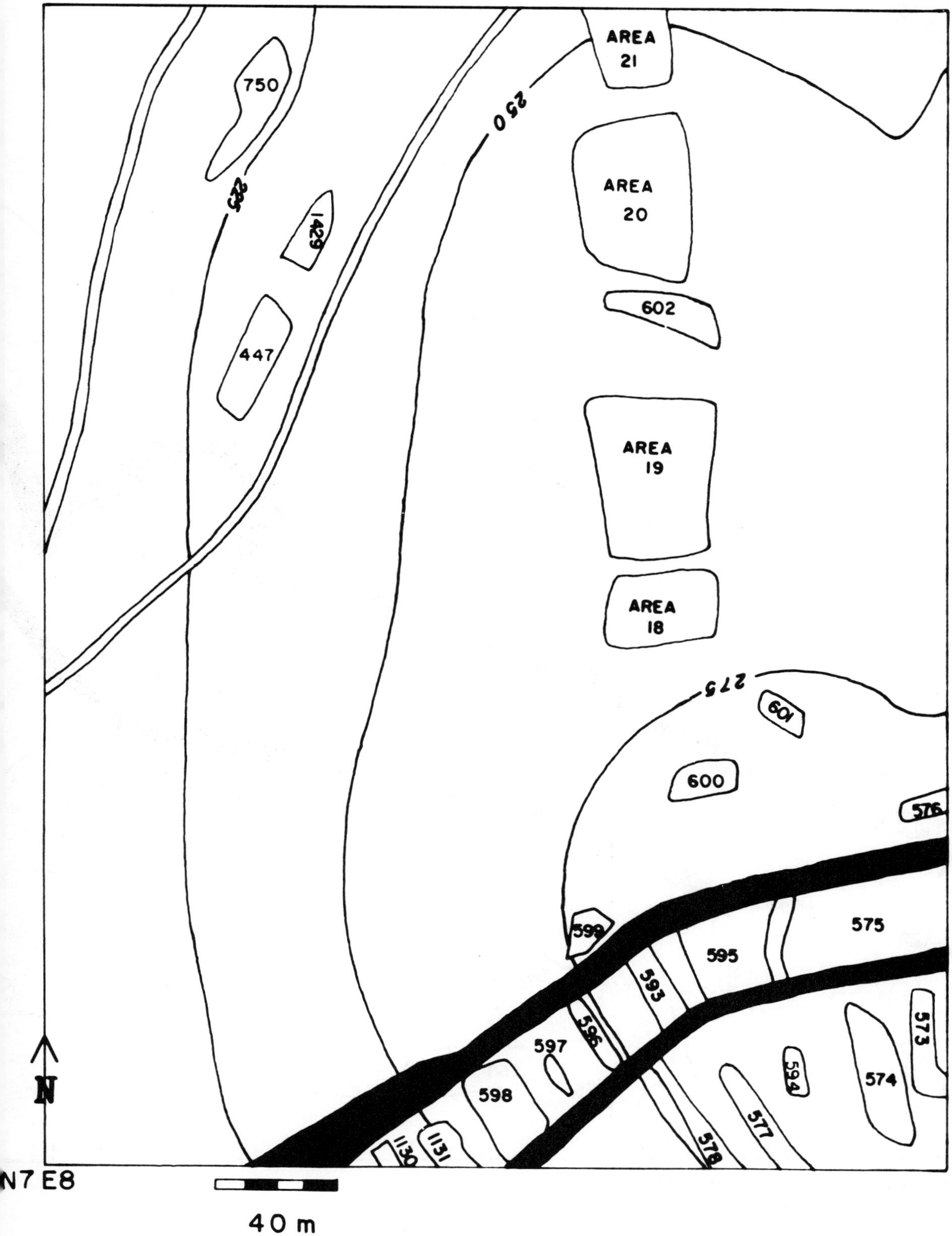

AREA 21
AREA 20
AREA 19
AREA 18
250
225
275
750
1429
447
602
601
600
576
599
575
595
593
596
597
598
1130
1131
578
577
594
574
573
N
N7 E8
40 m

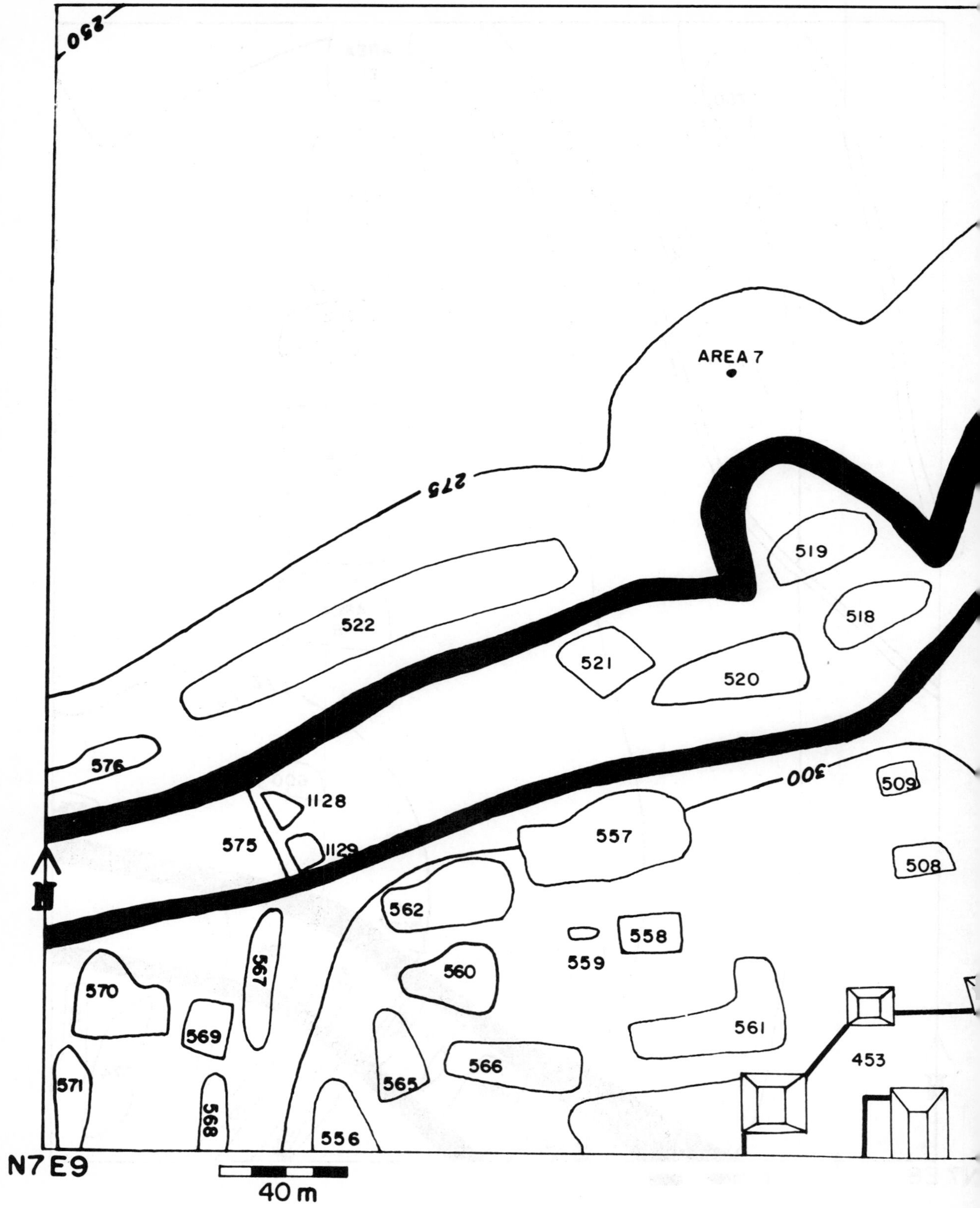

250
275
300
AREA 7
522
519
518
521
520
576
575
1128
1129
557
509
508
562
558
559
560
567
570
569
561
453
566
565
571
568
556
N7E9
40 m

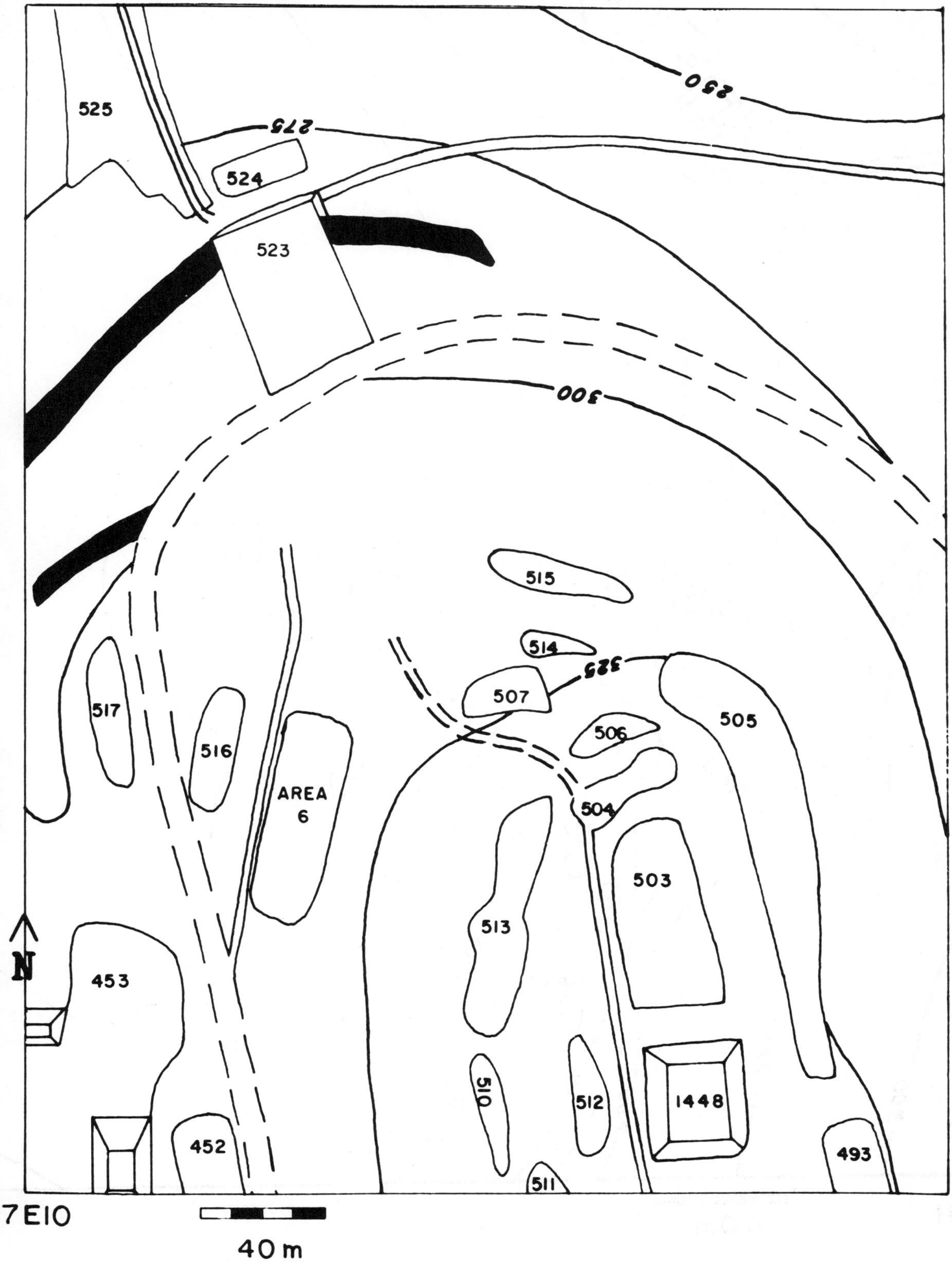

525
275
250
524
523
300
515
514
325
507
506
505
517
516
AREA 6
504
503
513
N
453
510
512
1448
452
511
493
40 m

N7E10

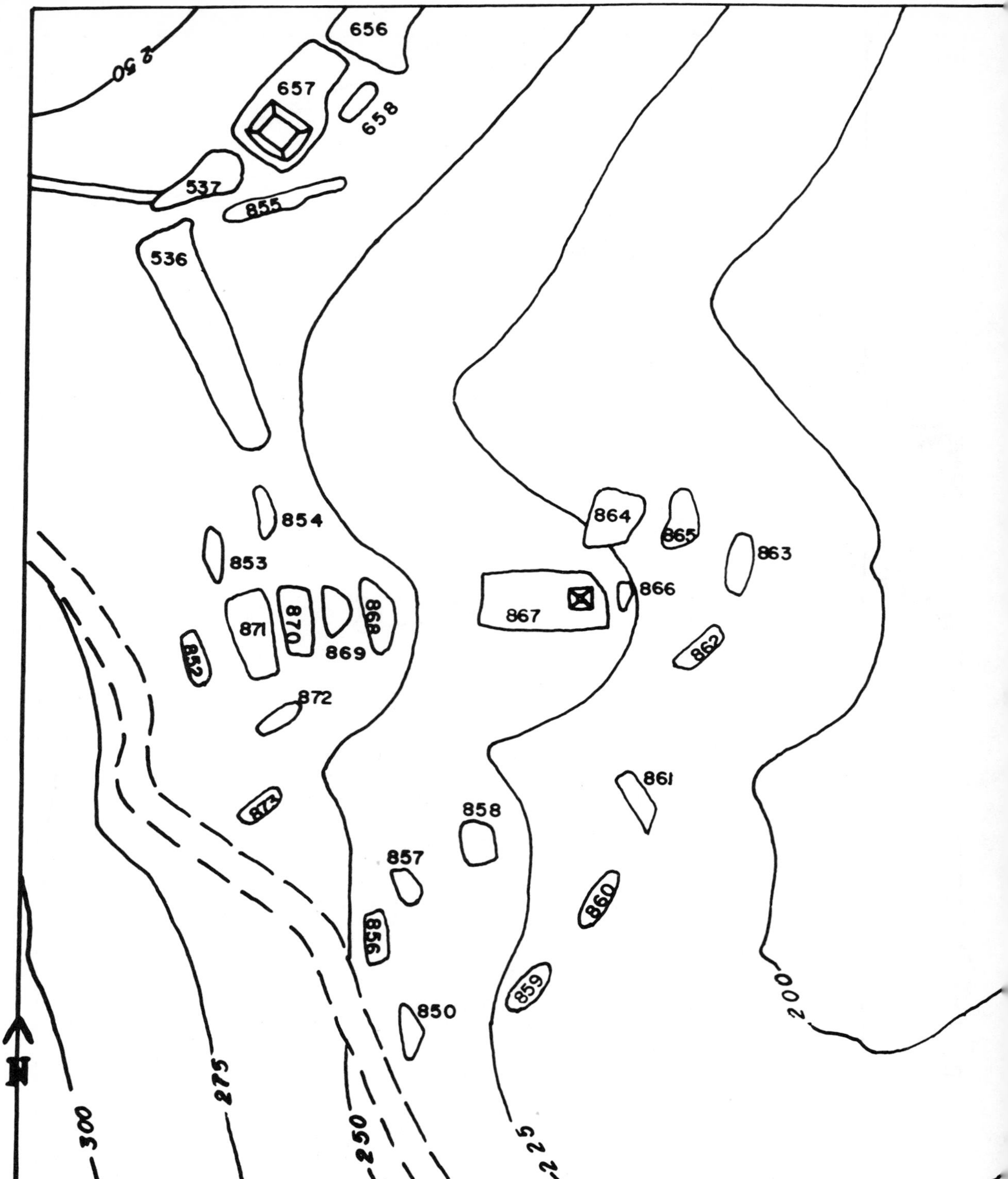
656
657
658
250
537
855
536
854
853
871
870
869
868
852
872
873
864
865
863
866
867
862
861
858
857
856
860
859
850
200
300
275
250
225
N

N7E11

40m

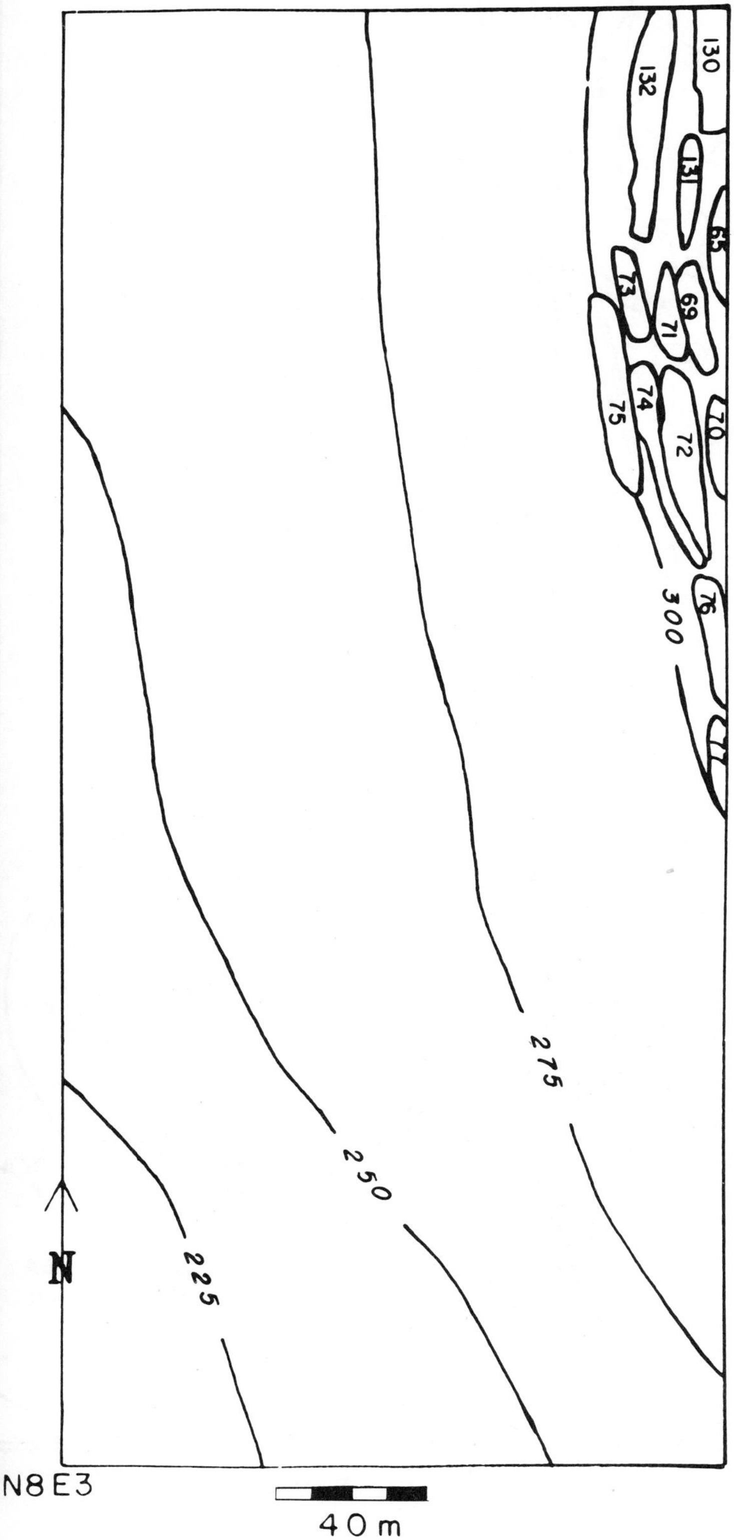

130
132
131
65
73
69
71
75
74
72
70
76
300
275
250
225
N
N8E3
40 m

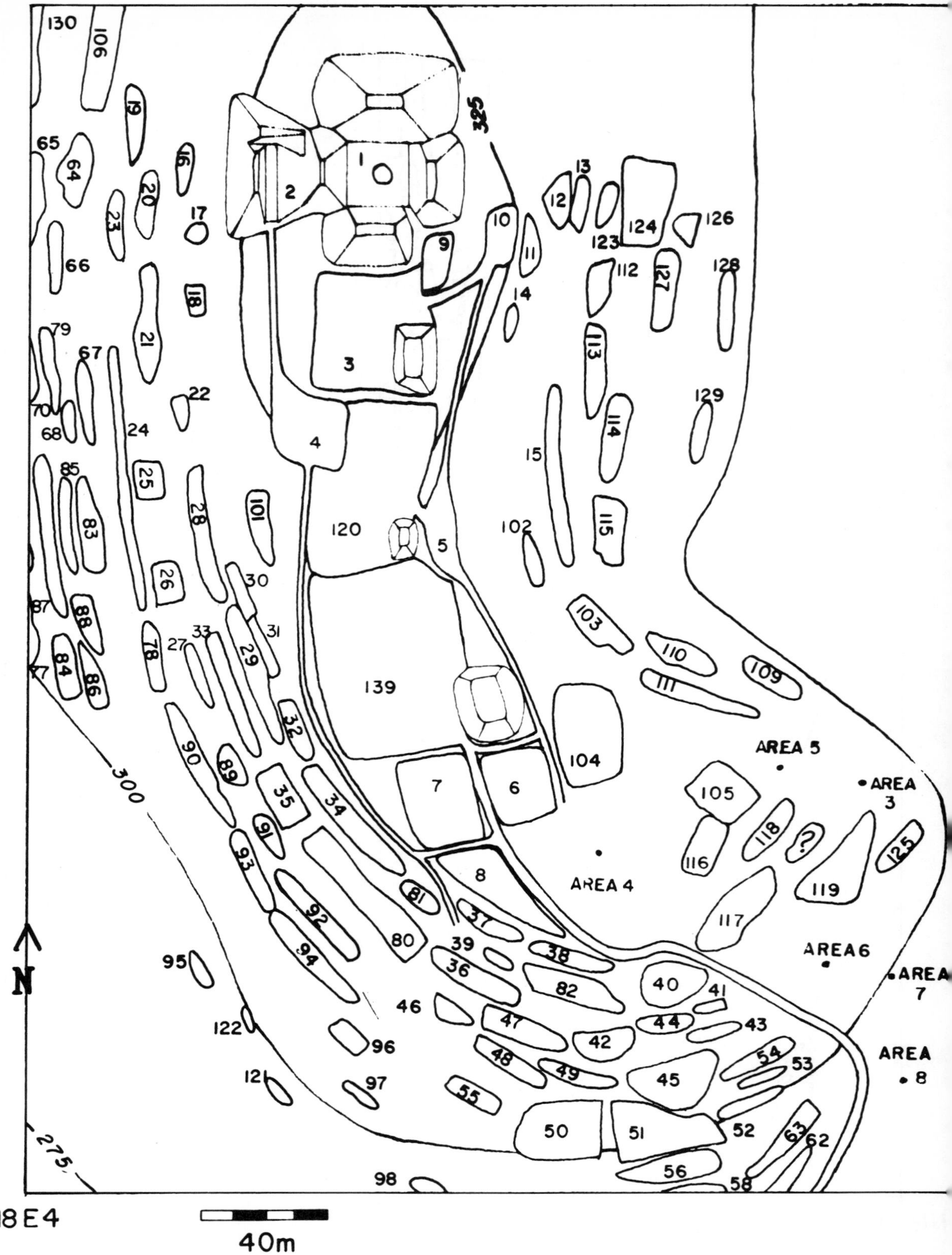

AREA 3
AREA 4
AREA 5
AREA 6
AREA 7
AREA 8
395
300
275
N
N8 E4
40m

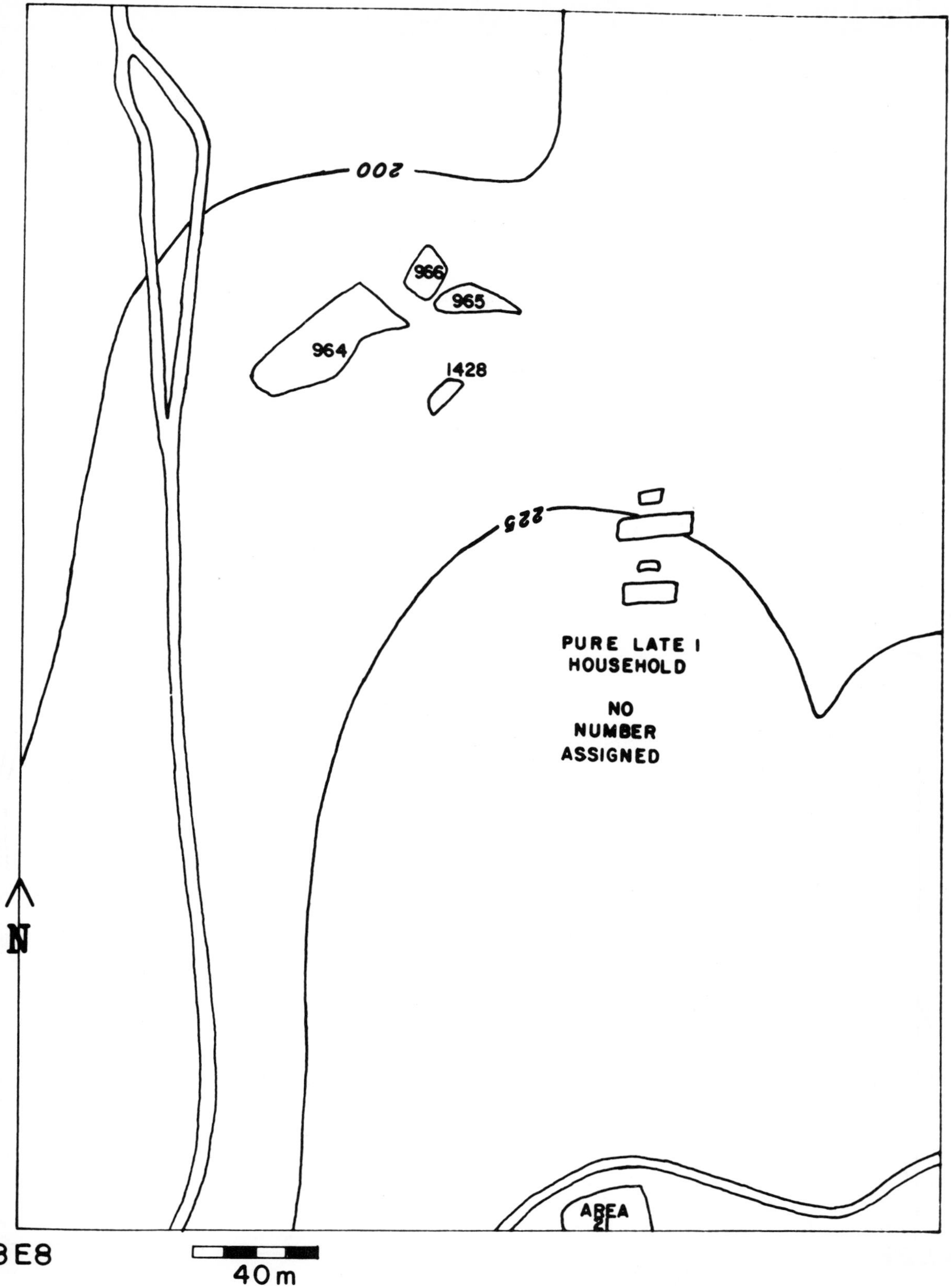
200
966
965
964
1428
225
PURE LATE I
HOUSEHOLD
NO
NUMBER
ASSIGNED
AREA
21
N
40m

N8E8

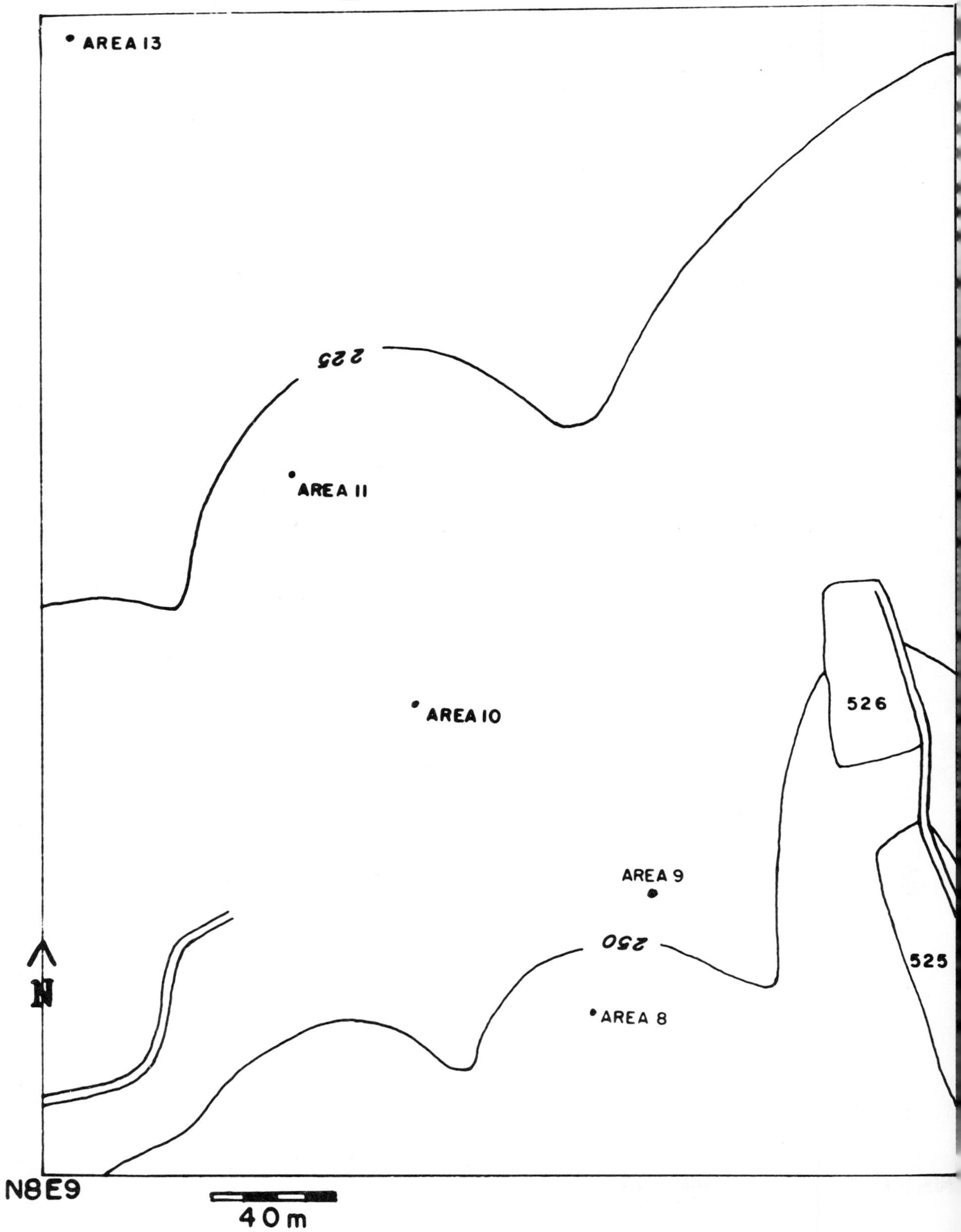

AREA 13
225
AREA 11
AREA 10
526
AREA 9
250
AREA 8
525
N
N8E9
40 m

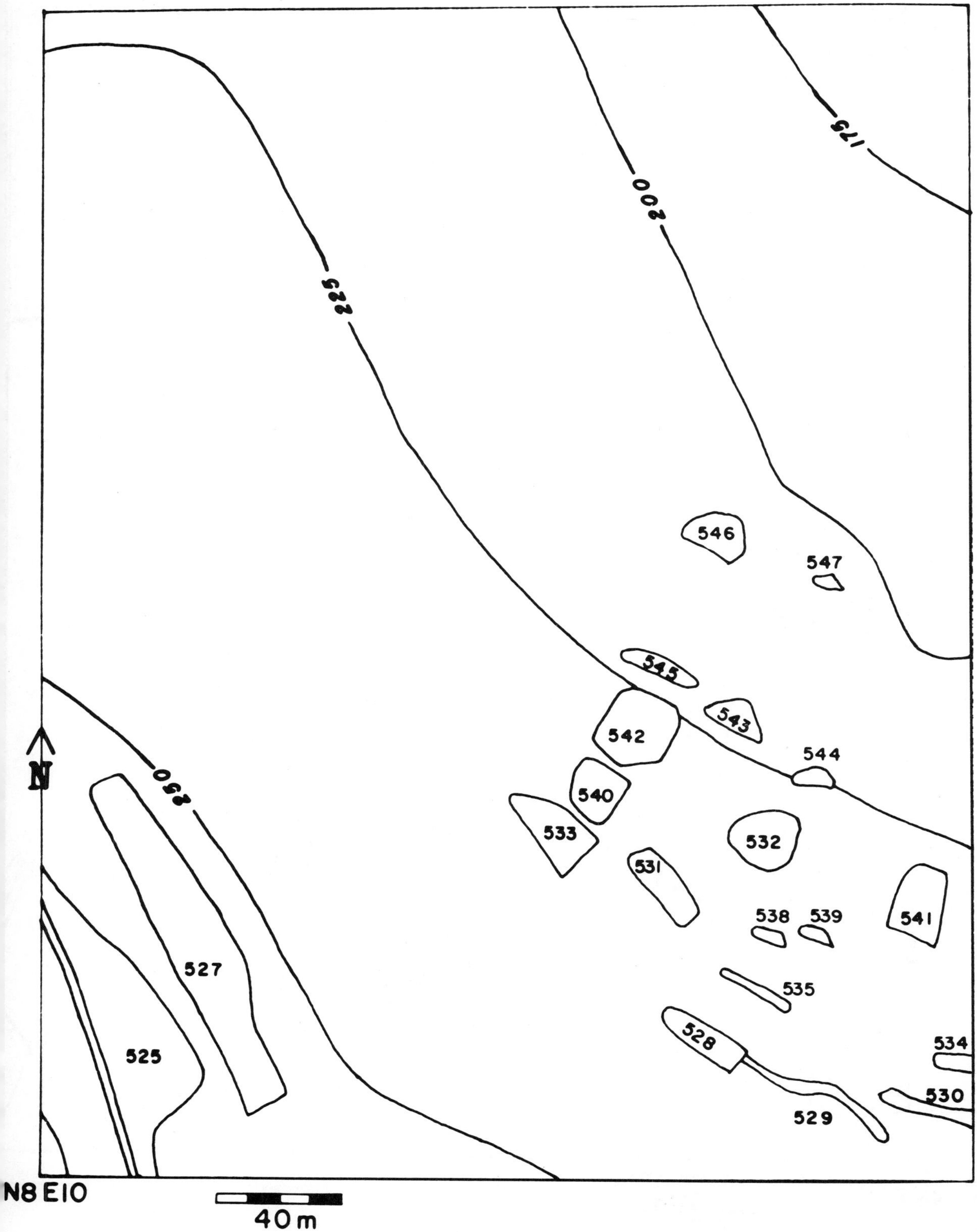

175
200
225
250
N
546
547
545
542
543
544
540
533
532
531
538
539
541
527
535
528
534
525
530
529
N8 E10
40 m

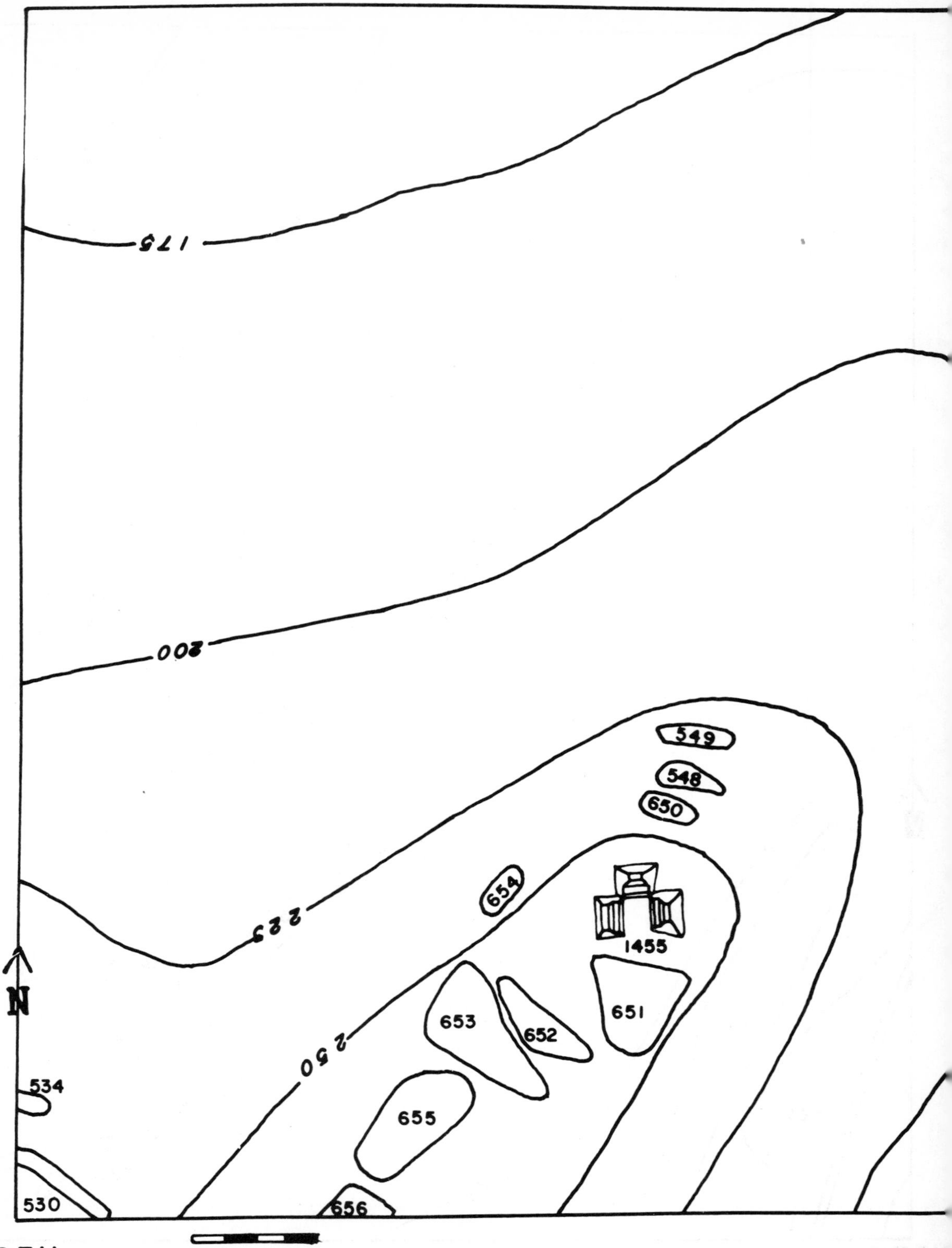
175
200
225
250
549
548
650
654
1455
651
652
653
655
656
534
530
N
40m

N8E11

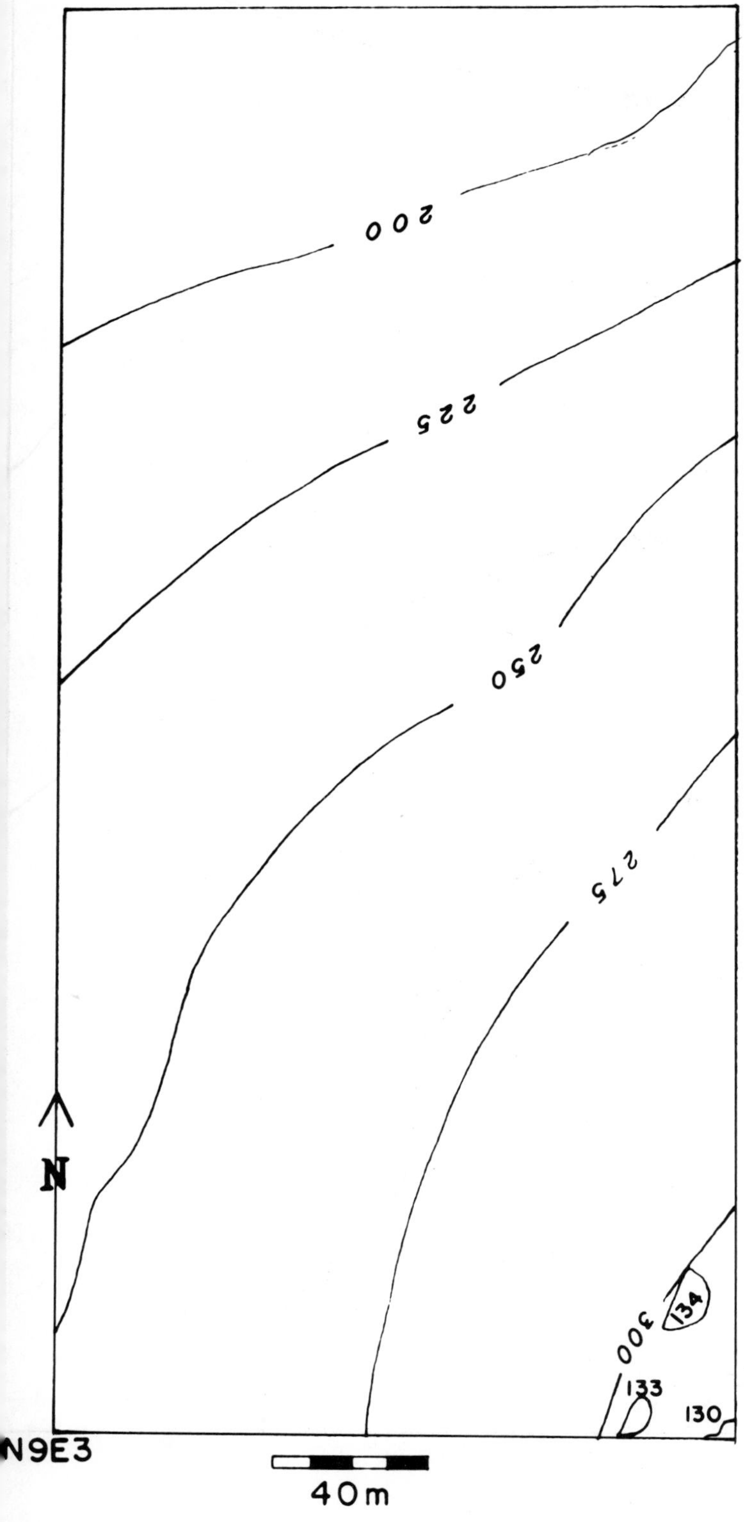
200
225
250
275
300
134
133
130
N
N9E3
40m

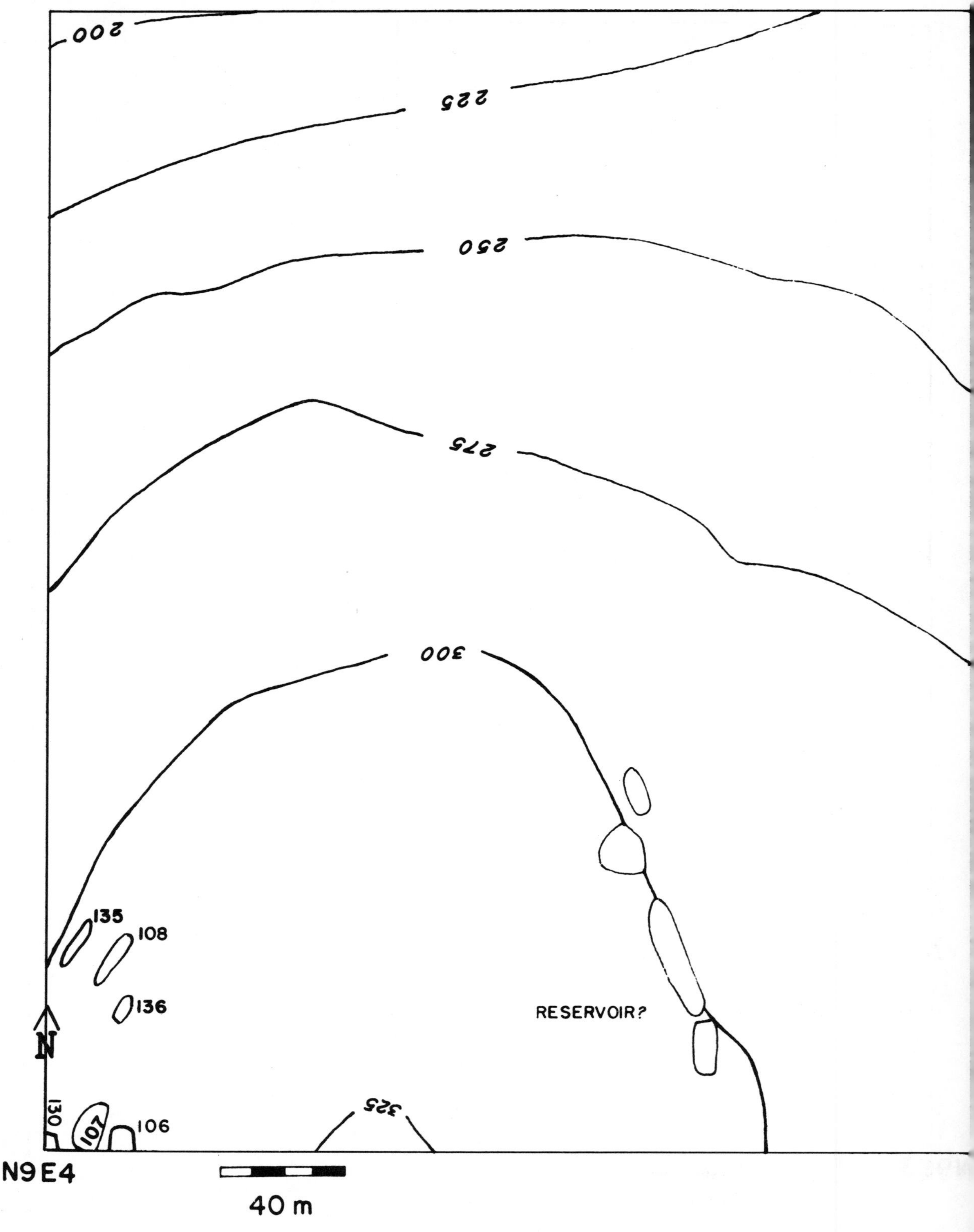
200
225
250
275
300
325
135
108
136
130
107
106
RESERVOIR?
N
N9 E4
40 m

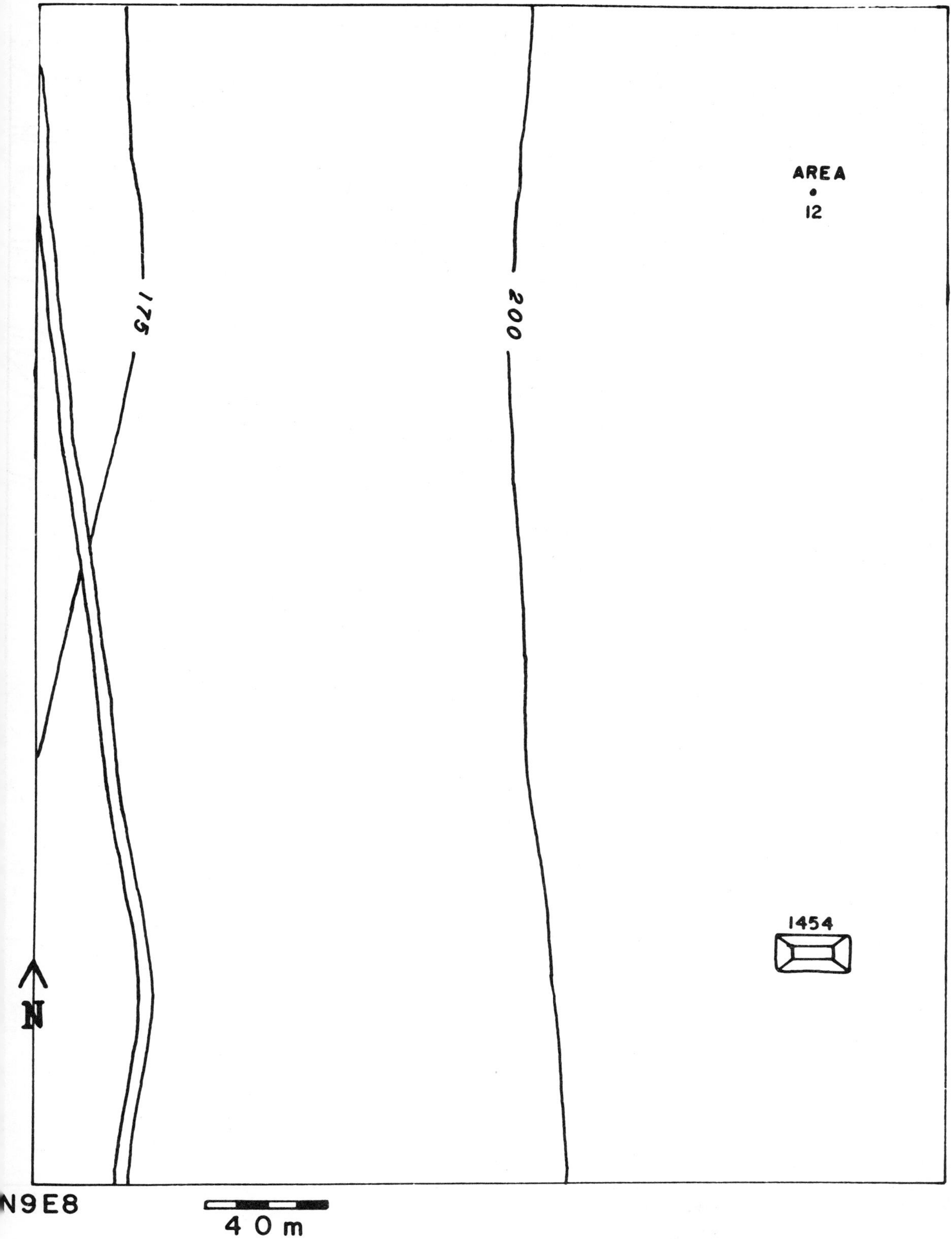

AREA
12
175
200
1454
N
N9E8
40m

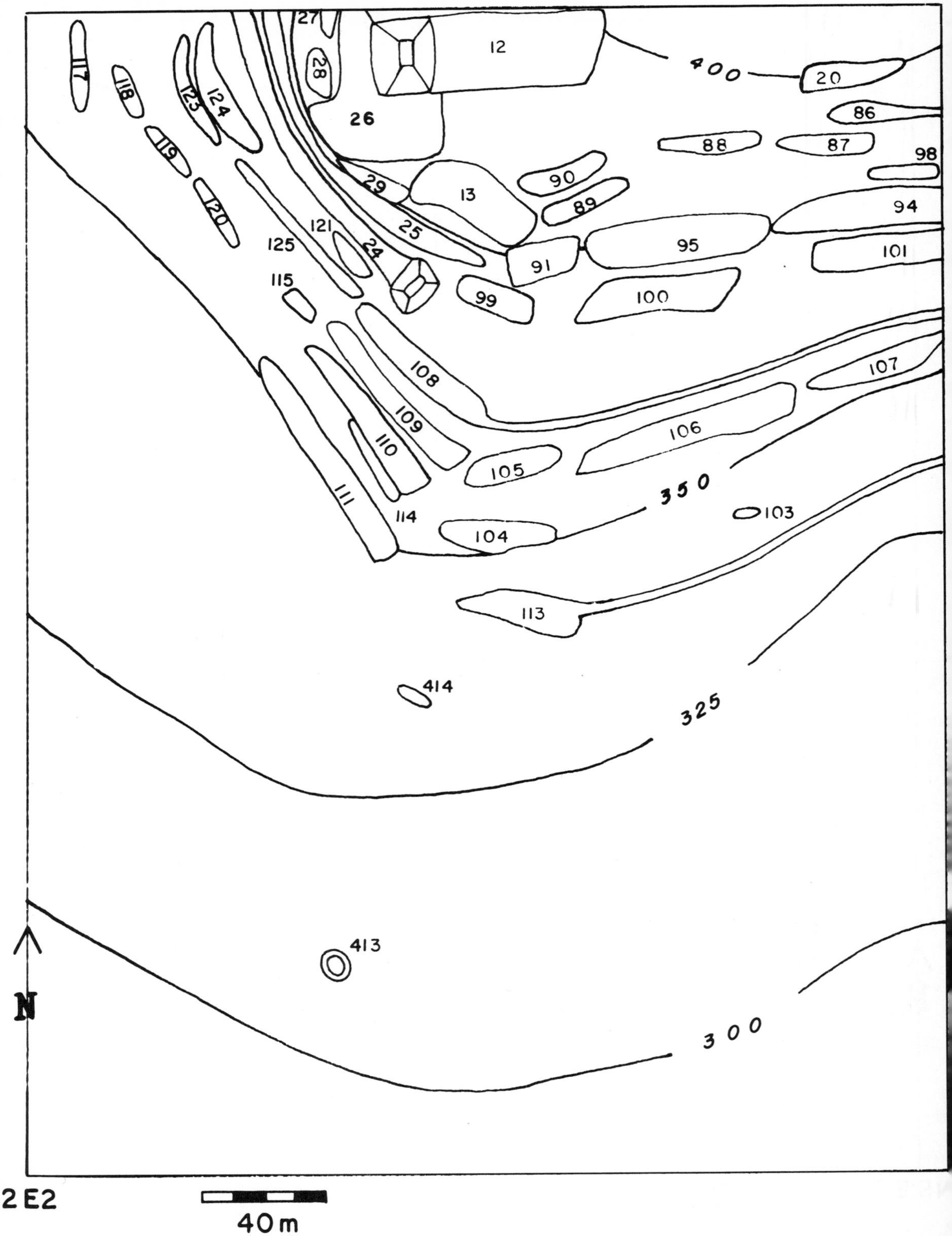

12
20
86
88
87
98
90
89
94
13
28
27
26
29
25
95
101
91
24
121
125
115
99
100
7
118
123
124
119
120
108
107
106
109
110
105
111
114
104
350
103
113
414
325
413
N
300
400
40m

N12 E2

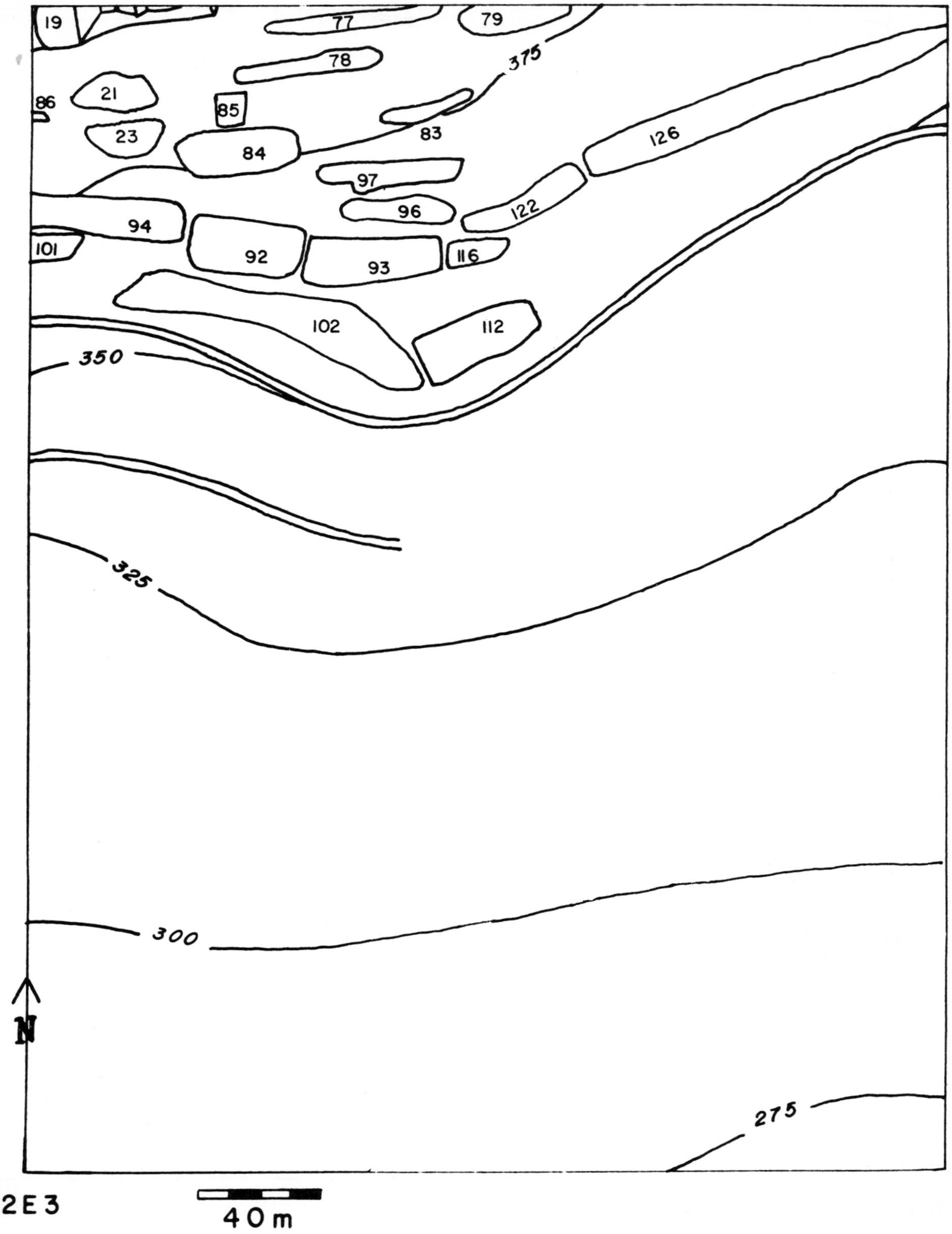

19
77
79
78
375
21
86
85
23
83
84
126
97
96
122
94
101
92
93
116
102
112
350
325
300
N
275

N12E3

40 m

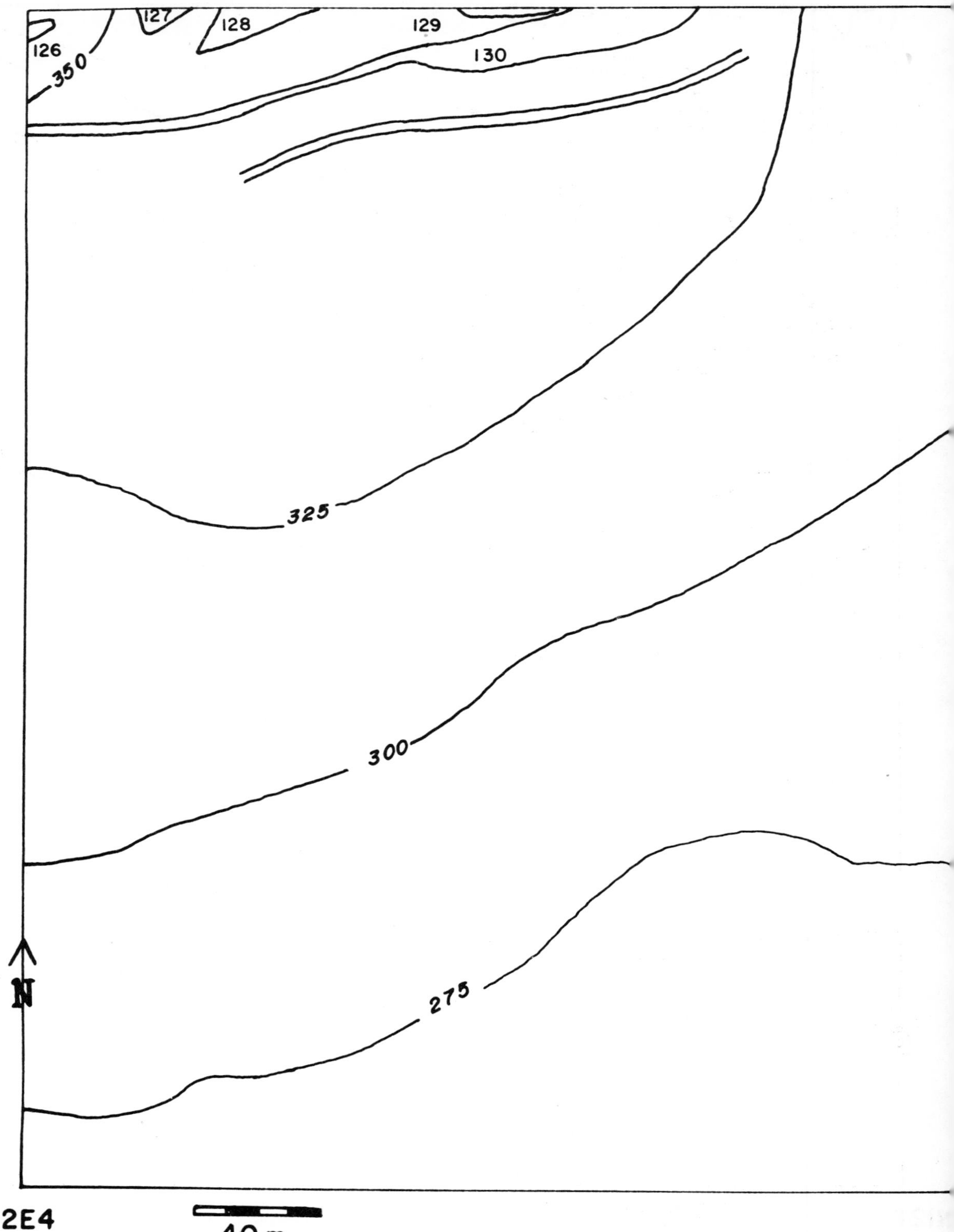
126
127
128
129
130
350
325
300
275
N
N12E4
40 m

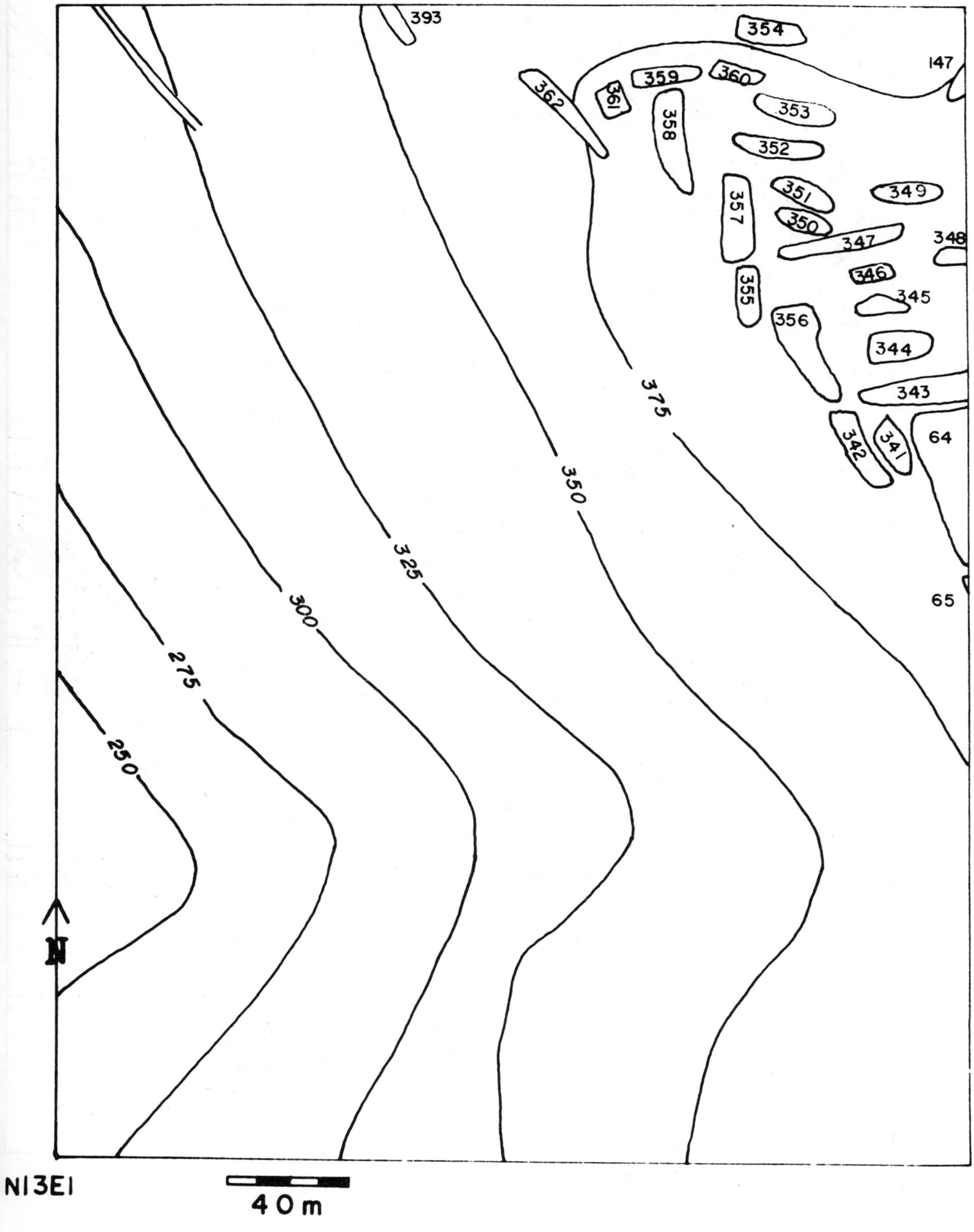

393
354
147
359
360
362
361
353
358
352
351
349
357
350
347
348
346
355
345
356
344
375
343
342
341
64
350
325
65
300
275
250
N
N13E1
40m

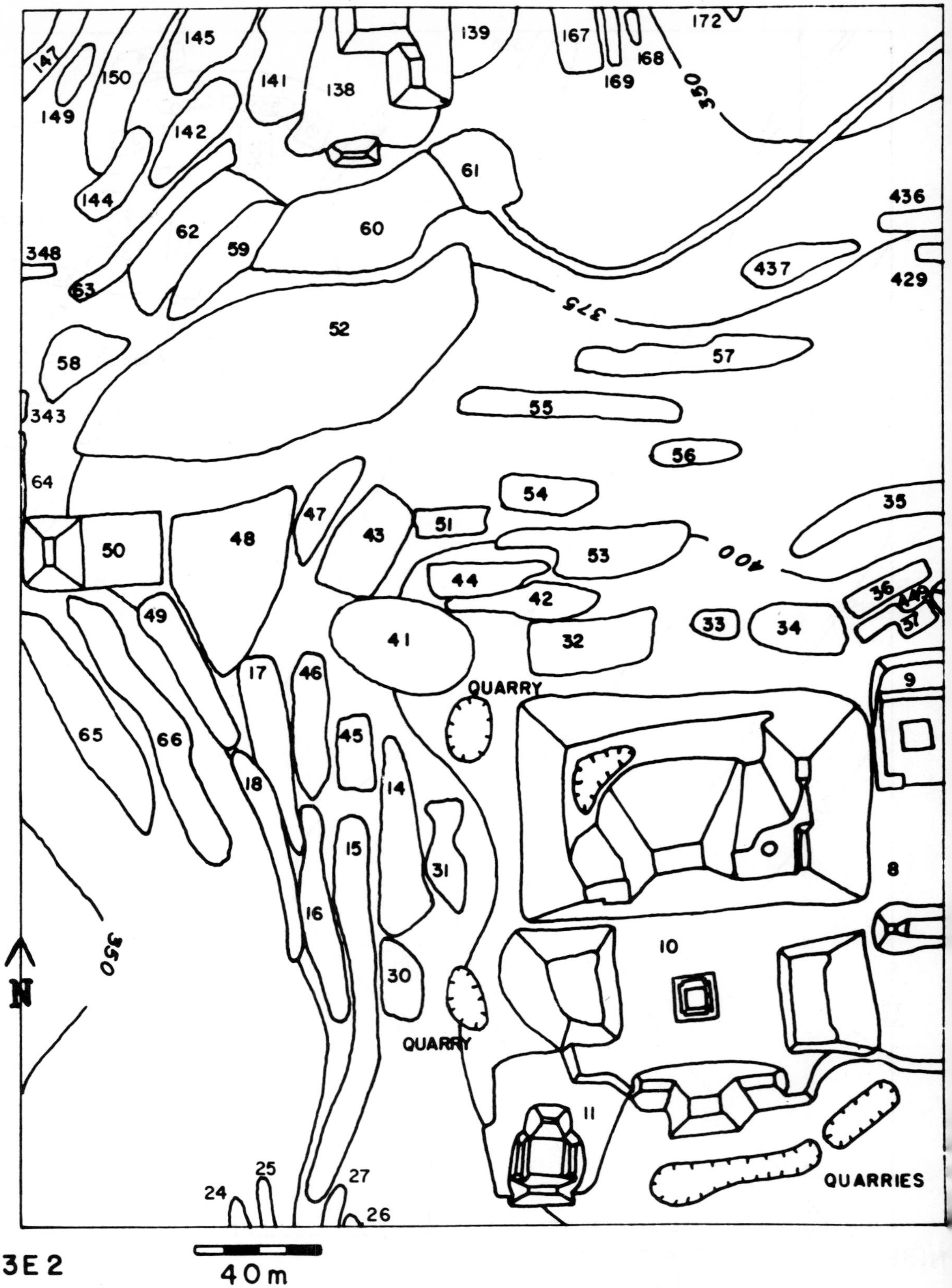
147
145
139
167
172
168
150
141
138
169
350
149
142
61
144
436
62
60
59
348
437
429
63
375
52
57
58
55
343
56
64
54
35
51
47
43
48
50
53
400
44
36
42
49
33
34
32
41
9
QUARRY
17
46
65
66
45
18
14
15
31
8
16
10
N
350
30
QUARRY
11
25
27
24
26
QUARRIES
40m

N13E2

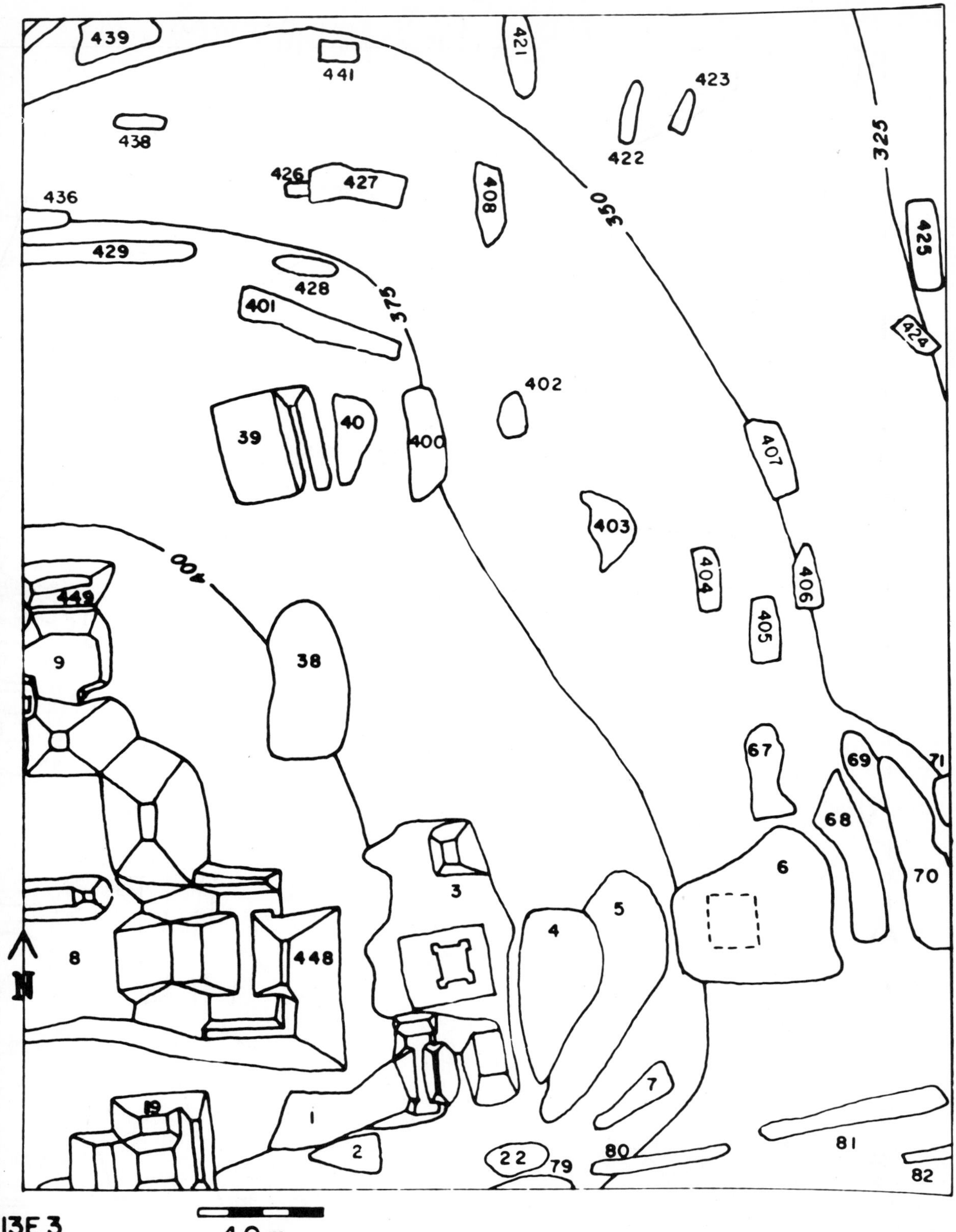
439
441
421
423
438
422
325
426
427
436
408
350
425
429
428
401
375
424
402
39
40
400
407
403
404
406
400
449
405
9
38
67
69
71
68
6
3
70
5
4
8
448
7
1
19
2
22
79
80
81
82

N13E3

40 m

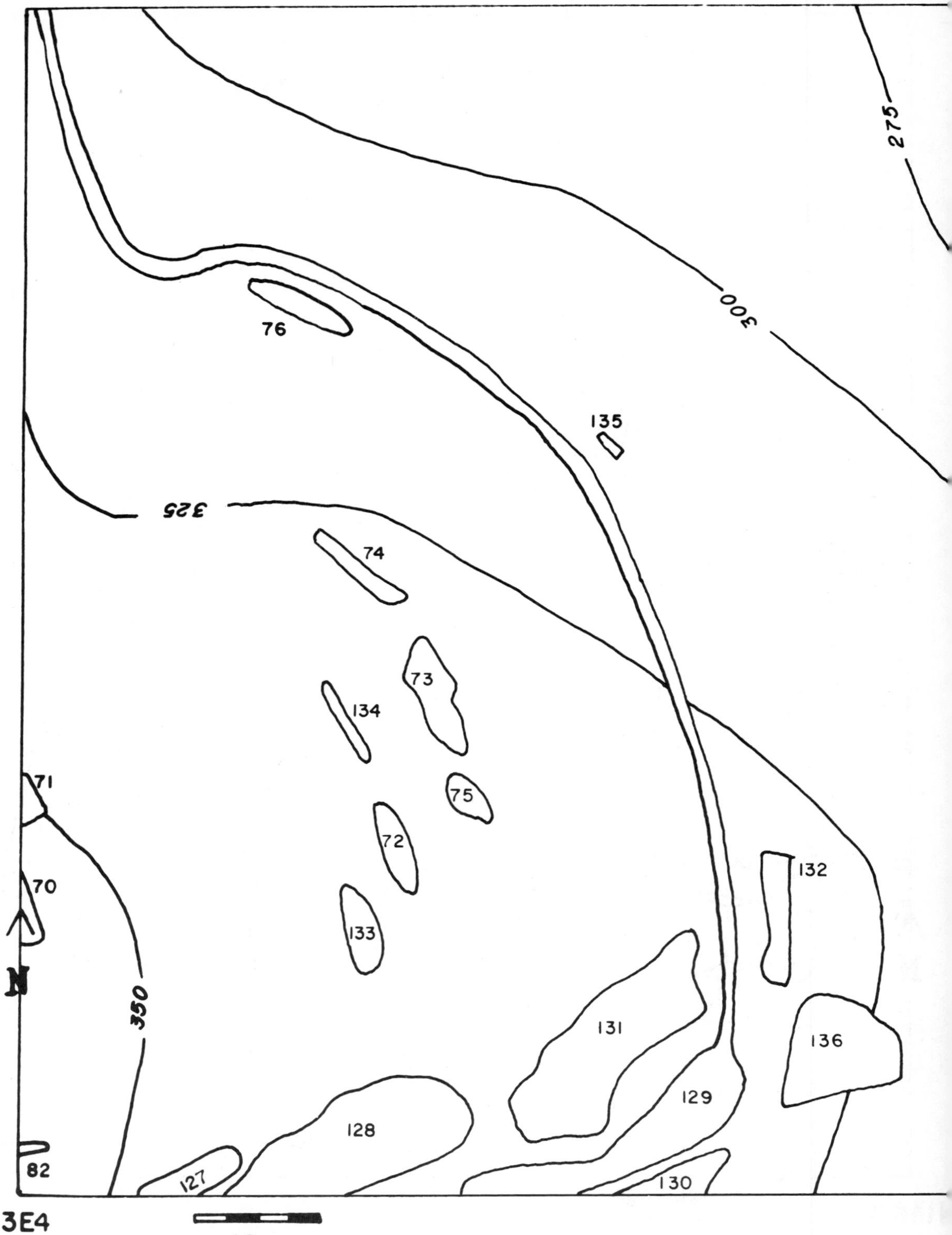

275
300
325
350
76
135
74
73
134
75
72
71
70
133
132
131
136
129
128
127
130
82
N

N13E4

40 m

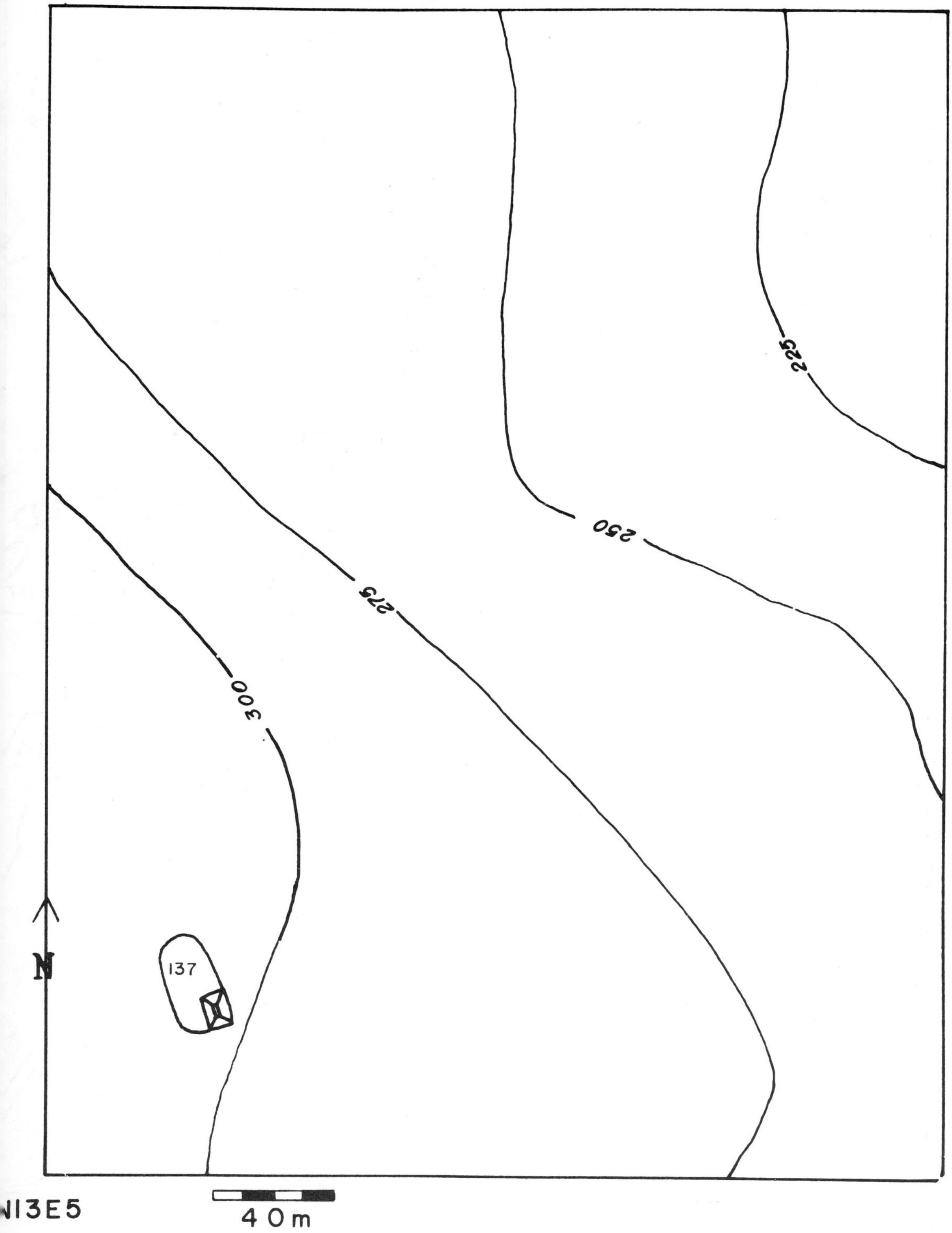

300
275
250
225
137
N
40m
N13E5

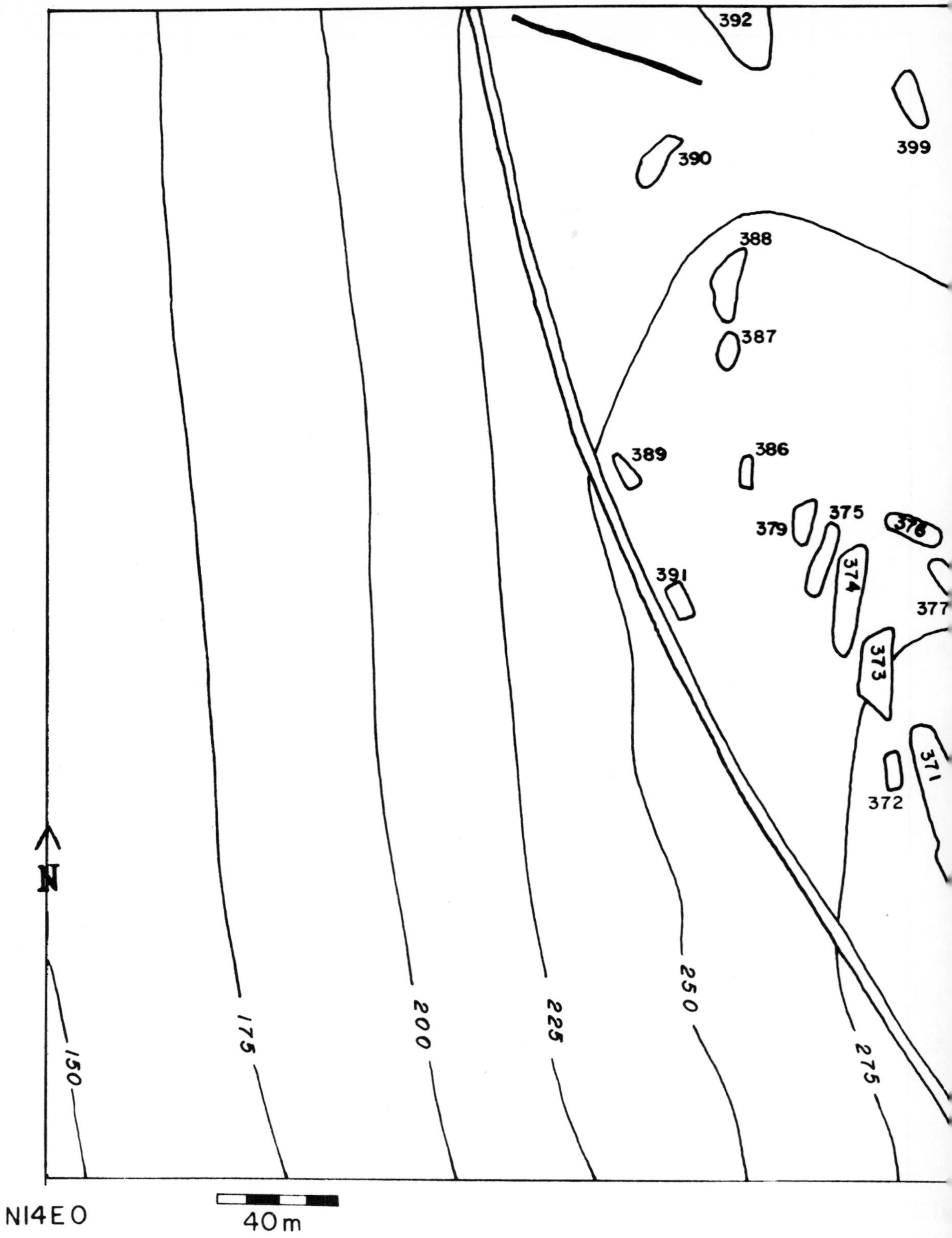
392
399
390
388
387
389
386
375
379
376
374
391
377
373
371
372
N
150
175
200
225
250
275
N14E0
40m

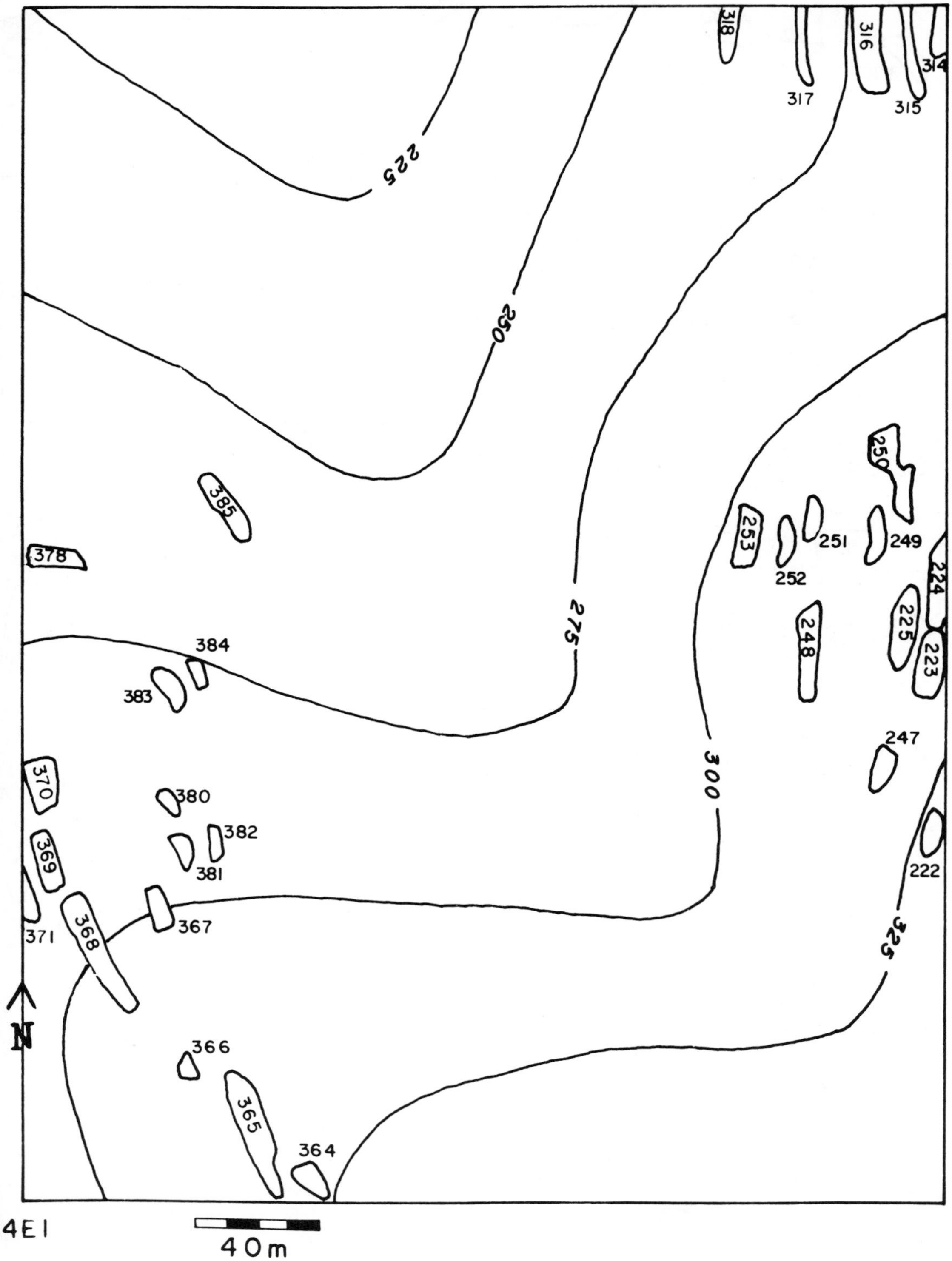
225
250
275
300
325
318
317
316
315
314
253
252
251
250
249
248
247
225
224
223
222
385
378
384
383
380
381
382
370
369
371
368
367
366
365
364
N
40m

N14E1

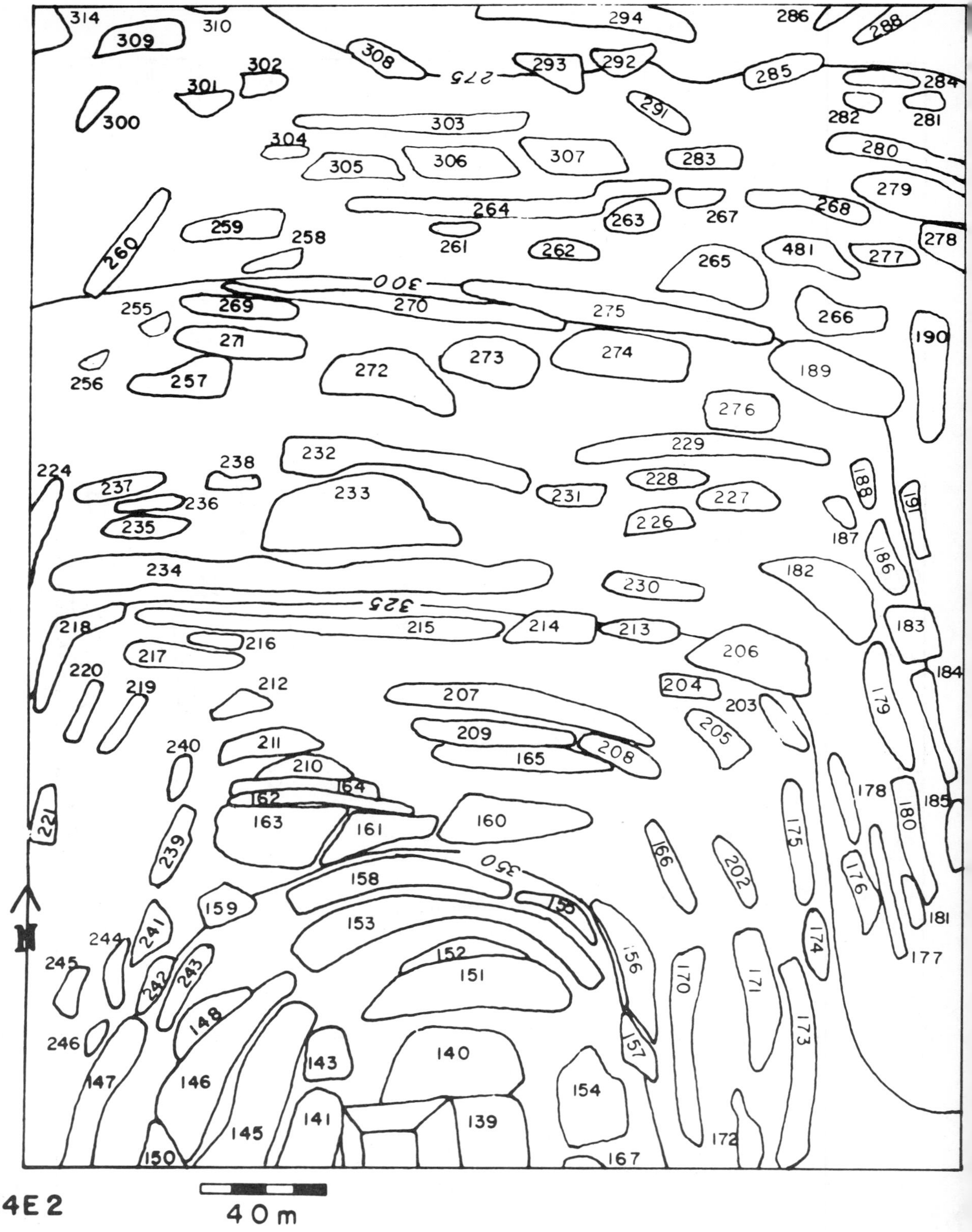

314
309
310
308
294
286
288
302
301
300
293
292
275
285
284
291
282
281
303
304
305
306
307
283
280
279
264
263
267
268
259
258
260
261
262
481
277
278
265
300
255
269
270
275
266
190
271
256
257
272
273
274
189
276
232
229
224
238
237
236
235
233
231
228
227
226
188
191
187
186
234
182
230
325
218
215
214
213
183
206
216
217
184
220
219
212
207
204
203
179
205
209
208
165
240
211
210
164
162
163
161
160
178
180
175
185
221
239
166
202
176
350
158
155
159
153
181
174
244
241
177
245
152
151
156
170
171
242
243
173
148
157
246
140
143
147
146
154
141
139
145
172
167
150
N
40 m

N14E2

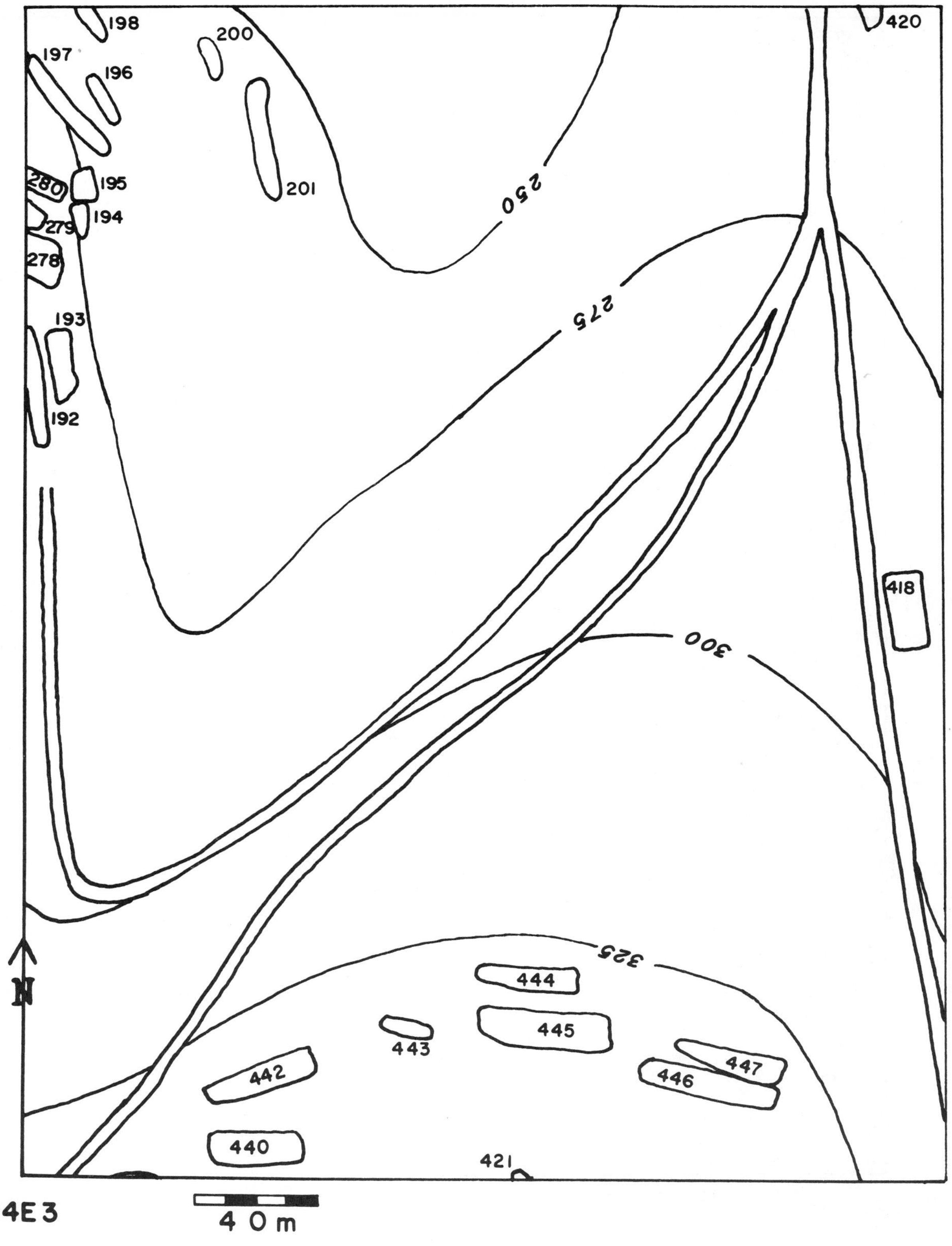

198
200
420
197
196
280
195
194
279
278
201
250
275
193
192
418
300
325
N
444
445
443
442
447
446
440
421
40 m

N14E3

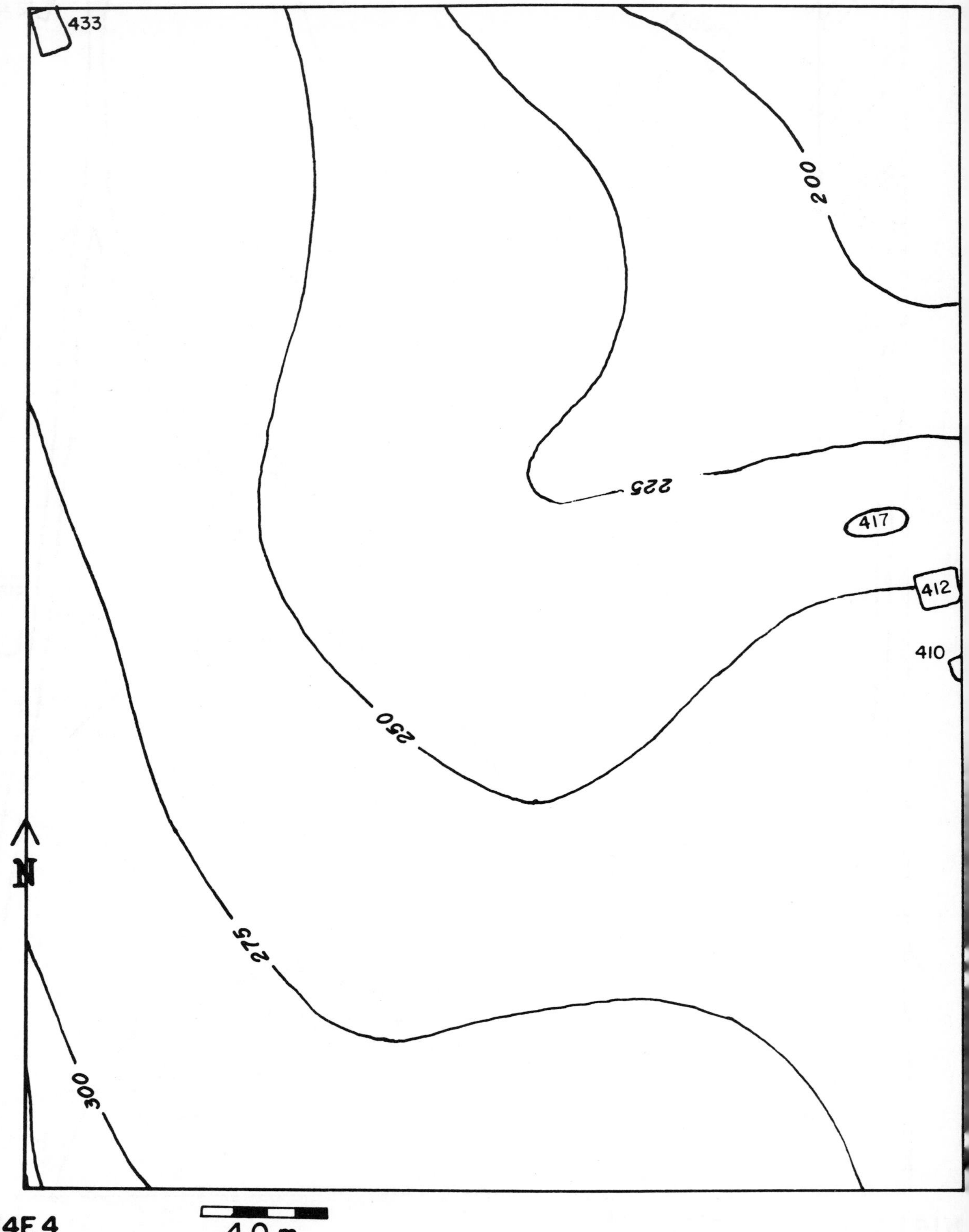

N 14E 4

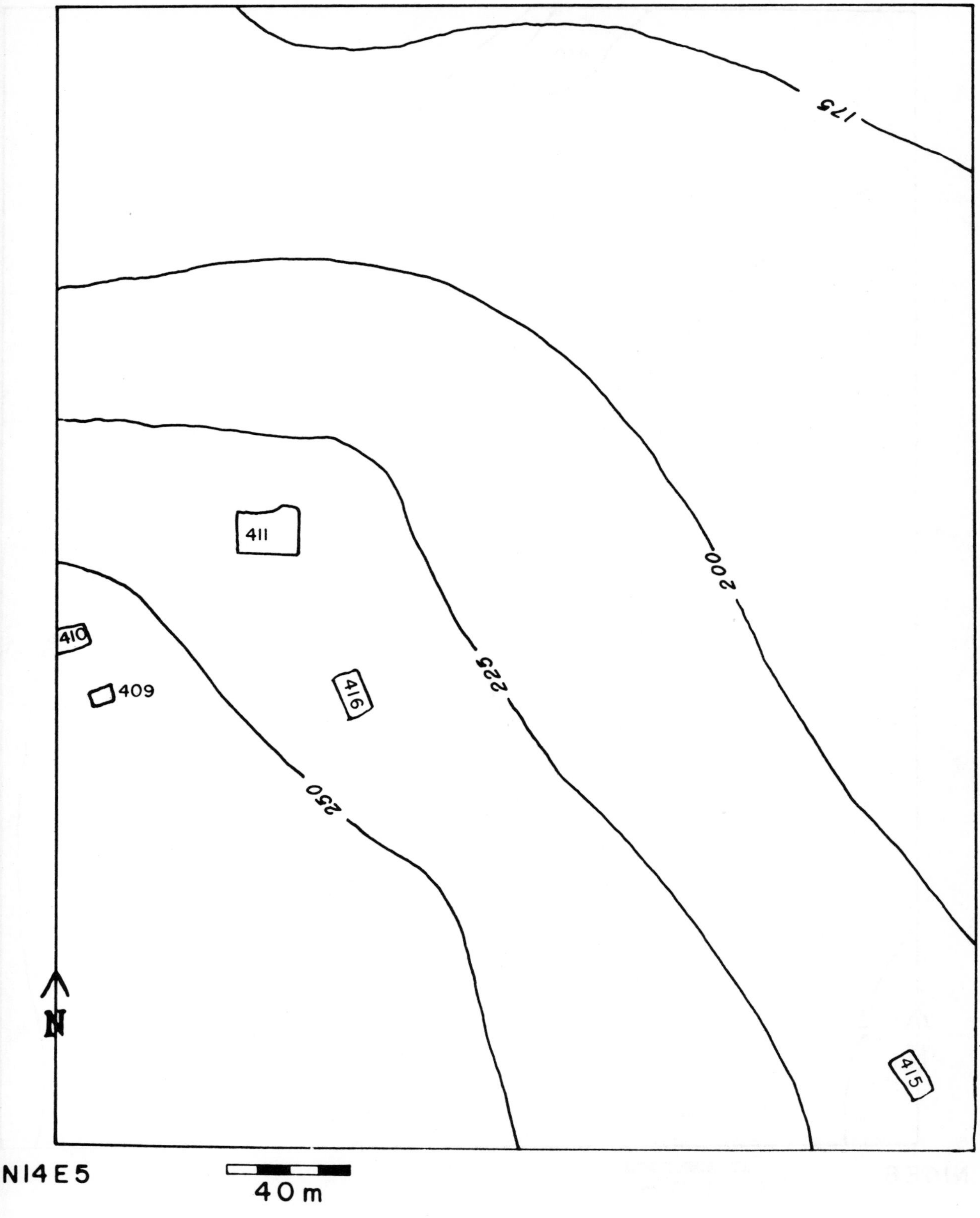

175
200
225
250
411
410
409
416
415
N
N14E5
40 m

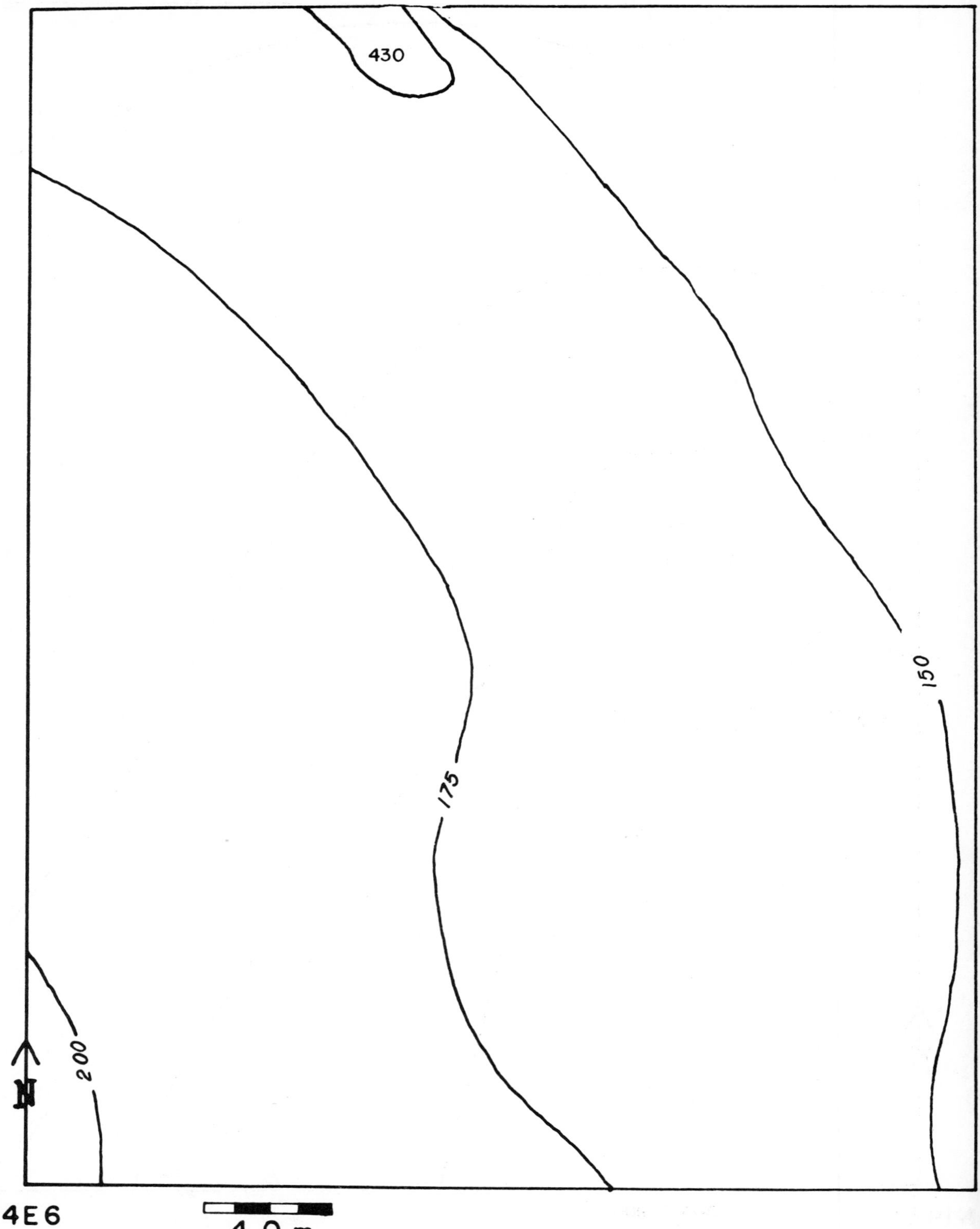

N14E6

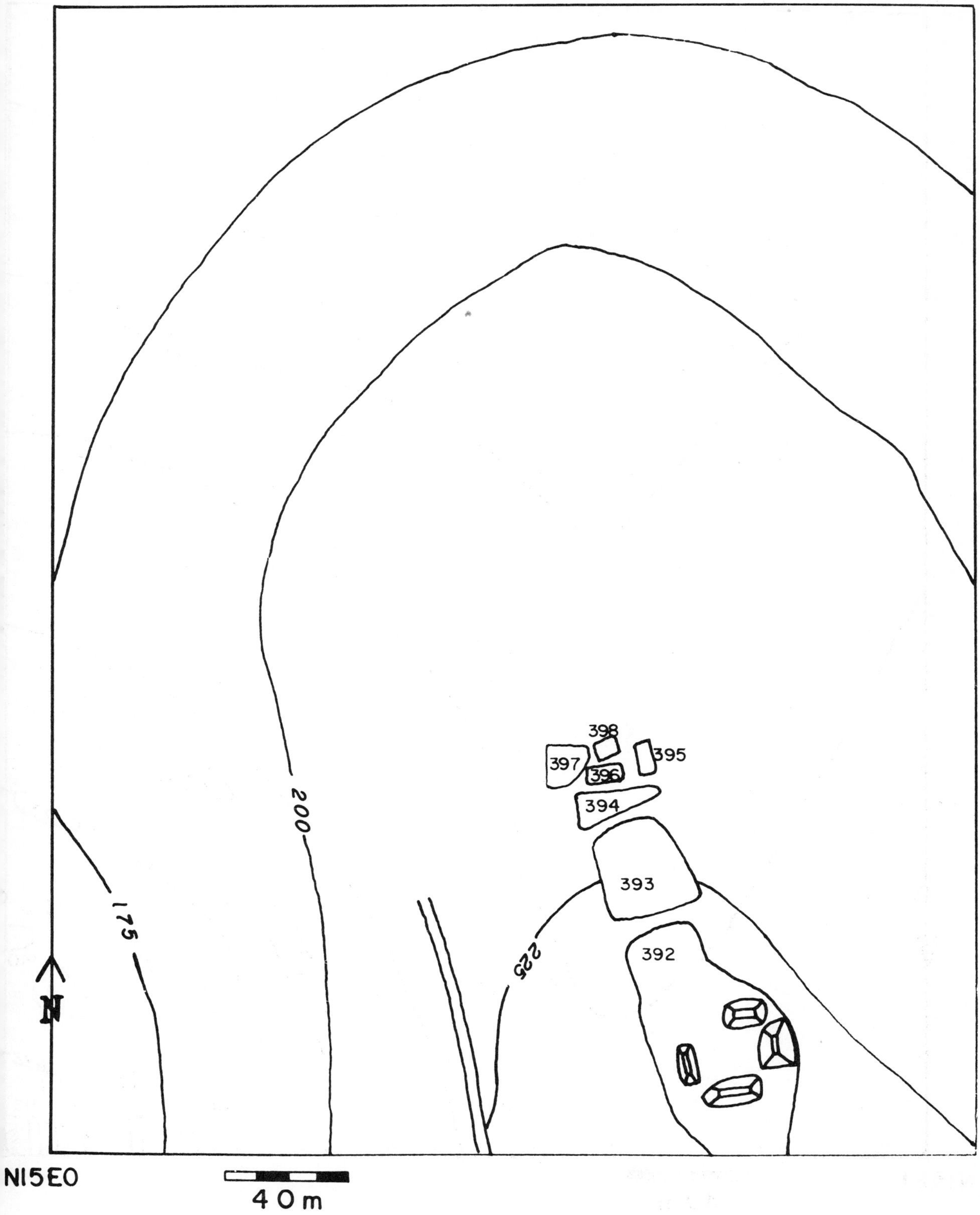

398
397
395
396
394
393
392
175
200
225
N
N15E0
40m

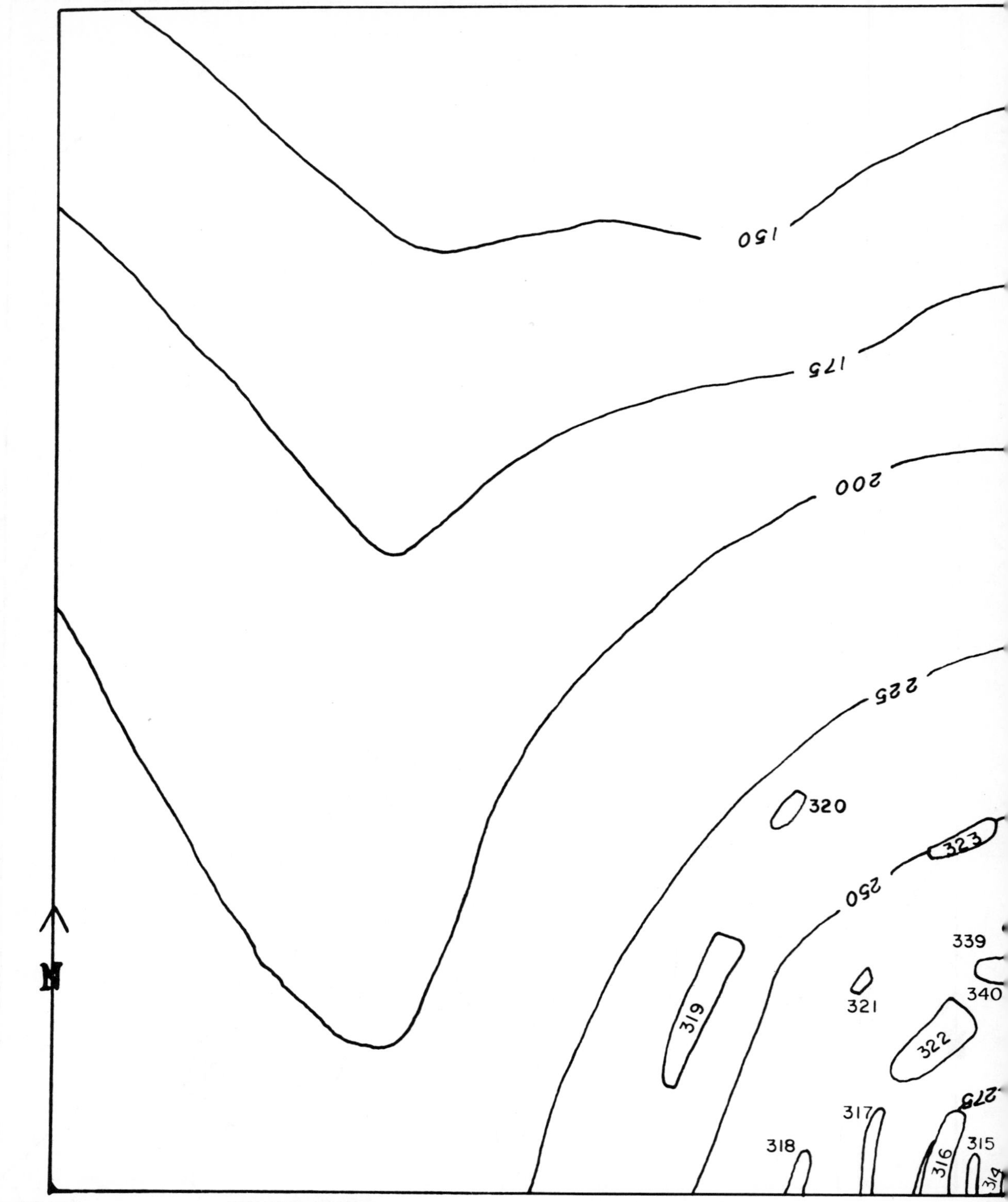
150
175
200
225
250
275
320
323
339
340
321
322
319
317
318
316
315
314
N
N15E1
40 m

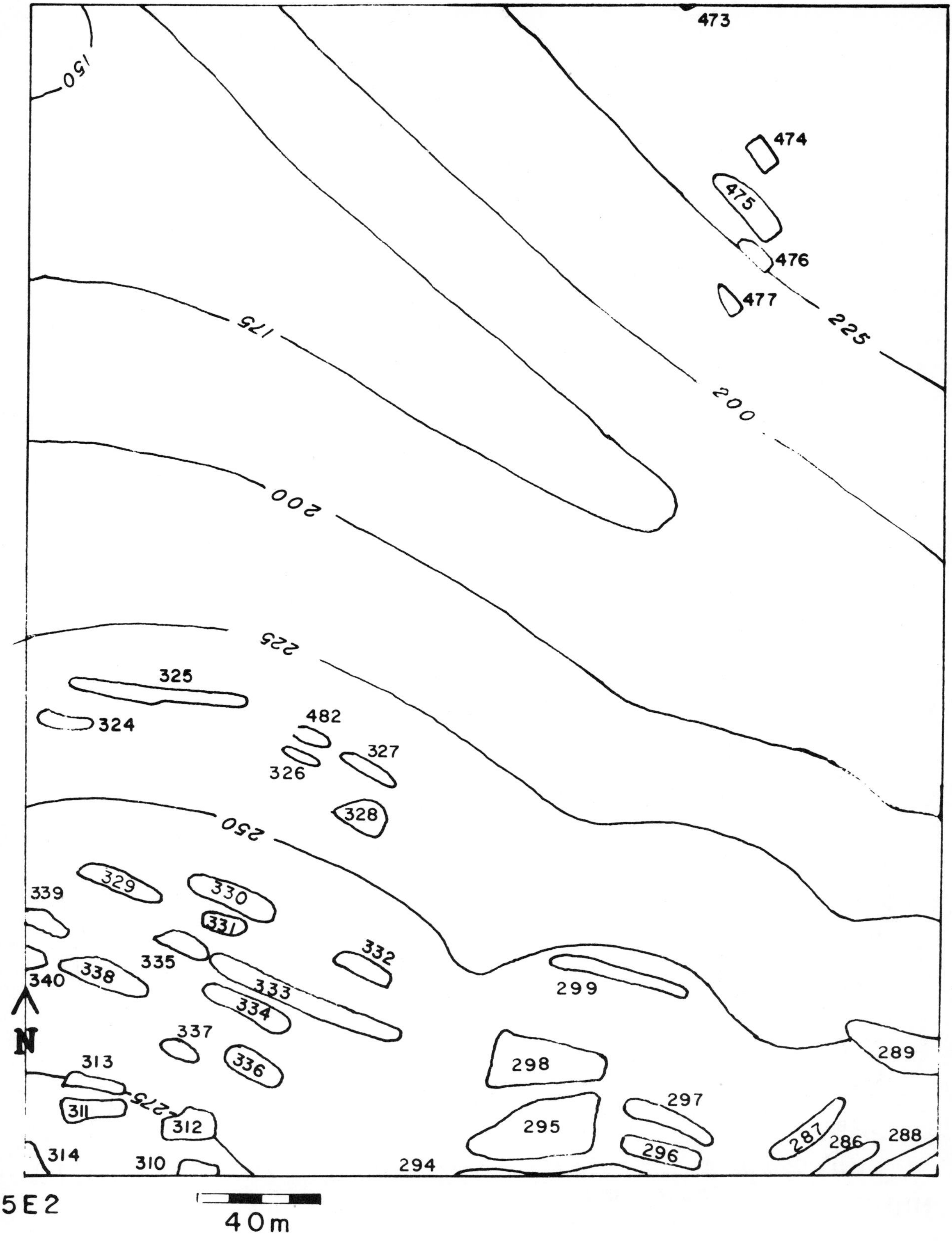
150
175
200
225
200
225
250
275
473
474
475
476
477
325
324
482
327
326
328
329
330
331
339
332
335
338
340
333
334
299
337
336
298
289
313
311
312
297
295
287
286
288
296
314
310
294
N
40m

N15E2

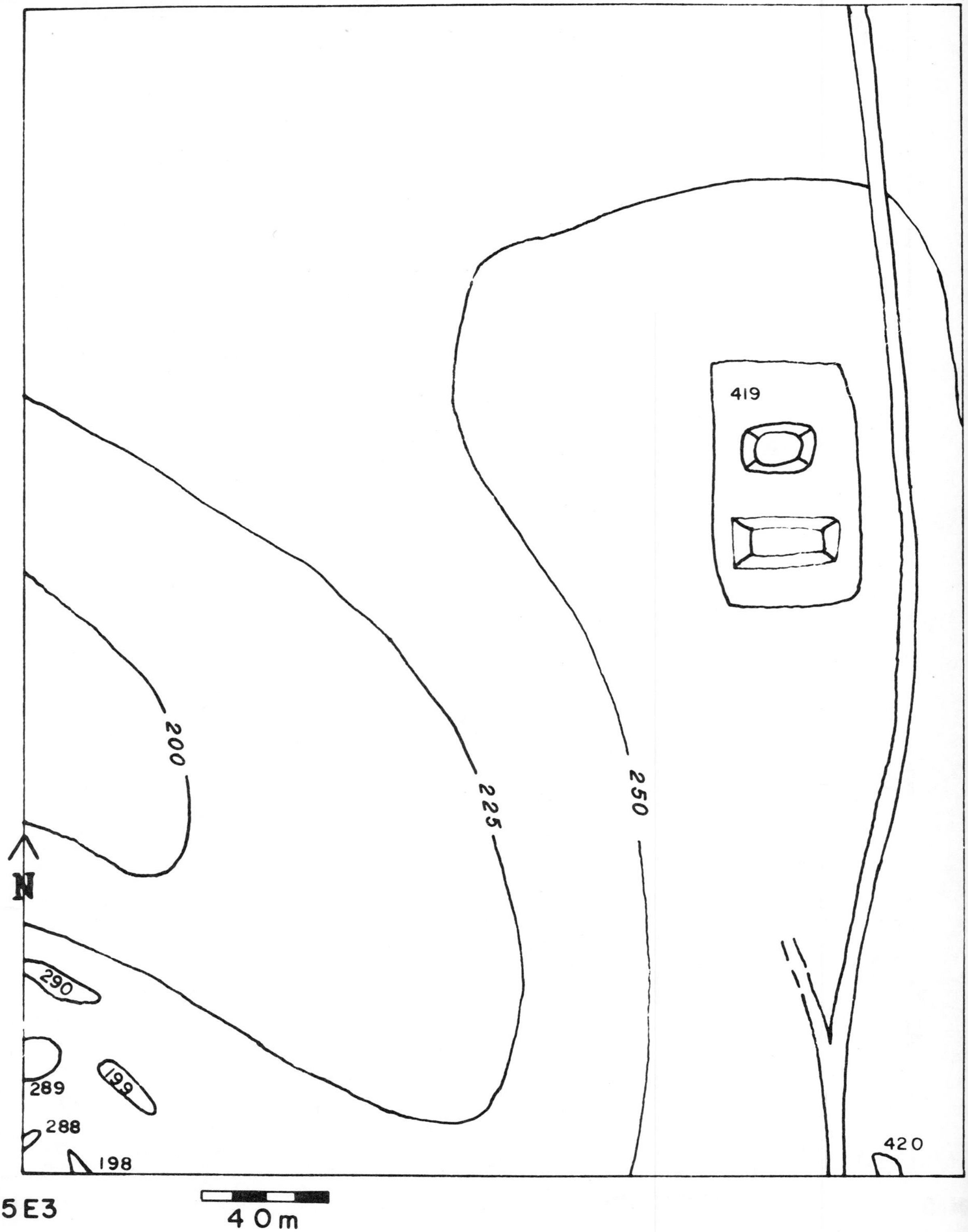

N15E3

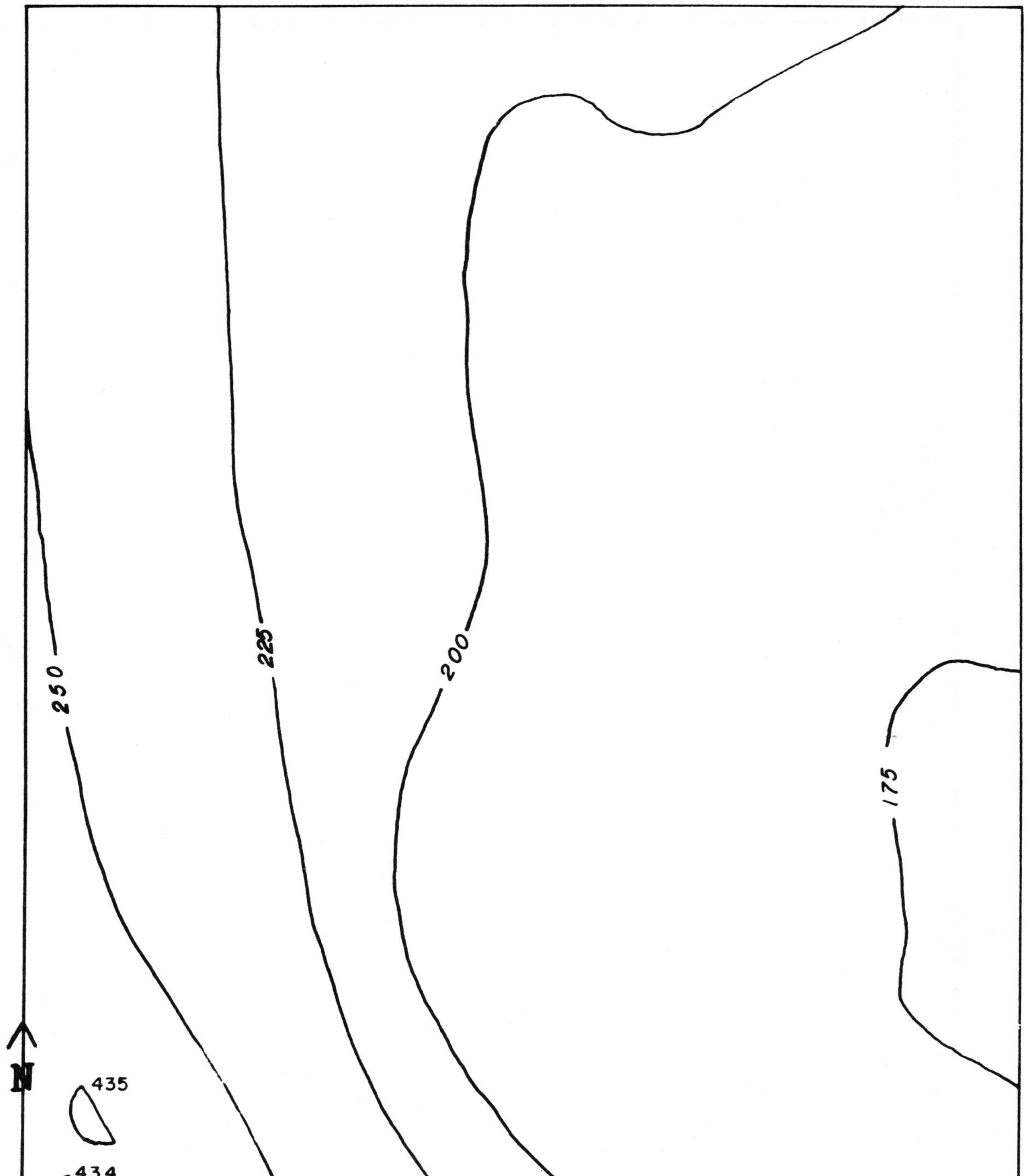

N15E4

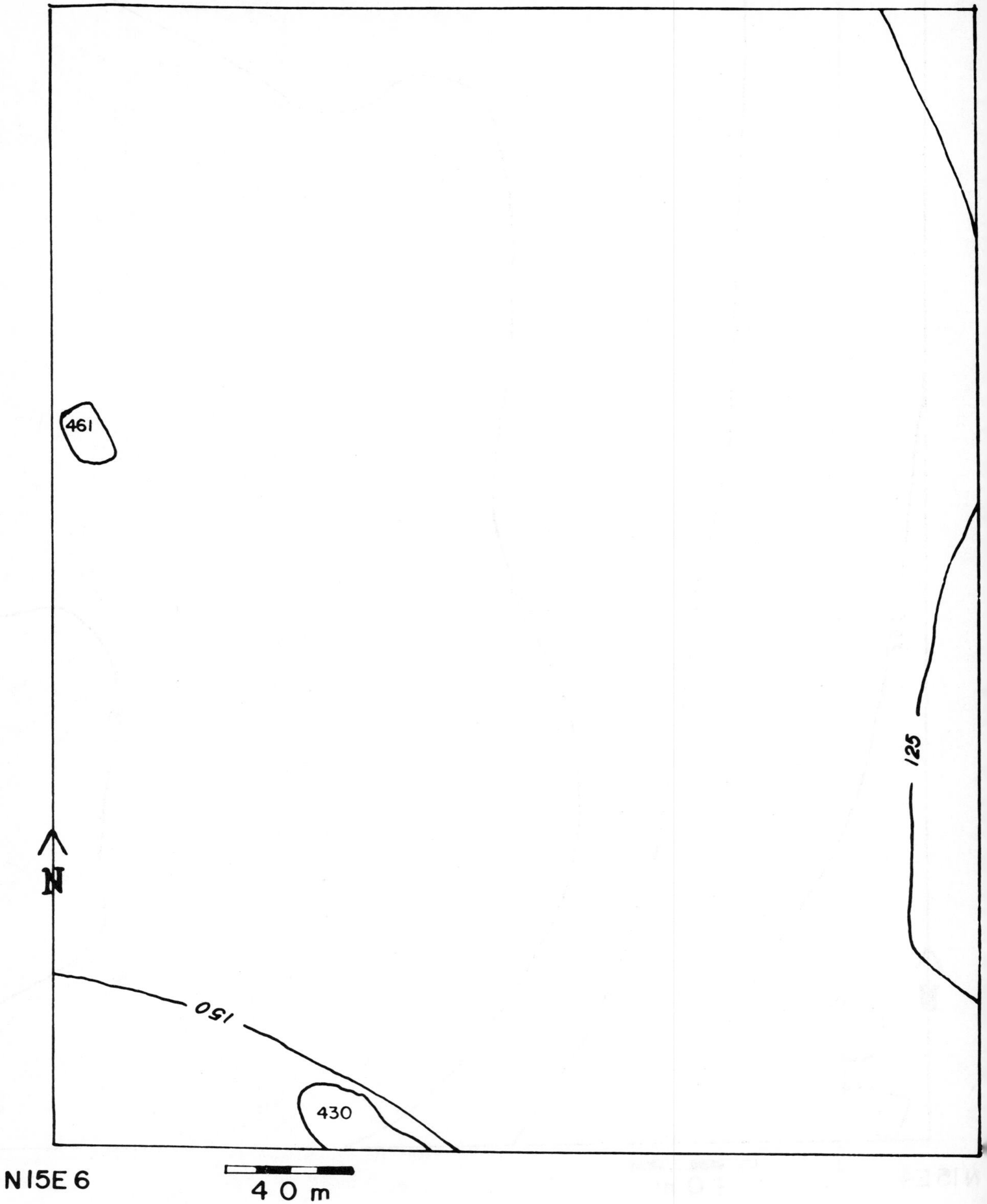
461
N
150
430
125
N15E6
4 0 m

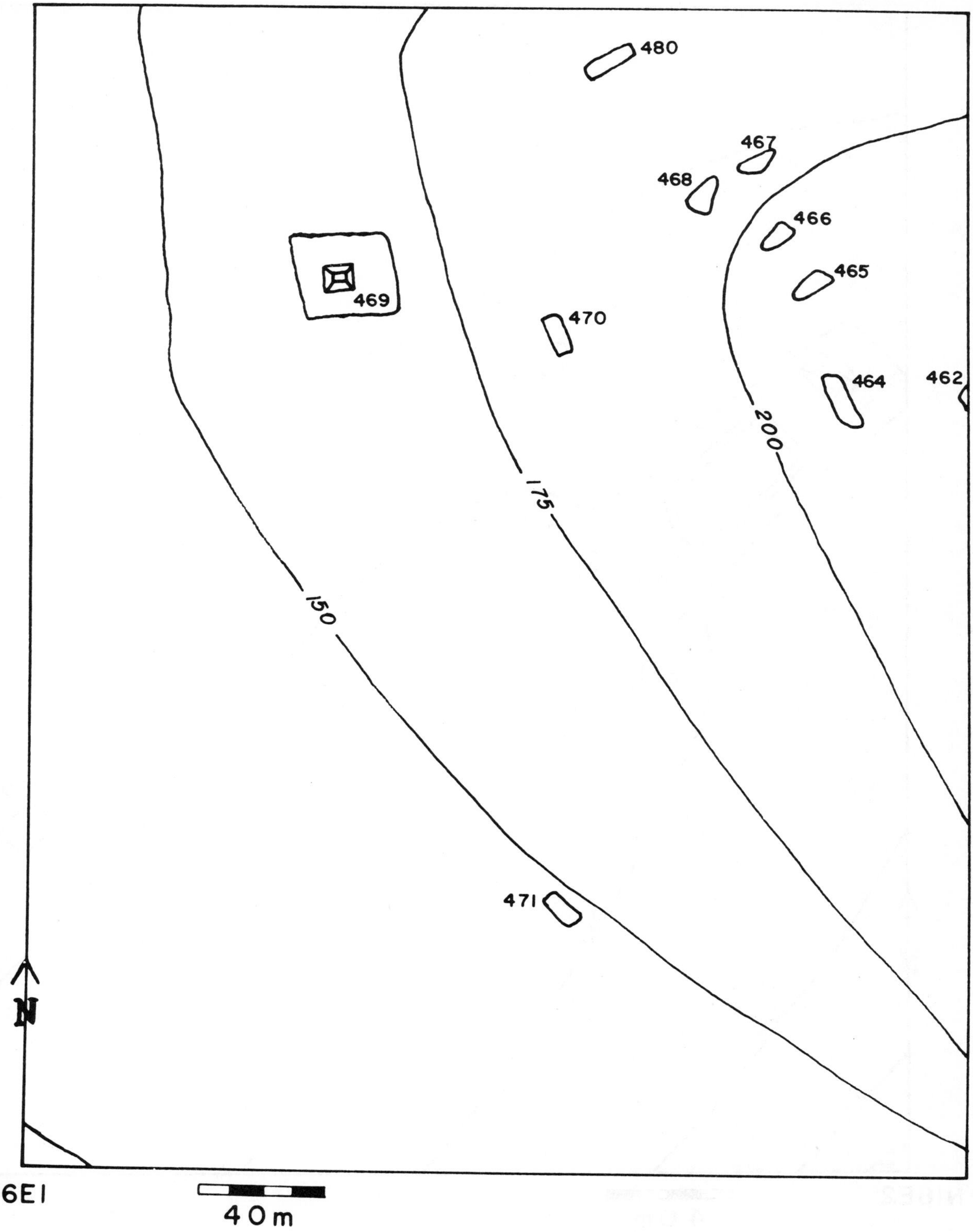

N16E1

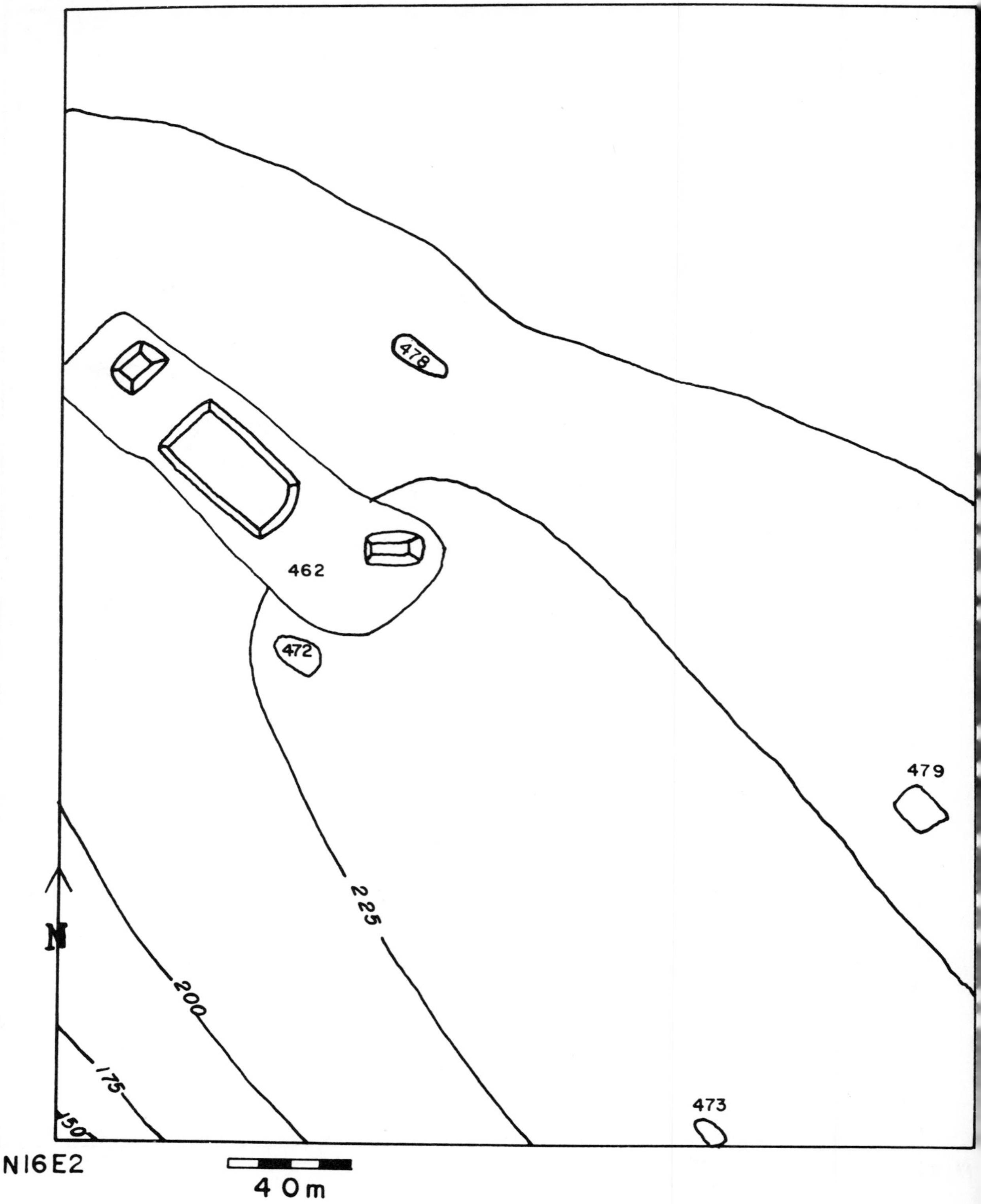

478
462
472
479
225
200
175
150
473
N
N16E2
40m

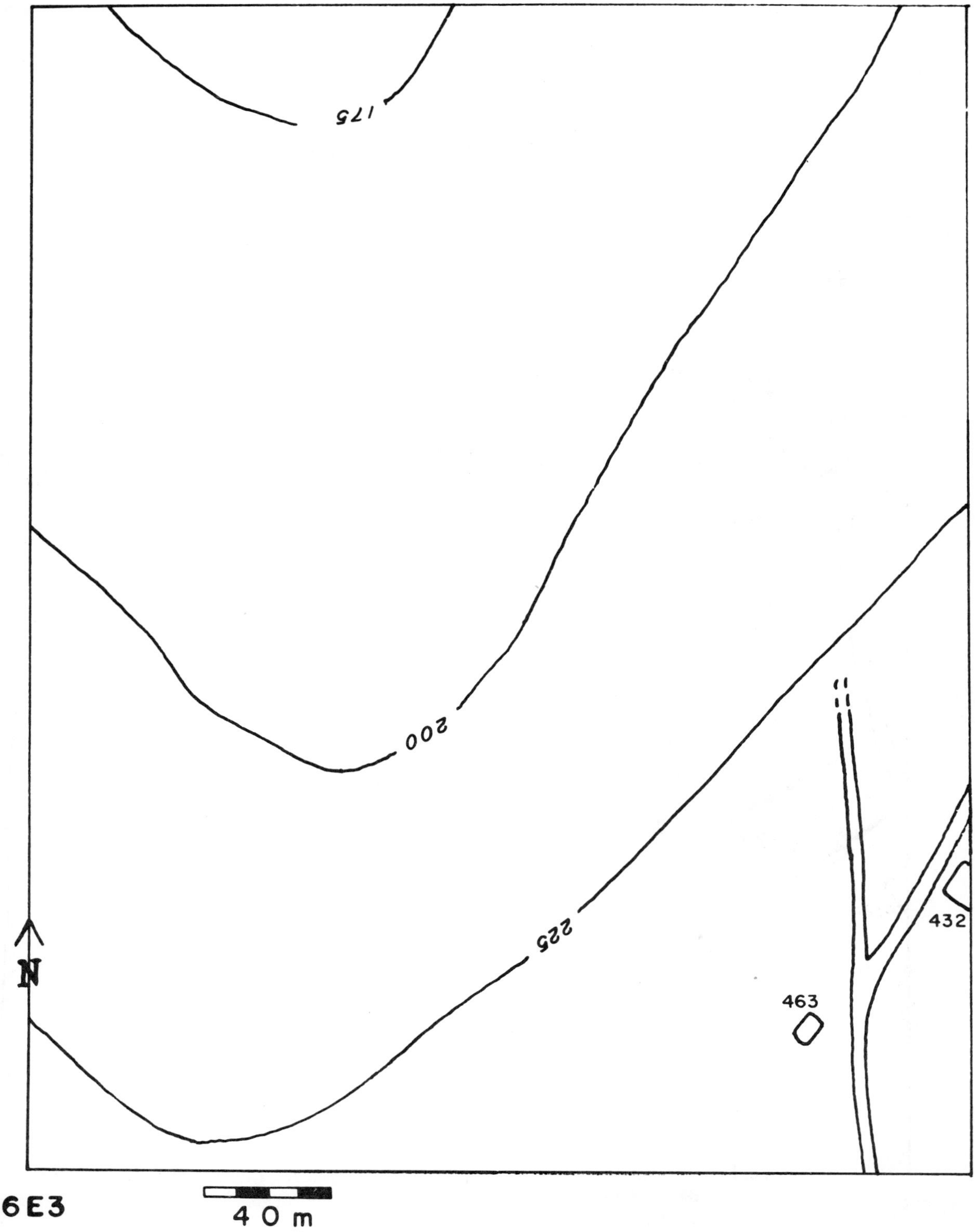

N16E3

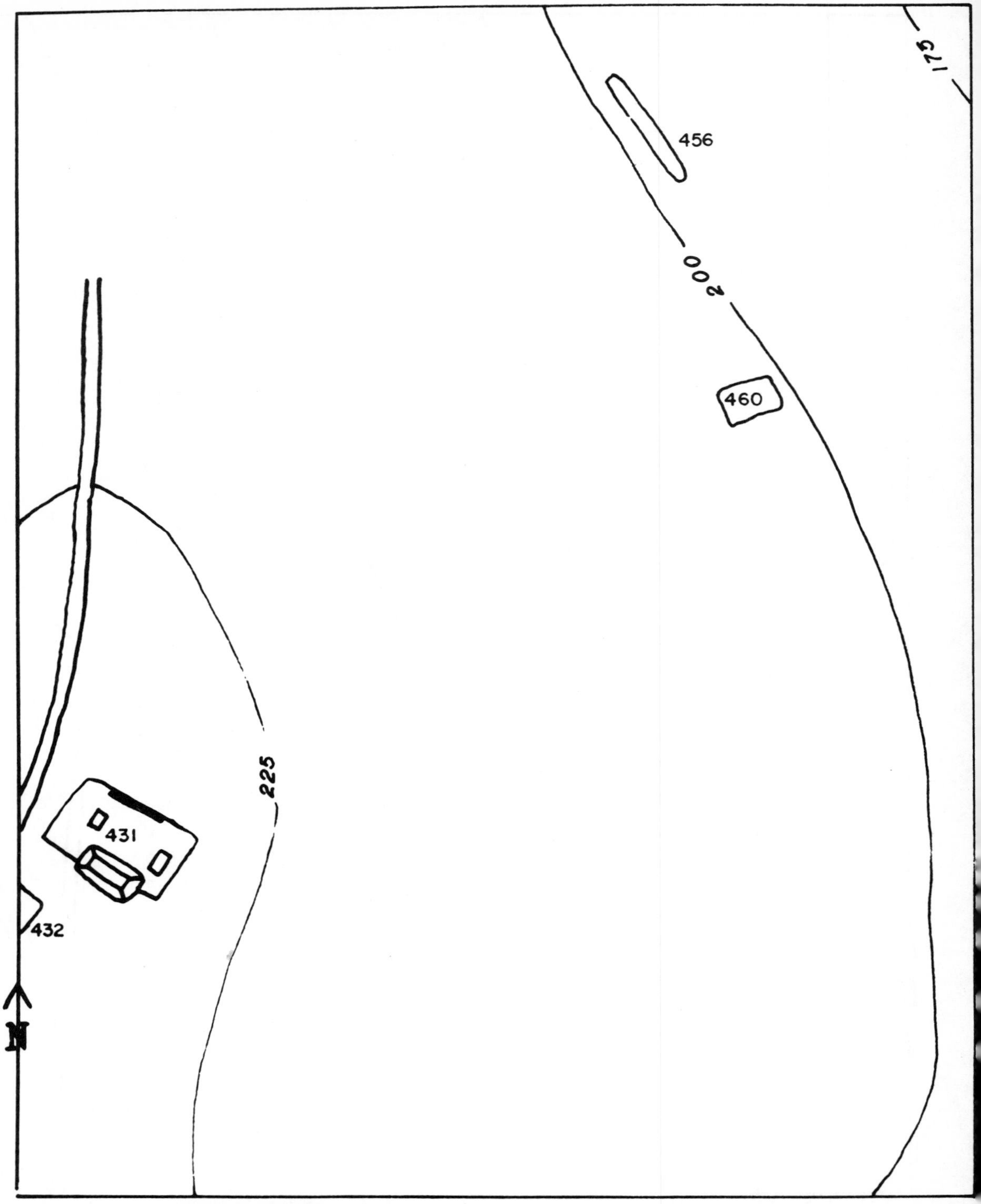

N16 E4

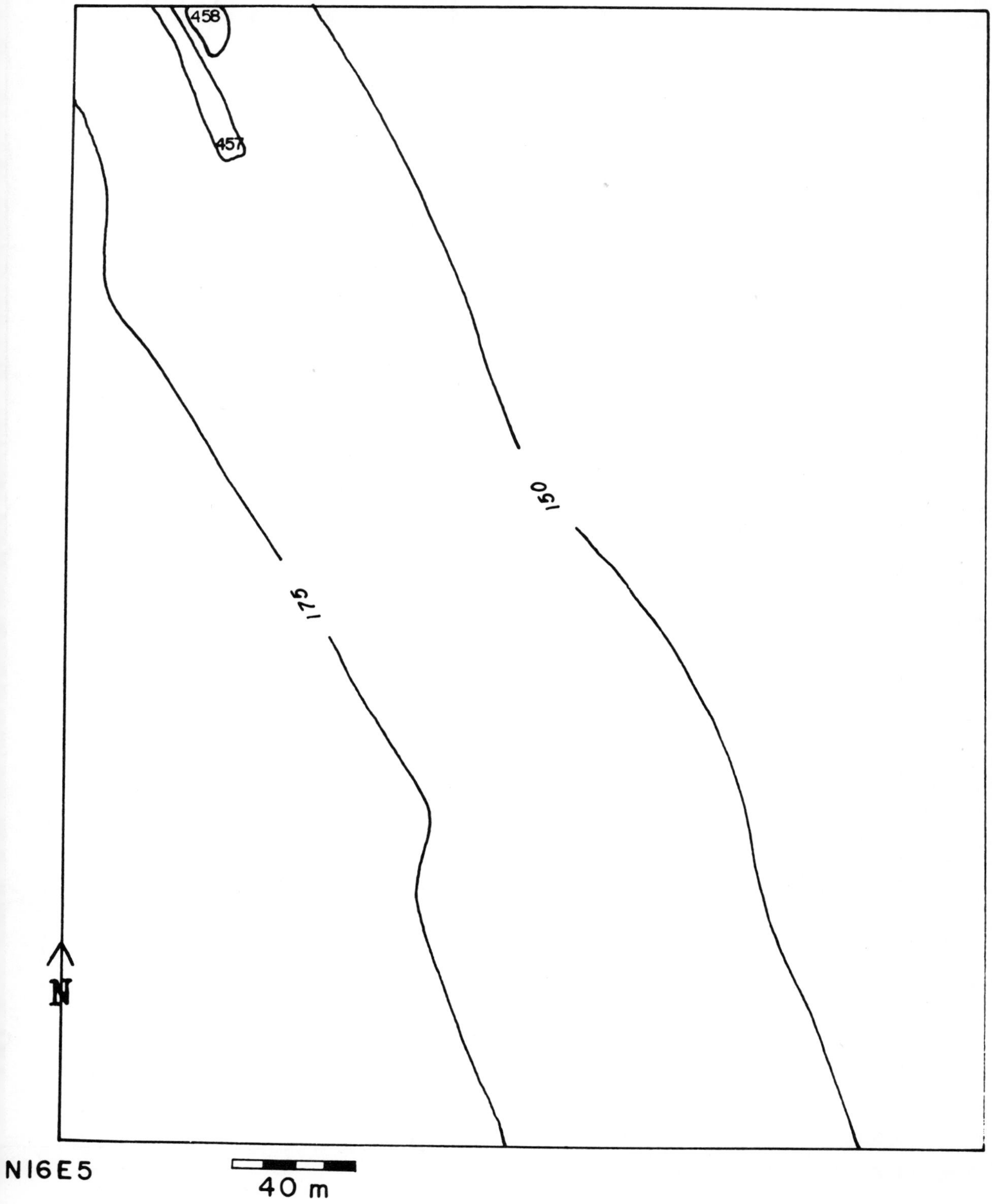
458
457
175
150
N
N16E5
40 m

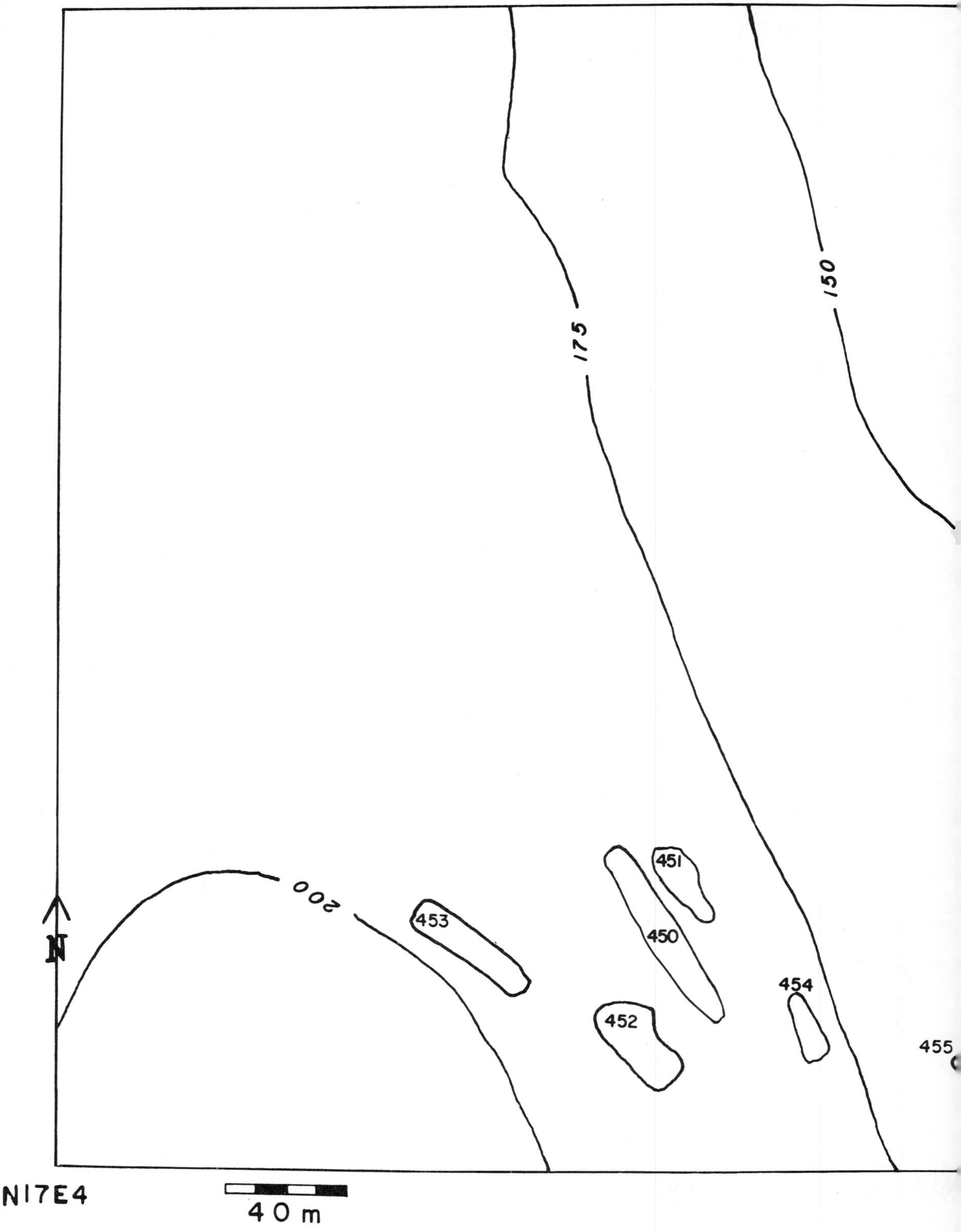
175
150
200
453
451
450
452
454
455
N
N17E4
40 m

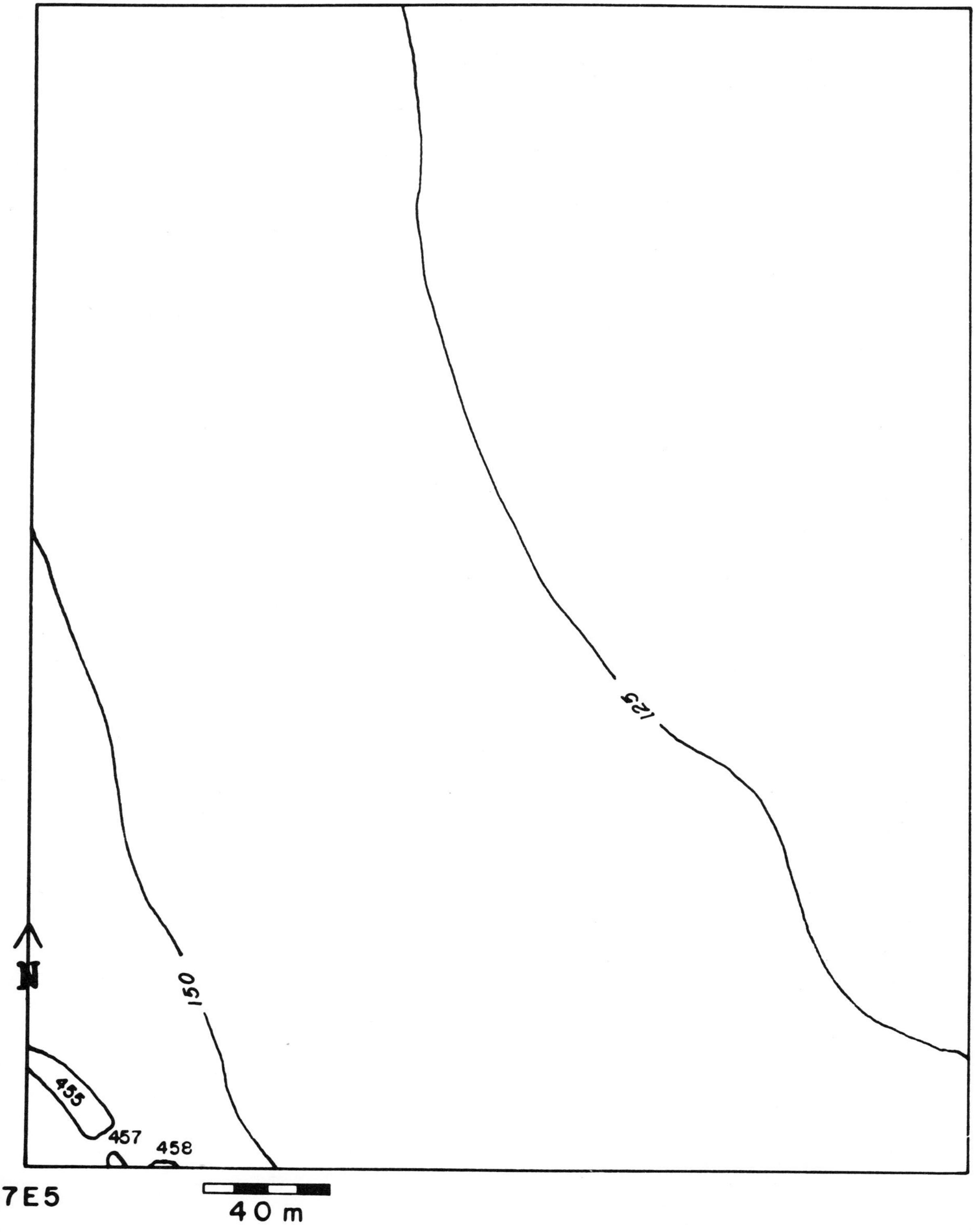

N17E5

APPENDIX VIII

Figurines and Urn Fragments from the Monte Albán Survey

CARL KUTTRUFF

Introduction

This appendix is structured to provide a descriptive catalogue of the figurine and urn fragments that were recovered from the site of Monte Albán during the Monte Albán Survey Project. This study generally classifies the figurine fragments according to the categories that were established by Caso and Bernal in *Urnas de Oaxaca* (1952). Certain modifications have been made, and insofar as possible, correlations of the various elements of the figurines have been pointed out. This task was hampered mainly by the fragmentary nature of the collections and the accuracy of the sample for distributional studies of particular figurine types was thought to be highly questionable. The site has almost certainly been collected for years for figurines, and there may have been some inconsistencies in recording and collecting figurines during the very early stages of the survey.

The dating of the figurines generally is based on Caso and Bernal's assignments. Attempts to correlate various head and headdress types with types of bodies, and other combinations of attributes have been pointed whenever possible. These correlations are based on the survey collections, published illustrations of complete or more complete figurines, photographs of the figurines from Monte Albán Terraces 634 and 635, excavated by Marcus Winter in 1972 and 1973, and examination of the figurine collections at the Museo Frissel in Mitla.[1]

Figures A.VIII–1 through A.VIII–4 show examples from the survey collections of the figurines discussed. Figure A.VIII–5 indicates the total distribution of the figurines and fragments by grid area, and Figure A.VIII–6 the distribution by site subdivision.[2]

The section on the urn fragments lists and describes the various urn elements that were recov-

[1] Appreciation is extended to Mr. Bruce Byland who furnished the photographs of the figurines from Monte Albán Terraces 634 and 635, and to Dr. John Paddock for his kindness in allowing us to examine and photograph the figurine collections at the Museo Frissel. Thanks are also extended to Mr. William O. Autry, Jenna Kuttruff, Ella Mae Stewart, and Carlyle McCulloch who aided the preparation of this report in many ways.

[2] Differences between the totals on the distribution sheets for the figurines and urns and the text are due to the loss of provenience of some of the artifacts, and the inability to correlate certain artifact numbers with terraces, grid areas, or site subdivisions. In some cases it was possible to plot site subdivision and not the grid area.

ered during the survey. These are generally grouped into basal, body, head and headdress elements. Brief descriptions of each element are given, survey examples are illustrated, and a reference to at least one published example, where possible, is provided showing that particular type of element on a complete urn. Possible dating of the elements is indicated whenever possible. This was difficult because of the fragmentary nature of many of the elements, and the use of the same element on urns of different periods. In most cases the elements by themselves were not accurate time markers.

Figures A.VIII–7 through A.VIII–11 provide examples of elements from the survey collections, and Figure A.VIII–12 shows the total distribution of urn elements by grid area. Figure A.VIII–13 gives the total distribution of urn fragments by site subdivision.

Figurines

SOLID MODELED FIGURINES

This category includes a total of 118 anthropomorphic figurines and fragments. They are hand modeled with the heads, arms, and legs attached to the bodies. Decoration and representation of body features is by punctation, incising, or appliqué decoration. For descriptive purposes this category has been subdivided into three groups, each with several variants based primarily on certain body shape characteristics.

Solid Rounded Body Figurines (Total 62)

The bodies of this group of figurines are modeled with a round, elongated body. Legs are rounded, tend to taper toward the end, and are usually spread slightly. Arms are also short, rounded and tapered and either extend straight out from the shoulder or slope slightly downward (Figure A.VIII–1A–F). The bodies represent male, female, and neuter figures. Breasts may be appliqué. The figures are naked except for necklaces that are appliqué, ones that are punctated (Figure A.VIII–1A,B,D,F), or consist of a combination of an appliqué band and incised lines. Three have an appliqué belt around the waist. One variant of this group are those figurines that have bulging stomachs. This protrusion is often broken showing a hollow area for the stomach (Figure A.VIII–1G), and probably originally represented a pregnant woman. Another variant is distinguished by the use of incised lines and punctations on the bodies representing necklaces, nipples, navels, genitals, and body decorations. The incised lines and punctations are also used to divide the body from the arms and legs, to separate the legs and feet and the arms and hands, and to demarcate the toes and fingers (Figure A.VIII–1H,I,J; Caso and Bernal 1952:323 and 325, Figures 476b and 479). Some of these also represent pregnant women (Figure A.VIII–1J). Two examples are classified as miniatures, since they are less than one-half the height of the other figurines in this category. Otherwise they are basically the same figurine (Figure A.VIII–1K). A third variant of body fragments has a series of incised vertical lines covering the torso and upper legs (Figure A.VIII–1L).

Heads associated with solid rounded bodies are solid and hand-modeled with broad noses, thick lips (usually appliqué) and coffee bean or pinched eyes. Sometimes a circle is incised around the head above the forehead (Figure A.VIII–1M and Caso and Bernal 1952:325, Figure 479), perhaps representing a headband (*maxtlatzontli*). All of these figurines probably date to Monte Albán I, particularly the incised and punctate body variant. The simpler rounded, modeled bodies may be from Late Monte Albán I or Early Monte Albán II. They appear to form a continuum between the incised variant and the flattened body form that is characteristic of Monte Albán II.

Flat Solid Body (Total 55)

These figurines have the distinguishing characteristic of the appearance of "gingerbread men" (or women) with wide flat bodies and outstretched arms and legs and are probably good markers for Monte Albán II. Elaboration of body details is minimal consisting of appliqué breasts and the only decorative treatment is appliqué necklaces

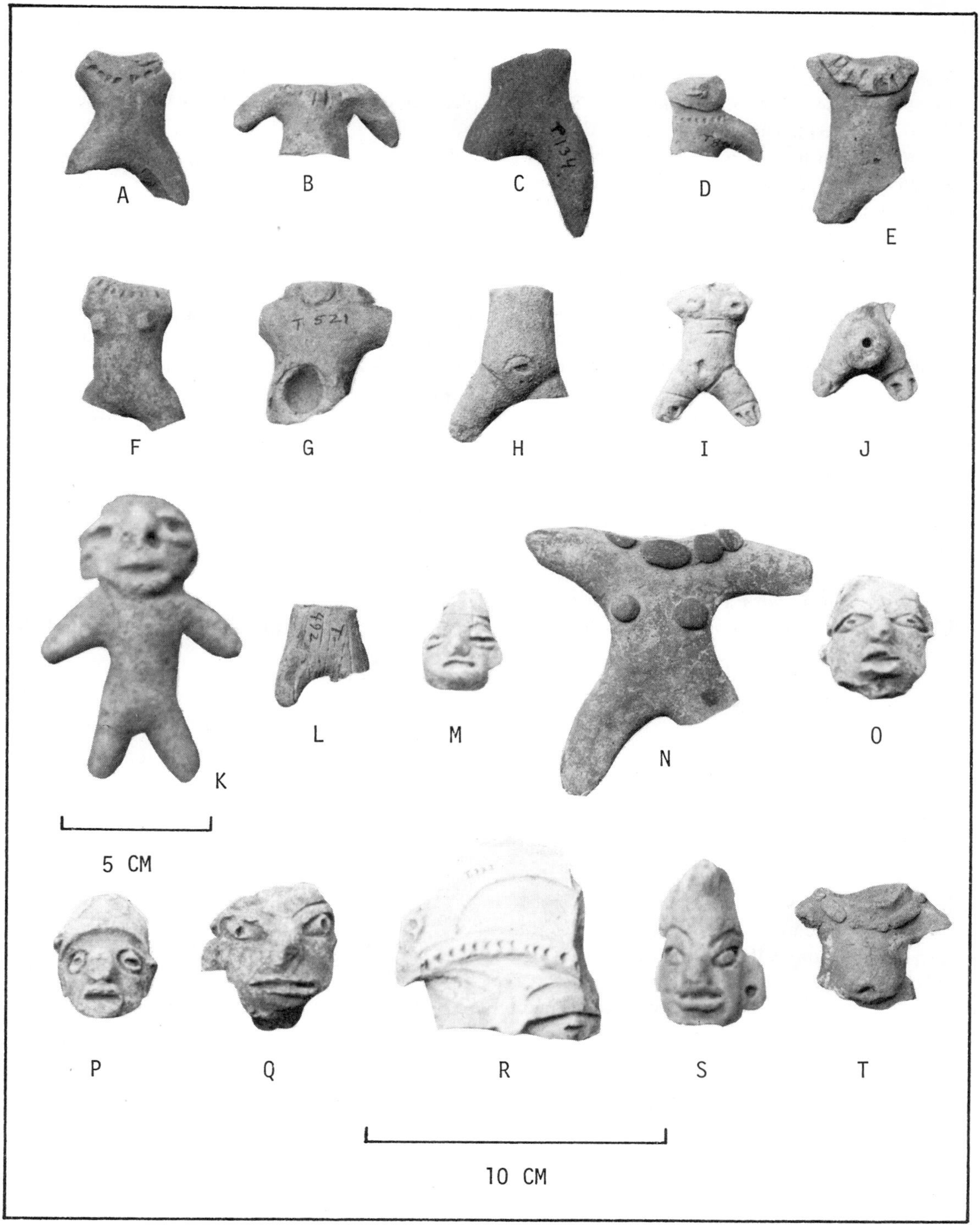

Figure A.VIII–1. Solid modeled figurines.

(Figure A.VIII–1N; Caso and Bernal 1952:338, Figure 500; Caso 1969:32, Figure 21; Spores 1974:46, Figure 31). The heads have broad noses, pronounced mouths, high-arched incised eyebrows, and incised almond-shaped eyes, sometimes with punctate pupils (Figure A.VIII–10P,Q,R). Headdresses, when present, are wide and rectangular with a series of punctations and/or incised lines around the periphery and sometimes with broad incised lines in the large central panel of the headdress.

Another type of head that may be associated with the flat solid body and possibly with the rounded solid body is a lengthened head with a broad nose, pronounced lips, high-arched incised eyebrows, and incised, almond-shaped eyes. Tall foreheads or headpieces are common. Ears are represented as flanges on the side of the head with punctations to represent the earspools (Figure A.VIII–1S). There is also at least one association of this type of head with a Monte Albán II plain bird body *silbato* (Caso and Bernal 1952:304, Figure 455).

Solid Body with Protruding Stomach (Total 1)

One figurine recovered has a rounded solid body with a protruding stomach, probably representing a pregnant woman. The navel was formed by a punctation, and there was an appliqué necklace (Figure A.VIII–1T). This figurine resembles those that have been excavated from Formative Period sites in the Valley of Oaxaca and the Tehuacan Valley (Flannery *et al.*, n.d.:97; MacNeish, Peterson, and Flannery 1970:162, Figure 98). The figurine would probably date to the *Guadalupe* phase (800–500 B.C.) in the Valley of Oaxaca; or it might be an unusual variant of the solid body figurines of Monte Albán I and II described above.

MOLD-MADE FIGURINES

Figurines in this group were produced by pressing wet clay into a fired clay mold. Often the fronts are quite elaborate, but the figurines are generally quite thin. The reverse sides show marks of being pressed wet into a mold. Apparently, the body, head, and headdress were molded in one piece. A total of 206 fragments are included here.

Body Fragments with Quechquemitls (Total 57)

A total of 57 flat mold-made figurines wearing a *quechquemitl* were collected. The arms are usually along the side, although seven fragments have the arms folded across the chest. The *quechquemitls* are either plain or have a series of different border decorations (see Caso and Bernal 1952: 295, Figure 446). A skirt often tied with a belt is worn below the *quechquemitl*. Legs and feet are rudimentary, although some do have toes (Figure A.VIII–2A–D). The bodies with skirt and *quechquemitl* are associated with the *Diosa 13 Serpiente* headdress, the *Diosa 13 Serpiente* braided hair variant, the *tocado de gran pluma*, and probably the *tocado de Yalateca*. However, the *tocado de gran pluma* is apparently exclusively associated with the body with folded arms. This group can probably be assigned to Monte Albán IIIa and IIIb.

Diosa con Tocado Trenzado (Total 13)

This form is probably a Monte Albán IIIb variant of the *Diosa 13 Serpiente* and is characterized by an elaborately braided headdress or hairpiece (Figure A.VIII–2E,F; Caso and Bernal 1952:294–295, Figure 446). Legs and feet, like other mold-made figurines, are very simply made and only occasionally show details of the feet or toes. At least one figurine of this category in the survey collection was covered with red paint. The complete figurines illustrated by Caso and Bernal (1952) show a female figure, usually with large earspools, elaborate necklace, *quechquemitl* and a skirt tied with a herringbone weave belt. The hands are usually at the sides, although crossed arms do occur.

Diosa con Tocado de Gran Pluma (Total 3)

These three figurine fragments consist of the readily distinguishible headdress portion of a mold-made figurine that has a horizontal feather

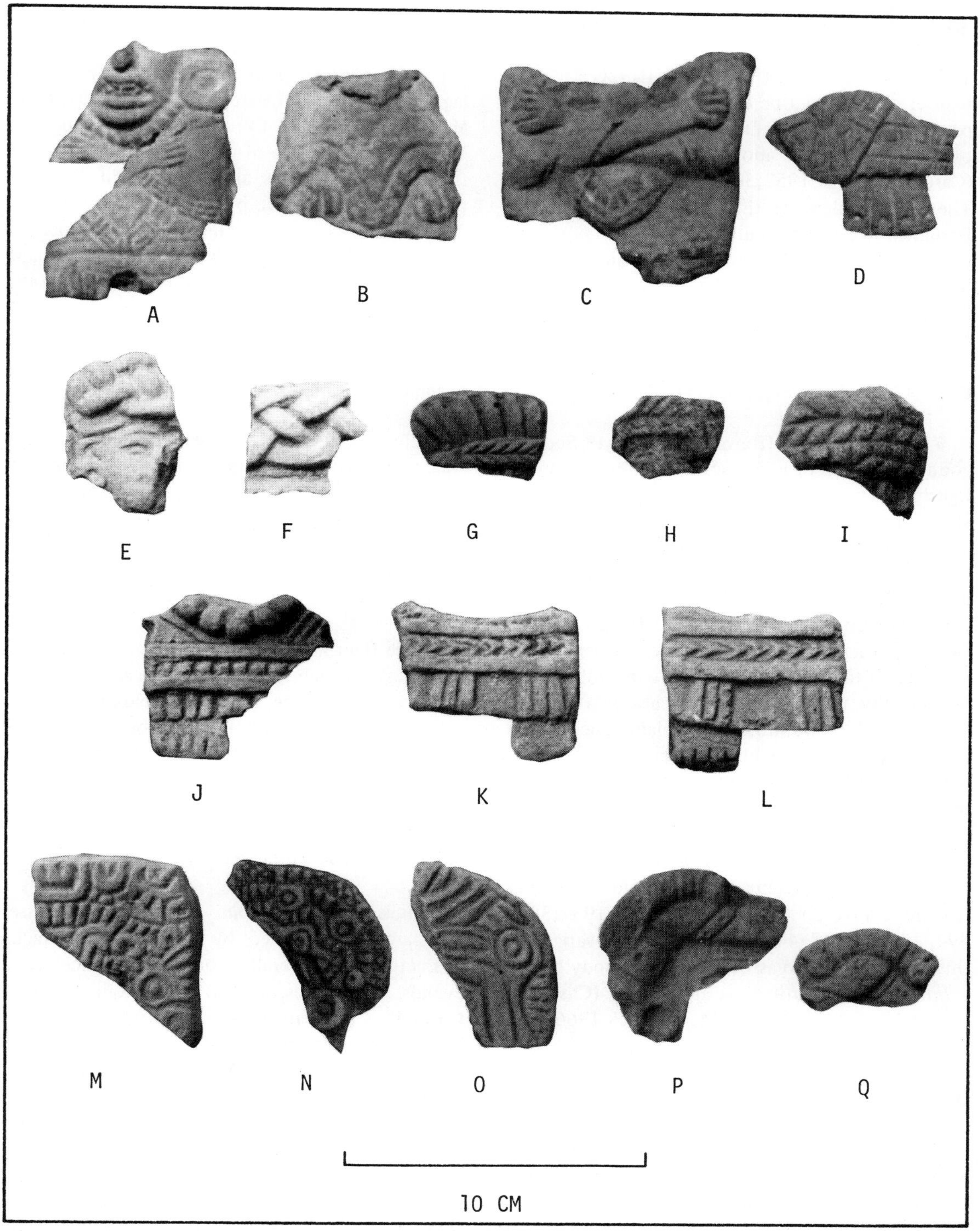

Figure A.VIII–2. Mold-made figurines.

above the forehead (Figure A.VIII–2G–I). This feather element can be either the entire headdress or part of one, the remainder consisting of a row of vertical feathers above the horizontal plume (Caso and Bernal 1952:300, Figures 452 and 453). The one complete figurine illustrated by Caso and Bernal shows a woman in a *huipil* or *quechquemitl* with the hands folded at the chest. Short stubby legs with the toes depicted are also present. This figurine category probably dates to Monte Albán IIIb or IV.

Diosa 13 Serpiente Figurines (Total 87)

This Monte Albán IIIa variant of the 13 Serpent goddess consists of a flat, solid, mold-made female figurine. The bodies are wide and have short stubby arms extending straight out from the shoulders. A belt tying the skirt is decorated with a central section composed of a row of squares (Figure A.VIII–2J), a row of chevrons, or a row of herringbonelike angles (Figure A.VIII–2K,L). The two ends of the belt hang down on either side of the base of the skirt. Legs and feet are stubby, and occasionally there is some indication of toes although the legs are more often plain. The body is invariably, and probably exclusively, associated with a smoothed faced person with an often elaborate appliqué necklace of beads and a complex headdress composed of a series of curvilinear elements and circles and dots which are probably highly stylized portraits of snakes and snake eyes (Figure A.VIII–2N,O; Caso and Bernal 1952:384–394, Figures 443–445). A slightly later variant of this headdress is also associated with a body having a *quechquemitl* with arms at the side (Caso and Bernal 1952:292, Figure 444; Paddock 1966:214, Figure 267).

Diosa con Tocado de Yalateca (Total 6)

This Monte Albán IIIa group of figurine fragments is characterized by the representation of the Yalalag headdress or hairpiece (Figure A.VIII–2P,Q). The headdress is a *rodete* of either yarn or a vine around which the hair is wrapped. This manner of dressing the hair is also known from Yalalag, Oaxaca, the Huasteca, and other parts of Mexico (Cordry and Cordry 1968:125 and 263). No complete figurine of this type is represented in the collection and few are illustrated in the literature. An urn illustrated by Caso and Bernal (1952:297, Figure 446) shows this headdress associated with a female wearing a *quechquemitl* (Caso and Bernal 1952:296–299, Figures 446, 447 and 448–451).

Miscellaneous Mold-Made Figurine Fragments (Total 40)

Included here are 26 head and 14 necklace fragments that were from mold-made figurines. It was difficult to accurately associate them specifically with any of the above categories because of their fragmentary natures.

SILBATOS

These figurines consist of mold-made heads and headdresses which were attached to a hollow body which may also be partially mold-made. They served as whistles, and had a short mouthpiece attached to the base. A total of 218 fragments of these figurines were in the survey collection, most of which are head and headdress fragments.

Silbato Diosa Joven (Total 26)

This is a group of *silbato* heads and headdresses that are characterized by well-developed facial characteristics, generally young appearance, eyes, eyelids, wide noses, and an open mouth showing teeth. Ears and earspools are also usually present. The headdresses are generally asymmetrical, with two or three horizontal bands centered above the forehead. These are flanked by a plain vertical bar and/or plain rectangular areas. Above the horizontal bands is a vertical plain area separating a figure of a *Quetzal* or a head of *Tlaloc* on the right hand side and a series of feathers on the left (Figure A.VIII–3A–F; Caso and Bernal 1952:310–312, Figure 461). These heads and headdresses

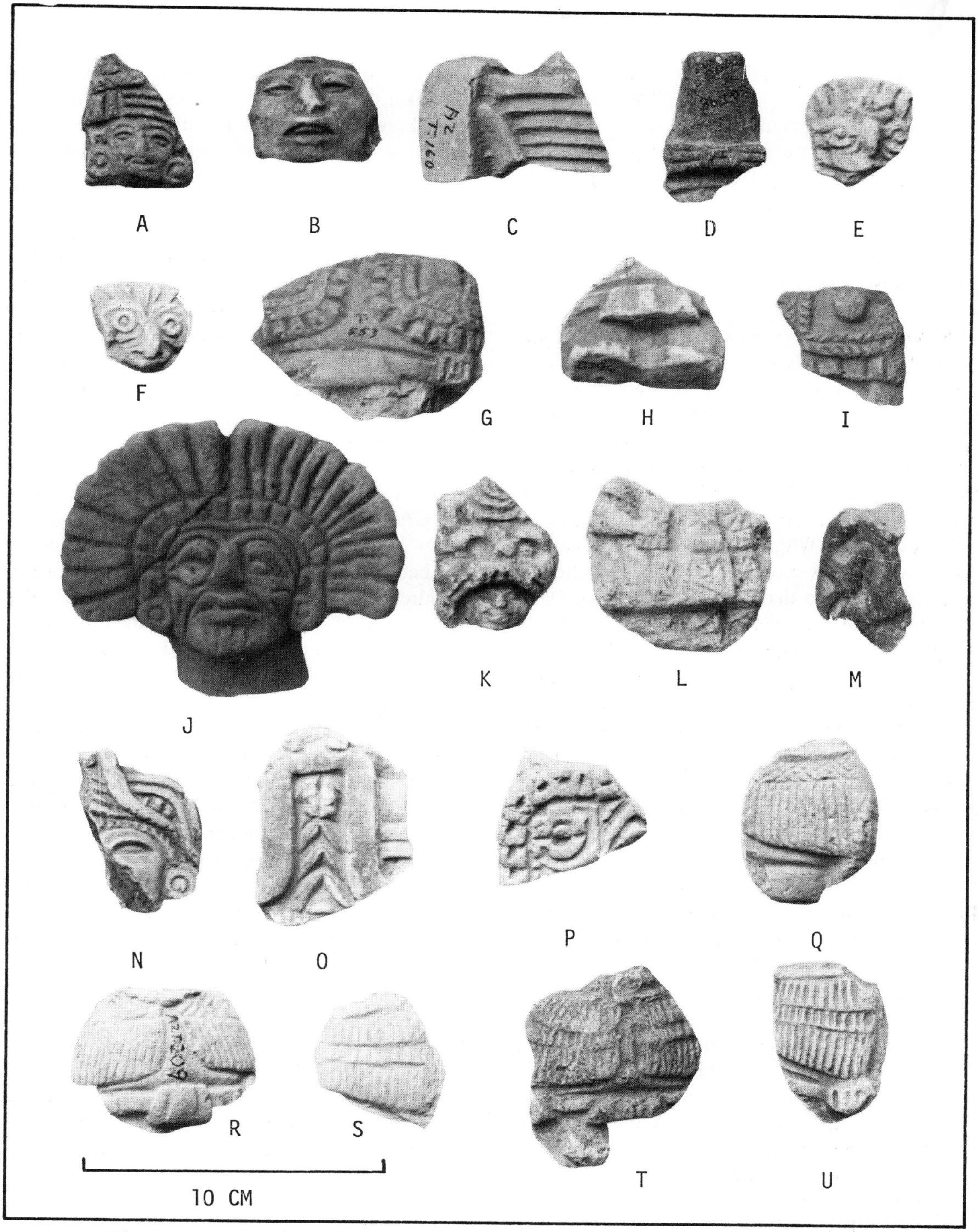

Figure A.VIII–3. *Silbatos.*

may have an appliqué necklace and are associated with several different body forms, predominately those wearing feathered capes (Figure A.VIII–3O–U), and more rarely with a *quechquemitl* (Caso and Bernal 1952:311, Figures 461a and c), the cape described below and probably with a plain bird body.

Silbato with Cape (Total 21)

Several different *silbatos* dating from Monte Albán IIIb have this body form. It consists of a man's body, short legs, and stubby feet often with the toes depicted. The characteristic feature is an elaborate cape that covers both shoulders and closes at the neck, but remains open down the front of the figure. The outside edge of the cape is decorated with a series of appliqué nodes, or incised rectangles. Within this border is a parallel decoration that is probably a stylized feather, or feathers, similar to that in the headdress of *Diosa con Tocado de Gran Pluma* described above (Caso and Bernal 1952:300, Figures 452 and 453). Within the second band of decoration there is an appliqué node on the cape near each shoulder, but on the front of the cape (Figure A.VIII–3G–I; Caso and Bernal 1952:306, Figure 457; 307, Figure 458, 311, Figure 461c). This cape and body form is found associated with *Diosa Joven* with the assymetrical headdress (Caso and Bernal 1952: 311, Figure 461c), with a *viejo* with an asymmetrical headdress (Caso and Bernal 306, Figure 457), and with a *joven* with a serpent headdress (Caso and Bernal 1952:168, Figure 294g).

Viejo Silbatos (Total 10)

These are a series of heads from *silbatos* that are in the form of an old man's face (*Huehuetcauh*). Wrinkles are prominent particularly around the eyes, forehead and on the cheeks. The nose is generally broad and the mouth is often open enough to show the teeth (Figure A.VIII–3J). These heads and associated headdresses are probably mold-made and were attached at the neck to a hollow body. Just above the forehead there is usually a band of squares which continues around the side of the head to the ear and earspool which complete this band. Extending straight out from the ear and over the top of the head is a row of feathers. Invariably they are asymmetrical with a different feather treatment on each side (Caso and Bernal 1952:308–309, Figures 459 and 460a–d). Apparently these heads are only associated with plain bird bodies. Although there are no illustrations from the survey collections, the headdress that is associated with the *viejo* described above may also be associated with a *joven* face.

Diosa 5 Flor (Total 9)

A man's face within a bat's mouth characterizes this *silbato* type, or more likely it is the representation of a man wearing a bat mask or headdress. The bat head is generally complete, with a feather headdress minimally containing the glyph D, the flower, located centrally on the front of the headdress (Figure A.VIII–3K,L,M). This glyph consists of a circle or a raised dot with three petals radiating upward and outward. This motif is often repeated three times on the headdress (Caso and Bernal 1952:84–86, Figures 135 and 136).

The bodies associated with this head form are hollow, short and stubby with an elaborate cape and generally with a choker down the front. The arms are positioned around the sides towards the front. The right hand holds what is probably an ear of maize. The left hand holds an undetermined object. Short legs and stubby feet protrude below the cape in some attempt to portray the toes. These date to Monte Albán IIIb.

Silbatos con Tocado de Serpiente (Total 60)

This Monte Albán IIIb or IV *silbato* form has a headdress that represents a serpent (Caso and Bernal 1952:167–169). It is stylized such that the palate is visible, extending vertically from the forehead to the top of the headdress. In some cases the nose detail is elaborated at the center top of the headdress. The eyes are shown on either side of the palate, often in the form of a *Cocijo* eye (Figure A.VIII–3N–P; Caso and Bernal 1952:168, Figure 294g and h). Faces are usually those of *Diosa Joven*, are well made and smooth, and the facial features reasonably well executed. Mouths are usually open with the teeth showing. Ears are often present, and nearly all have a circular ear spool (Caso and Bernal 1952: Figures 294 and 296). These heads are nearly always on a hollow, plain, rounded to pear-shaped bird body. At least one example occurs with a human body wearing a cape similar to those described above (Caso and Bernal 1952, Figure 294g).

Silbatos with Feather Capes (Total 37)

These are probably the bodies that are most associated with the *Diosa Joven* heads previously described. No other association has been illustrated. The body is hollow, short and wide, with stubby legs and feet with an occasional illustrated toe. The cape is around the shoulders, and arms, which are not shown, and pulled together in the front. Of the figurines recovered, and where it could be determined, 8 had one tier of feathers (Figure A.VIII–3Q,R), 2 had two tiers (Figure A.VIII–3S), and 26 had three tiers (Figure A.VIII–3T,U). At least 1 had red paint remaining on the cape (Caso and Bernal 1952:311, Figure 461b).

Miscellaneous Silbato Fragments (Total 55)

Several figurine fragments are grouped here. These could not be included accurately in one of the other described categories because of their fragmentary nature. In this collection there are 8 hollow body fragments that had appliqué or punctated necklaces, 18 basal fragments, 6 unidentifiable decorated *silbato* body fragments, 13 ear and earspool elements, and 5 *joven*-like solid heads that were obviously attached to *silbato* bodies. These could possibly have been grouped with the *joven*, but no headdress elements were present making this association much less certain. Additionally, there were 5 mouthpieces that probably served as the third support on the lower back of the bird effigy *silbatos*.

ANIMAL FIGURINES

This category is composed of all figurines that are zoomorphic figures, such as dog, jaguars, frogs, monkeys, and others. A total of 236 are analyzed.

Dogs (Total 86)

This category of figurines is modeled in the form of stylized dogs. They have a flat bodies with attached legs. Tails are shown as small nubs applied to body sections; legs are generally circular in cross section, and curved with a rounded or pointed end. There is no effort to indicate any detail of the feet. The heads are highly stylized, consisting of a pointed nose with a carved or incised line for the mouth, and two large protruding ears (Figure A.VIII–4A–C. Caso and Bernal 1965:886, Figure 17f; MacNeish *et al.* 1970:228, Figure 138). Eyes are generally appliqué buttons with the pupil shown by an incised circle or a punctation made with a tubular object. Placement of the eyes is on the ears, varying from the tip of the ears to a point near the nose.

Three variants of this generalized dog form were recovered in the surface survey. All were similar to the above in their basic form. One was decorated with a series of arc-shaped punctations, probably fingernail, down either side of the back (Figure A.VIII–4D). Another had a series of punctations on the underside of the body, and the third had an incised cross on the back (Figure A.VIII–4E). This group of figurines is usually a marker for Monte Albán IIIa.

Jaguars (Total 10)

This category consists of three realistically executed solid jaguar heads (Figure A.VIII–4F,G; Caso and Bernal 1952:57, Figure 83) and seven bodies. Those bodies that have been classified as

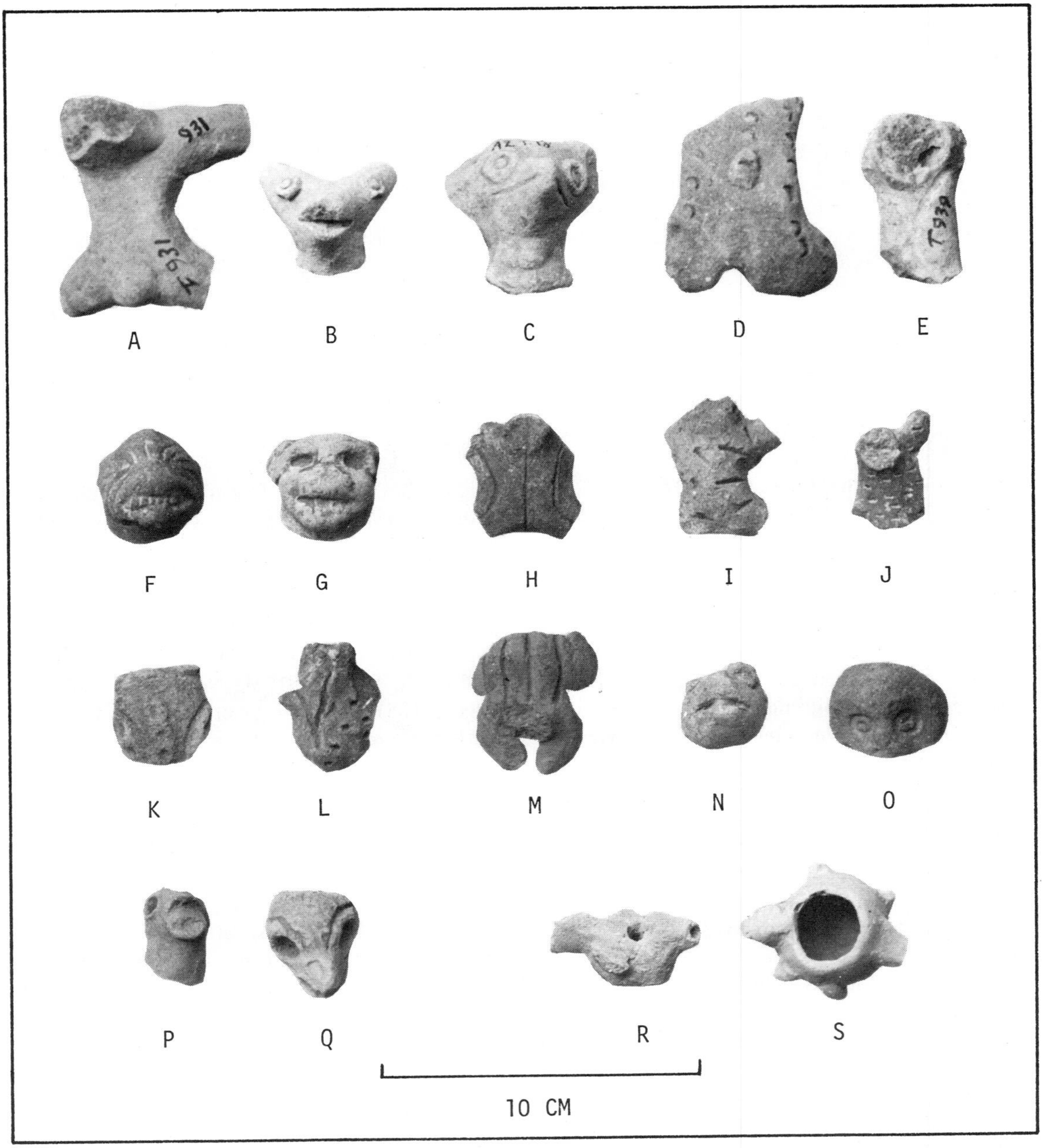

Figure A.VIII–4. Animal figurines.

jaguars are made similarly to those of the dog category but are consistently decorated with linear incised lines along the back (Figure A.VIII–4H), or in one case with a series of slashes over the back and sides (Figure A.VIII–4I). Another was covered with linear punctations (Figure A.VIII–4J).

Frogs (Total 5)

Two heads and three bodies, all solid figurines, and made similarly to the dogs and tigers were identified as frogs (Figure A.VIII–4K–N). The bodies are decorated with incised lines, which probably delineate the hind legs in a seated position. Spots on the legs and down the middle of the back are shown by circular punctations. One frog has three stripes down the back and the legs are partially extended (Figure A.VIII–4M).

Monkey (Total 1)

One animal figurine head fragment probably represents a monkey (Figure A.VIII–4O). It is a solid head with a convex facial area around the eyes. The eyes are formed by punctations with a tubular object, then punctated in the center to illustrate the pupil.

Birds (Total 3)

Two heads made similarly to those of the dogs probably represent birds (Figure A.VIII–4P,Q; MacNeish *et al.* 1970:228, Figure 138). Also included in this category is a whistle in the form of a stylized bird (Figure A.VIII–4R) which is similar to one illustrated for the *Palo Blanco* phase (A.D. 200–700) of the Tehuacan Valley (MacNeish *et al.* 1970:175, Figure 105).

Turtle (Total 1)

One miniature vessel in the form of a turtle was recovered (Figure A.VIII–4S).

Animal Legs (Total 130)

Numerous leg fragments from various animal figurines are included in the collections. These were generally attached to solid body figurines as described in the foregoing sections. They are usually circular in section, tapered toward the ends, and are slightly curved with pointed ends. One variant is flattened on the end, possibly the result of placing the soft, unfired figurine on a flat surface. Three examples of legs show some attempt to illustrate toes or claws with incisions, but they are rather poorly executed.

MISCELLANEOUS FIGURINE FRAGMENTS (Total 167)

These are figurine fragments which could not be put into the categories described above. Included are 59 feather elements and 34 head or face fragments from mold-made figurines or *silbatos*; three solid body fragments; 36 arms and leg fragments from either the rounded body or flat body figurines; 2 animallike forms and 33 indeterminate fragments.

Urns

URN BASES (TOTAL 21)

These fragments are from the bases or pedestals of urns. One is a simple base that has a rectangular depressed panel in the center front (Figure A.VIII–7A; Caso and Bernal 1952:195, Figure 328). Seven have a depressed rectangular panel on the front of the base with a lightninglike motif modeled in low relief within the panel (Figure A.VIII–7B,C; Caso and Bernal 1952:47, Figure 64). Two panels on the base of urns are similar to the above except that the motif consists of modeled diagonal lines. Two bases have a series of incised lines and carved motifs on the front (Fig-

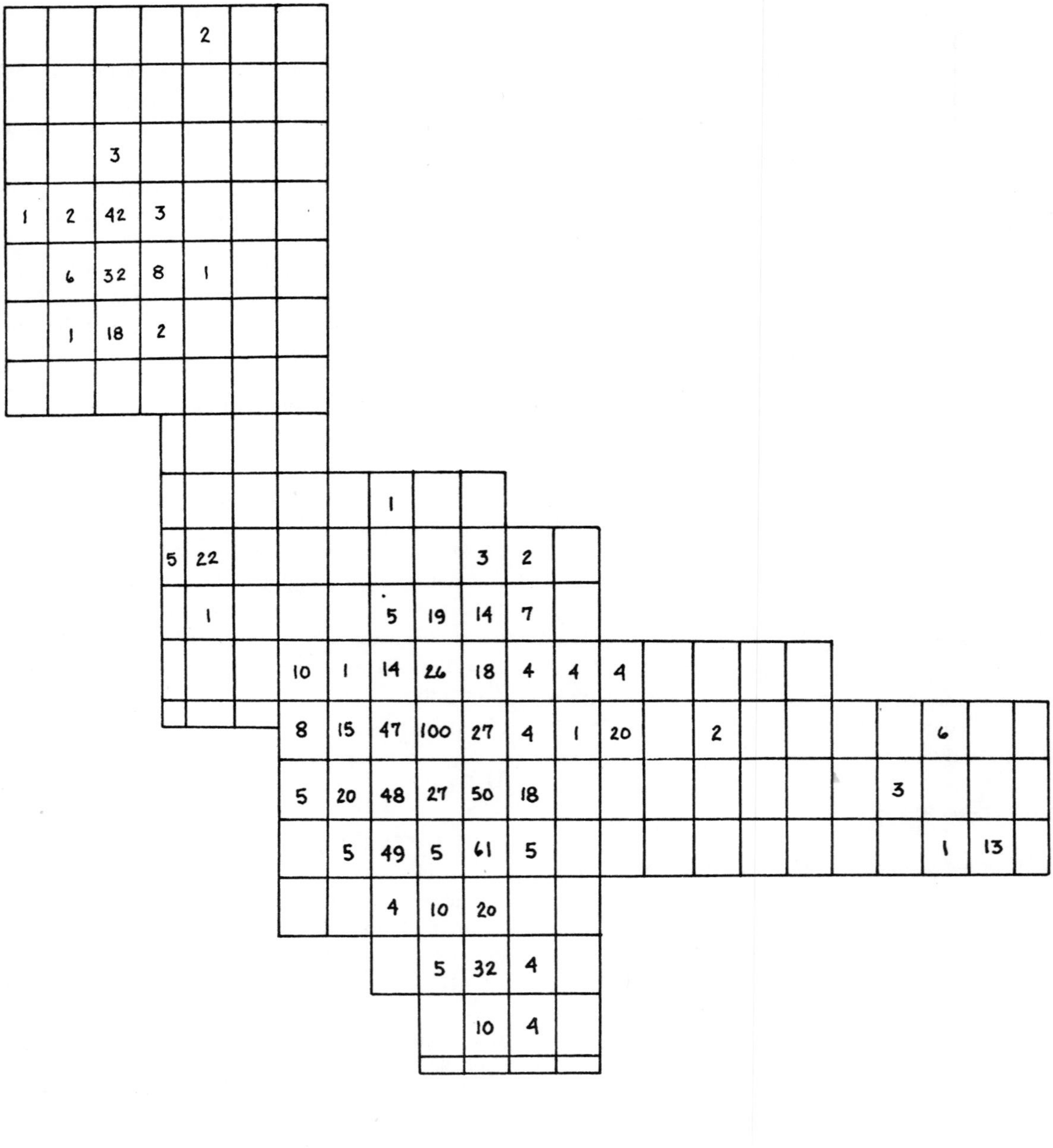

Figure A.VIII–5. Distribution of figurine fragments by grid area.

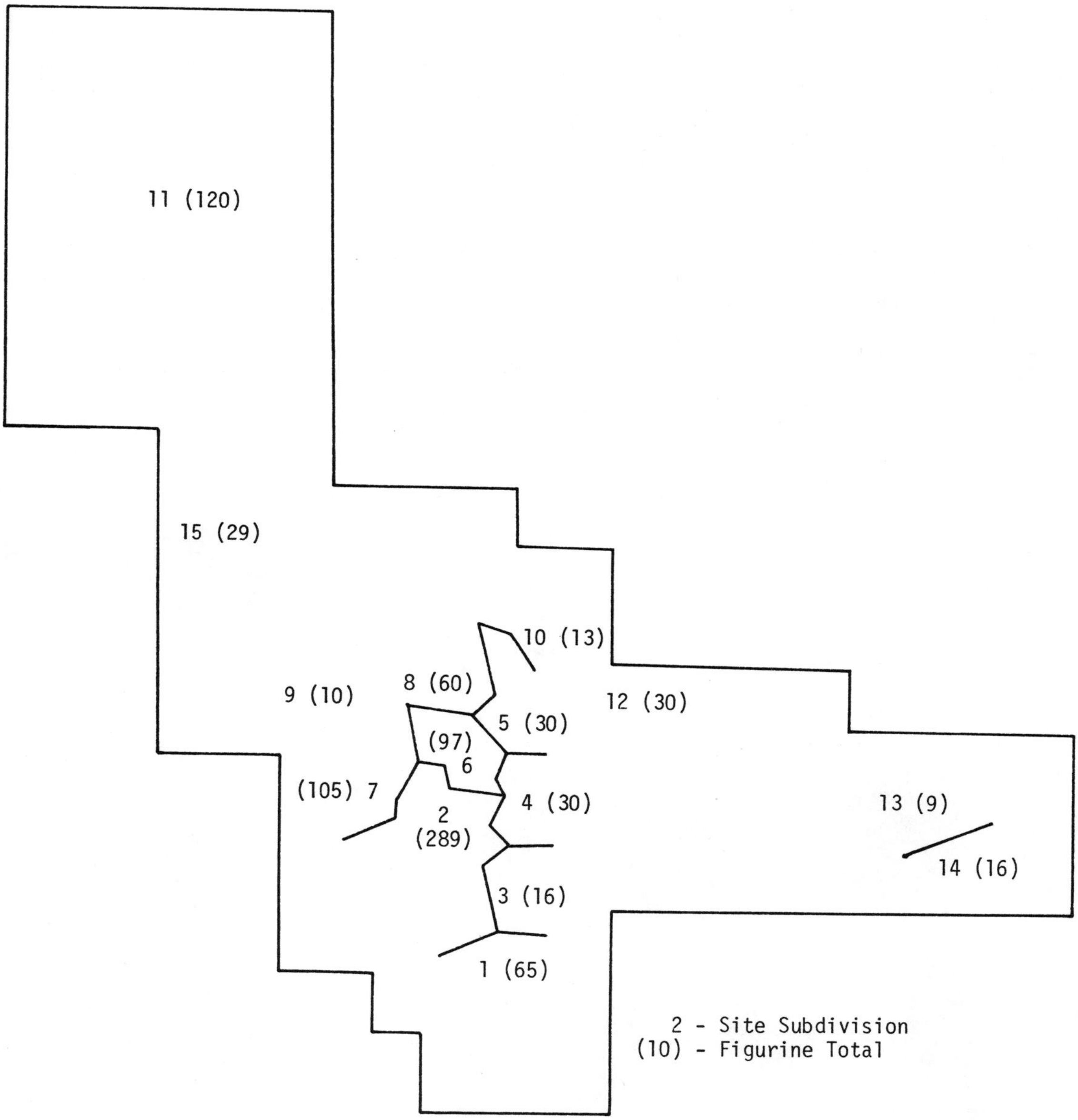

Figure A.VIII–6. Distribution of figurine fragments by site subdivision.

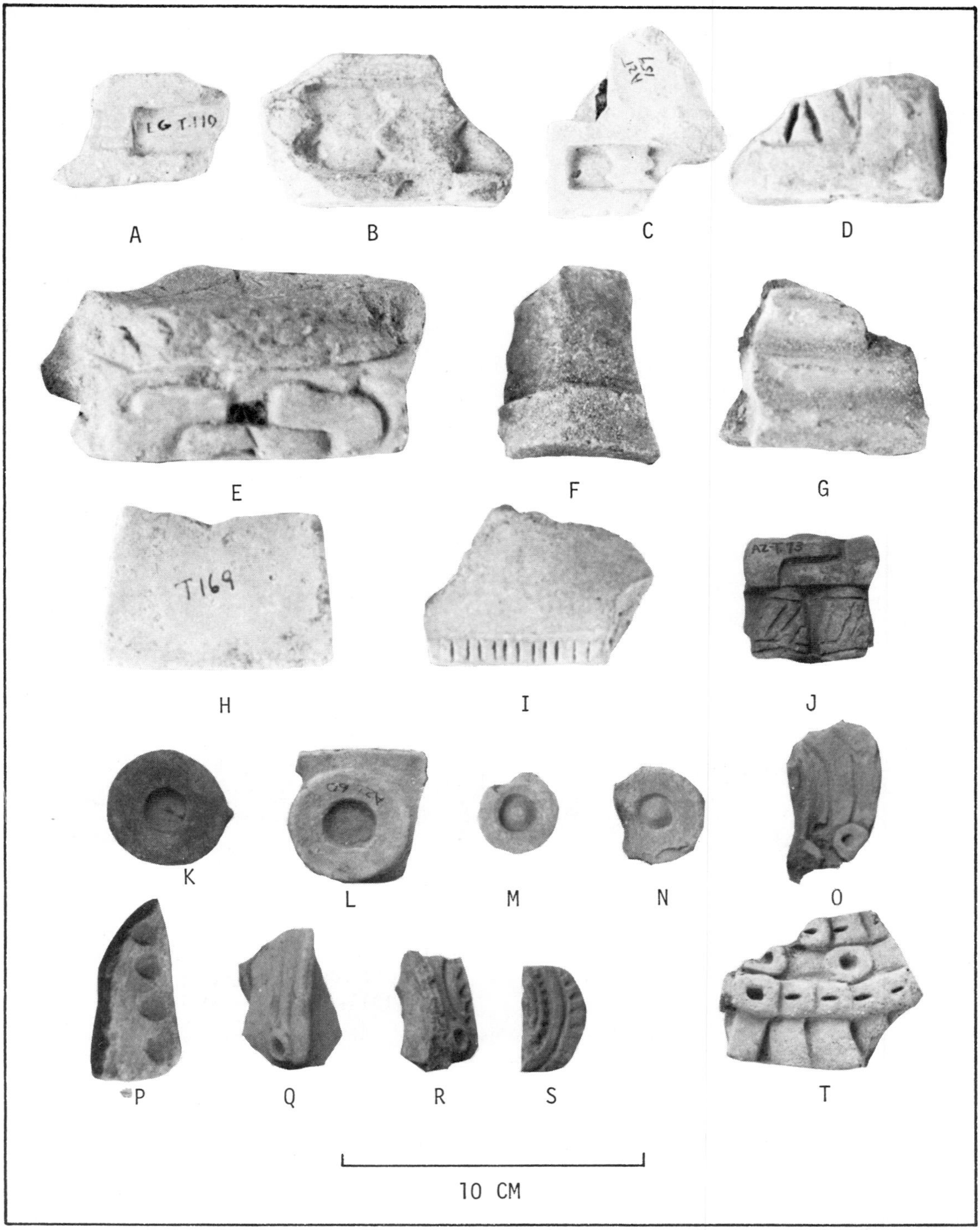

Figure A.VIII–7. Urn fragments.

ure A.VIII–7D,E). Seven basal fragments are plain except for a flange around the bottom of the pedestal (Figure A.VIII–7F). Finally, two pedestal fragments represent steps, and may be part of a pedestal in the form of a temple (Figure A.VIII–7G; Caso and Bernal 1952:76, Figure 123; Paddock 1966:118, Figure 65).

SKIRTS OR MAXTLATL (Total 2)

Two examples of breechcloths or *maxtlatl* were recovered. They appear to have lapped over the crossed knees of the figure (Caso and Bernal 1952: 137, Figures 234 and 235). One is plain and the other has a lower border of vertically incised lines separated from the rest of the skirt by a horizontal line. This decorative element probably represents a fringe along the lower edge of the skirt or breechcloth (Figure A.VIII–7I).

BELLS (Total 2)

Two urn elements in the collection illustrate what are probably bells attached to a belt, waistband, or necklace of a Monte Albán IIIa or IIIb urn. The bells are decorated with several incised lines around the circumference of the bell and diagonal incised lines fill the space between the horizontal incisions (Figure A.VIII–7J; Caso and Bernal 1952:180, Figure 306; 199, Figure 333; 209, Figure 346; Paddock 1966:168, Figure 174).

EARSPOOLS (Total 28)

A total of 28 earspools from urns were recovered. Basically, all are circular with a depressed center section. Some have flat centers (Figure A.VIII–7K,L; Caso and Bernal 1952:190, Figure 320; 286; Figure 434), and others have a convex to cone-shaped raised area in the central depression (Figure A.VIII–7M,N; Paddock 1966:145, Figure 142). Most of these are probably earspools. However, their use in other parts of an urn, particularly in the elaborate headdresses, is not unknown; for an example, see the headdress of an elaborate Monte Albán IIIb urn in the Leigh collection (Paddock 1966:168, Figure 174). One earspool fragment has four appliqué buttons around the raised rim of the earspool (Paddock 1966:129, Figure 92).

EARS (Total 35)

Thirty-five urn fragments consist of ears from various urns. They are decorated with incised lines, circles, punctations and appliqué ear spools (Figure A.VIII–7O–S).

NECKLACE FRAGMENTS (Total 2)

Two necklace fragments were recovered that are comparable to an elaborate necklace on a Monte Albán IIIa or IIIb urn that is illustrated (Caso and Bernal 1952:132, Figure 223; Paddock 1966:168, Figure 174). They consist of a number of rows of what are probably rectangular and circular beads and a lower row of feathers (Figure A.VIII–7T).

BOWS AND KNOTS (Total 6)

Six fragments of urn elements are identified as parts of bows or knots. These may occur in the headdresses, or on the front part of the figurine as part of the necklace or waistband. They may also appear as bows on *braseros* or vases. The ones in the survey collections are plain coils of clay that are either formed into a knot or tied with some type of band (Figure A.VIII–8A,B; Caso and Bernal 1952:33, Figure 33; 103, Figure 169; 109, Figure 179).

ROPES (Total 62)

A total of 62 fragments in the form of ropes are in the collection. Most of these are either from urns or *braseros*. These fragments varied from stylized ropes consisting of a thickened rim on a *brasero* with incised lines to represent the coils of the rope (Figure A.VIII–8E,D) to actual coils of clay that had been twisted together to form the rope (Figure A.VIII–8E–G). Some were made to

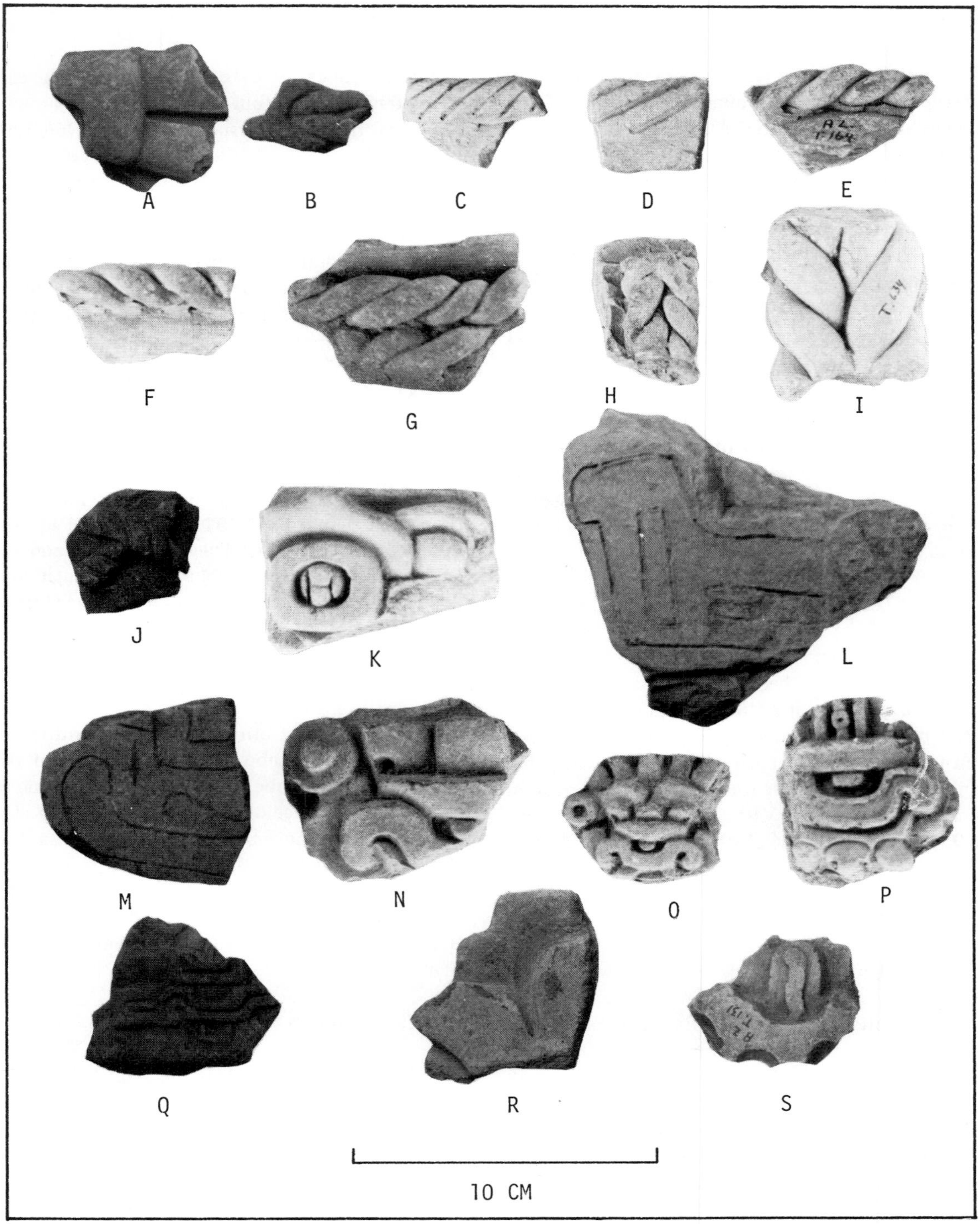

Figure A.VIII–8. Urn fragments.

look more like braiding than rope (Figure A.VIII–8H,I). Ropes, other than those that were free-standing and not attached to the urn, were attached to the rim, near the rim, or to the base of the *braseros* (Caso and Bernal 1952:89, Figures 144 and 145; 108, Figure 178). They generally ran parallel to the rim of the vessel, although several were attached vertically. On urns these ropes are used as necklaces, as well as decorative elements on clothing of the figures (Caso and Bernal 1952: 102, Figure 168; Paddock 1966:138, Figure 131 and 145, Figure 141). One urn fragment in the collection (Figure A.VIII–8J) consisted of a pair of crossed appliqué ropes or cords, and may represent part of a headdress of a Yalalag figure (Caso and Bernal 1952:102, Figure 168).

GLYPH A (Total 1)

One urn headdress fragment probably represents the glyph A as described by Caso (1928:27, Figure 3VII). Caso describes this glyph as the representation of a knot. This element is much more common as a necklace element (Figure A.VIII–8K; Caso and Bernal 1952:21, Figures 11 and 12).

GLYPH C (Total 67)

Fragments of various C glyphs were recovered in the survey. The range of the ones collected is shown in Figure A.VIII–8L–Q). They are all generally comparable to those that are illustrated by Leigh (1966) and Caso (1928). Monte Albán I or II through IIIb or IV are represented in this group of glyphs, with the fine-line incised ones (Figure A.VIII–8L,M) representing the earlier parts of the sequence. Most of the glyphs are from rather elaborate urns, and would have formed the central part of the headdress. For examples, see Caso and Bernal (1952); Paddock (1966:169, Figures 176–177; 93, Figure 5).

Two glyph fragments located in the survey are grouped here as a varient of the C glyph (Figure A.VIII–8R,S). These are apparently not described elsewhere as a separate glyph, and do resemble the C glyph. Leigh (1966:267, Figure 90) includes them with the C glyph. They consisted of the same basic form, except that instead of the water flowing out of the vase they have either a plain central upright section, one with a curved incised line, or an appliqué on this central panel (Figure A.VIII–8S). These appear primarily as part of a larger glyph that is generally worn as a necklace, but they are also utilized as part of a headdress, located either centrally, or symmetrically to either side of the central element of the headdress (Caso and Bernal 1952:209, Figure 346). As part of the necklace, this element regularly appears with what is probably the glyph A.

GLYPH E (Total 2)

Two urn fragments that were part of an urn headdress or a necklace element were in the form of what Caso describes as the glyph E (Figure A.VIII–9A,B). This consists of a cross within a circle, or a square border with rounded corners (Caso 1928:32, Figure 8; 1965:394, Figure 8).

GLYPH J (Total 2)

These two fragments are probably variants of the glyph C (Figure A.VIII–9C,D). Leigh shows an example of this glyph with illustrations of C glyphs, but does not discuss the relationship between the two. Caso (1928:36, Figure 13) and Caso and Bernal (1952) classify it as a glyph J. This glyph is similar to the glyph C except that the central element contains a *mazorca* rather than the usual water sign element. This glyph is generally associated with the *Diosa 2J* (Caso and Bernal 1952:79, Figure 127).

MISCELLANEOUS GLYPHS (Total 10)

One element is probably part of a headdress and consists of a circle which contained a wide incised U (Figure A.VIII–9E,F; Paddock 1966: 136, Figures 120 and 123). Two other urn fragments have a glyphlike form consisting of one or two concentric squares with rounded corners and a

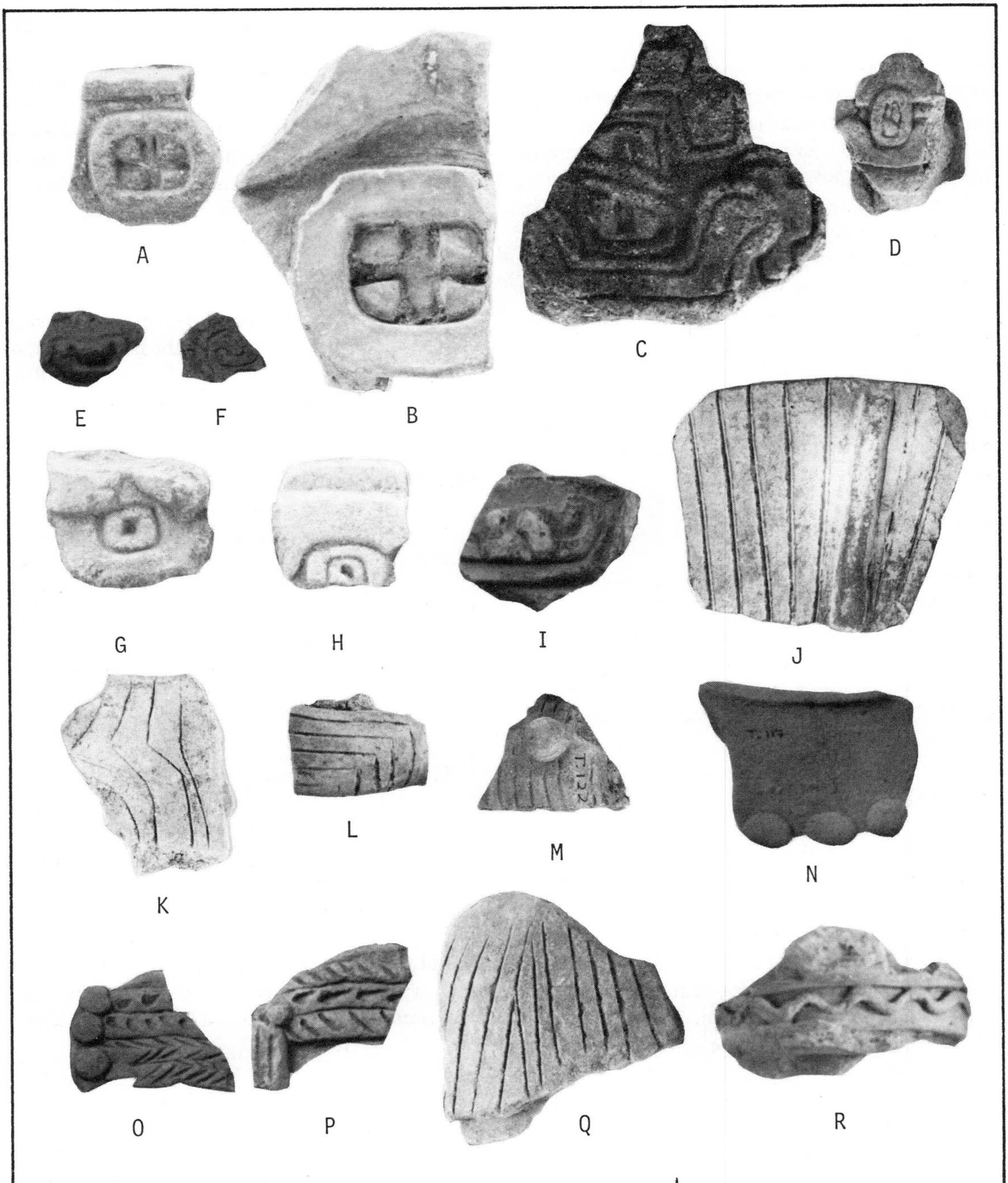

Figure A.VIII–9. Urn fragments.

central square dot in the center (Figure A.VIII–9G,H; Caso and Bernal 1952:134, Figure 225). One other urn element probably represents part of the glyph *Bolso* (Figure A.VIII–9I and Caso 1928: 134, Figure 225). Five others are too fragmentary to be grouped in any specific category.

INCISED HAIR OR HAIRPIECES (Total 57)

Fifty-seven fragments with parallel incised lines are from urn hairpieces (Figure A.VIII–9J–P; Caso and Bernal 1952:43, Figure 51; Paddock 1966: 137, Figure 127). Two of the fragments are parts of rolled hair buns on the top of the head. One has appliqué buttons or beads (Figure A.VIII–9M; Caso and Bernal 1952:102, Figure 168). A variant of this category is a series of hair elements that have the incised lines, but are also combined with appliqué beads or buttons, punctations and incised as well as punctated decorated treatment within the larger panels marked by the parallel incised lines (Figure A.VIII–9N–P; Caso and Bernal 1952: 155, Figure 267; 188, Figure 317).

INCISED CAPES (Total 9)

This is a group of nine urn fragments that are incised similarly to those of the hair or hairpieces above, except that they are part of a cape or collar of the urn and worn around the neck or shoulder (Caso and Bernal 1952:270, Figure 420).

HEADDRESS BAND WITH WATER SIGN (Total 1)

One narrow band from an urn headdress had an appliqué water sign along the center of the band. These are generally located above the forehead or to either side of a large glyph that is centrally located on the headdress (Figure A.VIII–9R; Caso and Bernal 1952:44, Figure 56; Paddock 1966:169, Figure 177).

MAIZE COBS (Total 5)

This category contains five accurate representations of corn ears with the husks removed and the kernals in place (Figure A.VIII–10A,B). They appear as headdress elements as well as parts of necklaces. At least one urn illustrated had two large ears of corn flanking either side of the figure (Caso and Bernal 1952:98, Figure 163; 100, Figure 166; 107, Figure 176; Paddock 1966:169, Figure 177).

HEADDRESS FEATHERS (Total 65)

A series of 65 various modeled feathers are in the survey collection. Most are elements of the headdresses of Monte Albán IIIa and IIIb urns and vary from plain feathers to ones that are more elaborately decorated. The most common is simply a series of plain modeled feathers (Figure A.VIII–10C,D). In other cases they are elaborated with incised lines either perpendicular to the length of the feather, or along the length, probably representating different colors on the feathers, or the shaft of the feather (Figure A.VIII–10E,F). At least two show the barbs of the feather radiating outward from the central shaft (Figure A.VIII–10G,H). Often the feathers are set in a band of beads (Figure A.VIII–10I).

A major variant is a set of eight featherlike elements that are common in Monte Albán IIIb or IIIa headdresses. These usually have a bar element across the feather, and an element that may be a very highly stylized *cerro* glyph (Figure A.VIII–10J–K); Caso and Bernal 1952:199, Figure 333; 209, Figure 346). One example of this group was decorated on both sides and would have protruded outward from the front of the headdress (see Caso and Bernal 1952:299, Figure 334).

SERPENT PALATE (Total 1)

One urn headdress fragment is part of a serpent palate, and probably formed part of the front of a

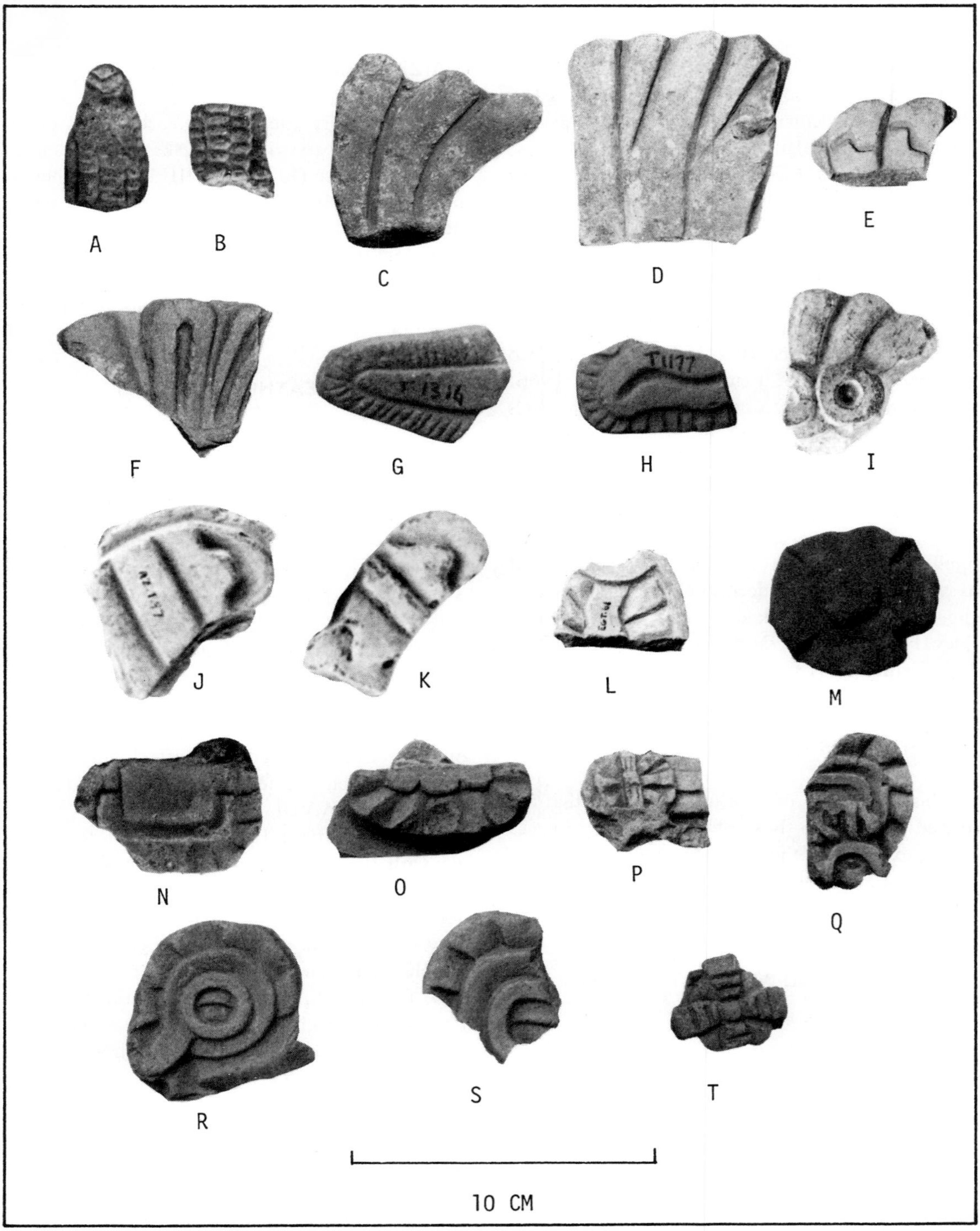

Figure A.VIII–10. Urn fragments.

headdress similar to those on the *silbatos* with serpent headdresses (Figure A.VIII–10L; Caso and Bernal 1952:168, Figure 294; 165, Figure 288; Paddock 1966:137, Figure 125).

ROSETTES (Total 28)

Twenty-eight rosettes were found which were originally parts of headdresses, necklaces, or *braseros*. Most are generally circular, or in some cases slightly rectangular. They have a central circular or square area and radiating panels, which probably represent feathers or flowers (Figure A.VIII–10M–Q; Caso and Bernal 1952:102, Figure 168; 109, Figures 179–180; 221, Figure 262). Three fragments are variants of the rosette (Figure A.VIII–10R,S) and may represent the eye of a bird (Caso and Bernal 1952:174, Figure 297). Another variant of the rosette has a Maltese cross as the main element. This may be a version of the glyph I (Figure A.VIII–10T; Caso and Bernal 1952:102, Figure 168; Caso 1928:35, Figure 12).

COCIJO EYES (Total 6)

Six urn fragments were in the form of *Cocijo* eyes. These elements can appear as the actual eyes of the figure on the urn (Figure A.VIII–11A,G;

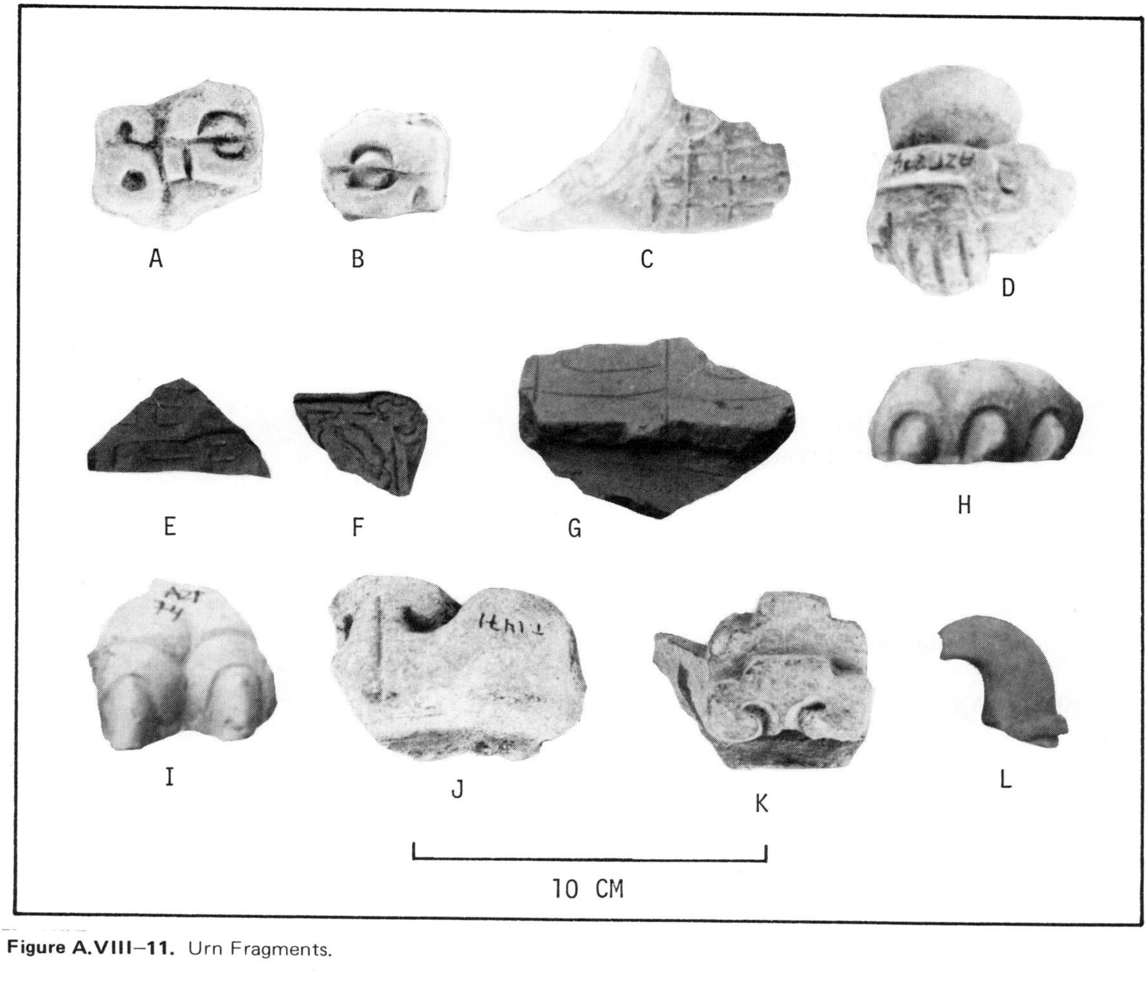

Figure A.VIII–11. Urn Fragments.

Caso and Bernal 1952:18, Figures 3 and 4) or as symmetrical elements in an elaborate headdress (Paddock 1966:138, Figure 132).

COCIJO FACE (Total 1)

One excellent example of a Monte Alban IIIa *Cocijo* face was recovered in the survey. It is virtually identical to one illustrated by Caso and Bernal (1952:38, Figure 42a). This fragment, like the referenced one was probably attached to the side of a *cajete*.

FACES, HANDS, ARMS, FEET (Total 65)

A total of 65 fragments including hand (9), feet (6), arm (33), hand and foot (1), and face (16) fragments were recovered from urns. Most were from large seated urns and were not sufficiently distinctive for comparison with similar forms on illustrated urns. Two specific exceptions are examples of hands. One consisted of an outstretched hand with incised lines forming a series of squares across the palm (Figure A.VIII–11C). The ends of the fingers were in the shape of a *cerro* glyph. The other is a well modeled hand with a bracelet that is also a *cerro* glyph (Figure A.VIII–11D); Caso and Bernal 1952:98, Figure 163).

INCISED URN FRAGMENTS (Total 3)

Three urn fragments have fine incised designs on the surface of the pieces. Two may be skirt fragments (Figure A.VIII–11E,G), and the other is probably from a box (Figure A.VIII–11F; Paddock 1966:118, Figure 60).

JAGUAR CLAWS (Total 11)

Eleven of the distinctive toe and claw portions of jaguar urns were recovered (Figure A.VIII–11H,I). These could be from either a jaguar foot vase (Caso and Bernal 1952:61, Figures 91–113) or the feet of a zoomorphic figure (Paddock 1966:173).

JAGUAR NOSES (Total 3)

These three elements (Figure A.VIII–11J,K) represent the stylized noses of jaguars or bats. They may appear as part of the face of the animal (Paddock 1966:133, Figure 109) or as a separate element in the headdress of an urn where they may closely resemble a three-petal flower (Paddock 1966:138–139, Figures 131 and 133). Leigh (1966:265, Figures 67–69) shows a similar element as an integral part of the glyph C. A very similar element is also used as the tongue of a serpent god (Paddock 1966:134, Figure 112).

BAT CLAWS (Total 3)

Three claws were recovered which were from the very distinctive bat claw vases that are associated with Monte Albán IIIb–IV (Figure A.VIII–11L; Caso and Bernal 1952:74, Figure 119).

MISCELLANEOUS URN FRAGMENTS (Total 230)

In addition to the urn fragments that have been described above there were numerous urn fragments in the survey collections that could not be classified. These consisted primarily of large plain sherds from bases and backs of the urns. While they are not included in the aforementioned categories of urn elements, they were used in the plot of the total distributions of urn fragments.

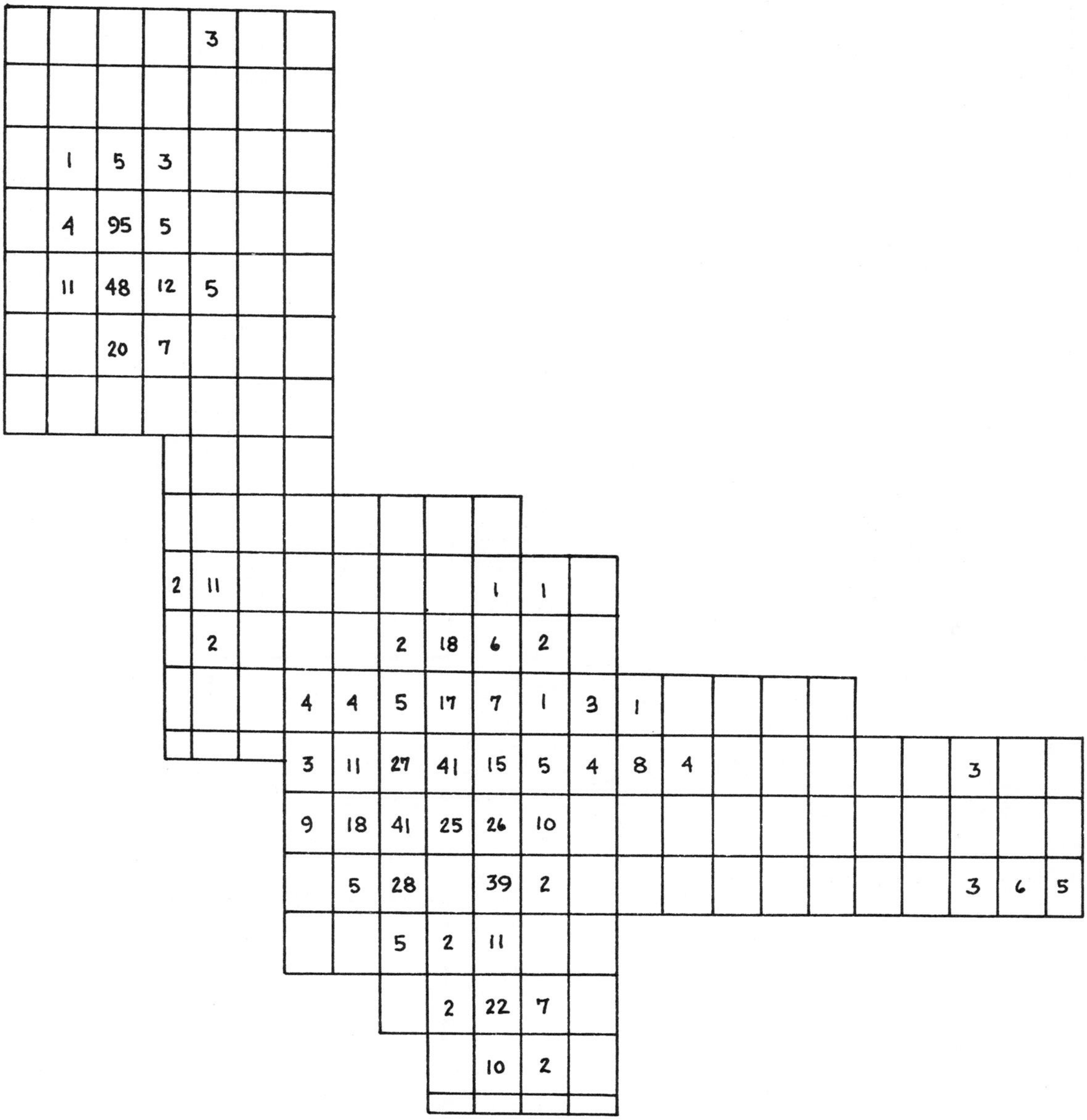

Figure A.VIII–12. Distribution of urn fragments by grid area.

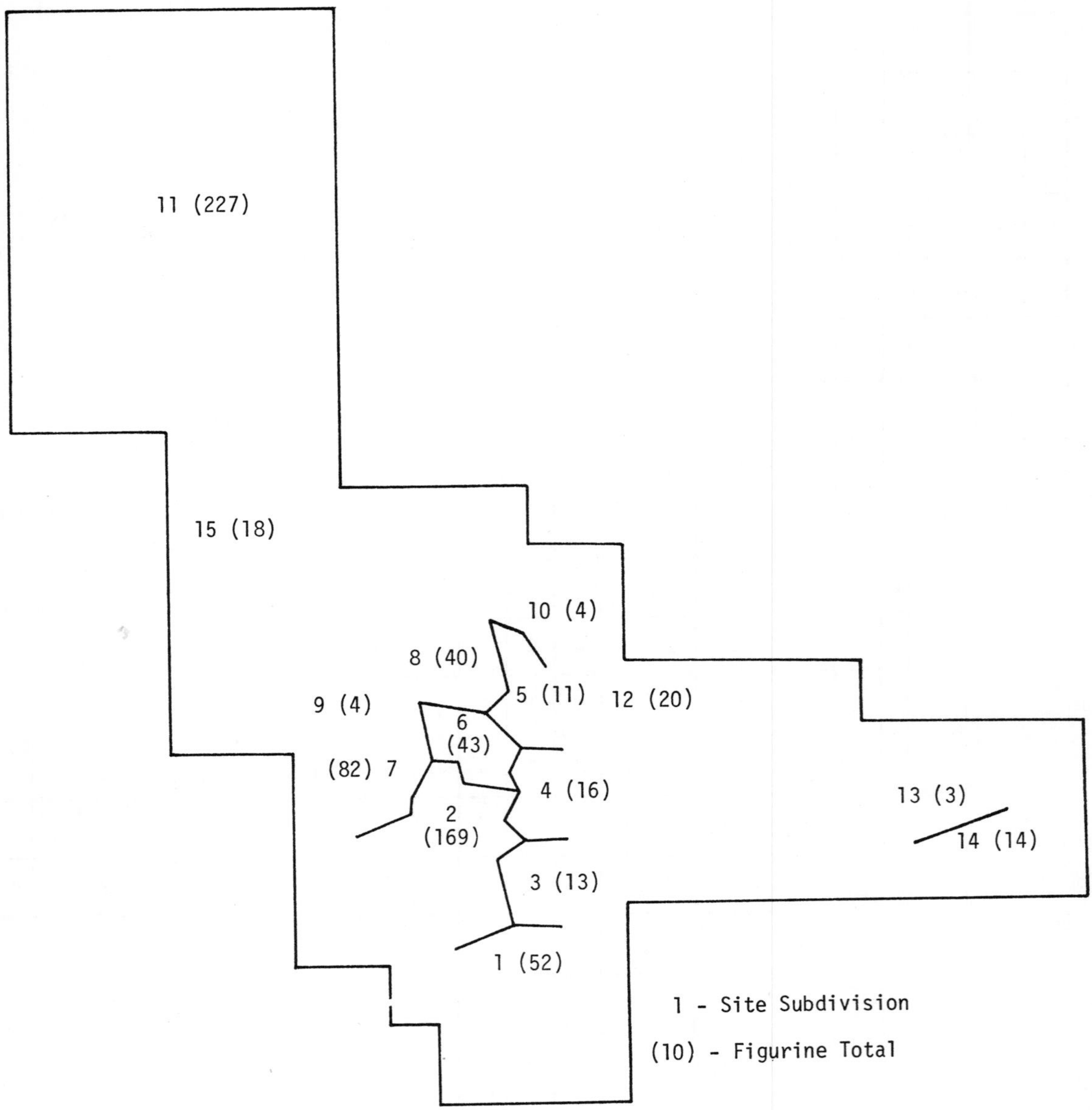

FigureA.VIII–13. Distribution of urn fragments by site subdivision.

APPENDIX IX

Test Excavations at Terrace 1227

CARL KUTTRUFF
WILLIAM O. AUTRY, JR.

Introduction

During the last two weeks of June 1973 limited test excavations were undertaken on Terrace 1227 at the site of Monte Albán. This terrace, mapped by the Monte Albán Survey Project[1] is located approximately 1200 m northwest of the North Platform (Main Plaza area) and along the outer limits of the main occupation zone of the site. The excavations were designed to cut across the lower defensive wall which surrounds Monte Albán on the north and west sides (See Figure 1.3 on p. 4). This wall forms the lower, or western, edge of Terrace 1227. The specific purposes of the test were (*a*) to define the nature of the wall construction, (*b*) to obtain a ceramic sample in order to date the wall construction, and (*c*) to establish the relationship between the defensive wall and the adjacent terrace.

A trench, 1 m in width, was established perpendicular to the defensive wall along an azimuth of 138° magnetic north approximately 75 m from the northwest corner of the terrace. The trench extended 6 m to the east from the top of the defensive wall onto the terrace and down the slope of the defensive wall to the west to a point just beyond a line of retaining stones at the base of the slope. Located and excavated in this manner, the trench was to have provided information on the constructions behind the lower retaining wall, the slope of the wall, and the area behind the crest of the wall. The plan and profile of this trench are illustrated in Figure A.IX–1. The excavations were carried to bedrock in the first 4 m east of the edge of the terrace, but were abandoned in the easternmost two squares. In the trench along the terrace slope and defensive wall, only the area around the retaining wall and a 1-m square located halfway up the slope were excavated to bedrock.

In addition to providing the expected data on the wall and terrace constructions, the excavations also exposed a Monte Albán II (200 B.C.–A.D. 200) tomb and a Monte Albán V (post A.D. 900) bell-shaped pit. These cultural features are described following a discussion of the stratigraphy of the terrace.

Summary of Stratigraphy

The stratigraphy of the terrace and slope consisted of an underlying limestone bedrock in all

[1] This paper is based on research sponsored in part by National Science Foundation Grant Numbers GS-28547 and GS-38030 to Richard E. Blanton.

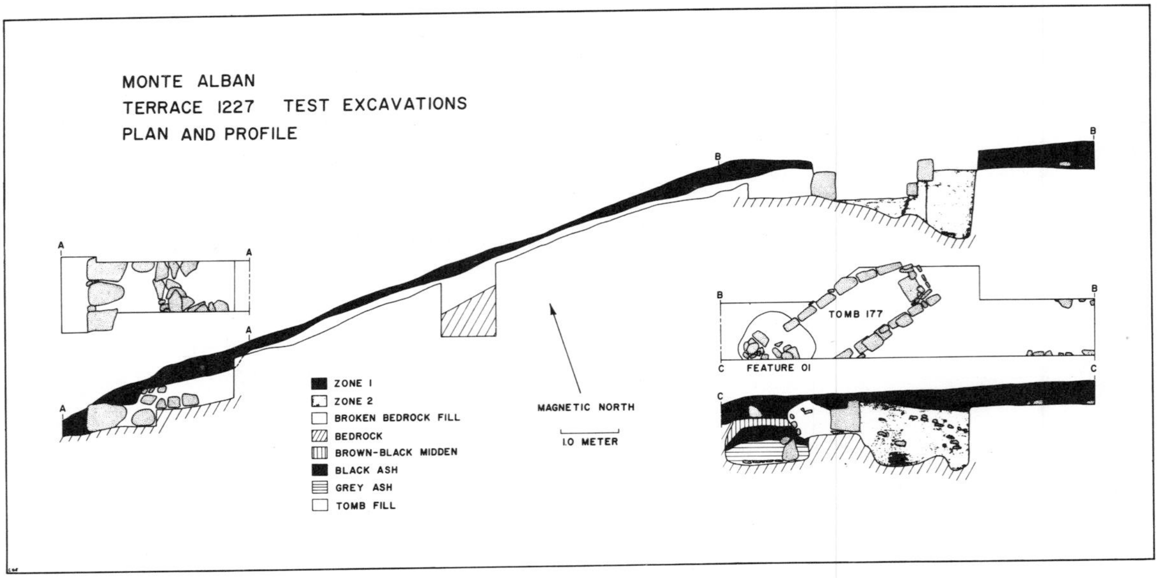

Figure A.IX–1. Plan and profile of Terrace 1227 excavations.

parts of the excavation overlaid by one or more layers of construction fill, cultural refuse, or some mixture of the two. The soft, white-to-yellow limestone bedrock had apparently been modified to some extent on the terrace surface as well as on the terrace slope. It is quite possible that the bedrock on the slope had been leveled so that it presented a rather even and smooth appearance. About 2 m behind what would have been the top of the wall, or the edge of the terrace, the bedrock had been gouged out to a depth approximately .50 m below the original grade. The actual areal extent of these modifications was not determined because of the limited scope of the excavations.

A retaining wall of faced blocks was set on the bedrock at the base of the slope, providing a straight face along the outside of this row of stones. The area behind the retaining wall and the entire slope of the defensive wall was then filled and covered with what appears to be a broken bedrock fill. Presumably this material was removed from the depression in the bedrock, and others like it, that was revealed in the trench just east of the edge of the terrace. This construction fill extended east from the edge of the terrace except where interrupted by the construction of such features as Tomb 177[2] and the later, intrusive Feature 1. No artifacts were recovered from this zone of broken bedrock fill. Therefore, we would infer that this episode of construction was completed prior to any heavy occupation of the immediate area.

The third major zone of deposition was a tan-to-light brown fill above the bedrock on the terrace itself (Zone 2, Figure A.IX–1). This fill contained midden debris, stone rubble, and other construction remains including several fired and unfired adobe fragments. The matrix, for the most part, appeared to be eroded adobe. Tomb 177 was located within this fill zone. We assume that the tomb was constructed at the same time the area was filled, and it might have been located beneath a patio or floor of a structure that has been obliterated by modern cultivation. The upper parts of the rocks forming the sides of the tomb extended

[2] Tomb 177 has been assigned by Marcus C. Winter, Centro Regional de Oaxaca, I.N.A.H. in order to place the tomb in the already established Monte Albán tomb sequence (personal communication from M. Winter: 22 September 1975).

into the present-day plow zone of the terrace. The eastern part of the floor of the tomb was of the same material as the fill in the squares adjacent to the tomb on the east, indicating that the area may have been filled at the same time the tomb was constructed. Alternatively, the tomb was intrusive to this zone of redeposited materials; however, there was no evidence outside the tomb to suggest that a pit was dug for its construction. Artifacts from this zone included 326 sherds ranging from Monte Albán I through Monte Albán V times, with Monte Albán II sherds predominating (See Table A.IX–1). The small number of Monte Albán IIIb–IV and V sherds are most likely intrusive, or included in this zone before Feature 1 was defined. Lithic debris included one large chert chopper, three chert or quartzite flakes, and one green obsidian blade fragment.

Located above the previously described construction fill (Zone 2, Figure A.IX–1) and Tomb 177 was a dark brown-to-black zone (Zone 1, Figure A.IX–1) varying in thickness from 10–40 cm. This zone was present in all squares on the terrace and continued over the edge to cover the broken bedrock fill on the slope of the wall. Cultural materials were generally confined to the terrace surface and limited in number on the slope. The upper 10–15 cm of this zone were disturbed on the terrace surface by recent plowing. A total of 368 sherds were recovered from this zone and ranged in time from Monte Albán I through V (Table A.IX–1). Lithic materials included 11 chert or quartzite flakes, one green obsidian flake, 6 gray obsidian blade segments, and 1 gray obsidian core.

Tomb 177

Tomb 177 was located approximately 1.5 m east of the terrace edge. The tomb was immediately below the plow disturbed soil at a depth of approximately 10 cm. The architecture of the

Table A.IX-1

Provenience:	Zone 1	Zone 2	Tomb fill	Feature 1
Ceramics				
MA V	12	04		11
MA IIIb–IV	05	02		02
MA IIIa	06		01	
MA II	119	136	61	19
Late MA I–II	19	20	09	05
Early MA I	16	31	07	04
Indeterminate[a]	149	175	66	44
Total	326	368	144	85
Artifacts				
Chert/quartzite flakes	11	03	01	01
Chert chopper		01		
Quartzite crystal bead			01	
Green obsidian blade	06	01		01
Green obsidian flake	01			
Green obsidian blade core	01			
Gray obsidian blade			01	
Gray obsidian flake			01	
Adobe fragments		03		

[a]This category also includes sherds that were not specific to a given period.

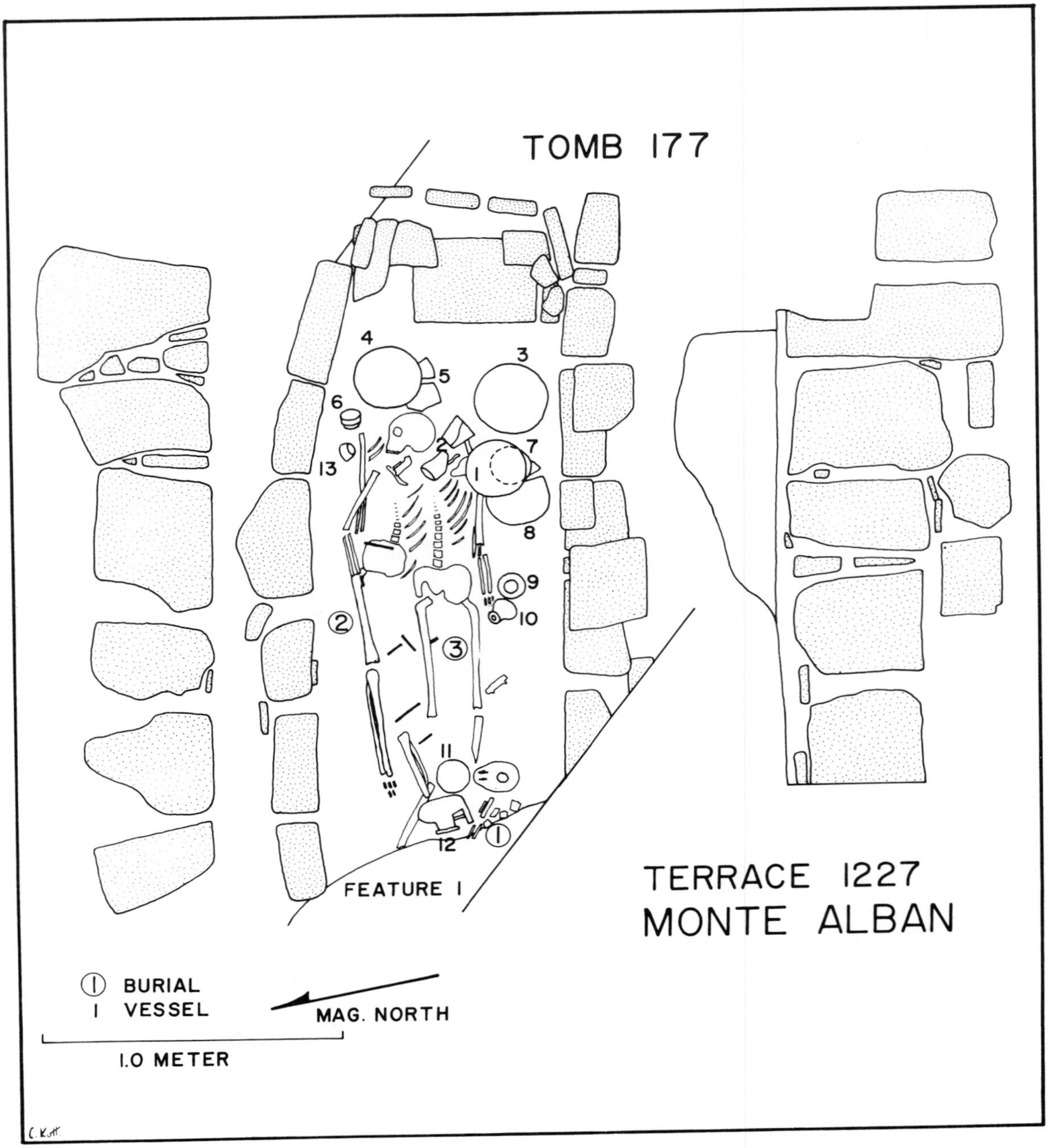

Figure A.IX–2. Detail of Tomb 177.

tomb was simple, consisting of a rectangular chamber with a simple entrance/antechamber on the east end. The tomb was constructed of large, rectangular, roughly shaped blocks placed on end (see Figure A.IX–2) with the spaces between the larger rocks chinked or filled with small irregular stones. The wall stones in the western half of the tomb had been set on bedrock, whereas those making up the tomb walls rested upon a surface of fill material which was described for the terrace outside the tomb (Zone 2). At the east end of the tomb there was a large rectangular stone threshold flanked by two thin rectangular stone slabs set vertically near the ends of the threshold to form the entrance or antechamber (Figures A.IX–2,3,5). The entrance had been sealed at one time with a large oval stone, probably after the placement of Individual 2, but this stone had fallen into the tomb prior to the interment of Individual 3 or it was pulled in at the time of the last burial.

The tomb was approximately 2^+ m along the longest axis (104° magnetic north), with a maximum width of .84 m. The maximum depth of the tomb from the top course of the wall stones to the bedrock floor was .79 m. The tomb conforms generally to the description of Monte Albán II tombs given by Acosta (1965:818–819, Figure 5d,e). The stones of the walls were unusually large, and the tomb was filled with rubble in a tan-to-brown matrix rather than having a slab roof and open chamber. If it previously had a slab roof as perhaps might be expected, these stones had apparently been removed since none of the stones in the tomb fill were large enough to have functioned as roofing slabs.

At least two and probably three individuals were interred in the tomb. The skeletal remains designated Individual 1 consisted of displaced rib fragments, humeri, radii, carpuls, a few phalanges and parietal and occipital fragments of the skull.[3] Parts of this individual remained unexcavated in the south profile near Feature 01, in what would have been the southwest corner of the tomb, because of lack of time. The remains of this individual, an old male, were also disturbed by the digging of Feature 01 during Monte Albán V times. This feature was intrusive into the west end of the tomb. A femur head and other fragments were located near the base of Feature 01, and these most likely belong with Individual 1. From placement and subsequent disturbance we assume that these remains are the first use of the tomb. The bones and grave goods were merely pushed to the

Figure A.IX–3. Tomb 177 after clearing, view east.

[3] Richard Wilkinson kindly examined the skeletal materials from the tomb and provided ages and sexes for the three individuals.

rear of the tomb when the second person was interred. This practice of reusing tombs with earlier remains displaced to the rear or sides of the tomb is well known from other excavated tombs at Monte Albán. Tomb 7 is probably one of the best-known examples (Caso 1970). So this appears to be a reasonable explanation for the disturbed remains within Tomb 177. It is possible, although not demonstrable, that Vessels 11 and 12 (all grave goods described below), may have been offerings associated with this first interment. Equally possible is the alternative that these two vessels were associated with one of the later burials, probably Individual 3, since the vessels were located between his feet. This idea is also supported by a tendency to include bridge-spout vessels with adult male burials in Late Formative times (Autry 1973:54–55).

Individual 2 was extended supine in the tomb with arms at his sides. The skeleton was relatively complete except for thoracic vertebrae, some carpals and phalanges, and ribs. The left leg was also missing. It was probably disturbed when the third individual was placed into the tomb. The skull had been displaced to the rear of the tomb near vessels 11 and 12 and was missing the maxillary sections as well as the mandible. A left femur head was located in the rubble fill 5–10 cm above the third individual during the course of excavating the tomb; and this femur is probably part of the missing left leg from Individual 2. This individual was also an old male. Several vessels are thought to be associated with this individual. Vessel 5 was located near where the head would have been located if the skeleton had been completely articulated. Part of this vessel was inside the tomb, and the remaining part was located in the antechamber, further emphasizing the disturbance of this individual when Individual 3 was placed in the tomb. Vessels 6 and 13 were located near the right shoulder; Vessels 11 and 12, mentioned above, were located near the feet and may also have been associated with this interment. Also accompanying the second individual were seven green obsidian blades (Figure A.IX–4) which had been scattered over the pelvic and leg regions of the burial. These blades were definitely stratified below Individual 3 (see Figure A.IX–2).

Individual 3, an old man, was the last to be interred in the tomb and the best preserved. Bones missing, probably due to poor preservation, included ribs, phalanges, and some vertebrae. Included as grave goods with this burial are Vessels 3 and 4, which were located just above and to the sides of the head; and Vessels 7, 8, and 1, located at the left shoulder of Individual 3 and partially over the upper arm of Individual 2. Also accompanying as offerings with this burial were Vessels 9 and 10, which were located around and under the hand of the last burial. Vessels 1 and 2 were located about 10 cm above Vessels 7 and 8 and separated from the latter by dirt and rubble fill. These may have been placed in the tomb with Individual 3, but it is also possible that they were associated originally with an earlier burial, and placed, or replaced, in the fill when the tomb was covered.

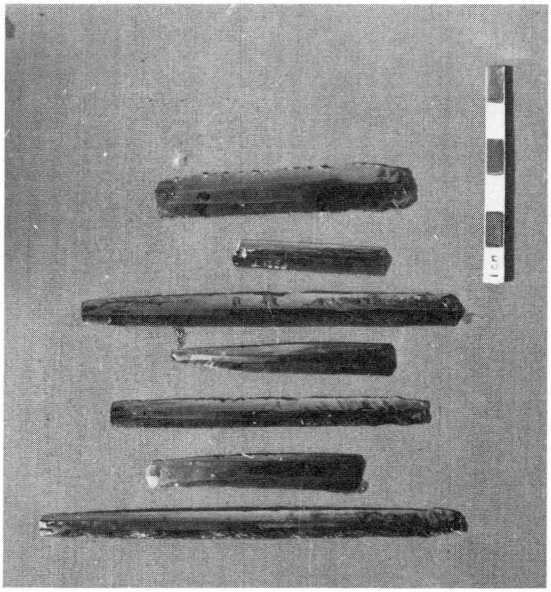

Figure A.IX–4. Obsidian blades associated with Interment 2.

Although the first two burials were probably placed into the tomb through the entrance, it is probable that the third was interred through the top. It may have been that the tomb collapsed sometime after the interment of Individual 2. After the interment of Individual 3, the large door stone (Figure A.IX–5) was pulled into the tomb as fill, and the burial was sealed with earth and rubble (Figure A.IX–6). Also included in the tomb fill were 144 sherds, one quartzite pebble, one chert or quartzite flake, a quartzite crystal bead, one gray-banded obsidian flake and one gray-banded obsidian blade (Table A.IX–1).

All of the ceramic offerings that were interred with the three individuals in Tomb 177 have been classified as Monte Albán II, rather firmly establishing the period of utilization for that structure. In addition, the sherds that were recovered from the tomb fill above the interments were predominantly Monte Albán II or earlier, with the occurrence of only two that date later then Monte Albán II. A brief description of the ceramic grave goods follows.[4]

Vessel 01 *Gris*, flat-based bowl with outleaned walls, burnished interior and exterior, wide double-line incising around the interior of the rim (Figure A.IX–7). Diameter: 21.5 cm; height: 5.6 cm. Category 1227.

Vessel 02 *Gris*, cylinder, "Xipe Totec" effigy (Figure A.IX–8). It is similar to those illustrated by Caso and Bernal (1952:258–259, Figures 409 and 410). This vessel is probably Period II since it has the eyes formed by incised lines, rather than the characteristic appliqué coffee bean eyes of Monte Albán IIIa. Not in our typology.

Vessel 03 *Crema*, flat-based bowl with outleaned walls, streaky orange finish, burnished interior and exterior (Figure A.IX–9). Diameter: 24.5 cm; height: 5.3 cm. Category 0057.

Vessel 04 *Crema*, flat-based bowl with outleaned walls, streaky orange finish, burnished interior and exterior (Figure A.IX–10). Diameter: 21.2 cm; height: 4.4 cm. Category 0057.

[4]Marcus Winter examined the ceramics and these descriptions are based upon his comments and observations about possible chronological placement.

Vessel 05 *Gris*, flat-based bowl with outleaned walls, burnished interior and exterior (Figure A.IX–11). Diameter: 19.0 cm; height: 5.0 cm. Not in our typology.

Vessel 06 *Crema*, small flat-based bowl with inleaned walls and a shelf for a lid (Figure A.IX–12). Nearly identical to those illustrated by Caso *et al.* (1967:241, Figure 218[b,d]) although not as well burnished. Diameter: 7.8 cm; height: 4.4 cm. Category 0023.

Vessel 07 *Crema*, flat-based bowl with outleaned walls and burnished interior, wiped around exterior rim (Figure A.IX–13). Diameter: 16.0 cm; height: 3.4 cm. Category 0375.

Vessel 08 *Gris*, flat-based bowl with outleaned walls, wide-line comb on interior bottom, burnished

Figure A.IX–5. Tomb 177 after partial excavation, view east.

Figure A.IX–6. Tomb 177 before excavation, showing rubble and earth fill, view east.

interior and exterior (Figure A.IX–14). Diameter: 20.0 cm; height: 7.2 cm. Category 1194.

Vessel 09 *Gris*, small *olla* with straight neck and handle (missing), burnished exterior and inside of neck (Figure A.IX–15). Rim diameter: 6.0 cm; maximum diameter: 10.8 cm; height: 8.8 cm. Not in our typology.

Vessel 10 *Gris*, asymmetrical *olla* with outflaring neck, burnished exterior and interior of neck (Figure A.IX–16). Similar to that illustrated by Caso *et al.* (1967:219, Figure 185). Rim diameter: 7.0 cm, maximum diameter 10.0 cm; height: 8.0 cm. Not in our typology.

Vessel 11 *Gris*, hemispherical bowl, burnished interior and exterior, except on base (Figure A.IX–17). Diameter: 10.2 cm; height: 5.0 cm. Not in our typology.

Vessel 12 *Gris*, bridge-spout vessel burnished on exterior, including neck and rim (Figure A.IX–18). Rim diameter: 10.2 cm; maximum diameter: 17.0 cm; height: 11.0 cm. Category 5084.

Vessel 13 *Gris*, small bowl with incurved rim, burnished exterior, wiped interior (Figure A.IX–19). Rim diameter: 4.9 cm; maximum diameter: 6.3 cm; height: 5.8 cm. Not in our typology.

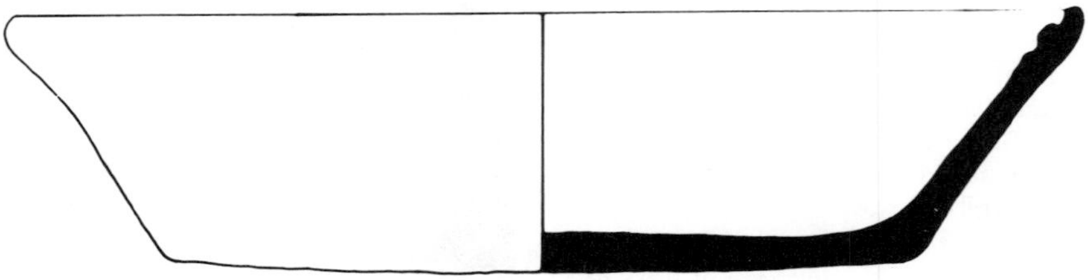

Figure A.IX–7. Vessel 1, reduced by one-half.

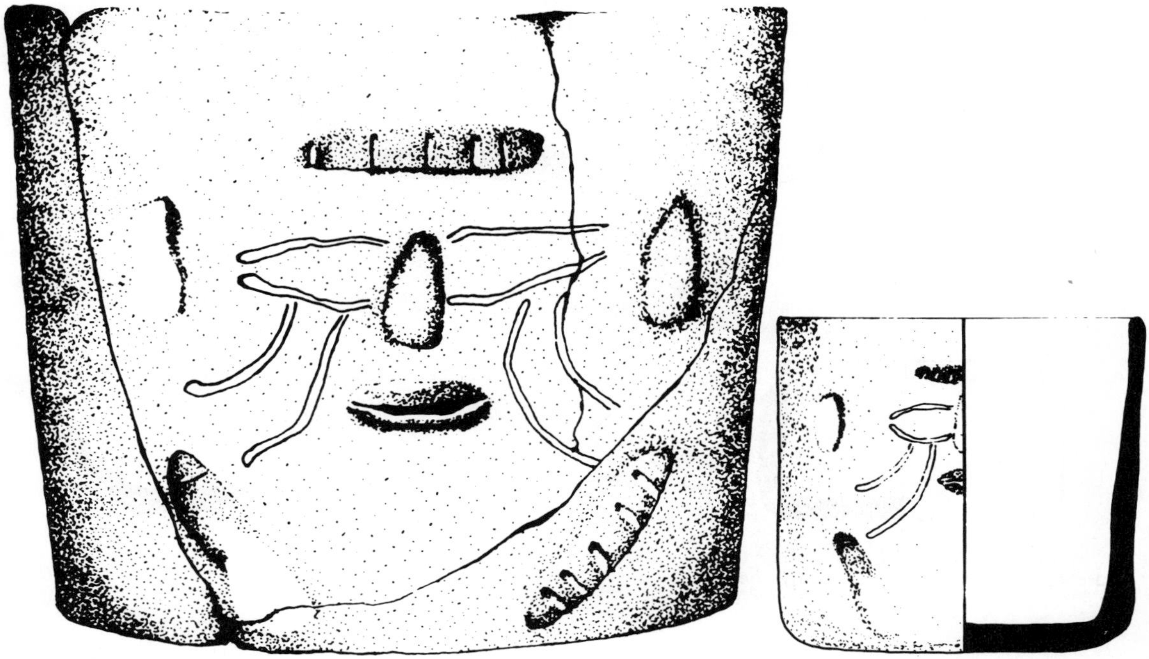

Figure A.IX–8. Vessel 2. Whole vessel is actual size, cutaway version is reduced by one-half.[5]

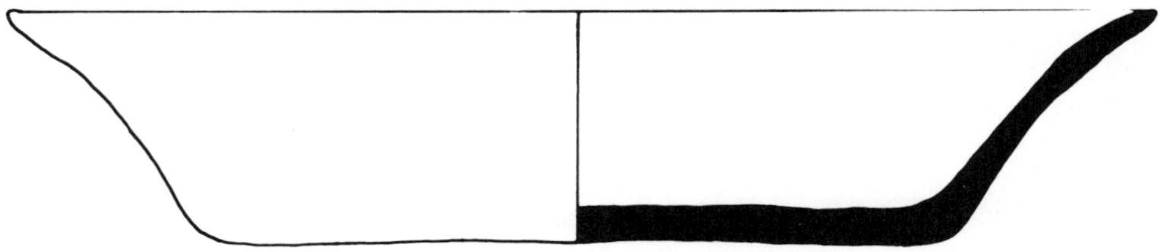

Figure A.IX–9. Vessel 3, reduced by one-half.

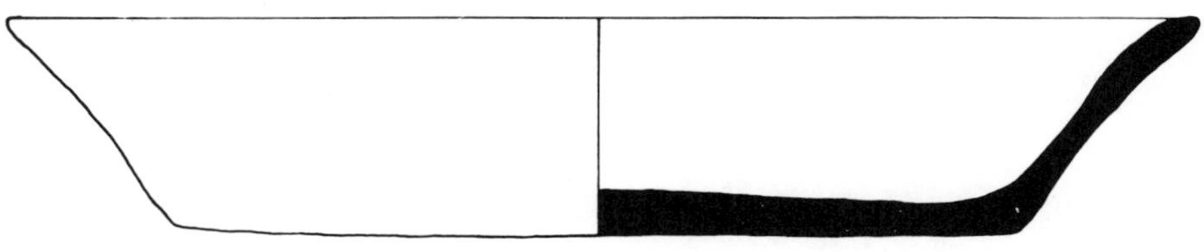

Figure A.IX–10. Vessel 4, reduced by one-half.

[5] Figure A.IX–8 drawn by Betty Brown, Illinois State University.

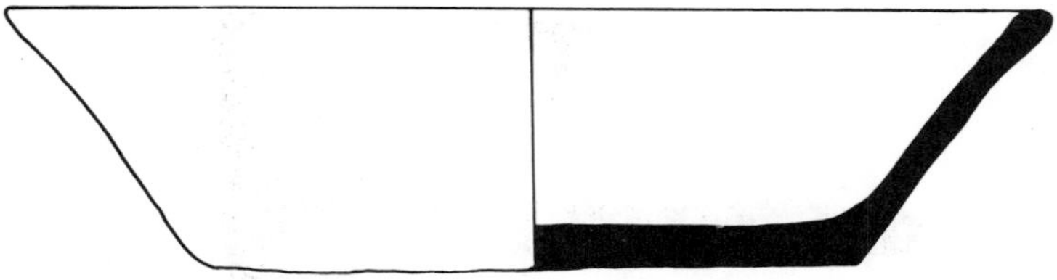

Figure A.IX–11. Vessel 5, reduced by one-half.

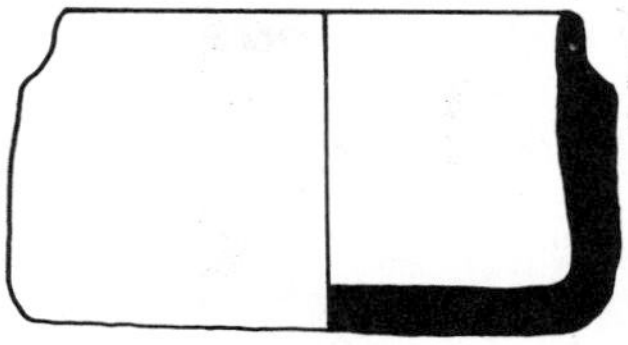

Figure A.IX–12. Vessel 6, reduced by one-half.

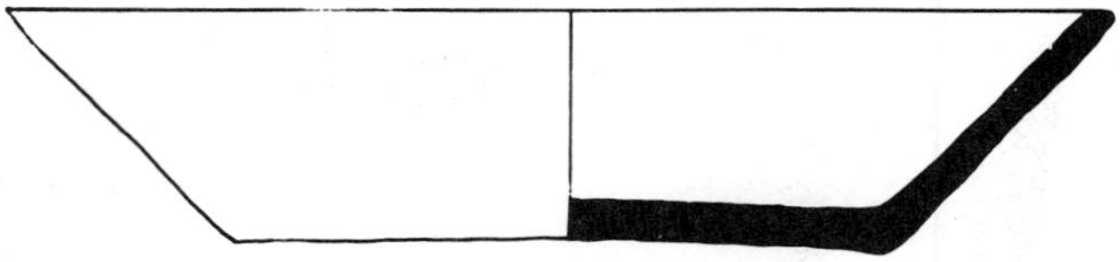

Figure A.-IX–13. Vessel 7, reduced by one-half.

Figure A.IX–14. Vessel 8, reduced by one-half.

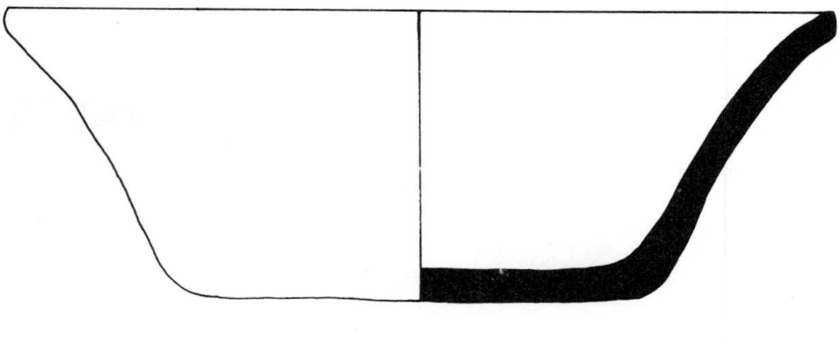

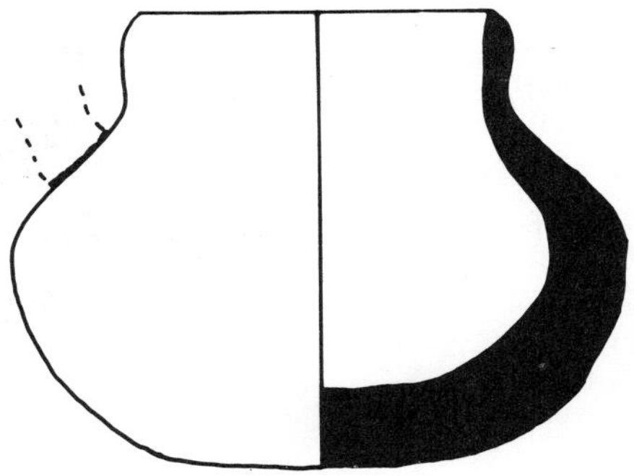

Figure A.IX–15. Vessel 9, reduced by one-half.

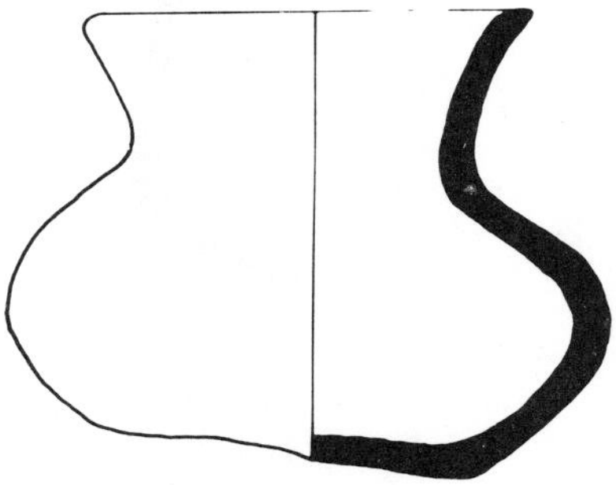

Figure A.IX–16. Vessel 10, reduced by one-half.

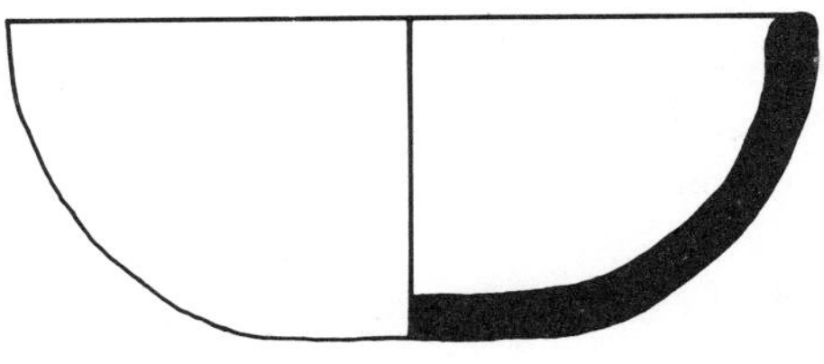

Figure A.IX–17. Vessel 11, reduced by one-half.

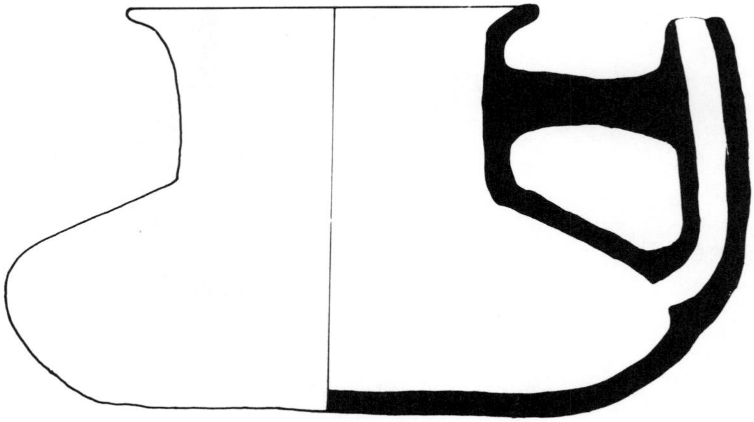

Figure A.IX–18. Vessel 12, reduced by one-half.

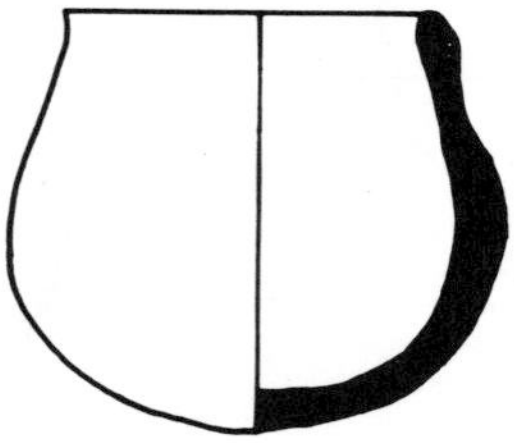

Figure A.IX–19. Vessel 13, reduced by one-half.

Feature 1

A bell-shaped pit was located and defined in the test trench near the edge of the terrace, just east of the crest of the defensive wall. The base was slightly concave. This feature was defined at the base of Zone 1 and had an opening of approximately .95 m and a depth from that point of .80 m. The base of the feature was 1.45 m in diameter. The pit was probably cut down from the terrace surface, but it was not defined until the point where it had been cut into the rock fill of the wall and the underlying bedrock. The pit, as previously noted, intruded into the western part of Tomb 177.

The internal stratigraphy of the pit consisted of at least three distinct layers (see Figure A.IX–1). On the floor of the pit were several flat stone slabs that apparently had been used as flagging in the base of the feature. The lowest layer of fill was a gray ashy lens with a few small rocks and sherds, probably refuse from cleaning a hearth or some other heating or cooking facility. The next zone was a black ashy layer with some small inclusive rocks, and was probably also the debris from a hearth that had been discarded into the pit. The last zone of the pit fill was a dark brown-to-black layer with numerous sherds and rubble.

Several fragments of human bone were found in the lower levels of the pit, along with one large stone that had probably served as a wallstone in the tomb. Other materials that were recovered in this feature included a chert or quartzite flake and one green obsidian blade fragment. On the basis of the ceramics, including several polychrome sherds,

Feature 1 has been assigned to a Monte Albán V occupation (see Table A.IX–1), which was probably the final prehispanic utilization of the terrace. We assumed that the pit had originally been dug and used as a storage facility. Possibly after the collapse of the side of the pit that was composed of tomb fill, the use of the pit for storage was discontinued and subsequently utilized for the disposal of waste.

Summary

The results of the test excavations on Terrace 1227 reveal a lengthy utilization of that area from Monte Albán I through V times. The predominant occupation appears to have been during Late Monte Albán I and Monte Albán II, with the latter dominating. Monte Albán phases IIIa and IIIb–IV are nominally represented. Materials and the one feature excavated which were assigned to Monte Albán V probably represent the reoccupation of the terrace area during that time. Several small households would probably make up such a settlement.

The initial construction of the lower defensive wall probably took place before any real occupation of the terrace area. This suggests that the wall would have been constructed during a late Monte Albán I or Early Monte Albán II phase. After the construction of the wall there was a substantial Monte Albán II occupation with large deposits of midden, the construction and utilization of Tomb 177, and presumably its associated structure.

APPENDIX X

Structure Summary and Ink Drawings of Field Maps

This appendix is designed to supply metric data that cannot be measured easily, or at all, from the 1:2000 map squares. In some cases patios, rooms, and other features were measurable from the surface, but are at a scale not practical to include in the 1:2000 maps. Field drawings made of terraces are included here where I thought the information would facilitate measurement. Obviously only selected terraces with architectural features exposed are included. These are the terraces where I felt the most accurate measurements of rooms and/or patios could be made. Most other architectural features visible on the surface are more fragmentary and so detailed drawings are not included. Some terraces with exposed architecture that can be drawn are not included here because they have already been published, or are obviously excavated, and therefore will, at some time be published by the excavators. Any drawings included here of excavated features must be considered to be preliminary, and will be superseded by the more accurate drawings made by excavators.

Structure Summary

Terrace number	Site sub-division	Terrace area (m²)	Structures–probable function	Structure	(m³)	Total structure area (m²)	Total room area (m²)	Patio area (m²)	Estimated total number of residences	Terrace area per house (m²)	Appendix X Figure number
1	2	480	One residence visible			?	?	10.2	?	?	A.X–1
2	2	2,602	Four probable structures,	A		115	–	–	4	651	
			one fragmentary	B		115	–	–			
				Possible structure		156					
5	2	3,750	Elaborate residence	A	1,404	709	159				A.X–2
				B	971	571	100	588	1	3,750	
				C	76	70	36				
				D	37	36	16				
				(*adoratorio*)							
9	2	1,157	One residence partially exposed			?	?	?	?	?	A.X–3
13	2	1,677	One probable residence with patio?			488	?	?	?	?	A.X–4
14	2	1,726	Low mound–residential?		133	186	88	?	?	?	
15	2	573	Two residences exposed				16.1				A.X–5
							6.8				
16	2	625	One partially excavated residence				20.25				A.X–6
17	2	2,568	Elaborate residence	A	278	180	56				A.X–7
				B	1,442	504	121	765	1	2,568	
				C	426	286	80				
18	2	1,387	Elaborate residence on platform		5,976	1,387	437	84	1	1,387	A.X–8
19	2	1,495	Includes one residence exposed by excavation								A.X–9
20	2	6,357	Several probable	A		175	130	45			
			residences exposed	B		391	294	97			
21	2	17,976	At least six residences exposed by excavation, stratigraphy complex				10.89				
							10.89				
							5.3				
							10.89				
24	2	2,113	Mound X, function unknown[a]								
27	2	11,750	Possibly as many as 10 residences[b]								

				Sistema Y							
				A	1,894	550	172				A.X–10
				B	1,332	411	105	625	10?	1,306	
				C	3,454	660	67				
				H			33				
				K			37.5				
				Q			85.6	14.4			
				W	3,530	825	588.4	11.6			
				X	338	300	139.5	18.5?			
				Z	130	163	100 (w/ patio)				
				Y	335	360	88.9	21.1			
28	2	2,304	One residence exposed					25			
29	2	825	Two residences exposed					52.3			A.X–11
								20.3			
30	2	684	Three residences exposed					14.4			A.X–12
								14.6			
								13			
31	2	3,136	Four residences exposed					10.5			A.X–13
								9.8			
								10.5			
32	2	924	Three residences exposed					28.9 (?)			A.X–14
								9 (?)	3	308	
								16 (?)			
								23 (?)			
35	2	268	Patio exposed					9			
36	2	212	One or two residences partially exposed					9			A.X–15
37	2	495	Two probable patios exposed					10.2			A.X–16
								7.8			
38	2	490	One residence exposed					15.36	1	490	A.X–17
39	2	621	Two patios exposed					16			A.X–18

(Continued)

[a]See Appendix I, Part 2, and published sources.
[b]The structure with Tomb 7 is difficult to interpret. See Appendix I, Part 2, and published sources.
[c]See Appendix I, Part 2.
[d]Dimensions of the mound.
[e]Structure built so that the slope closes the patio on its south edge.
[f]See reference to published plans in Appendix I, Part 2.
[g]See Appendix I, Part 2, for references to published plans.
[h]Excavated by I.N.A.H.
[i]Slope closes patio on south and west sides.
[j]The terrace has some evidence for walls and a patio, apart from the mound, but interpretation is difficult.

Structure Summary (Continued)

Terrace number	Site sub-division	Terrace area (m²)	Structure–probable function		(m³)	Total structure area (m²)	Total room area (m²)	Patio area (m²)	Estimated total number of residences	Terrace area per house (m²)	Appendix X Figure number
								32			
40	4	958	"Weird structure"[c]–one patio exposed above					12.3			
41	2	460	One residence partially exposed					16	1	460	A.X–19
43	2	1,793	Four patios exposed					17.6			
								10.2			
								10.2			
								10			
44	2	448	One patio exposed					12.8			
51	2	2,234	Elaborate residence	A	1,216	283	84				A.X–20
				B	961	359	25.6	441.6			
				C	970	308	72				
78	2	464	One residence exposed			336 (?)	251 (?)	85	1	464	A.X–21
79	2	3,480	Single mound		5,117	999	47.5				A.X–22
85	2	572	Single mound		93	120	16				
92	3	1,050	Single mound		460	168	25				A.X–23
104	4	284	One residence exposed			132	115.2	16.8	1	284	A.X–24
155	4	307	One residence exposed					19.1	1	307	A.X–25
156	4	917	One patio exposed					21.4			
160	6	2,587	Isolated mound		509	252	49				
161	6	3,040	One or two residences					23			A.X–26
			and two mounds		205		27	77			
					2,706		120	354			
165	6	6,484	Elaborate residence		1,996						
					637						
					1,029						
						1,905	265	725			
169	2	2,490	Two platforms, function unknown								
					368		64				
					127		65				
170	6	1,960	One residence exposed			90 (?)	60 (?)	30			A.X–27
171	6	437	One patio exposed					15.2			
174	6	8,513	Elaborate residence		260		64				
					2,104		169				
					909		118	725			
					993		152				
					294		83				

					2,457					
							12.9			
			Includes two small patios				14.4			
175	6	810	One residence partially exposed				25			
205	1	2,340	One residence exposed		70.4 (?)					A.X–28
207	1	2,563	Isolated mound	298	256	67.5				
211	1	1,313	Isolated mound	107	90	25				
242	1	4,351	Isolated mound plus two				12.9			A.X–29
			residences	68	40	5				
243	1	2,304	Three small structures		45					
			visible, one not		120					
			measurable							
256	2	8,762	One mound	908	400	56				
			Two unmeasurable mounds							
			One patio exposed				16			
264	2	3,744	One mound well preserved–may be an elite residence with the following approximate dimensions:			1,002	1,134	1 (?)	3,744 (?)	
				336	192	12[d]				
278	7	1,856	Elaborate residence	767	255	48				
				266	138	58				
				42	108	15	375	1	1,856	
				972	244	36				
					1,120	157				
294	7	1,696	Isolated mound	115	140	93				
320	1	131	Probably one residence					1	131	
333	1	3,320	Four possible residences,		190					
			slightly mounded		48					
					192					
					90					
337	1	1,604	Two mounds	216	202	38				
				202	255	158				
350	2	627	Two patios exposed				5			
							5			
378	2	2,400	One residence exposed		90					
388	2	178	One residence partially exposed				36	1	178	
424	7	520	One residence partially exposed		83			1	520	

(Continued)

Structure Summary (Continued)

Terrace number	Site sub-division	Terrace area (m²)	Structure–probable function		(m³)	Total structure area (m²)	Total room area (m²)	Patio area (m²)	Estimated total number of residences	Terrace area per house (m²)	Appendix X Figure number
430	7	120	One residence partially exposed			26 (?)			1	120	
453	8	15,200	Mound group cluster	*El Pitahayo*							
				A	395	440	360				A.X–30
				B	1,869	528	192				
				C	443	270	100				
				D	262	280	72	2,652			
				E	1,281	760	132				
				F	3,558	740	160				
				G	1,232	880	448				
455	8	2,762	Isolated mound		52	40	26				
464	5	3,375	One residence partially exposed			72 (?)	56 (?)	16			
491	5	4,417	Isolated platform–two unmeasurable low mounds along west edge of terrace		117	125	39				
657	10	878	Isolated mound		380	224	90				
659	12	2,040	Isolated mound		167	145	46				
703	12	946	Elaborate residence?		185	146	90				
					118	116	39	197	1 (?)	946 (?)	
					37	45	30				
800	6	2,452	Double-mound group		337	433	25				
					371	433	25				
867	7	790	Isolated mound		51	46	22				
879	5	1,695	Isolated mound		763	512	180				
938	5	6,050	Double-mound group		1,053	471	50				
					796	362	25				
992	5	392	Isolated mound		45	30	30				
1170	14	5,015	Two-mound group		1,944	1,070	192				
					1,427	608	73	1,188			
1214	7	1,003	Isolated mound		535	285	90				
1273		2,778	Two small mounds		210	173	6				
					71	75	24				
1306	7	1,434	Elaborate residence		1,232	531	80				
					363	211	39				
					495	224	114	326	1	1,434	
					82	142	24				

1327	7	1,856	Isolated mound		500 (estimate)	414	60		
1447	2	160,500	*Main Plaza*					39,986	A.X–32
				z	110	252	64		
				w	688	196	676		
				South Platform	152,912	13,420	7,040		
				S.P. x	6,260	1,088	224		
				S.P. y	1,694	675	396		
				S.P. y (upper)	218	36	144		
				t	597	80	320		
				m	9,611	952	572		
				o	1,920	760	128		
				u	1,102	648	648		
				(lower)					
				u	414	168	64		
				(upper)					
				l	6,423	1,824	690	47.6	
				v	4,314	2,555	1,782		
				n	1,300	476	240		
				Syst. IV	8,128	1,122	240		
				s	2,994	1,938	1,590		
				J	4,003	720	380		
				i	3,844	728	270		
				h	8,836	1,800	1,000		
				(lower)					
				h	1,024	320	320		
				(upper)					
				g	3,455	720	198		
				q	4,290	676	252		
				Plataforma Este	3,896	2,106	1,794	92	
				p	13,702	1,564	912		
				r	7,726	1,152	630		
				rr	3,248	1,152	884		
				Ball court	7,699	2,576	2,240		
				North Platform	448,802	48,160	34,750		
				A	2,271	576	72		
				B	1,800	612	147	3,364	
				I	3,931	1,064	40		
				e	2,010	546	130		
				d	2,582	858	84	575	
				Vertice Geodesico	3,049	540	144		
				c	1,120	960	240		
				a	900	396	28		

(Continued)

Terrace number	Site sub-division	Terrace area (m²)	Structure–probable function		(m³)	Total structure area (m²)	Total room area (m²)	Patio area (m²)	Estimated total number of residences	Terrace area per house (m²)	Appendix X Figure number
1448	5	1,220	Isolated mound		3,443	1,220	546				
1449	14	1,102	Elaborate residence		386	140	33				
					438	190	45.6				
					196	129	32.4	402	1	1,102	
					672	241	37.4				
1450	13	2,379	Two-mound group		1,111	410	233				
					1,111	410	233				
1451	13	605	Elaborate residence[e]		296	188	41				
					87	127	30	289	1	605	
1452	13	656	Elaborate residence		702	153	63				
					147	106	19				
					53	98	19	172	1	656	
					181	125	25				
1453	12	1,147	Elaborate residence		634	288	58				
					519	194	35				
					32	21	6.2	375	1	1,147	
					89	83	15				
					12	14.4	2.2				
					60	62	7				
1454		333	Isolated mound		381	333	81				
1455	10	468	Elaborate residence		22	107	70				
					82	119	34	127	1	468	
					97	129	33				
1456	4	2,200	Small ball court		2,096	1,008					
1457	4	5,136	Two measurable patios exposed					16			
			One possibly whole house exposed[f]			227 (?)	202 (?)	25			
1458	1	13,275	Elaborate residence	*Siete Venado*							
					4,797	1,050	116				
					6,020	1,103	68				
					664	378	96	1,105			
					1,353	632	244				
					465	281	44				
					336	247	100				
1459	4	1,763	Elaborate residence		215	147	17.5				
					1,357	510	90	476	1	1,763	
					1,697	630	117				

1460	5	1,696	Elaborate residence	406	259	23			
				1,663	527	66			
				190	284	30	351	1	1,696
				458	275	44			
1461	1	2,016	Elaborate residence	1,860	616	85			
				126	120	36	736	1	2,016
				54	67	42			
1462	4	2,931	Elaborate residence[g]		453	354	99		
1463	3	3,969	Elaborate residence	3,861	889	227			
				234	147	43			
				1,954	772	199	650		
				1,173	533	533			
1464	9	5,400	Mound group cluster						
			Elaborate residence?	85	194	147			
			Civic building?	236	233	33			
			Long platform	27	70	41			
Az.Terraces									
3	11	2,490	Elaborate residence[h]		695	536	159		
			Isolated mound	358	205	40			
			Ball court		ca. 600				
8	11	6,421	Two large plazas or				1,760		
			patios elaborate				1,760		
			residence[h]		891	796	95		
			Three mounds						
			Staircase divider	957	689	432			
			between two major	3,071	936	90			
			plazas	869	361	40			
10	11	14,300	Elaborate residence	31,324	6,336	918			
				4,674	900	90			
				6,639	1,418	444	2,160	1	14,300
				3,253	990	140			
11	11	2,918	Elaborate residence	563	285	36			
				250	192	68			
				366	216	48	351		
				261	187	81			
12	11	1,800	Isolated mound	745	572	34			
19	11	1,194	Elaborate residence	254	486	80			
				117	216	41			
				438	420	68	135		
				341	405	88			
			Small attached residence		225	202	23		
24	11	910	Isolated mound	206	171	48			
39	11	1,088	Elaborate residence[i]	224	384	96	640		

(Continued)

Terrace number	Site sub-division	Terrace area (m²)	Structure–probable function	(m³)	Total structure area (m²)	Total room area (m²)	Patio area (m²)	Estimated total number of residences	Terrace area per house (m²)	Appendix X Figure number
50	11	1,104	Isolated mound	696	450	30				
137	11	420	Isolated mound	78	119	7.6				
138	11	3,220	Two-mound group with a small mound along the south edge of the plaza	2,347	1,275	378				
				651	378	21				
				263	160	21				
154	11	520	Residence		286	250	36	1	520	A.X–31
206	11	545	Two patios exposed				11.2	2	273	A.X–33
							3.6			
274	11	569	Two residences partially exposed		≅ 66			2	285	
					≅ 158					
301	11	187	Residence partially exposed					1	187	A.X–34
302	11	126	Residence partially exposed					1	126	A.X–34
309	11	170	Residence partially exposed					1	170	A.X–35
392	11	2,964	One patio exposed				65			
			One elaborate residence	46	54	12				
				177	136	48				
				103	112	33	389			
				211	178	18				
413	11	(difficult to estimate)	Isolated mound	15	61	26				
419	11	3,520	Two-mound group	1,080	634	230				
				679	708	194				
431	11	1,664	Isolated mound[j]	251	225	48	432 (?)			
432	11	210	Residence partially exposed		195	150	ca. 45	1	210	A.X–36
448	11	3,575	Ball court		3,575					
449	11	1,152	Small ball court		1,152					
462	11	5,600	Terrace with two small mounds and one low platform (functions unknown)							

				110	230	63			
				262	219	60			
				960	1,200	1,200			
469	11	840	Isolated mound	69	100	42			
E.G.Terraces									
1	15	3,028	Elaborate residence	3,135	1,013	68			
				956	480	63	513	1	3,028
				581	360	22			
				1,256	662	68			
2	15	800	Ball court		800				
3	15	1,600	Isolated mound	192	290	108			
120	15	1,881	Isolated mound	186	135	32			
139	15	3,600	Isolated mound	613	520	135			

Ink Drawings of Field Maps

KEY:

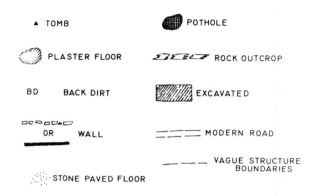

- TOMB
- POTHOLE
- PLASTER FLOOR
- ROCK OUTCROP
- BD BACK DIRT
- EXCAVATED
- OR WALL
- MODERN ROAD
- VAGUE STRUCTURE BOUNDARIES
- STONE PAVED FLOOR

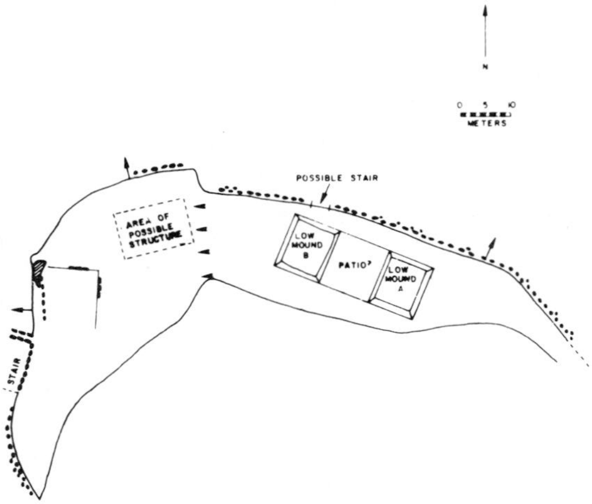

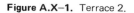

Figure A.X–1. Terrace 2.

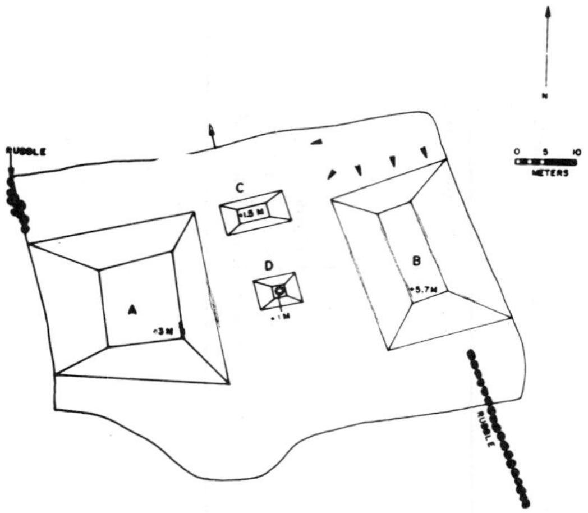

Figure A.X–2. Terrace 5.

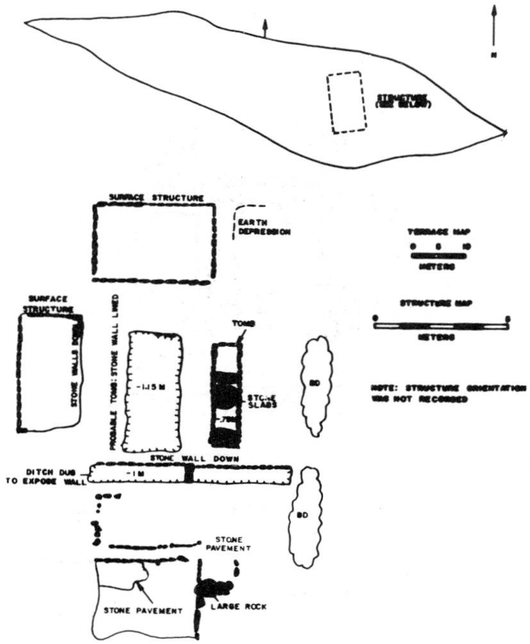

Figure A.X–3. Terrace 9.

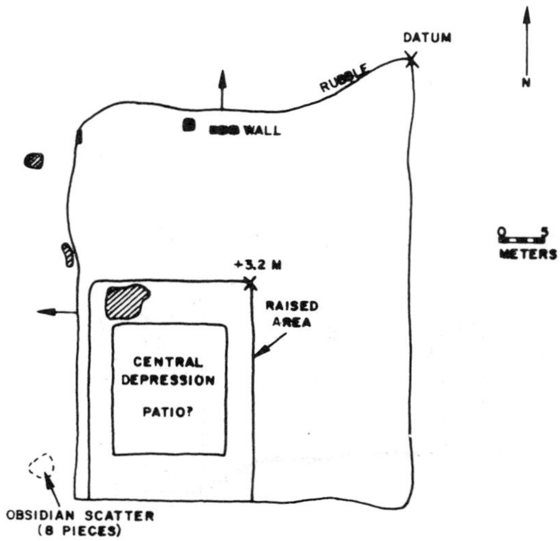

Figure A.X–4. Terrace 13.

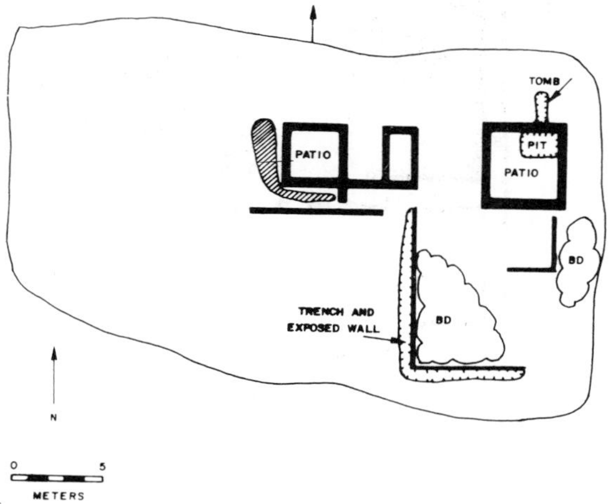

Figure A.X–5. Terrace 15.

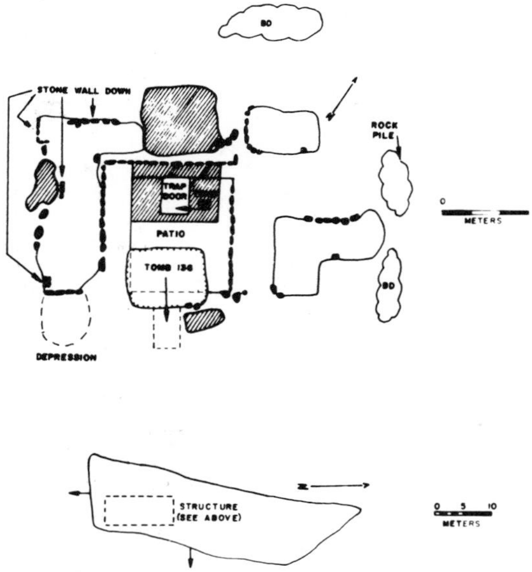

Figure A.X–6. Terrace 16.

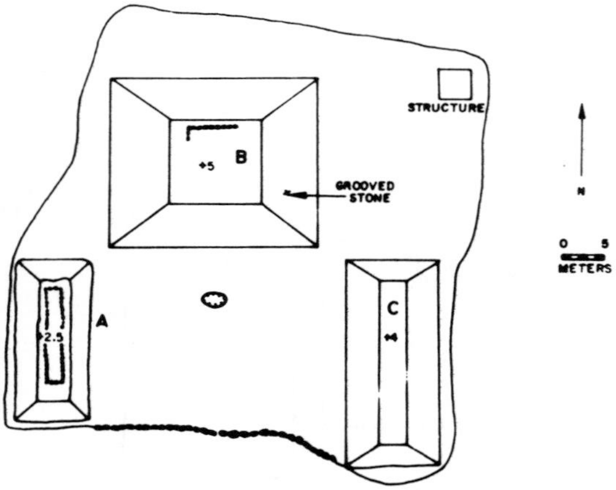

Figure A.X–7. Terrace 17.

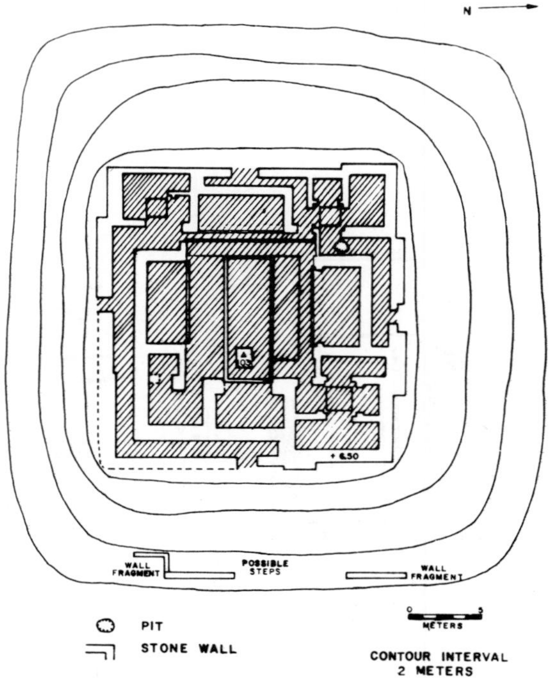

Figure A.X–8. Terrace 18.

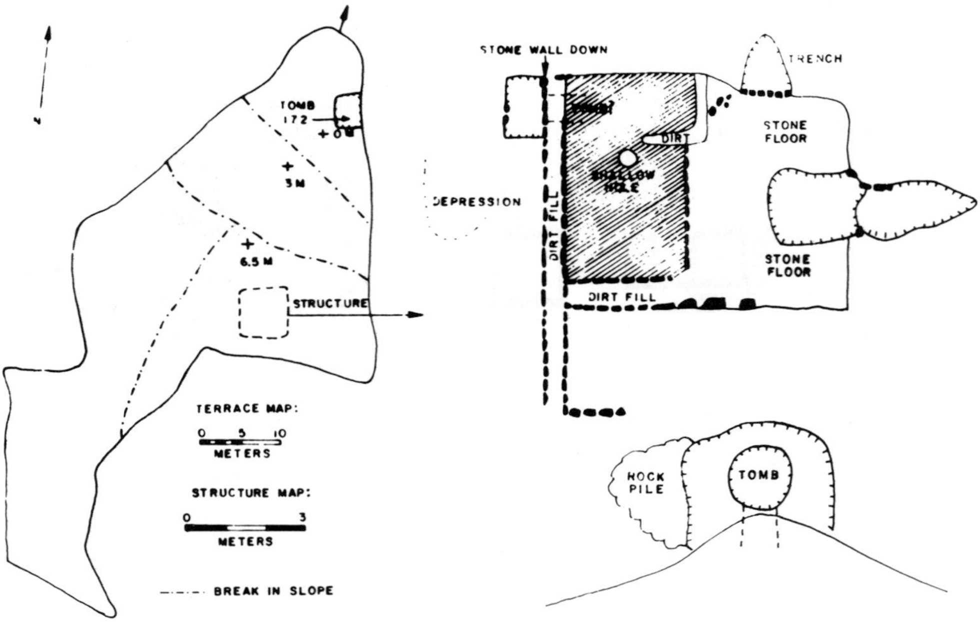

Figure A.X–9. Terrace 19.

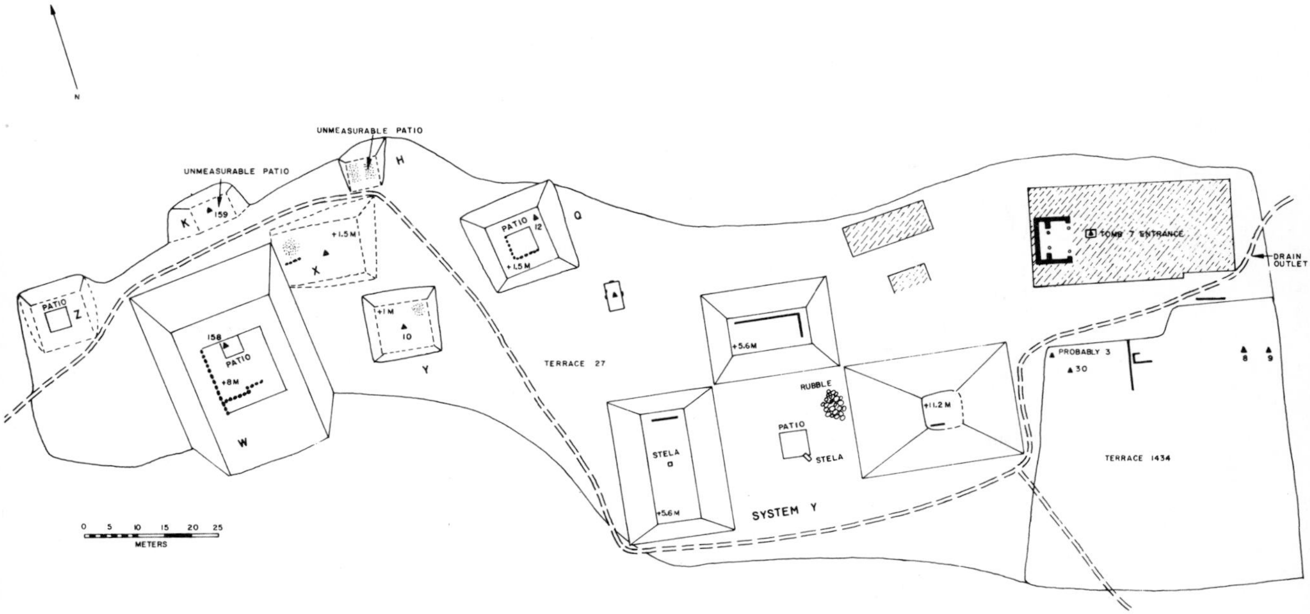

Figure A.X–10. Terrace 27.

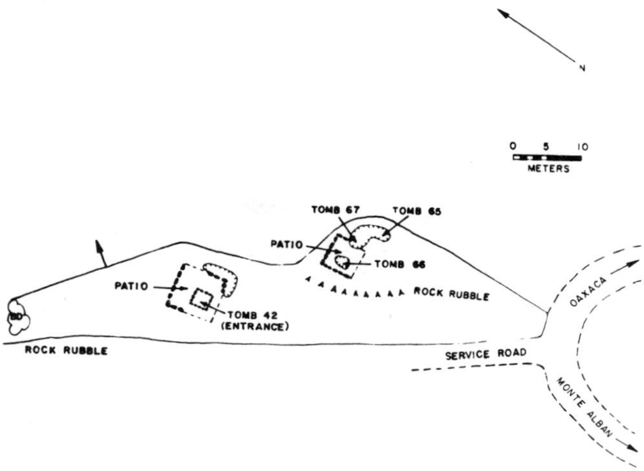

Figure A.X–11. Terrace 29.

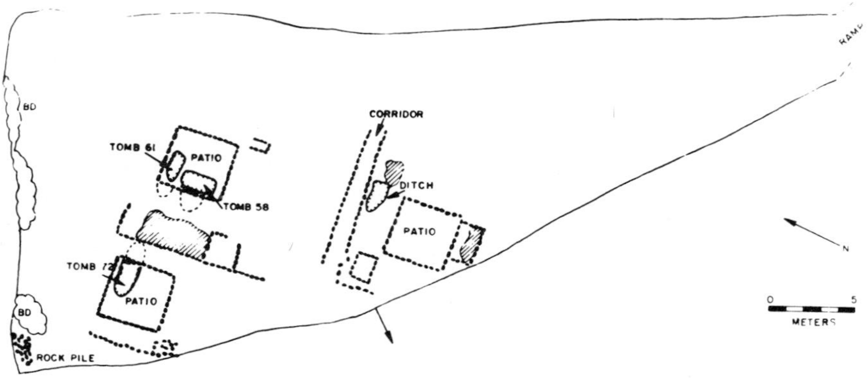

Figure A.X–12. Terrace 30.

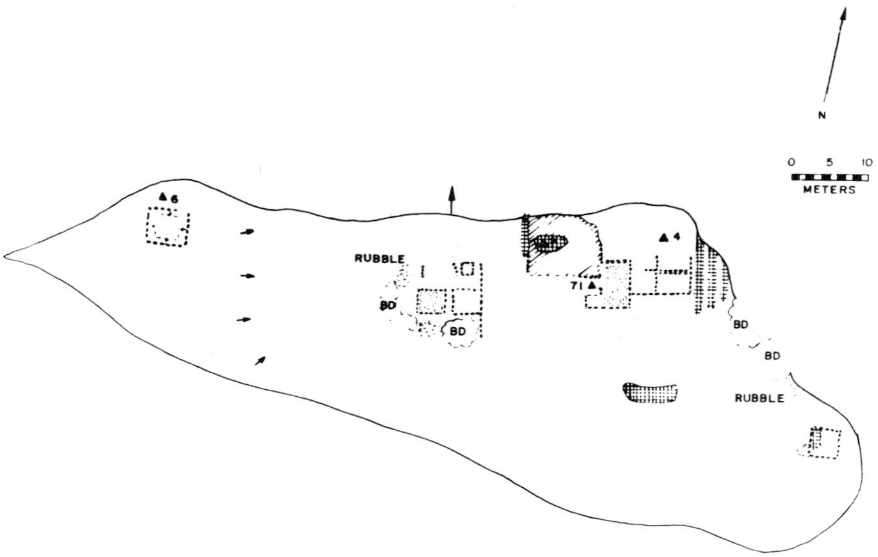

Figure A.X–13. Terrace 31.

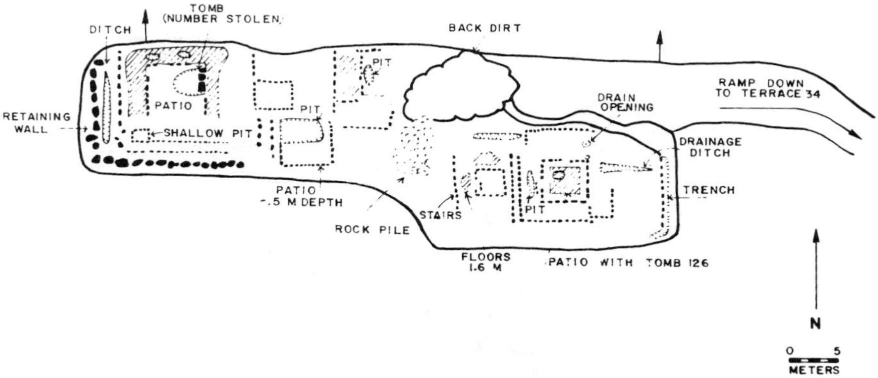

Figure A.X–14. Terrace 32.

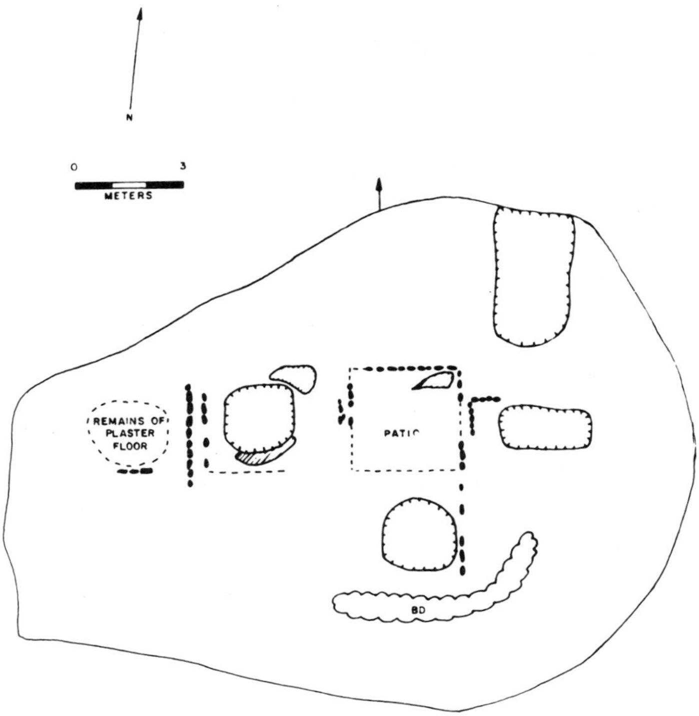

Figure A.X–15. Terrace 36.

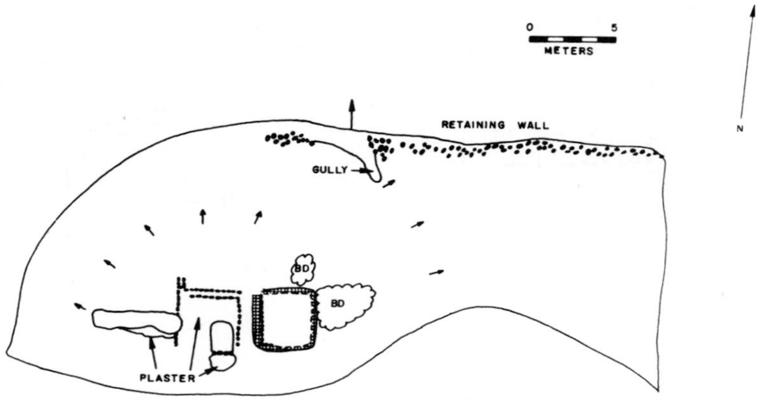

Figure A.X–16. Terrace 37.

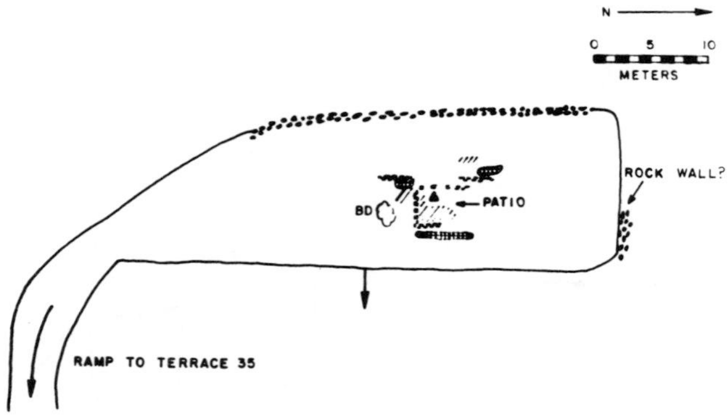

Figure A.X–17. Terrace 38.

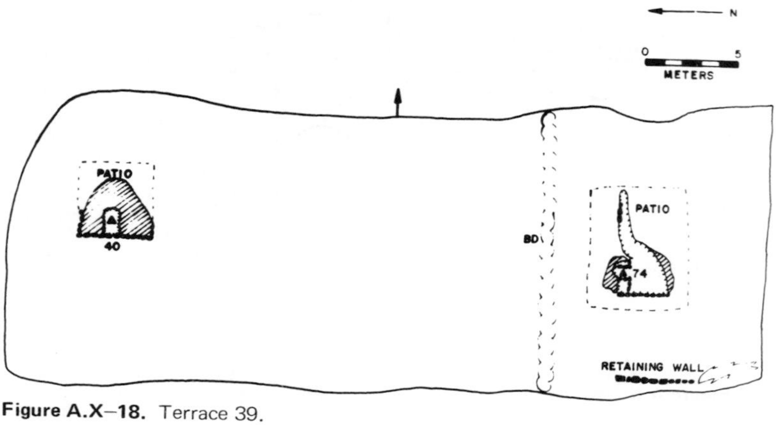

Figure A.X–18. Terrace 39.

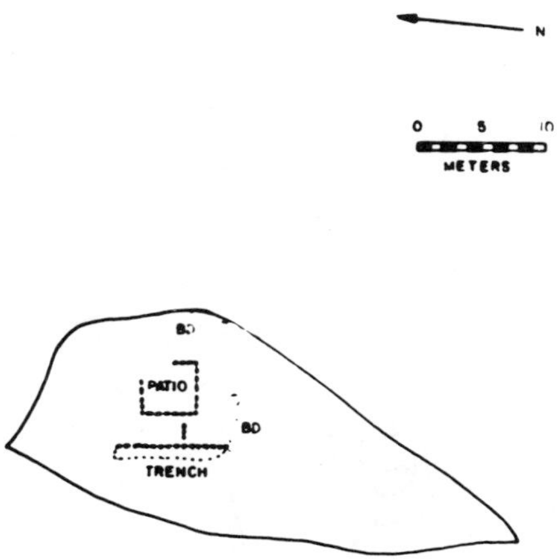

Figure A.X–19. Terrace 41.

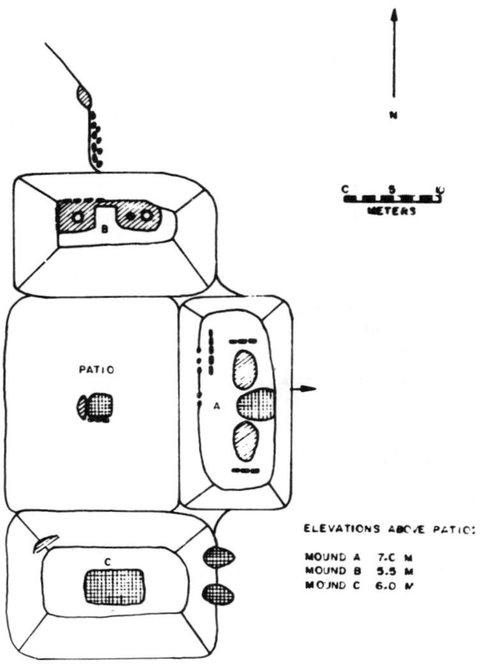

Figure A.X–20. Terrace 51.

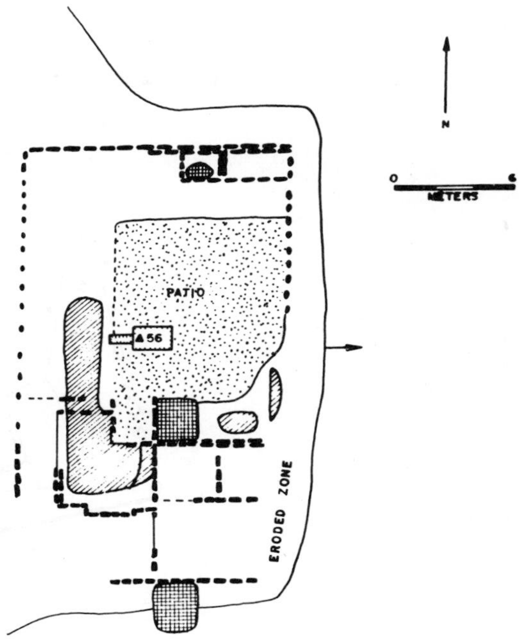

Figure A.X–21. Terrace 78.

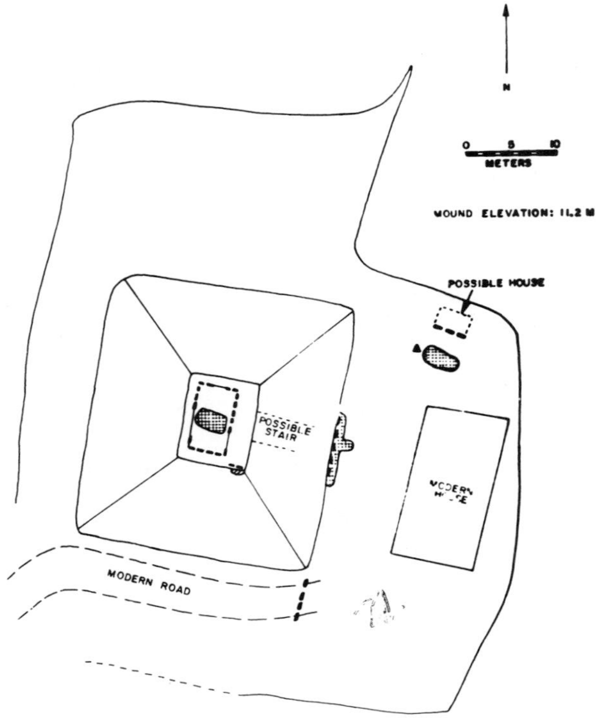

Figure A.X–22. Terrace 79

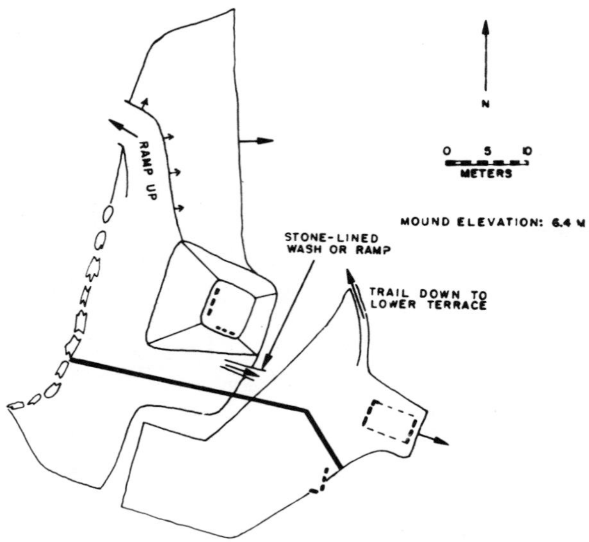

Figure A.X–23. Terrace 92 and 93.

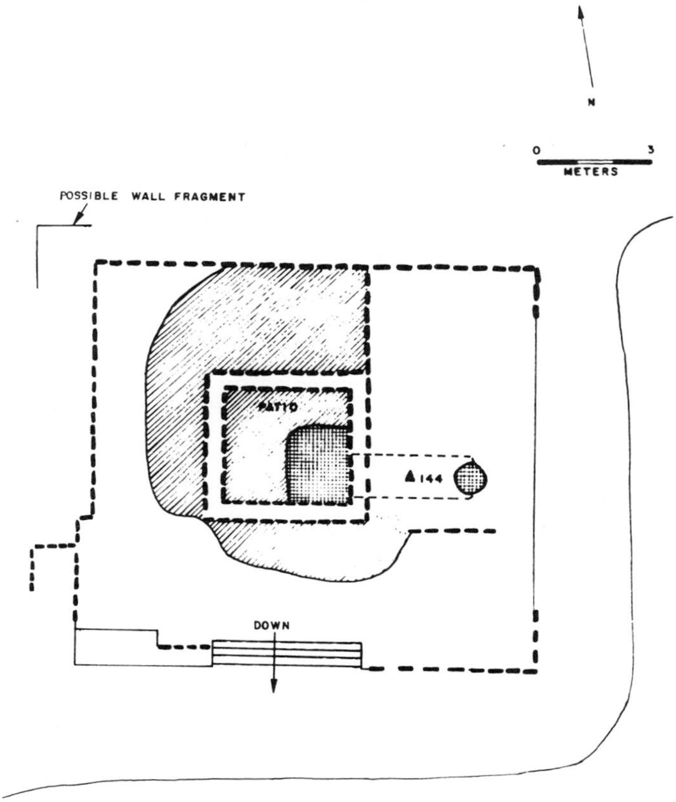

Figure A.X–24. Terrace 104.

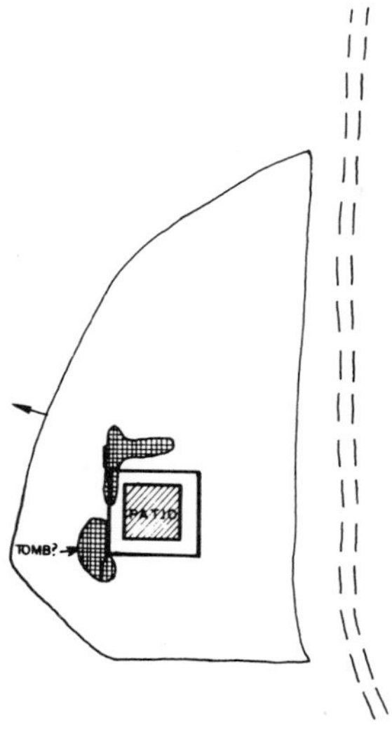

Figure A.X–25. Terrace 155.

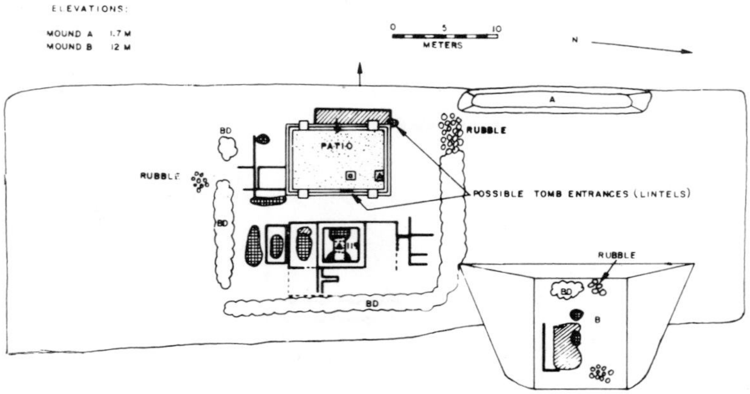

Figure A.X–26. Terrace 161.

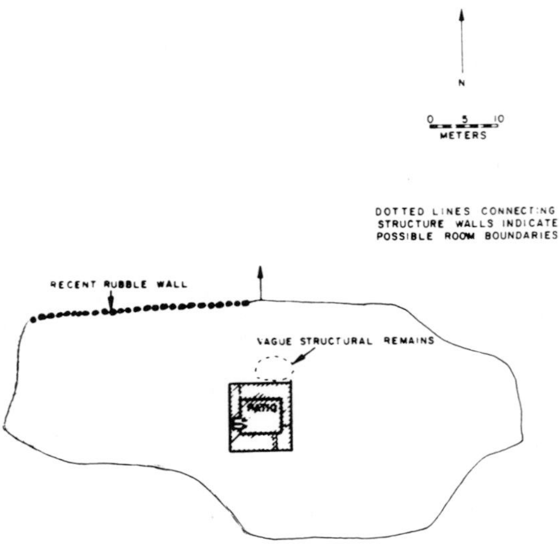

Figure A.X–27. Terrace 170.

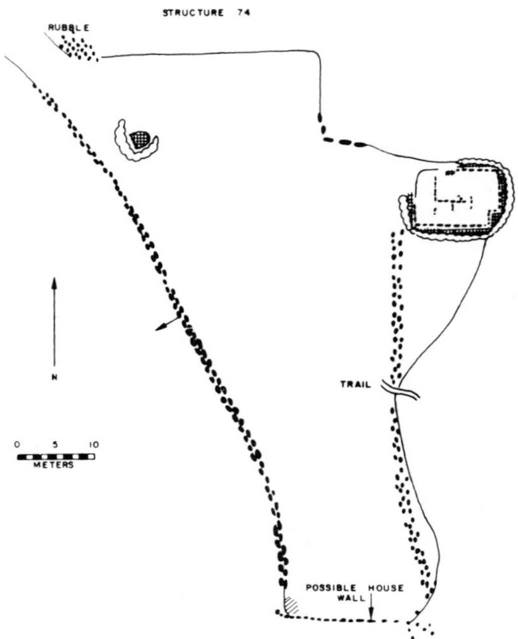

Figure A.X–28. Terrace 205.

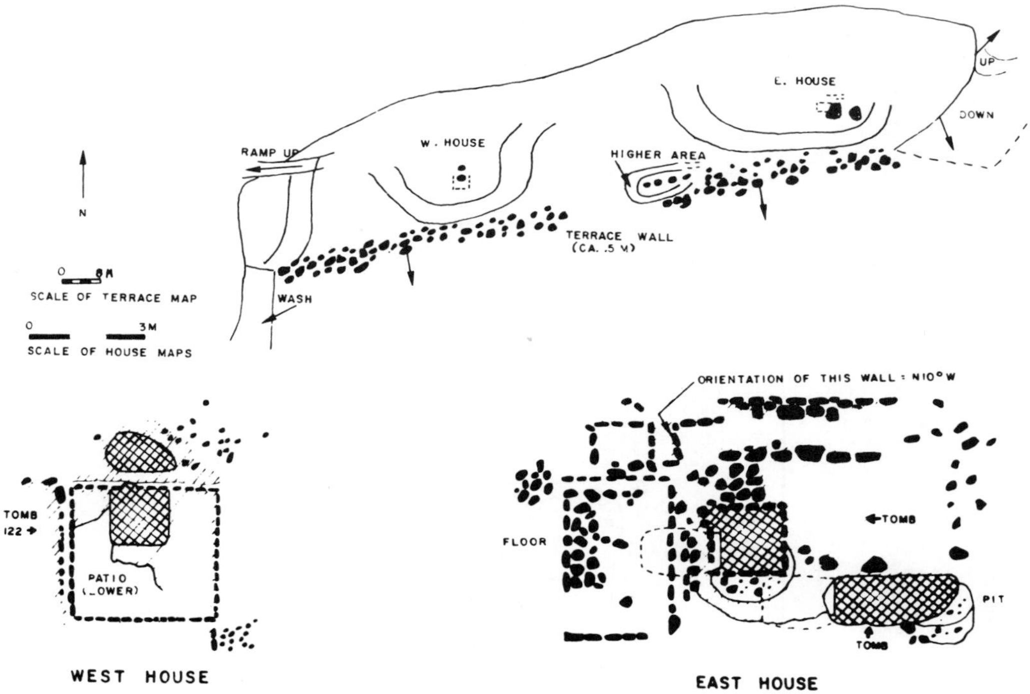

Figure A.X–29. Terrace 242.

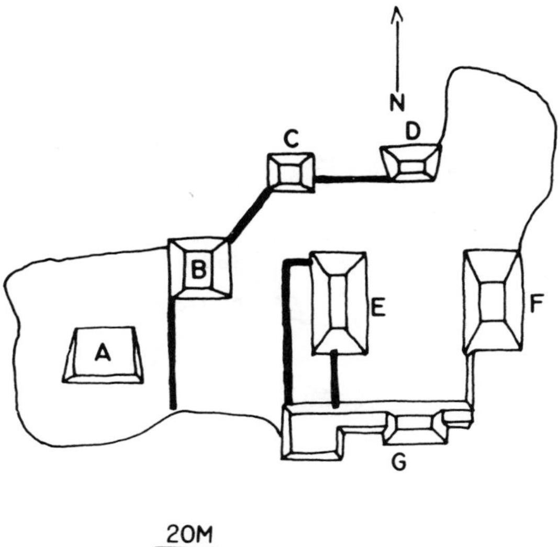

Figure A.X–30. Terrace 453.

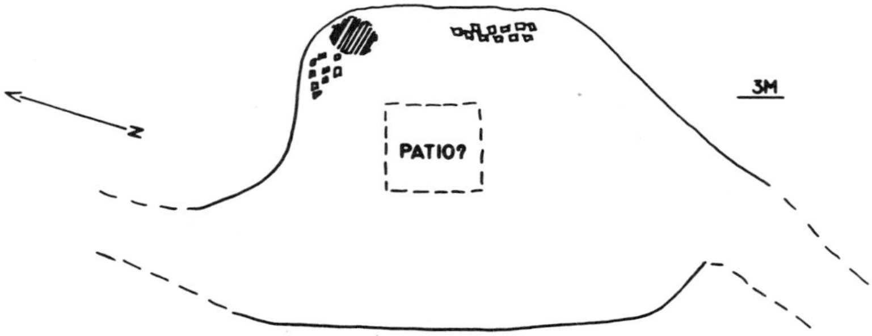

Figure A.X–31. Az. Terrace 154.

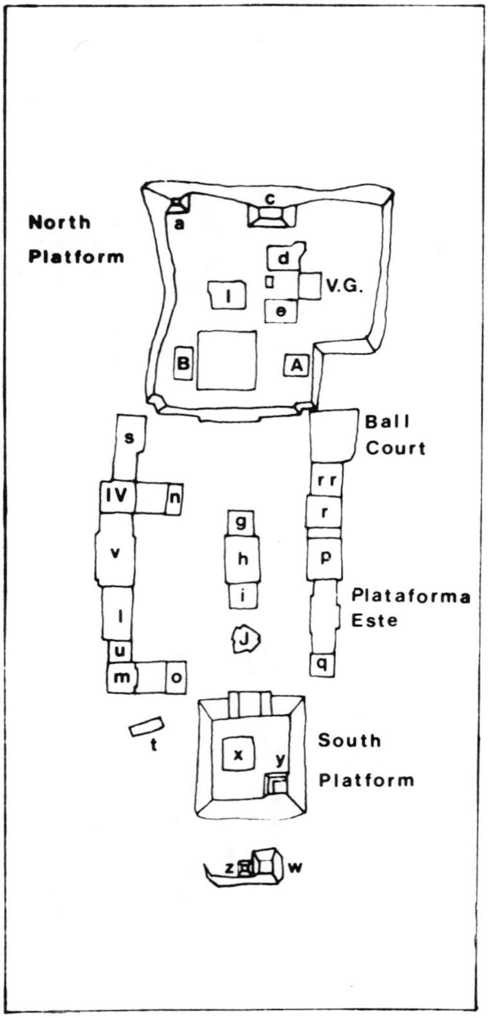

Figure A.X–32. Terrace 1447.

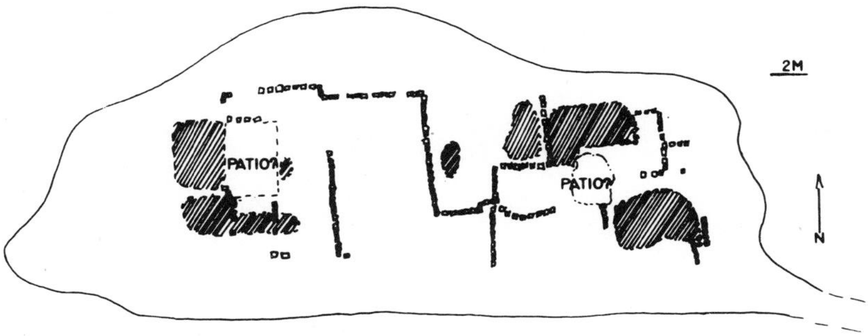

Figure A.X–33. Az. Terrace 206.

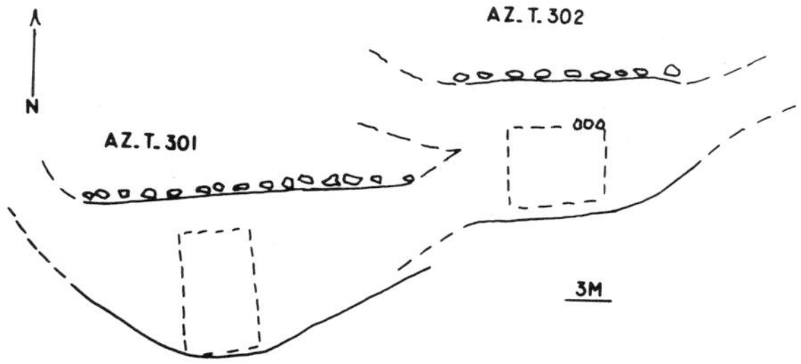

Figure A.X–34. Az. Terrace 301 and Az. Terrace 302.

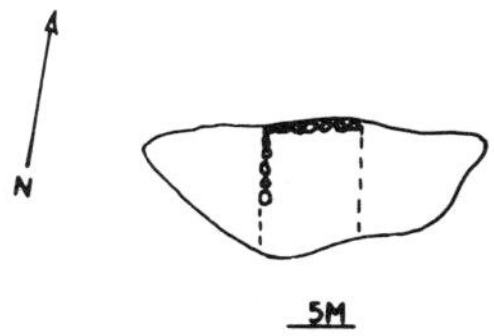

Figure A.X–35. Az. Terrace 309.

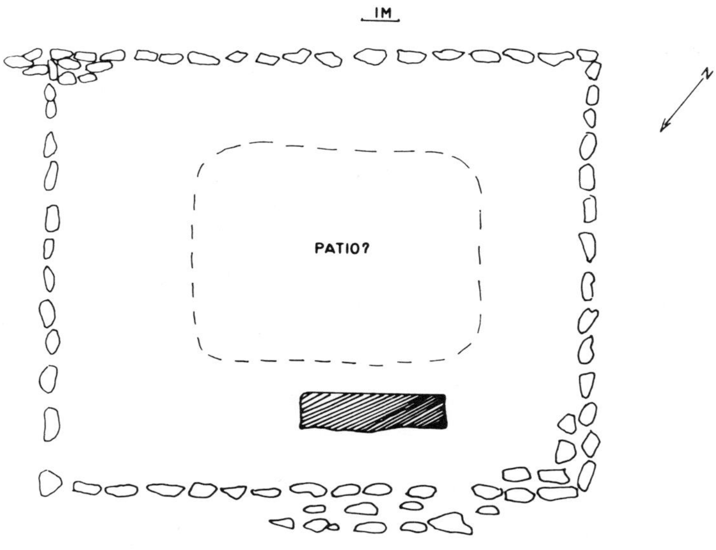

Figure A.X–36. Az. Terrace 432.

References

Acosta, Jorge R.

1949 El Pectoral de jade de Monte Albán. *Anales del Instituto Nacional de Antropología e Historia III*: 17–25.

1958 Exploraciones arqueológicas en Monte Albán, XVIII Temporada. *Revista Mexicana de Estudios Antropológicos, 15*, 7–50.

1965 Preclassic and classic architecture of Oaxaca. *Handbook of Middle American Indians*, Vol. *3*, Part 2, (Gordon Willey, ed.), pp. 814–836. Austin: University of Texas Press.

Armillas, Pedro

1971 Gardens on swamps. *Science 174*, 653–661.

Aswad, Barbara

1970 Social and ecological aspects in the formation of Islam. In *Peoples and cultures of the Middle East*, Vol. *1* (Louise Sweet, ed.), 53–73. Garden City: The Natural History Press.

Autry, William O., Jr.

1973 *Post Formative burial practices: Valley of Oaxaca, Mexico*. Unpublished Honors Thesis. University of North Carolina, Chapel Hill.

Aveni, A.F., and R.M. Linsley

1972 Mound J, Monte Albán: Possible astronomical orientation. *American Antiquity 37*, 528–540.

Batres, Leopoldo

1902 *Explorations of Monte Albdn, Oaxaca, Mexico*. Mexico: Dante Street Press.

Bernal, Ignacio

1949 La cerámica grabada de Monte Albán. *Anales del Instituto Nacional de Antropología e Historia III*: 59–77.

1965 Archaeological synthesis of Oaxaca. *Handbook of Middle American Indians* Vol. *3*, Part 2 (Gordon Willey ed.), pp. 788–813. Austin: University of Texas Press.

1966 Teotihuacan: Capital de emperio?, *Revista Mexicana de Estudios Antropológicos 20*, 95–110.

Berry, Brian J.L.

1961 City size distribution and economic development. *Economic Development and Culture Change 9*, 573–588.

Blalock, Hubert M., Jr.

1972 *Social statistics*, 2nd ed. New York: McGraw-Hill.

Blanton, Richard E.

1972 *Prehispanic settlement patterns of the Ixtapalapa Peninsula region, Mexico*. Occasional Papers of the Department of Anthropology, The Pennsylvania State University, No. 6, University Park.

1973 *The Valley of Oaxaca Settlement Pattern Project: A Progress Report to the NSF*. Mimeographed.

1976a The origins of Monte Albán. In *Cultural Change and Continuity* (Charles Cleland, ed.), pp. 223–232. New York: Academic Press.

1976b Anthropological studies of cities. *Annual Review of Anthropology, 5* 249–264.

1976c The role of symbiosis in adaptation and sociocultural change in the Valley of Mexico. In *The Valley of Mexico, studies in prehispanic ecology and society* (Eric Wolf, ed.), 181–202. Albuquerque: The University of New Mexico Press.

1976d *The Valley of Oaxaca Settlement Pattern Proj-*

ect: A report to the NSF and the INAH. Mimeographed.

Blanton, Richard E., and Jeffrey R. Parsons
1971 Ceramic markers used for period designations. Appendix I in *Prehistoric settlement patterns in the Texcoco Region, Mexico* (Jeffrey R. Parsons). Memoirs of the Museum of Anthropology, No. 3, the University of Michigan, Ann Arbor.

Bogue, Donald
1949 *The structure of the metropolitan community*. Horace H. Rackham School of Graduate Studies, The University of Michigan, Ann Arbor.

Boserup, Ester
1965 *The conditions of agricultural growth*. Chicago: Aldine, Atherton Inc.

Carrasco, Pedro
1964 Family structure of sixteenth-century Tepoztlan. In *Process and pattern in culture* (Robert A. Manners, ed.), 185–210. Chicago: Aldine.

Caso, Alfonso
1928 *Las Estelas Zapotecas*. Publicaciones de la Secretaría de Educacion Pública, Monografías del Museo Nacional Arqueología, Historia y Etnología, Mexico.
1932 Las Exploraciones en Monte Albán, Temporada 1931–2. *Instituto Panamericano de Geografía e Historia 7*.
1935 Las Exploraciones en Monte Albán, Temporada 1934–5. *Instituto Panamericano de Geografía e Historia 18*.
1938 Exploraciones in Oaxaca, quinta y sexta temporadas, 1936–7. *Instituto Panamericano de Geografía y Historia 34*.
1942 Resumen del informe de las exploraciones en Oaxaca durante la 7a y la 8a temporadas, 1937–1938 y 1938–1939. *Actas del XXVII Congreso Internacional de Americanistas, México, 1939*, II, pp. 159–187.
1947 "Calendario y escritura de las antiguas culturas de Monte Albán". In *Obras Completas de Miguel Othón de Mendizábal 1*, 115–143.
1965a Sculpture and mural painting of Oaxaca. *Handbook of Middle American Indians*, Vol. *3*, Part 2 (Gordon Willey, ed.), 849–870. Austin: University of Texas Press.
1965b Lapidary work, goldwork, and copperwork from Oaxaca. *Handbook of Middle American Indians*, Vol. *3*, Part 2 (Gordon Willey, ed.), 896–930. Austin: The University of Texas Press.
1965c Zapotec writing and calendar. *Handbook of Middle American Indians*, Vol. *3*, Part 2 (Gordon Willey, ed.), 931–947. Austin: The University of Texas Press.
1965d Mixtec writing and calendar. *Handbook of Middle American Indians*, Vol. *3*, Part 2 (Gordon Willey, ed.). Austin: The University of Texas Press.
1970 *El Tesoro de Monte Albán*. Memorias del Instituto Nacional de Antropología e Historia *III*.

Caso, Alfonso, and Ignacio Bernal
1952 *Urnas de Oaxaca*. Memorias del Instituto Nacional de Antropología e Historia *II*.
1965 Ceramics of Oaxaca. *Handbook of Middle American Indians*, Vol. *3*, Part 2 (Gordon Willey, ed.), 871–895. Austin: The University of Texas Press.

Caso, Alfonso, Ignacio Bernal, and Jorge R. Acosta
1967 *La Ceramica de Monte Albán*. Memorias del Instituto Nacional de Antropología e Historia *XIII*.

Clark, P.J., and F.C. Evans
1954 Distance to nearest neighbor as a measure of spatial relationships in populations. *Ecology 35*, 445–453.

Coe, Michael D.
1962 *Mexico*. New York: Praeger.

Cordry, Donald and Dorothy Cordry
1968 *Mexican Indian costumes.* University of Texas Press. Austin.

Cowgill, George
1974 Quantitative studies of urbanization at Teotihuacan. In *Mesoamerican Archaeology: New Approaches* (Norman Hammond, ed.), 363–396. London: Duckworth and Co.

Cruz, Wilfrido
1946 *Oaxaca recóndita: Razas, idiomas, costumbres, leyendas, y tradiciones del Estado de Oaxaca, México*. Mexico.

Deetz, James
1965 *The dynamics of stylistic change in Arikara ceramics*. Urbana: University of Illinois Press.

Drennan, Robert
ms Oaxaca radioarbon dates associated with ceramic phases. To be included in *The Cloud People* (Kent Flannery, ed.). Albuquerque: University of New Mexico Press.

Dupaix, Guillermo
1834 *Antiquités Mexicaines*. Paris: Bureau des Antiquités Mexicaines.
1969 *Expediciones acerca de los antiguos monumentos de la Nueva España, 1805–1808* (José Alcina Franch, ed.). Madrid: Ediciones José Porrúa Turanzas.

Esparza, Manuel (ed.)
1975 El Centro de Huaxyacac Azteca. Comment in the *Boletín del Centro Regional de Oaxaca, I.N.A.H.*, 5–6.

Flannery, Kent V, and Joyce Marcus
1976a Evolution of the public building in Formative

Oaxaca. In *Cultural Change and Continuity* (Charles Cleland, ed.), pp. 205–22. New York: Academic Press.

1976b Formative Oaxaca and the Zapotec cosmos. *American Scientist 64*, 374–383.

Flannery, Kent V., M.C. Winter, S. Lees, J. Neely, J. Schoenwetter, S. Kitchen, and J.C. Wheeler

n.d. *Preliminary archaeological investigations in the Valley of Oaxaca, Mexico*. A report to the NSF and INAH. Mimeographed.

Flannery, Kent V, Anne V.T. Kirkby, Michael Kirkby, and Aubrey Williams, Jr.

1967 Farming systems and political growth in Ancient Oaxaca. *Science 158*, 445–454.

Gorenstein, Shirley

1975 *Not forever on earth: Prehistory of Mexico*. New York: Charles Scribner's Sons.

Haggett, Peter

1965 *Locational analysis in human geography*. New York: St. Martin's Press.

Heizer, Robert, and James Bennyhoff

1958 Archaeological investigations at Cuicuilco, Valley of Mexico. *Science 127*, 232–233.

Holmes, William

1897 *Archaeological studies among the ancient cities of Mexico. Part II, Monuments of Chiapas, Oaxaca, and the Valley of Mexico*. Field Columbian Museum, Publication 16.

Hull, Richard

1976 *African cities and towns before the European conquest*. New York: W.W. Norton and Co.

Kirkby, Anne

1973 *The use of land and water resources in the past and present Valley of Oaxaca, Mexico.* Memoirs of the Museum of Anthropology. The University of Michigan, No. 5, Ann Arbor.

Kowalewski, Stephen

1976 *Prehispanic settlement patterns of the central part of the Valley of Oaxaca, Mexico*. Dissertation submitted to the department of anthropology, the University of Arizona.

in press Sections in *The cloud people* (Kent V. Flannery, ed.). Albuquerque: The University of New Mexico Press.

Krapf-Askari, Eva

1969 *Yoruba towns and cities.* Oxford Monographs on Social Anthropology. Oxford.

Lees, Susan

1973 *Socio-political aspects of canal irrigation in the Valley of Oaxaca, Mexico*. Memoirs of the Museum of Anthropology, the University of Michigan, No. 6, Ann Arbor.

Leigh, Howard

1966 The evolution of the Zapotec Glyph C. In *Ancient Oaxaca* pp. 256–269.

MacNeish, Richard S., Frederick A. Peterson and Kent V. Flannery

1970 *The prehistory of the Tehuacan Valley: Ceramics*. Volume 3. The University of Texas Press. Austin.

Marcus, Joyce

1974 The iconography of power among the Classic Maya. *World Archaeology 6*, 83–94.

1976a The iconography of militarism at Monte Albán and neighboring sites in the Valley of Oaxaca. In *The Origins of Religious Art and Iconography in Preclassic Mesoamerica* (H.B. Nicholson, ed.). Latin American Center, the University of California, Los Angeles, pp. 123–139.

1976b The origins of Mesoamerican writing. *Annual Review of Anthropology, 5*, 35–67.

Marquina, Ignacio

1964 *Arquitectura prehispánica.* Memorias del Instituto Nacional de Antropología E Historia *I*.

Mason, Roger, Dennis Lewarch, Michael O'Brien, and James Neely

n.d. Irrigation and the development of Monte Albán: The Xoxocotlan irrigation system, Oaxaca, Mexico. Manuscript.

Michels, Joseph

1973 Radiocarbon and obsidian dating: A chronometeric framework for Kaminaljuyu. In *The Pennsylvania State University Kaminaljuyu Project, 1969, 1970 Seasons, Part I–Mound Excavations* (Joseph Michels and William Sanders). Occasional Papers in Anthropology, the Department of Anthropology, the Pennsylvania State University, No. 9, pp. 21–65, University Park.

Millon, René

1967 Extensión y población de la ciudad de Teotihuacan en sus diferentes periodos: Un calculo provisional. *Teotihuacan, Onceava Mesa Redonda*, Sociedad Mexicana de Antropología, pp. 57–78.

1973 *Urbanization at Teotihuacan, Mexico, Volume I.* Austin: The University of Texas Press.

1976 Social relations in ancient Teotihuacán. In *The Valley of Mexico: Studies in Pre-Hispanic Ecology and Society* (Eric Wolf, ed.). Albuquerque: University of New Mexico Press.

Millon, René, Bruce Drewitt, and James Bennyhoff

1965 *The Pyramid of the Sun at Teotihuacan: 1959 investigations*. Transactions of the American Philosophical Society *55*. Philadelphia.

Morrison, Samuel

1965 *The Oxford history of the American people.*

New York: Oxford University Press.

Neely, James
1972 Prehistoric domestic water supplies and irrigation systems at Monte Albán, Oaxaca, Mexico. Paper presented at the 37th annual meeting of the Society for American Archaeology.

Nie, Norman, C. Hadlai Hull, Jean Jenkins, Karen Steinbrenner, and Dale Bent
1975 *Statistical package for the social sciences*, 2nd ed. New York: McGraw-Hill.

Olsson, G.
1965 *Distance and human interaction: A review and bibliography*. The Regional Science Institute, Philadelphia.

Paddock, John (ed.)
1966 *Ancient Oaxaca*. Stanford: Stanford University Press.

Paddock, John. Joseph Mogor, and Michael Lind
1968 Lambityeco Tomb 2: A preliminary report. *Boletín del Instituto de Estudios Oaxaqueños*, No. 25. Mitla Oaxaca, Mexico.

Palerm, Angel
1961 Sistemas de Regadío Prehispánicos en Teotihuacan y en el Pedregal. In *La Agricultura y el Desarollo de la Civilizacion en Mesoamerica* (Angel Palerm and Eric Wolf, eds.). Pan American Union, Revista Interamericana de Ciencias Sociales, Segunda Epoca, Vol. 1, pp. 297–302, Washington, D.C.

Palerm, Angel, and Eric Wolf
1957 Ecological potential and cultural development in Mesoamerica. In *Studies in Human Ecology*. Anthropological Society of Washington and Pan American Union Social Science Monograph No. 3, pp. 1–37, Washington, D.C.

Parsons, Jeffrey
1971 *Prehistoric settlement patterns of the Texcoco Region, Mexico*. Memoirs of the Museum of Anthropology, the University of Michigan, No. 3, Ann Arbor.

Saalman, Howard
1968 *Medieval cities*. New York: George Braziller.

Sanders, William T.
1965 *The cultural ecology of the Teotihuacan Valley*. The Department of Sociology and Anthropology, the Pennsylvania State University, University Park. Manuscript.

Sanders, William T., Jeffrey Parsons, and Michael Logan
1976 The valley as an ecological system: Summary and conclusions. In *The Valley of Mexico: Studies in prehispanic ecology and society* (Eric Wolf ed.), pp. 161–178. Albuquerque: The University of New Mexico Press.

Sanders, William T., and Barbara Price
1968 *Mesoamerica: The evolution of a civilization*. New York: Random House.

Sejourné, Laurette
1960 El Simbolismo de los rituales funerarios en Monte Albán. *Revista Mexicana de Estudios Antropológicos XVI*, 77–90.

Shepard, Anne
1968 *Ceramics for the archaeologist*. Carnegie Institution, Publication 609, Washington, D.C.

Skinner, G.W.
1964 Marketing and social structure in rural China: Part I. *Journal of Asian Studies 24*, 3–43.
1965a Marketing and social structure in rural China: Part II. *Journal of Asian Studies 24*, 195–228.
1965b Marketing and social structure in rural China: Part II. *Journal of Asian Studies 24*, 363–99.

Smith, Carol
1974 Economics of marketing systems: Models from economic geography. *Annual Review of Anthropology 3*, 167–203.
1975 Examining stratification systems through peasant marketing arrangements: An application of some models from economic geography. *Man 10*, 95–122.

Smith Carol (ed.)
1976 *Regional analysis* (2 volumes). New York: Academic Press.

Spores, Ronald
1972 *An archaeological settlement survey of the Nochixtlan Valley, Oaxaca*. Vanderbilt University Publications in Anthropology, No. 1, Nashville.

Spence, Michael
n.d. *The development of the Teotihuacan obsidian production system*. Manuscript.

Steward, Julian
1955 *Theory of culture change*. Urbana: University of Illinois Press.

Varner, Dudley
1974 *Prehispanic settlement patterns in the Valley of Oaxaca, Mexico, the Etla Arm*. Dissertation submitted to the Department of Anthropology, the University of Arizona.

Villagra, Agustin
1942 "Los Danzantes," piedras grabadas del Montículo "L," Monte Albán, Oaxaca. *Vigesimoseptimo Congreso Internacional de Americanistas, México II*, pp. 143–58.

Warner, R.
1954 *Thucydides: The Peloponnesian War*. Penguin: Harmondsworth.

Willey, Gordon

1953 *Prehistoric settlement patterns in the Viru Valley, Peru*. Bureau of American Ethnology, Bulletin 155, Washington, D.C.

1966 *An introduction to American archaeology*, Volume One: *North and Middle America*. Englewood Cliffs: Prentice-Hall.

Winter, Marcus

1972 *Tierras Largas: A formative community in the Valley of Oaxaca, Mexico*. Dissertation submitted to the Department of Anthropology, the University of Arizona.

1974 Residential patterns at Monte Albán, Oaxaca, Mexico. *Science 186*, 981–987.

Winter, Marcus, and William Payne

1976 Hornos para cerámica hallados en Monte Albán. *Boletín del Instituto Nacional de Antropología E Historia*, No. 16, pp. 37–40.

Wittfogel, Karl

1938 *New light on Chinese society*. Institute of Pacific Relations, New York.

1957 *Oriental despotism*. New Haven: Yale University Press.

Wolf, Eric

1959 *Sons of the shaking earth*. Chicago: University of Chicago Press.

1969 *Peasant wars of the twentieth century*. New York: Harper and Row.

1976 Introduction. In *The Valley of Mexico: Studies in prehispanic ecology and society* (Eric Wolf, ed.). Albuquerque: The University of New Mexico Press.

INDEX

A
B
C 8
D 9
E 0
F 1
G 2
H 3
I 4
J 5

STUDIES IN ARCHEOLOGY

Consulting Editor: Stuart Struever

Department of Anthropology
Northwestern University
Evanston, Illinois

Charles R. McGimsey III. **Public Archeology**

Lewis R. Binford. **An Archaeological Perspective**

Muriel Porter Weaver. **The Aztecs, Maya, and Their Predecessors: Archaeology of Mesoamerica**

Joseph W. Michels. **Dating Methods in Archaeology**

C. Garth Sampson. **The Stone Age Archaeology of Southern Africa**

Fred T. Plog. **The Study of Prehistoric Change**

Patty Jo Watson (Ed.). **Archeology of the Mammoth Cave Area**

George C. Frison (Ed.). **The Casper Site: A Hell Gap Bison Kill on the High Plains**

W. Raymond Wood and R. Bruce McMillan (Eds.). **Prehistoric Man and His Environments: A Case Study in the Ozark Highland**

Kent V. Flannery (Ed.). **The Early Mesoamerican Village**

Charles E. Cleland (Ed.). **Cultural Change and Continuity: Essays in Honor of James Bennett Griffin**

Michael B. Schiffer. **Behavioral Archeology**

Fred Wendorf and Romuald Schild. **Prehistory of the Nile Valley**

Michael A. Jochim. **Hunter-Gatherer Subsistence and Settlement: A Predictive Model**

Stanley South. **Method and Theory in Historical Archeology**

Timothy K. Earle and Jonathon E. Ericson (Eds.). **Exchange Systems in Prehistory**

Stanley South (Ed.). **Research Strategies in Historical Archeology**

John E. Yellen. **Archaeological Approaches to the Present: Models for Reconstructing the Past**

Lewis R. Binford (Ed.). **For Theory Building in Archaeology: Essays on Faunal Remains, Aquatic Resources, Spatial Analysis, and Systemic Modeling**

James N. Hill and Joel Gunn (Eds.). **The Individual in Prehistory: Studies of Variability in Style in Prehistoric Technologies**

Michael B. Schiffer and George J. Gumerman (Eds.). **Conservation Archaeology: A Guide for Cultural Resource Management Studies**

Thomas F. King, Patricia Parker Hickman, and Gary Berg. **Anthropology in Historic Preservation: Caring for Culture's Clutter**

Richard E. Blanton. **Monte Albán: Settlement Patterns at the Ancient Zapotec Capital**

in preparation

R. E. Taylor and Clement W. Meighan. **Chronologies in New World Archaeology**

Bruce D. Smith. **Prehistoric Patterns of Human Behavior: A Case Study in the Mississippi Valley**

Barbara L. Stark and Barbara Voorhies (Eds.). **Prehistoric Coastal Adaptations: The Economy and Ecology of Maritime Middle America**

Lewis R. Binford. **Nunamuit Ethnoarchaeology**

Charles L. Redman (Ed.). **Social Archeology: Beyond Subsistence and Dating**

Bruce D. Smith (Ed.). **Mississippian Settlement Patterns Sarunas Milisauskas. European Prehistory.**